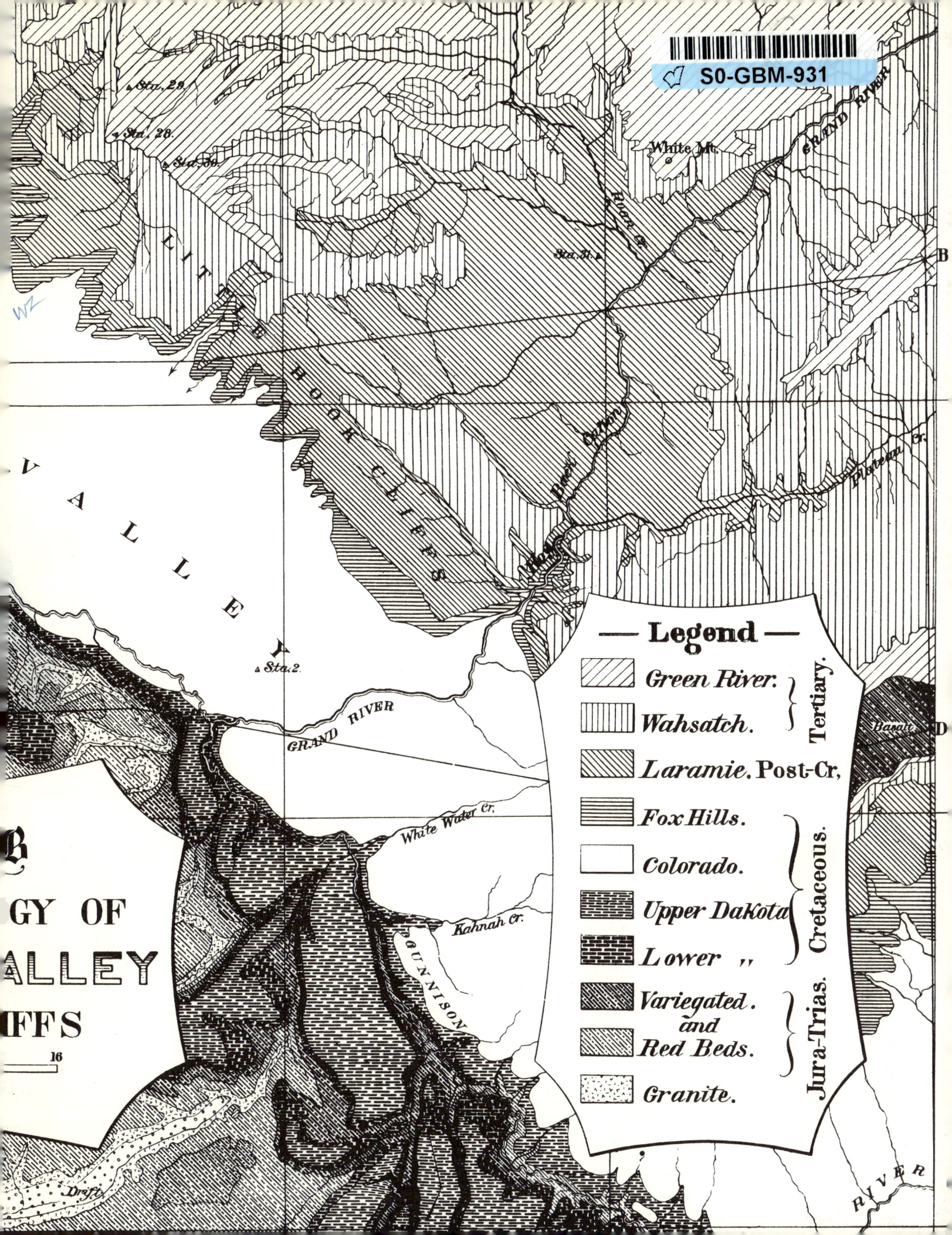

West Elk Breccia volcaniclastic facies in amphitheatre on north side of Mill Creek Canyon, West Elk volcanic field. Courtesy D. L. Gaskill, U.S. Geological Survey.

> "The hills west of Ohio Creek are composed mainly of breccia . . . eroded in the most fantastic fashion. The breccia is stratified, and there are huge castle-like forms, abrupt walls, spires, and towers."
>
> A. C. Peale, Hayden Survey, 1876

Western Slope Colorado

Western Colorado and Eastern Utah

Editors
RUDY C. EPIS and
JONATHAN F. CALLENDER

Managing Editor
JONATHAN F. CALLENDER

CONTENTS

President's Message vi
Editors' Message vi
Committees vii
Field Conference Schedule viii
Field Trip Routes ix
LANDSAT Photograph of Conference Area x

ROAD LOGS

First Day: Road Log from Grand Junction to Whitewater, Unaweep Canyon, Uravan, Paradox Valley, La Sal, Arches National Park, and Return to Grand Junction via Crescent Junction, Utah . . . . C. M. Molenaar, L. C. Craig, W. L. Chenoweth, and J. A. Campbell   1

Second Day: Road Log from Grand Junction to Glenwood Canyon and Return to Grand Junction . . . . R. G. Young, C. W. Keighin and J. A. Campbell   17

Third Day: Road Log from Grand Junction to Crested Butte via Delta, Montrose and Gunnison . . . . C. S. Goodknight, R. D. Cole, R. A. Crawley, B. Bartleson and D. Gaskill   29

Supplemental Road Log No. 1: Montrose to Durango, Colorado . . . . . K. Lee, R. C. Epis, D. L. Baars, D. H. Knepper and R. M. Summer   48

Supplemental Road Log No. 2: Gunnison to Saguache, Colorado . . . . R. C. Epis   64

ARTICLES

Stratigraphy and Tectonics

Stratigraphic Correlation Chart for Western Colorado and Northwestern New Mexico . . . . M. E. MacLachlan   75

Summary of Paleozoic Stratigraphy and History of Western Colorado and Eastern Utah . . . . John A. Campbell   81

The Middle Jurassic San Rafael Group and Related Rocks in East-Central Utah . . . . Robert B. O'Sullivan   89

Bedrock Geology of the Ridgway Area, Northwestern Flank, San Juan Mountains, Colorado . . . . Paul Weimer   97

Tectonic Evolution of Western Colorado and Eastern Utah . . . . D. L. Baars and G. M. Stevenson   105

Geomorphology

Glacial Moraines, Terraces and Pediments of Grand Valley, Western Colorado . . . . Scott Sinnock   113

Pleistocene Surficial Deposits of the Grand Mesa Area, Colorado . . . . Rex D. Cole and John L. Sexton   121

Pleistocene Drainage Changes in Uncompahgre Plateau–Grand Valley Region of Western Colorado, including Formation and Abandonment of Unaweep Canyon: A Hypothesis . . . . Scott Sinnock   127

Ancient Drainage Changes in and South of Unaweep Canyon, Southwestern Colorado . . . . S. W. Lohman   137

Geologic and Physiographic Highlights of the Black Canyon of the Gunnison River and Vicinity, Colorado . . . . Wallace R. Hansen   145

Quaternary Glacial and Slope-Failure Deposits of the Crested Butte Area, Gunnison County, Colorado . . . . Charles H. Robinson and Peter A. Dea   155

Uranium and Vanadium Resources

The Uranium-Vanadium Deposits of the Uravan Mineral Belt and Adjacent Areas, Colorado and Utah . . . . William L. Chenoweth   165

General Geology of Uranium-Vanadium Deposits of Salt Wash Sandstones, La Sal Area, San Juan County, Utah . . . . Anthony A. Kovschak, Jr. and Robert L. Nylund   171

Geology of the Lisbon Valley Uranium District, Southeastern Utah . . . . Gary C. Huber   177

Uranium in the Gunnison Country, Colorado . . . . Craig S. Goodknight   183

Geology of Dolomite-Hosted Uranium Deposits at the Pitch Mine, Saguache County, Colorado . . . . J. Thomas Nash   191

Oil Shale—Piceance Creek Basin

Cretaceous and Tertiary History and Resources of the Piceance
　Creek Basin, Western Colorado . . . . Ronald C. Johnson and C. William Keighin　199
Rio Blanco Oil Shale Company Tract C-a, Rio Blanco County,
　Colorado: Summary of Geology and Current Development . . . . E. A. Ziemba　211
Comparative Petrology of Tertiary Sandstones of Southern Piceance
　Creek Basin, Colorado . . . . Allan M. Ochs and Rex D. Cole　219
Uncertainties of Oil Shale Development . . . . Glen D. Weaver　229

Coal Resources

Upper Cretaceous (Campanian) Coal Resources of Western Colorado . . . . D. Keith Murray　233
Methane in Cretaceous and Paleocene Coals of Western Colorado . . . . C. M. Tremain, D. L. Boreck and B. S. Kelso　241
Coking Coals of Western Colorado . . . . L. R. Ladwig　249

Oil and Gas Resources

Potential Petroleum Resources of Northeastern Utah and Northwestern
　Colorado . . . . Albert F. Sanborn　255

Geology and Ore Deposits of the Gunnison Mineral Belt

Precambrian Geology Along Parts of the Gunnison Uplift of
　Southwestern Colorado . . . . D. C. Hedlund and J. C. Olson　267
Precambrian Sulfide Deposits in the Gunnison Region,
　Colorado . . . . Douglas M. Sheridan, William H. Raymond, and Leslie J. Cox　273
Proterozoic Syngenetic Massive Sulfide Deposits in the Gunnison
　Gold Belt, Colorado . . . . P. A. Drobeck　279
Stratigraphy, Petrology, and Structure of Precambrian Metavolcanic
　Rocks in the Iris District, Gunnison and Saguache Counties,
　Colorado . . . . Abdulkader M. Afifi　287
The Complex of Alkaline Rocks at Iron Hill, Powderhorn District,
　Gunnison County, Colorado . . . . Theodore J. Armbrustmacher　293
Structure and Petrology of Cochetopa Pluton and Its Metamorphic
　Wallrocks, Saguache County, Colorado . . . . Robert M. Hutchinson　297

Tertiary Volcanism and Ore Deposits

West Elk Volcanic Field, Gunnison and Delta Counties,
　Colorado . . . . D. L. Gaskill, F. E. Mutschler and B. L. Bartleson　305
Igneous Rocks of the Elk Mountains and Vicinity, Colorado—
　Chemistry and Related Ore Deposits . . . . Felix E. Mutschler, David R. Ernst, David L. Gaskill and Patty Billings　317
Geology of the Mount Emmons Molybdenum Deposit, Crested
　Butte, Colorado . . . . F. R. Dowsett, Jr., M. W. Ganster, D. E. Ranta, D. J. Baker and H. J. Stein　325

Geothermal Resources

Hydrothermal Resources of Western Colorado . . . . Richard H. Pearl　333

The Hanging Flume

The Hanging Flume of Dolores River Canyon, Montrose County,
　Colorado . . . . Elizabeth A. Learned　337

COPYRIGHT © 1981 by the New Mexico Geological Society, Inc.

The articles and road logs in this guidebook were prepared for presentation at the 32nd annual field conference of the New Mexico Geological Society, held on the Western Slope, Colorado and Utah on October 8–10, 1981. No part of this publication may be reproduced, stored in a retrieval system, or transmitted, in any form or by any means, electronic, mechanical, photocopying, recording, or otherwise, without the prior written permission of the copyright owner.

PRESIDENT'S MESSAGE

Once again, welcome to the annual field conference of the New Mexico Geological Society. This is the thirty-second consecutive, annual field conference sponsored by the Society. Each Fall this minor miracle springs from the efforts of an all volunteer force. Don Baars, Rudy Epis, Jack Campbell and Bill Chenoweth have sacrificed time and sanity so that the Society and its guests can enjoy the "geology and the good times" so intimately mixed in each field conference.

This year's guidebook is different from those of the past, in that the Society has not solicited any external financial support either in the form of advertising or as contributions from individuals and corporations. The Society continues to maintain a high scientific standard in which all contributions are carefully reviewed. I extend the special thanks of the Society to Jon Callender. Jon has not only served as the President, Vice-President and Secretary of the Society, but he also has been an author, editor or managing editor for seven guidebooks since 1974. As the Managing Editor for this guidebook, he has been at the focus of the pressure and panic of producing the final product that you hold in your hands.

Enjoy the Field Conference and make your plans to join us next year in Albuquerque Country.

Rod Ewing
President

EDITORS' MESSAGE

Since the days of the Hayden Survey more than a century ago, the part of Colorado west of the continental divide generally has been referred to as the western slope. Together with adjoining parts of eastern Utah and southwestern Wyoming, the western slope of Colorado long has been known to contain vast deposits of uranium, vanadium, coal, oil and gas, and oil shale. Equally well-known and documented in the literature are base and precious metal deposits related to volcanic and subvolcanic environments of Laramide and middle to late Tertiary age. During the past decade, significant geological effort has been focused on Precambrian volcanogenic metallic deposits of the Gunnison uplift and on Tertiary molybdenum deposits north of the Gunnison River. Likewise, encouraging assessments of the geothermal resources of the western slope of Colorado have been completed. Clearly, in the perspective of present-day and predictable national and international scenarios, the western slope of Colorado and neighboring segments of the Rocky Mountain West are destined for major, commercial exploration and production of metallic and non-metallic resources. Already in the news are forecasts of small, western slope communities with populations of less than a few hundred mushrooming to over 25,000 people, together with new cities of similar or larger size, within the next 10 to 20 years.

Most of the papers in this volume address the general or local geological framework of known or anticipated economic deposits as outlined above. However, the western mountainous slope of Colorado and adjacent province of plateaus and canyonlands of eastern Utah, which merge imperceptibly, are endowed with some of the most spectacular physiography and scenery in the nation. They are the result of repeated tectonic uplift and volcanism, and attendant erosion by the Colorado River and its major tributaries such as the Gunnison, Uncompahgre, Dolores and San Miguel Rivers, including of course, the renowned abandoned river valley of Unaweep Canyon atop the Uncompahgre Plateau, and the Black Canyon of the Gunnison River National Monument. The several papers in the geomorphology section of this volume are intended to decipher and explain the impressive landscapes we will enjoy during the field conference.

It is a pleasure to express our sincere appreciation to each author and co-author of articles and roadlogs in this volume. As every editor of such a volume knows, there could be no guidebook without the dedication of time and effort by individual contributors. We thank you all.

Although partly acknowledged in the credits for this book, we also wish to express our special thanks to the following individuals who supplied extra illustrative materials used throughout the volume: D. L. Baars, W. L. Chenoweth, C. P. Epis, D. L. Gaskill, W. R. Hansen, C. W. Keighin, S. W. Lohman, C. M. Molenaar, J. D. Moore, and S. Sinnock.

Rudy C. Epis
Jonathan F. Callender

COMMITTEES

EXECUTIVE COMMITTEE

R. C. Ewing, *President*	University of New Mexico
J. E. Mueller, *Vice-President*	New Mexico State University
R. W. Jentgen, *Treasurer*	U.S. Geological Survey, Farmington
D. I. Norman, *Secretary*	New Mexico Institute of Mining and Technology
J. E. Cunningham, *Past President*	Western New Mexico University

FIELD CONFERENCE

D. L. Baars, *General Chairman*	Consulting Geologist, Denver

GUIDEBOOK

R. C. Epis, *Editor*	Colorado School of Mines
J. F. Callender, *Co-Editor and Managing Editor*	University of New Mexico

REGISTRATION

W. L. Chenoweth	U.S. Department of Energy, Grand Junction

PUBLICATIONS

J. M. Robertson, *Chairman*	New Mexico Bureau of Mines and Mineral Resources
J. F. Callender	University of New Mexico

CARAVAN

J. A. Campbell	Fort Lewis College

ROAD LOGGING

J. A. Campbell, *Chairman*	Fort Lewis College
D. L. Baars	Consulting Geologist, Denver
B. L. Bartleson	Western State College
W. L. Chenoweth	U.S. Department of Energy
R. D. Cole	Multi Mineral Corporation
L. C. Craig	U.S. Geological Survey
R. A. Crawley	U.S. Department of Energy
R. C. Epis	Colorado School of Mines
D. L. Gaskill	U.S. Geological Survey
C. S. Goodknight	Bendix Field Engineering
R. M. Hutchinson	Colorado School of Mines
C. W. Keighin	U.S. Geological Survey
D. H. Knepper	University of Colorado
K. Lee	Colorado School of Mines
C. M. Molenaar	U.S. Geological Survey
R. M. Summer	University of Colorado
R. G. Young	Consultant, Grand Junction

TECHNICAL ASSISTANCE

Schlumberger Well Services	Beverages, en route
Welex, a Division of Haliburton	Mobil Sound Equipment
Judy Salas	Drafting

1981
FIELD CONFERENCE SCHEDULE

WEDNESDAY, October 7   **REGISTRATION DAY**

     3:00–9:00 p.m.   Registration: Grand Mesa Room, Holiday Inn, Grand Junction, Colorado
     6:00–9:00 p.m.   Cocktail party (cash bar)

THURSDAY, October 8   **FIRST DAY**

     6:30–7:00 a.m.   Board chartered buses in parking lot of Holiday Inn for tour of Uncompahgre Uplift, the fold and fault belt of the Paradox basin, via Unaweep Canyon, and Arches National Park. **(Bring your own lunch.)**

FRIDAY, October 9   **SECOND DAY**

     7:30–8:00 a.m.   Board chartered buses in parking lot of Holiday Inn for tour of stratigraphy and structure of west-central Colorado as seen from I-70 between Grand Junction and the east end of Glenwood Canyon, and presentation at Paraho Oil Shale Demonstration Plant. **(Bring your own lunch.)**

     6:30–7:30 p.m.   Cocktail party (cash bar), Holiday Inn.

     7:30–9:30 p.m.   Prime rib banquet with surprise speaker, Holiday Inn.

SATURDAY, October 10   **THIRD DAY**

     6:30–7:00 a.m.   Assembly of auto caravan at Holiday Inn, Grand Junction. **Please follow directions of flagmen.** Conference will follow U.S. Highway 50 to Gunnison and then tour the Crested Butte region north of Gunnison. Featured will be the mining activity of the Crested Butte area, a side trip to the Black Canyon of the Gunnison, and spectacular scenery. Conference will end at about 5:00 p.m. at Gunnison, Colorado. **(Bring your own lunch.)**

CREDITS

Front Cover: Black Canyon of the Gunnison; pen and ink drawing by Charlene P. Epis.

End Sheets: (Front) Geologic map of Grand Valley, F. D. Owen, Hayden Survey, 1876, courtesy W. L. Chenoweth; (Back, left) Looking northeast from Fruita Canyon at west entrance of Colorado National Monument toward Grand Valley, Book Cliffs (dark), and Roan Cliffs (light), courtesy S. W. Lohman; (Back, right) The Narrows of the Black Canyon of the Gunnison (width at river 12 m; depth 530 m; width at rim 350 m), courtesy W. R. Hansen.

Frontispiece: West Elk breccia volcaniclastic facies in Mill Creek Canyon, courtesy D. L. Gaskill.

Title Page: Mount Garfield, in Book Cliffs on northeastern side of Grand Valley; infrared photograph courtesy of S. W. Lohman.

Ink Drawings: P. Chenoweth, C. P. Epis, J. D. Moore.

Photography: D. L. Baars, W. L. Chenoweth, R. C. Epis, D. L. Gaskill, C. S. Goodknight, W. R. Hansen, C. W. Keighin, K. Lee, S. W. Lohman, C. M. Molenaar, S. Sinnock, R. J. Weimer.

Printer: University of New Mexico Printing Plant.

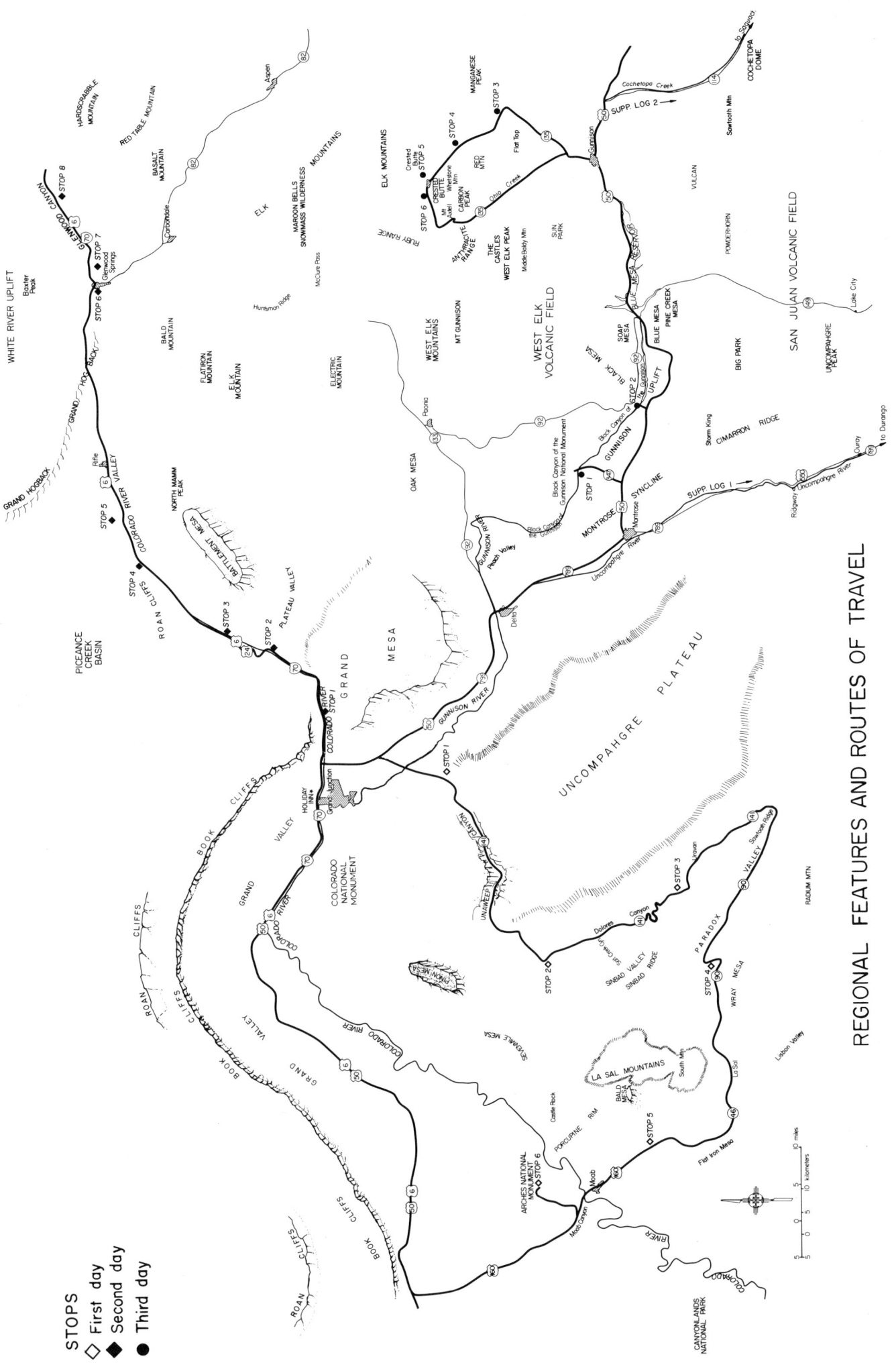

REGIONAL FEATURES AND ROUTES OF TRAVEL

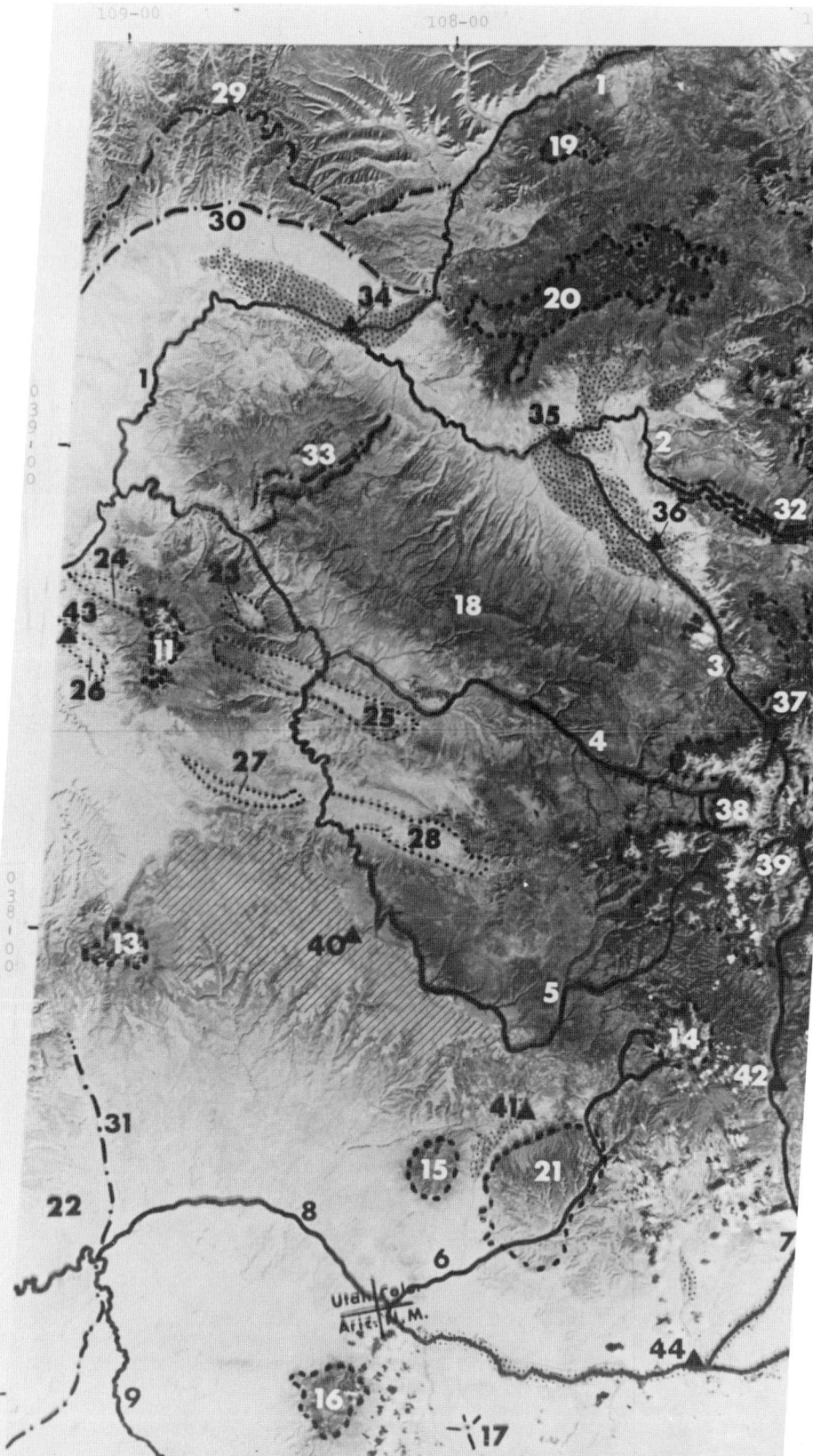

LANDSAT photograph of southwestern Colorado and southwestern Utah showing most of the localities to be visited on the field conference. Courtesy of Scott Sinnock, Sandia National Laboratories.

FIRST DAY
ROAD LOG FROM GRAND JUNCTION TO WHITEWATER, UNAWEEP CANYON, URAVAN, PARADOX VALLEY, LA SAL, ARCHES NATIONAL PARK, AND RETURN TO GRAND JUNCTION VIA CRESCENT JUNCTION, UTAH

by C. M. MOLENAAR, L. C. CRAIG, W. L. CHENOWETH, and J. A. CAMPBELL

THURSDAY, OCTOBER 8, 1981

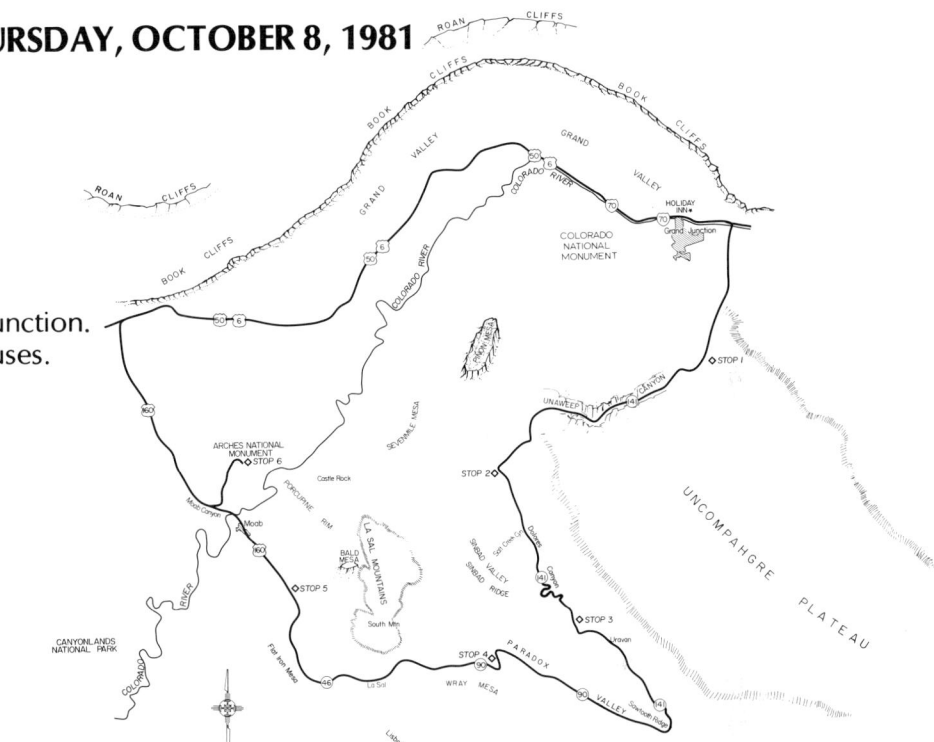

Assembly Point: Holiday Inn, Grand Junction. Park cars and board buses.

Departure Time: 7:00 a.m.

Distance: 324.6 miles

Stops: 6

SUMMARY

Today we will traverse part of the Uncompahgre Uplift and the fold and fault belt of the Paradox basin. The Uncompahgre Uplift has been a major factor in the geology of western Colorado. On this day we will see the western flank of this uplift and on the third day the eastern flank. The structure and stratigraphy of the salt anticlines in the Paradox basin will be a main feature of today's journey. This area of western Colorado and eastern Utah is rich in history and lore, much of it associated with mining. We will see gold, silver, copper, coal, uranium, vanadium and oil and gas operations. A stop in Arches National Park for photographs will be a final highlight.

Mileage

0.0 Holiday Inn, proceed south on Horizon Drive.
   0.1
0.1 **Turn left** onto I-70 at the Horizon Drive interchange.
   1.2
1.3 Walker Field control tower at 9:00, Mt. Garfield at 12:00. On the left the escarpment of the Little Book Cliffs marks the north edge of the Grand Valley and the south rim of the Piceance Basin. These cliffs occur westward from Grand Junction to the vicinity of Price, Utah. In 1875, Henry Gannett, topographer of the U.S. Geological and Geographical Survey noted that these cliffs were named "from the characteristic shape of the cliff, which with its overhanging crest and slight talus, bears considerable resemblance to the edge of a bound book."

THE HAYDEN SURVEY IN WEST-CENTRAL COLORADO

The United States Geological and Geographical Survey of the Territories was better known as the "Hayden Survey." This survey is noteworthy in the geological exploration of the west because of the remarkable exploits

Figure 1.3. Mt. Garfield, elevation 2062 m (6765 ft). Lower slope is Upper Cretaceous Mancos Shale; cliff is in the Mesaverde Group (Chenoweth photo).

and achievements during the groups's nine-year existence. After three years of reconnaissance in Nebraska, Wyoming, Colorado, and New Mexico for the General Land Office, Professor Ferdinand Vandiveer Hayden presented a plan to Congress for systematic geological and geographical mapping of the Western Territories. The plan was accepted, and field work began in Wyoming in August 1870.

In 1873 mapping commenced in Colorado using Denver as headquarters. This activity led to the publishing of the Atlas of Colorado in 1877. In 1874 work began in west-central Colorado. That year the Survey was divided into seven divisions: four topographical and geological divisions, a primary triangulation division, a photographic division, and a quartermaster division. The Second or Middle Division was under the command of Henry Gannett, topographer. Dr. Arthur C. Peale, M.D., served as geologist. Other members of the party included three assistants, two packers, and a cook. Although other Hayden divisions mapped in western Colorado, only the accomplishments of the Gannett party is summarized here as it covered the region of this field conference.

During the 1874 and the following two field seasons, the Gannett party mapped some 50,000 km² of western Colorado and adjacent parts of Utah at a scale of 1:250,000. The area covered by the survey was roughly bounded by these present-day cities: Gunnison on the east, Ouray on the south, Moab on the west, and Glenwood Springs on the north. The only inhabitants of this large region were Ute Indians.

Topographic mapping was the primary concern of the Hayden Survey; however, agriculture and mineral possibilities were considered. Every significant stream was gauged. The gradients of all rivers were measured. Lands suitable for irrigation were noted. During the three field seasons a total of 216 topographic stations were established for geodetic control. The elevation, latitude, and longitude were determined for each station.

Dr. Peale mapped the geology in a reconnaissance manner and drew cross-sections to show the stratigraphy and structure. He noted that "coal is more widely distributed in the district than either gold or silver," although gold-bearing gravels along the San Miguel River were noted. The survey also recorded malachite in Unaweep Canyon and the commercial possibilities of the salt in Sinbad's Valley. Peale was intrigued by the LaSal Mountains and wrote, "the Sierra la Sal presents one of the most promising fields for future detail investigation to be found in any part of the West."

The work of Gannett and Peale is all but forgotten; however, they left their mark upon the region. Gannett named Paradox Valley, Grand Mesa, the Little Book Cliffs, Plateau Creek, and the Grand River Valley (the Grand Valley). He also named Atkinson Creek for his assistant topographer, William R. Atkinson, Dallas Fork (Creek) for general assistant, L. Dallas, and the highest peak of the LaSals for his geologist, Peale. Dr. Peale can be credited with naming Gypsum Valley, Naturita Creek, and Disappointment Creek. He also named Rio Escalante and Rio Dominguez after the Spanish padres who were in the region in 1776. The highest point in Wyoming, Gannett Peak in the Wind River Range, bears witness to Gannett's early work in Wyoming for the Hayden Survey.

Professor Hayden was so impressed with the survey of the Colorado Territory that on March 15, 1877 he wrote the Secretary of the Interior, "When finished, Colorado will have a better map than any other State in the Union, and the work will be of such a character that it will never need to be done again. Colorado will never support so dense a population that a more detailed survey will be required."

0.4

1.7 Milepost 33. On I-70 in Colorado these markers record the mileage from the point the highway entered the state.

0.2

1.9 29 Road underpass. Mesa County has an alphabetic-numeric grid system for county roads. North-south roads are numbered

FIRST DAY ROAD LOG

with respect to their distance from the Utah line. Hence 29 Road is 29 miles east of the state line. East-west roads are lettered with respect to their distance from the 39th parallel. Thus, F Road is 6 miles north of the point of origin.

0.3

2.2 Highline Canal on the right. This is the northernmost system that brings irrigation water to the Grand Valley. Water is diverted from the Colorado River at the Highline Dam in DeBeque Canyon. Grand Mesa at 12:00. Note the northeast dipping beds of the Mesaverde Group on the west face of Grand Mesa. Rocks of the Green River Formation are present on Grand Mesa but are not visible due to the talus from the cap of basalt.

0.5

2.7 Milepost 34. Chalk Mountain capped with Green River Formation at 11:00.

1.7

4.4 Road cut in Mancos Shale.

0.5

4.9 Road cut in Mancos.

0.2

5.1 Road cut in Mancos.

0.3

5.4 **Turn right onto the Clifton exit** to I-70 Business Loop. Road cuts in Mancos.

0.2

5.6 Cross the Highline Canal and enter Clifton, Colorado, a rapidly growing suburb of Grand Junction.

0.6

6.2 Traffic light at Patterson Road (F Road); **continue straight ahead.** Uncompahgre Plateau on the skyline at 10:00 to 12:00. Uncompahgre is a distortion of the Ute Indian word "Ancapogari" meaning red lake. The Uncompahgre River was given this name by the Utes because near its source was a spring of hot, reddish water, disagreeable to the taste.

0.5

6.7 Traffic light at 32 Road, **turn left.**

0.2

6.9 Cross main line of the Denver and Rio Grande Western Railroad. Excellent view of Mt. Garfield at 9:00.

0.2

7.1 Note new subdivisions on the left for the next mile. Energy development is responsible for recent growth in the Grand Junction area.

0.2

7.3 Cross the Grand Valley Canal, the central system that distributes irrigation water to the Grand Valley. Water for this system is diverted from the Colorado River at Palisade.

1.1

8.4 Intersection with D Road. Office of Corn Construction Company on southwest corner. Warehouses and yard are to the south.

0.3

8.7 Clifton sewer lagoons on the left.

0.1

8.8 Gravel pit, now stocked with trout, on the right.

0.1

8.9 Bridge over the Colorado River. Outcrops of Mancos Shale on south bank. This river was known as the Grand River as early as 1842. The Green and the Grand joined in eastern Utah to form the Colorado. The Grand River was renamed the Colorado River by an act of the Colorado State Legislature approved March 24, 1921, and by an act of Congress approved July 25, 1921.

0.1

9.0 Road cut in Mancos Shale overlain with river gravels.

0.4

9.4 Intersection with C Road. In the Grand Junction-Palisade region the higher area between the Colorado and Gunnison Rivers is known as Orchard Mesa. This particular high spot is the Central Orchard Mesa. Several orchards can be seen along both sides of the road for the next 2 km. In an average year, the Clifton-Palisade area will produce 175,000 bushels of peaches.

0.4

9.8 Cross Orchard Mesa Canal No. 1. Water for this system is diverted from the Colorado River at the Highline Dam in DeBeque Canyon.

0.9

10.7 Cross Orchard Mesa Canal No. 2. Note house on small hill of Mancos at 12:00.

1.1

11.8 Steel buildings on small Mancos hill at 12:30 are water filtration plant and water tank for Orchard Mesa area. Water for domestic use comes from reservoirs on Grand Mesa.

0.3

12.1 Junction with U.S. Highway 50. **Turn left** at stop sign. The area of Unaweep Canyon, which cuts across the Uncompahgre Plateau, at 10:30.

2.6

14.7 Whitewater. Junction of U.S. 50 and Colorado 141. **Turn right on Colorado 141.**

0.4

15.1 Bridge over Gunnison River. This river was originally known as the Rio Javier, or by the Indian name Tomichi. After the death of Captain

	Gunnison in the fall of 1853, it was renamed the Gunnison.
	0.3
15.4	Outcrop of Dakota Formation on the right. Dip is to the east. Cotter Corporation uranium crushing and sampling plant ahead on left.
	0.6
16.0	Top of Burro Canyon Formation on right. Road to Cotter's plant on left.
	0.1
16.1	Cross East Creek, and enter East Creek Canyon, and start up 9-Mile Hill ahead. Cliffs are sandstones in the Dakota Formation, which are dipping east.
	0.8
16.9	Contact of Burro Canyon and underlying Brushy Basin Member of the Morrison Formation on the left.
	0.7
17.6	Cattle guard. Road is on the Brushy Basin, cliffs are the Burro Canyon, top ledge on skyline at 3:00 is the Dakota Formation.
	2.5
20.1	The Salt Wash Member of the Morrison is exposed in bottom of East Creek gorge at 2:00.
	2.6
22.7	About the top of 9-Mile Hill. Cliffs are sandstones in the Dakota Formation.
	1.0
23.7	Cactus Park turn-off. **Turn left.** Road on Entrada Sandstone. **Prepare to stop.**
	0.6
24.3	**STOP 1.** Gravel pits in Cactus Park. Entrada through Burro Canyon exposed on hills. Discussion of geomorphology and formation of Unaweep Canyon. **(See Lohman; Sinnock, this guidebook.) Return to Colorado 141.**
	0.6
24.9	Colorado 141, **turn left.**
	0.4
25.3	Bridge over Cactus Park drainage.
	0.3
25.6	Cattle guard. Cross-bedded Wingate Sandstone on both sides of the road.
	0.5
26.1	Contact of Wingate and Chinle on the left.
	0.3
26.4	Road on Precambrian. Abandoned site of Copper City at 10:00.
	0.5
26.9	Bridge across East Creek. Precambrian outcrops on the right. The oldest Precambrian rocks are a series of metamorphic rocks that were intruded by a gneissic granodiorite dated at 1670 m.y.b.p., a quartz monzonite batholith dated at 1480 m.y.b.p. and a granite dated at 1400 m.y.b.p.
	0.5
27.4	Small workings along road on right is an amethyst mine in the Precambrian.
	0.4
27.8	Bridge over Nancy Hanks Draw. Copper was mined from the Chinle Formation up Nancy Hanks Draw.
	2.2
30.0	Taylor Ranch on the left. Numerous northwest-trending faults and diabase dikes are present in this area. Based on paleomagnetic data, these dikes are probably Cambrian-Ordovician in age.
	0.2
30.2	Divide Road turns off to the left.
	0.8
31.0	View of broad, flat-floored Unaweep Canyon ahead. U-shaped due to debris accumulated along valley walls. Unaweep is a Ute Indian word meaning "canyon with two mouths."
	0.5
31.5	Smooth surface developed on Precambrian under Chinle evident on south wall of canyon.
	4.3
35.8	Unaweep Divide. Elevation 2148 m (7048 ft). Sign on the right. Starting down West Creek, with view of LaSal Mountains ahead. Cliffs of Wingate and about 30 m of Chinle on Precambrian on both sides of canyon.
	4.7
40.5	Ruins of Driggs Mansion on left. Built by an Englishman named Driggs as an elegant hunting lodge in 1916-1918; it was never used.
	1.8
42.3	Road cut in Precambrian.
	1.6
43.9	Craig Ranch on the left.
	5.8

Figure 31.0. Unaweep Canyon looking west. Note flat floor and U-shape (Baars photo).

Figure 49.7. View to the west down West Creek in Unaweep Canyon (Baars photo).

49.7 Entering West Creek narrows. Creek is incised into very coarse valley fill in the upper part of the narrows and Precambrian in the lower part.

0.4

50.1 Bridge over West Creek. The marshy area on the north (right) side of West Creek is the principal habitat for the rare Great Basin Silverspot butterfly, *Speyeria nokomis nokomis*. This butterfly has been reported at only two other localities in western Colorado. It is planned to set aside 32 hectare here to protect this species.

4.1

54.2 Bridge over West Creek.

0.4

54.6 Contact between Permian Cutler Formation and the Precambrian. This contact marks the western boundary of the Uncompahgre uplift. A major high-angle fault system is present along this contact. We will look at the eastern boundary of the Uncompahgre uplift on the third day of this field conference.

0.3

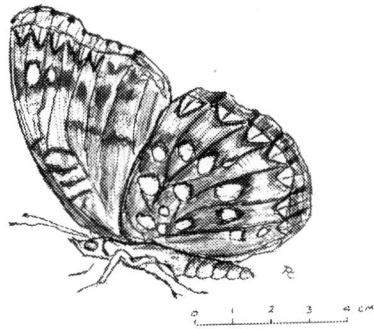

Figure 50.1. Speyeria nokomis nokomis, the rare butterfly of Unaweep Canyon (P. Chenoweth drawing).

54.9 Calamity Mesa road to the left. Mine dumps at 12:00 are on Beaver Mesa in the Salt Wash Member of the Morrison Formation. Uranium and vanadium were discovered on Beaver Mesa in 1913, and mining for radium began about 1916 or 1917. Between 1948 and 1970, 1,225,000 tonnes of ore averaging 0.29% U_3O_8 and 0.98% V_2O_5 were produced. LaSal Mountains ahead at 12:00. This part of the trip will circle the LaSal Mountains.

1.2

56.1 Good exposure of purple-red Cutler Formation on the right. Large, dark-colored boulders are in the Cutler. The lighter colored boulders are from thick Tertiary gravels that overlie the Cutler.

0.4

56.5 Cutler exposed in bluff on the right.

0.5

57.0 The Palisade at 3:00. From the base to top the Palisade consists of Permian Cutler Formation; Triassic Moenkopi and Chinle Formations; the cliff-forming Wingate Sandstone and overlying Kayenta Formation, both of Triassic age; the Jurassic Summerville; and Salt Wash Member of the Jurassic Morrison Formation, which caps the butte.

1.6

58.6 Entering Gateway Colorado. Elevation 1400 m (4595 ft), the lowest settlement in western Colorado. In 1875, Gateway was the site of a supply camp for the U.S. Geological and Geographical Survey (Hayden Survey) parties in western Colorado.

0.7

59.3 Bridge across the Dolores River. Remains of old vanadium mill up river at 8:00. **Prepare to stop.**

0.4

Figure 57.0. The Palisade at Gateway, Colorado (Baars photo).

59.7	**STOP 2.** Road to right goes up John Brown Canyon to mines on Beaver Mesa. Discussion of geology of Gateway area. Return to Colorado 141; **turn right** for drive up Dolores River.
	4.7
64.4	Gypsum bed at 3:00 marks the base of the Moenkopi Formation in this area.
	0.7
65.1	Cattle guard. Small strip mine in gypsum at 3:00. Road in top of Cutler Formation.
	0.6
65.7	Moenkopi at road level.
	3.8
69.5	Bridge over Salt Creek that drains Sinbad Valley to the right. Valley was named by miners from the San Juan region who undoubtedly saw a resemblance to the valley of diamonds that Sinbad the Sailor encountered on his second voyage in the book *The Thousand and One Nights*. Sinbad Valley is a small collapsed salt anticline.
	1.5
71.0	Lower part of red slope at road level is Moenkopi, upper part is Chinle Formation. Cliff is Wingate Sandstone with ledges of Kayenta Formation on top.
	1.7
72.7	Blue Creek enters Dolores River from the east on the right. Base of Chinle about at river level.
	2.5
75.2	Enter Montrose County.
	0.3
75.5	Blue Mesa at 12:00.
	1.4
76.9	Chinle-Wingate contact about at road level.
	1.3
78.2	Section exposed at 12:00 includes Wingate, Kayenta, Navajo(?), Entrada, and Salt Wash Member of the Morrison Formation at the top.
	1.2
79.4	Spring at the base of the Wingate at 3:00.
	0.6
80.0	Chinle again at road level.
	0.9
80.9	Chinle-Wingate contact at road level. Blue Mesa at 12:00 with Burro Canyon at top.
	0.8
81.7	Top of Wingate with Kayenta at road level, with thin Navajo Sandstone(?) at 9:00.
	0.9
82.6	Bridge over Dolores River at the mouth of Roc Creek, the giant bird that carried Sinbad to the valley of diamonds.
	0.1
82.7	Entrada Sandstone at road level overlain by Summerville Formation. Blue Mesa at 9:00.
	1.8
84.5	Lone Tree gold placer on the left at 9:00.
	1.0
85.5	Mesa Creek bridge. Entrada Sandstone at road level overlain by red Summerville slope and ledges of the Salt Wash Member of the Morrison.
	0.1
85.6	Union Carbide gravel pit at 3:00.
	1.4
87.0	On right, bridge over Dolores to gravel pit; on left at 9:00 the Bancroft gold placer.
	0.7
87.7	Old coke oven on the right built in the 1880's.
	0.4
88.1	Road on top of Kayenta Formation.
	0.4
88.5	Mine dumps at 12:00 in the lower, "first rim," of the Salt Wash Member.
	0.5
89.0	Uranium mines in "upper rim" of Salt Wash on Atkinson Mesa at 12:00. **Prepare to stop.**
	0.5
89.5	**STOP 3.** Hanging Flume was built to bring water to placer mines. **(See Learned, this guidebook.)** Discussion of geology and history of this area.
	1.1
90.6	Confluence of the Dolores and San Miguel Rivers at 3:00. We will be driving up the San Miguel River for the next 25 km.
	2.8
93.4	Bridge across the San Miguel River on the right. Road goes up the Dolores River to Paradox Valley.
	0.1
93.5	Atkinson Creek bridge.
	0.2
93.7	Evaporation ponds for Union Carbide uranium mill on the right.
	0.6

Figure 89.5. Hanging Flume along the Dolores River (Chenoweth photo).

94.3	Enter Uravan, a Union Carbide company town.
	0.8
95.1	Union Carbide uranium mill at 3:00.
	1.8
96.9	Leaving Uravan. San Miguel River bridge.
	0.3
97.2	Summerville Formation at road level.
	1.4
98.6	Upper Entrada at road level at 3:00. Road is in lower part of Salt Wash Member just ahead.
	3.1
101.7	Brushy Basin Member of the Morrison Formation forms variegated slope at 11:00. Slope capped by Burro Canyon Formation.
	1.6
103.3	Dakota Formation capping rim at 10:00.
	1.7
105.0	Salt Wash-Brushy Basin contact at road level.
	0.8
105.8	View of Uncompahgre Plateau at 11:00.
	1.0
106.8	Road and bridge to the left go to Nucla.
	1.0
107.8	On the left is the site of the old Vanadium Corporation of America's Naturita mill which processed vanadium and/or uranium ores from 1939 to 1958. Now General Electric's Nuclear Division buying station is located on this site.
	0.2
108.0	Coal mine in the Dakota at 9:00.
	0.7
108.7	Junction of Colorado 141 and 90. **Turn left onto highway 90** to Paradox, Colorado, and LaSal, Utah. The stone marker on the left, southwest side of intersection, commemorates the fact that the Dominguez and Escalante expedition camped near here on August 21, 1776.
	0.2
108.9	West Vancoram at 9:00. Vanadium Corporation of America's company housing of the 1940's.
	0.7
109.6	At 10:00 top of Salt Wash Member overlain by Brushy Basin Member and Burro Canyon Formation.
	1.4
111.0	Dakota-Burro Canyon contact. Entering southeast end of Paradox Valley. Valley is a large northwest-trending salt anticline that has collapsed after solution of the salt. Flanks of valley are highly faulted and folded due to salt flowage and/or solution collapse. Reverse dip on Burro Canyon at 3:00 is an example.
	0.1
111.1	Coke Ovens Ranch at 9:00. The Coke Ovens

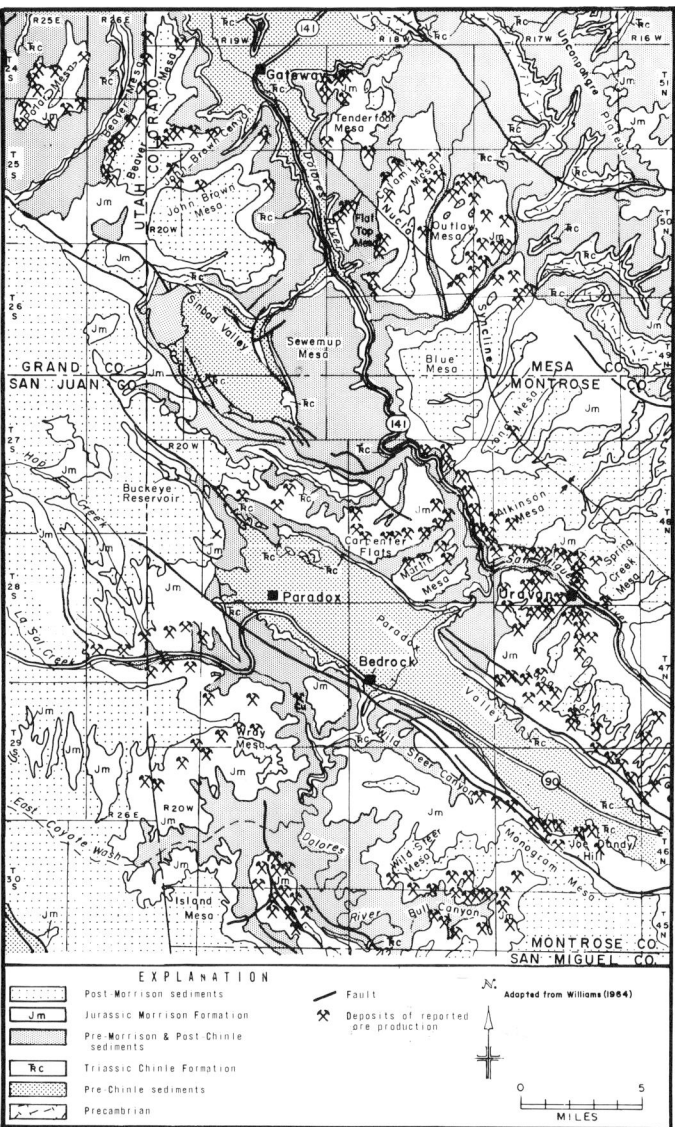

Figure 109.6. Geologic map of the area between Gateway and Paradox Valley, adapted from P. L. Williams, U.S. Geological Survey Miscellaneous Investigations Map I-360, 1964.

Figure 111.1. Aerial view of Dry Creek anticline (left foreground) and Paradox Valley (middle background). Looking west toward La Sal Mountains (Molenaar photo).

basin is the collapsed southeast end of the Paradox structure. Ranchers uranium leaching mill at 9:00. Across valley, Dry Creek emerges from the breached Dry Creek anticline also at 9:00.
0.7

111.8 Note dip reversal at 8:00 on southwest flank of valley. This is the Montrose Dome produced by salt flowage. This structure was drilled (the Kirby Dyer No. 1) and produced 17,840 m³ (630 MCF)/day from the Upper Honaker Trail–lower Cutler sands, but is now abandoned.
0.4

112.2 Sawtooth ridge along northeast rim of valley at 1:00 is Dakota on Burro Canyon.
0.9

113.1 LaSal Mountains at 12:00. Collapse structures in Salt Wash at 3:00.
0.8

113.9 Road junction. Road to the Bitter Creek uranium mining area.
0.6

114.5 Highly faulted north rim at 3:00.
0.5

115.0 Road junction. Road to Bull Canyon uranium mining area.
0.9

115.9 Road junction. Road to Thunderbolt Mine which produces from the upper part of the Salt Wash Member.
0.8

116.7 Paradox Formation (evaporites) of the Hermosa Group crops out in low hills at 3:00.
0.6

117.3 Road junction. Road to the right goes to the Joe Dandy Hill uranium area and Monogram Mesa. The Joe Dandy Hill area, on the southwest side of Paradox Valley (9:00), has been the site of considerable mining since 1910, from the upper part of the Salt Wash Member. First claims were staked in 1906 and by 1970 had produced 1,705,500 tonnes of ore averaging 0.27% U_3O_8 and 1.24% V_2O_5.
0.8

118.1 A hundred meters or so to the right is the location of American Liberty dry hole which bottomed in salt at 3306 m (10,846 ft).
0.8

118.9 Cotter Corporation open-pit uranium mine at 8:00. Completed pit will be 760×460×110 m deep (about 650 acres), producing from the upper part of the Salt Wash Member. About 65 million cubic meters of overburden will be removed to recover one million tonnes of uranium ore. Ore will be shipped to Cotter's mill at Canon City, Colorado. Operation was shut down in April 1981 due to depressed uranium market.
0.8

119.7 Entrada Sandstone cut out by faulting along cliffs at 2:00.
1.6

121.3 Road cut in Paradox gypsum.
0.3

121.6 Cutler Formation exposed in gully to right.
1.0

122.6 Low gray hills of Paradox at 3:00. This is the type area for the Paradox Formation.
1.7

124.3 Cutler Formation exposed at base of valley along the Dolores River to the right. The section on the northeast flank of the valley includes: Cutler, Moenkopi, Chinle, Wingate, Kayenta, Entrada, Summerville, Morrison, and Burro Canyon. The Paradox gray hills are mostly leached gypsum and black shale; however, unleached salt underlies the valley at a depth of 150 to 300 m.
0.9

125.2 Road junction. Road to right goes down Dolores River to confluence with the San Miguel River.
2.3

127.5 Bridge over Dolores River. The name Paradox was first applied to this valley in 1875 by Henry Gannett, a topographer with the Hayden Survey. Gannett noted that the river crossed the valley rather than flowing down it, thus making irrigation difficult!
0.4

127.9 The big town of Bedrock. Ahead, North Mountain, in the LaSals, has intruded in the center of the salt structure. This salt valley lines up with Castle Valley salt anticline on the other side of North Mountain.
0.9

Figure 121.6. Aerial view of the northwest end of Paradox Valley salt anticline. Note collapse area on plunge (Molenaar photo).

128.8 Continental Scorup No. 1 was drilled about 2.5 km to the right in the valley. This well penetrated the base of the salt at 4471 m (14,670 ft) and bottomed in the Mississippian at 4572 m (15,000 ft).

3.0

131.8 Collapse structures at 12:00 at the end of the valley. Road to the town of Paradox to the right.

THE HEADLESS CARETAKER AT PARADOX

In 1921, a flamboyant character named Lemuel "Slim" Hecox was employed as the caretaker of the Cashin Mine. Hecox always carried from $3000 to $4000 in a money belt and claimed he had obtained it while a member of the Jesse James Gang. He bragged no one could take the money away from him because he was "fast on the draw" and a good shot.

A few days after Thanksgiving in 1921, Hecox's decapitated body, without the cherished money belt, was found in his cabin at the Cashin Mine. The hideous act presumably was carried out by a gang of outlaws terrorizing the area, whose weird trademark was cutting off their victims' heads. In due time, the outlaws were captured and they revealed the location of Hecox's head. It was recovered up LaSal Creek about 25 km from the site of the murder, buried in an irrigation ditch.

Hecox's body had been buried in a crudely made coffin in the Paradox Cemetery, minus his head. After the recovery of his upper anatomy, the coffin was dug up and opened; however, since the coffin could not accommodate the length of the newly found extremity in its rightful place, it was put in the curvature of the caretaker's bended arm. "Slim" Hecox lies buried in the cemetery at Paradox, holding his head in one arm like the headless horseman in the "Legend of Sleepy Hollow."

1.4

133.2 Highway ascends the southwest side of Paradox Valley. Bleached Wingate Sandstone is repeated in fault slivers along road.

2.7

135.9 **STOP 4.** Road cut in Chinle overlain by Wingate. **Watch out for traffic!** Discussion of Paradox Valley. In the distance to the northeast is the Uncompahgre Plateau. The maximum structural relief on the basement between the Uncompahgre and Paradox basin is about 7600 m.

0.7

136.6 At 12:00 the section consists of Kayenta, Navajo, Entrada, Summerville, and Salt Wash Member of the Morrison. Note the thickness of the Navajo here as compared to zero thickness on the flank of the Paradox structure.

0.7

137.3 Driving down Spring Creek drainage to Junction with LaSal Creek. Cliffs at bottom of Spring Creek at 9:00 are Wingate Sandstone.

0.7

138.0 Junction with LaSal Creek. About 5 km down LaSal Creek to the left is the Cashin copper-silver mine. Deposits occur in a faulted zone in the Wingate Sandstone. Ore minerals consist chiefly of chalcopyrite, and native copper with some bornite, covellite and luzonite. Silver occurs in argentiferous covellite. The deposits were discovered about 1896 and were worked intermittently until 1945. About 350,000 ounces (10,000 kg) of silver and 1,700,000 pounds (770,000 kg) of copper have been produced.

1.5

139.5 Floor of LaSal Creek Canyon. Road in the Navajo Sandstone.

3.4

142.9 Utah-Colorado state line. Entrada Sandstone at road level. Uranium mines are in Salt Wash Member.

1.1

144.0 Firefly Pigmy uranium mine at 12:00. Uranium is in the upper part of the Salt Wash Member.

0.5

144.5 Vanadium Queen uranium mine at 3:00. Again uranium in upper Salt Wash.

2.0

146.5 Top of grade. Thick Burro Canyon forms cliffs on both sides of the road.

0.5

147.0 Wray Mesa road to left.

0.1

Figure 144.0. Firefly Pigmy uranium mine in the upper part of the Salt Wash Member (Chenoweth photo).

147.1	Entering Pine Ridge Valley. This valley is underlain at about 900 m by a salt anticline.
	0.4
147.5	Good view of the LaSals to the right. South Mountain is at 1:00; Mt. Peale (3877 m, 12,721 ft) at 2:00; and North Mountain at 3:00. These are middle Tertiary laccolithic intrusions dated at 23.5 m.y.b.p.
	0.3
147.8	Pine Ridge at 9:00. The Tenneco Redd Ranch No. 1 well site on the side of the hill at 9:00. This well penetrated a normal Mesozoic section, then 2740 m of salt. Well bottomed in the Mississippian at 3832 m (12,572 ft). About 2½ km southwest of here, Tide Water drilled a Mississippian test that penetrated 1829 m of Cutler and only 46 m of salt.
	3.6
151.4	Outcrops of Burro Canyon-Dakota along the road.
	1.6
153.0	Leaving LaSal-Manti National Forest. Crest of Pine Ridge salt anticline about here.
	0.4
153.4	Crest of hill. View southwest at 12:00 of Lisbon Valley and Abajo Mountains, another Tertiary laccolith complex.
	0.9
154.3	Head frame of the Rio Algom Lisbon Valley mine at 11:00. Mine produces from the Moss Back Member of the Chinle Formation at about 790 m. Mine is on the northeast, down-dropped side, of the Lisbon Valley fault and is one of the deepest uranium mines in the U.S.
	1.2
155.5	Entering LaSal, Utah. Union Carbide Corporation Beaver Creek shaft at 3:00. Uranium-vanadium is being mined at 195 m from the upper part of the Salt Wash Member. This mine is part of a new east-west LaSal Salt Wash trend of significant size outside the old Uravan uranium mineral belt.
	0.9
156.4	Rattlesnake open-pit uranium mine at 11:00. Mine in upper Salt Wash is one of the largest in this area and is on the southwest, upthrown side of the Lisbon Valley fault.
	1.4
157.8	Union Carbide's Redd shaft at 3:00 and Hecla shaft, ahead about 2 km, are part of the new LaSal trend. Both are 245-275 m shafts to reach ore in the upper part of the Salt Wash.
	0.3
158.1	Road junction to left to Lisbon Valley. The Lisbon Valley oil field is located in the southwest flank of the Lisbon surface anticline on the other side of the Wingate cliffs. The field had produced about 32 million barrels as of 1971, 99% of which was from a Mississippian carbonate reservoir. The discovery well, however, was completed in the Devonian McCracken Sandstone. Production has been as high as 11,000 bbls/day but has gradually declined to 7,000 bbls/day. The oil is piped to Aneth station about 100 km to the south. The trap is a faulted structure with vertical closure of about 500 m. The carbonate reservoir is vuggy and characterized by intercrystalline dolomite porosity. (One bbl equals 159 liters.)
	The Lisbon Valley uranium district has accounted for about 10% of the nation's total uranium production as of January 1980. The ore is in an arcuate belt, 24 km long and 0.8 km wide, in the Moss Back Member of the Chinle Formation, with some ore in the upper part of the Cutler Formation. Uraninite is the principal ore mineral in the Moss Back. The most famous mine is the Mi Vida which was discovered by Charley Steen during the 1950's boom. **(See Huber, this guidebook.)**
	0.9
159.0	Hecla shaft on the left.
	1.2
160.2	Road is about on Dakota, with alluvial-covered Dakota slope up to right toward the LaSal Mountains.
	0.1
160.3	Road cut in Brushy Basin Member of the Morrison Formation. Road is descending through the section.
	1.0
161.3	Top of Salt Wash at 3:00.
	0.5
161.8	Entrada at 3:00. West Coyote Wash on the left.
	0.9
162.7	Crossing the Lisbon fault. About 16 km to the south, this fault has a maximum displacement of about 1525 m but is dying out here. This is a collapse feature due to salt flow and solution.
	0.8
163.5	Entrada, Moab Tongue (upper member) at 3:00 overlain by Summerville.
	1.2
164.7	LaSal Junction. **Turn right on U.S. 163.**
	1.8
166.5	Pacific Northwest Pipeline compressor station on the left. This is on a 66-cm (26-in.) gas pipeline that supplies gas to the Pacific Northwest.
	1.0
167.5	Road follows along the Dewey Bridge (basal) Member of the Entrada (used to be the Carmel). Top of the Navajo Sandstone exposed in washes for next few kilometers.

FIRST DAY ROAD LOG

	3.9
171.4	Hole-in-the-Rock. Man-made caves in the Entrada Sandstone.
	0.3
171.7	Kane Springs campground on the right.
	0.5
172.2	Fault at 3:00 with Entrada against the Salt Wash.
	0.8
173.0	Top of hill at 9:00 is the Blue Hill uranium mining area. Salt Wash is host for ore.
	0.5
173.5	Summerville Formation overlying Entrada in road cuts.
	1.5
175.0	Entering Spanish Valley, another collapsed salt anticline. Morrison slumping into Spanish Valley in road cuts.
	4.2
179.2	Junction of road to the right that goes up Pack Creek. **STOP 5** (if there is time). Discussion of Spanish Valley geology. At 4:00 note dip reversal into Pack Creek graben, a continuation of Spanish Valley. Mancos Shale is exposed below pediments up valley. Section on the left, west flank of the structure is Chinle, Wingate, Kayenta, and Navajo on top.
	1.2
180.4	Entering Grand County.
	3.9
184.3	Low, gray knobs on the left at the base of the slope are Paradox gypsum and black shale.
	1.9
186.2	Moab city limits. Elevation 1219 m (4000 ft). Population about 5000.
	0.7
186.9	Ramada Inn on left. Stay on U.S. 163, **straight ahead.**
	1.2
188.1	Mi Vida Restaurant at 3:00 high. This was Charley Steen's house.
	0.7
188.8	Local L.P. gas company has a storage reservoir in the salt at about 610 m. Top of unleached salt is about 245 m deep.
	0.3
189.1	Note dip reversal at 11:00 at end of valley, with Navajo, Kayenta, and Wingate exposed.
	0.9
190.0	Junction with Utah 128 which goes up Colorado River to Castle Valley and Fisher Towers.
	0.1
190.1	Bridge over Colorado River. Collapse structures along the road on the right.
	0.5
190.6	Atlas Minerals Corporation uranium-vanadium mill on the left. This mill is rated at 1270 tonnes of ore per day. It has two circuites; an acid leach with solvent extraction for low lime/high vanadium ores of the Salt Wash; and a carbonate leach with caustic precipitation for the high lime/low vanadium ores of the Chinle Formation.
	1.0
191.6	Road to the left follows the river to the Texas Gulf Sulfur potash mine at the Cane Creek anticline. **Prepare to turn.**
	0.6
192.2	Entrance to Arches National Park. **Turn right.**
	0.3
192.5	Visitors center on the right.
	0.3
192.8	Entrada, Dewey Bridge Member, and Navajo contact on the right.
	1.0
193.8	Road cuts in the Navajo.
	1.0
194.8	South Park Avenue turn-out in the Dewey Bridge.
	0.4
195.2	LaSal Mountain viewpoint on right. Road continues near Dewey Bridge-Navajo contact. Arch on the skyline to the east (right).
	1.0
196.2	Courthouse Tower viewpoint turnoff.
	0.8
197.0	Courthouse Wash bridge.
	0.8
197.8	Dewey Bridge-Navajo contact well exposed along the road.
	0.8
198.6	Petrified dunes viewpoint.
	2.9
201.5	Balanced rock. **Prepare to turn.**
	0.2
201.7	Road junction, **turn right.** Road to left goes to Cach Creek graben.
	0.5
202.2	View to the left, 9:00, of Salt Valley salt anticline, another collapse structure.
	1.9
204.1	Turnout at end of loop, **STOP 6.** Brief discussion of geology, but mainly a picture stop. Arches have formed in the Entrada Sandstone. Return to U.S. 163 at entrance to park.
	0.2
204.3	Double Arch and Parade of the Elephants on right.
	2.3
206.6	Salt Valley salt anticline at 1:30.
	0.1
206.7	Road junction, **turn left to visitors center.**
	9.3

Figure 201.5. Balanced Rock, Arches National Park. Dewey Bridge Member at the base with the Slick Rock Member of the Entrada Formation forming "the rock" (Baars photo).

Figure 217.4. View to the northwest along the Moab fault (Molenaar photo).

216.0	Visitors Center.
0.2	
216.2	Road junction with U.S. 163, **turn right.**
0.8	
217.0	At about this point road crosses Moab fault, a high-angle normal fault caused by salt flowage. The Entrada is in contact with the upper part of the Honaker Trail Formation, with a throw of about 610 m on the fault.
0.2	
217.2	Section exposed here includes top 122 m of the Honaker Trail; 130 m of Cutler, then Moenkopi, Chinle, and Wingate cliff.
0.2	
217.4	Highway parallels Moab fault and goes up Moab Valley. Well location at wide spot on right ahead is Delhi Tayor No. 2 which was a potash stratigraphic test. This well went into salt at 713 m and bottomed near the base of the salt at 2872 m (9424 ft). The Cutler at the north end of Moab Valley is 230 m thick.
1.6	
219.0	Moenkopi-Cutler contact on left is at color break between brighter red Cutler and red-brown Moenkopi.
2.3	
221.3	Green hillside at 1:00 in distance is green shale of the Brushy Basin. At 11:30 is fault contact of Moab fault with Chinle on left and Brushy Basin on the right, a stratigraphic throw of 610 m.
1.1	
222.4	Bridge. At 3:00 sandstone channel in Salt Wash Member.
0.3	
222.7	Road junction. Dead Horse Point road to the left. **Stay on U.S. 163.**
0.3	
223.0	At 9:00 basal sandstone of the Chinle Formation is exposed near base of green shale where a uranium road has been cut. Uranium was mined from lenses of carbonaceous sandstone and mudstone pebble conglomerate in the basal Chinle. The Moss Back Member of the Chinle is not recognized here. Dark-colored sandstone in upper part of Chinle is locally called the "black ledge."
0.1	
223.1	Road for next 6 km is on westward-dipping Morrison Formation. Salt Valley salt anticline is to the northeast.
3.0	
226.1	Road is in Brushy Basin Member of the Morrison Formation.
0.8	
226.9	Approximate contact between Brushy Basin and Burro Canyon (Cedar Mountain). Road in the Burro Canyon.
1.1	
228.0	Burro Canyon (Cedar Mountain)-Dakota contact about here.
0.2	
228.2	Road is on Mancos Shale from here to Crescent Junction with west-dipping Dakota-Burro Canyon (Cedar Mountain) on the right.
1.6	
229.8	Airport Road on the left.
1.2	
231.0	Ferron Sandstone Member of Mancos at 9:00. Entrada dip slope at 3:00.
8.2	
239.2	Crossing the Salt Valley graben which is the north end of the Salt Valley anticline. Looking down Salt Valley at 5:00.
4.1	
243.3	**Turn right onto I-70 at the Crest Junction**

interchange. Book Cliffs on the left are formed by the rocks of the Mesaverde Group which overlie the Mancos Shale. In this area, the Mesaverde is composed of the Blackhawk Formation, Castlegate Sandstone, Sego Sandstone, Neslen Formation, Farrer Formation, and the Tuscher Formation. The Buck Tongue of the Mancos occurs between the Castlegate and Sego Sandstone. A sandstone of the upper Blackhawk and the Castlegate Sandstone form the lowest rim of the Book Cliffs. The escarpment formed by these cliffs marks the north side of the Grand Valley, and extends all the way to Grand Junction.

3.4

246.7 Tunnel under Interstate. At 9:00 the Sego Sandstone is visible above the Blackhawk-Castlegate rim. The Buck Tongue of the Mancos separates the Castlegate from the Sego. Above the Sego are rocks of the Neslen Formation.

1.4

248.1 Thompson exit. Settlement of Thompson at 11:00. Formerly known as Thompson's Springs, this was a watering point for the railroad. Until the spur line of the railroad was built to the Moab area, Thompson was the railhead for the Moab-Monticello area. Sego Canyon in the Book Cliffs is north of Thompson. Eight kilometers up the canyon is the coal-mining camp of Sego where large dinosaur tracks have been found.

0.7

248.8 Road cuts in the Mancos Shale.

0.4

249.2 Good view of the LaSal Mountains at 12:00.

1.4

250.6 Road cuts in Mancos Shale, Uncompahgre Plateau on the skyline straight ahead; Utah Tourist Information Center on the left.

1.1

251.7 The northwest nose of the Uncompahgre Plateau at 12:00, Sagers Wash syncline at 12:30 and Castle Valley at 1:00. Castle Valley is a salt anticline, on the north side of the LaSals, which is on trend with Paradox Valley. The prominent rims of the valley are formed by Wingate Sandstone.

2.5

254.2 Exit on the right goes to the Thompson mining district. Uranium-vanadium deposits occur in the Salt Wash Member of the Morrison Formation.

1.4

255.6 Northeast flank of Salt Valley exposed from 2:30 to 5:00.

4.0

259.6 Bridge over Pinto Wash. This particular area of the Grand Valley is known as Sagers Flats.

2.2

261.8 Red-colored cliffs at 11:00-12:00 are the Wingate Sandstone dipping northwest off of the nose of the Uncompahgre Plateau.

1.0

262.8 Good view of the Sagers Wash syncline at 1:00. This structure is formed between the Uncompahgre Plateau and the Salt Valley-Castle Valley-Paradox Valley salt anticlines. Good view of the Richardson amphitheater at 2:30. The amphitheater is adjacent to Castle Valley on the northeast. The monuments of Fisher Towers are barely visible on the northeast rim of the amphitheater. They are formed by coarse clastics of the Cutler Formation capped with Moenkopi.

2.6

265.4 Utah Highway 128 exit on the right. This highway goes to Moab, crossing the Colorado River at the Dewey Bridge, the only bridge on the Colorado River between Fruita, Colorado and Moab.

0.7

266.1 Bridge over Nash Wash. This is the approximate axis of the Sagers Wash syncline.

0.5

266.6 Overpass over the main line of the Denver and Rio Grande Western Railroad.

0.8

267.4 Bridge over Nash Canyon road. Cliffs of Wingate Sandstone dipping to the northwest at 12:00 to 1:00.

2.3

269.7 Bridge over Cisco Wash. Approximate axis of the Cisco dome. Settlement of Cisco at 2:00. In the past, Cisco was an important shipping point for sheep and cattle with water being pumped from the Colorado River 10 km to the south. Charlie Steen was living at Cisco when he discovered the Lisbon Valley uranium district and became a millionaire. Cliff dwellings have been found in the Book Cliffs north of Cisco.

0.8

270.5 Oil well on right of highway. A series of shallow, 300- to 600-m gas and oil wells are present along the route for the next 25 to 35 km. These are producing from both the Brushy Basin and Salt Wash Members of the Morrison and from the Entrada Sandstone. Small structures are the traps, such as Cisco and Harley domes.

1.7

272.2 Wingate Sandstone exposed in mesas and buttes at 1:00 to 2:00. High point of the

Uncompahgre Plateau at 2:30 is Pinon Mesa, capped by the Salt Wash Member of the Morrison Formation.

1.2

273.4 Dakota Sandstone exposed at 1:00 to 3:00 in floor of valley.

1.1

274.5 Road cut in Mancos shale. Roan Cliffs on the skyline at 12:00.

0.7

275.2 Exit right goes to Cisco and connects with Utah Highway 128.

1.5

276.7 Area of Westwater Canyon of the Colorado at 1:00 to 3:00. Here, the Colorado has cut a deep gorge into the Precambrian core of the Uncompahgre Plateau. The rapids in Westwater Canyon have become very popular for raft trips in recent years. Wingate Sandstone forms the red-colored cliffs of the canyon's tributary to the Colorado River.

2.6

279.3 Tree-covered slopes at 2:00 to 3:00 are formed by the upper Dakota Sandstone.

0.6

279.9 Bridge over Cottonwood Wash. Approximate axis of the northwest-plunging nose of the Uncompahgre Plateau.

2.8

282.7 Ranch exit on right. Tree-covered slopes at 11:00 to 2:30 are formed by the Dakota Sandstone on Harley dome.

1.3

284.0 Bridge over Westwater Wash.

1.6

285.6 Tree-covered slopes of Dakota Sandstone from 11:00 to 5:00 on the southwest flank of Harley dome.

1.7

287.3 Outcrops of Dakota Sandstone on both sides of highway.

0.6

287.9 Westwater exit. Westwater boat ramp of the BLM, 13 km south, is the launching point for raft trips through Westwater Canyon. Settlement of Harley Dome, Utah, at 9:00.

0.9

288.8 Road cuts in Dakota Sandstone. Highway descends the east flank of Bitter Creek anticline.

0.5

289.3 Road cut in Brushy Basin Member of the Morrison Formation.

0.2

289.5 Road cut in Burro Canyon Formation.

0.3

289.8 Road cut in Mancos Shale.

0.5

290.3 Dakota dip slopes from 12:00 to 3:00.

0.2

290.5 Road cut in Mancos Shale.

1.0

291.5 Bridge over West Bitter Creek. Exposures of Dakota on the right.

1.4

292.9 Colorado state line, enter Mesa County. Dip slope of Dakota on right.

0.8

293.7 Highway descends through the Dakota Sandstone into Rabbit Valley.

0.7

294.4 Rabbit Valley exit. Geologic section of the Dakota Sandstone, Burro Canyon Formation, Brushy Basin and Salt Wash Members of the Morrison Formation exposed in Rabbit Valley. A 21-km section of I-70 from the state line to Mack, Colorado, which includes this interchange, won first place in the Federal Highway Competition in 1974 for "the outstanding section of highway in the rural environment."

1.4

295.8 Exposures of sandstones of the Salt Wash Member on both sides of the highway. Dakota Sandstone caps mesa at 11:00 to 12:00.

0.9

296.7 Road cut in a sandstone of the Salt Wash.

1.2

297.9 Milepost 5. Roan Cliffs on skyline at 12:00. Highway ascends Brushy Basin section.

1.6

299.5 Dakota exposed in wash at 2:30.

2.4

301.9 Milepost 9. Dip slope of Dakota Sandstone on right. Settlement of Mack, Colorado at 10:00. This is the western limit of irrigation in the Grand Valley. Mack was the southern terminus of the old Uinta Railroad, a narrow-gauge line which hauled gilsonite from the Uinta Basin in Utah. The line, built about 1904, was abandoned in 1939. It also carried supplies to coal mining camps in the Book Cliffs. Grand Valley is eroded in Mancos Shale between Book Cliffs and Uncompahgre Plateau. It was named the Grand River Valley by Henry Gannett of the Hayden Survey in 1875.

0.7

302.6 Bridge over Salt Creek and main line of the D&RGW Railroad. Railroad follows Salt Creek to the Colorado River and parallels river through Ruby Canyon to Westwater.

0.1

302.7 Landslide areas on the right. Slide is caused by a sandstone in the Dakota which overlies a coal bed. Prospect trenches into the coal have allowed moisture to enter the coal bed causing the overlying sandstone to slip. Coal

FIRST DAY ROAD LOG

storage area at 10:00. Coal is produced from Mesaverde rocks in the Book Cliffs to the north.

1.0

303.7 Mack exit. Roan Cliffs, composed of the Paleocene-Eocene Wasatch Formation and the Eocene Green River Formation, visible above the Book Cliffs at 9:00 to 10:00. Colorado River at 1:00. Note steep dip of the Dakota Sandstone, marking the northeast flank of the Uncompahgre Plateau, on the right.

3.0

306.7 Steeply dipping Dakota hogback on right. Massive, red cliffs of Wingate Sandstone at 12:00 to 2:00.

1.1

307.8 Loma exit. Colorado Highway 139 provides access to northwestern Colorado over the Book and Roan Cliffs via Douglas Pass. Refinery at 12:00. This plant was operated by American Gilsonite Company from 1957 to 1974 and produced gasoline and other petroleum products from gilsonite. Powdered gilsonite was transported from mines near Bonanza, Utah, to the refinery via a 115-km slurry pipeline. In 1977, the plant and pipeline were acquired by the Gary Western Company and were converted to processing crude oil. The pipeline supplies oil from the Roosevelt, Utah area, and crude from the Rangely, Colorado area is trucked via Douglas Pass. In 1978 the refinery had a capacity of 14,000 barrels (2,226,000 l) per day.

0.9

308.7 Bridge over Reed Wash. Cliffs of Wingate Sandstone at 12:00 to 2:00; high point at 2:00 is Black Ridge capped by the Dakota Sandstone. Massive, salmon-colored cliffs across the Colorado River on the right are formed by the Entrada Sandstone.

0.7

309.4 Refinery at 9:00. Entrada Sandstone exposed in canyons at 3:00.

0.4

309.8 Bridge over north channel of the Colorado River; highway is located on an island between the two channels.

0.5

310.3 Bridge over north channel of the Colorado. Grand Mesa on skyline ahead.

1.1

311.4 Plant of Pabco Insulation on the left.

0.2

311.6 Bridge over Big Salt Wash.

0.6

312.2 Fruita exit. Colorado Highway 340 provides access to the Colorado National Monument to the south. This monument, containing 18,121 acres, was established May 24, 1911. It includes the dissected northeast flank of the Uncompahgre Plateau between Fruita and Grand Junction. The geologic section exposed in the monument includes Precambrian schist, gneiss, and granite, Chinle Formation, Wingate Sandstone, Kayenta Formation, Entrada Sandstone, Summerville Formation, Salt Wash and Brushy Basin Members of the Morrison Formation, Burro Canyon Formation, and the Dakota Sandstone. At this exit is a good view of the Colorado National Monument (3:00 to 4:00). Steeply dipping, massive cliffs of Wingate Sandstone exposed on right on the Lizard Canyon monocline. A few kilometers to the southeast the monocline becomes the Redlands fault with a maximum displacement of 245 m.

3.8

316.0 Frontage road overpass. Mt. Garfield at 10:00; Monument Canyon, in the Colorado National Monument, at 3:00.

1.7

317.7 Independence Monument in Monument Canyon at 4:00. This monument stands 137 m above the floor of Monument Canyon. It is formed by Wingate Sandstone and is capped by a thin remnant of the Kayenta Formation.

0.8

318.5 I-70 Business Loop exit. The Redlands area of Grand Junction is located at the foot of the Colorado National Monument at 2:00 to 5:00. The Entrada Sandstone is the principal aquifer for flowing artesian wells in the Redlands area.

1.9

320.4 24 Road exit. Note some remaining agricultural areas which have not been absorbed by recent growth in the Grand Junction area.

1.2

321.6 Refinery on the left. Refinery of Gardner Refinoil products processes used motor oil and new crude to make product known as Refinoil.

0.6

322.2 Cross the main Grand Valley Canal, one of three major systems that bring irrigation water to the Grand Valley.

1.8

324.0 Book Cliffs Country Club golf course on the right.

0.3

324.3 **Turn right onto the Horizon Drive exit.**

0.2

324.5 **Turn left** onto Horizon Drive.

0.1

324.6 Parking lot at the Holiday Inn. **End of First Day Road Log.**

Oblique aerial photographic view of the Roan Cliffs and Anvil Points experimental mine, Piceance Creek basin. U.S. Army Air Force photograph. (Courtesy C. W. Keighin, U.S. Geological Survey.)

SECOND DAY
ROAD LOG FROM GRAND JUNCTION TO GLENWOOD CANYON AND RETURN TO GRAND JUNCTION

by R. G. YOUNG, C. W. KEIGHIN, and J. A. CAMPBELL

FRIDAY, OCTOBER 9, 1981

Assembly Point: Holiday Inn, Grand Junction. Park cars and board buses.

Departure Time: 8:00 a.m.

Distance: 221.2 miles (road construction during logging may create errors in mileage).

Stops: 8

SUMMARY

The second day's field trip will cover the stratigraphy and structure of west-central Colorado. The stratigraphic sequence covered ranges from Proterozoic to Eocene in age and includes a wide variety of depositional environments. The major structural elements crossed include the east flank of the Uncompahgre Uplift, the Piceance Basin and the White River Uplift.

Mileage

0.0 Road log begins at intersection of I-70 and Horizon Drive in Grand Junction. **Turn from Horizon Drive onto I-70 east.** Basic geography:
- 9:00 Book Cliffs, average elevation 2150 m (7000 ft)
- 10:00 Little Book Cliffs, average elevation 2000 m (6500 ft)
- 11:00 Grand Mesa, average elevation 3050 m (10,000 ft)
- 2:00 San Juan Mountains, many peaks above 4250 m (14,000 ft)
- 3:00 Uncompahgre Plateau, average elevation 3050 m (10,000 ft)

GRAND JUNCTION

Prior to 1881 the Grand Valley of western Colorado was inhabited only by the Ute Indians. On September 4, 1881, the area was opened for settlement as the last of the Utes had been removed to reservations in eastern Utah. George A. Crawford, ex-governor of Kansas and a frontier capitalist and speculator, waited in Gunnison, Colorado while his associates William McGinley, O. D. Russell and J. C. Nichols rushed into the area to select a townsite for him. Their area of interest was the ford where the wagon road from the Uncompahgre Indian Agency to Salt Lake City crossed the Grand (Colorado) River near the confluence with the Gunnison River.

On September 26, 1881, the townsite was chosen on the north bank of the Grand River east of the junction with the Gunnison River and on October 10 a town company was formed. The settlers had difficulty in selecting a name for the settlement—proposed names included Ute, West Denver, and Bellyache Flats. The name Grand Junction finally was selected due to location of the junction of the Gunnison River with the Grand River. On June 22, 1882, the town of Grand Junction was officially incorporated.

Today, the tomb of George A. Crawford stands on a hill overlooking the junction of the two rivers. Crawford's settlement has now grown to a population of 58,000 and is the largest city between Denver and Salt Lake City.

1.8

1.8 Overpass. Exposures of Upper Cretaceous Mancos Shale, about 1525 m thick, on both sides of highway. Prominent salient of Little Book Cliffs at 12:00 is Mt. Garfield. Cliff formed by Upper Cretaceous littoral marine sandstones and marine and paludal shales of Price River Formation commonly referred to as Mesaverde Group. Notches on left mark positions of small faults. Mountain is on upper limb of small northeast-facing monocline. Regional dip of 8° to 10° to northeast increases to more than 27° on this flexure.

0.9

2.7 Light-colored outlier at 10:00 on horizon is Chalk Mountain, elevation 2466 m (8092 ft), formed mostly by marly units of Eocene Green River Formation.

1.8

4.5 Badlands at 10:00 formed by dissection of relatively weak upper half of Mancos Shale. Irrigation canal (Stub Ditch) to right of highway is highest canal in Grand Valley.

0.8

5.3 Clifton Interchange (I-70 Business Loop) and overpass.

0.4

5.7 Overpass. View of Mt. Garfield at 2:00. About halfway up Mancos slope is horizontal band of talus protecting underlying shale. Talus may be remnant of old "pediment" or upper portion of outwash terrace. Thin white sandstone at base of high cliff is littoral marine sandstone of Corcoran Member of Price River Formation that also includes overlying Palisade Coal and associated carbonaceous shale. A thin tongue of Mancos separates this unit from overlying littoral marine sandstone and associated mudstones of the Cozzette Member. Another thin Mancos tongue separates this Member from the "Rollins" sandstone and overlying Cameo Coal and carbonaceous shales of the Cameo Member. These three members here comprise the lower coal-bearing portion of the Price River (Mesaverde) Formation.

1.6

7.3 **STOP 1.** Discussion of local history and geology.

1.7

9.0 Milepost 40. Old Gearhart Mine dump and tram on left. Mine was in Palisade Coal bed above slump blocks and faults at base of high cliff.

0.3

9.3 Tram of old Garfield Mine at 9:00. Long-abandoned mine burned in about 1973 and resulting collapse caused large rock falls.

0.4

9.7 Approaching Palisade, elevation 1445 m (4740 ft). Good view of peach and pear orchards.

0.5

10.2 Exit 42 (Palisade). **Continue straight ahead.**

0.5

Figure 7.3a. Mt. Garfield, elevation 2062 m (6765 ft) (Chenoweth photo).

Figure 7.3b. Grand Mesa and the town of Palisade, looking southeast from Stop 1 (Chenoweth photo).

10.7	Masonry work on left designed to prevent erosion of Mancos.		
	0.4		
11.1	Town of Palisade on right has long been shipping point for pears, peaches, apples and other fruit. Ideally situated because of constant winds at mouth of DeBeque Canyon.		
	0.4		

10.7 Masonry work on left designed to prevent erosion of Mancos.

0.4

11.1 Town of Palisade on right has long been shipping point for pears, peaches, apples and other fruit. Ideally situated because of constant winds at mouth of DeBeque Canyon.

0.4

11.5 Old Palisade mines on left. Good view of Grand Mesa at 2:00. Mancos Shale, upper 150 m of formation, at base, overlain by Price River Formation, about 900 m thick, Wasatch Formation, about 450 m thick, Green River Formation, approximately 300 m thick, and Grand Mesa basalt, 60 m thick.

0.5

12.0 Portal of No. 3 Tunnel of Highline irrigation canal on right of roadway.

0.1

12.1 Palisade Greenhouse at 2:00.

0.2

12.3 Mt. Lincoln coal mine on left.

0.3

12.6 Old Farmers mine on left.

0.1

12.7 Cross Colorado River and D&RGW Railroad. Junction with U.S. 6-24 at east end of bridge. Enter DeBeque Canyon. We will traverse approximately 900 m of Price River (Mesaverde) strata between here and upper end of Canyon.

0.2

12.9 Old wier in river.

0.1

13.0 Tunnel No. 3 of Highline Canal back of outcrop on west side of river. Canal irrigates north side of Grand Valley. Landslide here on east side of Mt. Lincoln in spring of 1950 blocked tunnel, cut off irrigation water and interrupted railroad service. A special Congressional appropriation was rushed through, a contract awarded and 3 km of new tunnel driven in 19 days to save the valuable fruit crops. Small adits give access to tunnels.

0.5

13.5 Cameo coal exposed across river. Concrete structure along right side of highway is Orchard Mesa canal that irrigates part of south side of Grand Valley. Basalt boulders are from Grand Mesa basalt.

0.6

14.1 Cameo Exit. Roadside mine on right operated by GEX Colorado, Inc. Conveyor carries coal across river to loading facilities. All coal from mine is shipped to Pascagoula, Mississippi. Cameo Coal here is about 1.7 to 1.8 m thick with the 61-cm-thick Rider bed about 1 m above. About 15 m higher is Carbonara Coal, 1.8 to 2.1 m thick.

0.3

14.4 Cameo Power Plant of Public Service Co. of Colorado across river. Plant uses coal from Cameo mines and natural gas. Plant also is conducting test to determine effectiveness of nahcolite ($NaHCO_3$) for absorbing SO_2 from stack gas. Nahcolite is mined at Multi-Minerals shaft near C-b tract in Piceance Creek basin. Good view of landslide topography on east side of Mt. Lincoln behind power plant. Contact between lower coal-bearing and upper noncoal-bearing parts of Price River Formation on slope north of plant.

0.3

14.7 GEX open pit coal mine on right.

0.7

15.4 GEX coal stockpile and loading facilities across river along rail siding. Jerry Canyon enters from west.

0.2

15.6 Exit 47. State recreational area with swimming and camping facilities and small buffalo herd.

0.2

15.8 Overpass.

0.7

16.5 Good exposures of upper Price River (Mesaverde). High percentage of fluvial sandstone and minor amounts of carbonaceous shale and coal suggest deltaic environment.

0.2

16.7 Portal of Ute waterline from Plateau Creek at 2:00 high.

0.9

17.6 Exit 49. Highway 65 leads east up Plateau Creek to Mesa, Molina, Plateau City, Collbran and Grand Mesa.

0.1

17.7 Cross Plateau Creek. Lower reaches of this stream consist of a series of deeply incised meanders.

0.4

18.1 Steel Roller Diversion Dam, Grand Valley Project, U.S. Bureau of Reclamation (Water and Power Resource Service). Begun in 1912, completed in 1915. Dam is copy of first such type constructed in Germany using original plans with metric measurements. Dam supplies Highline (north) and Orchard Mesa No. 2 (south) canals. Diverts 900 million m³ (730,000 acre feet) per year for power and for irrigation of 14,000 hectares in Grand Valley. An additional 14,000 hectares are irrigated from private diversions downstream.

0.2

18.3 Enter two-lane highway. Price River

(Mesaverde) strata here dip 3° to 5° to northeast. Remnant of old stagecoach road across river.

0.5

18.8 Beavertail Tunnel on railroad across river. Twin tunnels of I-70 to be driven 100 m to right of railroad tunnel.

0.7

19.5 Shallow east-west syncline here marks south flank of Roberts Canyon anticline. Scattered juniper, pinon and serviceberry cover slopes. Sandbar willow and tamarisk thrive on river's edge. **Prepare to stop.**

0.5

20.0 **STOP 2.** Discussion of topography and geology.

0.2

20.2 Beavertail Tunnel exit on left. Note goose-nesting stands erected on islands by Colorado Department of Wildlife.

0.6

20.8 South flank of Roberts Canyon anticline. Fall of large rocks here appears related to faulting at DeBeque slide 300 m north.

0.2

21.0 DeBeque rock slide on right. Road cuts toe of slide causing instability. Movement of slide commonly coincides with movement on 3 small normal faults at head of slide mass. It has been suggested that fault movement occurs in response to withdrawal of natural gas from Dakota Sandstone reservoirs on Roberts anticline. Through 1979 Roberts Canyon unit had produced 10,641,890 m³ (375,773 MCF) gas. Cableway of Cameo gaging station (USGS) on left.

0.4

21.4 Strata on right dipping south.

1.0

22.4 Near axis of east-west-trending Roberts Canyon anticline. Also near northeast margin of ancestral Uncompahgre highland where onlapping Paleozoic strata dip northeast into Central Colorado basin.

1.1

23.5 Canyon entering from west is Jackson Canyon.

1.8

25.3 Sandstone quarry on left used by D&RGW to obtain ballast for protecting embankments. Note water seeping from sandstones on right.

0.4

25.7 Horseshoe Canyon enters from west across river. Cross East Horseshoe Creek. View ahead of Roan Cliffs (Tertiary strata).

0.4

26.1 Milepost 57. Excellent cross-bedding exposed in fluvial sandstones of Price River Formation on right.

0.6

26.7 Sandbars in river make popular habitat for local deer herd.

0.6

27.3 Uppermost Price River (Mesaverde) on right shows excellent cross-bedding in point bar deposits. Cliff capped by sandstone of uppermost Cretaceous Ohio Creek Formation.

0.6

27.9 Leave DeBeque Canyon and enter broad valley carved in Paleocene-Eocene Wasatch Formation (approximately 1525 m thick here). Roan Cliffs to north composed of upper part of Wasatch and overlying Eocene Green River Formation (about 1050 m thick) and Eocene Uinta Formation (approximately 120 m thick).

0.2

28.1 Milepost 59. Good view to the right (4:00) of contact of Cretaceous Price River with overlying Ohio Creek Formation. Brownish sandstone (about 5 m thick) of Ohio Creek rests disconformably on white sulfate encrusted Price River sandstone. Note honeycomb features of latter. Carbonaceous shale and thin coals in lower part of basal Atwell Gulch Member (Paleocene and Eocene) of Wasatch Formation poorly exposed in gravel-capped slope above Ohio Creek. Member is about 1050 m thick here.

1.2

29.3 Milepost 60. Cross Ashmead Draw. Horsethief Mt., elevation 2392 m (7846 ft), at 4:00.

1.1

30.4 **STOP 3.** Discussion of local geology and history.

0.4

30.8 Cross Little Horsethief Creek.

0.8

Figure 20.0. Price River (Mesaverde) Formation in DeBeque Canyon at Stop 2 (Chenoweth photo).

SECOND DAY ROAD LOG

31.6 DeBeque Interchange.
0.7
32.3 Cross Horsethief Creek. Note dark bands of carbonaceous shale and lignitic coal above river at 10:00.
0.5
32.8 Cross Colorado River. Mt. Logan, elevation 2574 m (8444 ft) straight ahead. Composed of Eocene Green River Formation capped by Eocene Uinta Formation.
0.6
33.4 Low hills ahead and on left formed by Molina Member (middle sandstone member) of Wasatch. Unit is about 120 m thick here and is mappable over a 500 km² area. Faunal remains indicate an Eocene age.
0.3
33.7 Battlement Mesa ahead. East-west elongate ridge averages 3170 m (10,400 ft) in elevation and is capped by late Miocene basaltic lava dated at 9.7 ± 0.5 m.y. (same age as lavas capping Grand Mesa). Note "pediment" or bajada surfaces merging with outwash terraces on south side of river.
1.2
34.9 Construction ends.
0.5
35.4 Milepost 66. Garfield/Mesa County line. Exposures here are of sandstones of Molina Member of Wasatch.
1.1
36.5 Occidental's Logan Wash in situ retort on skyline atop Mt. Logan at 9:00. Highway is on terrace supported by sandstones of Molina Member. Variegated beds above Molina are in Shire Member of Wasatch.
1.4
37.9 Excellent view (left) of Roan Cliffs. Lower slopes formed by reddish mudstones and sandstones of Shire Member of Wasatch. Shire is about 300 m thick here and grades upward and intertongues with Douglas Creek Member of Eocene Green River Formation. Douglas Creek is about 120 m thick and consists largely of cross-bedded, ripple-marked sandstone and algal and ostracodal limestone. Overlying the Douglas Creek Member is the Garden Gulch Member composed of about 180 m of gray shale and non-oil-bearing marls. Both are commonly lumped as Anvil Points Member. All the oil shales in this area are in the next higher unit, the Parachute Creek Member. This member is 300 m thick here and consists of interbedded oil shales, tuffs and marls. Most prominent of the oil shales is 29-m-thick Mahogany ledge about 58 m above the basal oil shale layer. Capping the Parachute Creek Member is the Eocene Uinta Formation composed of about 120 m of lenticular sandstone and siltstone beds with some interbedded marlstones.
1.0
38.9 Cross approximate axis of Crystal Creek anticlinal nose trending northwest.
1.3
40.2 Una siding on railroad.
0.5
40.7 Wallace Creek across river at 3:00 (south) was part of route reportedly traveled to Grand Mesa by Ute Indians with white women and children hostages taken during Meeker massacre of September 29, 1879.
2.0
42.7 Milepost 73. Mt. Callahan, elevation 2623 m (8607 ft), on the left rises 1100 m above Colorado River. The peak is capped by remnant of a basalt flow, probably once continuous with flows covering Battlement Mesa to south. Erosion by Colorado River since late Miocene time has isolated the flow remnant. Good exposures of stream channel deposits in Shire Member on left.
1.3
44.0 City limits of Parachute (formerly Grand Valley). Elevation 1553 m (5095 ft).
0.2
44.2 Cross Parachute Creek. Valley of Parachute Creek to north trends northwest approximately along the Eocene depositional axis of Piceance Creek Basin. The richest and thickest sequences of oil shale exposed along the southern margin of the basin are at the head of this valley. Ledges of oil shale beneath Mahogany ledge thicken to form a ledge in which the Colony Development Operation plant was located about 18 km up the valley. About 15 km up the valley is the site of the Union Oil pilot retort.
0.5
44.7 Leave Parachute. View south of High Mesa at 3:00 and site of new Exxon community (Battlement Mesa) across river at 2:00. **Prepare to stop.**
0.2
44.9 **STOP 4.** Discussion of Wasatch and Green River Formations.
0.2
45.1 Cross railroad spur leading to Union Oil retort 20 km up Parachute Creek. Spur not completed.
0.8
45.9 Good exposures (left) of color banding at Wasatch-Green River contact. Banding may reflect bleaching of red beds by reducing

Figure 44.9. Stop 4. Roan Cliffs northeast of Parachute Colorado. Lower slopes are in the Wasatch Formation and upper cliffs are in the Green River Formation (Baars photo).

waters percolating downward from organic-rich Green River beds.

1.8

47.7 Cottonwood Point at 9:00. Upper part of Wasatch and most of Green River well exposed here. Minor intertonguing between Shire Member of Wasatch and overlying Douglas Creek Member of Green River. At 4:00 across river is Battlement Creek. About 8 km up this creek is site of Rulison Project, a wholly contained 40 kiloton nuclear experiment conducted September 10, 1969. The device was exploded at a depth of 1654 m below the surface to test the use of nuclear explosives in fracturing and stimulating the production of natural gas from tight gas-bearing sandstones in upper Mesaverde. Subsequent tests indicated a cavity had formed and wellhead pressure had increased. However, the test demonstrated that the procedure is not economic, and the well remains shut, awaiting determination of radiation standards for marketing the slightly radioactive gas. The experiment was sponsored by the Atomic Energy Commission and Austral Oil Co. CER Geonuclear Corp. supplied engineering and project management for Austral.

0.4

48.1 New overpass (under construction).

1.8

49.9 Milepost 80.

1.4

51.3 Good exposures of Shire Member of Wasatch on left. Dominant plants on floodplain are greasewood, rabbitbrush and sage.

0.1

51.4 Rulison Interchange. Rulison gas field south of the river produces from fluvial sandstones in upper Mesaverde and lower Wasatch. Mesaverde production through 1979 was 104,642,286 m³ (3,694,351 MCF) gas and Wasatch production was 17,058,580 m³ (602,351 MCF) gas.

1.7

53.1 Anvil Points Interchange. Side trip to Paraho Oil Shale Demonstration Plant. **Prepare to turn.**

0.1

53.2 **Turn right onto exit. Turn left** toward Paraho Oil Shale Demonstration Plant and Naval Oil Shale Reserves 1 and 3.

0.3

53.5 View ahead of local section. Road ascends on sage-covered alluvium of Sharrard Park. Variegated beds of the Shire Member of the Wasatch Formation are exposed in juniper-pinon-covered hills at 9:00 and 1:00 and continue up slope to highest pinkish or reddish beds. Overlying the Wasatch and interfingering with it are siltstone, sandstone and marlstone beds of the Anvil Points Member (equivalent to Douglas Creek and Garden Gulch Members and lower part of Parachute Creek Member) of the Green River Formation. These beds weather to brown and tan and are overlain by whitish-weathering precipitous slopes of the Parachute Creek Member. This member contains the richest oil shale beds of the Piceance Creek basin. In this area Mahogany ledge occurs as first brown-weathering, projecting ledge above the base of the steep cliffs (note road leading to portals at 11:00). A 21-m-thick section of shale in the

Figure 53.5. Anvil Points area looking north at the Wasatch and Green River Formations (Baars photo).

Mahogany ledge averages about 93 l of oil/tonne (27 gal/ton), and of that section 18 m average 103 l (30 gal). Above the Mahogany ledge, about 140 m of oil shale average 34 to 52 l/tonne (10–15 gal/ton). The upper rounded portion of the cliffs is made by marlstone and sandstone of the Uinta Formation. Uinta supports cover of aspen, spruce and Douglas fir.

1.0

54.5 **Turn right** at sign pointing to Research Center.

0.4

54.9 Contact at 2:00 between Wasatch (below) and Green River (above) follows top of continuous red beds.

0.3

55.2 **STOP 5. Turn left** into parking lot. Guard station and gate to Paraho Research Center to the right. Entry is by permit only. Road log resumes at this gate after field trip stop. Discussion of stratigraphy of Green River Formation exposed in Anvil Points area, and general discussion of history and experimental methods of retorting oil shale at the Anvil Points Research Center. Road log resumes with vehicles returning south downhill to Anvil Points.

0.3

55.5 View south of Battlement Creek drainage and area of Project Rulison across river.

0.4

55.9 **Turn right** onto Anvil Points Circle Street. **Drive slowly.**

0.3

56.2 **Slow drive-by—on right.** Revegetation test plot of Colorado State University. Revegetation experiment on spent oil shale under controlled conditions of slope; soil to spent shale ratios; and irrigation. Spent shale was derived from earlier retorting experiments at the U.S. Bureau of Mines Anvil Points Research Center.

0.3

56.5 **Bear right (south) on road to return to I-70.** Ahead at 12:00 Battlement Mesa forms skyline.

1.0

57.5 **Return to I-70 to the right and continue east.**

2.0

59.5 Good exposures of Shire Member of Wasatch on left. White River Uplift at 12:00. Prominent River terraces at 3:00.

0.1

59.6 Crest of Webster Hill.

0.4

60.0 Major drainage at 3:00 across Colorado River is Porcupine Creek. Nearly 450 m of Wasatch, Green River and Uinta Formations are exposed in cirque-like features in upper reaches of the creek. Above Porcupine Creek, the highest knob on Battlement Mesa is North Mamm Peak, elevation 3390 m (11,123 ft), a remnant of a basalt flow.

1.7

61.7 Exit 87. West Rifle. At 11:00 is non-operating uranium-vanadium mill of Union Carbide Nuclear.

0.6

62.3 Cross railroad.

1.4

63.7 Cross Colorado River.

1.0

64.7 Bluff above floodplain on right probably mostly Pleistocene loess derived from floodplain.

0.6

65.3 Exit 90. Rifle-Meeker. Colorado Highways 13 and 789 give access to Piceance Creek basin oil shale development and to coal mining operations near Meeker and Craig. In August 1972, artist Cristo erected orange nylon curtain 900 m long across Rifle Gap, a watergap in the Grand Hogback about 10 km northeast of town.

0.6

65.9 At 9:00 (left), across river, is site of old Union Carbide uranium-vanadium mill and grassed over tailings pile. Note outwash gravels and loess in hill behind millsite.

2.1

68.0 View ahead (and left) of Grand Hogback on southwest flank of White River Uplift. Hogback is supported by vertical or near vertical beds of the Mesaverde Group. Beds of Paleocene and Eocene age southwest of the Grand Hogback dip at progressively lower angles up-section into the Piceance Creek basin. To the south, along the continuation of the fold, deep-seated thrusting has occurred.

1.1

69.1 Overpass and milepost 94. Note high "pediments" ahead at 12:00.

1.8

70.9 "Pediment" or bajada remnants at 9:00 still attached to hills.

0.6

71.5 Cross Colorado River. Note loess bluff on left. Harvey Gap at 10:00.

0.9

72.4 Exit 97 to Silt and to Divide Creek gas field.

1.3

73.7 Road cut on left shows Wasatch capped by outwash gravels.

1.5

75.2 Milepost 100.

0.7

75.9 Overpass.
1.3
77.2 On left at 9:00, yellowish-white sandstone below purplish-red Wasatch sandstone at 9:00 is Ohio Creek Formation.
0.4
77.6 Overpass.
0.1
77.7 New subdivision of town across river. Red slope on left formed of clinkers produced by burning of Wheeler and Allen coal beds at base of main part of Mesaverde. Contact with upper Mancos Shale tongue concealed here.
2.6
80.3 Exit 105 to Newcastle.
0.5
80.8 At 3:00 (south) is tipple formerly used to load coal mined from Wheeler and Allen coals. Small depressions along foot of slope mark position of mined and burned Wheeler coal.
0.2
81.0 Driving through Mancos Valley with main body of Mesaverde forming Coal Ridge to south and lower part of Mesaverde (Corcoran and Cozzette Members) exposed in low ridges to north. Natural gas is produced from sandstones in these latter units at Buzzard Creek and Divide Creek fields about 20 km south of the highway. Production at Divide Creek between August 1965 and the end of December 1979 was 1.246 billion m³ (43,998,657 MCF) natural gas; Buzzard Creek to that date had produced 125 million m³ (4,416,123 MCF) of gas. Two pale-red bands of the face of Coal Ridge to south are clinkers above burned coals. The lower band is the Wheeler bed, about 12 m thick, and the upper is the Allen coal bed about 6 m thick. Numerous explosions have occurred in coal mines in the Wheeler bed. The largest occurred on February 18, 1896 (49 dead), December 16, 1913 (37 dead) and November 4, 1918 (3 dead). On occasion smoke can still be seen rising from the burning beds and no snow lies here in winter.
1.2
82.2 Overpass.
0.3
82.5 Outcrop at 9:00 (north) of Mowry Shale capped by outwash gravel. River Bend village across river to south.
0.3
82.8 Dakota Sandstone forms hogback on right. Morrison Formation exposed below on north slope. Chinle Formation exposed on left of highway.
0.4
83.2 Chacra railroad signal house on left. Chain link fence across river at 3:00 (south) is dinosaur quarry in Morrison. Museum of Western Colorado (Grand Junction) removed some disarticulated bones of mixed dinosaur species. Nearby is an old prospect pit for uranium in the Morrison.
0.6
83.8 Excellent exposures at 1:00 (south) of a sequence of red beds overlain by tan and light-gray units. Four units comprise red slope: from bottom to top, they are the Maroon Formation (Permian); Weber Sandstone (Permian); the lower red beds member (Permian); the thin light-colored South Canyon Creek Member (Permian) and the overlying red beds of the upper member (Lower Triassic), all of the State Bridge Formation; and the Chinle Formation (Upper Triassic). The Entrada Sandstone (Upper Jurassic) overlies the Chinle and forms upper white band. The vegetated slope is formed on the Morrison Formation (Upper Jurassic) and the Dakota Sandstone (Upper Cretaceous) caps the ridge. The South Canyon Creek Member is correlative to part of Phosphoria Formation and equivalent strata of Utah, Idaho and Wyoming.
0.5
84.3 Overpass.
0.1
84.4 Exit 109. Canyon Creek.
0.5
84.9 Maroon Formation exposed on both sides of canyon. Light-colored Weber Sandstone caps slope on ridge to right (south).
0.4
85.3 Milepost 110.
0.2
85.5 Mud cracks and ripple marks exposed on parting surfaces of steeply dipping Maroon sediments on north (left) side of road.
1.0
86.5 Exit 111. South Canyon Creek.
0.4
86.9 South Canyon Creek at 3:00. Road to Coal Basin and to small hot springs now destroyed to prevent skinny-dipping.
0.4
87.3 Good exposure of Weber Sandstone at top of slope at 3:00. Maroon Formation about 1050 m thick here and dips steeply to southwest off White River Uplift, visible to northeast. White River Uplift, covering an area of more than 5200 km², is a domal upwarp covered by a blanket of Paleozoic sediments (commonly Leadville Limestone of Mississippian age). Volcanic extrusives of late Cenozoic age cover the northeastern part of the uplift and support

the highest area of the White River Plateau, the Flattops Wilderness area not visible here. The uplift is bounded on the north by a series of lesser folds including those of the Axial basin anticline. Bordering the uplift on the east is the Eagle River basin, a southeastward projecting tongue of the Sand Wash Basin, and on the west is the Piceance Creek basin. Dips on the east and north sides are relatively gentle; but on the west and southwest sides, along the Grand Hogback, the beds approach the vertical and in some places are somewhat overturned. Westward thrusting has been reported at depth along the Hogback, and large normal faults are common along the south flank near Glenwood Springs. Some uplift of this structure occurred in the Paleocene, but the major movement began in early-middle Eocene to produce the last of the Laramide mountains in the Colorado West.

1.7

89.0 Light-tan and gray Eagle Valley (Minturn Formation) evaporites of Pennsylvanian age exposed at 9:00 (left).

0.4

89.4 Exit 114. West Glenwood Springs. At 9:00 Leadville Limestone and Belden Formation (Pennsylvanian) dipping toward observer. At 11:00 are small Holly Sugar Co. quarries in cavernous Leadville. Note travertine terraces and spectacular exposures of outwash gravels on left. **Prepare to stop.**

0.8

90.2 **STOP 6.** Rest Area. Discuss geology. Broad fan at foot of red hill (right) on south side of Colorado River. Red beds in Maroon Formation (Pennsylvanian and Permian).

0.5

90.7 Good exposures of Belden Formation on left of highway.

0.1

90.8 Excellent view of Mt. Sopris up Roaring Fork valley (south). Mt. Sopris is a Tertiary stock intruded into Cretaceous beds. West Elk Mountains farther south on horizon are underlain by Oligocene and Miocene intrusive and extrusive rocks. **(See Gaskill and others, this guidebook.)**

0.2

91.0 Coal-loading facilities for Carbondale coal on right.

0.5

91.5 Leadville Limestone outcrops on left. Exit 116. Glenwood Springs-Carbondale-Basalt-Aspen. The town of Glenwood Springs, elevation 1751 m (5743 ft) at the confluence of the Colorado and Roaring Fork Rivers, was founded in 1882 by the Defiance Town and Land Co. It became the seat of Garfield County, organized the following year. The hot springs and mineral springs and the scenic beauty of the valley had long attracted the Ute Indians to this area because of the "miraculous healing powers" of the hot waters for both man and animals. It was not until 1882 that White man dreamed of turning the springs into a health spa. The Glenwood Hot Springs pool was constructed in 1888 after the Colorado River had been diverted from its original course north of the present Main Lodge to its present course. The original bathhouse was completed in 1891. The main spring has a daily flow of 16,350,000 liters of water at a temperature varying from 51 to 54°C (124–130°F). One of the most notorious of Glenwood Springs inhabitants was John Henry "Doc" Holliday, who came for the cure and is now buried here, having died of tuberculosis in 1887.

0.5

92.0 Vapor Springs Lodge and vapor caves in Leadville Limestone.

0.2

92.2 Excellent exposure of Molas Formation (Pennsylvanian red beds) resting on and filling sinks in karst in Leadville Limestone on left. A good section of Belden Formation, 185 m thick, is present across the river above the houses.

0.1

92.3 Road-cut in Leadville Limestone. Hot springs in river bed south of highway. Strong odor of H_2S.

0.1

92.4 Across river, Leadville Limestone forms massive cliff exhibiting solution cavities.

0.1

92.5 Chaffee Group (Devonian) exposed across river.

0.1

92.6 Across river, Dotsero Formation (Cambrian) and Manitou Formation (Ordovician) are exposed as thin-bedded units. Leadville Limestone at top of cliffs. Several normal faults with small displacements, down on northeast side, visible in cliff.

0.1

92.7 Leave Glenwood Springs.

0.1

92.8 Railroad tunnel across river in Sawatch Quartzite (Cambrian).

0.2

93.0 Cambrian-Precambrian contact.

0.1

93.1 Enter tunnel in Precambrian rocks (Idaho Spring Formation equivalent).

	0.2
93.3	Exit tunnel. Leadville Limestone in road cut. Precambrian on right. Normal fault crosses road near exit. Look for it on return trip!
	0.4
93.7	Molas Formation on left covering karst surface of Leadville Limestone Cliffs on south side of river contain all formations from Sawatch Quartzite to Leadville Limestone.
	0.3
94.0	No Name Exit. No Name Creek.
	0.3
90.3	Cross fault. Proceeding down section. **Prepare to stop.**
	0.4
94.7	**STOP 7.** Discussion of local geology.
	0.2
94.9	Across river, gray ledge of Leadville Limestone. High brush-covered slopes are formed on Belden Formation and lower part of Minturn Formation.
	0.2
95.1	Sawatch Quartzite exposed on both sides of canyon.
	0.6
95.7	White River National Forest boundary. Thin-bedded Sawatch Quartzite across river.
	0.9
96.6	Cross Grizzly Creek. Heart of river-rafting stretch of Colorado River. Precambrian rocks exposed here consist of granites, pegmatites and gneisses.
	0.4
97.0	Green epidote and pegmatites in exposures on left.
	0.6
97.6	Precambrian-Paleozoic contact at 12:00 high.
	0.8
98.4	Shoshone power plant. Penstocks bring water down from tunnel carrying water from Shoshone Dam 4 km upstream.
	0.7
99.1	Note potholes in polished gray granite in river bed.
	0.5
99.6	Pegmatites in road cuts.
	1.0
100.6	Big rapids on right (when river is running). Several fatalities among rafters have occurred here. Now off limits for boating. Impending construction of four-lane I-70 through Glenwood Canyon has caused much controversy. Current plans call for construction in the near future. Some of highway will be double decked to preserve canyon's beauty. This will be one of last sections of I-70 to be completed, but it will eliminate or at least reduce driving risks on a very hazardous stretch of highway.
	0.2
100.8	Shoshone dam and intake. At 1:00 is complete section from Sawatch Quartzite through Leadville Limestone.
	0.7
101.5	Hanging Lake Trail and Deadhorse Creek. Precambrian exposed on either side of river. Note coarse pegmatites as we approach Cambrian-Precambrian contact.
	0.3
101.8	On right is contact of Sawatch with Precambrian.
	0.5

Figure 94.7. Glenwood Canyon looking east from Stop 7 (Baars photo).

Figure 97.6. Glenwood Canyon looking east. Precambrian-Paleozoic contact at 12:00 high (Baars photo).

SECOND DAY ROAD LOG

Figure 102.3. Glenwood Canyon looking east. Sawatch Quartzite at road level and Belden Shale on top of hill (Baars photo).

102.3 Precambrian rocks on both sides of river. Inner canyon walls formed by Sawatch, Dotsero and Manitou Formations in a near-vertical cliff about 300 m high. Note that the upper 60 m of Sawatch Quartzite at base of sedimentary section consists of light-colored, dense, thin quartzite beds that give it a banded appearance. Notch in cliff below banded beds is formed by a glauconitic sandy dolomite 23 m thick. Total thickness of Sawatch Quartzite is about 150 m.
0.3

102.6 Contact between Precambrian and Sawatch Quartzite 3 to 4 m above highway.
0.8

103.4 Cliff of upper part of Sawatch Quartzite.
0.1

103.5 Cross French Creek. North of bridge cliff of Manitou Dolomite and upper part of Dotsero Formation. Clinetop algal limestone (upper unit of Dotsero Formation) is 1.2 m prominent bed, 50 m above valley floor. Dotsero Formation here is about 30 m thick.
0.3

103.8 Road cut in Dotsero Formation. Clinetop algal limestone member is thick, wavy bed at base of cliff, about 25 m above highway.
0.1

103.9 Brown cliff 30 m above road on left is Tie Gulch Member of Lower Ordovician Manitou Formation. Underlying beds are Dead Horse Member of Manitou containing thin beds of flat-pebble or edgewise conglomerate. In this area Tie Gulch Member is about 20 m thick and Dean Horse Member is about 30 m thick. Slopes below cliff are best collecting locality for Ordovician trilobites, brachiopods and gastropods.
0.4

104.3 Leave White River National Forest. Cliff north of road formed by Tie Gulch Member.
0.3

104.6 Belden Formation (Pennsylvanian) exposed in graben in hills north of road and in big hills south of river. Ahead is cliff of Leadville Limestone underlain by Chaffee Group consisting of Dyer Formation, 56 m thick, at top and Parting Formation, 30 m thick, at base.
0.3

104.9 Tie Gulch. Cliff east of gulch formed by Tie Gulch Member.
0.6

105.5 Sawatch Quartzite here slightly rose colored which is an unusual development. Note strongly developed northeast and northwest joint systems and prominent alteration along joints.
0.1

105.6 The notch in cliff above railroad tracks across the river is formed by 23-m-thick glauconitic dolomite in Sawatch Formation.
0.3

105.9 Road cut in Sawatch Quartzite. Here Sawatch makes main cliff above highway. Scrub junipers above Sawatch mark position of Dotsero Formation. Top brown cliff formed by Manitou Formation.
0.3

106.2 Note prominent joints in Manitou Formation, north side of road.
0.3

106.5 Cliff of Manitou Formation next to road.
0.1

106.6 Eagle County line. Contact between Manitou and Parting Formations.
0.1

106.7 Green shale overlain by black shale and in turn by light tan quartzite in Parting Formation.
0.1

106.8 Road cut in Broken Rib Member of Dyer Formation. **Prepare to stop.**
0.1

106.9 **STOP 8.** Discussion of geology.
0.2

107.1 Leave Glenwood Canyon.
0.2

107.3 Hills north of highway and south of river formed by Belden Formation.
0.1

107.4 Warm springs on both sides of Colorado River. Low ridge of travertine shows in bottomland across river. Large volume of salt enters river at this point. Salt is from Eagle Valley evaporites. Road cut on northwest side of highway exposes top of Leadville Limestone, a few meters of varicolored shale of Molas Formation and thin beds of gray limestone at base of Belden Formation.

0.7

108.1 Belden Formation north of highway.

0.8

109.7 Railroad cuts south of river expose dark gray shales and thin limestone in Belden Formation.

0.3

110.0 On north side of highway distorted gypsum beds of Eagle Valley evaporites cap low hills on steeply dipping south flank of Dotsero anticline, whose crest lies about 1 km north of highway. **Prepare to exit.**

0.6

110.6 **Take Exit 133.** Dotsero. Road leads north to Burns, McCoy, Oak Creek and Steamboat Springs. **Turn right. End of Road Log for Second Day. Return to Grand Junction via I-70. Banquet at Holiday Inn at 7:30 p.m.**

Figure 110.6. Dotsero, Colorado. Looking east. Low gray hills to the left of the highway are the Eagle Valley Evaporite Member of the Minturn Formation (Baars photo).

Mancos Shale badlands northeast of Montrose, Colorado, below Gunnison uplift on the skyline. (Courtesy W. R. Hansen, U.S. Geological Survey.)

THIRD DAY
ROAD LOG FROM GRAND JUNCTION TO CRESTED BUTTE VIA DELTA, MONTROSE AND GUNNISON

Grand Junction to Montrose
C.S. GOODKNIGHT, R. D. COLE and R. A. CRAWLEY

Montrose to Crested Butte
B. BARTLESON and D. GASKILL

SATURDAY, OCTOBER 10, 1981

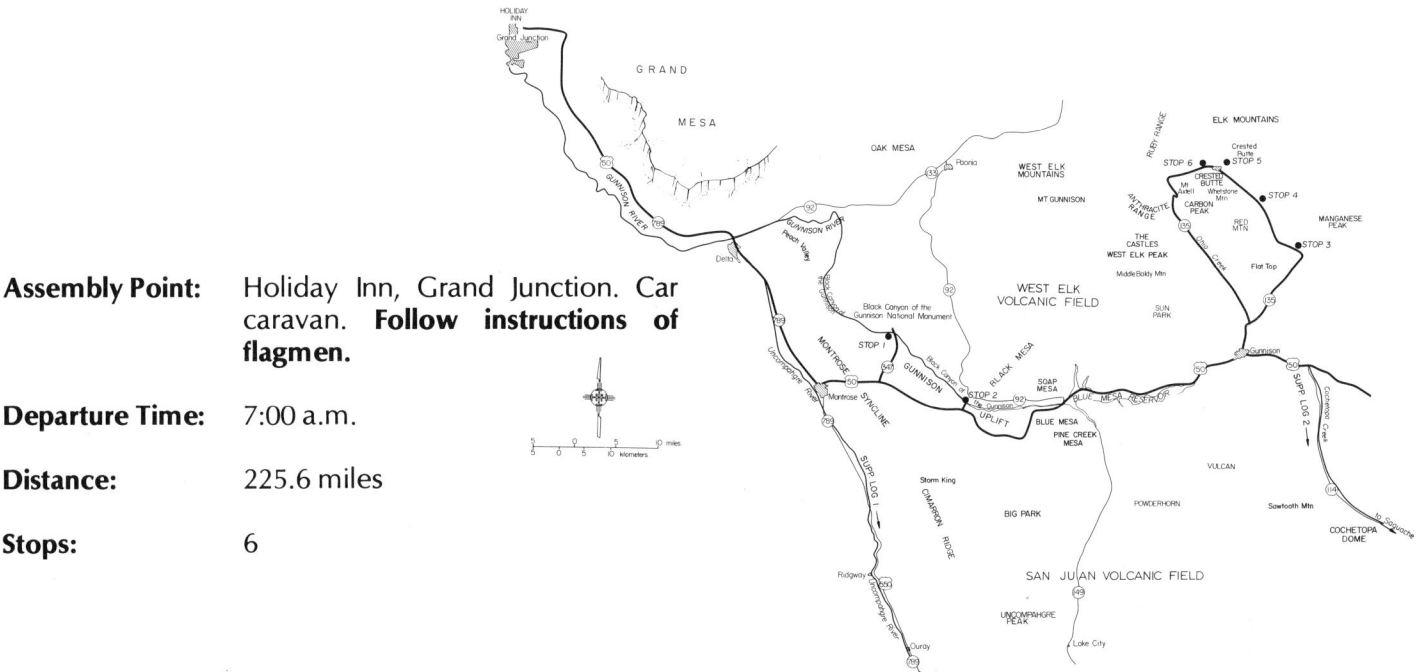

Assembly Point: Holiday Inn, Grand Junction. Car caravan. **Follow instructions of flagmen.**

Departure Time: 7:00 a.m.

Distance: 225.6 miles

Stops: 6

SUMMARY

Today's route leads southeast from Whitewater, Colorado, through the desolate Mancos Shale deserts surrounding Grand Junction to the alpine meadows of Crested Butte. The first 100 or so kilometers will traverse Cretaceous sedimentary rocks flanked on the east and west by Jurassic to Precambrian rocks. These older rocks constitute the cores of the Uncompahgre and Gunnison uplifts. Most of the softer sedimentary rocks between Whitewater and Montrose are veneered by Pleistocene terrace and pediment gravels. **(See Sinnock; Cole and Sexton, this guidebook.)**

Between Montrose and Gunnison, the route traverses Mesozoic and Cenozic sedimentary rocks with passages through canyons of the Precambrian Black Canyon schist and gneiss complex. Adjacent to the route, in the Blue Mesa Reservoir area, Oligocene volcanic and volcaniclastic units erupted from the San Juan and West Elk volcanic fields are conspicuous. **(See Gaskill and others, this guidebook.)**

Between Gunnison and Crested Butte the route will cross the east flank of the paleo-Uncompahgre uplift. The mining activity of the Crested Butte area will be the emphasis of this part of the trip. **(See Dowsett and others; Mutschler and others, this guidebook.)**

Mileage

0.0 Holiday Inn, **proceed south on Horizon Drive.**

0.1

0.1 **Turn left** onto I-70 at the Horizon Drive interchange.

1.2

1.3 Walker Field control tower at 9:00, Mt. Garfield at 12:00.

0.4

1.7 Milepost 33.

0.2

1.9 29 Road underpass.

0.3

2.2 Highline Canal on the right.

0.5

2.7 Milepost 34. Chalk Mountain capped with Green River Formation at 11:00.

	1.7
4.4	Road cut in Mancos Shale.
	0.5
4.9	Road cut in Mancos.
	0.2
5.1	Road cut in Mancos. **Prepare to turn.**
	0.3
5.4	**Turn right onto the Clifton exit to I-70 Business Loop.** Road cuts in Mancos.
	0.2
5.6	Cross the Highline Canal and enter Clifton, Colorado.
	0.6
6.2	Traffic light at Patterson Road (F Road), **continue straight ahead.**
	0.5
6.7	Traffic light at 32 Road, **turn left.**
	0.2
6.9	Cross main line of the Denver and Rio Grande Western Railroad. Excellent view of Mt. Garfield at 9:00.
	0.4
7.3	Cross the Grand Valley Canal.
	1.1
8.4	Intersection with D Road.
	0.3
8.7	Clifton sewer lagoons on the left.
	0.1
8.8	Gravel pit, now stocked with trout, on the right.
	0.1
8.9	Bridge over the Colorado River.
	0.1
9.0	Road cut in Mancos Shale overlain with river gravels.
	0.4
9.4	Intersection with C Road.
	0.4
9.8	Cross Orchard Mesa Canal No. 1.
	0.9
10.7	Cross Orchard Mesa Canal No. 2.
	1.1
11.8	Steel building on small Mancos hill at 12:30 is water filtration plant and water tank for Orchard Mesa area. **Prepare to turn.**
	0.3
12.1	**Junction with U.S. Highway 50. Turn left at stop sign.** The area of Unaweep Canyon, which cuts across the Uncompahgre plateau, at 10:30.
	2.6
14.7	Junction of U.S. Highway 50 and Colorado Highway 141; **continue straight ahead.** Highway 141 to the right crosses the Uncompahgre uplift (we went that way the first day).

The Gunnison River, visible at 3:00, exists in a shallow canyon on the northeastern flank of the Uncompahgre uplift. This canyon, which penetrates Precambrian crystalline rock near Bridgeport, parallels Highway 50 for the next 40 km.

At 2:00, about 3 km away, is the dam site of the proposed Dominguez Reservoir. The dam will flood the Gunnison River canyon and will form a narrow reservoir about 38 km long. The reservoir will have a storage capacity of 372 million m³ (302,000 ac-ft) and will support the municipal and agricultural needs of the Grand Valley as well as yield hydroelectric power.

	0.6
15.3	Bridge over Whitewater Creek.
	0.3
15.6	Roadcut in lower Mancos Shale.
	0.3
15.9	At 9:00 are large, rounded limonite-stained carbonate concretions exposed in two horizons along the left side (east) of the road most of the way to Delta.
	1.3
17.2	At 3:00 are three radio towers (KREX), and at 2:00 is Desert Reservoir.
	1.2
18.4	Two solar-powered houses in a small settlement of "Mancos dwellers" on both sides of the highway. The solar heating works quite well in late July.
	0.6
19.0	Road to left (Lands End Road) climbs to the top of Grand Mesa (switchbacks at 9:00), a basalt-capped plateau at an elevation of 3050 m (10,000 ft). The stratigraphic section beneath the basalt is comprised of the Green River, Wasatch, and Mesaverde Formations and the Mancos Shale.

Beneath the basalt cap are four levels of Pleistocene pediments. Examples are Purdy and Reeder Mesas. These pediments are Bull Lake and Pinedale in age and are capped by 5 to 10 m of poorly sorted gravel dominated by basalt clasts. These pediments will be quite evident to the east and northeast of Highway 50 as the route continues to Delta. **(See articles by Sinnock and Cole and Sexton, this guidebook.)**

	0.1
19.1	Bridge over Kannah Creek. At 9:00 is the "Kannah Creek Zoo," a collection of African mammals brought to the Mancos desert by an enterprising naturalist.
	1.2
20.3	Road climbs grade up onto a Pinedale pediment surface. At crest of hill are weathered roadcuts of pediment gravel made up of well-rounded basalt cobbles and boulders.

Figure 20.3. Grand Mesa and pediment surfaces, looking east (Goodknight photo).

Figure 20.6. Stinking Desert National Monument (Goodknight photo).

Gravel excavation operation at 3:00. Beneath pediment gravels are several horizons of fossiliferous siltstone in the Mancos Shale; small pelecypods are common. Pediments of the Kannah Creek embayment are very conspicuous at 8:00 to 11:00.

0.3

20.6 Cross Indian Creek. The panorama at 12:00 is of the famous "Stinking Desert National Monument" which stretches for the next 30 km or so. The monument (not shown on maps) is not sanctioned by any branch of the state or federal governments. The monument was created in 1979 by the "Friends of the Desert," a small group of zealots from Grand Junction. On Labor Day weekend, signs appear to notify passing pilgrims of the monument's existence. A pamphlet detailing all of the points of interest in the monument is available at the Fools' Hill Rest Area.

0.4

21.0 More exposures of limonite concretions visible at 10:00.

0.7

21.7 Extensive dip slope of Dakota Sandstone off of the Uncompahgre uplift visible at 1:00 to 4:00. This area is referred to as the Hunting Ground.

1.0

22.7 Route traverses a late Pinedale pediment surface. This pediment is covered by a one-pebble thick veneer of rounded basalt pebbles and cobbles.

2.1

24.8 Cross King Creek. At 10:00 is Indian Point (elevation of 3048 m, 10,000 ft), one of the two prominent basalt arms of Grand Mesa.

0.8

25.6 Road to right (west) leads to Bridgeport on the Gunnison River where Precambrian, Triassic, Jurassic and Cretaceous rocks are exposed.

1.1

26.7 Entering Delta County.

0.5

27.2 At 8:00 is "Paradox Mesa," a pre-Bull Lake pediment. Several tens of meters of yellow, weathered Mancos Shale are present beneath the pediment gravels.

At 4:00 is Dominguez Canyon, formed by deep entrenchment of Big Dominguez Creek into the east side of the Uncompahgre uplift. The red outcrops in the canyon are mainly Triassic Chinle Formation and Wingate Sandstone.

0.2

27.4 Distant panorama of the San Juan Mountains at 12:00.

1.1

28.5 Bridge over Beaver Gulch. The namesake for this creek is difficult to envision.

0.7

29.2 Uppermost Dakota Sandstone crops out in

roadcut to right; road rests on top of Dakota for next 1 km.
0.2

29.4 Juniper "Christmas Tree" along right shoulder of highway is decorated each holiday season following a tradition started in the 1930's. The tree was spared when Highway 50 was widened 20 years ago and now serves as the official forest preserve of the "Stinking Desert National Monument."
0.3

29.7 Roadcut at 9:00 exposes upper Dakota Sandstone and about 1 m of carbonaceous shale and shaly coal interbedded with sandstone and shale.
0.4

30.1 Wells Gulch at 3:00 exhibits exposures of Dakota Sandstone, Burro Canyon Formation and the Brushy Basin Member of the Morrison Formation (Jurassic).
0.1

30.2 Small-displacement normal fault exposed in roadcut at 9:00.
0.5

30.7 Turn off at 3:00 leads down Wells Gulch into Dominguez Canyon and the Gunnison River.
1.7

32.4 Rounded hills at 11:00 represent dissected remnants of former pediment surfaces.
0.7

33.1 Road to right (west) leads to the Gunnison River and Escalante Canyon beyond.
1.6

34.7 Dakota Sandstone is exposed at the heads of several canyons at 3:00.
0.8

35.5 Bull Lake age pediments at 10:00 on southwest flank of Grand Mesa. The West Elk Mountains in the distance at 11:00 are formed by Oligocene laccoliths and stocks. The northern end of the Gunnison uplift, at 12:00, developed during the Laramide and was rejuvenated during the late Tertiary and entrenched by the Gunnison River. **(See Hansen, this guidebook.)** At 1:00 and 2:00, Cimarron Ridge is capped by resistant Oligocene volcanic rocks erupted from the San Juan Mountains (2:00 to 3:00). South-trending fault crosses road.
1.4

36.9 Bridge over Alkali Creek.
0.9

37.8 Road to left (north) leads to Star Nelson Ranch.
0.6

38.4 At 3:00, the Gunnison River begins its entrenchment into the eastern flank of the Uncompahgre uplift. Pleistocene alluvial terraces appear along the Gunnison River. These terraces can be traced from here to Ridgway, Colorado.
1.4

39.8 Delta Speedway to the left (north).
0.2

40.0 Cross deep arroyo cut into Mancos Shale.
1.8

41.8 At 11:00 are the Ragged Mountains, the northernmost part of the West Elk Mountains. At 10:00 are several Pleistocene glacial outwash surfaces prograding southward off Grand Mesa.
0.7

42.5 Western Tanning to the right (south). Hold your nose!
1.1

43.6 Ute Council Tree is located down the road to the right.
0.8

44.4 Bridge over Gunnison River; entering Delta.
0.3

Figure 29.4. Stinking Desert National Forest (Goodknight photo).

Figure 29.7. Roadcut in upper part of the Dakota Sandstone (Goodknight photo).

THIRD DAY ROAD LOG

44.7 At 3:00 is a now-defunct sugar refinery operated previously by Holly Sugar Company. The tall silos are being considered for the storage of coal.
0.1

44.8 **Junction; continue straight ahead.** Colorado 92 to the left goes eastward up the North Fork Valley to Hotchkiss and Paonia. Entering business district of Delta, a small city founded at the juncture of the Uncompahgre and Gunnison Rivers, and supported primarily by agricultural activity.
1.2

46.0 Highway travels on Uncompahgre River floodplain. Denver and Rio Grande Western railway tracks to the right (west) parallel route for most of the way to Montrose.
0.4

46.4 Coors barley storage facility at 3:00.
1.0

47.4 Road to left (east) to Sweitzer Lake.
1.4

48.8 Delta-Montrose Vocational and Technical Center to the left.
0.4

49.2 On the horizon at 11:00 are dark, steep walls composed mainly of the Proterozoic Pitts Meadow Granodiorite (1730 ± 190 m.y.). The high walls represent the eastern side of the Black Canyon of the Gunnison, which reaches a maximum depth of 650 m.
1.0

50.2 Route passes through the broad Uncompahgre River Valley (up to 30 km wide), formed on the northwest-trending Montrose syncline.
1.7

51.9 Entering Montrose County. Road climbs up low alluvial terrace of Pleistocene age.
0.8

52.7 Bridge crosses Loutsenhizer Wash.
1.3

54.0 The Gunnison uplift at 9:00 is part of the more extensive Uncompahgre-San Luis highland. The uplift plunges to the northwest and is asymmetric; its west and south flanks dip the steepest and are bounded in part by faults **(see Baars and Stevenson; Hansen, this guidebook).**
0.4

54.4 Underground onion storage cellars at 3:00.
1.5

55.9 **Junction;** business route of Highway 50 to Olathe on the right. **Bear left on U.S. 50; stay on U.S. 50.**
1.3

57.2 At 3:00 are two Pleistocene alluvial terraces formed by the Uncompahgre River. The highest terrace is High Mesa.
0.9

58.1 Dip slope at 8:00 at the northwest side of the Gunnison uplift. Dark cliffs beyond red horizons are composed mainly of migmatitic gneiss of Precambrian X age. The Precambrian rocks have been uplifted along a major high-angle reverse fault called the Red Rocks Fault. The fault extends about 32 km and forms part of the southern margin of the Gunnison uplift. Vernal Mesa forms the horizon at 10:00.
3.5

61.6 Highway descends from East Mesa to the Uncompahgre River floodplain.
0.4

62.0 Deep road cut at 9:00 in Mancos Shale.
0.6

62.6 Horsefly Peak (elevation 3154 m, 10,348 ft) at 2:00 is the highest point on the Uncompahgre Plateau, near its southeastern end. The peak is capped and flanked by a pre-Wisconsin till. At 1:00 is Dallas Divide and the imposing north-facing range which marks the northwestern edge of the San Juan Mountains.
0.9

63.5 Terraces of the Uncompahgre River are represented by North Mesa at 9:00 and Spring Creek Mesa at 3:00.
2.5

66.0 Street to left (northeast) to Montrose County Airport.
0.4

66.4 City of Montrose.
0.6

67.0 Traffic light; **continue straight ahead. Stay on U.S. 50.**
0.2

67.2 Traffic light at highway intersection; **turn left on U.S. 50 toward Gunnison.** U.S. 550 proceeds straight ahead (south) through the San Juan Mountains to Durango. Colorado Highway 90 to the right leads southwest over the Uncompahgre Plateau to Naturita.
0.7

67.9 View straight ahead of the Red Rocks-Cimarron fault scarp which is formed by two en echelon faults trending northwest-southeast. The Cimarron fault can be traced for at least 64 km southeast to Powderhorn and has a vertical displacement of up to 1525 m. Motion has been recurrent, mainly in the Precambrian, late Paleozoic, and during the Laramide orogeny. These faults form the southern margin of the Gunnison uplift into which the Black Canyon of the Gunnison River is carved.
0.9

Mile	Description
68.8	Edge of town, yellow to gray slopes of Mancos straight ahead.
	0.2
69.0	View left (north) of the monoclinal fold of the west flank of the Gunnison uplift. The red rocks are the Entrada Sandstone dipping about 20° west and resting on the Precambrian. The mesa to the north in the foreground is Table Mountain and consists of Mancos shale capped by high terrace gravels.
	1.3
70.3	View of Cimarron Ridge capped by Oligocene volcanics at 2:00 in medium distance. Due south about 3:00 in far distance is the skyline of the San Juan Mountains with the high point being Mt. Sneffels (elevation 4313 m, 14,150 ft), glacially carved out of Oligocene volcanics.
	2.1
72.4	Cimarron fault scarp straight ahead. Northeast side is up. The mesa at 10:00, about a hundred meters above the level of the road, is Bostwick Park, a terrace which is the remnant of a stream that formerly flowed northward into the Gunnison, but erosion into the soft Mancos Shale by Cedar Creek, a westward flowing tributary of the Uncompahgre River, has captured the drainage of this older valley.
	2.6
75.0	Junction with Colorado Highway 347. **Turn left onto 347** for side trip to the Black Canyon National Monument.
	0.9
75.9	Road climbs to the north in the Mancos Shale.
	0.5
76.4	Top of terrace capped by reddish Quaternary gravels that floor Bostwick Park.
	0.8
77.2	Cross into zone of faults of the Cimarron fault zone. Road cuts in Morrison-Burro Canyon.
	3.2
80.4	Entrance sign to the Black Canyon National Monument.
	0.3
80.7	Junction with road to Crystal Dam site. **Stay to left.**
	0.2
80.9	Road to campground to the right.
	0.1
81.0	Grand Mesa at 12:00. Uncompahgre Plateau at 9:00.
	0.7
81.7	Tomchi Point turn-out to the right. **Prepare to stop.**
	0.4
82.1	**STOP 1.** Gunnison Point. Pull around and park close to the visitor's center for short discussion of the geology. **Return to Highway 50.**
	7.1
89.2	**Turn left on Highway 50 to Gunnison.**
	2.0
91.2	Beginning of large series of slide-flow complexes on right on south side of Cedar Creek. The steep slopes of Mancos capped by stream gravels above were relatively stable even after the Denver and Rio Grande railroad grade undercut them in the 1880's. However, an unlined irrigation ditch built later on the top of the mesa (Cedar Park) allowed seepage into the Mancos and this triggered the slope failures.
	0.5
91.7	Mud flow to right.
	0.5
92.2	Excellent example of rotational slump with conspicuous scarps above grading into an earth or mud flow below. The old D&RG railroad grade is clearly evident to right down low. Begin ascending Cerro Summit.
	1.3
93.5	Steep, narrow gully and slope failure in Mancos are evident straight ahead on left side of road.
	1.3
94.8	Talus blocks of volcanics on Mancos above road to left (9:00) are from Poverty Mesa on the upthrown side of the Cimarron fault.
	1.0
95.8	Good view of Poverty Mesa at 9:00 in distance.
	0.2
96.0	Cerro Summit, Mancos Shale in road cuts. Irrigation flume overhead.
	0.3
96.3	On right at 1:00-2:00 note abundant slope failures in covered Mancos slopes. Straight ahead is excellent view of the Cimarron fault with Precambrian schist and gneiss (dark colored) cut by granites and pegmatites faulted up adjacent to the covered Mancos slopes below. The conspicuous gap in the scarp at 12:30-1:00 is caused by the incision of Cimarron Creek, which enters the Black Canyon. This is where the D&RG railroad emerged from the Black Canyon on its route from Gunnison to Montrose. The light-colored "beds" just above and east of the gap are granite dikes and sills cutting the Precambrian metamorphics.
	1.0
97.3	Good view of debris flow in Mancos with slump scarp above at 1:00. Note aspen groves confined to gulches where water occasionally occurs.
	1.6

98.9 Abundant talus blocks of Precambrian pegmatite on Mancos on left from fault scarp. Some of these blocks appear to be incorporated in colluvium and are going for a ride in the mass-wasting forms.
0.9

99.8 Pink pegmatite talus blocks.
0.4

100.2 Slump block at right at 1:00, highly vegetated.
0.9

101.1 Cimarron, old railroad town.
0.2

101.3 Entrance to Morrow Point Dam. **Turn left** for side trip to dam site and good view of Black Canyon and Precambrian rocks.
0.1

101.4 Good exposure of Cimarron fault ahead. The Mancos Shale is overturned adjacent to the fault and the Precambrian rocks are gray mica schists on the limb of a north-trending antiform on the north, or upthrown side of the fault. About 5 km farther north along the road, dark gray layered quartzitic gneiss is exposed in the core of the antiform. These metamorphic rocks of medium to high grade are generally referred to as the Black Canyon Schist and have been folded into close limbed, plunging folds that trend northward.
0.5

101.9 Pegmatite sills intruded into the Black Canyon Schist.
0.3

102.2 Cross Cimarron Creek. The historic railroad exhibit along the road is one of the old engines on an original trestle that operated on the Denver & Rio Grande Railroad's old narrow gauge line that went through the Black Canyon from 1882 to 1949. The stretch through the Black Canyon was notorious for snow and rock avalanches and many lost their lives. **Prepare to stop.**
0.3

102.5 **STOP 2.** (Photo stop; no talk.) Parking area below Morrow Point Dam and power plant. The Morrow Point Dam is 143 m high; its power plant consists of two generating units with a total capacity of 120,000 kilowatts of hydroelectricity.
1.3

103.8 **Return to junction with U.S. Highway 50, turn left toward Gunnison.**
0.5

104.3 Note slump block on right in Mancos, followed by a slump-flow complex shortly beyond.
2.0

106.3 Silver Jack Reservoir turn off to right.
0.1

106.4 Note slope failures in Mancos to left—and for next several kilometers—some of these could be described as deep creep. Driving along the floodplain of the Cimarron River.
1.0

107.4 Little Cimarron road junction on right. Good view of broad valley formed by Little Cimarron and Cimarron Rivers.

Figure 102.5a. Morrow Point Dam (Baars photo).

Figure 102.5b. Downstream from Morrow Point Dam (Baars photo).

0.8
108.2 Gunnison County line.
0.5
108.7 Toe of a well-defined earth flow on left. Ascend hill.
0.6
109.3 Basaltic sill intruded into Mancos in foreground straight ahead forms small hogback.
0.3
109.6 Sharp curve to right.
0.1
109.7 Basaltic sill in roadcuts to right. Note conspicuous jointing and spheroidal weathering in sill. Ranch built on sill to left.
1.9
111.6 Abundant slope failures on right. Blue Mesa Tuff caps skyline to left (Fitzpatrick Mesa).
1.3
112.9 Blue Mesa Summit.
1.2
114.1 Turnoff to Arrowhead Ranch, the site of a proposed development, including a small ski area.
0.2
114.3 Exposures to right are volcanics in the West Elk Breccia, some of which are autobrecciated flows. **(See Gaskill and others, this guidebook.)**
0.2
114.5 Cross Cimarron fault and enter Precambrian rocks of Blue Creek Canyon. Migmatitic gneiss and schist of the Black Canyon Schist are cut by generally east-trending pegmatite dikes and larger east-trending bodies of Curecanti quartz monzonite, both of Precambrian Y age.
0.7
115.2 Cross Blue Creek and junction with Alpine plateau road. Abundant dikes for next 1.5 km.
0.7
115.9 Sharp curve to right. Thick, north-dipping pegmatite dikes on right just past curve.
0.7
116.6 Curve to left, leave Blue Canyon.
0.7
117.3 Soap Mesa on skyline to north (12:00) capped by series of welded tuffs.
0.8
118.1 Curve to right. Road cuts show good exposures of West Elk Breccia on the left and an irregular erosion surface with West Elk Breccia on Mancos Shale on the right. The West Elk is a volcaniclastic deposit composed of predominantly andesitic fragments in an ashey matrix, and much of it in this vicinity is of laharic origin. Lesser amounts of ash flow tuffs, pumice and crystal tuffs, rhyodacitic flows, and stream reworked conglomerates are all interbedded. These rocks were ejected from the West Elk volcano, a major Oligocene (approximately 35-50 m.y.b.p.), composite volcano with the main eruptive center being about 24-29 km north-northeast of here at the head of Soap and West Elk Creeks. Highway 50 is close to the southern limits of the West Elk Breccia. **(See Gaskill and others, this guidebook.)**
0.2
118.3 First view of Blue Mesa Reservoir and the east end of the Black Canyon. Blue Mesa Reservoir is Colorado's largest body of water when filled to capacity and is the main storage reservoir of the Curecanti system which consists of three dams on the Gunnison River, all part of the upper Colorado River storage project. Soap Mesa on the left across the Black Canyon is capped by four separate ashflow tuff sequences: Blue Mesa Tuff overlying the mostly covered slopes of West Elk Breccia, Sapinero Mesa Tuff, Fish Canyon Tuff and Carpenter Ridge Tuff at the top in the distance. Most of these show a well-developed basal vitrophyre underlain by gravels and average about 60 m thick here. These tuffs are of late Oligocene age and were erupted over the time span of approximately 30 to 26 m.y.b.p. Source areas for the ash flows were large cauldron complexes in the central and western San Juan Mountains to the south. Some of these ash flow sheets were enormous, spreading over 15,000 km².
1.0
119.3 Blue Mesa on right with good exposures of Blue Mesa Tuff forming prominent cliffs above covered slopes of West Elk Breccia.
0.9
120.2 Slopes to right are a major slide-flow complex developed in West Elk Breccia which con-

Figure 119.3. Blue Mesa Reservoir (Baars photo).

tinues for some distance. Directly ahead is Pine Creek Mesa also capped by Blue Mesa Tuff. The resistant welded tuff maintains a slope angle that is steeper than the less competent West Elk Breccia can withstand.

1.0

121.2 Intersection with Blue Mesa development road.

0.4

121.6 Cross Pine Creek, curve to left.

0.2

121.8 Excellent exposures of the Jurassic Junction Creek Sandstone (Bluff equivalent) in road cuts to right. The Junction Creek appears to be eolian in origin.

0.4

122.2 View of east entrance to Black Canyon.

0.5

122.7 Blue Mesa dam site to left. Good view of the Wanakah Formation (Summerville equivalent) and Junction Creek Sandstone lying unconformably on the Precambrian complex below on the north rim of the canyon just west of the dam site.

0.6

123.3 Intersection with Colorado 92. This is the Black Mesa road and access to the dam site.

0.2

123.5 Slopes at 8:00-10:00 across the reservoir are another huge slide-flow complex developed in the West Elk Breccia. Good slide-flow complex on right just before bridge.

0.6

124.1 Cross bridge over flooded mouth of the Lake Fork of the Gunnison, which heads near Lake City approximately 55 km due south. The path of the Lake Fork is controlled by a northwest-trending fault system.

0.9

125.0 Sapinero store on right. Exposures of Morrison Formation in road cuts. The old townsite of Sapinero, a railroad town, which was located at the confluence of Soap Creek and the Gunnison River, is now under water.

0.8

125.8 View left up the Soap Creek valley of the West Elks near the main vent center.

0.4

126.2 View left up West Elk Creek.

0.7

126.9 Spectacular view left across reservoir of pinnacles eroded into West Elk Breccia. The West Elk Breccia is underlain by Mancos Shale and overlain by Blue Mesa, Dillon Mesa and Sapinero Mesa Tuffs. The mesa just east of the pinnacles is Dillon Mesa. The West Elk Breccia commonly forms erosion remnants similar to this which are caused by resistant volcanic clasts acting as protective caps to the tuffaceous material below. The slopes below the pinnacles are Mancos (dusky yellow and abnormally thin due to mid-Cenozoic erosion), Dakota and Morrison. The unconformity below the West Elk Breccia is a very widespread, late Eocene erosion surface found throughout central Colorado and adjoining New Mexico. It developed prior to an outburst of volcanism in

Figure 122.7. Looking down Gunnison River from Blue Mesa Dam (Baars photo).

Figure 126.9. Pinnacles in the West Elk Breccia (Baars photo).

the Oligocene, of which the West Elk Breccia is the local representative. To the south, the San Juan Tuff is in a correlative position.
1.0

127.9 Lake City cutoff road (gravel) to right.
0.5

128.4 Cross bridge over Blue Mesa Reservoir; at 3:00 in far distance is Tomichi Dome, a very fine grained granite laccolith.
0.4

128.8 Exposures just past bridge are in Morrison Formation followed by colluvium developed from the West Elk Breccia.
1.1

129.9 Good exposures of West Elk Breccia straight ahead north of highway.
0.1

130.0 Red Creek road on left.
0.3

130.3 Cross Red Creek slump and temporary (since 1971) gravel road due to continuing slope failure. This is an old slump system which was reactivated by the fluctuating Blue Mesa Reservoir level alternately saturating and dehydrating the Morrison Formation. Highway 50 was relocated from stable ground to the south when the reservoir was constructed in the early 60's, but there was no geologic input on the new road bed. This problem area will cost over $1,000,000 to correct since extensive relocation of the highway north of the crown scarp is required. Another of these features which has been corrected at a cost of $300,000 will be seen in 2 km. Note old slope failure across reservoir to right.
0.6

130.9 Cliffs ahead are composed of Morrison, Burro Canyon and Dakota with thin Mancos section overlain by West Elk Breccia. Note black shales in Dakota.
0.4

131.3 Road cuts to left expose several good lenticular channel sands in the Morrison. Throughout southwestern Colorado the Morrison can be subdivided into the Brushy Basin and Salt Wash members. However, in this general vicinity, any subdivision breaks down and only the Morrison undifferentiated is recognized.
0.2

131.5 Curve in road and site of corrected slump. At one time the east-bound lane of the highway was 2 to 3 m below the west-bound lane as the slump scarp bisected the pavement.
0.5

132.0 Good road cuts in Morrison to left.
0.5

132.5 Good view of Dakota cliffs to north above gulch with Mancos slopes and West Elk Breccia above.
0.7

133.2 Channel in Morrison on left. Road up East Elk Creek on left. Good view of a basal vitrophyre at 9:00 to 10:00 on cliff in the Sapinero Mesa Tuff. Overlying crystal tuff at top of West Elk Breccia.
1.1

134.3 Elk Creek Marina and campground. This is the headquarters and visitor center for Blue Mesa Reservoir.
0.4

134.7 Road cuts to left show irregular erosion surface with West Elk Breccia resting on and scouring into Morrison Formation. Note that the West Elk Breccia may lie unconformably on a variety of units from the Precambrian to the Wasatch due to the late Eocene erosion.
0.4

135.1 Another view of basal vitrophyre of the Sapinero Mesa Tuff on mesas to left.
0.2

135.3 Rainbow Lake (Dry Creek) road to left.
1.2

136.5 Road cuts in Junction Creek Sandstone. The Junction Creek is resting on the Precambrian here and the older Jurassic units such as the Entrada and Wanakah have wedged out against the old Uncompahgre Highland.
0.3

136.8 Prairie dog town on right.
0.4

137.2 Cross Willow Creek. To the northeast, on the east side of Willow Creek, is an exposure of Morrison overlain by Dakota and capped by Blue Mesa Tuff. The ledge of Dakota can be followed for some distance in this area.
1.2

138.4 Cross Stevens Creek. Mesas at right (1:00 to 3:00) across reservoir are capped with the usual sequence of ash-flow tuff units. Exposure of Junction Creek can be seen at 3:00 across reservoir at sharp curve in road to Lake City.
1.2

139.6 West Elk Breccia in road cuts to left.
0.2

139.8 Enter Gunnison River Canyon cut into Precambrian rocks. Although no fault has been mapped here, the Precambrian surface rises abruptly and stays high for the next several kilometers. The broad valley we have just left was cut on the contact of the Precambrian and Junction Creek and the widening is due to the less resistant Mesozoic sediments. This contact also represents the surface of the Late

Paleozoic-Early Mesozoic Uncompahgre Highland. The Precambrian rocks in the canyon consist of older biotite schists, gneisses, and quartzites, cut by hornblende diorite and finally intruded by a medium-grained pink granite referred to as the granite of South Beaver Creek of Precambrian X age.

0.5

140.3 Steuben Creek on left; quartz biotite schist in road cuts on east and west sides of creek.

0.1

140.4 Lake City bridge, intersection with Colorado Highway 149.

0.6

141.0 Good exposures of hornblende diorite intruding the metamorphics and local pink granite bodies. This can be seen for the next 2 km, but exceptionally good exposures are found at Beaver Creek.

1.4

142.4 Beaver Creek enters the Gunnison canyon from the north. Beaver Creek heads in the West Elks and has cut some spectacular canyons.

0.6

143.0 This is the approximate level of the reservoir when it is full.

0.4

143.4 The large meadow across the river on the right is a major bird sanctuary and gray blue herons nest here.

0.6

144.0 Exposures of colluvium derived from the West Elk Breccia on left.

0.3

144.3 On right, former site of Neversink Resort now a picnic ground. The construction of Blue Mesa Reservoir also caused extensive flooding of the low-lying meadows in this area in midwinter due to ice jamming backing up from the high water mark.

0.8

145.1 Drab, sage-covered hills across irrigated meadows to north (left) are composed of West Elk Breccia. As discussed earlier, this is close to the southern margin of the West Elk volcanic field.

1.2

146.3 View straight ahead of "W" (Tenderfoot) Mountain, capped by welded tuff.

0.6

146.9 View straight ahead in distance of Fossil Ridge, with Precambrian capped by Paleozoic section. The presence of the Paleozoic section marks the limits of the Late Paleozoic Uncompahgre Highland, trending northwest several kilometers northeast of Gunnison. The low, rugged hills to the south across the Gunnison River are composed of the granite of South Beaver Creek which forms a ring dike approximately 8 km in diameter. The Aberdeen quarry, about 8 km to the south, furnished the granite from this body for the State Capitol building in the 1890's. A spur of the railroad proceeded south along South Beaver Creek to service the quarry.

1.2

148.1 Road cuts to left in Morrison, unconformably overlain by the West Elk Breccia. A small slump can be seen in the Morrison.

0.4

148.5 Cross Gunnison River.

0.1

148.6 Good view of "W" Mountain at 1:00 to 2:00.

0.5

149.1 City limits of Gunnison. Elevation 2348 m (7703 ft); population 8200 (including adjacent suburbs). Gunnison was founded in 1874 at the junction of Tomichi Creek and the Gunnison River, but did not become viable until the mining rush of 1879-1880. At one time, both the Denver & Rio Grande (1881-1954) and the Denver & South Park (1882-1911) Railroads serviced Gunnison and there was optimistic talk of this becoming the state capitol. But its boom was short lived and after the silver panic of 1893, Gunnison became a sleepy mountain village. Renewed growth occurred with the 1960's and 70's recreation boom and now Gunnison is once again a center of mining activity with molybdenum, uranium, titanium, other metals, and coal being actively explored. Two major mines, Amax's Mt. Emmons molybdenum project near Crested Butte and Homestake's pitch uranium mine near Monarch Pass, 64 km east, are prominent. **(See Dowsett and others, this guidebook.)**

0.2

149.3 View of the Palisades, with deep gullies carved into the West Elk Breccia.

0.8

150.1 Stop light at corner of Main, Highway 135, and Tomichi, Highway 50. **Go straight. Prepare to turn.**

0.5

150.6 **Turn left at east edge of town to Western State College.** Western State College of Colorado was founded in 1911 and now has an enrollment of approximately 3300 students.

0.2

150.8 **Turn right at caution light.**

0.1

150.9 **Turn left into parking lot.** Park and consolidate

	into as few vehicles as possible for trip to Crested Butte and return.
	0.8
151.7	Return to the corner of Main and Tomichi. **Turn right on Highway 135** toward Crested Butte.
	0.5
152.2	City limits of Gunnison.
	0.4
152.6	View of the "Palisades" of the Gunnison River at 9:00. These bluffs are composed of the Oligocene West Elk Breccia that are mostly laharic breccias. Note the crude stratification and a minor unconformity (dark above light). Sage-covered slopes to east are also composed of West Elk Breccia. You are now driving on alluvium of the Gunnison River floodplain which is over 30 m thick. The river is at the far west flank of the floodplain against the bluffs.
	0.2
152.8	View north (12:00), east of Ohio Creek valley, of Red and Flat Top Mountains capped with Miocene basalt flows (10 m.y.b.p.). Underlying the flows are interbedded Miocene volcaniclastics including rhyolitic and basaltic tuffs, associated epiclastics and thick boulder-sized unconsolidated gravels deposited on eroded Mesaverde Formation and Mancos Shale. The steep cliff below Red Mountain is the crown scrap of a series of composite slump blocks. Most of the slopes of Red and Flat Top Mountains are multiple debris-flow complexes of coarse angular volcanic rock fragments developed on Mancos Shale.
	0.2
153.0	View west (9:00) of slump-flow complex developed in Mancos Shale below cliffs of West Elk Breccia.
	0.2
153.2	View northwest (10:00). Yellow exposure of Mancos below West Elk Breccia forms prominent knob on west side of valley.
	0.4
153.6	Old railroad grade between Gunnison and Crested Butte is evident just west of highway.
	0.7
154.3	Cross Gunnison River.
	0.7
155.0	Good view up Ohio Creek valley of part of West Elk laccolith cluster. From east to west: Mt. Whetstone (just over west shoulder of Red Mountain), Mt. Axtell, Carbon Peak (conical mountain in center of valley), and the Anthracite Range, the serrated ridge. All of these are middle Cenozoic, fine-grained granodioritic porphyries. Flat Top completes the view to the east. The slope failures on the flanks of Red Mountain and Flat Top are especially evident here.
	0.2
155.2	Junction with the Ohio Creek Road; driving on high terrace gravels.
	0.3
155.5	View of Gunnison River floodplain incised into terrace gravels at 3:00.
	0.1
155.6	Gravel quarries and storage piles.
	0.8
156.4	Look up Ohio Creek Valley at 10:00 for view of East Beckwith Mountain, another laccolith, just west of the Anthracite Range. The old railroad grade is evident just west of the highway.
	1.2
157.6	Intersection to right to Rocky River Resort and Camp Gunnison. Exposures of Dakota Sandstone along gulch near Camp Gunnison water tower at 2:00.
	0.2
157.8	Small conical hill at 4:00 covered by spruce trees is Signal Peak. It is composed of Oligocene welded tuff capping West Elk Breccia.
	0.4
158.2	Exposures of Dakota Sandstone due east below Camp Gunnison water tank.
	0.4
158.6	View ahead on left side of road of Morrison-Burro Canyon-Dakota sequence dipping to southwest with covered slopes of Mancos Shale above.
	0.4
159.0	Slopes to west are Morrison-Burro Canyon-Dakota. The lower sandstone bench is the Burro Canyon Formation, while the top two are in the Dakota Formation.
	1.2
160.2	Excavated slopes in back of homesites to west show exposures of Morrison Formation.
	0.2
160.4	Junction Creek Sandstone crosses road, near large talus blocks of sandstone. The thinly bedded sandstone on top of the massive, white sandstone cliffs is a basal Morrison sandstone with green clay clasts.
	0.2
160.6	Excellent exposures of Junction Creek Sandstone dipping 7 degrees southwest, with partly covered slopes of Morrison Formation above. The Junction Creek (Jurassic) unconformably overlies Precambrian metamorphics. This white sandstone with major, wedge-tangential cross-bed sets also has been correlated with the Entrada Sandstone. However, examination of the Jurassic section in the Black

Canyon area where both sandstones are present shows that this unit more closely resembles the Junction Creek and further, the Entrada and Wanakah wedge out just east of Blue Mesa Reservoir. This exposure is close to the eastern margin of the late Paleozoic, Ancestral Rockies Uncompahgre Highland. During Ancestral Rockies time the pre-Pennsylvanian section was stripped and deposited into the Central Colorado Basin lying immediately to the east-northeast.

0.2

160.8 On left, toe of debris flow with abundant basalt fragments derived from the top of Flat Top Mountain.

0.3

161.1 Almont Campground entrance on right. Enter canyon cut into Precambrian rocks with Gunnison River on right.

0.4

161.5 The Junction Creek-Precambrian contact rises rapidly to the north due to the Almont fault and can be seen about 100 m above the river straight ahead. Note the fresh, large talus blocks scattered throughout this canyon.

0.4

161.9 Cross East River very close to the confluence with the Taylor River. The merging of these two rivers forms the Gunnison River. **Prepare to turn.**

0.1

162.0 Almont Resort-Intersection with Taylor River Road. **Turn right** and proceed up Taylor Canyon.

0.1

162.1 Cross Taylor River. The Almont fault strikes northwest with the southwest side upthrown. The trace of the fault crosses the road just past the bridge and proceeds southeast along the jeep road above the town of Almont. This fault runs parallel to, but about 7 km southwest of the Crested Butte lineament.

0.3

162.4 Enter Taylor River Canyon with walls composed of steeply dipping Precambrian metasediments and metabasalts cut by Precambrian X-aged granites. Studies in the area indicate that there is a thick sequence of metamorphics older than 1750 m.y.b.p., a metamorphic event at 1750 m.y.b.p. and a series of intrusions ranging from gabbro to granite from 1700 to 1360 m.y.b.p. Bighorn sheep often are seen on the slopes of the canyon.

1.7

164.1 Grassy slopes at top of canyon straight ahead are composed of a Mesozoic section capped by the Dakota.

0.7

164.8 Note very steep dip in Precambrian metasediments on left and continuing for next several kilometers. A complex of isoclinal folds seems the best explanation.

2.0

166.8 Cross Taylor River.

0.4

167.2 View of steeply dipping Dakota Sandstone straight ahead on left side of road. The steep dip is due to fault drag along the southwestern side of a small, wedge-shaped graben. The meadow or open part of the canyon here is caused by more easily eroded late Paleozoic and Mesozoic sedimentary rocks being juxtaposed against the more resistant Precambrian complex. The graben is only a little more than 1.5 km wide here.

0.1

167.3 Cross fault. The Dakota is also visible across the valley to the right in the lower tree-covered slopes. The high, tree-covered knob at 3:00 to 4:00 is the Precambrian on the upthrown side of the fault.

0.2

167.5 Road cuts on left are in the toe of debris flow developed on the Mancos Shale. This was recently excavated by the County Highway Department.

0.2

167.7 Tree-covered hogback ahead is held up by the Junction Creek Sandstone. **Prepare to turn.**

0.5

168.2 **Sharp turn to the left** on Jack's Cabin Cutoff Road, County 813. After completing the turn you have a good view of the fault scarp just described.

0.1

168.3 To right, road cuts of interbedded black shale and sandstone are in the Dakota, dipping steeply to the southwest.

0.2

168.5 Good view of debris flow to left—road is now in the Mancos Shale.

0.4

168.9 Good view of fault scarp to left marked by trees. **Prepare to stop.**

0.7

169.6 **STOP 3.** Jack's Cabin Divide. Discussion of Crested Butte lineament, Alkali basin and other local geologic features.

1.4

171.0 **DANGER, sharp curve to right and several more to follow.**

2.9

Figure 169.6. Jack's Cabin Divide looking northwest from Stop 3 (Baars photo).

Figure 177.9. Crested Butte Mountain from Cement Creek Road, Stop 4 (Baars photo).

173.9 Intersection with Colorado Highway 135. **Turn right** towards Crested Butte. This is the site of Jack's Cabin, an old toll road inn halfway between Gunnison and Crested Butte that became defunct after the coming of the railroad in 1881.
0.1

174.0 Good view of Round Mountain straight ahead. This is a rhyolitic laccolith dated at 11.7 m.y.b.p.
0.5

174.5 Circular slump in Morrison-Dakota to right at 3:00. Mud flow to left on the lower slopes of Red Mountain at 9:00.
0.5

175.0 Talus rampart ridge to right. Series of talus cones from Round Mountain, most of which appear to be inactive.
1.0

176.0 Cross East River.
0.3

176.3 View to right into Granite Basin. Prominent sandstone bench at mouth of basin is Junction Creek-Entrada(?); thick sequence of Paleozoic rocks up gulch.
0.5

176.8 Good view of Crested Butte, elevation 3711 m (12,175 ft), a laccolith of fine-grained granodiorite porphyry dated at 29 m.y.b.p., resting on Mancos Shale straight ahead. **Prepare to stop.**
1.1

177.9 **STOP 4.** Junction with Cement Creek Road on right. Mt. Whetstone with massive slope failures in Mancos below at 11:00; Mt. Emmons and Red Lady Basin at 11:45, Ruby Range at 12:30, Crested Butte Mountain at 1:00, debris flow at 2:00, Cement Creek canyon with Paleozoic section at 3:00. **(See Robinson and Dea, this guidebook.)** Note prominent light-gray cliffs of Leadville on north canyon wall, a short distance up Cement Creek (northeastern edge of Uncompahgre Uplift).
0.4

178.3 Good view of debris flow to right. The Dakota has slid on the Morrison and has turned into a classic flow below. Note 3 to 4 terrace levels along East and Slate Rivers cut into glacial outwash of Pinedale and Bull Lake(?) age. This is the approximate southern terminus of glacial advances, and associated deposits will be increasingly evident from this point north.
0.7

179.0 Cross Slate River bridge, note exposures of Mancos on left dipping about 7 degrees west. Abandoned railroad grade can be seen here.
0.3

179.3 Good view of Gothic Mountain (another laccolith) just to left of Crested Butte Mountain.
0.4

179.7 View northeast across valley of high peaks of the Elk Range, which consists of steeply folded and overturned Paleozoic and Mesozoic sediments intruded by several mid-Cenozoic stocks and overridden by the Elk Range thrust carrying flat-lying Pennsylvanian and Permian Gothic and Maroon Formations. Teocalli (elevation 4025 m, 13,208 ft) is the prominent, pyramid-shaped peak in the foreground at 2:00 with Castle Peak (elevation 4348 m, 14,265 ft) in the background, both composed of the Pennsylvanian-Permian Maroon Formation. The Maroon is as much as 3000 m thick in the region, although it is locally thinner due to erosion. Terminal moraines of Bull Lake(?) age forming lobes and hummocky ground rising above outwash (north and east).

0.5

180.2 On the left, a large mud-debris flow complex in the Mancos starting at the base of the Mt. Whetstone (elevation 3815m, 12,516 ft) laccolith. Some of these are active. The slope failure here and in similar settings throughout the region is partly caused by the loading of the laccolithic bodies on the incompetent Mancos below. The igneous caprock above also maintains a slope angle in the Mancos steeper than it can withstand. Crested Butte Mountain is apparently splitting by a series of blocklike steps on the north side due to the failure below (Ausgebirge-splitten). A series of major snow avalanche tracks from the top of Mt. Whetstone are conspicuous for the next few kilometers.

1.9

182.1 Road enters Pinedale terminal moraines (note rolling typography) opposite large debris flow apron at 9:00. Cliff with exposure of massive sandstone at 9:00 is the second regressive sandstone unit of the Mesaverde Formation overlain by thick beds of coal.

0.7

182.8 Intersection of Brush Creek Road on right followed shortly by Slate River bridge.

0.5

183.3 View southwest (7:00) up Baxter Gulch towards Bulkley No. 2 tramway coal mine 245 m above floodplain. At 9:00, portal and tramscar of Bulkley No. 1 coal mine, swept by periodic avalanches, rock falls and landslides. The Mesaverde strata at the top of the cliffs above the mine are separating along incipient landslide tension fractures.

0.4

183.7 View at 7:30 of Porter Pueblo coal mine workings and tram scar. Note landslide rubble and avalanche debris on slopes. View right of large meadow probably underlain by glacial lake sediments formed behind moraines.

0.2

183.9 Road cuts in recessional moraine. At 12:00 is Crested Butte ski area perched on incompetent Mancos Shale below the Crested Butte laccolith. Large granodiorite porphyry dikes trend northwest through the hill left of the ski area and are also exposed at the base of Crested Butte Mountain at 2:00. Dikes may represent conduits that fed the adjacent laccolith. Good view of Red Lady Basin and Red Lady Peak at 10:00 to 11:00 on the east shoulder of Mt. Emmons, the site of Amax's major molybdenum discovery.

0.4

184.3 Descend morainal hill. The town of Crested Butte lies directly ahead and is built on glacial outwash and on an alluvial debris fan. Beyond Crested Butte lies the U-shaped Slate River valley with the peaks of the northern Ruby Range in the distance. The Ruby Range consists of a series of mid-Cenozoic quartz monzonite porphyries intruded into the Mancos, Mesaverde, Ohio Creek and Wasatch formations. The Gothic Mountain laccolith can be seen at 11:30.

0.3

184.6 Crested Butte city limits. **Prepare to turn.**

0.3

184.9 Intersection of Crested Butte ski area road and Elk Avenue. **Turn right.** The caravan will proceed to the Slate River road approximately 1 km north of town for a good overview of the area and talks on the history and geology of the area. **Prepare to stop.**

0.9

185.8 **STOP 5. Turn around; return to road intersection for Stop 5.** The town of Crested Butte (1980 population 1164) was founded in 1879 as a supply center for the silver and gold mining camps in the area: Gothic, Irwin, Pittsburg and Schofield, etc. However the enormous coal reserves immediately surrounding the town are what attracted the Denver and Rio Grande railroad, which arrived in Crested Butte in November of 1881, only a few months after it had first come to Gunnison. The Crested Butte area first attracted prospectors perhaps as early as 1849 and a thriving placer

Figure 185.8. Mt. Whetstone from Crested Butte resort, Stop 5 (Baars photo).

gold camp was first noted in 1861 on upper Washington Gulch, with a reported million dollars in gold recovered by 1862. **Return to intersection of Elk Avenue and Colorado 135.**

0.9

186.7 Intersection of Elk Avenue and Colorado Highway 135. **Turn right on Elk Avenue,** for drive through historic downtown Crested Butte.

0.4

187.1 **Turn left on Second Street** just before bridge. A Mesaverde sandstone bench is visible at the end of Elk Avenue two blocks ahead.

0.2

187.3 **Turn right on White Rock Avenue,** Gunnison Co. Highway 12.

0.1

187.4 Proceed up hill which is a Mesaverde Sandstone bench with glacial debris on top. View to left across Coal Creek shows the portals of the Jokerville Mine. The mine opened in 1882 but a violent methane gas explosion on January 24, 1884 killed 60 miners. The mine never reopened. View ahead to northwest is the peak of Mt. Emmons with Red Lady Basin in the foreground. The Mt. Emmons molybdenum deposit lies 300 m beneath the western ridge. Red Lady Basin and the gulch which drains it is the site of a major snow avalanche chute which has run all the way across the road and 73 m up the other side of Coal Creek valley.

0.5

187.9 Road passes through Pinedale(?) moraine. To the south, forming a cliff above Coal Creek, is an outcrop of Mesaverde sandstones and siltstones which contain abundant plant fossils.

Figure 187.4. Crested Butte Mountain (Baars photo).

Dip of the beds is about 10 degrees west towards the axis of the southwest-plunging Coal Creek syncline.

0.9

188.8 Junction of road to Amax's Mt. Emmons project. **Proceed up Amax road.** Slopes of Coal Creek covered by glacial till over sediments of Cretaceous Mesaverde Formation and lower Tertiary Ohio Creek Formation.

0.2

189.0 Cross gulch from Red Lady Basin, which is the lower part of the avalanche chute discussed above. **Prepare to stop.**

1.0

190.0 **STOP 6.** Amax parking lot. Discussion of Mt. Emmons ore body. **(See Dowsett and others, this guidebook.) Return to junction of Kebler Pass road.**

1.2

191.2 Intersection of Kebler Pass road. **Turn sharp right.** Good view of Mt. Axtell laccolith overlying Wasatch and Ohio Creek Formation to south. Slopes of Coal Creek here have glacial debris on Ohio Creek Formation.

1.1

192.3 Uphill to right (north)—extensive area of bogs. Terraced spring deposits and bog iron deposits are cementing glacial and colluvial deposits. Springs feeding the area drain base metal veins along the northwest-trending Keystone-Union fault system.

0.7

193.0 Another good view of Mt. Axtell to left (south). Composition is similar to other laccoliths in area.

0.3

193.3 Look up stream bed to right (north) for outcrop of feldspathic, conglomeratic sandstone of the Ohio Creek Formation. West of the stream is the distal end of a complex of morainal deposits, rock glaciers, debris flows, and landslides which occupy the western part of Evans Basin.

0.7

194.0 Mouth of Elk Creek on right. The exposures of quartz latite porphyry at the north end of the Mt. Axtell laccolith thins to form a sill that was intruded near the base of the Wasatch Formation. North of Coal Creek the Axtell intrusive body is cut by numerous mineralized shears carrying silver, zinc, and lead. Note prospects and mine dumps. South of Coal Creek the rock is practically barren.

2.1

196.1 Junction with road to Lake Irwin and Irwin townsite. View of Ruby Peak (elevation 3854 m, 12,644 ft) and a quartz monzonite dike extending to the south. Ruby Peak is a granodiorite stock of Oligocene age which displays considerable textural and compositional variation. *Optional trip* (4.8 miles round trip) to old townsite of Irwin and Lake Irwin. **Turn right at first fork in road to Irwin townsite.**

0.4

196.5 Intersection of Kebler Pass road with Ohio Pass road. **Turn left onto Ohio Pass road.** View ahead of the northeast slopes of the Anthracite Range, another laccolith.

0.4

196.9 Junction with modern logging road to right and old railroad grade to Floresta, an abandoned anthracite coal mine and townsite on the north flanks of the Anthracite Range in a small, isolated valley about 3 km west of here. The Denver and Rio Grande Railroad came from Crested Butte. The mines operated from 1.2-m-thick bed from 1893 to 1919. Locally, where the coal is within a few meters of a laccolith, the coal is metamorphosed to a natural coke.

0.2

197.1 Another logging road to Floresta on right. Driving through morainal debris.

0.5

197.6 Large marsh with beaver lodge on right—glacial lake beds? Good view of east flank of Anthracite Range on right.

0.2

197.8 Ohio Pass, elevation 3071 m (10,074 ft). Fault zone through pass trending northwest drops Mesaverde and Wasatch strata about 200 m down to east. The Anthracite Range laccolith is cut by many north-northeast-trending shears, is locally mineralized and was probably emplaced subsequent to the Mt. Axtell laccolith just to the east (left).

0.3

198.1 View of upper Ohio Creek valley below. Ridge at 2:00 is composed of bedded West Elk Breccia.

0.2

198.3 Exposures of Wasatch underlying and intruded by Mt. Axtell laccolith in left roadcut.

0.3

198.6 Spectacular views of the "Castles" and West Elk Peak at 2:00 to 3:00. Both are composed of stratified West Elk Breccia, a series of andesitic volcaniclastic rocks. The Castles are joint-controlled erosion remnants. Note the folded outcrops of the Ohio Creek conglomeratic sandstone dipping 10 to 45 degrees southeast off the flanks of the Anthracite Range. The Anthracite Range is mantled with locally active, coalescing rock streams, landslides, debris flows, and colluvium. The tree-covered, dome-shaped mountain straight ahead is the northwest slope of the Carbon Peak laccolith overlain by 30-200 m of Mesaverde strata dipping 10 to 40 degrees west and northwest. The axis of the Coal Creek syncline trends southwest near the topographic low of Ohio Creek. The low, rolling topography visible in the upper Ohio Creek valley is mostly of morainal origin.

0.1

198.7 Talus from Mt. Axtell in left road cut.

0.2

198.9 Conspicuous curving gulch on the slopes of Carbon Peak is the Mesaverde intrusive contact.

0.1

199.0 Another good view of the Castles at 2:00.

0.2

199.2 **DANGER: Sharp curve to right.** Note rock tressels directly above, on the never-completed Denver and South Park Railroad grade from Gunnison.

0.6

199.8 Curve to left at end of aspen grove and cross upper Ohio Creek. Steep slopes ahead are the east flank of the Anthracite Range. A 15-cm-thick bed of coal is exposed in the creek at the right. Road for next few kilometers is in Pinedale tills.

0.6

200.4 View of west slope of Mt. Whetstone at 9:00 up valley. Carbon Peak from 10:00 to 12:00.

0.7

201.1 Beaver ponds picnic ground. **Stay left.**

0.5

201.6 View of remnants of rocky debris flow in gulch below to right.

0.1

201.7 Sharp curve to right.

0.1

201.8 Cross run-out fan of debris flow which ran in late spring, 1980. Debris flow was caused by failure of an abandoned beaver dam and resulting spill of large lake behind it. The dam is about 1600 m and 305 m vertically up gulch. As can be seen to the right, blocks up to 1.8-2.5 m diameter were carried by the flow. Numerous armored mud balls were formed by the flood. Exposures of Wasatch can be found a short distance up the gulch. Old coal mine portal and dump from late 1880's on left (east). Twenty coke ovens across creek south of mine portal can be seen.

0.2

202.0 Swampy Pass trailhead and parking area.

0.4

202.4	Cross Ohio Creek. Castle Creek ridge at 1:00 to 2:00 is composed of West Elk Breccia.
	0.1
202.5	Good view of the Castles at 3:00 and continuing for some distance. Meadow on right formed by floodplain of upper Ohio Creek.
	0.1
202.6	High peak at 3:00 to the right of the Castles is West Elk Peak, highest point of the West Elk Mountains (elevation 3973 m, 13,035 ft).
	0.5
203.1	Curve to left. Exposures of light-colored rock 30 to 60 m above road straight ahead are the Ohio Creek Formation, a latest Cretaceous(?) to Eocene alluvial fan deposit formed at the base of the Laramide Rockies. Source area was probably to the east near the site of the modern Sawatch Range. This is the type locality designated by Eldridge in 1894 and consists of a light-gray to white, friable, coarse, conglomeratic arkose with abundant pebbles and granules of chert and lesser amounts of quartz, quartzite, clay, and igneous rock fragments. Some of the chert pebbles contain Paleozoic fossils such as crinoids, bryozoans, and corals. Petrified wood fragments are found locally. The unit has minor amounts of interbedded sandstone, siltstone, and shale. The top contact with the Wasatch is eroded here, but the contact with the underlying Mesaverde Formation is arbitrarily placed at the base of the lowest chert pebble, conglomeratic sandstone. We will be driving through the Mesaverde Formation (mostly poorly exposed) for some distance from this point downstream.
	0.3
203.4	For the next 2 to 3 km note the various active and semi-active rock streams, debris and mud flows aproning Carbon Peak on your left. Some of these mass-wasting forms appear to be caused by igneous talus from Carbon Peak going for a ride on the underlying Mesaverde shales. Look back to your right (3:00-4:00) for a good view of the Anthracite Range. The high point on the range is named Ohio Peak (elevation 3740 m, 12,271 ft). Note the outwash terrace on right of possible Bull Lake age.
	1.1
204.5	Mouth of Castle Creek valley. Exposures of Mesaverde with thin coal beds on bluffs along Ohio and Castle Creeks. The road is now in the distal apron of a large slide-flow complex.
	0.3
204.8	Good view of major snow avalanche track on Carbon Peak to left at about 3:00.
	0.9
205.7	Faulted exposures of Mesaverde along road for next kilometer. A 1.5-m-thick coal bed underlies the terrace across Ohio Creek to the west.
	0.3
206.0	Baldwin—company town of the Alpine Fuel's Alpine coal mine, which operated from 1897 to 1946 from a 1.8-to-2.5-m-thick bed of bituminous coal (the no. 2 bed of this district) and produced about 2 million tonnes of coal. The shaft here is 46.6 m deep down to the coal bed. The Denver & South Park Railroad reached here in 1882 to service the coal mines in the area which had opened as early as 1874.
	0.6
206.6	Old stone house to right below is composed of blocks of Mesaverde sandstone presumably quarried from nearby outcrops. The coal dumps west in the Ohio Creek floodplain are the workings of the LaPlante mine, 1884-1885, and later mines (1922-1929) 200 m south on a 1.2-m-thick bed of coal, the no. 1 or oldest bed in this district. The coal directly overlies the basal regressive marine sandstone of the Mesaverde Formation and is probably equivalent to the Rollins Sandstone. The coal is associated with marine fossils here but east of Carbon Creek the horizon of the no. 1 coal bed is represented by thick carbonaceous shales. A fault trends west-northwest through the ranch buildings with the north side down about 75 m.
	0.2
206.8	Fault drops basal Mesaverde and Mancos/Mesaverde transition zone down to road level to left. This is the "Rollins" Sandstone discussed above and sparse Ophiomorpha burrows occur locally. Beds dip about 8° north here.
	1.2
208.0	**Sharp curve to right** and junction with Carbon Creek road (County Highway 737). Good exposures of the Rollins Sandstone, about 40 m thick, form a cliff on Star Hill back to the north behind you. The high peaks at 8:00 to 9:00 are Mt. Whetstone; Red Mountain is at 10:00 and Flat Top at 11:00 to 12:00. Amax's proposed mill site for the Mt. Emmons molybdenum deposit is in the saddle between Red and Flat Top Mountains. This would be reached by a tunnel under Mt. Axtell and proceeding south along the east slopes of Carbon Creek. Note the debris flow complexes coming from below Red and Flat Top. A number of coal mines operated in the vicinity around Carbon Peak and were formerly called the Mt. Carbon or

THIRD DAY ROAD LOG

Baldwin coal field. It includes some two dozen mines and total production exceeds 3.4 million tonnes of high volatile bituminous, some coking coal and some semi-anthracite. Only one mine is presently operating, the O.C. (Ohio Creek) No. 2, which is located about 2.5 km northeast of here.

0.7

208.7 Cross Carbon Creek. Another good view of the Castles at 3:00.

0.1

208.8 Ranch buildings mark the site of Castleton, founded in 1882 as a supply center for the nearby coal mines.

0.3

209.1 Good view of Red Mountain at 9:00. Cliffs are composed of oxidized basalt flows and are the headwall scarp for a series of toreva blocks. Note the debris flow complex coming from Flat Top straight ahead. To west (3:00) Mancos has failed below the covered slopes of West Elk Breccia in a series of flow complexes. Look back up Carbon Creek to north for a good view of Carbon Peak on left and Mt. Axtell beyond and just to east (right).

0.2

209.3 Note good sequence of earth and mud flows on slopes of Mancos to right at 3:00 (and continuing for next 2 km), caused by increased ground moisture resulting from irrigation ditch seepage.

1.0

210.3 Junction with O.C. Coal Mine road on left. Road cuts to left in toe of debris flow complex and continuing for next 3 to 5 km. View southwest (3:00-4:00) up Mill Creek. Several coal mines operated about 0.8 km north and approximately 185 m above Mill Creek about 4 km away. The Mesaverde is eroded away a short distance south of Mill Creek and all exposures to the west will be West Elk Breccia unconformably overlying Mancos shale. Two holes prospecting for oil were drilled a short distance north of here; the Signal Oil Field Service test, T.D. in the Dakota at 1460 m (4790 ft) in 1963 and the Vision Petrol Co. hole drilled into the Morrison Formation in 1962.

0.3

210.6 Terrace to right with earthflows below.

0.5

211.1 Confluence of Mill Creek and Ohio Creek to right. View up Mill Creek valley with steep cliffs of West Elk Breccia 8-11 km up valley at 3:00.

0.3

211.4 Begin paved road and junction with Mill Creek Road.

0.6

212.0 Good exposures of distal lobes of debris flows with large angular blocks of volcanics incorporated in them at left.

0.8

212.8 Good stream terrace to right across well-developed Ohio Creek floodplain.

2.1

214.9 Road climbs up onto terrace on east side of Ohio Creek valley and will remain on this feature for next several kilometers. Slope failures in Mancos Shale on either side of valley are common.

1.3

216.2 Small, cone-shaped hill at 12:00 is Signal Peak discussed earlier. In the distance at 1:00, the irregular, spruce-covered, dome-shaped mountain is Cochetopa Dome, a late-stage rhyolite dome-flow complex in the Cochetopa caldera.

1.4

217.6 View of Fossil Ridge in distance to east at 9:00 to 10:00.

1.0

218.6 Intersection with Allen Lane, County 8, to left.

2.0

220.6 End Ohio Creek road at intersection with Colorado 135 (Crested Butte Road). **Turn right to Gunnison.**

2.9

223.5 Cross Gunnison River.

1.1

224.6 Begin four-lane highway—view straight ahead in far distance (12:00) of Uncompahgre Peak, elevation 4361 m (14,309 ft), pyramid shaped with flat top sloping north. This is the highest peak in western Colorado and is composed of volcanics.

0.3

224.9 Curve to left. View of Tenderfoot or "W" mountain at 11:00—with slopes of West Elk Breccia and ash capped by welded tuff. The "W" on the mountain is (or was) the largest college letter in the world.

0.7

225.6 Gunnison city limits. **End of Third Day Road Log and Field Conference. See Supplemental Logs for exit routes.**

SUPPLEMENTAL ROAD LOG NO. 1
MONTROSE TO DURANGO, COLORADO*

K. LEE, R. C. EPIS, D. L. BAARS, D. H. KNEPPER, and R. M. SUMMER

INTRODUCTION

This road log runs from Montrose, Colorado, south along U.S. Highway 550 to Durango, Colorado, a distance of 110 mi (fig. 1). The route of the log crosses the San Juan Mountains along their western flank, crossing successively the Uncompahgre uplift, Sneffles horst, Silverton caldera, and the Grenadier highland (horst?) (fig. 2). Suggested stops along the way emphasize these geologic structures and the nature of the sedimentation and volcanism along the margins of the structures. Secondary emphasis is on geologic hazards, especially snow avalanches.

Mileage

0.0 Intersection of U.S. Highways 550 and 50 (Main Street) in Montrose. Start south on U.S. 550.
2.3

2.3 Montrose Valley and Montrose syncline.
1.0

3.3 Ute Museum.
3.7

7.0 View of Mount Sneffles on skyline at 1:00.
4.9

11.9 Ouray County line.
1.8

13.7 Dakota–Morrison contact (see fig. 3 for generalized stratigraphic column and also Weimer, this guidebook). Dakota Formation drops quickly beneath Mancos Shale to the north.
2.5

16.2 Sill intruded into Morrison on east side of Uncompahgre River; Dakota on skyline on both sides of valley.
0.5

16.7 Bridge across Uncompahgre River. Sill is green-gray, flow-layered, porphyritic-aphanitic, chloritized latite.
0.3

17.0 Chaffee Gulch.
0.1

17.1 Possible axis of proposed U.S. Bureau of Reclamation earth-fill dam (Dallas Divide Project). Sill very well exposed in cliffs on west side of valley; outstanding view of Mount Sneffles on skyline at 1:00.
0.6

17.7 Small erosional remnant of Morrison on west side of highway. Sill thickens and becomes locally discordant to bedding of Dakota and Morrison. Flow layering turns up abruptly and the intrusive trends northwest into Mancos Shale as a dike. Mancos is weakly hornfelsic at contact, with baked oysters (*Inoceramus*). Mancos visible on skyline south of intrusive contact.
1.2

18.9 Site of Ridgway Dam of the Dallas Creek Project of U.S. Bureau of Reclamation on right. Construction began in early 1980 and project is expected to be completed in late 1983. The earth fill dam will have a crest height above stream level of 69 m and a crest length of 725 m and contain 7,028,000 m^3 of material. Capacity of the reservoir will be 32,375 hectares (80,000 acre-feet). Main purpose of the dam is for irrigation in the Uncompahgre Valley, with secondary use for municipal water and recreation. Potential problems of faulting and landslides near the axis and abutments of the dam are currently under investigation (George F. Babits, personal communication, U.S. Bureau of Reclamation, Montrose, Colorado, July, 1981). Note: New section of highway circumvents the dam on the west and leaves road log for the next 3.5 miles and joins log approximately at mileage 23.0.
0.7

19.6 Alkali Creek.
1.5

21.1 Small fault in Dakota, down-to-east, on east side of road.
0.3

21.4 View straight ahead of fault, down-to-east.
1.6

23.0 **Stop 1.** Panoramic view to south of San Juan Mountains on skyline. Highest, horn-shaped peak in center is Mount Sneffles (4309 m; 14,143 ft) from which the Sneffles horst derives its name. The skyline mountains consist mostly of the Potosi and Silverton volcanic

---
*Road log is, in part, a synthesis of previously published materials. Reprinted and modified from: Epis, R. C., and Weimer, R. J., eds., 1976, Studies in Colorado field geology: Professional Contributions of the Colorado School of Mines, no. 8, 552 p.

SUPPLEMENTAL ROAD LOG NO. 1   49

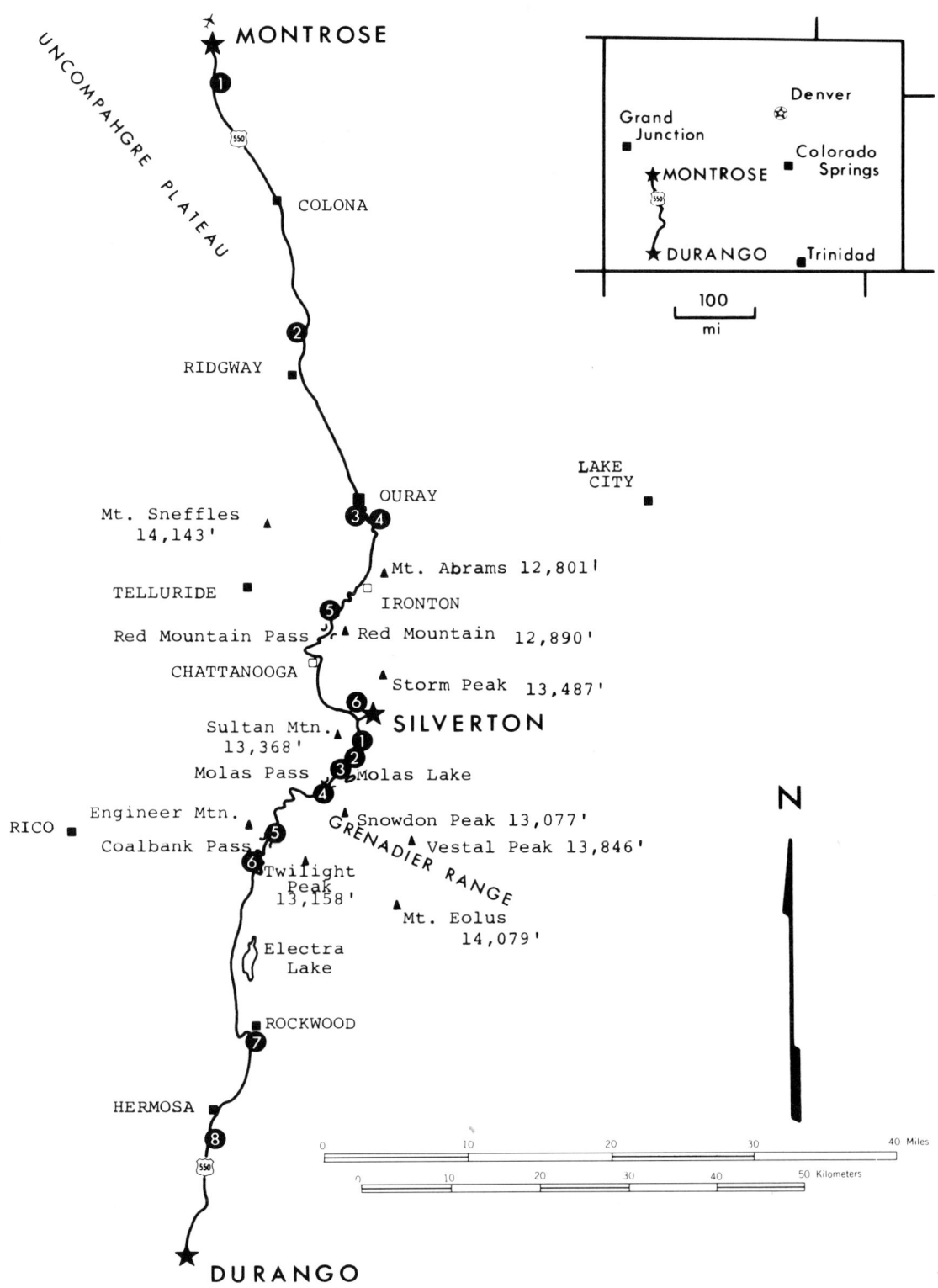

Figure 1. Index and route map for field trip from Montrose to Durango. Key for circled numbers from Montrose to Silverton: 1, Montrose syncline (mile 2.3); 2, Stop 1 (23.0); 3, Stop 2 (37.5); 4, Stop 3 (38.9); 5, Idarado Mine (47.5); and 6, Stop 4 (59.2). Key for circled numbers from Silverton to Durango: 1, Stop 5 (mile 62.5); 2, Stop 6, (64.5); 3, Stop 7 (65.4); 4, Stop 8 (67.0); 5, Stop 9 (74.4); 6, Stop 10 (76.8); 7, Stop 11 (94.1); and 8, Stop 12 (101.9). Circled numbers are keyed to road sections (fig. 2).

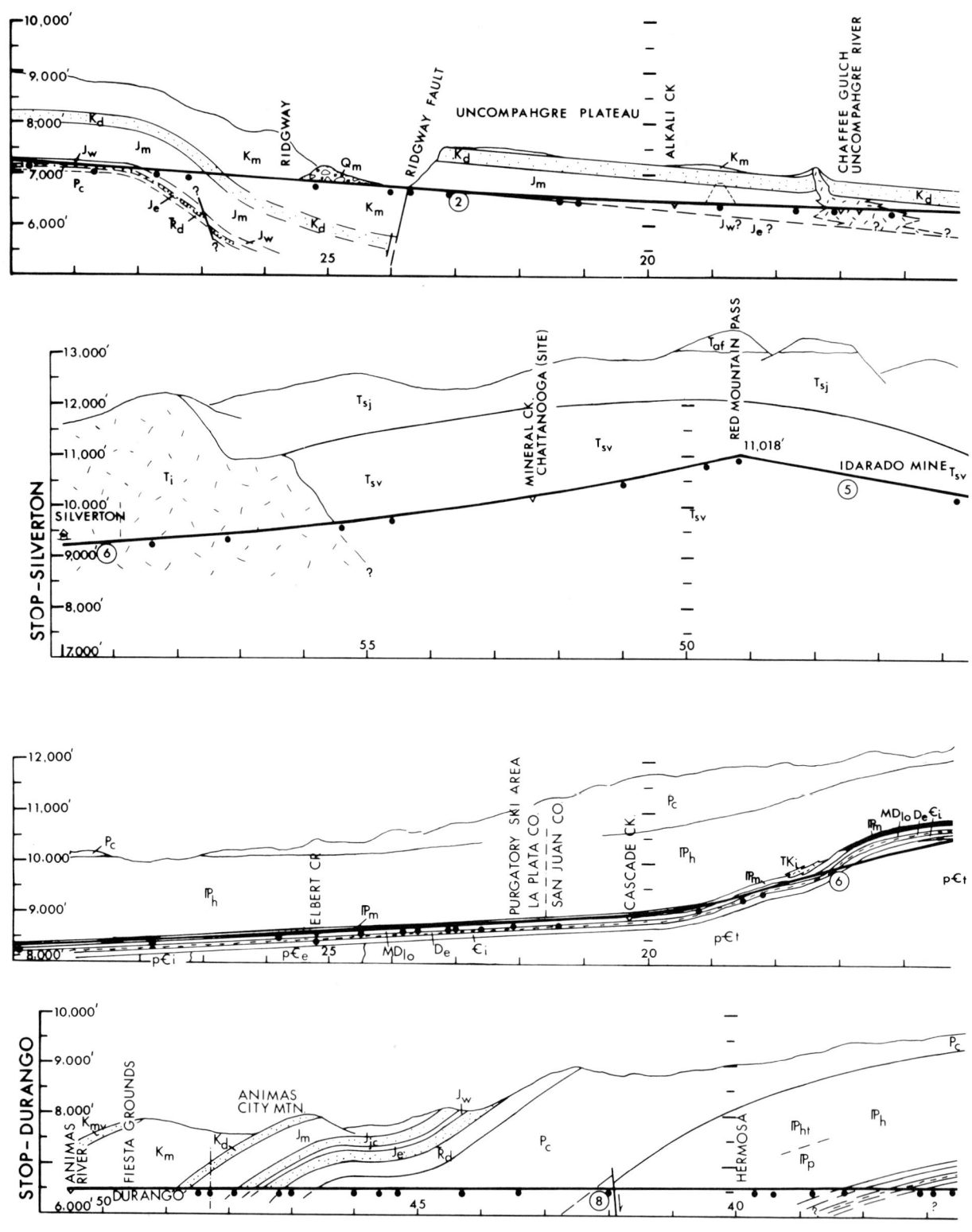

ROAD SECTIONS FROM MONTROSE

Figure 2. Road sections along the route of Montrose–Durango field trip. (These are not true cross-sections because the line
See Figure 1 for key to circled numbers on sections.

SUPPLEMENTAL ROAD LOG NO. 1

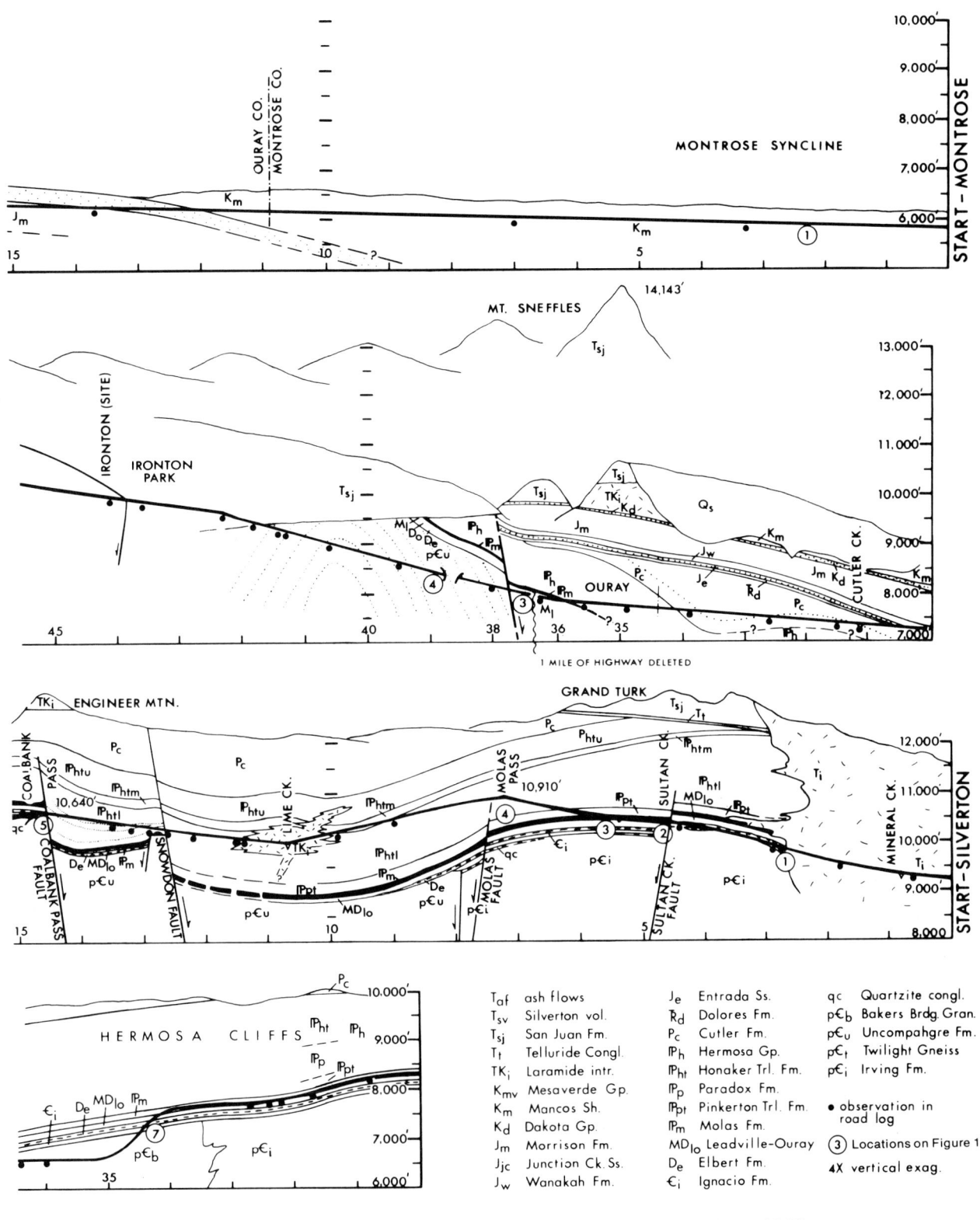

TO DURANGO, COLORADO
KEENAN LEE – 1976

of section is U.S. Highway 550, and the section shown is approximately the view seen above the highway to the west.)

series, a sequence of Oligocene ash-flow tuffs, erupted from the Silverton and Lake City cauldrons, lying on the intermediate lavas and breccias (about 612 m thick) of the San Juan Formation (32.1 m.y.). Mount Sneffles itself is a later intrusive, probably of latest Oligocene or earliest Miocene age. On this side of the horst, the volcanics lie on the Mancos Shale (Cretaceous), or locally on the upper Eocene Telluride Conglomerate; but, immediately southeast of Mount Sneffles, the Precambrian Uncompahgre Formation is exposed beneath the San Juan Formation. Because of elevation (greater than 4250 m) and precipitation (> 50 cm/yr, more than half of which falls as snow), snowfall can occur on the high peaks at any time of year. Snow avalanching is prevalent, both above and below timberline, from October to June.

Yellow-gray cliffs of Miller Mesa in middle distance, to southwest (2:00), are in the Mancos Shale. The resistant ledge-former in the middle is a group of calcareous shales and argillaceous lime mudstones that probably correlate with limestones of the Niobrara Formation. The apex of the triangular cliff face is San Juan Formation; immediately below are exposures of the Telluride Conglomerate and the "Ridgway Till," a probable mudflow.

Log Hill Mesa, immediately west of the Uncompahgre River, consists of Dakota and Morrison Formations, with local patches of Mancos Shale preserved by a gravel cap. The south end of Log Hill Mesa marks the trace of the east-west, down-to-south Ridgway fault, generally considered to be the southern edge of the (Laramide) Uncompahgre uplift. Throw on the fault here is about 460 m, juxtaposing Morrison and Mancos shales, but offset decreases rapidly to the east. Several oil tests, drilled on the south side of the fault, encountered natural gas and flowing hot water (see Weimer, this guidebook).

Low, rounded ridge to southwest (12:00), in foreground, is an end moraine of the Wisconsinian Uncompahgre glacier. The moraine has been breached by the Uncompahgre River (east) and Dallas Creek (west). The original plan for the Dallas Divide Project called for filling these two cuts with earth-fill, effectively recreating the probable late Wisconsinian glacial lake behind the end moraine (and inundating the post-Wisconsinian town of Ridgway).

0.1

23.1 Good exposures of Morrison in road cut on left (east).
0.6

23.7 Ridgway fault.
0.3

24.0 Junction with road to Owl Creek Pass and Silver Jack Reservoir. Cimarron Ridge, the skyline to east, shows jagged pinnacles of San Juan Formation (for example, Courthouse Mountain) resting on Upper Cretaceous, coal-bearing, Fruitland and Kirtland Formations.
1.2

25.2 Road cut in end moraine.
0.5

25.7 Junction with Colorado Highway 62. Road goes west into Ridgway and beyond to Placerville on the San Miguel River.
1.5

27.2 Crossing east-west, down-to-north, normal fault-monocline. Light cliffs of Dakota on either side of valley dip gently northward and are sharply folded-faulted across this structure and brought down to level of valley floor. Hot springs in valley mark probable trace of fault-monocline axis. This structure is of the same sense as the Box Canyon structure at Ouray but is of Laramide age. Morrison exposed below Dakota along west side of valley.
0.5

27.7 Excellent view southward of Uncompahgre Valley toward Ouray, with Mount Abrams on skyline.
1.1

28.8 To the east, above road level, is white Entrada Sandstone (Jurassic) between the Wanakah (Jurassic) and Dolores (Triassic) Formations. A small dike forms wall-like outcrop, cutting Entrada and Dolores. This location is along another east-west, down-to-north monoclinal flexure of Laramide age. The Permian Cutler Formation is at road level; Triassic is very thin.
0.9

29.7 Cliffs to east are Cutler Formation, overlain by very red, more shaley, Dolores Formation. Distinct white sandstone is Entrada; skyline is Morrison Formation.
0.5

30.2 Cedar Hill Cemetery. Gentle folding of Cutler visible.
0.9

31.1 Cutler Creek. Good exposures of the type section of the Cutler Formation in local domes. Lower part of Cutler is red, calcareous and sandy shales and red sandstones, similar to the upper Hermosa Group, but with fewer coarse detrital units. Cobble conglomerates, about 300 m above the base of the Cutler, may record Sneffles horst movements. Total exposed Cutler section is greater than 600 m thick.
0.4

SUPPLEMENTAL ROAD LOG NO. 1

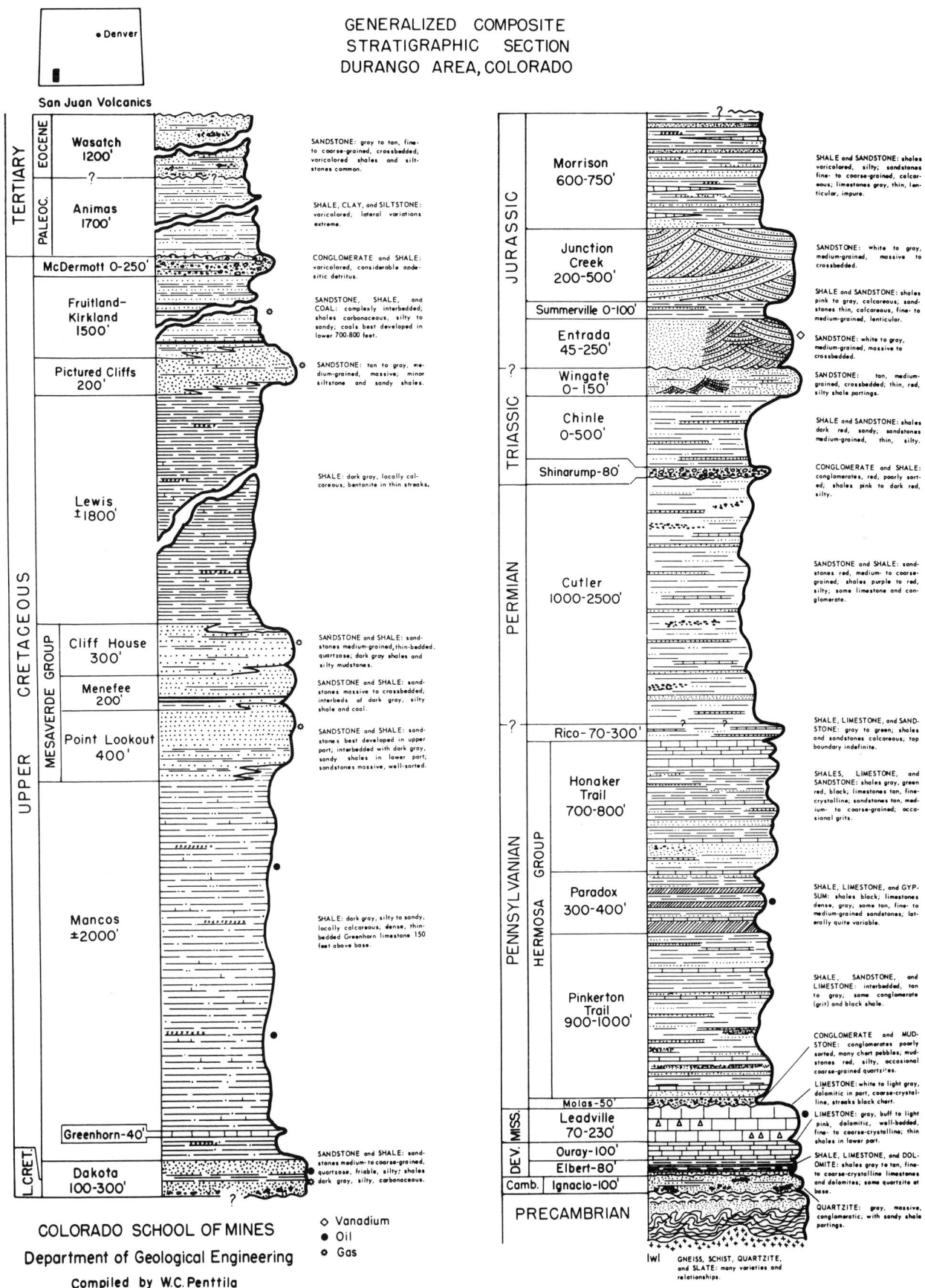

Figure 3. Generalized composite stratigraphic section, Durango area, Colorado.

31.5	To northeast, brush-covered, high slopes above Cutler are Dolores Formation. Mine dump is from base-metal replacement ores in limestone in Jurassic Summerville Formation. **1.1**
32.6	Good exposure of Cutler Formation on either side of valley. Distinct southward dip reversal of regional northward dip. **1.3**
33.9	Dexter Creek road. Near axis of syncline. **0.5**
34.4	Ouray city limits, the "Switzerland of America." Excellent exposures of Hermosa Group (Pennsylvanian) on either side of valley. Down-to-north monoclinal structure is evident in west wall of valley in Hermosa and Cutler formations (fig. 34.4). In the Hermosa Group, angular unconformities are evidence of Pennsylvanian uplift and deformation of the ancestral Uncompahgre uplift, or more specifically, uplift of the Sneffles horst immediately to the south. Several greenish-gray Laramide dikes cut Hermosa in lower limb of monocline and are accompanied by hydrothermal alteration. **0.5**
34.9	Intense hydrothermal alteration along east side of valley at "the Blowout," a Laramide granodiorite porphyry intrusive. Alteration is restricted to the intrusive and its wallrock; the overlying San Juan Formation (Oligocene) is unaltered. **0.7**
35.6	Hot springs swimming pool at Ouray. **0.7**
36.3	Mississippian Leadville Limestone in south side of road cut. **0.3**
36.6	**Turn off** (south) to Box Canyon and Camp Bird Mine. **0.5**
37.1	**Sharp turn.** Rounded, tree-covered hill, on left, with light gray rocks in roadcut, is underlain by moraine. Main highway roadcut on left is brecciated Leadville Limestone. **0.2**
37.3	Turnoff to Amphitheather Campground. **0.2**
37.5	**Stop 2.** Lookout Point. General view of Ouray and surroundings. The Blowout is just east of north (Ouray's streets are north-south). Northeast is Cascade Falls, with an exposed stratigraphic section from the Hermosa Group to the Dakota Sandstone, above which are the Laramide intrusive rocks of the Blowout, and a cap of San Juan Formation.

Section seen to the south-southwest shows Devonian Elbert Formation lying with sharp angular unconformity upon Precambrian quartzites of the Uncompahgre Formation (fig. 37.5). A thin Devonian Ouray carbonate overlies the Elbert, and the bench-former is the Leadville Limestone. The Hermosa Group is seen above the Leadville (a thin section of Molas Formation is out of sight); the skyline is San Juan Formation. A thin layer of Telluride Conglomerate is at the base of the San Juan, lying on a late Eocene erosion surface. This section is on the upthrown (south) side of the Ouray fault, which is the northern boundary of the Sneffles horst.

The Ouray fault trends west-northwest and is down-to-north. The trace of this fault is at the south end of the parking area, where Precambrian Uncompahgre quartzites and Mississippian Leadville limestones are juxtaposed. The fault is better seen at Box Canyon Falls. |

Figure 34.4. Permian–Triassic unconformity in west wall of Ouray Canyon. Formation symbols same as Figure 2 (R. J. Weimer).

Figure 37.5. Base of Paleozoic section, Devonian Elbert Formation, unconformably overlying Precambrian Uncompahgre Formation in Box Canyon, Ouray.

The section exposed to the northwest is on the north (down) side of the Ouray fault, off of the Sneffles horst. The Hermosa Group is seen at the base of the section [faulted against (unseen) Precambrian quartzites of the horst]; successive units are: Cutler Formation; Dolores Formation; Entrada Sandstone; Wanakah Formation; Morrison Formation; and Dakota Sandstone, overlain by a Laramide granodiorite porphyry sill, and capped by San Juan Formation.

0.2

37.7 Highway crosses Ouray fault, with Leadville Limestone on north, and steeply-dipping metasediments of the Uncompahgre to south.

0.3

38.0 Glacial striae along highway roadcut.

0.6

38.6 Tunnel in Uncompahgre Formation.

0.3

38.9 **Stop 3.** Bear Creek Falls. View to north of Uncompahgre River valley.

View to south of Mount Abrams (3902 m; 12,801 ft). Plaque to Otto Mears, builder of the original toll road over which the Million Dollar Highway was later built.

Outcrops of the Uncompahgre Formation show slaty argillites and quartzites, derived from sediments deposited and metamorphosed between 1,720 m.y. and 1,460 m.y. ago. Total thickness of the formation is unknown, but probably exceeds 2450 m. The outcrops north of the parking area show good examples of slaty cleavage and sedimentary structures: graded bedding, ripples, feeding trails (?). For the next 4.1 km, the highway is in strongly folded Uncompahgre metasediments, mostly slates.

This point is on the Sneffles horst, where the Paleozoic section is thin or absent. The canyon wall, immediately to the west (seen from previous stop), shows about 245 m of section (Elbert–Hermosa), below the Telluride and San Juan Formations; whereas, to the east, the San Juan rests directly on the Uncompahgre Formation.

Glacial till southeast of bridge over Bear Creek may be a remnant of a lateral moraine. Glacial cirque headwalls within Tertiary volcanics serve as excellent catchment basins for snow to accumulate and move down the steep, sparsely vegetated slopes. Snow avalanches have formed chutes on the slopes and commonly build debris cones or fans on the valley floor. These chutes can be observed on both sides of the valley from here to Silverton. Looking south-southeast at the prominent peak of Mount Abrams, the western flank forms the starting zone for the famed East Riverside Slide (referred to at mile 41.4).

0.6

39.5 Steeply dipping, massive Uncompahgre quartzite on west, with glacial striae.

1.1

40.6 Crest of large anticline to west (plunging west) in the Uncompahgre Formation. Slaty cleavage and graded bedding at Stop 4 (38.9) are consistent with the north flank of an upright anticline. San Juan Formation on crest of anticline.

0.7

41.3 Contact of San Juan Formation and Uncompahgre on east. Hydrothermal alteration along possible fault contact or breccia pipe.

0.1

41.4 Snow avalanche chutes descend into canyon from both valley walls. These are the Riverside avalanche tracks; both classified as large, frequent avalanches. Both can, and do, run at the same time. The West Riverside has a catchment basin of 60 hectares (150 acres) and has run at least seven times in a ten-year period. East Riverside has a catchment basin of 30 hectares with a spectacular shooting track across the highway that averages 63 percent slope. This avalanche crosses U.S. 550 three to four times a year and has been clocked at speeds of 400 k.p.h. Among the more recent casualties were a pastor and his two daughters, swept to their deaths on 3 March 1963.

0.7

41.8 Switchback causes the highway to cross the track of the Slippery Jim avalanche twice. This is another large, frequent avalanche that has run at least five times in ten years. In fact, the Red Mountain Pass section of U.S. 550 is one of the worst avalanche sections in Colorado. After a heavy snowfall, potential avalanche areas that are hazardous to travel and that could unexpectedly bury the highway are artificially released in a controlled manner by the highway department. Artillery, fired into starting zones to trigger the snow, is used with limited success.

0.5

42.3 Entering lower end of Ironton Park. Over the next several kilometers, numerous avalanche paths descend over 1070 m of relief from both east and west slopes. Aspen often revegetate avalanche paths; stands of different-aged timber, within individual paths, denote past size and frequency of avalanching. Classic examples of aspen "trimlines" outlining paths are expressed on the west slope of Ironton Park.

1.3

43.6 (Unseen) Contact of Ouray Limestone and San Juan Formation east of highway along break in slope. These are the last Paleozoic rocks along the highway until after we have passed through the Tertiary Silverton caldera. Several mines here worked replacement deposits in the Ouray Limestone.

0.5

44.1 Site of former town of Ironton. Entering the north portion of ring-fault zone of Silverton caldera. Red Mountain No. 1 is to the southeast; Red Mountain No. 2 to the south. Ouray Formation overlies Uncompahgre Formation in wooded slope to the east.

1.7

45.8 Leaving Ironton Park. Many switchbacks up road to Red Mountain Pass.

1.7

47.5 Idarado Mine.

1.7

49.2 Red Mountain Pass, San Juan County line (elevation 3358 m; 11,018 ft). Gold-ore wagons crossed here in 1878. Caldera ring-zone is a series of arcuate, down-to-east, high-angle faults, concentric to the Silverton caldera, whose geographic center is near Storm Peak (4111 m; 13,487 ft) to southeast. Along these faults, San Juan Formation, outside the caldera, is against younger Burns and Henson Formations of the Silverton volcanics. Red Mountain No. 3 to east.

0.5

49.7 Narrow gauge railroad crossing. Railroad was also constructed by Otto Mears, pretty much along the route of his toll road. It was originally planned to run from Silverton to Ouray, but the steep grades below Ironton Park were too great for normal trains, and the line stopped at Ironton. The first train came through Red Mountain Pass, at that time the highest railroad pass in the United States, on 17 September 1888.

0.3

51.0 Excellent view down glaciated Mineral Creek Valley. Numerous avalanche tracks on northeast side. These tracks commonly follow gullies that appear to be controlled by fractures and faults associated with the Silverton caldera ring-faulting. Mineral Creek follows Silverton caldera ring-zone.

1.4

52.4 Crossing Mineral Creek at the site of the former town of Chattanooga. In 1884, a snow avalanche started on the northwest slope, above the hairpin turn, and reportedly ran down the main street of town. Looking northwest from Chattanooga, two sections of the debris fan at the base of the Eagle Avalanche path are exposed in roadcuts along the highway.

2.2

54.6 Bear Mountain straight ahead. Excellent display of glacial geomorphology and avalanche chutes.

0.8

55.4 View of Sultan Mountain, just southeast of Bear Mountain. Sultan Mountain is part of a large silicic intrusion along south-southwest margin of Silverton caldera.

1.8

57.2 Junction with road to south Mineral Creek.

1.2

58.4 Intensely altered Henson–Burns volcanics along Silverton caldera ring-zone. Rapid physical and chemical weathering produces a supply of material that is being actively transported downslope by debris flows, debris slides, rockfalls, and snow avalanches.

0.5

58.9 Silverton City limits.

0.3

59.2 Junction U.S. 550 and Colorado 110. **Turn east on Colorado 110 to Silverton.**
Stop 4. Viewpoint of Silverton and surroundings.

Snow avalanches are rapid, violent forms of snow movement, caused by the acceleration of a failed mass of snow in steep terrain. Avalanches are active geologic agents of erosion and deposition, often transporting snow, organic, and inorganic debris to the runout zone, a gently-sloping area at the bottom of the slope. The destructive effects of avalanching in this zone constitute a serious hazard to lives and property within the San Juan Mountains.

Idaho Gulch (directly southeast) is a confined avalanche path, running off the northwest slope of Kendall Mountain. In the winter of 1913–1914, it reportedly crossed the ballpark and highway, running over 765 m from the break in slope of the runout fan. Idaho is known to have run more than 10 times in the past 70 years. Sorges Slide, directly south of Idaho Gulch, runs on an unconfined slope. Hence, the snow is not channelized in a particular track like Idaho Gulch. Sorges was first known to have run in approximately 1943, when it wiped out a virgin stand of conifers and deposited them within its path and on the Animas floodplain, serving as Silverton's winter fuel supply. It was not known to have run again until 1961, depositing a stand of aspen in the runout zone. Looking southwest, two paths (Gladstones, North and South) start as points and run down Sultan Mountain to the mining tailings. These are examples of point-source avalanches that begin below timberline from a point or spot within the timber.
0.6

59.8 Grand Imperial Hotel, Silverton. Leaving Silverton, there is a view of Sultan Mountain straight ahead. Mine dumps are visible on the lower slopes of Sultan Mountain and along the contact zone of the intrusion.
0.6

60.4 Junction U.S. 550 and Colorado 110.
0.2

60.6 Bridge across Mineral Creek. View north, along Mineral Creek toward Red Mountain Pass, shows caldera ring-zone and intense red-ocher alteration.
1.0

61.6 Roadcuts in Sultan Mountain intrusive.
0.9

62.5 **Stop 5.** Elevation 3048 m (10,000 ft). View back to northeast of Silverton; junction of Mineral Creek and Animas River; alteration and mineralization along caldera ring-zone. Mount Kendall, immediately east across the Animas River; outcrop in roadcut of Sultan Mountain intrusive in contact with Paleozoic sedimentary rocks. Contact metamorphism of sediments to quartzites, hornfelses, marbles and skarns. This is the first appearance of the Paleozoic section (Elbert, Ouray, and Leadville Formations) south of the Silverton caldera.
0.2

62.7 Roadcuts in Cambrian Ignacio and Devonian Elbert Formations for the next 2.5 km.
1.5

64.2 Contact of Ouray and Elbert Formations to west.
0.3

64.5 **Stop 6.** Sultan Creek. Excellent exposure of section from Ignacio Formation to Leadville Formation (fig. 64.5).
0.7

65.2 North turn-off to Molas Lake.
0.2

65.4 **Stop 7.** Molas Lake. Borrow-pit excavations show the relationship between the Leadville Limestone (Mississippian) and the lower Molas Formation (Pennsylvanian). The quarry has excavated into the west side of a paleokarst tower (kegelkarst, mogote, hum) and exposed paleokarst breccias. The Leadville here is a light blue-gray, partly recrystallized, bryozoan-coralline-brachiopodal-crinoidal lime wackestone to packstone. The lower part of the Molas Formation is a red, nonbedded terra rosa residuum that fills solution openings and breccia voids in the Leadville Limestone. The Middle Member of the Molas is a poorly stratified mixture of quartz sand and transported terra rosa material; the Upper Member shows marine reworking. The Molas–Hermosa contact appears to be gradational, and many of the fossils are common to both formations.

Vista toward south is dominated by Snowdon Mountain (3986 m; 13,077 ft) directly to the south (highway runs northeast-southwest), and the Grenadier Range of the Needle Mountains to the south-southeast. West-to-east, the Grenadier peaks are:

Mount Garfield—3982 m; 13,065 ft
Graystone Peak—4111 m; 13,489 ft
Electric Peak—4023 m; 13,200 ft;
  (at first look appearing to be a single peak, is actually three aligned peaks)
Arrow Peak—4207 m; 13,803 ft
Vestal Peak—4220 m; 13,846 ft

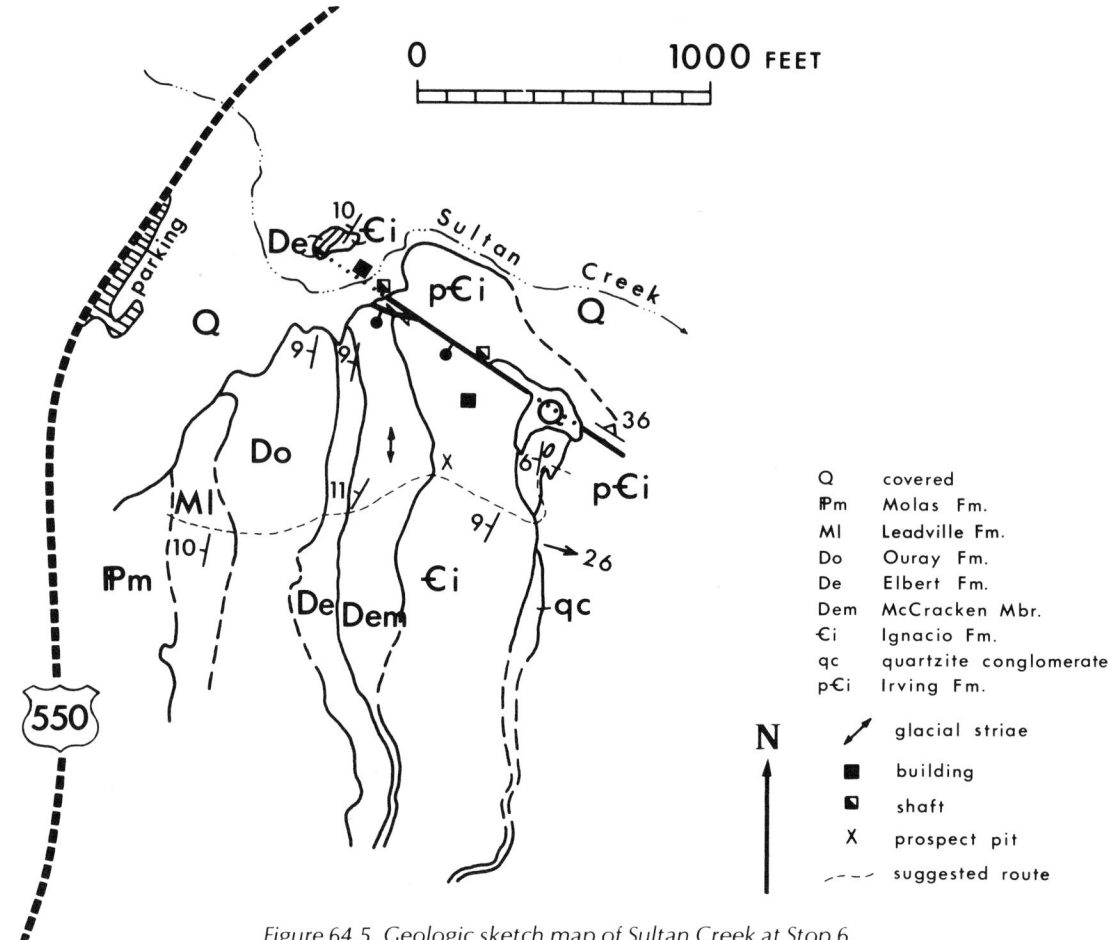

Figure 64.5. Geologic sketch map of Sultan Creek at Stop 6.

Trinity Peaks—4192 m; 13,752 ft
                4207 m; 13,804 ft
                4189 m; 13,745 ft
Storm King Peak—4189 m; 13,742 ft
Mount Silex—4152 m; 13,627 ft

Why is there such a marked concordance of peaks?

0.4

65.8 South entrance road to Molas Lake. Road cut in Pinkerton Trail Formation limestones and shales. Contact of the Honaker Trail–Pinkerton Trail formations is picked at the base of the first detrital sequence with thick arkose sandstones, which occurs in the covered area west of the highway.

1.2

67.0 **Stop 8.** Molas Pass, elevation 3325 m (10,910 ft). Highway is cut in the detrital facies of the Lower Member of the Honaker Trail Formation. Molas Lake is below to northeast (highway runs north-south) at elevation 3197 m (10,488 ft). Grand Turk Mountain, to north, is capped by the San Juan Formation, resting on a thin layer of Telluride Conglomerate, which, in turn, lies on the late Eocene erosion surface. The erosion surface bevels the gently westward-dipping Paleozoic strata, so that the Tertiary conglomerate lies on Cretaceous rocks to the northwest; Triassic Dolores Formation to the north-northwest; Permian Cutler Formation to the north; and Pennsylvanian Honaker Trail Formation to the northeast.

This area has been extensively glaciated during the Pleistocene, as is everywhere apparent. The terraces below are scoured Paleozoic rocks; Storm Peak, beyond Silverton, shows a hanging valley; well-displayed cirques, glacial valleys, and hanging tributaries can be seen east of the Animas Valley. Especially note the west-southwest-trending glacial striae that are common right in the pass itself, evidence that surely is suggestive of icecap conditions in the San Juans.

From this vantage, structural elements of the Paleozoic Grenadier highland (horst?) can be seen in the present topography: the Molas–Andres Lake fault, trending east-northeast and down-to-south, is about on line with Molas Pass; the Snowdon fault, trending east and passing along the north slope of Snowdon

Peak, is down-to-north, with the intervening Molas graben (present-day) represented by the modern Molas Creek Valley. The Molas graben was a high area during the early Paleozoic.

Viewpoint is on a carbonate bed of the carbonate-detrital sequences in the Lower Member of the Honaker Trail Formation. This bed is a gray, fossiliferous, lime wackestone to packstone, slightly sandy at the base and intraclastic at top. Fossils include phylloid algae, pelecypods, crinoids, fusulinids, gastropods, forams and brachiopods. Locally, the unit is a coralline boundstone made up of *Chaetetes*.

View ahead of Engineer Mountain.

2.7

69.7 Digits of Lime Creek quartz latite intrusion (Tertiary) here extend into the Honaker Trail Formation as sills, but the intrusion crosscuts the bedding as a dike and continues up to the top of the ridge to north.

0.8

70.5 Lime Creek. Numerous snow avalanches (bank slides) from here to Coalbank Pass.

0.7

71.2 Hill to the east (highway runs north-south) is the main part of the Tertiary Lime Creek intrusion, probably a laccolith, that intruded and deformed the Honaker Trail Formation. Minor hydrothermal alteration and pyrite mineralization are associated with the intrusion.

0.1

71.3 Lime Creek Road. Unfortunately, this is the road shown on the Durango 2° geologic map, rather than the present highway.

0.7

72.0 Highway crosses axis of a syncline in the Honaker Trail Formation, formed by drag folding along the Snowdon fault (to south) and laccolithic (?) intrusion (to north). The doubly-plunging syncline has its nadir just to the east of Lime Creek. Roadcut here shows carbonate solution features and channel scour in Lower and Middle members of the Honaker Trail Formation.

0.4

72.4 Highway crosses Snowdon fault.

0.3

72.7 Sharply flexed limestone beds in the lower Honaker Trail Formation, north of the Snowdon fault, are against Uncompahgre slates and quartzites to south. The Snowdon fault extends from here about 3.3 km west and at least 10 km east to the Animas River. The fault may connect with the Elk Park faults that extend another 16 km or so along the north flank of the Grenadier Range.

The area, from Lime Creek to slightly beyond Molas Pass, was burned in 1879, in a fire that cleared 10,400 hectares (26,000 acres). The 101-year period, since the fire, has been insufficient to re-establish a forest cover, despite replanting that began in 1911.

Outcrop of Cambrian (?) quartzite conglomerate overlying Precambrian quartzite on small hill below highway.

0.3

73.0 Sharply flexed beds of the Honaker Trail Formation, this time with a reverse dip to the south. This flexure, down-to-south, makes a small horst of the hill with the quartzite conglomerate. Angular unconformities in the flexure indicate vertical movement during deposition of the lower Honaker Trail Formation (Desmoinesian).

0.3

73.3 Peak ahead is Twilight Peak (4011 m; 13,158 ft), type area of the Twilight Gneiss.

1.1

74.4 **Stop 9.** Coalbank Pass, elevation 3243 m (10,640 ft). The old stage road, from Durango to Silverton, passed about here, and dropped down into Lime Creek nearly along route of present highway. With the advent of the automobile, the stage road was abandoned; the first auto road from Cascade Creek was made around the south and east flanks of Potato Hill into Lime Creek Canyon. There, for a considerable distance, the road is a narrow ledge blasted out of the face of the cliff. This caused many a faint heart to waver, especially in winter. The new Coalbank Hill road, which we are traveling, reverted back to the old stagecoach line. There is no coal at Coalbank Pass, on Coalbank Hill, or along Coal Creek.

Fault trending northwest, along drainage northeast of pass, is the Coalbank fault, down-to-northeast. Honaker Trail beds are against Precambrian rocks of the Twilight Gneiss with about 230 m of stratigraphic separation. On the upthrown block, the gneisses are overlain by the Devonian McCracken Member of the Elbert Formation in outcrops along the fault; whereas, at the parking area, a quartzite boulder-cobble conglomerate is between the two units (fig. 74.4a).

West of the highway, the Cambrian Ignacio Formation sandstones are between the quartzite conglomerate and the McCracken. Above the McCracken are thin shales and shaly carbonates of the Elbert Formation, overlain by thin carbonates of the Leadville-Ouray, and several meters of red Molas Formation terra rosa materials. The Pinkerton

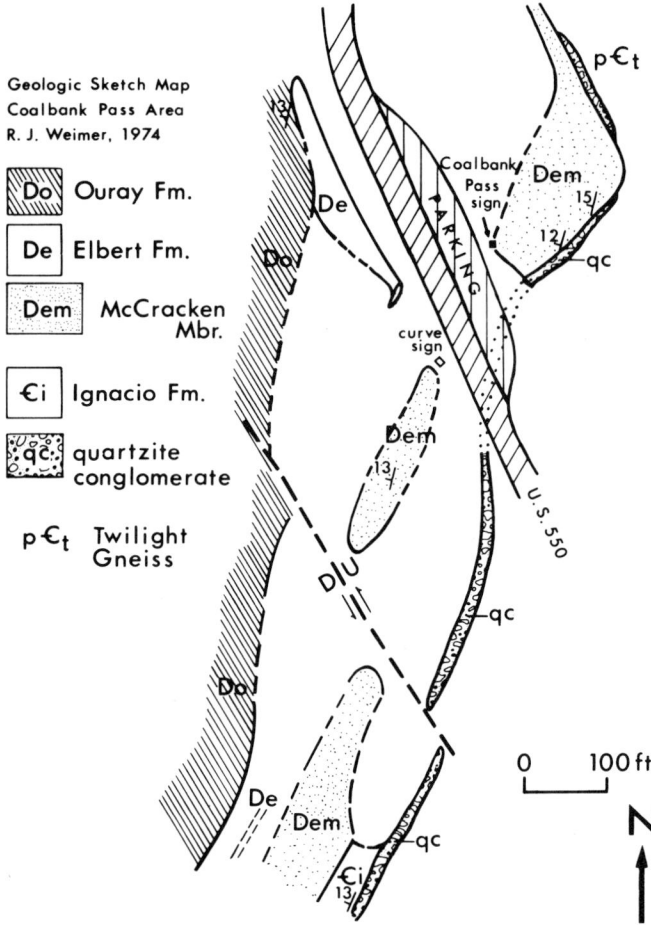

Figure 74.4a. Geologic sketch map of Coalbank Pass at Stop 9.

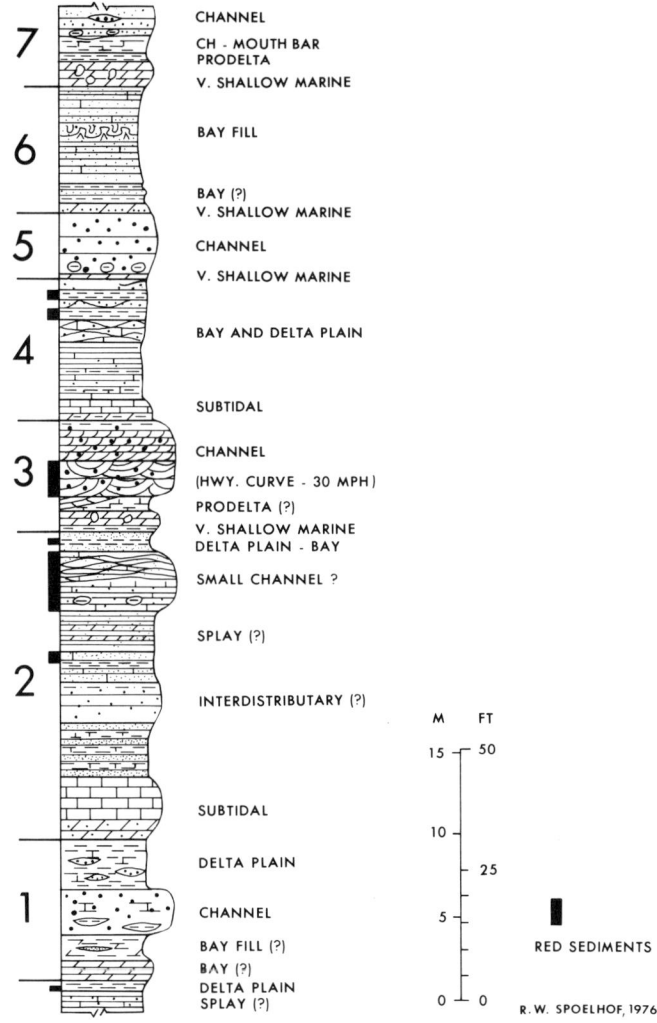

Figure 74.4b. Stratigraphic section of the Lower Member of the Honaker Trail Formation at Coalbank Pass.

Trail Formation apparently is absent at this locality; lower Honaker Trail carbonates and detrital rocks are the first rocks exposed above the Molas Formation. Middle Member limestone benches are at the top of the cliff, with 466 m of stratigraphic section above the Molas Formation.

Cyclic detrital and carbonate (here mostly dolomitic) deltaic and shallow-marine deposits in the lower Honaker Trail Formation are exposed at road level north of the Coalbank Pass fault (fig. 74.4b).

2.4

76.8 **Stop 10.** Cambrian–Precambrian contact. Road cut exposes lower part of Leadville, and all of Ouray, Elbert, and Ignacio Formations and Precambrian gneiss. Clean exposure of Elbert Formation in road cut. Farther downgrade, the Molas Formation is intruded and blackened by a Tertiary (?) sill.

1.2

78.0 Ouray Formation in road cut.

0.3

78.3 Mill Creek Lodge. Barrier gates across highway are used in winter (mid-November?) when avalanches close the road.

0.7

79.0 Glacially sculpted slopes to west are underlain by the lower Paradox Formation.

1.1

80.1 Cross Cascade Creek. Excellent exposures (but rugged cliffs) of the entire lower Paleozoic section. Ignacio Formation here contains numerous Cambrian obuloid brachiopods.

1.1

81.2 Roadcut in red siltstones of Molas Formation.

0.2

8.14 Leave San Juan County, enter La Plata County.

0.3

81.7 Purgatory Ski Area.

0.2

81.9	Cliffs ahead on the west rim of the valley are the Hermosa ("Beautiful") Cliffs.		are along Elbert Creek that enters the lake from the northwest.
	0.5		**2.1**
82.4	Columbine Ranger Station to west. Purgatory campground and trail to east; contact of Molas calcareous shales and basal Pinkerton limestone across ditch to west.	89.7	Entrance to Haviland Lake.
			0.9
		90.6	Cliffs of Leadville Limestone to east, showing knobby karst surface.
	0.4		**0.9**
82.8	Sedimentary breccia in west roadcut is the weathered top of the Leadville Limestone, with terra rosa material of the Molas as infilling matrix.	91.5	View of Hermosa Cliffs to west. Highway level is about at the Leadville–Molas contact; above, to the west, are the Pinkerton Trail Formation, and the higher cliffs of the Honaker Trail Formation. These three formations constitute the Hermosa Group. Glaciers in this part of the canyon were more than 600 m thick and reached nearly to the top of the Hermosa Cliffs.
	0.1		
82.9	Columbine Camp.		
	0.5		
83.4	Highway is following the karst surface that developed in late Mississippian–early Pennsylvanian time on the Leadville–Ouray carbonates; was covered and protected by the thick soils of the Molas, and was recently (Pleistocene) exhumed by the Animas glaciers. The closed depressions, on the east side of the highway, are paleokarst features.		
			0.5
		92.0	Exposure on west side of road is fossiliferous, dark gray, siliceous limestone and calcareous shale of the Pennsylvanian Pinkerton Trail Formation. Molas Formation underlies road and Pinkerton Trail.
			0.2
	0.2	92.2	Paradox Formation in slopes west of highway.
83.6	Basal Pinkerton Trail in roadcut. The dark gray limestones and shales here contain *Fusulina* and other Atokan fauna; whereas, at Molas Lake, the formation is probably Desmoinesian, suggesting northeastward transgression onto the Uncompahgre uplift.		**0.3**
		92.5	Road to Rockwood, now a near-ghost town, but formerly a booming town in the heyday of the railroad and mining.
			1.6
	0.7	94.1	**Stop 11.** Denver and Rio Grande Western Railroad. This narrow-gauge line runs 75.3 km from Durango to Silverton, where it dead-ends. The railroad was completed in 1882 to serve the mining industry at Silverton, but, at present, it is operated only for tourist excursions (round trip from Durango) during the summer. A geologic railroad log for this trip was prepared by Caswell Silver (New Mexico Geological Society Guidebook 8, 1957).
84.3	Collapse (?) breccia of Leadville Limestone, infilled by Molas terra rosas.		
	0.7		
85.0	Elbert Creek. Type section of the Elbert Formation is about 800 m downstream (east).		
	0.6		
85.6	The East Needle Mountains, dominated by Mount Eolus, 4291 m (14,079 ft), are to the northeast (highway is north-south), and the West Needle Mountains, with Twilight Peak, 4011 m (13,158 ft), the highest mountain, are to the north-northeast. The East Needles are composed mostly of Eolus Granite (1460 m.y.), and the West Needles are Twilight Gneiss (1780 m.y.).		
			Walk north along railroad tracks to see the Precambrian–Cambrian nonconformity, with Ignacio Formation on Baker's Bridge Granite (1720 m.y.). Northwest of the highway–railroad intersection is the abandoned Rockwood quarry, dug in the Leadville Limestone. The underlying Ouray Formation is exposed in the cliffs below and east of the quarry. The McCracken Sandstone Member of the Elbert is exposed along the railroad. The uppermost part of the Leadville Limestone, exposed in the rim of the quarry, is a coarse breccia, composed of fragments of Leadville Limestone cemented with red clay of the overlying Molas Formation. Solution channels and cavities deep in the limestone are filled with Molas red clay.
	2.0		
87.6	Entrance to Electra Lake (Ignacio Reservoir). Electra Lake is the source of water for the hydroelectric plant at Tacoma. A dam across Elbert Creek forms the lake which is supplied chiefly by a flume from Cascade Creek about 8 km north. The water from the lake drops about 150 m to a penstock; then enters the pipeline and plunges 60 m to the turbines, with a 204.5 kg pressure at the plant. Type sections for the Ignacio and Elbert Formations		

The quarry floor lies about 3 m above the base of the Leadville. Quarrying was carried no deeper stratigraphically because the underlying beds are too siliceous. The upper half of the Leadville, below the breccia, is composed of massive beds of white, coarsely crystalline limestone, containing crinoid stems and other fossils. Some beds are oolitic and others, particularly in the lower part, contain lenses and nodules of dark-gray chert. The oolitic strata are rich in endothyrid foraminifera.

The thickness of the Leadville is about 30 m. It is separated from the underlying Ouray Formation by a bed of limy shale, 90–150 cm thick, that forms a notch in the cliff face, exposed in the cliffs east of the quarry. Late Devonian fossils are present in the Ouray; and Mississippian fossils are present in the Leadville. The Ouray is about 21 m thick; it is similar to the Leadville but somewhat more siliceous. The lower 4–6 m of Ouray Limestone is thin bedded and contains thin shale partings.

1.7

95.8 Highway follows approximate contact of Precambrian (east) and Ignacio Formation (west). Slopes above Ignacio are formed on shales and argillaceous carbonates of the Elbert Formation. Giant glacial step, trending eastward across heavily glaciated Animas Valley, is developed in Precambrian granites.
0.4

96.2 Leadville–Ouray carbonate cliffs to west. Note (paleo?) caverns in Leadville.
0.2

96.4 Road to Baker's Bridge. The first mining camp in southwest Colorado was established here in 1861, on the east bank of the river, by a group of about 100 people under the leadership of Charles Baker. Little gold was found, however, and the Indians were a constant hazard. When the Civil War started, the party disbanded and returned east. Baker later returned and was killed by Indians as he was preparing to lead an exploring party into the Grand Canyon.
0.3

96.7 Golden Horseshoe Restaurant.
0.2

96.9 The gravel operation on the valley bottom was once a placer mine. On the east side of the valley, a road zigzags up through the Hermosa beds to Missionary Ridge.
1.2

98.1 Whispering Pines apartments.
0.5

98.6 Good view to west of Hermosa Group. The lower, wooded slopes are on black shales and gypsum of the Paradox Formation, while the upper cliffs are carbonates and sandstones of the Honaker Trail Formation.
0.6

99.2 The knob to east, with trees and a small house, is a drumlin. The redbeds to the southwest are in the Permian Cutler Formation.
0.3

99.5 The very flat floor of the Animas Valley, from here to Durango, is the result of lacustrine sedimentation in a glacial lake, which was formed when end moraines, at the north end of Durango, dammed the Animas Valley.
0.2

99.7 Cross D&RGW railroad tracks at Hermosa.
2.1

101.8 Trimble Lane to Trimble Hot Springs. A north-east-trending, down-to-northwest fault crosses the Animas Valley here. The hot springs along the fault discharge sulfurous water at 32–43°C.
0.1

101.9 **Stop 12.** View of Permian and Pennsylvanian strata. Hermosa Mountain, to the north, is in the center of the area of the Pennsylvanian Hermosa type section. The prominently exposed, light-colored ledge is a massive arkosic sandstone ("gritstone") in the Hermosa. Above this ledge are 252 m of interbedded white, arkosic sandstones; gray fossiliferous limestones; dolomites; and shales of the Honaker Trail. Above this, and capping the mountain, are more than 100 meters of red Permian Cutler arkose. The contact of the Honaker Trail and the underlying Paradox black shales and anhydrites is at the base of a limestone, 42 m below the "gritstone." On the east wall, the "gritstone" is just above the talus, and light-colored Honaker Trail is exposed up to the overlying red Permian Cutler arkose.
1.3

103.2 Red rocks of the canyon walls are Cutler Formation, 765 m thick here.
0.9

104.1 Waterfall Ranch, with waterfall in upper Cutler.
1.0

105.1 The structural terrace crossing the Animas Valley is the Durango anticline, a northeast trending structure.
0.3

105.4 Just above the houses and trailers west of the highway, the gray ledge-former is a fluvial, cross-bedded, conglomeratic sandstone (Shinarump-type) that marks the base of the Triassic section. The redbeds below are the uppermost Cutler Formation; the redbeds above are sandy shales and sandstones of the Triassic Dolores (Chinle) Formation.

0.4

105.8 **Slow** for look at section exposed in walls of Animas Valley. View toward southwest of the northern end of Animas City Mountain. The south-sloping mesa is capped by the resistant Dakota and Burro Canyon formations, consisting of two cliffy sandstones, separated by a dark gray shale with thin coals. Below the upper cliffs is a wooded and brush-covered slope, formed by 150 m of Jurassic Morrison Formation, which consists of interbedded, light green and maroon mudstone; white sandstone; and thin, light gray limestone. Below the Morrison, the upper of the two massive white sandstones is the Junction Creek Sandstone (45 m thick), which is separated from the underlying Entrada Sandstone (about 60 m), by the Wanakah formation (15 m), consisting of interbedded, gray-red sandstone and shale, and a basal, dark gray limestone (60–90 cm). Immediately below the rounded Entrada, is a 12-m thick, pinkish sandstone that weathers into a vertical cliff. It has been suggested that this unit is equivalent to the Triassic Wingate Sandstone. The underlying redbeds are Triassic Dolores sandy shales.

1.0

106.8 Prominent road cut on west in Dolores redbeds.

0.2

107.0 Sandstones in roadcut are Entrada Sandstone.

0.7

107.7 **Slow** for view of glacial features to southeast (highway runs southwest) that record several cycles of glaciation. Below the Mesa Verde hogback, on the skyline, can be seen three distinct levels of moraine; each of which represents a successively younger end moraine. The oldest (highest level with a few large houses) moraine is the "Durangoan" glacial, probably of Illinoisan age. Just to the right of this moraine is an extensive flat outwash plain (on which Ft. Lewis College is situated) associated with the Durangoan glacier. The next youngest moraine (middle-level ridge) is Wisconsinian Bull Lake, and the youngest (lower-level ridge) is Pinedale. These three end moraines are perfectly nested at this location. Inside, and upstream from the Pinedale end moraine, are the latest glaciofluvial and glaciolacustrine deposits.

0.4

108.1 Durango City Limits. View to south shows Cretaceous section. Skyline ridge is the Mesaverde Group, the upper part of which is the Cliff House Sandstone; the short slope below is the Menafee Formation; and the prominent sandstone below is the Point Lookout Sandstone. The gray slope below, and all around Durango, is the Cretaceous Mancos Shale.

0.2

108.3 Slopes to west are Morrison Formation capped by Dakota–Burro Canyon Sandstone.

1.1

109.4 Fiesta Grounds, middle entrance.

0.9

110.3 Animas River bridge.

End of Supplemental Log 1.

SUPPLEMENTAL ROAD LOG NO. 2
GUNNISON TO SAGUACHE, COLORADO

RUDY C. EPIS
(Information on Cochetopa pluton, mileage 20.4–25.8, contributed by Robert M. Hutchinson)

Mileage

0.0 Gunnison: Intersection U.S. Highway 50 (Tomichi Avenue) and Colorado State Highway 135 (Main Street). Proceed east on U.S. 50.
0.5

0.5 Western State College campus at 9:00. Old narrow gauge station of Denver and Rio Grande Railroad immediately south of highway. Rocks on either side of highway just above river level are predominantly regionally metamorphosed metavolcanic and interlayered metasedimentary gneisses of Precambrian X age (∼1700 m.y.) overlain locally by Jurassic Junction Creek Sandstone and Morrison Formation. Local tongues of early Oligocene, intermediate-composition, volcanic West Elk Breccia **(see Gaskill and others, this guidebook)** overlie all older rocks. At 1:00 on skyline about 35 km east is rhyolitic-granitic Tomichi Dome of mid-Tertiary age.
2.0

2.5 Road cut through laharic tongue of West Elk Breccia.
0.5

3.0 Resistant ledge-forming beds on left (north) are sandstones of the Dakota Formation overlying softer, reddish mudstones of the Morrison Formation.
1.3

4.3 Road cut on left in mudflows of the West Elk Breccia.
0.3

4.6 Pinnacles of West Elk Breccia on left.
0.3

4.9 **Stop 1.** Tongues of laharic West Elk Breccia filling channels carved into the Morrison Formation very well-exposed in road cuts on left for the next 2 km (Figs. 4.9a, 4.9b, 4.9c).
1.6

6.5 Road cut through Morrison Formation.
0.5

7.0 Road cut on left in Precambrian amphibolites.
0.4

7.4 Yellow-tan Junction Creek Sandstone overlying steeply foliated, metabasic Precambrian rocks on left of highway.
0.4

7.8 Excellent view of Tomichi Dome at 12:30. High peaks of the Sawatch Range on skyline at 1:00
0.6

Figure 4.9a. Contact of laharic West Elk Breccia in channel on right with thinly bedded Morrison Formation on left, west of channel wall.

Figure 4.9b. Closer view of lahar near center of channel, the walls of which are shown in Figures 4.9a and 4.9c. The large andesitic clast in the upper center is about 2 m in average diameter. The laharic breccias were shed from the West Elk volcanic field to the northwest and north.

Figure 4.9c. Gently dipping contact of West Elk Breccia above bedded Morrison Formation along eastern margin of channel.

SUPPLEMENTAL ROAD LOG NO. 2

8.4 Junction U.S. Highway 50 with Colorado State Highway 114; **turn right** (south) on Highway 114. The highway follows the valley of Cochetopa Creek carved into Precambrian foliated metavolcanic and metasedimentary rocks for the next 21.2 km. The Precambrian rocks are locally capped along the rim of the valley by flat-lying Junction Creek Sandstone or Oligocene ash-flow tuffs derived from the San Juan volcanic field to the south (Olson, 1976; Olson and Steven, 1976).
0.2

8.6 Bridge across Tomichi Creek.
0.2

8.8 Bridge across Cochetopa Creek. Excellent view of Tomichi Dome, about 21 km to the east (fig. 8.8).
1.3

10.1 Vader Ranch. **Beware of very sharp, blind curves for the next 27 km.** Along this stretch of Cochetopa Creek, its canyon displays many excellent examples of incised meanders cut by a relatively small stream into very resistant, crystalline rocks. The course of Cochetopa Creek has been superposed in the Precambrian rocks from a combined pre-Junction Creek Sandstone, pre-volcanic (late Eocene), and post-Oligocene ash-flow surface of relatively low relief. In this regard, its geomorphic history is akin to that of the Gunnison River, to which it is an eventual tributary **(see Hansen, this guidebook)**.
0.9

11.0 Good view of Razor Creek Dome just north of the rim of the Cochetopa Park caldera.
0.7

11.7 Flat-lying ledge of Oligocene ash-flow tuff at 12:00.
1.6

Figure 8.8. View from bridge across Cochetopa Creek eastward up valley of Tomichi Creek with Tomichi Dome in center skyline rising above intruded Mancos Shale. Slopes of Tomichi Valley in the middle distance are underlain by Precambrian plutonic rocks and Jurassic sedimentary rocks.

13.3 Bridge across Cochetopa Creek.
1.0

14.3 Numerous uranium prospect pits and dumps of the 1950's in Precambrian amphibolite on either side of valley. Some of the workings are older and are along gold- and base metal-bearing quartz veins.
0.9

15.2 Entrance to Kreuger Fishing Resort on right. We are in the middle of a 1.5 km wide zone of felsic metavolcanic rocks with steeply dipping, north-northeast-trending foliation. **Very sharp, blind curve in highway coming up.**
0.4

15.6 **Stop 2.** Excellent outcrops on left, near road, of Precambrian, weakly metamorphosed, pyroclastic felsic volcanic rocks. They are both foliated and lineated and give the impression of eutaxitic compaction layering of welded tuffs. They clearly contain relicts of flattened and stretched pumice lapilli. However, the origin of the planar and linear fabrics may be partly the result of regional metamorphic processes **(see Hedlund and Olson; Afifi; Drobeck, this guidebook;** and Olson, 1976). This stop is approximately in the center of the Precambrian metavolcanic belt described by the authors cited above.
0.9

16.5 Leaving Gunnison County, entering Saguache County.
0.9

17.4 **Stop 3.** Good exposures in left road cut of Precambrian metabasalt pillow lavas described and illustrated by Hedlund and Olson **(this guidebook)**. Dynamic metamorphic effects are weak and many pillows are discernible. Approximately 500 m south of this stop is the probable eastward extension of the Lulu fault of Afifi **(this guidebook)**. From the Lulu fault (?) southward for the next 6.8 km the road is in predominantly dense, fine-grained micaceous metaquartzites.
2.8

20.2 Junction with dirt road RDVV13 on left to Lost Ocho uranium mine and district **(see Goodknight, this guidebook)**. Stay on paved Colorado 114.
0.2

20.4 Bridge across Cochetopa Creek.
0.1

20.5 Series of impure metaquartzites, tightly folded and plastically deformed. Varying amounts of potash metasomatism and migmatitic layering occur throughout. This is the (qz) lithologic unit referred to by Hutchinson **(this guide-**

book). Other Precambrian lithologic symbols that follow refer to the same paper.

1.1

21.6 Contact with metagabbro (mgb) unit. Note relict blasto-ophitic and blasto-subophitic textures. Metagabbro extends for 300 m.

0.2

21.8 **Stop 4.** Contact of metagabbro with the Cochetopa Granite (Cgr) to the right (west). The northwest flank of the pluton dips approximately 75° northwest with a moderate igneous foliation visible within 90–150 m of the contact. In some places the metagabbro is absent and the granite lies in concordant contact with the quartzite unit. Lit-par-lit injection of the Cochetopa Granite has occurred locally where it intrudes the quartzite unit.

0.3

22.1 Xenolith of impure quartzite wallrock. Xenolith strikes about N.50–60°E. and is vertical. Three prominent joint sets are evident, but the presence of several shear zones complicates the jointing. Shear zones average a N. 30°E. strike and dip 65–70°SE.

1.1

23.2 Contact of Cochetopa Granite to the north and the porphyroblastic gneiss to the south. There is some intermixing of the two. Contact is generally in the gulley to the right (west).

0.2

23.4 Good road cut exposure of jointing in the Cochetopa Granite (fig. 23.4).

0.3

23.7 Contact of porphyroblastic gneiss and granite aplite dike to south. This is a large dike probably derived from Cochetopa Granite. It dips about 60° southeast.

0.2

23.9 Contact of granite aplite and the Cochetopa granite-gneiss (Cgn) phase of the Cochetopa Granite. The Cochetopa Granite is increasingly foliated to the next contact.

0.7

24.6 Contact of Cochetopa granite-gneiss and the metadiorite (mdi). There is a weak streaking and foliation developed in the metadiorite best seen in the outcrop from a distance of 10 m or more.

0.1

24.7 Considerable amounts of granite injection and pegmatization of the metadiorite, probably derived from Cochetopa Granite pluton to the north.

0.9

25.6 Contact of metadiorite and the granite-gneiss unit to the south.

0.1

25.7 Excellent overview or panoramic view of pinkish granite pegmatite dikes cutting through the metadiorite unit. Note the clearly defined evidence of joint-control of injection of the pegmatites by pre-existing joints in the metadiorite wallrocks. The pegmatites dip 10–50° northwest toward the Cochetopa Granite (fig. 25.7).

0.1

25.8 Contact of mixed zone (mz_2) and the granite-gneiss unit to the south (ggn). This is a massive, uniform moderately foliated quartzofeldspathic unit. Foliations are near vertical, sometimes dipping steeply northwest and sometimes steeply southeast.

1.2

27.0 **Stop 5.** Vicinity of contacts of Junction Creek Sandstone and early Oligocene volcanic rocks of the San Juan volcanic field with Precambrian basement rocks. Cochetopa Creek and highway emerge from the canyon into Cochetopa Park at essentially the level of the late

Figure 23.4. Jointing in Cochetopa Granite. View is looking west. Note the marginal fissure-type joint set dipping right to left (north to south).

Figure 25.7. Large granite pegmatite dikes cutting metadiorite. Note joint control of intrusion of the pegmatites.

Figure 27.0a. View looking northward down the canyon of Cochetopa Creek showing its incision into the Precambrian basement rocks. Note the relatively smooth, flat surface carved into the Precambrian rocks. This is the compound surface referred to at mileage 10.1 from which Cochetopa Creek was superposed into the basement rocks.

Figure 27.0b. View of Cochetopa Dome from road to Doyleville just above and west of Stop 5. In the right center is Cochetopa Creek meandering in the moat section of the Cochetopa Park caldera west of the dome. Hills on right side of photograph are mostly blocks of ash-flow tuff dropped into the caldera.

Eocene, pre-volcanic surface (fig. 27.0a). From here to Saguache the highway traverses several segments and stratigraphic units of the northeastern part of the San Juan volcanic field. At this mileage, the highway enters the Cochetopa Park caldera. The caldera is about 24 km in diameter and is an example of one of many ash-flow-related calderas in the San Juan field. The caldera collapsed primarily as a result of the eruption of the Nelson Mountain Tuff (Steven and others, 1974). For the next 10 km the highway will be in the moat section of the caldera, curving and paralleling the northern topographic rim. The moat is filled with stratified, light colored tuffaceous siltstones and sandstones interbedded with lesser air-fall and ash-flow tuffs. These deposits are visible in many road cuts and natural exposures. The central part of the Cochetopa Park caldera is topographically dominated by Cochetopa Dome (1:00) which rises about 500 m above the level of the moat (fig. 27.0b). The dome is a non-resurgent, late-stage, exogenous dome-flow complex of quartz latitic lava (Tweto and others, 1976). See Table 1 for terminology, ages, and correlation of stratigraphic units of the northeastern San Juan volcanic field.

0.6

Table 1. Summary and correlation of stratigraphic terminology of the San Juan volcanic field and the Bonanza center. Established correlations are shown by horizontal dotted lines. (After Bruns and others, 1971.)

MODIFIED AFTER LARSEN AND CROSS (1956)	OLSON, HEDLUND, AND HANSEN (1968)	MODIFIED AFTER LIPMAN, STEVEN, AND MEHNERT (1970)	THIS REPORT	BURBANK (1932)
Hinsdale Formation Basalt and Rhyolite	Hinsdale Formation	Hinsdale Formation Basalt (4.7-23.4 m.y.) and Rhyolite (4.8-22.4 m.y.) ASH-FLOW TUFFS AND RELATED ROCKS	Hinsdale Formation	
Piedra Rhyolite	Carpenter Ridge Tuff	Carpenter Ridge Tuff-Bachelor Mtn. Rhyolite	Carpenter Ridge Tuff	
Alboroto Rhyolite Sheep Mtn. Quartz Latite	Fish Canyon Tuff	Fish Canyon Tuff-La Garita Qtz. Latite (27.8 m.y.)	Fish Canyon Tuff Andesite of Saguache Creek Water-laid and air-fall tuffs of Saguache Creek	Porphyry Peak Rhyolite Brewer Creek Latite
Treasure Mtn. Rhyolite	Sapinero Mesa Tuff Dillon Mesa Tuff Blue Mesa Tuff	Tuff of Masonic Park (28.2 m.y.) Treasure Mtn. Rhyolite (29.8 m.y.) EARLY INTERMEDIATE LAVAS AND BRECCIAS	Sapinero Mesa Tuff Andesite of Ford Creek Bonanza Tuff	Squirrel Gulch Latite Bonanza Latite
Conejos Quartz Latite Bonanza volcanic pile	"OLDER VOLCANICS" Conejos Quartz Latite, Lake Fork Formation, and West Elk Breccia	Conejos Formation (31.1-34.7 m.y.), Lake Fork Formation, West Elk Breccia and San Juan Fm. (Included Bonanza volcanic pile)	Rawley Andesite	Hayden Peak Latite and Rawley Andesite

27.6	Junction with road 14PP to Doyleville (left). Stay on paved Colorado 114. Excellent view of Cochetopa Dome at 12:30 and of western topographic rim of Cochetopa Park caldera on right. At 9:00, excellent view of Razor Creek Dome composed of pre-caldera, early intermediate lavas and clastic volcanic rocks equivalent to the Conejos Formation and the West Elk Breccia (fig. 27.6).
0.7	
28.3	Excellent view at 3:00 of high peaks of the central San Juan volcanic field.
0.6	
28.9	Junction with road NN14 on right heading along west side of Cochetopa Dome and following Cochetopa Creek into the caldera. Stay on paved Highway 114.
1.5	
30.4	Bedded, light colored, moat-fill tuffaceous sediments of the caldera in road cuts and exposures to left (north). Outcrops of the northern margin of Cochetopa Dome on right, immediately south of West Pass Creek.
2.4	
32.8	Pits in moat-fill deposits date to mid-1950's uranium exploration.
1.7	
34.5	Junction with national forest access road to Archuleta Creek and Saguache Park. Road follows eastern and southeastern moat of Cochetopa Park caldera. Stay on paved Highway 114. Highway begins ascent up the eastern topographic rim of the caldera and eventually crosses the continental divide outside and east of the caldera at North Cochetopa Pass.
5.6	
40.1	North Cochetopa Pass, elevation 3093 m (10,149 ft). Highway descends eastward into the valley of Saguache Creek, eventually to enter the northern part of the San Luis Valley (northern part of the Rio Grande rift system) at the town of Saguache, about 45 km distant. The highway intersects outcrops of several regional and many local stratigraphic units of the northeastern portion of the San Juan volcanic field. The units have a regional tectonic dip eastward toward the San Luis Valley. Major stratigraphic units include the Conejos Formation, and ash-flow tuff formations with caldera sources indicated in parentheses, as follows: Fish Canyon Tuff (La Garita), Carpenter Ridge Tuff (Bachelor), Sapinero Mesa Tuff (San Juan and Uncompahgre), and Bonanza Tuff (Bonanza).
2.3	
42.4	Excellent road cut of well-developed columnar jointing in biotite, hornblende dacite dome within the Conejos Formation (fig. 42.4). High cliffs on skyline above (9:00) are Fish Canyon Tuff resting on the Conejos. Watch for Rocky Mountain Bighorn Sheep on the cliffs! The Fish Canyon Tuff descends eastward at a greater rate than the highway and is at road level 4.2 km to the east.
0.8	
43.2	**Stop 6.** Good road-cut exposures of local, light colored, bedded, tuffaceous sediments, air-fall and water-laid tuffs, and mudflows within the Conejos Formation. These rocks were deposited in local channels formed during periods of erosion and little if any volcanism. There are many such scattered accumulations within the Conejos and between

Figure 29.3. View looking south along eastern topographic rim of the Cochetopa Park caldera along the left half of photograph with the caldera moat in foreground. Rim rocks are similar to the pre-caldera rocks of Razor Creek Dome.

Figure 27.6. Razor Creek Dome, part of the northern topographic rim of the Cochetopa Park caldera. It is composed of pre-caldera, early intermediate volcanic rocks of Conejos Formation or West Elk Breccia age.

Figure 42.4. Columnar jointing in biotite, hornblende dacite dome in Conejos Formation. Columns average about 10–15 cm in diameter and can be seen to fan eastward and westward along the length of the road cut in a cross-sectional view of part of the dome.

other major stratigraphic units throughout the entire sequence (fig. 43.7).

0.9

44.1 Entrance to Buffalo Pass Campground of Rio Grande National Forest on right. Knobby outcrops of monolithic, dark gray andesitic flow breccia occur near road level on the left side of road for the next 1.3 km. This is yet another lithology within the Conejos Formation. The Conejos is a complex assemblage of lithogenetic units that are difficult to trace and map because of their sudden changes in thickness and lateral extent. The units are generally related to many scattered, local quartz latite to andesite volcanic centers and thin associated outflow facies. The flow breccia is overlain by the salmon pink-weathering Fish Canyon Tuff.

0.9

45.0 Outcrops of Fish Canyon Tuff on either side of highway. The Fish Canyon is a crystal-rich, quartz latite ash-flow sheet distributed throughout much of the northern and northeastern San Juan volcanic field. It reaches thicknesses in excess of 300 m to the southwest.

0.4

45.4 **Stop 7.** Intersection with Road 31CC to North Park and Spanish Creek on left. Good exposures close by of Fish Canyon Tuff showing crude, wide columnar jointing and wavy compaction layering resulting in "beehive" structure (fig. 45.4).

0.9

46.3 **Stop 8** (very poor parking for buses or large caravans). Approximate contact of Carpenter Ridge and Fish Canyon tuffs in road cut on right. To the left (northeast) across valley of East Pass Creek are excellent exposures of massive, crudely layered and jointed Fish Canyon Tuff overlain by well-layered, cliff-forming, densely welded zone of the Carpenter Ridge Tuff forming the skyline (fig. 46.3a). At the road cut one can observe very good examples of welding zonation, devitrification, and vapor phase crystallization in the Carpenter Ridge Tuff (figs. 46.3b and 46.3c). Over a vertical distance of a few meters the tuff grades from a white, basal unwelded zone through a gray, moderately welded zone, showing excellent vitroclastic texture under the hand lens, into a densely welded black

Figure 43.7. Tuffaceous siltstones, sandstones and volcanic conglomerates interbedded with ashes, lapilli tuffs and volcanic mudflows within the Conejos Formation. Two distinct, graded laharic breccias are visible in the central part of the figure. The mudflows are characteristically heterolithic, consisting of a variety of intermediate volcanic rock types. The regional dip of about 15 degrees to the right (east) is clearly visible. Man's cap on large block in center of photograph is size 58 (7¼) for scale.

Figure 45.4. So-called "beehive" structure in Fish Canyon Tuff is probably the result of intersection of widely spaced columnar joints and wavy eutaxitic layering because of abundant crystal content of the tuff.

Figure 46.3a. Carpenter Ridge Tuff overlying Fish Canyon Tuff along north side of East Pass Creek. Locally the densely welded, black vitrophyre zone of the Carpenter Ridge can be seen near the base of the cliffs.

Figure 46.3c. Spherulitic and lithophysal zone in devitrified Carpenter Ridge Tuff. Many spherulites and lithophysae are up to 15 cm in diameter.

vitrophyre zone. The densely welded zone is locally devitrified to reddish-purple, lithoidal tuff, and eventually grades upward into a post-emplacement, coarse spherulitic and lithophysal zone. Study from across the road reveals two such zones, indicating a compound cooling unit is present at this locality. From here one can view the eastward-dipping tuffs along the north side of East Pass Creek where, near the mouth of the creek, they are faulted against older rocks on the east side of the Sheep Creek fault zone (fig. 46.3d). Highway declines eastward toward Saguache Creek, generally on the dip slope formed by the densely welded zone of the Carpenter Ridge Tuff.

1.7

48.0 Cliffs of Carpenter Ridge Tuff immediately north of highway show slight reversal of dip to the west and define the Sheep Creek syncline formed by drag along the Sheep Creek fault zone. Higher ridge at 9:00–11:00 is Fish Canyon Tuff brought up on east side of the fault zone (Bruns and others, 1971).

0.3

48.3 Intersection of road to Upper Saguache Guard Station on left. Stay on paved Highway 114. At 11:00–12:00 in the distance are cliff-forming ledges of Sapinero Mesa Tuff step-faulted upward to the east along the Sheep Creek fault zone east of Saguache Creek.

1.0

49.3 Good exposures of Carpenter Ridge Tuff on left.

0.5

Figure 46.3b. Gray to black, moderately to densely welded Carpenter Ridge Tuff showing eutaxitic, fiamme structure of flattened and stretched pumice lapilli. The Carpenter Ridge is a crystal poor quartz latitic ash flow.

Figure 46.3d. Eastward dipping Carpenter Ridge Tuff overlying the Fish Canyon Tuff along north side of East Pass Creek. The tuffs are faulted against older rocks at the mouth of the creek along the Sheep Creek fault zone. The older rocks are dominantly andesitic and make up the unnamed hill on the right skyline and Trickle Mountain in the center skyline.

49.8	Bridge across Saguache Creek. Cliffs at 1:00–2:00 are Carpenter Ridge Tuff.
	1.0
50.8	Flying X Cattle Ranch on left. View back to the northwest (7:00–9:00) of cliffs of Fish Canyon Tuff overlying mixture of white tuffaceous rocks and darker breccias of the Conejos Formation (fig. 50.8). Note: From this general area northeastward into the Bonanza volcanic center, rocks of Conejos age have been called Rawley Andesite (Bruns and others, 1971). Trickle Mountain on skyline at 10:00 is underlain in its upper part by local, intermediate lavas of Saguache Creek which are younger than the Fish Canyon Tuff.
	1.4
52.2	Excellent view at 9:00 northward up Alkali Gulch of cliff-forming exposures of Sapinero Mesa Tuff near center skyline. Cliff in right foreground is Fish Canyon Tuff resting on local tuffaceous sediments of Saguache Creek (fig. 52.2).
	1.5
53.7	Dabney Ranch on left. Lower cliff-forming ledge on left, north of Saguache Creek and nearly at creek level, is densely welded zone of Sapinero Mesa Tuff. It is overlain by slope-forming, local volcaniclastic rocks and upper cliff-forming andesitic lava of Saguache Creek (fig. 53.7).
	0.7
54.4	**Stop 9.** Excellent exposure on right side of highway of cliff of densely welded, devitrified, spherulitic and lithophysal, reddish-purple quartz latitic Sapinero Mesa Tuff. The Sapinero Mesa is megascopically very similar to the Carpenter Ridge Tuff, and the two easily can be mistaken for each other in isolated outcrops (fig. 54.4).
	1.0
55.4	High peaks on skyline at 10:00 are part of the Bonanza volcanic center.
	0.3
55.7	Intersection with Road RD41G to La Garita. Stay on paved Highway 114.
	0.1
55.8	Hodding Creek.
	0.9
56.7	Old stage coach station on right side of highway. Good view of rocks of the Bonanza volcanic center at 12:00 on skyline and cross-

Figure 52.2. View northward up Alkali Gulch of cliff-forming, densely welded zone of the Sapinero Mesa Tuff just to right of center skyline. Cliff in right foreground, just north of Saguache Creek, is Fish Canyon Tuff resting on local tuffaceous sediments of Saguache Creek. Conejos Formation is in lower slopes on west side of Alkali Gulch.

Figure 50.8. Sloping, wooded cliffs of Fish Canyon Tuff north of confluence of Sheep and Saguache Creeks resting on light colored tuffaceous rocks and darker breccias of the Conejos Formation. Note onlap thinning of Fish Canyon at right (northern) edge of photo.

Figure 53.7. Lower cliffs of densely welded Sapinero Mesa Tuff, essentially at creek level on north side of Saguache Creek, overlain by local volcaniclastic rocks and upper cliff of andesite lava of Saguache Creek.

Figure 54.4. Densely welded, devitrified, spherulitic and lithophysal Sapinero Mesa Tuff very similar to the Carpenter Ridge Tuff of Figure 46.3c.

section view of Mill Creek syncline plunging toward Saguache Creek (fig. 56.7).

0.4

57.1 Bridge across Saguache Creek. Excellent exposure of Sapinero Mesa Tuff overlain by volcaniclastic rocks of Saguache Creek.

0.2

57.3 Road cut on left exposes cross-stratified water-laid tuffaceous sediments beneath black, welded vitrophyre zone of the Sapinero Mesa Tuff.

0.5

57.8 Intersection with Trickle Mountain Road on left. Lower cliffs on left are Sapinero Mesa Tuff. Large flat-topped mountain on right (south) is Houghland Hill.

1.7

59.5 Road to Flickinger Ranch on right. Highway road cut through densely welded Bonanza Tuff.

0.6

60.1 Intersection with Road EE38 on left up Jacks Creek. Dipping, dark-colored andesitic rocks of the Jacks Creek volcano of Conejos (Rawley) age are clearly visible in middle distance at 7:00–10:00 (Bruns, 1971).

0.5

60.6 Middle Creek. Good exposures of Bonanza Tuff in cliff-like outcrops at road and creek level on either side of highway and Saguache Creek for the next 4 km.

2.2

62.8 **Stop 10.** Good exposure of moderately to densely welded, reddish brown, devitrified Bonanza Tuff showing eutaxitic structure. This member of the Bonanza Tuff is a moderately crystal-rich biotite latite with characteristic purple-gray lithic lapilli. The Bonanza Tuff is the oldest known, major ash-flow sheet in the northeastern part of the San Juan volcanic field (Table 1 and fig. 62.8).

0.5

Figure 56.7. Looking to the northeast at southwestern rim of the Bonanza volcanic center on skyline and Mill Creek syncline in right middle distance plunging toward Saguache Creek in foreground.

Figure 62.8. Exposure of Bonanza Tuff on left side of road showing crude columnar jointing and eutaxitic compaction foliation. This is probably the basal cooling unit of at least five such units that comprise the Bonanza Tuff near Findley Gulch about 5 km to the east.

63.3	Road cut exposure on left of Precambrian metamorphic and granitic rocks and associated pegmatites. There are a number of similar, sub-volcanic exposures of Precambrian basement rocks in the vicinity of upper Jacks Creek. Cliffs in slopes at 9:00–11:00 are multiple ash-flow units of the Bonanza Tuff in a compound cooling relationship. View back to west of northern end of Houghland Hill (fig. 64.1).
	0.9
64.2	Entering lower Saguache Creek Valley. View on distant skyline straight ahead of the Sangre de Cristo Mountains, a horst block bounding the eastern side of the San Luis Valley graben of the northern Rio Grande rift system. At 12:30, notch in the range outline is Mosca Pass, at the western base of which is Great Sand Dunes National Monument.
	2.3
66.5	Ridge spur at 9:00 on west side of Findley Gulch exhibits 5 cooling members of the Bonanza Tuff unconformably overlying grey latite of Conejos age. The 5 members form a compound cooling unit here, but toward the Bonanza caldera, about 26 km to the north, the members coalesce into one or two cooling units and the Bonanza Tuff thickens markedly as it approaches the caldera source (fig. 66.5).
	1.4
67.9	Intersection with Road RD43BB to left up through Findley Gulch and northward to the Bonanza volcanic center and mining district.

Figure 66.5. Five ash-flow members of a compound cooling unit form the Bonanza Tuff at the ridge spur on the west side of Findley Gulch. View is to the north.

	At 2:00–4:00 dark colored lavas and breccias of andesite south of Saguache Creek are associated with a small, local volcanic center within the Conejos Formation (fig. 69.7).
	1.2
69.1	Entrance to Saguache Airport on right.
	0.6
69.7	Mergence of lower Saguache Creek Valley with the San Luis Valley at the outskirts of Saguache.
	0.8
70.5	Saguache city limits.
	0.2
70.7	Junction of Colorado State Highway 114 with U.S. Highway 285. **End of Supplemental Log 2.**

Figure 64.1. View looking west along Colorado State Highway 114 at northern end of Houghland Hill. The northern base of Houghland Hill on right side of photograph is underlain by Bonanza Tuff which is overlain in succession by local andesite of Ford Creek, Fish Canyon Tuff, Carpenter Ridge Tuff and capped by thin Hinsdale Basalt in the upper left of photograph. The conspicuous, long flat ridge on right skyline is underlain by Fish Canyon Tuff.

Figure 69.7. View to the south of dark andesitic lavas and breccias of local volcanic center within the Conejos Formation south of Saguache Creek. Note distinct dip of lavas to left (east). Central part of the dissected volcano begins on right side of photograph and extends to the west of view.

REFERENCES

Bruns, D. L., 1971, Geology of the Lake Mountain Northeast quadrangle, Saguache County, Colorado [Unpub. M.Sc. thesis]: Golden, Colorado School of Mines, 79 p.

Bruns, D. L., Epis, R. C., Weimer, R. J., and Steven, T. A., 1971, Stratigraphic relations between Bonanza center and adjacent parts of the San Juan volcanic field, south-central Colorado, in James, H. L., ed., Guidebook of the San Luis Basin, Colorado: New Mexico Geological Society Guidebook 22, p. 183–190.

Burbank, W. S., 1932, Geology and ore deposits of the Bonanza Mining District, Colorado: U.S. Geological Survey Professional Paper 169, 166 p.

Larsen, E. S. and Cross, W., 1956, Geology and petrology of the San Juan region, southwestern Colorado: U.S. Geological Survey Professional Paper 285, 303 p.

Lipman, P. W., Steven, T. A., and Mehnert, H. H., 1970, Volcanic history of the San Juan Mountains, Colorado, as indicated by potassium-argon dating: Geological Society of America Bulletin, v. 81, p. 2329–2352.

Olson, J. C., 1976, Geologic map of the Iris quadrangle, Gunnison and Saguache Counties, Colorado: U.S. Geological Survey Geological Quadrangle Map GQ-1286.

Olson, J. C., Hedlund, D. C., and Hansen, W. R., 1968, Tertiary volcanic stratigraphy in the Powderhorn–Black Canyon region, Gunnison and Montrose Counties, Colorado: U.S. Geological Survey Bulletin 1251-C, p. C1–C29.

Olson, J. C. and Steven, T. A., 1976, Geologic map of the Sawtooth Mountain quadrangle, Saguache County, Colorado: U.S. Geological Survey Miscellaneous Field Studies Map MF-733.

Steven, T. A., Lipman, P. W., Hail, W. J., Jr., Barker, Fred, and Luedke, R. G., 1974, Geologic map of the Durango quadrangle, southwestern Colorado: U.S. Geological Survey Miscellaneous Investigations Series Map I-764.

Tweto, Ogden, Steven, T. A., Hail, W. J., Jr., and Moench, R. H., 1976, Preliminary geologic map of the Montrose 1° × 2° quadrangle, southwestern Colorado: U.S. Geological Survey Miscellaneous Field Studies Map MF-761.

STRATIGRAPHIC CORRELATION CHART FOR WESTERN COLORADO AND NORTHWESTERN NEW MEXICO

M. E. MacLACHLAN
U.S. Geological Survey
Denver, Colorado 80225

INTRODUCTION

The stratigraphic nomenclature applied in various parts of western Colorado, northwestern New Mexico, and a small part of east-central Utah is summarized in the accompanying chart (fig. 1). The locations of the areas, indicated by letters, are shown on the index map (fig. 2). Sources of information used in compiling the chart are shown by numbers in brackets beneath the headings for the columns. The numbers are keyed to references in an accompanying list. Ages where known are shown by numbers in parentheses in millions of years after the rock name or in parentheses on the line separating two chronostratigraphic units.

No Quaternary rocks nor small igneous bodies, such as dikes, have been included on this chart. Because space is limited, all the accepted formal stratigraphic-rank endings for each of the units are abbreviated (Cgl, Conglomerate; Dol, Dolomite; Fm, Formation; Gb, Gabbro; Gp, Group; Gn, Gneiss; Gr, Granite; Ls, Limestone; M, Member; Monz, Monzonite; Qtz, Quartz; Qtzite, Quartzite; Ss, Sandstone; Sh, Shale; T, Tongue). Other abbreviations used are Can for Canyon, Cr for Creek, and pt for part. Dashed lines where used as boundaries for stratigraphic units on the chart indicate that the upper and (or) lower time span is uncertain.

EXPLANATORY NOTES FOR COLUMNS

Col. A.–F.
The age of the Burro Canyon Formation is middle to late Early Cretaceous. The underlying Morrison Formation is considered to be of Late Jurassic age and the overlying Dakota Sandstone of Late Cretaceous age (cols. A–D). In northwestern Colorado (cols. E and F), the age of the Dakota is probably Late Cretaceous but it may also be Early Cretaceous.

Cols. A.–B.
The correlation of the Telluride Formation (or Conglomerate) and Blanco Basin Formation with the San Jose Formation is uncertain. All three are considered to be early Eocene age. The San Jose may be younger than the Telluride or Blanco Basin (Baltz, 1967, p. 56–57).

Col. A.
The Chuska Sandstone of Eocene(?) to early Oligocene age occurs on the west side of the San Juan basin (Hackman and Olson, 1977).

The Middle Jurassic Cow Springs Sandstone is present beneath the Morrison Formation on the west side of the San Juan basin (Hackman and Olson, 1977).

Two older members of the Chinle are recognized beneath the Petrified Forest. These are the Shinarump (base) and the Monitor Butte (top). One younger member, the Owl Rock, is also present above the Petrified Forest. These three members are of more limited areal extent than the Petrified Forest (O'Sullivan, 1977).

De Chelly Sandstone (or De Chelly Sandstone Member of the Cutler Formation) of the west side of the basin is thought to correlate with the Glorieta Sandstone of the south side of the basin.

Cols. B.–C.
Age determinations on the Hinsdale Formation in parts of the volcanic field range from 4.7 to 23.4 m.y. on basalts and 4.8 to 22.4 m.y. on rhyolites (Lipman, 1975, p. 6, p. 90–100).

The early intermediate-composition volcanics and related rocks include several named units of limited areal extent, but of similar age and petrology—the West Elk Breccia at Powderhorn; the Conejos Formation in the vicinity of Conejos River canyon, southeastern part of the field; and the Lake Fork Formation in vicinity of Lake Fork of the Gunnison River, and the San Juan Formation near Telluride, both in the western part of the volcanic field. Still other names are applied to units in the northeastern part of the volcanic field (Lipman, 1975, p. 8).

Col. C.
The name Black Canyon Schist has been used in the Black Canyon of the Gunnison River, its type area, for Precambrian schists and gneisses but the stratigraphic and (or) lithologic significance of this name is questionable (Tweto, 1977; see also Hansen, this guidebook; Hedlund and Olson, this guidebook).

Col. D.
The Entrada Sandstone near Moab, Utah can be divided into the Moab Tongue (top), Slick Rock and Dewey Bridge Members (O'Sullivan, this guidebook).

Outliers of Page Sandstone have been recognized as far east as the Colorado River, near Moab, Utah (O'Sullivan, this guidebook).

In the deeper parts of the Paradox Basin, the Hermosa is considered by many to be a group divisible into the Honaker Trail (top), Paradox, and Pinkerton Trail (base) Formations (Wengerd and Matheny, 1958; Baars, 1962). The Paradox, the middle formation, has been separated into 29 evaporitic cycles (Hite and Cater, 1972). These cycles have been combined into five zones—the Ismay (top), Desert Creek, Akah, Barker Creek, and Alkali Gulch.

Col. E.
The members of the Green River Formation in the Piceance Basin are, successively downward, Parachute Creek (includes Mahogany oil-shale bed), Garden Gulch, Douglas Creek, and Anvil Points Members. Six tongues of the Green River, stratigraphically above the Parachute Creek, have also been mapped in the central and northern parts of the basin. These are, in sequence, youngest to oldest, the Stewart Gulch, Coughs Creek, Black Sulphur, Thirteenmile Creek, Dry Fork, and Yellow Creek (Hail, 1977; Duncan, and others, 1974; O'Sullivan, 1975).

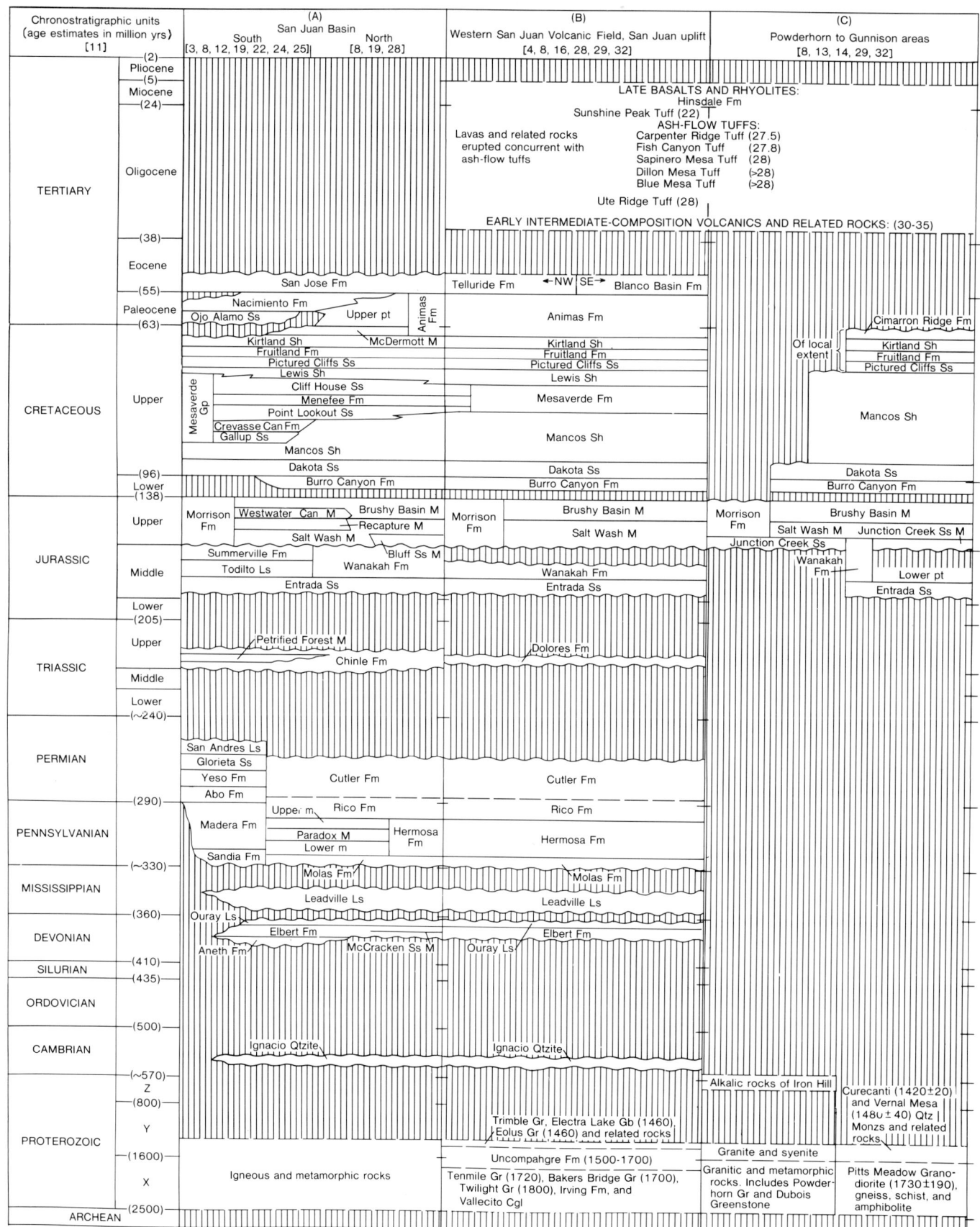

Figure 1. Stratigraphic correlation chart for western Colorado and northwestern New Mexico and east-central Utah.

STRATIGRAPHIC CORRELATION CHART

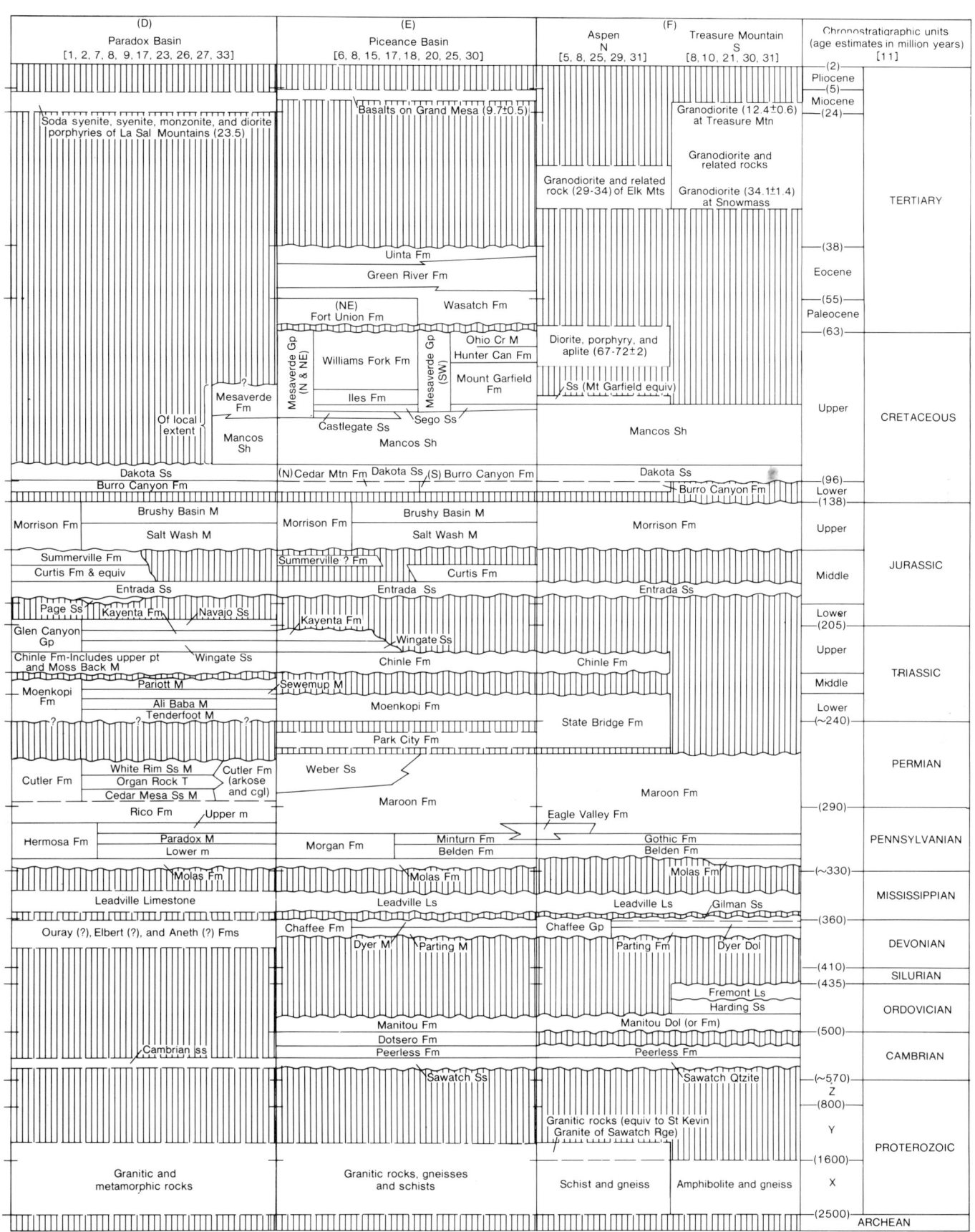

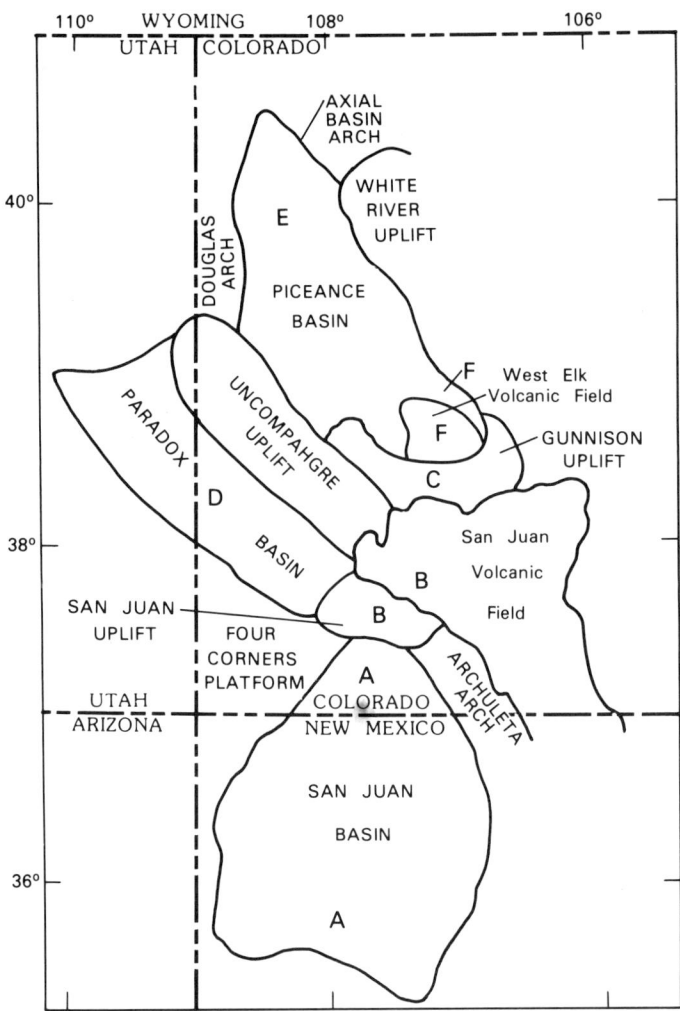

Figure 2. Index map showing areas referred to in stratigraphic columns and the tectonic provinces in western Colorado and northwestern New Mexico (from Grose, 1972, figure 1, p. 37).

In the southern part of the Piceance Basin, the Wasatch has been divided into the Shire (top), Molina, and Atwell gulch Members (Donnell, 1969).

The Burro Canyon and Cedar Mountain Formations are considered to be correlatives. The type locality of the Burro Canyon is in San Miguel County, Colorado, and that formation name is used generally south and east of the Colorado River. The type locality of the Cedar Mountain is in Emery County, Utah and that formation name is used generally north and west of the Colorado River.

The Ohio Creek is recognized as a white, kaolinitic unit 50 to 150 m thick beneath the Tertiary-Cretaceous unconformity. It is assigned as the upper member of the Hunter Canyon Formation, or, where the Mesaverde cannot be divided into formations, to the Mesaverde Formation (Johnson and May, 1980; Johnson and Keighin, this guidebook).

Col. F.
Basalt, tuff, breccia, and related igneous rocks of late Tertiary age are present west of Aspen.

Rocks called Summerville(?) in this column were mapped as Summerville Formation by Lohman (1965) in the Grand Junction area. These rocks may belong in the lower part of the Morrison Formation instead. The Summerville is shown as having been truncated west of Moab by O'Sullivan (this guidebook).

Placement of the Mississippian boundary is uncertain. It may be within the Dyer Dolomite or within the Gilman Sandstone of the Chaffee Group (Tweto and Lovering, 1977).

REFERENCES IN EXPLANATORY NOTES

Baars, D. L., 1962, Permian System of the Colorado Plateau: American Association of Petroleum Geologists Bulletin, v. 46, p. 149–218.

Baltz, E. H., 1967, Stratigraphy and regional tectonic implications of part of Upper Cretaceous and Tertiary rocks east-central San Juan Basin, New Mexico: U.S. Geological Survey Professional Paper 552, 101 p.

Donnell, J. R., 1969, Paleocene and lower Eocene units in the southern part of the Piceance Creek Basin Colorado: U.S. Geological Survey Bulletin 1274-M, 18 p.

Duncan, D. C., Hail, W. J., Jr., O'Sullivan, R. B., and Pipiringos, G. N., 1974, Four newly named tongues of the Eocene Green River Formation, northern Piceance Creek Basin, Colorado: U.S. Geological Survey Bulletin 1394-F, 13 p.

Grose, L. T., 1972, Tectonics, in Geologic Atlas of the Rocky Mountain region, United States of America: Denver, Colorado, Rocky Mountain Association of Geologists, p. 35–44.

Hackman, R. J. and Olson, A. B., 1977, Geology, structure, and uranium deposits of the Gallup 1° × 2° quadrangle, New Mexico and Arizona: U.S. Geological Survey Miscellaneous Investigations Series Map I-981.

Hail, W. J., Jr., 1977, Stewart Gulch Tongue—a new tongue of the Eocene Green River Formation, Piceance Creek Basin, Colorado: U.S. Geological Survey Bulletin 1422-E, 8 p.

Hansen, W. R., 1981, Geologic and physiographic highlights of the Gunnison River and vicinity, Colorado: New Mexico Geological Society Guidebook 32, this volume.

Hedlund, D. C. and Olson, J. C., 1981, Precambrian geology along parts of the Gunnison uplift of southwestern Colorado: New Mexico Geological Society Guidebook 32, this volume.

Hite, R. J. and Cater, F. W., 1972, Pennsylvanian rocks and salt anticlines, Paradox Basin, Utah and Colorado, in Geologic Atlas of the Rocky Mountain region, United States of America: Denver, Colorado, Rocky Mountain Association of Geologists, p. 133–138.

Johnson, R. C. and Keighin, C. W., 1981, Cretaceous and Tertiary history and resources of the Piceance Creek Basin, western Colorado: New Mexico Geological Society Guidebook 32, this volume.

Johnson, C. and May, Fred, 1980, A study of the Cretaceous-Tertiary unconformity in the Piceance Creek Basin, Colorado; The underlying Ohio Creek Formation (Upper Cretaceous) redefined as a member of the Hunter Canyon or Mesaverde Formation: U.S. Geological Survey Bulletin 1482-B, 27 p.

Lipman, P. W., 1975, Evolution of the Platoro caldera complex and related volcanic rocks, southeastern San Juan Mountains, Colorado: U.S. Geological Survey Professional Paper 852, 128 p.

Lohman, S. W., 1965, Geology and artesian water supply, Grand Junction area, Colorado: U.S. Geological Survey Professional Paper 451, 149 p.

O'Sullivan, R. B., 1975, Coughs Creek Tongue—A new tongue of the Eocene Green River Formation, Colorado: U.S. Geological Survey Bulletin 1395-G, 7 p.

O'Sullivan, R. B., 1977, Triassic rocks in the San Juan Basin of New Mexico and adjacent areas: New Mexico Geological Society Guidebook 28, p. 139–146.

O'Sullivan, R. B., 1981, The Middle Jurassic San Rafael Group and related rocks in east-central Utah: New Mexico Geological Society Guidebook 32, this volume.

Tweto, O., 1977, Nomenclature of Precambrian rocks in Colorado: U.S. Geological Survey Bulletin 1422-D, 22 p.

Tweto, O. and Lovering, T. S., 1977, Geology of the Minturn 15-minute quadrangle, Eagle and Summit Counties, Colorado: U.S. Geological Survey Professional Paper 956, 96 p.

Wengerd, S. A. and Matheny, M. L., 1958, Pennsylvanian system of the Four Corners region: American Association of Petroleum Geologists Bulletin, v. 42, p. 2048–2106.

REFERENCES USED IN COLUMNS

1. Armstrong, R. L., 1969, K-Ar dating of laccolithic centers of the Colorado Plateau and vicinity: Geological Society of America Bulletin, v. 80, 2081–2086.

2. Baars, D. L., 1972, Devonian System, *in* Geologic Atlas of Rocky Mountain region, United States of America: Denver, Colorado, Rocky Mountain Association of Geologists, p. 90–99.
3. Baltz, E. H., 1967, Stratigraphy and regional tectonic implications of part of Upper Cretaceous and Tertiary rocks east-central San Juan Basin, New Mexico: U.S. Geological Survey Professional Paper 552, 101 p.
4. Bromfield, C. S., Williams, F. E., and Popenoe, P., 1972, Mineral resources of the Wilson Mountains Primitive area, Colorado: U.S. Geological Survey Bulletin 1353-A, 79 p.
5. Bryant, B., 1980 (1979), Geology of the Aspen 15' quadrangle, Pitkin and Gunnison Counties, Colorado: U.S. Geological Survey Professional Paper 1073, 146 p.
6. Cashion, W. B., compiler, 1973, Geologic and structure map of the Grand Junction quadrangle, Colorado and Utah: U.S. Geological Survey Miscellaneous Investigations Series Map I-736.
7. Cater, F. W., 1970, Geology of the salt anticline region in southwestern Colorado: U.S. Geological Survey Professional Paper 637, 80 p.
8. Cobban, W. A. and Reeside, J. B., Jr., 1952, Correlation of the Cretaceous formations of the western interior of the United States: Geological Society of America Bulletin, v. 63, p. 1011–1044.
9. Foster, N., 1972, Ordovician System, *in* Geologic Atlas of the Rocky Mountain region, United States of America: Denver, Colorado, Rocky Mountain Association of Geologists, p. 76–85.
10. Gaskill, D. L. and Godwin, L. H., 1966, Geologic map of Marcellina Mountain quadrangle Gunnison County, Colorado: U.S. Geological Survey Geologic Quadrangle Map GQ-511.
11. Geologic Names Committee (U.S.G.S.), 1980 edition, Major geochronologic and chronostratigraphic units (chart).
12. Hackman, R. J. and Olson, A. B., 1977, Geology, structure, and uranium deposits of the Gallup 1° × 2° quadrangle, New Mexico and Arizona: U.S. Geological Survey Miscellaneous Investigations Series Map I-981.
13. Hansen, W. R., 1971, Geologic map of the Black Canyon of the Gunnison River and vicinity, western Colorado: U.S. Geological Survey Miscellaneous Investigations Series Map I-854.
14. Hedlund, D. C. and Olson, J. C., 1975, Geologic map of the Powderhorn quadrangle, Gunnison and Saguache Counties, Colorado: U.S. Geological Survey Geologic Quadrangle Map GQ-1178.
15. Johnson, R. C. and May, Fred, 1980, A study of the Cretaceous-Tertiary unconformity in the Piceance Creek Basin, Colorado; The underlying Ohio Creek Formation (Upper Cretaceous) redefined as a member of the Hunter Canyon or Mesaverde Formation: U.S. Geological Survey Bulletin 1482-B, 27 p.
16. Lipman, P. W., 1975, Evolution of the Platoro caldera complex and related volcanic rocks, southeastern San Juan Mountains, Colorado: U.S. Geological Survey Professional Paper 852, 128 p.
17. Lochman-Balk, C., 1972, Cambrian Systems, *in* Geologic Atlas of the Rocky Mountain region, United States of America: Denver, Colorado, Rocky Mountain Association of Geologists, p. 60–75.
18. Lohman, S. W., 1965, Geology and artesian water supply, Grand Junction area, Colorado: U.S. Geological Survey Professional Paper 451, 149 p.
19. Molenaar, C. M., 1978, Stratigraphic nomenclature charts for San Juan and Paradox Basins oil and gas fields of the Four Corners Area, v. 1: Four Corners Geological Society, p. 40–41.
20. Murray, D. K. and Haun, J. D., 1974, Introduction to the geology of the Piceance Creek Basin and vicinity, northwestern Colorado: Rocky Mountain Association of Geologists, 25th Field Conference, Energy resources of the Piceance Creek basin, Colorado, p. 29–39.
21. Mutschler, F. E., 1970, Geologic map of the Snowmass Mountain quadrangle Pitkin and Gunnison Counties, Colorado: U.S. Geological Survey Geologic Quadrangle Map GQ-853.
22. O'Sullivan, R. B., 1977, Triassic rocks in the San Juan Basin of New Mexico and adjacent areas: New Mexico Geological Society Guidebook 28, p. 139–146.
23. O'Sullivan, R. B., 1981, The Middle Jurassic San Rafael Group and related rocks in east-central Utah: New Mexico Geological Society Guidebook 32, this volume.
24. O'Sullivan, R. B. and Beikman, H. M., compilers, 1963, Geology, structure, and uranium deposits of the Shiprock quadrangle, New Mexico and Arizona: U.S. Geological Survey Miscellaneous Investigations Series Map I-345.
25. Ross, R. J. and Tweto, O., 1980, Lower Paleozoic sediments and tectonics in Colorado; *in* Colorado Geology: Rocky Mountain Association of Geologists p. 47–56.
26. Shawe, D. R., Simmons, G. C., and Archbold, N. L., 1968, Stratigraphy of Slick Rock district and vicinity, San Miguel and Dolores Counties, Colorado: U.S. Geological Survey Professional Paper 576-A, 108 p.
27. Shoemaker, E. M. and Newman, W. L. 1959, Moenkopi formation (Triassic? and Triassic) in salt anticline region, Colorado and Utah: American Association of Petroleum Geologists Bulletin, v. 43, p. 1835–1851.
28. Steven, T. A., Lipman, P. W., Hail, W. J., Jr., Barker, F., and Luedke, R. G., compilers, 1974, Geologic map of the Durango quadrangle, southwestern Colorado: U.S. Geological Survey Miscellaneous Investigations Series Map I-764.
29. Tweto, O., 1977, Nomenclature of Precambrian rocks in Colorado: U.S. Geological Survey Bulletin 1422-D, 22 p.
30. Tweto, O. and Lovering, T. S., 1977, Geology of the Minturn 15-minute quadrangle, Eagle and Summit Counties, Colorado: U.S. Geological Survey Professional Paper 956, 96 p.
31. Tweto, O., Moench, R. H., and Reed, J. C., Jr., 1978, Geologic map of the Leadville 1° × 2° quadrangle, northeastern Colorado: U.S. Geological Survey Miscellaneous Investigations Series Map I-999.
32. Tweto, O., Steven, T. A., Hail, W. J., Jr., and Moench, R. H., compilers, 1976, Preliminary geologic map of the Montrose 1° × 2° quadrangle, southwestern Colorado: U.S. Geological Survey Miscellaneous Field Studies Map MF-761.
33. Williams, P. L., compiler, 1964, Geology, structure, and uranium deposits of the Moab quadrangle, Colorado and Utah: U.S. Geological Survey Miscellaneous Investigations Series Map I-360.

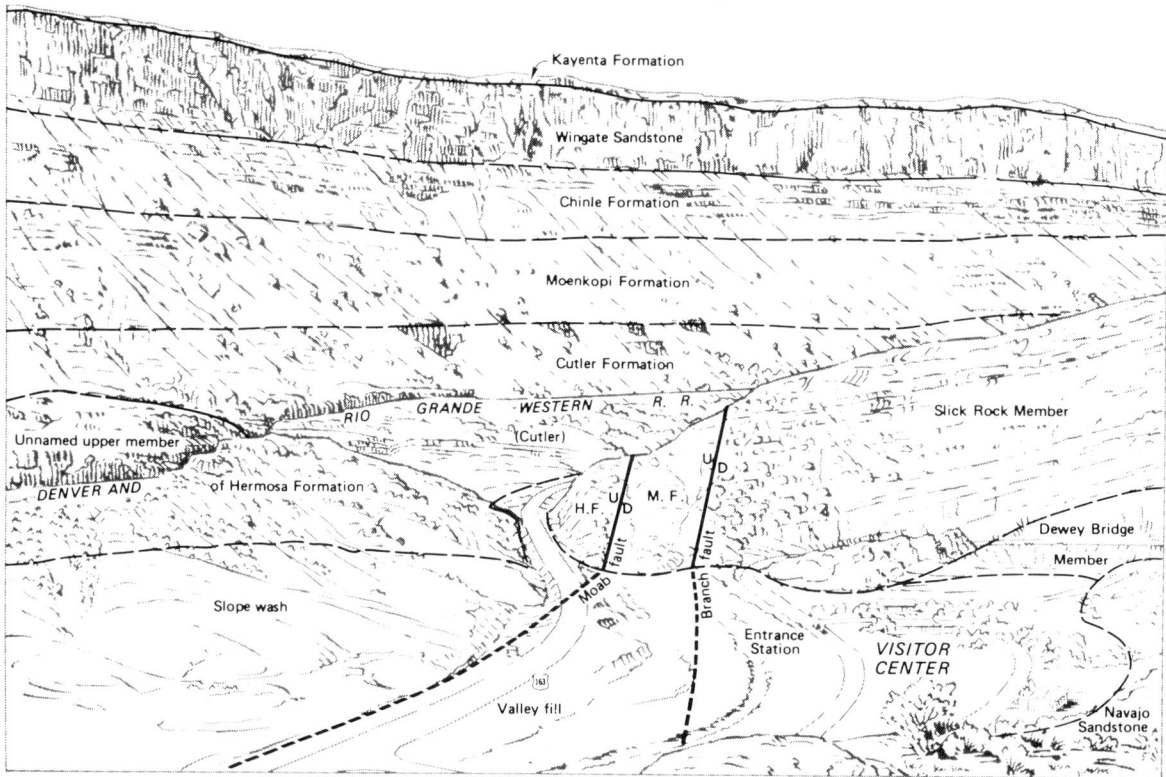

Faulted Seven Mile–Moab Valley anticline, viewed toward southwest from park road about 1.6 km above entrance to Arches National Park. U.S. Highway 163 at lower left is being renumbered U.S. 191. From color photograph by S. W. Lohman, U.S. Geological Survey, sketch by John R. Stacy shows geologic interpretation by Lohman and Edwin T. McKnight. **H.F.**, unnamed upper member of Hermosa Formation; **M.F.**, Moenkopi Formation. Total vertical displacement along both faults is about 760 m. Original sequence of strata may be visualized by placing Navajo Sandstone (lower right) atop Kayenta Formation on skyline. The Pacific Northwest (gas) Pipeline is buried beneath the slice of the Moenkopi Formation between the two faults, which accounts for the disturbed appearance of the rock. The two faults unite just beyond low ridge of the Slick Rock Member.

SUMMARY OF PALEOZOIC STRATIGRAPHY AND HISTORY OF WESTERN COLORADO AND EASTERN UTAH

JOHN A. CAMPBELL
Department of Geology
Fort Lewis College
Durango, Colorado 81301

and

U.S. Geological Survey
Box 25046, MS 916
Denver, Colorado 80225

INTRODUCTION

The area covered by this report extends from about Moab and Blanding, Utah on the west to Glenwood Springs and Gunnison, Colorado on the east (fig. 1). The Paleozoic Systems in this area are characterized by two different tectonic styles of sedimentation. The lower Paleozoic, Cambrian through Mississippian, consists of thin, stable shelf deposits that are commonly separated by major unconformities. The upper Paleozoic, Pennsylvanian and Permian, consist of thick basin deposits, a result of active tectonism.

The major structural elements of the region are shown on Figure 2. These structural elements are largely the product of Laramide deformation; however, the Paradox basin is a Paleozoic feature, and the Uinta and Uncompahgre Uplifts have influenced sedimentation throughout various parts of the Paleozoic (Baars, 1966; Baars and See, 1968; Lochman-Balk, 1972; Spoelhof, 1976; Weimer, 1980).

The stratigraphic terminology (fig. 3a, b) is from the San Juan Mountains for the area west of the Uncompahgre Uplift and from the White River Uplift for the area east of the Uncompahgre. East of the area discussed in this report in central Colorado, the stratigraphic sequence and terminology is somewhat different (Ross and Tweto, 1980; and DeVoto, 1980, a, b).

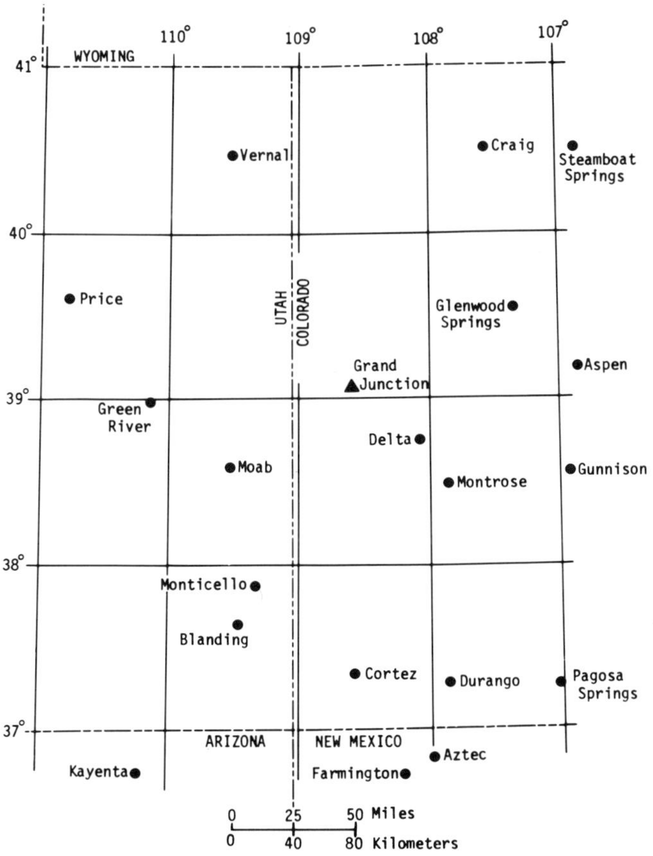

CAMBRIAN SYSTEM

The oldest Paleozoic rocks are in the subsurface along the western edge of the area. These are largely clastic rocks, medium to coarse quartz sandstones and some conglomerate, of probable Middle Cambrian age. To the east, the oldest Paleozoic rocks are of the same general lithology but are Late Cambrian, Dresbachian, age (Lochman-Balk, 1972). In the San Juan Mountains, these rocks are called the Ignacio Quartzite (fig. 3a) and in the White River

Figure 1. Index map, western Colorado and eastern Utah, showing area covered by this report.

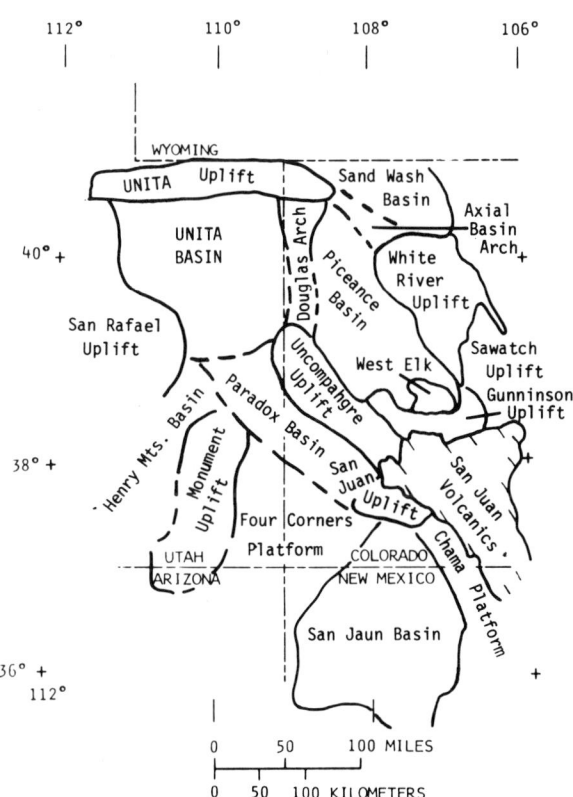

Figure 2. Major structural elements in western Colorado and eastern Utah (modified from Grose, 1972).

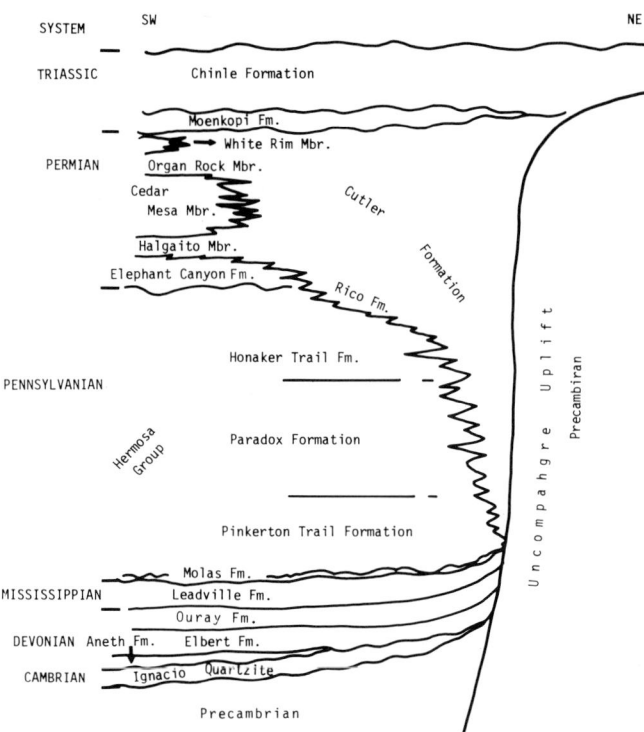

Figure 3a. Schematic stratigraphic section showing Paleozoic formations for the Four Corners area. No scale; thickness exaggerated for thinner units.

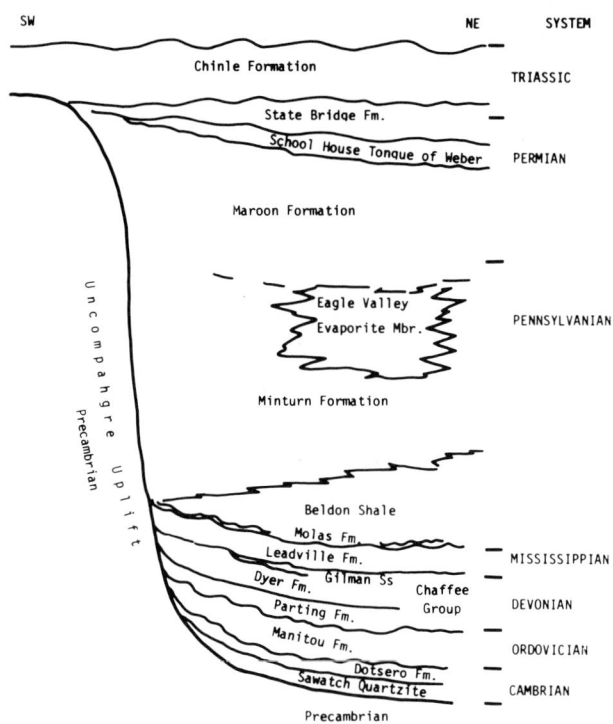

Figure 3b. Schematic stratigraphic section showing Paleozoic formations for the White River Uplift area. No scale; thickness exaggerated for thinner units.

Uplift and across the rest of Colorado, the Sawatch Quartzite (fig. 3b). These rocks are probably in part Franconian age (Lochman-Balk, 1972).

Late Cambrian, Trempealeauan, age rocks have been removed by erosion from most of western Colorado and eastern Utah except in the area of the White River Uplift (fig. 2). Here, the latest stage of the Cambrian is represented by the Dotsero Formation (Bass and Northrop, 1963). The Dotsero is composed of dolomites and dolomitic limestone with abundant flat-pebble conglomerate, and an upper algal limestone member, all of intertidal and supratidal origin (Tyler and Campbell, 1975; Tyler, 1976; Campbell, 1976).

The deposition of this sequence is a product of a slow, west to east transgression of the Cambrian sea across low-lying, weathered Precambrian terrain. At the time of maximum transgression, the shoreline was to the east near the present Gore Range (Tweto and Lovering, 1977; Tweto, 1977). A series of low islands probably persisted to the north along the Colorado-Wyoming border (Lochman-Balk, 1972; Bickford, 1974; Campbell and Bickford, 1976) along the axis of the Uinta peninsula (Lochman-Balk, 1972). During the maximum advance of the sea, the supply of detritus was curtailed and a vast tidal flat existed across this area in which carbonate sedimentation dominated (Campbell, 1972a; Tyler and Campbell, 1975). A minor regression occurred at the end of Trempealeauan (Lochman-Balk, 1972; Campbell, 1976) to close Cambrian history in this area. The present thickness and extent of the Cambrian System are shown in Figure 4.

ORDOVICIAN SYSTEM

Figure 5 shows the present thickness and distribution of the Ordovician System in eastern Utah and western Colorado. Ordovician rocks are not present in most of this area largely because of

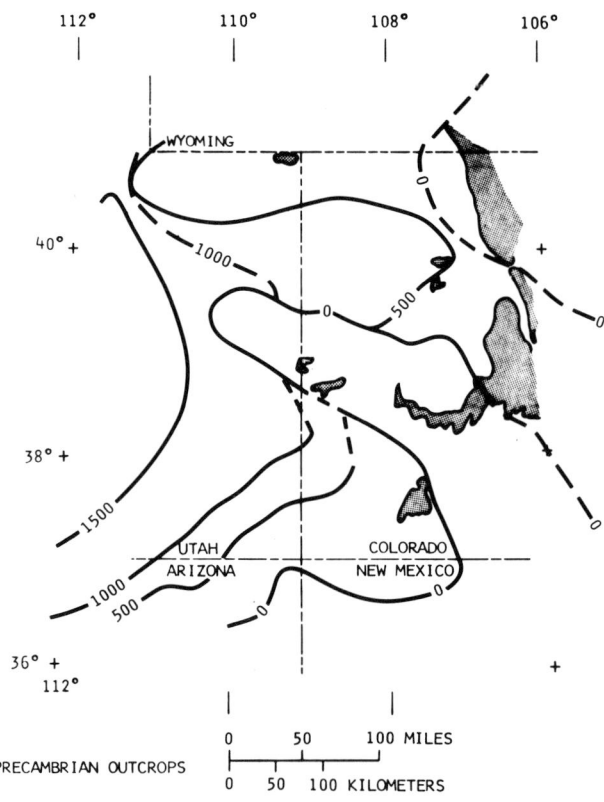

Figure 4. Isopach map of Cambrian System (modified from Lochman-Balk, 1972). Contour interval 500 ft (152 m).

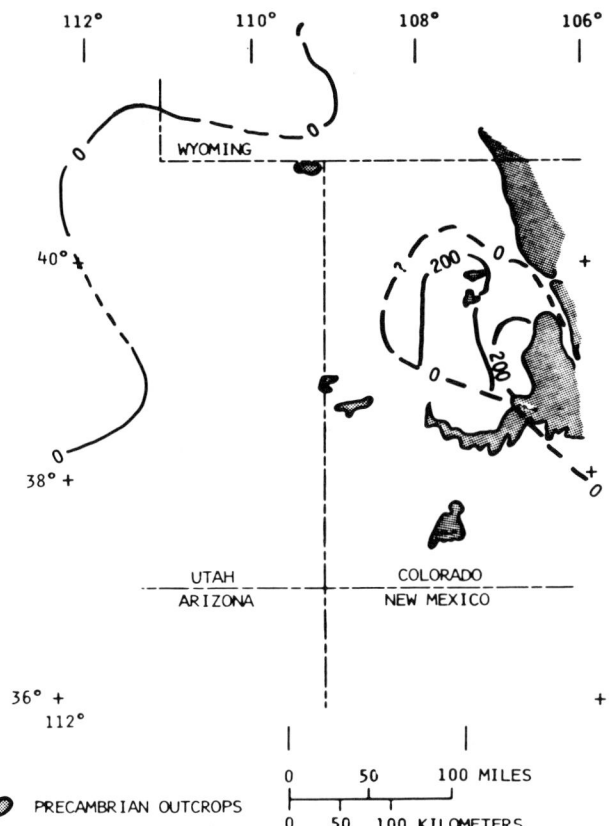

Figure 5. Isopach map of Ordovician System (modified from Foster, 1972). Contour interval 200 ft (61 m).

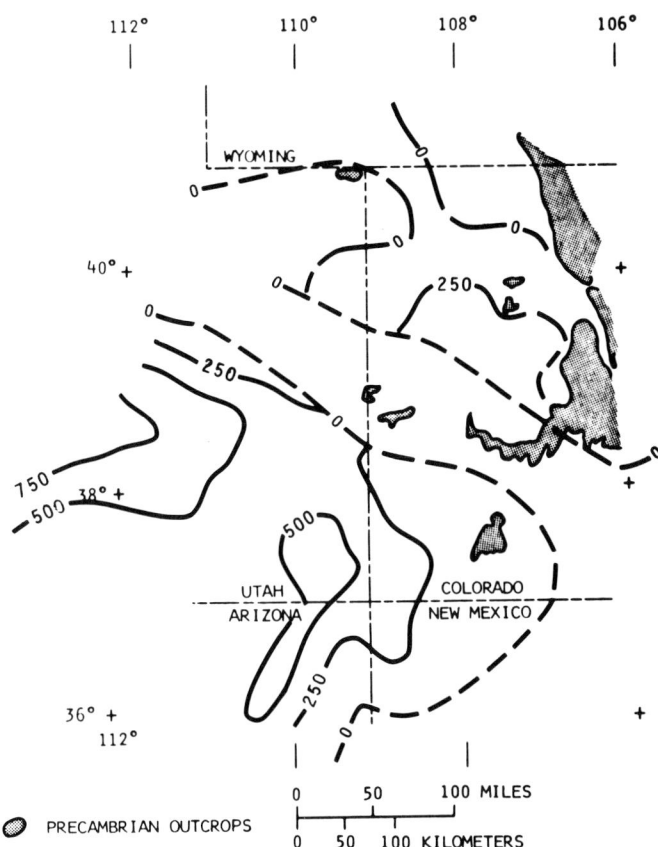

Figure 6. Isopach map of Devonian System (modified from Baars, 1972). Contour interval 250 ft (76 m).

several periods of pre-Devonian erosion. The lower Ordovician Manitou Formation is present in the White River Uplift area (Bass and Northrop, 1963), and Lower, Middle and Upper Ordovician rocks are present just east of the area of this report (Ross and Tweto, 1980).

The Manitou Formation is composed of dolomite and dolomitic limestone with abundant flat-pebble conglomerate very similar to the lithologies in the Dotsero Formation. The thickness of the Manitou varies considerabley in the White River uplift area due to pre-Devonian erosion. Fossils found by Bass and Northrop (1953) in the lower part of the Manitou indicate equivalence to zone B of the Canadian Series (Ross, 1951).

The fragmentary Ordovician record in Colorado indicates three periods of marine sedimentation separated by three periods of erosion. Only the earliest marine sequence is present in the White River Uplift area, and the nature of the carbonate sediments of the Manitou suggests intertidal and supratidal carbonate mud flats as the predominate environment (Campbell, 1972).

SILURIAN SYSTEM

The unconformity at the base of the Devonian represents about 100 million years, including all of Middle and Late Ordovician and Silurian and Early and Middle Devonian time. Rocks of Silurian age, as well as the other systems, could have been deposited and later removed by erosion. Although no Silurian rocks are known in this area, blocks of limestone that contain Middle and Upper Silurian brachiopods have been found in diatremes along the Colorado-Wyoming border south of Laramie, Wyoming (Chronic and others, 1969). No Silurian rocks are known within 480 km of these diatremes.

DEVONIAN SYSTEM

The oldest Devonian rocks in eastern Utah and westen Colorado are Upper Devonian, representing most of the Frasnian and Famennian Stages (Baars, 1971). Their present distribution and thickness across the area are shown in Figure 6.

The oldest Devonian stratigraphic unit southwest of the Uncompahgre Uplift is the Aneth Formation (fig. 3a). The Aneth is a dark colored, dense, argillaceous dolomite sequence that is present only in the subsurface in the Four Corners area (Baars, 1972). Conformably overlying the Aneth in the subsurface, and disconformably overlying the Cambrian Ignacio in exposures in the San Juan Mountains, are the sandstones, shales, and sandy dolomites of the Elbert Formation. The basal sandstone of the Elbert Formation is the McCracken Member. This sandstone is considered to be a product of a marine transgression with the source for the sand from local paleotectonic high areas (Baars and Campbell, 1968). Salt casts and stromatolitic dolomite suggest that much of the Elbert was deposited in an intertidal environment.

The oldest Devonian stratigraphic unit in the White River Uplift area consists of the sandstones, shales and thin stromatolitic dolomites of the Parting Formation, which is the basal formation of the Chaffee Group (Campbell, 1970a). Like the Elbert, the Parting consists of a basal sandstone unit, informally designated as Unit A, that is a product of marine transgression (Campbell, 1970a). Shallow marine to intertidal depositional environments are represented by the lithologies in the Parting (Campbell, 1967, 1970a, 1972b). The Aneth, Elbert and Parting Formations are of Frasnian age (Baars, 1972).

Conformably overlying the Elbert Formation in southwestern

Colorado is the Ouray Formation, and conformably overlying the Parting Formation in the White River Uplift area is the Dyer Formation (figs. 3a, b). Both the Ouray and Dyer are considered Famennian in age (Baars, 1972) with the upper part of Early Mississippian age (Baars, 1966; Baars and Campbell, 1968). The Ouray Formation is lime mudstone, pelletal lime mudstone and skeletal limestone that is locally dolomitized, and which formed in a quiet-water marine environment (Baars, 1966). The Dyer Formation consists of two carbonate members. The lower shallow marine fossilferous limestone is the Broken Rib Member and the upper intertidal to supratidal stromatolitic dolomite is the Coffee Pot Member (Campbell, 1970a, b). The Dyer Formation represents a regression of the Late Devonian–Early Mississippian sea from the White River Uplift area (Campbell, 1970a, b).

Unconformably above the Dyer Formation on the White River Uplift is a sandy dolomite that grades into a sandstone farther east, and which is unconformably overlain by the Leadville Formation. This is the Gilman Sandstone which Tweto and Lovering (1977) reassigned from the Leadville Limestone to the Chaffee Group because it is more closely related to the Dyer in composition and origin. The Chaffee Group thus consists of the Parting and Dyer Formations with the Gilman Sandstone at the top.

The depositional history of the Devonian consists of an initial west to east marine transgression over a highly weathered and eroded older Paleozoic terrain. Sources for sediment included local highs and the Front Range area to the east. With maximum transgression, sediment sources were covered or very low, and carbonate deposition prevailed. A minor regression occurred in the White River Uplift area with an influx of some sand which formed the Gilman Sandstone. At about this time, the diatremes in northern Colorado were formed (Naeser and McCallum, 1977).

MISSISSIPPIAN SYSTEM

The present distribution and thickness of rocks of Mississippian age are shown in Figure 7. These rocks, the Leadville Formation, are Early Mississippian in age, Kinderhookian and Osagean (Baars, 1966; DeVoto, 1980a). The Late Mississippian was a time of exposure, weathering and erosion of Lower Mississippian rocks across the area.

The Leadville Formation in southwestern Colorado consists of two informal members separated by an unconformity (Baars, 1966). The lower Kinderhookian-age member consists of stromatolitic dolomites, lime mudstones, and pelletal lime mudstones that are more fossiliferous to the west, and locally includes crinoidal biogenic banks adjacent to the Uncompahgre Uplift (Baars, 1966). It rests conformably on the Ouray Formation except in the vicinity of paleo-structures where local unconformities are present (Armstrong and Mamet, 1976). This member was deposited in intertidal to subtidal environments that persisted and expanded from Ouray time. Locally, over paleotectonic highs, the lower member thins or has been removed by pre-Osagean erosion (Baars, 1966; Armstrong and Mamet, 1976).

The upper member of Osagean age unconformably overlies the lower member, and consists of fossiliferous pelletal and oolitic limestone, and lime and dolomitic mudstone, with scattered crinoidal debris. As in the lower member, the carbonate facies changes on the flanks of the paleotectonic highs in the area (Baars, 1966).

Late Mississippian and Early Pennsylvanian time in this area was one of extensive weathering and erosion. Humid-climate solution erosion across the exposed Leadville Formation produced an extensive karst topography (DeVoto, 1980a). A residual *terra rosa*

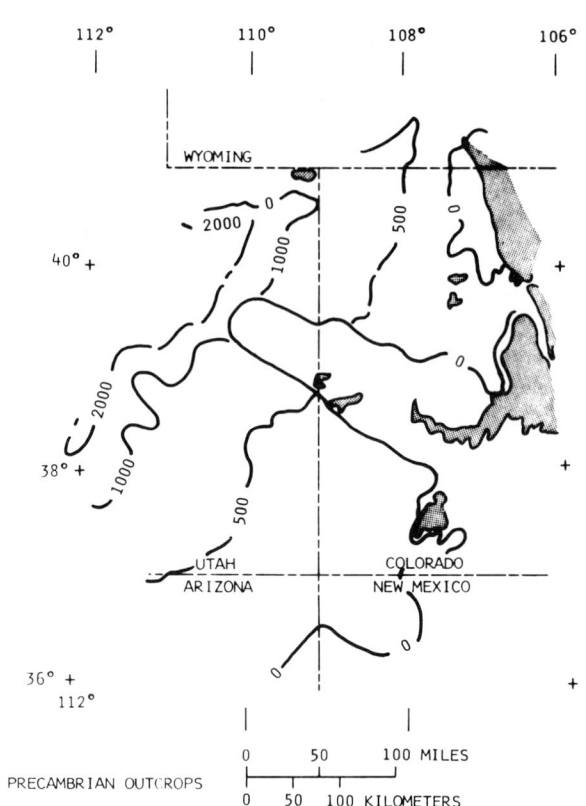

Figure 7. Isopach map of Mississippian System (modified from Craig, 1972). Contour interval 500 to 1000 ft (152 to 305 m).

developed on the karst surface (Merrill and Winar, 1958). This regolith is the Molas Formation which is dated in part as Early Pennsylvanian (Merrill and Winar, 1958) but must have begun to form during Late Mississippian time.

A similar but simpler Mississippian sequence is present in the White River Uplift area. The lower part of the Leadville Formation, probably Kinderhookian in age (Conley, 1972; DeVoto, 1980a), consists of thin-bedded stromatolitic dolomite that is of intratidal to supratidal origin (Conley, 1972). The upper unit is Osagean in age (Conley, 1972; DeVoto, 1980a), and consists of oolitic limestone to the east and fossiliferous limestone to the west with increasing amounts of lime mudstone to the west (Conley, 1972). This sequence represents a single easterly transgressive sequence (Conley, 1972), in contrast to the two transgressive sequences separated by a period of erosion noted in southwestern Colorado. Solution weathering, erosion and the formation of a regolith over a karst surface developed over this area during Late Mississippian and Early Pennsylvanian time. This paleosoil also is called the Molas Formation (Bass and Northrop, 1963).

In the subsurface of the far western and northwestern part of the area covered by this report, a thicker and more complete sequence of Mississippian rocks is present. For a complete and detailed report on these rocks, see Craig (1972) and Craig and others (1979).

PENNSYLVANIAN SYSTEM

Mountain building, and the development of flanking basins that received almost 4000 m of fluvial and marine sediment, are the characteristics of the Pennsylvanian Period in western Colorado and eastern Utah (fig. 8). The Uncompahgre Uplift was activated

SUMMARY OF PALEOZOIC STRATIGRAPHY

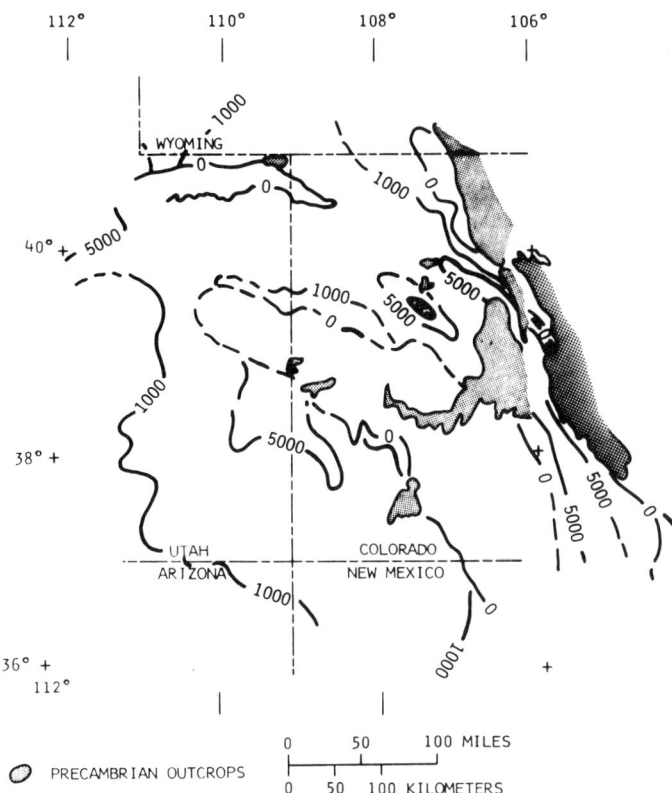

Figure 8. Isopach map of Pennsylvanian System. Central Colorado Trough is northeast of the Uncompahgre Uplift (modified from Mallory, 1972). Contour interval 1000 to 4000 ft (305 to 1219 m).

into a prominent mountain system, the Paradox Basin developed to the south and west, and the Central Colorado Trough developed to the north and east (figs. 2, 8). A number of excellent detailed reports are available on the tectonics and deposition in both of these basins including McKee and others (1967), Mallory (1972), McKee and others (1975), and DeVoto (1980b). A short summary of events is presented here.

Continued emergence and karst development characterized the early Pennsylvanian, most of Morrowan time, throughout the region (DeVoto, 1980b). Marine deposition commenced in Morrowan time in the Central Colorado Trough with the deposition of the black shales of the Beldon Shale (fig. 3b). This deposition continued into Atokan time, but coarse arkose became interbedded with the black shales in the upper part of the Beldon Shale as the Uncompahgre Uplift was slowly activated.

In southwestern Colorado, the Molas Formation continued to form during early Atokan time. However, the Atokan sea advanced across the weathered terrain reworking the upper Molas (Merrill and Winar, 1958). Thus the Atokan strata include the upper Molas, and dark colored shales and limestone and dolomite of the Pinkerston Trail Formation of the Hermosa Group, which were deposited in the Paradox Basin as a product of this marine invasion.

In southwestern Colorado, the Paradox Basin contains a thick sequence of evaporites and black shales that formed during Desmoinesian time. Along the flanks of the Uncompahgre Uplift, thick sequences of arkose of the lower part of the Cutler Formation (fig. 3a) were deposited in response to tectonic activity (Wengerd, 1962; Mallory, 1972; Hite and Cater, 1972).

Desmoinesian strata in the Central Colorado Trough consist of thick arkoses of the Minturn Formation, deposited along the flanks of the Uncompahgre as well as the flanks of the Front Range Uplift to the east (fig. 3b). In the middle of the trough, in the White River Uplift area, a marine seaway persisted in which evaporites were deposited along with black shale and a few thin limestones. These deposits are called the Eagle Valley Evaporite Member of the Minturn Formation (Murray, 1958). This evaporite deposition occurred at about the same time as that in the Paradox Basin but the two basins were not connected (Mallory, 1972).

Evaporitic deposition ceased and normal marine deposition of limestones, with minor shale and sandstone, returned to the Paradox Basin in Late Desmoinesian time and continued through Missourian into Virgilian time (Mallory, 1972). Coarse fluvial arkose of the Cutler Formation continued to accumulate along the flanks of the Uncompahgre Uplift. These arkose sediments were deposited farther to the west late in Pennsylvanian and into early Permian time (fig. 3a). The transition between marine and fluvial sediments has been mapped by some geologists as the Rico Formation.

In the Central Colorado Trough, fluvial deposition dominated as the sea withdrew and the Maroon formation was deposited over the Eagle Valley Evaporite Member (fig. 3b). The lower part of the Maroon is considered to be Missourian and Virgilian in age; however, deposition of the Maroon continued into the Permian.

PERMIAN SYSTEM

The depositional patterns that were established in the Late Pennsylvanian in eastern Utah and western Colorado continued into the Early Permian. Although the depositional patterns are similar, an unconformity is present between the Pennsylvanian and Permian Systems in the Paradox Basin (Baars, 1962). Deposition close to the Uncompahgre Uplift and in the Central Colorado Trough was probably continuous, however. The fluvial sediments of Wolfcampian age in the trough are the upper part of the Maroon Formation (fig. 3b). Overlying the Maroon in the White River Uplift area is the School House Sandstone which is a tongue of the Weber Sandstone (Brill, 1952). Fryberger (1979) considers the Weber Sandstone in northwestern Colorado to be of eolian origin. The Weber thickens to the northwest, intertongues with and grades eastward into the Maroon, and represents Late Pennsylvanian, (Missourian and Virgilian) as well as Early Permian (Wolfcampian) time in northwestern Colorado and northeastern Utah (Rascoe and Baars, 1972).

The final Paleozoic deposition in the Central Colorado trough occurred during Guadalupian time. Shales, siltstones, fine grained sandstones and a thin dolomite unit comprise the State Bridge Formation which unconformably overlies the Maroon Formation. Most of Leonardian time is represented by the erosional unconformity between the Maroon and the State Bridge. The thin dolomite unit is the South Canyon Creek Member (Bass and Northrup, 1962) which probably correlates with the Park City Formation of southwestern Wyoming (Rascoe and Baars, 1972). The deposition of the State Bridge Formation was evidently in a shallow marine to intertidal environment representing a marine invasion of the trough from the north. An eolian sandstone is present at the base of the State Bridge in the White River Uplift area (Freeman, 1971), indicating initial continental deposition. Paleozoic history closes in the Central Colorado trough with erosion of part of the State Bridge Formation before Triassic deposition.

Southwest of the Uncompahgre Uplift, deposition of the fluvial Cutler Formation continued into Wolfcampian time. This deposition consisted of three large fluvial, or wet alluvial, fans (Campbell, 1979, 1980). In the southeastern and central part of the Paradox

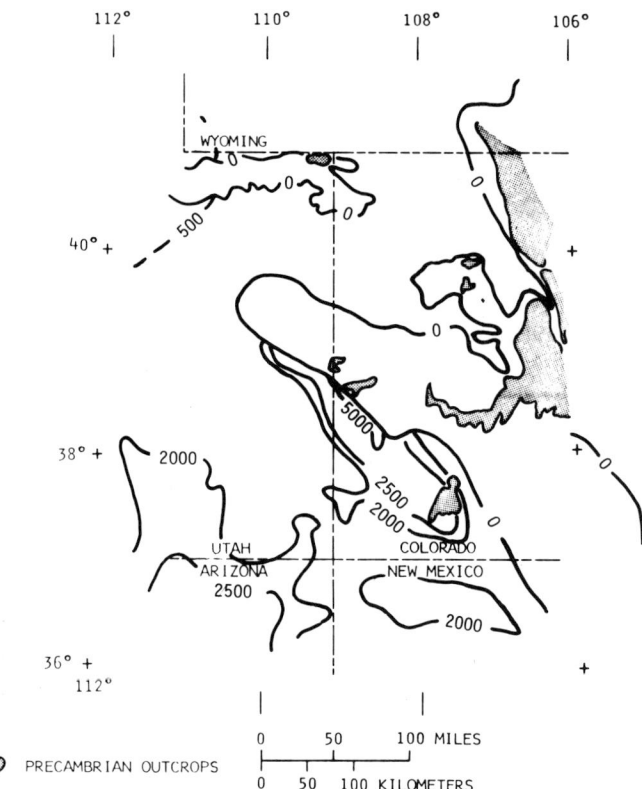

Figure 9. Isopach map of Permian System (modified from Rascoe and Baars, 1972). Contour interval 500 to 2500 ft (152 to 762 m).

Basin this fluvial deposition persisted, filling the basin. In the northwest during Early Wolfcampian, a sea was present to the west in which limestones, shales and sandstones of the Elephant Canyon Formation (Baars, 1962) were deposited. Rocks that were deposited along the distal margins of the northern fan are interbedded with the marine deposits (Campbell, 1979, 1980). Later in Wolfcampian time, a second sea was present in the northwestern part of the basin. Sandstones, shales and a few thin limestones of the Cedar Mesa Member of the Cutler Formation were deposited in shallow marine, marginal marine and eolian environments (Mack, 1977; Campbell, 1979, 1980). Once again, marine rocks are interbedded with distal fluvial sediments that were deposited along the margins of a large fluvial fan (Campbell, 1980). Red fluvial shales and sandstones that are present to the west between the Elephant Canyon Formation and the Cedar Mesa Member are the Halgaito Shale member of the Cutler, and fluvial red shales and sandstones that overlie the Cedar Mesa Member are the Organ Rock Shale Member of the Cutler Formation (fig. 3a). Final marine, and coastal dune deposition, probably in Leonardian time, along the western margin of the basin, produced the White Rim Sandstone Member of the Cutler Formation (Baars and Seager, 1970; Steele-Mallory, 1981). The basin was exposed to erosion during the remainder of Permian time and Paleozoic history for the Paradox Basin closes with an erosional unconformity. Present thickness and distribution of the Permian System are shown in Figure 9.

By the end of the Paleozoic, the Uncompahgre Uplift had been eroded, the basins filled, and the relief between the structural elements greatly reduced. Early Triassic erosion and deposition completed the leveling such that the fluvial Upper Triassic Chinle Formation was deposited across the area (MacLachlan, 1972).

REFERENCES

Armstrong, A. K. and Mamet, B. L., 1976, Biostratigraphy and regional relations of the Mississippian Leadville in the San Juan Mountains, southwestern Colorado: U.S. Geological Survey Professional Paper 985, 25 p.

Baars, D. L., 1962, Permian System of Colorado Plateau: American Association of Petroleum Geologists Bulletin, v. 46, p. 149–218.

———, 1966, Pre-Pennsylvanian paleotectonics-key to basin evolution and petroleum occurrences in Paradox Basin, Utah and Colorado: American Association of Petroleum Geologists Bulletin, v. 50, p. 2082–2111.

———, 1972, Devonian system, in Geologic Atlas of the Rocky Mountain Region: Denver, Colorado, Rocky Mountain Association of Geologists, p. 90–99.

Baars, D. L. and Campbell, J. A., 1968, Devonian Systems of Colorado, northern New Mexico and the Colorado Plateau: Mountain Geologist, v. 5, p. 31–40.

Baars, D. L. and See, P. D., 1968, Pre-Pennsylvanian stratigraphy and paleotectonics of the San Juan Mountains, southwestern Colorado: Geological Society of American Bulletin, v. 79, p. 333–350.

Baars, D. L. and Seager, W. R., 1970, Stratigraphic control of petroleum in White Rim Sandstone (Permian) in and near Canyonlands National Park, Utah; American Association of Petroleum Geologists Bulletin, v. 54, p. 709–718.

Bass, N. W. and Northrop, S. A., 1953, Dotsero and Manitou Formations, White River Plateau, Colorado, with special reference to Clinetop Algal Limestone Member of Dotsero Formation: American Association of Petroleum Geologists Bulletin, v. 37, p. 889–912.

———, 1963, Geology of the Glenwood Springs Quadrangle and vicinity, northwestern Colorado: U.S. Geological Survey Bulletin 1142-J, 74 p.

Bickford, H. L., 1974, Petrology of the upper Sawatch Formation (M.S. thesis): Fort Collins, Colorado State University, 104 p.

Brill, K. G., 1952, Stratigraphy in the Permo-Pennsylvanian zeugogeosyncline of Colorado and northern New Mexico: Geological Society of America Bulletin, v. 63, p. 809–880.

Campbell, J. A., 1967, Dispersal patterns in Upper Devonian in west-central Colorado, in International Symposium on the Devonian System, v. 2: Alberta Society of Petroleum Geologists, p. 1131–1138.

———, 1970a, Stratigraphy of the Chaffee Group (Upper Devonian) west-central Colorado: American Association of Petroleum Geologists Bulletin, v. 54, p. 313–325.

———, 1970b, Petrology of Devonian shelf carbonates of west central Colorado: Mountain Geologist, v. 7, p. 89–97.

———, 1972a, Lower Paleozoic systems, White River Plateau: Colorado School of Mines Quarterly, v. 67, no. 4, p. 37–62.

———, 1972b, Petrology of the quartzose sandstones of the Parting Formation in west-central Colorado: Journal of Sedimentary Petrology, v. 42, p. 263–269.

———, 1976, Upper Cambrian stromatolitic biostrome, Clinetop Member of the Dotsero Formation, western Colorado: Geological Society of America Bulletin, v. 87, p. 1331–1335.

———, 1979, Lower Permian depositional system, northern Uncompahgre basin: Four Corners Geological Society Guidebook, 9th Field Conference, p. 13–21.

———, 1980, Lower Pemian depositional systems, and Wolfcampian Paleogeography, Uncompahgre basin, eastern Utah, and southwestern Colorado, in T. D. Fouch and E. R. Magathan, eds., Paleozoic paleogeography of west-central United States: Society of Economic Paleontologists and Mineralogists, Rocky Mountain Section, Paleogeography Symposium 1, p. 327–340.

Campbell, J. A. and Bickford, H. L., 1976, Petrology of the Sawatch Sandstone, White River Plateau, west-central Colorado (abs.): Geological Society of America, Abstracts with Programs, v. 8, p. 573–574.

Chronic, John, McCallum, M. E., Ferris, C. S., Jr., and Eggler, D. H., 1969, Lower Paleozoic rocks in diatremes, southern Wyoming and northern Colorado: Geological Society of America Bulletin, v. 80, p. 149–156.

Conley, C. D., 1972, Depositional and diagenetic history of the Mississippian Leadville Formation, White River Plateau, Colorado: Colorado School of Mines Quarterly, v. 67, no. 4, p. 103–135.

Craig, L. C., 1972, Mississippian System, in Geologic Atlas of the Rocky Mountain Region: Denver, Colorado, Rocky Mountain Association of Geologists, p. 100–110.

Craig, L. C., Connor, C. W., and others, 1979, Paleotectonic Investigations of the Mississippian System in the United States: U.S. Geological Survey Professional Paper 1010, 559 p.

DeVoto, R. H., 1980a, Mississippian stratigraphy and history of Colorado, in H. C. Kent and K. W. Porter, eds., Colorado Geology: Denver, Colorado, Rocky Mountain Association of Geologists, p. 57–70.

———, 1980b, Pennsylvanian stratigraphy and history of Colorado, *in* H. C. Kent and K. W. Porter, eds., Colorado Geology: Denver, Colorado, Rocky Mountain Association of Geologists, p. 71–101.

Foster, N. H., 1972, Ordovician System, *in* Geologic Atlas of the Rocky Mountain Region: Denver, Colorado, Rocky Mountain Association of Geologists, p. 76–85.

Freeman, V. L., 1971, Stratigraphy of the State Bridge Formation in the Woody Creek Quadrangle, Pitkin and Eagle Counties, Colorado: U.S. Geological Survey Bulletin, 1324-F.

Fryberger, S. G., 1979, Eolian-fluviatile (continental) origin of ancient stratigraphic trap for petroleum in Weber Sandstone, Rangely field, Colorado: Mountain Geologist, v. 16, p. 1–36.

Grose, L. T., 1972, Tectonics, *in* Geologic Atlas of the Rocky Mountain Region: Denver, Colorado, Rocky Mountain Association of Geologists, p. 35–44.

Hite, R. J. and Cater, F. W., 1972, Pennsylvanian rocks and salt anticlines, Paradox basin, Utah and Colorado, *in* Geologic Atlas of the Rocky Mountain Region: Denver, Colorado, Rocky Mountain Association of Geologists, p. 133–138.

Lochman-Balk, C., 1972, Cambrian System, *in* Geologic Atlas of the Rocky Mountain Region: Denver, Colorado, Rocky Mountain Association of Geologists, p. 60–75.

Mack, G. H., 1977, Depositional environments of the Cutler–Cedar Mesa facies transition (Permian) near Moab, Utah: Mountain Geologist, v. 14, p. 53– 68.

MacLachlan, M. E., 1972, Triassic System, *in* Geologic Atlas of the Rocky Mountain Region: Denver, Colorado, Rocky Mountain Association of Geologists, p. 166– 176.

Mallory, W. W., 1972, Regional synthesis of the Pennsylvanian System, *in* Geologic Atlas of the Rocky Mountain Region: Denver, Colorado, Rocky Mountain Association of Geologists, p. 111–127.

McKee, E. D., Oriel, S. S., and others, 1967, Paleotectonic Investigations of the Permian System in the United States: U.S. Geological Survey Professional Paper 515, 271 p.

McKee, E. D., Crosby, E. J., and others, 1975, Paleotectonic Investigations of the Pennsylvanian System in the United States: U.S. Geological Survey Professional Paper 853, 349 p.

Merrill, W. M. and Winar, R. M., 1958, Molas and associated formations in San Juan basin–Needle Mountains area, southwestern Colorado: American Association of Petroleum Geologists Bulletin, v. 42, p. 2107–2132.

Murray, H. F., 1958, Pennsylvanian stratigraphy of the Maroon trough, *in* Curtis, B. F., ed., Symposium on Pennsylvanian rocks of Colorado and adjacent areas: Denver, Colorado, Rocky Mountain Association of Geologists, p. 47–58.

Naeser, C. W. and McCallum, M. E., 1977, Fission-track dating of kimberlitic zircons: Second International Kimberlite Conference, Santa Fe, New Mexico.

Rascoe, B., Jr., and Baars, D. L., 1972, Permian System, *in* Geologic Atlas of the Rocky Mountain Region: Denver, Colorado, Rocky Mountain Association of Geologists, p. 143–165.

Ross, R. J., Jr., 1951, Stratigraphy of the Garden City Formation in northeastern Utah, and its trilobite faunas: Yale University, Peabody Museum of Natural History Bulletin 6, 161 p.

Ross, R. J., Jr., and Tweto, O., 1980, Lower Paleozoic sediments and tectonics in Colorado, *in* H. C. Kent and K. W. Porter, eds., Colorado Geology: Denver, Colorado, Rocky Mountain Association of Geologists, p. 47–56.

Spoelhof, R. W., 1976, Pennsylvanian stratigraphy and paleotectonics of the western San Juan Mountains, southwestern Colorado, *in* R. C. Epis and R. J. Weimer, eds., Studies in Colorado field geology: Colorado School of Mines Professional Contribution 8, p. 159–179.

Steele-Mallory, B. A., 1981, White Rim Sandstone Member of Permian Cutler Formation: coastal dune field Utah (abs): American Association of Petroleum Geologists Bulletin, v. 65, p. 570.

Tweto, Ogden, 1977, Tectonic history of west-central Colorado, *in* H. K. Veal, ed., Exploration frontiers of the central and southern Rockies: Denver, Colorado, Rocky Mountain Association of Geologists, p. 11–22.

Tweto, Ogden and Lovering, T. S., 1977, Geology of the Minturn 15-minute Quadrangle, Eagle and Summit Counties, Colorado: U.S. Geological Survey Professional Paper 956, 96 p.

Tyler, T. F., 1976, Glenwood Canyon Member of the Dotsero Formation, west-central Colorado (abs.): Geological Society of America, Abstracts with Programs, v. 8, p. 641.

Tyler, T. F. and Campbell, J. A., 1975, Dotsero Formation, western Colorado: Mountain Geologist, v. 12, p. 113–118.

Weimer, R. J., 1980, Recurrent movement on basement faults, a tectonic style for Colorado and adjacent areas, *in* H. C. Kent and K. W. Porter, eds., Colorado Geology: Denver, Colorado, Rocky Mountain Association of Geologists, p. 23–35.

Wengerd, S. A., 1962, Pennsylvanian sedimentation in Paradox basin, Four Corners region, *in* C. C. Branson, ed., Pennsylvanian System in the United States: Tulsa, Oklahoma, American Association of Petroleum Geologists, p. 264– 330.

Panorama of north end of Paradox Valley (C. M. Molenaar photo).

Panorama along and across Paradox Valley (C. M. Molenaar photo).

THE MIDDLE JURASSIC SAN RAFAEL GROUP AND RELATED ROCKS IN EAST-CENTRAL UTAH

ROBERT B. O'SULLIVAN
U.S. Geological Survey
Denver, Colorado 80225

INTRODUCTION

The San Rafael Group of Middle Jurassic age is widely exposed in the uplands of the San Rafael Swell (fig. 1) and throughout much of the lowlands of the Green River Desert. Eastward from the Green River, the San Rafael Group is well displayed in high escarpments that form an almost continuous line of outcrop to Westwater Canyon. Between Courthouse Rock and Salt Valley the line of outcrop is interrupted and concealed by faulting. In the San Rafael Swell the group consists of five formations, in ascending order, Page Sandstone, Carmel Formation, Entrada Sandstone and the Curtis and Summerville Formations. In the Westwater Canyon area near the eastern border of Utah, the San Rafael Group is represented

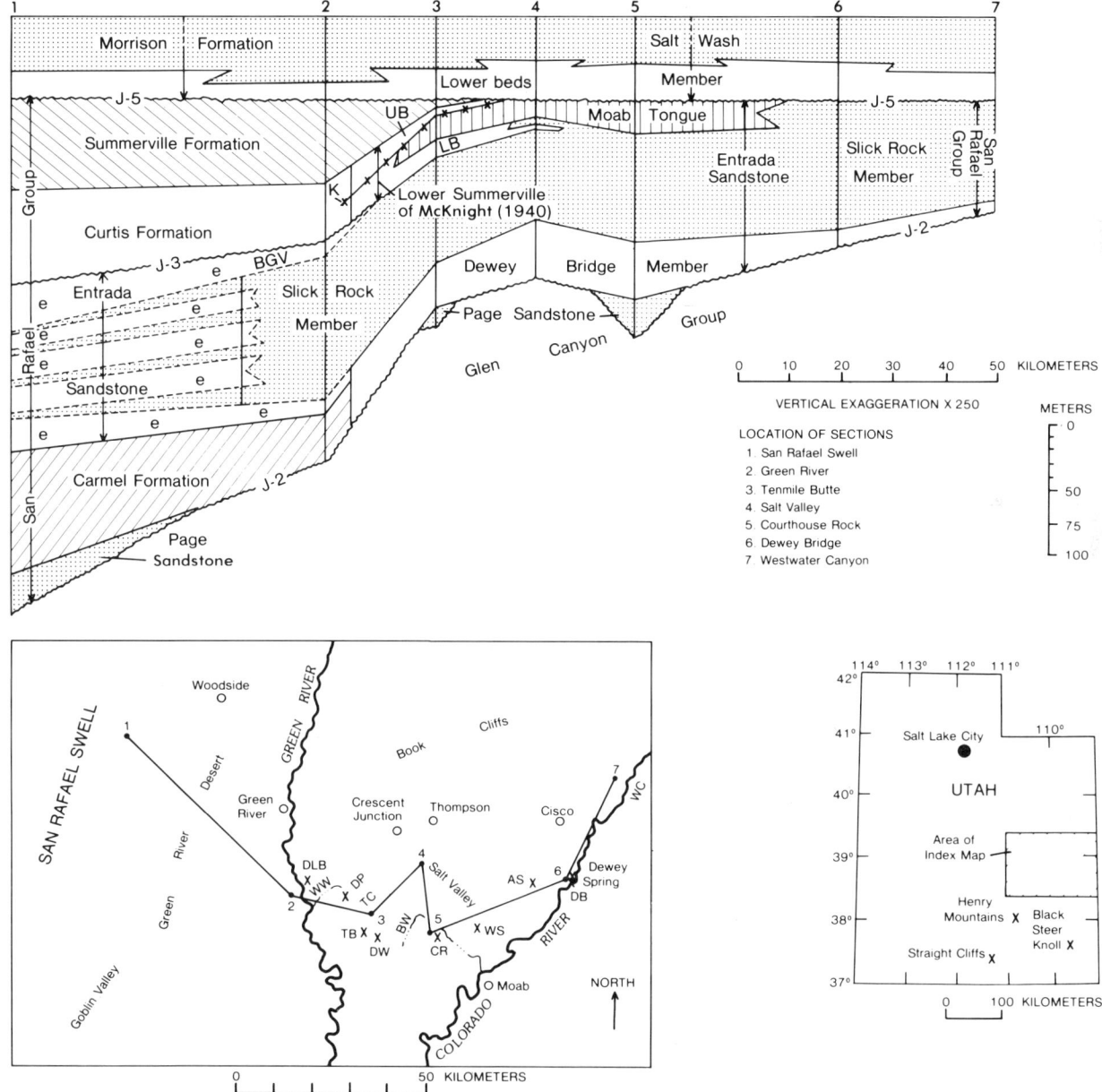

Figure 1. Index map and stratigraphic diagram showing correlation of San Rafael Group and related rocks. Symbols on diagram include: earthy facies of Entrada (E); bed at Black Steer Knoll (K); beds at Goblin Valley (BGV); and upper (UB) and lower (LB) beds of lower Summerville of McKnight (1940). Symbols on the map include: Auger Spring (AS); Bartlett Wash (BW); Courthouse Rock (CR); Dellenbaugh Butte (DLB); Dewey Bridge (DB); Dubinky well (DW); Duma Point (DP); Tenmile Butte (TB); Tenmile Canyon (TC); Willow Spring (WS); and White Wash (WW). J-2, J-3, and J-5 are unconformities discussed in the text.

solely by the Entrada Sandstone. Throughout the area the group is underlain by the Glen Canyon Group of Triassic and Jurassic age and is overlain by the Morrison Formation of Late Jurassic age.

STRATIGRAPHY

The distribution of the various parts of the San Rafael Group and their relationship to overlying and underlying rocks is shown on Figure 1. The stratigraphic diagram, as well as most of this report, is primarily a summary of two separate investigations (O'Sullivan, 1980 and 1981) describing Jurassic rocks from the Green River eastward about 74 km to Dewey Bridge. Some additional observations to the west in the San Rafael Swell and to the east near Westwater Canyon are included.

Sources of Data

The stratigraphic diagram (fig. 1) is derived from several sources. Most of the section in the San Rafael Swell (sec. 1) is from Wright and others (1979, p. 43-56) and was measured in secs. 3 and 4, T. 19 S., R. 12 E. The Page Sandstone in the San Rafael Swell (sec. 1) was measured by G. N. Pipiringos (oral commun., 1964) in sec. 18, T. 19 S., R. 11 E. The Carmel Formation and Entrada Sandstone in the composite section at the Green River (sec. 2) is from Wright and others (1962, fig. 2, no. 1 sec.) and was described from exposures in sec. 4, T. 24 S., R. 16 E. The upper part of the Green River section was measured by the writer near Dellenbaugh Butte in secs. 12 and 13, T. 23 S., R. 16 E. The Entrada Sandstone at Tenmile Butte is from Craig and others (1959, no. 204 sec.) and was described in sec. 23, T. 24 S., R. 18 E. The upper part of the Tenmile Butte section was measured by the writer in secs. 1 and 12, and the Page Sandstone was measured in sec. 27, T. 24 S., R. 18 E. All the other measurements are by the writer and the locations of the stratigraphic sections are as follows: Salt Valley (sec. 4) in secs. 30 and 32, T. 22 S., R. 20 E.; Courthouse Rock (sec. 5) in secs. 20, 28 and 29, T. 24 S., R. 20 E.; Dewey Bridge (sec. 6) in sec. 7, T. 23 S., R. 24 E.; and Westwater Canyon (sec. 7) in secs. 9 and 16, T. 20 S., R. 25 E.

Unconformities

Three unconformities are associated with the San Rafael Group in east-central Utah. Two of these unconformities—termed J-2 at the base of the San Rafael and J-5 at the top—are also recognized throughout much of the Western Interior of the United States. The J-2 erosion surface is also informally termed the "chert pebble unconformity" because basal beds of the San Rafael Group nearly everywhere are characterized by ubiquitous chert pebbles and granules (fig. 2A). An unconformity within the San Rafael referred to as J-3 at the top of the Entrada Sandstone is much less widespread and is difficult to recognize east of White Wash. The J-4 unconformity above the J-3 surface is truncated southward by the J-5 unconformity far to the north of Moab and is absent in east-central Utah. The unconformities and their regional stratigraphic significance are discussed more completely in a report by Pipiringos and O'Sullivan (1978).

Page Sandstone

The Page Sandstone (Peterson and Pipiringos, 1979, p. B20-B30) crops out primarily in a broad belt 65-80 km wide that trends about N. 15° E. and extends from the Straight Cliffs area of south-central Utah through the San Rafael Swell and into northern Utah. relatively small outliers of the Page Sandstone are recognized between the Green River and Salt Valley in east-central Utah. The Page is a light gray to reddish-tan fine-grained sandstone. In the San Rafael Swell, the Page is a highly crossbedded eolian sandstone (fig. 2B) about 30 m thick. In the swell, the Page is very similar to the underlying Navajo Sandstone in bedding and lithology, because it was undoubtedly derived from the Navajo and deposited in a similar environment. Near Tenmile Butte (sec. 3) the Page is 10 m thick and consists of a series of interdune flat beds as much as 1.5 m thick alternating with eolian crossbedded units as much as 3 m thick. At Courthouse Rock (sec. 5), the gray Page Sandstone is locally at least 30 m thick and consists almost entirely of flat-bedded units (fig. 2C) with only one crossbedded unit near the middle which is less than 1 m thick. Most of the Page of Courthouse Rock in all probability represents deposition in water. The Page Sandstone in east-central Utah appears to have been deposited in broad erosional depressions formed in the top of the Navajo Sandstone, possibly during the time the J-2 unconformity developed.

Carmel Formation

The Carmel Formation is of diverse lithology. In the stratigraphic section at the San Rafael Swell (sec. 1) about 75 percent of the Carmel Formation consists of greenish-gray and minor reddish-brown siltstone and shale in units as much as 10 m thick (Wright and others, 1979, p. 52-56). Limestone, sandstone and gypsum form a subordinate lithology. Gypsum is present in massive beds as much as 3.6 m thick, as a disseminated constituent and in veins and thin seams that cut other lithologies. Gypsum is most con-

---

Figure 2. Views of San Rafael Group and Morrison Formation.
  A Closeup of pebbles on J-2 unconformity near Courthouse Rock in NW¼ sec. 28, T. 24 S., R. 20 E.
  B Page Sandstone in San Rafael Swell in sec. 18, T. 19 S., R. 11 E. Feet of the geologists are on J-2 unconformity, which is basal unconformable contact of Page and underlying Glen Canyon Group. Photograph by G. N. Pipiringos.
  C Lower part of Page Sandstone near Courthouse Rock in SW¼ sec. 28, T. 24 S., R. 20 E.
  D Jurassic rocks near Duma Point in NW¼ sec. 30, T. 23, S., R. 18 E. Top of Slick Rock Member (SR) of Entrada Sandstone; lower Summerville of McKnight (1940) includes lower beds (LB), bed at Black Steer Knoll (K) and upper beds (UB); the basal red ledge (RL) of Summerville Formation; bed A (A) at base of Morrison Formation overlies the J-5 unconformity. The lower beds of the Salt Wash Member are 10.8 m thick and extend from the J-5 unconformity to the thick fluviatile sandstones on upper part of mesa. About 2.5 km to the east, the Moab Tongue appears beneath the bed at Black Steer Knoll.
  E Lower beds of Salt Wash Member unconformably overlying Moab Tongue about 4.8 km west of Auger Spring in SW¼SE¼ sec. 10, T.23 S., R. 22 E. Bed B (B) makes ledge at top of slope. Compare with fig. 2D. Strata at Duma Point from bed A through the bed at Black Steer Knoll have been removed by erosion along the J-5 unconformity.
  F Morrison Formation unconformably overlying Entrada Sandstone in SW¼NW¼ sec. 8, T. 23 S., R. 24 E. near Dewey Spring. Bed A (A) makes ledges at top of Slick Rock Member; bed B (B) is 0.5 m thick at top of lower cliff. Lower beds of Salt Wash are 30 m thick and extend from base of bed A to base of thick fluviatile sandstone in upper part of cliff. J-5 unconformity is at base of bed A.

Figure 2.

spicuous in the upper two-thirds of the formation. Gray, oolitic, ledge-forming limestone beds containing marine fossils are as much as 2.5 m thick. The limestone beds are found mainly in the lower one-third of the formation. Sandstone beds are commonly gray and as much as 2.5 m thick. Eastward from the San Rafael Swell, sandstone beds increase in abundance, and near the Green River (sec. 2) most of the Carmel consists of about equal amounts of sandstone and shale or siltstone (Wright and others, 1979, p. 83–87). Marine limestones and gray sandstone beds in the lower part of the Carmel disappear eastward towards the Green River by progressively onlapping the J-2 unconformity. The upper part of the Carmel Formation grades laterally into the lower part of the Entrada (Dewey Bridge Member) in a zone of transition extending from 3.2 to 8 km east of the Green River. The intergrading relationship of Carmel Formation and Entrada Sandstone are discussed in detail by Wright and others (1962, p. 2057–2062).

Entrada Sandstone west of the Green River

The Entrada Sandstone consists of siltstone and sandstone in differing proportions which vary regionally. In the San Rafael Swell (sec. 1), the Entrada Sandstone is mostly very fine grained sandstone to siltstone with only four clean partly crossbedded sandstone units, all less than 4.7 m thick (Wright and others, 1979, p. 49–51). The amount of siltstone diminishes eastward as succinctly described by Baker and others (1936, p. 7): "The Entrada sandstone in the San Rafael Swell is a deep red fine grained earthy sandstone that weathers into small bosses, "stone babies," and other rounded forms and at many localities is not much more resistant than shale. . . . Eastward from the San Rafael Swell this earthy facies passes into less earthy, irregularly bedded sandstone. . . . This in turn passes eastward into a sandstone composed of clean, fine- to medium-sized lime-cemented quartz grains, red, orange-red, or gray, banded at many places with conspicuous zones of color . . . with intricate cross bedding between horizontal bedding planes. . . ." The earthy facies of the Entrada Sandstone in the San Rafael Swell area is considered of nearshore marine origin (Baker, 1946, p. 80) marginal to marine rocks elsewhere in Utah.

Siltstone or earthy sandstone units near the base and top of the Entrada Sandstone are noteworthy. Over wide areas in an adjacent to the Green River Desert, siltstone beds at the top of the Entrada are referred to as the beds at Goblin Valley. Near the Green River (sec. 2), red siltstone in the lower part of the Entrada Sandstone can be traced eastward into the upper part of the Dewey Bridge Member (Wright and others, 1962, p. 2059).

The siltstone unit referred to as the beds of Goblin Valley has been discussed previously. McKnight (1940, p. 92) described these beds east of the Green River as ". . . a brownish-red muddy sandstone that weathers into rounded "rock baby" surfaces. The bedding is poor but appears to be largely horizontal. . . . This facies of the Entrada resembles the typical Entrada of the San Rafael Swell and is unlike anything developed to the east." In the Green River Desert, Baker (1946, p. 76) recognized the beds at Goblin Valley in the Entrada Sandstone as a ". . . zone of earthy sandstone 60 to 100 feet thick at the top of the formation . . . across the area. . . ." At places in the Henry Mountains, Hunt (1953, p. 71) reported that ". . . the upper beds of the Entrada have eroded very irregularly and give rise to clusters of small grotesquely shaped buttes." In Goblin Valley, a locality southeast of San Rafael Swell, the beds at Goblin Valley are eroded into a particularly bewildering maze of spheroidal forms termed "hoodoos," "stone-babies," or "goblins." A part of the valley has been set aside as Goblin Valley State Park because of these interesting and peculiar erosional features.

Entrada Sandstone east of the Green River

East of the Green River, three formal subdivisions are recognized in the Entrada Sandstone. The Dewey Bridge Member at the base overlain by the Slick Rock Member are present throughout the area. The Moab Tongue at the top of the Entrada is found only over a more limited area (fig. 1).

Dewey Bridge Member

The Dewey Bridge Member over much of east-central Utah is the basal subdivision of the San Rafael Group. The member is a rather uniform dark-reddish-brown, very fine grained silty sandstone with a scattering of coarse grains particularly near the base. Throughout most of the area the basal part of the Dewey Bridge is a reworked zone, of variable thickness, which consists of nondescript, light-colored sandstone and intermixed chert pebbles associated with the J-2 unconformity. The member, particularly the upper part, tends to weather to rounded spheroidal forms known as hoodoos, stone babies or goblins. Here and there, the strata of the Dewey Bridge Member are deformed into convoluted folds of various dimensions. The Dewey Bridge is in part equivalent to, but is lithologically unlike the Carmel Formation. The member lacks the marine limestones, gypsum beds, green siltstone and shale units and gray sandstone beds typical of the Carmel Formation. The Dewey Bridge closely resembles the silty beds of the earthy facies of the Entrada in the San Rafael Swell and similarly is probably of nearshore marine origin.

Slick Rock Member

The Slick Rock Member is present throughout most of east-central Utah. The member is recognized to a point about 16 km west of Green River where much of it grades into earthy sandstone or siltstone (Wright and others, 1962, p. 2062). To the west over most of the Green River Desert and the San Rafael Swell, the Slick Rock is not differentiated and consequently the Entrada Sandstone is not subdivided into separate members. The Slick Rock Member consists of gray, reddish-tan and reddish-brown sandstone arranged in a series of crossbedded and massive or flatbedded units or beds separated by horizontal bedding planes. In the 4 sections at Salt Valley (sec. 4), Courthouse Rock (sec. 5), Dewey Bridge (sec. 6) and Westwater Canyon (sec. 7), where the entire Slick Rock was measured, the member consists of a total of 141 individual beds or units: of this total 78 are flatbedded units as much as 15.2 m thick averaging 2.02 m, and 63 are crossbedded units as much as 19.2 m thick averaging 2.64 m. The crossbedded units are of eolian origin and the flatbedded units represent interdune deposits.

Moab Tongue

The Moab Tongue is the youngest part of the Entrada Sandstone. At Courthouse Rock (sec. 5) and east of Salt Valley (sec. 4), the Moab Tongue rests directly on the Slick Rock Member, but the two units can be distinguished from each other by bedding characteristics. Near courthouse Rock (sec. 5) the Moab Tongue forms a single unit consisting solely of crossbedded eolian sandstone about 27 m thick that is unbroken by any flatbedded sandstone units. In contrast, the underlying Slick Rock Member consists of numerous flat and crossbedded units all of much lesser thickness. As thus defined, the Moab can be traced almost to Auger Spring, a locality about 30 km east of Salt Valley (sec. 4). At Auger Spring a flatbedded unit lies within the sequence of beds that are laterally equivalent to the Moab Tongue. From Auger Spring eastward to Westwater Canyon, the strata between the Dewey Bridge Member and the J-5 unconformity are all assigned to the Slick Rock Member. It is obvious, however, that stratigraphic representatives of the Moab Tongue are in the upper part of the Slick Rock Member east of Auger Spring. The vertical jagged line on the stratigraphic diagram (fig. 1) that separates Moab Tongue from the Slick Rock Member indicates a lateral gradation and reflects the close affinity of the two units. The Moab Tongue as used herein joins the main body of the Entrada near Auger Spring; using different criteria Dane (1935, p. 94) and Wright and others (1962, p. 2067) traced the Moab from Auger Spring to Westwater Canyon.

West of Bartlett Wash the bedding characteristics of the Moab are different. In the Tenmile Butte area (sec. 3), the Moab contains flatbedded sandstone units, but the tongue can be easily distinguished because it is separated from the Slick Rock Member by an underlying westward-thickening wedge of red beds. The flatbedded units in the Moab Tongue above the red beds reflect a lateral westward gradation into red beds. A short distance west of Tenmile Canyon the Moab Tongue cannot be differentiated. The intermixed flatbeds and crossbeds in the Moab west of Bartlett Wash record a progressive change from the thick eolian sandstone in the east to the marginal marine red beds in the west.

Curtis Formation

The Curtis Formation overlies the Entrada Sandstone. The formation consists principally of gray to greenish-gray fine- to very fine grained sandstone and interbedded green siltstone. Sandstone is generally glauconitic and is in beds less than 2 m thick which commonly are ripple marked or crossbedded. Conglomeratic sandstone beds are present sparsely thoughout the Curtis but generally are concentrated near or at the base of the formation and locally fill depressions cut into the top of the Entrada along the J-3 unconformity. Gypsum and sandy limestone in thin beds constitute a minor lithology. At Dellenbaugh Butte, 21 dark-reddish-brown to purple shales are interspersed through the Curtis Formation in beds all less than 100 mm thick. Similar clay beds occur elsewhere. Viewed from a distance, the Curtis shows two different weathering aspects; a lower ledge-forming part and an upper slope-forming part. Fossils in the Curtis formation indicate that it is of marine origin.

The Curtis Formation changes color where its outcrop crosses White Wash. E. T. McKnight mapped the Curtis eastward from the Green River and in his report states (McKnight, 1940, p. 98): "In the San Rafael Swell, the Curtis is a well-defined unit, differing from the Summerville not only in its light-greenish-gray to whitish color but also in its constitution, being more nearly a true sandstone as compared with the muddy sandstones and shales of the Summerville. In the area covered by this report, however, the distinction between the two is rather artificial and would never have been made had this area alone been considered. The Curtis here has about the same physical constitution as the Summerville, from which it differs in showing a general greenish-gray rather than reddish tone. All the Curtis sections east of the Green River show some red coloration, which gradually increases in amount to the east until the red color predominates, whereupon the Curtis loses its identity and becomes lower Summerville." McKnight (1940, pl. 1), for convenience, arbitrarily did not extend the Curtis Formation east of the NW¼ sec. 15, T. 23 S., R. 17 E., a locality on the west side of White Wash.

Lower Summerville of McKnight (1940)

Although the Curtis Formation is no longer recognized by McKnight east of White Wash, laterally equivalent strata are referred to as the lower Summerville of McKnight (1940). The lower Summerville of McKnight (1940), which is what the Curtis becomes, can be traced for some distance to the east of White Wash and consists of lower and upper beds separated by the bed at Black Steer Knoll. The lower Summerville of McKnight (1940) is undoubtedly a marginal marine deposit because of its position between the marine Curtis Formation to the west and the eolian Entrada Sandstone to the east.

Bed at Black Steer Knoll

The bed at Black Steer Knoll is a useful marker that is recognized over wide areas of east-central and southeastern Utah. The bed varies laterally somewhat in thickness, topographic expression, bedding structures, and lithology. Between White Wash and the Green River, it thins and passes westward into the Curtis Formation. From White Wash to Duma Point the bed at Black Steer Knoll generally weathers to a prominent double ledge of flatbedded sandstone and minor siltstone 1.2 m to 2.0 m thick, which can be visually traced for long distances. Farther east in the Tenmile Canyon area, the bed at Black Steer Knoll is as much as 3.8 m thick and is in part crossbedded. In the Bartlett Wash area, the bed at Black Steer Knoll is thinner than it is in the Tenmile Canyon area and is commonly well indurated with yellowish-gray limonitic cement.

Upper and lower beds

The units referred to as the upper and lower beds of the lower Summerville of McKnight (1940) consist largely of reddish-brown siltstone to sandy siltstone. The beds generally crop out in steep covered slopes in which bedding structures are absent or obscured. Thin dark reddish-brown to purple clay beds are a lithologic feature of the lower Summerville of McKnight (1940) and are particularly abundant in the lower beds. These thin clay beds are the same as those in the Curtis Formation at Dellenbaugh Butte. At places east of White Wash, the upper beds contain one or more conspicuous white sandstone beds, which lithologically resemble sandstone beds in the Curtis Formation. These white sandstones in the upper beds of the lower Summerville of McKnight (1940) east of White Wash reflect an intermixing of lithology typical of the Curtis Formation to the west with equivalent red bed lithology to the east.

Summerville Formation

The Summerville Formation, overlies the Curtis Formation and is considered a marginal marine unit. The Summerville consists of red siltstone and lesser amounts of sandstone and shale, all in very thin beds. Gypsum is present in the upper part of the Summerville as thin beds, nodules, and seams, that cut across bedding. A noteworthy feature of the Summeville described by many geologists is the thin even bedding. Near the type locality in the northern part of the San Rafael Swell, Gilluly (1929, p. 109 stated that ". . . the bedding is very even and continuous. . . ." In the Green River Desert, A. A. Baker noted that the Summerville is ". . . in very thin regular beds" and also noted the ". . . thin regular bedding of the Summerville . . ." (Baker, 1946, p. 84 and 86, respectively).

The selection of the base of the Summerville Formation is arbitrary. At Dellenbaugh Butte, the contact, for convenience, is placed at the rather abrupt color change from the gray Curtis Formation to the red Summerville Formation. Eastward from White Wash, the contact is placed beneath a unit recognized as the red ledge (fig. 2D), a prominent rough ledge that can be traced from White Wash to Bartlett Wash. The red ledge and overlying strata assigned to the Summerville Formation form an eastward thinning wedge of red beds.

In the region between the Green and Colorado Rivers, all the red beds of the upper part of the San Rafael Group terminate in the Dubinky well-Salt Valley area. The Summerville Formation and the upper beds of the lower Summerville of McKnight (1940) as well as the bed at Black Steer Knoll are truncated beneath the J-5 unconformity at the base of the Morrison Formation. The lower beds of the lower Summerville of McKnight (1940) pass laterally eastward into the Entrada Sandstone near Salt Valley (sec. 4).

Morrison Formation

The Morrison Formation unconformably overlies the San Rafael Group throughout east-central Utah and is mostly of terrestrial origin. The Morrison is about 156 m thick near Duma Point and 188 m thick near Dewey Bridge (Craig and others, 1959, no. 64, and 52 secs. respectively); only the basal part of the Salt Wash which is the lower member of the Morrison is discussed herein. The Salt Wash member consists of a sequence of light-colored sandstone ledges interbedded with slope-forming shale and siltstone. A unit termed the lower beds forms a red siltstone slope in the basal part of the Salt Wash Member. The lower beds lie between the lowest prominent, very light gray, ledge-forming channel sandstone, and the top of the San Rafael Group. Thin dense gray limestone beds typical of the Morrison Formation in other parts of Utah are common in the lower beds. Gray ledge-forming sandstones, in which bedding is absent or not apparent, crop out at many localities. The lower beds also contain rounded limestone nodules and chert in thin beds or nodules. Gypsum is also present in some abundance from the San Rafael Swell to the White Wash area. The lower beds from Salt Valley eastward to Westwater Canyon include a light-gray to reddish-tan ledge-forming sandstone termed bed B (fig. 2E and F). Bed B is 0.1 to 3.5 m thick and lies 3.6 to 20 m above the base of the lower beds. Coarse grains and ripple marks are conspicuous features of bed B. East of the Dubinky well area, the lower beds wholly or in part have previously been correlated with the Summerville Formation (Gilluly and Reeside, 1928, pl. 15; Dane, 1935, p. 102–106; McKnight, 1940, p. 99–102; Stokes, 1952, p. 10–11).

Bed A

A thin widespread sandstone arbitrarily termed bed A everywhere immediately overlies the J-5 unconformity and marks the base of the lower beds. Bed A is light gray to yellowish gray locally banded reddish-brown; less commonly bed A is reddish tan. The bed throughout east-central Utah is generally less than 0.5 m thick but locally it is as much as 2.5 m. thick. Here and there the bed is ripple marked and commonly forms a resistant ledge (fig. 2E) that overhangs underlying rocks. Coarse to very coarse grains of chert and quartz, ranging from 1.5 mm to 5 mm across, are a characteristic feature of bed A. Coarse grains are plentiful in bed A from the San Rafael Swell to Salt Valley, less plentiful from Salt Valley to Dewey Bridge and very sparse or absent east of Dewey Bridge. The largest clast noted is an isolated quartz pebble measuring 11.6 mm across at a locality 6.7 km northeast of Courthouse Rock in the NW¼NW¼SE¼ sec. 12, T. 24 S., R. 20 E. Green clay galls are found in bed A at many places, but are particularly abundant at a locality 7.2 km east of Courthouse Rock near the center of sec. 19, T. 24 S., R. 21 E., where the road to Willow Spring crosses the outcrop of bed A.

Tracks of dinosaurs are found in bed A at a locality about 0.5 km northwest of Courthouse Rock in the SW¼NE¼NE¼ sec. 20, T.24 S., R. 20 E. The footprints heretofore were assumed to be in the Moab Tongue (McKnight, 1940, p. 94). The stratigraphic description of the track locality, however, clearly indicates that the footprints are in bed A. The footprints are described by McKnight (1940, p. 94) as ". . . in the very top of the Moab . . . preserved on a bedding plane that was either horizontal or else foreset at a very low angle." McKnight (1940, p. 97) further states that ". . . the track-bearing sand was deposited . . . beneath a red-bed series. . . ." The "red-bed series" referred to are the red siltstones of the lower beds of this report which immediately overlie bed A. Ripple marks present elsewhere in bed A indicate deposition in water. McKnight (1940, p. 97) in this regard states that "The tracks . . . prove that the sand in which they are imprinted was deposited by water. They could not have been preserved in dry wind-blown sand unless its surface had recently been wetted by rain, and such a surface would present a different appearance from the smooth, even bedding plane that is shown." The description just cited obviously applies only to bed A and not to the crossbedded eolian sandstone that makes up the entire Moab Tongue at the track locality. The footprints are on a slab of sandstone and McKnight (1940, p. 94) reports that "the trails of two or three animals are shown, the most perfectly preserved one of which records a bipedal creature with three functional toes, a 2 and one-half-inch foot, and an 8-inch stride. . . . Charles W. Gillmore, of the United States National Museum . . . reports that the animal making the tracks was probably an ornithopod dinosaur. . . ."

The environment of deposition of Bed A is not completely understood. Ripple marks in bed A together with other bedding features obviously indicate currents in a body of water. The dinosaur foot prints were made under subaerial conditions after, probably soon after, the deposition of bed A. McKnight (1940, p. 97) discussed the implications of the conditions necessary to form and preserve the tracks and thought the necessary environment ". . . would certainly prevail in fluviatile or delta deposits." Green clay galls in bed A suggest nearby source areas because the clay galls could not have survived a long transport cycle. The clay pebbles might have been derived from dried up mud in nearby terrestrial playa lakes. Clay galls also result from a process of fluviatile or tidal channel migration against clay banks. Although the conditions of deposition are uncertain, some geologists (L. C. Craig, oral commun., 1980) would exclude bed A and locally some overlying parts of the lower beds from the Morrison Formation because the strata seem more closely related to the San Rafael Group.

Base of the Morrison Formation

The lower boundary of the Morrison, as used herein, is at the J-5 unconformity. This is a minor downward change in the basal contact of the Morrison as used by many previous workers. According to L. C. Craig (written commun., 1980), some geologists place the base of the Morrison at the lowest indication of terrestrial deposition, a contact that lies at the base of the lowest channel sandstone, or lowest limestone, or lowest lenticular bed of sandstone, mudstone, or siltstone. In east-central Utah, this contact generally lies one or more meters above the J-5 unconformity. Locally however, channel sandstones are at or are very close to the J-5 unconformity. At a locality 8.8 km northeast of Dubinky well in the NW¼NE¼ sec. 23, T. 24, S., R. 19 E. a crossbedded fluviatile sandstone at least 1 m thick (the top is eroded) scours into the Moab Tongue. The fluviatile sandstone contains abundant green clay galls and shows as much as 0.6 m of relief in less than 3 m laterally.

At this locality the lowest channel sandstone coincides with the J-5 unconformity. At another locality 4.8 km southeast of Dubinky well in the NE¼SE¼ sec. 32, T. 24 S., R. 19 E., bed A is 1.5 m thick and consists of 2 parts. The lower 0.6 m is flat bedded and contains abundant clay galls; the upper 0.9 m is a crossbedded fluviatile sandstone with abundant green clay galls. Locally the upper crossbedded part of bed A interfingers with the lower flat beds indicating a close affinity of the 2 parts. However, at this locality, the lowest unequivocal terrestrial sandstone is 0.6 m above the J-5 unconformity. About 6.7 km northeast of Courthouse Rock in the SW¼NE¼ sec. 12, T. 24 S., R. 20 E., the stratigraphic sequence above the Moab Tongue consists of bed A 0.6 m thick overlain by 0.6 m of red siltstone in turn overlain by a crossbedded fluviatile sandstone 1 m thick. At this locality, 1.2 m separates the J-5 unconformity from the lowest undoubted terrestrial sandstone.

The initial deposition of the Morrison Formation can be divided into two stages. During the time the lower beds of the Salt Wash Member were laid down, quiet water or sluggish streams must have prevailed as indicated by thin limestones and the fine-grained siltstone that make up much of the lower beds. Here and there a sporadic stream deposited thin fluviatile sandstones some near or on the J-5 unconformity. Later, after deposition of the lower beds, a well established stream system deposited thick, coarse fluviatile sandstones. The onset of the powerful stream system that characterized the later parts of Salt Wash time varied from place to place as shown by the intertonguing of the lower beds with overlying parts of the Salt Wash (fig. 1).

SUMMARY

Recent geologic investigations, briefly described herein, show some new and somewhat different interpretations of the stratigraphy of part of the Jurassic rocks of east-central Utah. The Page Sandstone is found as isolated lenses almost as far east as Moab. Tracing a key bed—the bed at Black Steer Knoll—reinforces the previous correlation of Moab Tongue with the Curtis Formation and additionally shows that the Moab is equivalent mainly to about the lower half of the Curtis. The Summerville Formation, which overlies the Curtis Formation, is completely truncated near Dubinky well and is therefore of much more limited extent than heretofore believed. Strata previously assigned to the Summerville Formation over large areas east and south of Dubinky well lie above the J-5 unconformity and are now recognized as part of the lower beds of the Salt Wash Member of the Morrison Formation. The J-5 unconformity forms a convenient—although not universally accepted—base of the Morrison Formation in east-central Utah.

ACKNOWLEDGMENTS

This report owes much to the helpful advice of George N. Pipiringos, who readily shared and discussed his broad knowledge of Jurassic rocks in the Western Interior of the United States.

REFERENCES

Baker, A. A., 1946, Geology of the Green River Desert–Cataract Canyon region, Emery, Wayne and Garfield Counties, Utah: U.S. Geological Survey Bulletin 951, 12 p.

Baker, A. A., Dane, C. H., and Reeside, J. B., Jr., 1936, Correlation of the Jurassic formations of parts of Utah, Arizona, New Mexico and Colorado: U.S. Geological Survey Professional Paper 183, 66 p.

Craig, L. C., Holmes, C. N., Freeman, V. L., Mullens, T. E., and others, 1959, Measured sections of Morrison and adjacent formations: U.S. Geological Survey Open-File Report.

Dane, C. H., 1935, Geology of the Salt Valley anticline and adjacent areas, Grand County, Utah: U.S. Geological Survey Bulletin 863, 184 p.

Gilluly, James, 1929, Geology and oil and gas prospects of part of the San Rafael Swell, Utah: U.S. Geological Survey Bulletin 806-C, p. 69–130.

Gilluly, James and Reeside, J. B., Jr., 1928, Sedimentary rocks of the San Rafael Swell and some adjacent areas in eastern Utah: U.S. Geological Survey Professional Paper 150-D, p. 61–110.

Hunt, C. B., 1953, Geology and geogrphy of the Henry Mountains region, Utah: U.S. Geological Survey Professional Paper 228, 234 p.

McKnight, E. T., 1940, Geology of area between Green and Colorado Rivers, Grand and San Juan Counties, Utah: U.S. Geological Survey Bulletin 908, 147 p.

O'Sullivan, R. B., 1980, Stratigraphic sections of Middle Jurassic San Rafael Group and related rocks from the Green River to the Moab area in east-central Utah: U.S. Geological Survey Miscellaneous Field Studies Map MF-1247.

O'Sullivan, R. B., 1981, Stratigraphic sections of Middle Jurassic Entrada Sandstone and related rocks from Salt Valley to Dewey Bridge in east-central Utah: U.S. Geological Survey Oil and Gas Investigations Chart OC-113.

Peterson, Fred and Pipiringos, G. N., 1979, Stratigraphic relations of the Navajo Sandstone to Middle Jurassic Formation, southern Utah and northern Arizona: U.S. Geological Survey Professional Paper 1035-B, p. B1–B43.

Pipiringos, G. N. and O'Sullivan, R. B., 1978, Principal unconformities in Triassic and Jurassic rocks, Western Interior United States—a preliminary survey: U.S. Geological Survey Professional Paper 1035-A, p. A1–A29.

Stokes, W. L., 1952, Uranium-vanadium deposits of the Thompsons area, Grand County, Utah—with emphasis on the origin of carnotite ores: Utah Geological and Mineralogical Survey Bulletin 46, 51 p.

Wright, J. C., Dickey, D. D., Snyder, R. P., Craig, L. C., and Cadigan, R. A., 1979, Measured stratigraphic sections of Jurassic San Rafael Group and adjacent rocks in Emery and Sevier Counties, Utah: U.S. Geological Survey Open-File Report 79-1317, 157 p.

Wright, J. C., Shawe, D. R., and Lohman, S. W., 1962, Definition of members of Jurassic Entrada Sandstone in east-central Utah and west-central Colorado: American Association of Petroleum Geologists Bulletin, v. 46, p. 2057–2070.

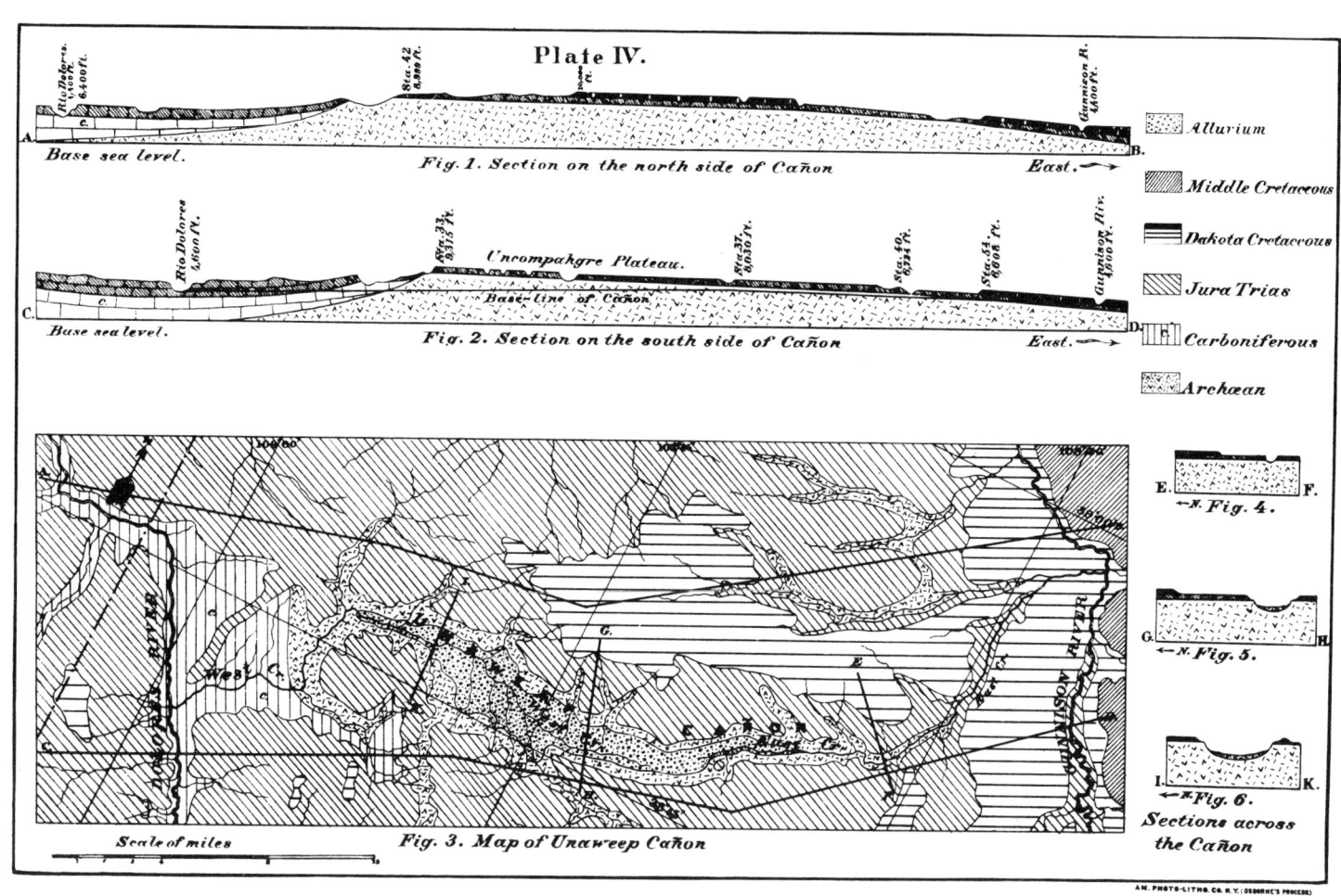

Geologic map and sections of Unaweep Canyon by A. C. Peale, Hayden Survey, 1874–75.

BEDROCK GEOLOGY OF THE RIDGWAY AREA, NORTHWESTERN FLANK, SAN JUAN MOUNTAINS, COLORADO

PAUL WEIMER
Sohio Petroleum Company
San Francisco, California 94111

INTRODUCTION

The Ridgway area is located on the northwestern flank of the San Juan mountain uplift in southwestern Colorado (fig. 1). The Uncompahgre River flows through the area, and the town of Ridgway is near the center. The local stratigraphic section consists of beds from Devonian through Late Jurassic in age in the subsurface. On the surface, the Upper Jurassic Morrison Formation, the Cretaceous Dakota Formation and Upper Cretaceous Mancos Group are exposed. Several wells have been drilled in the area and a small gas field is located in the eastern part. Regional high heat flow and structure resulting from Cenozoic uplift of the San Juan Mountains to the south have induced convective circulation of local ground water, resulting in several small hot springs.

The Ridgway area borders the southwestern margin of the late Paleozoic and early Mesozoic Uncompahgre Highland, which influenced the thickness and facies of late Paleozoic strata (fig. 2). The patterns of late Paleozoic and early Mesozoic tectonics and sedimentation are described here. The Dakota and Mancos Formations, which have not been previously studied in detail in this area, also are described. Finally, the origins of the Ridgway gas field and hot springs are explained.

GENERAL STRATIGRAPHY

Sedimentary rocks of Jurassic through Cretaceous age are exposed in the area. Beds of Devonian through Jurassic age rest unconformably on Precambrian granites and gneisses in the subsurface. A stratigraphic column for the area is shown in Figure 3.

The Elbert and Ouray Formations (Upper Devonian) consist of shales, sandstones, and limestones. The lower Mississippian Leadville Limestone rests unconformably on the Devonian strata. The Molas and Hermosa Formations (Pennsylvanian) and the Cutler Formation (Permian) are predominantly conglomerates, sandstones, shales, and limestones. These formations were deposited on the flank of the Pennsylvanian Uncompahgre uplift. The Upper Triassic Dolores Formation, consisting of red sandstones and shales, rests unconformably on the Cutler Formation. The Dolores Formation is overlain by the Entrada Formation, an Upper Jurassic sandstone.

The Morrison Formation, Late Jurassic in age, is exposed on the surface and consists of alternating layers of shale, siltstone, sandstone, and limestone. The overlying Dakota Formation and Mancos Group (Cretaceous) are described more fully in the section on Cretaceous stratigraphy.

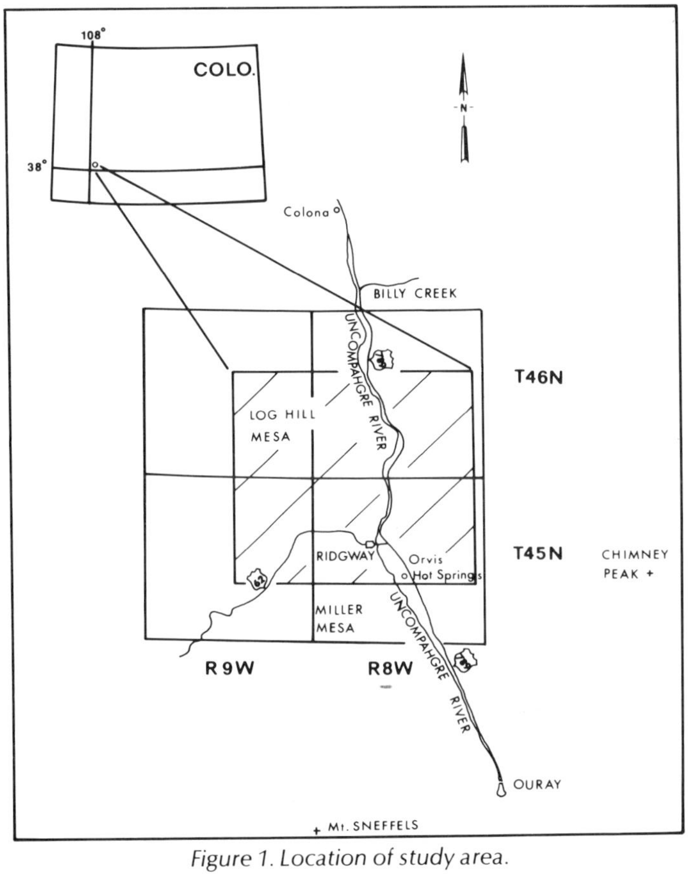

Figure 1. Location of study area.

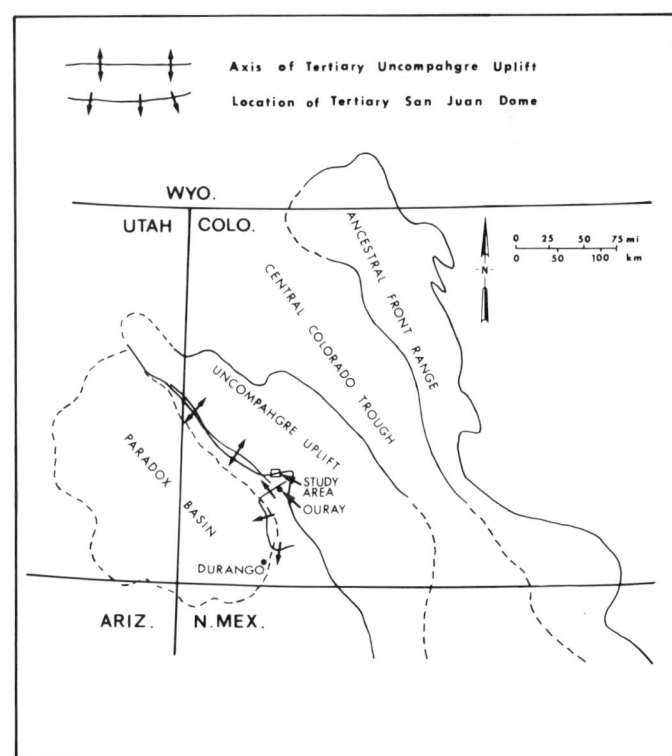

Figure 2. Location of study area relative to Pennsylvanian structural elements, and to the Tertiary Uncompahgre uplift and San Juan dome (after Mallory, 1960; Kelley, 1955).

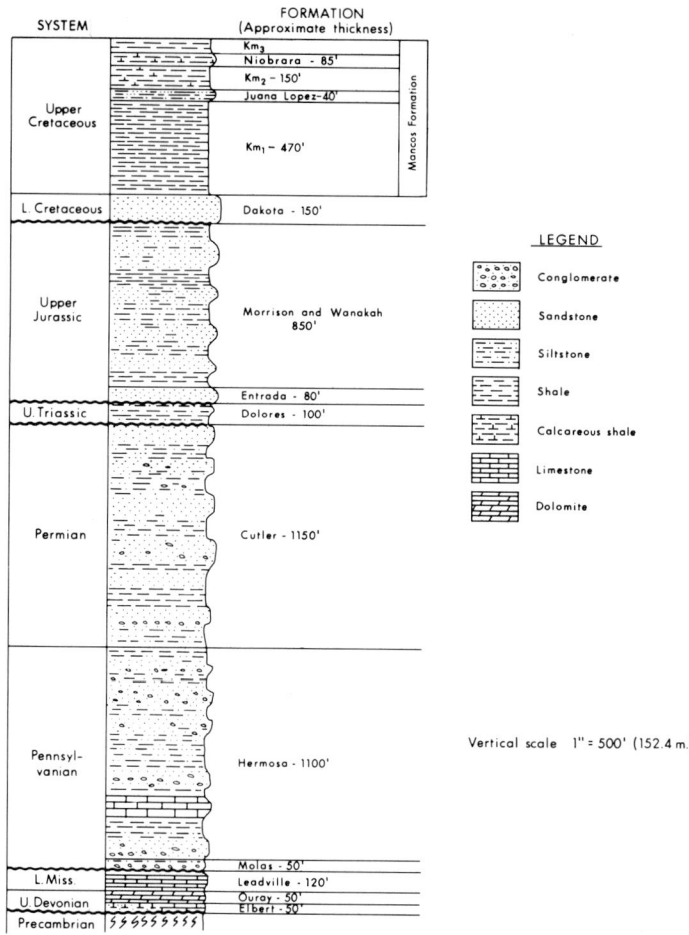

Figure 3. Generalized stratigraphic section of Ridgway area. Thicknesses obtained from Whitlock Swanson 1A well and surface measurements.

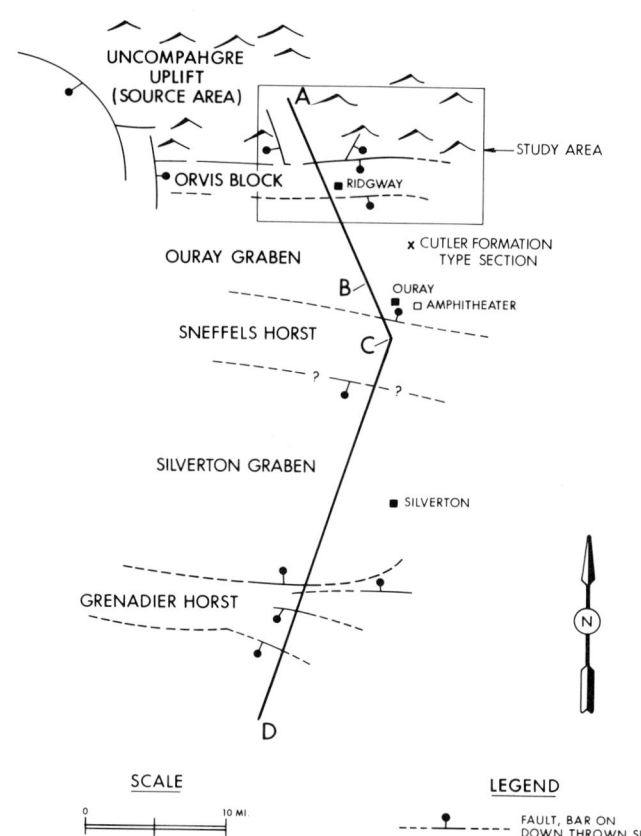

Figure 4. Map showing Paleozoic paleotectonic elements on west and northwest flank of San Juan dome in relation to the study area (after Weimer, 1980). A-B-C-D is line of section shown in Figure 6.

STRUCTURAL GEOLOGY

North-dipping Mesozoic strata on the northwestern flank of the San Juan dome are interrupted by west-striking faults and folds in the Ridgway area. The Laramide structures observed on the surface are related to three basement fault blocks—the Ouray graben, Orvis terrace, and Uncompahgre horst (fig. 4). Recurrent movement on these fault blocks has occurred throughout the Phanerozoic.

The most prominent structural feature in the area is the Ridgway fault, which strikes west across the northern part of the area (fig. 5). The Ridgway fault separates the Uncompahgre fault block from the Orvis fault block. At Loghill Mesa, where the stratigraphic separation on the fault is 350 m, the Morrison and Dakota Formations are exposed on the northern, upthrown side. The dip of the Uncompahgre block is a fairly uniform 3-4° to the north. The Morrison Formation, where in fault contact with the Benton Formation below Loghill Mesa, dips steeply to the south. This zone of high dip in the Morrison is mapped as "fault zone" in Figure 5 and is the result of the strata forming a drape fold over basement faults (see section on structural interpretations below). The fault trace immediately south of Loghill Mesa is covered by colluvium and is considered to lie at the most southerly outcrop of the Morrison Formation. The throw on the Ridgway fault decreases toward the east, and the fault dies out in Sec. 1 of T.45N., R.8W. Figure 9 shows throw on the fault is 46 m at this locality.

Two faults striking north-northwest across Loghill Mesa offset the Dakota Formation in the northwestern part of the area (fig. 5). Between the two faults is a monocline in the Dakota. These faults are believed to be Paleozoic faults reactivated during the Laramide orogeny.

Two northeast-trending fault blocks in the Uncompahgre River Valley north of the Ridgway fault have acted independently from movement on the Ridgway fault. Topographic expression of these faults is best seen in the displacement of the Dakota Formation in Sec. 27, T.46W., R. 8W. The outcrop patterns indicate that the fault blocks acted in a stair-step manner (fig. 5). However, the Dakota outcrop located in the south in Sec. 3, T.45N., R.8W. is in a graben. This indicates the eastern fault block has had a scissor-like movement. The northern extent of these faults is not known due to Quaternary cover.

Two other fault blocks are associated with the northeast-trending blocks. One fault in Sec. 34, T.46N., R.8W. strikes due north and joins a northwest-striking fault. To the south, the fault dies out in Sec. 3, T.45N., R.8W. The fault joins the northeast-striking fault at a place where the relative displacement changes on the northeast-striking fault.

A small, west-trending graben joins the north-striking fault in Sec. 34, T.46N., R.8W. The only surficial evidence of this block is where the Niobrara Formation is faulted against the Benton Shale. The eastern extent of this block is not known and is arbitrarily interpreted because of poor exposure.

An anticline formed north of the Ridgway fault, apparently in association with the uplift of the Uncompahgre fault block. The anti-

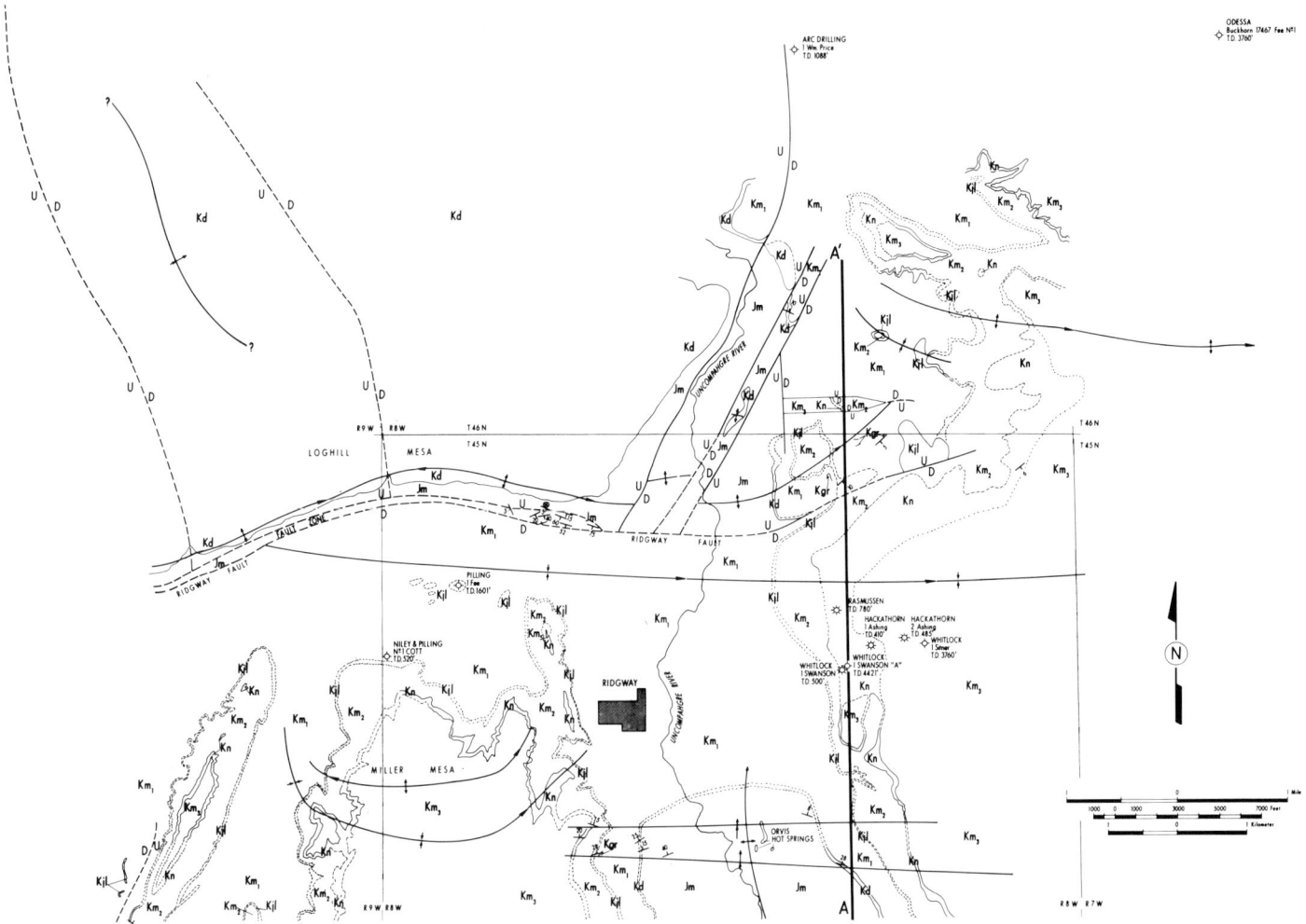

Figure 5. Bedrock map of the Ridgway area. Formation symbols are: Jm=Morrison; Kd=Dakota; Km₁=Mancos 1; Kjl=Juana Lopez; Km₂= Mancos 2; Kn=Niobrara; Km₃=Mancos 3. Sections along A-A' shown in Figures 8 and 9.

clinal axis trends east-west across Loghill Mesa and is apparently displaced by the rotation of the fault blocks along the Uncompahgre River. The trend of the axis in the eastern part of the area is the same as on Loghill Mesa, indicating the eastern and western parts of the Uncompahgre fault block remained horizontally stable with respect to one another during uplift.

In the northeastern part of the area, a small syncline and a larger anticline trend west. These structures are seen in outcrops of the Niobrara and Juana Lopez members of the Mancos Formation.

In the southern part of the study area there is a north-trending anticlinal axis (fig. 5), which is a continuation of a feature mapped by Luedke and Burbank (1962) in the Ouray quadrangle. Of greater importance is the monocline in the same area. At the southern edge of Figure 5, the Morrison through Niobrara Formations have low north dip on both sides of the Uncompahgre River. The beds dip steeply for 1 km northward, then flatten to gentle dip (3-4°). This monocline corresponds with the location of Orvis hot springs and is interpreted to have formed in response to basement faulting at depth (see structural interpretations below). The monocline dies out to the west in Sec. 20, T.45N., R.8W.

On Miller Mesa, the Km₂ and Niobrara members of the Mancos are deformed into an anticline and syncline. Mapping indicates the anticline has structural closure (fig. 5). Both the anticline and syncline have an arcuate trend.

A syncline lies south of the Ridgway Fault and parallel to it. The best surface expression of the syncline is north of the Ridgway gas field where the Niobrara forms a southward dip slope in Sec. 2 of T.45N., R.8W. and is dipping northerly at the southeastern corner of Sec. 10, T.45N., R.8W. (fig. 5).

PALEOTECTONIC AND STRUCTURAL INTERPRETATIONS

In the Ridgway area, most of the deformation apparently is related to basement tectonics, mainly by drape folding of strata (force folding) over basement fault blocks. The study area is important for evaluating Paleozoic tectonics of the San Juan Mountains. Although no Paleozoic strata are exposed in the area, thickness variations are known from subsurface data. Where exposed in the San Juan Mountains, the Paleozoic beds have been described in detail. To assist accurate structural interpretations, Paleozoic outcrop data are reviewed here.

Drape Folding and Basement Faulting

The concept of drape folding of sedimentary beds over basement-controlled fault blocks has been discussed in detail in the past sixteen years (Prucha and others, 1965, Stearns, 1971, 1975, 1978, Mathews, 1978, Mathews and Work, 1978), primarily to explain Laramide and post-Laramide structural features in the Wyoming province (Prucha and others, 1965). In drape folding, the structural basement reacts to stresses by faulting and rigid-body rotation (brittle deformation). The overlying sedimentary layers are then deformed primarily by forced folding (ductile deformation). The final geometry of the fold is controlled by various factors, including the degree of welding of the strata to the basement and the physical nature of the sedimentary sequence.

Stearns (1978) presented three general classes of sedimentary sections that deform differently in response to basement block movement: 1) a non-welded sedimentary section containing a stiff or non-thinning stratigraphic unit; 2) a welded, stiff, non-thinning controlling member; and 3) a section which is welded to the forcing member but is ductile and capable of thinning during the folding process. The Middle Paleozoic section in the Ridgway area is best classified as a welded, stiff, non-thinning stratigraphic section, whereas the younger upper Hermosa and Cutler formations contain enough ductile shales so that they are susceptible to thinning during deformation.

Regional Paleozoic Tectonics

The Paleozoic sedimentary rocks presently exposed in the San Juan Mountains were deposited in the Paradox basin. Mallory (1960) described two major Pennsylvanian highland areas in Colorado, the Uncompahgre highland and Front Range highland, both of which trended generally northwest (fig. 2). Baars (1965, 1966), Baars and See (1968), Spoelhof (1974, 1976), and Weimer (1980) described three major Paleozoic positive elements in the San Juan Mountains region (figs. 4, 6), the Grenadier horst, Sneffels horst, and Uncompahgre horst; and two intervening grabens, the Silverton graben and the Ouray graben. Recurrent relative movement of these fault blocks occurred throughout the Paleozoic, affecting both sediment thicknesses and facies distribution. Strata of Cambrian through Mississippian age are about 100 m thick in the Silverton and Ouray grabens, and thin to 30 m over the Sneffels and Grenadier horsts.

Spoelhof (1974, 1976) described in detail several episodes of Paleozoic movement of fault blocks bounding the Grenadier horst (figs. 4, 6): post-Late Cambrian–pre-Late Devonian, Late Devonian and Early Missippian, Late Mississippian, and throughout the Pennsylvanian.

Recurrent movement along the Sneffels horst also has been documented. The Cutler Formation at its type section (Sec. 12, T.44N., R.8W.) is 610 m thick (fig. 4) (Cross and others, 1905). The Cutler Formation thins to the south, and in one area near the Amphitheater east of Ouray (fig. 4), the Dolores Formation (Upper Triassic) rests on the Hermosa Formation (Luedke and Burbank, 1962). The entire Cutler section has been beveled across the top of the Sneffels horst. Lee and others (1976; see also Supplemental Log 2, this guidebook) described the angular unconformity existing between the dipping beds of the Cutler Formation and the overylying Dolores Formation (fig. 4 in their article). The steep dip of the Cutler Formation is due to drape folding over recurrently moving basement faults bordering the Sneffels horst. The regional thinning southward of the Cutler Formation and the angular relationship between the Cutler and Dolores formations suggest that movement of the Sneffels horst occurred in post-Cutler and pre-Dolores time (Late Permian or Early Triassic). This time period previously was considered to be one of tectonic quiescence.

The Ridgway area lies at the edge of the Uncompahgre highland. Data from wells #1 and #2 (fig. 7; Table 1) indicate that about 9.1 m of Dolores Formation rests on Precambrian basement. Data from well #8 indicate the Elbert Formation overlies the Precambrian. About 760 m of Paleozoic strata present in well #8 are absent in wells #1 and #2. Mallory (1960) projected the edge of the ancient Uncompahgre Uplift along the Ridgway fault. This writer agrees with his interpretation. However, data from well #4 indicate that a minimum of 61 m of Permo-Pennsylvanian strata occur below the Dolores Formation on Loghill Mesa. This change in thickness in strata is probably fault bounded and would correspond with the western-most fault striking northwest across Loghill Mesa. This evidence suggests that the boundary trend of the Uncompahgre highland changes in the Ridgway area (fig. 4) from west to northwest.

A restored Paleozoic cross section was constructed in the Ridgway area (fig. 8). To the north of the Ridgway fault, 10 m of Dolores Formation rests on the basement. The Dolores Formation is 33.5 m thick in wells #5, #6, #8, #11, and #12, suggesting that the ancient Uncompahgre uplift remained a positive element in the Ridgway area until late in the time of deposition of the Dolores Formation. The Orvis fault block is bounded on the north by the Ridgway fault and on the south by the Orvis fault. The Orvis fault is

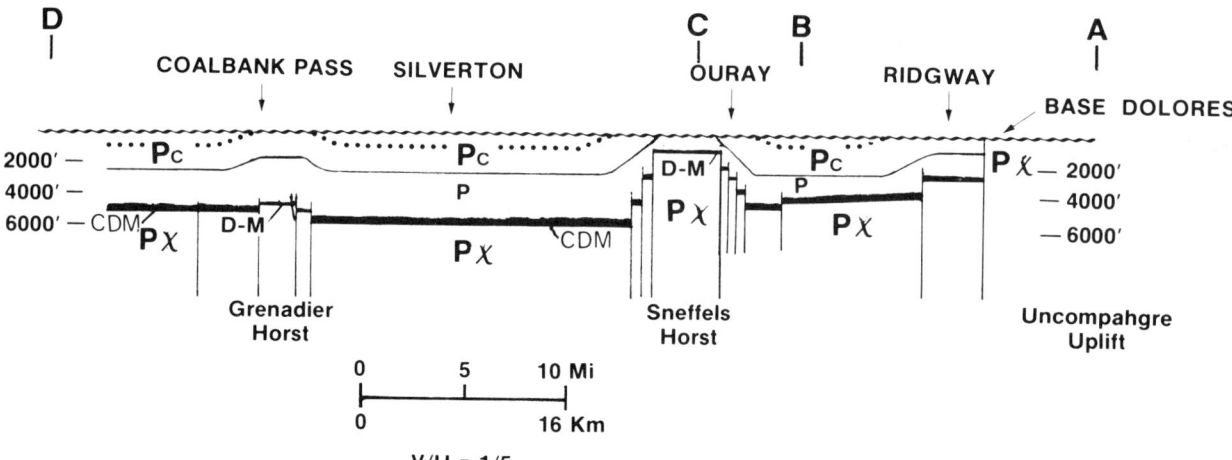

Figure 6. Regional north-south section restored to base of Dolores Formation showing thinning of Paleozoic section and erosion of the Cutler Formation across top of paleotectonic elements. Formation symbols are: Px=Precambrian; CDM=Ignacio, Elbert, Ouray, and Leadville; D-M=Elbert, Ouray and Leadville; P=Molas and Hermosa; Pc=Cutler. Line of dots in Pc is phantom horizon to show truncation at base of Dolores (after Weimer, 1980). See Figure 4 for location of line of section.

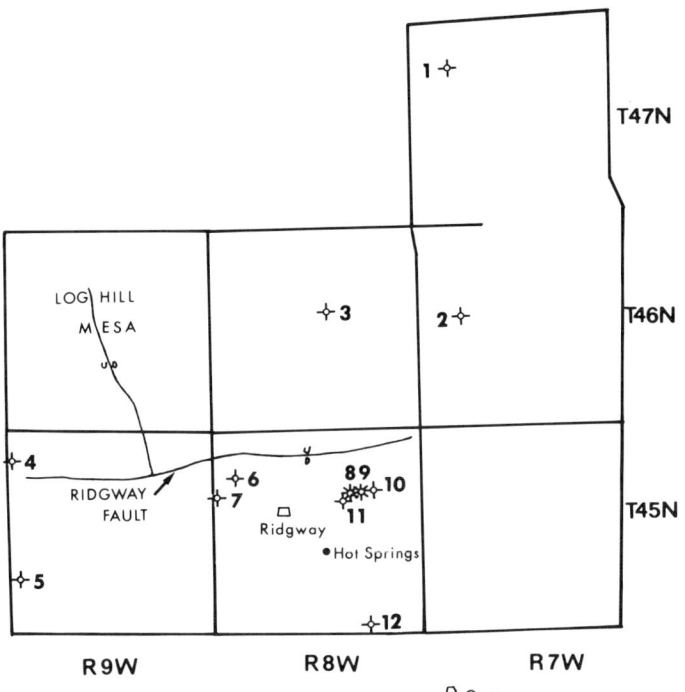

Figure 7. Location map of wells drilled in the Ridgway area. Well information in Table 1.

Table 1. Wells in the Ridgway area.

Well No.	Name	Thickness of Permo-Pennsylvanian (Hermosa and Cutler Fms).	Thickness of pre-Pennsylvanian Strata
1	Odessa Buckhorn 8477 Fee 1 SW NW Sec. 8, T. 47N, R. 7W. T. D. 4895 ft (1492 m) Precambrian	0	0
2	Odessa Federal 1746-7 Fee 1 NE SW Sec. 17, T. 46N., R. 7W. T. D. 3760 ft (1146 m) Precambrian	0	0
3	Arc Drilling 1 William Price C., Sec. 15, T. 46N., R. 8 W. T. D. 1088 ft (332 m) Wanakah	0 (est.)	0
4	Cheyenne Oil Ventures Hall Bros. 1 SW SW Sec. 6, T. 45N., R. 9W. T. D. 2506 ft (763 m) Penn.-Perm. (probably Cutler)	200 ft	?
5	Davis McClure 1 SE NW Sec. 30, T. 45N., R. 9W. T. D. 5539 ft (1688 m) Miss. or Dev.	3870 ft (1180)	324 ft (99 m)
6	Pilling Fee 1 C SW NE, Sec. 7, T. 45N., R. 8W. T. D. 1601 ft (488 m) Cutler	2400 ft (est.) (732 m)	220 ft (est.) (67 m)
7	Niley and Pilling 1 Cott SW SW Sec. 7, T. 45N., R. 8W. T. D. 520 ft (158 m) Benton	2400 ft (est.) (732 m)	220 ft (est.) (67 m)
8	Whitlock Swanson 1-A NE NE Sec. 15, T. 45N., R. 8W. T. D. 4421 ft (1348) Dev.	2400 ft (732 m)	220 ft (est.) (67 m)
9	Hackathorn Drilling 1 Ashing Ranch NE SE SW Sec. 11, T. 45N., R. 8W. T. D. 410 ft (148 m) Benton	2400 ft (est.) (732 m)	220 ft (est.) (67 m)
10	Hackathorn Drilling 2 Ashing Ranch NE SE SW Sec. 11, T. 45N., R. 8W. T. D. 485 ft (148 m) Benton	2400 ft (est.) (732 m)	220 ft (67 m)
11	Whitlock 1 Sittner C SW SE, Sec. 11, T. 45N., R. 8W T. D. 3760 ft (1146 m)	2400 ft (est.) (732 m)	220 ft (67 m)
12	Intex Halls 1 SE SW Sec. 35, T. 45N., R. 8W. T. D. 2413 ft (736 m) Tertiary Intrusive in Hermosa (Penn.)	3500 ft. (est.) (1016 m) (surface exposure plus well data)	---

not visible at the surface; however, field observations and well data suggest its existence. The Paleozoic strata in the Ouray graben are about 365 m thicker than in the Orvis block. Most of this thickness increase is within the Cutler Formation. By analogy, increases in stratigraphic thickness in the Upper Paleozoic sediments in the San Juan Mountains are fault bounded.

On the surface, a zone of steep dip occurs in the Dakota and Morrison Formations in the southern part of the study area (figs. 5, 9). This writer has interpreted this feature as drape folding of strata over a Laramide basement fault.

The thickness of strata in the Ouray graben is taken from surface measurements (Luedke and Burbank, 1962) and from subsurface

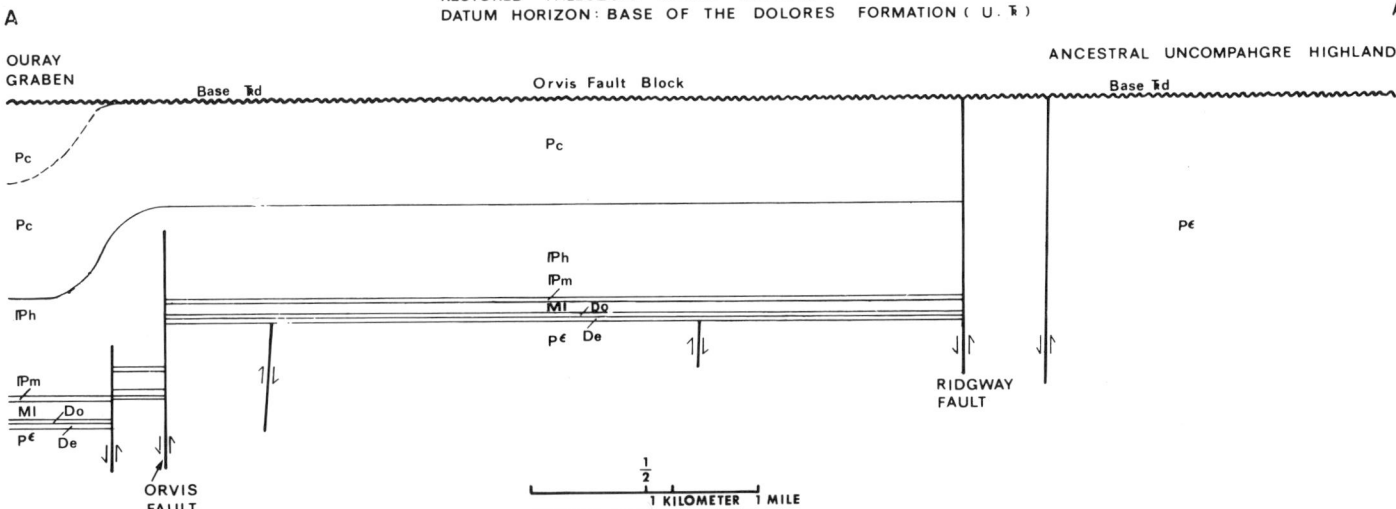

Figure 8. Local north-south section (A-A', fig. 5) restored to base of Dolores Formation ($\mathbb{T}$ d) showing thinning of Cutler Formation across the Orvis fault. Formation symbols are: P€=Precambrian; De=Elbert; Do=Ouray; Ml=Leadville; ℙm=Molas; ℙh=Hermosa; Pc=Cutler. Dashed line in Pc is phantom horizon to show truncation at base of Dolores.

data (wells #5 and #12). The thicknesses of strata on the Orvis block is from well #8. The thicknesses of the Elbert, Ouray, Leadville, Molas, and Hermosa all increase slightly in the Ouray graben. This evidence suggests the fault blocks were active at the time of deposition of Middle Paleozoic sediments. The Cutler Formation is 320 m thicker in the Ouray graben than in the Ridgway block. This disparity is due to at least two factors. Significant movement on the faults north and south of the Orvis block may have occurred during Cutler deposition and controlled the thickness variations. In addition, significant movement of the Orvis block may have occurred in post-Cutler, pre-Dolores time (similar to that of the Sneffels horst), causing beveling of the Cutler Formation on the Orvis block. Both of these factors probably affected Cutler thickness, although recurrent movement of the Orvis block after Cutler deposition probably caused most of the thickness variation.

The major faults in the restored Paleozoic cross section have all been drawn as vertical. Several authors (Barker, 1969; Spoelhof, 1974, 1976; Weimer, 1980) have demonstrated that most major Precambrian fault zones in this region are vertical. Where the faults are exposed south of the study area (near Ouray and the Grenadier horst), the fault planes are vertical (Spoelhof, 1974, 1976). Non-vertical faults in the cross section are minor, and their existence is inferred from present topography.

The total displacement on the Orvis fault during the Paleozoic is 245 m. Strata of Devonian through Early Pennsylvanian age probably acted as a welded, non-thinning section. Under vertical stresses, these strata deformed in a brittle manner and faulted with the basement. The upper Hermosa and Cutler Formations deformed as a welded, thinning section and responded to block movement by drape folding. A similar response is seen in the "paleodrape" of Hermosa and Cutler Formations in the Ouray Valley (Lee and others, 1976, Fig. 4). The total fault block displacement is great enough that an intermediate fault block is interpreted to exist 400 m south of the Orvis fault. Analogous intermediate fault blocks exist on the north side of the Sneffels horst and Grenadier horst (fig. 6) (Spoelhof, 1974, 1976; Weimer, 1980).

Structural Interpretation

The zone of steeply dipping Dakota and Morrison beds in the southern part of the area (fig. 9) apparently formed in response to Laramide movement on basement faults. This monoclinal feature is interpreted as a drape folding of strata over the upward moving Ouray graben fault block. The movement on the bounding faults is opposite to the direction of the Late Paleozoic movement. Similar reversals in movement on fault blocks in the San Juan region have been noted by Spoelhof (1974, 1976) and Weimer (1980). Thus, in Figure 9, two generations of drape folding are predicted—Permo–Triassic and Laramide. The relative directions of the two forced folds would be in opposite directions, reflecting the reversal in movements on the fault blocks.

Two other faults are inferred to exist on the Orvis fault block. One fault is placed where the steeply monoclinal dipping strata change to gentle dip. Associated with this fault, a rotated block is inferred just north of the Orvis fault. This tilted fault block is then responsible for the dip of the surficial strata. The basement is interpreted to be rotated largely in keeping with Stearns' models (1978). The change in dip on the monocline does not fit well into any one of Stearns' three general classes of sedimentary section. The entire sedimentary section probably reacted partly as in his welded-thinning and partly as in his welded-non-thinning model. When a welded non-thinning section (such as the mid-Paleozoic strata) is folded over basement blocks, minor draping in fact occurs over the subsidiary fault blocks. The overlying strata would react as a welded, ductile section. Hence, the change in dip of the strata would be compensated for by the ductile response of the strata. However, if the fault block beneath the monocline was not rotated, drape folds would occur at the edges of the block. The fault block is interpreted as tilted with minor offset of the lower sedimentary section occurring along the fault.

The strata have a uniform northerly dip across the Orvis fault block until reaching the syncline 1.6 km south of the Ridgway fault (figs. 5, 9). The basement is also believed to follow this regional dip. The syncline could be caused by Laramide movement on the Ridgway fault.

A problem arises, however, in explaining the gross thickening of the sedimentary section near the Ridgway fault (fig. 9). Enough ductile material exists in the middle to upper part of the sedimentary section to accommodate in part this spatial problem. A fault proposed at the basement level is believed to be partially responsible for the syncline, and a rotation of the basement would compensate for the spatial problem. On the Uncompahgre block the regional attitude is displayed by the uniformly northerly dipping Dakota beds. In Sec. 3 of T.45N., R.8W., the Dakota and Juana Lopez Formations dip steeply to the south just north of the Ridg-

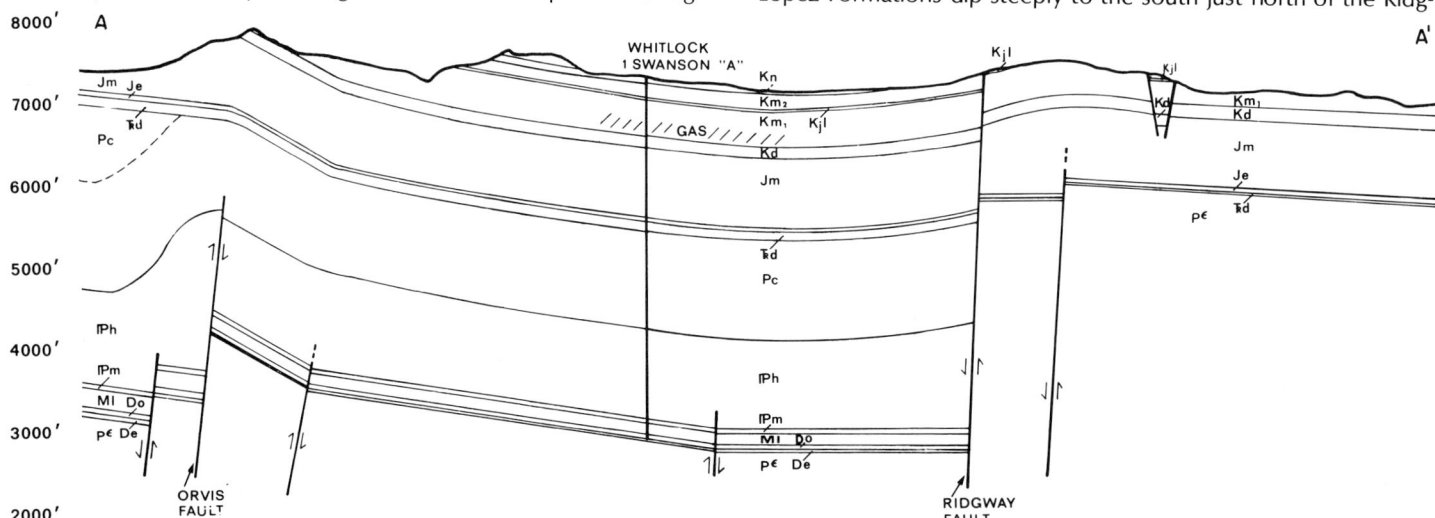

Figure 9. Local north-south section (A-A', fig. 5) showing northerly dipping monocline, Orvis fault, Ridgway gas field, and Ridgway fault. Symbols same as Figures 5 and 8.

way fault. The abrupt change in dip of these strata is interpreted as a drape fold over a basement fault. Hence, a fault has been inferred, north of the Ridgway fault, along the line of dip inflection. Displacement across this flexure is about 107 m. The shales in the Morrison Formation probably acted in a ductile manner and flowed into the area above the downthrown block.

The northernmost structural feature in Figure 9 is a small fault block within the Uncompahgre block. The surficial expression of this small block is in the Niobrara and Benton Formations. This fault block trends west and is attached to the north-trending fault (fig. 5).

The small fault block is interpreted to have formed by extensional faulting in relation to the drape fold 1.6 km to the south. The bounding faults probably die out in Morrison shales. Clement (1977) states that the apparent lengthening of a sedimentary section over a basement fault can be compensated for by normal extensional faulting close to or within the drape region. This normal fault would require a detachment of the sedimentary cover over the basement.

CRETACEOUS STRATIGRAPHY

The Dakota Formation crops out throughout the Ridgway area as a resistent ledge-forming unit. It varies in thickness from 38 to 54 m. Figure 10 is a reference section. The Dakota can be divided into four units based on lithology and depositional environment. The basal unit (unit 1) consists of sandstones and conglomeratic sandstones, poorly to moderately sorted, trough cross-stratified, commonly graded and fining upward. The overlying unit (unit 2) consists of interbedded sandstones, siltstones, shales and coals. The sandstones are medium grained. All lithologies contain abundant coalified plant fragments. The siltstones are flaser bedded and commonly bioturbated. The next overlying unit (unit 3) consists of interbedded sandstones and shales. The sandstones are fine to medium grained, trough cross-stratified, and extensively burrowed. Both lithologies contain carbonaceous material. The uppermost unit (unit 4) consists of interbedded sandstones and shales. The sandstones are cross-stratified to ripple bedded and contain carbonaceous imprints.

The Dakota Formation was deposited in the meander-channel and delta-plain parts of a fluvial system in the latter part of the Early Cretaceous. Unit 1 probably was deposited in a point-bar setting in a meander-channel. Units 2 and 3 were deposited in a delta-plain setting. The deposits resemble those of distributary channels, marshes, splays, lakes, fresh water bays, tidal channels and flats (LeBlanc, 1972). Unit 4 was deposited in a shoreline setting.

Armstrong (1968) identified the source of the clastic material for the Dakota Formation as the Sevier orogenic belt in central Utah. From this area rivers flowed eastward to the Mowry Sea in Colorado and Wyoming. The vertical changes in depositional setting reflect an overall basin deepening or transgression of the Mowry Sea.

Detailed mapping and stratigraphic studies indicate that, based upon two units of distinctive lithology, the Mancos Formation can be subdivided into five units. From oldest to youngest, they are the Km_1, Juana Lopez member, Km_2, Niobrara, and Km_3 (figs. 3, 5). The Juana Lopez and Niobrara members have similar lithologic and paleontologic content to their equivalents in the San Juan and Denver basins, respectively.

The Km_1 (time equivalent to the Benton Formation) consists of 143 m of black shale that includes the Greenhorn Limestone beds (3.8 m thick) 91.4 m above the base. The guide fossil *Pycnodonte newberryi* and several species of foraminifera were collected from

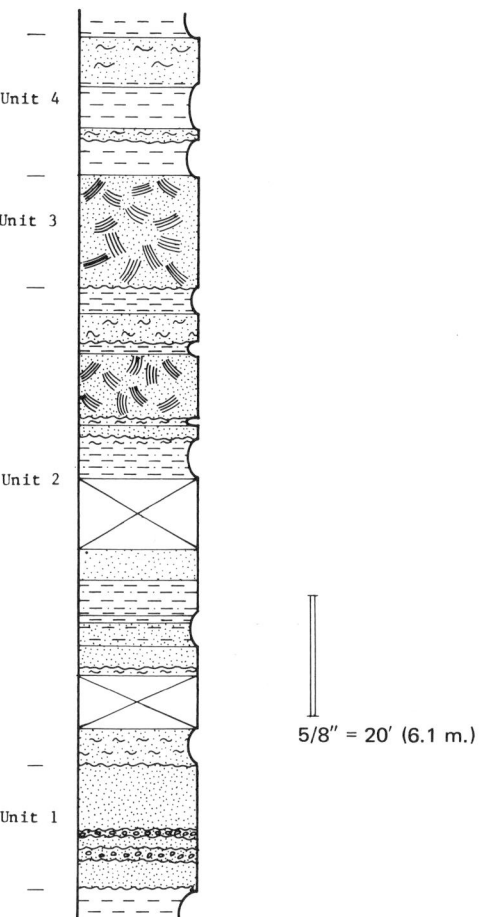

Figure 10. Reference section for the Dakota Formation in the Ridgway area. Symbols as in Figure 3.

the Greenhorn. The Km_1 is Cenomanian through middle Turonian in age. The overlying Juana Lopez is 12.2 m thick and consists of alternating layers of calcareous siltstone and black shale. The ammonites *Scaphites warreni, Prioncyclus Wyomingenesis,* and *P. macombi,* and the bivalve *Lopha lugubris* were found in the Juana Lopez. It is late Turonian in age and equivalent to the middle and lower part of the upper parts of the Juana Lopez in the San Juan Basin. The succeeding Km_2 is a 47-m thick, calcareous shale unit containing small, ellipsoidal (1 mm) white specks which increase in abundance upward. Km_2 is late Turonian through early Santonian in age and equivalent to the upper Carlile, Fort Hays Limestone, and Lower Smoky Hill Member of the Niobrara of the Great Plains. The Niobrara Formation is 25.9 m thick, consisting of gray, calcareous shales interbedded with white-speckled, gray, calcareous shale. Hattin (1975) described the occurrence of the white specks in carbonate deposits of the Upper Cretaceous in the western interior and found them to be coccoliths and coccolith debris. The bivalve *Inoceramus platinus* encrusted by the oyster *Pseudoperma congesta* is found throughout the Niobrara. The Niobrara is middle to late Santonian in age. Km_3 is a calcareous shale which weathers yellow. The main body of the Mancos Shale (Km_3) is above the Niobrara, although only 60 m is present in the Ridgway area. No section was measured of this unit.

RIDGWAY GAS FIELD

The Ridgway gas field is located 1.6 km east of the town of Ridgway (fig. 7). Production is limited to two wells, the #1 and #2 Ashing Ranch, which were originally completed for 2800 and 5600 m³ per day of gas, respectively. The producing interval is from fractures in the Km₁ member of the Mancos. Several other wells drilled in the area were dry (Table 1). Gas shows have been noted in several water wells in the area: Rasmussen (Sec. 10. T.45N, R.8W.), Bauer (NW¼ Sec. 11, T.45N., R.8W.), and Dude Ranch (SW¼ NE Sec. 14, T.45N., R.8W.). Figure 9 indicates the producing reservoir lies between the monocline to the south and the synclinal axis paralleling the Ridgway fault to the north.

Mallory (1977) describes occurrences of oil and gas in fractured shale reservoirs in Colorado and New Mexico, listing six types of structural expression associated with fractured reservoirs: 1) sharply arched anticline; 2) plunging anticlinal nose; 3) fault control in a major anticline; 4) simple homoclinal dip; 5) change of strike on a monoclinal flexure; and 6) abrupt dip change in a monocline. The last feature best describes the structural setting of the Ridgway gas field.

The Florence-Canon City oil field in Fremont County, Colorado, has a structure similar to the Ridgway gas field. At Florence, about 14 million barrels of oil have been produced from fractured lower Pierre Shale. Oil accumulation occurs in a north-trending syncline with a sharp monoclinal flexure on its east flank (Weimer, 1980). The 4.8 km-wide belt of fractured Pierre shale in which oil has accumulated lies on the gently dipping east flank of the syncline bordering the monoclinal trend on the west. The monocline overlies a basement fault and fracturing is responsible for the reservoir permeability and is related to the faulting and monoclinal bending of the rocks.

The immediate area around Ridgway appears unattractive for further petroleum exploration because suitable structural and stratigraphic configurations are absent. There may be better possibilities in the Cretaceous and older formations to the east of the map area, but a cover of Tertiary volcanic rocks renders exploration difficult.

GEOTHERMAL FEATURES

Geothermal occurrences have been known for a long time in the Uncompahgre River Valley. The word Uncompahgre, a Ute word meaning hot (unca)—water (pah)—spring (gre), is named for the hot springs near Ouray (Borneman and Lampert, 1978). In the Ridgway area, the only surficial occurrences of hot springs are on the Orvis Ranch (Sec. 22, T.45N., R.8W.). The temperature of the water is 52°C. Hot water also is encountered in many of the wells drilled in the area. The Pilling 1 Fee (TD=488 m is now a flowing artesian hot water well. The Whitlock 1 Swanson A (TD=1348 m) is used as a water well by Fred Bussey. The Bauer well (NW¼ Sec. 11, T.45N, R. 8W) has 33°C water.

The hydrology of Orvis Hot Springs has never been fully explained. Reiter and others (1975) studied the variation in heat flow across southern Colorado and concluded that the heat flow value is greater than 100 mw/m² in the Ridgway area. Barret and Pearl (1978) studied geothermometer parameters and concluded that the best estimate of the water's subsurface temperature is from 60° to 90°C.

The Orvis hot spring is located close to the monoclinal feature, which suggests fracturing of the rocks in the drape fold probably has created a conduit to permit upward passage of deep ground water.

ACKNOWLEDGMENTS

I wish to thank Drs. Rudy Epis, Robert Weimer, Don Eicher, Bruce Curtis, and William Cobban for their help on this project. Frank Johnson and Deborah Moss drafted several figures, and Susan Warren typed the manuscript. To all of them, I am grateful.

REFERENCES

Armstrong, R. L., 1968, Sevier orogenic belt in Nevada and Utah: Geological Society of America Bulletin, v. 79, p. 429–458.

Baars, D. L., 1965, Pre-Pennsylvanian paleotectonics of southwestern Colorado and east-central Utah (Ph.D. dissertation): Boulder, University of Colorado, 170 p.

———, 1966, Pre-Pennsylvanian paleotectonics—key to basin evaluation and petrolem occurrences in Paradox Basin, Utah and Colorado: American Association of Petroleum Geologists Bulletin, v. 50, p. 2080–2111.

——— and See, P. D., 1968, Pre-Pennsylvanian stratigraphy and paleotectonics of the San Juan Mountains, southwestern Colorado: Geological Society of America Bulletin, v. 79, p. 333–350.

Barker, F., 1969, Precambrian geology of the Needle Mountains, southwestern Colorado: U.S. Geological Survey Professional Paper 633-A.

Barrett, J. K. and Pearl, R. H., 1978, An appraisal of Colorado's geothermal resources: Colorado Geological Survey, Bulletin 39, p. 160–162.

Borneman, W. R. and Lampert, L. J., 1978, A climbing guide to Colorado's Fourteeners: Boulder, Colorado, Pruett Publishing Company, 280 p.

Cross, W., Howe, E., and Ransome, F. L., 1905, Description of the Silverton quadrangle: U.S. Geological Survey Geology Atlas, Folio 120.

DeFord, R. K., 1929, Surface structure, Florence oil field, Fremont County, Colorado, in Structure of typical American oil fields, V. II: Tulsa, Oklahoma, American Association of Petroleum Geologists, p. 75–92.

Hattin, D. E., 1975, Petrology and origin of fecal pellets in Upper Cretaceous strata of Kansas and Saskatchewan: Journal of Sedimentary Petrology, v. 45, p. 686–696.

Kelley, V. C., 1955, Tectonics of Four corners region: Four Corners Geological Society Guidebook, 1st Field Conference, p. 108–117.

Lee, K., Epis, R. C., Baars, D. L., Knepper, D. H., and Summer, R. M., 1976, Road log: Paleozoic tectonics and sedimentation and Tertiary volcanism of the western San Juan Mountains, Colorado, in Epis, R. C., and Weimer, R. J., Studies in Colorado Field Geology: Colorado School of Mines Professional Contributions, no. 8, p. 139–158.

Luedke, R. G. and Burbank, W. S., 1962, Geologic map of the Ouray Quadrangle, Colorado: U.S. Geological Survey, Geological Quadrangle Map GQ-152.

Mallory, W. W., 1960, Outline of Pennsylvanian stratigraphy of Colorado, in Weimer, R. J., and Haun, J. D., eds., Guide to the Geology of Colorado: Denver, Colorado, Rocky Mountain Association of Geologists, p. 22–33.

———, 1977, Oil and gas from fractured shale reservoirs in Colorado and northwest New Mexico: Denver, Colorado, Rocky Mountain Association of Geologists Special Publication 1, 38 p.

Mathews, V. E., III, 1978, ed., Laramide folding associated with basement block faulting in the western United States: Geological Society of America Memoir 151, 370 p.

———, and Work, D. F., 1978, Laramide folding associated with basement block faulting along the northeastern flank of the Front Range, Colorado: Geological Society of America Memoir 151, p. 101–124.

Prucha, J. J., Graham, J. A., and Nickelsen, R. P., 1965, Basement-controlled deformation in Wyoming province of Rocky Mountains foreland: American Association of Petroleum Geologists Bulletin, v. 49, p. 966–992.

Reiter, M., Edwards, C. L., Hartman, H., and Weidman, C., 1975, Terrestial heat flow along the Rio Grande rift, New Mexico and southern Colorado: Geological Society of America Bulletin, v. 86, p. 811–818.

Spoelhof, R. W., 1974, Pennsylvanian stratigraphy and tectonics in the Lime Creek–Molas Lake area, San Juan County, Colorado (Ph.D. dissertation): Golden, Colorado School of Mines, 193 p.

———, 1976, Pennsylvanian stratigraphy and paleotectonic of the western San Juan Mountains, southwestern Colorado, in Epis, R. C., and Weimer, R. J., 1976, Studies in Colorado Field Geology: Colorado School of Mines Professional Contributions, no. 8, p. 159–179.

Stearns, D. W., 1971, Mechanics of drape folding in the Wyoming province: Wyoming Geological Association, 23rd Annual Field Conference Guidebook, p. 125–143.

———, 1975, Laramide basement deformation in the Big Horn Basin—the controlling factor for structures in the layered rocks: Wyoming Geological Association, 27th Annual Field Conference Guidebook, p. 149–158.

———, 1978, Faulting and forced folding in the Rocky Mountains foreland: Geological Society of America Memoir 151, p. 1–37.

Weimer, R. J., 1980, Recurrent movement on basement faults, a tectonic style for Colorado and adjcent areas, in Kent, H. C. and Porter, K. W., ed., Colorado Geology: Denver, Colorado, Rocky Mountain Association of Geologists.

TECTONIC EVOLUTION OF WESTERN COLORADO AND EASTERN UTAH

D. L. BAARS
Consulting Geologist
Evergreen, Colorado 80439

and

G. M. STEVENSON
Tierra Petroleum Corp.
Denver, Colorado 80200

INTRODUCTION

The boundary between the Colorado Plateau and Southern Rocky Mountain provinces lies somewhere within the western Colorado–eastern Utah region, and is arbitrary in the geological sense, because the stratigraphy and tectonic relationships remain relatively constant throughout the area.

The area of this report lies astride the Uncompahgre Uplift segment of the Ancestral Rockies orogenic system (see fig. 2). To the west of the ancient Uncompahgre fault block lies the northwest-trending Paradox basin and to the east is the strikingly similar Eagle evaporite basin, both of late Paleozoic age. Bounding the region on the east are the marginal Gore and Mosquito faults of the Front Range segment of the Ancestral Rockies. Within this vast area the early Paleozoic stratigraphy is similar and essentially uniform within the paleotectonic basins, suggesting that the two downwarps were not so distinctly separated until after Mississippian time. However, in Pennsylvanian time the main uplift of fault blocks of the Ancestral Rockies abruptly separated and accentuated the Paradox and Eagle evaporite basins, although the stratigraphy of the two depressions remained remarkably similar. Both the Uncompahgre and Front Range uplifts became high topographic features and shed untold cubic kilometers of coarse, arkosic sediments into the eastern reaches of the structural basins. Whether the two salt basins were interconnected in a common sea is still a matter of personal interpretation.

The margins of the Paradox basin usually are defined by the geographic extent of salt deposited during Middle Pennsylvanian time in the Paradox Formation. Consequently, there is little or no reflection of the buried basin at the surface, except for the salt diapirs in the "Paradox fold and fault belt." The basin is bounded on the northeast and east by the Uncompahgre Uplift and is surrounded elsewhere by paleotectonically controlled shallow-water shoals. The ovate basin has a northwesterly orientation, extending from Durango, Colorado and Farmington, New Mexico on the southeast to Green River, Utah on the northwest.

The Uncompahgre Uplift, which is best known for its exposures on the Uncompahgre Plateau and Black Canyon of the Gunnison River, extends for some 700 km northwestward from near Santa Fe, New Mexico almost to Provo, Utah. It is complexly fault-bounded on its southwestern margin and tilts gently eastward into the Eagle basin. Where exposed, the crest of the tilted fault block is Precambrian metamorphic and igneous rocks, overlain by various Mesozoic formations. Although it has a complex growth history, the Uncompahgre Uplift was a dominant feature throughout most of Permo-Pennsylvanian time.

The Eagle evaporite basin lies generally between the tilted eastern margin of the Uncompahgre Uplift and the fault-bounded Front Range Uplift on the east. The generally northwest-trending structural depression is a diminutive copy of the Paradox basin. The Eagle Valley Evaporites in the central part of the basin include gypsum and halite interbedded with drab-colored clastic rocks (Lovering and Mallory, 1962) that interfinger eastward with shelf carbonates and clastics of the Minturn Formation and arkose of the Maroon Formation. As in the Paradox basin, salt diapirs are present at a reduced scale near Glenwood Springs and Eagle, Colorado (see also Campbell, this guidebook).

BASEMENT FRAMEWORK

Although much has been said about the Laramide deformation of the Colorado Plateau and Southern Rocky Mountain provinces, the fact is that the structural fabric of the region was fixed by Late Precambrian time and repeated rejuvenations of the basement structure, including the Ancestral Rockies and Laramide episodes, only modified the original framework.

It was sometime around the summer of 1,700 m.y.b.p. that activity got underway on two major shear systems that transect the Paradox basin and Uncompahgre Uplift as we know them today (fig. 1). One, the dominant northwest-trending swarm of faults that passes through the San Juan Mountains of southwestern Colorado and on into the subsurface of the eastern Paradox basin, may extend as far to the northwest as Vancouver Island, B.C. and toward the southeast into Oklahoma's Wichita aulacogen (Baars, 1976). The subordinate northeasterly swarm of faults forming the conjugate set of fractures extends from Grand Canyon, Arizona through the Colorado Mineral Belt to Lake Superior (Warner, 1978). The northwest-trending set, called the Olympic-Wichita lineament by Baars (1976), appears to have had right-lateral strike-slip displacement; movement took place between 1,720 m.y. and 1,460 m.y. in the San Juan Mountains. The northeast-trending Colorado lineament, dated at 1,700 m.y. by Warner (1978), displaced the basement rocks in a left-lateral sense. The two continental-scale shear systems form a conjugate set that intersect in the vicinity of Moab, Utah.

The basic fracture pattern outlined above could be formed when compressive forces were directed from the north (or south) in Precambrian time. Perhaps a more reasonable solution would be a right-lateral wrenching stress imposed on the western United States that Wise (1963) proposed as his "outrageous hypothesis." Whether the underlying mechanism is the "outrageous hypothesis" of Wise or north-south compression as proposed by Moody and Hill (1956) is irrelevant for this discussion. Recognition of the basic tectonic fabric provides a basis for understanding the "peculiar" structural features of the Colorado Plateau and Southern Rockies.

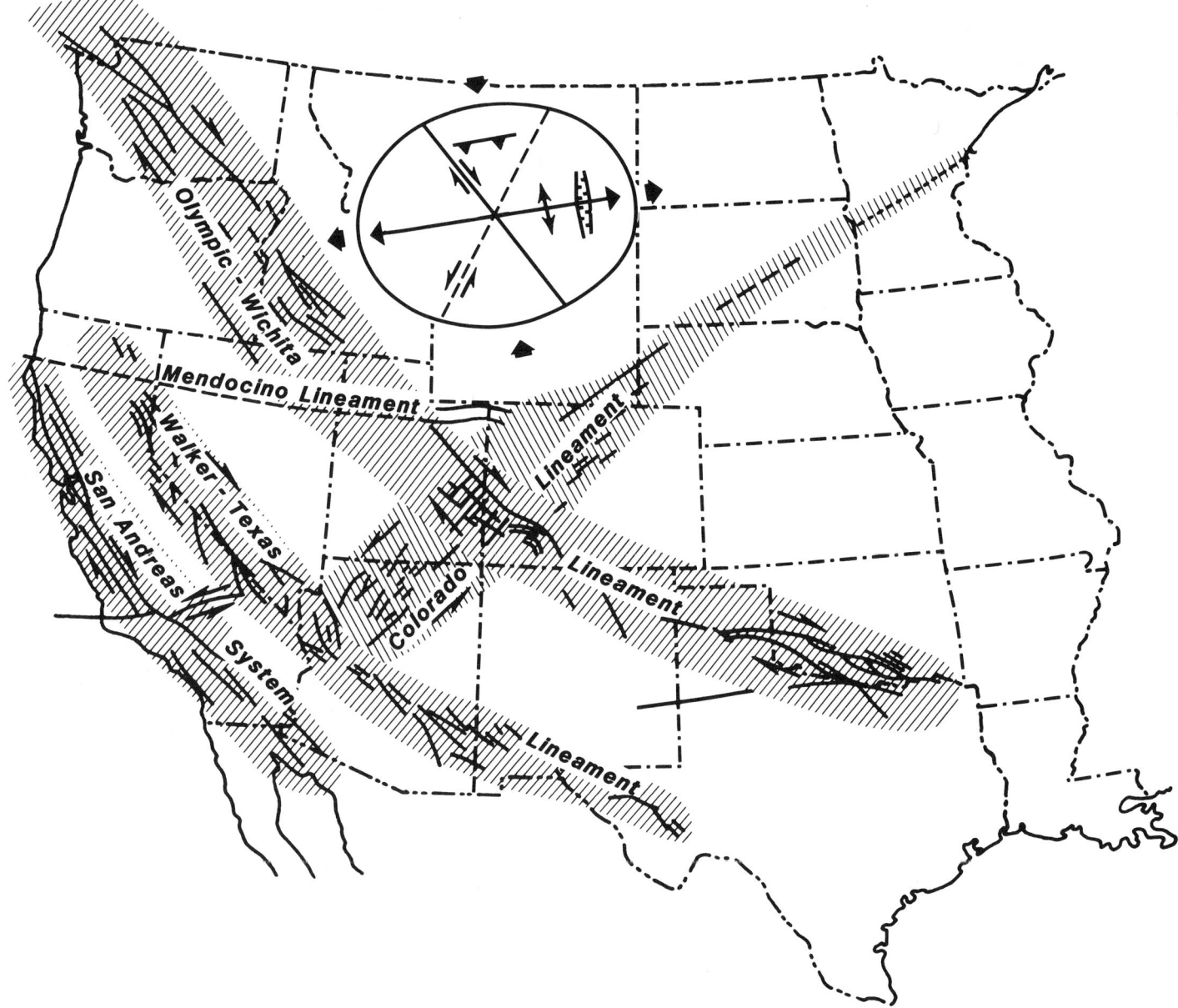

Figure 1. Location of major basement lineaments of the western United States. The sense of strike-slip offset is shown by arrows; northwesterly lineaments are right lateral, northeasterly lineaments are left lateral. The stress-strain ellipsoid is oriented such that maximum compressive stress is directed from the north.

A review of the strain ellipsoid oriented to properly represent the conjugate fractures described above (fig. 2) indicates that northerly-trending normal faults (east-west extension) should occur in conjunction with the wrench faults. It has been well established that the large monoclinal folds of the Colorado Plateau are drape structures over normal basement faults of Precambrian age; thus the monoclines originated as third-order features of the stress field. Furthermore, the large bounding faults of the Colorado Rockies (the Gore and Mosquito faults along the Front Range Uplift and the Cotopaxi fault that bounds the Wet Mountains Uplift farther south) are north-northwest normal faults that originated in Precambrian time (Tweto, 1980a, 1980b) and appear to have resulted from the same basic mechanism. Baars (1972, 1975) demonstrated early Paleozoic rejuvenation of these features. We should also expect to have easterly-trending folding and thrusting (north-south compression) which readily explains the "maverick" east-west trending thrusted anticlines of the Uinta Mountains. At least the very large Uinta Mountain arch had a Precambrian origin and fits the stress field described. Thus, the tectonic stage was set long before the Ancestral Rockies and Laramide orogenies, and most likely by about 1,700 m.y.b.p.

FAULT REJUVENATIONS

The Colorado Plateau and Southern Rockies were relatively quiescent during early Paleozoic time; however, Baars (1966) and Baars and See (1968) presented evidence that minor rejuvenations along the Olympic-Wichita lineament in the Paradox basin occurred during Cambrian, Devonian and Mississippian times. Baars (1972, 1975) described similar rejuvenations of tectonic activity along major structures in the vicinity of the Eagle basin and Front Range and Wet Mountains uplifts. Although early Paleozoic displacement on the faults was minor, sufficient vertical movement

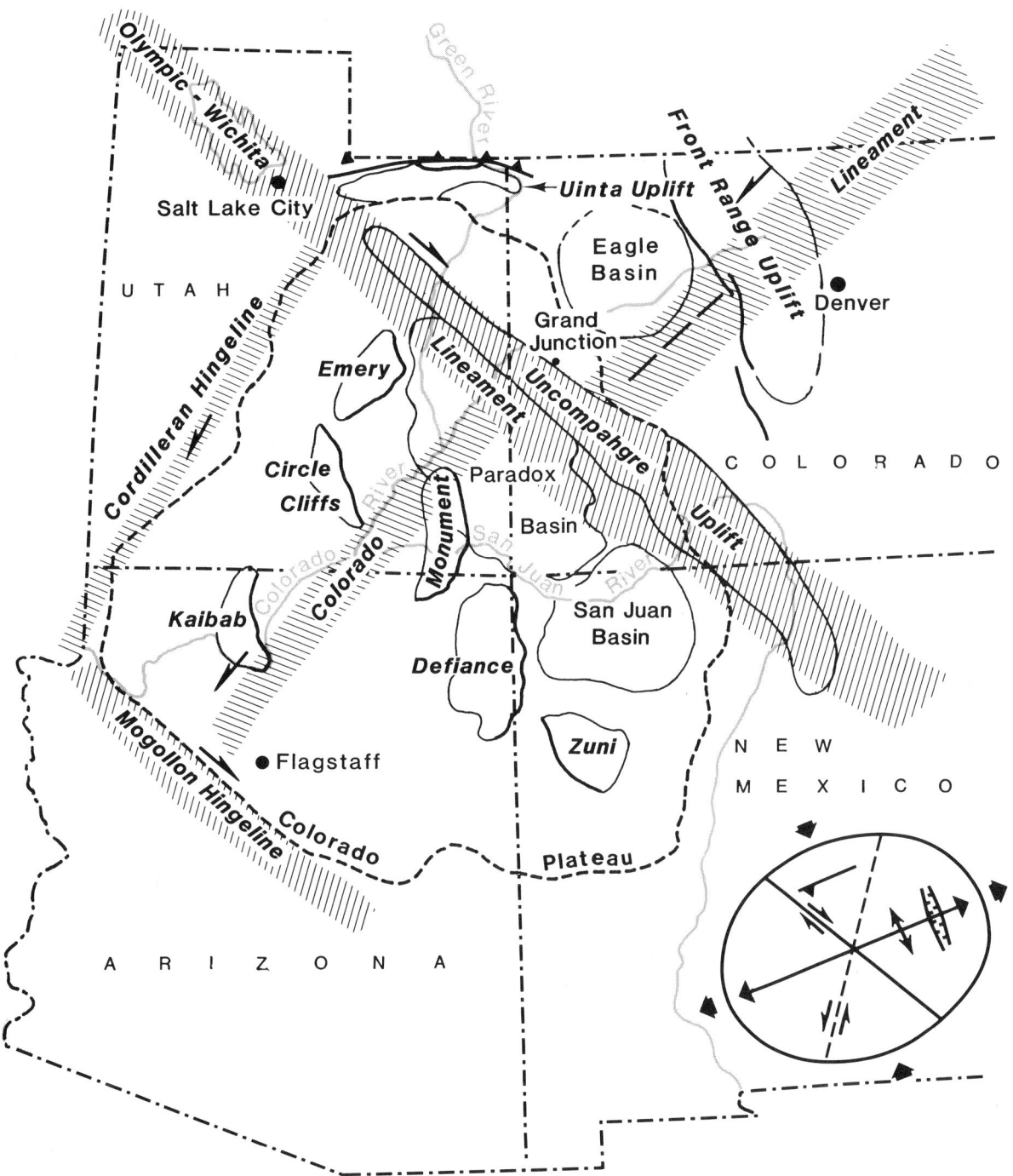

Figure 2. Location of Colorado Plateau and relationship to major orthogonal set of basement lineaments. Northwesterly lineaments are right lateral, northeasterly lineaments are left lateral. Stress-strain ellipsoid oriented such that maximum compressive stress is directed from the north.

occurred to create local shoaling conditions and alter sedimentary facies on a local scale. This structural activity was responsible for isolating local reservoir facies in Late Devonian and Early Mississippian rocks of the central Paradox basin. Similar potential reservoir facies in Mississippian strata of the southern Eagle basin have been reported by Nadeau (1972) in close proximity to basement structures. It appears that repeated paleotectonic rejuvenation on a minor scale is favorable to the development of petroleum reservoirs prior to Pennsylvanian time.

UPRISING OF ANCESTRAL ROCKIES

The relatively mild nature of the early Paleozoic tectonic activity took a dramatic change by the beginning of Middle Pennsylvanian (Atokan) time. Vertical displacement along the basement faults of the Paradox basin and Southern Rockies began slowly, but picked up momentum as Middle Pennsylvania (Desmoines) time progressed. The major uplifts of the Ancestral Rockies developed during this time as tilted fault blocks rising from Precambrian wrench faults and major normal faults became major source areas for coarse, arkosic clastic sediments. The Uncompahgre, Front Range and Wet Mountains uplifts arose to considerable heights, shedding hundreds of cubic kilometers of coarse clastics to the adjacent basins. More than a thousand meters of arkosic debris accumulated along the eastern flanks of the Paradox and Eagle (Maroon) basins in Permo-Pennsylvanian time. Although vertical displacement definitely dominated the earlier wrenching stress field, the structural fabric of the basement remained essentially unchanged, and east-west extension of the crust was greatly enhanced. Kluth and Coney (1981) have postulated that the increased tectonic activity resulted from the collision of the North American and South American-African plates at this time. However, the basic fabric remained essentially unchanged from the Precambrian pattern.

Uplifts

Uncompahgre-San Luis Uplift

The Uncompahgre Uplift had a complex history that is not completely understood because of poor exposures and limited subsurface data. Major uplift of the faulted highland began in Atokan time in a southern segment that extends from just east of Santa Fe, New Mexico northwestward to Ouray, Colorado. Relatively thick Atokan clastics in north-central New Mexico and southwestern Colorado attest to the early growth. This segment, the San Luis Uplift of early workers, continued its relatively modest rate of uplift well into Permian time, supplying clastic sediments to the Sangre de Cristo, Hermosa and Abo formations along the adjacent lowlands.

A pronounced westerly arc, or flex, occurs in the highland just east of Ouray, paralleling a similar westward flex in the adjacent Sneffels and Grenadier grabens of the San Juan Mountains (Baars and See, 1968). This arcuate bend in the basement faults is interpreted to be a left-lateral drag fold of enormous proportion caused by the Colorado lineament. It also appears to occur at the northwestern termination of the San Luis (Atokan) positive feature. From Ouray northwestward to the northwestern plunge of the surface Uncompahgre Plateau near Cisco, Utah, the middle (or Uncompahgre) segment of the uplift did not begin shedding massive amounts of arkose until Desmoinesian (Middle Pennsylvanian) time, but continued its positive tendencies well into Permian time. This northwesterly termination of the Uncompahgre Plateau also marks the emergence of the Colorado lineament into the Paradox basin. In other words, the Uncompahgre Uplift appears to have been segmented by the coupling of the Colorado and Olympic-Wichita lineaments.

The northwestern element of the Uncompahgre Uplift, perhaps best termed the Book Cliffs segment, extends from about Cisco to the overthrust belt in the Wasatch Mountains east of Provo, Utah in the subsurface. Its existence is known from geophysical and subsurface data underlying the southern flank of the Uinta Basin beneath the Book Cliffs. Thus, the rigid basement block provides a sill over which the structural basin sagged, creating the peculiar triangular shape of the basin. It did not shed significant amounts of arkosic debris until Early Permian time.

Front Range-Wet Mountains Uplifts

The complex growth history of the numerous individual segments of the Front Range-Wet Mountains uplifts of the Ancestral Rockies has been thoroughly documented and summarized by De Voto (1972). It will suffice here to reiterate that the history of the tectonic activity east of the Uncompahgre Uplift is similarly segmented and variably dated as that described for the Uncompahgre Uplift (see De Voto, 1972).

Complimentary Basins

Paradox Basin

The Paradox basin formed adjacent to the southwestern bounding faults of the Uncompahgre Uplift as a complimentary faulted depression (fig. 3). The deepest part of the basin lies immediately adjacent to the uplift, having stepped down structurally in a series of half-grabens from the western and southwestern shelves, or hingeline (fig. 4). Restricted marine circulation resulted in evaporite sedimentation throughout most of Desmoinesian (Middle Pennsylvanian) time. Salt deposition began in early Desmoinesian time in the deeper faulted troughs (Hite, 1960) and slowly filled the basin, burying the basement faults by the close of the epoch. Simultaneously, the Uncompahgre Uplift was supplying ever increasing amounts of arkosic sediments to the northeastern margin of the basin. The highland was continuously, or episodically, rising throughout the remainder of Pennsylvanian time, as the basin sank along the continuously active basement faults.

Most, if not all, of the smaller structural features of the Paradox basin were in place and growing during Paradox time. These folds exist at the surface today, having been enhanced by Laramide compression, but they were sufficiently prominent in Middle Pennsylvanian time to significantly impede open circulation of marine waters and to control salt thickness. Figure 3 shows the generalized surface structure of the region from Kelley (1955) overlain with Paradox salt isoliths. It is clear that the modern surface structures were actively developing around the periphery of the salt basin during the deposition of the salt and were actively affecting salt depositional patterns, as well as restricting marine circulation. These are all basement-related structures, and pre-date the Laramide orogeny.

Perhaps the most obvious and certainly the most interesting structural features of the Paradox basin are the large salt diapirs of east-central Utah and west-central Colorado (fig. 3). This broad region, termed the "Paradox fold and fault belt" by Kelley (1955), overlies the deeper structural depression of the Paradox basin where depositional salt thickness may have reached 1500 to 2400 m. The oldest and thickest salt deposits lie in the basement-controlled half grabens described above, but massive salt flowage has totally obscured other depositional characteristics.

The salt anticlines are strongly elongated northwesterly, paralleling the Uncompahgre frontal faults and overlying deep-seated basement faults (Cater and Elston, 1963; Joesting and Byerly, 1958;

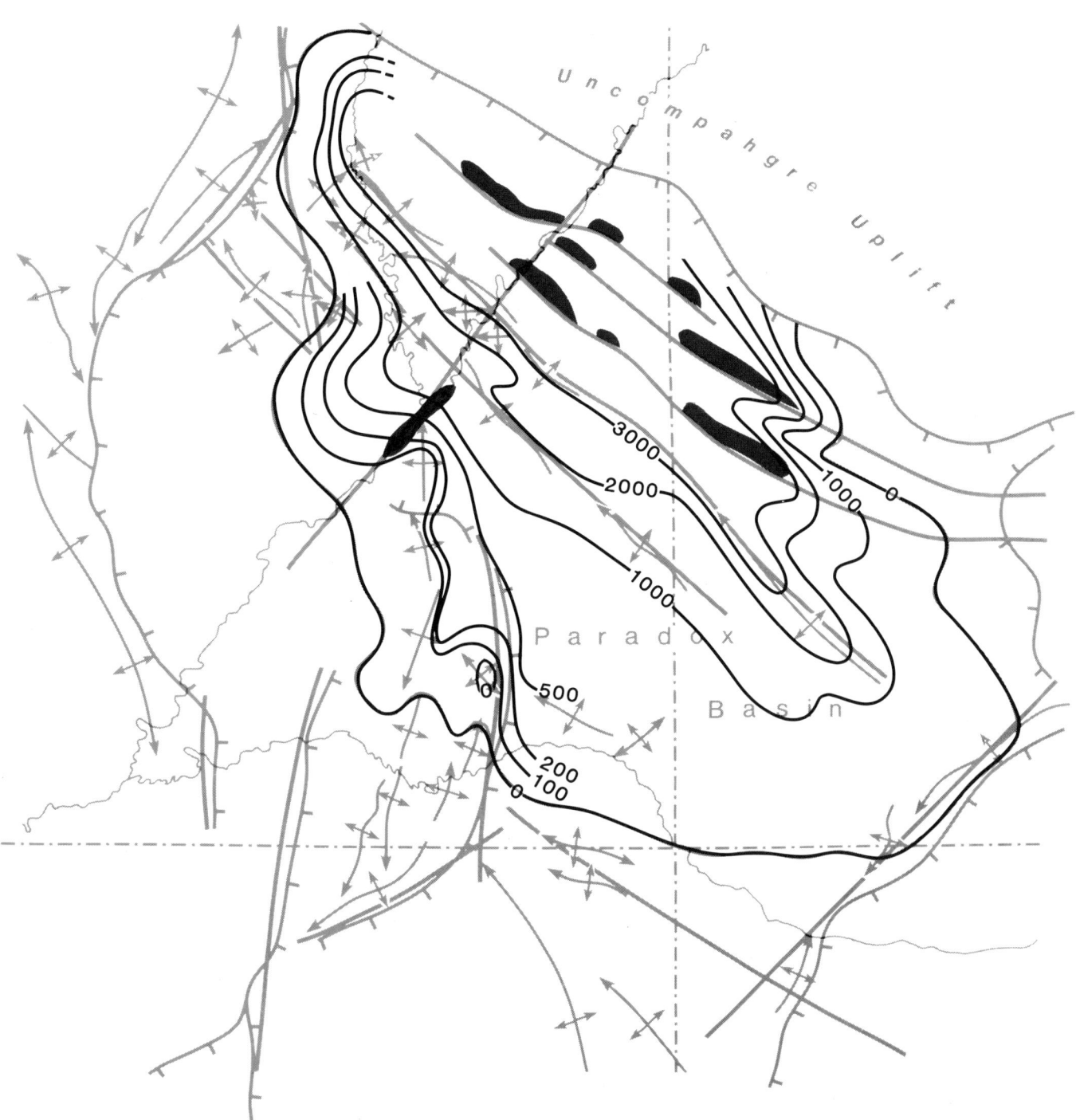

Figure 3. Location map of Paradox basin. Contours are net salt isoliths in feet from Kelley (1955). Salt anticlines shown in black with related northwest-trending basement faults (from Baars, 1966). Salt diapir on right is Paradox Valley; structure at left is Lisbon Valley.

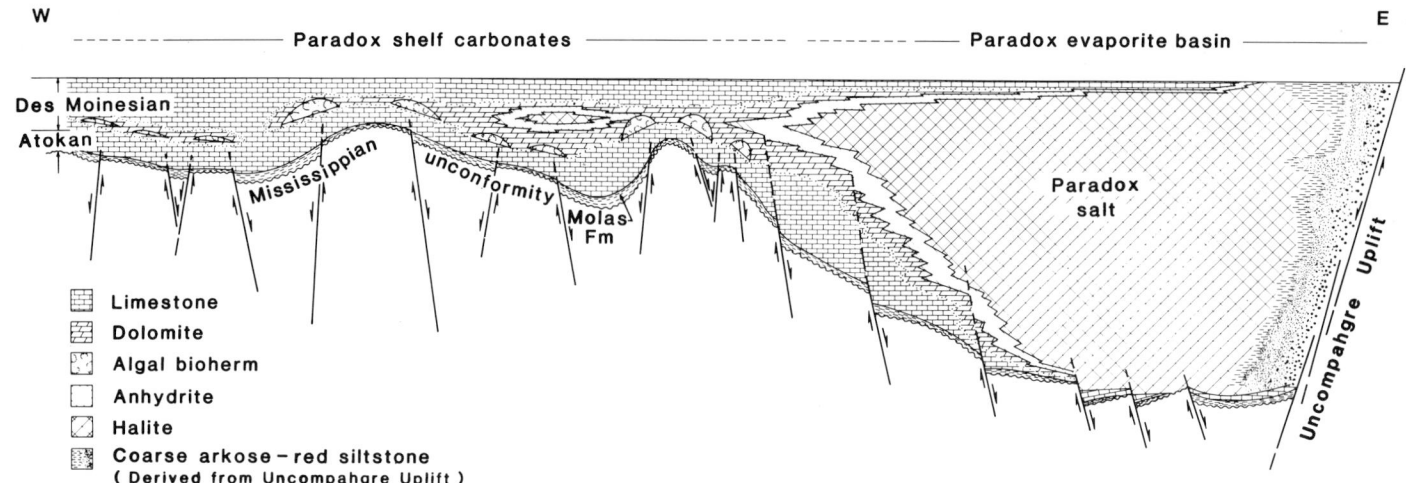

Figure 4. Schematic cross-section across Paradox basin at late Middle Pennsylvanian time, showing relationship of shelf carbonate to evaporite facies. Algal bioherms are shown in general relationships to basement structures. Salt diapirs are not shown.

Baars, 1966). As salt thickness reached about a thousand meters over the half-grabens, thick wedges of arkose were being deposited along the transition between the Uncompahgre highlands and the low-lying evaporite basin. The directional nature of the clastic overburden was a large factor in the initiation of salt flowage toward the southwest and the large basement faults, which are known to have vertical displacements of over 1800 m in Paradox Valley (fig. 5). Thus, the deep-seated faults were major buttresses to lateral salt movement. As the mobilized salt encountered the fault "scarps," flowage was directed upward and diapirism was initiated. Continued deposition of clastic overburden to the northeast caused salt to flow continuously or episodically until the supply was depleted in Late Jurassic time, as shown by repeated angular unconformities and pinchouts along the flanks of the structures. The source of the ever-thickening clastic overburden on the Uncompahgre Uplift was buried by Late Triassic and Jurassic sedimentation as the supply of salt diminished, marking the close of the diapiric activity.

Eagle Evaporite Basin

The poorly known Eagle evaporite basin, lying between the Uncompahgre and Front Range uplifts, has a similar history of subsidence and sedimentation as the Paradox basin. A paucity of subsurface data and limited exposures of Middle Pennsylvanian deposits provide only limited data, and interpretations are therefore highly generalized.

As previously outlined, basement faulting with a history of repeated rejuvenation is similar, if not identical, to the Paradox basin. Coarse clastic deposits were derived from the Front Range Uplift, and perhaps others, to the east and southeast, and interfingered with marine clastics and carbonates of the Minturn Formation of the Central Colorado Trough and the Eagle Valley Evapo-

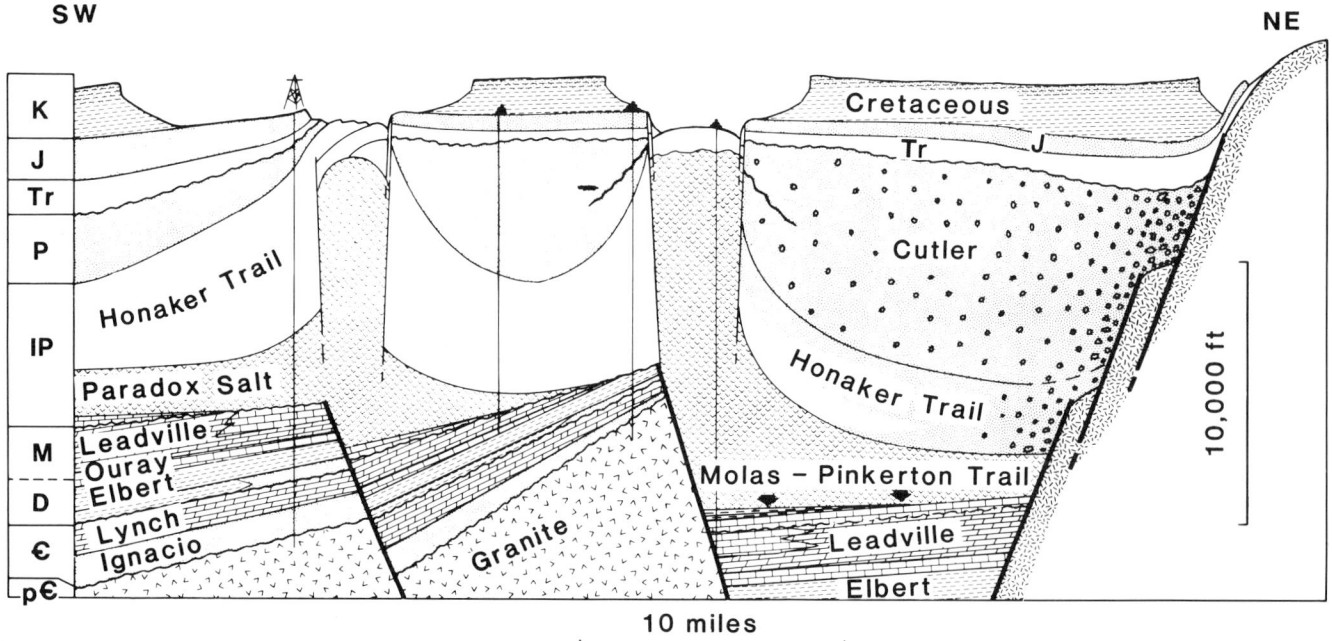

Figure 5. Schematic structural cross-section drawn normal to tectonic strike in eastern Paradox basin through Lisbon field and Wray Mesa region, showing relation between pre-salt faults and flowage structures (from Baars, 1966).

rites in the northwestern Trough (Lovering and Mallory, 1962). As in the Paradox basin, algal bioherms of Middle Pennsylvanian age grew along the margins of the evaporite basin (Walker, 1972). The extent and thickness of salt deposits in the restricted basin are only poorly known, and the nature of sub-salt structure is unknown due to the limited number of deep wells.

Two northwesterly trends of Eagle evaporite exposures in the vicinity of Glenwood Springs and the Eagle-Gypsum area have the characteristics of salt diapirs similar to the Paradox structures. Drilling indicates that salt is present in the structures, but their size and growth histories have not been determined. These salt anticlines may be more similar to the Paradox structures than is generally realized, and further deep exploration of the pre-salt section is certainly warranted.

DEMISE OF THE ANCESTRAL ROCKIES

The Ancestral Rockies had probably reached their zenith by Early Permian time; they underwent denudation for about the first half of the period, supplying great quantities of arkosic sediments to the lowlands during their demise. The Permian red beds from the uplifts finally buried many of the long-existing positive features of the region, such as the Zuni, Defiance, Kaibab, and Nacimiento uplifts of the Colorado Plateau. The Monument Upwarp remained sufficiently positive to cause major facies changes along its flanks and crests, while marine Permian deposits buried the Late Pennsylvanian erosional surface on the Emery uplift underlying the San Rafael Swell.

Fine-grained red beds and eolian sandstones dominated the Triassic and Jurassic systems, with little evidence of structural growth having played a significant role. By Late Cretaceous time, the intracratonic seaways shifted eastward, effectively burying the present day Colorado Plateau and Southern Rockies in marine muds and sands.

LARAMIDE DISTURBANCE

The Laramide orogeny is generally considered to have been the wave of compressional tectonism that reshaped the western North American continent from the west toward the east during latest Cretaceous through early Eocene time. During this event, the Colorado Plateau and Southern Rockies, as a whole, resisted the extensive thrust faulting that occurred to the west and south. The Colorado Plateau acted as a semi-rigid "mini-plate," rejecting intensive deformation along its western margin, the Cordilleran hingeline or Wasatch line, and along its southern border at the Texas-Walker Lane lineament. Pre-existing basement-related structures of the Plateau and Southern Rockies invariably pre-date the Laramide in origin, but were somewhat modified by the westerly compressive forces.

The primary effects of the Laramide on the Colorado Plateau and Southern Rockies were the enhancement of pre-existing structures and the overturning of drape folds, generally toward the east. The amplitude of virtually all of the folded structures was increased considerably by westerly compressive stress (σ_1), changing minor, low amplitude folds into major structures. Major monoclines formed over the larger north-oriented basement normal faults on the Plateau, and vertical throw was increased on similar faults in the Rockies. The net effect was to overturn the basement faults toward the east, and to create east-facing monoclines. There are a number of west-facing monoclines on the eastern Plateau and White River uplift (Kelley, 1955), but most of these occur as drape folds over the primary basement wrench faults rather than third-order normal faults. In spite of a flurry of extraordinary explanations of the Laramide origin of the Uinta Mountain arch by various structural geologists in recent years, the easterly trending fold was present in essentially its present configuration prior to Cambrian time, as shown by angular unconformities at that horizon. The Uinta-Piceance basin is a negative fold, draping off the Uinta Mountain arch on the north and the Uncompahgre Uplift under its southwest flank.

The multitude of problems encountered when the structural configuration of the Colorado Plateau and Southern Rockies is interpreted on the basis of Laramide stress fields are essentially eliminated when it is realized that these structures originated in a totally different stress regime in Precambrian time. The basement tectonic fabric of the region was fixed before Phanerozoic time and repeatedly rejuvenated during the various ensuring tectonic events, including the Ancestral Rockies and Laramide episodes. Bodily clockwise rotation of the provinces invoked by many authors to explain the observed relationships is unnecessary and unjustified by field relationships, except along basement shear zones.

AFTERMATH

Tectonic events following the Laramide disturbance have more effect on the geomorphology than anything else. Beginning shortly after the termination of Laramide time (probably during the Eocene) the entire Colorado Plateau Province was gently, but bodily, uplifted and tilted toward the north. A regional vertical doming of central Arizona seems to have been the cause of the tilting. The end result was that surface drainage gained potential energy and surface erosion was accelerated. The early denudation of the Province provided considerable amounts of sediments that were carried northward into a large lake (Lake Uinta) that formed between the structural buttresses of the northwestern Uncompahgre Uplift and the Uinta Mountain arch on the north. The Paradox basin region was merely subjected to surface erosion.

The most prominent topographic features on the Plateau are the so-called laccolithic ranges that stand to elevations exceeding 3,900 m. There are eight in all, and they appear to have been emplaced along basement lineaments (Kelley, 1955) or more likely at intersections of northwest and northeast basement lineaments (Witkind, 1975). Within the individual ranges, intrusive igneous rocks are exposed in the form of stock, dikes, sills, laccoliths and cactoliths. They appear to have been emplaced at two distinct times. One group, including the Ute, Carrizo, La Plata and Rico ranges, have been dated at between 61 and 84 m.y., or about Laramide time. The others, including the Henry (48 m.y.), LaSal (24 m.y.) and Abajo (28 m.y.) ranges were intruded around middle Eocene and early Miocene times (Witkind, 1975). It is interesting that the LaSal Mountains east of Moab were intruded along the basement faults underlying Paradox and Castle Valley salt structures and actually pierced the heart of the salt anticline. The resulting igneous rocks are peculiar aegirine-augite-rich syenite prophyries (soda-enriched) as a result of intrusion through halite. The range was named LaSal (salt) Mountains by the early Spanish explorers, because they found salt water springs in the mountains.

Late in the episode of regional tilting during the intrusion of the younger laccoliths, general elevation of the Plateau and Southern Rockies occurred. Surface and ground water drainage intensity increased and was gradually diverted toward the southwest along the Colorado River system, perhaps by a series of stream piracies along the route. Ground waters began to remove near-surface salt by solution on the larger salt diapirs; consequently, solution collapse of the crests of the anticlines began. Overlying strata of all ages from Permian to Cretaceous slumped into the weakened crests of the salt anticlines, leaving them with gravity faults along the high flanks and jumbled slump folds depressed into the terminations of the anticlines as we see them today. Superimposed streams cut downward into the structures, sometimes at right angles to the anticlines, creating "paradoxical" river courses that cut across the structures rather than flow along the axial valleys. Thus, the name was derived for Paradox Valley, from which the name was derived for the Paradox Formation and subsequently the Paradox basin.

CONCLUSIONS

The tectonic evolution of the Paradox basin and Southern Rockies may be summarized as follows:

1. A conjugate set of shear zones transected the region at about 1,700 m.y.b.p. The northwesterly shear has been named the Olympic–Wichita Lineament; the northeasterly set the Colorado Lineament. They probably resulted from relative compression from the north.

2. Related basement fractures were northerly oriented normal faults (extension) and easterly oriented folds (compression).

3. Small-scale vertical relief along the fracture system was rejuvenated throughout Cambrian, Devonian and Mississippian time, creating localized reservoir facies on the high, shoaling fault blocks.

4. The Uncompahgre and Front Range Uplifts and the compensatory Paradox and Eagle basins formed along the basement fractures in Pennsylvanian time from extreme east-west extension of the crust.

5. Salt thickened and diapiric structures formed in Pennsylvanian through Jurassic time from clastic overburden on the eastern margins of the basins, causing the salt to flow against and upward along the basement faults.

6. Laramide compressional forces from the west in Late Cretaceous to early Eocene time enhanced the existing structures and overturned them toward the east in most cases. The salt structures were little affected. Monoclines were formed over the northerly oriented normal faults in the basement, and the easterly trending Uinta Mountain arch was enhanced.

7. Regional tilting of the Plateau province toward the north caused surface drainage to fill Lake Uinta with sediments stripped from the south in early Tertiary time.

8. Intrusive igneous laccolithic magmas were implaced during Laramide and middle Tertiary times at intersections of basement lineaments.

9. Major surface structures of the Colorado Plateau and Southern Rockies were not formed in Laramide times, only enhanced from rejuvenation of basement structure. They resulted from a continuum of tectonic activity originating about 1,700 m.y.b.p. and continuing to the present.

REFERENCES

Baars, D. L., 1966, Pre-Pennsylvanian paleotectonics—Key to basin evolution and petroleum occurrences in Paradox basin, Utah and Colorado: American Association of Petroleum Geologists Bulletin, v. 50, p. 2082–2111.

———, 1972, Pre-Pennsylvanian paleotectonic framework of Ancestral Rockies of Colorado (abs.): Colorado School of Mines Quarterly, v. 67, n. 4, p. 137.

———, 1975, Pre-Pennsylvanian reservoir rocks of the eastern Colorado Plateau and Southern Rocky Mountains, in P. Bolyard, ed., Deep Drilling Frontiers of the Central Rocky Mountains: Denver, Colorado, Rocky Mountain Association of Geologists, p. 71–74.

———, 1976, The Colorado Plateau aulacogen—Key to continental-scale basement rifting: Proceedings of Second International Conference on Basement Tectonics, p. 157–164.

Baars, D. L. and See, P. D., 1968, Pre-Pennsylvanian stratigraphy and paleotectonics of the San Juan Mountains, southwestern Colorado: Geological Society of America Bulletin, v. 79, p. 333–350.

Baars, D. L. and Stevenson, G. M., 1981 (in press), Subtle stratigraphic traps in Paleozoic rocks of the Paradox basin: American Association of Petroleum Geologists Memoir.

Cater, F. W. and Elston, D. P., 1963, Structural development of salt anticlines of Colorado and Utah: American Association of Petroleum Geologists Memoir 2, Backbone of the Americas, p. 152–159.

De Voto, R. H., 1972, Pennsylvanian and Permian stratigraphy and tectonism in central Colorado: Colorado School of Mines Quarterly, v. 67, n. 4, p. 139–186.

Hite, R. J., 1960, Stratigraphy of the saline facies of the Paradox Member of the Hermosa Formation of southeastern Utah and southwestern Colorado: Four Corners Geological Society Guidebook, 3rd Field Conference, p. 86–89.

Joesting, H. R. and Byerly, P. E., 1958, Regional geophysical investigations of the Uravan area, Colorado: U.S. Geological Survey Professional Paper 316-A, p. 1–17.

Kelley, V. C., 1955, Regional tectonics of the Colorado Plateau and relationships to the origin and distribution of uranium: Albuquerque, University of New Mexico Press, 120 p.

Kluth, C. F. and Coney, P. J., 1981, Plate tectonics of the Ancestral Rocky Mountains, Geology, v. 9, p. 10–15.

Lovering, T. S. and Mallory, W. W., 1962, The Eagle Valley Evaporite and its relation to the Minturn and Maroon formations, northwest Colorado: U.S. Geological Survey Professional Paper 450-D, p. 45–48.

Moody, W. D. and Hill, M. J., 1956, Wrench fault tectonics: Geological Society of America Bulletin, v. 67, p. 1207–46.

Nadeau, J. E., 1972, Mississippian stratigraphy of central Colorado: Colorado School of Mines Quarterly, v. 67, n. 4, p. 77–102.

Tweto, Ogden, 1980a, Tectonic history of Colorado, in Colorado Geology, H. C. Kent and K. W. Porter, eds.: Denver, Colorado, Rocky Mountain Association of Geologists, p. 5–9.

———, 1980b, Precambrian geology of Colorado: in Colorado Geology, H. C. Kent and K. W. Porter, eds.: Denver, Colorado, Rocky Mountain Association of Geologists, p. 37–46.

Walker, T. R., 1972, Bioherms in the Minturn Formation (Des Moinesian Age), Vail–Minturn Area, Eagle County, Colorado: Colorado School of Mines Quarterly, v. 67, n. 4, p. 249–278.

Warner, L. A., 1978, The Colorado Lineament: a middle Precambrian wrench fault system: Geological Society of America Bulletin, v. 89, p. 161–171.

Wise, D. U., 1963, An outrageous hypothesis for the tectonic pattern of the North American cordillera: Geological Society of America Bulletin, v. 74, p. 357–362.

Witkind, I. J., 1975, The Abajo Mountains: an example of the laccolithic groups on the Colorado Plateau: Four Corners Geological Society, 8th Field Conference, p. 245–52.

GLACIAL MORAINES, TERRACES AND PEDIMENTS OF GRAND VALLEY, WESTERN COLORADO*

SCOTT SINNOCK
Sandia National Laboratories
Albuquerque, New Mexico 87185

INTRODUCTION

This paper discusses a set of late Pleistocene landforms in the Grand Valley of western Colorado (fig. 1). More detailed discussion is available in Sinnock (1978).

The Grand Valley is a broad lowland underlain by Mancos Shale and stretching from near Montrose, Colorado to Price, Utah. The floor of Grand Valley is ubiquitously characterized by multileveled pediments and/or terraces veneered with thin Pleistocene gravels. Within the study area, the Book Cliffs, Grand Mesa, West Elk Mountains, Black Canyon uplift, and San Juan Mountains form the northeastern boundary of the valley and the Uncompahgre Plateau gently rises from the southwestern edge of the valley. Locally the valley is the site of master drainage lines and associated glacial moraines and terraces; in other places only ephemeral drainage channels and associated pediments characterize the valley floor.

LATE PLEISTOCENE TILLS

Glacial moraines in the Ridgway Basin are the most useful chronologically determinative landforms in the study area. Three distinct

---
*Field activities were performed during the summers of 1976 and 1977 while the author was attending Purdue University. Preparation of this manuscript was supported by the U.S. Department of Energy

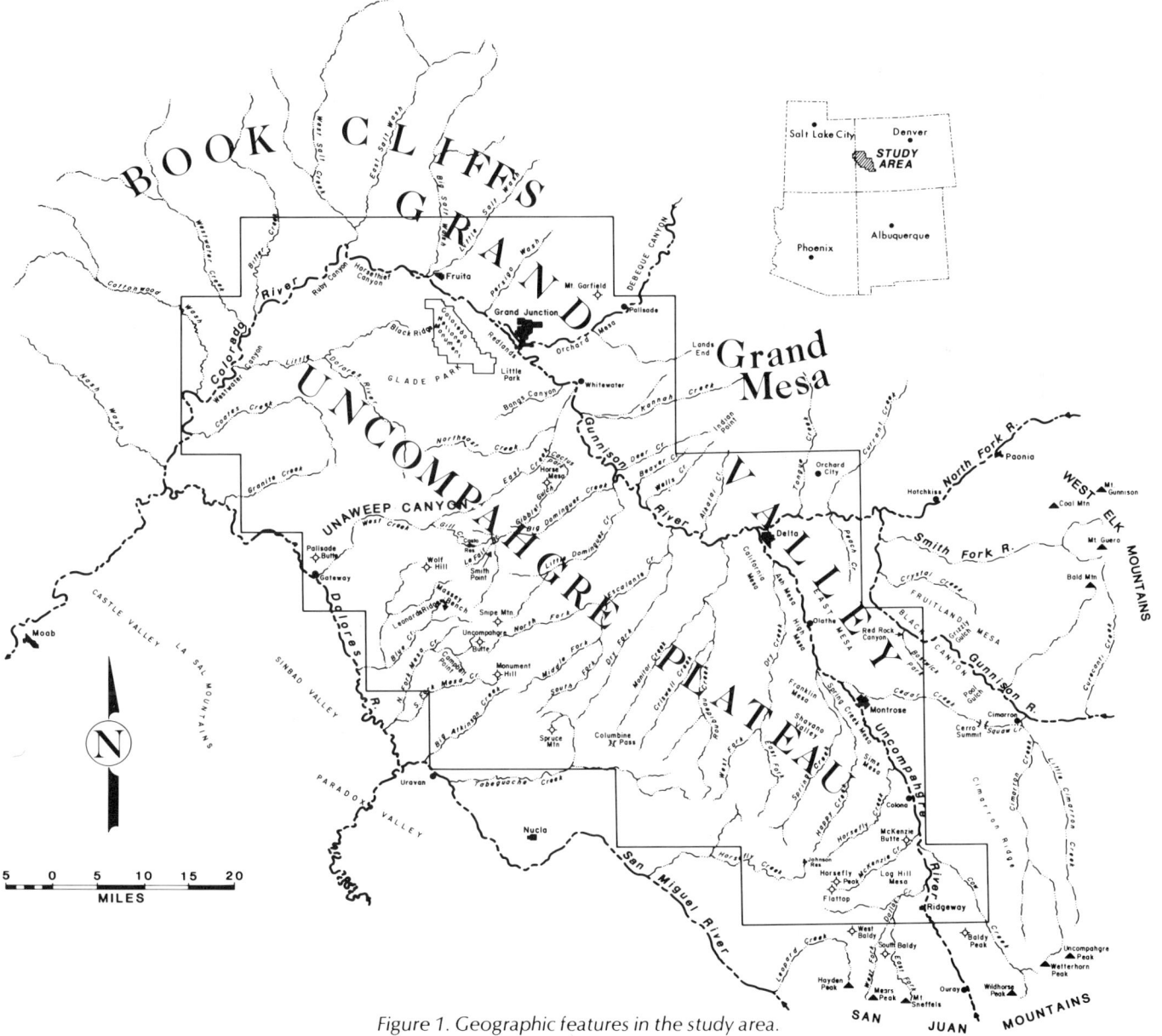

Figure 1. Geographic features in the study area.

Figure 2. Youngest Pinedale moraine and associated terrace near Ridgway. View is south from SE ¼, Sec. 4, T.45N., R.8W.

and a fourth indistinct moraines are located north of the town of Ridgway. The two lowest, and presumably youngest, are located about one mile* north of town. Two higher and older morainal deposits terminate one to two miles farther north.

The younger two moraines are relatively undissected, possess hummocky topography, kettles, kames, and eskers, and sit 50 to 200 ft above the river (fig. 2). The youngest is a thin (50 to 100 ft), broad, rather flat belt of till that surrounds 200 ft-high hills of the next older moraine. Two correlative lateral moraines extend south from Ridgway along the slopes of Baldy Peak on the east side of the Uncompahgre Valley. The younger lateral moraine is "nested" within the older. However, the fact that the younger terminal moraine surrounds the base of the older and extends farther down the valley suggests that the last glacial advance breached the older moraine, perhaps during an ice surge. The thickness of the ice was probably less than during the previous advance because the top of the younger till deposits occurs at lower elevations than the older till. Similar dissection and weathering on the two young moraines suggests that they were deposited at about the same general time.

Original depositional forms such as hummocky terrain, kettles, and so forth, do not occur on the older sets of moraines in the Ridgway Basin. These moraines are dissected by small streams and gullies and are significantly modified by mass wasting. The older moraines are 400 to 600 ft above the present river level and are difficult to distinguish from one another. A deposit mapped as outwash by Atwood and Mather (1932) caps a small hill one mile north of the largest deposit of the older till. Recent gravel-pit operations on the hill exposed an ice-contact mixture of till and outwash. This hill is therefore believed to represent the fourth and oldest moraine in the Ridgway Basin. A till deposit along the southeast edge of Log Hill Mesa on the Uncompahgre Plateau is thought to be a lateral moraine of this oldest till. No correlative lateral moraines have been identified upstream from Ridgway.

The Ridgway area tills were first described by Howe and Cross (1906) as a single suite of relatively recent moraines. Richmond (1954) mapped two Pinedale and two Bull Lake moraines along Dallas Creek, upstream from Ridgway. Tweto and others (1979) mapped all of the moraines near Ridgway as Bull Lake and Pinedale in age. Moraines in the Animas Valley near Durango were formed by glaciers flowing southward from the same ice caps above Ridgway. These till assemblages have been correlated (Richmond, 1965) with Pinedale, Bull Lake and the Sacagawea Ridge glaciations of the Wind River Mountains in Wyoming (Blackwelder, 1915; Holmes and Moss, 1955; and Richmond, 1948). Atwood and Mather (1932) also believed that three major glacial episodes are recorded in the tills around the San Juan Mountains. They mapped the resultant deposits, from youngest to oldest, as "Wisconsin," "Durango," and "Cerro" tills. Atwood and Mather's (1932) map shows both the Pinedale and Bull Lake moraines of Richmond (1965) in the Durango area as Wisconsin age and his Sacagawea Ridge moraine as Durango age. At Ridgway, Atwood and Mather mapped the two youngest tills as Wisconsin and the two older as Durango.

Thus, it is fairly certain that the moraines of the Ridgway Basin are Pinedale and Bull Lake deposits. The two freshest represent two separate Pinedale advances; the older two, Bull Lake advances.

PRE-BULL LAKE TILL

Another much older set of till deposits occurs on Horsefly Peak, Flat Top, West Baldy and South Baldy along a line from the San Juan Mountains to Horsefly Peak and along the flank of Cimarron Ridge in the Cerro Summit area. Howe and Cross (1906) described the deposit at Horsefly Peak and noted the absence of quartzites, paucity of San Juan Tuff breccias, and abundance of Potosi and Hinsdale volcanic clasts. Exposures of Hinsdale basalt presently are absent in drainage basins of the western San Juan Mountains. The Potosi Series is a thin, narrow ridge former, almost completely eroded from the region. San Juan Tuff currently comprises the greatest area of surface exposure in the Mt. Sneffels region. Howe and Cross concluded, and I concur, that the till on Horsefly Peak was deposited when most slopes of the San Juan Mountains were formed on volcanic units now absent or significantly reduced in surface area.

Atwood and Mather (1915) named this deposit the Cerro Till and later (1932) cited Hills (1884) as first recognizing its glacial origin. This interpretation seemed generally acceptable until Dickinson (1965a, 1965b) concluded that the Cerro till at this type locality at Cerro Summit was landslide debris. At about the same time Mather and Wengerd (1965) described massive Bull Lake-age landslide deposits in the Ridgway area. However, agatized rhyolite, granite, and basalt clasts occur at the surface throughout the region mapped as landslide by Dickinson. These same clasts, especially agatized rhyolite and basalt, are abundant at Horsefly Peak. Certainly the northern and western slopes of Cimarron Ridge (the Cerro Summit region) have wasted by downhill slumping, sliding and argilliturbatonal creep, but the material that is landsliding is mostly till.

Because of confusion surrounding the name "Cerro Till," I herein informally refer to the deposit as the Horsefly Peak Till. It is the only till of pre-Bull Lake age noted in the study area. At Cerro Summit, it occurs about 1,000 ft above the lowest nearby graded pediments. At Horsefly Peak, it is about 3,000 ft above the Ridgway Basin and rests on a fault-produced ridge probably formed after deposition of the till. Richmond (1965) mapped glacial deposits only 300 to 350 ft above the Animas River near Durango as Sacagawea Ridge age. Topographic form and weathering characteristics of the "Sacagawea Ridge" moraines resemble in many respects morainal material near Ridgway considered herein as Bull Lake. However, if Richmond's age assignments near Durango are correct, the older moraines in the Ridgway basin may be as old as Sacagawea Ridge age, making the Horsefly Peak Till at least as old as Cedar Ridge events in the Wind River Mountains. Descriptions of the Sherwin Till (Blackwelder, 1931) on the east flank of the

---

*English units of measurement are used throughout this paper because the source data from topographic maps are so expressed.

Sierra Nevada indicate similarity between the Sherwin and Horsefly Peak tills. Both are found on upland surfaces, deeply weathered, sparsely strewn with very large boulders, and considerably more extensive than younger, in-valley tills. The Bishop Tuff which overlies the Sherwin Till has been dated as 0.7 m.y. old (Dalrymple and others, 1965). If the Horsefly Peak Till correlates with the Sherwin, it is probably older than the Sacagawea Ridge, supporting correlation with Cedar Ridge glaciation. If true, and if the older moraines in Ridgway Basin are Bull Lake, then moraines of Sacagawea Ridge age are absent from the northwest flank of the San Juan Mountains.

This discussion indicates some uncertainty concerning stratigraphic correlation of Pleistocene events in the Rocky Mountain region. However, a set of relative age relationships in the northwest San Juan Mountains is evident: four "younger" in-valley tills and associated outwash terraces and at least one "older," upland till occur. All "younger" tills are about the same general order of magnitude in terms of moraine size, vertical separation, and down-valley extent. The Horsefly Peak Till, on the other hand, is quite different from the younger tills in all these respects. It is vertically separated from the other tills by thousands rather than hundreds of feet and covers broad areas, suggesting piedmont glaciation.

TERRACES

Each glacial advance produced an outwash train of downstream terraces. Near Montrose four distinct terrace levels are apparent. These terraces merge with similar terraces along the Gunnison and farther, with those along the Colorado River. The terraces thus correlate with Pinedale and Bull Lake glacial events.

The Uncompahgre River flows northward from the moraines near Ridgway and enters a small canyon entrenched through the southeastern tip of the Uncompahgre Plateau at McKenzie Butte, a dome formed around an intrusive dike. Near the town of Colona, Grand Valley heads and rapidly expands to nearly 12 mi in width, a dimension maintained for about 80 mi in a downstream direction. From Colona to Delta the Uncompahgre River flows along the approximate center of the valley. Outwash terraces from the glacial moraines of Ridgway form broad mesas (Sims, High, Spring Creek, Ash, and California) that rise southwestward from the river as four steps, the uppermost lapping onto the flank of the Uncompahgre Plateau. Terrace gradients parallel the northwest trend of the valley (fig. 3), and their surfaces comprise one of the largest irrigated row crop regions in western Colorado.

The four terrace levels are easily recognized between Delta and the moraines. Near the moraines, they are separated by sharp 100 to 150 ft-high interterrace scarps. The terraces merge toward Delta, where they are only about 50 to 75 ft apart, a separation generally maintained downstream along the Gunnison and Colorado rivers to Moab and perhaps beyond. The lowest terrace merges with the present floodplain of the Uncompahgre River near Olathe. From Colona to Delta converging terrace gradients average about 50 ft per mile; from Delta to Grand Junction, they slightly diverge and slope about 5 to 10 ft per mile.

Terrace surfaces are generally underlain by a layer of fine-grained, windblown or slackwater deposits resting on coarse-grained fluvial sand and gravels, which, in turn, rest on Mancos Shale and older rocks. The uppermost, fine-grained deposits are absent in some places. In others, they are overlain by slopewash, fan or pediment deposits. Along the Uncompahgre River, the terrace gravels and cobbles are entirely comprised of San Juan Mountain-provenance volcanic, carbonate and quartzite clasts. Rounding of originally joint-controlled triclinic forms toward triaxial indicatrices generally occurs in a downstream direction along with size diminution of the clasts. Downstream from Delta, terrace

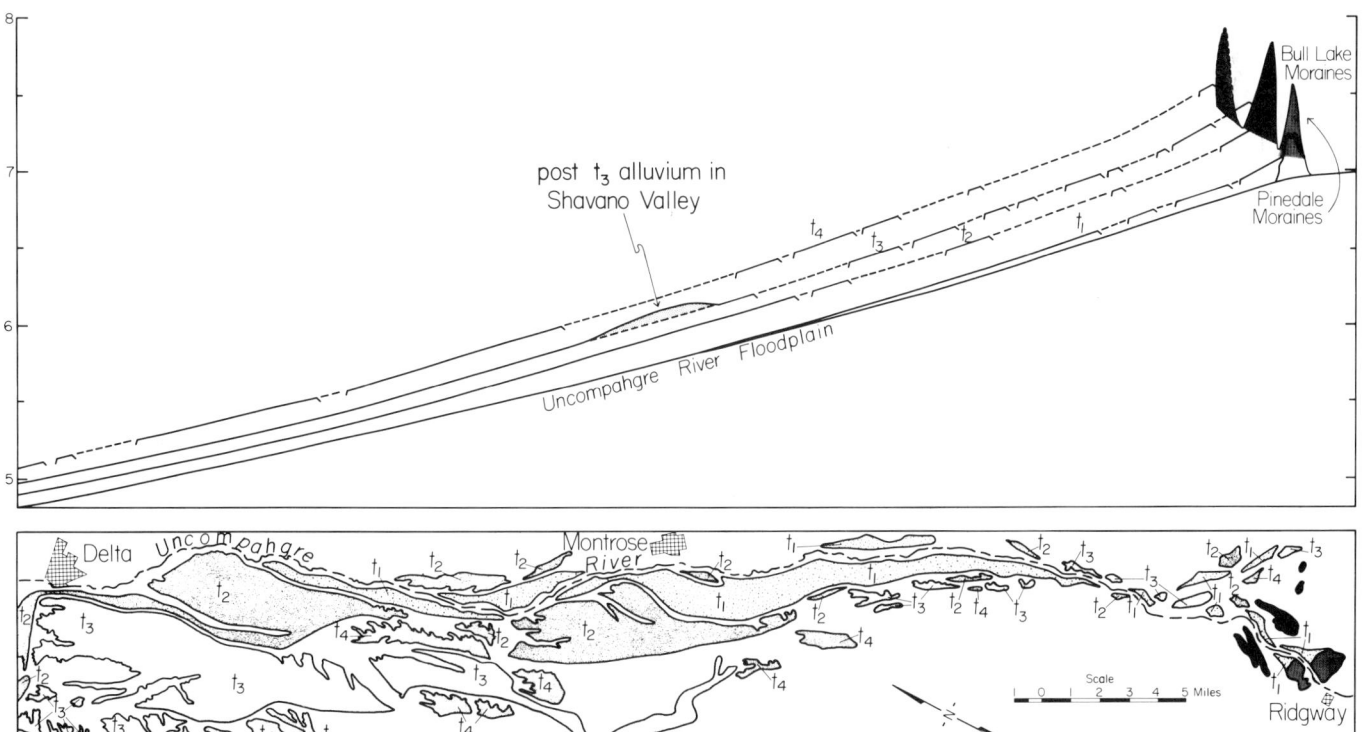

Figure 3. Profiles and surface distribution of terraces from Ridgway to Delta; vertical exaggeration of profile is 30×. Vertical axis is elevation in thousands of feet.

gravels include more varied rock types from the headwaters of the Gunnison and North Fork Rivers. Thickness of terrace deposits ranges from about 2 to 30 ft along the Uncompahgre River.

Terraces and pediments similar to those along the main trend of Grand Valley occur in a large embayment extending up the Gunnison and its North Fork from Delta to Paonia.

Below Delta the Gunnison flows east, out of the center of Grand Valley, and cuts into the flank of the Uncompahgre Plateau. There it bends back to the northeast and enters a canyon 600 to 800 ft deep along the lower slopes of the plateau. Scattered patches of terrace remnants are perched on the canyon walls throughout the canyon. The river emerges at Whitewater before reoccupying a smaller canyon for about five more miles downstream. Where the Gunnison reemerges into the Grand Valley, it joins the Colorado River, which flows into the study area from the northeast.

In the apex of the confluence broad outwash terraces again are found and join terraces entering the area along the southeast side of the Colorado River. South of the confluence, the terraces lap onto the plateau's dipping flank (fig. 4) in a manner similar to those between Delta and Colona. Along the Colorado National Monument fault zone, the terraces sharply truncate drag folds below the fault scarp (fig. 5) and comprise the Redlands region near Grand Junction.

On the right bank of the Colorado near Grand Junction, a 2.5 mi-wide, very flat, undissected slip-off plain slopes gradually toward the river. The river hugs the southern edge of this broad lowland where it flows at the base of an 80 ft-high cliff separating the river from the first terrace level. The towns of Grand Junction and Fruita are sited on this low, sloping plain. Along with the terraces, this area comprises another major irrigated region in Grand Valley.

Four miles west of Fruita, the Colorado crosses the northwest extension of the Monument uplift zone and occupies a canyon entrenched 1,000 ft below walls capped with Dakota Sandstone. As along the canyon of the Gunnison River between Delta and Whitewater, isolated terrace patches occur on the canyon walls (fig. 6).

The valley terraces have long been recognized. Nelson and Kolbe (1910) mapped the soils of the terraces along the Uncompahgre Valley as the Mesa Series. From geologists' perspectives Atwood and Mather (1932) described and mapped the terraces as outwash trains from Wisconsin through Cerro glacial episodes. Knobel and others (1955) mapped the Mesa, Hinman, and Genola soil series near Grand Junction and described them as derived terrace material from old river alluvium. Lohman (1965) recognized

Figure 5. Terrace sands (Ts) and gravels (Tg) truncating tilted Jurassic sandstones and shales (Jm) and overlain by pediment gravels (Pg) derived from the Colorado National Monument. View is northwest from CO-340 south of Fruita.

and briefly mentioned the terraces in the Redlands but chose not to include surficial deposits on his geologic map of the Grand Junction area. Tweto and others (1979) mapped the terraces throughout Grand Valley as Pinedale and Bull Lake age alluvium.

Terrace outwash associated with the Horsefly Peak Till occurs throughout the uplands of the Uncompahgre Plateau northwest of Horsefly Peak. Old outwash gravels occur at Columbine Pass, in the headwaters of Dry Creek and Roubideau Creek and in Cactus Park (Cater, 1965; Lohman, 1961). All these deposits are interpreted as remnants, perhaps reworked, of an outwash train associated with the Horsefly Peak Till. Their origin is discussed in more detail in the companion paper of this guidebook (Sinnock, this guidebook).

Howe and Cross (1906) first recognized the gravel deposits on the uplands of the Uncompahgre Plateau and thought they were outliers of the Horsefly Peak Till. Atwood and Mather (1932) agreed. Hunt (1969) interpreted the Horsefly Peak Till and associated outwash gravels as Miocene-age fluvial gravels. Richmond (1965) described the Bridgetimber, Bayfield and Oxford gravels of Atwood and Mather (1932) as evidence of very early glaciations in the San Juan Mountains. Marshall (1959), Williams (1964), and Tweto and others (1979) mapped them as Mancos Shale. Cater (1965) and Lohman (1961) interpret the gravels in Cactus Park as reworked Plio-Pleistocene gravels of the Gunnison River.

Figure 4. Terrace gravels lapping onto Dakota Sandstone (Kd) along the lower flank of the Uncompahgre Plateau near Grand Junction. Note pediments at the base of the Book Cliffs. View is northwest from SE ¼, Sec. 18, T.15N., R.1W.

Figure 6. Terrace gravels resting on Entrada Sandstone (Je) just south of Westwater Canyon. ℞kw is Triassic Kayenta and Wingate formations. View is northwest in NE¼, Sec. 36, T.21S., R.24E.

Terrace Genesis

The terraces between Ridgway and Fruita correlate with glacial episodes in the San Juan Mountains. The two older terraces and pediments are Bull Lake age, the two younger are Pinedale. Yeend (1969) maps and assigns identical ages to terraces and pediments along the Colorado River Valley upstream from De Beque Canyon. Local variations of glacial behavior make resulting terrace and pediment sequences difficult to correlate among the headwater regions of glacial valleys in the Southern Rocky Mountains, but those along the master streams are buffered from the effects of these variations and permit a glimpse at the nature of regional, fluvio-glacial events.

Homoclinal migration of master drainage inherited from pre-Bull Lake time (Sinnock, this guidebook) continued into the late Pleistocene. Episodic glacio-fluvial regime changes superposed their effects on this continuing landform evolution. The result created a situation ideal for preservation of terraces along the Uncompahgre River.

At the outbreak of late Pleistocene glaciation, the Uncompahgre River was at the present position of the highest terrace (see Figure 11, companion Sinnock paper). Thereupon commenced a sequence of events similar to those outlined by Richmond (1962) for terrace formation during glacial cycles.

As the climate cooled, precipitation in the highlands increased but did not yet form ice. Desert valleys remained dry, but master streams swelled and the rivers incised. As ice began to form in the highlands, frost-riving and other periglacial phenomena increased sediment production. Streams were required to carry greater loads and began to spread out as anastamosing channels and alluviate the valleys, forming the terrace deposits. Blocked by the 2° dip slope of the Uncompahgre Plateau to the southwest, the widening terraces spread to the northeast on low, pediment slopes graded to the river. This tended to block the river's return to its former position. The permeable gravels deposited in the wake of the shifting river tended to absorb enough of the river's flow to cause additional sediment to be dropped, nudging the river to continue migrating northeastward onto lowermost pediment slopes.

At glacial maxima, end moraines formed and a general equilibrium obtained whereby neither significant erosion nor alluviation occurred along the terraces, though both sediment load and runoff were at their greatest levels during the glacial maxima. The river maintained its position along the northeast edge of the newly formed outwash plain. During the retreating phases of glacial pulses, discharge decreased, exposing more sandbars. Loess deposits and sand dunes formed upon the terrace surfaces. At glacial minima, equilibrium between sediment supply and transport capacity again obtained but along a meandering stream with attendant slackwater areas which locally deposited finer grained fluvial sands upon the coarser terrace gravels. Major incision awaited readvance of the ice, which is consistent with the fact that the elevation difference between the merging lowest terrace and present floodplain is small even near the moraines. The merger of the low terrace with floodplain along the Uncompahgre River also may be due in part to retarded incision rates of the Gunnison River where it encounters the Precambrian surface in the middle part of its canyon along the plateau flank.

Incision attendant with glacial cycles lowered the floodplain and created the elevated terraces southwest of the river. Incision passed through the outwash gravels and into the underlying Mancos Shale. If the Dakota Sandstone were encountered during incision, the river shifted northeast along the resistant sandstone surface. However, perhaps by coincidence, the ratio of the width of the terraces to interterrace vertical separation is approximately equal to the cotangent of the angle of structural dip. Hence, incision during each episode returned the riverbed almost exactly to the level of the Dakota-Mancos contact.

Between Delta and Whitewater, remnants of all four terraces are found within the Gunnison Canyon, demonstrating that this canyon began forming before the first advance of late Pleistocene glaciers. Similar terrace deposits indicate pre-glacial incision along Horsethief–Ruby–Westwater Canyon of the Colorado River.

Terraces near Grand Junction tell a slightly different story of late-Pleistocene river wanderings. The Colorado River, in contrast to the Uncompahgre River, did not significantly change its geographic position in the Grand Junction area throughout the Pleistocene. It maintained its position and general elevation during early uplift of the Uncompahgre Plateau, but only its position during and after the final uplift phases. Another difference is that the Colorado River flowed (and flows) almost normal to strike, and sustained lateral migration upon a resistant stratigraphic horizon could not occur. Therefore, lateral movement of the river tended to be oscillatory rather than directional. The relations between the terraces and slip-off plain from Palisade to Fruita support this inference.

The higher terraces along this stretch are reduced to very small patches. Remnants of the higher terraces are restricted to a band about one mile wide south of the lowest terrace. Only the lowest terrace occupies significant area. It follows the river on the southeast between Palisade and Grand Junction, and on the southwest between Grand Junction and Fruita. Two levels of slip-off plain extend along the north side of the river as distinct belts, each about 2.5 mi wide. Although the upper one is highly dissected by small arroyos, its boundaries are clear. Thus, the slip-off slopes rather than the terraces form the broad expanse of late Pleistocene surfaces in the Grand Junction area.

This situation was caused by geographic oscillation of the Colorado River at the same time that the four broad terraces formed near Montrose as the Uncompahgre River migrated northeastward. The Colorado River deposited outwash on its valley floor during glacial advances and migrated northward onto the lower reaches of pediments below the Book Cliffs in a manner similar to that described for the Uncompahgre River. This forced the river northward as it emerged from De Beque Canyon. Because no stratigraphic surface disposed continued migration in a northward direction after alluviation ceased, the river returned to its former course during incision by sliding back toward the south, cannibalizing its own terrace deposits and shaving into the Mancos Shale. The net result is a suite of small, uncannibalized terrace patches south of the river and gentle, riverward sloping slip-off surfaces on Mancos Shale north of the river. Because incisional slip-off commenced from the northern edges of the terraces, elevations at the upper parts of the slip-off slopes match the terrace elevations south of the river. Current incision by the Colorado River has not completely cannibalized the lowest terrace, so a broad remnant remains northeast of the river. Earlier terraces were almost completely consumed, thus their widths are diminished to very narrow bands.

Near Montrose the second terrace level above the river is about one and one-half to two times as wide as the first. Near Grand Junction, the upper slip-off plain extends twice the distance from the Colorado River as the lower. This suggests that the second terrace near Grand Junction was originally about twice as wide as the first. Therefore, it is reasoned that the first Pinedale glacial advance was more intense than the second, an inference supported by the

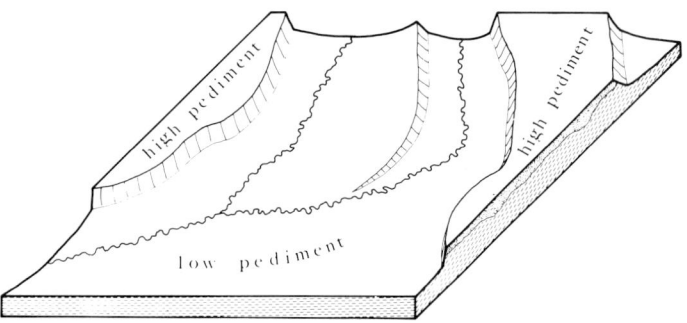

Figure 7. Schematic diagram demonstrating how scarp may separate parts of the same (low) pediment level and be as high as interpediment scarps separating pediments (high and low) of different ages.

relative sizes of the two Pinedale moraines in Ridgway Basin. Because the relationship among terrace widths is similar along both the Colorado River and Uncompahgre River, the relative intensity of separate Pinedale advances was probably regional, at least in the Southern Rocky Mountains.

PEDIMENTS

Four pediment levels occur northwest of the rivers in Grand Valley and are counterparts to the four valley terraces. Local differences in pediment elevations make precise correlations difficult. For example, pediments may form simultaneously along a stream and one of its tributaries (fig. 7). If pedimentation consumes the uplands between the streams, separate pediments graded to the same level will meet along a divide separating the two streams. If one stream is closer to the divide than the other, an interpediment scarp will separate the two correlative pediments. Such a scarp may be almost as high as one which separates pediments formed during two separate epochs. Conversely, two pediments of different ages may have the same general elevation. Notwithstanding, the overall association of four major pediment levels with the four terrace levels is evident. The lowest and still active pediment merges locally with the lowest terrace and floodplain. Higher pediment surfaces merge with the elevations of corresponding terraces (fig. 8).

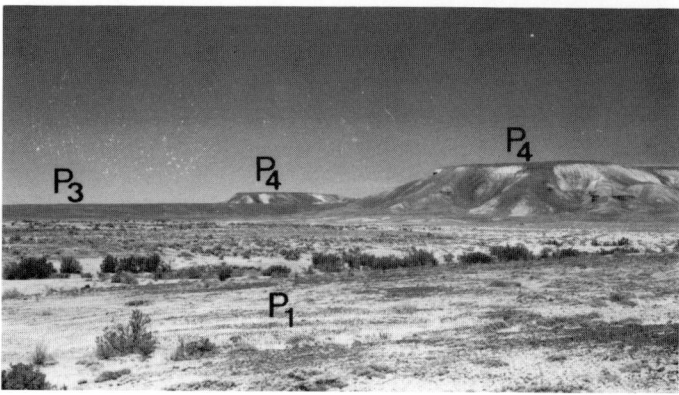

Figure 9. Pediments between Delta and Whitewater; dark layer of basalt gravel caps higher pediments. Lower pediment (P_1) has no gravel cap. View is northwest from NE ¼, Sec. 36, T.4S., R.97W.

From Delta to Colona the cliffs along the northeastern side of Uncompahgre River Valley are capped by Mesozoic shales and sandstones and possess no source rocks amenable to survival as pediment gravel deposits. Therefore, pediment gravel veneers are thin or absent and Mancos Shale generally forms the pediment surfaces. Remnants of older pediments are reduced to narrow ridge crests, many of which have been eroded below their original levels, yielding extensive badland terrain devoid of old pediment surfaces. The lowest pediment near Montrose grades to the floodplain or lowest terrace of the Uncompahgre River and creates an extensive lowland known as East Mesa. At the south end of Grand Valley near Colona, a few high-level pediments are well preserved where they are capped with a protecting gravel derived from volcanic rocks of Cimarron Ridge.

Between Delta and Grand Junction the upper pediments slope toward the river from the southern flank of Grand Mesa as wide, smooth, concave surfaces (figs. 9, 10). Pediment surfaces are commonly capped with a layer of permeable gravels composed of poorly sorted clay to boulder-sized deposits about 0 to 40 ft thick. Basalt clasts derived from Grand Mesa are sub-angular to well-rounded and range from about one inch to three feet in diameter. Pediments in Grand Valley are generally best preserved where

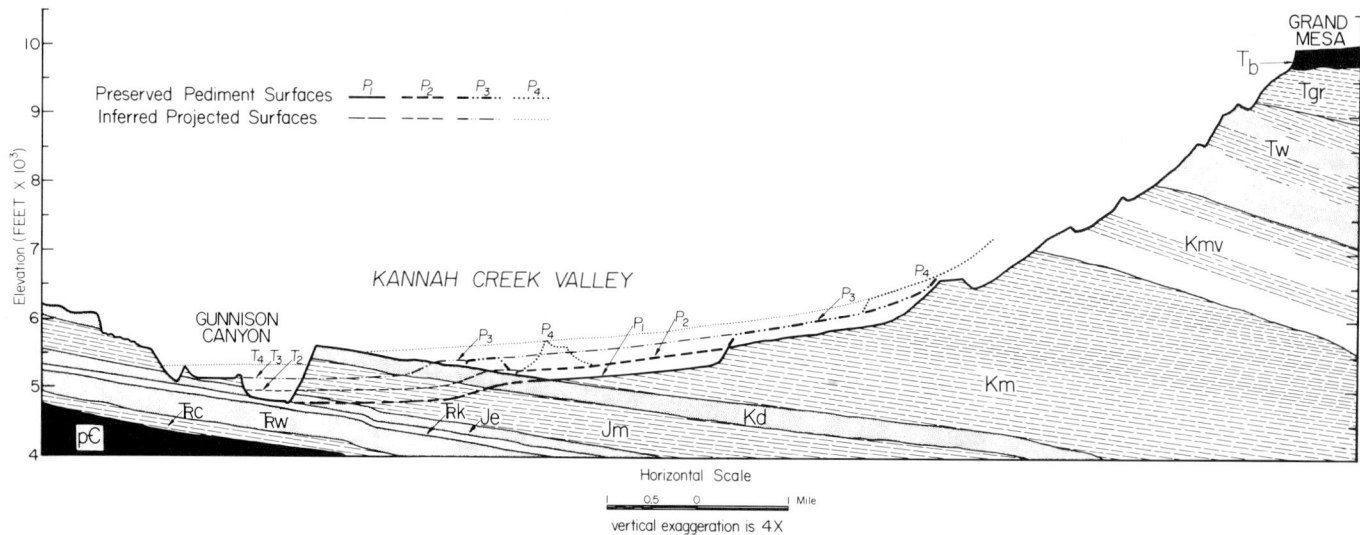

Figure 8. Projected pediment profiles between Delta and Whitewater. Bedrock units include p₵ Precambrian undifferentiated, ℞c Chinle, ℞w Wingate, ℞k Kayenta, Je Entrada, Jm Morrison, Kd Dakota, Km Mancos, Kmv Mesaverde, Tw Wasatch, Tgr Green River, and Tb Tertiary basalts.

Figure 10. Pediments at the base of Grand Mesa. View is north from NW ¼, Sec. 23, T.3S., R.2E.

such permeable, thick deposits mantle their surfaces, causing local inversions of topography during successive periods of pedimentation.

The lowest pediment possesses no basalt-gravel cover. It forms a strike valley nestled at the contact between the Dakota Sandstone and Mancos Shale and grades topographically and stratigraphically upward into the lower slopes of Grand Mesa. The strike valley is two to three miles northeast of, parallel to, and perched 200 to 300 ft above the Gunnison River where it is entrenched into the flank of the Uncompahgre Plateau. Wells, Beaver, Deer, and Kannah creeks drain the lower pediment along short, steep ravines that breach the canyon wall. A small cuesta formed by the Ferron Sandstone Member of the Mancos Shale rises 50 ft above the surrounding pediment, bifurcating it into a pair of parallel, strike valleys graded to the same level. Near Delta and Whitewater, the lower pediment merges along strike with the Gunnison floodplain. Northwest of Kannah Creek, the pediments swing around the Lands End promontory of Grand Mesa, eventually grading toward terraces along the southeast side of the Colorado River downstream from De Beque Canyon.

Northwest of the river, pediments occur between the Book Cliffs and the slip-off plain at Grand Junction and are poorly preserved. Badlands in Mancos Shale dominate the landscape. The badlands and dissected pediments commence abruptly at the base of the Book Cliffs and grade to the slip-off slope where they are equally abruptly truncated at their lower ends. For about five to eight miles northeast from Mt. Garfield, the Book Cliffs are very smooth and conspicuously devoid of deep serration by obsequent streams. Incision by the streams increases to the northwest, together with better preservation of higher pediments. Northeast of Fruita, the upper pediments are well preserved, although extensive badland areas still occur (fig. 4). This pattern continues essentially unchanged as the valley and bounding Book Cliffs swing to the southwest around the northwestern end of Uncompahgre Plateau and out of the study area. The pediment terrain drains south to the river along ephemeral streams which breach the rim of Westwater Canyon, a situation analogous to that between Whitewater and Delta.

The pediments in Grand Valley have not been so clearly recognized as distinct landforms as have the terraces. Because they generally are not used for irrigated row crops, soils mapping in Grand Valley has not included much of the pedimented terrain. Yeend (1969) concluded that pediments west of Grand Mesa were either terraces or low lying moraines. Tweto and others (1979) map the pediments as pre-Bull Lake surficial deposits of unspecified origin.

Pediment Genesis

Pediments flanking Grand Mesa indicate an alluviation-incision cycle similar to that of the terraces. Grand Mesa was covered by an ice carapace during four late Pleistocene events correlated with two Bull Lake and two Pinedale episodes (Yeend, 1969). Meltwater flowed from Grand Mesa to the Gunnison River along many pedimented washes in Grand Valley. Clasts from the basalt cap of Grand Mesa were mixed with meltwater and detritus from underlying shales and sandstones to form a muddy slurry of clays, sand, gravel, and large basalt boulders. This slurry oozed down the slopes of Grand Mesa and onto the pediments as pro-glacial mudflows forming the deposits that mantle all but the lowest pediment. Local depressions on the pediment surfaces suggest that ice blocks were incorporated in the slowly moving slurries, which upon melting created small kettle-like depressions.

During both the major rivers' incisional phase and interglacial times, the lowest pediment eroded headward along the washes graded to the rivers. Because pediment development occurred during inter-glacial conditions, no large mudflow deposits were supplied to the headward-expanding pediments. During subsequent glacial conditions, the mudflow deposits accumulated upon the pedimented surfaces. This accounts for the absence of mudflow deposits on the lowest pediment surface which is veneered only with sand and a very thin layer of small broken basalt cobbles derived from the mudflow deposits on older pediments.

Near Montrose and Grand Junction, no mudflow deposits comparable to those below Grand Mesa occur on the upper pediments because no glaciers or resistant caprocks existed in headwater regions. In these regions, pedimentation probably has occurred continuously throughout the late Pleistocene and perhaps earlier. Incisional episodes along the master streams formed pediment knickpoints that migrated headward by processes described by Bryan (1932, 1940). Thus, the graded pediment levels simultaneously migrated headward. This generally creates a situation whereby older pediments occur near the cliffs and younger pediments near the master stream.

CONCLUSION

A distinct set of landforms composed of river terraces and cliff-flanking pediments characterizes the floor of Grand Valley from Colona to Fruita. The terraces form four separate levels that generally rise toward the lower slopes of the Uncompahgre Plateau, whereas the correlative four pediments are dispersed throughout the lowlands at the base of the Book Cliffs, Grand Mesa, Black Canyon uplift and Cimarron Ridge. The four levels correspond, from oldest to youngest, to two separate glacial advances during each of Bull Lake and Pinedale times. The degree of preservation of the terrace and pediment forms is directly related to the infiltration capacity of the gravels veneering their surfaces. When the gravels are at least in part derived from headwater igneous or metamorphic terrain, the resulting deposits predispose the forms to preservation, contrary to those surfaces veneered with thin gravels derived from sedimentary rocks. The general northeastward migration of the landform assemblage (terraces, river, pediments, and cliffs from southwest to northeast) contributed to conditions which facilitated the formation and preservation of the four terraces and associated pediments.

REFERENCES

Atwood, W. W., 1915, Eocene glacial deposits in southwestern Colorado: U.S. Geological Survey Professional Paper 95, p. 13–25.

Atwood, W. W. and K. F. Mather, 1932, Physiography and Quaternary Geology of the San Juan Mountains, Colorado: U.S. Geological Survey Professional Paper 166, 176 p.

Blackwelder, E., 1915, Post-Cretaceous history of the mountains of central western Wyoming: Journal of Geology, v. 25, p. 97–117, 193–217, 307–340.

———, 1931, Pleistocene glaciation in the Sierra Nevada and Basin and Ranges: Geological Society of America Bulletin, v. 42, p. 865–922.

Bryan, K., 1932, Pediments developed in basins with through drainage: Geological Society of America Bulletin, v. 43, p. 128–129.

———, 1940, The retreat of slopes: Annual Association of American Geographers, v. 30, p. 254–268.

Cater, F. W., Jr., 1966, Age of the Uncompahgre Uplift and Unaweep Canyon, west-central Colorado: U.S. Geological Survey Professional Paper 550-C, p. C86–C92.

Dalrymple, G. B., A. Cox, and R. R. Doell, 1965, Potassium-argon age and paleomagnetism of the Bishop Tuff, California: Geological Society of America Bulletin, v. 76, p. 665–674.

Dickinson, R. G., 1965a, Geologic map of the Cerro Summit quadrangle, Montrose County, Colorado: U.S. Geological Survey Geologic Quadrangle Map GQ-486.

———, 1965b, Landslide origin of the type Cerro Till, southwestern Colorado: U.S. Geological Survey Paper 525-C, p. C147–C151.

Hills, R. C., 1884, Extinct glaciers of the San Juan Mountains, Colorado: American Journal of Science, 3rd Series, v. 27, p. 391–396.

Holmes, G. W. and J. H. Moss, 1955, Pleistocene geology of the southwestern Wind River Mountains, Wyoming: Geological Society of America Bulletin, v. 66, p. 629–654.

Howe, E. and W. Cross, 1906, Glacial phenomena of the San Juan Mountains, Colorado: Geological Society of America Bulletin, v. 17, p. 251–274.

Hunt, C. B., 1969, Geologic history of the Colorado River, *in* The Colorado river region and John Wesley Powell: U.S. Geological Survey Professional Paper 669-C, p. C59–C130.

Knobel, E. W., R. K. Dansdill, and M. L. Richardson, 1955, Soil Survey of the Grand Junction area, Colorado: U.S. Department of Agriculture, series 1940, no. 19, 118 p.

Lohman, S. W., 1961, Abandonment of the Unaweep Canyon, Mesa County, Colorado, by capture of the Gunnison and Colorado rivers: U.S. Geological Survey Professional Paper 424-B, p. B144–B146.

———, 1965, Geology and artesian water supply Grand Junction area, Colorado: U.S. Geological Survey Professional Paper 451, 149 p.

Marshall, C. H., 1959, Photogeologic map of the Norwood-1 quadrangle, Montrose and Ouray counties, Colorado: U.S. Geological Survey Miscellaneous Investigations Map I-283.

Mather, K. F. and S. A. Wengerd, 1965, Pleistocene age of the "Eocene" Ridgway Till, Colorado: Geological Society of America Bulletin, v. 76, p. 1401–1408.

Nelson, J. W. and L. A. Kolbe, 1910, Soil map of the Uncompahgre Valley, Colorado: U.S. Department of Agriculture, Bureau of Soils.

Richmond, G. M., 1948, Modification of Blackwelder's sequence of Pleistocene glaciation in the Wind River Mountains, Wyoming (abs.): Geological Society of America Bulletin, v. 59, p. 1400–1401.

———, 1954, Modification of the glacial chronology of the San Juan Mountains, Colorado: Science, v. 119, p. 177.

———, 1962, Quaternary stratigraphy of the La Sal Mountains, Utah: U.S. Geological Survey Professional Paper 324, 135 p.

Sinnock, S., 1978, Geomorphology of the Uncompahgre Plateau and Grand Valley, western Colorado, USA (Ph.D. dissertation): W. Lafayette, Indiana, Purdue University, 201 p.

Tweto, O. and others, 1979, Geologic map of Colorado: U.S. Geological Survey Map, Denver, Colorado.

Williams, P. L., 1964, Geology, structure, and uranium deposits of the Moab quadrangle, Colorado and Utah: U.S. Geological Survey Miscellaneous Investigations Map I-360.

Yeend, W. E., 1969, Quaternary geology of the Grand and Battlement Mesas area, Colorado: U.S. Geological Survey Professional Paper 617, 50 p.

PLEISTOCENE SURFICIAL DEPOSITS OF THE GRAND MESA AREA, COLORADO

REX D. COLE
Multi Mineral Corporation
715 Horizon Drive
Grand Junction, Colorado 81501

and

JOHN L. SEXTON
Department of Geosciences
Purdue University
West Lafayette, Indiana 47907

INTRODUCTION

Grand Mesa, with an average surface elevation of about 3050 m, is a basalt-capped plateau that forms one of the most prominent physiographic features in west-central Colorado (fig. 1). Basalt flows capping Grand Mesa have protected the underlying weaker sedimentary rocks from erosion. Progressive erosion of Grand Mesa since the outpouring of basalt 10 million years ago (K/Ar date of 9.7 ± 0.5; Marvin and others, 1966) has produced an impressive array of pediments, alluvial fans, glacial outwash fans, landslides, and colluvial deposits which now flank the mesa on all sides.

The Grand Mesa area has been a topic of study since the Hayden Surveys (Hayden, 1876). Most recent studies have focused on the glacial geology of the area (Henderson, 1923; Nygren, 1935; Retzer, 1954; Yeend, 1969). Sinnock (1978; this guidebook) addressed the geomorphology of the western front of Grand Mesa in his study of the Uncompahgre Plateau and Grand Valley. General treatment of the geology of Grand Mesa is given by Young and Young (1968, 1977). Detailed mapping of parts of the Grand Mesa area has been done by Yeend (1969), Donnell and Yeend (1968a, b, c, d, e), Yeend and Donnell (1968), Hail (1972a, 1972b), and Sinnock (1978).

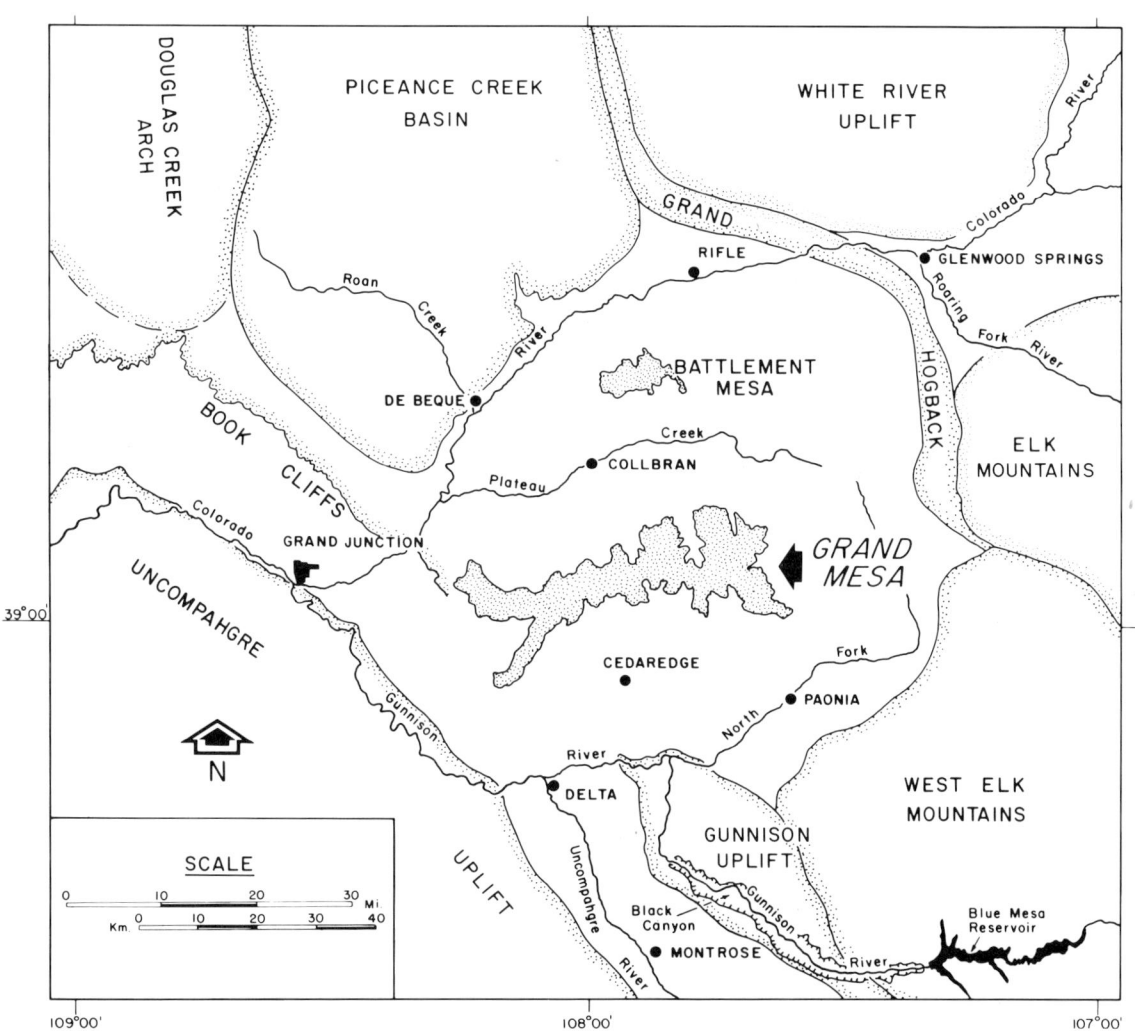

Figure 1. Index map of western Colorado showing positions of Grand Mesa and other physiographic features.

In this paper we briefly address the general geology of the Grand Mesa area, and then we provide a more detailed description of the Pleistocene surficial deposits. Our intent is to illustrate the complexity and diversity of the surficial deposits, and to bring together for the first time an overview of the depositional processes that were active during their formation.

GEOLOGIC SUMMARY

Grand Mesa is a conspicuous landform visible from many parts of western Colorado. It is separated from adjacent landforms, such as the Book Cliffs, Uncompahgre uplift, Gunnison uplift, West Elk Mountains, Huntsman Hills and Battlement Mesa by the Colorado River, the Gunnison River, North Fork of the Gunnison River, Muddy Creek and Plateau Creek (fig. 1). The Mesa is situated in the southern Piceance Creek basin. Several smaller structural flexures, such as the Montrose syncline, the axial extension of the Gunnison uplift, and the West Elk Mountain uplift, are also present in the area. Several small-displacement normal faults are also present.

The oldest rocks in the area (fig. 2) are the sandstones and variegated shales of the Morrison Formation (Jurassic). The Morrison is overlain by 1,500 to 2,500 m of drab-colored Upper Cretaceous shale, sandstone and coal that comprise the Dakota Sandstone, Mancos Shale and Mesaverde Formation (and equivalents). The Mesaverde and Mancos make up most of the stratigraphic section visible on the west and south slopes of Grand Mesa. Cretaceous rocks are overlain by a variable thickness of Tertiary sandstone, shale, marlstone, lean oil shale and claystone that make up the Wasatch Formation (Paleocene-Eocene), Green River Formation (Eocene), Uinta Formation (Eocene) and the North Park Formation (Miocene).

Tertiary sedimentary rocks are overlain by up to 240 m of basalt flows and intercalated tuff, baked soil horizons, and volcanic conglomerate. The Grand Mesa basalt is part of the bimodal suite of late Cenozoic alkali basalts that are scattered throughout northwestern Colorado (Larson and others, 1975). The area of basalt extrusion was probably near the east end of the Grand Mesa in an area of dikes and small plugs. As many as 20 basalt layers may be present; individual flows range in thickness from 15 to 60 m. The quantity of basalt that was released is unknown. Yeend (1969) speculates that the flood lavas extended from the vent area outward over much of southern Piceance Creek basin and over the northern part of the Uncompahgre uplift. Young and Young (1968) contend, however, that the original area of basalt coverage was limited, more or less, to the basalt's present-day extent. Their hypothesis is that basalt eruption occurred near or within Miocene stream valleys with the subsequent flows being confined to the

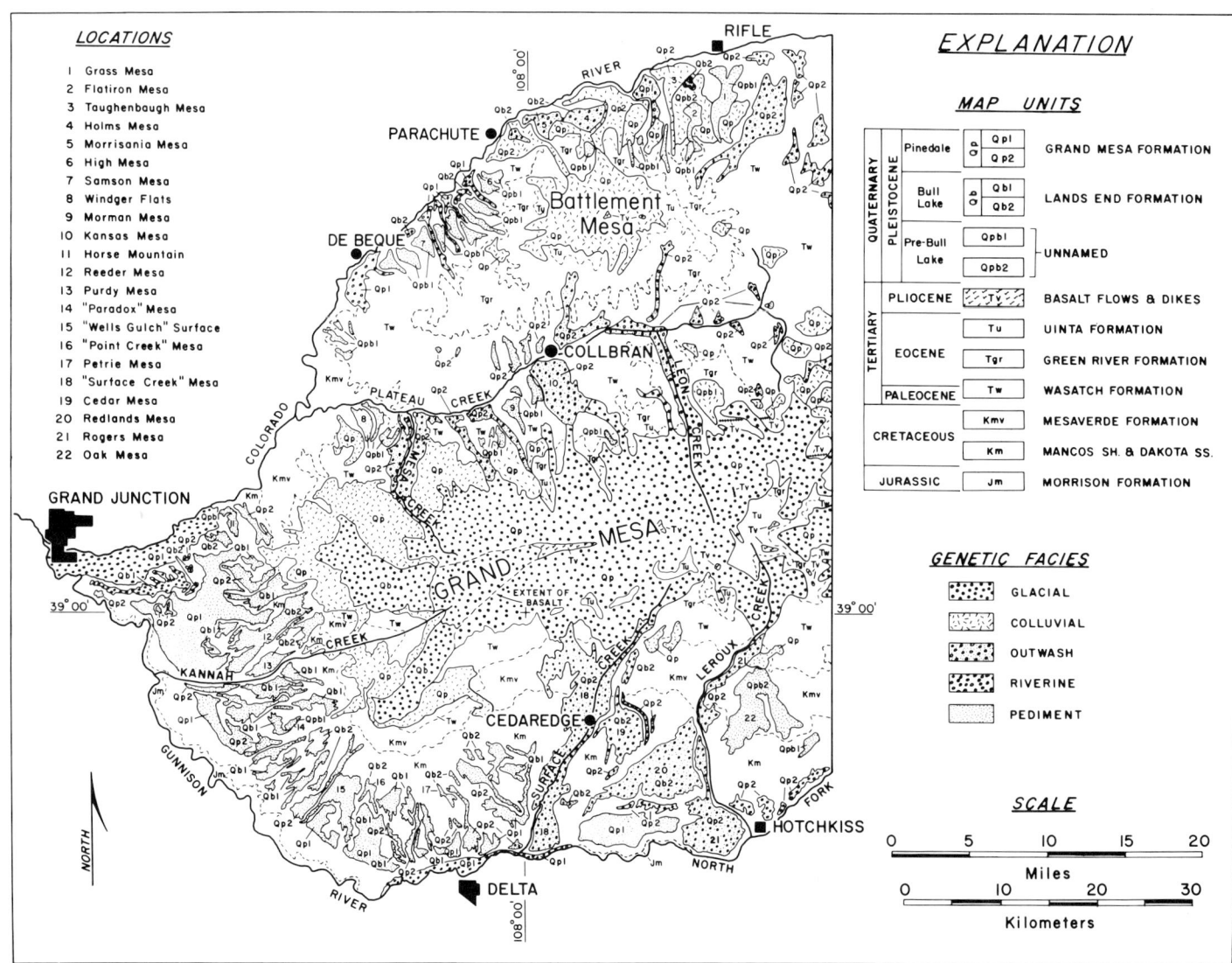

Figure 2. Geologic map of Grand Mesa area. Compiled from Yeend (1969), Sinnock (1978), Hail (1972a, 1972b) and unpublished mapping.

valleys. This could explain the "Y" shaped aerial extent of the basalt that makes up the western prongs of Grand Mesa (fig. 1).

The most recent deposits in the Grand Mesa area are Pleistocene tills, alluvial gravels, pediment gravels, and colluvial deposits. In the northern half of the area (Yeend, 1969), the bulk of these deposits have been grouped into either the Lands End Formation (Bull Lake) or the Grand Mesa Formation (Pinedale). The remainder of this paper will address these deposits more fully.

PLEISTOCENE SURFICIAL DEPOSITS

At the time of Grand Mesa volcanism, it is likely that much of the uplift of the Colorado Plateau region had not yet occurred (Young and Young, 1968; Yeend, 1969; Sinnock, 1978). As uplift did occur, progressive incision by the ancestral Colorado, Gunnison and Uncompahgre rivers and their tributaries produced an ever-changing panorama of erosional, transportational and depositional surfaces. Some of the younger surfaces are nearly intact while many of the older ones are badly dissected and poorly preserved.

Classification

Yeend (1969) has provided a detailed classification of the various surficial deposits exposed from the crest of Grand Mesa north to the Colorado River. This classification (fig. 3) depicts three major episodes of gravel and till deposition, each of which was produced by a late-Pleistocene glacial event: Pinedale, Bull Lake or pre-Bull Lake. Yeend (1969) further classifies the surficial deposits on the basis of depositional processes into three facies: glacial, alluvial and colluvial. The alluvial facies is further subdivided into either terrace or pediment types. All of the facies of Pinedale age are collectively designated the Grand Mesa Formation, while all facies of Bull Lake age are designated as Lands End Formation. Pre-Bull Lake deposits are divided on the basis of suspected process; however, Yeend (1969) did not designate a formal stratigraphic name.

Sinnock (1978) provides a classification of the various surficial deposits exposed on the western and southwestern flanks of Grand Mesa. Four major levels of terraces and pediments are designated. Sinnock (1978) assigns a Pinedale age to the two lowest levels of terraces and pediments, a Bull Lake age to the upper two levels.

Hail (1972a, 1972b), in his mapping of the Cedaredge and Hotchkiss areas on the southern flank of Grand Mesa, recognized three major levels of fan and pediment gravels and one sheet of glacial till (fig. 3). He assigned a pre-Bull Lake age to the highest gravel-covered surfaces, and Bull Lake and Pinedale ages to the lower two levels, respectively. Hail (1972a, 1972b) does not directly correlate the three major levels of fan and pediment gravel with those of Yeend (1969); however, he does (1972a) equate the glacial drift with the lower till horizon of the Grand Mesa Formation.

In Figure 2 we have summarized the mapping of surficial deposits by Yeend (1969), Sinnock (1978) and Hail (1972a, 1972b). The classification of the various units is shown on Figure 3. Like previous workers, we make the initial subdivision on the basis of age, and recognize that at least six major periods (elevational levels) of gravel deposition are preserved on the flanks of Grand Mesa and Battlement Mesa. Following subdivision by age, we further classify the deposits on the basis of suspected genesis into five dominant subtypes: glacial (till and drift), outwash, pediment, riverine, and colluvial.

For the most part, our genetic subdivision of surficial deposits is similar to that of Yeend (1969), with one exception. We have subdivided Yeend's (1969) alluvial facies into riverine-type gravels and outwash-type gravels. Both types tend to be well sorted; however, outwash gravels have clasts of local provenance, whereas riverine gravels have clasts of both local and distant provenance.

Because of the similarity in position, gravel composition and depositional characteristics of gravel-veneered surfaces on the west and south flanks of Grand Mesa and those mapped and classified by Yeend (1969) to the north, we have applied the usage of the

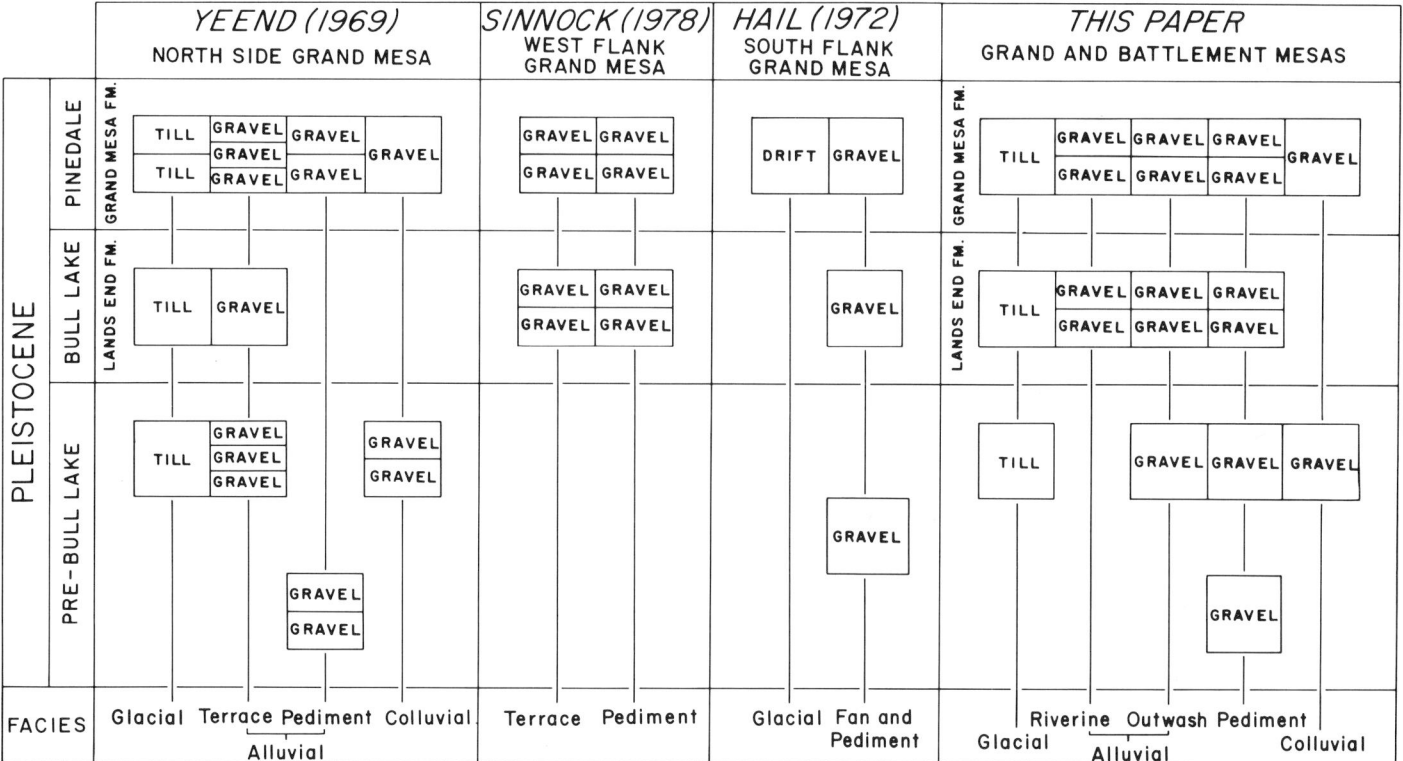

Figure 3. Classification of surficial deposits in the Grand Mesa area.

Grand Mesa and Lands End Formations to all Pinedale-aged and Bull Lake-aged deposits in the Grand Mesa area. Older surficial deposits are not designated by a formal stratigraphic name.

Description of Deposits

The five genetic types of surficial deposits (fig. 3) reflect the major depositional processes responsible for the transportation and deposition of sediment. In Figure 2, each depositional surface is designated according to its most dominant sediment type. It is certainly recognized that a given surface may have been formed by one or more transportational/depositional process. Indeed, this is the rule rather than the exception.

Glacial Deposits

Yeend (1969) recognized four separate horizons of glacial till, two of Pinedale age, one of Bull Lake age, and one of pre-Bull Lake age (fig. 3). The tills are typically poorly sorted and have weak stratification (fig. 4). The clasts are dominated by basalt, and range in size from pebbles to boulders with a matrix of sand and silt. Till horizons are generally less than 30 m thick; however, Yeend (1969) reports a 41-m thick, pre-Bull Lake till sequence at a location on the east end of Grand Mesa. The tills of the Grand Mesa and Lands End Formations are generally capped by thin soil horizons, 0.5 to 1.0 m thick. Inner-till soils are also reported.

The most extensive tills are those of the Grand Mesa Formation (fig. 2), covering most of the top of Grand Mesa, the landslide bench, and extending down various stream valleys onto the flanks of Grand Mesa. Yeend (1969) mapped till down to an elevation of 1,646 m in the vicinity of Plateau Creek. This low elevation is unusual for the Rocky Mountain area and several subsequent workers (e.g., Sinnock, 1978) have challenged the concept. In actuality, the lower limit of Pinedale till deposition is difficult to place because clearly defined terminal and recessional moraines are not present, and because the tills have been locally reworked into outwash or colluvial deposits. In Figure 2, the lower limit of Pinedale till occurrence is placed at about 2,000 m on the north side of Grand Mesa, and at about 2,300 m on the south side (Hail, 1972a, 1972b).

The Bull Lake till of the Lands End Formation is present over most of the western half of Grand Mesa; however, it is exposed at the surface only on the two western prongs of the Mesa. Elsewhere it is buried by till of the Grand Mesa Formation. Yeend (1969) reports that Bull Lake till was deposited down to an elevation of 1,768 m on the north flank of Grand Mesa. Again, this is difficult to verify because of the lack of terminal moraines and the lateral gradation of till into outwash and colluvial gravels.

The pre-Bull Lake till is present at a single location near Chalk Mountain on the eastern end of Grand Mesa at an elevation of more than 3,050 m (Yeend, 1969). This small exposure is not shown on Figure 2.

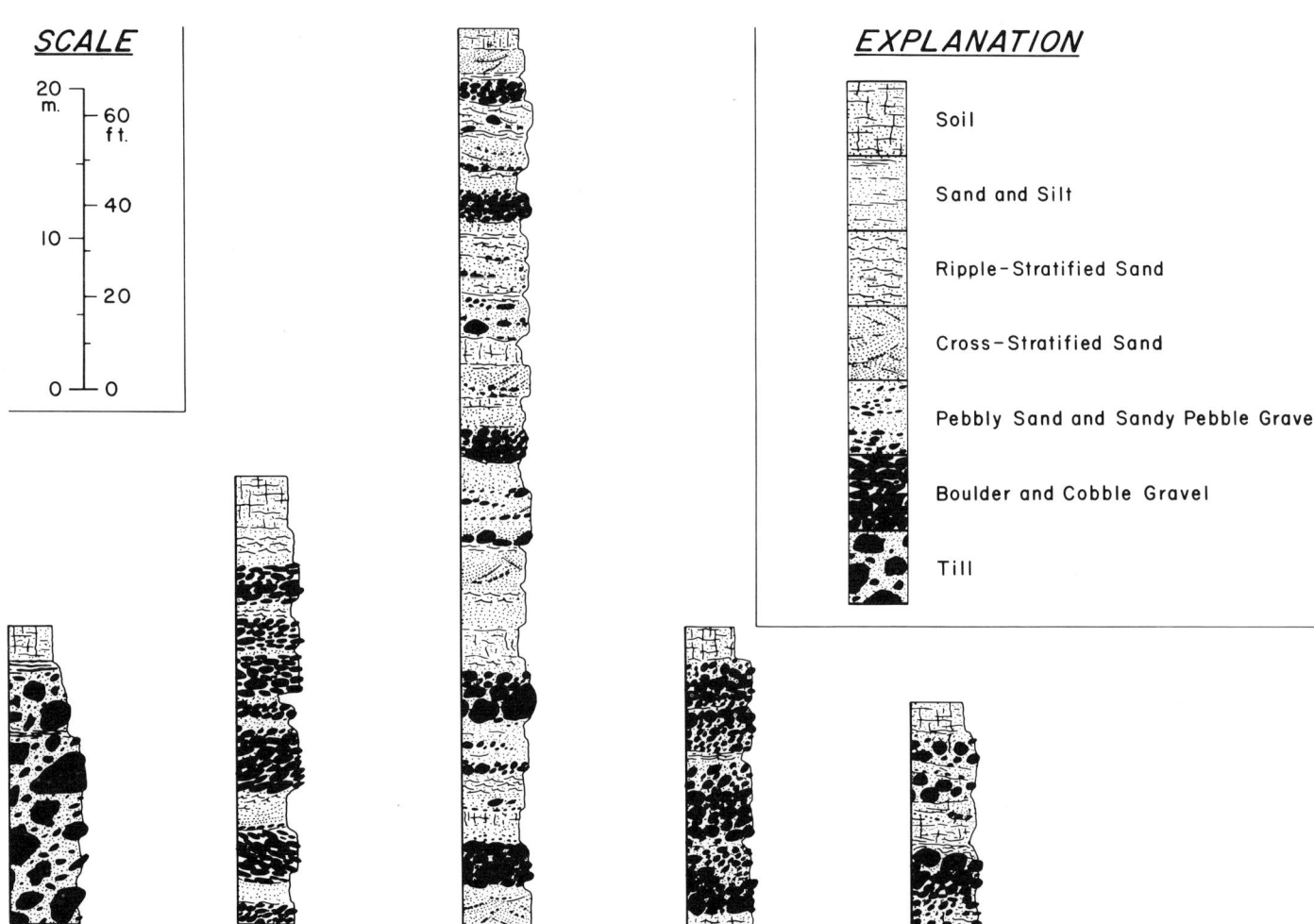

Figure 4. Sedimentologic characterization of surficial deposits in the Grand Mesa area.

Riverine Deposits

Pleistocene alluvial gravels associated with the major rivers lateral to Grand Mesa and Battlement Mesa are designated as riverine facies. As mentioned in a previous section, this term is applied to well-sorted sands and gravels which have clasts of mixed provenance, as compared to outwash and pediment gravels which have clasts of local provenance.

Riverine deposits occur in four distinct levels: two of Pinedale age, and two of Bull Lake age (fig. 3). The various levels are conspicuous near Delta and Grand Junction (fig. 2) where they form well-preserved terraces lateral to the Gunnison and Colorado rivers. Riverine gravels are generally 10 to 25 m thick and are comprised of alternating beds of well-sorted, imbricated pebble and cobble gravel, and cross-stratified and ripple-stratified sand and silt (fig. 4). The highest Bull Lake riverine terraces are generally about 170 m above local baselevel, while the lowest Pinedale terraces are usually less than 20 m above baselevel. The stratification sequences (fig. 4) of riverine deposits suggest deposition in a meandering fluvial environment.

Outwash Deposits

Outwash deposits formed by glacial meltwaters are common on both the north and south sides of Grand Mesa and also on the north and south flanks of Battlement Mesa. Typically, they are found in close proximity to the modern-day streams (Leroux, Surface, Mesa, and Leon Creeks). Outwash surfaces have the largest dimensions of all the surfaces exposed in the study area. For example, the Pinedale outwash surface associated with the Surface Creek drainage system is nearly 27 km long and has a surface area of about 80 km².

The longitudinal profiles of the more prominent outwash and pediment surfaces flanking Grand Mesa and Battlement Mesa are shown on Figure 5. The major Pinedale outwash surfaces on the south side of Grand Mesa are Rodgers Mesa (fig. 5 f) and "Surface Creek" Mesa (fig. 5 e), whereas on the north side, the major surfaces are in the Mesa Creek (fig. 5 c) and Leon Creek drainages (fig. 2). Depositional gradients for these surfaces average about 90 m/km and the distal portions of the surfaces project about 70 m above the present-day baselevel (Gunnison River, North Fork of Gunnison River, and Plateau Creek). Bull Lake outwash surfaces, such as Redlands Mesa (fig. 5 f) and Cedar Mesa (fig. 5 e), have depositional slopes averaging 135 m/km, and project to an elevation 340 m above local baselevel.

The outwash deposits are comprised of gravel, sand and silt, and range in thickness from 15 to 60 m. On the south side of Grand Mesa, the pebbles, cobbles and boulders are predominantly basalt with rare sandstone and mudrock, whereas on the north side, clasts of basalt, sandstone and marlstone are more equally abundant. Statification of the outwash sediment is generally quite striking (fig. 4), and is strongly suggestive of deposition in a braided-river environment. Gravel horizons representative of channel-bar deposition are interbedded with channel-fill cross-stratified sand, pebbly sand, and coarse silt. Cross-stratification is dominated by high-angle, medium-scale planar and trough types. Ripple-stratified sand and silt are locally common, including climbing ripples. For the most part, the stratification and textural sequences are similar

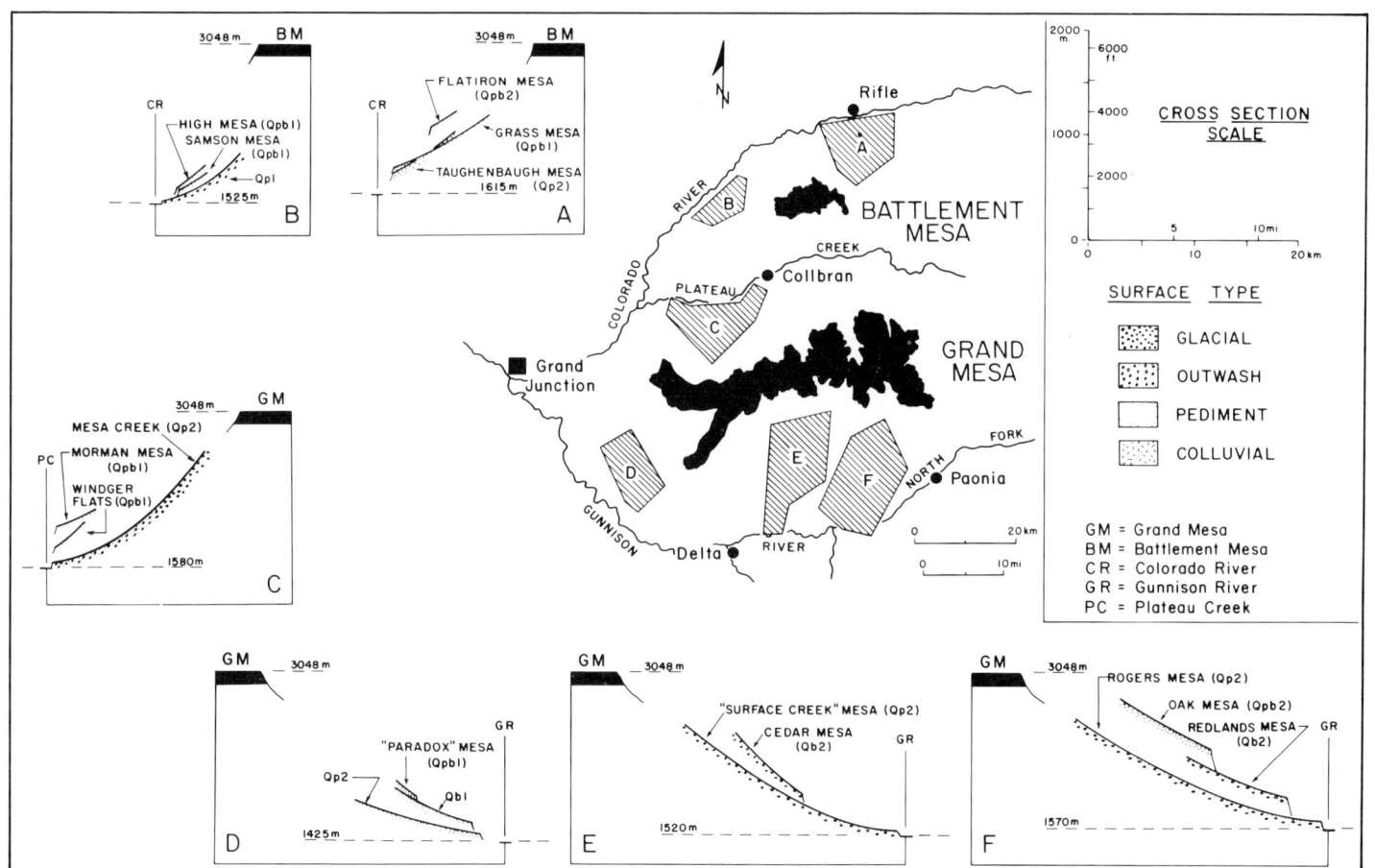

Figure 5. Topographic profiles of pediment, outwash and colluvial surfaces flanking Grand Mesa and Battlement Mesa.

to the "Donjek type" braided river deposits described by Miall (1977) from the Yukon Territory, Canada.

Clast size increases proportionally upslope in all of the outwash gravels studied. In the most proximal portions, basalt clasts as large as 5 m in diameter have been observed. On the distal ends of the outwash surfaces, maximum clast size rarely exceeds 0.5 m. At these locations, the outwash sequence commonly rests unconformably upon well-sorted, well-stratified, imbricated riverine gravels. This suggests that the outwash detritus prograded outward from the mountain front onto the alluvial plains of the major rivers.

Pediment Deposits

Pedimentation during the Pleistocene and possibly Pliocene produced a distinctive array of gravel-veneered surfaces on the western flanks of both Grand Mesa and Battlement Mesa (fig. 2). These surfaces are numerous and conspicuous in the area between Delta and Grand Junction, and between Parachute and DeBeque. For the most part, the pediments formed only on weak Mancos Shale or Wasatch Formation.

Six levels of pediments are present (fig. 3). The oldest surficial deposits in the study area, Oak Mesa near Hotchkiss (fig. 5 f), and Flatiron Mesa near Rifle (fig. 5 a), are thought to have formed by pedimentation. Oak and Flatiron Mesas are clearly pre-Bull Lake in age and may be as old as Pliocene. Their distal ends project to an elevation about 400 m above present-day baselevel. Younger, pre-Bull Lake pediments have also been recognized (Yeend, 1969). These surfaces are most abundant northwest of Battlement Mesa (e.g., High Mesa and Sampson Mesa (fig. 5 b)). They project to an elevation about 160 m above present-day baselevel.

Two levels of Bull Lake pediments and two levels of Pinedale pediments are present between Delta and Grand Junction (Sinnock, 1978). The Pinedale pediments generally project to an elevation 20 to 60 m above local baselevel, while the Bull Lake pediments project to between 150 and 250 m.

Sediment deposited on the pediment surfaces rarely exceeds 20 m in thickness, and is dominated by pebble- to boulder-sized gravel clasts composed predominantly of basalt, sandstone and marlstone. Gravel clasts are generally poorly sorted and commonly are partially supported by a sand matrix (fig. 4). Stratification is weakly developed, and where present, generally occurs as graded and reverse-graded bedding. These sedimentologic characteristics suggest that the dominant depositional agents accompanying pedimentation were mudflows and debris flows with some local reworking by sluggish streams. Sinnock (1978) noted "kettle-like" depressions on some pediment surfaces flanking the west side of Grand Mesa, suggesting that glacial ice blocks were possibly rafted to low elevations (1,650 to 2,100 m) during deposition of sediment on the pediment surfaces.

Colluvial Deposits

Colluvial deposits are common high on the flanks of Grand Mesa (beneath the basalt cap), and make up nearly all of the top of Battlement Mesa (fig. 2). The majority of these deposits are thought to be of Pinedale age, although several pre-Bull Lake colluvial surfaces have been mapped near Vega Reservoir (Yeend, 1969). On the north slope of Battlement Mesa, mudflows and debris flows have moved downslope from the solifluction mantle capping the mesa, over pre-existing pediment and outwash fans and surfaces, and onto riverine gravels of the Colorado River. Examples of this situation are Taughenbaugh, Holms, and Morrisania Mesas (fig. 2). The gravels beneath the Pinedale colluvial deposits are usually Bull Lake in age. This explains why surfaces like Taughenbaugh Mesa project to a higher elevation above local baselevel (fig. 5 a) than would ordinarily be expected for Pinedale surfaces.

Colluvial deposits are quite variable in thickness, ranging from more than 100 m in local pockets on the landslide bench of Grand Mesa to 10 to 20 m on the distal portions of fan-shaped mudflows. Hetergeneous clast compositions and textures prevail, although well-stratified sands and gravels may be locally common. Dominant processes appear to have been landsliding and slumping high on Grand and Battlement Mesas, and dominantly mudflows and debris flows at lower elevations. Solifluction was very active on the crest of Battlement Mesa during all glacial periods, but most noticeably during Pinedale time.

ACKNOWLEDGMENTS

We wish to thank R. G. Young and J. D. Powell for reading the manuscript and offering suggestions for its improvement. C. Lepp was very helpful in compiling data for this paper. S. Rex typed the manuscript, and we thank her for this assistance.

REFERENCES

Donnell, J. R. and Yeend, W. E., 1968a, Geologic map of the North Mamm Peak Quadrangle, Garfield County, Colorado: U.S. Geological Survey Open-File Map.

———, 1968b, Geologic map of the South Mamm Peak Quadrangle, Garfield and Mesa Counties, Colorado: U.S. Geological Survey Open-File Map.

———, 1968c, Geologic map of the Hawxhurst Creek Quadrangle, Garfield and Mesa Counties, Colorado: U.S. Geological Survey Open-File Map.

———, 1968d, Geologic map of the Grand Valley Quadrangle, Garfield County, Colorado: U.S. Geological Survey Open-File Map.

———, 1968e, Geologic map of the Housetop Mountain Quadrangle, Garfield and Mesa Counties, Colorado: U.S. Geological Survey Open-File Map.

Hail, W. J., Jr., 1972a, Reconnaissance geologic map of the Hotchkiss area, Delta and Montrose Counties, Colorado: U.S. Geological Survey Miscellaneous Geologic Investigations Map I-698.

———, 1972b, Reconnaissance geologic map of the Cedaredge area, Delta County, Colorado: U.S. Geological Survey Miscellaneous Geologic Investigations Map I-697.

Hayden, F. V., 1876, Report of progress of the exploration for the year 1874: U.S. Geological and Geographical Survey of the Territories, 8th Annual Report (Hayden), 151 p.

Henderson, Julius, 1923, The glacial geology of Grand Mesa, Colorado: Journal of Geology, v. 31, p. 676–678.

Larson, E. D., Ozima, Minoru, and Bradley, W. C., 1975, Late Cenozoic basic volcanism in northwestern Colorado and its implications concerning tectonism and the origin of the Colorado River system: Geological Society of America Memoir 144, p. 155–178.

Marvin, R. F., Mehnert, H. H., and Mountjoy, W. M., 1966, Age of basalt cap on Grand Mesa, in Geological Survey Research for 1966: U.S. Geological Survey Professional Paper 550-A, p. A81.

Miall, A. D., 1977, A review of braided-river depositional environments: Earth Sciences Review, v. 13, p. 1–62.

Nygren, W. E., 1935, An outline of the general geology and physiography of the Grand Valley district, Colorado (M.S. thesis): Boulder, University of Colorado.

Retzer, J. L., 1954, Glacial advances and soil development, Grand Mesa, Colorado: American Journal of Science, v. 252, p. 26–37.

Sinnock, Scott, 1978, Geomorphology of the Uncompahgre Plateau and Grand Valley, western Colorado, U.S.A. (Ph.D. dissertation): West Lafayette, Indiana, Purdue University, 196 p.

Yeend, W. E., 1969, Quaternary geology of the Grand and Battlement Mesas area, Colorado: U.S. Geological Survey Professional Paper 617, 50 p.

Yeend, W. E. and Donnell, J. R., 1968, Geologic map of the Rulison Quadrangle, Garfield County, Colorado: U.S. Geological Survey Open-File Map.

Young, R. G. and Young, J. W., 1968, Geology and wildflowers of Grand Mesa, Colorado: Wheelright Press, Ltd., 155 p.

———, 1977, Colorado West: Land of geology and wildflowers: Wheelwright Press, Ltd., 239 p.

PLEISTOCENE DRAINAGE CHANGES IN UNCOMPAHGRE PLATEAU-GRAND VALLEY REGION OF WESTERN COLORADO, INCLUDING FORMATION AND ABANDONMENT OF UNAWEEP CANYON: A HYPOTHESIS*

SCOTT SINNOCK
Sandia National Laboratories
Albuquerque, New Mexico 87185

INTRODUCTION

This paper presents a model for geomorphic changes that culminate in the present landforms of the Uncompahgre Plateau and Grand Valley region of western Colorado (fig. 1). This model is but one of an infinite number of possible solutions to the problem of geomorphogenesis in the study area; it can be no more.

Figures 2, 5 and 7 through 11 present the landform development as a series of schematic cross sections and maps representing a seven-stage evolutionary sequence. The following narrative outlines the evolutionary hypothesis as a continuum of changes and stresses the conditions represented on the figures. More detailed discussion is available in Sinnock (1978). See Figure 1 of companion paper (Sinnock, this guidebook) for a location map of geographic names referred to in the following discussion.

---

*Field activities were performed during the summers of 1976 and 1977 while the author was attending Purdue University. Preparation of this manuscript was supported by the U.S. Department of Energy

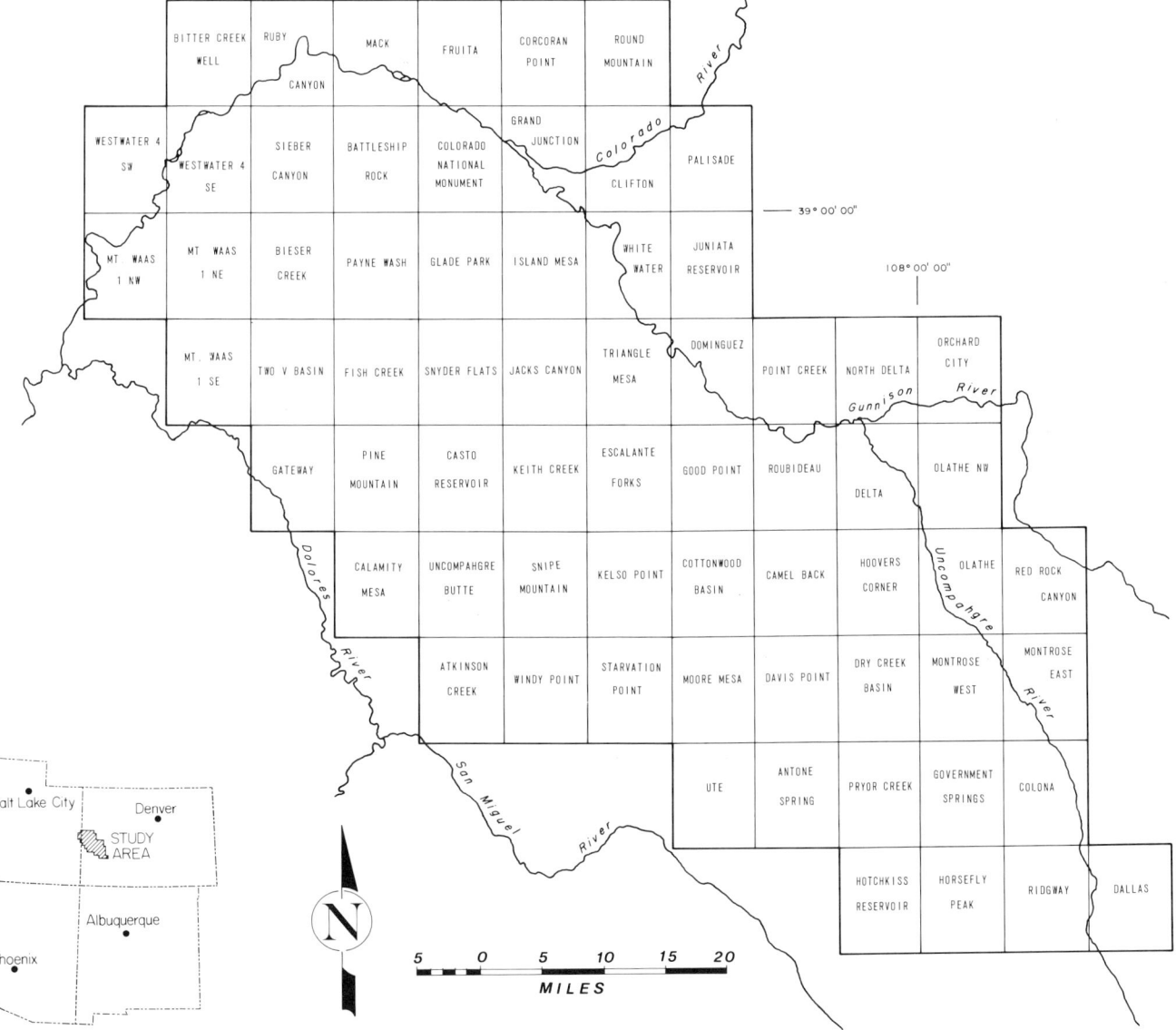

Figure 1. Study area, including an index of 7½ minute topographic quadrangles. The dashed outlines on Figures 2, 5, and 7–11 correspond to the boundary of the index map.

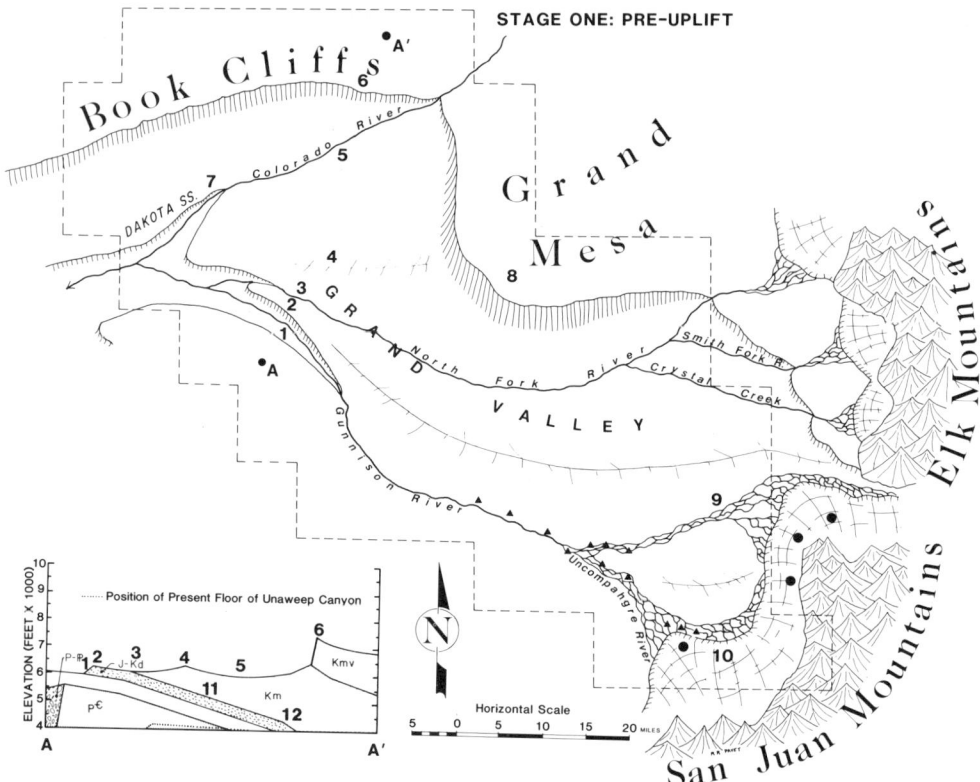

Figure 2. Physiographic diagram and cross section of conditions at the time of Stage One: pre-uplift.

GEOMORPHOGENESIS

The analysis begins before the Uncompahgre Plateau existed as a structural or topographic feature. At this time, the Grand Valley, San Juan and West Elk mountains, Colorado, Uncompahgre, Gunnison, and North Fork rivers, Grand Mesa and the Book Cliffs were present, though not in their current forms nor locations (fig. 2).

Piedmont glaciers flowed from the San Juan Mountains onto a gentle slope of Mancos Shale at the head of ancestral Grand Valley. One glacial lobe terminated near present-day Horsefly Peak on the Uncompahgre Plateau and deposited the till preserved there today (figs. 2, 3). Another lobe deposited correlative till in the Cerro Summit area and perhaps near Paonia. Glacial meltwater poured from the ice front along anastomosing outwash channels of the ancestral Gunnison, Uncompahgre and North Fork Rivers. The ancient Gunnison flowed from the Sawatch Mountains, past the Cerro Summit ice front and joined the ancestral Uncompahgre River near the present bifurcation of the two forks of Dry Creek on the flank of the Uncompahgre Plateau. The Uncompahgre River flowed to its Gunnison confluence from the ice front located in the Horsefly Peak region. At this time, the ancestral Colorado River emerged from the Book Cliffs near the present townsite of Grand Junction. The Colorado flowed up-dip through about 600 m of Mancos Shale, breached a cuesta capped by Dakota Sandstone, and flowed out of the study area on a surface of Triassic sandstone.

Outwash terrace gravels of the ancestral Gunnison and Uncompahgre rivers are partly preserved on low hills, some cored with Mancos Shale, rising above the present Dakota Sandstone surfaces of the Uncompahgre Plateau (figs. 2, 4). The Uncompahgre outwash occurs near Johnson Reservoir and east of Dry Creek; the Gunnison gravels are found between the two forks of Dry Creek and at the upper end of Roubideau Creek. Presumably outwash was deposited along the entire courses of the ancient anastomosing Gunnison and Uncompahgre meltwater channels. However, in the region between the ancient Cerro Summit and Horsefly Peak glaciers, the gravels were deposited on thick Mancos Shale and were subsequently cannibalized as the rivers cut into the underlying shales.

Figure 3. Till deposits on Horsefly Peak. View is to the north from SE ¼, Sec. 35, T.46N., R.10W.

Figure 4. Outwash gravel-capped hill on uplands of Uncompahgre Plateau. View is to the northeast from Colorado State Road 90, NE ¼, Sec. 10, T. 47N., R.11W.

Downstream from the confluence, the ancestral Gunnison River flowed northwest, along the Dakota-Mancos contact while descending from an elevation of about 8,000 ft near the ice front to about 6,500 ft 30 mi downstream*. Upstream from the confluence the ancestral Gunnison transected about 450 m of Mancos Shale.

A Triassic sandstone bench occurred along the ancestral Gunnison River below its embayment into the Dakota-capped cuesta. Remnants of this bench are preserved southwest of the present Uncompahgre fault scarp at Massey Bench, Leonards Ridge and similar areas and northeast of the fault between outliers of Dakota

---
*All elevations are expressed in terms of present day sea level. True elevations of past times are unknown, but relative heights defined by elevation differences are unaffected by the chosen reference horizon. English units are used because the source data from topographic maps are so expressed.

Sandstone such as Uncompahgre Butte and Monument Hill. This bench is preserved also at the southern end of Palisade Butte, 1,500 ft above the present Dolores River near Gateway. The confluence of the Gunnison and Colorado rivers was near the present confluence of Granite Creek and the Colorado River north of Moab. Hence, the ancestral Gunnison River crossed the inactive Uncompahgre fault zone near the present location of Columbine Pass.

North Fork River flowed around Grand Mesa, whose cliffs were approximately where the present Gunnison River is entrenched into the flank of the Uncompahgre Plateau. Upstream from its embayment through the Dakota Sandstone cuesta, North Fork stripped the lower part of the Mancos Shale from the Dakota surface. Downstream from the embayment the North Fork joined the Gunnison on the Triassic sandstone bench near Gateway. Just above the confluence, the North Fork flowed across the inactive Uncompahgre fault zone near the present mouth of Unaweep Canyon.

At the time of these conditions no Precambrian rocks were exposed in the study area and uplift of the Uncompahgre Plateau had not yet begun. An isostatic monocline similar to the one today occurred southwest of the Book Cliffs and Grand Mesa. Stresses from isostatic compensation migrated northeastward with the retreating cliffs. After the cliffs migrated past the southwestern edge of the late Paleozoic Uncompahgre Highland, compensating stresses were focused along the ancient Uncompahgre fault zone contributing to its renewed movement.

When uplift began (fig. 5), the part of the ancestral Gunnison River above Columbine Pass was trapped on the raised side of the fault. The reentrant into the Dakota Sandstone cuesta was abandoned as tilting associated with the uplift forced the river to pond and spill northeastward to a new position along the Dakota-

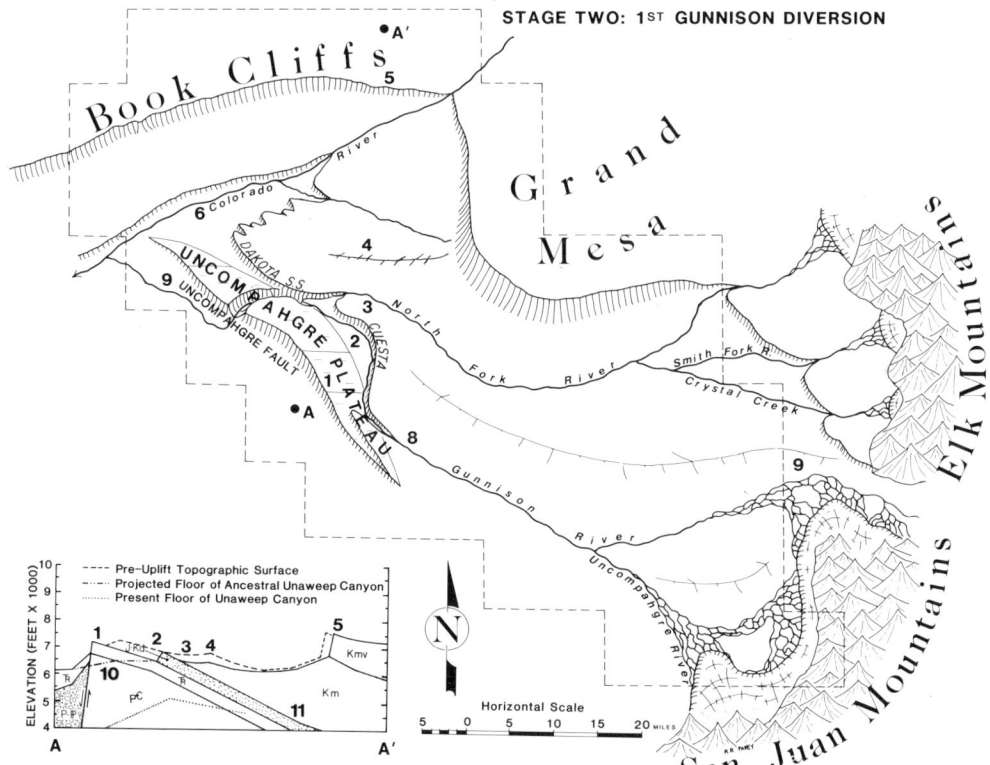

Key to map and cross section:
1. Uncompahgre fault becomes active and raises crest of Uncompahgre Plateau about 1,000 ft.
2. Gunnison River has migrated northeastward in response to rising plateau. River bed elevated slightly, but slips down Triassic dip surface in attempt to regain pre-uplift level. Dakota cuesta shaved to northeast by sliding river.
3. North Fork River joins Gunnison and becomes antecedent across rising plateau fault block, carving upper part of inner gorge of Unaweep Canyon.
4. Divide between North Fork and Colorado rivers is low pediment ridge on Mancos Shale.
5. Book Cliffs have migrated slightly to northeast.

Key to map only:
6. Colorado River begins migrating northward around rising fault block.
7. Downstream from Unaweep Canyon, Gunnison follows approximate course of present Dolores River.
8. Gunnison River spills around southeast end of fault block and cuts new embayment into Dakota cuesta.
9. Low pediment divide near present Bostwick Park separates Gunnison and North Fork basins.

Key to cross section only:
10. Unaweep Canyon is cut into Precambrian crystalline rocks.
11. Rotational axis for uplift occurs about 30 mi northeast of fault scarp.

Figure 5. Physiographic diagram and cross section of conditions at the time of Stage Two: 1st Gunnison Diversion.

Figure 6. Perched ancestral Gunnison River Valley near Smith Point on the Uncompahgre Plateau uplands. View is to the north from NW ¼, Sec. 13, T.15N., R.16W.

Mancos contact. A new reentrant through the cuesta formed near the present location of a perched valley between Snipe Mountain and Uncompahgre Butte. Below the cuesta the river migrated to the northeast on the Triassic sandstone, shaving Morrison shales and Dakota Sandstone from its northeastern valley wall (fig. 6).

The North Fork joined the Gunnison on the Triassic sandstone bench where they began cutting the upper parts of Unaweep Canyon. As uplift continued, antecedence deepened and extended the Unaweep gorge headward. After 600 to 700 ft of uplift, the Precambrian surface was encountered and entrenched (fig. 5). Upstream from the gorge the Gunnison migrated down-dip on the Triassic bench to the vicinity of Gill Creek. After headward extension of the gorge passed the ancestral Gunnison–North Fork confluence, entrenchment into the Triassic rocks occurred along the present stretch of Gill Creek between Casto Reservoir and Unaweep Canyon. The current anomalous up-dip flow of this small, ephemeral stream is inherited from the course of the Gunnison at this time.

The Colorado River was relatively unaffected during the initial phases of uplift. Its embayment into the Dakota Sandstone cuesta expanded by normal headward migration. Below the cuesta the Colorado shaved the cuesta scarp, enlarging the Triassic Sandstone bench in Glade Park.

An axis of structural rotation during uplift was located at the approximate site of the present Dakota Sandstone-Mancos Shale contact in Grand Valley. Thus 1000 ft of uplift at the plateau crest corresponded to only a few hundred feet near the head of the cuesta embayment along the ancestral Gunnison River. Similar reductions in the amount of uplift occurred along all transects from the crest of the rising plateau to the Dakota–Mancos contact in Grand Valley. The ancestral Colorado River and other master streams in the area approximately maintained a constant elevation during uplift. The Colorado flowed quasi-normal to strike, and eroded vertically a few hundred feet into the rising shales of Grand Valley. The Gunnison and North Fork rivers flowed quasi-parallel to strike and shifted laterally along the contact between the Dakota Sandstone and Mancos Shale in order to remain graded to the Colorado. Downstream from Gateway, the ancestral Gunnison River retained its former course along the present position of the Dolores River, but flowed about 1500 ft above the present river level.

Glaciated headwaters of the master streams were relatively unaffected by the Uncompahgre fault. Figure 5 indicates a slight retreat of the Cerro Summit–Horsefly Peak glaciers only because glaciation in general is characterized by alternating advance and retreat of the ice, and it is inferred that a glacial event as significant as the Horsefly Peak glaciation was characterized by more than one advance-retreat episode.

When the plateau crest had risen about 1,000 ft, the ancestral

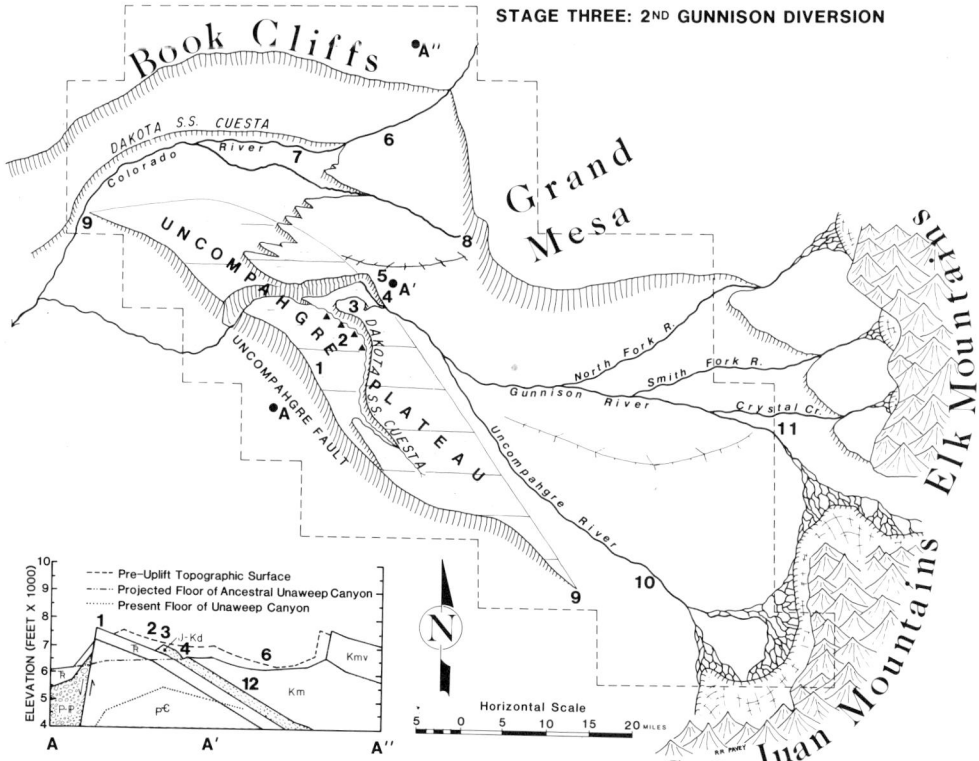

Key to map and cross section:
1. Crest of plateau has risen about 1,500 ft.
2. Gunnison River abandons course along plateau crest. Ancestral Gill Creek occupies abandoned valley.
3. Salient develops along Dakota cuesta north of abandoned Gunnison Valley, as
4. Embayment into cuesta migrates headward along new Gunnison's course.
5. Distance decreases between Gunnison River and pediment divide separating Gunnison and Colorado basins.
6. Colorado River incises into Mancos Shale while remaining at about same elevation above sea level.

Key to map only:
7. Colorado River migrates northward around rising plateau and planes Triassic sandstone bench in Glade Park.
8. Ancestral Kannah Creek begins notching embayment into Grand Mesa.
9. Uncompahgre fault laterally expands to northwest and southeast.
10. Uncompahgre River headwaters are isolated from Gunnison River because
11. Gunnison River spills across low pediment divide into upper North Fork basin.
    Triangles represent deposits of agatized gravels eroded from Dakota cuesta deposited in valley of underfit Gill Creek near modern Casto Reservoir.

Key to cross section only:
12. Thickness of Mancos Shale is decreasing in area of present Uncompahgre Plateau.

Figure 7. Physiographic diagram and cross section of conditions at the time of Stage Three: 2nd Gunnison Diversion.

PLEISTOCENE DRAINAGE CHANGES

Gunnison and North Fork basins were separated only by a low divide perched upon a thin layer of Mancos Shale upstream from their respective reentrants through the Dakota Sandstone cuesta. Below the cuesta the Gunnison was impeded from rapid homoclinal migration by the cuesta scarp and was ponded because it was unable to maintain grade by lateral migration down the dip slope of the Triassic surface as the plateau rose. In response, the Gunnison abandoned its course along present Gill Creek by spilling into the North Fork basin upstream from the cuesta (fig. 7). A new confluence with the North Fork formed near the lower end of present Dominguez Canyon. The resulting embayment into the Dakota Sandstone cuesta extended headward at a position up-dip from present Horse Mesa, isolating a ridge of Dakota Sandstone between two regions of Triassic sandstone benches. The remnants of this ridge are now low hills rising above the Triassic sandstone bench northeast of Casto Reservoir. Downstream from the cuesta the river turned southwest and eased into the deepening and lengthening inner gorge of Unaweep Canyon.

The abandoned Gunnison Valley near the plateau crest was occupied by ancestral Gill Creek. Where it crossed the cuesta scarp, Gill Creek eroded agatized clasts from Dakota conglomerates and deposited them along its underfit course below the cuesta. These deposits are preserved near Casto Reservoir and shown by triangles on Figure 7.

As the plateau rose it also impeded the flow along the upper courses of the Gunnison River. As a result the partially dammed Gunnison spilled across a low divide on Mancos Shale upstream from its confluence with the Uncompahgre River and occupied the lower parts of the North Fork basin, where it captured the lower courses of ancestral Crystal Creek and Smith Fork River (fig. 7).

As uplift proceeded, the Gunnison and Uncompahgre rivers continued to homoclinally migrate northeastward, stripping the Dakota Sandstone surface of the Uncompahgre plateau. Retreat of the Book Cliffs and Grand Mesa accompanied the river migrations, but at a lesser rate, resulting in steepened slopes.

At some time after the ancestral Colorado River had planed a considerable part of the Glade Park surface, uplift commenced along the fault at the Colorado National Monument. During early stages of this uplift, the Colorado was able to maintain its course across the newly uplifted terrain and planed the Dakota and underlying Jurassic rocks from the Triassic sandstones in the vicinity of present Little Park (fig. 8). This brief period of antecedence separated the Dakota-capped uplands northwest of Unaweep Canyon from those northeast of Glade Park, while preserving the continuity of Dakota Sandstone down-dip from the fault. A tributary, ancestral Kannah Creek, flowed to the Colorado from Grand Mesa and through a notch into the Dakota cuesta at the location of present headwaters of Northeast Creek.

The embayment into the Dakota cuesta along the Gunnison River likewise migrated northeastward. Below the cuesta, the river stripped Jurassic and Cretaceous rocks from the present outer valley of Unaweep Canyon. The inner Unaweep gorge concurrently lengthened headward. The ridge of Dakota Sandstone down-dip from Gill Creek was reduced in area by headward abstraction

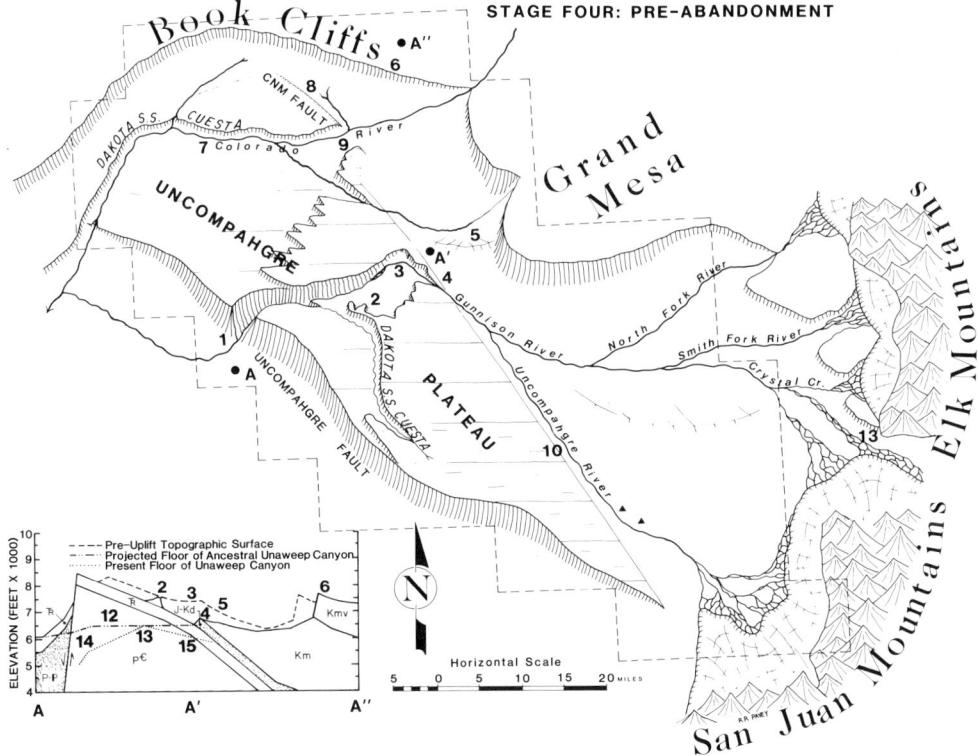

Key to map and cross section:
1. River in Unaweep Canyon is graded to Triassic sandstone surface on present Palisade Butte.
2. Salient along Dakota cuesta between old courses of Gunnison River is eroded at heads of dip-slope tributaries to Gunnison.
3. Head of inner Unaweep gorge has migrated about 4 mi northeastward.
4. Embayment into Dakota cuesta has likewise migrated northeastward to southwest edge of modern Horse Mesa.
5. Only low pediment divide on Mancos Shale separates Colorado and Gunnison basins.
6. Book Cliffs continue to retreat to northeast.

Key to map only:
7. Colorado River continues to migrate northward in Glade Park area, but
8. Monument fault begins to lift northern corner of plateau.
9. Colorado River becomes antecedent across Monument uplift zone, stripping Jurassic and Dakota rocks from Little Park.
10. Uncompahgre River migrates northeastward across Dakota surface, stripping remaining Mancos Shale.
11. Gunnison is blocked by readvance of Horsefly Peak–Cerro Summit glaciers and diverted to its approximate present course.
   Triangles represent volcanic provenance fluvial deposits presently resting on Uncompahgre Plateau uplands along Dry Creek.

Key to cross section only:
12. Just prior to abandonment, Gunnison River in Unaweep Canyon possessed essentially flat gradient.
13. Present divide between East and West creeks is only point of pre-abandonment floor of Unaweep Canyon not significantly lowered by erosion along the two creeks.
14. West Creek has cut maximum of about 1,700 ft, and
15. East Creek has cut maximum of about 500 ft below abandoned valley floor.

Figure 8. Physiographic diagram and cross section of conditions at the time of Stage Four: Pre-abandonment.

along developing dip-slope tributaries to the Gunnison. Similar tributaries developed on the newly stripped Dakota surface of the rising plateau and formed precursors of Dominguez, Escalante, Roubideau and Dry Creek canyonlands.

River gravels presently about 1,000 ft below those discussed earlier (fig. 2) were deposited on the stripped plateau surface at about this time by the ancestral Uncompahgre River (fig. 8). These gravels are possibly outwash from a readvance of the Horsefly Peak glaciers or perhaps from an intermediate age glaciation not evidenced by preserved till deposits.

The glacial readvance in the Cerro Summit area dammed the ancestral Gunnison River and forced it to escape along a new course near the present location of Black Canyon. The abandoned course of the Gunnison below the ice dam was occupied by an outwash channel that flowed quasi-parallel to the Gunnison in the vicinity of Bostwick Park and Red Rock Canyon.

Conditions represented on Figure 8 occurred just prior to the abandonment of Unaweep Canyon and Glade Park by the ancestral Gunnison and Colorado rivers, respectively. Figure 9 illustrates conditions just after both abandonments occurred. The timing of these major river diversions relative to each other is uncertain.

A few assumptions regarding the inferred geomorphogenesis of the Uncompahgre Plateau should be made explicit:

1) the river that abandoned Unaweep Canyon possessed an essentially flat gradient at the time of abandonment;
2) as a result, the Gunnison River was ponded and spilled across a low divide on Mancos Shale and into the adjacent basin of the Colorado River*;
3) the gradient of the river in Unaweep Canyon at the time of abandonment steepened near the Uncompahgre fault zone and merged with the bench on Kayenta Sandstone near Palisade Butte;
4) canyon deepening has occurred along East and West Creeks since abandonment;
5) the present divide between these creeks occurs in the only vicinity of Unaweep Canyon that has not been significantly lowered by post-abandonment erosion;
6) 1,000 ft of uplift has occurred along the plateau crest since abandonment of Unaweep Canyon;

---

*These first two assumptions apply to all antecedent river diversions. However, diversion occurs only if ponding raises the river bed or a resultant lake surface to the height of a basin-defining divide upstream from the rising structure. Hunt (1956) considers a combination of antecedence and superposition from ponded deposits immediately upstream from the uplift zone meritorious of a special name, "anteposition." Actually, "anteposition" is normal during antecedance.

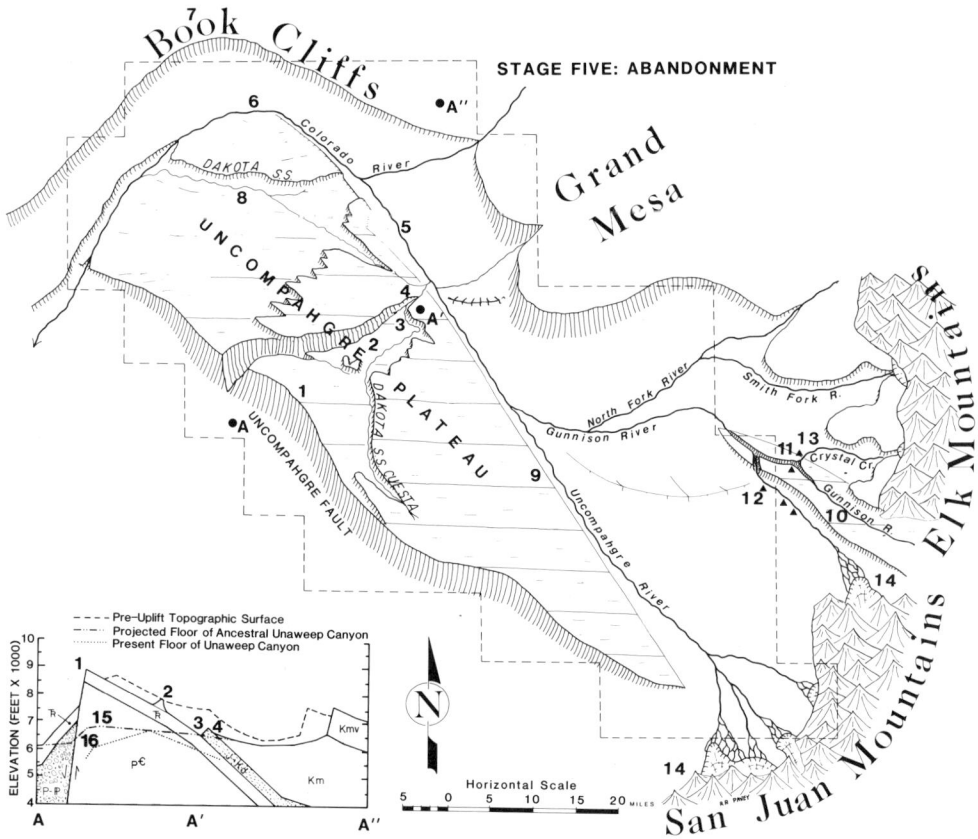

Key to map and cross section:
1. Crest of plateau has risen about 500 ft since abandonment of Unaweep Canyon.
2. Old salient along Dakota cuesta is breached as Gibbler Gulch captures headwaters of Gill Creek, isolating Dakota-capped outlier northeast of modern Casto Reservoir.
3. Gibbler Gulch impinges down-dip against Dakota cuesta and scours its southwest facing edge.
4. Northeast Creek and East Creek begin flowing to Gunnison.

Key to map only:
5. Ponded Gunnison spills across low, pre-abandonment pediment divide into Colorado basin.
6. Ponded Colorado River spills around north end of rising Monument Uplift zone, causing
7. Book Cliffs to rapidly retreat, accentuating their arcuate trend around north end of plateau.
8. Little Dolores River occupies abandoned Colorado Valley in Glade Park.
9. Uncompahgre River continues to migrate across Dakota surface, stripping Mancos Shale from Uncompahgre Plateau.
10. Black Canyon Uplift commences, creating Fruitland Mesa which is still largely covered with Mancos Shale, except where
11. Antecedent Gunnison River breaches Dakota Sandstone and begins cutting Black Canyon.
12. Antecedent tributary cuts Red Rock Canyon; another,
13. Crystal Creek, flows up-dip through Grizzly Gulch.
14. Last remnants of early Pleistocene glaciers are rapidly disappearing.
    Triangles represent volcanic provenance fluvial deposits presently resting on upland surfaces along rim of Black Canyon, in Grizzly Gulch, and below pediment deposits in Bostwick Park and Shinn Park.

Key to cross section only:
15. Divide between East and West creeks forms on abandoned floor of Unaweep Canyon.
16. West Creek plunges across post-abandonment-produced fault scarp, causing divide between East and West Creeks to migrate to northeast.

Figure 9. Physiographic diagram and cross section of conditions at the time of Stage Five: Abandonment.

7) because uplift was rotational, post-abandonment uplift has raised the present East-West creek divide about 500 ft;
8) just before abandonment the Gunnison River flowed in ancestral Cactus Park near the southwest edge of present Horse Mesa; and
9) the Bangs Canyon monocline had not formed at the time of abandonment.

Uplift following the conditions shown in Figure 8 caused the Gunnison River to pond and overtop the low divide that separated it from the Colorado River basin. The spillover occurred downdip from the former river course and at about the same elevation as the head of the Gunnison's reentrant into the Dakota Sandstone cuesta. After diversion, the Gunnison joined the Colorado in Grand Valley near the east entrance to the Colorado National Monument (fig. 9).

Post-abandonment uplift soon rotated the plateau block and reversed the previous southwesterly slope of the canyon floor. A divide between East and West Creeks formed near the crest of the fault scarp and then rapidly migrated northeastward due to headward capture caused by steeper gradients along West Creek in the vicinity of the fault scarp. East Creek was unable to significantly erode into the abandoned canyon floor because its low gradient was determined by post abandonment tectonic rotation.

The upper reaches of ancestral Gill Creek were captured by headward erosion along ancestral Gibbler Gulch which eventually cut through the Dakota Sandstone ridge formed by the earlier diversion of the Gunnison River to the North Fork basin. Later erosion of the Dakota caprock outliers formed the present small, Jurassic-sandstone-capped hills rising above the stripped Triassic surface north of Gill Creek. Gibbler Gulch occupied the abandoned course of the Gunnison through ancestral Cactus Park where it scoured the southwest side of the cuesta scarp, eventually causing Cactus Park to migrate to its present location.

Diversion of the ancestral Colorado River from Glade Park occurred because the river was ponded upstream from the Colorado National Monument fault and overflowed to the northwest (fig. 9). The river escaped around the northwestern end of the expanding uplift along a new route generally corresponding to its present course downstream from Fruita. In response, the Book Cliffs rapidly migrated northward, accentuating their arcuate form around the northern corner of the plateau.

Uplift in the Black Canyon area also commenced about this time, forcing the ancestral Gunnison River to entrench the Dakota Sandstone and begin carving Black Canyon (fig. 9). Ancestral Crystal Creek cut through the Mancos Shale and into the Dakota Sandstone along Grizzly Gulch. The pre-ice-dammed course of the Gunnison became antecedent across the rising monoclinal scarp and carved the upper slopes of Red Rock Canyon. Upstream from the uplift this stream deposited the gravels which are found today at Bostwick Park beneath locally derived pediment deposits. Penecontemporaneous fluvial gravels are preserved along the rim of Black Canyon and in Grizzly Gulch (fig. 9). During uplift of the Black Canyon area Smith Fork River homoclinally shifted northward across the rising slopes of Fruitland Mesa.

The early glaciers in the San Juan and West Elk Mountains disappeared about this time. Uplift along the Uncompahgre Fault ended after raising the crest of the plateau more than 3,000 ft (fig. 10). However, movement along the Colorado National Monument

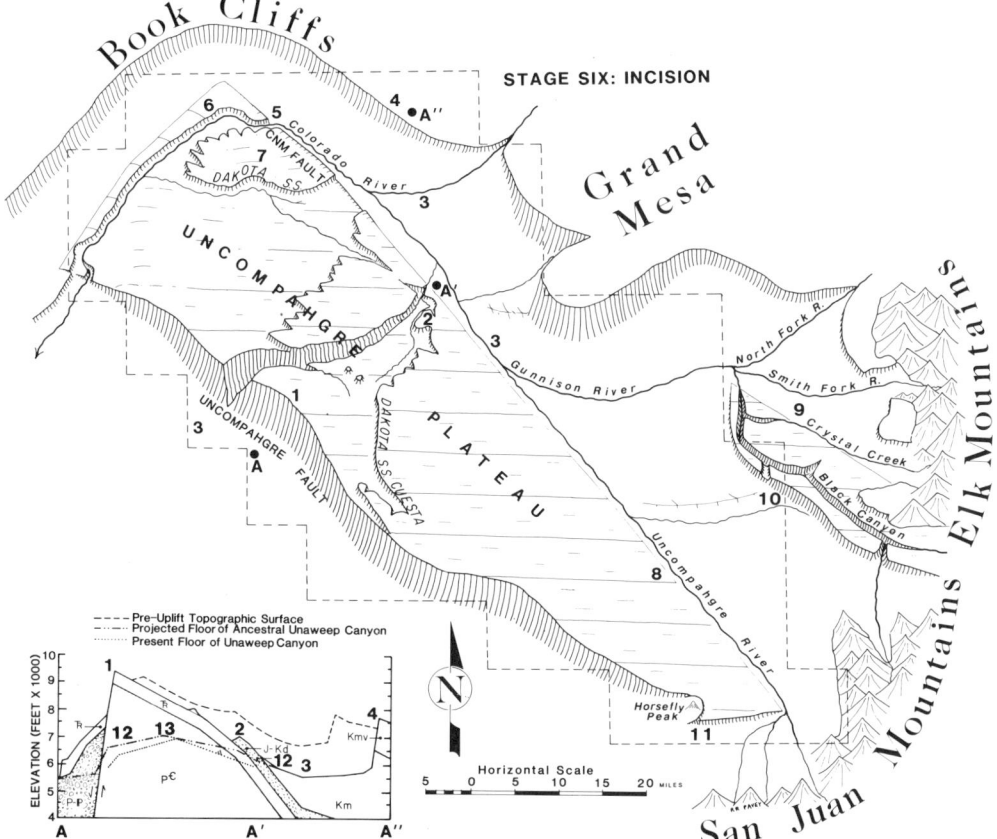

Key to map and cross section:
1. Uplift is complete, plateau crest has risen to more than 9,000 ft.
2. Dakota cuesta is eroded by Gibbler Gulch and tributary of East Creek.
3. Gunnison, Dolores, and Colorado rivers vertically incise about 700 ft.
4. Book Cliffs increase in height.

Key to map only:
5. Colorado River antecedently incises across Monument Uplift for second time, forming Horsethief-Ruby-Westwater Canyon and separating Dakota capped uplands of
6. Westwater Cuesta and
7. Black Ridge.
8. Uncompahgre River continues sliding down plateau dip slope and stripping Mancos Shale from Dakota surface.
9. Crystal Creek abandons Grizzly Gulch for easier strike-trending course.
10. Red Rock Canyon is abandoned because antecedence is unable to keep pace with continuing uplift of Fruitland Mesa.
11. Uncompahgre Uplift extends to Ridgway Basin; thrust faulting near Horsefly Peak accompanies last stage of uplift.

Key to cross section only:
12. East and West creeks steepen as they incise to maintain grade to master streams.
13. Divide between two creeks becomes sharper and migrates northeast.

Figure 10. Physiographic diagram and cross section of conditions at the time of Stage Six: Post-Abandonment Incision.

fault zone continued, and the Colorado River again became antecedent, carving the upper slopes of the present canyon downstream from Fruita. This canyon may have formed by superposition from the Mancos Shale during regional incision of the drainage net after uplift ceased.

Stream profiles before and after abandonment of Unaweep Canyon support the fact that regional drainage incision followed the abandonment. A projection of the Unaweep Canyon floor profile to Grand Valley at the time of abandonment (fig. 9) indicates that about 1,500 ft of vertical incision has occurred since abandonment (fig. 11). Stream bed lowering relative to an arbitrary horizon is assumed to have been minimal or nonexistent during antecedent sculpting of Unaweep Canyon. Erosional and sediment transport energy of the drainage system was consumed by rapid homoclinal shifting across the rising plateau slopes and antecedant incision of Unaweep Canyon. After uplift, the tectonic impetus for continued rapid homoclinal migration was removed, and available erosional energy was redirected to regional incision. The increased flow of the Colorado River owing to the addition of the Gunnison's flow volume also may have assisted incision. In either event, the master rivers began to lower their beds through the shales of Grand Valley (fig. 10).

The lower course of East Creek steepened toward the deepening Gunnison. Streams in the Colorado National Monument began flowing across the fault scarp to the Colorado river, carving the canyons of the Monument. West Creek continued cutting into Precambrian rocks below the abandoned floor of Unaweep Canyon as the creek's base level, the Dolores River, deepened at the same rate as the Colorado. The Triassic sandstone bench preserved on Palisade Butte became perched at this time. Gibbler Gulch continued to notch the Dakota cuesta near the present upper edge of present Horse Mesa. Eventually, this notch intersected the course of a small northwest flowing tributary to East Creek and Horse Mesa was separated from the Dakota-capped uplands of the Dominguez Creek canyonlands (fig. 11). Gibbler Gulch then flowed in present Cactus Park where it deposited reworked ancestral Gunnison River gravels derived from near the plateau crest. Similar volcanic provenance gravels are presently found near Smith Point and also are interpreted as deposits from ancestral Gunnison River gravels reworked by this dip-slope flowing stream (fig. 10).

As incision occurred along the lower course of the Gunnison River, compensation was accomplished upstream as the Uncompahgre River continued to homoclinally migrate across the Dakota Sandstone surface in the vicinity of Dry Creek, stripping the remaining Mancos Shale from the Uncompahgre Plateau. The Gunnison likewise migrated across lower parts of the present Dominguez, Roubideau and Escalante creeks. At a certain point, the Gunnison crowded the oversteepened slopes along Grande Mesa and was unable to shift farther. To maintain its vertical component of erosion, the Gunnison was forced to lower its course through the Dakota Sandstone, carving the upper part of the present canyon along the flank of the Uncompahgre Plateau between Delta and Whitewater. Simultaneously, the Colorado River deepened its gorge along the north end of the plateau, etching Horsethief, Ruby and Westwater canyons.

Development of deeply incised canyonlands along Dominguez,

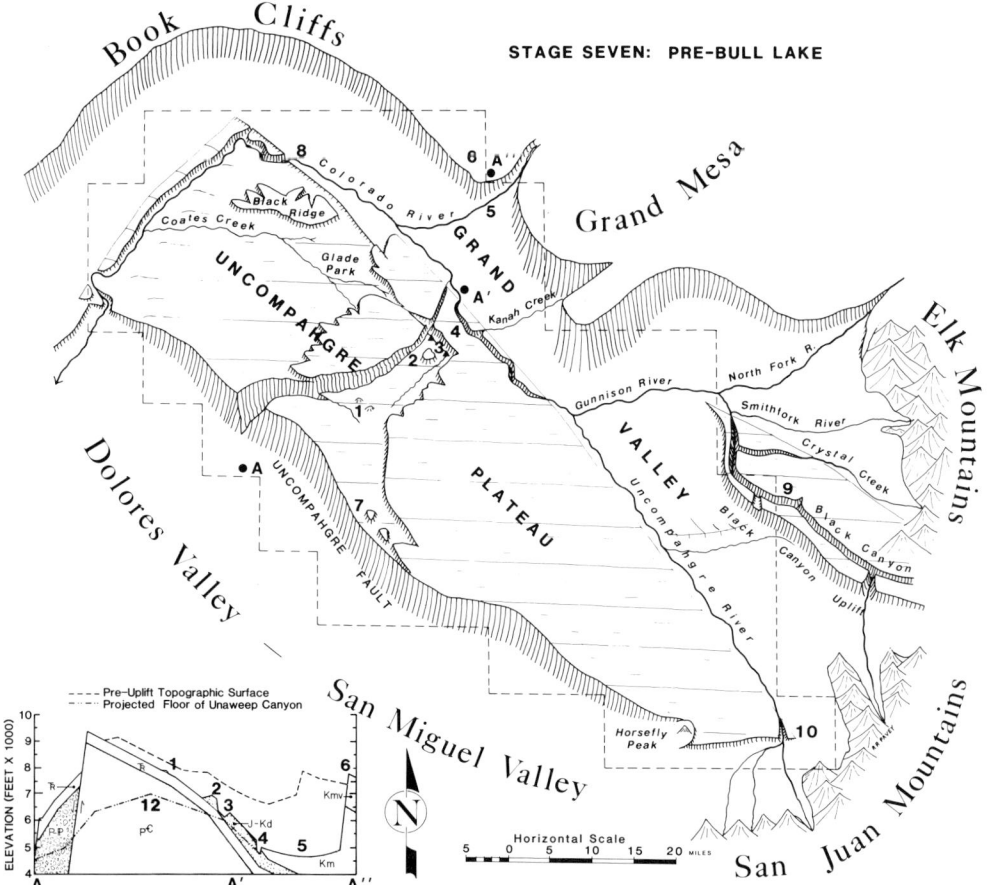

Key to map and cross section:
1. Jurassic-capped hills northeast of Gill Creek remain as small cuesta outliers.
2. Horse Mesa is detached from Dakota uplands of Escalante Canyonlands.
3. Cactus Park is excavated by Gibbler Gulch.
4. Gunnison River incises along lower flank of Uncompahgre Plateau.
5. Colorado River deepens De Beque Canyon and flows across Grand Valley on reduced thickness of Mancos Shale.
6. Book Cliffs continue to retreat and increase in height.

Key to map only:
7. Uncompahgre Butte and Monument Hill are isolated as outliers from Dakota cuesta by dip-slope drainage (not shown) of Escalante Canyonlands.
8. Horsethief–Ruby–Westwater Canyon is deepened along Colorado River.
9. Gunnison River continues deepening Black Canyon.
10. Uncompahgre River begins to entrench southeast corner of Uncompahgre Plateau near Colona.

Triangles represent volcanic-provenance Gunnison River gravels reworked by Gibbler Gulch and deposited in Cactus Park.

Key to cross section only:
11. Divide between East and West creeks approaches present position. Both streams have eroded Precambrian rocks to attain their approximate present position and gradients.

Figure 11. Physiographic diagram and cross section of conditions at the time of Stage Seven: Pre-Bull Lake.

Escalante, and Roubideau drainage nets accompanied entrenchment of the Gunnison. These streams eroded deeply into the plateau in order to join the Gunnison at stratigraphic levels below the Dakota. Concommitant retreat of the Dakota-capped valley sides caused widening of the canyons and resulted in the distribution throughout the study area of volumetrically comparable erosional rates. As entrenchment of West and Middle forks of Escalante Creek extended to the crest of the plateau, it captured the upper drainage of ancestral Gibbler Gulch (formerly Gill Creek and still earlier the Gunnison River). Headward abstraction through the old salient on the Dakota Sandstone cuesta resulting from the first diversion of the Gunnison River, created Uncompahgre Butte, Monument Hill, and other Dakota-capped outliers on the present plateau crest. Big Dominguez Creek worked headward to the outer valley of Unaweep Canyon and captured the middle section of ancestral Gibbler Gulch. The process of capture is continuing. Present Gill Creek is about to be pirated by the LaFair branch of Little Dominguez Creek. Meanwhile, the Little Dolores River and Coates Creek drainage nets deepened the canyons of Glade Park. Their headwaters reduced the surface area of Dakota Sandstone northwest of Unaweep Canyon and at Black Ridge while their main channels incised to the Precambrian surface in Glade Park.

In the Black Canyon area, the Gunnison cut more deeply into the rising Black Canyon Uplift. Incision along the stream flowing to the Gunnison through Bostwick Park and Red Rock Canyon eventually was unable to keep pace with uplift, and escaped around the eastern edge of the uplift zone (fig. 10). Continued uplift caused antecedence along this new course, forming Pool Gulch north of present Cerro Summit (fig. 11). A similar diversion occurred later, Pool Gulch was abandoned, and the present course of Squaw Creek to Cimarron was established. Crystal Creek was blocked in Grizzly Gulch by the rising slope of Fruitland Mesa and escaped along its present course.

The conditions shown on Figure 11 occurred immediately prior to the Bull Lake glacial episode. At this time, all drainage lines were approximately in their present positions. Regional incision had progressed to within a few hundred feet of the present valley floors. A companion paper (Sinnock, this guidebook) details succeeding events with emphasis on terrace and pediment development in Grand Valley. This paper concludes with a few general comments about the outlined early to mid-Pleistocene adjustments.

DISCUSSION

It is proposed that significant changes occurred during the Pleistocene in the geographical position, arrangement, and elevation of the major drainage channels throughout the western Colorado region.

If 500,000 years were required for the events outlined in this paper, then the maximum deepening of 3000 ft along Unaweep Canyon required only about 0.1 in. of abrasion per year from the floor of Unaweep Canyon. This task would be quite easy for the ancestral Gunnison River considering the hard milling agents of large volcanic, granitic, and metamorphic clasts and abundant grit (quartz, zircon, garnet, etc.) that comprised its bedload. Similarly, if concurrent uplift along the Uncompahgre fault occurred from about 500,000 to 300,000 years ago, only the same general rate of uplift ($\sim$0.1 in./year) is required. In general terms, this rate of tectonism is compatible with occurrence of an earthquake on the scale of that at Hegben Lake, Montana (Morisawa, 1975) or Wonder, Nevada (Slemmons and others, 1959) once every few hundred to a thousand years; this is a reasonable assumption for an active uplift zone.

Cliff migrations inferred herein as the dominant erosional events must have occurred on an annual basis of about one inch per year to produce ten miles of cliff retreat in 500,000 years. These rates of scarp retreat are the same general order of magnitude as those estimated by Gustavsen and others (1980a, b) for the Caprock Escarpment along the Little Red River Basin in Texas. Gustavsen and his colleagues measured sediment yields and changing erosion pin positions along the Caprock and estimated a scarp retreat rate of 110 mm (about 4 in.) per year for the past 380,000 years.

Many features produced by these changes have been discussed by others, and most previous studies concluded that the events producing the current landform features are older, perhaps much older, then Pleistocene. Hunt (1956, 1969) summarized earlier works on the erosional history of the Colorado River Basin and concluded that gravels at Horsefly Peak and on the Uncompahgre Plateau uplands were deposited during the Miocene by the ancestral Uncompahgre River. He believed, as do I, that the Uncompahgre River homoclinally migrated to its present position from the vicinity of the gravel deposits on the plateau uplands, but thought this migration was essentially accomplished by the beginning of the Pleistocene. Hunt agrees with Cater (1966) that Unaweep Canyon was abandoned in late Pliocene or earliest Pleistocene and that uplift accordingly commenced in early to mid-Pliocene. Lohman (1961, 1965) suggests, and Hunt (1956) and Yeend (1969) agree, that Unaweep Canyon was formed by superposition of the Colorado River from Grand Mesa basalts and early Tertiary sediments. Cater (1966) concludes that only 100 to 200 ft of deepening along the Dolores River occurred during the entire Pleistocene. Hunt (1969) concurs, and extends the same order of magnitude of deepening to the Black Canyon, where he allows 400 ft of incision during the Pleistocene. He draws on Hansen (1965), who places the beginning of Black Canyon incision in mid- to late Pliocene. Hansen suggests that the Black Canyon formed by superposition upon a pre-existing uplift from a synclinal axis developed in San Juan and West Elk volcanic deposits.

These previous studies, in effect, have assumed that tectonic activity essentially stopped before or shortly after the Pleistocene began. Additionally, these studies require that most or all Plio-Pleistocene erosion along the master streams was essentially vertical, with the exception of Hunt's mention of homoclinal migration by the Uncompahgre River.

Another group of workers agrees somewhat more with the assumptions presented in this paper by concluding that tectonic activity continued well into the ice ages and perhaps continues unabated even today. Shawe (1968) describes tectonic warping of Pleistocene outwash terraces in Disappointment Valley south of the study area. Similar synclinal warping can be observed on the highest terrace along the Roaring Fork River between Glenwood Springs and Carbondale northeast of the study area. Atwood and Mather (1932) concluded that Black Canyon represents an ice-dammed diversion of the Gunnison River by Horsefly Peak–Cerro Summit glaciers. However, they correlate the highest terrace in Montrose Valley, rather than the gravels on the plateau uplands, with this early glaciation.

If, as proposed by Cater (1966), only 200 ft of vertical incision has occurred in the region during the entire Pleistocene (I will assume about two million years), then only about 0.001 in. of drainage net lowering occurred per year. This corresponds to about 6,000 ft in 60 million years, an amount compatible with removal of the entire Mesozoic section since regression of the Mesaverde seas. However, the 200 ft of vertical erosion cited by Cater was based on an "in-canyon" environment. Volumetrically, this reduces the inferred erosion rate several orders of magnitude, because canyons are merely linear gashes cut below broad regional surfaces which once supported thick overlying Cretaceous and early Tertiary deposits. Also, throughout much of the early and perhaps middle Cenozoic, deposition rather than erosion characterized the region. Thus, 30 million years is a more likely time period for post-Cretaceous erosional activity in the study area (Hunt, 1956; Dutton, 1882).

Migration rates for the Book Cliffs of about 0.25–1 in. per year would yield about 120–480 mi of stripping in the 30 million years since erosion of the region began in earnest. Assuming stripping of the Book Cliffs occurred in two directions from a central area, this reduces to only 60–240 mi in the same time period. The equivalent of the Book Cliffs at Mesa Verde National Park near Cortez is about 130 mi from those in the study area.

Erosional rates postulated by previous workers for the Pleistocene would remove only about one-half of the Mesozoic and none of the Tertiary section presumed to have been deposited in western Colorado. Additionally, it is reasonable to presume that denudation rates have accelerated throughout the middle and late Tertiary and into the Quaternary due to increasing river gradients associated with epeirogenic uplift. Thus, Pleistocene erosion rates probably represent a maximum during the Cenozoic. Considering these facts, the erosion rates postulated in this paper are consistent with the erosional work that has been accomplished during the past 30 million years or so.

It is evident that most denudation in the study region (and most probably elsewhere in the Colorado Plateau) occurred along fine-textured, low-order drainage nets of steep, retreating scarps. The processes by which cliffs retreat and the morphologic forms developed upon and below them are well described by Smith (1958) and Bryan (1932, 1940). Cliff retreat occurred along small tributaries to consequent streams of the Uncompahgre Plateau and along obsequent streams of the Book Cliffs and Grand Mesa. Similar retreat of the Uncompahgre fault scarp was precluded by the relation between available erosional energy and the erosional resistance of the uplifted wedge of Precambrian crystalline rocks. This helps explain the absence of large pediment or fan deposits along the base of the fault scarp, because the existing entrenched tributaries to the San Miguel River were capable of transporting the material eroded from the southwest side of the plateau. Material eroded from Book Cliffs and Grand Mesa was transported to the appropriate master stream along concave pediments cut on Mancos Shale. Pediment erosion lowered the valley floor between the cliffs and the river. The pediment surfaces merged with Dakota Sandstone at the rivers, so the master streams were required to remove only a thin layer of Mancos Shale while migrating northeastward. Volumetrically, the master streams eroded very little, but transported much. They provided only the final polishing touches to the stripping of the great structural plains so abundant throughout the study area. The process of cliff-pediment-river migration exemplified in the study area was probably common throughout the Colorado Plateaus, but the foregoing discussion of erosion in the Uncompahgre Plateau–Grand Valley region suggests that it is unwise to call upon "regional" processes to describe the formation of local landforms.

ACKNOWLEDGMENTS

I extend my gratitude to W. N. Melhorn of the Purdue Geosciences Department for his continual support and encouragement during the field investigations and writing in support of my dissertation (Sinnock, 1978), which, in part, forms the basis for this report. Also, I thank R. R. Pavey and D. Garcia for their help in graphically rendering the concepts presented on the physiographic diagrams and accompanying cross sections. Finally, appreciation is extended to the Waste Management and Environmental Programs Department, Sandia National Laboratories, for its patience and secretarial support during preparation of this manuscript.

REFERENCES

Atwood, W. W. and K. F. Mather, 1932, Physiography and Quaternary geology of the San Juan Mountains, Colorado: U.S. Geological Survey Professional Paper 166, 176 p.

Bryan, K., 1932, Pediments developed in basins with through drainage: Geological Society of America Bulletin, v. 43, p. 128–129.

———, 1940, The retreat of slopes: Annual Association of American Geographers, v. 30, p. 254–268.

Cater, F. W., Jr., 1966, Age of the Uncompahgre Uplift and Unaweep Canyon, west-central Colorado: U.S. Geological Survey Professional Paper 550-C, p. C86–C92.

Dutton, C. E., 1882, The Tertiary history of the Grand Canyon district: U.S. Geological Survey Monograph 2, 264 p.

Gustavsen, T. C. and others, 1980a, Nuclear Waste Isolation Studies of the Palo Duro and Dalhart Basins, Texas Panhandle, FY 1980, in Proceedings of the 1980 National Waste Terminal Storage Program Information Meeting: ONWI-212, Battelle Memorial Institute, Columbus, Ohio, p. 269–272.

———, 1980b, Geology and Geohydrology of the Palo Duro Basin, Texas Panhandle: Geological Circular 80-7, University of Texas, Bureau of Economic Geology, Austin, Texas.

Hansen, W. R., 1964, The Black Canyon of the Gunnison, today and yesterday: U.S. Geological Survey Bulletin 1191, 76 p.

Hunt, C. B., 1956, Cenozoic geology of the Colorado Plateau: U.S. Geological Survey Professional Paper 279, 95 p.

———, 1969, Geologic history of the Colorado River, in the Colorado River region and John Wesley Powell: U.S. Geological Survey Professional Paper 669-C, p. C59–C130.

Lohman, S. W., 1961, Abandonment of the Unaweep Canyon, Mesa County, Colorado, by capture of the Gunnison and Colorado rivers: U.S. Geological Survey Professional Paper 424-B, p. B144–B146.

———, 1965, Geology and artesian water supply, Grand Junction area, Colorado: U.S. Geological Survey Professional Paper 451, 149 p.

Morisawa, M., 1975, Tectonics and Geomorphic Models, in Theories of Landform Development, W. M. Melhorn and R. C. Flemal (eds.): Proceedings of the Sixth Annual Geomorphology Symposia Series, Binghamton, New York, p. 199–216.

Shawe, D. R., 1968, Stratigraphy of the Slick Rock district and vicinity, San Miguel and Dolores counties, Colorado: U.S. Geological Survey Professional Paper 576-A, 104 p.

Sinnock, S., 1978, Geomorphology of the Uncompahgre Plateau and Grand Valley, western Colorado, USA (Ph.D. dissertation): W. Lafayette, Indiana, Purdue University, 201 p.

Slemmons, D., K. V. Steinbrugge, D. Tocher, G. B. Oakeshott, and V. P. Gianella, 1959, Wonder, Nevada Earthquake of 1903: Bulletin of the Seismological Society of America, v. 49, p. 251–265.

Smith, K. G., 1958, Erosional processes and landforms in the Badlands National Monument, South Dakota: Geological Society of America Bulletin, v. 69, p. 975–1007.

Yeend, W. E., 1969, Quaternary geology of the Grand and Battlement Mesas area, Colorado: U.S. Geological Survey Professional Paper 617, 50 p.

ANCIENT DRAINAGE CHANGES IN AND SOUTH OF UNAWEEP CANYON, SOUTHWESTERN COLORADO

S. W. LOHMAN
U.S. Geological Survey
Denver, Colorado 80225

INTRODUCTION

On the first day of the field trip our route takes us through spectacular Unaweep Canyon athwart the high Uncompahgre Plateau—the now "high and dry" abandoned gorge that I believe once carried the combined flows of the ancestral Colorado and Gunnison rivers. From Gateway, at the southwestern end of the canyon, we will go up the Dolores and San Miguel rivers to Uravan and Vancorum, then traverse Paradox Valley along most of its northwestward trending longitudinal axis. At about the middle of the valley, near Bedrock, Colorado, we will cross the Dolores River, which "paradoxically" cuts across the roughly canoe-shaped valley instead of following the longitudinal axis, as do most normal streams, hence the name Paradox Valley.

Evidence to be presented strongly suggests: that the Dolores River once joined the ancestral San Juan River to the southwest but was diverted northward from about the present town of Dolores, Colorado, to join the ancestral San Miguel River; that the combined flows of these two ancestral rivers once joined with the ancestral Colorado River at the southwestern end of ancestral Unaweep Canyon, near the present town of Gateway, Colorado; and that the ancestral upper Colorado River then joined the present Colorado River southwest of the present confluence of the Dolores and Colorado Rivers near Dewey Bridge, in eastern Utah.

Although most of the details of these suggested drainage changes have already been published, it is hoped that this brief summary, which includes some new findings, will be of interest to most participants on the field trip. As these possible drainage changes probably span more than 50 million years, they will be discussed in approximate chronological order.

As will be noted below, there is not universal agreement concerning some of these suggested drainage changes, and a new and quite different interpretation of the changes in and near Unaweep Canyon is given in this guidebook by Sinnock.

DIVERSION OF THE ANCESTRAL DOLORES RIVER

Early Diversion

The present Dolores River heads on the south side of Lizard Head Pass in the San Miguel Range, in Dolores County, Colorado, and flows southwestward in a relatively straight consequent course to the town of Dolores in Montezuma County. There it abruptly turns about 135 degrees to the north and flows in an entrenched meandering course some 110 km north to its confluence with the San Miguel River in Montrose County.

When I worked in the Dolores–Dove Creek area during the 1940's, this abrupt change in the direction of the Dolores River appeared to me to be quite anomalous, but I did not know the reason for this about face until Hunt (1956a, p. 45) suggested that the headward part of the ancestral Dolores River once flowed southwestward to join the ancestral San Juan River, but was diverted northward by the doming and uplift that accompanied the intrusion of the laccolithic Sleeping Ute Mountain*, about 30 km southwest of Dolores (see Ekren and Houser, 1965).

The drainage patterns of the Dolores River and other streams, and Hunt's concept (1969, fig. 63) of the possible ancestral patterns, are shown in Figure 1.

Hunt (1956a, p. 45) first postulated that most of the laccolithic mountains were of late Miocene or early Pliocene age, but later (1969, p. 81) he assumed an early Miocene age for the Sleeping Ute and La Sal Mountains, and other laccolithic mountains in the Colorado Plateau. Radiometric age determinations by the K-Ar (potassium-argon) method by Armstrong (1969) for rocks from seven of the eight groups of laccolithic mountains on the Colorado Plateau (Witkind, 1975, p. 245) indicated a Miocene or older age for the La Sal Mountains, but indicated a Late Cretaceous age for Sleeping Ute Mountain. Fission-track and K-Ar dating by Cunningham and others (1977, p. 5) determined an average age of about 70 million years for 5 samples of rock from Sleeping Ute Mountain, indicating a Late Cretaceous age.

Regardless of the exact age of the rocks involved, I am in entire agreement with Hunt that the ancestral Dolores River once flowed southwestward, probably to the ancestral San Juan River, but was later diverted to its present northward course. If Sleeping Ute Mountain was intruded as early as the Cretaceous, the downcutting of the ancestral Dolores may have been impeded by the resistant igneous rocks, and the diversion may have been aided also by warping that accompanied later epeirogenic uplift of the Colorado Plateau. Regardless, the diversion allowed the meandering stream to cut downward into relatively flat-lying Cretaceous sediments, oblivious to the structures that lay beneath.

In a series of eight cross sections, Cater (1970, fig. 13) has clearly shown the gradual growth and eventual erosion and collapse of the Gypsum Valley and Paradox Valley salt anticlines, the products of erosion and solution having been carried away by the Dolores River and its tributaries. Additional geologic and hydrologic data on the salt anticlines, including the Spanish Valley–Moab–Seven Mile faulted anticline, which we will traverse near Moab, Utah, are given by Hite and Lohman (1973, p. 53–57; see also Lohman, 1975).

Later Diversion

Figure 1 shows not only Hunt's concept of the diversion of the ancestral Dolores River, but also the slight monoclinal slip of the San Miguel River southwestward off the flank of the embryonic Uncompahgre arch (fig. 2), the confluence of the Dolores and San Miguel rivers, and in turn their confluence with the combined flows of the ancestral Gunnison and Colorado rivers heading southwestward through ancestral Unaweep Canyon to the Colorado River near its confluence with the Green River.

It is perhaps interesting to note that even though the San Miguel probably is older than the diverted reach of the Dolores River, the

---

*This group of mountains was first referred to as the El Late Mountains by Holmes (1877, p. 237–276). Later the name was changed to Ute Mountain when the range became the principal part of the Ute Mountain Indian Reservation. Still later the name was changed to Sleeping Ute Mountain because when viewed from the east it resembles a human body lying on its back, complete with head, folded arms, knees, and toes. The geology of the mountain has been mapped by Ekren and Houser (1965).

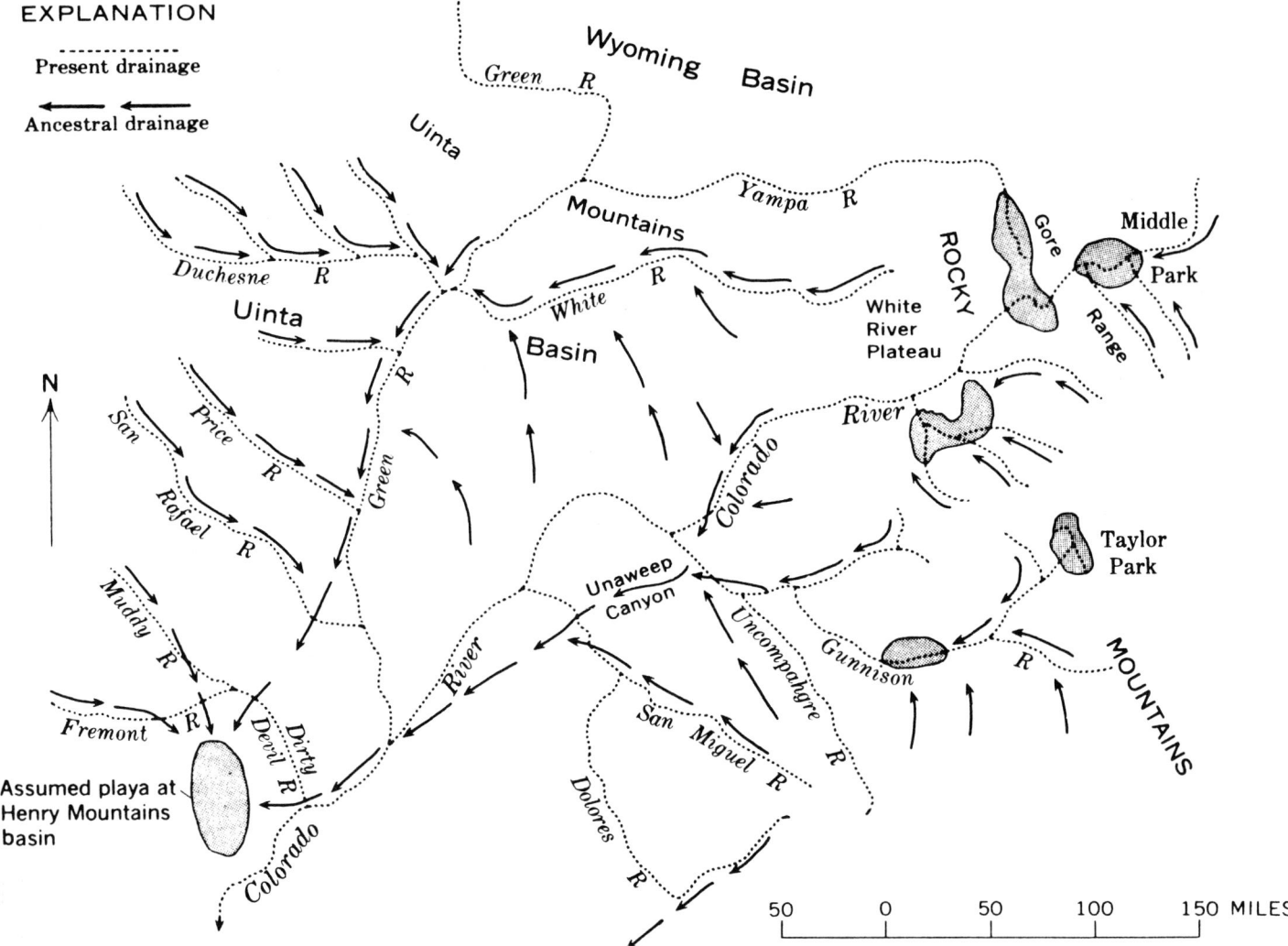

Figure 1. Possible drainage system in the upper Colorado River basin before intrusion of Sleeping Ute Mountain and other laccolithic mountains, and present drainage system (from Hunt, 1969, fig. 63).

name of the latter was applied to the lower reach between the confluence and the Colorado River, presumably because the longer Dolores had the greater flow.

The flow of the Dolores River has been reduced somewhat by a small diversion dam about 1.7 km west of the town of Dolores, from which water flows southward through a tunnel and aqueduct to supply the city of Cortez and westward in canals to irrigate croplands. If and when the McPhee Dam is completed about 15 km downstream from the town of Dolores, the flow of the Dolores will be reduced still more. According to Herb Hand (U.S. Water and Power Resources Service, oral communication, Jan. 1981), the 82-m high dam will impound about 494 million m³, which hopefully will supply full service irrigation to about 14,000 hectares and supplemental irrigation to about 10,500 hectares, mostly by pumping.

According to Hunt (1956a, p. 82; 1969, p. 103) the detour of the Dolores River around the north side of the La Sal Mountains suggests that the river may have once traversed across or north of the site of these mountains, but later was shifted monoclinally northward after the laccolithic intrusion of the La Sal Mountains. I am in general agreement with his views, which are depicted in Figure 1, but I suggest that the ancestral course or an intermediate course may have been between the old and new routes shown in Figure 1, possibly along a route connecting the present Fisher Valley salt anticline, the faulted salt anticline along the Onion Creek Canyon, and the broad Professor Valley of the Colorado River (Lohman, 1975, fig. 7).

A search of the route has revealed no residual gravels, so if any were present they have long since been removed by erosion, as would be expected. The bedrock geology of the La Sal Mountains has been studied by Hunt (1958) and the surficial geology was studied by Richmond (1962), neither of whom found any residual gravels.

DIVERSION OF THE ANCESTRAL COLORADO AND GUNNISON RIVERS

Unaweep Canyon

Unaweep Canyon is a spectacular deep canyon, or windgap, that crosses the Uncompahgre Plateau, or arch, for a distance of about 70 km between the towns of Whitewater and Gateway, Colorado. It is occupied by paved Colorado Highway 141, which we will traverse on our trip. The inner gorge of the central part of the canyon, which is cut in resistant Proterozoic crystalline rocks and is nearly vertical walled, is from 300 to about 370 m deep and from 400 to 800 m wide in most places and about 1,600 m wide locally.

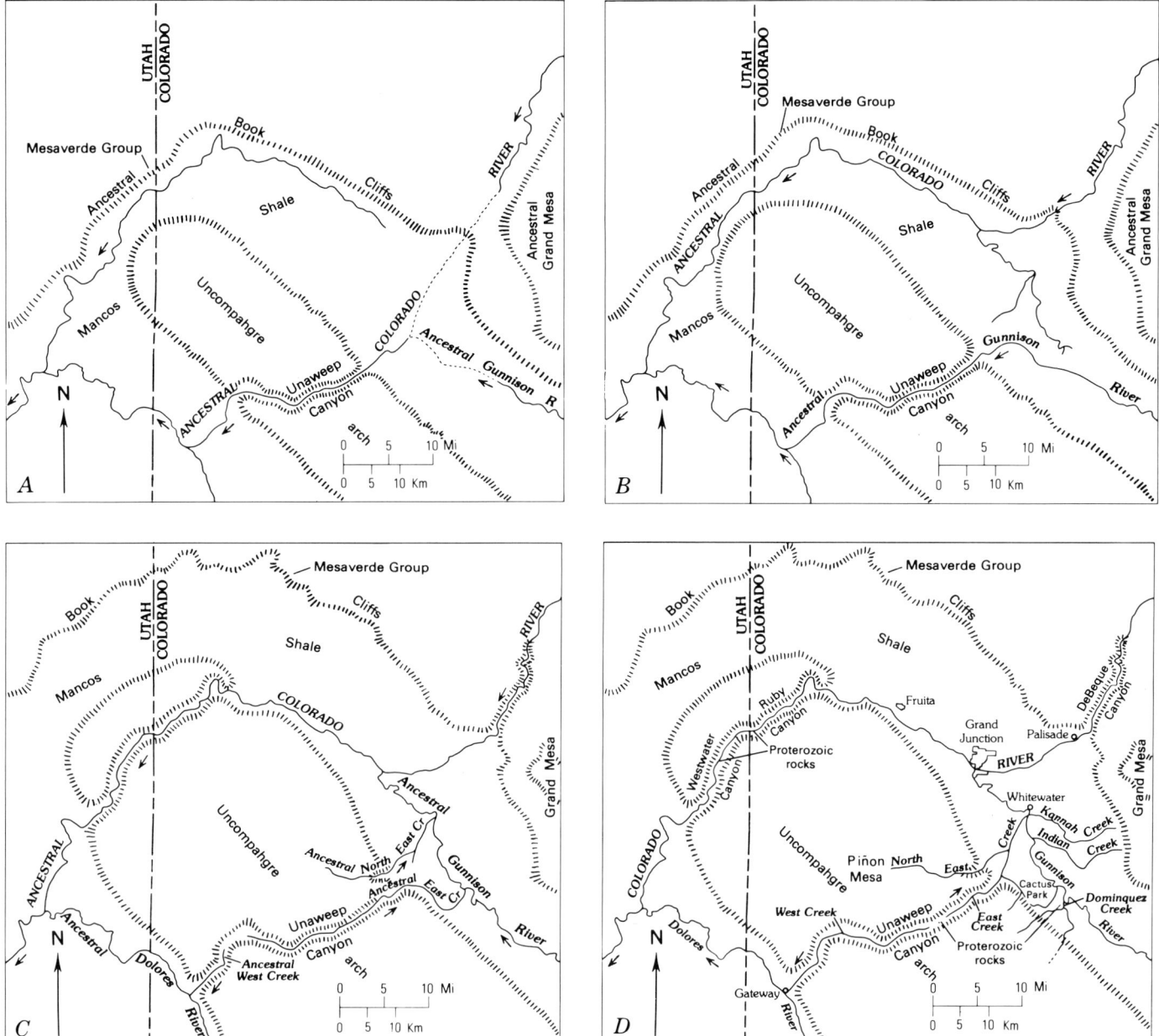

Figure 2. Probable drainage pattern and topographic features at northwestern end of ancestral Uncompahgre arch at four successive stages of development. Solid drainage lines taken from Moab and Grand Junction Quadrangles, Colorado and Utah, scale 1:250,000; dashed drainage lines are as I believe them to have been. **A**, just prior to capture of ancestral Colorado River; **B**, after renewed uplift of the Uncompahgre arch and capture of ancestral Colorado River, and just prior to capture of ancestral Gunnison River; **C**, after probable additional uplift and after abandonment of Unaweep Canyon following capture of ancestral Gunnison River; and **D**, present drainage pattern after latest uplift, shift of Unaweep Divide, and capture of ancestral East Creek (from Lohman, 1981, fig. 34).

The entire canyon, including the gentler slopes of the overlying Mesozoic sedimentary rocks, has maximum depths of 600–1,000 m and widths at the top of 6 to 8 km.

The canyon is now drained by two small streams, one of which flows northeastward (East Creek) and the other southwestward (West Creek) from a barely perceptible divide in the bottom of the gorge (fig. 2-D). The divide, known as Unaweep Divide, has an altitude of about 2,140 m and stands about 760 m higher than Grand Junction and Gateway.

That such an immense canyon could not have been cut by such puny streams flowing in opposite directions was recognized more than 100 years ago by A. C. Peale and Henry Gannett, members of the Hayden Survey. They each concluded correctly that the canyon was cut by a large river, but Peale (1877, p. 58, 59) attributed the cutting to the Gunnison River alone, whereas Gannett (1882, p. 785) attributed it to the Grand* (Colorado) River. Most later workers have agreed with Gannett that the canyon was once oc-

---

*The present Colorado River northeast from its confluence with the Green River in the middle of Canyonlands National Park in Utah, formerly was called the Grand River, and the Grand and Green rivers joined at the confluence to become the Colorado River. The Grand River was renamed the Colorado River by act of the Colorado State Legislature approved March 24, 1921, and by act of Congress approved July 25, 1921, but the older name Grand is still used for many other features in Colorado and eastern Utah.

cupied by the Colorado River (including its large tributary, the Gunnison River): (Stokes, 1948, p. 38; Shoemaker, 1954; Cater, 1955; Hunt, 1956a, fig. 60; and Lohman, 1961, 1965a, 1965b, 1981). Cater (1966; 1970, p. 71), mainly on the basis of river gravels and overlying fanglomerates near Gateway, later changed his mind and concluded among other things that "Unaweep Canyon was carved by the Gunnison River, and the Colorado River never flowed through it . . ." and that ". . . the rise of the modern Uncompahgre uplift probably began in mid- or late Pliocene time," not in early Tertiary time as contended by Hunt (1956a, fig. 54) and by me in the four reports cited above. In later reports, Hunt (1969, table 2, fig. 50, 63) and I (Lohman, 1981, and this guidebook) still contend that Unaweep Canyon was cut and occupied by the flow of both the Colorado and Gunnison rivers.

Canyon Cutting

Hunt's (1969, fig. 63) ideas of the possible drainage pattern in early Miocene time, when a somewhat smaller combined flow of the ancestral Colorado and Gunnison rivers flowed through Unaweep Canyon, are shown in Figure 1. If the intrusion of Sleeping Ute Mountain is as old as Late Cretaceous, as noted above, then a comparable drainage pattern may have existed earlier than Hunt indicated, but it may have been less extensive. In Figure 1, some of the headwater streams are shown flowing into temporary playas or lakes. My concept of the major drainage and topographic features just prior to the capture of the ancestral Colorado River is shown in Figure 2A. After having cut through more than a thousand meters of soft Mesozoic and probably also early Tertiary sedimentary rocks, the superposed ancestral river had encountered the hard core of the Uncompahgre arch, which had been uplifted beginning in early Tertiary time. At the time depicted in Figure 2A, probably in mid- to late Pliocene, the river had cut through more than 300 m of Proterozoic granite, gneiss, and schist in Unaweep Canyon. Because of the hardness of these old rocks, downcutting in and upstream from Unaweep Canyon was greatly retarded for a long time.

Not so with the tributary shown at left in Figure 2A, however, which, though carrying much less water than the master stream, had only the soft Mancos Shale to cut. Note that at this time the band of Mancos Shale extended much farther up the flanks of the northwestward-plunging Uncompahgre arch than at present, and some parts of the plateau probably still were covered by the Mancos and possibly by even younger strata. Note also that the ancestral Book Cliffs and Grand Mesa then were closer to the plateau.

Capture of Ancestral Colorado River

Probably in latest Pliocene time additional uplift of the Uncompahgre arch, accompanied perhaps by an unusually large flood, caused the ancestral Colorado River to overflow its banks and spill across a low shale divide into the headwaters of the tributary. As a consequence of the renewed uplift, the river probably was ponded just prior to the spillover.

With this enormously increased supply of water, the tributary cut down rapidly into the soft shale, captured the waters of the ancestral Colorado, and isolated the ancestral Gunnison River, as shown in Figure 2B. Stream capture of this type is appropriately called stream piracy.

Capture of Ancestral Gunnison River

Note in Figure 2B that soon after the capture of the ancestral Colorado River, a tributary was cutting southeastward into the soft shale, and was about to capture the ancestral Gunnison River. The positions of the three streams depicted in Figure 2A suggest that it was most unlikely that both rivers could have been captured simultaneously.

Figure 2C depicts my concept of what the drainage pattern may have been after capture of the ancestral Gunnison River by a tributary of the newly formed and rapidly downcutting ancestral Colorado River. Map C, taken from my 1981 report, differs from that shown in my three earlier reports in that I have shown the divide between ancestral East and West creeks farther southwest. I did so because the repeatedly uplifted Uncompahgre arch was asymmetric in that the crest, at the time Unaweep Canyon was abandoned by the two rivers, was not in the middle of the arch but was near the southwest side. As described by Cater (1970, p. 67), this resulted from the facts that although sharp locally faulted monoclines are found on both sides of the arch, in general the northeastern flank has a rather gentle northeastward dip (Lohman, 1963; 1965a, pl. 1), whereas the southwestern flank of the arch also is bordered by normal faults of considerable vertical displacement (Cater, 1955).

Capture of East Creek

Ample evidence indicates that after abandonment of Unaweep Canyon by the ancestral Colorado and Gunnison River, ancestral East Creek joined the ancestral Gunnison River along the course shown in Figure 2C, but that later, probably in the Pleistocene, East Creek was captured by a tributary of North East Creek to form the present drainage pattern shown in Figure 2D. By comparing Figures 2B and 2C, it is apparent that about 10 km of the old course of East Creek, in what is now known as Cactus Park (fig. 2D), was a part of the former course of the ancestral Gunnison River. Examination of aerial photographs or topographic maps* shows that the remainder of the former course of the ancestral Gunnison River was southeastward and eastward, and probably deviated from the present course of the river near the railroad siding of Huff, about 10 km west of Delta. The northwestern part of this old course probably was at least in part of structural origin, for it lay just southwest of two monoclines of probable early Tertiary age (see Lohman, 1963; 1965a, pl. 1).

The capture of East Creek probably was caused by what may have been the latest uplift of the Uncompahgre arch, probably in early Pleistocene time, which increased the northeastward dip of the strata and the gradient of North East Creek on the northeastern flank of the Uncompahgre arch. This allowed a tributary of North East Creek to cut rapidly headward and capture the smaller East Creek near the top of what is now called Ninemile Hill—the steepest part of Colorado Highway 141 northeast of Unaweep Divide. The gradient of East Creek now averages about 17 m per km in a generally flat-bottomed valley from Unaweep Divide to the northeastern end of Cactus Park, about 60 m per km in a deep V-shaped canyon from there to the confluence with North East Creek, and about 25 m per km in a shallower V-shaped canyon from the confluence to the Gunnison River near Whitewater. A very gentle divide in the NE ¼ sec. 16, T. 14 S., R. 99 W., at an altitude of about 1930 m, now separates the two parts of beheaded ancestral East Creek—one part draining westward to East Creek and the other draining first southeastward then northeastward to the Gunnison River (fig. 2D).

A small outcrop of terrace deposits containing cobbles and pebbles of basalt, quartzite, granite and other crystalline rocks covers

---

*See for example the Moab Quadrangle, Colorado and Utah, scale 1: 250,000.

the crest of a small hill in Cactus Park in the NE ¼ NW ¼ sec. 6, T. 14 S., R. 99 W. These deposits are about 23 m above East Creek only 1 km to the west, and about 265 m below Unaweep Divide. Although the gravels could have been deposited directly by the ancestral Gunnison River, it seems more likely that they were brought into Unaweep Canyon by either of the two ancestral rivers, then later were reworked and deposited by ancestral East Creek, when it followed the old course shown in Figure 2C. East Creek probably carried much more water during the Pleistocene than it does now.

Studies of the alluvium in Unaweep Canyon in sec. 1, T. 14 S., R. 100 W., by Hunt (1956b, p. 66), made in connection with an archaeological investigation, afforded additional evidence that the capture of East Creek probably occurred in Pleistocene time. He found three successive deposits of alluvium, which he believed range in age from late Pleistocene to early historic. As the oldest layer was deposited after East Creek had cut down about 23 m below the old gravel deposit, the capture obviously took place earlier—probably in the early Pleistocene.

As pointed out earlier, Cater (1966, 1970, p. 71) believed that Unaweep Canyon was cut and occupied solely by the ancestral Gunnison River and that the ancestral Colorado River never flowed through it. Cater further stated (1966, p. C88, C89) that those of us who believe Unaweep Canyon to be the abandoned channel of the Colorado River have based our assumptions largely on the alignment of the canyon with the course of the Colorado River upstream from Grand Junction. Moreover he noted ". . . the small size and different topographic characteristics of the valley of East Creek north of Cactus Park as compared with Unaweep Canyon and the old channel of the Gunnison in and southeast of Cactus Park." Finally, Carter stated, "No residual river gravels have been found on the slopes and shoulders of this segment of East Creek valley; their presumed absence supports this [his] argument."

I believe there are ample answers to all these objections, including some additional evidence. First of all, the alignment of the Colorado River in DeBeque Canyon upstream from the Grand Valley with its former course in Unaweep Canyon is indeed striking, as shown in Figure 2, and surely is more than coincidental. After studying the Quaternary geology of Grand and Battlement Mesas, Yeend (1969, p. 19) concluded in part: "If, in fact, the Colorado [River] at one time flowed across the Uncompahgre Plateau through Unaweep Canyon (Lohman, 1961), then the Colorado was even more discordant with the underlying structure than it is now, as it flows in the soft Mancos Shale around the north end of the Uncompahgre uplift. The preglacial drainage on Grand Mesa, along which the high-level gravels are concentrated, lines up closely with the trend of Unaweep Canyon. This fact seems to lend support to the hypothesis that the Colorado River may have flowed through Unaweep Canyon, and that it was superposed upon the Uncompahgre structure from a capping of virtually flat-lying basalts (Hunt, 1956a)."

In several discussions during the last few years with John R. Donnell, U.S. Geological Survey, who mapped Grand and Battlement Mesas, it was learned that a small remnant of the lava on the crest of the Roan Cliffs just southwest of the present town of Parachute (formerly Grand Valley) indicates that the lava flows crossed this part of the ancestral Colorado River valley. However, Donnell reported that although the flows are about 245 m thick on the eastern part of Grand Mesa they thin to only about 60 m along the western rim of the mesa, hence it is not certain whether they reached as far southwest as Unaweep Canyon.

I have already contrasted the striking differences in shape, character and gradient between the gentle flat-bottomed remnant of Unaweep Canyon upstream from Cactus Park with the steep V-shaped canyon of East Creek downstream; it remains to account for the absence of residual gravels on the slopes of the steep "capturing" segment of East Creek canyon north of Cactus Park—a major objection raised by Cater (1966, p. C89).

Unaweep Canyon actually comprises three distinctive segments: 1) A mature central U-shaped, relatively flat bottomed, "fossil" remnant extending about 16 km southwest from the north end of Cactus Park to a reservoir about 6 km west of Unaweep Divide; 2) between the reservoir and Gateway is the generally steep youthful V-shaped lower canyon of West Creek; and 3) northwest from Cactus Park, as noted above, is the steep V-shaped youthful lower canyon of East Creek.

Prior to the renewed uplift of the Uncompahgre arch that brought about the abandonment of Unaweep Canyon, the bottom of the mature northeastward extension of the old canyon was in the Mancos Shale more than 100 m above the present site of Whitewater, and the later uplift that brought about the capture of East Creek increased the difference in altitude still more. Naturally, any gravels in the old mature channel of the ancestral Colorado River have long since been carried away by the rapidly degrading East Creek. Moreover, for similar reasons, no trace of the old mature channel remains between the north end of Cactus Peak and the mouth of DeBeque Canyon (fig. 2D).

Character of Central Remnant of Unaweep Canyon

The U shape of the beautiful, mature, central section of Unaweep Canyon (fig. 3) has prompted many geologists to ponder if the canyon was carved by a glacier. The nearest glaciers, however, were atop towering Grand Mesa to the east, in the San Juan Mountains far to the southeast, and in the La Sal Mountains to the southwest.

The abandonment of Unaweep Canyon discussed above removed the gigantic storm sewer that for millions of years had carried off the erosion products from the canyon walls, resulting from the action of frost, water, wind, and gravity. Since abandonment, rock materials that have fallen from the cliffs of the inner gorge and from the gentler slopes above simply have piled up at the foot of the cliffs to form a canyon equally as U shaped as those actually cut by glaciers.

There has been some speculation as to the depth of fill in the central segment of Unaweep Canyon. I have always considered that it probably is relatively shallow—a few meters at most, but thick enough to supply domestic and stock wells at several of the ranches.

On the basis of geophysical studies by both seismic refraction and electrical resistivity methods, done as a part of a master's thesis, Oeslby (1977, 1978) suggested, among other things, that the valley fill beneath Unaweep Divide is 330 to 395 m thick, and that it becomes thinner both to the southwest and northeast. However, he went on to state (1978, p. 65) that: "Because of the numerous problems encountered in measuring the thickness of fill in Unaweep Canyon by geophysical techniques, . . . a simple graphical method was devised to estimate the thickness. The method consists of projecting both bedrock canyon slopes downward until they intersect at the presumed ancient valley-bottom."

Oeslby assumed the canyon sides to be V shaped and that all the fill was derived from the canyon walls and sides. Some of his downward projections coincided with geophysical soundings; others did not.

Figure 3. Unaweep Canyon, looking southwest from rim of inner gorge cut in hard Proterozoic rocks, just to the right of first cattle guard on Divide Road, near the middle of sec. 16, T. 14 S., R. 100 W., about 9 km north of Unaweep Divide, which is just around the corner to the right of the most distant part of the canyon visible. Slope above rim of inner gorge on right are Triassic strata capped by flat bench of the Jurassic Entrada Sandstone. For 4-color reproduction, see Lohman (1981, fig. 36).

I agree that such material as does underlie the floor of the canyon was derived locally, but its derivation would have altered the shape and size of the canyon. Moreover, such canyon walls could be V shaped, vertical, or shaped like the cross section of a boat, so that their downward projection as straight lines might prove quite fallacious; for example, downward projection of vertical walls would extend to infinity. Oesleby finally concluded (p. 77) that a few boreholes are needed to really solve the problem, and I fully agree.

Post Diversion Changes

Unaweep Divide now stands about 760 m above the Dolores River at Gateway and also above the confluence of the Colorado and Gunnison rivers at Grand Junction. It is not certain how much of this interval is due to the several uplifts of the Uncompahgre arch and how much is due to downcutting by the Colorado, Gunnison, and Dolores rivers since the uplifts and the last stream capture. However, in an earlier study of dissected pediments and other old surfaces in the Colorado River valley and Grand Valley between the town of Silt and Grand Junction, I estimated that in the area northeast of the Uncompahgre arch the valleys may have been deepened by erosion as much as 180 to 240 m; if so, the remaining 520 to 580 m may be attributable to the uplifts. The details leading to these conclusions, which are beyond the scope of this paper, are given in the earlier report (Lohman, 1965a, p. 72–74).

POSSIBLE FUTURE STREAM CAPTURES NEAR THE UNCOMPAHGRE ARCH

As stated in earlier reports (Lohman, 1965a, p. 79, 80; 1965b, p. 55; and 1981, p. 83), the Colorado River did not necessarily solve its problems by abandoning its hard rock course in Unaweep Canyon in favor of a soft rock course around the northwestern end of the plunging Uncompahgre arch—it may have just postponed them. As shown in figure 2D, the river has again cut down into its old nemesis—the resistant Proterozoic rocks—in Ruby Canyon at and near the Colorado–Utah border and in nearby Westwater Canyon in eastern Utah, and the Gunnison River has just reached the hard rocks at its confluence with Dominquez Creek, not far upstream from Whitewater. Thus once again hard rock is slowing the downcutting of the river, and will slow it down for a long time to come. Someday, Ruby and Westwater Canyons will be deep gorges like the central segment of Unaweep Canyon. Then it is quite possible that another young tributary may "sneak" around the Uncompahgre arch some distance northwest of these canyons and capture the river into a new soft-rock course. Similarly, when a deep gorge in Proterozoic rocks has been cut by the Gunnison at the mouth of Dominquez Creek, a tributary, such as Indian Creek or Kannah Creek, could cut headward to the east of the canyon and capture the Gunnison upstream from the canyon. Of course, other possible future events, such as renewed uplift, volcanism, or climatic changes could alter, hasten, or prevent such stream diversions.

ACKNOWLEDGMENTS

I am greatly indebted to Charles B. Hunt and James E. Weir, Jr., both formerly with the U.S. Geological Survey for many years, for their kindness and expertise in reviewing this paper. I also wish to thank Ogden Tweto of the Survey, and John R. Donnell, formerly with the Survey, for profitable discussions of some of the problems. Finally, I am indebted to Professor J. C. Harrison, of the Institute for Research in Environmental Sciences, University of Colorado, for kindly loaning me the master's thesis of Oesleby (1978).

REFERENCES

Armstrong, R. E., 1969, K-Ar dating of laccolithic centers of the Colorado Plateau and vicinity: Geological Society of America Bulletin, v. 80, p. 2081–2086.

Cater, F. W., 1955, Geology of the Gateway Quadrangle, Colorado: U.S. Geological Survey Geologic Quadrangle Map GQ-55.

―――, 1966, Age of the Uncompahgre uplift and Unaweep Canyon, west-central Colorado: U.S. Geological Survey Professional Paper 550-C, p. C86–C92.

―――, 1970, Geology of the salt anticline region in southwestern Colorado: U.S. Geological Survey Professional Paper 637, 80 p.

Cunningham, C. G., Naeser, C. W., and Marvin, R. F., 1977, New ages for intrusive rocks in the Colorado mineral belt: U.S. Geological Survey Open-File Report 77-573, 7 p.

Ekren, E. B. and Houser, F. N., 1965, Geology and petrology of the Ute Mountains area, Colorado: U.S. Geological Survey Professional Paper 481, 74 p.

Gannett, Henry, 1882, The Unaweep Canyon [Colorado]: Popular Science Monthly, v. 20, p. 781–786.

Hite, R. J. and Lohman, S. W., 1973, Geologic appraisal of Paradox basin salt deposits for waste emplacement: U.S. Geological Survey Open-File Report, 75 p.

Holmes, W. H., 1877, Report of the San Juan district, Colorado: U.S. Geological and Geographical Survey of the Territories (Hayden), 9th Annual Report, p. 237–276.

Hunt, C. B., 1956a, Cenozoic geology of the Colorado Plateau: U.S. Geological Survey Professional Paper 279, 99 p.

―――, 1956b, Geology of the Taylor site, Unaweep Canyon, Colorado, in Archaeological Investigations on the Uncompahgre Plateau in west-central Colorado: Denver Museum of Natural History Proceedings, no. 2, p. 64–68.

―――, 1958, Structural and igneous geology of the La Sal Mountains, Utah: U.S. Geological Survey Professional Paper 294-I, p. 305–364.

―――, 1969, Geologic history of the Colorado River, in the Colorado River Region and John Wesley Powell: U.S. Geological Survey Professional Paper 669-C, p. 59–130.

Lohman, S. W., 1961, Abandonment of Unaweep Canyon, Mesa County, Colorado, by capture of the Colorado and Gunnison Rivers: U.S. Geological Survey Professional Paper 424-B, p. B144–B146.

―――, 1963, Geologic map of the Grand Junction area, Colorado: U.S. Geological Survey Miscellaneous Geologic Investigations Map I-404.

―――, 1965a, Geology and artesian water supply of the Grand Junction area, Colorado: U.S. Geological Survey Professional Paper 451, 149 p.

―――, 1965b, The geologic story of Colorado National Monument [with graphics by John R. Stacy]: Fruita, Colorado, Colorado and Black Canyon Natural History Association, 56 p.

―――, 1975, The geologic story of Arches National Park, with graphics by John R. Stacy: U.S. Geological Survey Bulletin 1393, 113 p.

―――, 1981, The geologic story of Colorado National Monument, with graphics by Arthur L. Isom and John R. Stacy: U.S. Geological Survey Bulletin 1508, 142 p.

Oesleby, T. W., 1977, Geophysical determination of valley-fill thickness in Unaweep Canyon, Colorado [abs.]: Geological Society of America, Abstracts with Programs, v. 9, p. 753–754.

―――, 1978, Uplift and deformation of the Uncompahgre Plateau: Evidence from fill thickness in Unaweep Canyon, west-central Colorado [M.S. thesis]: Boulder, University of Colorado, 122 p.

Peale, A. C., 1877, Geological report on the Grand River district: U.S. Geological and Geographic Survey of the Territories (Hayden), Annual Report 9, p. 31–102.

Richmond, G. M., 1962, Quaternary stratigraphy of the La Sal Mountains, Utah: U.S. Geological Survey Professional Paper 324, 135 p.

Shoemaker, E. M., 1954, Structural features of southwestern Utah and adjacent parts of Colorado, New Mexico, and Arizona: Utah Geological Society Guidebook 9, p. 48–69.

Stokes, W. L., 1948, Geology of the Utah–Colorado salt-dome region, with emphasis on Gypsum Valley, Colorado: Utah Geological Society Guidebook 3, 50 p.

Witkind, I. J., 1975, The Abajo Mountains: An example of the laccolithic groups on the Colorado Plateau: Four Corners Geological Society Guidebook, Canyonlands, p. 245–252.

Yeend, W. E., 1969, Quaternary geology of the Grand and Battlement Mesas area, Colorado: U.S. Geological Survey Professional Paper 617, 50 p.

Plunge of Gunnison uplift, looking north toward Grand Mesa.

GEOLOGIC AND PHYSIOGRAPHIC HIGHLIGHTS OF THE BLACK CANYON OF THE GUNNISON RIVER AND VICINITY, COLORADO

WALLACE R. HANSEN
U.S. Geological Survey
Denver, Colorado 80225

GEOGRAPHIC SETTING

The Black Canyon of the Gunnison straddles the boundary between two physiographic provinces, the Southern Rocky Mountains to the east and the Colorado Plateau to the west. Inasmuch as the boundary there is ill defined, the area shares characteristics of both provinces—sharp ridges, broad mesas, precipitous canyons, complex geology, and vegetation communities that range from desert shrub to boreal forest. The ultimate cause of this dramatic setting is the Gunnison River which, down through time, has carved the Black Canyon out of the heights of the Gunnison uplift. The river and its reservoirs separate the West Elk Mountains on the north from the San Juan Mountains on the south (fig. 1).

Physiographically and geologically, the Black Canyon is divisible into three sections—lower, middle, and upper—which merge gradually with one another but have marked differences. Common to all three, and imparting a certain unity, is an inner gorge of

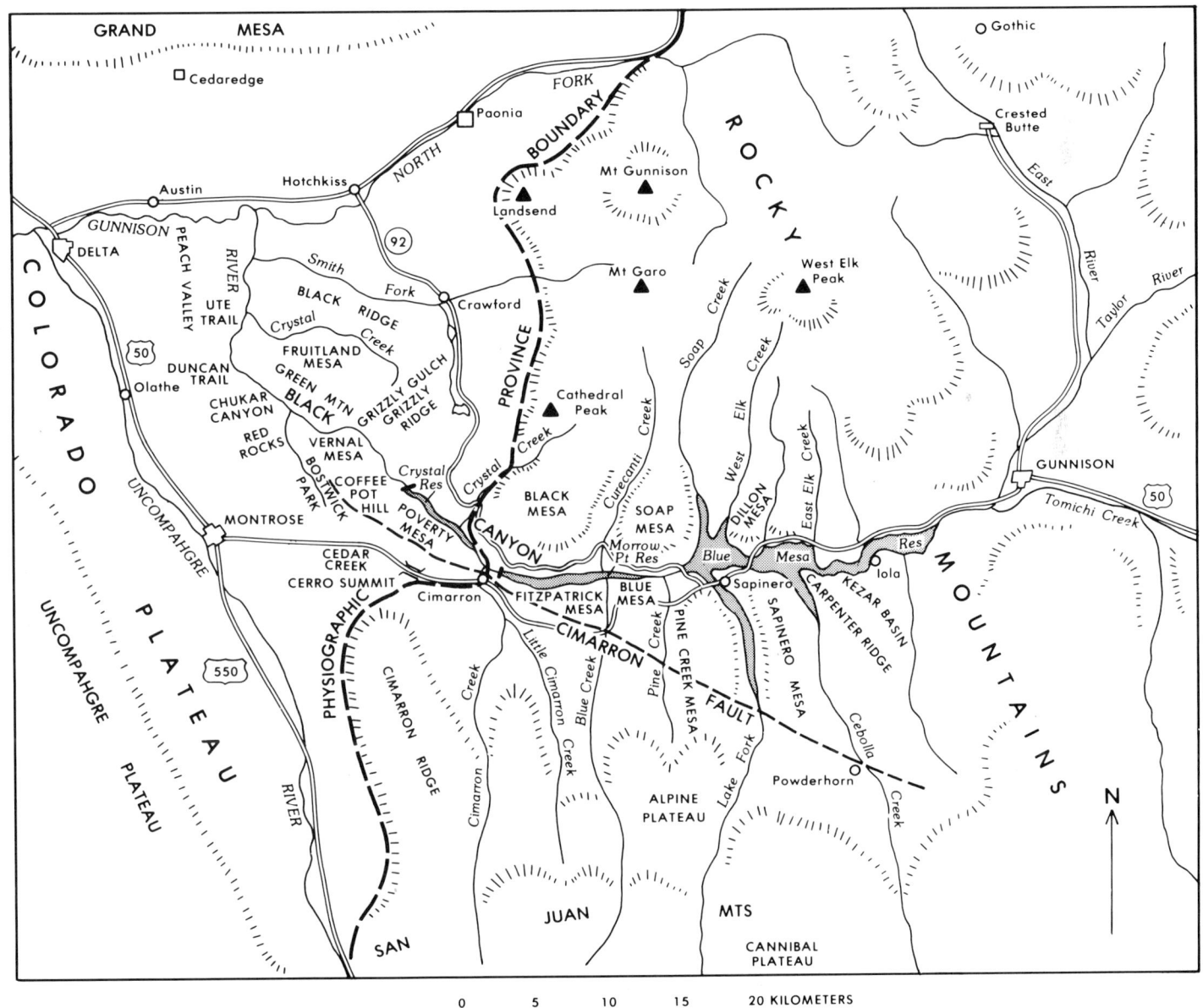

Figure 1. Location map of the Black Canyon area, western Colorado.

crystalline rock renowned for its sheer walls, startling depths, and awesome countenance. At one time the entire canyon area was covered by a capping of middle Tertiary volcanic rocks. This capping, which provided the means for subsequent superposition of the river, has been differentially eroded, so that none remains in the lower section of the canyon and most is gone from the middle, but in the upper it is well preserved on the high mesas above Morrow Point and Blue Mesa reservoirs.

In the lower section, flaring walls of bright-colored Mesozoic sedimentary rocks, 300 m thick and nearly free of soil, surmount a narrow inner gorge of dark Pitts Meadow Granodiorite (fig. 2). The lower section is eroded into the plunging crest of the Gunnison uplift, and resistant Dakota Sandstone forms the outer canyon rim, sloping away in long, barren dip slopes. Successively older strata—the Burro Canyon, Morrison, Wanakah, and Entrada Formations—underlie the Dakota above the inner gorge. At the top of the Precambrian, the well-exposed Uncompahgran unconformity truncates the roots of the old Uncompahgre highland, formed in Pennsylvanian time with the rise of the Ancestral Rocky Mountains.

In the middle section, which contains Black Canyon of the Gunnison National Monument and Crystal Reservoir, the rim view is dominated by a rather flat skyline formed of hard Precambrian rocks on the south rim and poorly exposed sedimentary rocks on the north. Most of the sedimentary capping has been stripped from the south rim, exhuming the Uncompahgran surface. The sedimentary section, though preserved on the north rim, is largely concealed by soil and shrubbery. Here the inner gorge attains its greatest depth and grandest development, particularly between Pulpit Rock and Painted Wall (fig. 3), where it is 1½ times deeper than wide (fig. 4), rimmed by the highest cliffs in Colorado.

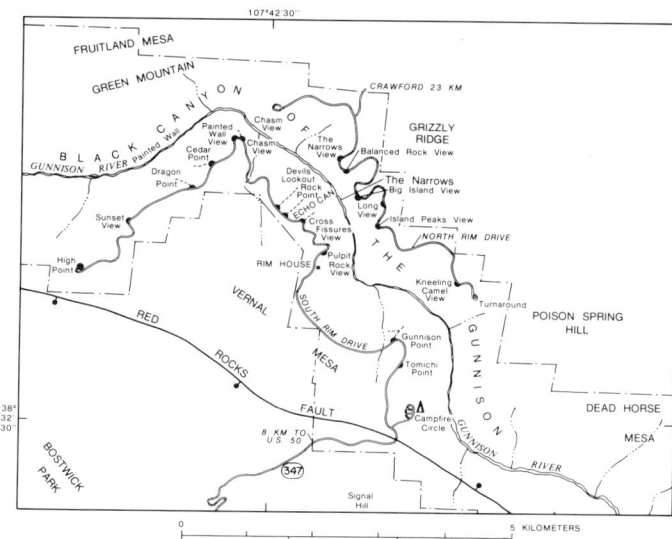

Figure 3. Road access and rim overlooks, Black Canyon of the Gunnison National Monument.

Figure 2. Inner gorge of the lower Black Canyon about 5 km upstream from Smith Fork. Walls of Pitts Meadow Granodiorite are topped with Entrada Sandstone. Dakota Sandstone at the skyline.

Figure 4. The Narrows of the Black Canyon, looking downstream toward Green Mountain. The canyon here, 12 m wide at river level, is about 520 m deep. Note the well-formed joints parallel to canyon walls, and the lineations plunging gently to the left (west). The abrupt rim at the top of the Precambrian is the old Uncompahgran erosion surface. The outer rim on the skyline is capped by Dakota Sandstone.

GEOLOGIC AND PHYSIOGRAPHIC HIGHLIGHTS

Figure 5. Palisade-like cliff of Blue Mesa Tuff forming outer rim of Upper Black Canyon at Soap Mesa. Inner gorge 300 m deep is out of view just behind the aspen grove in the foreground. Distant slopes are mostly West Elk Breccia.

Table 1. Rock formations of the Black Canyon area.

SUBDIVISION	FORMATION	THICKNESS (m)	AGE (m.y.)[1]
Quaternary System	Alluvium, talus, landslides	<>25	<>1
Tertiary System	Hinsdale Formation	<45	18.5
	Carpenter Ridge Tuff	<70	27.5
	Fish Canyon Tuff	<90	27.8
	Sapinero Mesa Tuff	<70	28
	Dillon Mesa Tuff	<25	>28
	Blue Mesa Tuff	<80	>28
	West Elk Breccia	<>300	<>32
Cretaceous System	Mancos Shale	<>680	~80
	Dakota Sandstone	<30	~105
	Burro Canyon Formation	<35	~110
Jurassic System	Morrison Formation		~145
	Brushy Basin Member	<120	
	Salt Wash Member	35-55	
	Wanakah Formation	<80	~155
	Junction Creek Member	<30	
	Pony Express Member	<2	
	Entrada Sandstone	<30	~170
Ordovician or Cambrian System	Diabase	<90	510±60
Precambrian (Proterozoic Eon)	Pegmatite	<100's	<>1700
	Curecanti Quartz Monzonite		1420±15
	Vernal Mesa Quartz Monzonite		1480±40
	Pitts Meadow Granodiorite		1730±190
	Metamorphic rocks	>1000's	>1700

[1] Tertiary ages from Lipman and others, 1973
Mesozoic age based on Van Eysinga, 1978

In the upper section, remnants of the once broader volcanic cover rest directly on the Precambrian basement and form the heights of the canyon walls, although a thin wedge of Mesozoic rocks intervenes toward the head of the canyon. The rim is uneven and indefinite, merging with higher rolling back country or, locally on the south, becoming a serrated ridge. But its chief attribute is a nearly continuous palisade of resistant welded Blue Mesa Tuff 15–100 m thick, forming a line of cliffs 300–600 m above the canyon floor and rising toward the west (fig. 5). The canyon has the V-shaped profile of a typical, though exceptionally rugged, mountain stream valley modified by fjord-like Morrow Point Reservoir. At Morrow Point Dam, the north rim is 1,000 m above the river.

Clearly, the middle section is the most dramatic reach of the Black Canyon, and few gorges in the world are its peer. The more verdant upper section is impressive in its own right, especially in autumn as seen from Colorado Highway 92, when the frosted oaks, choke cherries, and aspens herald the coming of winter. So far as the rocks are concerned, the lower section is the most colorful, and it best displays the sedimentary capping of the Gunnison uplift, the geologic setting of the canyon, and the regional structural framework.

THE ROCKS

The rocks of the Black Canyon area are summarized in Table 1. Precambrian rocks of varied types are exceptionally well exposed along the full length of the canyon (Hunter, 1925; Hansen, 1965 and 1971). The name Black Canyon Schist, sometimes applied to these rocks, has little stratigraphic or lithologic significance. Age and general relations are given by Hansen and Peterman (1968). Sedimentary rocks of Jurassic and Cretaceous age (fig. 6) are best exposed along the lower section (Hansen, 1965, 1968, and 1971), accessible, however, only by rough jeep roads and trails. Volcanic rocks of Tertiary age on the high mesas along the upper canyon (Olson and others, 1968; Hansen, 1971) are readily seen at close range along Colorado Highway 92. These rocks were erupted from volcanic centers in the West Elk and San Juan Mountains (Gaskill and others, 1977; Lipman and others, 1978).

Precambrian

Metamorphic Rocks (>1,700 m.y.)*

Metamorphic rocks of the Black Canyon—largely metasedimentary and metamorphosed to the almandine-amphibolite grade—range widely in composition and texture. Some variations must

*All ages are taken from Hansen and Peterman (1968), based on whole-rock Rb-Sr analyses.

reflect original differences, but others likely reflect metamorphic changes accompanied by the introduction of feldspar, either by injection or, perhaps more commonly, by metasomatism, including extensive migmatization between Morrow Point and Blue Mesa Dam. Rocks of the staurolite subfacies crop out in the eastern part of the Monument. Sillimanite is prevalent in the migmatites near Morrow Point. The original rocks probably were mostly impure arkosic sandstone, graywacke, and sandy shale, although some may have been volcanic, as Hunter (1925, p. 28) suggested. Bedding is well preserved in a few rocks, particularly the more quartzitic varieties. Primary sedimentary structures other than bedding generally are lacking, although crossbedding is suggested in some places, and metaconglomerate is present locally but is rare. Chemically some rocks approach rhyolite (fig. 7), but primary textures that might indicate a volcanic origin are lacking.

Figure 6. Outer wall of the lower Black Canyon. Dark Precambrian rock, lower right, capped by 300 m of Jurassic and Cretaceous rocks: Entrada, Wanakah, Morrison (Salt Wash and Brushy Basin Members), Burro Canyon (forming cliff), and Dakota at the rim.

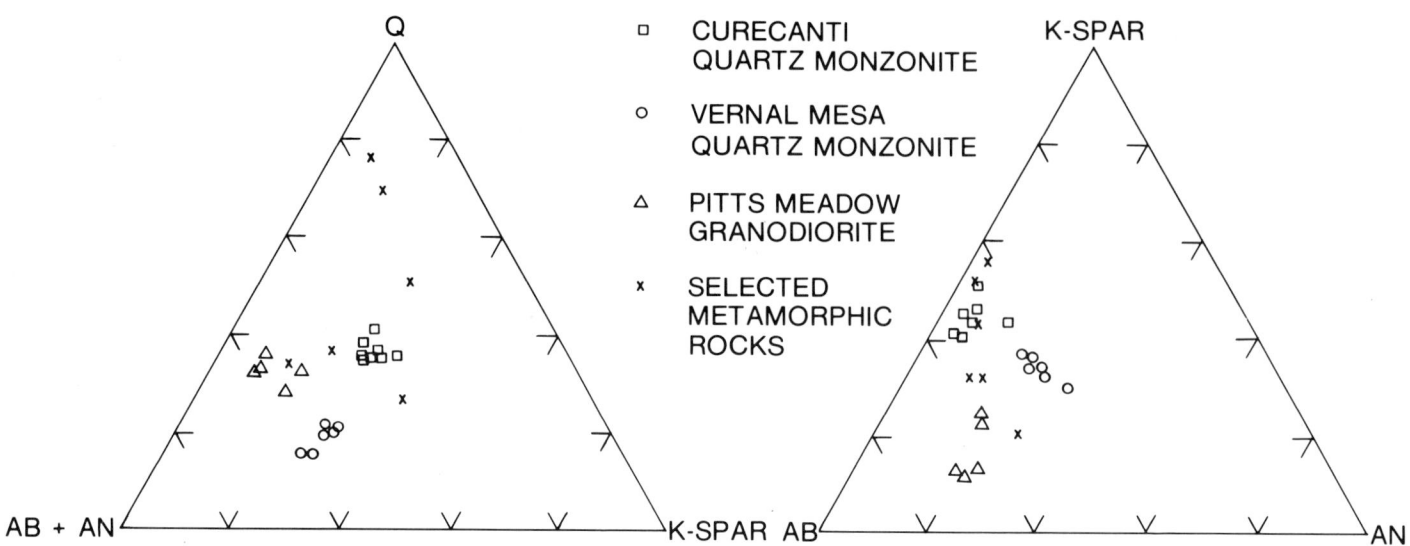

Figure 7. Triangular diagrams of chief plutonic and metamorphic rocks of the Black Canyon area, showing quartz and feldspar ratios.

Rather abundant amphibolites are problematical; zoned plagioclase in some specimens suggests an igneous parentage, possibly basaltic tuff or flows. Some masses seem to have been intruded as podlike or waferlike bodies, and a few are clearly metamorphosed dikes. Some plutonic breccias (pipes?) are amphibolitized. Former pyroxenite (?) pods have been amphibolitized also.

Pitts Meadow Granodiorite (1,700 ± 190 m.y.)

The Pitts Meadow Granodiorite (Hansen, 1968; Hansen and Peterman, 1968) crops out along the lower Black Canyon and its tributaries in a pluton that probably is batholithic in size. Exposed 13 km north to south and 6½ km west to east in the narrow canyon walls, its outcrop is limited to the few square kilometers of the lower canyon, but there is no reason to believe that it does not extend much farther under cover of overlapping sedimentary rocks. In fact, similar rocks crop out near the north end of the Uncompahgre Plateau (Hedge and others, 1968).

Though locally massive, the Pitts Meadow generally is gneissic—being well foliated and lineated and, in places, having two sets of lineations concordant with those in the adjacent wallrocks. It contains abundant oriented inclusions, some of which contain sillimanite. Streaky schlieren look like disintegrated xenoliths smeared out by flowage.

Complex wallrock relations suggest both metasomatism and magmatic intrusion: where the wallrock is paragneiss or metaquartzite, the boundary commonly is gradational over many meters; where the wallrock is amphibolite, the contact may be sharp but nearly concordant; vaguely bounded "skialiths" deep within the pluton include ghostlike masses several meters long. Such field relations suggest parautochthonous emplacement at katazonal depth (Buddington, 1959), contemporaneous with the deformation and high-grade regional metamorphism of the enclosing rocks.

The composition of the Pitts Meadow ranges from predominant granodiorite or sodic quartz diorite (trondhjemite) to diorite and highly mafic border phases that are mostly hornblendite. Most of the rock is about 45–55 percent plagioclase (An_{22-26}), 25–35 percent quartz, 2–18 percent microcline, 5–15 percent biotite, and from less than 1 to about 5 percent hornblende. Quartz and feldspar ratios are given in Figure 7.

Vernal Mesa Quartz Monzonite (1,480 ± 40 m.y.)

The Vernal Mesa Quartz Monzonite crops out in and near the Black Canyon of the Gunnison National Monument, where it forms a moderately large semiconcordant pluton, probably phacolithic in shape but modified by faulting and partly hidden by overlapping sedimentary rocks. Locally it is sharply discordant.

In most places, the rock is moderately well foliated parallel to its near-vertical walls but locally lacks obvious foliation. Abundant inclusions of country rock are oriented parallel to the foliation. Foliation, in fact, is due chiefly to a preferred orientation of the wall-rock inclusions and of large microcline phenocrysts. This relation suggests magmatic flowage late in the cooling history of the rock. Some phenocrysts have granulated margins, seemingly caused by protoclasis. Wallrock relations, form, and fabric together suggest emplacement in a late-syntectonic mesokatazonal environment, shallower than the inferred emplacement of the Pitts Meadow.

Analyzed specimens of Vernal Mesa are mostly very coarse grained porphyritic biotite-quartz monzonite, but they range from quartz monzonite to granodiorite to subordinate nonporphyritic biotite-hornblende diorite. Owing to the coarseness of the rock, an accurate modal composition is difficult to obtain. Point counts in the field and in the laboratory indicate 20–30 percent (volume) microcline phenocrysts 15–40 mm long. The normative composition of four typical samples averages about 15 percent quartz, 22 percent orthoclase (microcline), 43 percent plagioclase (An_{32-38}), and 17 percent femic minerals (mostly biotite).

Curecanti Quartz Monzonite (1,420 ± 15 m.y.)

The Curecanti Quartz Monzonite forms one major pluton in the Black Canyon and many minor ones. Named and first described by Hunter (1925, p. 49), it has more recently been discussed by Hansen (1964, 1965, and 1971) and by Hansen and Peterman (1968). Curecanti plutons are sharply discordant. The major body, which has the shape of a thick subhorizontal sheet or wedge rooted on the west, cuts across steeply dipping gneiss. Both its roof and its floor are exposed in the canyon walls. Minor bodies are mostly lenticular or irregular, short thickened dikes or pipes. Most of them are slightly foliated, and they appear to be late syntectonic. The major pluton lacks foliation and appears to be nontectonic, even though its emplacement was forcible.

An epimesozonal environment of emplacement is suggested by the uniform granularity of the rock, isotropic fabric, and discordant wallrock relations. The plutons lack chilled borders, but they rose to shallow enough depths for the major body to lift its roof in a somewhat laccolithic fashion.

Fresh rock is light-gray to light-orange-pink, medium-grained sodic-potassic quartz monzonite or albite-microcine granite. Its modal composition is about 34 percent quartz, 33 percent plagioclase (An_{8-22} commonly An_{12}), 26 percent microcline, 4 percent biotite, and 3 percent muscovite. A trace of garnet is ubiquitous in the major pluton but is lacking from most of the minor ones. Analyzed samples from the minor plutons are appreciably more calcic than samples from the major one.

Pegmatite (ranges widely in age)

Pegmatite is exceedingly abundant in the Black Canyon, and the countless dikes, sills, and irregular bodies of all sizes aggregate a very large total volume (fig. 8). Nearly all the pegmatite is mineralogically simple, consisting of microcline (much of it perthitic), quartz (much of it graphic), muscovite, and local albite. Biotite, hematite after magnetite, tourmaline, garnet, hornblende and rarely, beryl are local accessories.

The largest single mass of pegmatite is a stocklike body nearly 2½ km long and nearly a kilometer across, just southeast of the national monument at Coffee Pot Hill. Bodies almost as large crop out on Poverty Mesa north of U.S. Highway 50 near Cerro Summit.

Black Canyon pegmatite obviously ranges widely in age. Most of it, however, seems to be related in time and origin to the Curecanti Quartz Monzonite. A quarried sample near the Curecanti pluton was dated at 1,360 ± 40 m.y. by Rb-Sr (feldspar) analysis; a biotite sample from another dike had a K-Ar age of 1,290 ± 40 m.y.; both these ages probably are minimums (Hansen and Peterman, 1968). Few pegmatites actually cut the Curecanti, although some vaguely bounded masses grade transitionally into it. Many pegmatites, on the other hand, intrude the Vernal Mesa Quartz Monzonite. Thus, an important period of pegmatite injection followed emplacement of the Vernal Mesa and accompanied or preceded emplacement of the Curecanti.

Figure 8. Painted Wall in Black Canyon of the Gunnison National Monument, Colorado's highest cliff (700 m). Metasedimentary gneiss interlaced with pegmatite. The sloping rim is an exhumed part of the old Uncompahgran erosion surface. The deep cleft to the right is a widened joint.

Many small pegmatite dikes are associated with the Pitts Meadow Granodiorite. Two or three separate injections cut across earlier-formed aplite, as well as across the granodiorite itself.

The oldest pegmatite forms small irregular pods emplaced along the foliation of the country rock, deformed along with it, and truncated by younger rocks.

Lamprophyre (>1,430 m.y. but <1,700 m.y.)

Two types of lamprophyre, reminiscent of those in the Sawatch Range and described by Pearson and others (1966, p. 1113), have been noted in the Black Canyon. One type, a plastically deformed, weakly to strongly foliated hornblende-biotite-microcline metavogesite, crops out sparsely in widely scattered localities and forms small northwest-trending dikes that, in the upper canyon, are cut by the Curecanti pluton. Despite metamorphism, these dikes retain porphyritic textures and chilled borders that together suggest hypabyssal emplacement. Similar dikes cut the Pitts Meadow Granodiorite, thereby bracketing their time of injection.

The other type of lamprophyre, also a vogesite, is not obviously deformed or metamorphosed but forms straight-walled dikes and pipes in the headward part of the canyon and adjacent Lake Fork. It has not been observed in contact with any other igneous rock.

Cambrian or Ordovician

Diabase (510 ± 60 m.y.)

Diabase is the youngest known intrusive rock in the Black Canyon, cutting all adjacent crystalline rocks, although a pre-Laramide camptonite sill (Larsen and Cross, 1956, p. 234; Hansen, 1971) intrudes Mancos Shale just south of the Black Canyon at U.S. Highway 50 near Little Cimarron Creek. Diabase dikes of this age in the Black Canyon are of special interest, inasmuch as they are among the few igneous rocks as yet so dated in Colorado and are the only diabases. Alkalic plutons of Early Cambrian or late Proterozoic age have been dated from the Wet Mountains and from Iron Hill in the Powderhorn District (Z. E. Peterman, oral communication, 1968). A recently discovered tephritic leucitite dike in Lodore Canyon in the Uinta Mountains (Hansen, 1977) has been dated at 483 ± 29 m.y. by Sambhudas Chandhuri of Kansas State University.

Most diabase dikes in the canyon area trend N. 60°–70° W., and dip steeply south. They form a zone or set as much as 3 km across that extends an exposed distance of about 26 km from the mouth of Red Rock Canyon southeastward to and beyond Powderhorn, where they cut the alkalic complex. Some of the larger dikes reach 60 m across, have gabbroic cores, and can be traced for several kilometers. All have chilled borders. The smaller ones—down to a centimeter or so across—are dense and aphanitic.

Radiometric dating of the diabase by the Rb-Sr method has been possible because the rock contains appreciable K-feldspar in interstitial micropegmatite. The diabase in turn is helpful in placing a minimum time on the first movement of a system of conjugate fractures that moved before and after the diabase was emplaced, including such major fractures as the Red Rocks fault.

GEOLOGIC STRUCTURE

The dominant structural feature of the region is the Gunnison uplift (fig. 9), the upraised block through which the river has carved the Black Canyon. Though the Gunnison uplift is fundamentally a Laramide structure, its bounding elements began to take form in Precambrian time. It is outlined by old Precambrian faults that readjusted themselves to renewed earth movements during the Uncompahgran and Laramide orogenies. The uplift thus is mainly a composite tilted fault block rather than an updomed fold, but it is

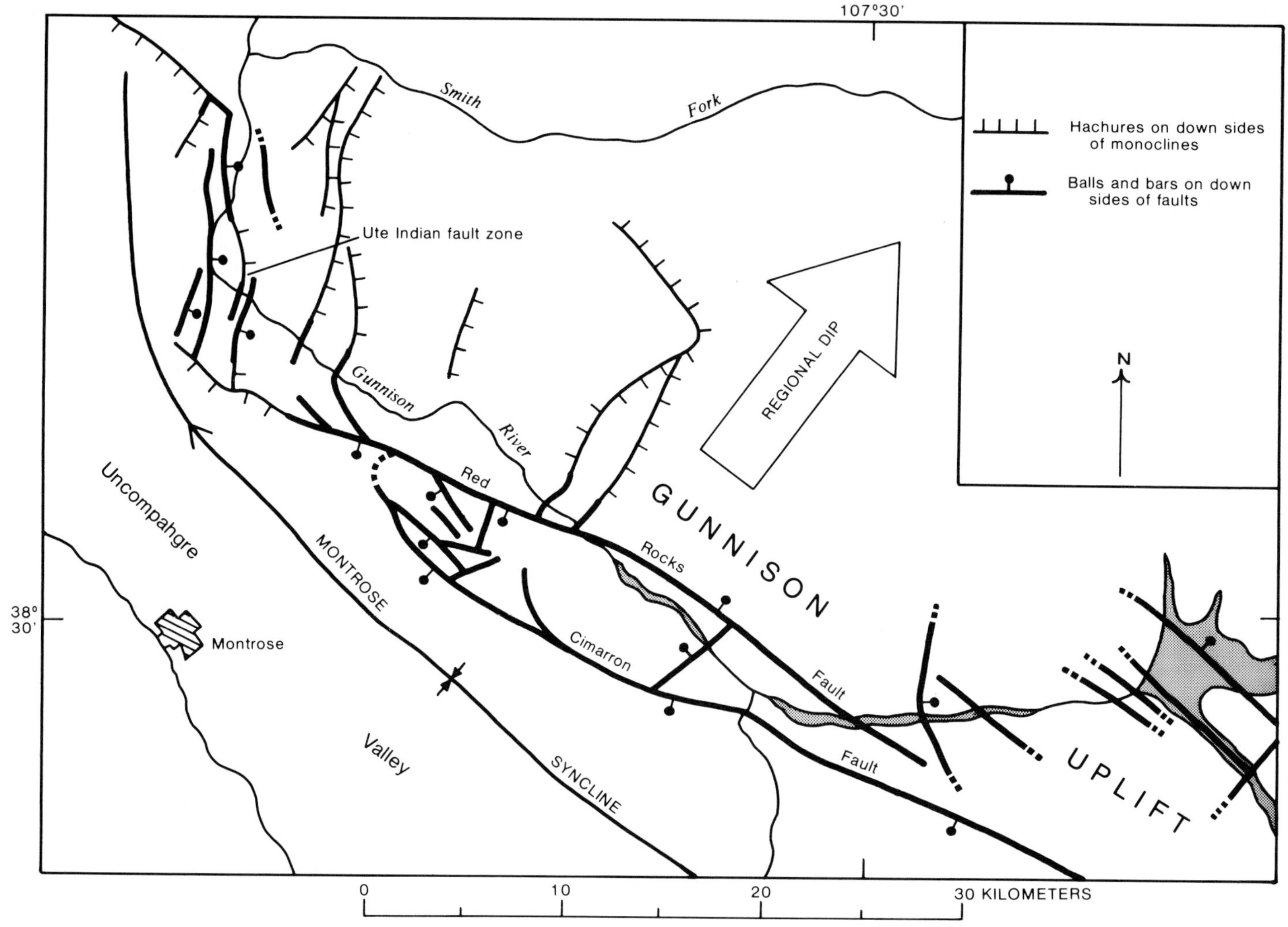

Figure 9. Sketch map showing faults and monoclines of the Black Canyon region.

sharply folded locally along faults and is gently flexed across the crest. To the northwest, the uplift passes into a plunging anticlinal nose, skirted by Colorado Highway 92 east of Austin, almost surely controlled by faulting at depth. Overall, the Gunnison uplift slopes off to the northeast into the Piceance Creek Basin. On the southwest and west it is bounded by faults and (or) monoclines.

If minor fractures and displacements are ignored, the Gunnison uplift is thus seen as a broad tilted block, still partly capped by the Dakota Sandstone but stripped down to the Precambrian basement along the canyon rims and overlapped toward the southeast by volcanic rocks. The sloping tops of Fruitland Mesa, Grizzly Ridge, Vernal Mesa, Poison Spring Hill, Dead Horse Mesa, Poverty Mesa, and the several mesas near the head of the canyon are manifestations of this great block. The steep south slopes of Vernal Mesa and Poverty Mesa coincide with lines of faulting.

Precambrian Folds

Precambrian rocks of the Black Canyon have been intricately and repeatedly folded and faulted, both at large scales and small. As one wag aptly put it:

> The greater folds have lesser folds
>   upon their flanks to right 'em
> And these, in turn, still smaller folds
>   and so ad infinitum
> (With apologies to Robert Burns)

Large-scale Precambrian folds range from a few to several kilometers across the limbs (fig. 10). Anticlines tend to be broad and flat topped, the limbs steep or overturned. Many minor folds are isoclinal. Major axes trend and plunge within a few degrees of north except in the middle section of the canyon, where they trend generally southwestward. Plutonic activity accompanied and followed deformation.

Large-scale folding is discernible directly on the ground in only a few places where it is not masked by details. One such place is Morrow Point, where a north-trending anticlinal axis crosses the Black Canyon about a kilometer below the mouth of Cimarron Creek. This fold is visible from Cimarron; from Poverty Mesa or Crystal Reservoir one can see the west limb gradually steepen and

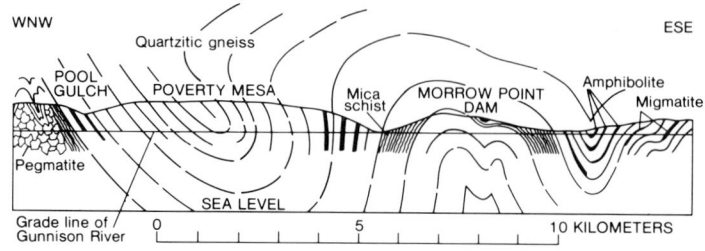

Figure 10. Sketch section along the Black Canyon near Cimarron, showing style and scale of folding.

overturn. Morrow Point Dam is built on the east limb, about at the axis of a subordinate syncline a few score meters across.

Joints

Joints vary greatly in age, size, attitude, and origin, and a detailed description of their many variations is beyond the scope of this paper. They are, however, among the more spectacular manifestations of past earth stresses in the Black Canyon, and large well-formed sets contribute greatly to the character of the canyon scenery, particularly in the steep-walled sections of the national monument (see figs. 4, 8).

Two main high-angle joint sets extend throughout the canyon area, one trending northwestward, the other northeastward. The northwesterly set is the more prominent in the national monument where some individual fractures extend more than 2 km. These fractures are regarded as shear joints. A few large low-angle joints are also visible from the canyon rims. In the upper canyon, well-formed exfoliation joints, best seen by boat, add distinction to the Curecanti pluton.

Faults

Most faults of the area are ancient fractures that have had several periods of displacement. The largest displacements, which produced mylonite, were pre-Laramide, either Precambrian or Uncompahgran. Some have had no Laramide displacement, and no fault in the area offsets the Tertiary volcanics. The large Red Rocks fault, which bounds Vernal Mesa on the southwest, arises near the head of Red Rock Canyon and trends east-southeast 30 km or so toward Blue Creek (see figs. 3, 9). This fault has a pre-Laramide strike-slip displacement of about 5½ km, offsetting the Vernal Mesa pluton and several large diabase dikes. Its Laramide habit was scissors-like—up about 1,200 m on the south, toward the west, and down about 120 m on the south, toward the east. Its hinge or node is just south of the south-rim campground in the Monument. As the Red Rocks fault dies out toward the southeast, its displacement is taken up by the Cimarron fault, which extends about 64 km from Bostwick Park to Powderhorn. These faults together form the southwest boundary of the Gunnison uplift. The Cimarron fault has a high-angle reverse habit, clearly shown by wall relations at Cimarron, where its dip is about 60 degrees and its throw is about 1,200 m.

The best-exposed faults in the area are in the lower reach of the canyon, and their large escarpments dominate the local scenery. Access, unfortunately, is poor. The Ute Indian fault zone is a north-trending line of fractures along which Pitts Meadow Granodiorite has been thrust at least a hundred meters up and over the Entrada Sandstone. Field evidence indicates repeated offset. Pre-Jurassic movements caused local mylonitization. Laramide movements produced no mylonite, but caused considerable shattering and brecciation, especially in the hanging wall. Like most other faults in the Black Canyon, the faults of the Ute Indian zone are reverse faults; measured dips on well exposed fault planes are as low as 32 degrees.

Monoclines

The remarkable monoclines of the Black Canyon area are Laramide features caused by the draping of sedimentary rocks across the previously faulted crystalline basement, owing in large part to plastic flowage of the gypsiferous Wanakah Formation and warping in the overlying strata. Monoclinal folding is best exemplified in the lower section of the Black Canyon (fig. 11), particularly along the well-exposed vertical and lateral extensions of the Ute Indian

Figure 11. View west from Green Mountain across the lower Black Canyon toward the Uncompahgre Valley and Plateau, showing monoclinal draping over the Ute Indian fault zone. Fault here, increasing rapidly in throw toward the right (north), dips west about 26–30°. Note inner gorge in middle distance at left and far right.

fault zone. Elsewhere, monoclines expressed as warps or bends in the Dakota Sandstone on top of Green Mountain and Grizzly Ridge can be seen passing downward into faults in the wall of the Black Canyon. The large Red Rocks fault passes laterally into a monocline west of Bostwick Park, where it becomes the steep northeast limb of the Montrose syncline.

GEOLOGIC HISTORY
Precambrian Events

Prior to about 1,700 million years ago, a thick sequence of arkosic sandstones, graywackes, sandy shales, and perhaps rhyolitic to basaltic volcanic rocks was deposited across the area on an unexposed basement. Subjected to intense folding and amphibolite-grade metamorphism, this sequence was then transformed essentially to its present metamorphic character. At about the same time, the Pitts Meadow batholith (cf., Boulder Creek intrusions of the Front Range) and its associated pegmatite and aplite dikes were intruded into the lower Black Canyon area.

Renewed crustal movements 1,500–1,400 m.y. ago accompanied the intrusion of the Vernal Mesa and Curecanti plutons (cf., Silver Plume of the Front Range). The Vernal Mesa pluton, which has no exact Front Range counterpart, was strongly foliated by protoclastic flowage, but deformation had died out by the time the main body of the Curecanti was emplaced. A few small lamprophyric dikes (metavogesite) were intruded after the Pitts Meadow but before the Curecanti and probably before the Vernal Mesa. Countless pegmatite dikes were injected during or soon after emplacement of the Curecanti pluton. Another metamorphic event in the range of 1,300–1,200 m.y. ago is suggested by altered mica ages (Giffin and Kulp, 1960). Possibly this event accompanied early fault movements.

Intrusion of Diabase

Diabase dikes were injected into the east-southeast-trending fracture zone in Cambrian or Ordovician time—probably Late Cambrian. Subsequent movements along the fracture zone deformed and displaced some of them. In the Powderhorn District the same dike swarm cuts the alkalic complex there, according to D. C. Hedlund and J. C. Olson (oral communication, 1967).

Late Paleozoic Events

The balance of Paleozoic history prior to Pennsylvanian time has been obscured by the Uncompahgran orogeny and the erosion that followed. Judging from what happened in adjacent areas, we can assume that shallow Paleozoic seas covered the Black Canyon area in much of pre-Pennsylvanian time. In Pennsylvanian and later time, thick wedges of clastic sediment, stripped from the old Uncompahgre highland, were deposited in the adjacent Paradox and Eagle River basins. Ultimately the ancestral Uncompahgre highland was reduced to a low featureless plain, broadly archlike in cross section, with an apex near the town of Gunnison. The Black Canyon area was just west of the crest. Segments of the old plain are well preserved in cross section along rims of the Black Canyon in the conspicuous unconformity between the Precambrian and the overlying rocks.

Mesozoic Time

The roots of the old Uncompahgre highland persisted as a subaerial plain over the Black Canyon until Middle Jurassic time, when sedimentation resumed. The eastward overlap of Jurassic rocks onto the unconformity indicates that the surface sloped westward in the Black Canyon area in Jurassic time, at a gradient of about 0.75 m/km. Mostly nonmarine sediments, deposited by the wind, in brackish lakes, and on river flood plains, accumulated during the Jurassic Period. These are the Entrada, Wanakah, and Morrison Formations. Lapping against the old highland, the Entrada is well represented in the lower Black Canyon, but it thins eastward and wedges out completely in the national monument. The Wanakah Formation persists throughout the canyon but thins markedly toward the east; only its Junction Creek Member extends into the Blue Mesa Reservoir area, where it rests directly on the Precambrian. First fluvial, then littoral, and finally true marine conditions evolved in Cretaceous time—represented by the Burro Canyon Formation, the Dakota Sandstone, and the Mancos Shale. Younger formations, if deposited, were stripped away in the mountain building that followed.

Laramide Orogeny

Near the close of Cretaceous time the Gunnison uplift took form as renewed movements along the old faults raised the uplift above its surroundings. Erosion attacked the heights, slowly reducing them to a common level, so that streams flowing west from the newly risen Sawatch Range were finally able to flow almost unhindered across the beveled crest of the uplift, by then eroded to its Precambrian core. Projecting above the widening plains were scattered hills a few score meters high, now fossil monadnocks buried by Tertiary volcanic eruptions.

Tertiary Volcanism

Volcanic eruptions began in the nearby West Elk and San Juan mountains in middle Tertiary (Oligocene) time, covering the beveled core of the Gunnison uplift with successive blankets of volcanic debris. Eruptions of intermediate lavas and volcanic breccias (West Elk Breccia and San Juan Formation) from both volcanic centers were succeeded in late Oligocene time by more-silicic pyroclastic eruptions of welded tuff out of the San Juan Mountains and, finally, by localized Miocene outpourings of mafic alkalic lava—the Hinsdale Formation (Olson and others, 1968; Lipman and others, 1978). If earlier Cretaceous or Tertiary volcanism in the San Juan Mountains affected the Gunnison uplift, it left no recognized evidence. As the volcanic piles grew, the west-flowing drainage through the area became channeled between the two volcanic centers. Drainage was curtailed from time to time by volcanic outbursts, but between eruptions it left sheets of gravel of Sawatch provenance. Some of these are well exposed along Highway 92. Volcanism persisted in the San Juan Mountains long after it had ended in the West Elks. Great sheets of pyroclastic tuff poured north from the San Juans across the Gunnison uplift and onto the flanks of the West Elks (Table 2). Concomitantly, synclinal warping began along the axis of the present Black Canyon, probably caused by unloading and doming of the West Elk Mountains (fig. 12). Consequently, each ash flow acquired a synclinal structure and, because of ponding, was thickened over the Black Canyon (fig. 13). Warping continued until after the eruption of the Hinsdale Formation.

Erosion of the Black Canyon

The stage was now set for the cutting of the Black Canyon. Volcanic activity affecting the area ended with the eruption of the Hinsdale Formation, and the Gunnison River began to cut its canyon. When its course became fixed, the river was thus flowing on a thick fill of volcanic rock and gravel and was positioned along the axis of the late Tertiary syncline. Fortuitously, its course also crossed the buried Gunnison uplift, so that when the uplift was finally again breached by erosion, the river—held in by its own steep banks—had no alternative but to erode downward into the Precambrian core. Had its course been only a few kilometers to the south, beyond the bordering faults of the Gunnison uplift, the river would have met only soft sedimentary rocks and today, instead of the Black Canyon, there would be just another broad valley, like the Uncompahgre or perhaps the North Fork.

Formation of the syncline was absolutely critical to the ultimate cutting of the Black Canyon. Because volcanic activity in the West Elk Mountains had largely ceased by the onset of ash-flow eruptions in the San Juan Mountains, erosion was unloading the West Elks all the while that the ash flows were spreading north across the Black Canyon area. Updoming of the West Elks, probably caused by unloading, reversed the dips in the distal parts of the ash flows, one after another, producing the growing syncline along the Black Canyon axis. Without the syncline, drainage would have migrated down dip, locating the Gunnison River far to the north, off the Gunnison uplift, and we would have no Black Canyon.

Late Quaternary Deformation

Although there is no known Quaternary movement on any fault in the Black Canyon area, some regional late Quaternary deformation is probable. The best evidence is in the well-formed terracing along the North Fork and the Uncompahgre River downstream from the Gunnison uplift, contrasted with the near lack of terrac-

Table 2. Ash-flow tuffs of the Black Canyon–Blue Mesa Reservoir area (from Lipman and others, 1973).

Formation	Age (m.y.)	Original Volume (km^3)	Caldera Source
Carpenter Ridge	27.5	1,200–1,500	Creede–La Garita
Fish Canyon	27.8	3,000+	Creede–La Garita
Sapinero Mesa	28	1,000+	Uncompahgre–San Juan–Silverton
Dillon Mesa	>28	50–100	Uncompahgre (?)
Blue Mesa	>28	400+	Lost Lake (?)

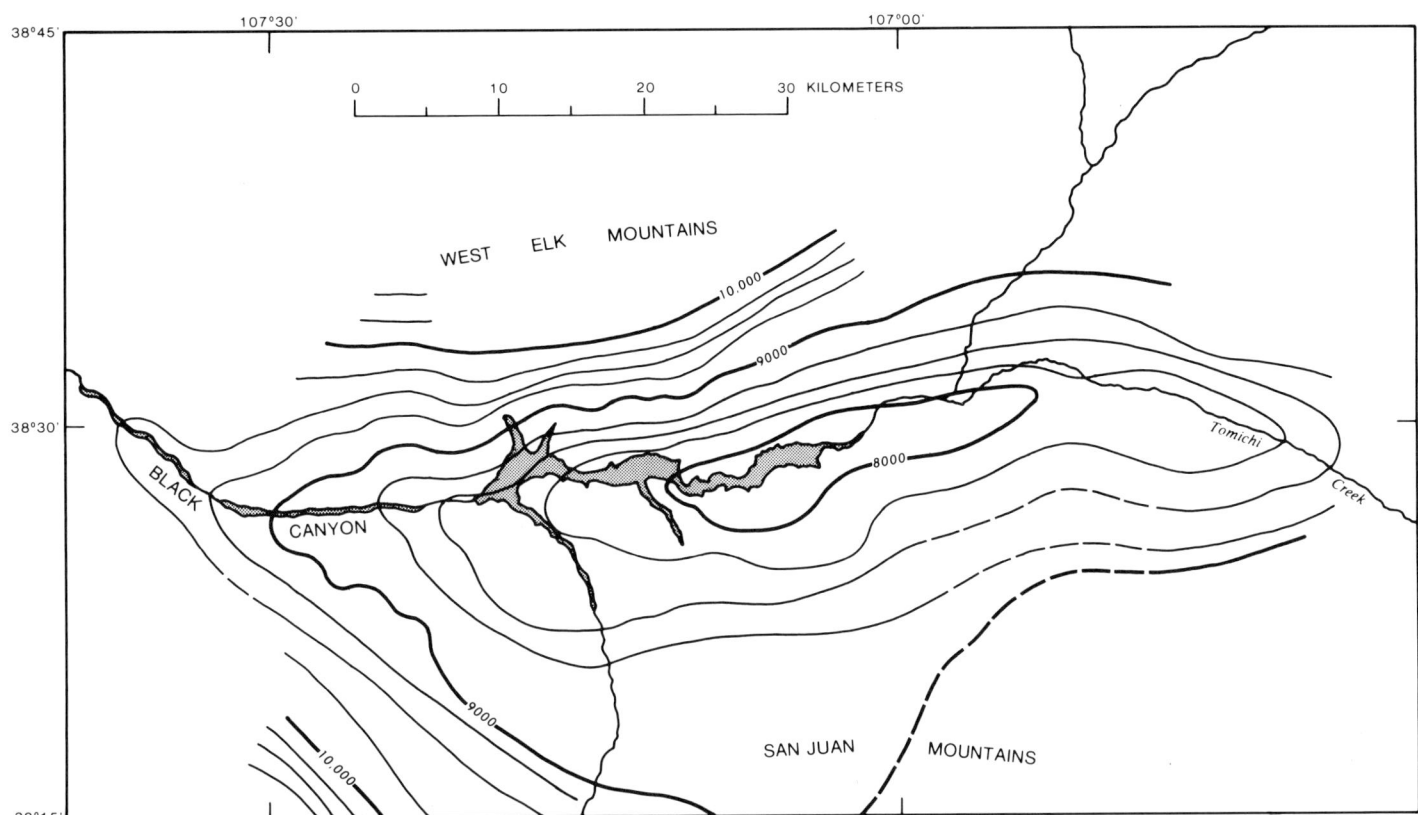

Figure 12. Structure contours drawn at the base of the ash-flow tuff volcanic sequence. Dashed contours indicate area of probable nondeposition. Based on geologic maps by Hansen (1971), Hedlund and Olson (1973), Hedlund (1974), and Tweto and others (1976). Contour interval 250 feet (about 78 m).

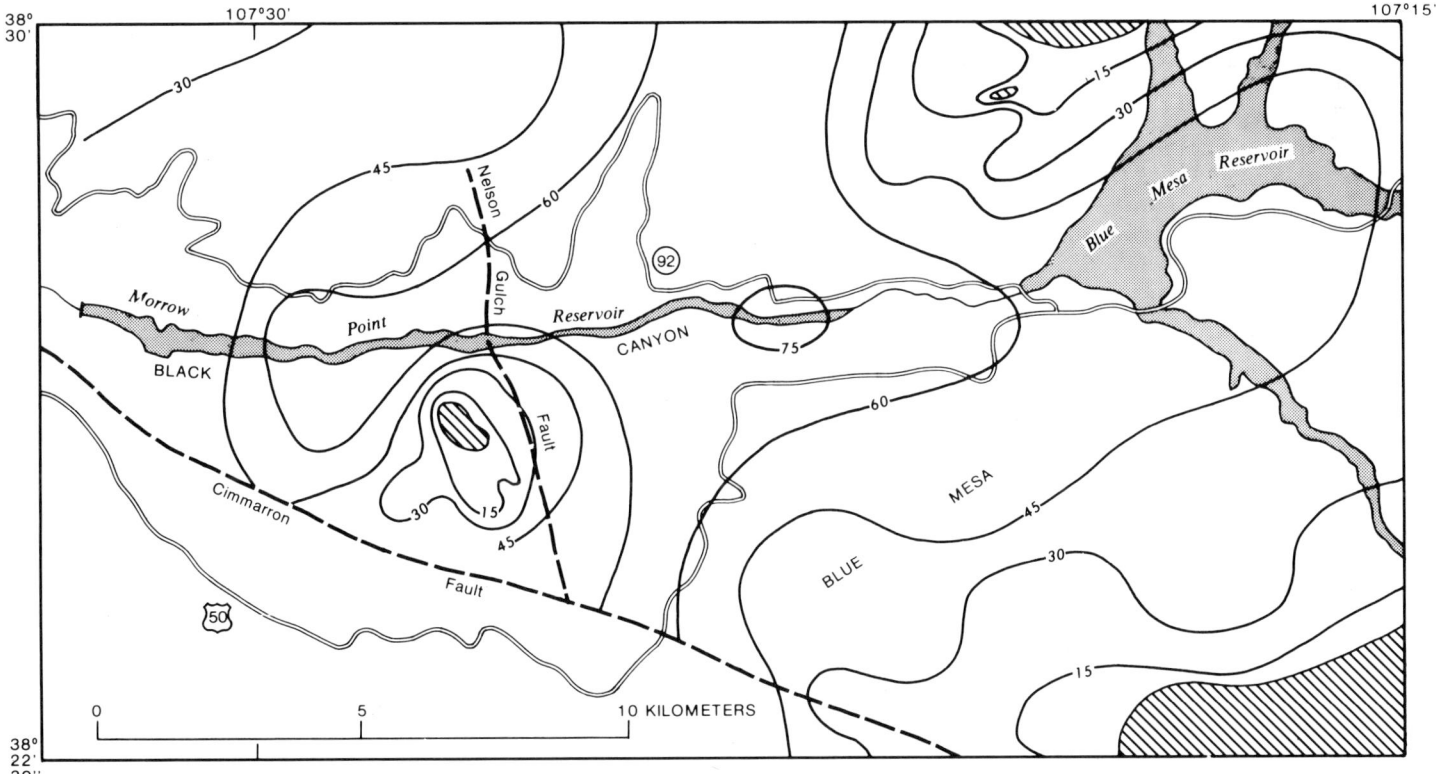

Figure 13. Thickness map of the Blue Mesa tuff. Thickening over the Black Canyon area coincides with the axial region of the syncline shown in Figure 12. Ruled pattern indicates area of nondeposition—either topographic highs ("islands") at the time of eruption or the distal edge of the ash flow. Contour interval 15 m.

ing on the Gunnison River itself immediately upstream of the canyon. The hard-rock core of the uplift has been a local base level to the upstream drainage, and a continued slow rise of the uplift—up toward the southwest, as indicated by the rise of the volcanic rims in that direction—would restrain downcutting and terracing by the river. The lack of terracing is especially pronounced just upstream of the uplift along the river and its tributary Tomichi Creek, at the town of Gunnison and vicinity. Indeed, wintertime lowland flooding in the fields below Gunnison, owing to ice blockage of the channel, is aggravated by the absence of confining terraces.

REFERENCES

Buddington, A. F., 1959, Granite emplacement with special reference to North America: Geological Society of America Bulletin, v. 70, p. 671–747.

Gaskill, D. L., Rosebaum, J. G., and King, H. D., 1977, Mineral resources of the West Elk Wilderness and vicinity, Delta and Gunnison Counties, Colorado: U.S. Geological Survey Open-File Report 77-751, 111 p.

Giffin, C. E. and Kulp, J. L., 1960, Potassium-argon ages in the Precambrian basement of Colorado: Geological Society of America Bulletin, v. 71, p. 219–222.

Hansen, W. R., 1964, Curecanti pluton, an unusual intrusive body in the Black Canyon of the Gunnison, Colorado: U.S. Geological Survey Bulletin 1181-D, p. D1–D15.

———, 1965, The Black Canyon of the Gunnison, Today and Yesterday: U.S. Geological Survey Bulletin 1191, 76 p.

———, 1968, Geologic map of the Black Ridge quadrangle, Delta and Montrose counties, Colorado: U.S. Geological Survey Geologic Quadrangle Map GQ-747, scale 1:24,000.

———, 1971, Geologic map of the Black Canyon of the Gunnison River and vicinity, western Colorado: U.S. Geological Survey Miscellaneous Geologic Investigations Map I-584, scale 1:31,680.

———, 1977, Geologic map of the Canyon of Lodore South quadrangle, Moffat County Colorado: U.S. Geological Survey Geologic Quadrangle Map GQ-1403, scale 1:24,000.

Hansen, W. R. and Peterman, Z. E., 1968, Basement-rock geochronology of the Black Canyon of the Gunnison, Colorado: U.S. Geological Survey Professional Paper 600-C, p. C80–C90.

Hedge, E. E., Peterman, Z. E., Case, J. E., and Obradovich, J. D., 1968, Precambrian geochronology of the northwestern Uncompahgre Plateau, Utah and Colorado: U.S. Geological Survey Professional Paper 600-C, p. C91–C96.

Hedlund, D. C., 1974, Geologic map of the Big Mesa quadrangle, Gunnison County, Colorado: U.S. Geological Survey Geologic Quadrangle Map GQ-1153, scale 1:24,000.

Hedlund, D. C. and Olson, J. C., 1973, Geologic map of the Carpenter Ridge quadrangle, Gunnison County, Colorado: U.S. Geological Survey Geologic Quadrangle Map GQ-1070, scale 1:24,000.

Hunter, J. F., 1925, Precambrian rocks of Gunnison River, Colorado: U.S. Geological Survey Bulletin 777, 94 p.

Larsen, E. S., Jr., and Cross, Whitman, 1956, Geology and petrology of the San Juan region, southwestern Colorado: U.S. Geological Survey Professional Paper 258, 303 p.

Lipman, P. W., Steven, T. A., Luedke, R. G., and Burbank, W. S., 1973, Revised volcanic history of the San Juan, Uncompahgre, Silverton, and Lake City calderas in western San Juan Mountains, Colorado: Journal of Research, U.S. Geological Survey, v. 1, p. 627–642.

Lipman, P. W., Doe, B. R., Hedge, C. E., and Steven, T. A., 1978, Petrologic evolution of the San Juan volcanic field, southwestern Colorado: Pb and Sr isotope evidence: Geological Society of America Bulletin, v. 89, p. 59–82.

Olson, J. C., Hedlund, D. C., and Hansen, W. R., 1968, Tertiary volcanic stratigraphy in the Powderhorn–Black Canyon region, Gunnison and Montrose Counties, Colorado: U.S. Geological Survey Bulletin 1251-C, p. C1–C29.

Pearson, R. C., Hedge, C. E., Thomas, H. H., and Stern, T. W., 1966, Geochronology of the St. Kevin Granite and neighboring Precambrian rocks, northern Sawatch Range, Colorado: Geological Society of America Bulletin, v. 77, p. 1109–1120.

Tweto, Ogden, Steven, T. A., Hail, W. J., Jr., and Moench, R. H., 1976, Preliminary geologic map of the Montrose 1° × 2° quadrangle, southwestern Colorado: U.S. Geological Survey Miscellaneous Field Studies Map MF-761, scale 1:250,000.

Van Eysinga, 1978, Geologic time table: Amsterdam, Elsevier Publishing Co.

QUATERNARY GLACIAL AND SLOPE-FAILURE DEPOSITS OF THE CRESTED BUTTE AREA, GUNNISON COUNTY, COLORADO

CHARLES H. ROBINSON
and
PETER A. DEA
Converse Ward Davis Dixon, Inc.
Lakewood, Colorado 80215

INTRODUCTION

During the Quaternary Period, the region near Crested Butte, Gunnison County, Colorado was subjected to alpine glaciation. Glacial, periglacial and alpine processes have produced surficial deposits that are involved in the development of the area. The proposed molybdenum mine on Mount Emmons and expansion of the recreational industry have imposed strong development pressures. The genesis of the surficial deposits, on which much of the development will occur, has a profound impact on the engineering considerations for development.

Feasibility studies of the Mount Emmons molybdenum deposit by AMAX, Inc. are being conducted in the area around Crested Butte, Colorado. Engineering and environmental geologic mapping at scales ranging from 1:24,000 to 1:2,400 has been conducted over a three-year period beginning in June 1978 by Charles S. Robinson and Associates, now Converse Ward Davis Dixon, Inc., as part of these feasibility studies (fig. 1). The study of the surficial deposits led to a basic understanding of the late Pleistocene and Recent geologic history of the region.

Bedrock geologic studies of the area were conducted by Gaskill and others (1976, 1977) of the U.S. Geological Survey and by exploration geologists with Climax Molybdenum Company and AMAX, Inc. Geologic hazards were recognized by Soule (1976) of the Colorado Geologic Survey.

GENERAL GEOLOGY

The Crested Butte area is underlain by sedimentary rocks of Cretaceous and Tertiary age. The sedimentary rocks have been folded, faulted, and to different degrees indurated, hydrothermally altered, and metamorphosed by the intrusion of several Tertiary igneous bodies. Sedimentary rocks include the Mancos Shale and the Mesaverde Formation of Cretaceous age overlain by the Ohio Creek and Wasatch Formations of Tertiary age.

Numerous igneous bodies, including sills, dikes and laccoliths, have intruded the sedimentary rocks. The composition of the intrusives ranges from granodiorite to quartz monzonite. The intrusives are commonly porphyritic containing large euhedral phenocrysts of feldspars. The prominent geomorphic features, Crested Butte, Gothic Peak, Mount Whetstone, Carbon Peak and Mount Axtell, are formed by these intrusives. Basaltic flows of Miocene age cap Red Mountain and Flat Top Mountain.

Many faults dissect the sedimentary and igneous rocks. Faults show two predominant trends, northwest and northeast, and dip steeply to vertically. Offset, where recognizable, is usually normal with few lateral displacements recognized.

The Crested Butte area is within the Colorado Mineral Belt, and includes a wide variety of metallic elements that have been mined in the past. These include gold, silver, lead, zinc and copper. AMAX is currently conducting feasibility studies on a major molybdenum deposit under Mount Emmons. High quality coal has been mined from beds in the Mesaverde Formation throughout the area.

GLACIAL GEOLOGY

High cirque basins, deep trough-shaped valleys and deposits of till and erratics throughout the Colorado Rocky Mountains show the predominance of glaciers during Quaternary time. Large mountain ice caps covered much of the high mountains and fed valley glaciers that commonly flowed into valleys to form large piedmont lobes. Multiple glaciations are indicated by nested mo-

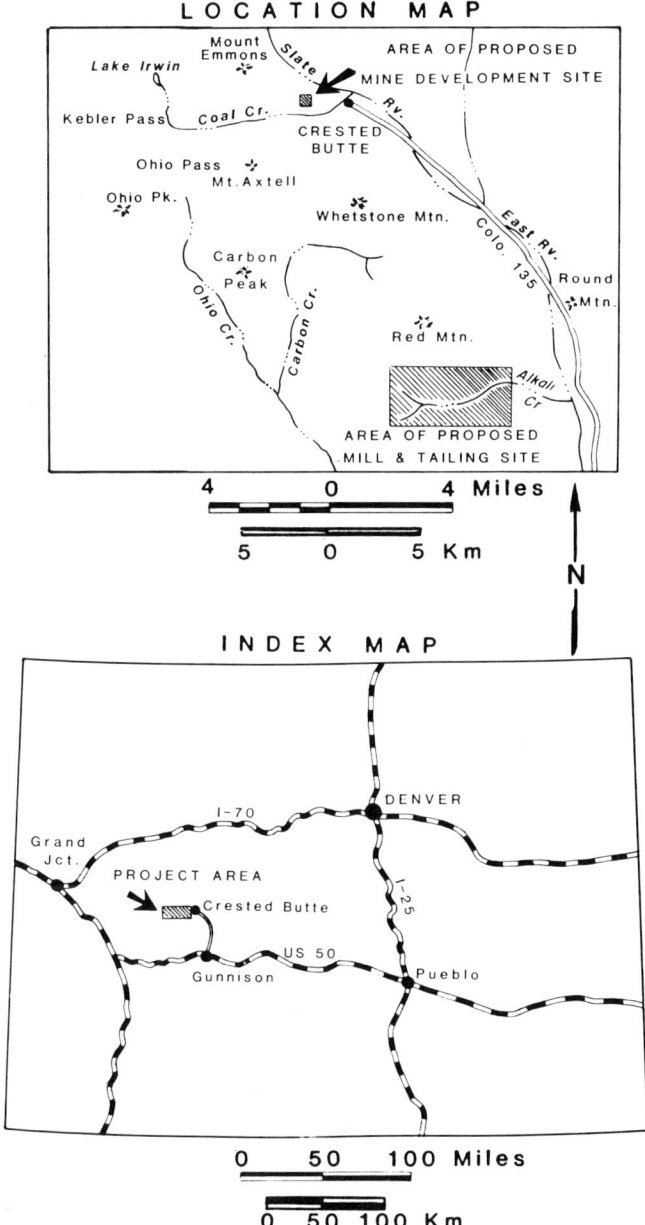

Figure 1. Index and location maps of the Crested Butte area.

raines, till sequences, relative age-dating and radiocarbon-dating techniques (Meierding and Birkeland, 1980). Four periods of major glaciation are recognized in Colorado: pre-Bull Lake, Bull Lake, Pinedale and Holocene, with at least the latter three characterized by several stades of advance and retreat.

Meierding and Birkeland (1980) offer a thorough review of the most recent studies on characteristics and ages of glacial deposits in Colorado. Much work is still needed to more confidently define ages of the deposits and especially to correlate deposits and glacial events throughout Colorado and the Rocky Mountain region. Lack of dates makes correlation difficult, and many factors may cause nonsynchroniety in glacial advances even within the same mountain range. These factors include equilibrium-line altitudes, size of ice accumulation areas, differing response times for glaciers of different size, gradient, exposure and local climate. Prevalence of several rock glaciers and small cirque glaciers indicate that glacial events may have occurred throughout the Holocene and be continuing at present.

Although no definite ages are yet available from glacial deposits in the Crested Butte area, lateral moraines indicate the presence of two to three stades of glaciation of probable Pinedale age. Relationships between moraines of two valley glaciers show that the two valley glaciers flowed together. However individual stades or advances of each glacier were not synchronous.

Glacial Deposits

Glacial deposits that blanket much of the Crested Butte area are ground moraines and lateral moraines of presumed Pinedale age. In the cirque basins, where erosion dominated, only a thin veneer of ground moraine and erratics remain. Till is up to 60 m thick in the valley bottoms. Moraines consist of till containing poorly sorted clay, silt, sand and gravel with subangular to well rounded cobbles and boulders and angular boulders up to 3 m in diameter.

Moraines along Coal Creek and the lower Slate River (fig. 1) form the most conspicuous glacial deposits in the area and are the moraines examined in this study. Lateral moraines form broad, rounded to flat-topped benches and sharp-crested ridges perched along steep bedrock slopes. Erosional processes have significantly modified the moraines—streams and runoff have dissected and rounded many of the once crested moraina1 ridges; and saturated

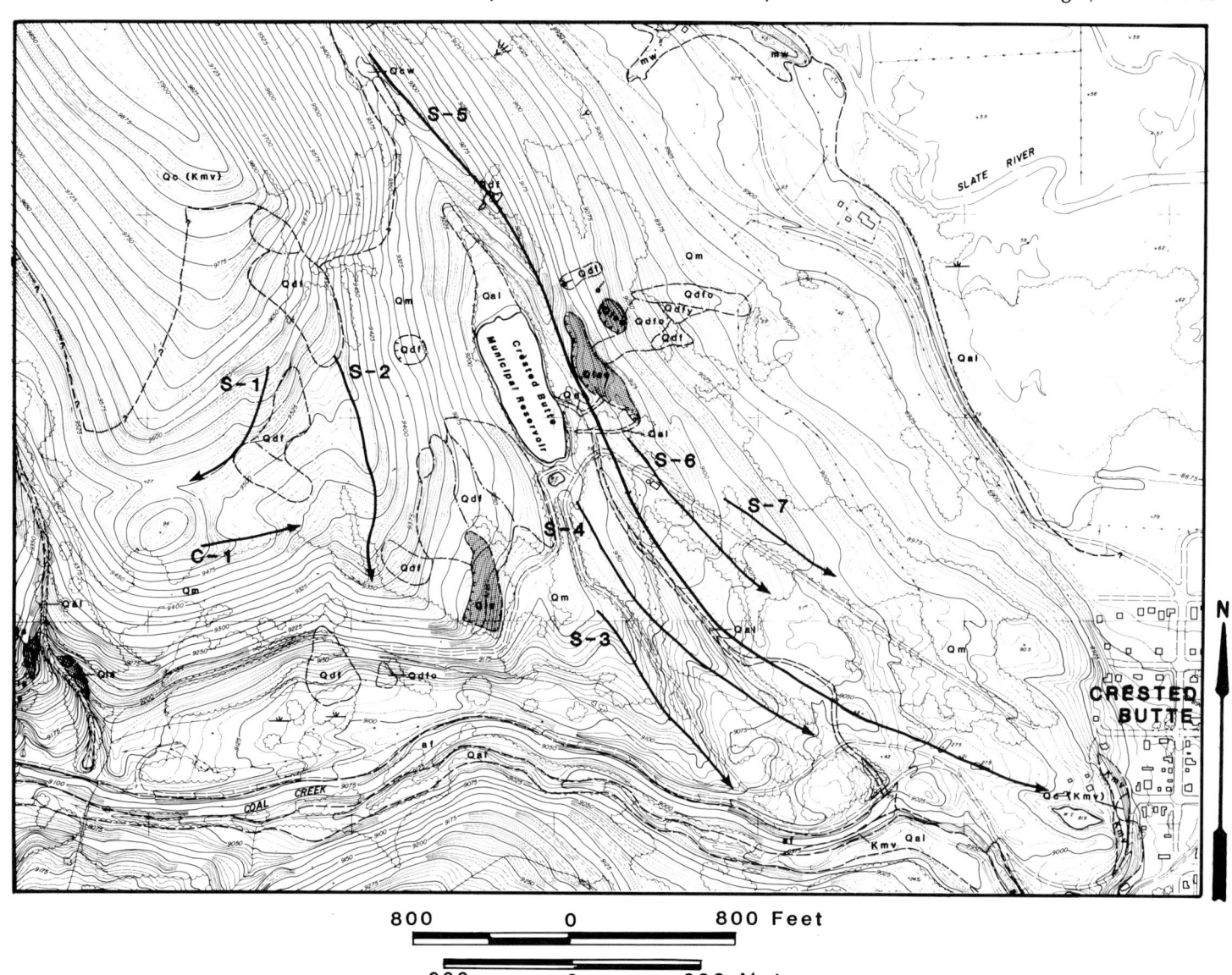

Figure 2. Geologic map of Crested Butte municipal reservoir area, showing crestlines of lateral moraines deposited by Coal Creek glacier (C-1) and Slate River glacier (S-1 to S-7) (see Figure 3 for explanation).

conditions combined with oversteepening by stream bank erosion have caused many debris flows. Due to erosional modifications it often is difficult to differentiate between ground moraine and what were once well formed lateral moraines.

Ground moraines occur in the valley bottoms and on the floors of the cirque basins. They are recognized by low rolling, hummocky topography and lack the ridge-like form indicative of lateral moraines. Many large boulders or glacial erratics cover the surface of ground moraine. The till comprising ground moraines also contains many large boulders as seen in roadcuts along Coal Creek.

The best preserved sequence of lateral moraines is near the Crested Butte municipal reservoir (fig. 2). The sharp crest and steep sides of the moraines, covered with many unweathered surface boulders, strongly support correlation to Pinedale-age deposits (Meierding and Birkeland, 1980; Richmond, 1965). Although it is likely that there are pre-Bull Lake and Bull Lake-age glacial deposits in the Crested Butte area, their age has not been documented yet.

The upper extent of moraines, regardless of type, define a minimum upper ice elevation of the last glacier that occupied the valleys. The upper limit of till deposited by the main valley glacier in Coal Creek can be traced along the north side of Coal Creek on ridges separating four cirque basins. From west to east the cirque basins are Elk, Evans, Red Lady and Coon basins. Where the valley glacier began to narrow from the broad catchment area surrounding Lake Irwin (fig. 1), the ice rose to an altitude of at least 10,800 ft (3292 m). This is shown by morainal material on and slightly above the flat bench retaining Copley Lake located 1.6 km east of Lake Irwin. The ice level may have been higher here, as evidenced by a step-like series of flat benches on the ridge northeast of Copley Lake. The upper bench is at 11,275 ft (3437 m), due west of Elk Basin. Lack of significant well-preserved glacial deposits suggests that an older glacial event eroded the flat benches. Down valley to the east, between Elk and Evans basins, the highest deposit of till is at an altitude of 10,850 ft (3307 m). The ice is believed to have been higher than this, probably during an older glaciation, as suggested by erosional benches located upslope. The highest and most prominent bench is at an altitude of 11,150 ft (3399 m). A huge post- or periglacial landslide complex above the moraine and surrounding the erosional benches limits interpretation of the glacial deposits.

The minimum upper ice limit between Evans and Red Lady Basins is at 9,950 ft (3033 m). Limited deposits of till occur at this altitude as debris flows have removed most of the moraine. The upper limit of the glacial deposits in this area most commonly is defined by the presence of large glacial erratics of sandstone and latite porphyry up to 3 m in diameter. The minimum upper ice limit farther down valley is well marked by till on the slope between the creeks draining Red Lady and Coon Basins. From west to east the upper till limit extends from approximately 9,800 to 9,600 ft (2987 to 2926 m) over about 1 km. A thin veneer of till and many glacial erratics of latite porphyry clearly define the upper altitudes of glacial deposits across the entire kilometer distance.

The best preserved lateral moraines in the area are between the outlet of Coon Basin and the Slate River Valley (fig. 1). Here the glaciers flowing from the Coal Creek and the Slate River valleys met and deposited lateral moraines. The cross cutting relationship between the linear sharp crested lateral moraines in each valley shows the sequence of advances of the most recent Coal Creek and Slate River valley glaciers. A well defined lateral moraine deposited by the Coal Creek glacier extends from the southeast side of a bedrock knob at 9,525 ft (2903 m) about 120 m eastward to an altitude of 9,475 ft (2888 m) (C-1, fig. 2). This moraine truncates a lateral moraine (S-1, fig. 2) deposited by the Slate River glacier that slopes southerly from an altitude of 9,650 ft (2941 m) to the Coal Creek lateral moraine. The elevation of this upper Slate River moraine above the Coal Creek lateral moraine indicates that the Slate River glacier must have initially been higher than the Coal Creek glacier, causing its ice to spill southwest into the Coal Creek Valley. The trend and slope of this moraine clearly indicates a source from the north—the Slate River valley glacier. Till and erratics cover the bedrock slopes above the moraines to an altitude

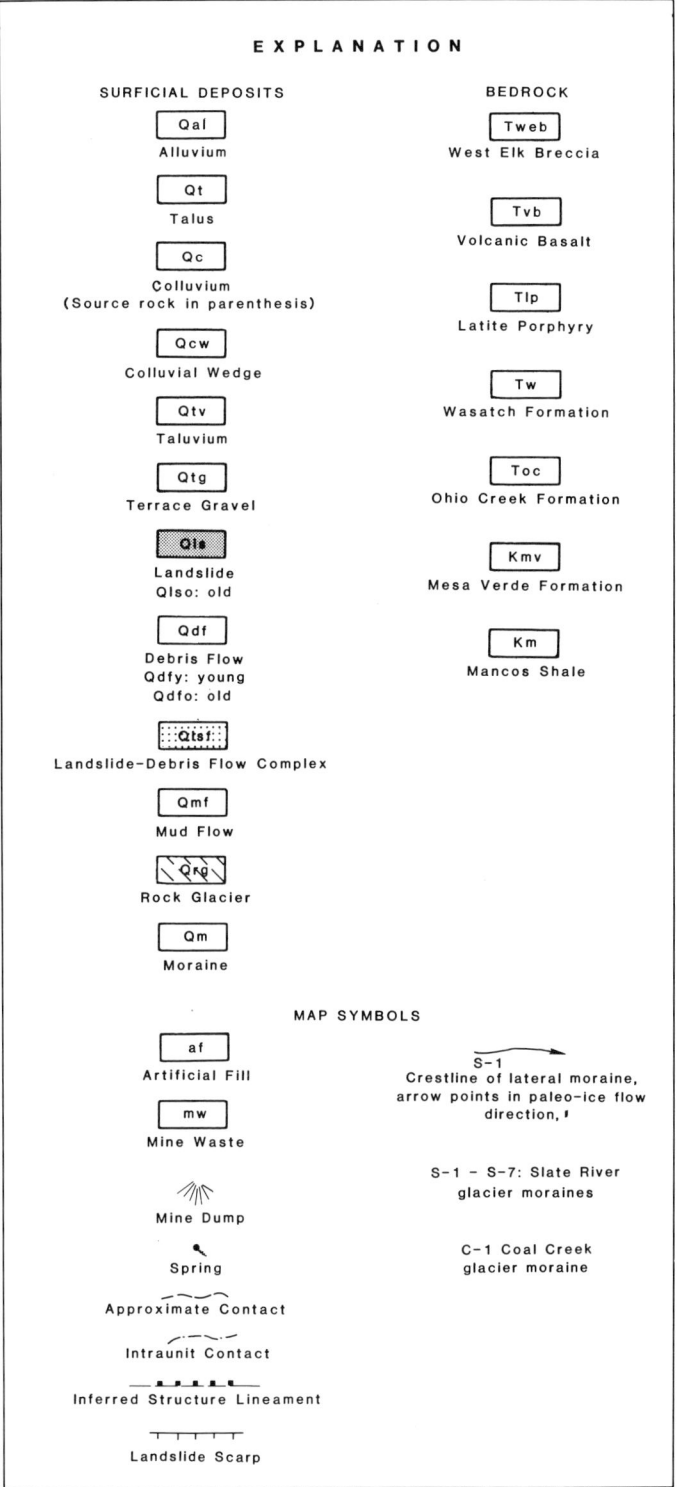

Figure 3. Explanation of geologic maps for Figures 2, 5 and 8.

of 9,825 ft (2995 m). This till also is believed to have been deposited by the Slate River glacier. Near the top of this slope, at 9,580 ft (2920 m), is a bedrock bench sprinkled with small erratics, which curves and slopes from the Slate River valley toward lower Coon Basin. This bench is also evidence of the Slate River valley glacier, and its higher altitude above the Coal Creek glacier. As the Slate River ice surface was lowered, and/or the Coal Creek glacier rose higher, the Coal Creek glacier dominated, as evidenced by the truncation of the upper Slate River lateral moraine (S-1) by the Coal Creek lateral moraine (C-1). The Coal Creek moraine was in turn truncated by the Slate River glacier during a readvance. This is indicated by another south-trending lateral moraine (S-2, fig. 2) that slopes from north to south and cuts off the Coal Creek moraine. This moraine forms the crest of the high ridge west of the Crested Butte municipal reservoir.

Extending from the south end of the reservoir are several more lateral moraines deposited by the Slate River glacier. The most prominent begins at 9,350 ft (2850 m) and passes along the east side of the reservoir trending southerly to the western limits of Crested Butte at an altitude of 8,995 ft (2742 m). This moraine is over a kilometer long and forms and dams the town reservoir (S-5, fig. 2). The location of the four smaller lateral moraines are shown in Figure 2 as S-3, S-4, S-6 and S-7. They parallel the Slate River valley and represent recessional stades of the Slate River glacier.

Below the Coal Creek–Slate River valley junction the glaciers coalesced and flowed southeasterly through the present location of Crested Butte. As ice bypassed the present townsite it scoured out an arcuate face on the north side of Gibson Ridge, south of Crested Butte. The upper altitude of the steep arcuate slope is compatible with that of the erosional bench above the town reservoir. This indicates a minimum ice thickness of 180 m. Between the base of Gibson Ridge and the town of Crested Butte the ice deposited a large moraine, a kilometer long and 300 m wide. The ice eventually flowed 6.5 km south of Crested Butte to the present site of the Crested Butte airport, where it deposited a large hummocky terminal moraine. Ice also flowed from the mountains northeast of Crested Butte into the East River and Brush Creek valleys. The relationship between these glaciers and the Slate River glacier has not yet been documented.

The relative ages of the Coal Creek and Slate River glaciers can be determined from the relationships of the moraines at the Coal Creek–Slate River Valley junction. This sequence of moraines indicates that although the two adjacent glaciers were present simultaneously, their individual advances were not always in phase. The originally higher elevation of the Slate River glacier may have been due to its source areas being higher and much larger, with less southern exposure than the source area of the Coal Creek glaciers. Truncation of the Coal Creek lateral moraine by the Slate River moraine may be due to the more rapid deterioration of Coal Creek ice related to two reasons: 1) quick response time of a small ice mass to climatic changes; and 2) more southern exposure of the source areas. These differences must have been significant factors in ice accumulation. The Slate River Valley is much broader than the Coal Creek Valley, and would require more ice to fill it. Ice in the Coal Creek Valley also was able only to reach a limited elevation as ice near the upper valley spilled over ice passes to the south and west—Ohio and Kebler Passes which regulated the ice elevation in the valley. This is evidenced by deposits of till in the Kebler Pass area ranging from altitudes of 9,980 to 10,175 ft (3042 to 3101 m), and in the broad area between Ohio Pass and Splains Gulch to the east ranging from altitudes of 10,074 to 10,690 ft (3071 to 3258 m) (fig. 1). The Lake Irwin area is the only possible significant source area for ice that deposited the till with only a minor contribution from Ohio Peak on the east end of the Anthracite Range (fig. 1).

The age of the glacial deposits in the Crested Butte area is not known, yet their similarity to other deposits in the Rocky Mountains suggests a late Pinedale age. Benedict (1973), Andrews and others (1975), and Carrara and Andrews (1973) have dated late Pinedale glaciation as ending at approximately 10,000 years B.P. (before present). This is compatible with a radiocarbon age date of 7,100 ± 255 years B.P. from iron bog sediments cored from west of the Keystone Mine on Mount Emmons (Fall, 1981, personal communication). This does not represent the oldest date of the bog since full penetration of the bog was not made.

One to three stades of glaciation are recognized in the Crested Butte area. Only one glacial stade is recognized in the Coal Creek Valley by the one lateral moraine. At least two, possibly three, stades of glacial advance are recorded by the Slate River glacial deposits. The upper lateral moraine (S-1) marks the first stade and the second highest lateral moraine (S-2) marks the second stade. The second stade moraine indicates a readvance of ice. It is differentiated from a recessional moraine, as it truncates the Coal Creek moraine. It is possible that the kilometer-long moraine (S-5) that dams the Crested Butte municipal reservoir marks a third stade as it appears to truncate the southeast end of a smaller recessional moraine (S-4). Three stades of Pinedale glaciation have commonly been recognized in Colorado in and near Rocky Mountain National Park (Richmond, 1960; Madole, 1969; Meierding, 1977). No definitive correlation of glacial stades between the Crested Butte area and other glaciated regions of Colorado has been confirmed to date.

Rock Glaciers

Rock glaciers are conspicuous features in the Crested Butte area. They flow or have flowed from cirque basins on mountains such as Mount Whetstone, Mount Axtell, and Mount Emmons. The rock glaciers occur at the base of cirque headwalls or steep valley sides and tongue down valley in a lobate form. The hummocky surfaces are covered with large angular blocks of rock. Studies by White (1971), Wahrhaftig and Cox (1959), Potter (1967) and many others, indicate that only the upper one-fourth to one-fifth thickness of the rock glacier is coarse blocky rubble. The inner parts are generally finer grained and resemble till. The coarse size provides large voids that allows rapid drainage of rain and melt water.

The rock glaciers on Mount Emmons in Evans, Red Lady and Wolverine basins show only minor intra-flow features and appear relatively inactive, while those on the flanks of Mount Axtell and Whetstone Mountain show curvilinear transverse ridges and furrows indicative of dynamic movement (fig. 4). No flow-rate data have been collected on these rock glaciers. Annual flow rates on active rock glaciers in the Front Range, which appear similar to those on Mount Axtell and Whetstone Mountain, range from 5 to 9.7 cm in the Arapahoe Mountain area (White, 1971) and up to 60 cm at upper west Maroon Creek, less than 9 km north of Crested Butte (Bryant, 1971). Rock glaciers in the Crested Butte area have not been dated. However the rock glacier in Evans Basin (fig. 5) postdates the last major glacial occupation of the basin and the massive slope failure complex.

Many rock glaciers, some of which show activity, closely correlate to Late Pleistocene (Pinedale) and early Holocene glacial advances in Colorado (Benedict, 1973; Carrara and Andrews, 1973; Birkeland, 1973). It is tempting to conclude that rock glaciers and glacial advances are synchronous, but rock glaciers have a lower

Figure 4. Rock glacier on east side of Mount Axtell.

response time to climatic change. Fewer rock glaciers have originated in the last few thousand years in Neoglacial time than in Pleistocene time. A few Neoglacial rock glaciers, however, have been recognized in Colorado (Meierding and Birkeland, 1980).

SLOPE-FAILURE DEPOSITS

Slope-failure deposits in the Crested Butte area are the result of mass wasting of surficial deposits and bedrock during glacial and periglacial climatic conditions. Three different relationships of the glacial-periglacial processes to slope failures processes have been recognized: 1) failures comprised of material such as till deposited by glaciers; 2) failures comprised of colluvium weathered during freeze-thaw cycle during glacial and periglacial times; and 3) slope failures related to the retreat and removal of glacial ice that left steep slopes of surficial materials or rock unsupported. Slope failure deposits have resulted from debris flows and landslides. Debris flow deposits commonly consist of till derived from slope failure of moraines. Many of these occurred when retreating glaciers left saturated till unsupported on steep slopes. Cool and moist periglacial and Holocene climates also saturated the moraines causing slope failures. Slope failure deposits of till occur commonly along Coal Creek.

In certain areas weathering and freeze-thaw cycles, related to periglacial and alpine climates, weathered bedrock to form deposits of colluvium. Subsequent moist conditions and possible stream undercutting resulted in mobilization of large deposits of colluvium. They generally flowed as fluid to viscous debris and mudflows, commonly incorporating large blocks of bedrock. Most colluvium-related flows were derived primarily from the easily weathered Mancos Shale as in Alkali Creek area. Slope failures of colluvium, derived from the Mesaverde and Ohio Creek formations, occurred on the ridges between Elk, Evans and Red Lady basins.

Where bedrock was weathered by glacial processes and oversteepened by glacial erosion, or where talus deposits or lateral moraines formed margins to the ice, final retreat of the glaciers left

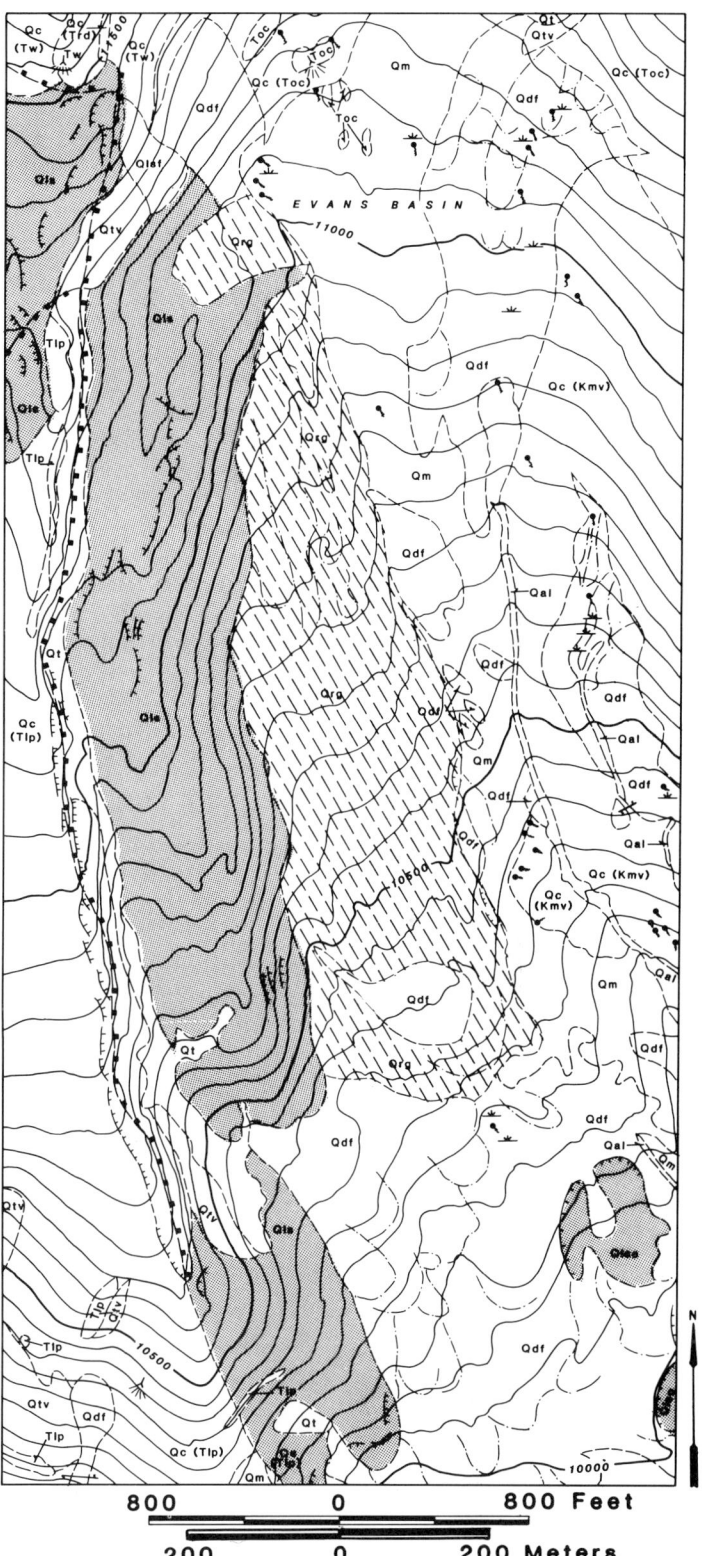

Figure 5. Surficial geologic map of Evans Basin landslide (see Figure 3 for explanation).

the bedrock or surficial deposits relatively unsupported, and failure occurred. Exposure of oversteepened bedrock slopes caused large landslides in Evans basins.

Two areas of massive slope failure in the Crested Butte area, Evans Basin and Alkali Creek, are discussed below. Although they are two of the more massive slope-failure deposits in the area, their nature and origin typify landslide-flow complexes in the Crested Butte area. The engineering implications of such deposits are briefly described.

Evans Basin Landslide-Flow Complex

The Evans Basin area was mapped at a scale of 1:2,400 to provide engineering geology for the proposed mine site (fig. 5). The slope-failure complex encompasses an area of approximately 700 m by 1,890 m ranging from 10,000 ft to 11,500 ft (3048 to 3505 m) in altitude. Evidence from drill holes indicates that at an altitude of approximately 10,250 ft (3125 m) the complex is over 61 m thick near its center. The slope failures include landslide deposits and debris flow deposits. A rock glacier has modified part of the landslide deposits. Figure 6 shows the headscarp area of the major landslide mass. The slope-failure complex is a result of the mass erosion of siltstone and sandstone that was intruded by a latite porphyry sill. The sedimentary rocks were removed by glacial ice that eroded the area and, as a result, there was a loss of lateral support of the sill. In addition, a strong joint set in the latite porphyry parallels the axis of the basin and the head scarp. From bedrock geologic mapping there is no evidence of offset related to the joints except as the results of the slope failure.

The slope-failure complex represents several movement events. The major failure occurred during the last stage of ice occupation. Steep sided margins of the complex indicate that there was still some ice in the basin during failure. This failure included the movement of blocks of latite porphyry, up to a few hundred meters on a side, eastward and downslope from the sill (figs. 6, 7).

During a period shortly after the last of the glacial ice left the basin, periglacial processes were still quite active and a rock glacier developed on the failed mass of latite porphyry. The front of the lobe-shaped rock glacier is a steep concentric ridge that is 3.6 to 7.6 m high. The eastern side is a steep continuous slope with blocks of latite porphyry up to 3 m in diameter nearly at the angle of repose. The surface of the deposit is marked by transverse and longitudinal ridges and furrows. Lengthwise, near the center of the rock glacier, is an irregular and meandering furrow with pits or depressions that indicates the rubble mass has deflated due to the melting of an ice core. Along the eastern side, and extending to about midway around the front, the rock glacier is in sharp contact with the underlying moraine, which indicates the rock glacier overran the material deposited by the ice.

The last event was the development of debris flow deposits that were the result of a more fluid failure of unconsolidated material. Large debris flows occurred at the toe of the rock glacier. These debris-flow deposits are primarily till that was saturated by the meltwaters from the snow and ice pack upslope. The debris flows range in volume from a few tens of cubic meters to many thousands of cubic meters. They flowed downslope a short distance and were deposited where the slope flattened. Within any large debris flow deposit many individual flow units are recognized. These indicate that the large flows were a composite of many smaller failures. There are only minor failures, mostly as debris flows, presently occurring. The failures occur along the small creek that drains Evans Basin. The failures occur during periods of heavy spring runoff and during torrential summer thundershowers, and involve only a few cubic meters of material.

The large slope-failure complex was of concern in the siting of the Mount Emmons Project mine buildings and the disposal of mine development rock. Through detailed surficial geologic mapping it was determined that the large slope failures occurred during the last stages of glacial activity and soon after melting of the glacial ice. Only small debris flow failures occur under present climatic conditions and the occurrence of a large failure is considered unlikely. Engineering recommendations for the proposed mine site located in lower Evans Basin included minimizing cuts in the toes of old, stabilized slope-failures and minimizing fills at the heads of the slope-failure deposits. The complex nature of the slope failures and the material involved leads to an extreme heterogeneity of materials at the construction site. This makes the testing and evaluation of ground-water flow conditions difficult. Of primary importance to the planning for construction in the area is the consideration of ground and surface water.

Alkali Creek Landslide-Flow Complex

The Alkali Creek area was mapped at a scale of 1:2,400 to provide engineering geologic information for the proposed tailing disposal site. The area of slope-failure complexes is in a large basin at the headwaters of Alkali Creek immediately south of Red Mountain, 19 km south of Crested Butte (fig. 1). The types of slope-failure complexes that have occurred in the Alkali Creek area reflect the difference in materials and geomorphic processes between the Alkali Creek and the Evans Basin areas (fig. 7). The bedrock in much of the Alkali Creek area is the Mancos Shale. The weathering of the Mancos Shale results in predominantly fine-grained colluvium consisting of clay, silt and fine sand. As a result

Figure 6. Evans Basin landslide.

Figure 7. Headscarp and landslide blocks of Evans Basin landslide.

of the fine-grained nature of the colluvium, earthflows and slumps are the predominant failure modes. Also, the Alkali Creek area is below the lower limit of glaciation and the predominant geomorphic processes are periglacial and alpine. There is palynological evidence that ice has not occupied the Alkali Creek area in the past 15,000 years (Markgraf and Scott, 1981).

Landslides in Alkali Basin are slope-failure complexes consisting of block rotation and/or translation and flow of earth materials. The designation "landslide-flow complex" has been given to these deposits. Landslide-flow complexes occur at the rim of the basin. Figure 8 shows the headscarps of the complexes at the eastern edge of the basin. Carbonized wood, taken from the debris-flow section of the landslide-flow complex in the southwest corner of the basin, has shown different periods of slope movement. The dates obtained indicate that wood was incorporated in a flow event approximately 6,500 years B.P. and 3,000 years B.P.

Mudflow deposits are deposits of fine-grained materials that have been flushed down gullies, or large saturated masses of fine-grained material with local boulders and gravels that have flowed downslope. The mudflows in the Alkali Creek area contain a small proportion of gravels and boulders as do all surficial deposits in this area, but are generally finer-grained than the debris flows. The

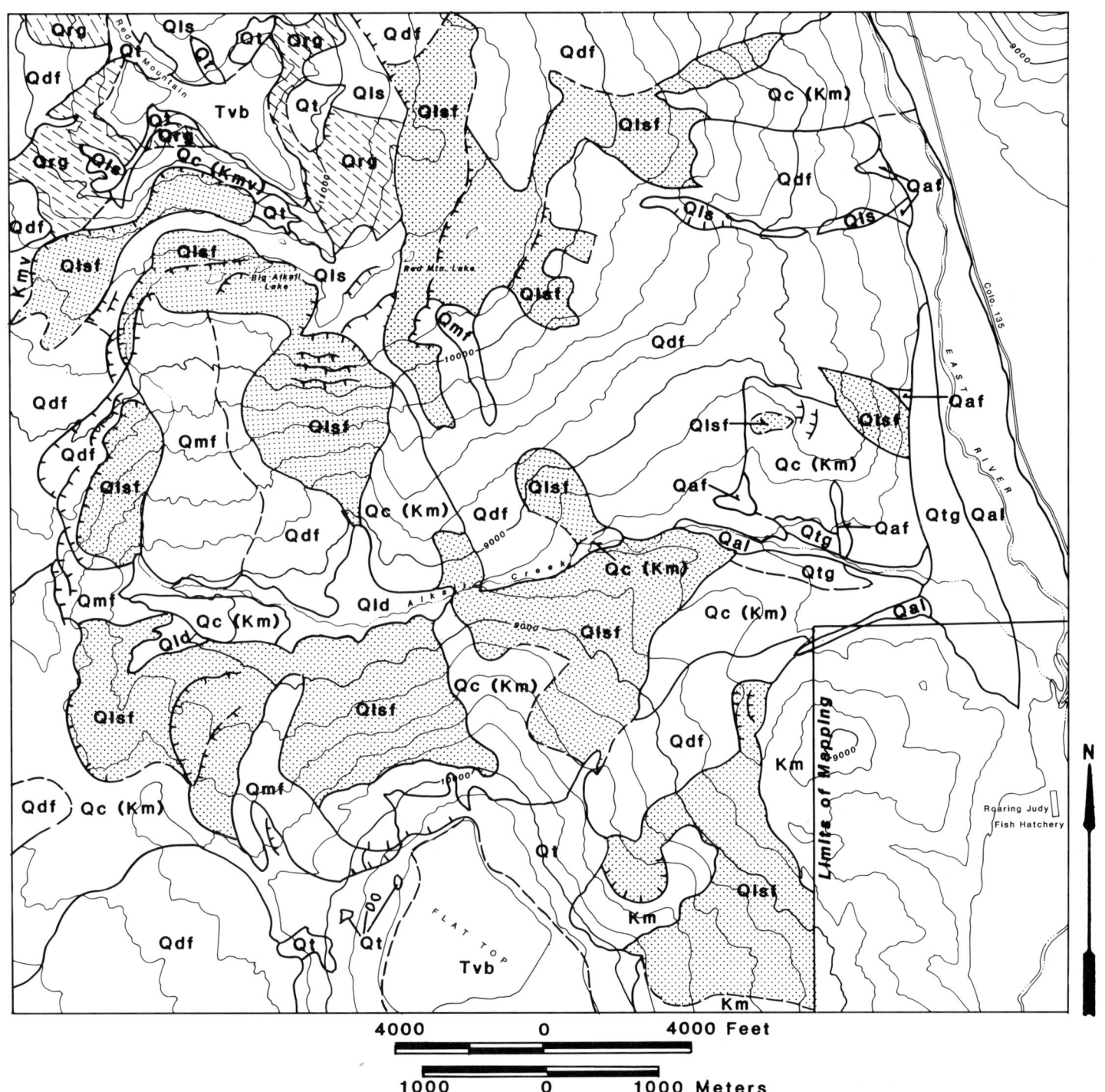

Figure 8. Surficial geologic map of the Alkali Creek area (see Figure 3 for explanation).

Figure 9. Headscarps and landslide–flow complex of Alkali Creek area looking north toward Red Mountain.

present morphology of the mudflows (Fig. 9) indicates that these masses had a greater degree of saturation and greater velocity at the time of failure than the debris flows. The large mudflows are believed to have occurred at a time of significantly higher precipitation than today. Small mudflow events have occurred in recent years, but these are restricted to small (less than 77 m³) flows that have resulted from oversteepened scarp slopes and along creek banks.

Debris flows are the most extensive of the slope-failure complexes in the Alkali Creek area. The debris flows consist of deposits of boulders and gravels from the basalt caps of Red Mountain and Flat Top Mountain intermixed with fine-grained colluvium derived from the Mancos Shale. These materials, when saturated with water, probably flowed downslope as a viscous fluid at a moderate rate (1.5 m/day). The debris flows may contain blocks of Mancos Shale up to 1 m in diameter near the heads of the flows. An exploration drill hole in the center of a large debris flow below Big Alkali Lake, north of Alkali Creek, at approximately 9,200 ft (2800 m) altitude revealed the deposit is over 61 m thick. Carbonized wood taken from the core of the hole at a depth of approximately 49 m was dated at about 8,000 years B.P.

The location of the proposed tailings dam is approximately in the center of the basin between two bedrock ridges. The stability of the slope failures was of concern when location of the tailings dam was proposed. Because of the size and complexity of the slope failures, traditional slope-failure analysis was inadequate and not applicable for planning purposes. Fortunately, lake sediments were discovered covering the toes of the large slope-failure that would be impacted by the tailings impoundment. The lake sediments consist of clay, silt and sand with interbedded organic materials and gravels near the margins of the former lake. On-going palynological studies of the lake sediments have given relatively reliable information as to the stability of the slope failures (Fall, 1981, personal communication). The study of pollen and carbonized wood preserved by the lake sediments has shown that a lake existed from at least 15,000 years B.P. to 3,000 years B.P. (Markgraf and Scott, 1981). The lake was probably formed when the drainage was blocked by at least one slope failure east of the proposed tailings dam alignment. The record shows that for the 12,000 years studied there was a constant rate of accumulation of sediment in the lake of approximately 30 cm/1,000 years. The constant sedimentation rate indicates that there have not been any slope failures into the lake for the past 15,000 years.

Periglacial and alpine geomorphic processes are postulated for the occurrence of such extensive slope failures. The paleoclimatic reconstruction based on the vegetation changes, as interpreted from the pollen sequence preserved in the lake sediments (Markgraf and Scott, 1981), is as follows: from at least 15,000 to 10,000 years B.P. a cool-moist climate with a spruce forest growing at an elevation of 9,000 ft (2750 m). From 10,000 to 4,000 years B.P. a slightly warmer drier climate dominated with a growing pine forest, somewhat less spruce and increased fir plus some additional steppe plants. Since approximately 4,000 years B.P. the climate has been essentially the same as it is today, again slightly warmer and dryer than the time of the slope failures with sagebrush steppe vegetation dominating the area at approximately 9,000 ft (2750 m).

The stability of the slopes in the Alkali Creek area has been enhanced by the existence of the lake in the basin. If water was impounded over the toes of the slope failures in the past the saturated conditions would have created failures that reached equilibrium under those conditions. Furthermore the deposition of up to 18 m of fine-grained material on the toes of these failures would buttress them. The probability of large catastrophic failures appears to be very small. Partial filling of the basin with tailings from the milling process will further stabilize the slopes. Construction of roads, buildings and the water diversion structures above the tailings impoundment will require particular attention to the ground water and surface water.

SUMMARY

Detailed geologic mapping has shown the presence of deposits of till in the Crested Butte area that are of probable Pinedale age. Three stages which are comparable to glaciated mountains elsewhere in the Rocky Mountains appear likely. Deposition of saturated till on steep slopes resulted in many slope failure complexes. Many of these probably occurred as ice retreated from the cirque valleys and basins. Other slope failure deposits consist of thick deposits of colluvium that formed from periglacial and alpine processes. Bedrock has also failed as massive landslides and was related to ice retreat.

Slope failure deposits are of utmost concern to developmental activities in the Crested Butte area and throughout the Rocky Mountains. An understanding of the processes is essential in their identification. Detailed geologic mapping and air photograph interpretation cannot only aid in identifying the deposits but can provide evidence to determine their stability. Often many slope-failure deposits can be proven to be old and stable. The slope-failure deposits require detailed soil and geologic engineering examination to design for proper construction and development.

ACKNOWLEDGMENTS

We wish to thank the personnel of the Mount Emmons Project of Climax Molybdenum Corporation for their cooperation, with special thanks to Dr. Willis H. White, Daniel R. Stewart, Reese W. Ganster and Fred R. Dowsett. We appreciate the help of Dr. Charles S. Robinson, Dale M. Cochran and William A. Gallant for reviewing the paper. We also thank Mary Jane Kendall for drafting the illustrations and Dori Darrow for typing the paper. Converse Ward Davis Dixon, Inc. provided facilities for the paper preparation for which we are grateful.

REFERENCES

Andrews, J. T., Carrara, P. E., King, F. B. and Suchenrath, R., 1975, Holocene environmental changes in the alpine zone, northern San Juan Mountains: Evidence from bog stratigraphy, and palynology: Quaternary Research, v. 5, p. 173-197.

Benedict, J. B., 1973, Chronology of cirque glaciation, Colorado Front Range: Quaternary Research, v. 3, p. 584-599.

Birkeland, P. W., 1973, Use of relative age dating methods in a stratigraphic study of rock glacier deposits, Mt. Sopris, Colorado: Arctic and Alpine Research, v. 5, p. 401-416.

Bryant, Bruce, 1971, Movement measurements on two rock glaciers in the eastern Elk Mountains, Colorado: U.S. Geological Survey Professional Paper 750-B, p. B108-B116.

Carrara, P. E. and Andrews, J. T., 1973, Problems and applications of lichenometry to geomorphic studies, San Juan Mountains, Colorado: Arctic and Alpine Research, v. 5, p. 373-384.

Gaskill, D. L. and Goodwin, C. H., 1966, Geologic map of the Marcellina Mountain quadrangle, Gunnison County, Colorado: U.S. Geological Survey Geological Quadrangle Map GQ-578.

――――, ――――, and Mutschler, F. E., 1967, Geologic map of the Oh-be-joyful quadrangle, Gunnison County, Colorado: U.S. Geological Survey Geologic Quadrangle Map GQ-578.

Madole, R. F., 1969, Pinedale and Bull Lake glaciation in upper St. Vrain drainage basin, Boulder County, Colorado: Arctic and Alpine Research, v. 1, p. 279-287.

Markgraf, V. and Scott, L., 1981, Lower timberline in central Colorado during the past 15,000 yrs: Geology, v. 9, p. 231-234.

Meierding, T. C., 1977, Age differentiation of till and gravel deposits in the upper Colorado River basin (Ph.D. dissertation): Boulder, University of Colorado, 235 p.

――――, and Birkeland, P. W., 1980, Quaternary glaciation of Colorado, in Colorado Geology, H. C. Kent and K. W. Porter: Denver, Colorado, Rocky Mountain Association of Geologists, p. 165-173.

Potter, N. Jr., 1967, Rock glaciers and mass-wastage in the Galena Creek area, northern Absaraka Mountains, Wyoming: U.S. Army Article Laboratories, Natick, Massachusetts, Technical Report, 75 p.

Richmond, G. M., 1960, Glaciation of the east slope of Rocky Mountain National Park: Geological Society of America Bulletin, v. 71, p. 1371-1382.

――――, 1965, Glaciation of the Rocky Mountains, in Wright, H. E. Jr., and Frey, D. G., eds., The Quaternary of the United States: Princeton, N.J., Princeton University Press, p. 217-230.

Soule, J. M., 1976, Geologic hazards in the Crested Butte—Gunnison area, Gunnison County, Colorado: Colorado Geological Survey Information Series 5, 34 p.

Wahrhafig, C. and Cox, A., 1959, Rock glaciers in the Alaska Range: Geological Society of America Bulletin, v. 70, p. 383-436.

Kodels Canyon fault, looking northwest across mouth of Fruita Canyon, at west entrance of Colorado National Monument. Here, along a normal fault dipping steeply northeastward, the 107-m cliff of Wingate Sandstone at upper left has been sheared and squeezed into only a few meters of broken rocks overlain by a steep slope of the Kayenta Formation covered by piñon and juniper. The 45-m cliffs at right are the Entrada Sandstone, which belong high atop the cliff at left. From color photograph by S. W. Lohman, U.S. Geological Survey.

THE URANIUM-VANADIUM DEPOSITS OF THE URAVAN MINERAL BELT AND ADJACENT AREAS, COLORADO AND UTAH

WILLIAM L. CHENOWETH
U.S. Department of Energy
Grand Junction, Colorado 81502

INTRODUCTION

The Salt Wash Member of the Morrison Formation of Jurassic age contains economic deposits of uranium and vanadium minerals in western Colorado, southeastern Utah, northeastern Arizona, and northwestern New Mexico. These deposits have accounted for nearly 13 percent of the United States' uranium production. The most productive deposits are in a relatively small area in southwestern Colorado that is referred to as the Uravan mineral belt. Included with the Uravan mineral belt in this overview are the following adjacent areas: Thompson, Moab, La Sal, and Dry Valley (fig. 1).

This paper is intended to present a brief overview of the geologic setting of the deposits, to review the geologic investigations, and to summarize the development of the mining industry in the area.

GEOLOGIC SETTING

The Uravan mineral belt, as defined by the U.S. Geological Survey (USGS) in 1952, is an elongate area in southwestern Colorado wherein uranium-vanadium deposits in the Salt Wash Member of the Morrison Formation "generally have closer spacing, larger size, and higher grade than those in adjacent areas and the region as a whole" (Fischer and Hilpert, 1952, p. 3). The belt in-

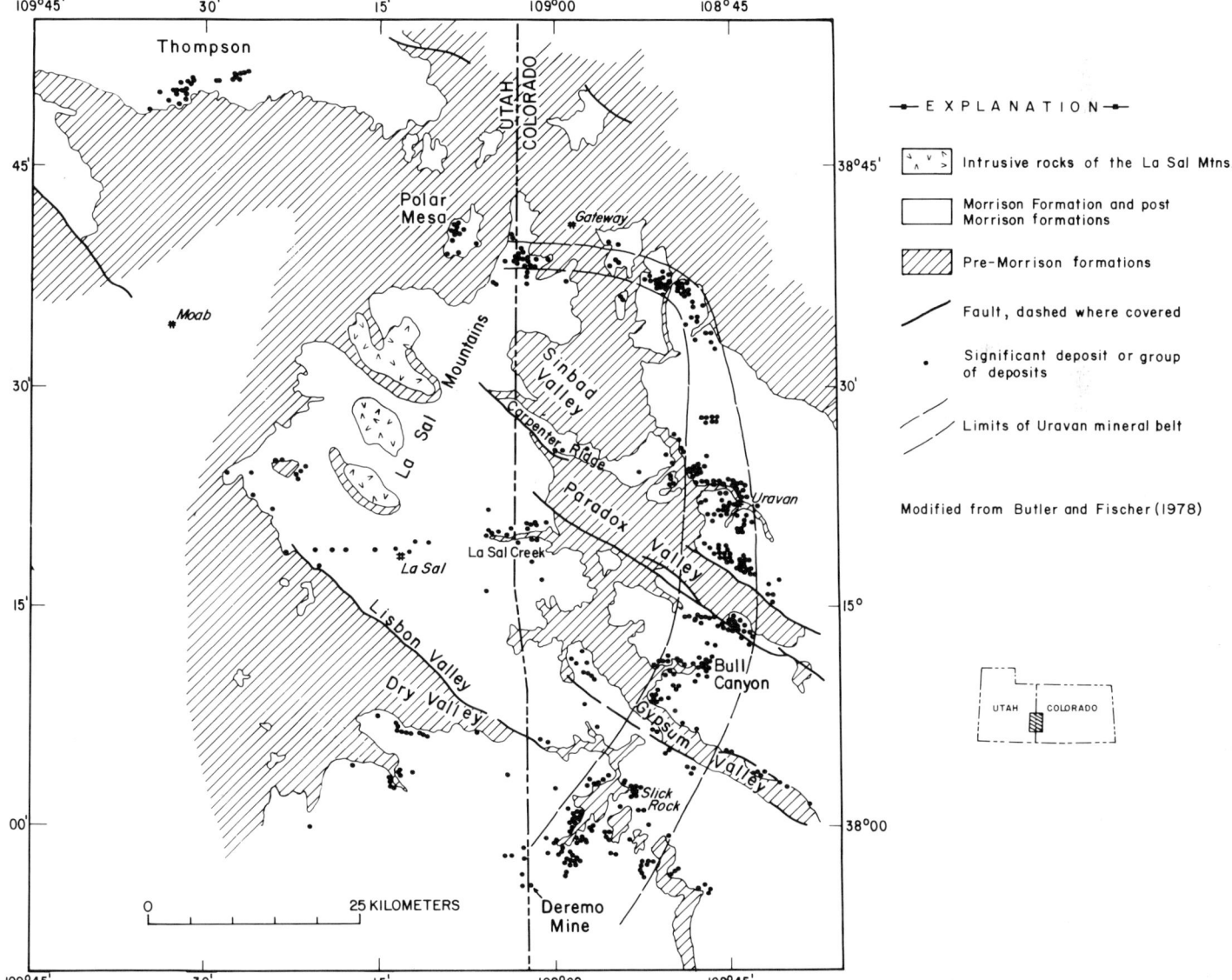

Figure 1. Index map of southwestern Colorado and southeastern Utah showing the location of uranium-vanadium deposits in the Salt Wash Member of the Morrison Formation.

cludes the Gateway, Uravan, Bull Canyon, Gypsum Valley, and Slick Rock districts (fig. 1).

The Salt Wash Member consists of interbedded fluvial sandstone and floodplain-type mudstone units. The sandstone beds crop out in three to eight cliffs or "rims" with the mudstone units forming slopes. The uppermost sandstone, or rim, contains the majority of the ore deposits, but deposits do occur in the lower sandstones. A few deposits occur in coarse conglomeratic sandstones in the lower part of the overlying Brushy Basin Member. Records of the Grand Junction Office of the U.S. Department of Energy (DOE) show that production has been derived from nearly 1,200 individual properties within the area.

Individual deposits or groups of deposits are localized within reduced permeable, carbonaceous Salt Wash sandstones. Many of the deposits in the Uravan area are within well-defined, sandstone-filled paleostream channels which are several hundred meters wide and up to a few kilometers long. The tabular ore bodies typically are elongated parallel to sedimentary trends, and are concordant with the bedding. The ore averages about 1.2 m thick, but in a few places ore thicknesses approaching 9 m have been mined. Individual ore bodies may be connected by weakly mineralized rock, but generally the boundary of ore and barren rock is abrupt. Figure 2, a plan view of the Deremo Mine in the Slick Rock area, illustrates the typically erratic distribution of ore bodies and the relatively small size of individual stopes. The mineralized area at the Deremo was defined by surface holes drilled on 61-m centers, but most of the ore has been found by mining and close-spaced underground drilling (Thamm and others, 1981, p. 36).

Ore bodies ranging from a few tons to large masses containing more than one million tonnes of ore tend to be clustered within elongated favorable areas a few kilometers long by several hundred meters wide. Average production from these elongated favorable areas has ranged from a few hundred thousand tonnes of ore to a few million tonnes of ore.

Although most of the mineralized zones in the Salt Wash are tabular and concordant with bedding, the ore in some deposits abruptly crosses bedding in smooth curves to form rolls. The rolls in plan view are generally narrow, not more than a few meters wide, sinuous, and decidedly elongated parallel to local sedimentary structures, major channels, or axes of greatest permeability. Most rolls are C- or S-shaped in cross section, but various other shapes have been reported.

The term "roll" was originally used by miners to describe mineralization that cuts sharply across bedding features, and was adopted by Fischer (1942). This use predated the discovery of the roll-type deposits in Wyoming, and its application to Salt Wash deposits is more descriptive than generic.

Some small, high-grade ore bodies consist of fossil logs and podlike accumulations of carbonaceous material replaced with uranium and vanadium minerals. Fossil logs may be as large as 15 m long and 1 m in diameter.

Sedimentary features exert a strong control on the shape and distribution of the Salt Wash deposits. On a broad scale, clusters or trends of deposits are associated with major sedimentary channels and tend to occur along their margins. On a more local scale, individual deposits or lenses of mineralization commonly terminate against shale horizons, channel margins, and other sedimentary features that produces permeability changes.

In most large ore bodies and clusters of smaller ore bodies, sediments adjacent to ore-bearing, reduced sandstone are oxidized. In general, the highest grade ore in any deposit occurs next to the oxidation-reduction boundary. Where narrow, gray unoxidized zones extend into red oxidized sequences, the grade and continuity of the ore improve dramatically. These zones, bounded above and below by red sediments, do not make major mines in themselves, but contain high-grade pods of ore within larger mines (Thamm and others, 1981, p. 47).

Within an ore body, uranium and vanadium minerals coat sand grains, fill interstices, and replace organic material, feldspar, calcite, and quartz. In unoxidized ore bodies, the principal uranium minerals are uraninite and coffinite. The main uranium minerals in oxidized ores are tyuyamunite, metatyuyamunite, and carnotite. Although the oxidized ores are called carnotite deposits, the mineral carnotite is not as abundant as tyuyamunite (S. R. Austin, personal communication, 1978). Vanadium clays, consisting largely of chlorite and/or hydromica, are the main vanadium minerals in both oxidized and unoxidized ores and deposits. Montroseite is present in the unoxidized ores and corvusite is common in the partly oxidized deposits. The oxidation of vanadium forms a series of vanadate minerals which include: tyuyamunite, metatyuyamunite, carnotite, hewettite, metahewettite, pascoite, rauvite, rossite, metarossite, fervanite, and hummerite. The mineralogy of the Salt Wash ores is summarized by Weeks and others (1959). Generally the amount of vanadium exceeds the uranium in ratios ranging from 3:1 to 10:1. Ores mined in the area have averaged 5:1. Within the Uravan mineral belt, the vanadium increases southward from Gateway (3:1) to Slick Rock (8:1). These ratios are based on uranium production since 1947 and include both oxidized and unoxidized ores. With a few local exceptions, both oxidized and unoxidized ores are in radioactive equilibrium.

GEOLOGIC INVESTIGATIONS

Geologic investigations of the uranium-vanadium deposits of southwestern Colorado and southeastern Utah began about 1900 and have continued to the present. As a result, an extremely large number of reports have been written on the area. The majority of these reports are the results of studies by the USGS and the U.S. Atomic Energy Commission (AEC) during the uranium boom of the 1950s. Nelson-Moore and others (1978) have compiled a bibliography of uranium reports in Colorado, which includes some reports in the adjacent parts of Utah.

During World War II, the Union Mines Development Corporation, contractor to the Army Corps of Engineers, systematically studied the deposits as part of a general uranium resource appraisal of the Colorado Plateau. This work resulted in a series of district reports complete with mine maps and detailed descriptions of individuals deposits. These reports were open-filed by the AEC in the 1950s and 1960s.

Subsequent district studies include: Thompson (Stokes, 1952), La Sal Creek (Carter and Gualtieri, 1965), and Slick Rock (Shawe and others, 1959).

One of the earliest regional summaries was written by Coffin (1921) during the radium era. Included with this report was a reconnaissance geologic map of the carnotite region of southwestern Colorado. In 1958, Wood and Lekas (1958) published a brief summary of the uranium geology and economics of the Uravan mineral belt. Included with this article was a mine location map of the belt. Eleven years later, Motica (1969) prepared a fairly detailed summary of the area. Recently, Thamm and others (1981) compiled an excellent summary of the geologic features of the Salt Wash deposits.

HISTORY AND PAST PRODUCTION

The history of the mining of carnotite deposits in southwestern Colorado and southeastern Utah reflects the importance of three

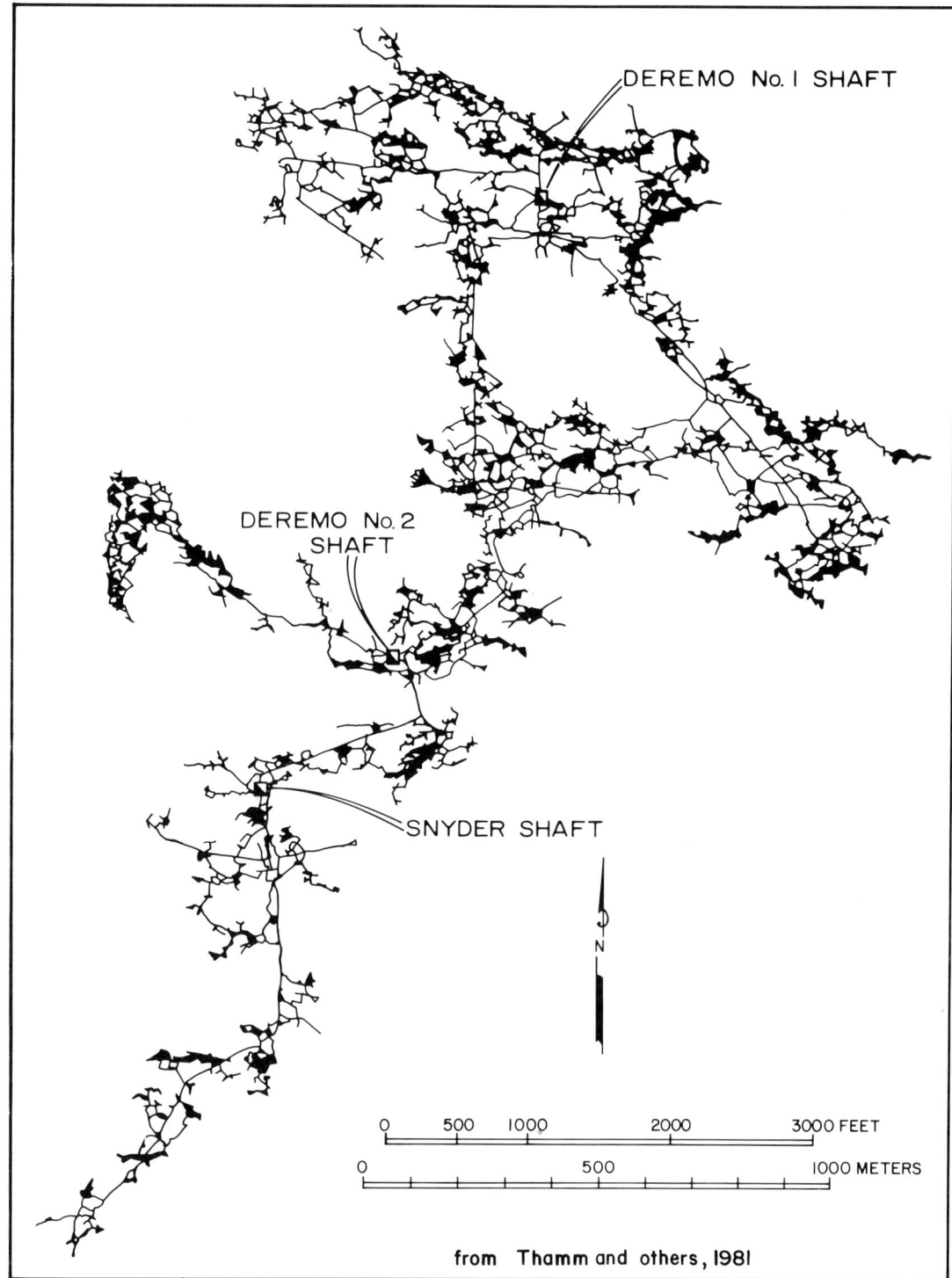

Figure 2. Plan map of the Deremo Mine, Slick Rock area, Colorado.

metals—radium, vanadium and uranium. All three are briefly reviewed in the following sections. Much of the historical material is taken from a staff report by the U.S. Atomic Energy Commission (1951).

Early Activities

The existence of a yellow substance in the Paradox Valley rimrock of Montrose County was known to the settlers prior to 1880. It is assumed that the Ute and Navajo Indians used this yellow powder as a pigment before the white settlers came to the region.

In 1881, a prospector named Tom Talbert sent some yellow material from the Roc Creek area of Montrose County to an assayer in Leadville to determine its content. This and other early attempts to detect the elements present in the yellow material were unsuccessful. About 1896 the claims on Roc Creek were relocated by Tom Dullan. Gordon Kimball and associates of Ouray, Colorado, leased the property in 1898 and sent some of the yellow material to Charles Poulot in Denver who found it contained uranium in sufficient quantity to make it valuable. During June 1898, Gordon Kimball shipped 9 tonnes of ore from the Roc

Creek property to Denver. This shipment averaged 21.5 percent uranium oxide (U_3O_8) and over 15 percent vanadium oxide (V_2O_5) for which Kimball was paid $2,600 (Kimball, 1904). The high vanadium content resulted in a penalty when the shipment was resampled in France. In 1899 Charles Poulot and another Frenchman named Voilleque sent mineral specimens to France where M. M. C. Friedel and E. Cumenge established the approximate composition of this mineral and named it carnotite, after the French mining engineer and chemist M. Adolphe Carnot.

Soon after the first shipment of carnotite it became known that the yellow mineral was marketable, and many claims were staked. Most of the claims were located along Roc Creek, along La Sal Creek, and in adjacent areas.

In 1900, Poulot and Voilleque conducted experimental work on extracting vanadium and uranium oxides from carnotite ores at the camp of the Cashin copper mine on La Sal Creek. The ores used in these experiments came from mines on Roc Creek, on La Sal Creek, and on the San Miguel River. As a result of these studies, a company formed by Poulot, Voilleque, and James McBride built an experimental mill at the mouth of Summit Creek in the Slick Rock area. About 6,800 kg of uranium-vanadium concentrates were produced at this plant before operations were transferred to the Western Refining Company in 1903 and to the Dolores Refining Company in 1904 (Lundquist and Lake, 1955). This activity created much interest in carnotite areas, and widespread claim staking occurred throughout the area between 1902 and 1905. According to Fischer (1968, p. 738), between 1898 and 1909 total production from the region was 8,200 tonnes of high-grade ore. With the exception of ore from the vicinity of the Summit Creek plant, all ore mined before 1906 was shipped either to the eastern part of the United States for vanadium recovery or to Europe for the recovery of radium.

The Radium Era

The discovery of radium by Marie and Pierre Curie in 1898 led to the realization that all uranium ores contained this new element. Experiments which showed that radium inhibited the growth of certain cancers so astonished the medical profession that an incentive to mine the carnotite ores was created.

Shortly before 1910, metallurgical processes for relatively large-scale recoveries of radium from carnotite ores were perfected. The improved processes resulted in greatly increased demands for carnotite and in accelerated prospecting in the entire area. About one gram of radium is present in every 180 to 275 tonnes of ore containing 2.0 percent U_3O_8. With development work being organized by the Radium Luminous Metals Company in 1910, and by the Radium Company of Colorado and the Standard Chemical Company in 1911, a mining rush resulted which affected the entire Colorado Plateau.

Shortly after 1910, the carnotite deposits in southwestern Colorado and southeastern Utah became one of the principal world sources of radium. For about 12 years, these deposits were mined for radium and yielded some byproducts of uranium and vanadium.

The Radium Company of Colorado treated its ore in a plant in Denver while the Radium Luminous Metals Company shipped ore to its plant in East Orange, New Jersey. The National Radium Institute built a dry-process plant in the Long Park area. This mill was later purchased by the Pittsburgh Radium Company and moved a few kilometers northwest to Saucer Basin. However, after treating some 1,814 mt of ore, the mill did not prove successful, and was dismantled.

The Standard Chemical Company treated most of its ore at the Joe Junior mill at the present-day site of Uravan. The American Rare Metals Company purchased the Summit Creek plant at Slick Rock and recovered some uranium and vanadium as well as radium. Operating costs were high because of the isolation of the mines; for example, Placerville, Colorado, about 105 km from the Joe Junior camp, was the nearest shipping point. Concentrates, ores, and supplies were hauled by freight wagon between Placerville and Joe Junior and to other points within the area. The freight rates between Joe Junior and Placerville were $27.00 per ton in 1914, but by 1922, rates had been reduced to $14.00 per ton as a result of road improvements and the introduction of motor trucks.

Because of the high freight rates, the Radium Company of Colorado and the Radium Luminous Metals Company found it unprofitable to mine and ship ore assaying less than 2.0 percent U_3O_8. The Standard Chemical Company could mine and mill ore running as low as 1.25 percent U_3O_8, although the average grade of ore treated in this plant was over 1.50 percent U_3O_8. The mill recovery varied between 65 and 70 percent.

The beginning of World War I in 1914 had little effect on the mining of carnotite ores though it did affect the European market. Because of the increasing demands for vanadium, radium plants were engineered to recover quantities of vanadium as a byproduct from carnotite. With the entry of the United States into the war in 1917, emphasis slowly began to shift away from the production of radium to the production of vanadium. By 1922 Colorado Plateau ores were no longer competitive with newly developed high-grade pitchblende ores in the Belgian Congo as a source of radium.

The end of the war caused both a drop in the demand for vanadium and a resumption of production from lower cost areas. Mining and milling of carnotite ores ceased around 1923 and was not resumed in most districts of southwestern Colorado and southeastern Utah until 1936.

From 1910 to 1923, the carnotite ores are estimated to have yielded 202 grams of radium with small amounts of vanadium and uranium recovered as byproducts (Fischer, 1968, p. 738). During this period, the price of the world market for the elemental radium content in purified salts, ranged from $70,000 to $180,000 per gram (Tyler, 1930, p. 41).

The Vanadium Era

Prior to 1930, most of the vanadium produced in the United States came from roscoelite deposits near Rifle and Placerville, Colorado. In 1928, U.S. Vanadium Corporation (USV), then a subsidiary of Union Carbide and Carbon Corporation, anticipated a growing market for vanadium, and purchased from Standard Chemical the Joe Junior concentrator and 14 km² of mining claims. Between 1934 and 1935, the assets of the Colorado Radium Company and the Radium Luminous Metals Company were acquired by the Vanadium Corporation of America (VCA).

After a period of comparative inactivity, the rising demand for vanadium by the alloy-steel industry renewed interest in the deposits. Most of the established mines were reopened by 1935. VCA built a new town and mill at Vancorum, west of Naturita, Colorado. USV moved its plant from Rifle to the Joe Junior site in 1936 and altered the metallurgical process to handle carnotite ores. The townsite of Uravan was thus founded. North Continent Mines Company built a mill in the Slick Rock area, as did International Vanadium Corporation in Dry Valley, Utah.

Prospecting continued, and many new mines were developed

throughout the area. A small mill was built at Gateway, Colorado, by Gateway Alloys, Inc. The United States' entry into World War II in 1941 gave the vanadium industry new impetus.

In order to stimulate the production of strategic materials, the federal government formed the Metals Reserve Company in 1942. Vanadium was one of the strategic materials, and Metals Reserve began an ore purchasing program and increased the base price paid for vanadium. Mills at Monticello, Utah, and Durango, Colorado, were built and operated for Metal Reserve by VCA and USV, respectively. To insure a steady supply of ore for the mills, Metals Reserve established buying stations and stockpiled ore for distribution.

The Metals Reserve program, which lasted from 1942 through February 1944, greatly stimulated prospecting, and many new deposits were found. After the termination of the program vanadium mining all but ended in the area.

Manhattan Engineer District Studies

To evaluate the uranium resources of the Salt Wash Member of the Morrison Formation of the Colorado Plateau, the Army Corps of Engineers, as part of the Manhattan Project, contracted with Union Carbide and Carbon Corporation to create a raw-materials appraisal group. This group, known as Union Mines Development Corporation (UMDC), was formed in 1943 and was active through 1946.

UMDC geologists systematically studied the uranium-vanadium deposits of the area. All of the known outcrops of uranium-vanadium minerals, prospects, and mines were mapped and described. Their work was thorough, and few outcropping occurrences of uranium-vanadium minerals known today were overlooked by UMDC.

As part of its study, UMDC determined the amount of vanadium ore that had previously been mined. For Uravan and adjacent areas, this amounted to 639,406 tonnes of ore, averaging 1.93 percent V_2O_5, and containing 12,328,144 kg of vanadium oxide. Details of this early vanadium production are given in Table 1. These vanadium ores also were estimated to have contained 1,781,207 kg U_3O_8, much of which went into the tailings at the vanadium mills.

In 1943 UMDC began the operation of acid leach plants at Durango and Uravan for the recovery of uranium from vanadium tailings. The concentrates produced in the tailing treatment plants were shipped to a refinery at Grand Junction where a low-grade uranium concentrate and a commercial-grade fused vanadium oxide were produced. The treatment plants and refinery were in operation until late 1946.

The Atomic Energy Commission Program

In May 1947, the newly created Atomic Energy Commission signed a contract with VCA for the purchase of uranium concentrates from the Naturita mill. Deliveries to the AEC started later that year. Another contract was signed with VCA to purchase concentrates from the Durango mill, and with USV to buy concentrates from the Uravan mill; deliveries began in 1949 and 1950, respectively. The Metals Reserve mill at Monticello was altered by the AEC to permit the recovery of uranium. Climax Uranium Company began operating the first mill in the United States designed primarily for the production of uranium with vanadium as a by-product at Grand Junction in 1951.

Ore-buying schedules and other AEC incentives stimulated prospecting throughout the area. During the 1950s, the AEC and the USGS carried out extensive geologic studies and exploration programs to assist the newborn nuclear industry. These investigations resulted in the discovery and development of many deposits, and by the mid-1950s nearly all surface and near-surface deposits had been discovered.

The yearly production of uranium oxide in ore from the area is shown in Figure 3. This chart was compiled from records of the Grand Junction Office of the U.S. Department of Energy. Starting in 1947, production increased yearly until 1960 when an all-time high of 2,102 tonnes of U_3O_8 in ore were produced. The AEC announced in 1961 that purchases of uranium ore after April 1, 1962, would be limited to annual quotas allocated to individual properties. Also, from that date until the end of 1966, instead of buying concentrate at the graduated prices previously in effect, the AEC would pay $8.00 per pound for U_3O_8 in concentrates produced mostly from reserves discovered before November 24, 1958. As a result of this change, the production of uranium ore in the Uravan area and in the United States, declined in 1961 for the first time since 1947 (fig. 3). In 1962, the AEC proposed to continue the purchase of uranium until 1971 from those suppliers who would agree to defer delivery of a part of their pre-1966 quotas until 1967

Table 1. Pre-1946 vanadium production, Uravan mineral belt and adjacent areas.

Area	Tonnes	Grade (%)	Kilograms V_2O_5
COLORADO			
Uravan	424,127	1.78	7,554,988
Slick Rock	89,541	2.38	2,133,734
Gateway	26,236	1.93	505,746
Gypsum Valley	18,779	1.90	356,802
Bull Canyon	16,928	2.18	369,212
Carpenter Ridge	2,722	1.90	51,710
UTAH			
Dry Valley	20,866	1.87	390,187
La Sal Creek	11,440	1.93	220,788
Moab	9,979	1.80	179,626
Thompson	9,616	2.79	268,295
Polar Mesa	9,172	3.24	297,057
TOTALS	639,406	1.93	12,328,145

Estimated contained kg U_3O_8—1,784,235

Modified from Webber, 1947, fig. 59

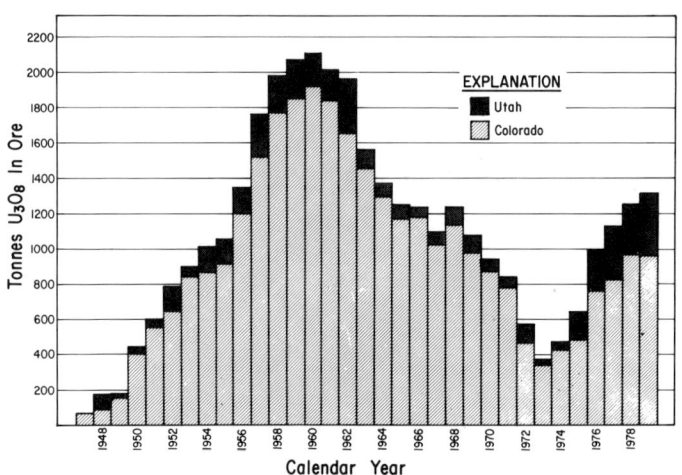

Figure 3. Uranium production, 1947–1979, Uravan mineral belt and adjacent areas.

and 1968. The price to be paid in 1969 and 1970 was not to exceed $6.70 per pound of U_3O_8. The Climax Uranium Company at Grand Junction elected not to participate in the AEC stretchout program and began producing uranium for private sales to utilities in 1966. The AEC procurement program ended December 31, 1970. During the period 1947 through 1970 the AEC purchased ores containing approximately 27,170 tonnes U_3O_8.

During the late 1940s and early 1950s, the AEC obtained mineral rights on 1,813 km² of land on the Colorado Plateau. Exploration was conducted on these lands by the AEC and the USGS, and when significant ore bodies were found, the land was leased for mining. By 1957, some 1,709 km² had been returned to the public domain. Of the 104 km² that were retained, 85 km² were in the Uravan area of Colorado and Utah. By March 1962, mining on these lands had terminated because of expired leases. During mid-1974, the lands were again leased, and mining and exploration commenced later that year. Since then, $42 million in production royalties have been paid to the federal government.

The Private Market

After the termination of the AEC purchasing program the only market for uranium was the electric utilities. Since nuclear power generation did not develop as rapidly as had been anticipated, uranium production continued to decline in the early 1970s. The demand for vanadium kept the industry in the Uravan area from collapsing completely. In 1970, the Climax mill at Grand Junction closed, and most of the Climax properties were acquired by Atlas Minerals.

Production in the Uravan area reached an all time low of 371 tonnes of U_3O_8 in ore in 1973. Following this, the rise in uranium prices to record levels by the mid-1970s resulted in a surge of activity and increasing production. New ore bodies were located by exploration on the DOE lease blocks and outside the mineral belt in the Gypsum Valley, Dry Valley, and La Sal areas.

A buying station was established by General Electric's Nuclear Division near Naturita for independent miners. A vanadium circuit was installed by Atlas at its Moab mill in 1976. The Cotter Corporation, a wholly-owned subsidiary of Commonwealth Edison, built a crushing and sampling plant at Whitewater, Colorado, in order to ship its ore by rail to the company mill at Canon City, Colorado. In June 1980, the Energy Fuels Nuclear mill near Blanding, Utah, began operating and now provides a market for the mines in the southern part of the area.

During the period 1947 through 1979, uranium production from Uravan and adjacent areas has amounted to 14,675,000 tonnes of ore averaging 0.24 percent U_3O_8 and containing 34,754,000 kg of U_3O_8. This represents 11 percent of the total United States' uranium production. Vanadium has been recovered from 14,589,600 tonnes with an average grade of 1.24 percent V_2O_5 and containing 187,443,300 kg of V_2O_5. This represents 80 percent of the total domestic production of vanadium from sandstone uranium ores. Mines within the confines of the Uravan mineral belt (fig. 1) account for 85 percent of the uranium that has been produced in the area.

OUTLOOK

Although poor market conditions and increased operating costs have forced many operations to close during the latter part of 1980 and the early part of 1981, the long term outlook for the area is favorable. An increase in the price of uranium and an expanded market would result in increased production. Significant reserves exist on the DOE lease blocks and in the La Sal trend (see paper by Kovschak and Nylund, this guidebook), and elsewhere in the area.

In addition to the known reserves, the possibilities of finding additional deposits in the Salt Wash are good. Studies of the Department of Energy's National Uranium Resource Evaluation Program have estimated 43,360,000 kg of U_3O_8 of probable potential resources may be present in the area at forward costs of $30 per pound U_3O_8, or less.

The known reserves and the favorable geology for undiscovered potential resources are expected to result in the Uravan area being a source of uranium and vanadium ore for many years to come.

ACKNOWLEDGMENTS

Publication of this paper is authorized by the U.S. Department of Energy, Grand Junction Office. The assistance of Elizabeth A. Learned in compiling the historical annual production deserves recognition.

REFERENCES

Butler, A. P., Jr., and Fischer, R. P., 1978, Uranium and vanadium resources in the Moab 1° × 2° quadrangle, Utah and Colorado: U.S. Geological Survey Professional Paper 988-B, p. B1–B21.

Carter, W. D. and Gualtieri, J. L., 1969, Geology of the uranium-vanadium deposits of the La Sal quadrangle, San Juan County, Utah, and Montrose County, Colorado: U.S. Geological Professional Paper 508, 82 p.

Coffin, R. C., 1921, Radium, uranium, and vanadium deposits of southwestern Colorado: Colorado Geological Survey Bulletin 16, 231 p.

Fischer, R. P., 1942, Vanadium deposits of Colorado and Utah, a preliminary report: U.S. Geological Survey Bulletin 936-P, p. 363–394.

———, 1968, The uranium and vanadium deposits of the Colorado Plateau region, in Ridge, J. D., ed., Ore deposits of the United States, 1933–1967: New York, American Institute of Mining, Metallurgical, and Petroleum Engineers, v. 1, p. 735–746.

Fischer, R. P. and Hilpert, L. S., 1952, Geology of the Uravan mineral belt: U.S. Geological Survey Bulletin 988-A, p. 1–13.

Kimball, Gordon, 1904, Discovery of carnotite: Engineering and Mining Journal, v. 77, p. 956.

Lundquist, A. Q. and Lake, J. L., 1955, History and trends of uranium plant flowsheet: Mining Congress Journal, v. 41, n. 11, p. 35–42.

Motica, J. E., 1968, Geology and uranium-vanadium deposits in the Uravan mineral belt, southwestern Colorado, in Ridge, J. D., ed., Ore deposits of the United States, 1933–1967: New York, American Institute of Mining, Metallurgical, and Petroleum Engineers, v. 1, p. 805–813.

Nelson-Moore, J. L., Collins, D. B., and Hornbaker, A. L, 1978, Radioactive mineral occurrences of Colorado and bibliography: Colorado Geological Survey Bulletin 40, 1,054 p.

Shawe, D. R., Archbold, N. L., and Simmons, G. C., 1959, Geology and uranium-vanadium deposits of the Slick Rock district, San Miguel and Dolores Counties, Colorado: Economic Geology, v. 54, p. 395–415.

Stokes, W. L., 1952, Uranium-vanadium deposits of the Thompsons area, Grand County, Utah, with emphasis on the origin of the carnotite ores: Utah Geological and Mineral Survey Bulletin 45, 51 p.

Thamm, J. K., Kovschak, A. A., Jr., and Adams, S. S., 1981, Geology and recognition criteria for sandstone uranium deposits of the Salt Wash type, Colorado Plateau province—final report: U.S. Department of Energy Report GJBX-6(81), 136 p.

Tyler, P. M., 1930, Radium: U.S. Bureau of Mines Information Circular 6312, 55 p.

U.S. Atomic Energy Commission, 1951, Uranium exploration on the Colorado Plateau, interim staff report: U.S. Atomic Energy Commission Report RMO-1000, 75 p.

Webber, B. N., 1947, Geology and ore reserves of the uranium-vanadium depositional province of the Colorado Plateau region: Union Mines Development Corp. Report RMO-437, 279 p.

Weeks, A. D., Coleman, R. E., and Thompson, M. E., 1959, Summary of the ore mineralogy, pt. 5, in Garrels, R. M., and Larsen, E. S., 3d, compilers, Geochemistry and mineralogy of the Colorado Plateau uranium ores: U.S. Geological Survey Professional Paper 320, p. 65–79.

Wood, H. B. and Lekas, M. A., 1958, Uranium deposits of the Uravan mineral belt, in Guidebook to the geology of the Paradox Basin: Intermountain Association Petroleum Geologists, Ninth Annual Field Conference, p. 208–215.

GENERAL GEOLOGY OF URANIUM-VANADIUM DEPOSITS OF SALT WASH SANDSTONES, LA SAL AREA, SAN JUAN COUNTY, UTAH

ANTHONY A. KOVSCHAK, JR.
Union Carbide Corporation
Grand Junction, Colorado 81501

and

ROBERT L. NYLUND
Union Carbide Corporation
Uravan, Colorado 81436

INTRODUCTION

Important uranium-vanadium deposits occur in the uppermost sandstone "rim" of the fluvial Salt Wash member of the Jurassic Morrison Formation in the La Sal area, approximately 50 km south of Moab, Utah. The deposits are concentrated in an east-west trending belt approximately 19 km in length. The mineralized trend is virtually continuous from the community of La Sal Junction, Utah, on the west to the Utah-Colorado state line on the east. Utah Highway 46 parallels the mineralized trend and provides easy access to either the Union Carbide uranium mill at Uravan, Colorado, 100 km to the east or to Atlas Minerals uranium mill at Moab, Utah, 50 km to the north (fig. 1). Uranium deposits are located in the southernmost sections of T.28S., R.24 and 25E. and the northernmost sections of T.29S., R.24 and 25E.

Mining and exploration activity have progressed both eastward and westward in recent years, from an early start in the La Sal Creek area on the east, and the La Sal Junction–Rattlesnake area on the west. The majority of the existing reserves lie in the central La Sal area between the Pine Ridge collapse and the old Continental Materials Corporation Rattlesnake Pit. Production grades for La Sal and La Sal Creek ores are somewhat higher in vanadium and uranium than production grades from other localities (Table 1). The La Sal–La Sal Creek district is the largest Salt Wash production area outside the main Uravan mineral belt with future forecasts calling for substantially more production. Union Carbide Corporation and Atlas Minerals control the overwhelming land position, and both have operating mines in the area: Beaver Shaft, Mike, Snowball, Heckla, La Sal; and Pandora, respectively.

GEOLOGY

The La Sal area lies within the Paradox Basin of southwest Colorado and southeast Utah. Four major structural features resulting from salt tectonics and Tertiary intrusive activity dominate: La Sal Mountains, Lisbon Valley anticline, Pine Ridge anticline, and Coyote Wash syncline (fig. 2).

The La Sal Mountains, a laccolithic intrusive of predominately diorite porphyry with lesser amounts of monzonite and syenite porphyries, are considered to be late Cretaceous to early Miocene in age (Carter and Gualtieri, 1965). Teritary gravel derived from the

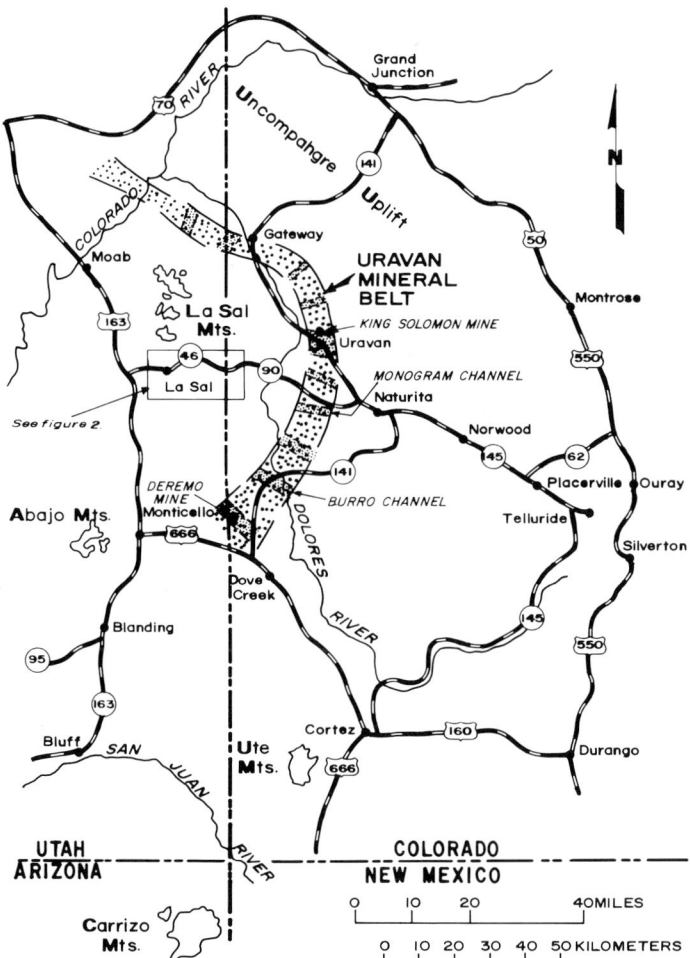

Figure 1. Index map of the Uravan Mineral Belt (modified from Chenoweth, 1978).

Table 1. Uranium ore production from the Salt Wash Member for the principal ore districts, based on U.S. Department of Energy records (modified from Thamm and others, 1981).

DISTRICT	Tons of Ore	Pounds U_3O_8	% U_3O_8	% V_2O_5
Uravan Mineral Belt	13,987,000	68,590,000	0.25	1.29
La Sal–La Sal Creek District	989,000	6,426,000	0.32	1.46
Lukachukai–Carrizo District	846,000	4,009,000	0.24	1.15
Green River District	670,000	2,632,000	0.20	0.19
Other Districts	1,153,000	4,254,000	0.18	1.21
TOTAL	17,645,000	85,911,000		
AVERAGE (weighted)			0.24	1.25

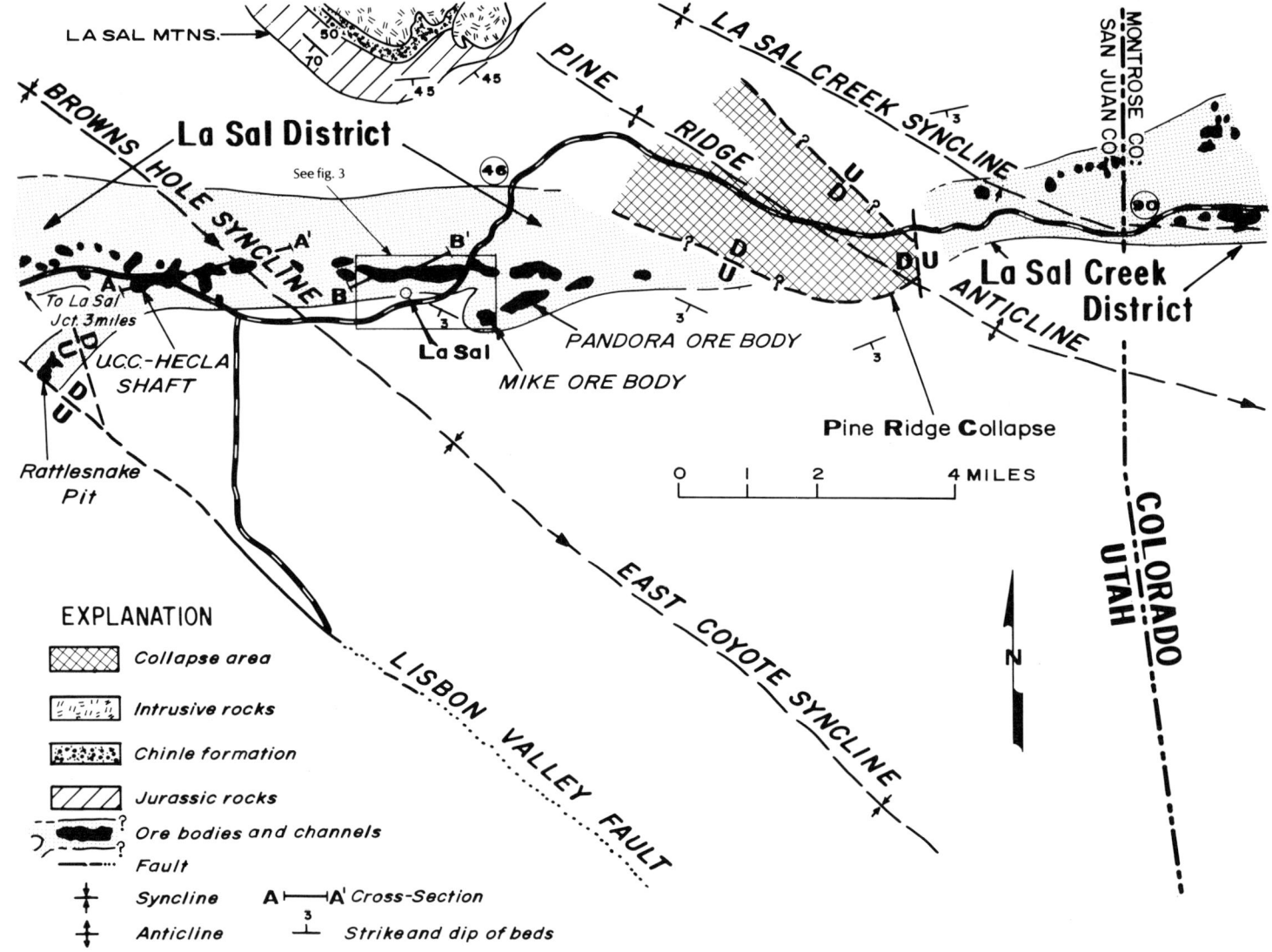

Figure 2. Map showing Salt Wash channels and mineralization of La Sal area; cross-section index.

La Sal Mountains covers a portion of the La Sal area with thicknesses up to 61 m.

The Lisbon Valley anticline, south of the La Sal area, is an elongated, breached salt anticline associated with the production of oil, gas, copper, and Triassic uranium ores. Lisbon Valley appears to have been a slightly salient feature during the time of lower Salt Wash deposition based upon interpretation of Salt Wash stratigraphic sections. Holes drilled by Union Carbide through the complete Salt Wash section on the western end of the major mineralized trend yield stratigraphic sections lacking lower Salt Wash sandstone development. In contrast, holes drilled by Union Carbide on the eastern end intersected a normal Salt Wash sequence. These data would seem to indicate that the Lisbon Valley anticline was slightly salient during lower Salt Wash deposition.

The Pine Ridge anticline in the eastern La Sal area is a large collapse feature with a vertical displacement of some 90 m (Carter and Gualtieri, 1965). The collapse separates an older and well-explored La Sal Creek mineral belt from the larger, more recently discovered deposits lying to the west (fig. 2). Exploration test holes drilled by Union Carbide in the collapse area intersected mineralized Salt Wash sandstones, although core recovery was hampered by highly fractured ground, and stratigraphic relationships of the mineralized sandstones are difficult to ascertain. More importantly, the information dates the collapse as post deposition and mineralization of the Salt Wash.

The Coyote Wash syncline trends northwesterly between the La Sal Mountains and the Lisbon Valley anticline. The La Sal mineral trend crosses the Coyote Wash syncline with the major portion of the trend lying on the north flank of the syncline where dips are approximately four degrees to the southwest. Test holes drilled across the syncline intersected a normal Salt Wash section which implies development of the synclinal flexure after deposition of the Salt Wash.

Salt Wash deposits of the La Sal area and La Sal Creek mineral belt are physically separated and lie west of the larger arcuate belt of collective mineralized Salt Wash channels that Fischer and Hilpert (1952) named the Uravan mineral belt (fig. 1). The La Sal and La Sal Creek deposits occupy a unique position in relation to the other mineral deposits in that they are located in a relatively straight channel west of and perpendicular to the main arcuate Uravan belt. The separate and centralized position of the La Sal Channel resembles the central hub of a wheel with the other mineral belt Salt Wash deposits representing the rims and spokes. Deposits from both mineralized belts are similar in ore habit, orebody configuration and sedimentological association, and are obviously part of the same overall depositional and genetic province.

LA SAL CHANNEL

The main La Sal mineralized trend was a late discovery. Carter and Gualtieri (1965) stated: The La Sal Creek mineral belt is a favorable zone 305 to 915 m in width and 8.0 km long, with the western extremity of this belt not clearly defined (p. 40). Exploration of the area between the La Sal Creek mineral belt on the east and the Rattlesnake Pit on the west may discover that mineralized ground is continuous between them (p. 73). The discovery of the Pandora orebody in eastern La Sal in the late 1960s and early 1970s marked the beginning of the definition of the extension and continuation of the mineralized belt.

The La Sal channel appears to afford an opportunity to understand the depositional and mineralizing systems of the Salt Wash by virtue of its uninterrupted linear and lateral extent. In a few cases, mineralization and channel sands are continuous for several kilometers (i.e., Burro, Monogram, Deremo channels), but none of these trends approach the 19.0 km length of the La Sal trend. The study of the relationships of mineralized channels and deposits within the Uravan mineral belt is complicated by the highly dissected topography of the belt.

The magnitude of the La Sal channel was unknown due to limited surface exposure. Channel sandstones in the La Sal townsite area exceed 37 m in thickness and have lateral continuity for over 1.6 km in width. In contrast, sandstones exposed on the eastern and western extremities of the trend are of a multiple, thin nature and average 12–15 m in thickness. The coalescing of channels on the western end and the bifurcation of the main channel on the eastern end illustrates the overall depositional regime common to channels of the Salt Wash, but does not explain the single channel deposition seen at La Sal townsite. The thick accumulation of sandstones along portions of the main trend and at the townsite can be interpreted as representing the coalescing and superimposition of two channels and not necessarily the deposition of a single channel. A thorough geologic reconstruction which would reveal the relative merit of either interpretation is tenuous. Immediately west of La Sal Junction, widespread erosion has stripped away the Salt Wash from all of the Canyonlands country. The next exposures are found on the east side of the Henry Mountains approximately 112 km to the west.

The La Sal channel shares many characteristics with other Salt Wash channels, although several characteristics are apparently more distinctive or are merely better developed and more observable in the La Sal channel: 1) coarser-grain size; 2) relatively straight configuration; and 3) unusual thickness. The main La Sal channel is designated as that channel system east of the Rattlesnake Pit and west of the Pine Ridge collapse. Salt Wash sandstones from Egnar Plains to Polar Mesa are typically characterized by fine to medium grain size, whereas La Sal sandstones are medium to coarse. Grain-size characteristics vary little from mineralized to unmineralized sandstones, or between red and gray-channel sandstones, which implies that grain size had little effect on the diagenetic preparation of the host rocks.

The La Sal channel is a large, gray, diagenetically reduced sandstone channel which displays small variations in color, grain size, carbonaceous debris, internal sedimentary structures, or other visually measurable parameters. Mudstones underlying the channel are a favorable greenish-gray color and reflect diagenetic alteration of red mudstones commonly found away from favorable channels.

The main La Sal channel appears to be unusually straight, void of numerous bends and meanders characteristic of braided and meandering fluvial channel sandstones. The apparent channel straightness may be a reflection of the ore body alignment and the undissected nature of the terrain at La Sal.

The La Sal channel can be interpreted to represent the junction of two channels: 1) one trending northeasterly which comprises the mineralized area surrounding the Rattlesnake Pit, and 2) the weakly mineralized channel system trending due east from La Sal Junction. The junction of the two channels results in the thick channel system referred to as the main La Sal channel. One conclusion that could be drawn is that the La Sal channel is a major trunk or distributary stream; therefore it is closer to the sediment source than other channel sandstones and feeds the majority of the channels which comprise the remainder of the Uravan mineral belt. Young's (1978) conclusion after studying the Salt Wash was that three distributary channels are found west of the Uravan mineral belt: Yellow Circle, La Sal, and Coyote Wash. Neither the Yellow Circle nor the Coyote Wash distributaries are found to be of the same magnitude as the La Sal channel and, therefore, the dominant role of the La Sal channel suggests that it is the principal distributary.

ORE DEPOSITS

Exploration of the channel proved somewhat frustrating due to the widespread favorable nature of the sandstones. Numerous holes were drilled exploring the central and northern portions of the channel with success being limited to several small isolated clusters of ore-grade intersections. Significant mineralization is concentrated on the southern downdip channel margin where the gray channel sandstones begin to interfinger with red and pink sandstones and red overbank mudstones. Significant mineralization appears proximal to red bordering sediments as described in recent published work on the Salt Wash (Thamm and others, 1981). Figure 2 illustrates the preferential characteristic of the orebodies and also demonstrates their pronounced linearity.

Salt Wash deposits resemble other epigenetic tabular sandstone uranium deposits found in the United States in that they are found entirely within reduced gray sandstones, and are not associated with tongues of oxidized sandstone as are roll-front type deposits. They are intimately associated with carbonaceous debris and are overlain by tuffaceous sediments. There appears to be no problem of remobilization of ore due to disequilibrium primarily because of the abundance of vanadium in the ores.

The La Sal uranium-vanadium deposits have a consistent black primary mineral suite comprised of uraninite, coffinite, montroseite, and vanadium aluminosilicates. The ore impregnates the matrix of the sandstone and replaces some detrital quartz and feldspar grains, and is homogeneously distributed, except for heterogeneities within the sandstone. Ores found in the central channel region are all primary ores, whereas oxidized ores are common to several mines in the La Sal Creek mineral belt. Primary mineral suites are modified by progressive secondary oxidation above the water table to form an oxidized mineral assemblage dominated by corvusite, carnotite and tyuyamunite (Weeks and others, 1959).

Shape of Deposits

Salt Wash deposits are normally elongated parallel to sedimentary trends and are roughly elliptical in plan view. Mineralization is typically tabular and concordant to bedding, although the ore can abruptly cross bedding to form "rolls" (Fischer, 1942).

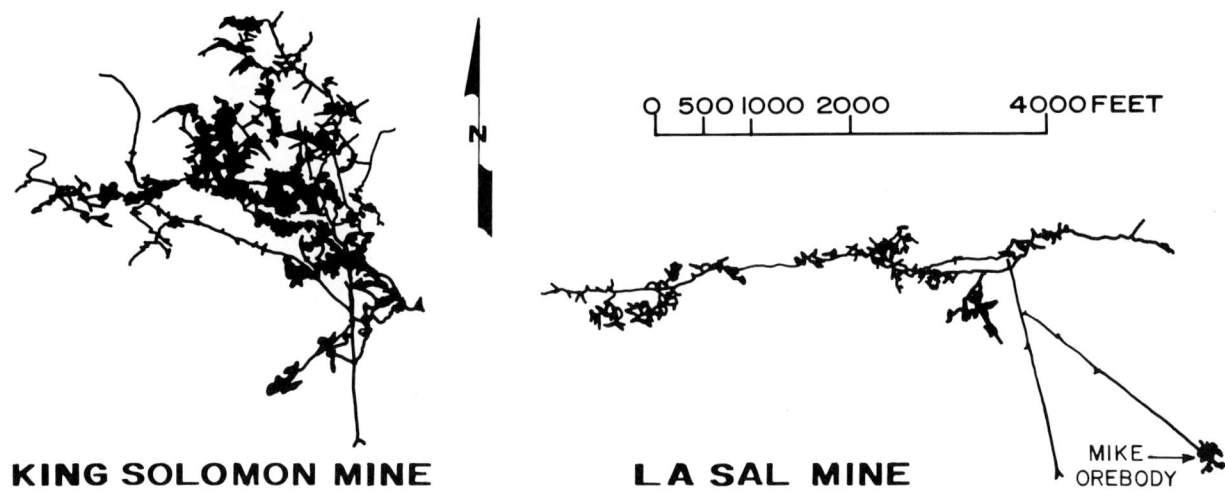

KING SOLOMON MINE   LA SAL MINE

Figure 3. Plan view maps of the King Solomon and La Sal Mines illustrating the pronounced linearity of the La Sal deposits.

Deposits found in the main La Sal channel tend to be similar although perhaps more strongly elongated than typical Salt Wash deposits found in other areas. The La Sal Mine (fig. 3) is much narrower and more noticeably elongated parallel to the channel direction than comparably large deposits such as the Deremo and King Solomon mines. The King Solomon Mine (fig. 3) is more amoeboid in plan view even though the ore is not continuous. Additional mining experience of La Sal deposits will perhaps alter this observation, although it seems compatible with the overall strong linearity of the deposits.

Mined areas of the La Sal Mine reveal certain unusual aspects of the ore when viewed in cross-section. As seen at the La Sal Mine, multiple vertical ore horizons are not a common characteristic of Salt Wash deposits, since the deposits tend to be strongly tabular with ore concentrated in tabular bodies in the lower one-third of the sandstone. The La Sal Mine has ore in tabular bodies which is distributed in multiple horizons through the sand (figs. 4 and 5) with barren sandstone occurring between horizons.

Cross sections drawn through most Salt Wash deposits reveal the strong concordant and tabular control of most mineralization.

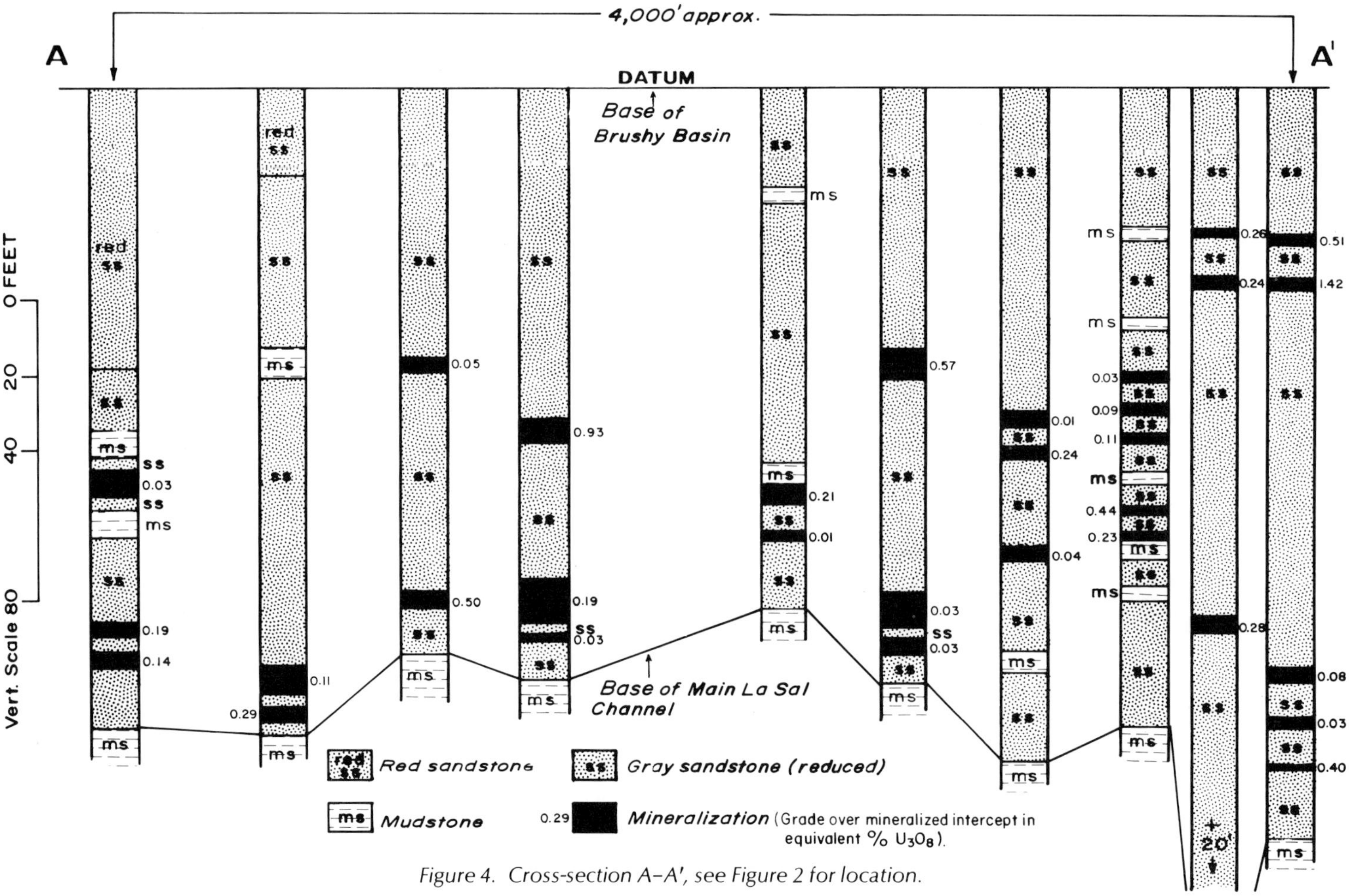

Figure 4. Cross-section A–A', see Figure 2 for location.

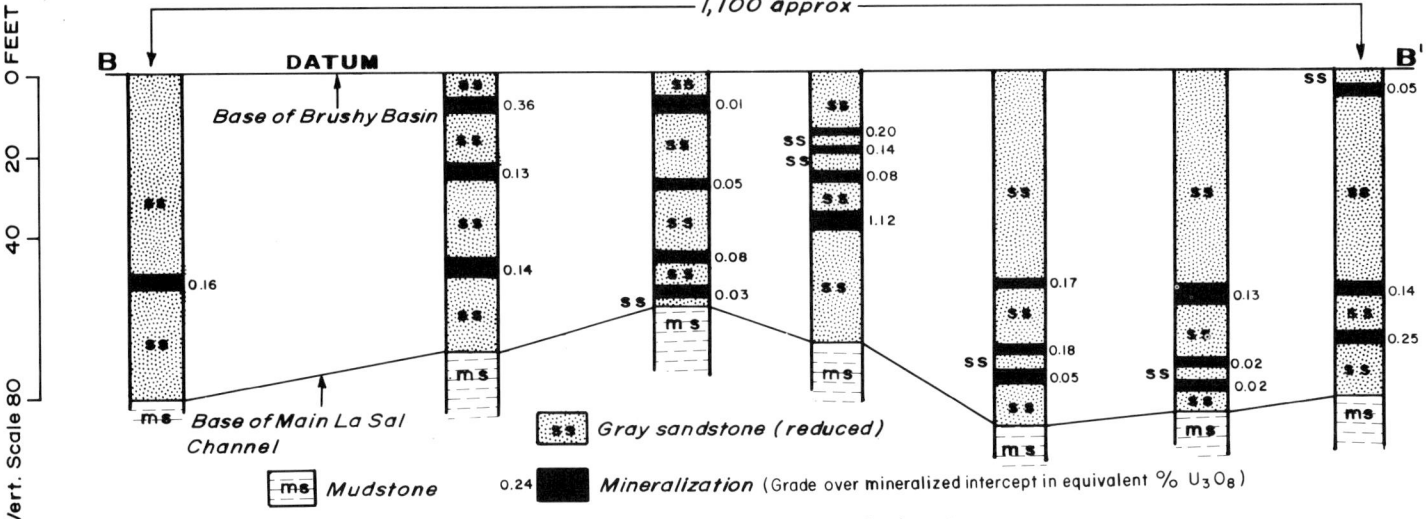

Figure 5. Cross-section B-B', see Figure 2 for location.

"Rolls" are certainly common to tabular orebodies, but the central La Sal ores appear to be atypical in that they are comprised of a high percentage of "roll ore." Shawe (1956, 1959) correlates the occurrence of "roll ore" with numerous well-defined mudstone layers interbedded with thin sandstone layers near the base of thick sandstone channels. While this observation is verifiable in many deposits, the La Sal channel appears in many areas as a thick homogeneous sandstone void of well-defined mudstone layers, but hosting a strong development of "roll ore." The coarser grain size and relative homogeneity of the sandstone may also play a role in determining the development of "roll ore" in addition to the well-defined mudstone layers.

Deposits found in the La Sal Creek mineral belt are more representative of the typical Uravan mineral belt deposit in that they are described as having an average ore thickness of 1 meter and are tabular, but are modified by "rolls." Like the majority of the deposits, they are intimately associated with carbonaceous trash and with depressions and scour surfaces within and along the margin of the channels. In general, the ore deposits are measured in tens of thousands of tons (Carter and Gualtieri, 1965).

One major meander has been interpreted to exist and is believed to host the Mike and Pandora orebodies (fig. 2). The Mike orebody lies to the southwest and is an extension of the much larger Pandora orebody. The Mike orebody is bounded on three sides by reddish-brown barren sandstones which quickly grade into red floodplain mudstones. Closure on three sides gives the Mike orebody a half circle appearance in plan view which probably mimics the curvature of the stream meander. Identification of this meander is due to the fact that it is mineralized and extensively drilled. There is a high probability that other meanders exist and they should be entertained as exploration targets.

CONCLUSIONS

The La Sal mineralized trend must certainly be considered as part of the same depositional and mineralizing systems that are responsible for the uranium-vanadium deposits of the Uravan mineral belt. Certain aspects of the deposits and of the host sandstones are unusual but not of sufficient magnitude to require alternative explanations.

Exploration potential of the La Sal area should be considered excellent. Targets include meander bends, possible bifurcating channels, and the north side of the channel. Additional large channels could be present to the south unless the Lisbon Valley Salt anticline deflected the deposition of channel sandstones away from the area.

Major production of ore from Salt Wash sandstones will gradually move westward with La Sal and Shootaring Canyon being dominant areas. La Sal will play an important role in the uranium future of the Canyonlands country.

REFERENCES

Carter, W. D. and Gualtieri, J. L., 1969, Geology of the Uravan vanadium deposits of the La Sal quadrangle, San Juan County, Utah, and Montrose County, Colorado: U.S. Geological Survey Professional Paper 508, 82 p.

Chenoweth, W. L., 1978, Uranium in Western Colorado: Mountain Geologist, v. 15, p. 89–96.

Fischer, R. P., 1942, Vanadium deposits of Colorado and Utah, a preliminary report: U.S. Geological Survey Bulletin 936-P, p. 363–394.

Fischer, R. P and Hilpert, L. S., 1952, Geology of the Uravan mineral belt; U.S. Geological Survey Bulletin 988-A, p. 1–13.

Shawe, D. R., 1956, Significance of roll orebodies in genesis of uranium-vanadium deposits on the Colorado Plateau, in Page, L. R., Stocking, H. E., and Smith, H. B., compilers, Contributions to the geology of uranium and thorium by the United States Geological Survey and Atomic Energy Commission for the United Nations International Conference of Peaceful Uses of Atomic Energy, Geneva, Switzerland, 1955: U.S. Geological Survey Professional Paper 300, p. 239–241.

Shawe, D. R., Archbold, N. L., and Simmons, G. C., 1959, Geology and uranium-vanadium deposits of the Slick Rock district, San Miguel and Dolores Counties: Economic Geology, v. 54, p. 395–415.

Thamm, J. K., Kovschak, A. A., Jr., and Adams, S. S., 1981, Geology and recognition criteria for sandstone uranium deposits of the Salt Wash type, Colorado Plateau province—final report: U.S. Department of Energy Report GJBX-6 (81), 136 p.

Weeks, A. D., Coleman, R. G., and Thompson, M. E., 1959, Summary of the ore mineralogy, in Garrels, R. M., and Larsen, E. S., III, compilers, Geochemistry and mineralogy of the Colorado Plateau uranium ores: U.S. Geological Survey Professional Paper 320, p. 65–79.

Young, R. G., 1978, Depositional systems and dispersal patterns in uraniferous sandstones of the Colorado Plateau: Utah Geology, v. 5, p. 85–102.

View across San Miguel River Valley toward Uncompahgre Plateau from Mill No. 2 mine on Club Mesa, near Uravan.

Uranium-vanadium mill of Union Carbide Corp., Uravan, Colorado.

GEOLOGY OF THE LISBON VALLEY URANIUM DISTRICT, SOUTHEASTERN UTAH

GARY C. HUBER
Canyon Resources Corporation
Golden, Colorado 80401

INTRODUCTION

The Lisbon Valley uranium district, or the Big Indian uranium district, is located in the east-central part of the Colorado Plateau (fig. 1). The district is approximately 50 km southeast of Moab, Utah. The majority of the uranium deposits occur in the Moss Back Member of the Chinle Formation (Triassic); however, minor amounts of ore have been produced from sandstones of the Cutler Formation (Permian).

Uranium was first discovered in the area in 1913 at the southern end of the district in Chinle sandstones (Wood, 1968). By 1948, a low-grade deposit had been developed in upper Cutler sandstones. In July of 1952, Charles A. Steen intersected 4 m of high-grade uranium in the lower sandstones of the Chinle Formation. The first ore produced from this discovery was on December 4, 1952 (Stocking, 1975), and in the following years the largest uranium district in southeast Utah was delineated.

GEOLOGIC SETTING

The oldest rocks which outcrop in the Lisbon Valley area are the Pennsylvanian-age Hermosa Group (fig. 2). The limestones and sandstones of the Hermosa are overlain by the Cutler Formation of Permian age. At this location, the Cutler is composed of red sandstones, siltstones, and minor limestones which were apparently deposited in environments which alternated between westward-flowing streams and eastward marine transgressions. The sedimentology of this formation is being reconstructed by Campbell (1978, personal communication) in an effort to relate the depositional environments to the occurrence of uranium in the Cutler Formation.

The upper contact of the Cutler Formation is an unconformity. The entire Moenkopi Formation is missing at Lisbon Valley due to erosion or nondeposition. Therefore, the Chinle Formation rests directly upon the Cutler Formation. The amount of angularity between the two formations varies but generally is under 5 degrees.

The Chinle Formation originally covered the entire region. This formation of Late Triassic age has been informally subdivided into two parts: a lower bentonitic sequence and upper red-bed sequence (Stewart and others, 1972). The bentonitic sequence, predominantly gray in color, is composed of claystone, clayey sandstone, and widespread sandstone and conglomerate ledge formers. Montmorillonitic clay, which is thought to have been derived from volcanic ash, comprises the claystones of this sequence. The continental deposits of the bentonitic sequence formed in rivers, flood plains, and associated lakes.

The red-bed sequence is composed of reddish-brown or reddish-orange siltstones with sparse sandstones and limestones (Stewart, 1969). The rocks which comprise this sequence are thought to have formed mainly in a large, shallow lake. However, part of this sequence in east-central Utah may have formed in a somewhat different environment as indicated by the larger percentage of sandstone in the section.

Regionally, the Chinle Formation is composed of seven formal members and several informal members which are generally equivalent to the named members. The seven units in ascending order are: Temple Mountain, Shinarump, Monitor Butte, Moss Back, Petrified Forest, Owl Rock, and Church Rock.

Several opinions exist as to what members of the Chinle Formation actually are present in the Lisbon Valley area. The Shinarump Member and the Monitor Butte Member are generally believed to be absent at the Lisbon Valley section (Stewart, 1969). The basal sandstone interval which rests unconformably on the Cutler Formation is generally called the Moss Back Member and the remaining part of the Chinle is called Churck Rock Member. Stewart and others (1972) suggested that the lower sandstones of the Chinle in this area may not, in fact, be the Moss Back Member but rather a younger sandstone. However, Young (1978, personal communication) suggested the lowermost sandstones of the area may be in fact the Shinarump Member. O'Sullivan and MacLachlan (1975) preferred not to use the traditional member names for the upper Chinle; instead, they adopted an informal lithologic breakdown of the claystone member, limy member, and siltstone member.

The Lisbon Valley uranium district is located on the southwestern flank of a faulted anticline. This structure, the Lisbon Valley anticline, is one of the main salt anticlines of the Paradox basin. However, the anticline is different from the majority of the others as the Pennsylvanian salts did not penetrate to the surface.

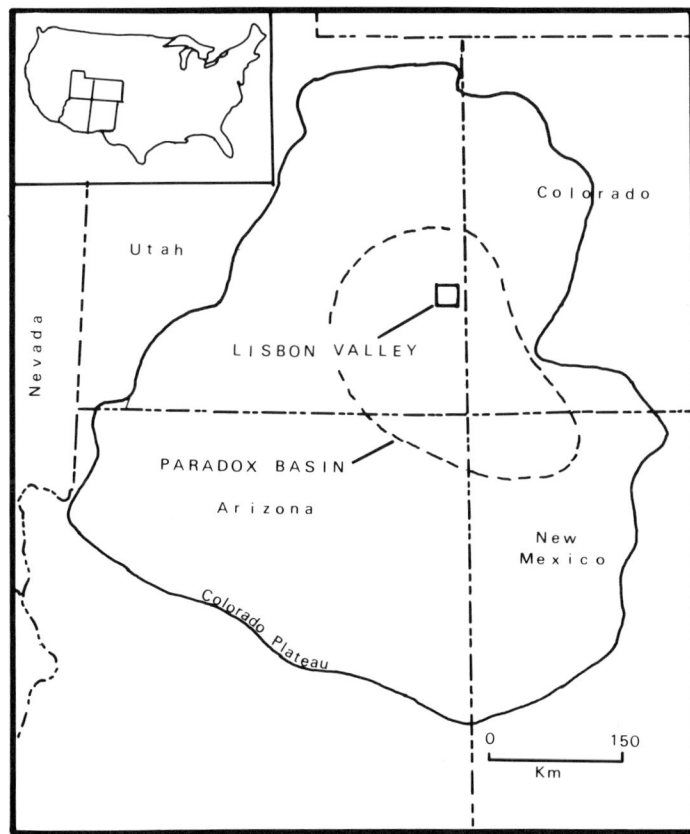

Figure 1. Index map of Lisbon Valley uranium district.

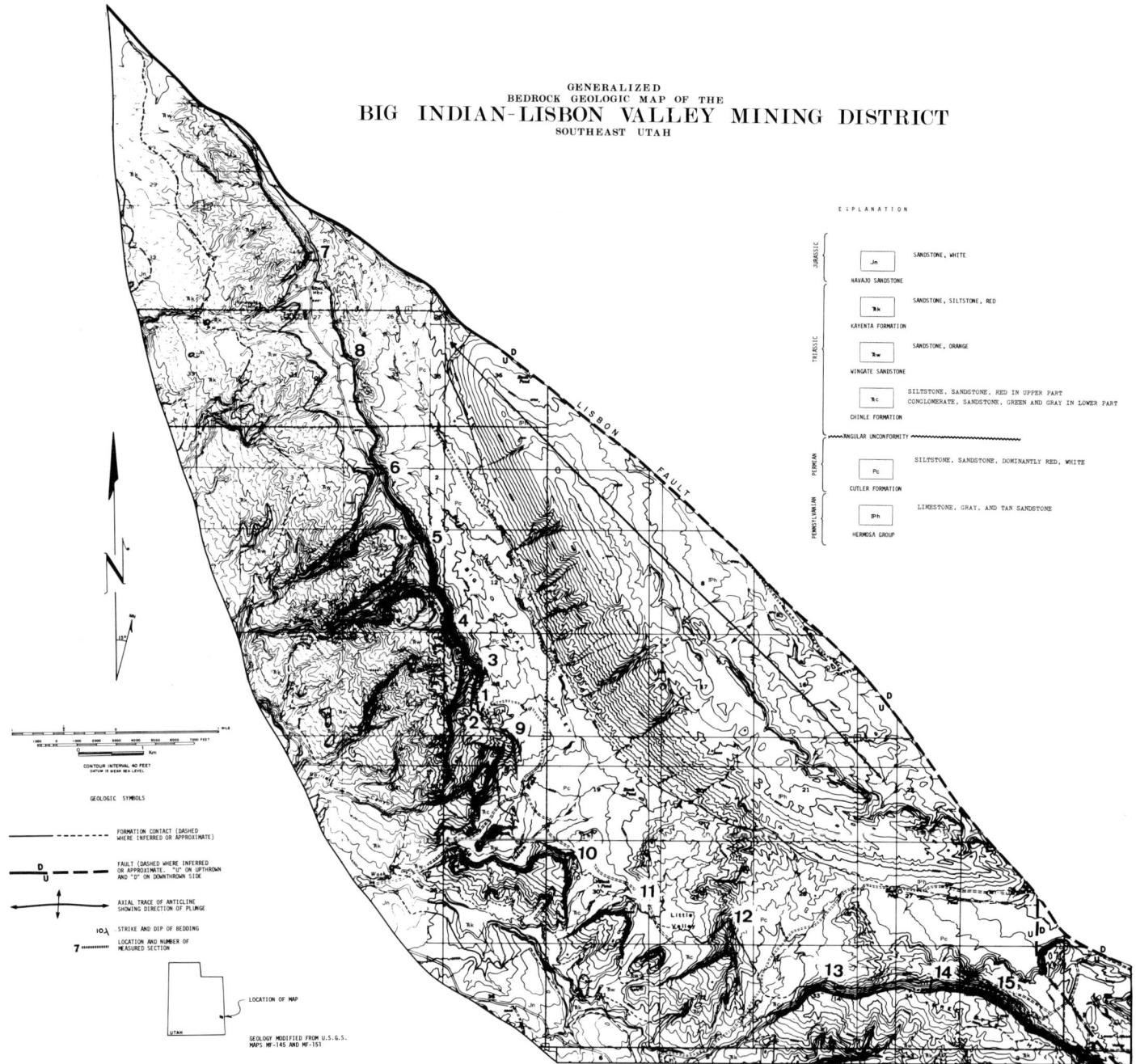

Figure 2. Geologic map of the Big Indian–Lisbon Valley district.

The northeastern side of the anticline has been faulted down along the Lisbon fault approximately 1,200 m along the crest and shows a displacement of about 606 m near the North Alice and Rio Algom (Lisbon) mines (Wood, 1968). Coyote Wash syncline is about 6.5 km northeast of Lisbon Valley and the Hatch Rock syncline is about 13 km west of the district.

It appears that the anticline was positive and an active feature at the beginning of the Triassic Period. This is indicated by the absence of the Moenkopi Formation in the Lisbon Valley area and its presence between the Chinle and Cutler strata in adjacent synclinal areas (Wood, 1968, and Budd, 1960). Butler and Fisher (1978) suggest that small variations of Chinle thickness along the outcrop of the southwestern flank of the Lisbon Valley anticline indicate that minor uplift of parts of the anticline may have occurred during Chinle sedimentation. Tectonic activity during Laramide time or later faulted the anticline along the axis and displaced the northeast block downwards along the Lisbon fault.

CHINLE FORMATION

Stratigraphic information, obtained from 15 measured sections in the Lisbon Valley area (numbered in fig. 2) and 22 drill holes west of the district, is shown on Figures 3 and 4. The Chinle Formation is composed of an upper siltstone and sandstone unit and a lower sandstone unit called the Moss Back Member.

The general vertical sequence of the upper unit in the northern part of Lisbon Valley consists of a lower greenish-gray siltstone, a middle reddish-brown to pale red sandstone, and an upper reddish-brown siltstone. Both siltstone intervals commonly are par-

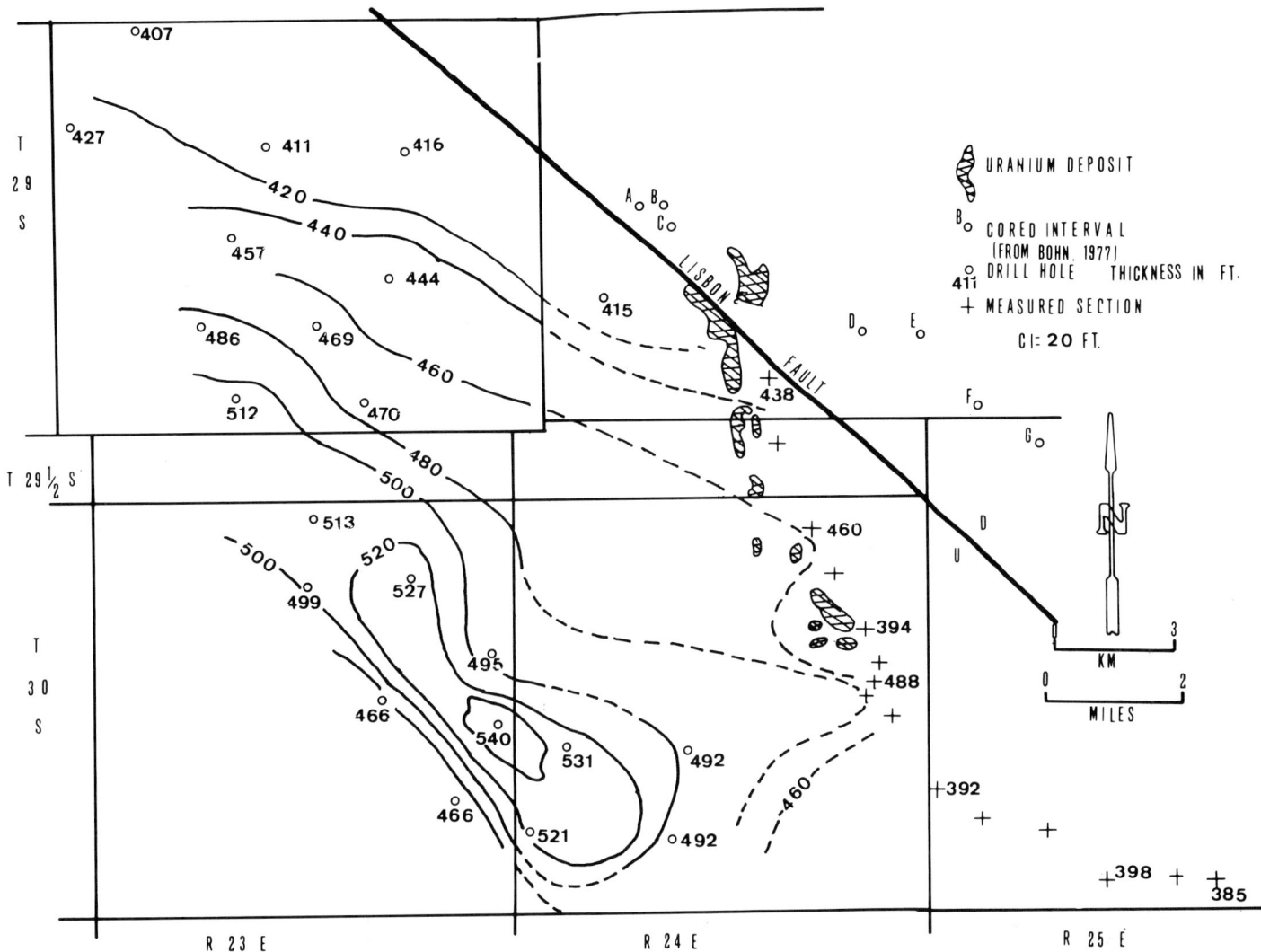

Figure 3. Isopach map of Chinle Formation in the Big Indian–Lisbon Valley district.

tially covered; however, small lenticular sandstones are believed to be present in the siltstones beneath the covered slopes. The middle sandstone interval generally is very fine- to fine-grained, well to moderately sorted, with subrounded grains. Locally, the basal part of the sandstones contain conglomerates composed of quartz pebbles. Stratification types include plane bedding, large-scale trough cross-bedding, some tabular cross-bedding, and ripple-marked zones. The upper sediments of the Chinle Formation along the south part of the district are also principally siltstones. However, the middle sandstones appear to be more discontinuous than those to the north.

In Lisbon Valley the Moss Back Member is composed of a lower sandstone unit and an upper sandstone unit. The main facies of the lower unit as calculated from the measured sections include: 15 percent parallel-bedded conglomerate, 15 percent trough cross-bedded sandstone, 66 percent interbedded siltstone and sandstone, and 4 percent other facies. The generalized depositional model for the lower unit starts with a scour surface upon which channel lag conglomerates were deposited. This facies is overlain by trough cross-bedded sandstone indicating overbank deposition. The large amount of fine-grained sediments (siltstones), the depth of scouring, abundant mudstone clasts in the conglomerate, and a poorly defined fining-upward sequence suggests deposition by a meandering stream. However, the lack of the upper point bar facies of parallel lamination and ripple-marked sandstones presents a problem. It is possible that the reason for this apparent absence of upper point bar sediments is that the river which deposited these sediments belonged to the coarse-grained, point bar, meander-belt model. In this type of river, the sediments of the upper point bar are removed by chute erosion. Conglomerate lenses overlain by trough cross-bedded sandstones locally were observed between the measured sections in the upper part of the unit and may represent chute fill. This model is not wholly satisfactory because large foreset bedding, characteristic of chute bars, was not observed at the outcrop. The Donjek-type braided river model (Miall, 1977) commonly contains point bar deposits similar to those described. However, the large amount of fine-grained overbank material associated with the lower unit is not common to the braided river model.

The main facies observed in sandstone of the upper unit as calculated from the measured sections include: 22 percent parallel-bedded and trough cross-bedded conglomerate, 32 percent trough cross-bedded sandstone, 32 percent parallel-bedded sandstone, 10 percent ripple-marked sandstone, and 4 percent other facies. These percentages do not include the siltstones which occur at the top of the sequence. The reason that the overlying silt-

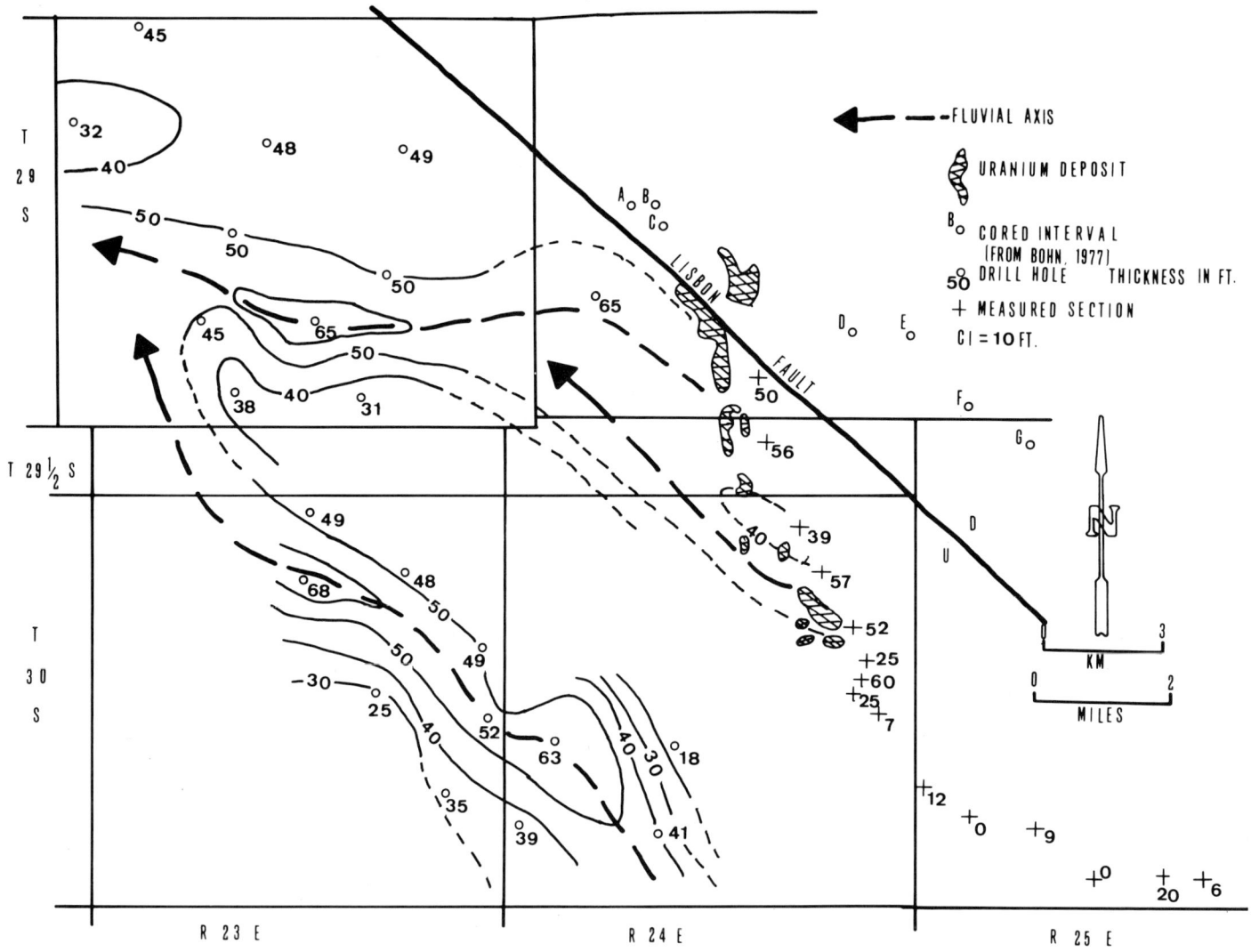

Figure 4. Isopach map of lower Chinle sandstones in the Big Indian–Lisbon Valley district.

stones were not incorporated into the breakdown of the facies is that it was not possible to ascertain what thickness of siltstones were deposited by the channels of the upper unit. The generalized depositional model of this unit starts with a channel lag conglomerate followed by channel-fill facies of trough cross-bedded and parallel-bedded sandstones. The upper part of the sequence contains ripple-marked sandstones capped by siltstones. This model is suggestive of point bar deposits. The abundance of siltstone at the top of the sandstone interval and vertical sequence of sedimentary structures suggests a fine-grained, point bar, meander-belt model. However, the occurrence of trough cross-bedding in the upper part of the interval and poorly defined upward fining of grain size suggests a coarse-grained, point bar, meander-belt model.

The geology of the mineralized area north of the Lisbon Fault (Lisbon mine) and along the southern part of the outcrop in T.30S., R.25E. (fig. 4) is different from the rest of the district. The dominant lithologies within these areas are siltstones, fine-grained sandstones, and mudstone-pebble conglomerates. These mudstone-pebble conglomerates are contained in a sandstone matrix which is fine- to medium-grained. The large amount of siltstone, flat-pebble conglomerate and thin sandstone beds suggests sedimentation in an environment different from the rest of the district. The depositional environment is interpreted as marginal to the main channel system, where the dominant sedimentation was in an overbank environment of crevasse-splay deposits into a flood basin. This is supported by the abundance of mudstone clasts and generally finer-grained sediments contained in the two areas. The mudstone clasts are composed of both reddish-brown and greenish-gray colored fragments. The reddish-brown clasts may have been derived from the higher, oxidized part of the natural levee and the greenish-gray clasts may have come from the lower and more reduced part of the levee.

Figure 3 is an isopach map of the Chinle Formation. The increase in total thickness in the region of the Hatch Rock syncline (southwestern part of the map) suggests that this structure may have been active during Chinle deposition and influenced sedimentation. In general, the formation appears to be thinning in a north and northeastern direction. It is possible that this reduction in total thickness could have been influenced by the Lisbon Valley anticline if it were a positive feature during Chinle time. Figure 4 is an isopach map of the lower Chinle sandstones in the area. Two main stream systems are indicated on this map. The northern one apparently swings to the north immediately west of Lisbon Valley and then turns to the west. The second stream system apparently flowed northwest along the Hatch Rock syncline where it joined the northern system and flowed westward. Based on the isopach map of the total lower Chinle sandstones, it appears that the small anticline may have influenced sedimentation, as indicated by the thinness of lower sandstones found in the northwest corner of T.28S., R.23E. A gravity low which may indicate the presence of a minor salt cell underlying this anticline has been reported by Byerly and Joesting (1959). If this area were slightly positive, then it may have acted as an intra-stream divide and most of the sediments at that locality would be the finer-grained overbank deposits.

The trend of the thickest part of the lower Chinle sandstones along Hatch Rock syncline also indicates the possibility of tectonic influence on sedimentation. In this area, the elongate nature of the sandstone isopach follows the synclinal axis.

The results of the outcrop study and the drilling program suggest that the Lisbon Valley area was the site of two main belts of fluvial sedimentation in the Moss Back Member. These northwesterly trending belts averaged about 6.5 km in width except in the area of T.29S., R.23E., where the width may be from 10 to 16 km. The nature of the vertical sequences of the sedimentary structures, and the various facies of fine-grained sediments and massive conglomerates, suggest the lower Chinle sandstones at Lisbon Valley were deposited by a river belonging to a coarse-grained, point bar, meander-belt model or a Donjek-type braided river model. It is interesting to note that the main Lisbon Valley uranium deposits appear to be located perpendicular to a fluvial belt that has been interpreted as characteristic of a coarse-grained, point bar, meander-belt model. This is in agreement with the observation of Rackley (1976) that most of the uranium deposits of the western United States occur in sediments deposited by coarse-grained, point bar, meander-belt rivers.

URANIUM OCCURRENCES

The Lisbon Valley district, also known as the Big Indian Valley district, can be subdivided into two areas of mineralization (fig. 5). The southern area, which is the smaller of the two, includes the Service Berry, Divide, and Continental mines. Atlas Minerals Corporation has recently announced the discovery of a new high-grade uranium deposit in this part of the district. The northern area contains the majority of the reserves in a narrow belt which is about 1 km wide and about 10 km long. The mines in this area include: Louise, Mi Vida, Ike-Nixon, La Sal, Cord, Radon, Far West, North Alice, and Rio Algom (Lisbon mine). Wood (1968) describes the ore bodies as irregular, amoeba-shaped masses that are concordant to bedding. The average thickness is about 2 m but ranges from a few centimeters to over 13 m in thickness with an average grade of 0.39 percent U_3O_8. The total production for the district is over 68 million pounds of uranium oxide (Chenoweth, 1981, personal communication).

The uranium deposits of Lisbon Valley occur in the lowest sandstone or conglomerate of the Moss Back Member. Sedimentological controls of the uranium mineralization were not recognized in the Moss Back Member in Lisbon Valley. However, the isopach map of the lower Chinle sandstones (fig. 4) shows a spatial relationship between sandstone thickness and uranium mineralization. The mineralized areas seem to occur where the thickness of lower sandstones exceed 12 m. The thinness of the sandstones in the middle of the belt suggests that an intra-stream divide may have existed during Moss Back deposition.

Based on the stratigraphic interpretation of the lower Chinle sediments, the uranium deposits in the northern part of the district, from the Mi Vida mine to the Rio Algom mine (fig. 5), are restricted to the lower unit of the Moss Back Member. Here, the main uranium deposits are spread out from the southern edge of the sandstone belt all the way across the channel deposits to the northern edge, and in the case of the Rio Algom mine, the mineralization spreads past the banks into the crevasse-splay deposits.

If the interpretation of the Rio Algom mine area is correct, then the northern extent of mineralization would be limited by the pinchout of the crevasse-splay sandstones into the flood basin deposits. The uranium deposits in the southern part of the district also are believed to be hosted in crevasse-splay deposits.

Geochemical zoning of several elements has been found to occur over the deposits. Kennedy (1961) found that a molybdenum halo extended up to about 3 m above the uranium mineralization in the northern part of the district. Calcium was also found to be concentrated above the ore for about 0.6 m. Recent work by Brooks (1978, personal communication) provides a detailed look at the mineral zoning. Sampling on approximately 15-cm spacing revealed the ore body at the Far West incline to have an upper molybdenum maximum value underlain by the uranium zone which in turn was underlain by a vanadium zone followed by a copper zone. This sequence of zoning is characteristic of the upper limb, or more generally the outer side of a geochemical cell (i.e. roll-type deposit), as described by Rackley (1976) and Harshman (1974).

SUMMARY

The sandstones of the lower part of the Chinle Formation at Lisbon Valley were deposited in a fluvial environment. Facies analysis of these sandstones suggests that this fluvial environment was of the coarse-grained, point bar, meander-belt type or possibly the Donjek-type braided stream of Miall (1977). Sedimentation during Moss Back time, as well as for the rest of the Chinle Formation, appears to have been influenced by tectonic activity. This is shown by the sub-surface geometry of the sandstones of the Moss Back Member as well as the thinning of the total Chinle Formation to the north towards the Lisbon Valley salt anticline.

Uranium mineralization in the Lisbon Valley district occurs in the basal sandstones and conglomerates of the Moss Back Member.

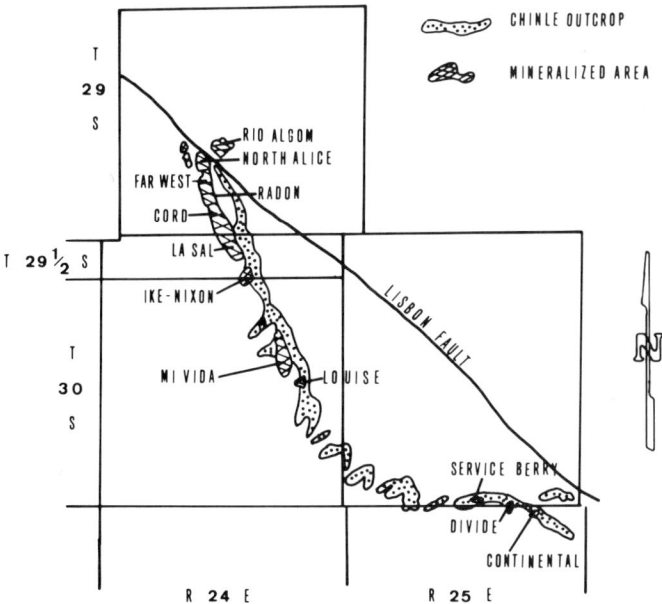

Figure 5. Uranium mineralized areas and mines in the Lisbon Valley district.

The long axes of the ore bodies are approximately perpendicular to the northwest-trending channel system as mapped in the subsurface. The uranium mineralization is not solely hosted by channel sandstones. In the Rio Algom mine (Lisbon mine), the host rock for the mineralization is believed to be of crevasse-splay origin. The geochemistry of the uranium deposits reveals similarities to the oxidation-reduction geochemical cell uranium deposits of the Wyoming basins. The distribution of elements in a vertical sequence from the top downward has been reported to be molybdenum, calcium, uranium, vanadium, and copper.

ACKNOWLEDGMENTS

The author wishes to express his appreciation to the numerous individuals and companies who were most helpful in this study. Energy Reserves Group provided financial support and granted permission to publish the results of this work. This paper has been summarized from an earlier publication (Huber, 1979) which treats the district in greater detail.

REFERENCES

Budd, H., 1960, Notes on the Pure Oil Company discovery at northwest Lisbon: Four Corners Geological Society Guidebook, Geology of the Paradox fold and fault belt, p. 121–124.

Butler Jr., A. P. and Fisher, R. P., 1978, Uranium and vanadium resources in the Moab 1° × 2° quadrangle, Utah and Colorado: U.S. Geological Survey Professional Paper 988-B, 22 p.

Byerly, P. E. and Joesting, H. R., 1959, Regional geophysical investigations of the Lisbon Valley area, Utah and Colorado: U.S. Geological Survey Professional Paper 316-C.

Harshman, E. N., 1974, Distribution of elements in some roll-type uranium deposits: International Atomic Energy Agency, Formation of uranium ore deposits, p. 169–184.

Huber, G. C., 1979, Stratigraphy and uranium deposits of the Lisbon Valley District, San Juan County, Utah (Ph.D. dissertation): Golden, Colorado School of Mines, 210 p. (also summarized in Colorado School of Mines Quarterly, v. 75, n. 2, 45 p.

Kennedy, V. C., 1961, Geochemical studies of mineral deposits in the Lisbon Valley area, San Juan County, Utah (Ph.D. dissertation): Boulder, University of Colorado, 157 p.

Miall, A. D., 1977, A review of the braided stream depositional environment: Earth Science Reviews, v. 13, p. 1–62.

O'Sullivan, R. B. and MacLachlan, M. E., 1975, Triassic rocks of the Moab-White Canyon area, southeastern Utah: Four Corners Geological Society, Canyonlands Country Guidebook, p. 129–142.

Rackley, R. I., 1976, Origin of western-states type uranium mineralization, in Handbook of stratabound and stratiform ore deposits: New York, Elsevier, p. 90–156.

Stewart, J. H., 1969, Major Upper Triassic lithogenetic sequences in Colorado Plateau region: American Association of Petroleum Geologists, v. 53, p. 1866–1879.

Stewart, J. H. and others, 1972, Stratigraphy and origin of the Chinle Formation and related Upper Triassic strata in the Colorado Plateau region: U.S. Geological Survey Professional Paper 690, 336 p.

Stocking, M., 1975, Charlie Steen—Prospector: Four Corners Geological Society, Canyonlands Country Guidebook, p. 51–54.

Wood, H. B., 1968, Geology and exploitation of uranium deposits in the Lisbon Valley area, Utah, in Ore deposits of the United States, 1933–1967: American Institute of Mining and Metallurgical Engineers, p. 771–790.

URANIUM IN THE GUNNISON COUNTRY, COLORADO*

CRAIG S. GOODKNIGHT
Bendix Field Engineering Corporation
P.O. Box 1569
Grand Junction, Colorado 81502

INTRODUCTION

Uranium prospecting spread eastward from the Colorado Plateau in the middle and late 1950s to a more hard-rock environment in the area surrounding Gunnison. Two major uranium districts (Cochetopa and Marshall Pass) were discovered during that time, as were numerous uranium occurrences elsewhere in the area. More recently, in the late 1970s, the Gunnison country experienced renewed and more intense uranium exploration and development.

Approximately 1.2 million kg of U_3O_8 have been produced from the Gunnison country; over 99 percent of this has come from the Cochetopa and Marshall Pass districts. Uranium in both districts and many of the other occurrences is associated closely with fault and shear zones which cut brittle host formations (dolomites and sandstones) of Paleozoic and Mesozoic age. Minor uranium occurrences are in pegmatites and shear zones in Precambrian rocks, Cambrian vein material, and sandstones of early Tertiary age.

Much of the information and basic data on the various uranium occurrences for this paper were collected from 1977–1979 during the evaluation of the Montrose (1°×2°) quadrangle by Bendix Field Engineering Corporation, under contract to the U.S. Department of Energy for the National Uranium Resource Evaluation (NURE) program. The reader is referred to the Montrose quadrangle evaluation report (folio) for additional information on uranium occurrences (many others having less than 0.01 percent U_3O_8) and favorability (Goodknight and Ludlam, 1981).

The area of Gunnison country for this paper is somewhat restricted to within the Montrose 1°×2° quadrangle boundary, and also excludes the area around Lake City; the boundary of the area described in this paper is shown in Figure 1. An index map (fig. 1) shows all the known occurrences of material containing at least 0.01 percent U_3O_8.

*Publication authorized by the U.S. Department of Energy, Grand Junction Office.

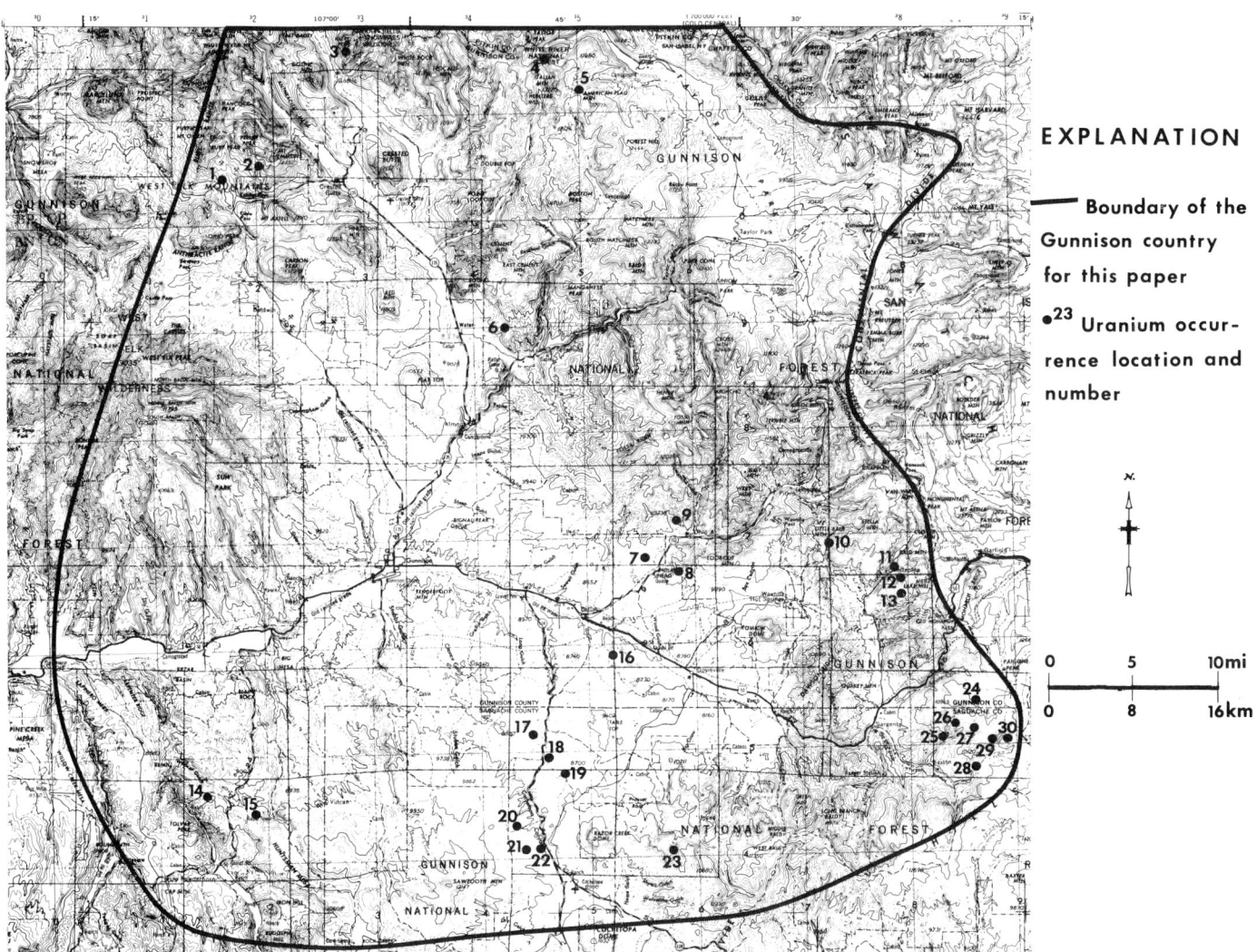

Figure 1. Index map of the Gunnison country showing locations of selected uranium occurrences (at least 0.01 percent U_3O_8).

DESCRIPTION OF URANIUM OCCURRENCES IN AREAS (OR DISTRICTS)

Ruby–Irwin District

Uranium has been found in the southeastern part of the Piceance Creek basin in the Ruby–Irwin base- and precious-metal mining district. In this district, centered about 10 km west of Crested Butte, uranium is in the Ruby Anthracite Creek area and at the Standard mine. Prospectors in the mid-1950s found uranium in the lower part of the Eocene Wasatch Formation along Ruby Anthracite Creek at the Yellowdog and Pearl B claims (locality 1, fig. 1 and Table 1). Workings on the claims in the E½ sec. 4, T. 14 S., R. 87 W. consist of several prospect pits and one short adit; no uranium was produced. During quadrangle evaluation (Goodknight and Ludlam, 1981) in 1978, high radioactivity was found in some dump material from the abandoned Standard mine in the SE¼ sec. 25, T. 13 S., R. 87 W. (loc. 2). The anomalously radioactive dump material came from the Paleocene Ohio Creek Formation and/or the Eocene Wasatch Formation; the exact location of the material was uncertain because the entrance to the mine (formerly a large producer of lead, zinc, and silver) was caved.

Uranium mineralization in the Ruby Anthracite Creek area is in iron-stained, fine- to medium-grained feldspathic sandstone that contains a moderate amount (up to several percent) of carbonaceous material and minor pyrite along bedding. Uranium is associated with carbonaceous material, mainly near the base of poorly developed stream channel systems that trend west or northwest. Samples of mineralized rock taken during quadrangle evaluation contain up to 0.035 percent U_3O_8; no uranium minerals have been identified.

The uranium occurrence at the Standard mine is in gray, fine-grained sandstone with clay and carbonaceous clasts, probably from a fluvial channel. A sample of radioactive material taken during quadrangle evaluation from the mine dump contained 0.59 percent U_3O_8 and uranium (uraninite?) is associated with carbonaceous material which composes about two percent of the rock. The mine is within the body of base-metal mineralization related to the Redwell Basin intrusive complex of Oligocene age, centered about 2–3 km to the east. Uranium was probably emplaced by groundwaters in the carbonaceous sandstone before the episode of base-metal mineralization which provided pyrite, sphalerite, argentiferous galena, chalcopyrite, and pyrrhotite.

Elk Mountains

The part of the Elk Mountains shown in Figure 1 extends from Gothic on the west to the Taylor River on the south and east. Four areas of uranium cocurrences have been found in this (southern) part of the Elk Mountains.

On the west side of Virginia Basin about 2.5 km north of Gothic in the NW¼ NE¼ sec. 34, T. 12 S., R. 86 W. (loc. 3), low-grade stratiform uranium enrichment occurs in a thin, gray, freshwater lime-

Table 1. Selected uranium occurrences (at least 0.01 percent U_3O_8) and their host formation(s) in the Gunnison country.

Locality Number (fig. 1)	Name	Formation
1	Yellowdog and Pearl B claims	Wasatch Formation
2	Standard mine	Ohio Creek and/or Wasatch Formation
3	Virginia Basin	Morrison Formation
4	Mt. Tilton	Parting Sandstone of Chaffee Group
5	Star Basin	Bog material and fault breccia
6	North Star claims (Jacks Cabin)	Altered Precambrian Y granite
7	Pegmatite No. 783	Precambrian pegmatite
8	Brown Derby mine	Precambrian pegmatite
9	Willow Creek mine	Precambrian pegmatite
10	Margo claim group	Precambrian YX(?) granite
11	Akron Tunnel	Paleozoic sedimentary rock
12	West Point Hill	Leadville Limestone
13	Big Red No. 22 mine and No. 39 prospects	Sawatch Sandstone
14	Spencer area	Iron-rich vein material
15	Mrs. Roberts deeded land	Thorium- and uranium-bearing vein
16	Surefire mining claims	Morrison Formation
17	Post claim group	Junction Creek Sandstone
18	Do Dah claim group	Fault zone in rocks of Precambrian X age
19	Los Ochos mine	Junction Creek Sandstone, Morrison Formation, and brecciated Precambrian rocks
20	Milbob claim group	Junction Creek Sandstone
21	La Rue claims	Dakota Sandstone
22	Bet claim group	Morrison Formation, Junction Creek Sandstone, and brecciated Precambrian rocks
23	Lucky Friday claim group	Junction Creek Sandstone and quartz monzonite of Precambrian X age
24	Little Indian No. 36 mine	Harding Sandstone
25	Apache No. 4 claim	Harding Sandstone
26	Little Indian No. 6 claim	Harding Sandstone
27	Pitch mine	Leadville Dolomite and Belden Formation
28	Chester Fault at Marshall Creek	Pegmatitic granite of Precambrian X age
29	Marshall Pass No. 5 claim and Lookout claim group	Fractured granite gneiss and quartz monzonite of Precambrian X age
30	Hidden Reserve claim group	Precambrian pegmatite

stone bed in the lower part of the Morrison Formation. This occurrence was discovered in the mid-1950s and was investigated in 1978 by Goodknight and Ludlam (1981). A sample from the limestone bed contained 0.01 percent U_3O_8; the highest radioactivity was along fractures or joint surfaces. The occurrence is probably epigenetic and may be either an efflorescent or a peneconcordant deposit.

Near the head of Cement Creek on the north side of Mt. Tilton in the SE¼ sec. 28, T. 12 S., R. 84 W. (loc. 4), another low-grade stratiform uranium enrichment occurs—this time in the lowr part of the Parting Sandstone of the Chaffee Group. This occurrence was found in 1978 during quadrangle evaluation (Goodknight and Ludlam, 1981); a sample of the Parting contained 0.017 percent radiometric uranium. High radioactivity occurs in a thin bed of dark brown, quartzose, medium- to fine-grained sandstone in the Parting, which represents a marginal-marine environment during transgression of a sea in Late Devonian time.

On the south side of Star Basin near the head of Italian Creek in secs. 1 and 12, T. 13 S., R. 84 W. are three closely-separated uranium occurrences (all shown by loc. 5, fig. 1). All three occurrences were found in 1978 during quadrangle evaluation and all may possibly be related. Two occurrences (in sec. 1) are in black, organic-rich bog material at the sites of highly-radioactive cold springs which overlie Precambrian YX(?) gneissic granite. The third occurrence (in sec. 12) is in limonite-cemented breccia along an east-trending normal fault separating shales of the Pennsylvanian Belden Formation to the south from gneissic granite of Precambrian YX(?) age. The area of the occurrences is along the Castle Creek fault zone of Laramide age bordering the west side of the Sawatch Range; the Oligocene Italian Mountain intrusive complex lies less than 2 km to the west (Cunningham, 1973).

Samples of the bog material at the two occurrences contained just over 0.01 percent U_3O_8; however, the radiometric uranium content of one of the samples was 1.3 percent. This high radioactivity at the springs is probably due to radium-226. A sample of the occurrence along the fault zone had 0.016 percent U_3O_8. Radium-226, a uranium daughter product that appears at the springs, is probably being transported from a vein-type uranium deposit somewhere along the hydrologic system supporting the springs. The occurrence in the fault breccia may represent a more extensive vein-type uranium deposit at depth or many other faults in the area may host vein-type uranium deposits responsible for high radium contents in the springs.

In the extreme southern Elk Mountains about 10 km north of Almont in the E½ sec. 17, T. 15 S., R. 84 W. (loc. 6), uranium occurs at the North Star claims in what is commonly referred to as the Jacks Cabin area. Uranium was discovered here in 1955 along the northwest-trending North Star (or Granite) reverse fault. The North Star fault in this area separates Precambrian Y granitic rocks to the northeast from the Belden Formation and younger Mesozoic sedimentary rocks to the southwest. The fault zone is 30–60 m wide and is developed mainly in altered and fractured granite. Uranium (autunite and meta-autunite) occurs along fractures; a sample of fractured granite contained 0.034 percent U_3O_8 (Goodknight and Ludlam, 1981). Numerous prospect pits and two caved adits occur along a 2-km length of the fault zone. In the past five years, several companies have conducted exploratory drilling along the fault in this area.

Quartz Creek District

Uranium occurrences are known from three of the numerous pegmatite bodies that compose the Quartz Creek mining district, about 24 km east of Gunnison. Uranium in these pegmatites is in small, widely scattered pods of uranium-bearing minerals. The simple and zoned pegmatites in the district are related to the Wood Gulch Granite of Precambrian X age exposed to the south.

Pegmatite No. 783, named on the map by Staatz and Trites (1955), was sampled by Goodknight and Ludlam (1981) in 1979 and found to contain the thorium minerals brockite and greyite and 0.011 percent U_3O_8; no uranium minerals were identified. This microcline-quartz-pegmatite is in the E½ sec. 32, T. 50 N., R. 3 E. (loc. 7).

The Brown Derby mine in the NE¼ sec. 3, T. 49 N., R. 3 E. (loc. 8) produced about 110 kg of U_3O_8 from 365 metric tons of lepidolite and microlite mined during World War II (Nelson-Moore and others, 1978). Chip samples taken during quadrangle evaluation in 1978 from the margin of the Brown Derby No. 1 pegmatite contained several percent U_3O_8 from the minerals pyrochlore and uranopyrochlore.

A sample taken during quadrangle evaluation in 1978 from a radioactive part of the Bucky pegmatite at the Willow Creek mine (loc. 9) contained 0.084 percent U_3O_8. This mine is near the northern end of the district in the NE¼ sec. 22, T. 50 N., R. 3 E. Radioactive minerals identified in 1978 from this occurrence include struverite, uranopyrochlore, and monazite.

Tomichi (Whitepine) District

Four areas of uranium occurrence have been found in the Tomichi (and Whitepine) base-metal mining district. The district is on the west flank of the Sawatch Range and is characterized by small remnants of Paleozoic sedimentary rocks bounded by Laramide reverse faults. The remnants have been mineralized by hydrothermal solutions from the nearby Oligocene Mount Princeton batholith to the northeast.

The prospects at the Margo claim group (formerly known as the Delores-Marie or Vicki Lee) along Canyon Creek, about 7 km northwest of Whitepine, are in the E½ sec. 25, T. 50 N., R. 4 E. (loc. 10). Uranium has been known in this area since the mid-1950s in shear zones and fractures in pegmatitic granite of Precambrian YX(?) age. The Bald Mountain reverse fault (Dings and Robinson, 1957), which bounds a Paleozoic remnant, is less than 1 km west of the occurrence. A sample taken at a prospect in 1979 during quadrangle evaluation had 0.029 percent U_3O_8 and uranium-bearing minerals were identified as euxenite-polycrase, zircon, and xenotime.

Uranium was found by Gallagher and others (1977) in small pieces of dump material from the Akron Tunnel (loc. 11), just south of Whitepine. The haulage tunnel, which has been caved for many years, connected with several mine workings to the east along the north-trending Star reverse fault where replacement deposits of silver, lead, and zinc occur in Paleozoic sedimentary rocks. A sample of radioactive dump material taken during quadrangle evaluation in 1979 had 0.45 percent U_3O_8.

In 1978 during quadrangle evaluation, uranium was found near the base of the Leadville Limestone about 1 km southeast of Whitepine on the top of West Point Hill (loc. 12). This occurrence (in the E½ sec. 3, T. 49 N., R. 5 E.) is in white to light gray dolomitic sandstone that is anomalously radioactive along strike for about 100 m. A sample of the dolomitic sandstone contained 0.014 percent U_3O_8 (Goodknight and Ludlam, 1981). Uranium in this occurrence may represent a stratiform deposit or it may be related to the Star reverse fault, about 150 m to the east.

Uranium was discovered in 1957 at the Big Red occurrences in secs. 10 and 11, T. 49 N., R. 5 E. (loc. 13), about 3 km south of

Whitepine. The Big Red No. 22 mine and No. 39 prospects are about 1 km apart in separate small remnants of Upper Cambrian Sawatch Sandstone along the footwall of a northwest-trending reverse fault. Extensive drilling occurred in the summers of 1978 and 1979 along several kilometers of the reverse fault system. The Sawatch in this area rests on granitic rocks of Precambrian YX(?) age.

About 250 kg of U_3O_8 of an average grade of 0.22 percent were produced in the later 1950s and early 1960s from the Big Red No. 22 mine (Nelson-Moore and others, 1978). During quadrangle evaluation in 1978, a sample was taken in fault gouge at the Big Red No. 39 prospects that contained 0.064 percent U_3O_8 and about 10 percent iron. Autunite is the main uranium mineral at the occurrences and, in addition, torbernite and parsonite are possibly present at the Big Red No. 22 mine (Goodknight and Ludlam, 1981).

A marked difference exists in the thorium contents of the two Big Red occurrences. Almost no thorium occurs at the Big Red No. 22 mine, whereas, the thorium-to-uranium ratio at the Big Red No. 39 prospects is between 2 and 3. Olson and others (1977) note that the high thorium content at the Big Red No. 39 may be an indication of alkalic magmatism in the area during Cambrian time. Other evidence for alkalic magmatism is a very small thorium-rich carbonatite body near Quakey Mountain, about 10 km to the southwest (Goodknight and Ludlam, 1981).

Powderhorn District

Two uranium occurrences in the Powderhorn district are known in thorium-bearing veins that were emplaced in shear or breccia zones in Precambrian rocks. The veins are numerous and occur 2–20 km north and northwest of the alkalic complex at Iron Hill (carbonatite stock) of Early Cambrian age to which the veins are related; see Armbrustmacher (this guidebook) for a description of the Iron Hill complex. Both occurrences are in the southern part of the Gunnison gold belt which contains gold-bearing quartz veins and thorium-bearing jasperoid veins; see articles about sulfide mineralization in the gold belt by Drobeck and Sheridan and others (this guidebook). It is not known why only a few of the thorium veins are enriched in uranium.

About 2 km southwest of the old townsite of Spencer in the NW¼ sec. 8, T. 47 N., R. 2 W. (loc. 14), uranium occurs in a northeast-trending, iron-rich vein that cuts a Precambrian leucosyenite plug. This occurrence, found during quadrangle evaluation in 1978, contained 0.23 percent U_3O_8 and over 10 percent of both calcium and iron (mainly as specular hematite).

The uranium occurrence known as (being on) Mrs. Roberts deeded land is about 7 km north of Powderhorn in the N½ NE¼ sec. 15, T. 47 N., R. 2 W. (loc. 15). Uranium was discovered there in the mid-1950s in a northeast-trending vein along a shear zone in Precambrian Dubois Greenstone. Malan (1955) took vein samples that contained up to 0.28 percent U_3O_8 and up to 5.35 percent equivalent thorium.

Cochetopa District

Approximately 650,000 kg of U_3O_8 (Nelson-Moore and others, 1978) have been produced from the Cochetopa uranium district, centered about 20 km southeast of Gunnison. This production is only slightly higher than that of the Marshall Pass district (which will soon surpass the Cochetopa in total production).

The Cochetopa district is about 20 km long from north to south; along this axis is Cochetopa Canyon, which splits the district into east and west halves. The geology of many of the uranium deposits in the district is described by Malan and Ranspot (1959). Uranium was first discovered in the district in 1954 at the Los Ochos mine (loc. 19) along the major fault of the same name. Nearly all the uranium produced in the district has come from this mine and several others along the Los Ochos fault, which cuts mainly the Upper Jurassic Junction Creek Sandstone and Morrison Formation and rocks of Precambrian X age. Minor production of about 13 kg of U_3O_8 (Nelson-Moore and others, 1978) came from the La Rue claims (loc. 21) in the Dakota Sandstone along the major Cochetopa fault in the southern part of the district.

Uranium mineralization in the district is mainly along normal fault zones (as the Los Ochos and Cochetopa faults) of Laramide to mid-Tertiary age. The width and magnitude of mineralization is controlled generally by the degree of brecciation and fracturing imposed on the wall rocks by faulting. Hydrothermal alteration is well developed and epigenetic marcasite is common at the uranium occurrences. Sandstones along faults are silicified, limonite-stained, and bleached; and Precambrian rocks are kaolinized, chloritized, and sericitized. The district was covered in Oligocene time by ash flows from calderas to the south. Although many characteristics are present to support a hydrothermal origin for uranium in the district, an origin (or enrichment) of uranium in these structures by supergene processes from a source in the overlying volcanic rocks is also likely (Olson, 1976).

The Los Ochos and four other mines are in the N½ secs. 2–4, T. 47 N., R. 2 E. along about 4 km of the Los Ochos fault. Ore that was produced from these mines from 1955 until the mid-1960s contained an average of 0.14 percent U_3O_8; these mines (as is much of the district) are on Homestake Mining Company claims. Uranium has been produced mainly from fault breccia in the Junction Creek Sandstone and the Morrison Formation. Uranium minerals in the deposit are uraninite, autunite, uranophane, torbernite, johannite, uranopilite, and zippeite.

The other area of production in the district in the mid-1950s was at the La Rue claims (mine) in the SW¼ sec. 29, T. 47 N., R. 2 E., where the average ore grade was 0.20 percent U_3O_8. Uraniferous asphaltite, uranociricite, and brannerite occur in this deposit. Samples of the deposit taken during quadrangle evaluation contained up to 0.76 percent U_3O_8 and had very high concentrations of arsenic, molybdenum, tungsten, chromium, titanium, yttrium, and lanthanum (Goodknight and Ludlam, 1981).

The Surefire mining claims (loc. 16) at the northern edge of the district reportedly contained autunite-rich float (from the Morrison Formation?) that had 1.0–2.0 percent U_3O_8 (Nelson-Moore and others, 1978). Farther south on the Post claim group (loc. 17), uranium mineralization was found in 1978 during quadrangle evaluation in Junction Creek Sandstone that is silicified and heavily impregnated with limonite and hematite. A sample from this occurrence in the NE¼ NW¼ sec. 29, T. 48 N., R. 2 E. contained 0.021 percent U_3O_8 and high concentrations of arsenic and molybdenum.

The Do Dah (also known as Belle Lode) claim group (loc. 18) is just east of Cochetopa Canyon in the NW¼ sec. 33, T. 48 N., R. 2 E. Here, uranium occurs in gouge material along a fault trending north-northeast that cuts metasedimentary rocks of Precambrian X age; a sample of the gouge taken in 1979 during quadrangle evaluation contained 0.042 percent U_3O_8. Another uranium occurrence is about 2 km to the north along the same fault. Samples from both occurrences contain very large amounts of arsenic and copper. Homestake Mining Company has claims in this area and conducted drilling at the Do Dah occurrence in the late 1970s.

Uranium occurs in three areas on the Milbob claim group (loc.

20) in the southwest part of the district. Two occurrences in the NE¼ sec. 19, T. 47 N., R. 2 E. are along the same normal fault that trends east-northeast. The other occurrence is along a fault of similar trend in the SE¼ sec. 13, T. 47 N., R. 1 E. All the occurrences are in Junction Creek Sandstone faulted against Precambrian X quartz monzonite of Cochetopa Creek. Samples taken in 1978 and 1979 during quadrangle evaluation had up to 0.056 percent U_3O_8 in the sec. 19 occurrences and 0.035 percent U_3O_8 at the sec. 13 occurrence.

At the south end of the district, the Bet claim group (loc. 22) (also called the Elisha group or Mercury mine area) contains three uranium occurrences along several fault systems. The faults trend generally east and may be related to subsidence of the Cochetopa Creek caldera to the south. One occurrence is in silicified sandstone of the Morrison Formation along a fault zone in the NE¼sec. 29, T. 47 N., R. 2 E., just east of the old Mercury mine. A small body of rhyolite (Oligocene?) intruded along the fault in the area of the occurrence. A sample of the sandstone taken in 1979 during quadrangle evaluation had 0.63 percent U_3O_8 and visible uranophane and autunite; the sample also had high concentrations of arsenic, lanthanum, and molybdenum.

A uranium occurrence was found during quadrangle evaluation in brecciated Cochetopa Creek quartz monzonite along a fault about 500 m east of the Morrison occurrence. A sample from this occurrence had 0.012 percent U_3O_8 and contained high amounts of thorium, barium, chronium, lanthanum, and lead. The third occurrence is in Junction Creek Sandstone along a fault on the east side of Cochetopa Canyon in the NW¼ sec. 28, T. 47 N., R. 2 E. A sample from this occurrence taken during quadrangle evaluation had 0.097 percent U_3O_8 (mainly in uraninite and brannerite) and high amounts of molybdenum and lead.

Uranium occurs in two areas on the Lucky Friday (also known as Anna) claim group (loc. 23) in the southeast edge of the district, east of Razor Creek Dome. Both occurrences are in the NW¼ sec. 27, T. 47 N., R. 3 E., one east of West Gismo Creek in altered Cochetopa Creek quartz monzonite along a northeast-trending fault zone and the other in silicified Junction Creek Sandstone west of West Gismo Creek. Samples taken for quadrangle evaluation in 1979 contained 0.01 percent U_3O_8 (from the quartz monzonite) and 0.023 percent U_3O_8 (from the sandstone). The quartz monzonite had high amounts of thorium, barium, lanthanum, lead, yttrium, and zinc, and the sandstone was high in lanthanum, molybdenum, and lead.

Marshall Pass District

From 1956 until 1972, about 600,000 kg of U_3O_8 at an average grade of nearly 0.6 percent U_3O_8 was produced from four mining areas in the Marshall Pass uranium district. Nearly all the production from the district, located about 60 km east of Gunnison, has come from the Pitch mine (loc. 27) along the Chester fault zone. Other areas of minor production are the Little Indian No. 36 mine (loc. 26) at the north end of the Chester fault and the Marshall Pass No. 5 claim and Lookout claim group, both about 2 km east of the Chester fault (loc. 29) (see Nash, this guidebook).

The Marshall Pass district (contained within T. 48 N., R. 6 E.) is split roughly into east and west halves by the north-trending Chester fault. The fault is an upthrust that developed during the Laramide along part of the western side of the Sawatch Range. Metasedimentary and metavolcanic rocks and pegmatitic granite, all of Precambrian X age, are east of the fault and sedimentary rocks of Cambrian to Pennsylvanian age are in a synclinal remnant west of the fault. Because the fault dip steepens with depth, the Precambrian rocks of the upthrust block have been placed above and west of footwall Paleozoic rocks that have been deformed into an overturned syncline (Nash, 1979). Oligocene volcanic rocks (ash flow and waterlaid tuffs) cover the south end of the Chester fault and at one time probably covered all of the district (Olson, 1979).

The Pitch mine (earlier called the Erie No. 28 claim or Pinnacle mine) produced about 550,000 kg of U_3O_8, mainly from 1956 to 1962. Homestake Mining Company gained control of the Pitch mine in the early 1970s (and now has claims over most of the district) and began an intensive drilling program around the mine that has established a reserve of about 3.2 million kg of U_3O_8 at an average grade of 0.17 percent U_3O_8 (Ward, 1978). Since 1978, Homestake has been developing an open-pit mine (on their recently-patented mining claims) along the Chester fault on and around the site of the old Pitch mine. This development, called the Pitch Project, also includes the construction of a mill south of the mine; ore production will eventually be 550 metric tons per day. The new open-pit mine is in the area where secs. 15, 16, 21, and 22 meet.

Uranium occurs at the Pitch mainly in brecciated Leadville Dolomite of Mississippian age in the footwall of the Chester fault zone. The dominant role of the Leadville Dolomite in hosting uranium at the Pitch mine is discussed by Nash (1979, and this guidebook). Other rocks hosting uranium along the fault are sandstone, siltstone, and carbonaceous shale of the Pennsylvanian Belden Formation (Pitch mine), the Ordovician Harding Sandstone (Little Indian No. 36 mine), and Precambrian rocks (both mines). Uranium minerals identified from the Pitch are uraninite, meta-torbernite, coffinite, and sabugalite (Ward, 1978). Epigenetic pyrite and marcasite are present in the deposit as are enriched amounts of lead and molybdenum. Hydrothermal alteration patterns are poorly developed along the Chester fault; only minor silicification and hematization are present. Nash (1979, 1980) and Olson (1979) conclude that the Oligocene volcanic rocks that once covered the Chester fault were viable sources of uranium which migrated down into the broad zone of structural permeability created by the upthrust and formed epigenetic uranium deposits.

The first uranium discovered in the district was in 1955 at the Little Indian No. 36 mine in the SE¼ sec. 9. Here, the brittle sedimentary unit present adjacent to the Chester fault is the steeply-dipping Harding Sandstone (in most places a quartzite) from which about 31,000 kg of U_3O_8 at an average grade of 0.44 percent U_3O_8 were produced during the late 1950s (Nelson-Moore and others, 1978). Uranium minerals present in this deposit are uranophane, uraninite, autunite, gummite, and boltwoodite.

The Chester Fault is exposed on the north side of Marshall Creek in the SW¼ sec. 27 (loc. 28), about 3 km south of the Pitch mine. Here, uranium occurs in pegmatitic granite on the west side of the fault. A sample taken during quadrangle evaluation contained 0.013 percent U_3O_8 and the minerals euxenite and ilmenorutile were identified (Goodknight and Ludlam, 1981). These radioactive minerals are normally associated with rare-earth pegmatites, indicating that uranium at this locality may not be related to the Chester fault.

In the Harry Creek area, about 2 km east of the Chester fault, are the small mines and numerous prospects on the Marshall Pass No. 5 claim (NE¼ sec. 22) and the Lookout claim group (NE¼ sec. 27 and SE¼ sec. 22). About 170 kg of U_3O_8 at an average grade of 1.06 percent U_3O_8 were produced in 1956 from the Marshall Pass No. 5 claim (Nelson-Moore and others, 1978). This high-grade uranium was mined from colluvium overlying quartz monzonite of Precambrian X age and the main ore mineral was uraninite. A sample of fractured quartz monzonite taken on the claim during quadrangle evaluation was enriched in copper, lead, and zinc and contained kasolite (lead uranyl silicate), and radioactive barite.

Production from all the Lookout claims (mainly in the late 1950s) was about 6300 kg U_3O_8 at an average grade of just over 1.0 percent U_3O_8 (Nelson-Moore and others, 1978). Most of this production was from the Lookout No. 22 claim (mine) where very high grade material was initially recovered from colluvium and veins were mined later. Samples of fractured granite gneiss and pegmatitic granite of Precambrian X age taken during quadrangle evaluation had up to 2.9 percent U_3O_8. These samples contained meta-autunite and kasolite (as fracture filling and surface coating), as well as enriched amounts of lead, zinc, arsenic, niobium, tungsten, yttrium, and zirconium. Uranium minerals identified by Gross (1965) from the Lookout No. 22 were uraninite, shoepite, epiianthinite, becquerelite, soddyite, boltwoodite, zeunerite, meta-zeunerite, and hydrated autunite. The fractures and minor faults that host uranium minerals at the Lookout claims (and the Marshall Pass No. 5 claim) may represent normal faults produced during arching of the upthrust block of the Chester fault (Nash, 1980); uranium could then have been introduced to these structures by supergene processes from overlying volcanic rocks.

The Hidden Reserve claim group was located in 1955 on a hilltop east of Harry Creek in the SW¼ sec. 23 (loc. 30). Thorium and uranium occur on the claims in biotite-rich pegmatites that contain rare-earth minerals. Samples taken during quadrangle evaluation from radioactive pegmatites on the claims contain yttrocolumbite and high amounts of lanthanum, lead, yttrium, zirconium, and niobium; these samples also contained up to 0.09 percent U_3O_8 and 0.17 percent equivalent thorium (Goodknight and Ludlam, 1981). These uranium occurrences are clearly pegmatite-related and probably not related to the Chester fault system.

Uranium occurs in the western part of the Marshall Pass district (in the Indian Creek area) in the upper Harding Sandstone of Middle Ordovician age. Ranspot and Spengler (1957) and Malan (1959) describe the uranium mineralization found in the Harding (and elsewhere in the district) during early development of the district. The Harding is part of a remnant of Paleozoic sedimentary rocks that has been preserved in a syncline west of the Chester fault. A "trashy," oxidized carbonaceous facies (probably deposited in a lagoon behind an offshore bar) about 1.5 m thick in the upper third of the Harding hosts uranium enrichment in this district and in several other areas to the east and southeast of Gunnison country. The carbonaceous facies contains abundant asphaltic pellets and phosphatic fossil fragments; and the uranium minerals uranophane and autunite (or meta-autunite) occur within or along the edges of the fragments. The widespread uranium enrichment in the carbonaceous facies of the Harding averages probably about 0.01 percent U_3O_8.

About 100 holes were drilled in the mid-1950s on the Apache No. 4 claim (loc. 25) in the S½ sec. 19; this claim was part of the Big Indian claim group. The holes encountered a 1.5 m-thick zone in the Harding containing 0.03 to 0.04 percent U_3O_8. A sample taken during quadrangle evaluation from an outcrop of the carbonaceous facies near the claim contained 0.10 percent U_3O_8. Drilling in 1955 on the Little Indian No. 6 claim (loc. 26) in the SE¼ SW¼ sec. 17 reportedly encountered 0.10 percent U_3O_8 (Ranspot and Spengler, 1957).

POSSIBILITIES FOR ADDITIONAL DISCOVERIES

The greatest potential for additional uranium discoveries is in the eastern part of the Gunnison country. Additional deposits, similar to that at the Pitch mine, are likely to exist in brittle, extensively fractured Paleozoic sedimentary rocks in the footwall of Laramide upthrust faults along the west side of the Sawatch Range. The most favorable areas are where these faults are or were once overlain by mid- to late-Tertiary volcanic rocks which were a major source of uranium. These and other types of faults may also be favorable if they are near plutons that are sources of uranium such as the uranium-enriched Oligocene Mount Princeton batholith and certain other plutons as old as Precambrian X age. The highest favorability must be assigned to those faults that cut both Precambrian rocks and Paleozoic sedimentary rocks; however, faults that cut solely Precambrian rocks may also host uranium deposits if these rocks are brittle. Some areas of faulting within the eastern part of Gunnison country that have some of the favorable characteristics mentioned above are: the Star Basin area near Italian Mountain (Castle Creek fault zone), North Star (Granite) fault, faults in the Texas Creek area, faults in the Cross Mountain to Broncho Mountain area, faults in the area from Canyon Creek to Pitkin, Crookton fault, and faults in the Whitepine area.

Information that could greatly enhance the possibility of new uranium discoveries in the eastern part of Gunnison country are the two detailed surveys done in addition to the Montrose quadrangle evaluation report (Goodknight and Ludlam, 1981). A detailed uranium hydrogeochemical and stream sediment reconnaissance (HSSR) (Maassen, 1981) was done for the Sawatch Range portion of the Montrose quadrangle, which includes most of the eastern Gunnison country. A detailed aerial gamma ray and magnetic survey was done for three areas within eastern Gunnison country; these were three of five areas chosen for surveys in the Montrose quadrangle (GeoMetrics, Inc., 1980). Two of the areas that have detailed aerial surveys also have detailed HSSR data.

REFERENCES

Cunningham, C. G., Jr., 1973, Multiple intrusion and venting of the Italian Mountain intrusive complex, Gunnison County, Colorado (Ph.D. dissertation): Palo Alto, California, Stanford University, 168 p.

Dings, M. G. and Robinson, C. S., 1957, Geology and ore deposits of the Garfield quadrangle, Colorado: U.S. Geological Survey Professional Paper 289, 110 p.

Gallagher, G. L., Edmond, C. L., and D'Andrea, R. F., Jr., 1977, Preliminary evaluation of the uranium favorability in the area northeast of Gunnison, Colorado: U.S. Energy Research and Development Administration, GJBX-61(77), Open-File Report, 26 p.

GeoMetrics, Inc., 1980, Aerial gamma ray and magnetic survey, Montrose detail projects, Colorado: U.S. Department of Energy GJBX-212(80), Open-File Report, 6 volumes, 1031 p.

Goodknight, C. S. and Ludlam, J. R., 1981, Uranium resource evaluation of the Montrose (1°x2°) Quadrangle, central Colorado: U.S. Department of Energy, GJQ-010, Open-File Report, in press.

Gross, E. B., 1965, A unique occurrence of uranium minerals, Marshall Pass, Saguache County, Colorado: American Mineralogist, v. 50, p. 909–923.

Maassen, L. W., 1981, Detailed uranium hydrogeochemical and stream sediment reconnaissance data release for the eastern portion of the Montrose NTMS Quadrangle, Colorado, including concentrations of forty-five additional elements: U.S. Department of Energy, Open-File Report, in press.

Malan, R. C., 1955, Mrs. Roberts Deeded Land: U.S. Atomic Energy Commission Preliminary Reconnaissance Report DEB-P-3-1752-1901, Open-File Report, 1 p.

———, 1959, Geology and uranium deposits of the Marshall Pass district, Gunnison, Saguache, and Chaffee Counties, Colorado: U.S. Atomic Energy Commission, TM-217, Open-File Report, 13 p.

Malan, R. C. and Ranspot, H. W., 1959, Geology of the uranium deposits in the Cochetopa mining district, Saguache and Gunnison Counties, Colorado: Economic Geology, v. 54, p. 1–19.

Nash, J. T., 1979, Geology, petrology, and chemistry of the Leadville Dolomite: Host for uranium at the Pitch Mine: U.S. Geological Survey Open-File Report 79-1566, 51 p.

———, 1980, Supergene uranium deposits in brecciated zones of Laramide upthrusts—concepts and applications: U.S. Geological Survey Open-File Report 80-385, 36 p.

Nelson-Moore, J. L., Collins, D. B. and Hornbaker, A. L., 1978, Radioactive mineral occurrences of Colorado and bibliography: Colorado Geological Survey Bulletin 40, 1061 p.

Olson, J. C., 1976, Uranium deposits in the Cochetopa district, Colorado, in relation to the Oligocene erosion surface: U.S. Geological Survey Open-File Report 76-222, 13 p.

———, 1979, Preliminary geologic map and structural maps and sections of the Marshall Pass mining district, Saguache, Gunnison, and Chaffee Counties, Colorado: U.S. Geological Survey Open-File Report 79-1473.

Olson, J. C., Marvin, R. F., Parker, R. L., and Mehnert, H. H., 1977, Age and tectonic setting of lower Paleozoic alkalic and mafic rocks, carbonatites, and thorium veins in south-central Colorado: Journal of Research, U.S. Geological Survey, v. 5, p. 673–687.

Ranspot, H. W. and Spengler, R. G., 1957, Uranium deposits of the Marshall Pass area, Gunnison and Saguache Counties, Colorado: U.S. Atomic Energy Commission DAO-3-TM-42, Open-File Report, 29 p.

Staatz, M. H. and Trites, A. F., 1955, Geology of the Quartz Creek pegmatite district, Gunnison County, Colorado: U.S. Geological Survey Professional Paper 265, 111 p.

Ward, J. M., 1978, History and geology of Homestake's Pitch Project, Saguache County, Colorado (abs.): American Institute of Mining, Metallurgical, and Petroleum Engineers, Program 107th Annual Meeting, p. 44.

GEOLOGY OF DOLOMITE-HOSTED URANIUM DEPOSITS AT THE PITCH MINE, SAGUACHE COUNTY, COLORADO

J. THOMAS NASH
U.S. Geological Survey
Denver, Colorado 80225

SUMMARY

Newly documented uranium ore in the Pitch mine occurs chiefly in brecciated Mississippian Leadville Dolomite along the Chester upthrust zone, and to a lesser extent in sandstone, siltstone, and carbonaceous shale of the Pennsylvanian Belden Formation and in Precambrian granitic rocks and schist. Uranium-mineralized zones are generally thicker, more consistent, and of higher grade in dolomite than in other hosts, and roughly 50 percent of the new reserves are in dolomite. Strong physical control by dolomite is evident, as this is the only rock type that is pervasively brecciated within the fault slices that make up the footwall of the reverse-fault zone. Other rocks tended to either remain unbroken or undergo ductile deformation. Chemical controls on uranium deposition are subtle and appear chiefly to involve coprecipitation of FeS_2 as pyrite and marcasite, suggesting that sulfide ion may be the reductant.

Leadville Dolomite in the area is about 130 m thick and is predominantly nonfossiliferous dolomicrite. In the Pitch mine, Leadville Dolomite is bound by faults and maximum known thickness is about 17 m. Mud texture, paucity of fossils and other allochems, thin laminations, and probable algal mat structures suggest sedimentation in a tidal-flat (possibly supratidal) environment. Preservation of mud texture and lack of replacement features indicate that dolomitization was an early, prelithification process, as in modern tidal flats, and produced a chemically and texturally uniform rock over tens of meters vertically with relatively few limestone beds surviving. Carbonate rocks of the Belden Formation, in contrast to those of the Leadville, contain calcite in great excess of dolomite, more than 5 percent silt-size quartz and clay, and abundant fossils and oolites. Belden limestones (sandy micrite and sandy wackestone) probably were deposited in an intertidal or subtidal environment. Not much uranium ore occurs in these rocks. Chemical aspects, such as the iron, sulfur, and organic carbon contents, are similar to those of Leadville dolomites, and hence seem favorable, but limestones in the Belden generally are only mildly fractured.

The content of most minor elements in ore-bearing dolomites is normal for rocks of this composition, but iron, sulfur, molybdenum, and lead are enriched in ore. One surface expression of ore in dolomite is ocher, leached, porous gossan that is characterized by residual silica and limonite and by high radioactivity but low uranium content.

INTRODUCTION

An important recent economic development on the Western Slope was the reopening of the Pitch mine as an open-pit uranium mine in 1979. The Pitch mine is in the Sawatch Range in Saguache County, Colorado, about 60 km east of Gunnison (fig. 1). The Pitch deposit (formerly known as the Pinnacle) and several other uranium prospects were located in 1955. Mining began in 1959 with the opening of two underground adits, and ceased in 1962 when the contract with U.S. Atomic Energy Commission expired. About 100,000 tons of ore averaging 0.50 percent U_3O_8 (1,000,000 lbs or 454,000 kg U_3O_8) was mined, and another 100,000 lbs (45,400 kg) U_3O_8 was recovered by solution mining (Ward, 1978). In 1972, Homestake Mining Company acquired the property and began to reevaluate the mine area for additional reserves amenable to open-pit mining, because the previous history had demonstrated that fault offsets of ore and unstable wallrocks made underground mining costly.

In the period 1972 to 1977, Homestake Mining Company documented a reserve minable by open-pit methods of 2.1 million tons of ore at an average grade of 0.17 percent U_3O_8 (7,140,000 lbs or 3,245,000 kg U_3O_8) (Ward, 1978). Rather than seek high-grade "vein-type" ore, Homestake explored for more dispersed ore. Success came in 1973 when the company recognized a "new" type of ore in brecciated dolomite of the Mississippian Leadville Dolomite. The dolomite was found to be complexly faulted between slices of sandstone, siltstone, and shale of the Pennsylvanian Belden Formation. Much of the ore mined in 1959–61 also was probably in Leadville Dolomite, but was not recognized as such (J. M. Ward, Homestake Mining Co., oral communication, 1979). Homestake is mining the deposit at a rate of about 600 tons per day from an open pit that ultimately will be about 1,500 m long and have an average depth of 120 m.

GEOLOGIC SETTING

Rocks ranging in age from Precambrian to Oligocene(?) are known in the Pitch mine area (Table 1). Precambrian rocks are chiefly pegmatitic granite, hornblende-biotite schist, hornblende gneiss, and pegmatite. A hematitic regolith was developed on the Precambrian rocks prior to the Cambrian. Above the Precambrian was deposited about 600 m of Paleozoic rocks. The lower half is

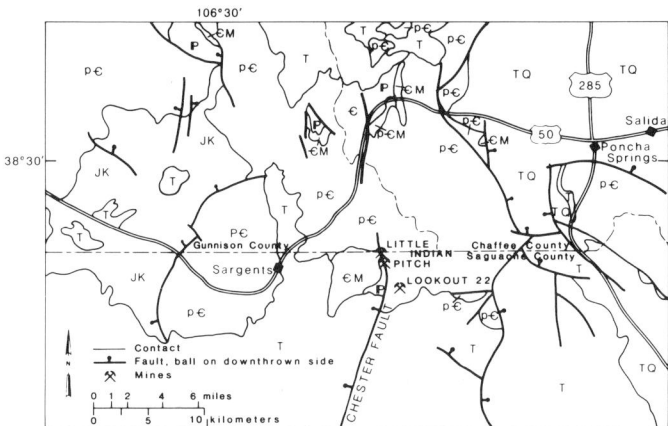

Figure 1. Generalized geologic map and location of Pitch Mine, Colorado (after Tweto and others, 1976). Note that more detailed mapping (Olson, 1979) does not show the Chester fault cutting Tertiary volcanics. Abbreviations: TQ, Tertiary and Quaternary sediments, mainly post-volcanic; T, Tertiary intrusive and volcanic rocks; JK, Jurassic–Cretaceous rocks; ₽, Pennsylvanian sedimentary rocks; ∈M, Cambrian to Mississippian sedimentary rocks; p∈, Precambrian rocks.

Table 1. Simplified stratigraphic column in the Pitch Mine area (Modified from Olson, 1979)

Oligocene(?) QUARTZ-LATITE FLOWS: light-colored felsic flows, 0–20 m thick
—unconformity—
Pennsylvanian BELDEN FORMATION: contains three units: upper green and brown sandstone and gray shale (200 m or more thick); middle blue-gray limestone with red shale and fine sandstone (30–60 m thick); and lower white sandstone and black shale (40–90 m thick)
—unconformity—
Mississippian LEADVILLE DOLOMITE: dark blue-gray to brownish-gray dolomite and minor limestone; contains calcite and chalcedony veinlets and local black chert zones; about 130 m thick
Devonian DYER DOLOMITE: tan to light-gray dolomite; about 50 m thick
Devonian PARTING QUARTZITE: varicolored shale and quartzite; about 5 m thick
—unconformity—
Ordovician FREMONT DOLOMITE: blue-gray limestone and dolomite; about 55 m thick
Ordovician HARDING QUARTZITE: white quartzite, commonly with limonitic stain, and some black shale; about 10 m thick
—unconformity—
Ordovician MANITOU DOLOMITE: light-pinkish-gray dolomite, 75–90 m thick
Cambrian SAWATCH QUARTZITE: vitreous quartzite less than 1 m thick
—unconformity—
Precambrian granitic and metamorphic rocks

predominantly dolomite, but it contains three units of quartzite that are useful stratigraphic markers between the similar-appearing dolomites. The Mississippian Leadville Dolomite is the darkest dolomite in the area, and generally is massive with faint laminations. The top of the Leadville Dolomite is locally limonitic, the result of a karst that was developed prior to deposition of the Pennsylvanian Belden Formation. The Belden Formation comprises diverse rock types, including coarse kaolinitic sandstone; green, clay-rich, fine sandstone; black and red shale; and gray and black limestone and minor dolomite. Abrupt facies changes are common over lateral distances of 300 m. A few erosional remnants of Oligocene(?) quartz latite flows are preserved topographically above and a kilometer north of the Pitch mine. About 6 km south of the mine, more than 300 m of Tertiary andesitic volcanics of the San Juan volcanic field cover Paleozoic rocks.

The major structural feature in the mine area is the Chester fault zone, which dips east at about 70°, strikes nearly due north, and places Precambrian rocks above and west of Paleozoic rocks (figs. 2 and 3). Net reverse movement along numerous faults is more than 600 m. The fault zone is about 100 m wide in the mine area (fig. 2). Paleozoic rocks immediately west of the Chester fault are folded into a south-plunging syncline whose east limb is probably overturned under the fault zone (fig. 3). Farther west, the Paleozoic rocks have a low dip and are gently warped in broad folds. East-trending faults cut the Chester fault zone and form rotated blocks. The faulting in the Chester fault zone is of Laramide age; Cretaceous rocks about 20 km to the west are displaced by similar reverse faults, and Oligocene(?) volcanic rocks show small displacement, probably from reactivation along the Chester fault. Younger north-trending faults displace volcanic rocks southeast of the mine (Olson, 1979).

URANIUM DEPOSITS

Uranium anomalies, occurrences, and deposits are known in five geologic settings in the Marshall Pass district. The following are arranged by decreasing age of host, but the ages of mineralization are not known.

(1) Precambrian biotite schist—several vein-type prospects and small mines occur in the Harry Creek area (Lookout 22, Marshall Pass No. 5 prospects) about 2 km east of the Pitch mine. Mineralization is probably pitchblende and some hexavalent uranium minerals. Near these vein-like deposits are high-grade concentrations of uranium in alluvium (type 5 below). The deposits are probably related, and the high concentrations mined probably reflect supergene processes (Malan, 1959; Gross, 1965).

(2) Precambrian pegmatite—shears in pegmatite in the Pitch mine area contain pitchblende, including the discovery outcrop for the Pitch mine (Ward, 1978).

(3) Ordovician Harding Quartzite—uranophane and other U^{+6} minerals fill fractures in the quartzite and generally are accompanied by limonite (Malan, 1959). A bed containing carbonaceous trash, organic pellets, and fish scales near the top of the Harding is radioactive. This bed guided prospectors to the Little Indian 36 deposit, where the Harding is fractured in the Chester fault zone 2 km north of the Pitch mine. Production from the Little Indian 36 mine from 1957 to 1959 was about 6,800 tons ore averaging of 0.48 percent U_3O_8 (65,000 lbs or 29,500 kg U_3O_8) (Ward, 1978).

(4) Mississippian Leadville Dolomite and Pennsylvanian Belden Formation—at the Pitch mine, oxidized and reduced uranium minerals occur in dark-gray dolomite, sandstone, black shale, and coaly shale. Oxidation occurs to depths of about 100 m. In oxidized zones, disequilibrium is great and radioactivity is much in excess of uranium content. Pyrite occurs in most unoxidized rocks, but many pyritic rocks have very low uranium content. Fractures, shears, and breccia zones carry the uranium ores. Past production from the Pitch (Pinnacle) mine was about 1,100,000 lbs (500,000 kg) U_3O_8 (Ward, 1978).

Carbonaceous shales of the Belden are radioactive in many places, as at the mouth of Indian Creek, 6 km southwest of the Pitch mine.

(5) Eocene(?) carbonaceous regolith—several unusual small but high-grade concentrations of uranium have been mined from "alluvium" (Gross, 1965) and carbonaceous regolith developed in Precambrian gneiss and schist and in places overlain by Tertiary volcanic flows (Malan, 1959). Mined localities were at the Lookout No. 22 claim, previously mentioned, and the Bonita claims east of the Continental Divide (about 11 km east of the Pitch mine). Pitchblende and a number of U^{+6} minerals have been identified from these deposits (Malan, 1959; Gross, 1965). Most of the several hundred tons of high-grade ore (about 3,900 lbs or 1,800 kg U_3O_8) produced from these deposits was from the pockets in alluvium, and a lesser amount from vein-like deposits within Precambrian host rocks (type 1, above) (Malan, 1959; Ward, 1978).

The ages and genetic relations of these various types of uranium

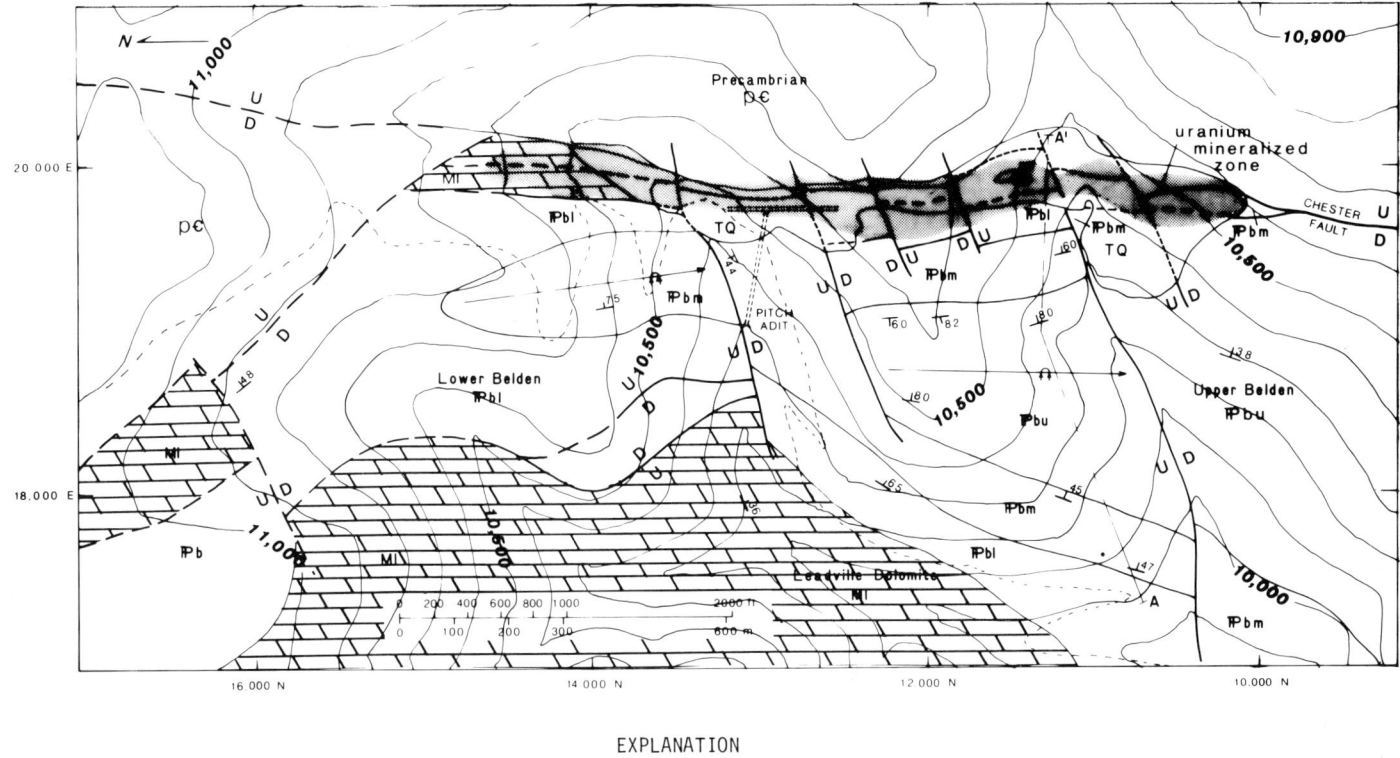

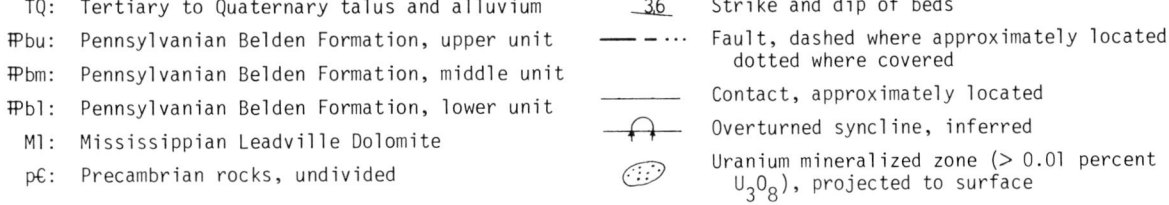

Figure 2. Geologic map of the Pitch Mine area. Cross section A-A' is shown on Figure 3. Geology in places adapted from mapping by Olson (1979) and J. M. Ward, Homestake Mining Co. (unpub. data, 1972–1977). Base generalized from 1:2,400 map of Homestake Mining Co. Grid is mine coordinate system used by Homestake Mining Co.

deposits are unresolved problems. Most observers suspect that the deposits share some fundamental geologic features, such as a common source.

PETROLOGY OF CARBONATE HOST ROCKS

Approximately 350 m of carbonate rocks in five formations occur in the mine area. Many of the carbonate rocks are lithologically similar to each other, especially the pinkish-tan-weathering dolomites of the Manitou, Fremont, and Dyer Dolomites. Dolomites and limestones of the Belden and Leadville Formations generally are darker than the underlying carbonates.

Dolomite is the predominant rock of the Leadville in the mine area, although limestone occurs in a few places. Typical dolomites are medium gray to black, often with brownish or reddish-brown tones, and tend to be a bit lighter and bluish on weathered surfaces. Bedding ranges from medium to massive, commonly with faint laminations (mm scale). Carbonaceous shale and sand layers are rare and are thin where present. Most Leadville dolomites are fetid when broken.

Brecciation of several types is common in the Leadville Dolomite. In a few places, the brecciation is associated with curved surfaces and bounded by undeformed beds, suggesting intraformational slumping. Some breccia at the top of the Leadville contains iron oxides and seems to reflect karst development. A large area of breccia 2 km south of the Pitch mine contains angular and subangular fragments but little sparry carbonate cement. This breccia, which probably formed in pre-Belden time, contains small amounts of iron oxides and does not seem to be related to karst.

Leadville Dolomite in the Chester fault zone at the mine is interpreted to be bound by faults (fig. 2). In some localities, the dolomite lies on a hematitic regolith of Precambrian rocks, which suggests a possible depositional contact, but other relations suggest that these are fault contacts. Maximum thickness of Leadville Dolomite in the mine is about 17 m, only a small fraction of the total Leadville section known in the area (about 130 m). It has not been possible to establish the stratigraphic position of the Leadville in the mine because it is highly deformed, and the outlying Leadville displays no obvious internal units useful for correlation.

Chert is common in the Leadville as veinlets, stringers, and concretionary nodules. The chert is generally black. In some well-exposed localities bed-like chert is faulted and cut by a breccia of recrystallized dolomite. Much of the chert is probably early diagenetic (Banks, 1970) although the occurrence of several cherty or "jasper" zones that crop out over an area of more than a thousand square meters adjacent to (under) the Chester fault zone suggests that some chert may be structurally controlled and of Tertiary age.

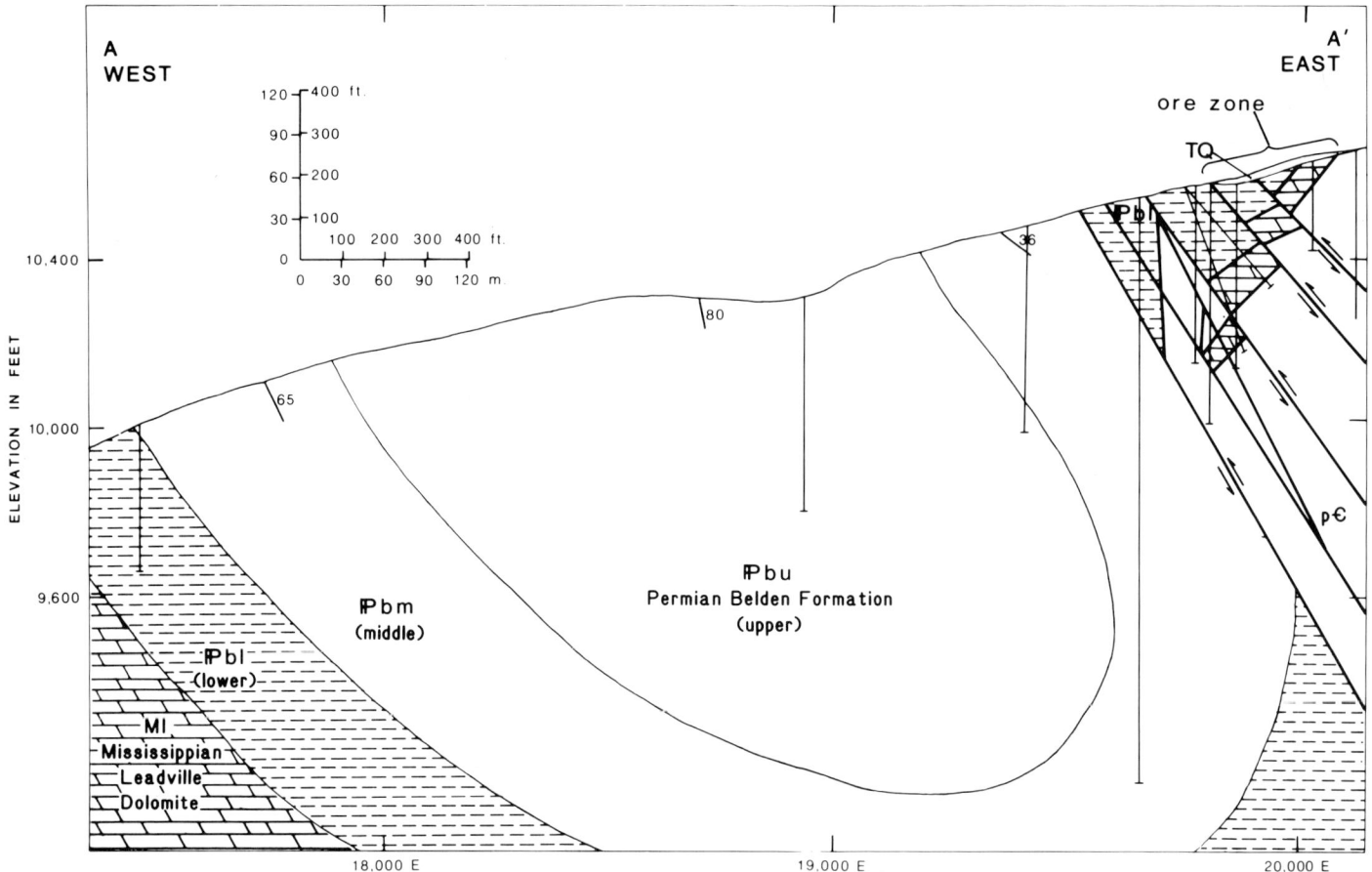

Figure 3. Schematic cross section A-A' of the Pitch Mine area. Line of section is shown on the geologic map (fig. 2). Structure in the Chester fault zone is known from drilling to be much more complex than shown. The overturned synclinal structure is inferred from sparse surface outcrops showing bedding attitudes. Symbols are same as on Figure 2.

Carbonate rocks in the Belden Formation generally are limestone, with rare dolomite, and have thick to massive bedding. Color is light gray or bluish gray in outcrop, and medium gray to black or brownish black on fresh surfaces or core. Terrigenous material is generally abundant in Belden carbonates; black or red shale laminae or enclosing beds are much more common than in the Leadville. White or pink calcite veinlets are common in the Belden carbonates, but chert and intraformational breccia have not been observed.

Petrographic studies (Nash, 1979) show that the Leadville Dolomite consistently contains more than 95 percent dolomite and rarely contains more than traces of terrigenous quartz and clay. However, chemical analyses and normative mineral calculations indicate more quartz and clay than are visible in thin sections. Pyrite is, or was, present in essentially all dolomites in amounts ranging from about 0.2 to 16 percent. Twenty percent of the dolomites display faint lamination, 7 percent contain intraclasts, 8 percent contain burrows or evidence of bioturbation, 3 percent contain sparse fossils (a few brachiopods), and 2 percent contain pellets. Sand grains are generally round and are probably windblown. Possible mudcracks are present in 5 percent of the dolomites, and possible "birdseye" textures (openings filled by sparry carbonate) are present in 3 percent. No gypsum, anhydrite, or halite were observed in thin sections or X-ray diffraction patterns, nor were any casts or pseudomorphs after these evaporite minerals detected.

Based on composition and texture, all the Leadville dolomites are classified as dolomicrites (Folk, 1959, 1962) or dolomite mudstone (Dunham, 1962). The dolomites formed from dolomite mud or dolomitized lime mud. The general absence of terrigenous grains or carbonate clasts testifies to a probable lack of strong currents or wave action, meaning that the environments were probably protected from the source by a barrier or by distance.

Samples from the Leadville collected about 1 km west of the mine are notably different from the typical carbonates described above. These samples show good bedding and crossbedding, are composed entirely of calcite, and contain 30 to 40 percent fossils (ostracods, gastropods, foraminifera, and brachiopods) and oolites supported in very fine calcite mud. They are classified as fossiliferous biomicrite (Folk, 1962) or packstone (Dunham, 1962). The locality 1 km west of the mine appears to be in the middle to upper part of the Leadville.

Carbonate rocks in the Belden Formation are compositionally and texturally more diverse than in the Leadville. In the Belden a continuum exists between essentially pure carbonate rocks and terrigenous rocks. Here we will consider only those samples containing more than 50 percent carbonate minerals. Of the 29 samples that meet this criterion, 60 percent contain 10 to 50 percent quartz sand and silt grains, 28 percent are fossiliferous, 18 percent are bioturbated, and 12 percent contain intraclasts. Most of the Belden carbonates contain calcite and little or no dolomite; 15 percent had dolomite in excess of calcite. Based on these compositional and textural data, most Belden carbonates are classified as sandy micrite (Folk, 1962) or sandy wackestone (Dunham, 1962). In a few samples, sparry calcite cements clasts; these rocks contained little mud and are classified as grainstone (Dunham, 1962).

Chert nodules and stringers in the Leadville are replacements of carbonate rock and are very finely crystalline chalcedonic quartz. Grain size typically is less than 15 microns. Specks of iron oxides and carbonaceous matter occur between chalcedony crystallites. Irregular veinlets or swaths of more coarsely crystalline quartz (50 microns to 1 mm size) cut or grade from the aphanitic chert. Textures of chalcedony and quartz in the broad, silicified "jasper" zones are similar to that in chert nodules.

The most important host for ore in the Pitch deposit is dark-gray dolomite of the Leadville. In the ore zone, this dolomite has a consistent composition. Calcite is a minor constituent, except in some near-surface-oxidized ocher dolomites that underwent some de-dolomitization. Silica content is the major variable and is chiefly chert, which probably is older than the ore. Fragments of chert are seen in breccia; hence that chert is pre-fault.

Carbonate breccias are extensive in the Chester fault crush zone. It is common to observe in drill core 5 to 10 m of uniformly and thoroughly brecciated dolomite. Such zones typically contain uniform and high ore grades, indicating that dark dolomite breccia is a favorable host, presumably for both physical and chemical reasons. The breccias generally are not well cemented, and fragments and matrix are not notably recrystallized. Extensive cementation of breccia by silica or sparry carbonate has not been recognized. Many breccias are a mixture of lithologies that must have originated in different formations. The mixing of breccia fragments is consistent with the extremely complex interfaulting of slivers of Precambrian, Leadville, and Belden rocks.

Dolomite in the ore zone, and in breccias along the Chester fault zone, shows remarkably little recrystallization. Many are essentially unrecrystallized (grain size less than 4 microns), and dolomite matrix between the breccia fragments typically is very finely crystalline (less than 16 microns). Crustified overgrowths have not been observed, even in fault breccia. Recrystallization of these carbonate rocks seems to be normal coalescive neomorphism, typical of diagenesis (Folk, 1965). Hence, most recrystallization probably occurred in the Paleozoic, long before the area was deformed and probably long before uranium was emplaced.

Pyrite occurs in all Paleozoic rocks in the ore zone. It is most conspicuous as coarse crystals in white Belden sandstones, but pyrite is also present as small crystals in siltstone, carbonaceous shale, and coal, and in dolomite and limestone of the Belden and Leadville. Pyrite in carbonate rocks occurs in three habits: (1) along silty bedding planes; (2) dispersed as tiny crystals, generally less than 50 microns in size, throughout the rock; and (3) along fractures and in breccia matrix. Fine dispersed pyrite probably accounts for as much as about 0.5 weight percent sulfur found in chemical analyses (Nash, 1979).

The distribution of uranium minerals in carbonate rocks is complex. Veinlets of pitchblende and coffinite a few millimeters wide are rarely seen. Much of the uranium is not in recognizable minerals in drill core or under the microscope in incident light. Many core samples containing 2 to 5 weight percent U_3O_8 have no visible uranium minerals. Most of the uranium is carried in the matrix of breccia and along numerous tiny cracks as very fine grained films of pitchblende or coffinite. Pyrite and marcasite generally are in the same openings.

Carbonate rocks in the Chester fault zone are oxidized to depths of more than 100 m along faults and can be pervasively oxidized in the upper 60 m of some breccia zones. In the most severe instances, near-surface carbonate rocks are oxidized and leached to a porous, friable, ocher rock composed of quartz and iron oxides with only traces of calcite. More common is an intermediate product—ocher dolomite that may have some voids and that has more quartz and calcite than normal. Under the microscope, the ocher dolomites seem to be only slightly modified, with the exception that original disseminated pyrite is oxidized to iron oxides and cracks are covered with a thin film of iron oxide. Hence, there seem to be two end-member situations: (1) dolomite that has been thoroughly leached and oxidized to form gossan, and (2) barely altered dolomite in which the only major change is oxidation of pyrite and transport of some iron to produce a strong color effect. Ocher dolomite of both types generally contains about 50 to 200 ppm uranium, but probably contained much more prior to oxidation. Most of this oxidation and uranium leaching must be relatively recent, because the oxidized rocks are badly out of radioactive equilibrium. Some reduced zones contain uranium in excess of daughter products, suggesting redeposition of recently leached uranium. Presumably the cause of the leaching is sulfuric acid generated by oxidizing pyrite. Radium is precipitated by sulfate, a factor contributing to the disequilibrium problem (Phair and Levine, 1954).

GEOCHEMISTRY OF CARBONATE ROCKS

Chemical analyses of 99 samples of carbonate rocks are reported by Nash (1979) and summarized in Table 2. Some general comments can be made.

Aluminum

Mean aluminum content of Leadville and Belden carbonates is 1.79 and 2.17 percent Al_2O_3, respectively, which is equivalent to 4.4 and 5 percent normative clay (Table 2). The clay in the Leadville samples generally is not evident in thin sections, possibly because of the contrasting optics of dolomite and very fine clay. The aluminum content of these carbonates is much higher than reported by Weber (1964) for primary dolomites or by Till (1970) for lagoonal carbonate sediment. However, the amount of normative clay, calculated from aluminum, is less than Roehl (1967) reported for supratidal dolomite. Till (1970) demonstrated that aluminum content correlates strongly with carbonate mud content in Holocene sediments and suggested that an environmental factor, probably quietness of water, controls the concentration of clay minerals and carbonate mud.

Iron

Total iron content of the Leadville Dolomite (2.84 percent Fe_2O_3; 1.99 percent Fe) appears to be abnormally high, approximately seven times the 0.40 percent Fe_2O_3 reported by Weber (1964). Belden carbonates contain about four times the amount of iron that Weber reports. Statistical tests on ore zone samples indicate that iron and normative FeS_2 correlate strongly with uranium, confirming the mineralogical associations seen under the microscope. Iron appears to be a key chemical component, but its behavior in sedimentation and diagenesis can not be specified well.

Organic carbon

Organic carbon content of Leadville Dolomite (mean 0.24 percent) is not as high as anticipated for these dark-gray rocks. This value matches the average reported by Gehman (1962) for his survey of carbonate rocks. Apparently the Leadville and Belden carbonates do not contain abnormal amounts of organic carbon, al-

Table 2. Statistical summary of petrochemical data for Leadville Dolomite and Belden Formation

Variable	Leadville Dolomite				Belden Formation				Mean Reference value[1]
	Average	Standard deviation	Minimum value	Maximum value	Average	Standard deviation	Minimum value	Maximum value	
SiO_2 (%)	22.67	26.93	0.20	97.70	21.37	20.57	2.90	92.20	--
Al_2O_3 (%)	1.79	2.65	0.03	13.70	2.17	2.21	0.33	11.60	0.34 (W)
Fe_2O_3 (%)	2.54	7.28	0.02	46.40	1.37	1.30	0.05	4.70	0.40 (W)
FeO (%)	0.27	0.30	0.00	1.40	0.33	0.48	0.00	2.50	--
MgO (%)	13.28	7.06	0.07	20.80	7.43	6.98	0.35	18.70	--
CaO (%)	23.92	11.64	0.15	53.10	31.98	12.82	2.00	53.00	--
Na_2O (%)	0.030	0.03	0.00	0.10	0.04	0.05	0.00	0.28	0.053 (W)
K_2O (%)	0.38	0.42	0.00	1.60	0.55	0.61	0.04	3.40	0.79 (W)
H_2O^+ (%)	0.98	1.56	0.16	9.10	0.80	0.61	0.24	2.60	--
H_2O^- (%)	0.39	0.84	0.01	5.50	0.28	0.22	0.03	0.89	--
TiO_2 (%)	0.088	0.11	0.00	0.53	0.13	0.13	0.00	0.69	0.034 (W)
P_2O_5 (%)	0.038	0.03	0.00	0.20	0.093	0.11	0.01	0.63	--
MnO (%)	0.074	0.06	0.00	0.31	0.078	0.05	0.01	0.19	0.032 (W)
CO_2 (%)	33.15	15.26	0.00	48.20	33.02	10.76	1.20	45.50	--
F (%)	0.032	0.02	0.00	0.08	0.038	0.03	0.01	0.21	0.032 (G)
S (%)	0.36	0.99	0.01	6.30	0.34	0.73	0.02	3.10	--
C total (%)	9.37	4.13	0.20	13.16	9.42	2.98	0.44	12.85	--
C organic (%)	0.25	0.22	0.00	0.88	0.34	0.66	0.00	4.20	0.24 (Ge)
Carbonate (%)	9.11	4.17	0.00	13.07	9.07	2.96	0.42	12.35	--
Cl (ppm)	143.6	125.7	25.0	550	82.5	53.8	25.0	230	207. (W)
Ba (ppm)	116.8	131.7	20.0	920	182.8	317.9	55.0	2100	86. (W)
Sr (ppm)	91.9	75.4	10.0	310	240.5	147.9	49.0	620	174. (W)
Pb (ppm)	20.9	34.9	0.8	220	22.7	39.9	1.0	200	68. (W)
Zn (ppm)	112.6	341.0	5.0	2600	127.7	236.4	5.0	1000	1100. (W)
Mo (ppm)	6.94	15.5	0.05	88.0	2.28	4.0	0.05	19.0	1.1 (G)
Hg (ppm)	0.187	0.49	0.005	2.6	0.050	0.099	0.005	0.56	0.07 (G)
U (ppm)	1506.8	5874.4	0.18	33500	116.4	217.9	1.56	1190	2.1 (G)
Dolomite XR[2]	5.8	3.1	0.0	10	4.3	2.8	0.00	9.0	
Calcite XR[3]	1.18	2.32	0.0	10	2.3	2.8	0.00	8.0	
Quartz XR	3.0	2.8	0.0	10	3.1	1.6	1.0	10.0	
Clay XR	0.2	0.46	0.0	2	0.3	0.6	0.00	0.0	
Hematite XR	0.08	0.5	0.0	4	0.0	0.0	0.0	0.0	
Dolomite NM	63.8	33.0	0.5	99.0	37.6	33.3	2.0	92.0	
Calcite NM	9.8	19.7	0.0	95.0	38.9	34.5	0.5	95.0	
Quartz NM	19.5	26.3	0.5	98.0	16.9	19.2	2.0	91.0	
Clay NM	4.4	7.6	0.0	39.0	5.02	5.5	1.0	31.0	
Hematite NM	1.8	6.8	0.0	44.0	0.58	0.8	0.0	3.2	
Pyrite NM	0.8	2.40	0.0	16.0	0.8	1.9	0.0	8.0	

[1]Reference values from Graf (1960), (G); Gehman (1962), (Ge); and Weber (1964), (W).
[2]Abundance determined by X-ray diffraction, in parts per ten.
[3]Normative minerals calculated from chemical analyses.

though the literature data base does not appear broad enough to be a reliable comparison. Preliminary correlation and R-mode factor analyses indicate that uranium is essentially independent of organic carbon content.

Sulfur and normative pyrite

Sulfur content of these rocks, about 0.35 percent for both Leadville and Belden samples, may be abnormal. However, I have been unable to locate any chemical data on sulfur content of carbonate rocks elsewhere. Normative pyrite and total S correlate extremely highly with uranium. Sulfur and iron in these rocks seem important in the formation of the uranium deposits.

Minor elements

Minor elements Ba, Ag, Cr, Cu, Hg, Mo, Pb, Sr, V, and Zn were investigated for use as possible pathfinder elements for uranium (Nash, 1979). Minor-element concentrations in the Leadville and the Belden appear to be at or below normal levels, compared to those in carbonate rocks elsewhere (Weber, 1964; Graf, 1960). Mo is the only minor element enriched in either formation: it has a mean concentration of about 6.7 ppm in Leadville samples, and it ranges as high as 88 ppm in a high-grade ore sample. Mo correlates strongly with U in statistical tests on ore sample subsets but does not form a halo beyond uranium ore.

INTERPRETATION

Sedimentation and diagenesis of Leadville Dolomite

The texture and the mineralogy of the dolomicrites and of their neomorphosed equivalents are consistent with numerous reports of ancient and Holocene dolomite termed "primary" or "early" dolomite. These rocks are generally believed to form from carbonate mud that accumulated in relatively quiet water, such as lagoons, or in beach areas beyond the reach of normal wave action (supratidal zone). Many features associated with supratidal environments are observed in the Leadville dolomite, particularly the thin laminae and the lack of fossils. Other features need comments. Algal stromatolites are either poorly developed or absent in the Leadville of this area. Nothing resembling stromatolite heads has been observed, but possibly the relatively common thin laminae are flat-laminated stromatolites or algal mats such as are present in some supratidal zones (Campbell, 1970; Gebelein and Hoffman, 1973; J. A. Campbell, oral communication, 1979). Although neomorphism could have obscured stromatolite structures, the apparent absence of stromatolites seems to be a problem if the Leadville was supratidal. Desiccation cracks and "birdseye" textures are rare if present at all, and no evaporite minerals have been confirmed or inferred.

Sedimentation of the finely laminated carbonate muds of the Leadville appears to have occurred in a tidal-flat or supratidal environment, based on comparisons with modern (e.g., Shinn and others, 1969) and ancient (Laporte, 1967; Roehl, 1967) examples. The same interpretation has been made for the Leadville and Dyer carbonates to the north (Conley, 1972; Nadeau, 1972; Campbell, 1970). Dolomitization probably started soon after the mud was deposited. This interpretation is based chiefly on the lack of replacement textures and preservation of micrite textures. The dolomite is texturally and chemically uniform over tens of meters vertically, and few limestone beds exist. The observed uniformity is not readily explained by any of the numerous dolomitization hypotheses in the recent literature.

Structural control of ore

The most important factor in producing the uranium deposits is the Chester fault. The Pitch orebody is within the zone of multiple fault strands and best ore zones are in thoroughly brecciated Leadville Dolomite. The brittle character of the dolomite is an important accessory factor. The Little Indian deposit likewise is along the Chester fault where brittle quartzites are broken and turned on end. Drilling in the intervening area between these two ore deposits reveals additional uraniferous zones in brecciated rocks along the Chester fault.

More specifically, the structural mechanism is forced faulting of brittle rocks above a rigid basement block in an upthrust (Stearns, 1978; Nash, 1980). In theory, experiment, and nature, brittle rocks (such as dolomite) develop abundant fractures and breccia when they occur immediately above upthrust basement blocks. At the Pitch mine, as in experiments (Friedman and others, 1976), maximum fracturing occurs where brittle beds intersect the reverse fault plane at angles near 70°. At lower angles of intersection, deformation is less intense, probably due to deflection of shears onto bedding planes. To explore for zones of maximum brittle deformation one must focus on brittle beds, changes in dip where beds are folded next to the fault zone, and anticipate concave-downward curvature of the fault surface.

Chemical control of ore

The chemistry of ore deposition in dolomite is not well understood, but there probably was some wallrock involvement. Organic carbon was suspected at first, but chemical analyses reveal relatively low and uniform organic carbon content and no correlation with uranium content. Iron and sulfur contents are anomalous, and FeS_2 as pyrite and marcasite occurs in most uraniferous breccia and veins. The presence of a large proportion of FeS_2 as marcasite may be an indication of formation from metastable sulfur compounds as in some sandstone-type uranium deposits (Goldhaber and Reynolds, 1979; Granger and Warren, 1969). A sulfur species, such as sulfite or thiosulfate, might be the reductant responsible for precipitating uranium and keeping it within the carbonate breccia.

Possible role of karst

Karst is well known in the Leadville Dolomite in central Colorado. Iron-stained karst localities in the Pitch mine area have been prospected for metals and are shown on the 7½-minute topographic map of the area. Recently, Dupree and Maslyn (1979) have proposed that uranium at the Pitch mine "largely occurs in the black organic-rich matrix material of carbonate breccias" that formed by sinkhole collapse and fill. My observations, particularly in the ore zone, do not agree with those interpretations. The carbonate breccias are classic tectonic breccias and are clearly related to faulting in the Chester fault zone. The breccia, and uranium grade, die out below and to the west of the faults. By inspection of numerous cores, new open-pit exposures, and thin sections I find no evidence for "organic-rich matrix" or washed-in clayey sinkhole fill. Chemical analyses do not indicate presence of unusual amounts of organic carbon or aluminum in uranium-bearing breccias. On close inspection and microscopic examination, black portions of some core are fragments of black shale of the Belden; their presence is consistent with tectonic mixing of breccia in a complex fault zone. Karst features that I have observed outside of the mine are characterized by iron oxide fillings, not black clays, and are only slightly radioactive.

ACKNOWLEDGMENTS

It is a pleasure to acknowledge the cooperation of Homestake Mining Company. This project obviously would not have been possible without their permission to examine surface and mine exposures, and to log and sample drill core and cuttings. Homestake also provided important base maps and geologic information. J. Mersch Ward, District Geologist, was a gracious host and offered stimulating discussion. Jerry C. Olson and John A. Campbell, both of the U.S. Geological Survey, offered helpful advice on regional geology and carbonate petrology.

REFERENCES

Banks, N. G., 1970, Nature and origin of early and late cherts in the Leadville Limestone, Colorado: Geologic Society of America Bulletin, v. 81, p. 3033–3048.

Campbell, J. A., 1970, Petrology of Devonian shelf carbonates of west central Colorado: Mountain Geologist, v. 7, p. 89–97.

Conley, C. D., 1972, Depositional and diagenetic history of the Mississippian Leadville Formation, White River Plateau, Colorado, in DeVoto, R. H., ed., Paleozoic Stratigraphy and Structural Evolution of Colorado: Quarterly Journal of the Colorado School of Mines, v. 67, no. 4, p. 103–135.

Dunham, R. J., 1972, Classification of carbonate rocks according to depositional texture, in Ham, W. E., ed., Classification of Carbonate Rocks: American Association of Petroleum Geologists Memoir 1, p. 108–121.

Dupree, J. A. and Maslyn, R. M., 1979, Paleokarst controls on localization of uranium at Pitch Mine, Sawatch Range, Colorado [abs.]: American Association of Petroleum Geologists Bulletin, v. 63, p. 826.

Folk, R. L., 1959, Practical petrographic classification of limestones: American Association of Petroleum Geologists, v. 43, p. 1–38.

———, 1962, Spectral subdivision of limestone types, in Ham, W. E., ed., Classification of Carbonate Rocks: American Association of Petroleum Geologists Memoir 1, p. 62–84.

———, 1965, Some aspects of recrystallization in ancient limestones, in Pray, L. C. and Murray, R. C., eds., Dolomitization and Limestone Diagenesis, A Symposium: Society of Economic Paleontologists and Mineralogists Special Publication No. 13, p. 14–48.

Friedman, M. and others, 1976, Experimental folding of rocks under confining pressure, Part III—Faulted drape folds in multilithologic layered specimens: Geological Society of America Bulletin, v. 87, p. 1049–1066.

Gebelein, C. D. and Hoffman, Paul, 1973, Algal origin of dolomitic laminations in stromatolitic limestone: Journal of Sedimentary Petrology, v. 43, p. 603–613.

Gehman, H. M., Jr., 1962, Organic matter in limestones: Geochimica et Cosmochimica Acta, v. 26, p. 885–897.

Goldhaber, M. B. and Reynolds, R. L., 1979, Origin of marcasite and its implications regarding the genesis of roll-front uranium deposits: U.S. Geological Survey Open-File Report 79-1696, 38 p.

Graf, D. L., 1960, Geochemistry of carbonate sediments and sedimentary carbonate rocks, Part III, Minor element distribution: Illinois State Geological Survey Circular 301, 71 p.

Granger, H. C. and Warren, C. G., 1969, Unstable sulfur compounds and the origin of roll-type uranium deposits: Economic Geology, v. 64, p. 160–171.

Gross, E. B., 1965, A unique occurrence of uranium minerals, Marshall Pass, Saguache County, Colorado: American Mineralogist, v. 50, p. 909–923.

Laporte, L. F., 1967, Carbonate deposition near mean sea-level and resultant facies mosaic: Manlius formation (Lower Devonian) of New York State: American Association of Petroleum Geologists Bulletin, v. 51, p. 73–101.

Malan, R. C., 1959, Geology and uranium deposits of the Marshall Pass District, Gunnison, Saguache, and Chaffee Counties, Colorado: Denver, National Western Mining Conference, Colorado Mining Association, p. 1–20.

Nadeau, J. E., 1972, Mississippian stratigraphy of central Colorado, in DeVoto, R. H., ed., Paleozoic Stratigraphy and Structural Evolution of Colorado: Quarterly Journal of the Colorado School of Mines, v. 67, no. 4, p. 77–101.

Nash, J. T., 1979, Geology, petrology, and chemistry of the Leadville Dolomite: Host for uranium at the Pitch Mine, Saguache County, Colorado: U.S. Geological Survey Open-File Report 79-1566, 51 p.

———, 1980, Supergene uranium deposits in brecciated zones of Laramide upthrusts—Concepts and applications: U.S. Geological Survey Open-File Report 80-385, 36 p.

Olson, J. C., 1979, Preliminary geologic and structural maps and sections of the Marshall Pass Mining District, Saguache, Gunnison, and Chafee Counties, Colorado: U.S. Geological Survey Open-File Report 79-1473, scale 1:24,000.

Phair, George and Levine, Harry, 1954, Notes on the differential leaching of uranium, radium, and lead from pitchblende in H_2SO_4 solutions: Economic Geology, v. 48, p. 358-369.

Roehl, P. O., 1967, Stony Mountain (Ordovician) and Interlake (Silurian) facies analogs of recent low-energy marine and subaerial carbonates, Bahamas: American Association of Petroleum Geologists Bulletin, v. 51, p. 1979–2032.

Shinn, E. A., Lloyd, R. M., and Ginsburg, R. N., 1969, Anatomy of a modern carbonate tidal-flat, Andros Island, Bahamas: Journal of Sedimentary Petrology, v. 39, p. 1202–1228.

Stearns, D. W., 1978, Faulting and forced folding in the Rocky Mountains Foreland, in Matthews, Vincent, III, ed., Folding associated with basement block faulting in the western United States: Geological Society of America Memoir 151, p. 1–38.

Till, Roger, 1970, The relationship between environment and sediment composition (geochemistry and petrology) in the Bimini Lagoon, Bahamas: Journal of Sedimentary Petrology, v. 40, p. 367–385.

Tweto, Ogden, Steven, T. A., Hail, W. J., Jr., and Moench, R., 1976, Preliminary geologic map of the Montrose 1° × 2° Quadrangle, southwestern Colorado: U.S. Geological Survey Miscellaneous Field Studies Map MF-761, 1 sheet (1:250,000).

Ward, J. M., 1978, History and geology of Homestake's Pitch Project, Saguache County, Colorado [abs.]: American Institute of Mining, Metallurgical, and Petroleum Engineers, Program of the 107th annual meeting, Denver, Colorado, February 26–March 2, 1978.

Weber, J. N., 1964, Trace element composition of dolostones and dolomites and its bearing on the dolomite problem: Geochimica et Cosmochimica Acta, v. 28, p. 1817–1868.

CRETACEOUS AND TERTIARY HISTORY AND RESOURCES OF THE PICEANCE CREEK BASIN, WESTERN COLORADO*

RONALD C. JOHNSON and C. WILLIAM KEIGHIN
U.S. Geological Survey
Denver, Colorado 80225

INTRODUCTION

The Piceance Creek Basin is a Late Cretaceous and Tertiary age sedimentary basin in west-central Colorado. It is bounded on the southeast by the Sawatch uplift, on the east by the White River uplift, on the north by the Uinta uplift, on the southwest by the Uncompahgre uplift, and on the west by the Douglas Creek arch (fig. 1). It is part of a larger complex of Laramide-age basins, including the Uinta Basin to the west and the greater Green River Basin to the north, which hold vast lacustrine oil-shale deposits of Eocene age. This paper is a general overview of the development of the Piceance Creek Basin starting in the Early Cretaceous time. Oil shale, and other resources, are discussed briefly.

GEOLOGIC HISTORY

Late Cretaceous

The Cretaceous epicontinental sea transgressed generally from northeast to southwest across the Piceance Creek Basin area in the Early Cretaceous, depositing about 60 to 90 m of marginal marine fluvial and paludal sediments of the Dakota Sandstone (called Dakota Group by Haun, 1959). As much as 1,700 m of marine Mancos Shale was deposited before the next marine regression, represented by the Castlegate Sandstone (fig. 2), reached the westernmost part of the area in the Campanian (Zapp and Cobban, 1960). A mixed sequence of marine, marginal marine, and paludal sediments comprise the next 210 to 600 m of section (fig. 3), as the shoreline regressed slowly across the area from northwest to southeast. This overall regressive sequence was interrupted by several relatively minor transgressions, but the Cretaceous seaway had retreated east of the area before the end of the Campanian (figs. 2, 4). At this time the Piceance Creek Basin did not exist, as such, because the surrounding Laramide uplifts that define the basin did not begin to rise until somewhat later. The area presently occupied by the Piceance Creek Basin was located along the western side of a seaway that extended from the Arctic Ocean to the Gulf of Mexico (fig. 5). Figure 2 shows an isopach of the interval from the top of the Dakota Sandstone to the top of the Rollins Sandstone member of the Mount Garfield Formation (west)-Trout Creek Sandstone Member of the Iles Formation (east), the youngest basinwide regressive marine sandstones. The interval thickens to the northeast, away from both the Uncompahgre uplift and the Douglas Creek arch. There is no evidence that either uplift was a positive area at this time, but that subsidence rates appear to have been influenced by the Uncompahgre and the Douglas Creek arch nonetheless. This sediment-thickening trend is similar to that found in younger sediments when the Uncompahgre uplift, as well as other uplifts, were actively rising.

Following the retreat of the Cretaceous seaway, more than 1,200 m of late Campanian, and possibly Maestrichtian age nonmarine sediments were deposited in the area (figs. 3,6). During this time interval, only one marine transgression, the Lewis transgression, migrated as far west as the Piceance Creek Basin area (fig. 1), and this transgression extended only to the northeast corner of the basin (Handcock, 1925; Zapp and Cobban, 1960). The Lion Canyon Sandstone Member of the Williams Fork Formation, west of Meeker, was deposited during this transgression or during the regression that followed.

The Sawatch uplift, southeast of the basin (fig. 1), began to rise during deposition of the nonmarine Cretaceous section (Obradovich and others, 1969; Tweto, 1975). The effects of this uplift on Cretaceous sedimentation are unknown. Chert pebbles, common in the upper part of the nonmarine Cretaceous section in the southern part of the basin, may have come from the rising Sawatch uplift, but overall, the section in the southeastern part of the basin near the uplift is similar to the section for the rest of the basin. The nonmarine Cretaceous section thickens toward the uplift at its nearest preserved exposure, about 15 to 25 km west (fig. 6). Apparently the uplift did not affect subsidence rates in the adjacent Piceance Creek Basin.

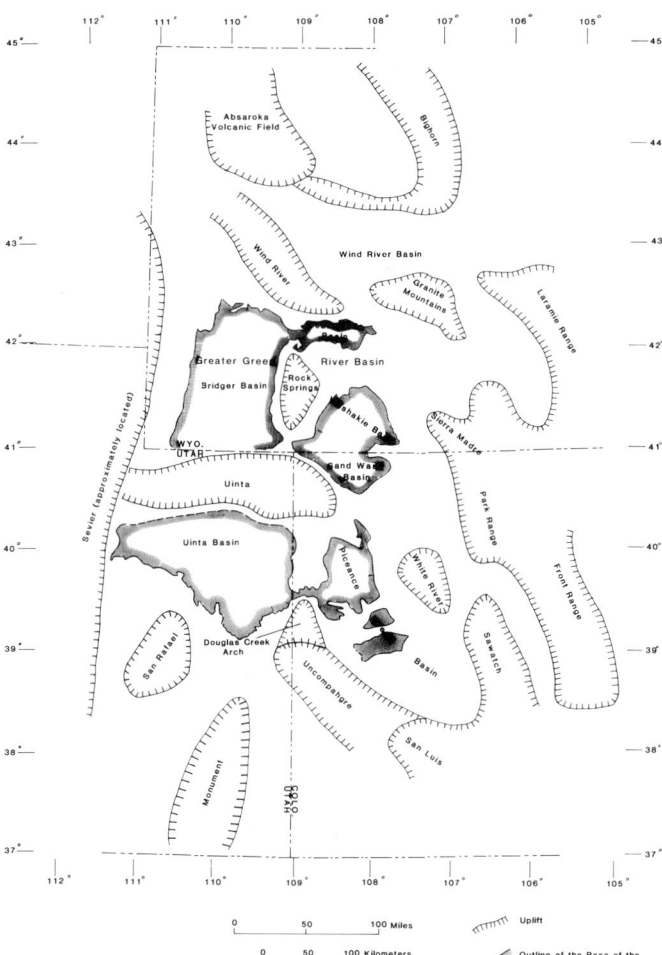

Figure 1. Map showing basins that contain Green River oil shale. Approximate extent of uplifts in Late Cretaceous and early Tertiary time are also shown.

---
*Part of this work was prepared in cooperation with the U.S. Department of Energy, Western Gas Sands Project.

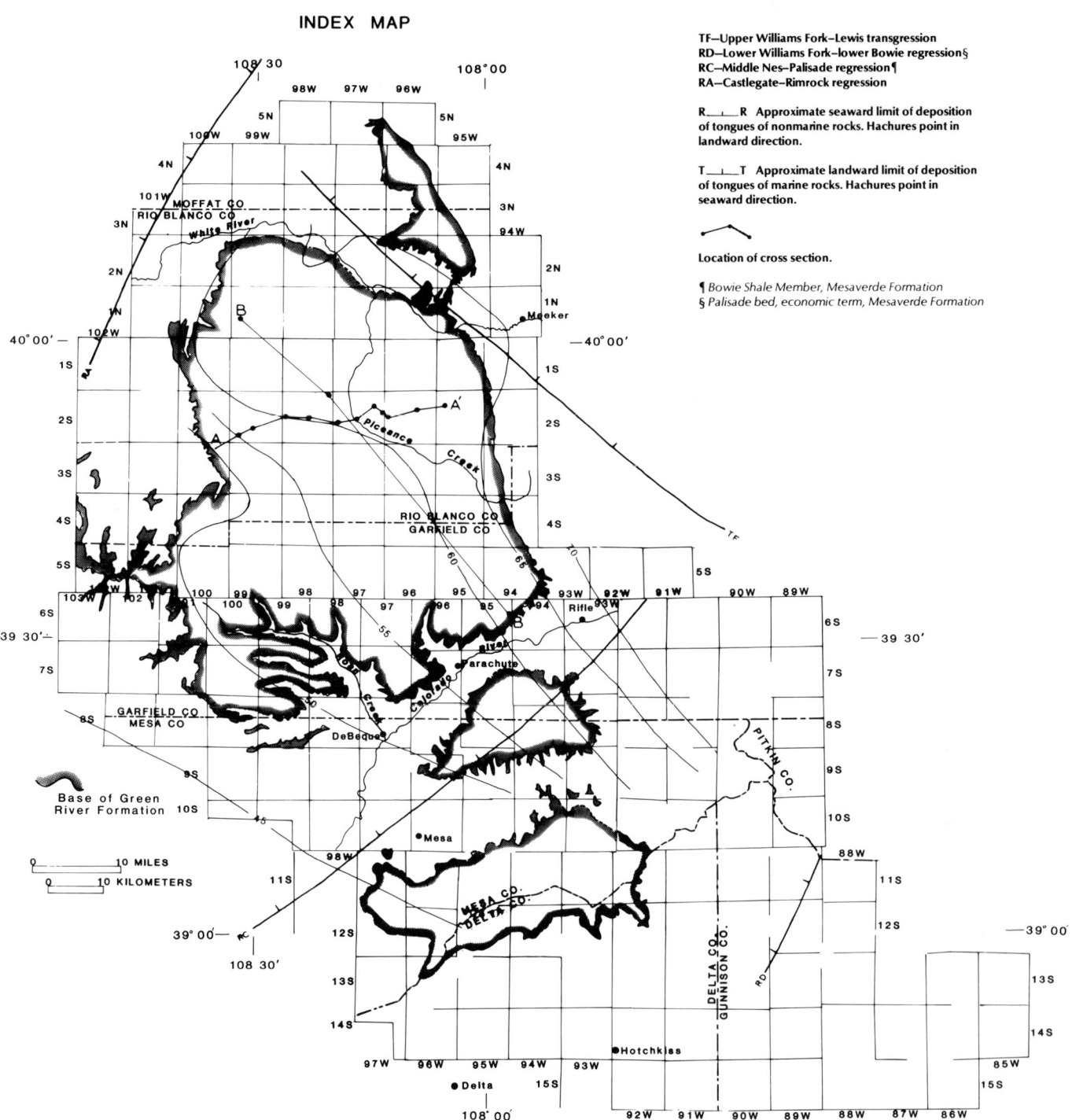

Figure 2. Index map showing the location of cross sections A-A' and B-B', the limits of selected Late Cretaceous transgressions and regressions (Zapp and Cobban, 1960), and a generalized isopach of the interval from the top of the Dakota Sandstone to the top of the Rollins Sandstone Member-Trout Creek Sandstone Member. Contour interval, 500 ft (152 m).

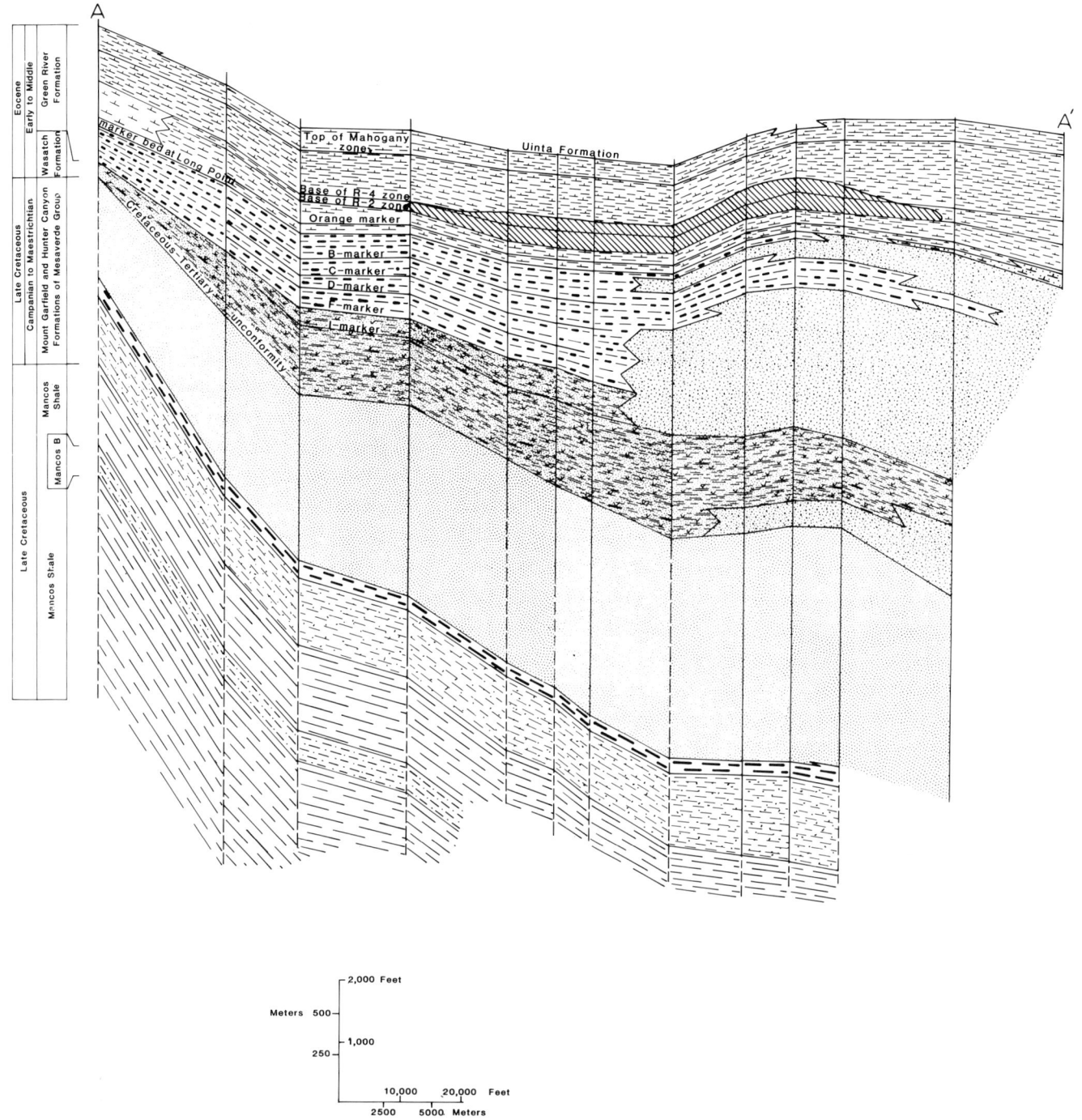

Figure 3. Generalized east-west cross section through the central part of the Piceance Creek Basin; modified from Johnson (1979). Key for cross section and correlation diagrams.

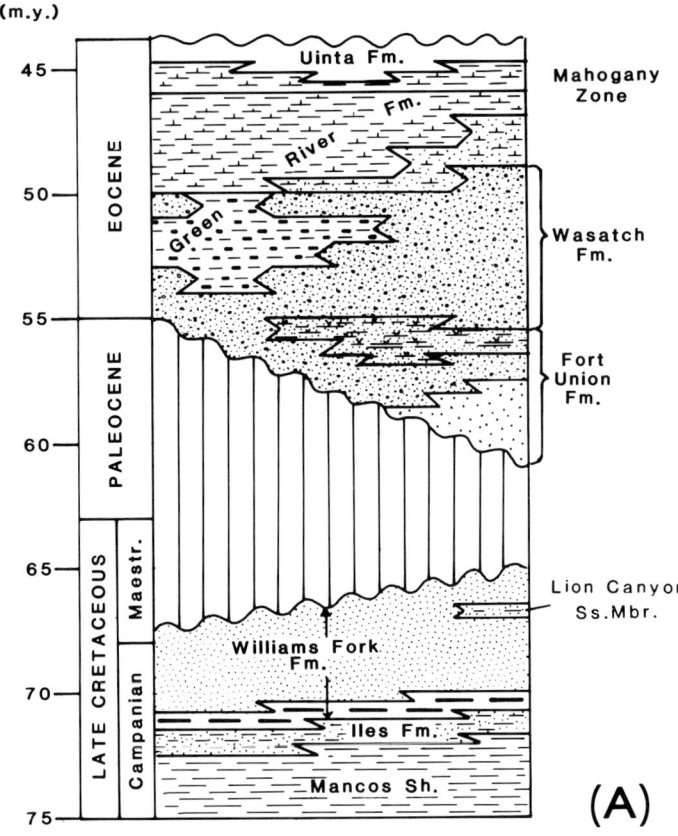

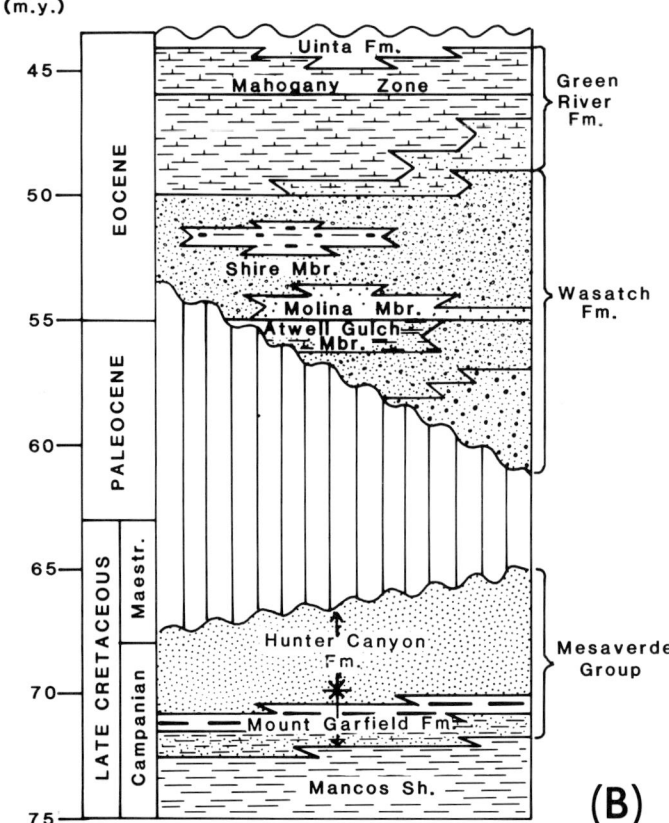

Figure 4. Correlation diagrams for the Piceance Creek Basin. **A,** *northern Piceance Creek Basin;* **B,** *southern Piceance Creek Basin.*

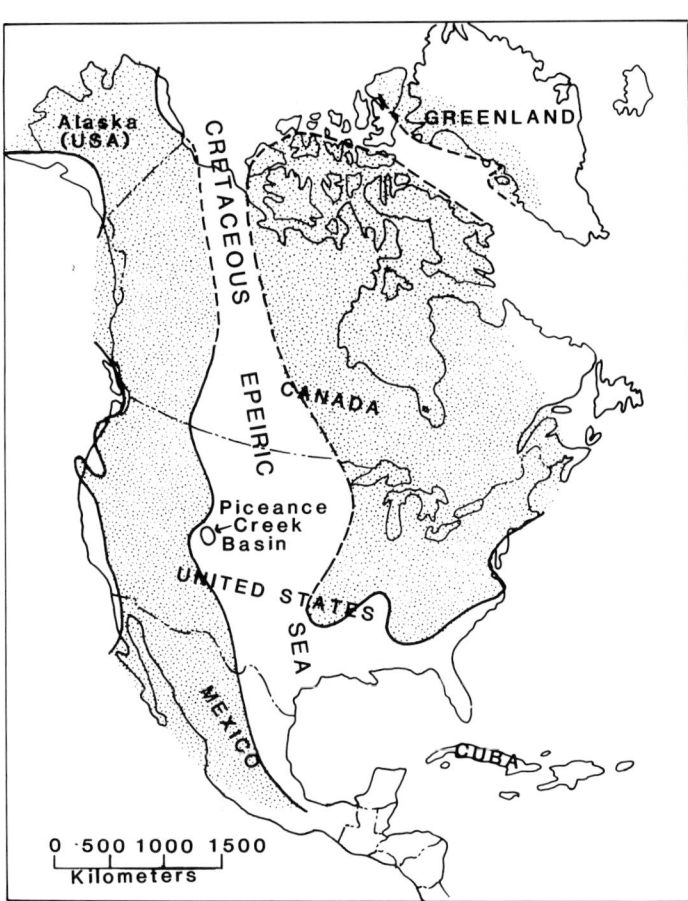

Figure 5. Approximate extent of Cretaceous epeiric sea during late Campanian time (from Obradovich and Cobban, 1976).

Cretaceous-Tertiary Unconformity

An unconformity between the Cretaceous and Tertiary sections probably is present throughout the basin. The youngest rocks below the unconformity are late Campanian to Maestrichtian (Johnson and others, 1980). The oldest rocks above the unconformity range in age from early to middle Paleocene in the northern and eastern parts of the basin (Hail, 1973; Newman, 1974), to late Paleocene and probably early or middle Eocene in the western and southwestern parts of the basin (Johnson and May, 1978). Several Laramide structures began to rise during this time, disrupting the old coastal-plain drainage system and establishing a new drainage system controlled largely by local uplifts.

The Cretaceous section beneath the unconformity is highly weathered, particularly in the southwestern part of the basin where a kaolinite-rich zone as much as 150 m thick is present (Johnson and May, 1980). Most of this weathering probably occurred prior to deposition of the unaltered overlying rocks. The amount of section removed by this period of erosion is unknown but much of the thinning of the nonmarine part of the Mesaverde from 1,400 m in the northeastern part of the basin to less than 600 m along the western margin (fig. 6) may be due to erosion at this time. Despite the evidence of intense weathering, local relief on the unconformity surface is minor, consisting only of shallow conglomerate-filled channels (Johnson and May, 1980). The kaolinitic zone formerly was called the Ohio Creek Formation and was thought to be Paleocene in age. The Ohio Creek recently was reduced in rank, its age and affiliation changed. It is a member of

INDEX MAP

Figure 6. Isopach of the interval in the Mesaverde Group from the top of the Rollins (west) or Trout Creek Sandstone Member (east) to the Cretaceous-Tertiary unconformity. Modified from Granica and Johnson (1980). Contour interval, 100 ft (30.5 m).

the underlying Upper Cretaceous Hunter Canyon Formation or locally of the Mesaverde Formation (Johnson and May, 1980).

Paleocene

Sediments first began to accumulate on the unconformity in the eastern part of the basin in early or middle Paleocene, and spread westward, eventually burying the Douglas Creek arch on the western margin of the basin in early to middle Eocene time. Westward onlapping of Paleocene sediments on the unconformity has been noted in the southern part of the basin (Johnson and May, 1978), and also probably is responsible for the westward thinning of the lower member of the Fort Union Formation noted by Hail (1973, 1974) along the White River in the northern part of the basin.

Paleocene sediments represent the intensity of activity and the composition of surrounding Laramide uplifts. A thick sequence of coarse andesitic debris from the Sawatch uplift accumulated in the southeastern part of the basin. This unit, originally called the "Ruby beds" (Hills, 1890; Eldridge, 1894), and later included in the Wasatch Formation, is about 750 m thick at Ruby Peak in the southeasternmost part of the basin (Eldridge, 1894), but thins to the north and is about 260 m thick at Rifle Gap. A sandstone section that ranges in thickness from 240 to 430 m, possibly derived from the Park Range to the northeast, is found at the base of the Fort Union Formation in the Meeker area in the northeastern corner of the basin. These sandstones pinch out to the west and southwest in the subsurface. Sandstones with sparse chert pebbles are found in the Fort Union at Fletcher Gulch in the northwestern corner of the basin. The Unita uplift to the northwest may have been the source area. The Paleocene section in the southwestern part of the basin is distinctly different. Onlapping of the Cretaceous-Tertiary unconformity occurred here in late Paleocene (Johnson and May 1978). However, with the exception of a thin basal chert and limestone-pebble conglomerate, the Paleocene section consists largely of gray to black shales with a few thin coals. The Uncompahgre uplift to the southwest was a positive feature during the Paleocene because sediments lap out on the Cretaceous-Tertiary unconformity to the southwest, but it was not a major source of coarse clastic sediments.

A paludal unit consisting mainly of dark-colored shales and thin coals with thin sandstones and siltstones represents most of the Paleocene section in the central part of the basin (Johnson, 1979a, b, c) and the late Paleocene section around the margins of the basin (Hail, 1973, 1974; Pipiringos and Rosenlund, 1977; Johnson and May, 1978). Most of the early to middle Paleocene are coarse clastic units restricted to the margins of the basin and are overlain by upper Paleocene plaudal rocks.

Eocene

In early Eocene time, a permanent freshwater or near freshwater lake formed in the central and northwestern part of the Piceance Creek Basin. Deposits from this earliest stage of Lake Uinta are characterized by low-grade oil shale, ostracodal limestone, mollusk-bearing sandstone, and kerogen-rich shale interbedded with thin coals. One tongue of this deposit, as much as 60 m thick, extends as far south as the lower part of the Roan Creek drainage, just north of DeBeque (Johnson, 1975, 1977).

At about the same time that a permanent freshwater lake formed in the central part of the basin, a shift in deposition from paludal rocks to oxidized alluvial mudstone occurred around the basin's perimeter (fig. 3). Discontinuous sandstones are more common in these sequences than in the underlying paludal rocks of the late Paleocene, but sandstone still generally comprises less than 20 percent of the section.

Clastic sediment entered the basin from at least two new directions during the Eocene, possibly indicating activity on uplifts that were not present, or were inactive, during the Paleocene. A thick pile of variegated mudstone and sandstone was deposited along the eastern margin of the basin (fig. 3), suggesting that the White River uplift began to rise during Eocene time. Farther basinward, a thick sandstone sequence was deposited along the eastern margin of Lake Uinta. More sandstone was deposited in this area of the lake than in any other.

A sand-dominated fluvial deposit as much as 150 m thick is found at approximately the base of the Eocene section in the southwestern part of the basin. This unit, named the Molina Member of the Wasatch Formation (Donnell, 1969), contains chert pebble lenses and is interpreted to be a braided-stream deposit (Johnson and May, 1978). The unit is in sharp contact with the underlying paludal rocks of late Paleocene age and grades upward into variegated mudstones. The Molina Member also grades laterally into variegated mudstones to the north, northeast, and east, and probably was deposited by streams flowing off the Uncompahgre uplift to the southwest. This is the only coarse clastic sequence in the Tertiary section that apparently had a southwestern source, despite the fact that several intervals in the Late Cretaceous and Tertiary thin toward the southwest (figs. 2,6,7).

Lake Uinta expanded rapidly to cover most of the basin in the late early to early middle Eocene. This transgression is marked throughout much of the basin by a distinctive gastropod-rich marker bed called the marker bed at Long Point (Johnson and May, 1978). Salinity began to increase after the transgression and eventually led to the precipitation of great quantities of nahcolite, dawsonite, and halite. These saline minerals were precipitated both on the lake floor and in the unlithified lake sediments (Dyni, 1974; Beard and others, 1974). Kerogen content of the sediments is much greater than in the earlier freshwater stage, and all the economically important oil shale is found in rocks of this age.

In the middle to late Eocene, a delta consisting largely of volcaniclastic debris prograded southward across the basin (Surdam and Stanley, 1980; Johnson, 1981), filling in the Piceance Creek Basin part of Lake Uinta. This deltaic complex, named the Uinta Formation, is the youngest stratigraphic unit preserved in the Piceance Creek Basin.

RESOURCES
Oil Shale

The shale-oil resource potential of the Green River Formation has been of interest for many years and has been discussed in several publications (Donnell, 1961; Donnell and Austin, 1971; Donnell and Blair, 1970; Keighin, 1975; Pitman, 1979; Pitman and Donnell, 1973; Pitman and Johnson, 1978). In general, Green River oil shale is a very fine-grained, carbonate-rich rock containing high but variable quantities of kerogen, which yields oil when subjected to destructive distillation. The center for oil-shale deposition is the north-central part of the basin, where there is as much as 550 m of nearly continuous oil shale (figs. 7,8). Rich oil shale is in two members of the Green River Formation, the older Garden Gulch member, which contains abundant clay, and the younger Parachute Creek member, which contains abundant saline minerals and more carbonate and authigenic feldspars than the Garden Gulch Member (Robb and Smith, 1974). In the center of the basin, the Garden Gulch Member extends from the marker bed at Long Point to the base of the R-2 oil-shale zone (fig. 3), and the overlying Parachute Creek Member extends up to the base of the Uinta Formation. Both members grade toward the basin margins into marginal lacustrine sandstone, mudstone, and limestone of the Anvil Points and Douglas Creek Members of the Green River. Both the Garden Gulch and the Parachute Creek contain significant oil-shale deposits; however, the Parachute Creek member has attracted the most attention, primarily because it is thicker and the overburden is less. Both members have been subdivided into persistent rich and lean oil-shale zones (fig. 8). Many of these time-stratigraphic zones can be traced into the Uinta Basin to the west (Cashion and Donnell, 1972). The richest and most widespread of these zones is the Mahogany zone (or Mahogany ledge in surface exposures). This is one of the few oil-shale zones that is rich enough to be mined on outcrop (fig. 9).

The mineralogy of the Green River oil shale is moderately complex and is variable throughout the oil-shale interval (Brobst and Tucker, 1973; Desborough and Pitman, 1974; Robb and Smith, 1974). The nonorganic fraction consists of variable quantities of dolomite, calcite, quartz, potassium and plagioclase feldspars, analcime, nahcolite, dawsonite, pyrite, and clay minerals, primarily illite. Study of oil shales by X-ray diffraction and scanning electron

Figure 7. Isopach of the interval in the Green River Formation from the base of the bed at Long Point in the Douglas Creek Member, to the top of the Mahogany zone. Note general east-northeast thickening trend. Rapid thickening in the northern and eastern parts of the basin are due to clastic influxes. Contour interval, 100 ft (30.5 m).

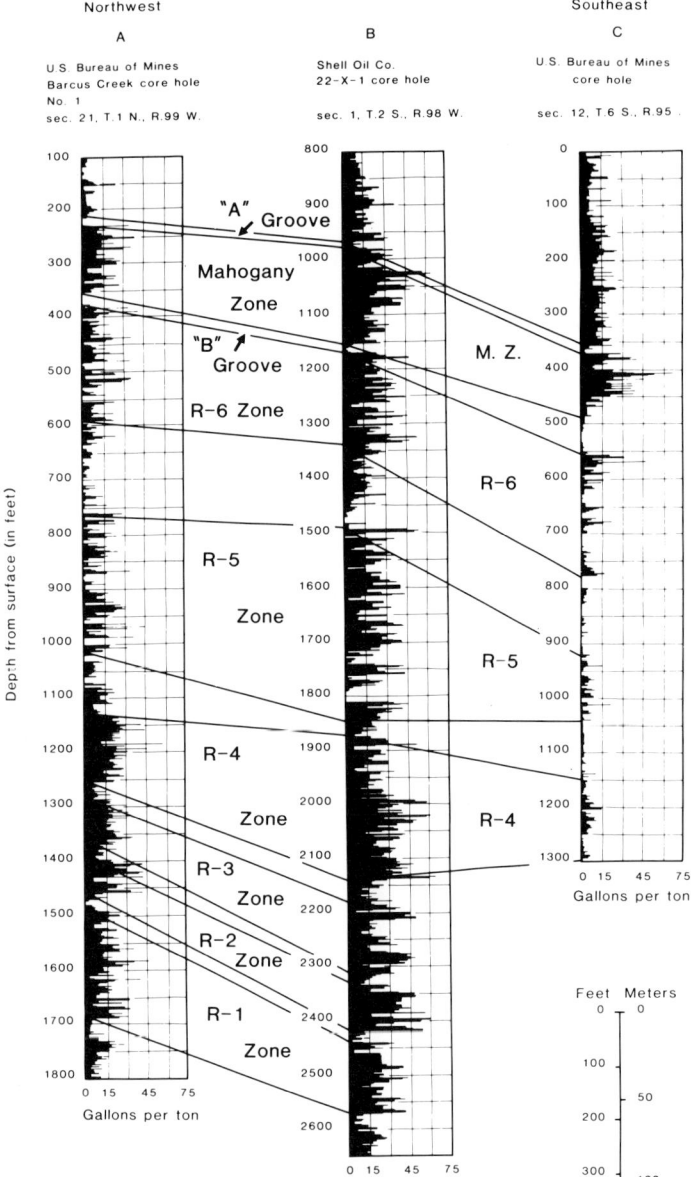

Figure 8. Northwest-southeast cross section showing oil-yield histograms of lower part of the Parachute Creek Member of the Green River Formation, and correlation of rich oil-shale zones labeled R-1 to R-6 and Mahogany zone. Location of core holes is shown in Figure 2 as B-B'.

microscopy demonstrates that most of the feldspars, and many of the other minerals, are authigenic. The nature and distribution of some of these minerals within a sample of oil shale are illustrated in Figure 10. Knowledge of the mineralogy and mineral distribution in the oil shale is important for planning the economic potential of the resources. For example, Ca-Mg-Fe carbonates, when associated with sodium bicarbonates, act as a flux during retorting, and have a significant effect on the thermal requirements for retorting (Desborough and Pitman, 1974). Some minor and trace elements may be deleterious if leached from spent shale; knowing the residence(s) of these elements is desirable.

In beds greater than 3.1 m thick and yielding 25 gallons (100 l) or more of oil per ton, there are an estimated 471 billion barrels of oil in place (Keighin, 1975). Work is in progress on evaluating, on a zone by zone basis, oil-shale resources (Pitman and Johnson, 1978; Pitman, 1979).

Saline Minerals

A saline facies of the Green River Formation is present in the central part of the Piceance Creek Basin (fig. 9) that contains nahcolite ($NaHCO_3$), dawsonite ($NaAl(OH)_2CO_3$), and halite associated with oil shale. The saline facies is found in the lower part of the Parachute Creek Member of the Green River Formation (fig. 3). It is overlain by a leached zone as much as 200 m thick (Hite and Dyni, 1967; Dyni, 1974; Beard and others, 1974) in which most of the nahcolite and halite have been leached by ground water. At the saline depocenter of the basin (eastern part of T. 1 S., R. 98 W.), the thickness of nahcolite-bearing oil shale reaches a maximum of approximately 345 m and is overlain by 430 to 600 m of overburden (Dyni, 1974, p. 112). Nahcolite occurrence is variable, and ranges between nonbedded crystalline aggregates and coarse-grained beds.

Nahcolite could serve as a raw material for a number of basic industrial chemicals, although this market is now dominated by the trona industry of Wyoming. Of more immediate potential value is the use of nahcolite to remove SO_2 from powerplant stack gases. Beard and others (1974, p. 108) estimated that approximately 29 billion tons of nahcolite are within the Piceance Creek Basin.

Dawsonite, a potential source of alumina, is associated with nahcolite. It is not easily leached by ground water and therefore has a somewhat greater lateral and vertical distribution than nahcolite or halite. Dawsonite is disseminated throughout an oil-shale matrix as fine crystals (Beard and others, 1974), where it may account for as much as 25 percent of the rock. Approximately 19 billion tons of dawsonite are estimated to be present in the Piceance Creek Basin (Beard and others, 1974, p. 108).

Other Commodities

Other major resources found in the Piceance Creek Basin include gas and oil from both the Cretaceous and Tertiary and coal from the Cretaceous. These resources are discussed by others in this guidebook and will be discussed here only briefly. Most sandstones in the Late Cretaceous appear to be capable of producing some gas over large areas of the basin. Major factors that have restricted development are, (1) limited size of individual reservoirs, (2) low permeability, (3) drilling depth, and (4) local water-bearing reservoirs. Structure does not appear to have a major influence on gas accumulation (fig. 11); however, reservoir permeability is generally better on structural highs and closures. The nonmarine part of the Mesaverde Group probably contains the greatest in-place gas reserves, but sandstones are discontinuous and reservoir quality is low. Sandstones in the marginal marine part of the Mesaverde are more persistent and generally have slightly better permeability. These reservoirs have been extensively developed in the southern part of the basin, in areas where the drilling depth is not too great.

Occurrence of gas at shallow drill depths has also contributed to the development of the "Mancos B," a silty and sandy zone in the Mancos Shale (Kellogg, 1977). The unit has been extensively developed in the western part of the basin on and adjacent to the Douglas Creek arch, where drilling depths are generally less than 1,500 m. The Dakota Sandstone is too deep throughout most of the basin to have attracted much attention thus far; however, production has been established in isolated areas throughout much of the southwestern and western parts of the basin, and areas of production are actively being extended. Drilling depth to the Dakota in this area ranges from about 2,000 to 3,000 m.

Figure 9. In-place oil resources for the Mahogany zone in barrels per acre. Contour interval, 50,000 barrels per acre. From Pitman and Johnson (1978). Stippled area is approximate limit of nahcolite occurrence (from Beard and others, 1974).

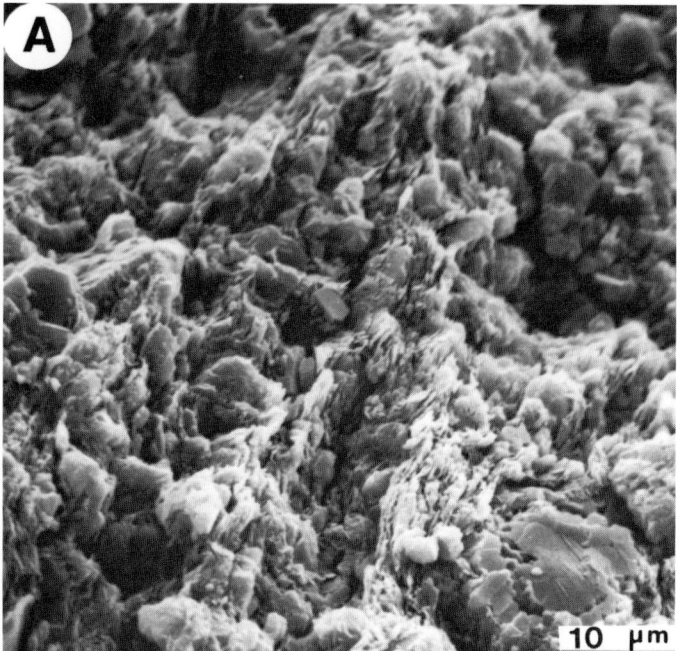

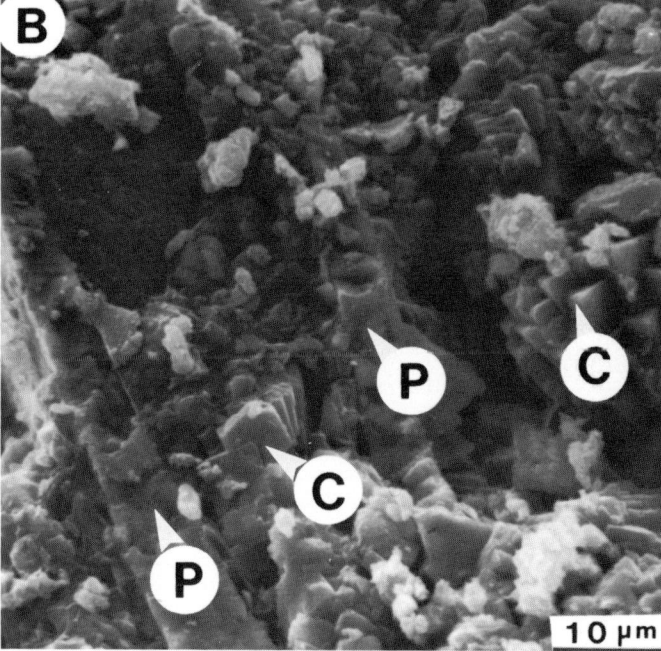

Figure 10. Scanning electron micrograph of oil shale that yields 25 gallons of oil per ton. **A,** Intimate mixture of very fine grained detrital, platey kerogen and clays, and euhedral to subhedral authigenic minerals; **B,** high concentration of authigenic minerals: P, iron sulfide (pyrite?) and C, calcite.

Tertiary gas and oil production has been established in the central part of the basin from the marginal lacustrine sandstone of the Douglas Creek Member of the Green River Formation, and in the Wasatch Formation, with most production coming from fluvial sandstones between the F and the I marker (fig. 3). Farther to the south, along the Colorado River, production recently has been established in the Molina Member of the Wasatch Formation.

Cretaceous coals have been mined in many parts of the basin where the marginal marine-fluvial transitional part of the Mesaverde Group crops out.

REFERENCES

Beard, T. N., Tait, D. B., and Smith, J. W., 1974, Nahcolite and dawsonite resources in the Green River Formation, Piceance Creek Basin, Colorado: Rocky Mountain Association of Geologists Guidebook, 25th Field Conference, Energy resources of the Piceance Creek Basin, Colorado, p. 101–109.

Brobst, D. A. and Tucker, J. D., 1973, X-ray mineralogy of the Parachute Creek Member, Green River Formation in the northern Piceance Creek Basin, Colorado: U.S. Geological Survey Professional Paper 803, 53 p.

Cashion, W. B. and Donnell, J. R., 1972, Chart showing correlation of selected key units in the organic-rich sequence of the Green River Formation, Piceance Creek Basin, Colorado, and Uinta Basin, Utah: U.S. Geological Survey Oil and Gas Investigations Chart OC-65.

Desborough, G. A. and Pitman, J. K., 1974, Significance of applied mineralogy to oil shale in the upper part of the Parachute Creek Member of the Green River Formation, Piceance Creek Basin, Colorado: Rocky Mountain Association of Geologists Guidebook, 25th Field Conference, Energy resources of the Piceance Creek Basin, Colorado, p. 81–89.

Donnell, J. R., 1961, Tertiary geology and oil-shale resources of the Piceance Creek Basin between Colorado and White Rivers northwestern Colorado: U.S. Geological Survey Bulletin 1082-L, p. 835–891.

——— 1969, Paleocene and lower Eocene units in the southern part of the Piceance Creek Basin, Colorado: U.S. Geological Survey Bulletin 1274-M, p. M1–M18.

Donnell, J. R. and Austin, A. C., 1971, Potential strippable oil-shale resources of the Mahogany zone (Eocene), Cathedral Bluffs area, northwestern Colorado: U.S. Geological Survey Professional Paper 750-C, p. C13–C17.

Donnell, J. R. and Blair, R. W., 1970, Resource appraisal of three rich oil-shale zones in the Green River Formation, Piceance Creek Basin, Colorado: Colorado School of Mines Quarterly, v. 65, no. 4, p. 73–87.

Dyni, J. R., 1974, Stratigraphy and nahcolite resources of the saline facies of the Green River Formation in northwest Colorado: Rocky Mountain Association of Geologists Guidebook, 25th Field Conference, Energy resources of the Piceance Creek Basin, Colorado, p. 111–122.

Eldridge, G. H., 1894, Anthracite-Crested Butte Folio 9: U.S. Geological Survey Geologic Atlas of the United States.

Granica, M. P. and Johnson, R. C., 1980, Structure contour and isochore map of the nonmarine part of the Mesaverde Group, Piceance Creek Basin, Colorado: U.S. Geological Survey Miscellaneous Field Studies Map MF-1189.

Hail, W., Jr., 1973, Geologic map of the Smizer Gulch Quadrangle, Rio Blanco and Moffat Counties, Colorado: U.S. Geological Survey Geologic Quadrangle Map GQ-1131.

——— 1974, Geologic map of the Rough Gulch Quadrangle, Rio Blanco and Moffat Counties, Colorado: U.S. Geological Survey Geologic Quadrangle Map GQ-1195.

Handcock, E. T. and Eby, J. B., 1930, Geology and coal resources of the Meeker Quadrangle, Moffat and Rio Blanco Counties, Colorado: U.S. Geological Survey Bulletin 812-C, p. 191–242.

Haun, J. D., 1959, Lower Cretaceous stratigraphy of Colorado: Rocky Mountain Association of Geologists, 11th Field Conference, Washakie, Sandwash, and Piceance Basins, p. 1–8.

Hills, R. C., 1890, Orographic and structural features of Rocky Mountain Geology: Colorado Scientific Society Proceedings, v. 3, p. 362–458.

Hite, R. J. and Dyni, J. R., 1967, Potential resources of dawsonite and nahcolite in the Piceance Creek Basin, northwest Colorado: Fourth symposium on oil shale, Colorado School of Mines Quarterly, v. 62, no. 3, p. 25–38.

Johnson, R. C., 1975, Preliminary geologic map, oil-shale yield histograms and stratigraphic sections, Long Point Quadrangle, Garfield County, Colorado: U.S. Geological Survey Miscellaneous Field Studies Map MF-588.

——— 1977, Preliminary geologic map and cross section of The Saddle Quadrangle, Garfield County, Colorado: U.S. Geological Survey Miscellaneous Field Studies Map MF-829.

——— 1979a, Cross section A-A' of Upper Cretaceous and lower Tertiary rocks, northern Piceance Creek Basin, Colorado: U.S. Geological Survey Miscellaneous Field Studies Map MF-1129-A.

——— 1979b, Cross section B-B' of Upper Cretaceous and lower Tertiary rocks, northern Piceance Creek Basin, Colorado: U.S. Geological Survey Miscellaneous Field Studies Map MF-1129-B.

——— 1979c, Cross section C-C' of Upper Cretaceous and lower Tertiary rocks, northern Piceance Creek Basin, Colorado: U.S. Geological Survey Miscellaneous Field Studies Map MF-1129-C.

——— 1981, Stratigraphic evidence for a deep Eocene Lake Uinta, Piceance Creek Basin, Colorado: Geology, v. 9, p. 55–62.

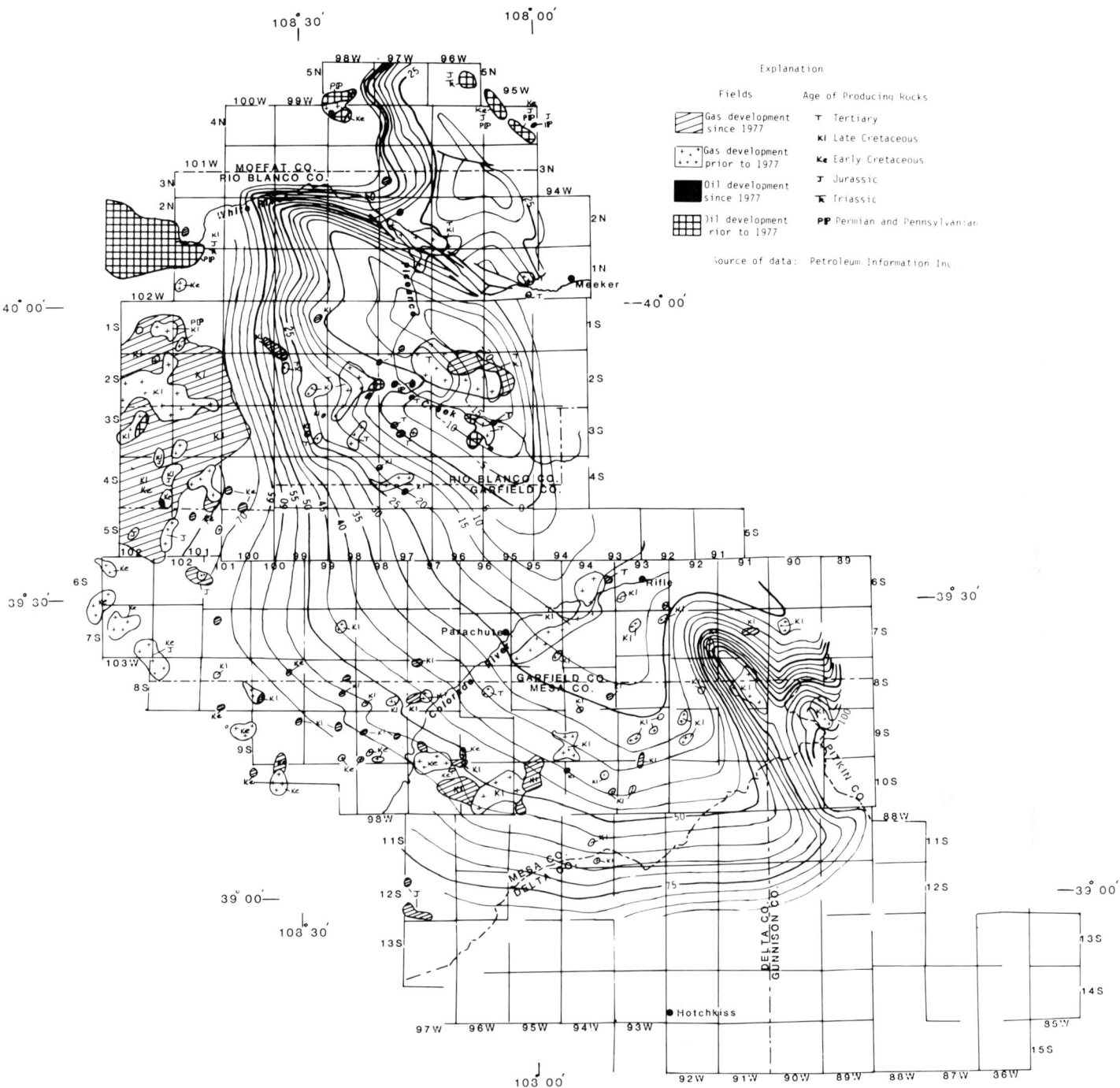

Figure 11. Oil and gas fields in the Piceance Creek Basin. Structure contours are on the Cretaceous-Tertiary unconformity, and are modified from Granica and Johnson (1980). Contour interval, 500 ft (152 m).

Johnson, R. C. and May, F., 1978, Preliminary stratigraphic studies of the upper part of the Mesaverde Group, the Wasatch Formation, and the lower part of the Green River Formation, DeBeque area, Colorado, including environments of deposition and investigations of palynomorph assemblages: U.S. Geological Survey Miscellaneous Field Studies Map MF-1050.

——— 1980, A study of the Cretaceous-Tertiary unconformity in the Piceance Creek Basin, Colorado: the underlying Ohio Creek Formation (Upper Cretaceous) redefined as a member of the Hunter Canyon or Mesaverde Formation: U.S. Geological Survey Bulletin 1482-B, 27 p.

Johnson, R. C., May, F., Hansley, P. L., Pitman, J. K., and Fouch, T. D., 1980, Petrography, X-ray mineralogy, and palynology of a measured section of the Upper Cretaceous Mesaverde Group in Hunter Canyon, western Colorado: U.S. Geological Survey Oil and Gas Investigations Chart OC-91.

Keighin, C. W., 1975, Resource appraisal of oil shale in the Green River Formation, Piceance Creek Basin, Colorado: Colorado School of Mines Quarterly, v. 70, no. 3, p. 57–68.

Kellogg, H. E., 1977, Geology and petroleum of the Mancos B. Formation, Douglas Creek Arch Area, Colorado and Utah: Rocky Mountain Association of Geologists, 1977 Symposium, Exploration frontiers of the central and southern Rockies, p. 167–179.

Newman, K. R., 1974, Palynomorph zones in early Tertiary formations of the Piceance Creek and Uinta Basins, Colorado and Utah: Rocky Mountain Association of Geologists Guidebook, 25th Field Conference, Energy resources of the Piceance Creek Basin, Colorado: p. 47–55.

Obradovich, J. D. and Cobban, W. A., 1976, A time scale for the Late Cretaceous of the Western Interior of North America: Geological Association of Canada Special Paper 13, p. 31–54.

Obradovich, J. D., Mitschler, F. E., and Bryant, Bruce, 1969, Potassium-argon ages bearing on igneous and tectonic history of the Elk Mountains and vicinity, Colorado—A preliminary report: Geological Society of America Bulletin, v. 80, p. 1749–1756.

Pipiringos, G. N. and Rosenlund, G. C., 1977, Preliminary geologic map of the White Rock Quadrangle, Rio Blanco and Moffat Counties, Colorado: U.S. Geological Survey Miscellaneous Field Studies Map MF-837.

Pitman, J. K., 1979, Isopach, structure contour, and resource maps of the R-6 oil-shale zone, Green River Formation, Piceance Creek Basin, Colorado: U.S. Geological Survey Miscellaneous Field Studies Map MF-1069.

Pitman, J. K. and Donnell, J. R., 1973, Potential shale-oil resources of a stratigraphic sequence above the Mahogany zone, Green River Formation, Piceance Creek Basin, Colorado: Journal of Research, U.S. Geological Survey, v. 1, p. 467–473.

Pitman, J. K. and Johnson, R. C., 1978, Isopach, structure contour, and resource maps of the Mahogany oil-shale zone, Green River Formation, Piceance Creek Basin, Colorado: U.S. Geological Survey Miscellaneous field Studies Map MF-958.

Robb, W. A. and Smith, J. W., 1974, Mineral profile of oil shales in Colorado core hole No. 1, Piceance Creek Basin, Colorado: Rocky Mountain Association of Geologists Guidebook, 25th Field Conference, Energy resources of the Piceance Creek Basin, Colorado: p. 91–100.

Surdam, R. C. and Stanley, K. O., 1979, Lacustrine sedimentation during the culminating phase of Eocene Lake Gosiute, Wyoming (Green River Formation): Geological Society of America Bulletin, v. 90, p. 93–110.

Tweto, O., 1975, Laramide (Late Cretaceous-early Tertiary) orogeny in the southern Rocky Mountains: Geological Society of America Memoir 144, p. 1–43.

Zapp, A. D. and Cobban, W. A., 1960, Some Late Cretaceous strand lines in northwestern Colorado and northeastern Utah: U.S. Geological Survey Professional Paper 400-B, p. B246–B249.

RIO BLANCO OIL SHALE COMPANY TRACT C-a, RIO BLANCO COUNTY, COLORADO: SUMMARY OF GEOLOGY AND CURRENT DEVELOPMENT

E. A. ZIEMBA
Rio Blanco Oil Shale Company
Aurora, Colorado 80014

STRATIGRAPHY

A generalized stratigraphic column of Tertiary Eocene rocks in the Piceance Creek basin is shown in Figure 1. The column makes no attempt to maintain vertical scale representative of individual stratigraphic unit thicknesses. Its primary function is to portray the relative stratigraphic positions of the basin's major and minor Eocene units, the position of the basin's main oil-shale interval within the Parachute Creek Member, Green River Formation, and the oil-shale interval as defined at Tract C-a. Also shown are key markers, both lithologic and electric log, which are important in oil-shale stratigraphic correlations.

Figure 2 is a southwest-northeast stratigraphic cross section across Tract C-a utilizing oil-grade logs of three of the 27 coreholes drilled on the tract. It is oriented approximately normal to depositional or isopach strike of the main oil-shale interval of the Parachute Creek Member. The section portrays the tract's principal stratigraphic oil-shale characteristics, including the positions of four key electric log markers (A- and B- grooves, Blue and Orange markers) and two key lithologic markers (Mahogany marker and Mahogany bed). These six stratigraphic markers are not only areally persistent within Tract C-a but also throughout most of the Piceance Creek basin.

The oil-shale zonation established by Rio Blanco Oil Shale Company within Tract C-a also is shown on the cross section of Figure 2. It is based on a zonation first established by the U.S. Geological Survey within the main oil-shale interval (A-groove to Blue marker) on a regional scale. The Rio Blanco zonation expands that of the U.S. Geological Survey stratigraphically above and below the main oil-shale interval resulting in 19 discrete oil-shale zones; 9 relatively rich and 10 relatively lean. These zones are designated L-00 through L-8 in stratigraphically ascending order with the alternating rich and lean zones identified "R" and "L", respectively. However, the Mahogany and A-groove (AG) zonal nomenclature is retained because of their well-established usage.

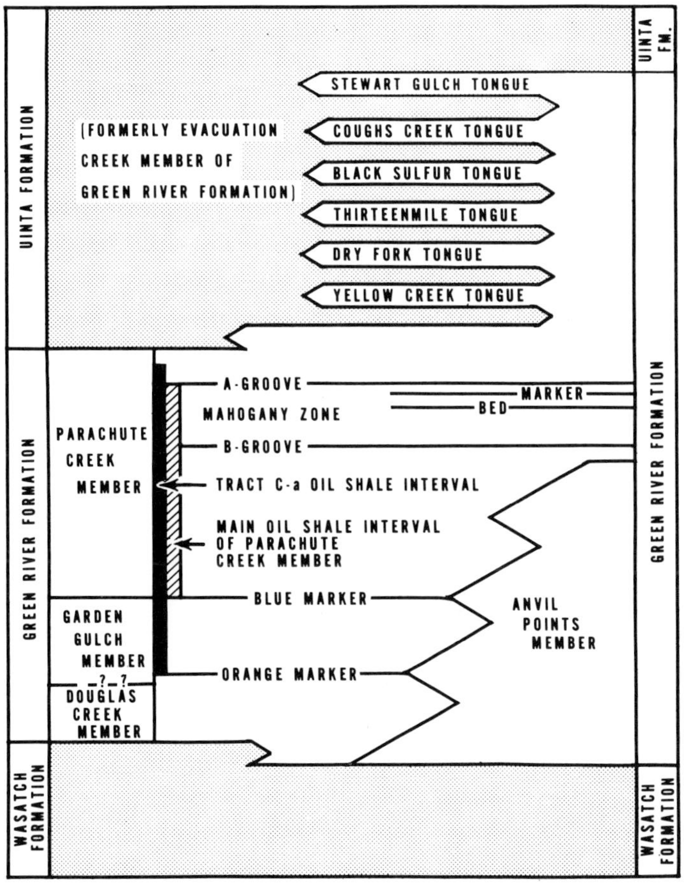

STRUCTURE

The regional setting of Tract C-a within the Piceance Creek basin is shown in Figure 3. The tract (approximately 5,100 acres) is situated on the basin's west flank where regional dip is basinward generally to the east and northeast.

Figure 4 portrays Tract C-a structure based on photogeologic mapping, surface geologic mapping and subsurface corehole and well control. The horizon mapped is the middle of the A-groove, the key electric log marker immediately above the Mahogany zone shown on the cross section of Figure 2 (corehole CE 702 log). In general, beds within the tract strike to the north and northwest and dip gently basinward to the east and northeast at slopes of 2–4° (37–66 m/km) except where locally disturbed by folds and faults.

The structural framework of Tract C-a is dominated by the low-relief southeast-plunging Sulfur Creek anticlinal nose and three en echelon grabens (fault systems) on its northeast flank. The trends of these grabens are all parallel or subparallel to the Sulfur Creek anticlinal axis. The northernmost graben is the most structurally complex of the three with up to 71 m of displacement mapped at the surface where it crosses Corral Gulch. Several minor folds and subsidiary faults complete the structural framework. All faults thus far mapped are high angle to vertical.

RESOURCES

A total of 27 coreholes have been drilled on Tract C-a to define its resources. Combined, these coreholes have yielded some 9900 m of core.

Shale Oil

The entire oil-shale interval underlying Tract C-a (L-8 zone through L-00 zone of Figure 2) increases in both thickness and grade across the tract basinward to the northeast. It averages 370

Figure 1. Generalized stratigraphic column of Tertiary Eocene series, Piceance Creek basin.

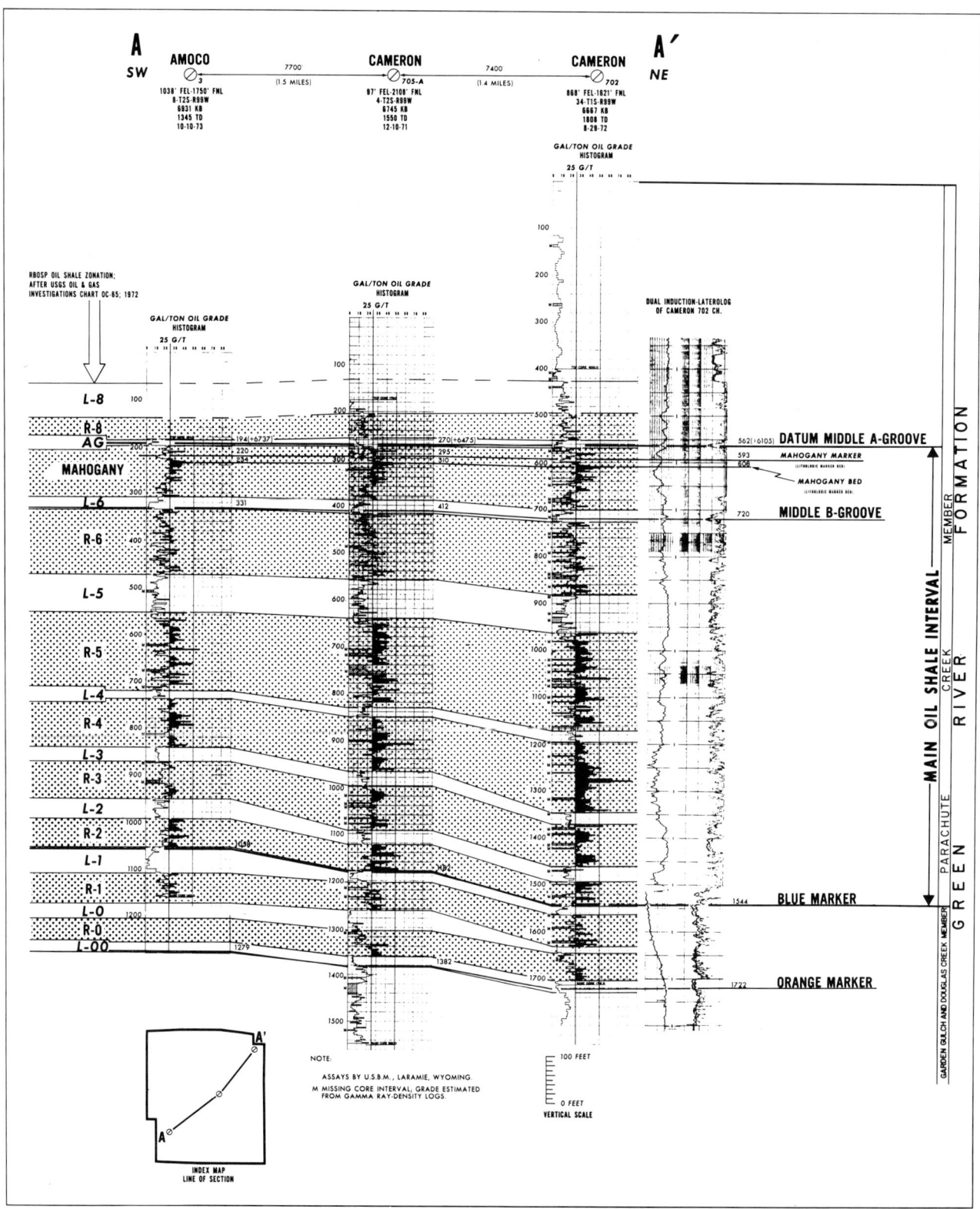

Figure 2. Southwest-northeast stratigraphic cross section, Tract C-a.

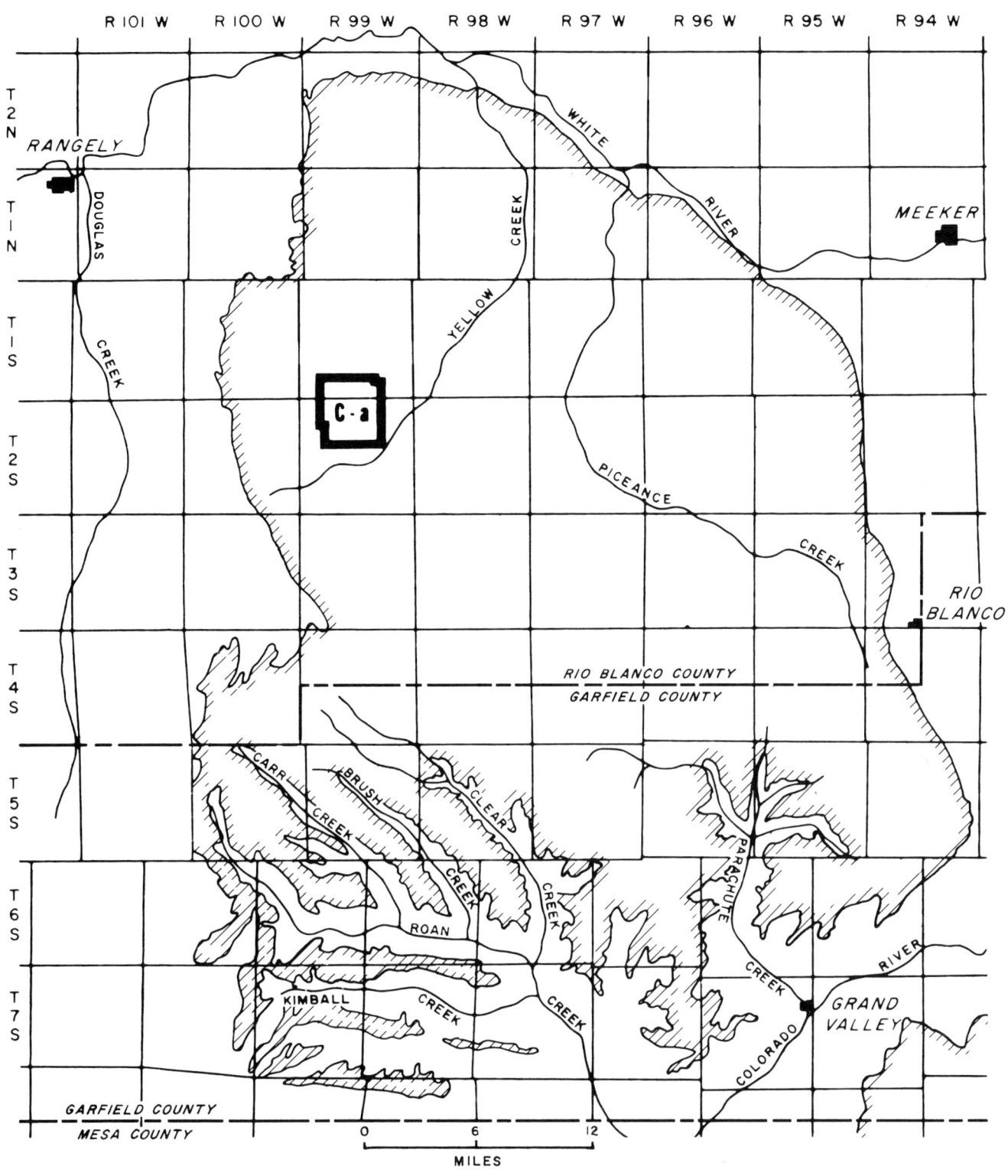

Figure 3. Regional map, Piceance Creek basin.

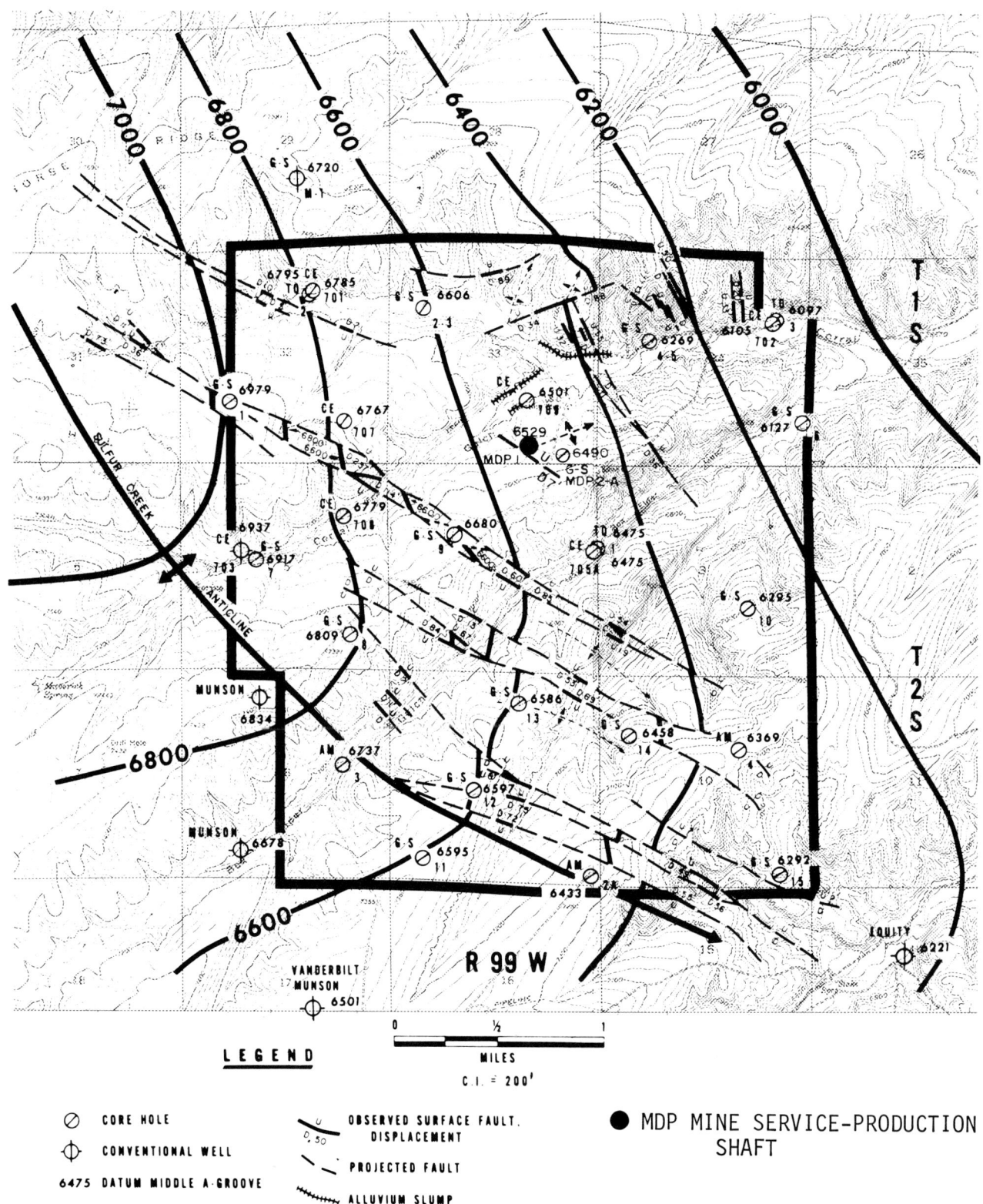

Figure 4. Tract C-a middle A-groove structure map; contours and elevations in feet.

m in thickness and 20.5 G/T oil in grade, and contains 9.1 billion barrels of shale oil in place. Overburden atop this interval averages 102 m in thickness. To put that shale grade into some perspective, a block of 20.5 G/T shale the size of an average office desk weighs 3.2 tons (2900 kg) and contains about 1.6 barrels of shale oil. In more familiar oil-field terminology, 20.5 G/T is equivalent to about 1,500 barrels of oil per acre-foot.

Of the total in-place resource of 9.1 billion barrels, about 80 percent, or 7.3 billion barrels, are contained within the main oil-shale interval (Mahogany through R-2 zones of Figure 2). This interval averages 270 m in thickness and 23.2 G/T in grade with an average overburden thickness of 144 m.

Recoverable shale oil at Tract C-a is highly dependent upon the method of development applied. Three methods have been considered by Rio Blanco Oil Shale Co., namely open-pit mining, underground mining (multi-level, room and pillar) and modified in situ. With a total in-place resource of 9.1 billion barrels, estimated recoveries for each of the three methods are as follows:

Method	Recoverable (Bill. Bbls.)	Recovery Factor (%)
Open-Pit Mining	5.2	57
Underground Mining	1.1	12
Modified In Situ (MIS)	1.7–2.5	19–27

Tract development by open-pit mining would exploit the total oil-shale interval present and result in a pit bottoming out at the base of the L-00 zone of Figure 2. Development by underground mining would be selectively confined to several of the richer oil-shale zones shown on Figure 2.

Tract developed by modified in situ methods (MIS) includes surface retorting of oil shale mined out in the preparation of underground retorts. The lower recovery values listed above reflect initial development of about the upper two-thirds of the total oil-shale interval (top R-8 through base R-4 zones of Figure 2). The higher values include potential additional recoveries in a second phase of development in which the lower one-third of the total shale interval might be exploited.

Of the three methods of development considered, open-pit mining clearly would result in the greatest shale-oil recovery at Tract C-a. This was the approach submitted in Rio Blanco's original 1976 detailed development plan. However, the plan called for off-tract lands for both the processing plant and spent-shale disposal. These lands were determined to be unavailable. MIS development of the tract offers the next best recource recovery and this is the approach now being pursued as outlined in our 1977 revised development plan.

Dawsonite

The mineral dawsonite [$NaAl(OH)_2CO_3$], a potential source of alumina, is present within the tract's R-2 through R-5 zones (fig. 2). It occurs as microscopic crystals finely disseminated throughout the oil shale and as thin laminations along bedding planes. About 360 million tons of dawsonite are estimated to be present under Tract C-a, containing about 125 million tons of alumina. Recoverable dawsonite has yet to be determined.

Nahcolite

The mineral nahcolite ($NaHCO_3$), a potential source of soda ash, is present within the tract in very minor amounts scattered throughout several of the oil-shale zones. It occurs as thin beds, stringers, nodules and crystal coatings on vug walls and on shale partings. Most of the nahcolite originally deposited within Tract C-a has been subsequently removed by groundwater leaching (dissolution). Its current very limited presence precludes its designation as a significant tract resource.

DEVELOPMENT

Rio Blanco Oil Shale Co. is currently in the modular development phase of MIS development of Tract C-a. The objectives of this phase are to gain operating experience, improve process efficiency and define capital and operating costs for a commercial-sized operation, termed the commercial phase. This development program consists of the sequential preparation and burn of three relatively small MIS retorts, the third and largest of which is 18 m × 45 m × about 120 m high as presently designed. The burn of the last retort in this phase is scheduled for completion in early 1982. Total shale oil to be produced from these three retorts is estimated at about 50,000 barrels. In the commercial phase, somewhat larger MIS retorts are envisioned. Coupled with surface retorting of mined-out shale, production of 76,000 barrels of shale oil per day is tentatively scheduled.

In basic terms, shale-oil production by the MIS method utilizes established mining methods to develop underground chambers whose function is essentially identical to conventional surface retorts. A fraction of each chamber's total contained shale volume is first drawn (excavated) to obtain a pre-designed void volume or porosity. The chamber's remaining shale volume is then fragmented by drilling and blasting. The resulting porous rubblized shale mass within the chamber is then retorted in place.

Based on a recently completed extensive review of MIS technology, Rio Blanco has made substantial changes in its originally designed modular development program. Figure 5 is an isometric drawing which shows the *previous* program and its mine plan to develop and burn five relatively small MIS retorts. These retorts ranged in size from 9 m × 9 m × 42 m high to 30 m × 30 m × about 120 m high. An extensive mine network consisting of seven levels (A through G) was required to develop the five retorts.

The *current* modular development program is shown in the isometric drawing of Figure 6. This new program reduces the number of MIS retorts from five to three and the number of mine levels to prepare and burn them from seven to two.

In the current modular development program, the preparation and burn of the three retorts is actually accomplished from both the mine and the surface. The drawn or excavated fraction of each retort is removed via the mine's G Level. The remaining fraction is then rubblized using blastholes drilled from the surface. Retort burn is initiated by a downhole burner lowered to the top of the retort from the surface. Fluids produced from each retort are conveyed via G Level for pumping to the surface. Sub-E Level surrounds the three MIS retorts and serves as a drainage gallery for upper aquifer groundwater. This level is positioned just below the base of the upper aquifer and longholes drilled from it upward into the aquifer are designed to dewater the entire three-retort area. The level's objective is to virtually "dry out" the retort line and prevent any upper aquifer water from flowing into the retorts to preclude their burn.

As previously described, the currently planned commerical phase of Tract C-a development consists of shale-oil production from both MIS retorting (underground) and surface retorting. Even if MIS retorting is successful, an efficient surface retorting method is needed to process the substantial quantities of oil shale mined out during the preparation of large-scale MIS retorts. Should MIS retorting be unsuccessful for any reason, then an efficient surface

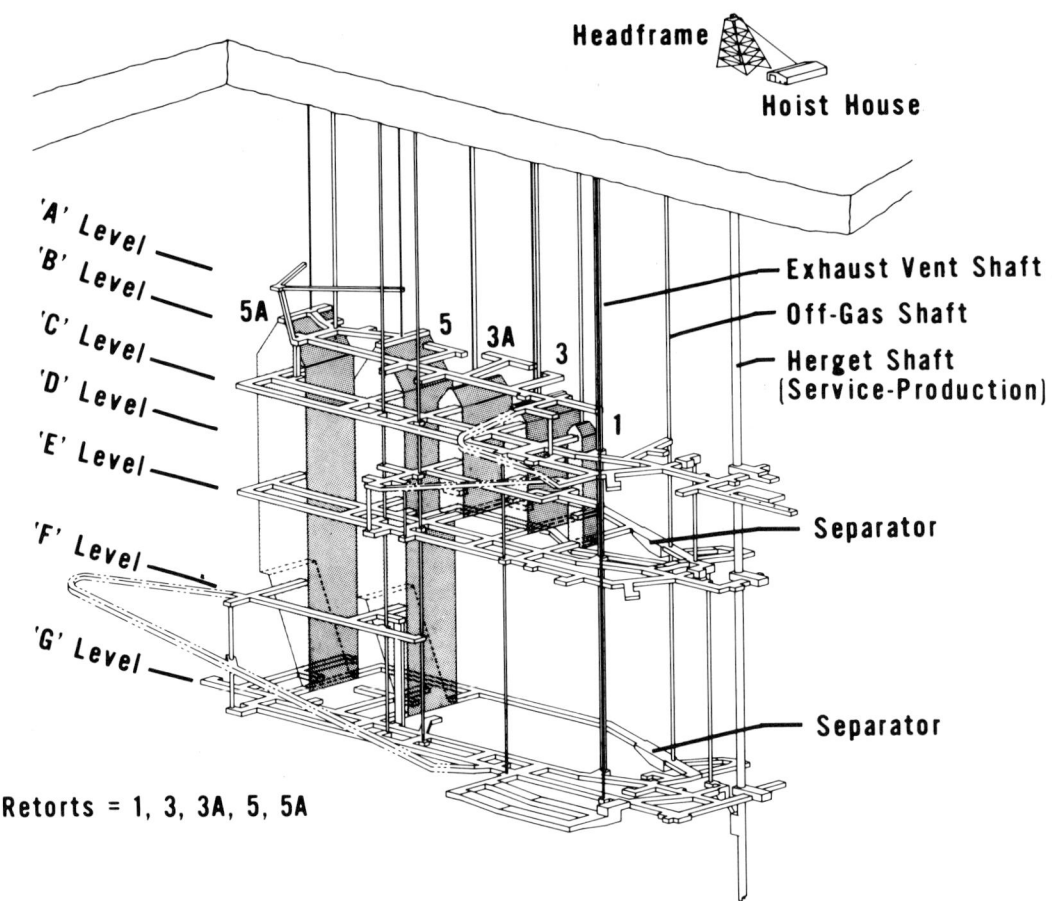

Figure 5. Modular development program, previous plan.

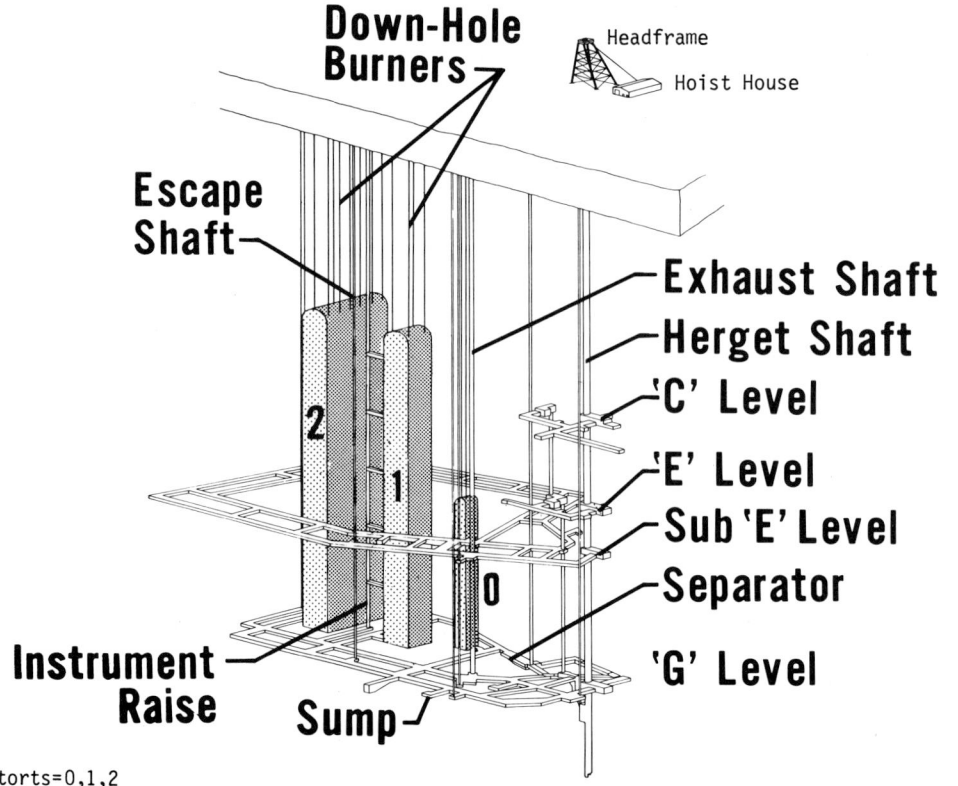

Figure 6. Modular development program, current plan.

retorting process is still critical as an integral part of alternative methods of tract development (open-pit or underground mining). Optimum surface retorting is therefore critical to any commercial development of the tract.

To determine the optimum surface retorting method for use at Tract C-a, Rio Blanco extensively reviewed several technologies and selected the Lurgi-Ruhrgas (L-R) process as the most promising. Planning is now underway for the construction of a 4,400 T/D L-R modular demonstration retort. Shale feed for the retort will be provided from both the underground MIS mine and a small open pit located near the northwest corner of the tract.

Lastly, the MIS method of shale-oil production on a commerical scale at Tract C-a has great potential but is recognized as risky at this point in time. Many questions related to its technical and economic feasibility require answers based on hard data. Rio Blanco Oil Shale Co. has committed over $90 million to the current modular development program to provide those answers.

Lizard Canyon monocline, forming part of northeastern border of Colorado National Monument. Looking southeastward across mouth of Lizard Canyon from southeasternmost loop of Rim Rock Drive just before it ascends Fruita Canyon. Strata range from upper Triassic Chinle Formation at lower right beneath sharp upper bend to upper Jurassic Morrison Formation forming gentle lower bend at left middle. Grand Mesa forms left skyline. From color photograph by S. W. Lohman, U.S. Geological Survey.

COMPARATIVE PETROLOGY OF TERTIARY SANDSTONES OF SOUTHERN PICEANCE CREEK BASIN, COLORADO

ALLAN M. OCHS
Southland Royalty, 410 17th Street, Suite 1000
Denver, Colorado 80202

REX D. COLE
2921 F ½ Road
Grand Junction, Colorado 81501

INTRODUCTION

Comparative petrographic analyses of channel-form and tabular sandstone bodies in the upper Wasatch Formation (Paleocene-Eocene) and lower Green River Formation (Eocene) in the southern Piceance Creek basin show that compositional and textural variability reflects the environment of deposition.

Sandstones from the sampled intervals are generally similar in texture and composition but have varying concentrations of (1) angular to well-rounded monocrystalline quartz grains, some with abraded overgrowths; (2) fresh and slightly altered potassic and sodic feldspars; and (3) volcanic-lithic fragments, mostly andesite. Wasatch sandstones generally contain slightly more lithic fragments than those of the Green River, which are more quartzose. The difference is attributed to the fluvial mode of deposition recognized in the Wasatch Formation which contrasts with the marginal-lacustrine nature of the sampled portion of the Green River Formation. Lacustrine sandstone also commonly contains accessory analcime and pyrite.

Paleocurrent data suggest a south, southwest, and southeasterly source for the lower Tertiary sediment. Petrographic evidence further suggests that the source terranes were compositionally consistent during the development of the lake and that the sediment was primarily derived from Mesozoic and Paleozoic sedimentary rocks and early Cenozoic silicic volcanics and intrusives.

This paper describes lacustrine and fluvial sandstones of the Wasatch and Green River Formations as they outcrop at several localities along the southern margin of the Piceance Creek basin. The description combined with petrographic analyses of thin-sectioned samples provide a basis for determining the provenance of the sand, as well as a crude comparison of compositional and textural features that resulted from differences in depositional processes.

Sandstones in marginal lacustrine settings in the Wasatch and Green River Formations are proven reservoirs for significant hydrocarbon reserves in the Uinta and Piceance Creek basins. Altamont–Bluebell field in the northern part of the Uinta Basin is a major field discovery with an estimated ultimate recovery of 250 million barrels (40 billion liters) (Lucas and Drexler, 1975). The trapping mechanism is stratigraphic in nature, comprising stacked lacustrine and fluvial sandstone bodies that are sealed by an updip prograding sequence of alluvial facies composed of red siltstones, shales, and sandstones. Similar traps are found in the Piceance Creek basin, although not as large as Altamont–Bluebell. Although the producing sandstones are fractured, production is greater from lacustrine sandstones than from fluvial sandstones. This sugests that lacustrine and fluvial sandstone porosity and permeability may be related to compositional and textural modifications of the sediment during deposition.

METHODS

Four sections were described and sampled in the southern portion of Piceance Creek basin (fig. 1): 1) Douglas Pass, on the Douglas Creek arch, 2) Red Pinnacle on the southwest edge of the basin, 3) Parachute Creek on the southeast margin of the basin, and 4) Rio Blanco along the eastern edge of the basin. Sampling was commonly restricted to the uppermost 50 m of the Wasatch Formation and from all sandstone-bearing members or facies in the lower part of the Green River Formation.

Outcrop descriptions provided information on sandstone body geometry; type, size and orientation of sedimentary structures; and lithologic sequence. Textural and compositional attributes of the sandstone were determined quantitatively from thin-sectioned samples. Average framework grain size was determined by measuring the apparent long axes of twenty-five grains per thin section. The relative amount of framework grains, matrix ($<30\mu$) minerals, cement, and porosity were assessed with two hundred counts per thin section. Framework grain mineralogy was evaluated by three hundred counts per thin section. Ten thin sections were randomly chosen and recounted confirming the reproducibility of the point count data. Approximately eighty other thin sections from samples taken from carbonate and mudrock portions of the sequence were also described.

Three sedimentary rock classifications are utilized: 1) Dunham's (1962) classification for carbonates, 2) Folk and others (1970) sandstone classification, and 3) Picard's (1971a) classification for fine-grained sedimentary rocks. Sedimentary structures were described in terms of their type, size, and orientation and directional data gathered from these were grouped into primary, secondary, and tertiary intervals using an adaptation of Tanner's (1959) technique developed by High and Picard (1972).

GEOLOGIC FRAMEWORK

The Piceance Creek basin is a structural basin that has been uplifted to a broad plateau (Donnell, 1961a, p. 835). Several structural features surround the basin: the Axial Basin uplift in the north, the White River uplift on the east, the Elk and West Elk mountains on the southeast and south respectively, the Uncompahgre uplift on the southwest, and the Douglas Creek arch on the west. Laramide development of these structures controlled the formation of the basin while post-Laramide, probably Pliocene, movement of the structures has resulted in the basin's present configuration (Murray and Haun, 1974, p. 33). The basin is asymmetrical with gently dipping limbs on the south and west, and steeply dipping limbs on the north and east (Donnell, 1961a). The axis of the basin trends northwest to southeast with a maximum depositional thickness located twelve kilometers northwest of Rio Blanco, Colorado (Smith, 1974). Tertiary rocks in the basin comprise alluvial, deltaic,

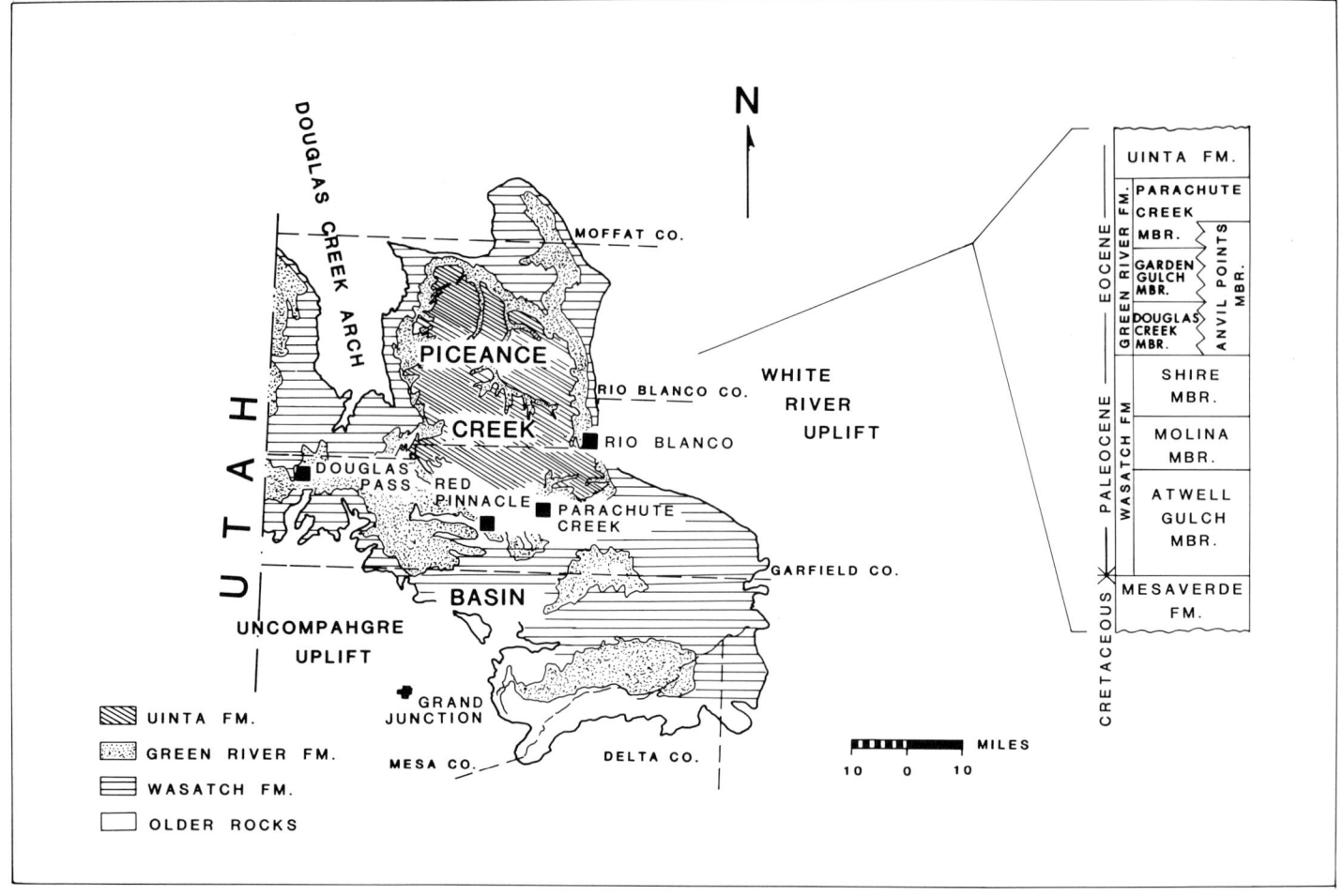

Figure 1. Geologic and location map of the Piceance Creek basin.

and lacustrine deposits of the Wasatch, Green River, and Uinta formations. The Tertiary rocks overlie thick Cretaceous sandstones and shales of the Mesaverde Group.

The Laramide Orogeny (Late Cretaceous–Eocene) in the southern Rocky Mountains was characterized by uplift of previously uplifted and eroded Paleozoic highlands and volcanic and igneous intrusive activity. From Late Cretaceous through Eocene, the Piceance Creek basin served as a catchment basin for both the eroded detritus of previously deposited sedimentary rocks and sediment derived from the volcanics, intrusives, and airfall pyroclastics. Initial sedimentary deposits were largely alluvial in nature, as illustrated by the Wasatch Formation. Extensive floodplains with northwestward flowing drainages were developed in contrast to the previous eastward flowing drainages of the underlying Mesaverde Group (McDonald, 1972, p. 254). Subsidence during the Eocene and formation of the Axial Basin anticline to the north restricted drainages which resulted in ponding and deposition of the lacustrine-dominated Green River Formation. Expansion of Lake Uinta during a supposed humid period of the Eocene merged the lakes of the Uinta and Piceance Creek basins across the Douglas Creek arch (Bradley, 1931; Cashion, 1967; Donnell, 1961a; Roehler, 1974). The lake was ultimately infilled, as recorded in the rocks of the Uinta Formation. Infilling and desiccation may have been initiated by the cutoff of inflowing drainages or a shift to a more arid climatic regime.

STRATIGRAPHY

The Wasatch Formation is the thickest Tertiary unit in the basin, thickening from approximately 120 m at Douglas Pass to more than 1700 m in the basin interior (Donnell, 1961a, p. 846). In the southern portion of the basin, Donnell (1961b, 1969) divided the formation into three members: (1) the Atwell Gulch Member at the base, (2) the Molina Member, and (3) the Shire Member at the top. However, farther basinward, these divisions become less distinct. Location of the Paleocene–Eocene contact within the Wasatch Formation is uncertain. Paleocene leaves and vertebrates have been found in the basal portion of the Atwell Gulch Member while Eocene mammal remains have been found in the Shire Member (Donnell, 1969, p. 13). The intervening Molina Member has not yielded fossil evidence to suggest an age. The Atwell Gulch Member varies from 200 m to 600 m in thickness and is composed of gray lenticular sandstone and siltstone, carbonaceous shale and thin lignite beds. The upper portion of the member consists of lenticular brown sandstone, variegated gray and red claystone, rare thin nonmarine limestone beds, and carbonaceous shale and lignite (Donnell, 1969). The Molina Member is a wedge of brown, thickly bedded, fine- to coarse-grained sandstones with some red and gray variegated claystone partings attaining a thickness of nearly 150 m (Donnell, 1969, p. 11). Basinward the member grades into siltstone and red and gray variegated claystone. The Shire Member is the uppermost and thickest member of the Wasatch

Formation. The member comprises purple and red claystones and some brown lenticular sandstones that intertongue with and are partial chronologic equivalents to the Douglas Creek Member of the Green River Formation (Donnell, 1969, p. 12). Thicknesses in excess of 1200 m are reported along the western margin of the White River uplift.

The Green River Formation conformably overlies and intertongues with the Wasatch Formation. The formation consists of fluvial-deltaic and lacustrine rocks thickening eastward from 300 m at Douglas Pass to more than 900 m in the center of the basin. Four members are recognized in the Green River Formation in this basin: (1) the basal Douglas Creek Member, (2) the Garden Gulch Member, (3) the Parachute Creek Member, and (4) the Anvil Points Member. Bradley (1931) initially described the first three members and Donnell (1953) later described the Anvil Points Member along the eastern margin of the basin. The Anvil Points Member is supposedly stratigraphically equivalent to the Douglas Creek and Garden Gulch Members and the lower portion of the Parachute Creek Member.

Roehler (1974) found the type sections of the Douglas Creek and Garden Gulch members described by Bradley (1931) to be largely temporal equivalents. The type Garden Gulch Member is now incorporated into the redefined Parachute Creek Member which includes all rocks between the black, flaky oil shale of the new Garden Gulch Member and the overlying Uinta Formation (Roehler, 1974). The Parachute Creek Member consists of fluvial-deltaic and lacustrine rocks including the rich oil shale and evaporite deposits of the basin interior.

The Uinta Formation occurs as an erosional remnant over most of the Piceance Creek Basin, attaining a maximum thickness of 450 m. The formation consists of marlstone, oil-shale, medium- to coarse-grained sandstone with some marlstone, and siltstone partings (Juhan, 1965; Cashion and Donnell, 1974; Ochs, 1978). The rocks in this unit represent the contraction and ultimate infilling of Lake Unita. The abundant reworked pyroclastics in the rocks were derived from a north-northeasterly source (Cashion and Donnell, 1974, p. 7).

SEDIMENTOLOGY

Rock sequences in both the Wasatch and Green River formations represent fluvial and lacustrine depositional processes. This was recognized by the earliest of workers in the region, W. H. Bradley (1931). However, not until recently have lithofacies been identified and assigned to specific depositional settings. In the Uinta basin, Ryder and others (1976) recognized three major lithofacies: 1) open lacustrine, 2) marginal lacustrine, and 3) alluvial. Each of the lithofacies is made of localized depositional settings in which a characteristic rock type dominates the rock sequence. In this order the major lithofacies form a progression from a core of open lacustrine oil shale and carbonate surrounded by marginal lacustrine sandstone, shale, and marlstone which in turn is haloed by sandstones, siltstones, shales and conglomerates of the outermost alluvial facies. The successive facies halos are characterized by increased abundance of clastic sediments, less carbonate, and a chemical change from reducing to oxidizing conditions toward the basin margin. In the adjoining Piceance Creek basin Roehler (1974) (fig. 2) identified ten depositional settings: 1) mountain front or pediment, 2) red-bed fluvial, 3) non-red-bed fluvial, 4) fresh-

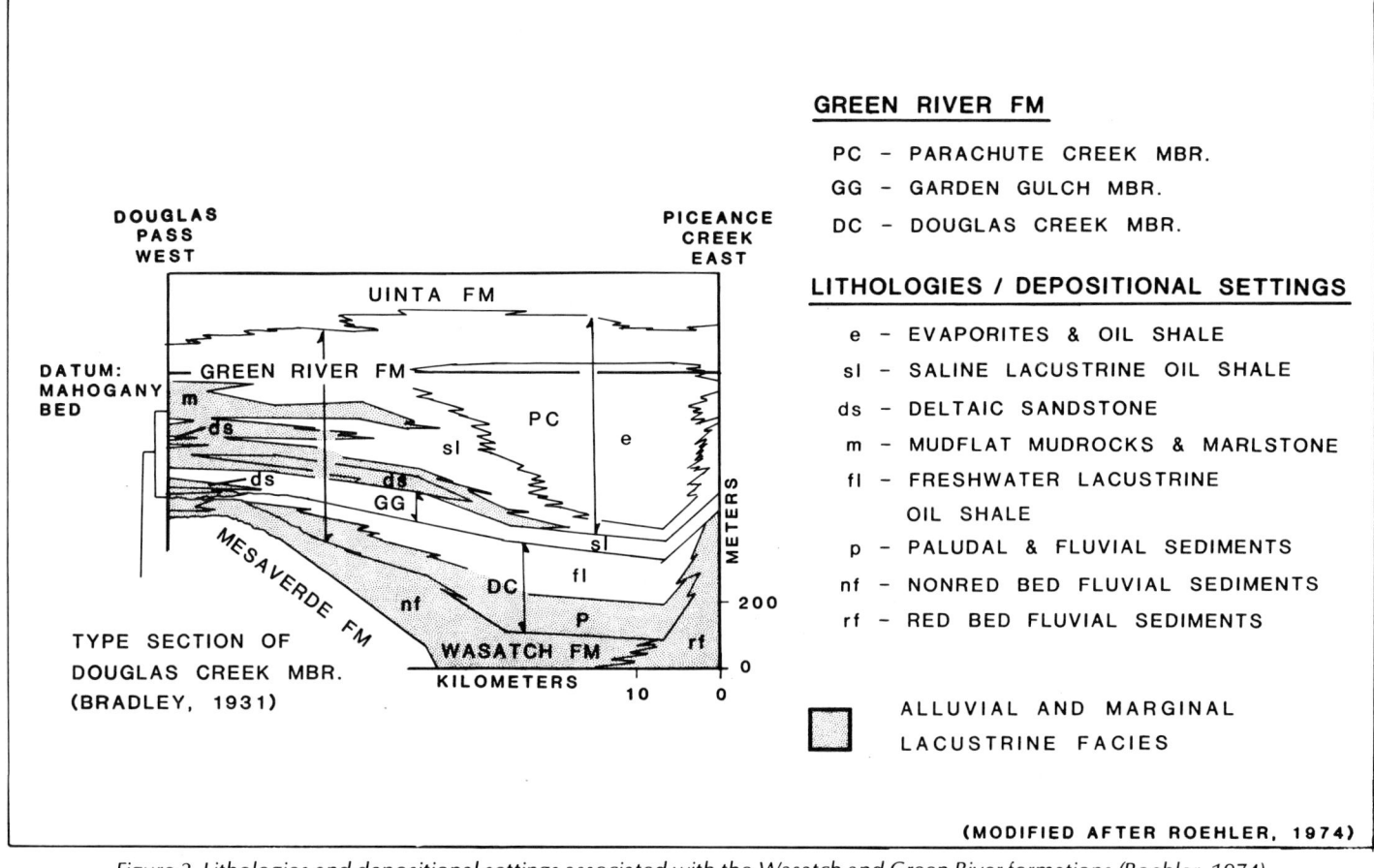

Figure 2. Lithologies and depositional settings associated with the Wasatch and Green River formations (Roehler, 1974).

water pond, 5) swamp or paludal, 6) shoreline or littoral, 7) freshwater lacustrine, 8) saline lacustrine, 9) mudflat, and 10) evaporite. Although differently named, this sequence of facies is similar to those described by Ryder and others (1976) and characterizes similar changes in depositional processes.

Marginal lacustrine facies represent an interface between fluvial and lacustrine processes which is manifested in the texture and compositon of the sandstones. Differentiating lacustrine from fluvial sandstone can be accomplished on the basis of the sandstone body geometry, sedimentary structures, and associated lithologies. Criteria for recognition of these sandstone types were developed largely by Picard and High (1970, 1972, 1972a) in portions of the Uinta basin. Although the criteria specifically referred to the P. R. Springs area of the southern Uinta basin, some features can be extrapolated to the rocks examined and discussed herein. Picard and High (1970) found that fluvial sandstone of the Wasatch Formation and the Douglas Creek Member of the Green River Formation to be lenticular and channel-form with erosional bases. The channel-fill deposits are made up of a fining-upward sequence commonly with a basal channel lag. Common sedimentary structures include abundant trough cross-stratification, parting lineations, and horizontal stratification. Lacustrine sandstones from the Douglas Creek Member are tabular, more laterally persistent (several kilometers) with flat or slightly undulatory bases (Picard and High, 1970, p. 16). Associated sedimentary strucutres include horizontal stratification, asymmetric ripple bedding, low-angle trough cross stratification (thinner than those measured in the fluvial sandstones), and some disturbed bedding (Picard and High, 1970, p. 16). Another attribute of lacustrine sandstone bodies, is the associated algal, oolite, and ostracode-bearing beds. Similar characteristics were also observed in the lacustrine sandstones of the Parachute Creek Member at Raven Ridge in the northeastern Uinta basin (Picard and High, 1972a).

LOCAL SECTIONS

At the four measured and sampled sections, the Wasatch Formation consists of gray and red variegated shale and siltstone and gray to white channel-form and lenticular sandstone. The sandstones were deposited as channel-fill, point bar, and overbank deposits. The presence of red shales suggests that the depositional setting was well drained leading to oxidation of the iron-bearing minerals. Common sedimentary structures found within the sandstone bodies include horizontal bedding, trough cross-stratification, asymmetric ripple marks, and climbing ripples. Channel-fill deposits commonly contain lag deposits at the base grading to trough cross-stratification and ultimately to ripple and horizontal bedding. This upward sequence of structure was accompanied by a general decrease in grain size. Lenticular sand bodies were usually horizontally stratified with occasional ripple marks. The section of Wasatch Formation described at Parachute Creek is a point bar deposit that infilled a meandering channel (fig. 3).

Conformably overlying the floodplain sequences of the Wasatch

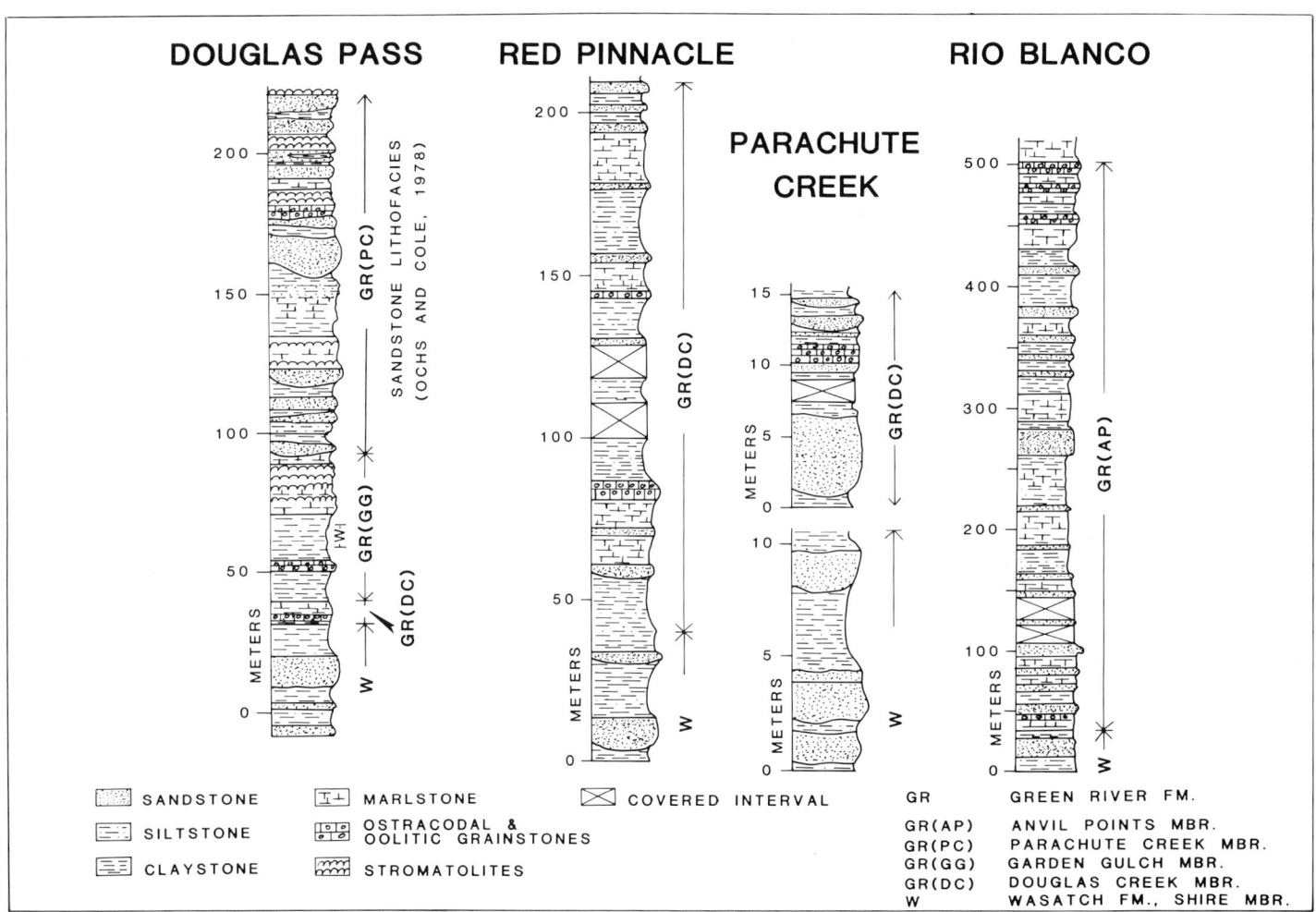

Figure 3. Measured sections from four principal localities along the southern margin of the Piceance Creek basin.

Formation at all sample localities are the various members of the lacustrine dominated Green River Formation. Sandstone-bearing marginal lacustrine facies occur in all members of the Green River Formation. At Douglas Pass the Wasatch Formation is overlain and intertongued with mudstones (dominately gray clayey siltstone and green claystone) of the Douglas Creek Member. These rocks grade upward into the more open lacustrine papery oil shale, ostracode-bearing shale, marlstone, and stromatolitic limestone, of the Garden Gulch Member (fig. 3). The Parachute Creek Member is in gradational contact with the underlying Garden Gulch Member and consists of gray sandstone (channel-form and tabular), gray to green claystone and mudstone, stromatolitic limestone, and lean oil shale. In this order, the sequence records expansion of the lake across the Douglas Creek Arch effectively merging the Uinta and Piceance Creek basins. The basal 130 m of this member comprises channel-form and tabular deltaic sandstone representing distributary channels and offshore bars respectively, of a lacustrine delta complex. Distributary channels are 1 to 2 m thick and 20 to 30 m wide (fig. 4) suggesting a low depositional gradient. Distributary channels clearly cross-cut and intertongue with underlying marlstone and claystone. The upper 50 m of this basal sandstone lithofacies (Ochs and Cole, 1978) is increasingly dominated by tabular sandstones and algal boundstones (fig. 5) indicating the influence of more open lacustrine processes.

The Douglas Creek Member of the Green River Formation at Red Pinnacle was the only sandstone-bearing member. In contrast to the proximal deltaic sandstone of the Parachute Creek Member at Douglas Pass the sandstones at Red Pinnacle suggest a more basinal position relative to distributary portions of a delta. Laterally persistent tabular sandstone and lenticular sandstone are intercalated with marlstone, ostracodal and oolitic grainstones, as well as green claystones and clayey siltstones. Sandstone bodies in the 130 m sequence seldom exceed 0.5 m thickness and are commonly ripple-bedded with nearly symmetric ripple marks. Horizontal stratification is common and occasional trough cross-stratification is encountered.

The small sampled section of the Douglas Creek Member at Parachute Creek (fig. 3) consists of channel-form and lenticular sandstone interbedded with green siltstone and claystone. The base of the channel contains rip-up clasts from the underlying gray-green shale. The stacked channel sequence is interpreted as distributary channels very proximal to the central portion of the delta lobe.

The Anvil Points Member is supposedly equivalent to most of the section described at the previous localities. At Rio Blanco (fig. 3) the member is composed of lenticular and tabular sandstone interstratified with green claystone, ostracodal and oolitic grainstones (fig. 6) and marlstone. These lithologies grade upward into saline lacustrine oil shale. The thin tabular and lenticular sandstones (<1 m thickness) belong in the distal portion of a delta where the sand is exposed to reworking by open lacustrine circulation. One small section (<30 m thickness) contains channel-form sandstone suggesting sporadic progradation of a delta.

PETROGRAPHY

Distinguishing lacustrine from fluvial sandstone on the basis of compositional and textural attributes is not a novel idea. Petrographic criteria were also developed by Picard (1976) in the P. R. Spring area of eastern Utah. In general, fluvial sandstone contains a few percent more terrigenous matrix, coarse mica, plagioclase, potassic feldspar and rock fragments than lacustrine sandstone. In contrast the lacustrine sandstones are texturally and mineralogically more mature, containing more authigenic carbonate grains,

Figure 4. Distributary channel, one of many, characterizing the "sandstone lithofacies" of the Parachute Creek Member at Douglas Pass (channel thickness approximately 1.2 m).

Figure 5. Laterally-linked hemispheroid stromotalites common in the "stromotalite lithofacies" and in the upper portion of the "sandstone lithofacies" of the Parachute Creek Member at Douglas Pass (keys for scale).

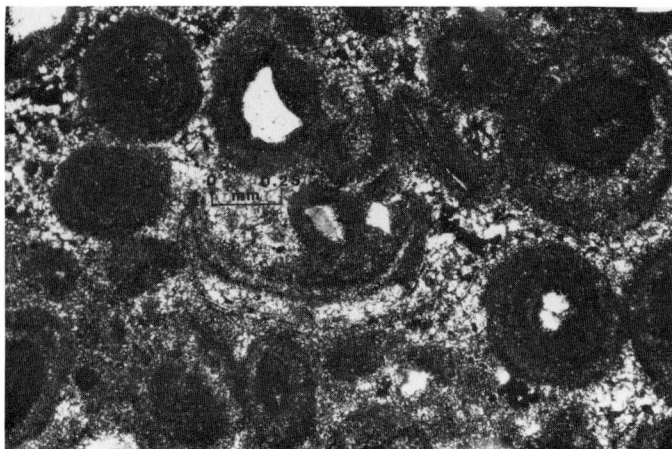

Figure 6. Photomicrograph of oolitic and ostracodal grainstone in the Anvil Points Member at Rio Blanco; also typical of other measured members of the Green River Formation.

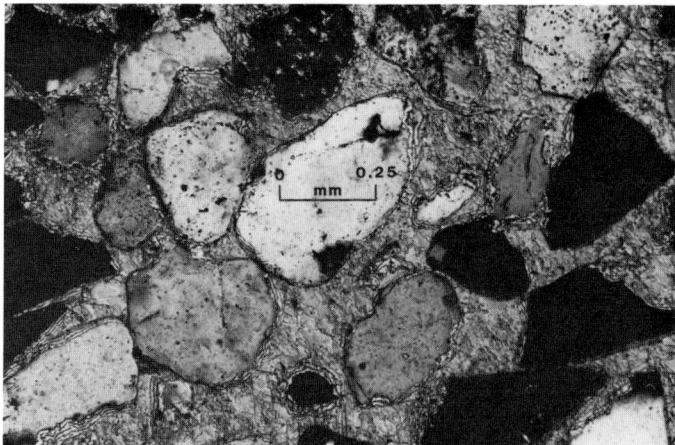

Figure 7. Photomicrograph of Douglas Creek Member sandstone from Red Pinnacle.

quartz, and accessory analcime. The common association of allochemical constituents, such as oolites, and shell fragments also characterize lacustrine sandstones.

All of the sandstone sampled in the Wasatch and Green River formations is moderately to well sorted and very fine- to medium-grained. Lacustrine sandstone in the Green River Formation tends to be fine- to very fine-grained. Comparison of the relative abundances of framework, matrix, cement, and porosity does not clearly distinguish lacustrine from fluvial sandstone. However, there is a tendency for lacustrine sandstone framework grains to be cement supported. Framework grains make up 54 to 90 percent of the sandstone.

Detrital matrix material is relatively scarce, constituting from only 1.0 to 10.0 percent of the sandstone. Three samples out of the entire sample population contained more than 15 percent matrix. Higher matrix values are usually found in the Wasatch Formation, especially at Douglas Pass where the average matrix content is 11.9 percent. Most Green River sandstone has less than 10 percent matrix, some of which is authigenic and is composed of reworked volcanic ash. At Parachute Creek there is more quartzose silt-sized material in the matrix of the Wasatch samples. In those samples of the Wasatch Formation where volcaniclastic grains make up a substantial portion of the framework mineralogy, volcanic lithic fragments are badly deformed and highly altered. This impairs the accurate discrimination of pseudomatrix from cementing agents. Devitrification of volcanic glass and the alteration of the andesite lithic fragments to analcime creates matrix material that fills in what may have been primary porosity. Surdam and Boles (1979) made similar observations in volcanic sandstones in New Zealand.

The type of cement, not the abundance, was found to be useful in distinguishing lacustrine from fluvial sandstone. Cement types and the time of cementation are critical factors in determining the resulting texture of the sandstone. There is strong correlation between lacustrine depositional settings and the occurrence of calcite as the principal cementing agent. When calcite occurs as the dominant cementing agent, the framework grains are commonly suspended in the calcite (fig. 7) suggesting early cementation or original deposition of micrite and subsequent recrystallization to spar. Silica cement is the second most abundant cement type associated with fluvial sandstone bodies. This is especially apparent in the Parachute Creek Member at Douglas Pass where calcite occurs only in tabular sandstones interstratified with oolite and ostracode grainstone beds. In contrast to the dominance of point-edge framework grain contacts of calcite-cemented sandstones, most fluvial sandstone is characterized by edge-edge contacts resulting in grain suturing as a product of pressure solution.

Quartz is the most abundant component of sandstone from the Wasatch and Green River formations averaging 56.0 and 62.0 percent, respectively. More than 95 percent of the quartz is monocrystalline "common" quartz. Most grains are angular with the remainder being rounded to subrounded. Quartz grains with quartz overgrowths are abraded (fig. 8). Polycrystalline quartz is present, in about one-third of the samples, in amounts less than 4.0 percent. The least abundant quartz variety is volcanic quartz, and it is found in amounts less than 2.0 percent.

The total feldspar content ranges from 6.3 to 45.0 percent with respective averages of 18.4 and 22.4 percent for Wasatch and Green River samples respectively. Orthoclase dominates in both formations. Plagioclase is the next most abundant feldspar variety which is followed by microcline. Orthoclase content commonly varies from 2.3 to 24.7 percent with Wasatch and Green River sandstone averaging 10.5 to 10.8 percent. Plagioclase concentrations range from 2.0 to 18.0 percent with respective averages of 5.5 and 7.8 percent for Wasatch and Green River sandstone. Anor-

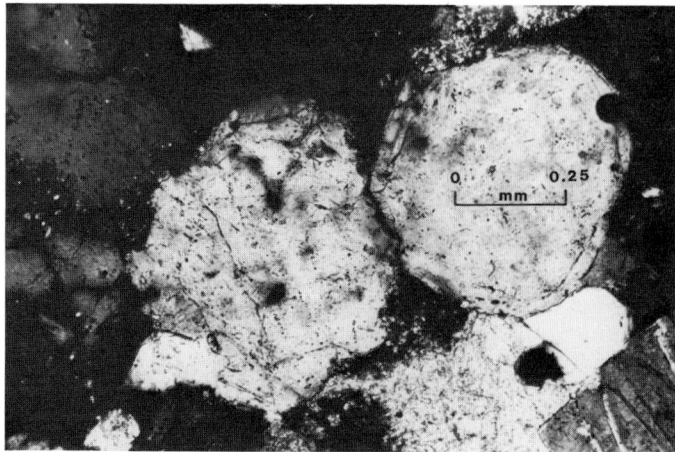

Figure 8. Photomicrograph of Wasatch Formation sandstone at Red Pinnacle but representative of many Wasatch sandstones.

thite contents of properly oriented plagioclase grains were determined using the Michel-Levy method as prescribed by Heinrich (1965). Anorthite values of plagioclase vary from AN_3 to AN_{53} (albite to andesine). Trace amounts (<1.0 percent) of sanidine are found in a few samples from both formations. Microcline content varies from 0.1 to 5.4 percent with Wasatch and Green River sandstone averaging 2.1 and 3.7 percent respectively. Feldspar grains are generally angular, however, a few grains are subangular to rounded (fig. 9).

More than 95 percent of the lithic fragments are of volcanic origin. The volcanic lithic fragments are composed of volcanic glass, andesite, and rhyolite. The remainder of the lithics are composed of claystone (possibly phyllite) fragments. Volcanic glass is the most abundant constituent of the volcanic fraction in both formations. Rhyolite and andesite grains have been distorted through compaction and subsequent alteration (fig. 9). Alteration is especially apparent in non-calcite cemented sandstones. Volcanic glass content varies from 3.3 to 37.3 percent with respective Wasatch and Green River sandstone averaging 19.1 and 10.0 percent. Andesite fragments are found in samples at all localities. Andesite concentrations range from 2.0 to 10.5 percent in Wasatch sandstone and 1.0 to 3.5 percent in Green River sandstone. Rhyolite fragments are found only in the sandstone at Parachute Creek where values vary from 0.3 to 2.7 percent with respective Wasatch and Green River sandstone averaging 0.7 to 0.3 percent.

Accessory minerals such as biotite, muscovite, analcime, and pyrite make up 0.3 to 14.0 percent of the framework grains. Mica (biotite and muscovite) content ranges from 0.3 to 8.0 percent of the framework grains with Wasatch and Green River sandstone averaging 1.3 and 1.7 percent respectively. Analcime is considered a framework mineral although it probably formed authigenically. Analcime concentrations range from 0.3 to 13.3 percent making up an average of 0.8 percent of the Wasatch framework grains and 1.6 percent of the Green River framework grains.

Allochemical constituents, such as shell fragments, oolites, and micrite chips, make up less than 5.0 percent of the framework grains and are restricted to lacustrine sandstone bodies. Oolites are concentric and commonly contain single quartz grains in their cores. Ostracode debris makes up most of the shell fragments (fig. 6). Abraded edges on some ostracode shells suggest transportation or agitation prior to deposition.

PROVENANCE

The mineralogy of framework grains in the Wasatch and Green River Formations reflect source terranes composed of (1) fine- to medium-grained clastics, (2) acid igneous intrusives, and (3) intermediate volcanics, probably andesites and rhyolites. Subangular to rounded monocrystalline quartz grains, some with abraded quartz overgrowths, indicate recycling of pre-existing sedimentary rocks, probably fine- to medium-grained sandstones. Transparent, angular, monocrystalline quartz may suggest a sedimentary origin, but this may infer an acid igneous source terrane as well. A plutonic source may also be implied from the relatively large size and freshness of the potassic and plagioclase feldspar grains. However, a feldspathic sandstone proximal to the site of deposition may have also contributed the feldspars. Volcanic lithic fragments are common constituents of the framework grain mineralogy. Although dominated by the abundance of volcanic glass, lithic fragment contents commonly contain andesite fragments. The source terrane for the volcanic material is likely andesitic in nature. The volcanic material was probably supplied to the basin directly as airfall pyroclastics.

Paleocurrent data (fig. 10) from the sample localities suggest sediment input from source areas to the southwest, south and east. A thick sequence of Mesozoic and Paleozoic clastic sedimentary rocks covered most of the area south and east of the Piceance Creek basin prior to and during the Larimide Orogeny. The clastic sediments were originally deposited in the Colorado Trough which received sediment shed from the strongly positive Uncompahgre and Front Range uplifts. King (1977) estimated Permian and Pennsylvanian thicknesses in the trough in excess of 3000 m. Erosion of the structures and exposure of the Precambrian core in the uplifts through the Permian was followed by deposition of fine-grained clastics during the Triassic, Jurassic and Lower Cretaceous. Rejuvenation of the structures along pre-existing Precambrian shear zones (Tweto, 1975) stripped much of the rock from the structures depositing the detritus in the intermontane basins. The White River uplift is an extension of the larger Sawatch

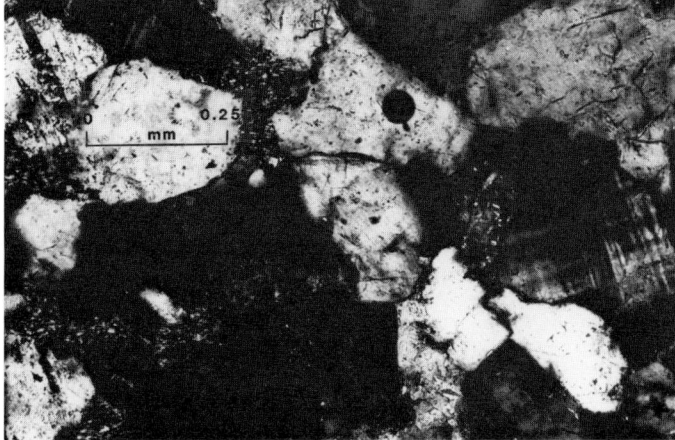

Figure 9. Photomicrograph of Douglas Creek Member sandstone from Parachute Creek.

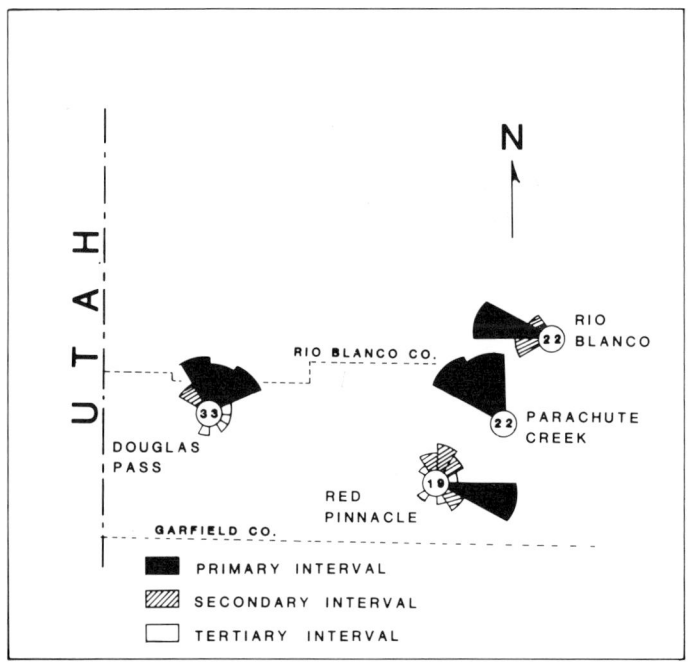

Figure 10. Paleocurrent data collected at sample localities.

uplift (McDonald, 1972; King, 1977) and was initially positive during the Paleocene. To the west, the Douglas Creek arch, an extension of the Uinta uplift (McDonald, 1972), was active prior to the Late Cretaceous which is recorded by the thinning of the Mesaverde Formation over the arch. This provided effective closure of the basin until the transgression of Lake Uinta over the arch during the Eocene.

Intrusion and volcanic activity occurred concurrently with the uplift of the surrounding areas. The presence of volcanic glass and andesitic volcanolithics in the sandstone within the basin suggest a large areal extent of this source terrane. Cenozoic volcanism and intrusive activity were generally restricted to the northeast trending Colorado Mineral Belt along the southern and eastern margin of the basin (Stevens and others, 1972). The strongest period of volcanism occurred during the Miocene (Stevens and others, 1967) in the San Juan Mountains of southern Colorado. Volcanic activity in this area during the late Cretaceous and Paleocene may also have occurred (Larsen and Cross, 1956). In the Elk and West Elk mountains intrusion was preceded by andesitic volcanism during the Paleocene (Stevens and others, 1972). Potassium-argon dating and cross-cutting internal relations of the dikes indicate emplacement at 65 to 72 million years ago (Obradovich and others, 1969). The volcanics and intrusives of the Elk and West Elk mountains probably supplied much of the lithic fragments in the sandstone units in the southern Piceance Creek basin. Although the activity may have ceased during the Paleocene, erosion of the source terrane throughout the Eocene continued to influence the composition of the sandstones. A source for the abundant volcanic ash are airfall pyroclastics which may have had their source farther north in the central Rocky Mountains. This is especially appealing when attempting to explain the source for the volcanic material in the Uinta Formation. The volcanic activity which occurred in the central Rocky Mountains; specifically the Absaroka Mountains, began in the Late Eocene (King, 1977). These centers of activity may have supplied airfall material to a rather large surrounding area.

SUMMARY

A comparison of averages of textural and compositional components of Wasatch and Green River sandstones reveals interesting though subtle differences (fig. 11) that are more than likely related to different environments of deposition. Almost all of the samples were fine- to very fine-grained, and therefore the textural and compositional attributes are not likely to be artifacts of different grain sizes.

As a group, the deltaic sandstones of the Green River Formation are texturally more mature than Wasatch sandstones. Matrix content is higher (usually 2.0 to 5.0 percent) in the floodplain-deposited Wasatch sandstones. This reflects the amount of energy applied to the sediment and the number of times the sediment has been exposed to reworking. The abundance of cement in the Green River sandstones is another criteria that distinguishes marginal-lacustrine from fluvial sandstones. Early cementation by carbonate cements in some sandstones resulted in the appearance of framework grains floating in the cement (fig. 7).

Compositional elements also reflect the relative difference in the amount of energy applied to the sediment. This is most apparent in the feldspar, lithic fragment, and quartz contents. Generally, Green River sandstone is more quartzose and feldspathic. The increased feldspar content may be an artifact of mechanical breakdown of larger feldspar grains along cleavage planes. Marginal lacustrine sandstones also contain less lithic fragments. Volcanic lithic fragments are almost the sole component of the total lithic fragment content, therefore, they are very sensitive to mechanical and chemical degradation. Quartz, being the most common framework constituent, is noticeably more abundant in marginal lacustrine sandstones, especially in those sandstone bodies further away from the active distributary portions of the delta. Fluvial sandstone quartz content is usually lower than in marginal lacustrine sandstones. Quartz overgrowths are also more common in fluvial sandstones, again reflecting the lesser total amount of energy applied to the sediment.

ACKNOWLEDGMENTS

This paper is an outgrowth of a study submitted as a master's thesis to Southern Illinois University at Carbondale. Partial financial support was provided by Sigma Xi. Acknowledgment is made to Dr. Charles F. Mansfield and Dr. Frank Ethridge for helpful criticisms in the evolution of this manuscript. Appreciation is also extended to Mr. Bill Berryman (of Southland Royalty) and Mrs. Delores Highsmith for technical expertise in drafting the figures. Finally, thanks are due to Ms. Barbara North, Ms. Sherry Westmoreland, and Ms. Debra Kleve for diligently typing the many revisions.

REFERENCES

Bradley, W. H., 1931, Origin and microfossils of the oil shale of the Green River Formation of Colorado and Utah: U.S. Geological Survey Professional Paper 168, 58 p.

Cashion, W. B., 1967, Geology and fuel resources of the Green River Formation, southeastern Uinta Basin, Utah and Colorado: U.S. Geological Survey Professional Paper 548, 48 p.

Cashion, W. B. and Donnell, J. R., 1974, Revision of nomenclature of the upper part of the Green River Formation of the Piceance Creek Basin, Colorado, and the eastern part of the Uinta Basin, Utah: U.S. Geological Survey Bulletin 1394-G, 9 p.

Donnell, J. R., 1953, Columnar section or rocks exposed between Rifle and Debeque Canyon, Colorado: Rocky Mountain Association of Geologists Guidebook, Field Conference to northwestern Colorado, facing p. 14.

Donnell, J. R., 1961a, Tertiary geology and oil shale resources of Piceance Creek Basin between the Colorado and White Rivers, northwestern Colorado: U.S. Geological Survey Bulletin 1082-L, p. 835-891.

Donnell, J. R., 1961b, Tripartition of the Wasatch Foramtion near Debeque in northwestern Colorado: U.S. Geological Professional Paper 424-B, p. B147-B148.

Donnell, J. R., 1969, Paleocene and lower Eocene units in the southern portion of the Piceance Creek Basin, Colorado: U.S. Geological Survey Bulletin 1274-M, 18 p.

Dunham, R. J., 1962, Classification of carbonate rocks according to depositional texture, in Ham, W. E., ed., Classification of Carbonate rocks: Tulsa, Oklahoma, American Association of Petroleum Geologists, p. 108-121.

Folk, R. L., Andrews, P. B., and Lewis, D. W., 1970, Detrital sedimentary rock classification and nomenclature for use in New Zealand: New Zealand Journal of Geology and Geophysics, v. 13, p. 937-968.

Heinrich, E. W., 1965, Microscopic identification of minerals: New York, McGraw-Hill, 414 p.

High, L. R. and Picard, M. D., 1972, Mathematical treatment of orientation data, in Carver, R. E., ed., Procedures in sedimentary petrology: New York, Wiley-Interscience, p. 573-596.

Juhan, J. P., 1965, Stratigraphy of the Evacuation Creek Member (Green River Formation), Piceance Creek Basin, northwestern Colorado: Mountain Geologist, v. 2, p. 123-128.

King, P. B., 1977, The evolution of North America, revised edition: Princeton, New Jersey, Princeton University Press, 197 p.

Larsen, E. S., Jr. and Cross, Whitman, 1956, Geology and petrology of the San Juan region, southwestern Colorado: U.S. Geological Survey Professional Paper 258, p. 55-58

Lucas, P. T. and Drexler, J. M., 1975, Altamont-Bluebell: A major fractured and overpressured stratigraphic trap, Uinta basin, Utah: Denver, Colorado, Rocky Mountain Association of Geologists, Symposium on Deep Drilling Frontiers in the Central Rocky Mountains, p. 265-273.

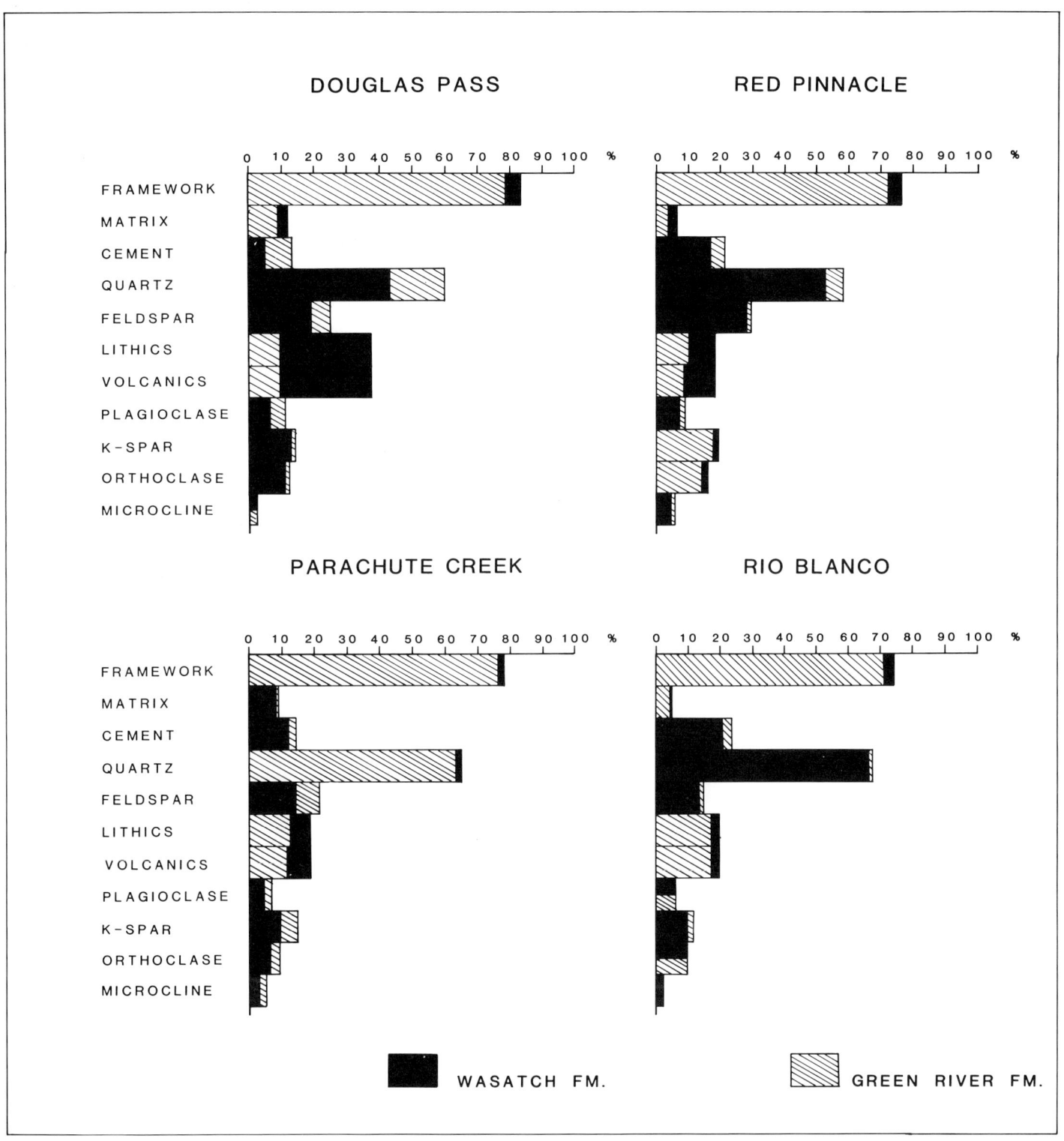

Figure 11. Comparison of averages of Wasatch and Green River sandstone textural and compositional features.

McDonald, R. E., 1972, Eocene and Paleocene rocks of the southern and central basins: Denver, Colorado, Rocky Mountain Association of Geologists, Geologic Atlas of the Rocky Mountain Region, p. 243-256.

Murray, D. K. and Haun, J. D., 1974, Introduction to the geology of the Piceance Creek Basin and vicinity, northwestern Colorado: Denver, Colorado, Rocky Mountain Association of Geologists, Energy resources of the Piceance Creek Basin, Colorado, p. 29-39.

Obradovich, J. O., Mutschler, F. E., and Bryant, B., 1969, Potassium-argon ages bearing on the igneous and tectonic history of the Elk Mountains and vicinity, Colorado—a preliminary report: Geological Society of American Bulletin, v. 80, p. 1749-1756.

Ochs, A. M., 1978, Comparative petrology of lower Tertiary sandstones, southern Piceance Creek Basin, Colorado: (M.S. thesis): Carbondale, Illinois, Southern Illinois University.

Ochs, A. M. and Cole, R. D., 1978, Depositional lithofacies of Parachute Creek Member of Green River Formation, Douglas Creek Arch, Colorado (abs.): American Association of Petroleum Geologists Bulletin, v. 62, p. 550.

Picard, M. D., 1971, Classification of fine-grained sedimentary rocks: Journal of Sedimentary Petrology, v. 41, p. 179-195.

Picard, M.D., 1971a, Petrographic criteria for recognition of lacustrine and fluvial sandstone, P. R. Spring oil-impregnated sandstone area, southeast Uinta Basin, Utah: Utah Geological and Mineralogical Survey, Special Studies 36, 24 p.

Picard, M.D. and High, L. R., Jr., 1970, Sedimentology of oil-impregnated lacustrine and fluvial sandstone, P. R. Spring area, southeast Uinta Basin, Utah: Utah Geological and Mineralogical Survey, Special Studies 33, 32 p.

Picard, M. D. and High, L. R., Jr., 1972, Paleoenvironmental reconstructions in an area of rapid facies change, Parachute Creek Member of Green River Formation (Eocene), Uinta Basin, Utah: Geological Society of America Bulletin, v. 83, p. 2689-2708.

Picard, M. D. and High, L. R., Jr., 1972a, Criteria for recognizing lacustrine rocks: in Recognition of Ancient Sedimentary Environments: Society of Economic Paleontologists and Mineralogists Special Publication 16, p. 108-145.

Robinson, Peter, 1972, Tertiary history: Denver, Colorado, Rocky Mountain Association of Geologists, Geologic Atlas of the Rocky Mountain Region, p. 233-242.

Roehler, H. W., 1974, Depositional environments of rocks in the Piceance Creek Basin, Colorado: Denver, Colorado, Rocky Mountain Association of Geologists, Energy Resources of the Piceance Creek Basin, Colorado, p. 57-64.

Ryder, R. T., Fouch, T. D., and Elison, J. H., 1976, Early Tertiary sedimentation in the western Uinta Basin, Utah: Geological Society of America Bulletin, v. 87, p. 496-512.

Smith, J. W., Beard, T. N., and Trudell, L. G., 1974, Stratigraphic framework of Green River Formation oil shales in the Piceance Creek Basin, Colorado: Denver, Colorado, Rocky Mountain Association of Geologists, Energy resources of the Piceance Creek Basin, Colorado, p. 65-69.

Steven, T. A., Mehnert, N. H., and Obradovich, J. D., 1967, Age of the volcanic activity in the San Juan Mountains, Colorado: U.S. Geological Survey Professional Paper 575-D, p. 47-55.

Steven, T. A., Smedes, H. J., Prostka, P. W., Lipman, P. W., and Christiansen, R. L., 1972, Upper Cretaceous and Cenozoic igneous rocks: Denver, Colorado, Rocky Mountain Association of Geologists, Geologic Atlas of the Rocky Mountain Region, p. 229-232.

Surdam, R. C. and Boles, J. R., 1979, Diagenesis of volcanic sandstones, in Aspects of diagenesis, Scholle, P. A. and Schluger, P. R., eds.: Society of Economic Paleontologists and Mineralogists Special Publication 26, p. 227-242.

Tanner, W. F., 1959, The importance of modes in cross-bedding data: Journal of Sedimentary Petrology, v. 29, p. 221-225.

Tweto, Ogden, 1975, Laramide (Late Cretaceous-Early Tertiary) orogeny in the southern Rocky Mountains: Geological Society of America Memoir 144, p. 1-44.

UNCERTAINTIES OF OIL-SHALE DEVELOPMENT

GLEN D. WEAVER
Department of Economics
Colorado State University
Fort Collins, Colorado 80523

INTRODUCTION

The present flurry of development activity in the Piceance Basin culminates more than sixty years of effort to commercialize the area's rich oil-shale resources (Russell, 1980). The first boom period began shortly before 1920 when dwindling supplies of domestic crude prompted the filing of 9,000 placer claims on federal oil-shale lands in the basin. Numerous companies were soon formed to exploit the deposits, on both public and private lands, but none succeeded even though the U.S. Bureau of Mines supported this early venture by operating a pilot plant near Rulison between 1925–1927. Optimism faded quickly following the discovery of large oilfields in eastern Texas.

Interest revived in 1944 when Congress passed the Synthetic Liquid Fuels Act (Matzick and others, 1966). Essentially a prototype of the Energy Security Act signed by President Carter in June 1980, this legislation authorized the construction of demonstration plants to produce synthetic fuels from oil shale, coal, agricultural crops, forestry products, and other substances. Under its authority, the Bureau of Mines established the Oil-Shale Research Laboratory at Laramie, Wyoming, and the Oil-Shale Experiment Station at Anvil Points, located about 11 km west of Rifle, Colorado. Room-and-pillar mining, surface retorting, and shale-oil refining experiments were conducted at Anvil Points until 1956.

Private research efforts also resumed in the 1950s and 1960s, first by Union Oil Company, then by Colony Development Operation, Equity Oil Company, a consortium of companies who leased the Anvil Points facility, and others (Office Tech. Assess., 1980, p. 128–153). The Department of the Interior (1968) also moved to promote development by formulating a program to lease federal oil-shale lands, but when offered in the fall of 1968, the test program drew little participation from private industry (Anonymous, 1968).

After a short lull, development activities proceeded once again, albeit not without further interruptions (Novak, 1975, 1976a). Prospects for commercialization appeared to reach an all-time high in early 1974. OPEC had increased world oil prices dramatically, the Arab oil embargo had created public awareness of the need to increase domestic energy supplies, the Paraho Development group had reopened the Anvil Points facility, and Interior's new prototype leasing program had been enthusiastically supported by private industry. The two Colorado lease tracts, C-a and C-b, had received bonus bids of $210 and $118 million, respectively, both far higher than what Interior had anticipated. Colony Development Operation, then considered to have the most advanced technology, had become leaseholder of tract C-b and also had announced plans to build a commercial facility on its Dow property at the head of Parachute Creek.

Within a few months, however, Colony unexpectedly cancelled plans for commercial production on its private lands, and in 1976 both Colony and the Rio Blanco group, operator of tract C-a, requested suspension of diligence requirements on their federal leases. All four of the Colony partners eventually withdrew from tract C-b, turning over control to Occidental Oil Shale, who had been developing a modified in-situ process at its Logan Wash site since 1972. Oxy appeared for a time to be the only company still committed to commercial production.

Currently another boom period is in full swing, with at least 7 projects in some phase of oil-shale or sodium-mineral development (Table 1). Construction and operation workforce on these projects is expected to reach 2,253 by the end of this year (Comm. on Oil Shale, 1981). Shale-oil production is targeted at about 250,000 b/d in 1990, with the possibility of additional output by Mobil Oil Company. Several projects are also ongoing in the nearby Uinta Basin of Utah (Callahan, 1981).

Table 1. Oil-shale projects in the Piceance Basin, circa March 1981

Project	Development Plans
Cathedral Bluffs Shale Oil Co. (Occidental Oil Shale, Inc., and Tenneco Shale Oil Co.)	Operator of federal lease tract C-b; presently sinking shafts for production of 55,000 b/d in 1985 using modified in-situ retorting.
Chevron Shale Oil Company	Conducting environmental baseline studies on its private lands and determining which permits are necessary; plans to construct mine and retort module, with possible production of 50,000 b/d by early 1990.
Colony Development Operation (Exxon Co., U.S.A., and Tosco Corp.)	Has acquired major permits for construction of 47,000 b/d surface retort on its private lands by 1985; also building a new community, Battlement Mesa, to house oil-shale workers.
Multi Mineral Corp.	Is developing an experimental nahcolite mine at Horse Draw in cooperation with U.S. Bureau of Mines to be used in designing a commercial mine on an existing federal sodium lease; also hopes to acquire federal lease for production of nahcolite, soda ash, alumina, and shale oil.
Occidental Oil Shale, Inc.	Operating a modified in-situ research facility on private lease lands at Logan Wash for use in developing the Cathedral Bluffs (tract C-b) property; no plans for commercial production at this site.
Rio Blanco Oil Shale Co. (Gulf Oil Corp. and Standard Oil Co. of Indiana)	Operator of federal lease tract C-a; engaged in modified in-situ demonstration program that could lead to production of 50,000 b/d by 1987; also examining proposal for open pit mine and surface retorting.
Union Oil Company	10,000 b/d module now under construction on private lands to be completed by 1983; 50,000 b/d facility using surface retorting to be onstream by 1988.

Data abstracted from Callahan (1981).

If history provides insight to the future, then current optimism regarding development must be tempered with caution. Oil shale remains a high-risk investment because of the large and possibly unreliable plant cost estimates, technical uncertainties, uncertainty of future world oil prices, and uncertainty of government support in the form of financial assistance or other incentives. A full discussion of these issues is contained in a report recently submitted to Congress by the Office of Technology Assessment (1980). Liberal use has been made of this report in the following sections.

TECHNOLOGY AND PLANT COSTS

The capital and operating costs of shale-oil production are known to be large, but just how large is still a matter of some speculation. Table 2 shows the experience of one company in estimating capital costs for a 46,000 b/d facility using underground mining and TOSCO retorting. Reasons for the tremendous escalation in plant costs include inflationary price increases, especially in the industrial sector supplying plant equipment, increased environmental regulations, and improved engineering knowledge (Office Tech. Assess., 180, p. 186–189). The large cost increase between early and late 1974, which prompted Colony Development to cancel plans for production on its Dow property, resulted primarily from more detailed evaluation of engineering design. The subsequent estimates represent updates of the late 1974 version.

First-generation developers are understandably reluctant to commit themselves to full-scale production without first proceeding through the modular phase. Past experimental activity has occurred only at the pilot-plant or semiworks level, at least for surface retorting systems, which means that scaleup by a factor of 10 or more is needed to achieve commercial output. Building a modular retort, one of several identical units that would be integrated in a commercial plant, is itself a costly enterprise, requiring an investment of several hundred million dollars (Office Tech. Assess., 1980, p. 173). The alternative is to risk significant cost overruns because of unreliable or ineffective equipment design. At present, only the Colony group appears to have enough confidence in its technology to proceed directly to full-scale production.

Early entry into commercial production conveys some benefits as well as risks. If the industry grows rapidly, then the first few plants will have contracted for a significant share of U.S. engineering, construction, and manufacturing capacity. Since carrying charges on capital investment represent almost half the unit costs of shale-oil production, project operators would be willing to bid up prices for key equipment to avoid construction delays. The resulting hyperinflation during a crash program could increase real prices by 50 percent or more (Office Tech. Assess., 1980, p. 63, 187–188).

An upward revision of plant cost estimates may also be needed if developers must underwrite part of the financial costs of community growth. Governor Lamm of Colorado has advocated raising the state's mineral severance taxes as one means of funding the socioeconomic costs of oil-shale and coal-related energy developments. So far the Republican-controlled Colorado General Assembly has resisted the governor's plea, but this could change if the financial burden on local and state government becomes too great. Large public investments will unquestionably be needed to accommodate growth in what is now an overwhelmingly rural area (Kilker, 1981; Office Tech. Assess., 1980, p. 419–473). The paucity of existing infrastructure has prompted Colony Development Operation to invest $60 million of its own money to build a new residential community for its workers (Anonymous, 1980). Other companies have aided local communities with smaller grants. How much assistance private industry may have to provide in the future, directly or through increased severance taxes, is unknown.

WORLD OIL PRICES

The strong revival of oil-shale activity over the past two years coincided with a doubling between January 1979–1980 of refinery costs for imported oil (Chase Manhattan Bank, 1979, 1980). In March 1980 the posted price of premium crude, which is the counterpart of upgraded shale oil, stood between $34 and $38 per barrel (Office Tech. Assess., 1980, p. 190). Shale oil is probably competitive within this price range, assuming that developers are willing to accept an aftertax profit of perhaps no more than 12 percent. A developer who commits nearly $2 billion to a shale-oil plant with a long payback period must be confident that future increases in production costs will lag behind the rising price of conventional crude. Chase Manhattan analysts (Emerson, 1980, p. 2) project that OPEC real prices will grow at just over 3 percent annually during the remainder of this decade, reaching an inflated $100 per barrel in 1990 or about $45 in constant 1980 dollars. Although this outlook should be encouraging to oil-shale developers, experiences of the 1970s demonstrate that production costs could escalate more rapidly than oil prices.

GOVERNMENT POLICIES

Oil-shale development occurs within an institutional framework of government policies that affect investment opportunities. Specific policies that have been criticized for delaying or discouraging investment include access to federal lands, unrealistic or uncertain environmental stipulations, bureaucratic permit requirements, lack of a coordinated national energy plan, and price controls on domestic oil. Only the price control issue has been resolved to date. First initiated under the general price freeze of 1971–1973, the controls evolved into a complex eight-tier system until abolished by President Reagan in early 1981, several months before they were scheduled to expire under existing law. Actually, part of the controls still persist in the form of the windfall profits tax enacted by Congress last year.

Access to federal lands is not a major impediment to first-generation plants, but additional leasing will be needed to encourage new entrants and to permit expansion of the industry much beyond the announced production level of existing developments. Although private lands comprise more than one-fifth of total acreage in the Piceance Basin (U.S. Dept. Interior, 1968, Tables A-1–A-2), their commercial potential is generally inferior to the federally-owned resources. Some tracts are too small to be commercially viable. Others contain thin or lean deposits, and almost none contain sodium minerals that could be recovered simultane-

Table 2. Capital costs of oil-shale processing

Date	Estimated Cost ($ Million)
1968	138
1973	250–300
Early 1974	400–500
Late 1974	850–900
1976	960
1977	1,050
Feb. 1980	1,700

Date provided by Tosco Corp. and Colony Development Operation (Office Tech. Assess., 1980, Table 22, p. 186).

ously to lower the cost of shale-oil production. The Interior Department presently is formulating a permanent leasing program and also may recommend changing the Mineral Leasing Act to allow leasing of larger tracts, allocation of more than 1 tract to a single company, and leasing of tracts solely for siting facilities or offsite waste disposal (Anonymous, 1981a).

Both plant costs and ultimate size of the industry will be affected by environmental regulations. To date, most attention has focused on the Clean Air Act, especially the Prevention of Significant Deterioration (PSD) component which limits new emissions in areas where the existing air is cleaner than that required by national ambient air quality standards. For oil-shale developers, this means meeting the Class II standards applicable to the Piceance Basin itself and the even more stringent Class I standards of the Flat Tops Wilderness, located some 30 kilometers to the east (Edmonds, 1981). The present system allots each facility a portion of the total allowable pollution increment on a first-come, first-served basis. Just how large an industry might be accommodated is problematical because of unreliable atmospheric dispersion models and uncertainty regarding emission levels from a mix of production technologies. EPA has established a provisional limit of 400,000 b/d based on certain simplifying assumptions. Congress is expected to modify the Clean Air Act later this year, with the PSD program receiving high priority (Crow, 1981).

Another environmental issue that could seriously impede oil-shale expansion is the existence of federally-listed endangered fish species in the White River, Green River, and Colorado River mainstem (Joseph and others, 1977). Protection of these species under provisions of the Endangered Species Act may prevent development or add materially to the costs of building water-storage facilities that will be needed to support shale-oil production. The Fish and Wildlife Service has already taken a very conservative stance on the White River Dam project, which could supply water to developers in Utah, and the Moon Lake Power Plant project on the Green River. The Service recently issued a negative biological opinion for the Moon Lake project even though it would deplete flows of the Green River by only 2 percent (U.S. Fish and Wildlife Service, 1980).

Environmental issues interface with another uncertainty, that of securing the multitude of local, state, and federal permits required at various stages of project development (Davidson, 1976; Novak, 1976b). Some government agencies issue both permits and regulations. Others give clearance to permit applications required by other agencies; for example, clearance from the National Park Service and State Historical Society regarding archaeological-historical sites must be obtained before the lead agency will issue its permit. Even after permits are issued, the possibility remains that stipulations may be changed at a later date. The resulting complexity and uncertainty provides opportunity for disruption of company planning schedules, contributes to inflationary costs when delays do occur, promotes additional costs if designs have to be altered, and poses the risk that insurmountable roadblocks will eventually be encountered. Congress tried unsuccessfully last year to resolve the permitting dilemma by proposing the creation of an Energy Mobilization Board. At the state level, Colorado has just established a voluntary Joint Review Process designed to expedite decisionmaking by coordinating permit applications and providing fuller public participation in the permitting process.

In the short term, the most crucial governmet policy would seem to be implementation of the Energy Security legislation enacted by Congress last year, which created a Synthetic Fuels Corporation empowered to assist private industry to develop oil shale and other synthetic sources by providing purchase agreements, loan guarantees, or direct loans. Provisional commitments of financial help have been made to the Union Oil project and to Tosco Corporation, one of the two Colony partners, under the program's initial phase (Anonymous, 1981b). This phase also included an unsuccessful application by Occidental Oil Shale, who may reapply as the program expands. However, the new Reagan administration opposes implementing the full scope of government aid. One of the President's first official acts was to fire the Corporation's chairman and board of directors (Anonymous, 1981c). Unless pushed by Congress, government financial assistance may languish rather than promote synthetic-fuel development.

CONCLUSIONS

Oil-shale development in the Piceance Basin has a long history of unfulfilled expectations. Most of the factors which discouraged commercialization in the past still remain; indeed, the uncertainties imposed by government regulation have increased rather than diminished. Nonetheless, the relatively large number of projects now poised to build modular or commercial facilities affords optimism that one or more first-generation plants will be constructed in the next few years. Only by taking this initial step will industry be able to clarify the technical and economic uncertainties that have plagued development for so long. Projections of how rapidly the industry might expand after this first endeavor, or at what production level it might eventually peak, are speculative issues better left to future analysts.

REFERENCES

Anonymous, 1968, Disinterest dulls U.S. oil-shale leasing: Oil and Gas Journal, v. 66, no. 53, p. 97.

———, 1980, Work starts on town for Colony project workers: Western Oil Reporter, v. 37, no. 10, p. 62.

———, 1981a, Alternate schedule submitted: Western Oil Reporter, v. 38, no. 2, p. 67.

———, 1981b, Three synfuels projects picked for financial aid: Oil and Gas Journal, v. 79, no. 4, p. 115–116.

———, 1981c, Policy questions cloud outlook for synfuels projects: Oil and Gas Journal, v. 79, no. 6, p. 43.

Callahan, K., 1981, Oil shale—when, where and how much?: Shale Country, v. 3, no. 1, p. 12–15.

Chase Manhattan Bank, 1979, United States petroleum highlights: The Petroleum Situation, v. 3, no. 3.

———, 1980, United States petroleum highlights: The Petroleum Situation, v. 4, no. 3.

Committee on Oil Shale, Rocky Mountain Oil and Gas Association, 1981, Committee on Oil Shale workforce estimates for the years 1981–1990 and the years 1990 & 2000: Denver, Rocky Mountain Oil and Gas Association, Quarterly Report, Feb. 12.

Crow, P., 1981, U.S. lawmakers poised to fine tune Clean Air Act: Oil and Gas Journal, v. 79, no. 11, p. 27–33.

Davidson, D., 1976, The permit procedure: many steps, many stops: Shale Country, v. 2, no. 11, p. 5–6.

Edmonds, C., 1981, The Clean Air Act—putting together a jigsaw puzzle: Shale Country, v. 3, no. 2, p. 14–17.

Emerson, J. D., 1980, Refiners in a changing world: The Petroleum Situation, v. 4, no. 8, p. 1–2.

Joseph, T. W., Behnke, R. J., and Holden, P. B., 1977, An evaluation of the status, life history, and habitat requirements of endangered and threatened fishes of the Upper Colorado River system: Washington, D.C., Government Printing Office, 183 p.

Kilker, C., 1981, The growth powder keg: is it ready to explode?: Shale Country, v. 3, no. 1, p. 18–20.

Matzick, A., Dannenberg, R. O., Ruark, J. R., Phillips, J. E., Lankford, J. D., and Guthrie, B., 1966, Development of the Bureau of Mines gas-combustion oil-shale retorting process: U.S. Bureau of Mines Bulletin 635, 199 p.

Novak, A., 1975, Oil shale—1976: review/preview: Shale Country, v. 1, no. 12, p. 4–9.

———, 1976a, Oil shale—1976/1977: Shale Country, v. 2, no. 12, p. 2–6.

———, 1976b, The shale paperwork maze of permits, clearances, regulations: Shale Country, v. 2, no. 11, p 4–5.

Office of Technology Assessment, 1980, An assessment of oil shale technologies: Washington, D.C., Government Printing Office, 517 p.

Russell, P., 1980, The history of Western oil shale: East Brunswick, N.J., Center for Professional Advancement, 176 p.

U.S. Department of the Interior, 1968, Prospects for oil shale development, Colorado, Utah, and Wyoming: Washington, D.C., U.S. Department of the Interior.

U.S. Fish and Wildlife Service, 1980, Memorandum, section 7 consultation on Deseret Generation and Transmission Cooperative, Moon Lake project: Salt Lake City, Utah, U.S. Fish and Wildlife Service, 6 p.

UPPER CRETACEOUS (CAMPANIAN) COAL RESOURCES OF WESTERN COLORADO

D. KEITH MURRAY
Colorado School of Mines Research Institute
Golden, Colorado 80401

INTRODUCTION

Colorado encompasses parts or all of eight distinct coal-bearing regions, which cover nearly 30 percent of the total area of the State (fig. 1). These eight regions, within which are located 21 designated coal fields, contain more than 10 percent of the total coal reserves of the United States above a depth of 1,830 m (6,000 ft), or at least 434 billion short (394 billion metric) tons of in-place coal. Of this resource, more than 273 billion short (248 billion metric) tons, or 63 percent of the total, have been estimated for the Green River, San Juan River, and Uinta coal regions of western Colorado (see Murray, 1980a, 1980b). Although most of this resource is believed to consist of coals of Cretaceous age, no data presently are available regarding the breakdown of coal resources in Colorado by geologic age or formation. However, based on the known distribution and thicknesses of the widespread, multiple (often numbering 20 to 30 or more) coal beds encountered in the Mesaverde Group and equivalents (essentially, Campanian in age), there is little doubt that the bulk of the coal resources of Colorado lies within this sequence. In the southeast part of the Uinta region, for example, total net thickness of Mesaverde coals in places exceeds 24 m, based on an evaluation of oil and gas well geophysical logs in the area (see Murray and others, 1977, p. 389). In the Dan-

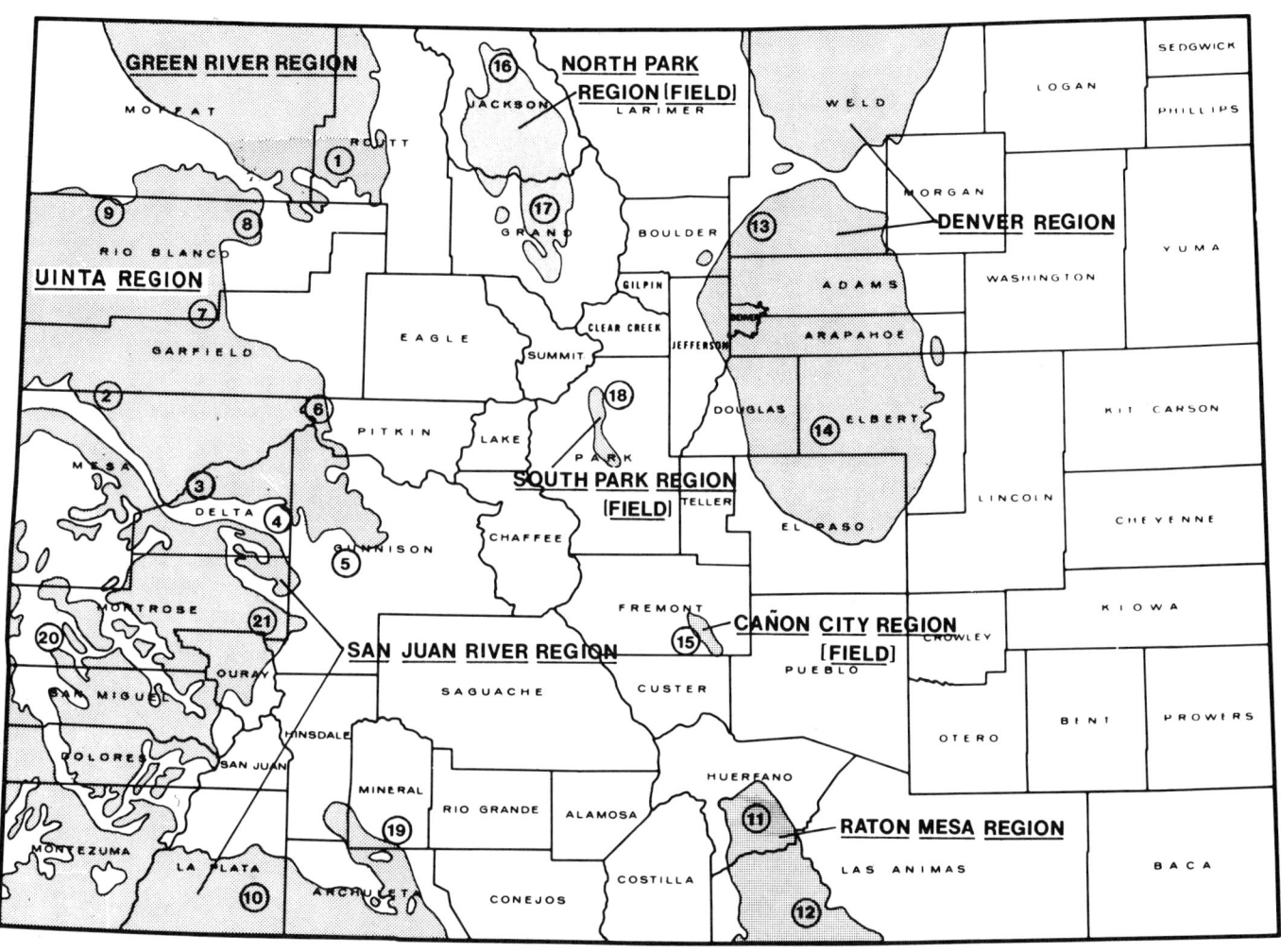

1. Yampa
2. Book Cliffs
3. Grand Mesa
4. Somerset
5. Crested Butte
6. Carbondale
7. Grand Hogback
8. Danforth Hills
9. Lower White River
10. Durango
11. Walsenburg
12. Trinidad
13. Boulder-Weld
14. Colorado Springs
15. Canon City
16. North Park
17. Middle Park
18. South Park
19. Pagosa Springs
20. Nucla-Naturita
21. Tongue Mesa

Figure 1. Coal-bearing regions and fields in Colorado.

forth Hills coal field, Rio Blanco and Moffat Counties (fig. 1), total coal thicknesses in the 30–47 m range have been noted, based upon subsurface information. To date, western Colorado coal fields have produced more than 224 million short (203 million metric) tons of coal, which amounts to nearly 33.5 percent of the State's cumulative production, from 1864 through 1980, of nearly 670 million short (608 million metric) tons. During 1980, the three western Colorado coal regions produced more than 17 million short (15.4 million metric) tons of coal, or 90 percent of the State's total. Virtually all of the historic coal production from western Colorado has come from Cretaceous-age sequences; and all of the present production consists of coals of this age. Based on preliminary data from the Colorado Division of Mines, nearly 12 million short (10.9 million metric) tons of coal was surface-mined in western Colorado during 1980, which comprises 70 percent of all coal mined in that region and nearly 93 percent of all surface-mined coal in Colorado.

COAL-BEARING ROCKS

Colorado coals range in age from early Late Cretaceous to Eocene. The higher rank bituminous coals, which comprise the largest reserves, generally are found in the Upper Cretaceous Dakota and Mesaverde Groups in western Colorado, especially in the region extending from Garfield County south to the New Mexico state line. The oldest coals in Colorado occur in the Dakota Group in the southwestern part of the State (northern San Juan River region, Durango to Nucla–Naturita field areas). Successively younger coals were laid down as the Late Cretaceous Western Interior sea retreated eastward and northeastward from the region (Murray, 1980a).

The youngest coals, generally of lower rank (subbituminous A to lignite), are found in latest Cretaceous and early Tertiary rocks in the Green River, North and South Park, Raton Mesa and Denver coal regions. Subbituminous coals occur in the Cretaceous Lance, Laramie, and Vermejo formations; in the Paleocene Fort Union and Raton formations; and in the Paleocene–Eocene Wasatch and Coalmont formations. Lignite is restricted to the Paleocene-age upper part of the Denver Formation in the central Denver coal region (Murray, 1980a).

The Cretaceous-age coal-bearing sequences (fig. 2) and coal ranks present in the western Colorado regions can be generalized as follows (units presently being mined are in bold-face type) (Murray, 1980a):

GREEN RIVER REGION:
  Lance Formation (Upper Cretaceous)—probably mostly subbituminous B and C.
  Mesaverde Group (Upper Cretaceous)—mostly high-volatile C bituminous, some high-volatile B bituminous and subbituminous A.

SAN JUAN RIVER REGION:
  Fruitland Formation (Upper Cretaceous)—high-volatile B and C bituminous.
  Menefee Formation of Mesaverde Group (Upper Cretaceous)—high-volatile A and B bituminous (locally of coking quality).
  Dakota Group (Upper Cretaceous)—high-volatile B and C bituminous (currently mined only in Nucla–Naturita field; may locally be of coking quality).

UINTA REGION:
  Mesaverde Group (Upper Cretaceous)—anthracite and semi-anthracite (restricted to areas of igneous activity in southeastern part of area, especially in Crested Butte field); medium-volatile bituminous (high-grade coking coal, chiefly in Coal Basin area of Carbondale field); high-volatile A, B, and C bituminous (of coking quality in parts of Carbondale and Somerset fields); subbituminous A and B(?) (only in local areas near outcrops).

STRUCTURE OF COAL-BEARING REGIONS

The San Juan River, Uinta and Green River coal regions, for the most part, are located within Laramide-age structural basins. The interior areas of these basins appear to be relatively free from structural complications; here the coal beds probably are not highly folded, faulted or otherwise disturbed. However, some margins of these structural basins are moderately to severely

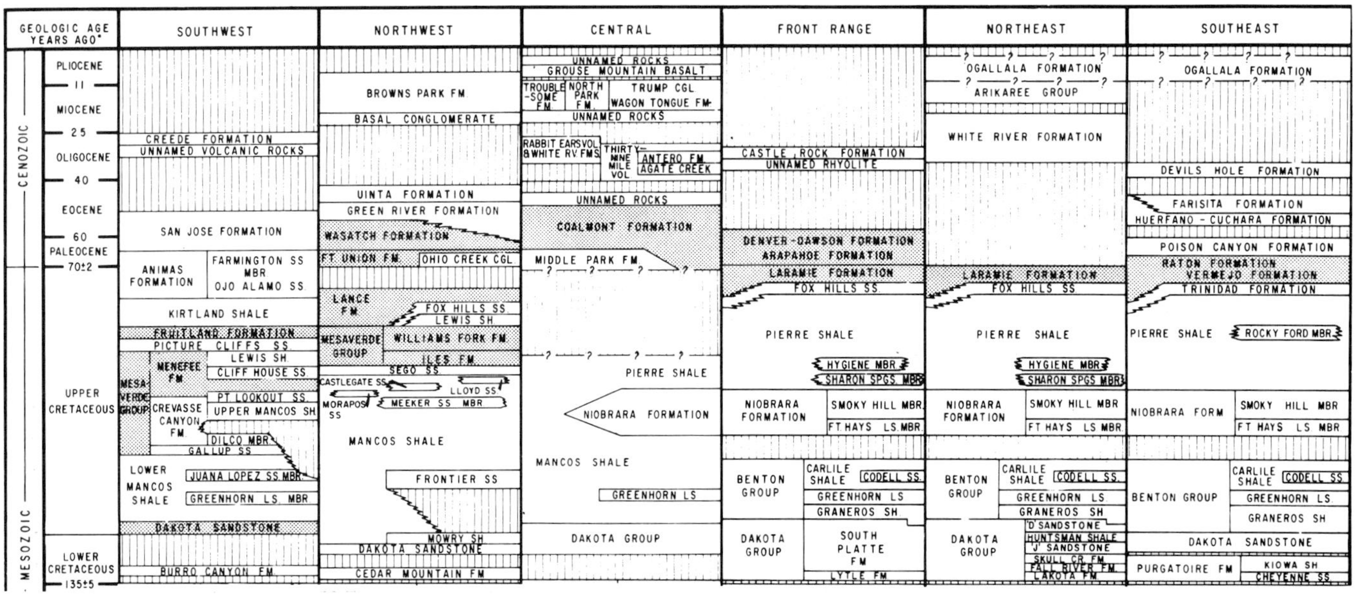

Figure 2. Colorado stratigraphic correlation chart, parts of Mesozoic and Cenozoic Eras. Coal-bearing units are shaded.

folded and faulted. In places, Tertiary igneous activity has metamorphosed the coal to anthracite, and even to coke. The Uinta region, which is located partially within the Piceance Creek basin, and the Green River region, the Colorado portion of which includes the Sand Wash basin, each contains significant coal resources to depths exceeding 3000 m. The Piceance Creek and Sand Wash basins are the deepest structural depressions in the State (Murray, 1980a).

Only a small part, possibly 5 to 10 percent, of the coal resources of Colorado today are considered to be surface-minable due to the limited areas within the coal-bearing regions in which the coal beds are both of gentle dip and under "shallow" cover (Murray, 1980a).

CHARACTERISTICS OF UPPER CRETACEOUS COALS

Coal Rank

Statewide, Colorado coals range in rank from lignite to anthracite; however, western Colorado coals vary from subbituminous to anthracite in rank, but are predominantly bituminous. More than 70 percent of the State's coal resources are bituminous, approximately 23 percent subbituminous, five percent lignite (in the Denver coal region), and less than 2 percent anthracite (Murray, 1980b).

Generally, the older a coal, the higher its rank. However, geologic factors such as above-normal geothermal gradient and burial to great depths (say, below 1500 to 3000 m) can significantly increase the rank of even the youngest coals. This is especially true in the relatively deep structural basins of western Colorado, parts of which are characterized by notably high geothermal heat flow resulting from Tertiary-age igneous activity.

Coal Analyses

Since 1975, the Colorado Geological Survey and the U.S. Geological Survey have been conducting cooperative programs to sample and analyze most of the producing coal mines in Colorado, together with coals likely to be mined in the future that have been cored by both Federal and private industry drilling programs.

Results of the first of these programs have been published (Boreck and others, 1977), and analytical results of additional coal sampling efforts by the Colorado Geological Survey are in press (Khalsa and others, 1981). A significant percentage of these analyses pertain to western Colorado coals. Table 1 compares certain chemical characteristics of coals from the Green River region, in northwest Colorado, with coals from the entire Rocky Mountain coal province (of which Colorado is a part), Interior province (Illinois, Iowa, Kansas, etc.), and Northern Great Plains province (Montana, North and South Dakota, and northeastern Wyoming).

None of the Colorado coals sampled to date, which include coals from all of the larger producing mines in the State, appears to contain significant quantities of toxic or radioactive elements (such as arsenic, mercury, selenium, strontium, thorium, and uranium). In fact, most appear to contain smaller amounts of these substances than do coals from other regions of the United States (Murray, 1980b).

Moisture, volatile matter, and fixed carbon contents of Colorado coals vary considerably with rank from region to region. Moisture content is generally in the 1- to 20-percent range, as-received. An overall average of about 12 percent moisture is a general value for Colorado coals. Statewide, volatile matter content varies from 6.9 percent (in anthracite in Crested Butte field) to approximately 45 percent, with most coals being in the 31–40 percent range. Fixed carbon content typically varies between 39 and 69 percent.

The ash content of coal beds in Colorado varies considerably as a result of different environments of deposition, even within the same coal "zone." The range typically is from approximately two to 20 percent, averaging about six percent. Locally, however, ash content may reach 25–30 percent, as-received (Murray, 1980b).

Sulfur content of most Colorado coal beds varies from 0.2 to 1.2 percent, as-received. More than 99 percent of the coals analyzed contain less than 1.0 percent, and more than 50 percent contain less than 0.7 percent sulfur. The bulk of the coal being surface-mined in Colorado at present contains between 0.2 and 0.5 percent sulfur; on the other hand, much of the underground-mined metallurgical-grade coal in Colorado contains 0.5–1.0 percent sulfur, still low in comparison with many Eastern coals.

In terms of pounds of sulfur per million Btu, most of the coal being surface-mined in Colorado today for use in steam-electric power plants contains between approximately 0.2 and 0.5 lb/million Btu (0.04 and 0.10 kg/million kJ), well within the definition of low-sulfur coal: specifically, one which contains 0.6 lb or less sulfur per million Btu (0.12 kg or less/million kJ) (Murray, 1980b).

Most of the subbituminous and bituminous steam coal being produced today in Colorado ranges from about 10,000 to 13,600 Btu/lb (23,260 to 31,634 kJ/kg); and coking coal, from 12,070 to over 14,000 Btu/lb (28,075 to over 32,564 kJ/kg), as-received. On a dry, ash-free basis, most Colorado coals vary between 13,300 and 14,500 Btu/lb (30,936 and 33,727 kJ/kg) in heat content. On a moisture- and ash-free basis, an average of approximately 14,000 Btu/lb (32,564 kJ/kg) is reasonable for most Colorado coals; and on an as-received basis, about 11,370 Btu/lb (26,447 kJ/kg) (Murray, 1980a).

Coking Coal

Studies indicate that the original, identified, in-place coking-coal reserves in the State of Colorado total over 4.3 billion short (3.9 billion metric) tons (Goolsby and others, 1979). These reserves include the highest quality and rank coking coals in the West, and account for Colorado's prominence as an important source of low-sulfur coking coal.

Coal produced from mines in Colorado has served as an important source of coking coal since the Nineteenth Century, when coal was coked in beehive ovens to fuel the State's early metal foundries. Production also was utilized by the railroads, and, eventually, in blast furnaces for the manufacture of steel. Economic and

Table 1. Arithmetic mean of proximate, ultimate, and heating value analyses for the Yampa coal field, Green River region, Colorado; compared with the arithmetic means for the Rocky Mountain, Interior, and Northern Great Plains coal provinces (modified from Boreck and others, 1977).

	Green River Region — Yampa Field	Rocky Mountain Province	Interior Province	Northern Great Plains Province
Moisture (%)	8.0	12.9	7.2	24.5
Volatile Matter (%)	37.4	36.0	32.2	31.7
Fixed Carbon (%)	45.9	42.0	48.0	35.4
Ash (%)	9.0	9.1	12.6	8.3
Hydrogen (%)	5.4	5.6	4.9	6.2
Carbon (%)	63.9	59.7	65.2	49.2
Nitrogen (%)	1.6	1.2	1.2	0.9
Oxygen (%)	19.8	23.8	12.2	34.2
Sulfur (%)	0.5	0.6	3.9	1.2
Heating Value (Btu/lb.)	11,203	10,480	11,580	8,480

environmental factors led to the gradual abandonment of beehive ovens in favor of modern byproduct processes for the production of coke. Today, Colorado coals are primarily coked in byproduct ovens operated by CF & I Steel Corporation (Pueblo, Colorado), United States Steel Corporation (Provo, Utah), and Kaiser Steel Corporation (Fontana, California).

Significant reserves of coking, or metallurgical, coal are located in the Raton Mesa, San Juan River, and Uinta coal regions (fig. 1). Although a large percentage of Colorado's historic coking coal production has come from the Trinidad coal field, in the Raton Mesa region, today more than 73 percent (or some 2 million short, 1.8 million metric tons) of the State's coking coal is produced in the Uinta region, from the Carbondale and Somerset fields. Nearly 30 percent of the coal mined in the Uinta region in 1980 was used to make steel or for smelting purposes. Western Colorado coal regions contain approximately 52 percent of the original identified in-place coking-coal reserves in the State, or 2.23 billion short (1.81 billion metric) tons, out of a total of 4.3 billion short (3.9 billion metric) tons (Goolsby and others, 1979). The San Juan River region contains 1.78 billion short (1.61 billion metric) and the Uinta region 0.45 billion short (0.41 billion metric) tons of this in-place reserve. All of the western Colorado coking coals are found in the Dakota and Mesaverde Groups (and equivalents), of Cretaceous age. The highest grade metallurgical coal mined in the western United Sta comes from the Mesaverde Group in the Coal Basin area, Pitkin County, in the Carbondale field of the Uinta region (Murray, 1980b).

Methane from Coal Beds

The Carbondale and Somerset coal fields, located in the southeastern part of the Uinta coal region, are characterized by being the sites of the gassiest producing coal mines in Colordo (fig. 1; see Fender and Murray, 1978; Boreck and Strever, 1980; and Murray, 1980a). According to U.S. Bureau of Mines records, active mines in these two fields emiited (i.e., wasted) a total of approximately 10.65 million cu ft (MMCF) (0.30 million m^3) of methane per day, diluted to approximately one percent by ventilated air (see Fender and Murray, 1977, Table 3). More than 8.2 MMCFPD (0.23 million m^3/day) methane was ventilated in 1977 from the five Mid-Continent Resources ccking coal mines located in the Coal basin area, near Redstone, Pitkin County, in the Carbondale field. Current methane ventilation figures probably exceed that amount. The Dutch Creek No. 1 mine in Coal Basin, scene of the recent tragic mine explosion that claimed 15 lives, is listed (Fender and Murray, 1977) as having the highest average daily methane emission—more than 2.23 MMCFGPD (0.06 million m^3/day)—of any coal mine in Colorado. This may well be the gassiest coal mine in the western United States. Dutch Creek No. 1 also experienced a "dust" explosion in 1957, and a severe gas explosion in 1965 that claimed several lives. The Coal Basin mines produce the highest grade (premium) coking coal (medium-volatile bituminous) in the West. The deeper portions of the Uinta (Piceance Creek basin), Green River (Sand Wash basin), and San Juan River (San Juan basin) coal regions in Colorado are believed to contain very large, in-place resources of coal-bed methane, numbering in the *trillions* of cubic feet (tcf). In the Piceance Creek basin, Colorado, this gas resource is believed to exceed 12 tcf (340 x 10^{9}m). An aggressive program of unconventional (i.e., methane-from-coal-beds) gas exploration by the petroleum industry, now just getting underway in this and several other coal-bearing basins in the Rocky Mountain region, is expected eventually to recover a signifiiant part of this valuable energy resource.

COAL-BEARING REGIONS

The coal-bearing regions of western Colorado—the Green River, San Juan River, and Uinta—all lie west of the Continental Divide and are included within the Rocky Mountain coal province. The Green River and Uinta regions fall within the Laramide-age Sand Wash and Piceance Creek basins, respectively (fig. 1). The San Juan River coal region occupies parts of the Chama platform, San Juan basin, Four Corners platform, and Paradox basin, and laps onto the San Juan and Uncompahgre uplifts.

Table 2 includes representative analyses of coal beds from each of the major coal fields in the three western Colorado coal regions.

Green River Region

The southeast arm of the large Green River coal region is located in Moffat and Routt Counties of northwestern Colorado (fig. 1). The larger part of this important coal region covers most of southwestern Wyoming (Averiit, 1972, fig. 3). The Colorado part of this region is comprised of the Sand Wash structural basin, of Laramide age, and the north flank of the Axial Basin uplift, which includes the Williams Fork Mountains and forms the southern edge of the basin. The perimeter of the Green River coal region is defined, except where faulted, by the base of the Upper Cretaceous Mesaverde Group. The oldest coals in the region are found in the Iles Formation, lower Mesaverde Group (fig. 2).

Coal-bearing Upper Cretaceous, Paleocene, and Eocene rocks crop out along the Yampa River-Williams Fork Mountains area, in the southeastern part of the region. This area constitutes the Yampa Coal field, the only named field in the region. The southern flank of the Sand Wash basin consists of gently northward-dipping sediments that are locally folded, especially in the southeastern part of the basin, and complicated by late Tertiary faults and igneous intrusives, which, in places, have upgraded some of the coals to anthracite.

Virtually all of the coals mined to date in the Green River region have come from the Iles and Williams Fork Formations of the Mesaverde Group (fig. 2). Younger coal-bearing rocks (Lance, Fort Union, and Wasatch formations) are preserved toward the interior of the basin, away from outcrops of the Mesaverde, on or near which most of the coal mining to date has taken place. A major part of the region contains multiple coal beds in several formations below a depth of 900 m; in the central part of the Sand Wash basin, coals are present to depths in excess of 3000 m (Jones and others, 1978).

The Mesaverde coals in the Green River region, for the most part, are high-volatile C bituminous in rank and vary in thickness from approximately 1 to 6 m. The younger Lance Formation coals, which have been only locally mined in the past (not mined at present), appear to be subbituminous B or C and range up to about 3 m in thickness.

This region to date has produced more than 114 million short (103 million metric) tons of coal (or approximately 17 percent of the State's coal) from nearly 200 mines. Most of the coal (all of it low-sulfur) currently being mined in the Green River region is burned in steam-electric generating plants located either within the region or elsewhere in Colorado, mostly in the Denver area. Some of the coal is exported to states such as Illinois, Iowa, Nebraska, and Texas.

Total in-place coal resources in the Colorado part of the Green River region probably far exceed 60 billion short (54 billion metric) tons above a depth of 1830 m, although very little work has been done to date in evaluating the coals below "minable" depths.

Table 2. Range of analyses of Cretaceous-age coals of western Colorado, as-received (modified from Murray, 1980b, Table 14).

REGION, Field, Formation (Coal bed)	Moisture (%)	Volatile Matter (%)	Ash (%)	Sulfur (%)	Heating Value (Btu/lb)	Ash Fusion Temperature (°F)	FSI
GREEN RIVER							
Yampa							
Lance Fm. (Lorella, Kimberly)	19.6-21.8	-	4.1- 6.5	0.5-0.7	9,660- 9,720	2,010-2,260	0
Williams Fork Fm., "Upper Coal Gp."							
(Dry Creek, Crawford, Fish Creek)	9.8-16.9	34.9-39.2	4.1-17.2	0.4-1.8	9,800-11,680	2,070-2,480	0
Williams Fork Fm., "Middle Coal Gp."							
(Lennox, Wadge)	6.4-11.8	33.8-39.0	3.0-20.2	0.3-0.9	9,871-12,440	2,140-2,890	0-0.5
Iles Fm., "Lower Coal Gp."							
(E,D,C,B,A or Pinnacle)	6.3-12.2	-	4.3-11.3	0.3-0.9	11,090-12,560	2,250-2,780	0
SAN JUAN RIVER							
Durango							
Fruitland Fm.	0.9- 2.3	20.8-23.6	19.5-26.6	0.7-0.8	11,230-12,140	-	-
Menefee Fm. (9 beds)	1.6-10.7	36.2-42.1	3.4-16.6	0.6-1.3	10,860-14,700	2,020-3,000	0.5.5
Nucla-Naturita							
Dakota Ss. (Fm.) (3 beds)	2.5-13.5	32.6-36.1	6.1-12.8	0.5-1.1	10,010-13,380	2,620-2,910	0-1.5
Tongue Mesa							
Fruitland Fm. (Cimarron)	14.2-16.0	36.0-47.3	6.7- 8.4	0.5-0.9	9,350-10,200	2,450-2,480	0
UINTA							
Book Cliffs							
Mt. Garfield Fm. (Mesaverde Gp.)							
(Carbonera, Cameo, Palisade, Thomas, Anchor Mine)	3.3-14.0	29.8-35.4	4.9-23.3	0.4-1.7	9,833-13,560	2,130-2,960	0-1.0
Carbondale							
Williams Fork Fm. ("South Canon Gp.", Dutch Creek, Allen, Anderson)	0.8- 3.4	22.0-28.1	3.4-10.0	0.3-1.3	12,470-15,190	2,140-2,505	8.5-9.0
("Fairfield Gp." or A,B,C,D, Coal Basin A-B)	0.8- 4.0	21.8-39.3	3.4- 6.7	0.4-1.5	12,609-15,088	2,180-2,455	1-9
Crested Butte							
Williams Fork Fm., Paonia Mbr.(6 beds)	2.5-13.3	-	3.2- 9.1	0.4-1.9	11,400-14,170	2,130-2,480	0
Danforth Hills							
Williams Fork Fm. (Lion Cyn., Goff, Fairfield Gps.)	8.9-15.5	-	2.2- 9.6	0.3-1.4	10,140-11,790	2,210-2,910	-
Iles Fm. ("Black Diamond Gp.")	9.2-13.4	-	3.7-10.0	0.4-0.6	11,200-11,970	2,210-2,990	-
Grand Hogback							
Williams Fork Fm. (E, Sunnyridge)	4.0- 4.8	37.2-39.8	6.1-10.4	0.6-0.7	12,060-12,581	2,230-2,910	1.0-1.5
Grand Mesa							
Mt. Garfield Fm. (Mesaverde Gp.) (6-8 beds)	3.1-19.5	30.4-35.0	2.1-17.9	0.5-2.2	8,298-13,489	2,060-2,970	-
Lower White River							
Williams Fork Fm.	11.2-14.1	-	4.4- 8.5	0.4-0.5	10,800-11,230	2,060-2,910	0-1.5
Somerset							
Williams Fork Fm. (F,E,D,C,B,A beds)	3.2-13.6	35.3-37.7	3.2-11.4	0.5-0.8	10,040-13,453	2,145-2,810	0-3.0

Speltz (1976) estimates that nearly one billion short (0.9 billion metric) tons of potentially surface-minable coal may exist in this part of the region.

San Juan River Region

The San Juan River coal region is located in southwestern Colorado and in part of west-central Colorado as far north as the Grand Valley–Grand Junction area and the southern part of Delta County (fig. 1; also see maps by Jones and others, 1978; and Averitt, 1972). The larger part of this region lies in northwestern New Mexico and includes the San Juan structural basin, the Red Mesa–Mesa Verde platform, the Cortez saddle, and the eastern part of the Paradox basin, which extends into Utah. The region also includes parts of the Gunnison and Uncompahgre uplifts in Colorado.

Since the late 1800's, the San Juan River region has produced more than 9.5 million short (8.6 million metric) tons of coal from nearly 200 mines, which represents 1.4 percent of the total production of Colorado.

Durango field (fig. 1) includes the Colorado part of the San Juan structural basin, the Hesperus–Red Mesa–Cortez area, and the Mesa Verde area, in La Plata and Montezuma Counties. Coals in the field are found in the Dakota Group, Menefee Formation, and Fruitland Formation, all of Cretaceos age (fig. 2).

Dakota coals are relatively thin, discontinuous, and of high ash content in and near the areas of outcrop (the Hogback) north and northeast of the town of Durango. In the subsurface to the south and west, Dakota coals have been mined to some extent at relatively shallow depths; the resource exists to a depth of 2440 m or more in the Colorado part of the San Juan basin.

Coal beds in the Menefee Formation comprise the most significant coal resource in the Durango field and are the only ones being mined at present. In local areas of structural complexity near Durango, they are of coking quality (Goolsby and others, 1979).

To date, La Plata and Montezuma Counties have produced more than 6.76 million short (6.13 million metric) tons of coal, which is more than 75 percent of the total for the Colorado part of the San Juan River region. Most of the coal currently being mined in the field is used locally for domestic and industrial purposes.

Nucla-Natura field (fig. 1) extends from Dolores County northward to just south of the Colorado River, in Mesa County. Throughout this large, highly dissected area (the "Dakota coal subregion" of Hornbaker and others, 1976), most of the post-Dakota coal-bearing rocks, and even much of the Dakota Group itself, have been stripped away by erosion. The single currently producing mine in this field furnishes approximately 100,000 short (90,700 metric) tons of coal per year to the nearby Nucla Power Plant. Three minable coal beds, 0.9 to 1.5 m thick, occur in the Dakota sequence in this area. The Nucla-Naturita coal field to date has produced over 2.1 million short (1.9 million metric) tons of coal, or about 24 percent of the total for the San Juan River region (Colorado portion).

Pagosa Springs field, located in Archuleta County (fig. 1), has produced a total of only 75,000 short (68,025 metric) tons of bituminous coal over the years. One small surface mine currently operates in the field.

Tongue Mesa field consists of an isolated erosional remnant of Upper Cretaceous sediments (equivalent to at least part of the Mesaverde Group) capped by volcanic rocks of Late Cretaceous and early Tertiary ages. The coal-bearing "Mesaverde" sequence has been eroded west of Tongue Mesa field.

The coals in this field occur within a 275-m thick sequence that correlates with the Kirtland–Fruitland–Pictured Cliffs Formations in the San Juan basin to the south (fig. 2). At least four coal beds, ranging from 0.6 to 12 m in thickness, occur on Tongue Mesa in the lower 60 m of the Fruitland Formation. The most persistent and thickest coal bed, the Cimarron (or Lou Creek), together with several thinner coals, were underground-mined intermittently from the 1890's until the 1940's. No mines presently are active in the field. Tongue Mesa coals generally are subbituminous B in rank and commonly are considerably oxidized and "bony."

Uinta Region

Approximately one-half of the large Uinta coal region lies in west-central Colorado; the remainder constitutes the main coal-bearing region of eastern Utah (fig. 1; Averitt, 1972). Most of that part of the region located in Colorado coincides with the Piceance Creek structural basin of Laramide age and is located in the eastern part of the Colorado Plateau physiographic province. The Uinta region in Colorado is bounded by the Grand Hogback monocline on the east, Axial Basin uplift on the north (which separates this region from the Green River coal region), the Utah State line on the west, Grand Valley and Colorado River on the southwest, and the North Fork Valley and Gunnison uplift on the south and southeast.

The Piceance Creek basin is the largest structural basin in western Colorado, covering an area exceeding 11,500 km^2, as defined by the base of the Upper Cretaceous Mesaverde Group. The basin is asymmetric in shape, with the steep flank on the east; its long axis trends northwest. This is one of the deepest basins in the Rocky Mountain region, with an estimated 7,600+ m of sediments filling its deepest part, which is located at the north end of the basin, in Rio Blanco county. The southeastern part of the region, in Gunnison and Pitkin Counties, is marked by the Elk and West Elk mountains igneous intrusive complexes of Tertiary age—sills, laccoliths, dikes, etc., and associated folds and faulting. The high geothermal heat flow characteristic of this part of the region has increased the rank of much of the coal that occurs here. As a result, the southeast part of the Uinta region contains large resources of coking coal, much of it of premium grade and high in methane content, and commonly lying under more than 300 m of overburden (Murray and others, 1977; Goolsby and others, 1979).

The eight coal fields in the Uinta region that exist around its periphery are briefly discussed below in alphabetical order (fig. 1). All of these fields are, or have been, productive from the Mesaverde Group (fig. 2). The Lower White River field is the only one not presently producing.

Since the late 1800's, this important region has produced more than 91.5 million short (83 million metric) tons of coal, which constitutes nearly 15 percent of the total for all of Colorado, from nearly 300 mines. Currently, the Uinta region is second only to the Green River region in annual production, and first in the State in the production of both underground-mined coal and coking coal.

Book Cliffs field contains a number of high-quality coal beds in the Mount Garfield Formation of the Mesaverde Group. These are mostly high-volatile C bituminous in rank, with some high-volatile B. Hornbaker and others (1976) have estimated total in-place resources in this field (in the 1,287 km^2 area considered) at approximately 7.2 billion short (6.5 billion metric) tons to a depth of 1,830 m.

Carbondale field, located at the eastern edge of the region, in Garfield and Pitkin Counties, produces high-quality coking coal from the Mesaverde Group. In the Coal Basin area, Pitkin County, in the southern part of the field, some of the coals have been metamorphosed to high-volatile A and medium-volatile bituminous; and, locally, to semianthracite and anthracite. Original in-place coal resources to a depth of 1,830 m in the 265 km^2 area considered have been estimated at more than 5.2 billion short (4.7 billion metric) tons.

Crested Butte field is located at the southeastern tip of the Uinta region, in Gunnison County, near the Crested Butte ski resort. Much of the field lies at elevations above 3,000 m. Coal-bearing Mesaverde strata in this area have been folded, faulted, and intruded by igneous rocks. The coals here range from high-volatile C bituminous to anthracite; some are of good coking quality. Coal beds in the field vary from about 0.6 to 4 m in thickness. Original in-place coal resources, to a depth of 1,830 m in the 386 km^2 area surveyed, are estimated at some 1.56 billion short (1.41 billion metric) tons (Hornbaker and others, 1976).

Danforth Hills field, which extends from Axial south to Meeker, is situated at the northeast limit of the Uinta region, in Rio Blanco and southern Moffat counties. This field is separated from the Yampa field, Green River region, to the north by Axial basin, a topographic low in which the coal-bearing Mesaverde Group, which crops out in hills both to the north and south, has been stripped away. Both subdivisions of the Mesaverde Group here (the Iles and Williams Fork formations) contain numerous good-quality bituminous coal beds, chiefly high-volatile C in rank. Some of these beds exceed 6 m in thickness. Original in-place coal resources to a depth of 1,830 m in the approximately 644 km^2 area for which the estimate was made, total more than 10.5 billion short (9.5 billion metric) tons (Hornbaker and others, 1976).

Grand Hogback field is located along the east rim of the Piceance Creek basin, the edge of which is sharply upturned to form the prominent Grand Hogback monocline. This feature extends south of Meeker for some 64 km to Rifle, then makes an abrupt bend to the southeast, through the old mining town of New Castle, where the hogback is cut through by the Colorado River, then to Glenwood Springs, where the structure again trends south, making the eastern edge of the Uinta region (fig. 1). Coal-bearing Mesaverde sediments crop out along the length of the Grand Hogback, with 40-degree to nearly vertical dips, where coal has been mined for many years. The Mesaverde coals in the northern part of the Grand Hogback field are mainly high-volatile C bituminous; these grade southward toward Glenwood Springs, in Garfield County, to high-volatile B bituminous. The major part of the coal mined from this field has come from the "Fairfield" and "South Canon" coal "groups" or "zones" in the lower part of the Williams Fork Formation. The "Black Diamond" coal group, in the upper part of the Iles Formation, also has been mined in this area, as has the "Keystone" coal group, in the upper part of the Williams Fork. The numerous coal beds in this sequence range from approximately 1 m to more than 5 m in thickness. Original in-place resources to a depth of 1,830 m in the 257 km^2 area considered is estimated at more than three billion short (2.7 billion metric) tons.

Grand Mesa field, situated on the south flank of the prominent Grand Mesa, a very large flat-topped feature over 3,000 m in elevation that is capped by Tertiary volcanic flows, lies primarily in Delta County. The northwestern part of the field, on the west flank of Grand Mesa and south of the Colorado River, is located in Mesa County (fig. 1). The Mesaverde coals in this field, as in the Book Cliffs field, are in the Mt. Garfield Formation. The coal beds in Grand Mesa field range from high-volatile C bituminous to subbituminous A and are typically 1.2–4.3 m thick. Original in-place resources, to a depth of 1,830 m in the 850 km² area for which the estimate was made, probably exceed 8.6 billion short (7.8 billion metric) tons (Hornbaker and others, 1976).

Lower White River field covers a large area that includes the western Piceance Creek basin and much of the Douglas Creek arch, westward to the Utah State line (fig. 1). Most of the field lies in Rio Blanco County; a small part, a few kilometers north of the giant Rangely oil field (the largest field in Colorado), is located in southern Moffat County. Coals in Lower White River field occur in both the Williams Fork and Iles formations. Most of the mining to date has taken place in the Rangely area, in the Mesaverde rimrock that defines the flanks of the large, breached Rangely anticline. Coal beds here vary from about 2.4 to 3.7 m or more in thickness and are high-volatile C bituminous in rank. In the 1,496 km² area surveyed, 11.76 billion short (10.67 billion metric) tons of in-place coal resources have been estimated to a depth of 1,830 m.

Somerset field is located in the valley cut by the North Fork of the Gunnison River and its tributaries, in Delta and Gunnison Counties. The coals in this area occur in the Bowie and Paonia Members of the Williams Fork Formation, are high-volatile B and C bituminous in rank, and range up to 7.6–9.1 m in thickness. In the eastern part of the field, near the settlement of Somerset, coking coal of relatively good quality is produced at mines that include United States Steel's Somerset Mine, the largest underground mine in Colorado (present capacity, approximately one million short, 0.9 million metric, tons per year). In-place coal resources to a depth of 1,830 m in the 515 km² area investigated are conservatively estimated at more than 8 billion short (7.3 billion metric) tons (Hornbaker and others, 1976).

REFERENCES

Averitt, Paul, 1972, Coal, *in* Geologic atlas of the Rocky Mountain region: Denver, Colorado, Rocky Mountain Association of Geologists, p. 297–299, Fig. 3 (map).

Boreck, D. L., Jones, D. C., Murray, D. K., Schultz, J. E., and Suek, D. C., 1977, Colorado coal analyses, 1975 (Analyses of 64 samples collected in 1975): Colorado Geological Survey Information Series 7, 112 p.

Boreck, D. L. and Strever, Mark, 1980, Conservation of methane from mined/minable coal beds, Colorado: Colorado Geological Survey Open-File Report 80-5, 95 p.

Goolsby, S. M., Reade, N. B. S., and Murray, D. K., 1979, Evaluation of coking coals in Colorado: Colorado Geological Survey Resource Series 7, 72 p.

Hornbaker, A. L., Holt, R. D., and Murray, D. K., 1976, Summary of coal resources in Colorado, 1975: Colorado Geological Survey Special Publication 9, 17 p.

Jones, D. C. and Murray, D. K., 1976, Coal mines of Colorado, statistical data: Colorado Geological Survey Information Series 2, 27 p.

Jones, D. C., Schultz, J. E., and Murray, D. K., 1978, Coal resources and development map of Colorado: Colorado Geological Survey Map Series 9, scale, 1:500,000.

Khalsa, N. S. and others, Colorado coal analyses, 1976–1979: Colorado Geological Survey Information Series 10 (in preparation).

Murray, D. K., 1980a, Coal, *in* Colorado Geology, H. C. Kent and K. W. Porter, eds.: Denver, Colorado, Rocky Mountain Association of Geologists, p. 205–216.

———, 1980b, Colorado—description of seams, *in* Keystone Coal Industry Manual, G. F. Nielsen, Ed.-in-Chief: New York, McGraw-Hill Mining Publications, p. 472–494.

Murray, D. K., Fender, H. B., and Jones, D. C., 1977, Coal and methane gas in the southeastern part of the Piceance Creek basin, Colorado, *in* Exploration frontiers of the Central and Southern Rockies: Rocky Mountain Association of Geologists Field Conference Guidebook, p. 379–405.

Speltz, C. N., 1976, Strippable coal resources of Colorado—location, tonnage, and characteristics of coal and overburden: U.S. Bureau of Mines Information Circular 8713, 70 p.

Independence Monument, separating the two entrances of Monument Canyon in Colorado National Monument. Looking north from Grand View; Colorado River, Grand Valley, and Book Cliffs in distance. Roan Cliffs are white cliffs at extreme distance on right skyline. Floor of canyon is Proterozoic metamorphic rocks; overlying strata are upper Triassic. Slopes at foot of cliffs are red Chinle Formation; cliffs are Wingate Sandstone (107 m); thin protective caprock on top of cliffs is lower sandstone of the resistant Kayenta Formation. Top of monument is nearly 137 m above canyon floor. Infrared photograph by S. W. Lohman, U.S. Geological Survey.

METHANE IN CRETACEOUS AND PALEOCENE COALS OF WESTERN COLORADO

C. M. TREMAIN, D. L. BORECK, and B. S. KELSO
Colorado Geological Survey
Denver, Colorado 80203

INTRODUCTION

Western Colorado is the site of coal, oil, and natural gas development in three principal areas: the San Juan River, the Uinta, and the Green River Regions (fig. 1). Evidence is accumulating that some of the coals in these regions both act as a source and potential reservoir for natural gas (methane). This paper details some of the evidence and describes work being done by the Colorado Geological Survey (CGS) to estimate the methane resources of these regions.

PROCEDURES

Only areas considered to have a high methane potential are included in this paper. These areas contained thick, high ranking coals at depth (Goolsby and others, 1981).

Net coal thicknesses were determined from the following logs: natural gamma, caliper, sonic or acoustic, neutron, and density. SP-resistivity logs were used only to pick formation tops or verify the presence of coals seen on the other logs or sample logs. The minimum seam thickness used in determining net coal thicknesses is 0.6 m (2 ft) for the San Juan Region, 1 m (3 ft) for the Uinta Region, and 1.2 m (4 ft) for the Green River Region.

SAN JUAN RIVER REGION

The San Juan River Coal Region of southwestern Colorado is that area underlain by the coal-bearing Dakota Formation (Goolsby and others, 1979, p. 38).

Within this region, the San Juan Basin offers the greatest methane potential. The basin, a deep assymetrical syncline, is approximately 160 km in diameter (fig. 1). Its arcuate axis lies just south of the Colorado–New Mexico border. The steeply dipping,

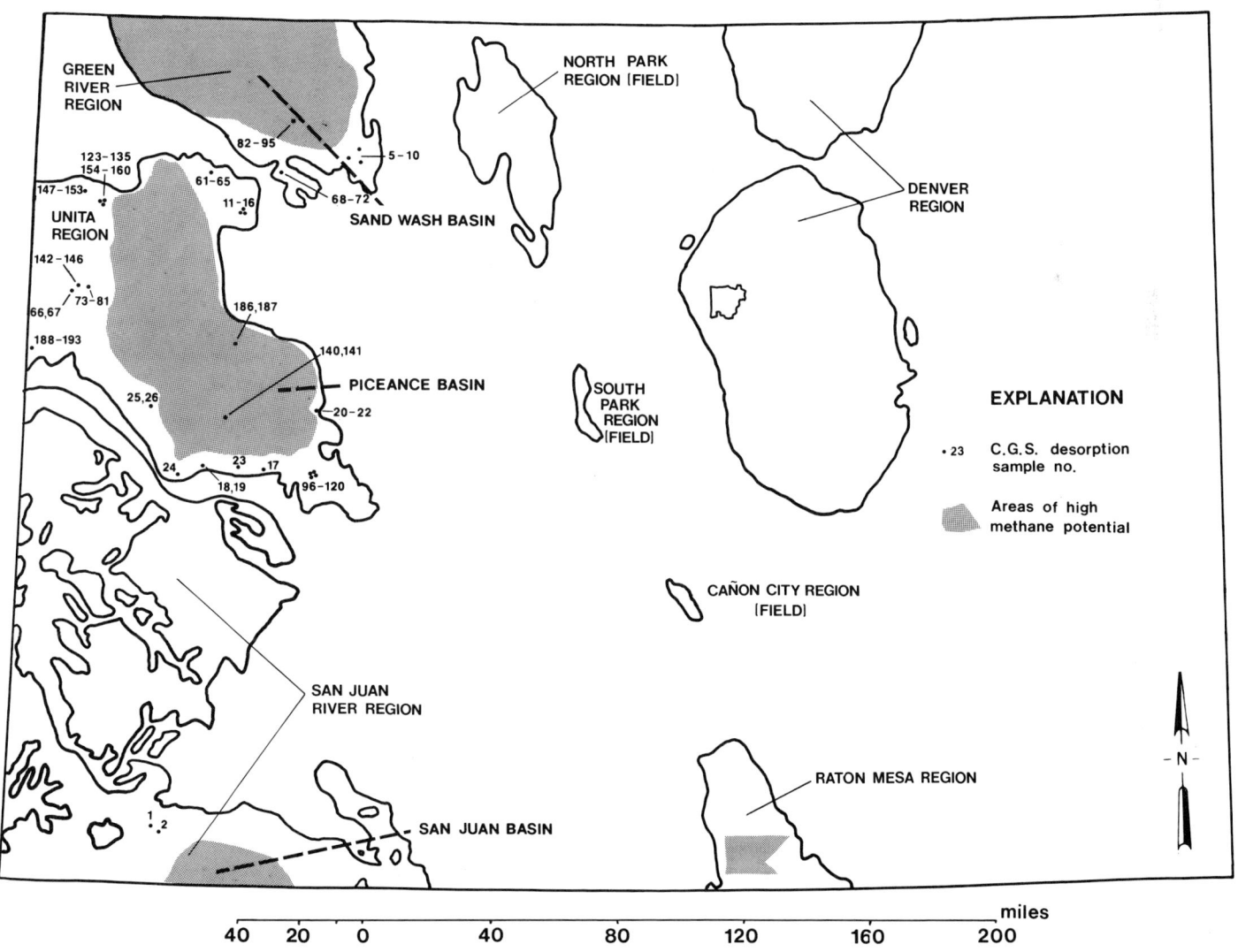

Figure 1. The coal regions of Colorado.

U-shaped Hogback Monocline forms the northern rim of the basin. To the east, the Gallina–Archuleta Arch and the Nacimiento Uplift bound the basin. To the south, the basin grades into the Chaco Slope. The southwestern boundary of the basin is formed by the Defiance Monocline (Woodward and Callender, 1977, p. 210).

En echelon northwesterly trending folds and northeasterly trending high-angle faults occur along the basin's eastern boundary. Around the basin's perimeter are radial folds plunging towards the basin's center and minor folds parallel to the basin's margins. These structures formed principally during Late Cretaceous Laramide times. The entire area was then epeirogenically uplifted. Igneous intrusions were emplaced along the basin's margins during Tertiary times.

The San Juan Basin contains sediments ranging in age from Cambrian to Quaternary. The Precambrian basement is encountered at depths of 1,428 m to 4,276 m below the surface.

The Upper Cretaceous sediments contain all of the coal-bearing formations in the basin (fig. 2). These sediments are a series of intertonguing marine and nonmarine deposits which resulted from three transgressive-regressive cycles of the Cretaceous epicontinental sea (Fassett and Hinds, 1971, p. 4). The final regression of the sea is represented by the Pictured Cliffs Sandstone.

The marine sediments are pro-delta and interdeltaic deposits of shoreline marine sands, offshore sandy silts, and deep water muds. The nonmarine deposits are lower delta or coastal-plain deposits, and upper delta or alluvial-plain deposits (Molenaar, 1977, p. 159). It is predominantly in these nonmarine, coastal-plain and alluvial-plain facies that coal sequences are found.

The coal-bearing formations of the San Juan Basin, in ascending order, are the Dakota, the Menefee (Mesaverde Group), and the Fruitland formations (fig. 2). The Dakota has coal seams ranging in thickness from 0.6 m to 2.4 m. All seams are discontinuous and grade laterally into carbonaceous shales. The coals were probably deposited in a flood-plain/braided stream environment. The Menefee coals, like the Dakota coals, are extremely lenticular and also range from 0.6 m to 2.4 m thick. It appears these coals were deposited on a delta plain between distributary channels.

The Fruitland Formation, which averages 122 m in thickness, has the thickest and most continuous coal seams in the region. Coals throughout the formation range from less than 0.3 m to 22 m. Thickest and most continuous seams in the Fruitland are found in the lowermost 21 m. These seams formed from peat deposited in brackish to fresh-water lagoons and marshes, behind a barrier coastline. The thinner seams in the Fruitland probably formed on upper coastal plains (alluvial plains).

Historically, the Fruitland Formation has been broken into three coal zones (Boreck and Murray, 1979, p. 56). The upper zone (Shamrock zone) may reach 6 m in thickness and is found near the middle of the formation. The middle zone (commonly called the Carbonera or Peacock zone) is located in the basal 21 m of the formation. The third zone (Fruitland tongue) is a shale and coal deposit which intertongues with the Pictured Cliffs Sandstone. This zone is not continuous throughout the basin and is difficult to locate on geophysical logs.

The Fruitland coals in the San Juan River Region vary in rank from subbituminous B (sub B) at the basin's perimeter, to medium volatile (mv) in the deeper parts of the basin. The medium volatile ranking coals may be due to local upgrading. The deepest Fruitland coals in the basin have overburdens of up to 1,200 m.

Methane

Evidence from mine data, oil and gas exploration, and desorption of coal cores and cuttings samples indicates that gas is present in the coals of the San Juan Basin.

Fender and Murray (1978, p. 8) reported three gassy mines in the San Juan region. The Burnwell No. 1 and the Hesperus (old) mines were sites of mine fires. The Champion was the site of a gas explosion.

A large number of wells had gas shows in coal zones or were tested and/or producing from Fruitland coal intervals. One well, T.32N., R.7W., recorded a gas "kick" over a 6.4 m interval, containing a 1.5 m coal at its base. A second well (T.33N, R.6W.) was drill-stem tested over a 49 m Fruitland interval containing three coal beds totaling 17 m. The interval tested 5,664 m³ per day (200 MCFD) with a flow pressure of 96 pounds in a 1 hour test. Well completion included 2.4 m of coal (Goolsby and others, 1981, Appendix B).

Lent (1980) gives the results of 10 desorption measurements (using the U.S. Bureau of Mines "direct method") from the San Juan River Coal Region of Colorado and New Mexico. The gas contents

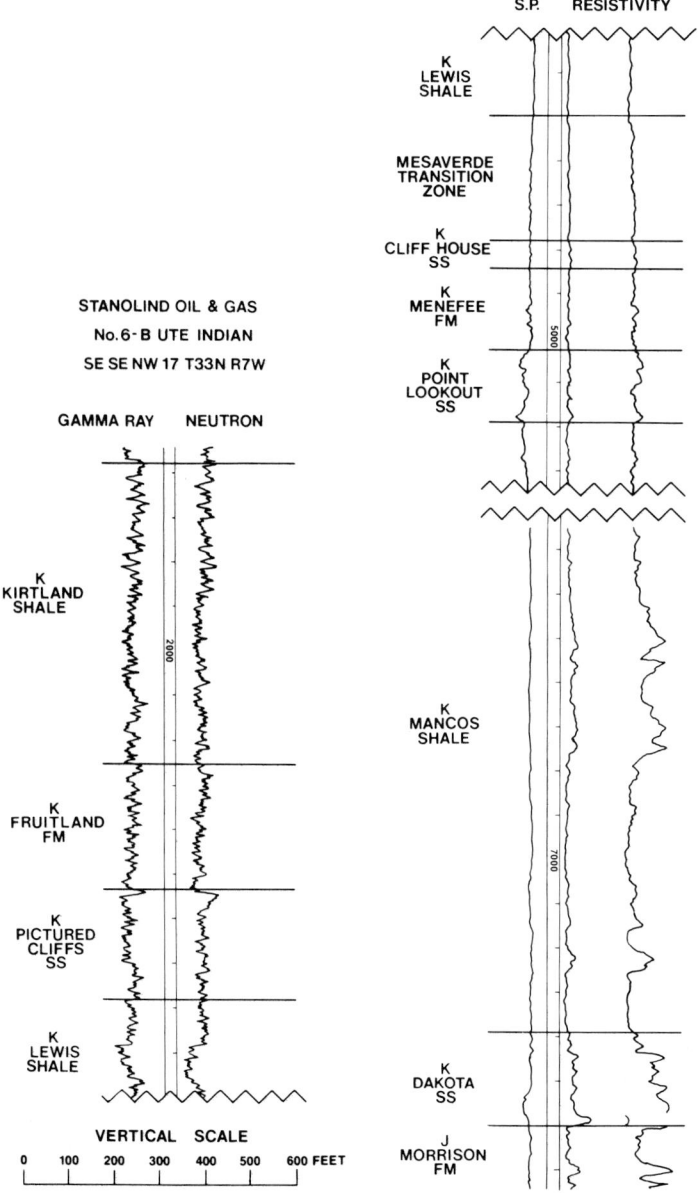

Figure 2. Log showing Cretaceous coal-bearing formations (Dakota, Menefee, and Fruitland) in the San Juan Basin.

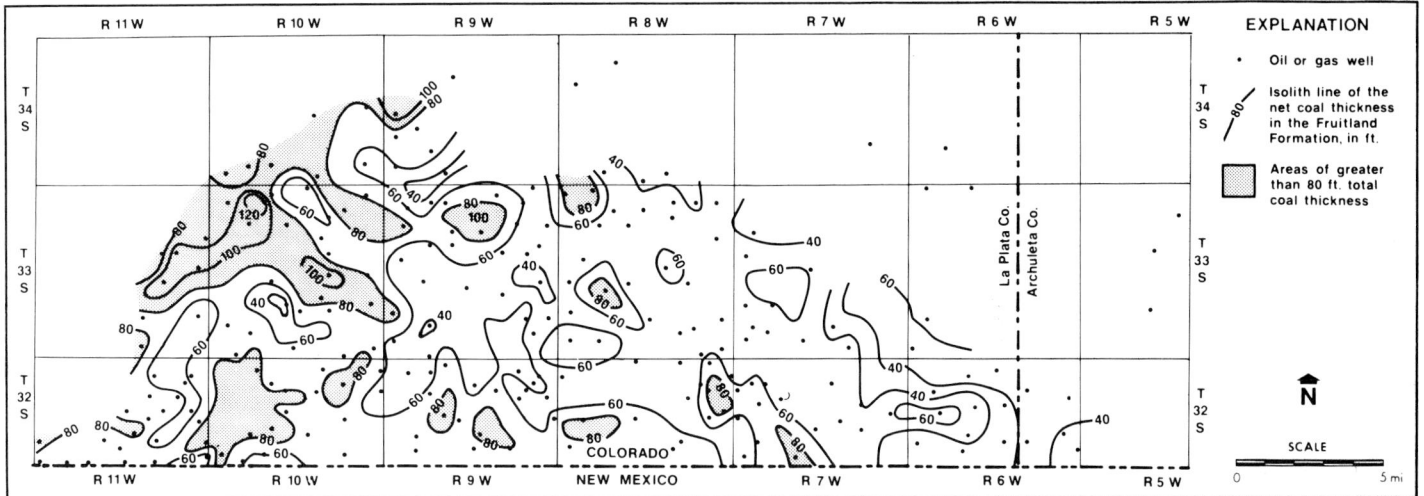

Figure 3. Net coal thickness map of the coal-bearing Fruitland Formation, San Juan Basin (from Goolsby and others, 1981).

range from 0.16 cubic centimeters per gram (cm³/g) [5.3 cubic feet per ton (ft³/t)] of coal to 4.2 cm³/g (134 ft³/t). The coals rank from high volatile C bituminous (hvC) to high volatile A bituminous (hvA). However, these data do not reflect the high methane potential of the region, since the samples were not from the highest ranking Fruitland seams.

Goolsby and others (1981) reported on an area in the Colorado part of the San Juan Basin characterized by thick, continuous, and high ranking Fruitland coals under sufficient overburden to prevent gas loss. This area covers 1,528 km² in T.32N.–T.34N. and R.5W.–R.11 W. Figure 3 is a net coal thickness map and Figure 4 is a structure map of this area.

The authors believe the gas contents of the coals in the study area are similar to those of coals in the Raton Mesa Coal Region. This belief is based on similarities in rank, overburden depths, stratigraphic position, and localized upgrading (Goolsby and others, 1981, p. 25; and Tremain, 1981, p. 34). The gas contents of the Raton Mesa region ranged from 2.25 cm³/g (72 ft³/t) in a high volatile B bituminous (hvB) sample to 16.0 cm³/g (514 ft³/t) in a medium volatile bitumunous (mv) sample.

A coal resource estimate of 19.7 billion short tons was obtained for the study area by planimetering the net coal thickness isopach (fig. 3). Multiplying this tonnage by the low and high gas contents stated above, gives a total coal bed methane resource estimate ranging from 40 billion m³ (1.4 trillion ft³) to 283 billion m³ (10.0 trillion ft³).

UINTA REGION

The Unita Coal Region (fig. 1) is the area in west-central Colorado and eastern Utah bordered by the base of the Mesaverde Group. The Colorado portion of the region covers 18,648 km² (Murray, 1980, p. 214).

The Piceance Basin, in the Colorado portion of the Uinta Region, has excellent methane potential. This basin is defined by the Cretaceous–Tertiary outcrop and covers approximately 10,360 km² (Dunn, 1974, p. 217). The basin is bounded by: the Axial Basin Uplift in the north; the Grand Hogback Monocline in the east; the Elk and West Elk mountains and the Gunnison Uplift in the south; the Uncompahgre Uplift in the southwest; and the Douglas Creek Arch in the west.

The basin itself is assymetrical with a steeply-dipping eastern and northeastern flank and a gentle western and southwestern flank.

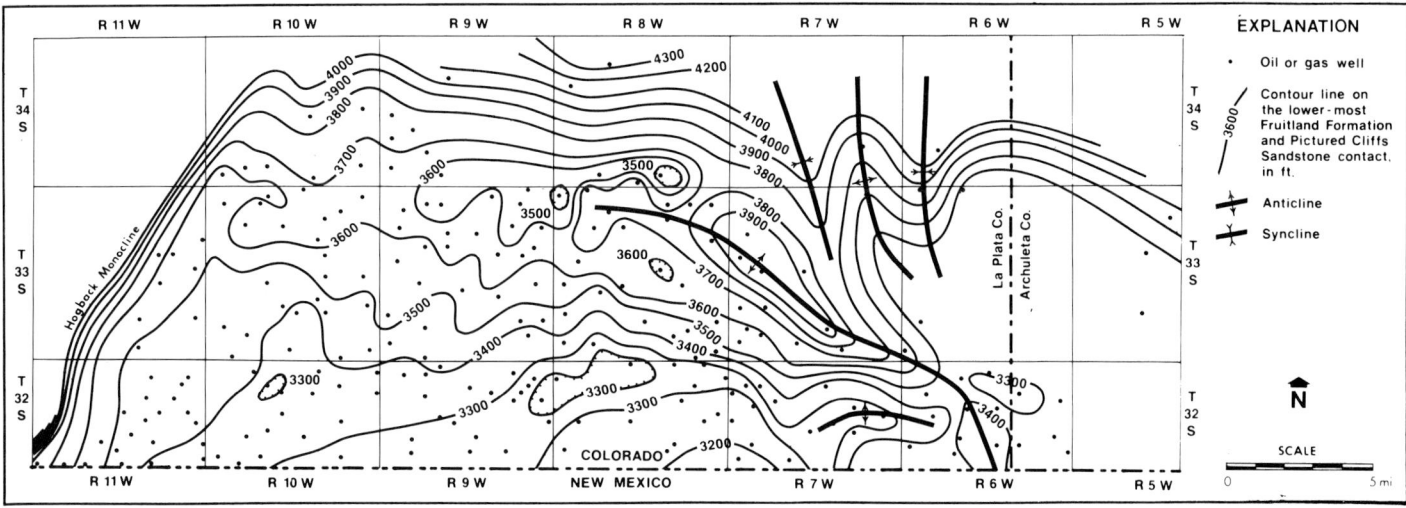

Figure 4. Structure map of the lower Pictured-Cliffs Sandstone–Fruitland Formation contact, San Juan Basin (from Goolsby and others, 1981).

The axis of the basin trends northwesterly and parallels the Grand Hogback Monocline on the eastern side of the basin. This axis is split by basinward plunging anticlines on its north and south ends (Dunn, 1974, p. 217). Other northwest-southwest trending anticlines dot the interior of the basin. Gas and locally oil is produced from a number of these anticlines and from structures in the adjoining Douglas Creek Arch.

The Precambrian basement is 5,500 m below sea level at the deepest point in the basin. There are over 7,620 m of Cambrian through Quaternary sediments at this point (Murray, 1980, p. 214). Cretaceous sediments constitute over 3,000 m of this sequence (Murray and Haun, 1974, p. 31). These sediments were deposited as the Cretaceous sea slowly and episodically regressed to the east. The marine Mancos Shale comprises the major portion of the lower Cretaceous sediments. Upper Cretaceous sediments are predominantly the non-marine sandstones, shales, and coals of the Mesavede Group (see fig. 5).

The Mesaverde coals occur as discontinuous beds throughout the formation. They show great variations in thickness and rank. In an outcrop at Newcastle, the total coal thickness reaches 33 m; an individual bed is reported as 15 m (Gale, 1910, p. 111). Subsurface data in the south central part of the basin show a maximum of 24 m of coal present in beds up to 9 m thick. The coals range from subbituminous B (sub B to anthracite (anth) in rank. Figure 6 is an isopach and rank map of Mesaverde coals. Figure 7 is a structure map of the Cozette Sandstone near the base of the Mesaverde Group.

Methane

Fender and Murray (1978) listed 47 coal mines in the region that reported gas occurrences. The gassiest mines are in the Carbondale coal field (T.7-10S., R.89W.) where the coal ranks medium volatile (mv). In this field, the L. S. Wood mine emitted 61,454 m³ per day (2,170 MCFD); the Dutch Creek #1 mine emitted 37,892 m³/d (1,338 MCFD); and the Dutch Creek #2 mine emitted 40,384 m³/d (1,426 MCFD) for the period 1974 through 1976.

At least two wells have produced methane from coal in the Piceance Basin area. A well on the Douglas Creek Arch produced an average of 283 m³/d (10 MCFD) for several months from a shallow coal bed. A well in the south-central part of the basin had an initial production of 12,461 m³/d (440 MCFD) and 17 m³/d (109 barrels) of water from perforations in three deep, medium volatile coals.

The gas contents of the 80 samples collected by the CGS from the region have ranged from 0 to 13.7 cm³/g (0 to 438 ft³/t) (Table 1). The quality of the gas of seven of these samples has ranged from 3,583 to 8,534 kcal/m³ (403 to 960 BTU/ft³). These and other samples taken by the U.S. Bureau of Mines and the CGS show an increase in gas contents with increasing rank and depth. Therefore, those areas with thick, high ranking coals at depths sufficient to prevent gas loss would be likely methane prospects. Study of coal rank, isopach, structure, and topographic maps should reveal such areas.

By planimetering the coal isopach map (fig. 6) and using gas contents averaged from Table 1, the CGS has estimated a coal bed methane resource of 878 billion m³ (31 trillion ft³) in the southern half of the Piceance Basin. The CGS is currently revising this map in order to estimate the methane resources for the entire basin.

GREEN RIVER COAL REGION

The Green River Coal Region in northwestern Colorado (fig. 1) is defined as the area bounded by the basal contact of the Upper Cretaceous Mesaverde Group (Murray, 1980, p. 211).

The main structure within the region is the Sand Wash Basin. The basin is bordered by the Cherokee Ridge to the north, the Sierra Madre Uplift to the east, the Axial Basin Arch to the south, and the Uinta Uplift to the west and southwest.

The basin's axis trends west-northwest. Depth to the top of the Precambrian rocks in the deepest part of the basin is approximately 5,300 m below sea level (Haun, 1962, p. 11). Folding and faulting is common in the basin. The major structures are usually found along the periphery. Upper Triassic intrusives occur in the eastern part of the basin.

Sedimentary rocks in the Sand Wash Basin–Green River Region range from Upper Cambrian to Tertiary in age. Coal-bearing rocks in the Green River Region are: the Upper Cretaceous Iles and Williams Fork formations (or Rock Springs and Almond formations) of the Mesaverde Group, the Upper Cretaceous Lance Formation, the Upper Cretaceous–Paleocene Fort Union Formation, and the Paleocene–Eocene Wasatch Formation (fig. 8).

The Iles and Williams Fork formations (Mesaverde Group) were deposited in a marginal marine environment bordering the Late Cretaceous epeirogenic sea. The formations are predominantly white to light brown sandstones, gray shales, and coals. The coals are found throughout the Mesaverde Group. Most individual coal beds are less than 3 m thick, although coals up to 7 m have been recorded. Net coal thicknesses for the Iles and Williams Fork formations range from 6 to 41 m.

The Lance Formation was deposited in a marginal marine to fluvial environment. The formation is made up of gray shales, light brown sandstones and coals. Lance coals are not as thick and well

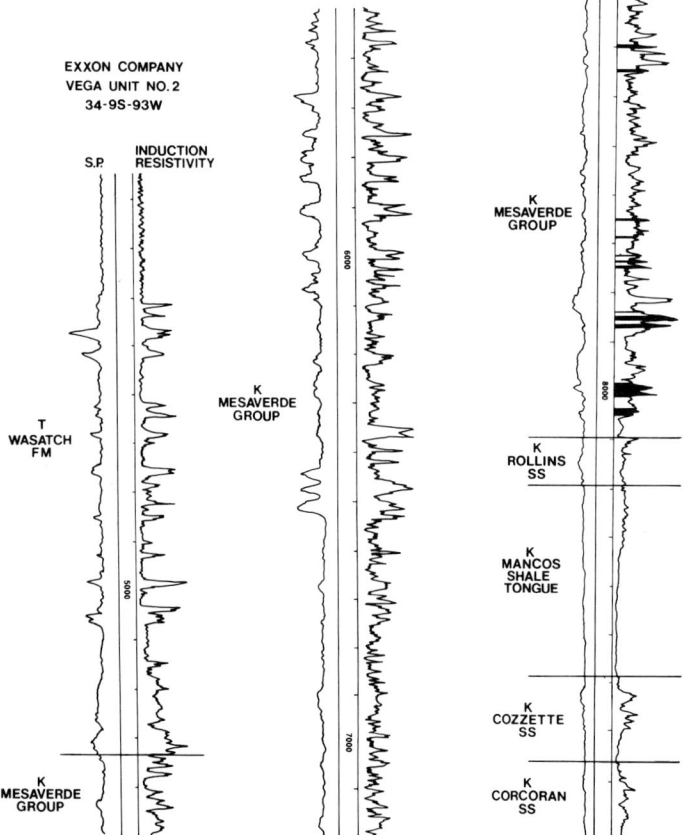

Figure 5. Type log for the southern Piceance Basin. Coals are shown in black.

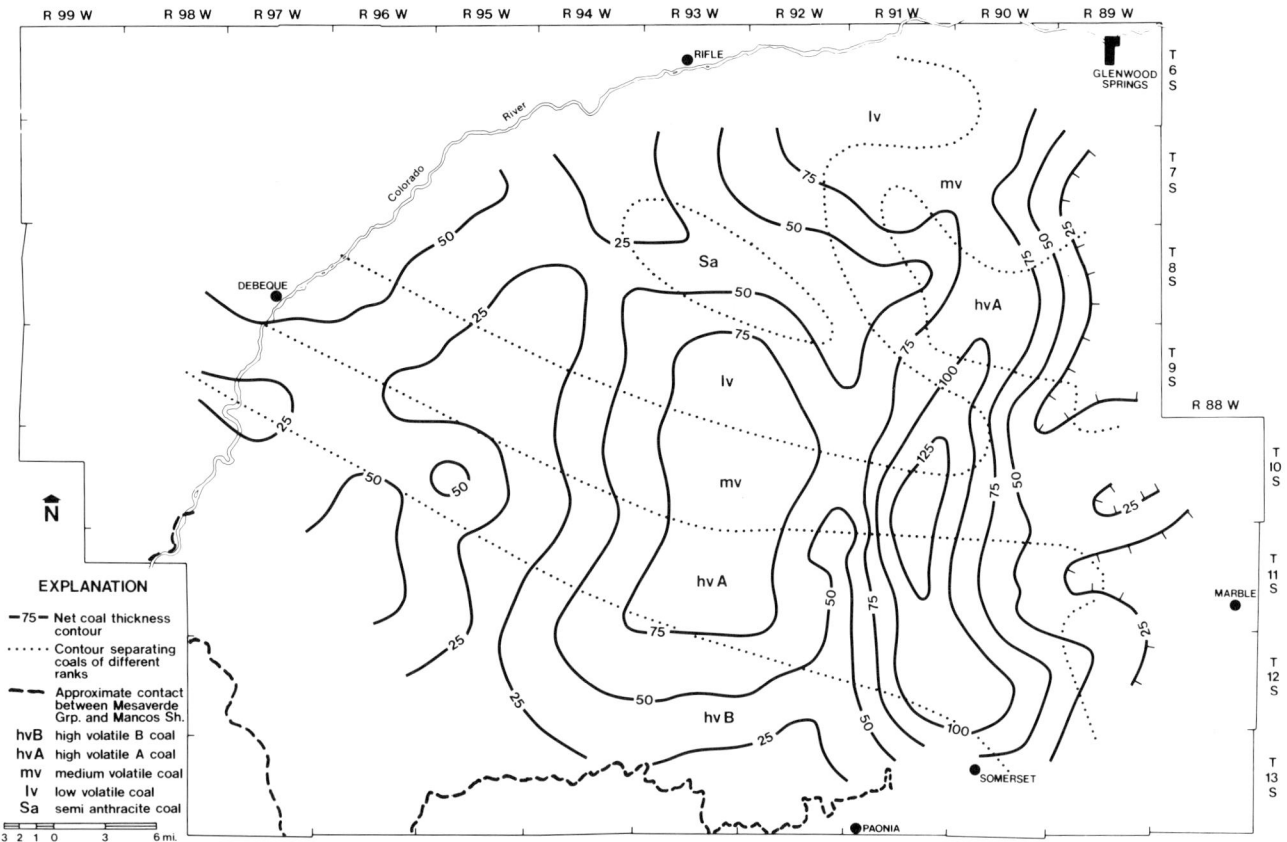

Figure 6. Net coal isopach and coal rank map of the Cretaceous Mesaverde coals, southern Piceance Basin (after Fender and Murray, 1978; Freeman, 1979). Isopachs in feet.

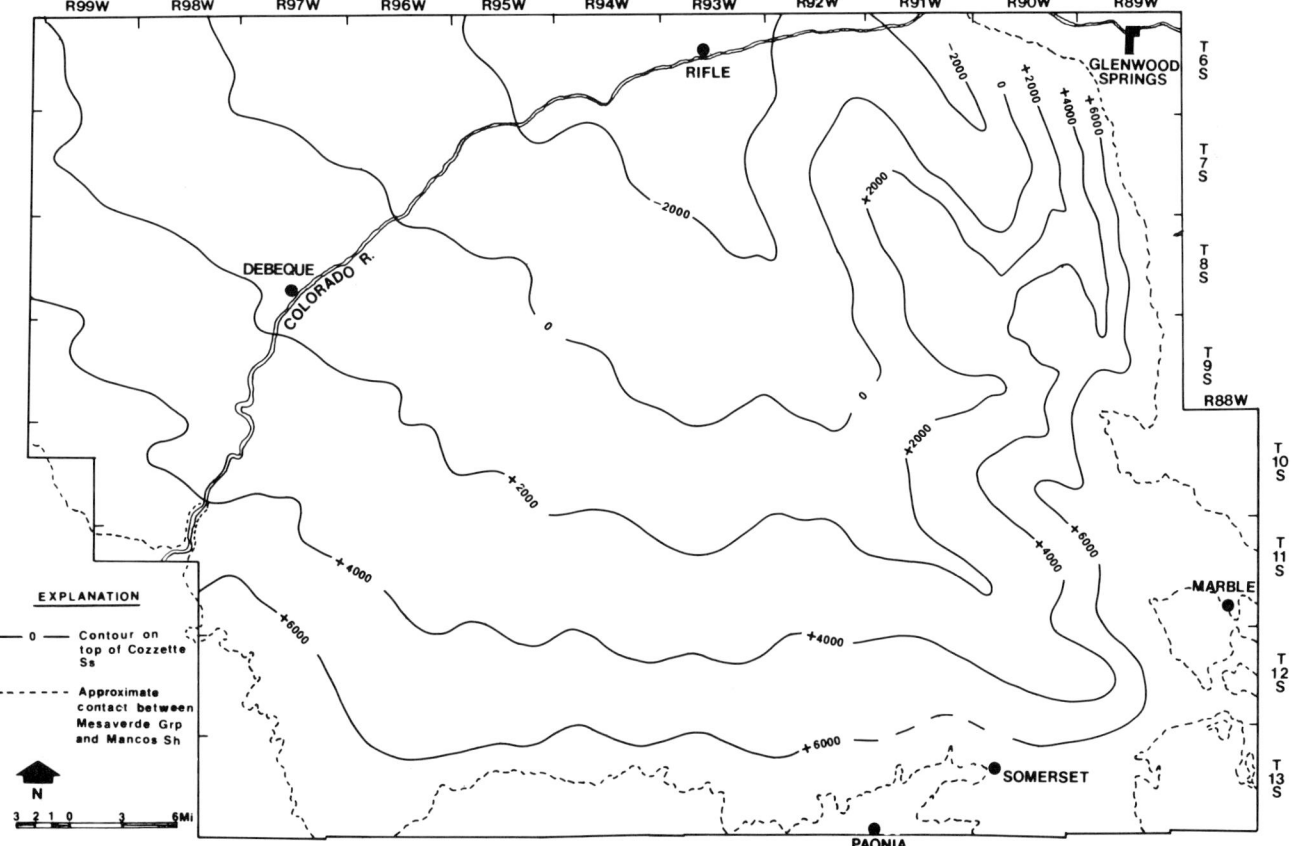

Figure 7. Structure on the top of the Cretaceous Cozzette Sandstone in the southern Piceance Basin (after Fender and Murray, 1978). Contours in feet.

Table 1. *Coal sample and desorption data.*

CCS no.	Formation name	Depth to coal bed (ft)	Bed thickness (ft)	Total gas (cm³/g)	(ft³/t)	Apparent rank of coal	% methane in gas	Heating value of gas (Btu/ft³)
		SAN JUAN RIVER COAL REGION						
1	Menefee	295	9+	.17	5	hvBb	[1]	
2	Menefee	310	7.5	.32	10	hvAb		
		GREEN RIVER COAL REGION						
5	Williams Fork	1283	11.5	NC [2]		hvCb		
6	Williams Fork	1393	11.0	?	?	hvCb		
7	Williams Fork	488	1.3	NC		hvCb		
8	Williams Fork	335	8.5	.24	8	hvCb		
9	Williams Fork	1104	4.5	NC		hvCb		
10	Williams Fork	1123	9.7	NC		hvBb		
68	Williams Fork	176.5	20.6	0.11	4	subA-hvCb		
69	Williams Fork	644.0	3.6	0.09	3	hvCb		
70	Williams Fork	720.9	3.0	0.0	0	hvCb		
71	Williams Fork	766.3	9.0	0.50	16	hvCb		
72	Williams Fork	799.8	7.3	0.18	6	hvBb		
82	Williams Fork	3660	3	7.84	251	hvBb	81.78	825
83	Williams Fork	3663	6	7.99	256	shale	53.21	538
84	Williams Fork	3684	4	3.77	121	hvBb		
85	Williams Fork	3929	5	3.86	124	hvBb		
86	Williams Fork	3947	.2	2.72	87	hvBb		
87	Williams Fork	3958	1	9.01	288	hvBb		
88	Williams Fork	4658	15.6	8.41	269	hvBb		
89	Williams Fork	4658	15.6	9.26	296	hvBb		
90	Williams Fork	4658	15.6	9.4	301	hvBb		
91	Williams Fork	4658	15.6	8.56	274	hvAb		
92	Williams Fork	4658	15.6	10.08	322	hvAb	74.41	769
93	Williams Fork	4658	10	10.50	336	hvAb		
94	Williams Fork	4716	10	11.76	376	hvAb	69.45	741
		UINTA COAL REGION						
11	Williams Fork	2216	15	.50	16			
12	Williams Fork	2243	4	1.31	42	--		
13	Williams Fork	2122	12	.98	31	--		
14	Williams Fork	2106	8	.10	3	hvCb		
15	Williams Fork	48.7	10.8	0	0	hvCb		
16	Williams Fork	502.6	12	.19	6	hvCb		
17	Williams Fork	504	5.8	5.62	179	hvCb		
18	Williams Fork	706.7	7.6	.82	26	hvCb		
19	Williams Fork	706.7	6.6	1.7 [3]	54	mvb		
20	Williams Fork	1500	8.7	.215 [3]	7	mvb		
21	Williams Fork	1300-1500	25	.22 [3]	7	hvCb		
22	Williams Fork	2000	20	.46 [3]	15	hvCb		
23	Mesaverde Gp. [4]	992.5	14.5	0	0	hvAb		
24	Mesaverde Gp.	579	5.5	2.5	80	hvAb		
25	Mesaverde Gp.	809	3.5	7	223	hvAb		
26	Mesaverde Gp.	1284.5	13	.36	12	subA-hvCb		
61	Williams Fork	144	13	0.39	13	subA-hvCb		
62	Williams Fork	144	19.5	0.24	8	subA-hvCb		
63	Williams Fork	163.5	4.3	0.15	5	subA-hvCb		
64	Williams Fork	287.5	20.7	0.116	4	subA-hvCb		
65	Williams Fork	294.8	3	0.667	21	hvBb		
66	Mesaverde Gp.	1588		0.489	16	hvCb		
67	Mesaverde Gp.	1607		3.58	115	shale		
73	Mesaverde Gp.	685.2	.4	6.68	214	shale		
74	Mesaverde Gp.	698.1	14.5	1.45	126	siltstone		
75	Mesaverde Gp.	772.35	.6	0.76	66	shale		
76	Mesaverde Gp.	770.88	.57	2.69	156	hvBb		
77	Mesaverde Gp.	759.2	.8	7.61	243	hvBb		
78	Mesaverde Gp.	809.3	.4	2.76	130	hvBb		
79	Mesaverde Gp.	835.?	4.7	4.31	138	hvBb		
80	Mesaverde Gp.	835.?	7.8	3.47	111	hvBb		
81	Mesaverde Gp.	962.?	4.8	2.49	80	hvAb		
97	Williams Fork	873	6.1	3.2	102	hvAb		
98	Williams Fork	896	1.6	3.74	120	hvAb		

CCS no.	Formation name	Depth to coal bed (ft)	Bed thickness (ft)	Total gas (cm³/g)	(ft³/t)	Apparent rank of coal	% methane in gas	Heating value of gas (Btu/ft³)
		UINTA COAL REGION						
99	Williams Fork	948	2.9	3.88	124	hvAb		
100	Williams Fork	1133	6.7	0.28	9	hvAb		
101	Williams Fork	1133	6.7	6.81	218	hvAb		
102	Williams Fork	1187	14	5.82	186	hvAb		
103	Williams Fork	1187	14	5.94	190	hvAb		
104	Williams Fork	1207	6.8	6.15	197	hvAb		
105	Williams Fork	1227	1.2	3.72	119	hvAb		
106	Williams Fork	782	13	6.06	194	hvAb		
107	Williams Fork	782	13	6.77	217	hvAb	73.09	739
108	Williams Fork	719	6	6.62	212	hvAb		
109	Williams Fork	1182	6.9	5.70	182	hvAb		
110	Williams Fork	1236	12.7	5.93	190	hvAb		
111	Williams Fork	1260	5.3	6.53	209	hvAb		
112	Williams Fork	1516	12	3.16	101	hvAb		
113	Williams Fork	1583	8	3.36	108	hvAb		
114	Williams Fork	1583	8	4.12	132	hvAb		
115	Williams Fork	1783	12	5.42	173	hvAb		
116	Williams Fork	1783	12	2.99	96	hvAb		
117	Williams Fork	1830	14.65	6.10	195	hvAb		
118	Williams Fork	1830	14.65	5.53	177	hvAb		
119	Williams Fork	1854	6.7	5.98	191	hvBb		
120	Williams Fork	1854	6.7	7.66	245	hvAb		
123	Mesaverde Gp.	1324.68	1.17	2.04	65	hvCb		
124	Mesaverde Gp.	1330.6	8.21	2.25	72	hvCb		
125	Mesaverde Gp.	1330.6	8.21	2.19	70	hvCb		
126	Mesaverde Gp.	1330.6	8.21	2.06	66	hvCb		
127	Mesaverde Gp.	1349.75	2.05	1.81	58	hvCb		
128	Mesaverde Gp.	741.75	6.43	0.64	20	hvCb	(47.63) [5]	610
129	Mesaverde Gp.	758.71	2.22	2.05	80	hvCb	(33.11)	506
130	Mesaverde Gp.	758.71	2.22	2.25	72	hvCb		
131	Mesaverde Gp.	764.92	2.5	2.50	80	hvCb		
132	Mesaverde Gp.	770	2.15	2.79	89	hvCb	(57.66) 58.6	610
133	Mesaverde Gp.	794.65	4.0	2.34	74	hvCb	(46.10) 49.2	506
134	Mesaverde Gp.	797.5	5.37	2.23	71	hvCb	(38.27) 39.3	403
135	Mesaverde Gp.	805.8		1.35	43	hvCb	(38.27) 37.8	388
140	Mesaverde	7598	18	13.69	438	mvb	(82.99) 82.1	942
141	Mesaverde	7598	18	11.90	381	lvb	(79.63) 78.3	854, 960
							85.9	
142	Mesaverde	1148.9	8	1.11	36	hvCb		
143	Mesaverde	1148.9	8	0.76	24	hvBb		
144	Mesaverde	1207	8.7	0.92	29	hvBb		
145	Mesaverde	1207	8.7	0.64	20	hvBb		
146	Mesaverde	1223	2	0.95	30	hvBb		
147	Mesaverde	878.75	.4	0.03	1	shale		
148	Mesaverde	879	3.3	0.29	9	hvCb		
149	Mesaverde	892.72	8.8	0.02	1	siltstone		
150	Mesaverde	898.45	8.8	0.02	1	siltstone		
151	Mesaverde	904.3	7.7	0.13	4	hvCb		
152	Mesaverde	904.3	7.7	0.20	6	hvCb		
153	Mesaverde	912.4	.95	0.01	0	shale		
154	Mesaverde	1186.5	1.88	0.02	1	sandstone		
155	Mesaverde	1190.96	2.74	0.03	1	shale		
156	Mesaverde	1197.15	3.05	0.02	1	siltstone		
157	Mesaverde	1198.65	8.4	1.32	42	hvCb		
158	Mesaverde	1208.34		1.19	38	hvCb		
159	Mesaverde	1187.7	3.5	0.01	0	siltstone		
160	Mesaverde			0.97	31	hvCb		
184	Green River	685.2						
185	Green River	1189.7				oil shale		
186	Williams Fork	7445	1			oil shale		
187	Williams Fork	7476.5				shale		

1. blanks indicate gas analyses not run
2. NC = not calculated
3. mine samples; gas contents probably higher
4. Gp. = group
5. heating value not measured if methane percentage in parentheses
6. the following blank spaces indicate data not yet available

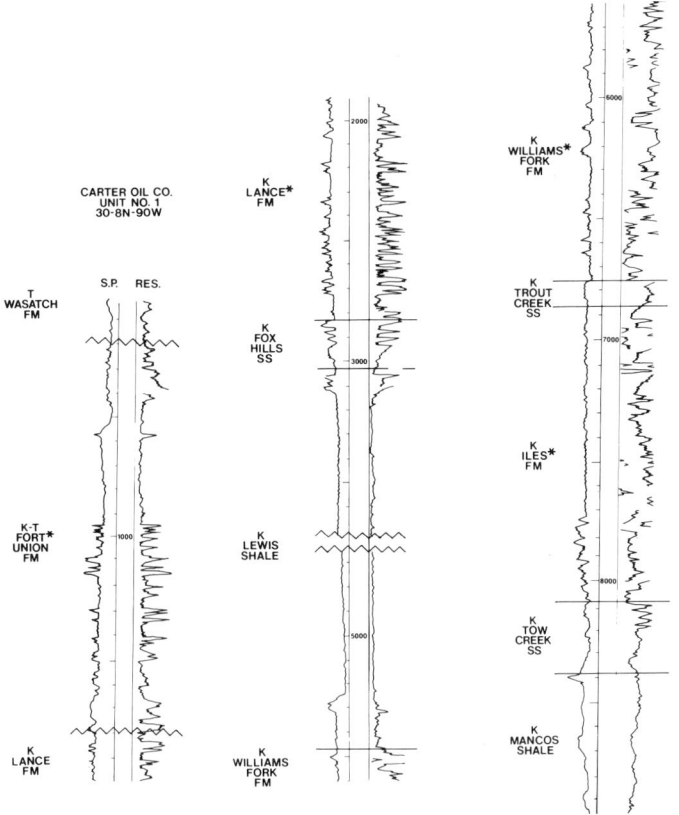

Figure 8. Log showing Upper Cretaceous and Tertiary coal-bearing formations in the Sand Wash Basin (modified from Rocky Mountain Association of Geologists, 1975). Coal-bearing formations marked by an asterisk.

developed as the Mesaverde coals. Net coal thicknesses range from 0 to 7.3 m, with the thickest individual coal bed attaining 3.6 m.

The Fort Union Formation rests unconformably on the Lance. It was deposited in a fluvial environment and is predominantly drab brown and gray sandstones, shales, and coals. Fort Union coals are the thickest reported in the five coal bearing formations. Individual coals are up to 15 m thick. Net coal thicknesses range from 0 to 33.5 m.

The Wasatch Formation overlies the Fort Union and consists of fluvial gray and pink arkosic sandstones, mudstones, conglomerates, and coals. Coals found in the Wasatch are, as a rule, thin and sparse.

Figure 9 is a net coal isopach map combining coal thicknesses from the Lance and Fort Union formations. Mesaverde coals were not included in the isopach due to scarcity of well log data and the Wasatch coals due to their sparseness. The mapped area is marked by the basal contact of the Wasatch Formation and by the Colorado state line. The isopach map should not be used to interpret specific depositional trends as the map is a composite of two formations deposited in two different environments.

Methane

Evidence for the presence of coal bed methane is found in both coal mine records and oil and gas data within the Green River Region–Sand Wash Basin. Coal mine records report the following: The Wadge No. 1, No. 2 mine complex (T.6N., R.97W.) was rocked by a gas explosion in 1942. Another mine, the Apex No. 2 Mine (T.4N., R.86W.), recorded an average gas emission of 322 m³/d (11.4 MCFD) in 1974 (Fender and Murray, 1978, table 1).

Well records obtained during oil and gas exploration offer conclusive evidence of the presence of coal bed methane at depths greater than 900 m. At these depths, mudlogs show gas kicks from coals; these kicks generally increase in strength with increasing depth. Gas buildups are often reported when drilling through coal sections. Coal cores bleeding gas have also been recovered.

Coal cores from four coal exploratory and one oil and gas test in the Green River Region have been desorbed (Table 1). The coal exploration core samples taken at depths of 53–427 m in T.5N., R.86–87W. yielded from 0 to 0.50 cm³/G (0–16 ft³/t). Core samples taken from the oil and gas test (T.7N., R.90W.) at depths of between 1,097 to 1,440 m, contained from 0.58 to 11.76 cm³/g (18 to 376 ft³/t).

The Sand Wash Basin of the Green River Region is believed to have a high potential as:

1) The amount of gas in the coals increases with increasing depth, and
2) Many of the thick coal sequences shown in Figure 9 occur under sufficient overburden to retain this gas.

The CGS will be calculating methane resources for the Sand Wash Basin in the near future.

CONCLUSIONS

The three regions of western Colorado contain basins with high methane potential. These areas may be found using coal rank,

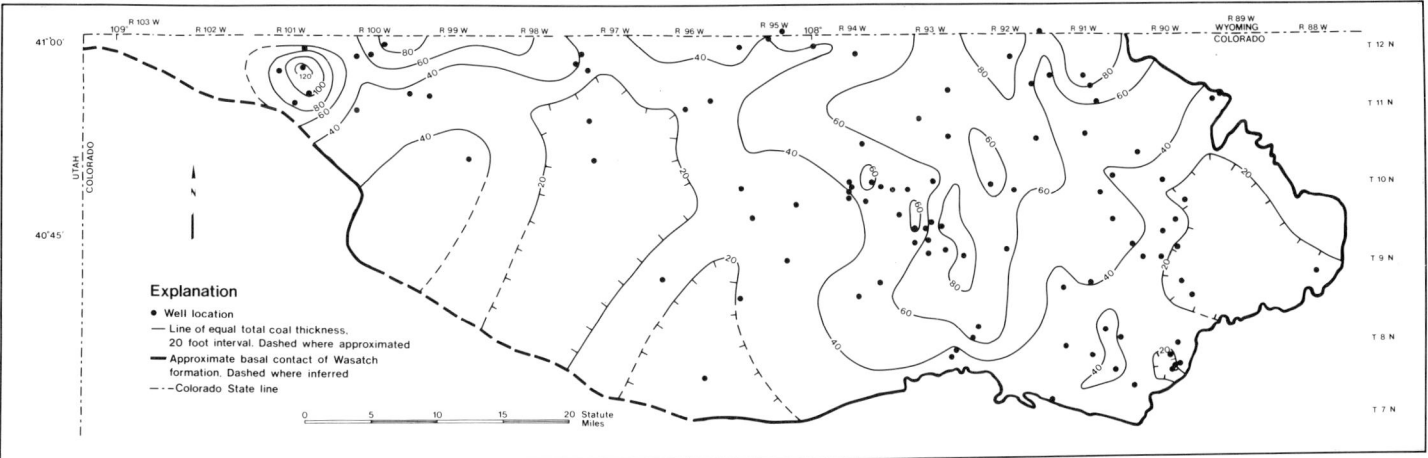

Figure 9. Net coal thickness map of the Lance and Fort Union formations, Sand Wash Basin.

depth, and desorption data obtained at little cost when drilling for coal reserve information or oil and gas. Potential coal reservoirs should be considered during all such exploration so they can be quickly developed when the economics so justify.

ACKNOWLEDGMENTS

This material was prepared with the support of the U.S. Department of Energy (DOE) Grant No. DE-FG21-80MC14256 and by funds from the Colorado Oil and Gas Conservation Commission. Special thanks go to S. M. Goolsby and H. B. Fender for data developed in previous CGS methane studies. Any opinions, findings, conclusions, or recommendations expressed herein are those of the author(s) and do not necessarily reflect the views of DOE.

REFERENCES

Boreck, D. L. and Murray, D. K., 1979, Colorado coal reserve depletion data and coal mine summaries: Colorado Geological Survey Open-File Report 79-1, 65 p.

Dunn, H. L., 1974, Geology of petroleum in the Piceance Creek Basin, northwestern Colorado, in Guidebook to the energy resources of the Piceance Creek Basin, Colorado: Rocky Mountain Association of Geologists, Denver, Colo., p. 217–223.

Fassett, J. E. and Hinds, J. S., 1971, Geology and fuel resources of the Fruitland Formation and Kirtland Shale of the San Juan Basin, New Mexico and Colorado: U.S. Geological Survey Professional Paper 676, 76 p.

Fender, H. B. and Murray, D. K., 1978, Data accumulation on the methane potential of the coal beds of Colorado: Colorado Geological Survey Open-File Report 78-2, 25 p.

Freeman, V. L., 1979, Preliminary report on rank of deep coals in part of the southern Piceance Creek Basin, Colorado: U.S. Geological Survey Open-File Report 79-725, 10 p.

Gale, H. S., 1910, Coalfields of northwestern Colorado and northeastern Utah: U.S. Geological Survey Bulletin 415, 265 p.

Goolsby, S. M., Kelso, B. S., and Tremain, C. M., 1981, Deep coal bed methane potential of the San Juan River Coal Region, southwestern Colorado: Colorado Geological Survey Open-File Report 80-2.

Goolsby, S. M., Reade, N. S., and Murray, D. K., 1979, Evaluation of coking coals in Colorado: Colorado Geological Survey Research Series 7, 72 p.

Haun, J. D., 1962, Introduction to the Geology of Northwest Colorado, in Exploration for oil and gas in northwestern Colorado: Rocky Mountain Association of Geologists, 1962, p. 7–14.

Lent, J., 1980, San Juan Basin Report—A study of the Upper Cretaceous geology, coal, and coal bed methane resources of the San Juan Basin, in Colorado and New Mexico: Prepared by TRW Energy Systems Planning Division, for the U.S. Dept. of Energy under contract number DE-AC21-78MCO8089.

McCulluch, G. M., Levine, J. R., Kissel, F. N., and Deul, 1975, Measuring the methane content of bituminous coalbeds: U.S. Bureau of Mines Report of Investigations 8043, 22 p.

Molenaar, C. M., 1977, Stratigraphy and depositional history of Upper Cretaceous rocks of the San Juan Basin area, New Mexico and Colorado, with a note on economic resources: New Mexico Geological Society Guidebook 20, p. 159–166.

Murray, D. K., 1980, Coal in Colorado, in Colorado Geology: Rocky Mountain Association of Geologists, Denver, Colo., p. 205–216.

Murray, D. K. and Haun, J. D., 1974, Introduction to the geology of the Piceance Creek Basin and vicinity, Northwestern Colorado, in Guidebook to the energy resources of the Piceance Creek Basin, Colorado: Rocky Mountain Association of Geologists, Denver, Colo., p. 29–39.

Rocky Mountain Association of Geologists, 1975, Subsurface cross-sections of Colorado: Rocky Mountain Association of Geologists Special Publication No. 2, p. 27–31, Fig. 20.

Tremain, C. M., 1981, The coal bed methane potential of the Raton Basin, south-central Colorado: Colorado Geological Survey Open-File Report 80-4, 39 p.

Woodward, L. A. and Callender, J. F., 1977, Tectonic framework of the San Juan Basin: New Mexico Geological Society Guidebook 28, p. 209–211.

COKING COALS OF WESTERN COLORADO*

L. R. LADWIG
Colorado Geological Survey
Denver, Colorado 80203

INTRODUCTION

Colorado is presently a major producer of coking quality coal. These resources are located in three Colorado coal regions, two of which lie within the western portion of the state. The Uinta Coal region produces high quality coking coal from a number of active mines while in the San Juan River region the production of coal for coking purposes is extremely limited although reserves appear to be adequate.

The coking coal resources of Colorado have been dealt with in the past by West (1874, 1875) and Weeks (1884) with state-wide coking coal data and by Lakes (1899a). Lakes specifically mentioned coke from coal mined at the Porter and San Juan mines in the "La Plata Field" and in a subsequent article (Lakes, 1899b) described the coal resources of the "Grand River Field," now called the Uinta region.

Numerous authors over the years have presented data on Colorado coking coal deposits; however, the most important publications in recent years are those of Averitt (1966), Jones and Murray (1978), and Goolsby and others (1979). These most recent publications indicate that the Uinta region with the Somerset, Crested Butte, Grand Hogback, and Carbondale fields is the most important western Colorado coking coal producer while the San Juan region has been of historic importance only. Figure 1 shows the outline of these two regions.

COKING COAL CLASSIFICATION

What makes a coking coal? Many classification systems have been devised for determining the desirability of any specific coal for its use in coke oven blends. The problems that are inherent in coal testing and reporting procedures which can lead to discrepancies within any coal classification system are discussed in Lowry (1963), Allen (1964), Rees (1968), Givens (1969) and Givens and Zarzab (1975). Although there are exemptions, few coal classification systems define coal property rigidly enough to adequately predict what the properties of the resultant coke over charge will be.

A complete review of various coking coal classification systems is too long for this paper but can be found in Goolsby and others (1979). The systems used by the Colorado Geological Survey are depicted in Table 1 and are based on ash and sulfur content, as proposed by William S. Sanner, Sr., in conjunction with ASTM coal rank designations.

GEOLOGIC HISTORY

The geologic history of a coal deposit, with all of its variables, governs the final feasibility of using it as a coke feedstock. Weimer (1977) has discussed thoroughly the principle factors that influence the formation of coal deposits in the western United States. Basic considerations of these depositional parameters can aid in the evaluation of potential coking coal resources. These include ash, sulfur, trace elements, thickness, geometry and geographic distribution.

The rank of the coal as shown in Table 1 is important in determining a coke feedstock. The rank is in part determined by the depositional history, i.e., greater depth of burial equals higher rank, for example as reported by Freeman (1979) that the rank of coals in the Uinta region increase to where semi-anthracite coals are found in the deeper parts of the basin. There are important exceptions to this general geothermal gradient relationship in that heat from igneous activity or abnormalities in the geothermal gradient may cause local increases in coal rank.

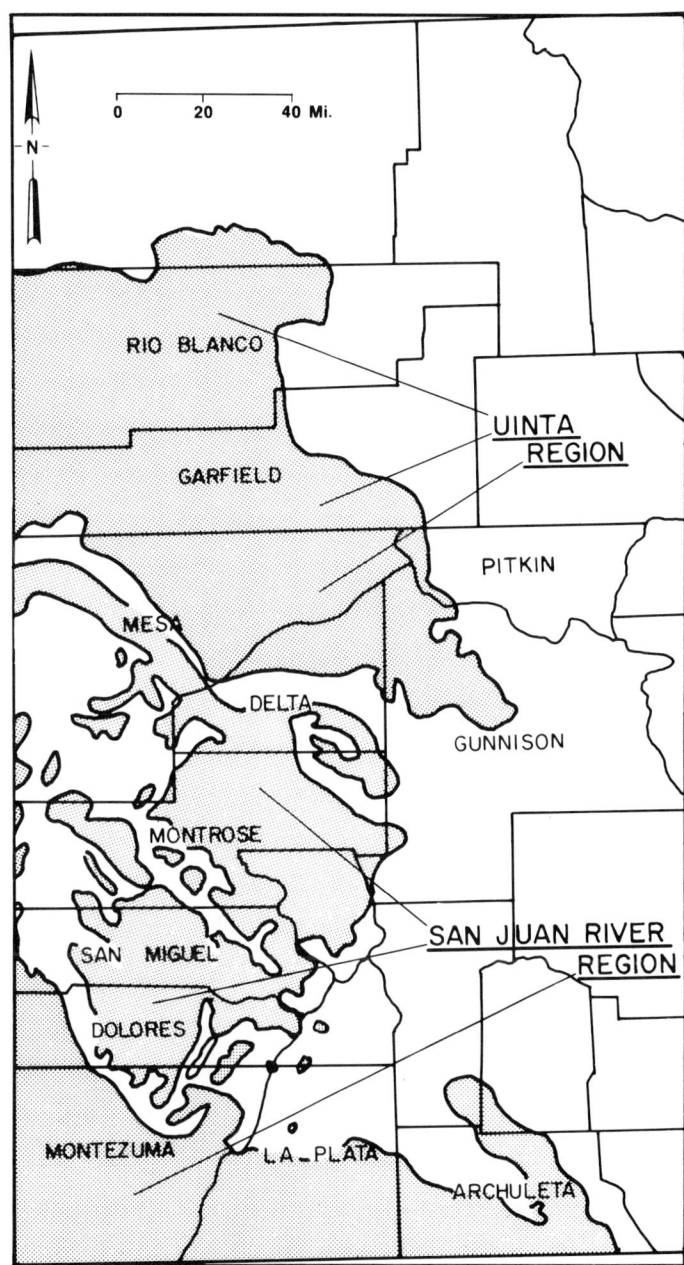

Figure 1. Outline of western Colorado coal regions (stippled) containing coking quality coal.

---
*Credit to Goolsby and others (1979) for the basis of this article.

Table 1. *Coking coal classification system used to evaluate coal resources in Colorado (from Goolsby and others, 1979).*

	ASTM COAL RANK (BITUMINOUS)					
COKING COAL GRADE	LOW-VOLATILE	MEDIUM-VOLATILE	HIGH-VOLATILE A	HIGH-VOLATILE B		
PREMIUM	PREMIUM GRADE LOW-VOLATILE BITUMINOUS COKING COAL	PREMIUM GRADE MEDIUM-VOLATILE BITUMINOUS COKING COAL	PREMIUM GRADE HIGH-VOLATILE A BITUMINOUS COKING COAL	PREMIUM GRADE HIGH-VOLATILE B BITUMINOUS COKING COAL	0-1.0% / 0-8.0%	GREATEST
MARGINAL	MARGINAL GRADE LOW-VOLATILE BITUMINOUS COKING COAL	MARGINAL GRADE MEDIUM-VOLATILE BITUMINOUS COKING COAL	MARGINAL GRADE HIGH-VOLATILE A BITUMINOUS COKING COAL	MARGINAL GRADE HIGH-VOLATILE B BITUMINOUS COKING COAL	1.1-1.8% / 8.0-12.0%	COKING COAL "DESIRABILITY"
LATENT	LATENT GRADE LOW-VOLATILE BITUMINOUS COKING COAL	LATENT GRADE MEDIUM-VOLATILE BITUMINOUS COKING COAL	LATENT GRADE HIGH-VOLATILE A BITUMINOUS COKING COAL	LATENT GRADE HIGH-VOLATILE B BITUMINOUS COKING COAL	1.9-3.0% / 12.1-15.0% SULFUR / ASH	LEAST
	GREATEST ← COKING COAL "DESIRABILITY" → LEAST					

In certain areas in Colorado, igneous dikes and sills have detrimentally affected the quality of the coal. They have either totally destroyed or have altered the properties of the coal within close proximity to the igneous dike. An example of this is the Crested Butte Field in Gunnison County, Uinta Region (fig. 2) and the Archuleta portion of the San Juan Basin (fig. 3), where numerous Tertiary igneous dikes have altered the coal beds. Because coal uniformity is of major concern to coke producers, coal found in close proximity to igneous dikes generally cannot be used as coke feedstock.

The intrusion of large igneous bodies such as inferred in the Pitkin County portion of the Uinta basin have had a beneficial effect, with resultant medium–volatile bituminous coal being of premium quality as coke feedstock (Goolsby and others, 1979).

COKING COAL REGIONS
San Juan River Region

The San Juan River coal region (fig. 3), as defined by the area underlain by the coal-bearing Dakota Formation, contains coal deposits in three formations of Upper Cretaceous age. These are the Dakota Formation, Menefee Formation of the Mesaverde Group and the Fruitland Formation.

Although large areas of southwestern Colorado are underlain by coals in the Dakota Formation, these coals are generally thin, lenticular and high in ash content. Limited analytical data for these coals indicate that the coal resources are predominantly marginal grade high-volatile B and C bituminous coking coal.

The coal deposits in the Menefee Formation range from premium grade high-volatile C bituminous to marginal grade high-volatile A bituminous coking coal. The rank generally increases to the northwest and along the western margin of the basin where it is premium grade high-volatile C bituminous coking coal. The coal bed stratigraphy of the Menefee Formation is shown on Figure 4; identified coking coal reserves for the entire region (all formations) are shown in Table 2.

Uinta Region

This coal-bearing region is defined as that portion of the basin marked by the contact of the coal-bearing Mesaverde Group with the underlying Mancos Shale. This region is divided into eight coal fields (Landis, 1959), of which four have important coking coal resources. These are the Somerset (Delta and Gunnison Counties), Crested Butte (Gunnison County), Grand Hogback (Garfield County) and Carbondale (Pitkin and Garfield Counties) fields (figs. 5 and 6).

The Somerset field contains premium to marginal high-volatile A and B bituminous coking coal. The Crested Butte field has been influenced heavily by Tertiary intrusions, folding and faulting and consequently the coal rank varies from high-volatile C bituminous to anthracite. The Grand Hogback field contains a high-volatile A bituminous coal in the vicinity of Township 5 South with non-coking coal both north and south of this area. The southern portion of the Carbondale field has the most "desirable" coking coal in the west with rank varying from high-volatile A bituminous to medium-volatile bituminous. Identified reserves for these fields are shown in Table 3.

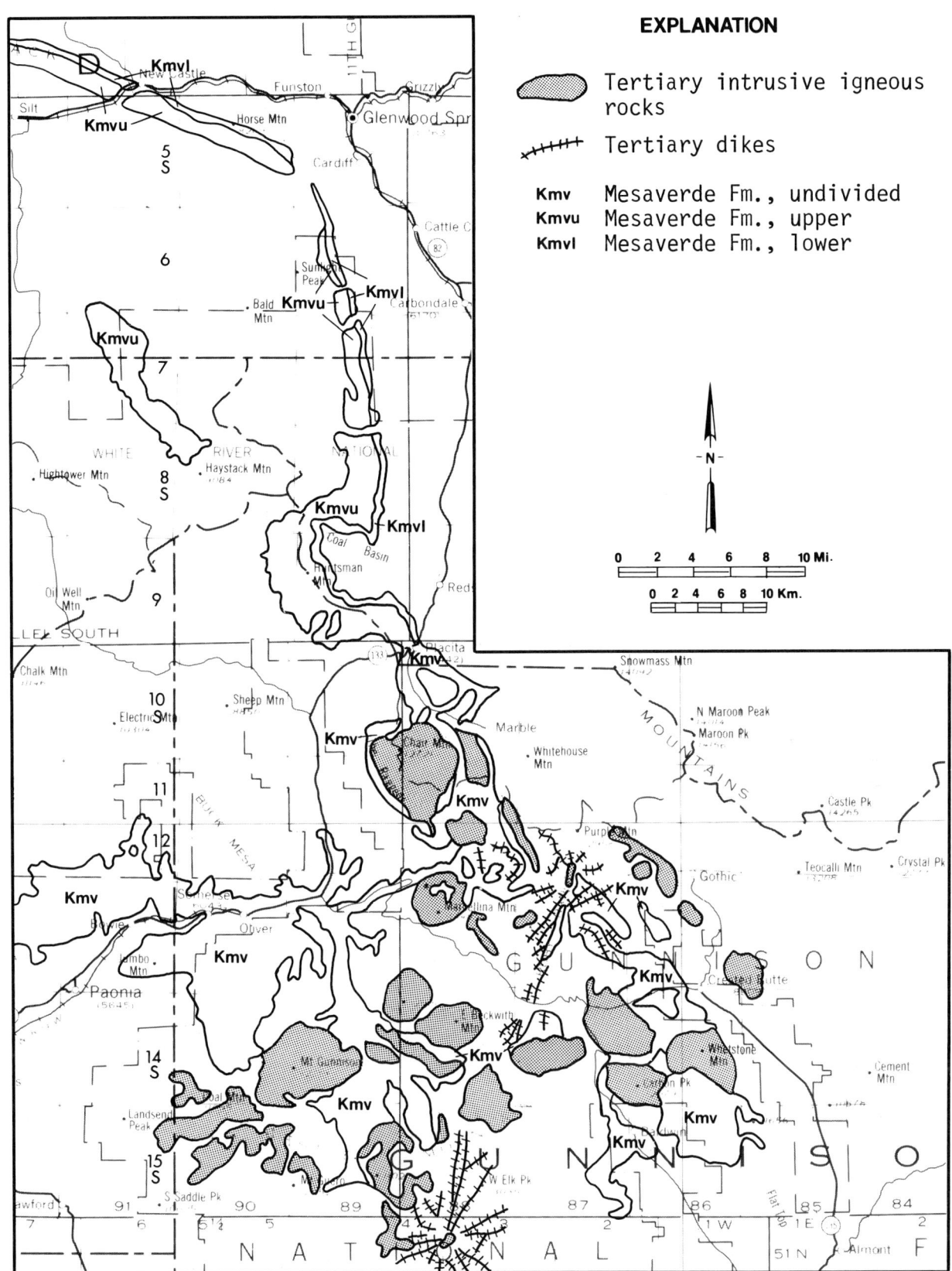

Figure 2. Location of Tertiary intrusions and dikes in the Crested Butte field, Uinta Region (revised from Goolsby and others, 1979).

Table 2. Identified original in-place coking coal reserves in the Durango, Nucla-Naturita, and Pagosa Springs fields, the San Juan River region (from Goolsby and others, 1979).

Coking Coal Classification	Short tons x 1,000,000	% of total
Premium to marginal grade high-volatile A bituminous	87.23	4.90
Premium to marginal grade high-volatile A to B bituminous	585.99	32.92
Premium to marginal grade high-volatile B bituminous	14.50	0.81
Marginal grade high-volatile A bituminous	155.37	8.73
Marginal to latent grade high-volatile A bituminous	365.26	20.52
Marginal to latent grade high-volatile B bituminous	7.73	0.43
Latent grade high-volatile A bituminous	171.71	9.65
Unclassified high-volatile bituminous	392.08	22.03
Total	1,779.87	99.99[1]

1) Does not equal 100% due to independent rounding.

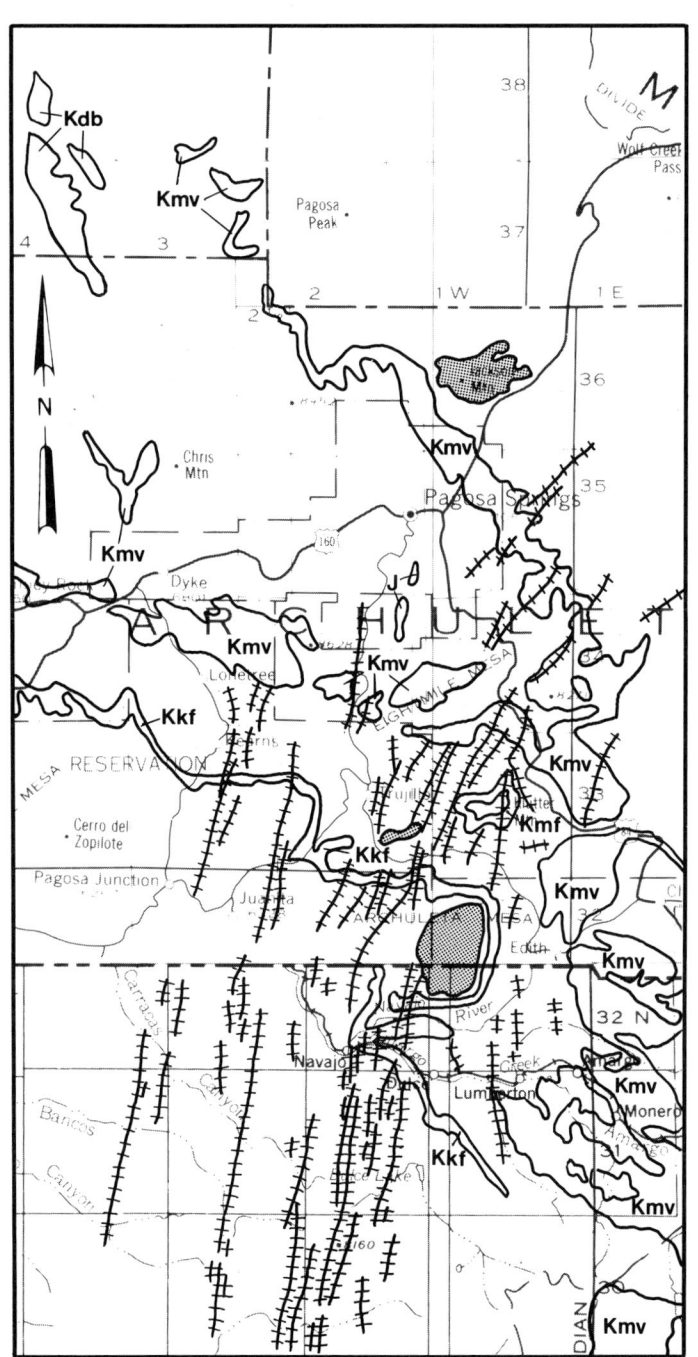
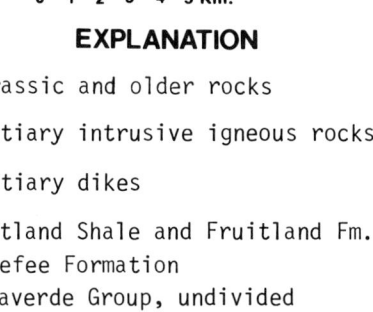

Figure 3. Location of Tertiary intrusions and dikes in the Archuleta County portion of the San Juan River region (revised from Goolsby and others, 1979).

Table 3. Identified original in-place coking coal reserves in the Grand Hogback, Carbondale, Crested Butte, and Somerset coal fields, the Uinta region (from Goolsby and others, 1979).

Coking Coal Classification	Short Tons x 10^6	% of Total
Premium grade high-volatile A to medium-volatile bituminous	21.23	4.75
Premium grade high-volatile A bituminous	128.05	28.66
Premium grade high-volatile B bituminous	78.86	17.65
Premium grade high-volatile A to B bituminous	129.37	28.96
Premium to marginal grade high-volatile B bituminous	54.04	12.10
Marginal grade high-volatile B bituminous	35.17	7.87
Total	446.72	99.99*

*Note: Total does not equal 100% due to independent rounding

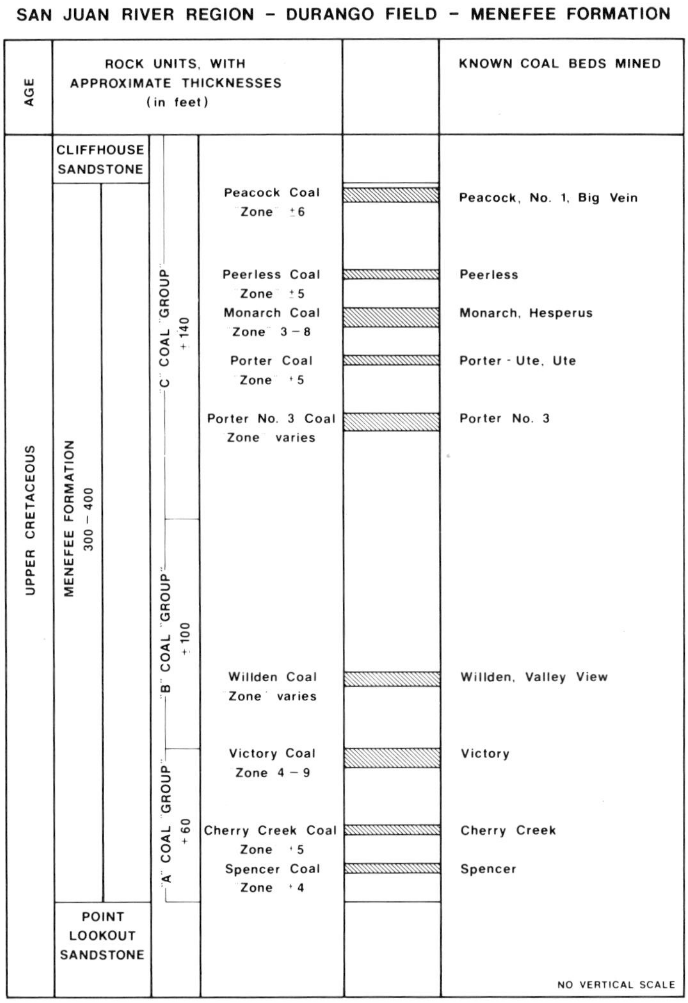

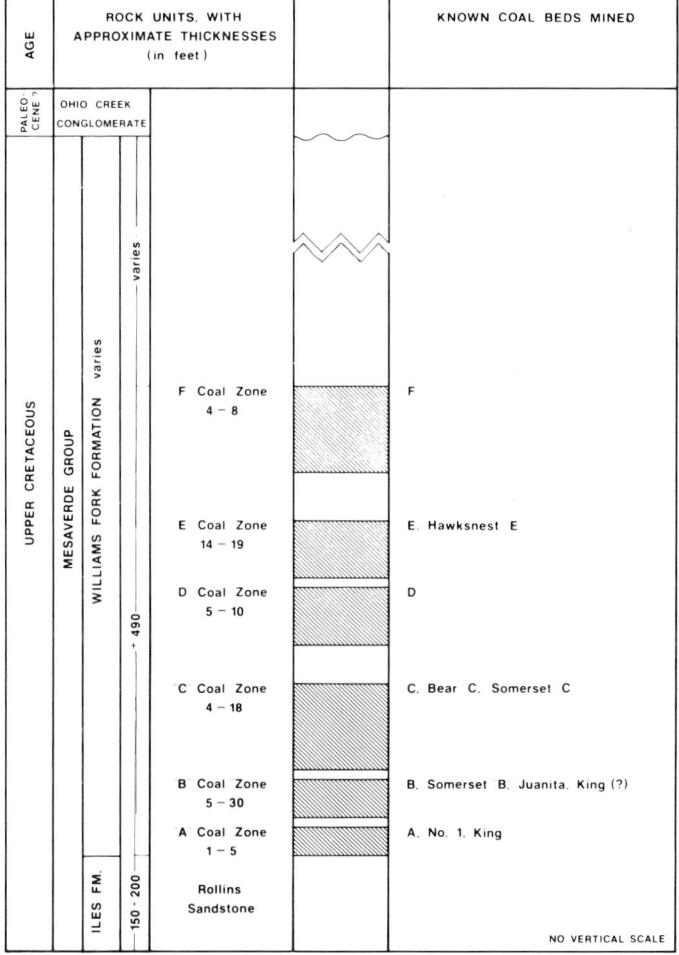

Figure 4. The stratigraphy of the Menefee Formation in the Durango field, San Juan River region, Colorado (from Boreck and Murray, 1979).

Figure 5. Coal-bearing formation, coal zone, and coal bed stratigraphy of the Somerset field, Colorado (from Boreck and Murray, 1979).

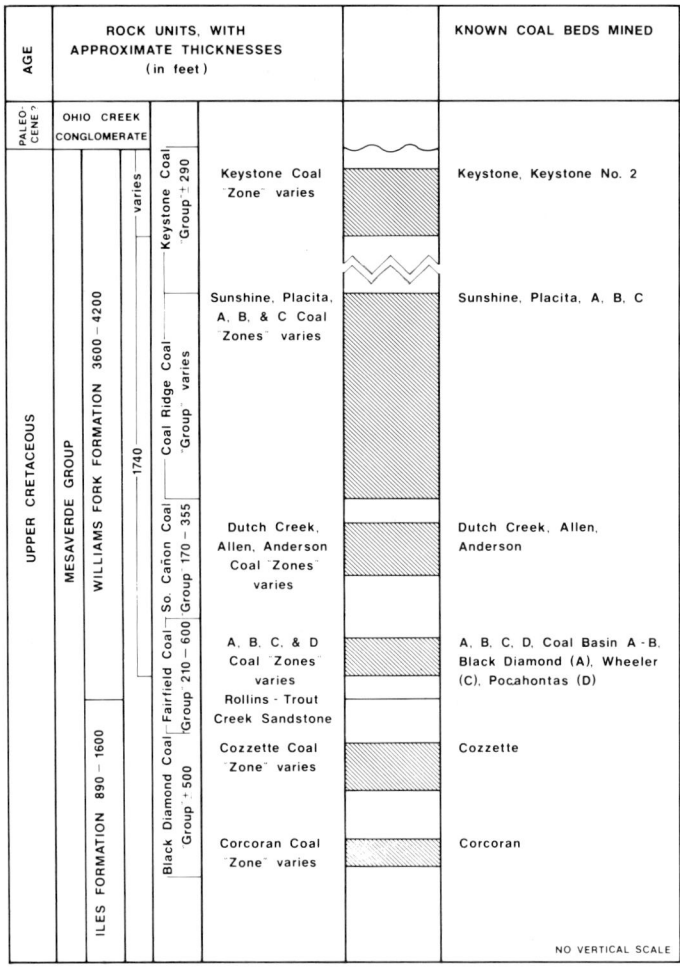

Figure 6. Coal-bearing formation, coal zone, and coal bed stratigraphy of the Grand Hogback and Carbondale fields, Colorado (from Boreck and Murray, 1979).

CONCLUSION

The coking coal resources of western Colorado have been exploited since the late 1800's and still make up a significant portion of total current coal production. These resources should continue to be a vital part of the Colorado coal industry for years to come as additional exploration pinpoints economically minable beds.

REFERENCES

Allen, R. R., 1964, Effects of retort-immersion depth on Gieseler plasticity determinations on Western coals: U.S. Bureau of Mines Report of Investigations 6559, 26 p.

Averitt, Paul, 1966, Coking-coal deposits of the western United States: U.S. Geological Survey Bulletin 1222-G, 48 p.

Boreck, D. L. and Murray, D. K., 1979, Colorado coal reserve depletion data and coal mine summaries: Colorado Geological Survey Open File Report 79-1, 65 p.

Freeman, V. L., 1979, Preliminary report on rank of deep coals in part of the southern Piceance Creek basin, Colorado: U.S. Geological Survey Open File Report 79-725, 10 p.

Given, P. H., 1969, Problems of coal analysis: Pennsylvania State University Report SROCR-9, submitted to U.S. Office of Coal Research, Contract No. 14-01-0001-390, 40 p.

Given, P. H. and Zarzab, R. J., 1975, Problems and solutions in the use of coal analyses: Pennsylvania State University Technical Report 1, 40 p.

Goolsby, S. M., Reade, N. B. S., and Murray, D. K., 1979, Evaluation of coking coal in Colorado: Colorado Geological Survey Information Series 11.

Jones, D. C. and Murray, D. K., 1978, First Annual report—evaluation of coking-coal deposits in Colorado: Colorado Geological Survey Open-File Report 78-1, 18 p.

Lakes, Arthur, 1899a, Coal fields of Colorado: Mines and Minerals, v. 19, p. 541–543.

―――, 1899b, Grand River coal fields of Colorado: Mines and Minerals, v. 20, p. 110–111.

Landis, E. R., 1959, Coal resources of Colorado: U.S. Geological Survey Bulletin 1072-C, p. 131–232.

Lowry, H. H., ed., 1963, Chemistry of coal utilization, supplementary volume: New York, John Wiley and Sons, 1142 p.

Rees, O. W., 1966, Chemistry, uses and limitations of coal analysis: Illinois State Geological Survey Report of Investigations 220, 55 p.

Weeks, J. D., 1884, The coke industry in Colorado: U.S. 10th Census, 1880, v. 10.

Weimer, R. J., 1977, Stratigraphy and tectonics of Western coals, in Murray, D. K., ed., Geology of Rocky Mountain coal, a Symposium, 1976: Colorado Geological Survey Resource Series 1, p. 9–27.

West, W., 1874, On the value of Colorado coals in metallurgy: Mining Review, v. 5, n. 2, p. 12–13.

POTENTIAL PETROLEUM RESOURCES OF NORTHEASTERN UTAH AND NORTHWESTERN COLORADO

ALBERT F. SANBORN
3759 E. Nobles Road
Littleton, Colorado 80122

INTRODUCTION

The area covered in this paper (fig. 1) contains more than 104,000 km² (40,000 mi²). It includes the Uinta, Piceance, Eagle, North Park, Middle Park, and South Park basins.

The region is rich in hydrocarbons. Commercial production of oil and gas is obtained from strata of the Paleozoic, Mesozoic and Cenozoic Eratherms. Thick sedimentary strata are present, and source and reservoir beds are amply distributed throughout the geologic section. Because of the thickness of sedimentary rocks, the range in age of reservoir rocks, and the abundant shows of hydrocarbons in much of the geologic section, prospects for development of substantial new reserves are excellent (fig. 2).

STRATIGRAPHY

Cambrian and Ordovician

Cambrian strata are present in the subsurface throughout the area except where eroded during pre-Late Devonian and mid-Triassic periods of exposure. They crop out along the southwestern and southeastern flanks of the Uinta Mountains in Utah and along the western flanks of the Colorado Rockies. They unconformably overlie Precambrian rocks and are progressively overlapped by Upper Devonian and Mississippian strata (Robison, 1964). In northwestern Colorado, Ordovician dolomite locally lies on Cambrian strata. The Cambrian, where preserved, ranges in thickness from 60–150 m.

The Cambrian consists of a basal marine quartzite or quartzitic, glauconitic sandstone, or dolomite. The rocks normally are well indurated and tightly cemented. No known source rocks are related to the Cambrian. For these reasons, and because of the unfavorable history of exposure and erosion, the Cambrian is not considered promising for future hydrocarbon reserves.

Ordovician strata are represented by the marine Manitou Dolomite, which has very limited distribution. Like the Cambrian, it has little reservoir capacity and is given no potential for hydrocarbons.

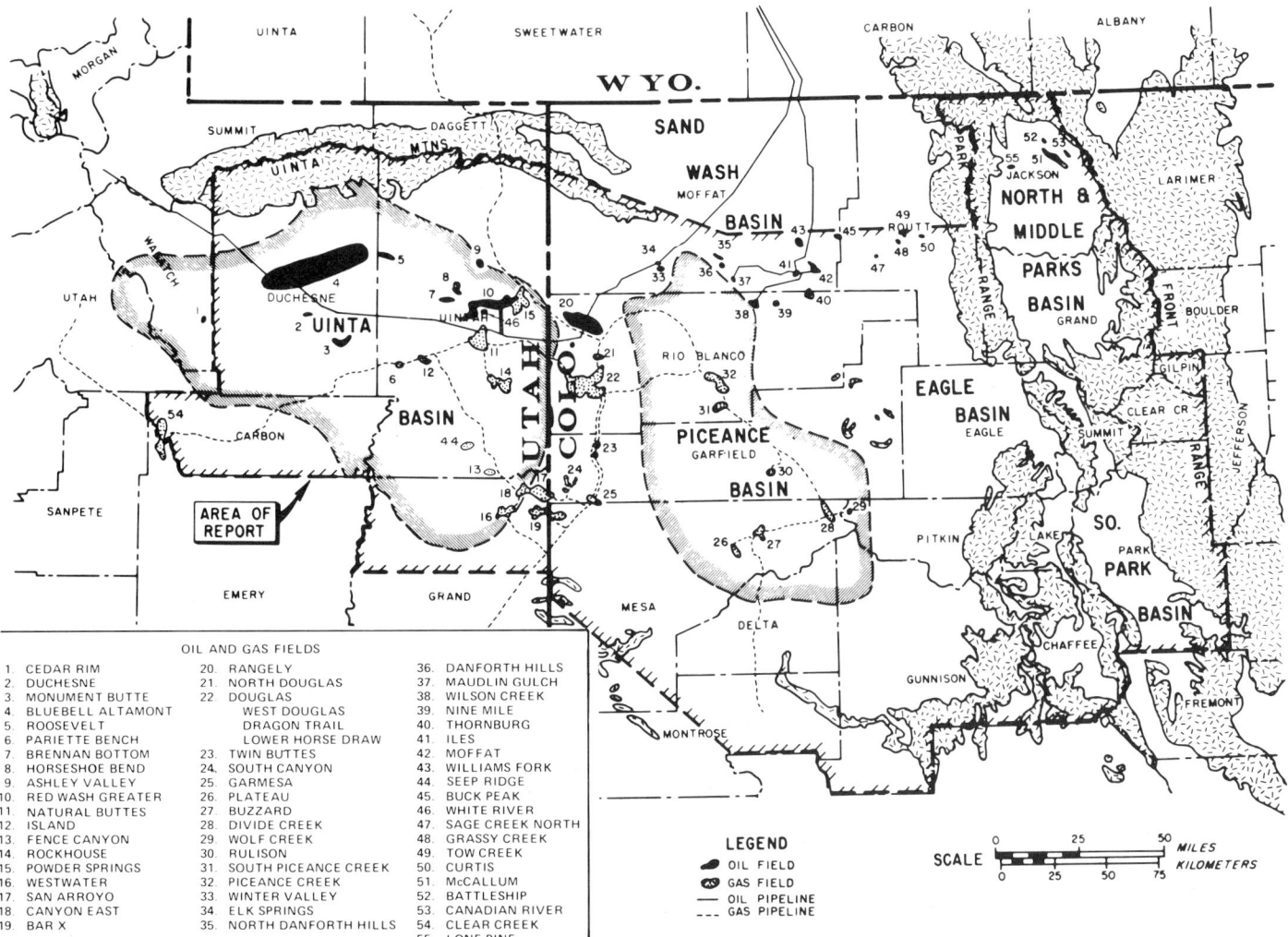

Figure 1. Index map showing principal oil and gas fields, northeastern Utah and northwestern Colorado.

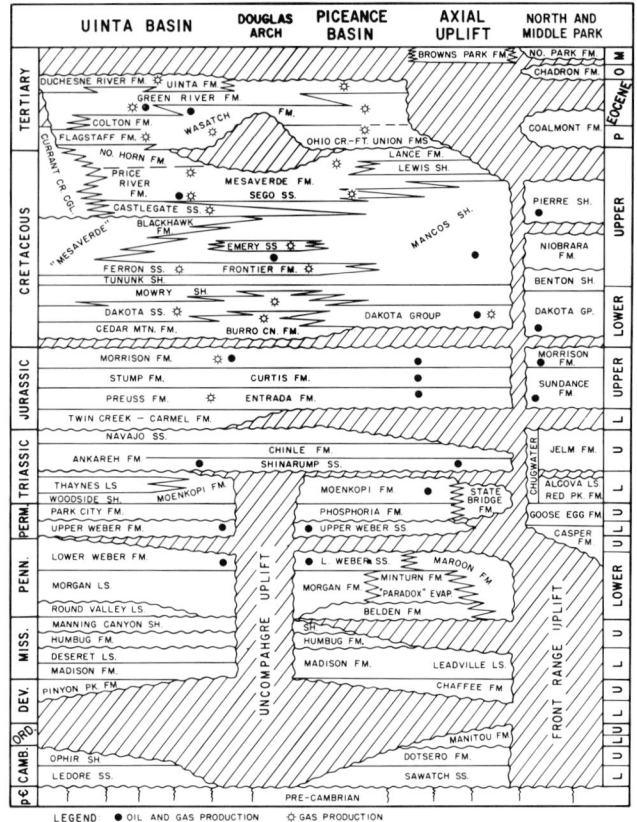

Figure 2. Correlation diagram, northeastern Utah and northwestern Colorado.

Devonian and Mississippian

After a long period of erosion, marine transgression began in Late Devonian time and continued into the Mississippian. Thus, Upper Devonian and Lower Mississippian strata progressively onlap eroded Ordovician, Cambrian, or Precambrian rocks. The Devonian of northwestern Colorado is composed of dolomite and quartzitic sandstone. Reservoir development is poor.

Rigby (1959) states that, in the western Uinta basin, "most Devonian sediments associated with the unconformity surface hold little possibility of petroleum production. In areas, however, where sands have been well washed there is a possibility of production."

Devonian and Mississippian strata range in thickness from zero to more than 900 m (fig. 3). Lithology is predominantly carbonate capped by dark shale. Some sandstone is present at the base and overlying the carbonate rocks. Much of the carbonate rock is dolomite which locally contains intercrystalline to vugular porosity. The sandstone commonly is cemented by carbonate and has limited porosity. Some of the carbonate rock and the overlying black shale facies are probably petroleum-generative strata. Shows of oil are common in the Mississippian, and noncommercial gas was produced from a sandstone lens in an upper shale bed in western Carbon County, Utah. Early Pennsylvanian emergence (Sadlick, 1957) resulted in widespread development of a karst surface on thin Lower Pennsylvanian strata or on eroded Mississippian strata. This history suggests that preservation of indigenous hydrocarbons is unlikely in much of the region. However, in the Uinta basin, and particularly in the western part where the section is thicker, the chance of preservation of hydrocarbons is somewhat better. Elsewhere, porous reservoir rocks would have to be charged from younger source strata by downward or lateral migra-

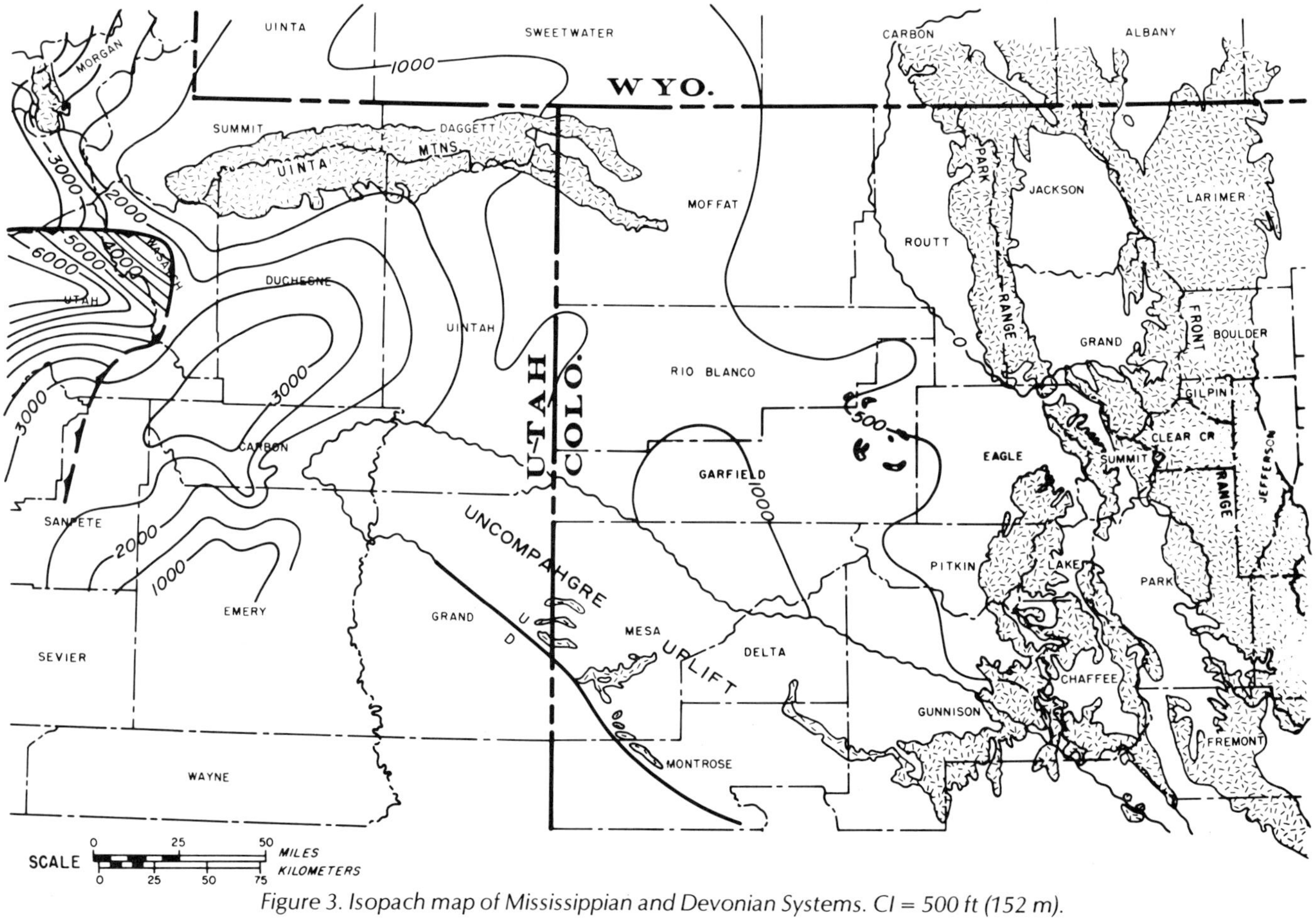

Figure 3. Isopach map of Mississippian and Devonian Systems. CI = 500 ft (152 m).

tion. Because Mississippian strata are 4750 m or deeper in half the area, the risk and cost of exploration are greatly increased.

Among the exploratory wells drilled, fewer than 20 have penetrated Mississippian strata. Largely because of the depth and unknown characteristics of reservoir rock, the Devonian–Mississippian interval has been given rather small future reserve potential.

Pennsylvanian and Permian

The Pennsylvanian and Permian are considered together because the source beds and reservoir rocks are interrelated. This section, which ranges in thickness from zero to more than 3000 m, was deposited during a period of great tectonic activity (fig. 4). Its complex geologic history is indicated by at least three, and probably four, major unconformities (fig. 2). The rising Ancestral Rockies shed large quantities of clastic sediment. In addition, considerable amounts of sand were transported into the area. The section is predominantly sandstone and arkose; interbedded carbonate is present locally, principally in northwestern Colorado (Murray, 1958). Also in northwestern Colorado, Lower Pennsylvanian rocks contain interbedded dark-gray organic shale and limestone, above which an evaporite basin developed locally (fig. 2). The evaporites are mostly gypsum and anhydrite (Katich, 1958; Lovering and Mallory, 1962). Some halite has been reported in the subsurface. These evaporites and related strata are of the same age as, and are similar in lithology to the Paradox evaporites of the Paradox basin, to the southwest. Because of this similarity, many geologists prefer to use the term "Paradox Formation" in northwestern Colorado. The strata contain excellent hydrocarbon source beds and numerous shows have been recorded in them, but no reservoir rocks have been found associated with them. However, the environment of deposition suggests that patch "reefs" or similar carbonate buildups may be present in the subsurface, and reef-like organic carbonate buildups have been reported on the surface. In addition, sandstone strata overlying and laterally equivalent to these beds may contain reservoir-quality porosity and permeability.

Sandstone, very prevalent in this unit, is of two types—mature quartzose sandstone and arkose. The arkose lies in thick wedges adjacent to the Precambrian granitic blocks of the Ancestral Rockies, which were the source for these beds (Mallory, 1958). Of the quartzose sandstone strata, the uppermost or Weber Sandstone is the most important economically, although some of the lower sandstone beds may hold future reserves. The Weber Sandstone of Pennsylvanian and Permian age is the producing formation in the giant Rangely field, from which more than 600 million barrels (95 billion liters) of oil have been produced. The Weber Sandstone ranges in thickness from zero at the eastern pinchout to more than 600 m at the western edge of the study area. It is well-sorted, mature sandstone of dominantly very fine to fine grain size (Bissell, 1964). Although the Rangely structure is a large Laramide (Late Cretaceous to early Tertiary) fold, the original trap appears to have been stratigraphic. It is probable that large undiscovered reserves are present in this formation, which has a subsurface extent of more than 34,000 km² (13,000 mi²).

Overlying the Weber is the Upper Permian Park City or Phosphoria Formation, a marine cyclic deposit rich in hydrocarbons (Cheney and Sheldon, 1959). This unit is not productive in the

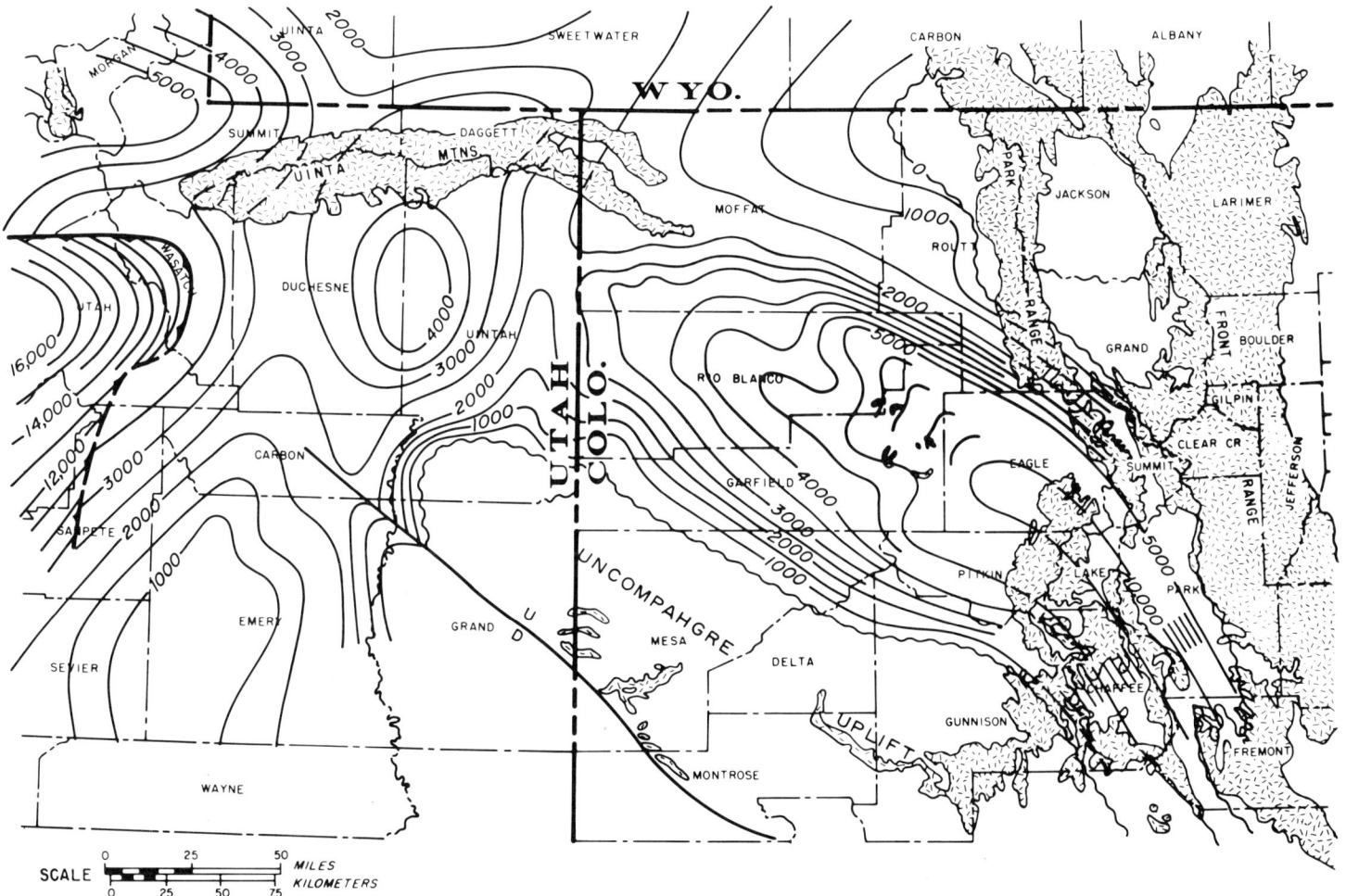

Figure 4. Isopach map of Permian and Pennsylvanian Systems. CI = 500 ft (152 m).

study area, but is a good potential source bed. These rocks are considered by many geologists to be the source of the oil in the Weber Sandstone at Ashley Valley field in Utah and Rangely field in Colorado. In Wyoming, several fields produce oil from the Phosphoria Formation. The reservoir rocks are pelletal and algal dolomites formed along an ancient strandline. Similar facies are present in the subsurface along a broad band extending northeasterly across the study area. In the Uinta Basin the top of this facies is mainly deeper than 4500 m. However, the possibility of finding an oil-filled reservoir in this formation must be considered.

Jurassic and Triassic

The Jurassic and Triassic are considered together because of similar histories. This section is composed of grossly interlayered marine and continental strata. Total thicknesses range from 150 to 1800 m (fig. 5). Three marine cycles of deposition are represented in the section, enclosed in envelopes of red and varicolored continental shale and red, orange, and white fluvial and eolian sandstone. Reservoir rock is mainly nonmarine sandstone. The Shinarump, Navajo, and Entrada strata (fig. 2) include regionally well-developed porous sandstones. Each provides reservoirs for several small fields of oil and (or) gas and one large field (Wilson Creek) in the area of this report. At Wilson Creek, more than 30 million barrels of oil have been produced from the Entrada Sandstone. In addition, the basal member of the Morrison Formation, the Salt Wash Member, is a good sandstone reservoir at Wilson Creek from which more than 60 million barrels (9.5 billion liters) of oil and 55 BCF (1.6 billion m³) of gas have been produced.

The Shinarump, Navajo and Entrada sandstones tend to be blanket deposits and require closed structures for accumulation. The Salt Wash Member of the Morrison changes thickness and varies laterally in lithology from interbedded nonmarine shale and tight thin fluvial sandstone to thicker porous sandstone. The potential for stratigraphic entrapment in the Salt Wash is good.

Cretaceous

Rocks of Cretaceous age are the most extensive in the study area; they cover more than 80,000 km² (31,000 mi²). Thickness ranges from 1800 to more than 3000 m (fig. 6). The section is characterized by complex interfingering of marine and continental strata. The environment was mainly marine in the eastern part and mainly continental in the western part. Nine principal transgressions and regressions are recognized in Cretaceous sedimentation (Hale and Van deGraaf, 1964). The seas were principally transgressive in Early and early Late Cretaceous time and predominantly regressive throughout the rest of Late Cretaceous. The complex intertonguing relations were described by Haun and Weimer (1960), Lane (1963), Walton (1957), Warner (1964), and Young (1959).

Substantial amounts of gas have been found in the Cretaceous in this area, and ultimate reserves are estimated to be about 2 trillion ft³ (57 billion m³). However, to date, the comparatively small amount of oil found in these rocks has come mainly from frac-

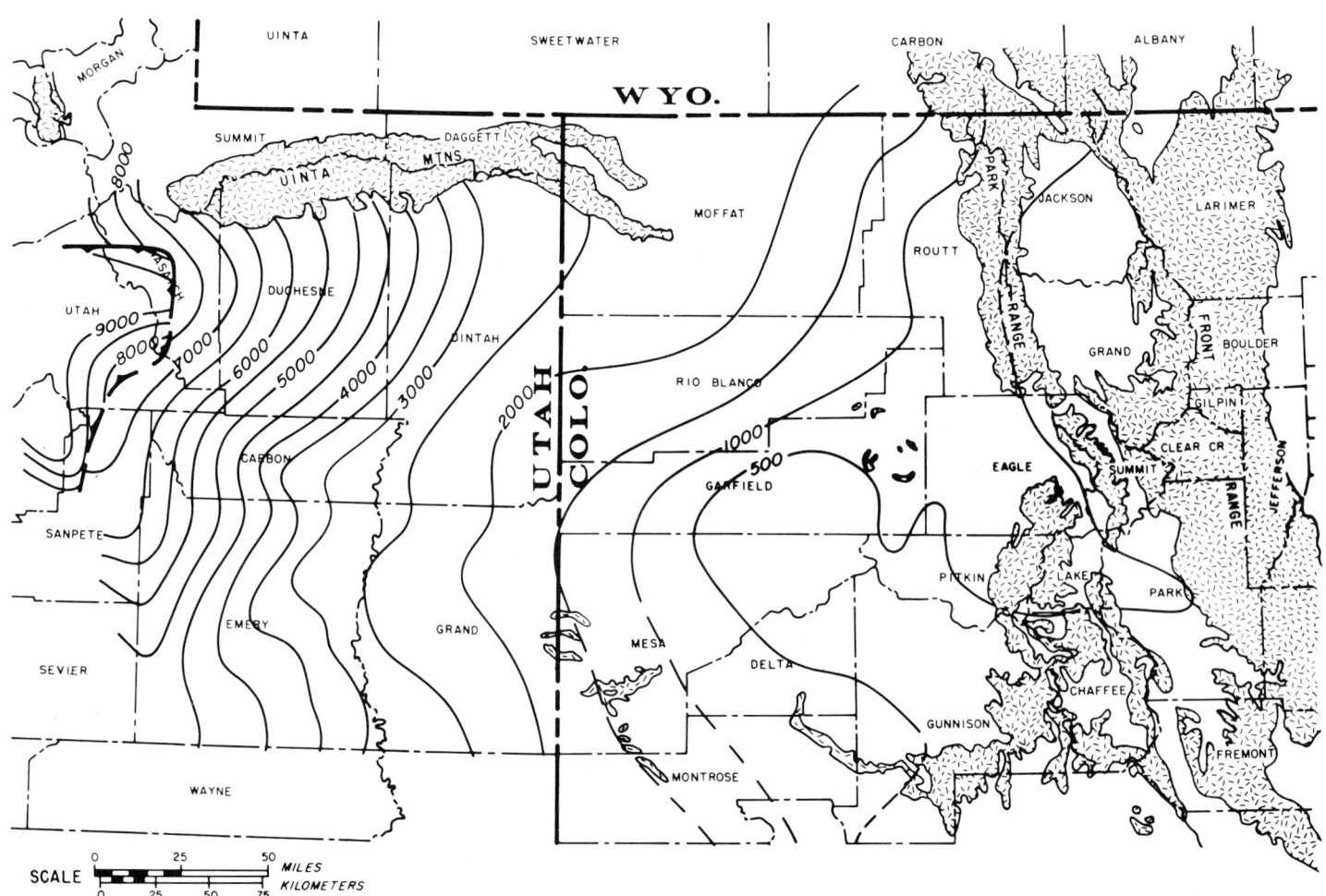

Figure 5. Isopach map of Jurassic and Triassic Systems. CI = 500 ft (152 m).

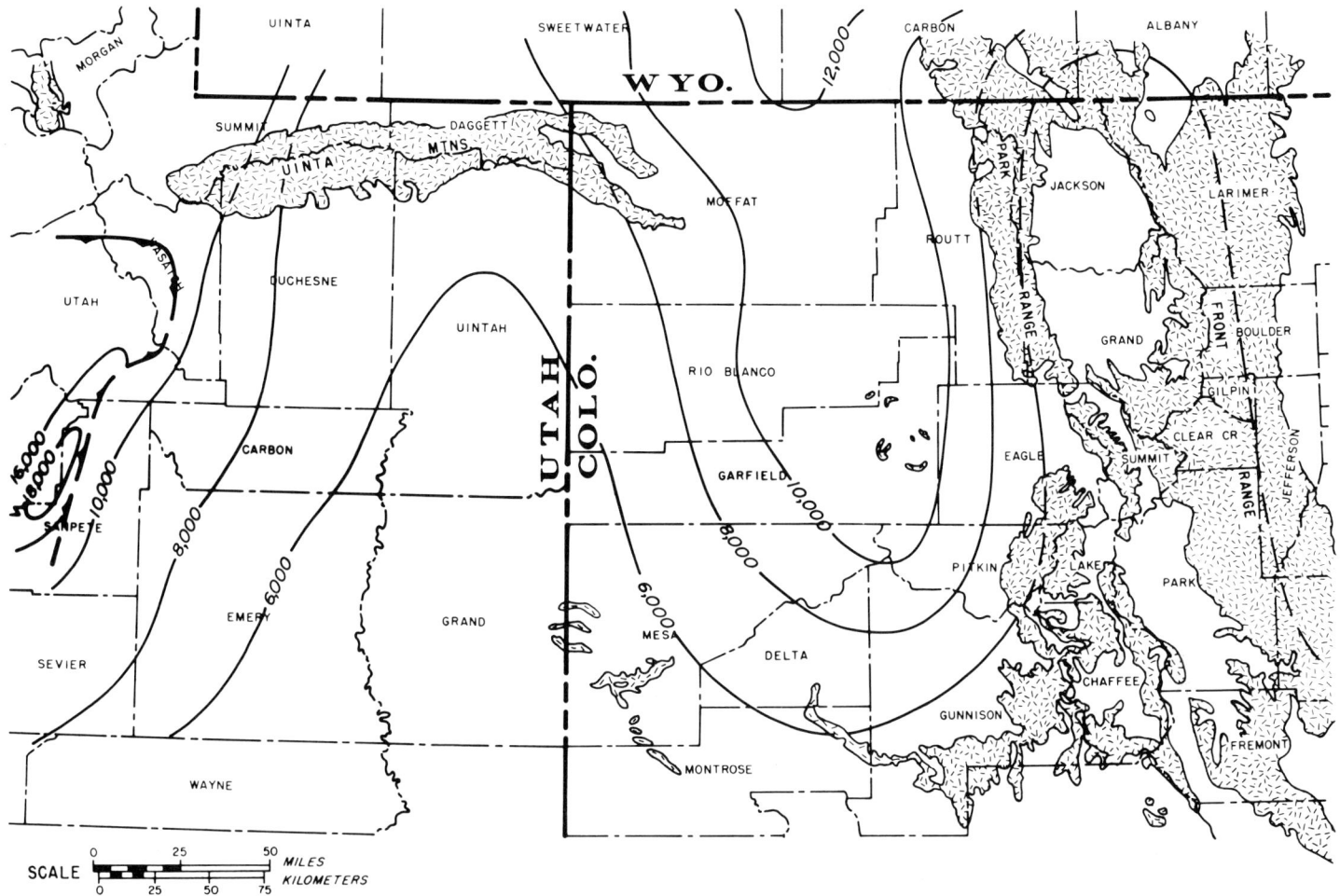

Figure 6. Isopach map of Cretaceous System. CI = 2,000 ft (610 m).

tured marine shale and the Dakota Sandstone. Reservoirs are sandstone developed as bar or beach deposits along the fluctuating strandline and as fluvial channel sands in the continental sediments. The Mancos Shale is a likely source for oil, and the carbonaceous beds in the lagoonal areas may be the source for gas.

Although great thicknesses of sandstone of Cretaceous age are present, effective porosity appears to be limited. The sandstone is either clay-filled or tightly cemented in much of the section. Thus, the main problem in exploration of the Cretaceous is locating effective porosity in trap position. There are enormous reserves of gas in these low-permeability reservoir rocks. Any technologic advance in production of gas from this tight sandstone will increase available reserves very substantially. It is not expected that very large accumulations of oil will be discovered, although one or two fields with reserves of 100 million barrels (16 billion liters) are possible. Most of the undiscovered hydrocarbons are expected to be in stratigraphic traps.

Tertiary

Potential hydrocarbon bearing Tertiary strata in this area are confined to the Paleocene and Eocene Series. Younger Tertiary nonmarine strata are present in part of this area, primarily on or near the surface and are not considered prospective for hydrocarbon accumulation. Paleocene and Eocene strata are nonmarine and range in thickness from 600 to more than 3300 m (fig. 7). This sequence is one of the most petroliferous deposits in the world, containing great quantities of gas, liquid petroleum, solid petroleum, "oil shale," and bituminous sand. Although the present evaluation excludes the last three types of accumulation, the Tertiary rocks in the Uinta and Piceance Basins stand high in potential for future oil and gas reserves.

An important oil-bearing formation, the Green River Formation, is a complex suite of lacustrine deposits which is enclosed in an envelope of fluvial-floodplain and interbedded lacustrine deposits. The underlying part of the envelope is the Wasatch Formation and equivalents, and the overlying strata are the Uinta and Duchesne River Formations. Green River sediments have yielded more than 130 million barrels (20 billion liters) of oil and 400 BCF (11 billion m^3) of gas.

The Wasatch Formation is also important for hydrocarbon production. More than 100 million barrels (16 billion liters) of oil and 300 BCF (8.5 billion m^3) of gas have been produced from these strata. The greater part of the oil has been produced since the discovery of Altamont field in 1970. The Wasatch Formation is Paleocene and Eocene in age. The basal part is equivalent to the Flagstaff Formation in the southwest part of the Uinta basin. The Wasatch Formation contains sediments deposited in lacustrine, fluvial, floodplain and lagoonal environments. The strandline of lacustrine deposition is the most important belt for the location of hydrocarbon reservoirs in both the Green River and Wasatch Formation.

During early Tertiary time, the present Uinta Mountains began to

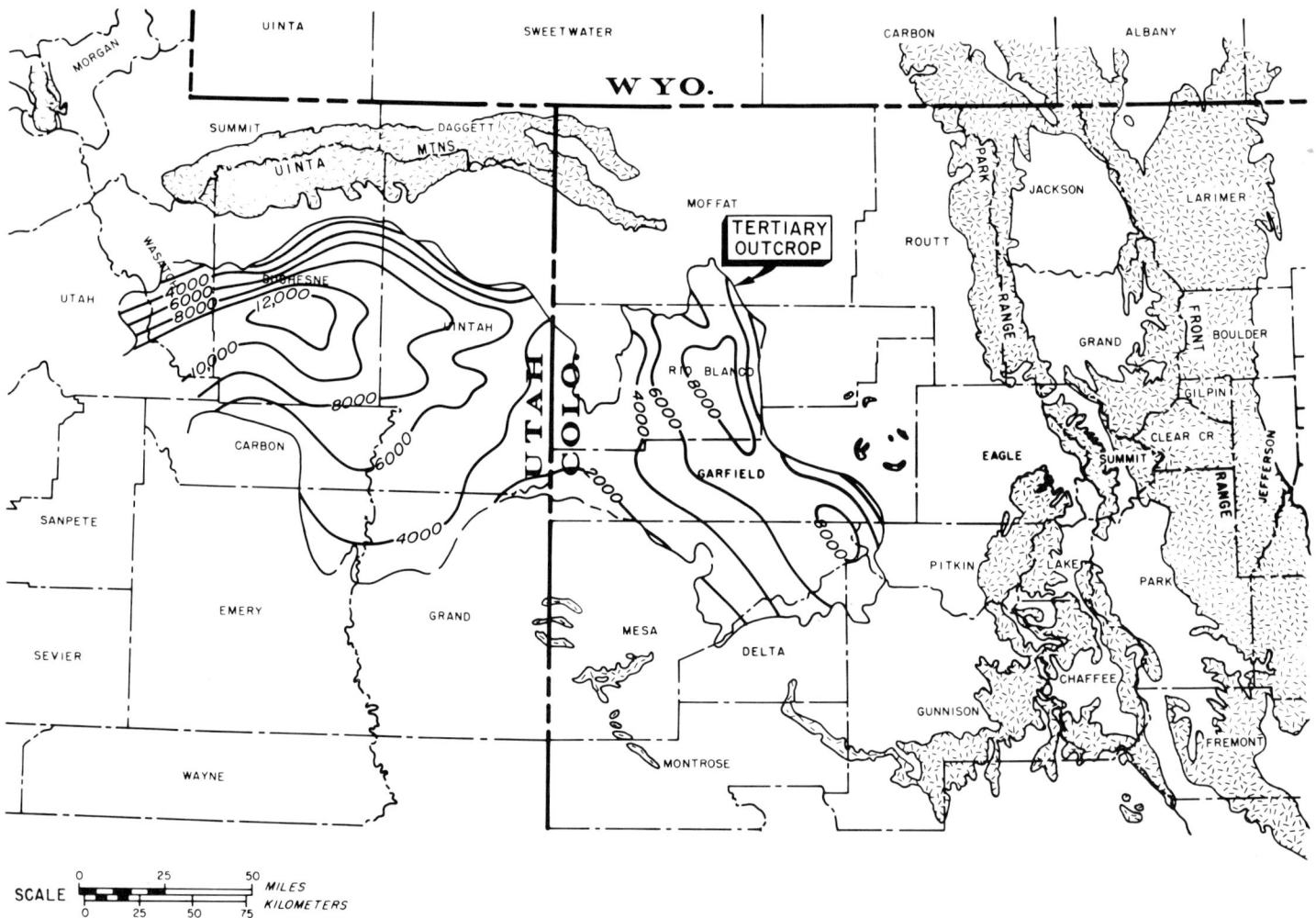

Figure 7. Isopach map of Tertiary strata (Paleocene and Eocene). CI = 2,000 ft (610 m).

rise, dividing the Tertiary basin into two parts; the southern part is the Uinta basin. Concurrently, the north-trending Douglas Creek arch (fig. 8) began to rise separating the Uinta basin from the Piceance basin. On the south, the Uncompahgre highland again became positive. Clastic material was contributed to the two Tertiary basins from these three positive features. By the end of Wasatch deposition, the Douglas Creek arch had been overlapped by red shale. The Douglas Creek arch, later covered by thin Green River sediments, was not subject to erosion during the rest of Eocene time.

Clastic sediments for the Green River Formation were derived from the Uinta Mountains on the north and the Uncompahgre highland on the southeast. Bar, beach, and deltaic sands were deposited along a rapidly fluctuating strandline. The central part of the lake received fine-grained clastic material augmented by a rain of orthochemical sediment and rich organic debris derived from the abundant biota of this unusual lake.

The resulting reservoir rocks are marginal lacustrine sands pinching out basinward into organically rich fine-grained sediments—a remarkable setting for the development of stratigraphic traps. The subsequent shifting of the basinal axis to the north gave the north-source sands an updip, southward pinchout into impermeable lacustrine fine-grained sediments (fig. 9).

The Red Wash field produces from multiple stratigraphic traps formed in an ancient delta complex. Production was at first believed to be confined to the Red Wash nose, a westerly dipping structure (fig. 8). Later a substantial accumulation was found in and south of the southerly syncline at the southwestern edge of the Red Wash feature. The area, the Wonsits Valley Unit, is a stratigraphic accumulation on northerly regional dip. The Wonsits Valley area and the Red Wash field are referred to as Red Wash Greater field.

Hydrocarbon production in the Bluebell–Altamont field is from reservoirs in marginal lacustrine strata from both Green River and Wasatch beds. Production is mainly confined to the area of the fluctuating strandline in dominantly fine siliceous clastics and carbonate strata. Porosity and permeabiltiy are greatly enhanced by intrastratal fracturing. Fracture production has become a substantial part of Tertiary production. Future reserves in the Uinta Basin Tertiary strata are expected to be very substantial.

Tertiary production in the Piceance basin is almost entirely gas. The Green River strata are thin, and the high pour point of the lacustrine oil, about 100°F (38°C), precludes production from strata shallower than about 1000 m. The Wasatch Formation, 30–1500 m thick, contains sandstone beds that produce gas in large amounts at Piceance Creek field.

Elsewhere in this basin smaller fields are producing from the Tertiary and additional gas discoveries are expected.

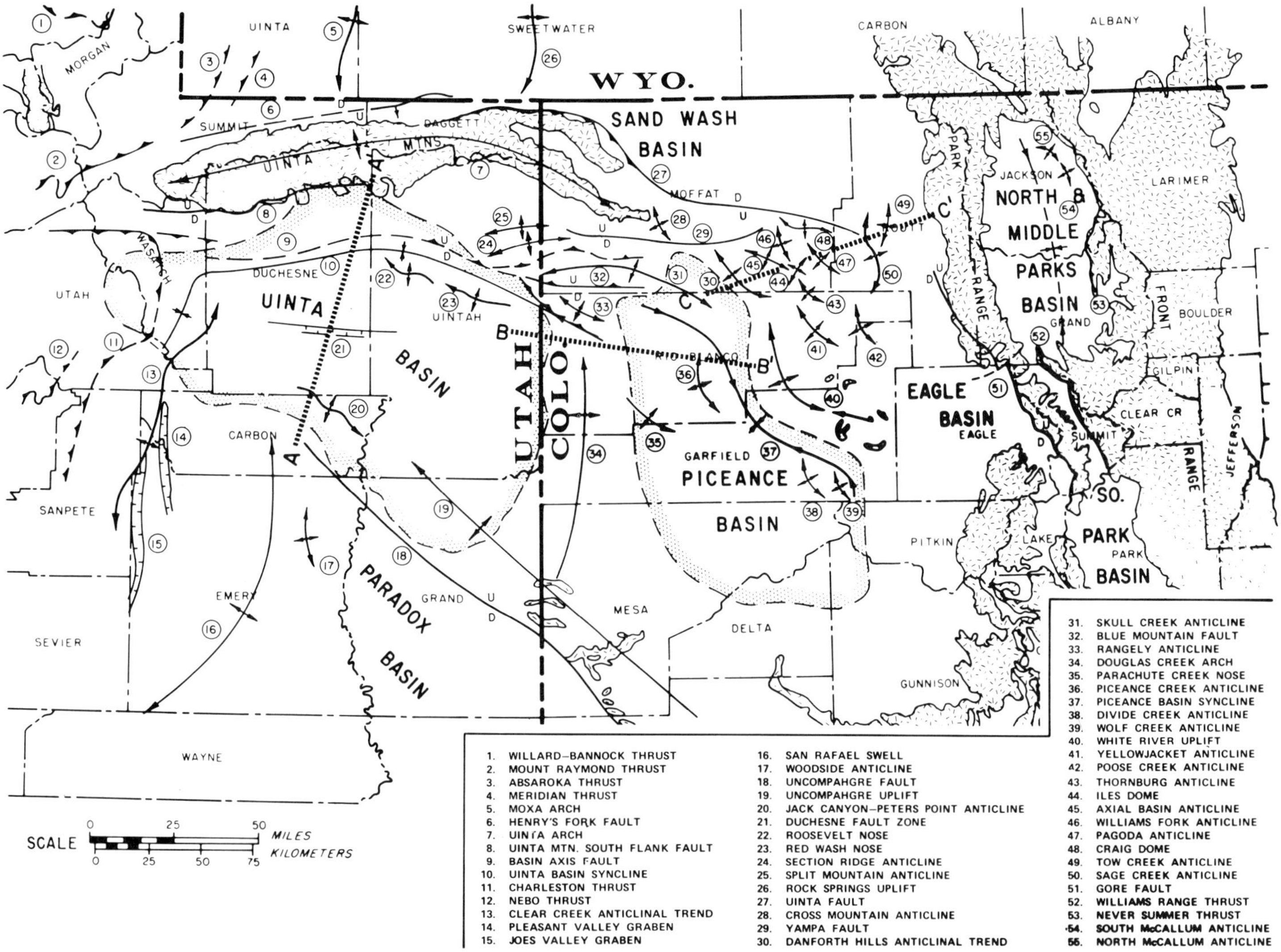

POTENTIAL PETROLEUM RESOURCES

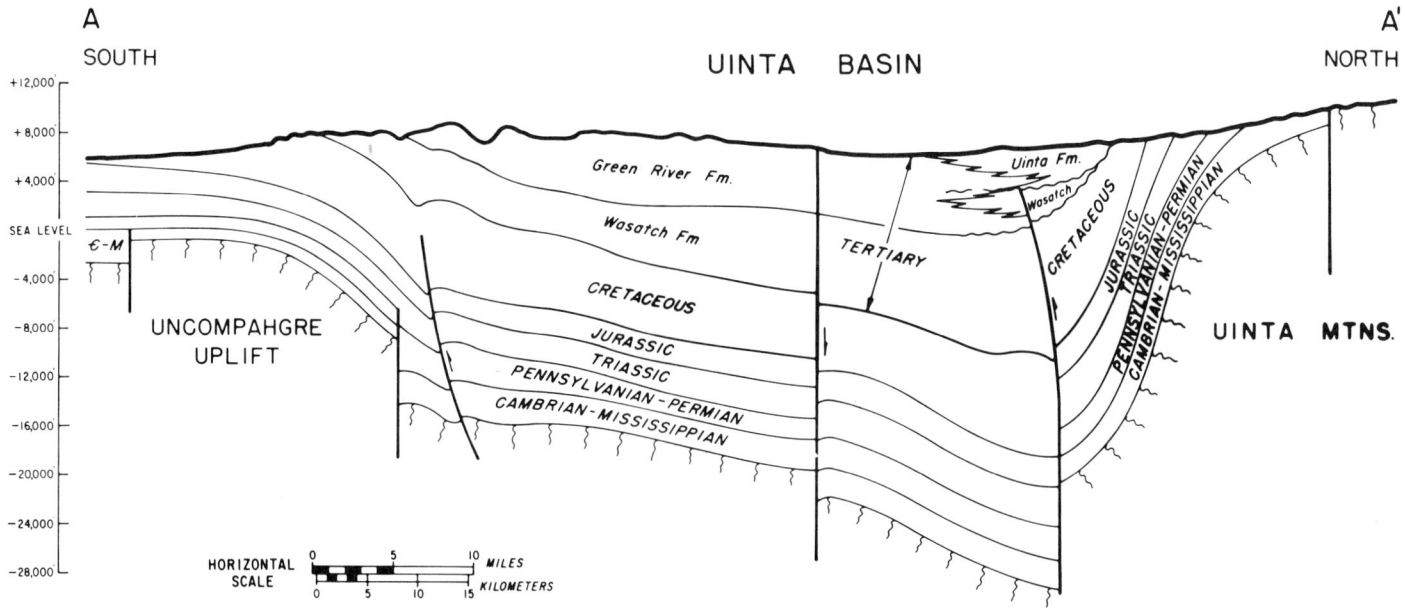

Figure 8. Tectonic map showing major or economically important features, northeastern Utah and northwestern Colorado.

1. WILLARD–BANNOCK THRUST
2. MOUNT RAYMOND THRUST
3. ABSAROKA THRUST
4. MERIDIAN THRUST
5. MOXA ARCH
6. HENRY'S FORK FAULT
7. UINTA ARCH
8. UINTA MTN. SOUTH FLANK FAULT
9. BASIN AXIS FAULT
10. UINTA BASIN SYNCLINE
11. CHARLESTON THRUST
12. NEBO THRUST
13. CLEAR CREEK ANTICLINAL TREND
14. PLEASANT VALLEY GRABEN
15. JOES VALLEY GRABEN
16. SAN RAFAEL SWELL
17. WOODSIDE ANTICLINE
18. UNCOMPAHGRE FAULT
19. UNCOMPAHGRE UPLIFT
20. JACK CANYON–PETERS POINT ANTICLINE
21. DUCHESNE FAULT ZONE
22. ROOSEVELT NOSE
23. RED WASH NOSE
24. SECTION RIDGE ANTICLINE
25. SPLIT MOUNTAIN ANTICLINE
26. ROCK SPRINGS UPLIFT
27. UINTA FAULT
28. CROSS MOUNTAIN ANTICLINE
29. YAMPA FAULT
30. DANFORTH HILLS ANTICLINAL TREND
31. SKULL CREEK ANTICLINE
32. BLUE MOUNTAIN FAULT
33. RANGELY ANTICLINE
34. DOUGLAS CREEK ARCH
35. PARACHUTE CREEK NOSE
36. PICEANCE CREEK ANTICLINE
37. PICEANCE BASIN SYNCLINE
38. DIVIDE CREEK ANTICLINE
39. WOLF CREEK ANTICLINE
40. WHITE RIVER UPLIFT
41. YELLOWJACKET ANTICLINE
42. POOSE CREEK ANTICLINE
43. THORNBURG ANTICLINE
44. ILES DOME
45. AXIAL BASIN ANTICLINE
46. WILLIAMS FORK ANTICLINE
47. PAGODA ANTICLINE
48. CRAIG DOME
49. TOW CREEK ANTICLINE
50. SAGE CREEK ANTICLINE
51. GORE FAULT
52. WILLIAMS RANGE THRUST
53. NEVER SUMMER THRUST
54. SOUTH McCALLUM ANTICLINE
55. NORTH McCALLUM ANTICLINE

Figure 9. Structural cross section, Uinta Basin. Line of section is shown in Figure 8.

New technology may be developed to remove the substantial reserves of high pour point oil trapped in the shallow sands of the Green River Formation.

STRUCTURAL SETTING

The dominant basins in the study area are outlined by major positive features, as shown on the tectonic map (fig. 8). The form of the basins is shown on the structure map (fig. 10) and three cross sections (figs. 9, 11, and 12).

Most of the structural features as now expressed are of "Laramide" (Late Cretaceous to early Tertiary) age or younger. However, where more information is available, it appears that many of the pronounced Laramide features had earlier and more subtle expression.

Most of the production is from combination structural and stratigraphic traps that have been discovered by drilling anticlinal features. Most of the exploratory drilling to date has been directed to the search for structural features. However, the Cretaceous and Tertiary intertonguing facies are ideal for stratigraphic entrapment. More stratigraphic accumulations will be found as the industry gives more attention to the search for stratigraphic traps.

PRODUCING ROCKS

As shown on the correlation chart (fig. 2), every system from Pennsylvanian through Tertiary produces oil and gas. Except for fracture reservoirs in the Tertiary and Cretaceous, the reservoirs are in sandstone strata. Some accumulations are in tabular beds but most are lenticular beds.

Gas production from the Wasatch Formation has been disappointing because of rapid decrease in productivity. The sandstone is clay-filled or tightly cemented, resulting in low effective porosity and a lower reservoir volume than might be expected. However, technologic advances may in time increase producibility of the Wasatch strata.

The high pour point of the Tertiary lacustrine oils (90–100°F; 32–38°C) presents special problems. To be transported, this oil must be heated or mixed with a low-pour point "carrier" crude. The Red Wash field Tertiary crude oil is mixed with Rangely field Pennsylvanian oil and transported by pipeline to Salt Lake City, Utah.

POTENTIAL FUTURE PRODUCTION

Future production in the area may be expected in large part from new fields and pools in the strata that are now productive. The reservoirs will be mainly lenticular sandstone bodies. It is probable that most of the new oil will be found in stratigraphic traps, inasmuch as the more readily determinable structures have been drilled. Geophysical methods will be used to locate deeper structural features, and certainly some of these structures will reward the explorer with significant new reserves.

Carbonate reservoir possibilities in the Mississippian and Penn-

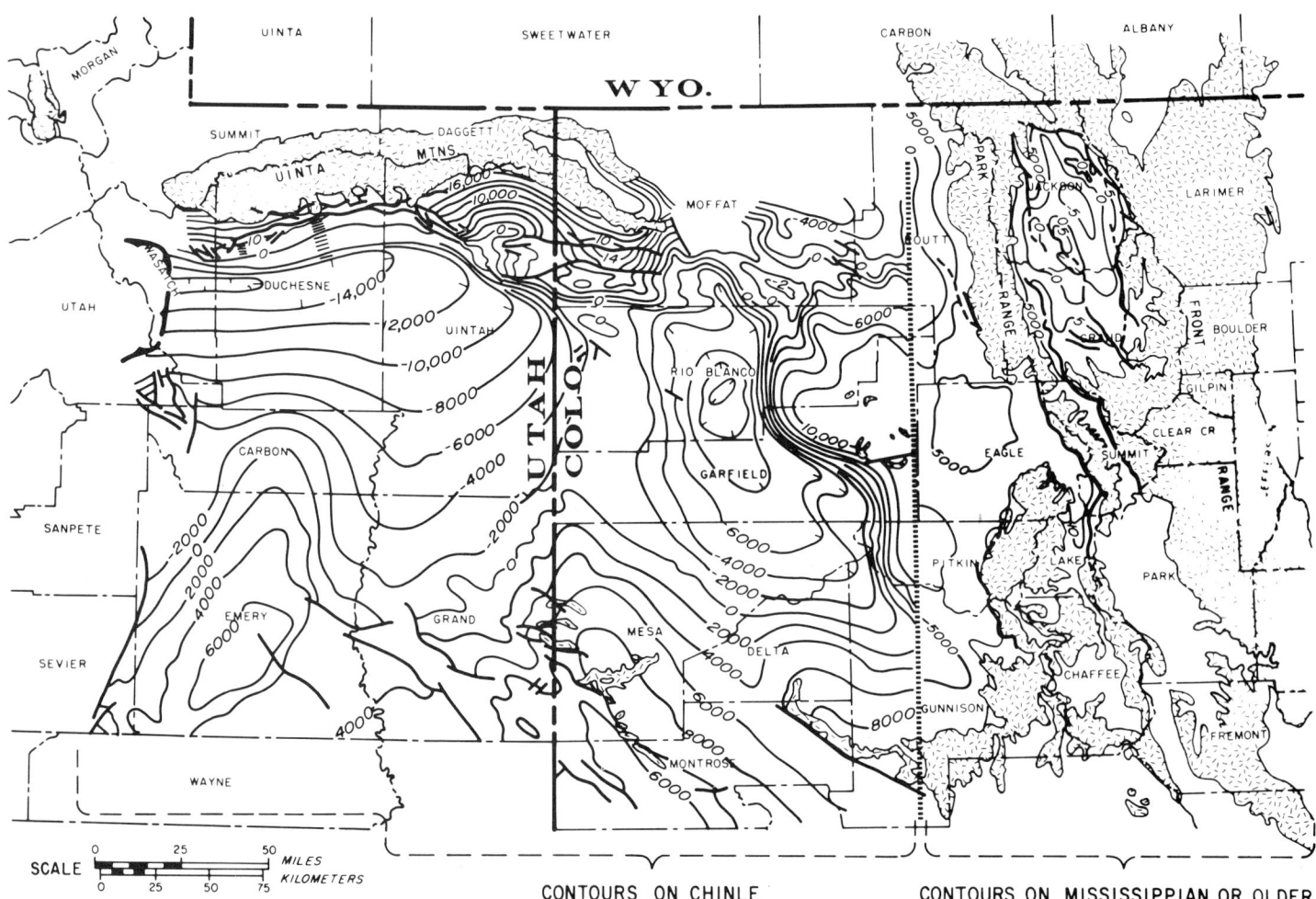

Figure 10. Structure contour map of top of Triassic Chinle Formation and Mississippian System or older rocks as indicated. Modified after Kelley (1955) and Anderman (1961). Elevation in feet from sea level.

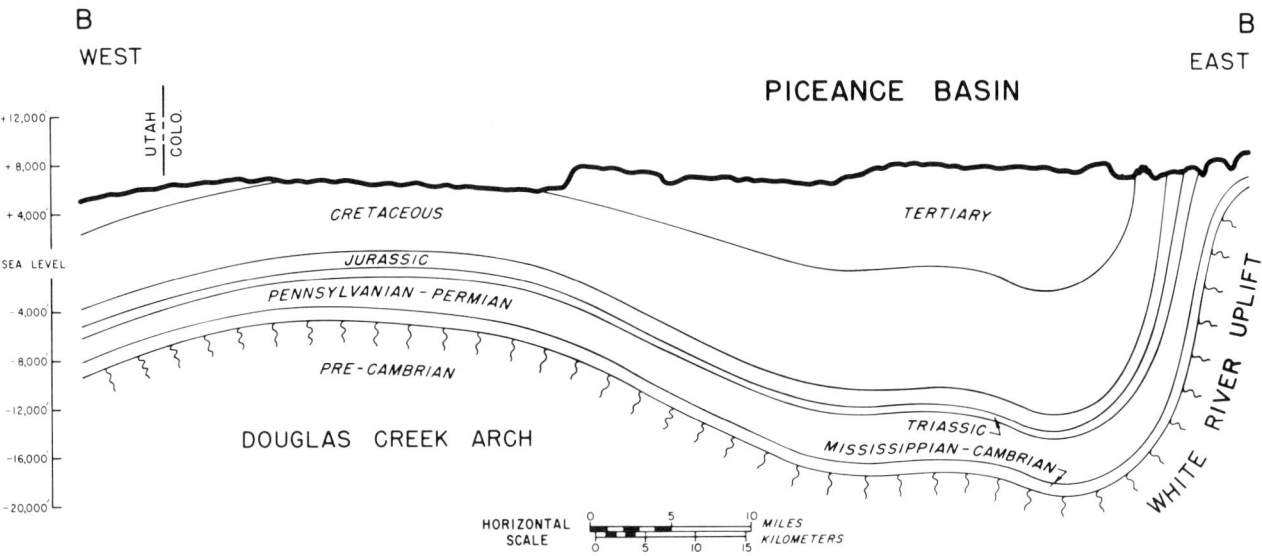

Figure 11. Structural cross section, Douglas arch and Piceance basin. Line of section is shown in Figure 8.

sylvanian are yet to be evaluated. The Mississippian has had few tests and is relatively unknown. On the average, there has been one Mississippian test for every 5000 km² (2,000 mi²) in the study area.

In the Pennsylvanian the presence of reefs adjacent to evaporites has been observed on the outcrop. These reefs may be found to have porosity and reservoir capacity in the subsurface, and there is ample associated source rock.

ESTIMATION OF FUTURE RESERVES

Estimation of undiscovered reserves is a highly speculative process. However, some assumptions can be based on knowledge of regional distribution of thickness of strata, amount of porous beds characteristic of an interval, and production experience in the area. Sufficient source rocks must be available to charge the section with hydrocarbons, and trapping conditions must be present. Furthermore, after a trap has been filled with hydrocarbons, structural history must be favorable for its preservation. Because we know only a few of these parameters and surmise the rest, numerical values for undiscovered reserves are conjectural at best. However, they do offer a means of comparison and they are a summation of present knowledge. Figures 13 and 14 present a graphic summary of the estimated hydrocarbon potential.

CONCLUSIONS

The area comprising the Uinta and Piceance basins and vicinity has excellent potential for future reserves. Estimated ultimate recoverable reserves of 3 billion barrels (500 billion liters) of oil and 5 trillion ft³ (150 billion m³) of gas are predicted.

Potential for new oil and gas exists in Paleozoic, Mesozoic, and

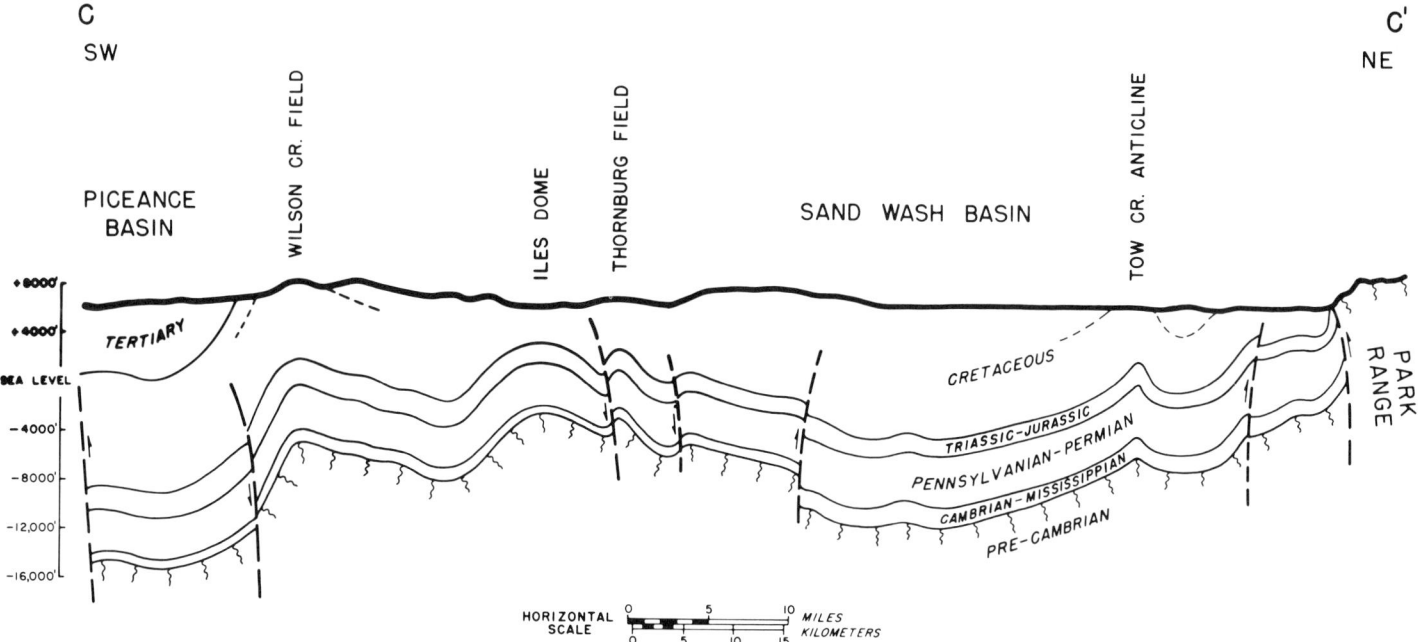

Figure 12. Structural cross section, Piceance basin to Park Range. Line of section is shown in Figure 8.

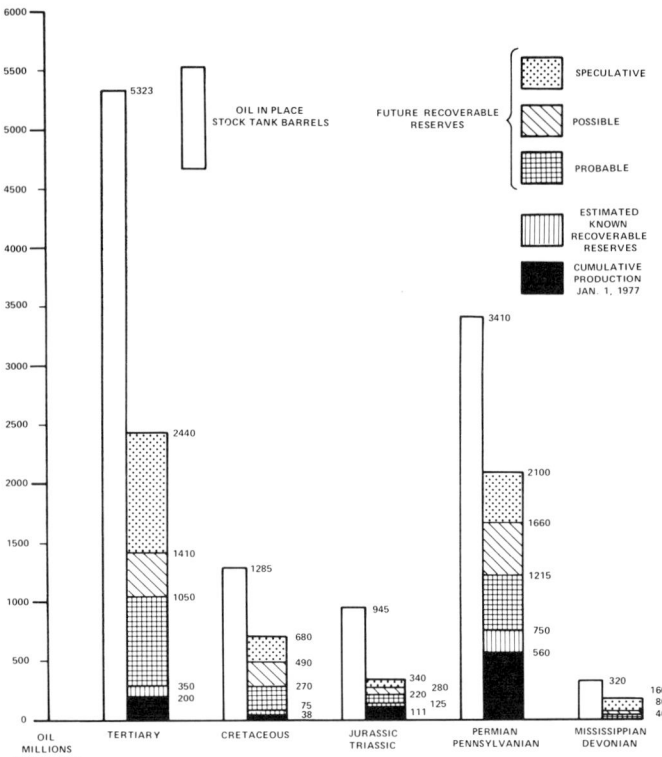

Figure 13. Present and future oil reserves, northeastern Utah and northwestern Colorado. Estimated oil in place is compared with estimated recoverable oil. Future reserves are rounded off to nearest 50 million barrels (7.95 billion liters).

Cenozoic rocks. Most of the future oil and gas reserves will be found in stratigraphic traps. The dominant reservoirs for future petroleum will be lenticular sandstone bodies.

ACKNOWLEDGMENT

This article is a revised and abridged edition of "Possible Future Petroleum of Uinta and Piceance Basins and Vicinity, Northeast Utah, and Northwest Colorado" by Albert F. Sanborn in Rocky Mountain Association of Geologists—1977 Symposium. Appreciation is expressed for permission to use this material for the present paper.

REFERENCES

Behrendt, J. C. and P. Papenoe, 1969, Basement structure contour map of North Park—Middle Park basin, Colorado: American Association of Petroleum Geologists Bulletin, v. 53, p. 678-682.

Bissell, H. J., 1964, Lithology and petrography of the Weber Formation in Utah and Colorado, in Guidebook to the geology and mineral resources of the Uinta basin: Intermountain Association of Petroleum Geologists 13th Annual Field Conference, p. 67-91.

Boggs, S., Jr., 1966, Petrology of Minturn Formation, east-central Eagle County, Colorado: American Association of Petroleum Geologists Bulletin, v. 50, p. 1399-1422.

Cheney, T. M. and R. P. Sheldon, 1959, Permian stratigraphy and oil potential, Wyoming and Utah, in Guidebook to the geology of the Wasatch and Uinta Mountains: Intermountain Association of Petroleum Geologists 10th Annual Field Conference, p. 90-100.

DeVoto, R. H., 1964, Stratigraphy and structure of Tertiary rocks in southwestern South Park: Mountain Geologist, v. 1, p. 117-126.

──────, 1965, Pennsylvanian and Permian stratigraphy of central Colorado: Mountain Geologist, v. 2, p. 209-228.

Donnell, J. R., 1960, Tertiary geology and oil shale resources of the Piceance Creek basin between the Colorado and White Rivers, northwestern Colorado: U.S. Geological Survey Bulletin 1082-L, p. 835-891.

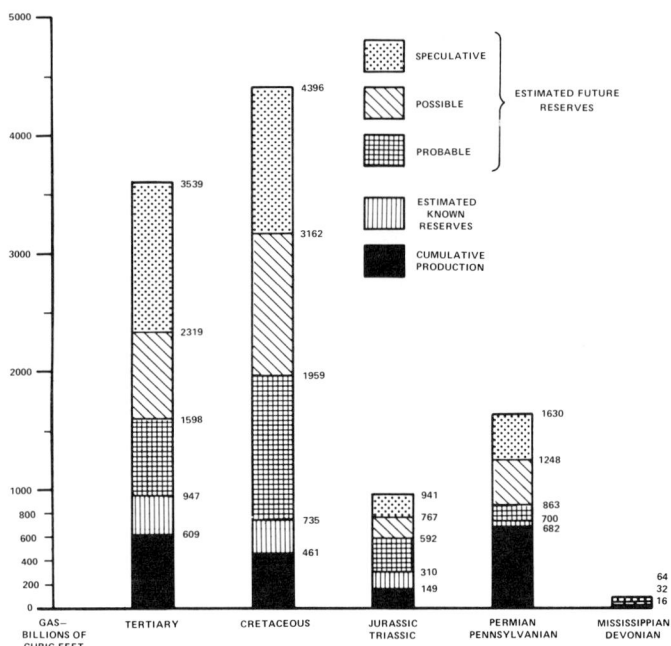

Figure 14. Present and estimated future gas reserves, northeastern Utah and northwestern Colorado. 1 BCF = 28 million m³.

Dunn, H. L., 1974, Geology of petroleum in the Piceance Creek basin, northwestern Colorado: Rocky Mountain Association of Geologists 25th Field Conference Guidebook, p. 217-224.

Ettinger, M., 1964, Geology of the Hartsel area, South Park, Park County, Colorado: Mountain Geologist, v. 1, p. 127-132.

Folsom, L. W., 1968, Economic aspects of Uinta basin gas development, in Natural gases of North America—a symposium: American Association of Petroleum Geologists Memoir 9, v. 1, p. 199-208.

Hale, L. A. and F. R. Van deGraaf, 1964, Cretaceous stratigraphy and facies patterns—northwestern Utah and adjacent areas, in Guidebook to the geology and mineral resources of the Uinta basin: Intermountain Association of Petroleum Geologists 13th Annual Field Conference, p. 115-138.

Hansen, A. R., 1963, The Uinta basin—structure, stratigraphy and tectonic setting, in Oil and gas possibilities of Utah, re-evaluated: Utah geological and Mineralogical Survey Bulletin 54, p. 175-176.

Haun, J. D., 1962, Introduction to the geology of northwest Colorado, in Exploration for oil and gas in northwestern Colorado: Denver, Colorado, Rocky Mountain Association of Geologists, p. 7-14.

────── and J. A. Barlow, Jr., 1962, Lower Cretaceous stratigraphy of Wyoming, in Symposium on Early Cretaceous rocks of Wyoming and adjacent areas: Wyoming Geological Association 17th Annual Field Conference Guidebook, p. 15-22.

────── and R. J. Weimer, 1960, Cretaceous stratigraphy of Colorado, in Guide to the geology of Colorado: Denver, Colorado, Rocky Mountain Association of Geologists, p. 58-65.

Hoffman, F. H., 1957, Possibilities of Weber stratigraphic traps, Rangely area, northwest Colorado: American Association of Petroleum Geologists Bulletin, v. 41, p. 894-905.

Jensen, F. S., 1958, Oil and gas in Permo-Pennsylvania rocks of the Maroon basin, northwestern Colorado and northeastern Utah, in Symposium on Pennsylvanian rocks of Colorado and adjacent areas: Denver, Colorado, Rocky Mountain Association of Geologists, p. 122-128.

Katich, P. J., Jr., 1958, Stratigraphy of the Eagle Evaporites, in Symposium on Pennsylvanian rocks of Colorado and adjacent areas: Denver, Colorado, Rocky Mountain Association of Geologists, p. 106-110.

Lane, D. W., 1963, Sedimentary environments in Cretaceous sandstone in northwestern Colorado: American Association of Petroleum Geologists Bulletin, v. 47, p. 229-256.

Lovering, T. S. and W. W. Mallory, 1962, The Eagle Valley Evaporite and its relation to the Minturn and Maroon Formations, northwest Colorado: U.S. Geological Survey Professional Paper 450-D, p. 45-48.

Millison, C., 1962, Accumulation of oil and gas in northwestern Colorado controlled principally by stratigraphic variations, in Exploration for oil and gas in northwestern Colorado: Denver, Colorado, Rocky Mountain Association of Geologists, p. 41-48.

Murray, D. K. and Haun, J. D., 1974, Introduction to the Geology of the Piceance Creek Basin and vicinity, northwestern Colorado: Rocky Mountain Association of Geologists 25th Field Conference Guidebook.

Murray, H. F., 1958, Pennsylvanian stratigraphy of the Maroon trough, in Symposium on Pennsylvanian rocks of Colorado: Denver, Colorado, Rocky Mountain Association of Geologists, p. 47-58.

Newton, W. A., 1957, North and Middle Parks as an oil province, in Guidebook to the geology of North and Middle Park basins: Denver, Colorado, Rocky Mountain Association of Geologists, p. 104-108.

Osmond, J. C., 1965, Geologic history of site of Uinta basin, Utah: American Association of Petroleum Geologists Bulletin, v. 49, p. 1957-1973.

———, and others, 1968, Natural gas in Uinta basin, Utah, in Natural gases of North America—a symposium: American Association of Petroleum Geologists Memoir 9, v. 1, p. 174-198.

Picard, M. D., 1956, Summary of Tertiary oil and gas fields in Utah and Colorado: American Association of Petroleum Geologists Bulletin, v. 40, p. 2956-2960.

Porter, L., Jr., 1963, Stratigraphy and oil possibilities of the Green River Formation in the Uinta basin, in Oil and gas possibilities of Utah, re-evaluated: Utah Geologic and Mineralogic Survey Bulletin 54, p. 193-198.

Quigley, M. D., 1965, Geologic history of Piceance Creek-Eagle basins: American Association of Petroleum Geologists Bulletin, v. 49, p. 1974-1996.

Rigby, J. K., 1959, Late Devonian erosional surface exposed in the Wasatch and Uinta Mountains, in Guidebook to the geology of Wasatch and Uinta Mountains: Intermountain Association of Petroleum Geologists 10th Annual Field Conference, p. 60-62.

Ritzma, H. R., 1962, Piceance Creek gas field, in Exploration for oil and gas in northwestern Colorado: Denver, Colorado, Rocky Mountain Association of Geologists, p. 96-103.

———, 1965, Piceance Creek sandstone, Basal Green River sandstone tongue, northeast Piceance Creek basin, Colorado: Mountain Geologist, v. 2, p. 103-107.

Robison, R. A., 1964, Cambrian of the Uinta Mountains, in Guidebook to the geology and mineral resources of the Uinta basin: Intermountain Association of Petroleum Geologists 13th Annual Field Conference, p. 63-65.

Sanborn, A. F., 1971, Possible future petroleum of Uinta and Piceance Basins and vicinity, northeast Utah and northwest Colorado, in Future Petroleum Provinces of the United States—Their Geology and Potential: American Association of Petroleum Geologists Memoir 15, v. 1, p. 489-508.

———, 1977, Possible future petroleum of Uinta and Piceance Basins and vicinity, northeast Utah and northwest Colorado: Denver, Colorado, Rocky Mountain Association of Geologists—1977 Symposium, p. 151-166.

——— and Goodwin, J. C., 1965, Green River formation at Raven Ridge, Uinta County, Utah: Mountain Geologist, v. 2, p. 109-114.

Sanlick, W., 1957, Regional relations of carboniferous rocks of northeastern Utah, in Guidebook to the geology of the Uinta basin: Intermountain Association of Petroleum Geologists 8th Annual Field Conference, p. 56-77.

Sawatzky, D. L., 1964, Structural geology of southeastern South Park, Park County, Colorado: Mountain Geologist, v. 1, p. 133-139.

Tweto, O., 1949, Stratigraphy of the Pando area, Eagle County, Colorado: Colorado Scientific Society Proceedings, v. 15, p. 149-235.

Walton, P. T., 1957, Cretaceous stratigraphy of the Uinta basin, in Guidebook to the geology of the Uinta basin: Intermountain Association of Petroleum Geologists 8th Annual Field Conference, p. 97-101.

Warner, D. L., 1964, Mancos-Mesaverde (Upper Cretaceous) intertonguing relations, southeast Piceance Basin, Colorado: American Association of Petroleum Geologists Bulletin, v. 48, p. 1091-1107.

Wells, L. F., 1958, Petroleum occurrence in the Uinta basin, in Habitat of oil: Tulsa, Oklahoma, American Association of Petroleum Geologists, p. 344-365.

Young, R. G., 1959, Cretaceous deposits of the Grand Junction area, Garfield, Mesa, and Delta Counties, Colorado, in Symposium on Cretaceous rocks of Colorado and adjacent areas: Denver, Colorado, Rocky Mountain Association of Geologists, p. 17-25.

Gunnison Gorge Recreation area, Black Canyon, looking northwest from Black Ridge toward Grand Mesa on skyline.

PRECAMBRIAN GEOLOGY ALONG PARTS OF THE GUNNISON UPLIFT OF SOUTHWESTERN COLORADO

D. C. HEDLUND and J. C. OLSON
U.S. Geological Survey
Denver, Colorado 80225

INTRODUCTION

The Gunnison Uplift of southwestern Colorado consists of extensive Precambrian rocks along the south side of the Gunnison River that extend for as much as 120 km from the Black Canyon area through the Powderhorn district and eastward to Cochetopa Creek (fig. 1). The part of the Gunnison Uplift discussed in this report occupies an area of about 60 by 30 km and is a part of the Uncompahgre–San Luis Highlands. The Cimarron fault bounds the Gunnison Uplift on the south and is well exposed in the valley of the Lake Fork of the Gunnison River, where the Upper Cretaceous Mancos Shale is faulted downward on the south against Precambrian rocks. The fault block in this region is tilted 5 to 10 degrees to the north-northeast. Along the Gunnison River, the Precambrian rocks dip under the cover of Upper Jurassic and Cretaceous sedimentary rocks, and the contact slopes northward forming a part of the south flank of the Piceance Creek Basin.

The Precambrian rocks have been separated into two major formations, the younger dominantly metasedimentary Black Canyon Schist and the older dominantly metavolcanic Dubois Greenstone. The Black Canyon Schist is at least 10,000 m thick, and in the Black Canyon W. R. Hansen (1971) recognized five different map units. In the Powderhorn region, the Dubois Greenstone is at least 8,000 m thick and the base of the formation is not exposed. Olson and Hedlund (1973) separated the Dubois Greenstone into three main rock types: (1) metabasalt and meta-andesite flows, (2) felsite porphyries and metatuffaceous rocks, and (3) epiclastic rocks derived from the older volcanic strata. The purpose of this paper is to give a review of the Precambrian stratigraphy, structure, and intrusive activity.

Uplift and erosion in the late Paleozoic and (or) Triassic resulted in the removal of all Paleozoic strata and peneplanation of the Precambrian basement prior to the deposition of the Upper Jurassic Junction Creek Sandstone. Laramide movement on the Cimarron fault resulted in at least 610 m of displacement. Subsequent erosion removed Upper Jurassic and Cretaceous sedimentary rocks from most of the area prior to the eruption of extensive Oligocene lavas, laharic breccias, ash-flow tuffs, and Miocene or Pliocene flows onto the stripped surface of Precambrian rock.

Numerous small gold and silver mines within the Dubois Greenstone gave rise to the term Gunnison Gold Belt, and such small

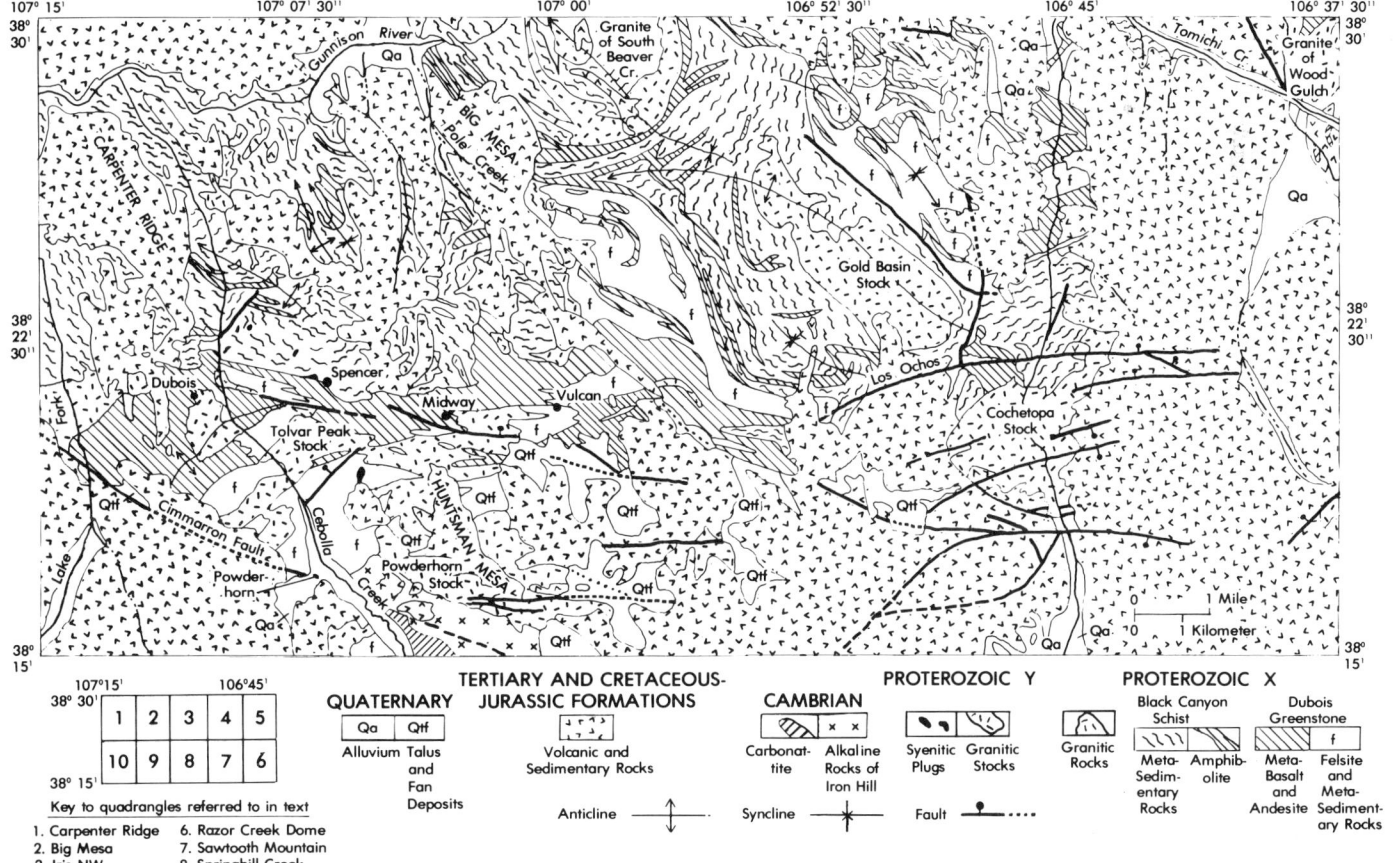

Figure 1. Generalized geologic map of part of the Gunnison Uplift, Colorado.

mining towns as Dubois, Spencer, Vulcan, and Midway were formed in the late 1880's. In the middle and late 1970's, with the recognition of volcanogenic massive sulfide deposits in the region, there was a renewed interest and exploration of the gold- and silver-bearing stratabound base-metal sulfides. D. M. Sheridan, W. H. Raymond, and L. J. Cox (this guidebook) discuss this type of mineralization in an accompanying paper (see also Drobeck, this guidebook).

PRECAMBRIAN STRATIGRAPHY
Dubois Greenstone

The Dubois Greenstone was first described by Hunter (1925, p. 28–36) who named the formation after the old mining camp of Dubois (fig. 1). The Dubois Greenstone can be divided into three parts: (1) metavolcanic hornblende schist, amphibolite, and chlorite-hornblende schist with intercalated purplish-gray metachert beds; (2) felsitic metavolcanic rocks including quartz porphyry flows and dikes and thinly interlayered muscovite-chlorite schists locally containing kyanite, staurolite, spinel, garnet, and sericitized andalusite; and (3) diverse metamorphosed epiclastic and pyroclastic rocks.

Amygdules and pillow structures are locally present in the hornblendic gneiss and schist (fig. 2). Chemical analyses of these metavolcanic rocks suggest a tholeiitic basalt composition (Table 1). Generally the Dubois Greenstone is more schistose in the Powderhorn–Lake Fork region and shows some retrograde chloritization, whereas to the east in the Cochetopa Creek area the

Figure 2. Pillow within metabasalt of the Dubois Greenstone.

greenstone is less deformed and relatively nondeformed pillows are still recognizable. Pillow lavas are well exposed in road cuts on the east side of Cochetopa Creek about 1,500 m south of the Gunnison–Saguache County line. Among the felsitic rocks are "quartz-eye" porphyries that represent rhyolitic flows and tuffs (fig. 3). The "quartz-eyes" are generally devoid of inclusions, are locally lensoid, and commonly display a bluish irridescence. A pronounced bimodal basalt-rhyolite series of flows is recognized within the Dubois Greenstone.

Table 1. Chemical analyses of Precambrian metamorphic rocks.

Sample No.—	150041	150040	3418	R82	3306-A
Rock type—	Amphibolite, Dubois Greenstone	Amphibolite, Dubois Greenstone	Felsite porphyry, Dubois Greenstone	Metatuff Felsite	Quartz biotite schist, Black Canyon Schist
SiO_2	51.0	47.5	73.2	77.0	73.3
Al_2O_3	15.3	17.9	12.2	12.0	13.3
Fe_2O_3	2.3	2.5	1.5	1.3	0.8
FeO	7.8	6.2	3.7	0.96	1.8
MgO	7.0	7.1	0.73	0.83	1.4
CaO	10.9	10.8	3.0	1.1	1.4
Na_2O	2.1	2.5	2.8	3.1	3.2
K_2O	0.37	0.81	0.94	2.2	3.2
TiO_2	0.80	0.36	0.34	0.17	0.22
P_2O_5	0.09	0.10	0.12	0.01	0.04
MnO	0.20	0.18	0.14	0.00	0.08
H_2O	1.3	2.0	0.90	0.07	0.65
CO_2	0.14	0.34	0.09	0.02	0.38
Sum	99.3	98.3	99.7	98.8	99.8

Analyses by P. L. D. Elmore and S. D. Botts, U.S. Geological Survey.

Figure 3. Microphotograph (15×) of "quartz-eyes" in felsite porphyry from the Dubois Greenstone.

This metavolcanic formation also contains a thick (>4,300 m) sequence of submarine pyroclastic flows with interbedded epiclastic rocks (Olson, 1976a; Afifi, 1980, this guidebook). Graded bedding, lithic and crystal clasts, and stretched and deformed shard and pumice fragments have been recognized and are especially well shown in the Iris quadrangle (Olson, 1976a).

Black Canyon Schist

The best exposures of the Black Canyon Schist* are along the walls of the Black Canyon where Hunter (1925, p. 10–22) described a thick section of quartz-biotite schist and gneiss, migmatite, sillimanitic quartz-muscovite-biotite schist and gneissic amphibolite. Migmatite is most common in the Carpenter Ridge and Big Mesa quadrangles (Hedlund and Olson, 1973, 1974) (fig. 1) and farther west in the Black Canyon (Hansen, 1971) where the migmatite is pervaded by pegmatite dikes and pods. Most of the Black Canyon Schist is of metasedimentary origin, and relict stretched pebbles and cobbles are present locally within discontinuous metaconglomerate beds (fig. 4). Chemical analyses indicate about 36 percent normative quartz and 2 percent normative corundum for some samples of schist. Thin layers of intercalated gneissic amphibolite within the quartz biotite schist commonly occur as boudins and locally are contorted or abruptly terminated. An alignment of the amphibolite layers generally indicates the strike or attitude of the original bedding within the schist, and most probably these layers are metamorphosed basaltic or andesitic flows.

AGE RELATIONS OF PRECAMBRIAN METAMORPHIC ROCKS

The metamorphism of the Black Canyon Schist occurred about 1.7 billion years ago based on Rb-Sr dating (Hansen and Peterman, 1968). Age determinations have not been made on the Dubois Greenstone, but the Dubois metavolcanic rocks were probably metamorphosed to amphibolite grade about 1.7 to 1.8 billion years ago as based on isotopic ages from similar rocks in other areas of southwestern Colorado (Hutchinson, 1976). The intrusion of large and small granite bodies, some of which are synkinematic

*The Black Canyon Schist is an accepted formational name of use in a restricted area, but of limited general application (Tweto, 1977).

Figure 4. Metaconglomerate in the Black Canyon Schist.

and associated with migmatization, probably occurred about the time of metamorphism, although some may be as young as 1.35 to 1.4 billion years. The granite of Tolvar Peak has some chemical and lithological similarities to the felsite porphyry in that the Na_2O/K_2O ratio (3–5/1) is relatively high and the quartz grains are similar (Tables 1 and 2). The granite of Tolvar Peak probably is approximately coeval with the felsitic and metabasaltic rocks of the Dubois Greenstone and intruded the volcanic pile shortly after extrusion of the mixed flows and clastics.

The metasedimentary schists of the Black Canyon are concordant with the metavolcanic rocks of the Dubois Greenstone except in areas where there has been intense shearing or intrusion along the formational contact by granite. Moreover, both formations are of similar metamorphic grade—that is, amphibolite facies—and except in the Gateview quadrangle show similar fold patterns. Where pillows have been observed in the Dubois Greenstone the flow tops indicate a younger flow sequence toward the contact with the Black Canyon Schist.

STRUCTURE
Folds

The Black Canyon Schist and the infolded felsite and amphibolite of the Dubois Greenstone in the northwestern part of the area form a large synclinorium with minor smaller folds striking northwest (fig. 1). The thick felsitic mass in the Pole Creek area in the southwestern part of the Iris NW quadrangle and another in the Milkranch Gulch area in the west-central part of the Powderhorn quadrangle (Hedlund and Olson, 1975), together with extensions from these folded masses toward the east, form the V-shaped outcrop pattern of the flanks of a synclinorium plunging northwestward. Younger rocks therefore occupy the trough of the synclinorium progressively northwestward, passing from felsite to the thick locally pillowed basaltic sequence of the Dubois Greenstone to the very thick metasediments of the Black Canyon Schist. Above and northwest of the Dubois metavolcanics, the first sedimentary rocks commonly are quartzofeldspathic schists, as found in the

Table 2. Chemical analyses of Precambrian igneous rocks.

Sample No.	D 100330	150044	150039	150045	150046
Rock type	Powderhorn granite	Granite of Tolvar Peak	Augite syenite	Augite syenite	Biotite syenite
SiO_2	73.15	73.2	48.5	53.8	44.7
Al_2O_3	13.45	14.2	10.4	11.9	9.2
Fe_2O_3	1.25	2.5	4.6	3.0	2.1
FeO	1.19	0.85	3.3	4.7	6.3
MgO	0.57	0.24	10.9	9.2	13.3
CaO	1.86	0.81	7.2	6.6	9.8
Na_2O	3.73	5.6	1.3	2.2	1.0
K_2O	3.43	1.2	8.4	5.8	4.8
TiO_2	0.16	0.25	0.81	0.82	1.5
P_2O_5	0.10	0.01	1.3	0.66	1.7
MnO	0.07	0.02	0.14	0.14	0.13
H_2O	0.11	0.62	0.71	0.56	1.4
CO_2	0.21	0.08	0.68	0.16	1.8
Sum	99.3	99.6	98.2	100	97.7

Analyses by P. L. D. Elmore and S. D. Botts, U.S. Geological Survey.

northwestern and northeastern corners of the Powderhorn quadrangle and the southeastern part of the Big Mesa quadrangle. The greater feldspar content of these metasedimentary rocks, compared to the more quartzose, micaceous, fine-grained character of typical Black Canyon Schist in a large area in the Carpenter Ridge and Big Mesa quadrangles, is interpreted as having been derived from nearby volcanic rocks.

The crescentic structure in the northwest corner of the Iris NW quadrangle is interpreted to be a northwest-plunging syncline that is about 10 km across, shows closure to the southeast, and has an axial plane that strikes N.35°W. The synkinematic granite of South Beaver Creek outlines the limbs and crest of the fold. The amphibolite layer that forms a crescentic band just southeast of the granite body is interpreted to be correlative with the similar unit in the southern half of the Iris NW quadrangle just east of the thick felsite mass of Pole Creek, where it is in part a pillow lava.

A relatively small anticlinal fold is well shown in the Dubois Greenstone and associated felsite layers just east of the Lake Fork of the Gunnison River (fig. 1). The foliation and layering are bent from their common N.40°E. strike to an east and slightly southeast strike. This flexing of the axial plane possibly is related in part to drag along a major shear zone with right-lateral displacement.

In the Iris quadrangle, epiclastic and metamorphosed rocks are folded into a tightly compressed syncline that plunges steeply southeast. The keel of the fold just northwest of Green Mountain is delineated by folded amphibolite layers (Olson, 1976a). (See also Afifi, this guidebook.)

Numerous other small folds make up a part of the large synclinorium, and some of the larger ones are represented in the northwestern part of Figure 1. In most places the foliation in the metamorphosed rock is approximately parallel to the bedding and is generally steep throughout the region, except for the relatively flat foliation surfaces within the Black Canyon Schist of the Carpenter Ridge quadrangle.

Faults

Faults of Precambrian, Cambrian, and Laramide ages are recognized in the region and most are dated by either association or displacement of known types of mineralization—for example, thorium veins and the stratabound massive sulfides—or by displacement of Mesozoic sedimentary rocks. The Precambrian faults are most difficult to date owing to the absence of a Paleozoic sedimentary rock cover and the local occurrence of Mesozoic sedimentary rocks.

Shearing and dislocation of probable Precambrian age is illustrated by one major zone that trends about N.80°W. across the northeastern part of the Gateview quadrangle and into the Powderhorn quadrangle. This fault displaces parts of the near-vertical northeast limb of a broad steep fold in the Dubois Greenstone. The shearing is distributed along many shear planes in a zone about 500 m wide. In this wide belt, chlorite- and sericite-rich schists are common and were formed by retrograde metamorphism of rocks that had attained the staurolite-kyanite grade of metamorphism (fig. 5).

Some Precambrian(?) faults are mineralized by veins that locally contain base-metal sulfides. One such fault about 0.5 km south of Midway in the Powderhorn quadrangle is at least 6 km long and trends west-northwest. Many of the base-metal sulfides are not clearly fault-controlled but show evidence of deformation, and the pyrite, pyrrhotite, arsenopyrite, and sphalerite grains are deformed. Many of the stratabound sulfide deposits are parallel to the foliation and layering in the Dubois Greenstone.

Cambrian faults are commonly dated by association with thorium veins that are along open and brecciated faults that strike dominantly either northwest or N.60°E. to due east. These faults and veins are reddened, jasperized, and commonly contain barite as well as thorogummite and thorite. Because many of these veins and coextensive faults are proximal to the alkaline intrusions of the complex at Iron Hill and to the thin trachyte porphyry dikes in the region, they are probably the same late Precambrian or Early Cambrian age as the intrusive at Iron Hill, about 570 m.y. old (Olson and others, 1977).

Laramide faults such as the Cimarron fault, the Los Ochos and several other unnamed faults in the Sawtooth Mountain quadrangle (Olson and Steven, 1976), a fault in the southeast corner of the Powderhorn quadrangle, and a fault in the northwest corner of the Big Mesa quadrangle all displace Upper Jurassic formations and (or) Mancos Shale of Late Cretaceous age. The Cimarron fault, the largest, has about 610 m of displacement, and may represent a rejuvenated Precambrian fault. Along the south side of Cebolla Creek near Powderhorn, its trend is marked by hot springs and travertine spring aprons. The Los Ochos fault can be traced for about 20 km, and east of Cochetopa Creek the fault has been the site of uranium mineralization (Malan and Ranspot, 1959). The Laramide fault in the southeast corner of the Powderhorn quadrangle and southwest corner of the Spring Hill Creek quadrangle contains breccias that were locally prospected for fluorspar (Olson and others, 1975).

Figure 5. View east to Vulcan mines. Steeply dipping chlorite schist within felsites of the Dubois Greenstone in the foreground.

METAMORPHISM

The metasedimentary and metavolcanic rocks are metamorphosed in the biotite-chlorite to epidote amphibolite facies. The grade of metamorphism is generally lowest in the eastern part of the area and increases northwestward to the sillimanite zone in the Carpenter Ridge quadrangle. In areas of migmatized quartz biotite schist in the northwest corner of the map area (fig. 1), a sparse amount of fibrolitic sillimanite is present within the more micaceous schist. The occurrence of sillimanite coincides with the presence of numerous pegmatitic dikes and pods along the Gunnison River in the Carpenter Ridge quadrangle. In small areas locally higher grades show varying amounts of staurolite, kyanite, garnet, and sparse spinel. One such area is in a belt 500 to 700 m wide that strikes N.75°W. in the northeastern corner of the Gateview quadrangle. The rocks in this area were originally sediments rich in quartz, alumina, and iron with interlayered rhyodacite tuffs or flows. In a typical quartz-chlorite-biotite-staurolite-kyanite schist the black layers, less than 3 mm thick, and containing biotite and staurolite porphyroblasts, alternate with grayish-green layers of quartz, chlorite, and locally kyanite. Dark-brown, twinned staurolite porphyroblasts commonly stand out in relief on weathered surfaces. The staurolite-kyanite rocks indicate medium- to high-grade metamorphism involving strong deformation under relatively high stress, as shown by crenulations, drag folds, and strong shear zones in some of the felsites and metasediments.

After regional metamorphism, a rather pervasive northeast-striking foliation, accompanied by shearing and retrograde metamorphism, was superimposed on the earlier formed structural features in some areas.

PRECAMBRIAN INTRUSIONS

Precambrian intrusives include a diverse group of rocks ranging from diorite to granite to syenite. Isotopic ages have been determined for the syenitic rocks, 1,330 to 1,390 m.y. old, but the other intrusive rocks are probably mostly 1,750–1,800 m.y. in age. Hunter (1925, p. 38, 39) named the "Powderhorn granite group" and considered them to be the oldest in the region. However, it is highly probable that the granite of Tolvar Peak, the smaller dioritic bodies in the Big Mesa quadrangle, and the synkinematic granite of South Beaver Creek are somewhat older. These various intrusives are discussed in order of probable age.

Dioritic Rocks

Some of the earliest rocks intrusive into the metavolcanic and metasedimentary rocks are the numerous small plutons and dikes that are mostly quartz diorite or metadiorite but range from gabbro to granodiorite in composition. These intrude all the older metamorphic rocks described above, but are cut by granites. About 50 such small bodies were mapped in the Big Mesa and Gateview quadrangles.

Granitic Rocks

The granitic rocks, including granodiorite, quartz monzonite, and granite, are exposed over an area of 78 km² within the Precambrian basement. These rocks occur in three principal belts that trend east-northeast throughout the region: (1) a belt along the south and southeast margin of the mapped area consists of extensive bodies of granitic rocks and only small areas of metamorphic rock. The belt contains the Powderhorn Granite, the quartz monzonite of Cochetopa Creek, and the granite of Wood Gulch; (2) a central east-northeast-trending belt dominated by metavolcanic and metasedimentary rocks, but containing small syntectonic granitic bodies that are generally concordant with the foliation of the enclosing metamorphic rocks. This belt contains the granite of Tolvar Peak, the granite and quartz diorite of Gold Basin, the granites of the Sugar and Pole Creek areas within the Big Mesa quadrangle, and the arcuate granitic bodies of South Beaver Creek; and (3) a group of leucogranite and biotite granite bodies that form irregular discordant stocks and dikes within areas of migmatite and quartz biotite schist in the northwest part of the mapped area, in the Carpenter Ridge and Big Mesa quadrangles.

Alkalic Rocks

About 20 small plugs of augite syenite, biotite syenite, and leucosyenite crop out in the region, many of them in an area just northwest of Spencer and east of Cebolla Creek. Some of the plugs have leucosyenite cores with marginal wall zones of biotite syenite; others are unzoned and are of augite syenite. The intrusives are characterized by a high K_2O content, which ranges from 5 to 8 percent, whereas the Na_2O values are generally less than 2 percent (Table 2). Relatively high values of TiO_2 and P_2O_5 can be attributed to the rutile inclusions in biotite and to the abundance of accessory apatite.

The alkalic plugs have intruded the Dubois Greenstone and the Black Canyon Schist and have yielded K-Ar ages of 1,330 to 1,390 m.y. (Olson and others, 1977). These alkalic plugs are clearly older than the 570-m.y. alkaline rocks of Iron Hill but are younger than the 1,700 to 1,800-m.y. regional metamorphism. Although there is some uralitization of the augite grains in the augite syenite, the other minerals or original texture show little modification.

REFERENCES

Afifi, A. M., 1980, Precambrian geology of the Iris area, Gunnison and Saguache Counties, Colorado [abs.]: Geological Society of America, Abstracts with Programs, v. 12, p. 265.

Hansen, W. R., 1971, Geologic map of the Black Canyon of the Gunnison River and vicinity, western Colorado: U.S. Geological Survey Miscellaneous Geologic Investigations Map I-584, scale 1:31,680.

Hansen, W. R. and Peterman, Z. E., 1968, Basement-rock geochronology of the Black Canyon of the Gunnison, Colorado, in Geological Survey Research 1968: U.S. Geological Survey Professional Paper 600-C, p. C80–C90.

Hedlund, D. C., 1974a, Geologic map of the Big Mesa quadrangle, Gunnison County, Colorado: U.S. Geological Survey Geologic Quadrangle Map GQ-1153, scale 1:24,000.

———, 1974b, Geologic map of the Iris NW quadrangle, Gunnison and Saguache Counties, Colorado: U.S. Geological Survey Geologic Map GQ-1134, scale 1:24,000.

Hedlund, D. C. and Olson, J. C., 1973, Geologic map of the Carpenter Ridge quadrangle, Gunnison County, Colorado: U.S. Geological Survey Geologic Quadrangle Map GQ-1070, scale 1:24,000.

———, 1975, Geologic map of the Powderhorn quadrangle, Gunnison and Saguache Counties, Colorado: U.S. Geological Survey Quadrangle Map GQ-1178, scale 1:24,000.

Hunter, J. F., 1925, Precambrian rocks of Gunnison River, Colorado: U.S. Geological Survey Bulletin 777, 94 p.

Hutchinson, R. M., 1976, Precambrian geochronology of western and central Colorado and southern Wyoming: Studies in Colorado field geology, Professional Contributions of Colorado School of Mines, no. 8, p. 73–77.

Malan, R. C. and Ranspot, H. W., 1959, Geology of the uranium deposits in the Cochetopa mining district, Saguache and Gunnison Counties, Colorado: Economic Geology, v. 54, p. 1–19.

Olson, J. C., 1976a, Geologic map of the Iris quadrangle, Gunnison and Saguache Counties, Colorado: U.S. Geological Survey Geologic Quadrangle Map GQ-1286, scale 1:24,000.

———, 1976b, Geologic map of the Houston Gulch quadrangle, Gunnison and Saguache Counties, Colorado: U.S. Geological Survey Geologic Quadrangle Map GQ-1287, scale 1:24,000.

Olson, J. C. and Hedlund, D. C., 1973, Geologic map of the Gateview quadrangle, Gunnison County, Colorado: U.S. Geological Survey Geologic Quadrangle Map GQ-1071, scale 1:24,000.

Olson, J. C., Marvin, R. F., Parker, R. L., and Mehnert, H. H., 1977, Age and tectonic setting of Lower Paleozoic alkalic and mafic rocks, carbonatites and thorium veins in south-central Colorado: Journal of Research, U.S. Geological Survey, v. 5, p. 673–687.

Olson, J. C. and Steven, T. A., 1976, Geologic map of the Sawtooth Mountain quadrangle, Saguache County, Colorado: U.S. Geological Survey Miscellaneous Field Studies Map MF-733, scale 1:24,000.

Olson, J. C., Steven, T. A., and Hedlund, D. C., 1975, Geologic map of the Spring Hill Creek quadrangle, Saguache County, Colorado: U.S. Geological Survey Miscellaneous Field Studies Map MF-713, scale 1:24,000.

Tweto, Ogden, 1977, Nomenclature of Precambrian rocks in Colorado: U.S. Geological Survey Bulletin 1422-D, p. D1–D22.

PRECAMBRIAN SULFIDE DEPOSITS IN THE GUNNISON REGION, COLORADO

DOUGLAS M. SHERIDAN, WILLIAM H. RAYMOND, and LESLIE J. COX
Central Mineral Resources Branch
U.S. Geological Survey
Denver, Colorado 80225

INTRODUCTION

Base-metal massive sulfide deposits are currently of considerable economic interest because they are characteristically high in grade. Such deposits are mined mainly for copper, zinc, and lead, but some also contain recoverable silver and gold. New exploration has been stimulated in many parts of the world by numerous studies during the last two decades concerning various syngenetic and exhalative processes of origin and the relation of stratabound sulfide deposits to certain types of host-rock lithology (King and Thompson, 1953; Horikoshi, 1969; Anderson, 1969; Matsukuma and Horikoshi, 1970; Sangster, 1972; Stanton, 1972; Hutchinson, 1973). Many massive sulfide deposits in various places in the world are now considered to be volcanogenic. Using the newer geologic concepts and newer, more refined guides to ore, mining companies have made some outstanding new discoveries, including, for example, the recent finding of two large Precambrian deposits: one containing more than 7 million tons* of zinc-copper-lead ore at Izok Lake in the Northwest Territories, Canada (Money and Heslop, 1976, p. 24–25), and another having 60 million tons of zinc-copper ore at Crandon, Wisconsin (Eyde, 1977, p. 51).

The search for minable Precambrian sulfide deposits has been extremely active in recent years in numerous areas in Colorado, New Mexico, and southern Wyoming. The initial stimulus for this renewal of interest likely was given by Giles' suggestion (1974) that a significant part of the Precambrian terrain in northern New Mexico and southern Colorado may be a "previously unrecognized volcanogenic massive sulfide metallogenic province." Data presented by Sheridan and Raymond (1977) indicated that representative samples from many long-ignored Precambrian sulfide deposits distributed throughout western Colorado are of a grade suggesting potential economic significance.

The present report is a brief description of the geology of Precambrian sulfide deposits in the Gunnison region, Colorado. In other reports in this guidebook, the Precambrian geology along parts of the Gunnison uplift is described by D. C. Hedlund and J. C. Olson, syngenetic sulfide mineralization in the Gunnison Gold Belt is described by P. A. Drobeck, and the stratigraphy, petrology, and structure of Precambrian metamorphic rocks in the Iris district are described by A. M. Afifi.

GEOLOGIC SETTING

Precambrian sulfide deposits occur in many localities in Colorado (Sheridan and Raymond, 1977) in metamorphic complexes about 1,800 million years in age (Tweto, 1980, p. 37), that is, Proterozoic X. The progenitors of these metamorphic rocks were sedimentary, volcanic, and subvolcanic intrusive rocks. The major period of Precambrian folding and regional metamorphism reached its peak in the period 1,700–1,775 m.y. ago, according to radiometric age determinations (Hedge and others, 1967; Hedge and others, 1968; Hansen and Peterman, 1968; Silver and Barker, 1968;

Stern and others, 1971). Isotopic data (Hedge, 1969) indicate that no great amount of time elapsed between the original deposition and the time of metamorphism. Lead isotope studies on galena samples from Precambrian sulfide deposits in Colorado indicate an age in the same 1,700–1,800 m.y. bracket (Bruce Doe, oral communication, 1979). The age data and the metamorphic textures of the ore-bearing rocks indicate that the sulfide deposits were metamorphosed at the same time as their host rocks during the major regional metamorphism.

Metamorphism was markedly less intense in the Gunnison region than in most other areas in Colorado that contain Precambrian sulfide deposits. J. C. Olson and D. C. Hedlund (oral communications, 1977) noted that most of the Gunnison region is in the lower amphibolite facies, but locally in the western part the grade is somewhat higher where the rocks contain staurolite, kyanite, or andalusite. They noted also that in the eastern part of the region near Cochetopa Canyon the rocks are in the greenschist facies, and that original features such as pillows in metabasalts and shardlike textures in felsic metavolcanics are still recognizable. In contrast, such original textures and structures have been largely obliterated in the Park Range, Front Range, Wet Mountains, and much of the Salida region where Precambrian sulfide deposits and their host rocks were metamorphosed to the upper amphibolite facies, that is, the sillimanite zone of regional metamorphism (Sheridan and Raymond, 1977).

DISTRIBUTION OF DEPOSITS

Precambrian sulfide deposits in the Gunnison region are spatially related to a Precambrian greenstone belt, long known as "the Gunnison gold belt" (Lakes, 1896). This belt of metavolcanic rocks, the Dubois Greenstone, trends northeasterly from the Lake Fork of the Gunnison River for about 50 km and is as much as 10 km wide (fig. 1). Shown on the map are nine Precambrian sulfide deposits that were examined during brief reconnaissance studies in 1975 and 1977. Eight of these are within the belt of metavolcanic rocks, but one is in metasedimentary terrain.

In addition to the mines at these deposits, there are numerous other mines and prospects throughout the greenstone belt. Many of these are in what appear to be stratabound Precambrian sulfide deposits similar to those described in this report. Others are in veins. According to J. C. Olson and D. C. Hedlund (written communication, 1981), gold-bearing quartz-chlorite veins are Precambrian in age, whereas thorite-bearing veins are Cambrian in age.

HOST ROCKS

Most of the Precambrian sulfide deposits mentioned in this report are in host rocks of the Dubois Greenstone. As described by Hedlund and Olson (1975; written communication, 1981), the Dubois Greenstone consists principally of two groups of metavolcanic rocks: (1) hornblende schist and amphibolite that probably originated as basaltic and andesitic lavas; (2) felsite and felsite porphyry—felsic metavolcanic rocks that originated as flows and tuffs

---

*Figures cited from published sources are in the units originally reported.

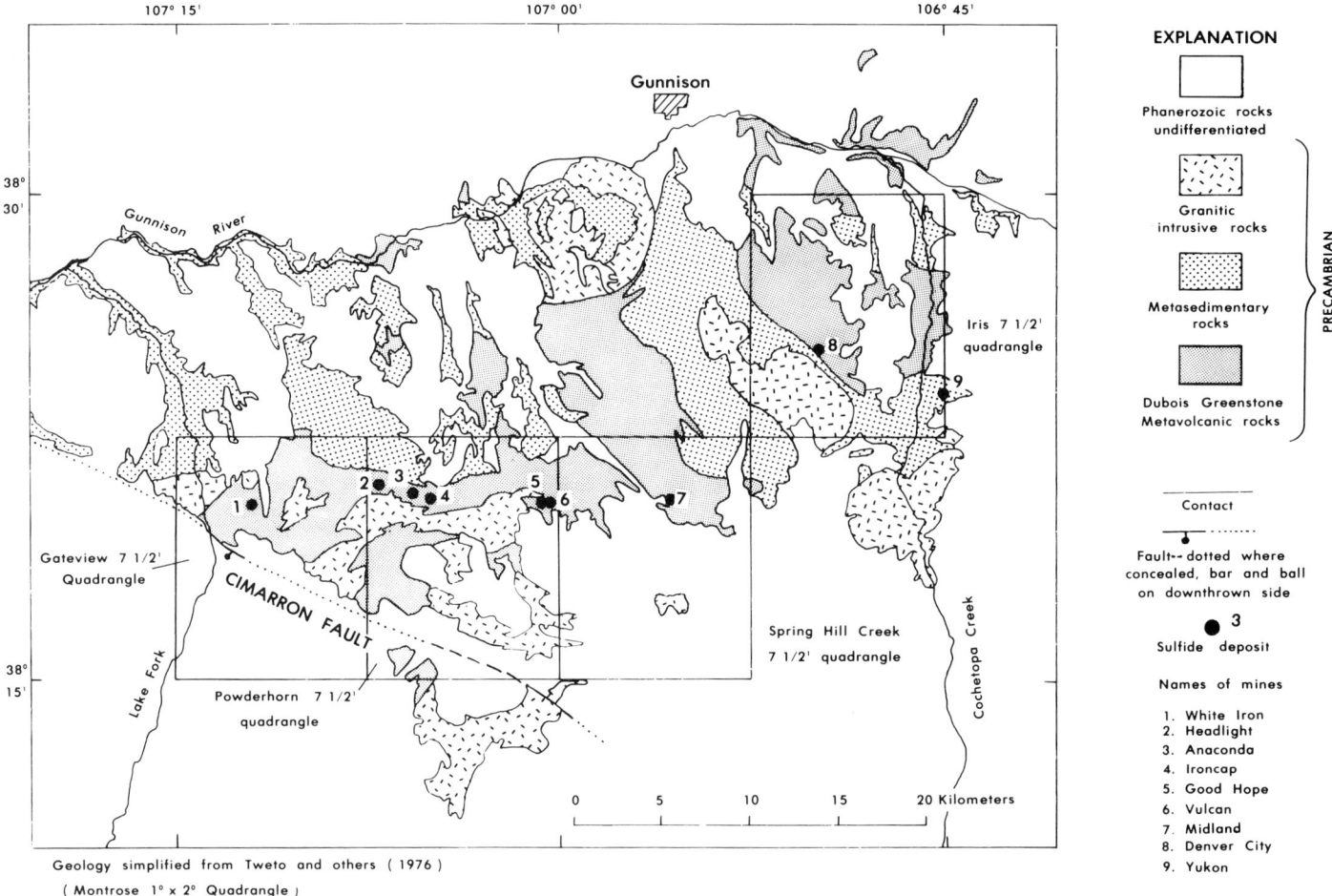

Figure 1. Distribution of Precambrian sulfide deposits in the Gunnison region, southwestern Colorado.

of rhyolite, quartz latite, and dacite. Intercalated with these are numerous beds of purplish-gray to gray, magnetite-bearing quartzite, commonly 2 to 7 m thick, that are inferred to have originated as sea-floor chert beds. Within the Dubois Greenstone in some areas are diverse metamorphosed epiclastic and pyroclastic rocks. In most places the foliation is approximately parallel to the lithologic layering.

The White Iron mine (fig. 1, no. 1) is in hornblende schist and amphibolite. The mine, although not designated by name on the geologic map of the Gateview quadrangle (Olson and Hedlund, 1973), is in the SW¼ sec. 10, T. 47 N., R. 3 W.

The geologic setting of the five mines in the Dubois Greenstone in the Powderhorn quadrangle (fig. 1, nos. 2-6) is delineated in greater detail on the geologic map by Hedlund and Olson (1975). The Headlight mine (fig. 1, no. 2) is in felsite and felsite prophyry near a contact with hornblende schist and amphibolite. Southeast of the mine, a lens of quartzite is along the contact. Westward from the mine, the unit of felsic metavolcanic rocks contains interlayered aluminous metasedimentary beds (Olson and Hedlund, 1973). The Anaconda mine (fig. 1, no. 3) is in hornblende schist, amphibolite, and a bed of quartzite. The Ironcap mine (fig. 1, no. 4) is in hornblende schist and amphibolite, and nearby are numerous beds of quartzite. Drobeck (1979, p. 103, 105) also noted abundant carbonate (marble) in the vicinity of the Ironcap mine. The Good Hope and Vulcan mines (fig. 1, nos. 5 and 6) are in the map unit of felsite and felsite porphyry, and nearby are thin lenses and layers of hornblende schist, amphibolite, and magnetite-bearing quartzite. The host rocks within about a kilometer of the Good Hope and Vulcan mines are considerably more schistose than elsewhere, and contain abundant fine muscovite and chlorite.

The geologic setting of the Midland mine (fig. 1, no. 7) is delineated in greater detail by Olson and others (1975) on their geologic map of the Spring Hill Creek quadrangle. The mine is in a bed of magnetite-bearing quartzite (metachert) within amphibole schist.

The geologic setting of the two mines shown in the Iris quadrangle on Figure 1 is delineated in greater detail by Olson (1976) on his geologic map of that quadrangle. The Denver City mine (fig. 1, no. 8) is in a unit of felsite and felsite porphyry. Nearby are elongate bodies of amphibolite and a few beds of magentite-bearing quartzite. About 1.8 km northeast of the mine is a volcanic breccia in a unit of lapilli tuff and crystal-lithic tuff. The Yukon mine (fig. 1, no. 9) is in terrain that is largely metasedimentary phyllite and schist.

SULFIDE DEPOSITS
General Character

The Precambrian sulfide deposits in the metavolcanic belt are stratabound and are elongate parallel to gradational and interfingering contacts between mafic and felsic metavolcanic rocks. Groups of deposits, such as those in the Powderhorn quadrangle, appear to be strung out parallel to the major contacts and to the abundant thin beds of magnetite-bearing quartzite. Some of the deposits are in or adjacent to a quartzite bed. The sulfides commonly are in laminae and elongate aggregates parallel to lithologic layering and foliation. Some specimens of ore are crudely banded. The sulfides are generally fine grained (less than 1 mm), but locally are medium grained (1–5 mm).

At some of the deposits, the ores consist mainly of base-metal sulfides alone or in a pyrite- or arsenopyrite-rich matrix. This type of ore is truly "massive sulfide," as defined by Sangster (1972, p. 11). Other deposits contain ores of a disseminated type, characterized by concentrations of base-metal sulfides in a matrix rich in silicate minerals. Locally, as at the Anaconda and Headlight mines, some of the ore is characterized by small rounded to angular fragments of rock enclosed in a matrix of sulfides. Whether this is a conglomerate or a fragmental rock of some other origin has not yet been determined.

The geology at the Vulcan and Good Hope mines differs from the geology at other deposits because a younger mineralizing event has been superimposed on the Precambrian sulfide deposits there. Modifications include the introduction of abundant tellurium and the formation of native sulfur. Abundant selenium is present also, some of which may have been redistributed from the Precambrian deposits.

Mineralogy and Texture

The principal sulfide minerals in the Precambrian deposits of the Gunnison region are sphalerite, chalcopyrite, pyrite, arsenopyrite, and galena. The predominance of one, two, or three of these major minerals, with or without abundant magnetite, characterizes each deposit. At the White Iron mine (fig. 1, no. 1) arsenopyrite is the principal sulfide. The Headlight mine (fig. 1, no. 2) in the western half of the Powderhorn quadrangle is characterized by assemblages of chalcopyrite, arsenopyrite, and sphalerite. The Anaconda mine (fig. 1, no. 3) is characterized by pyrite with minor sphalerite, and the Ironcap mine (fig. 1 no. 4) by chalcopyrite with minor pyrite. At the Vulcan district in the eastern half of the quadrangle, crudely banded pyrite and sphalerite are the predominant sulfides of the Good Hope and Vulcan mines (fig. 1, nos. 5 and 6). The gold-bearing deposit at the Midland mine (fig. 1, no. 7) is characterized by abundant pyrite and magnetite, whereas base-metal sulfides are present only in trace amounts. In the Iris quadrangle, the Denver City and Yukon mines (fig. 1, nos. 8 and 9) are characterized by sphalerite with lesser chalcopyrite and galena.

Metallic minerals occurring in minor to trace amounts with the principal sulfides include pyrrhotite, marcasite, tennantite, berthierite, molybdenite, ilmenite, magnetite, hematite, rutile, gahnite, and gassiterite(?). Native gold and native silver were not observed. Of the major and minor phases, sphalerite, chalcopyrite, pyrite, arsenopyrite, pyrrhotite, marcasite, ilmenite, and magnetite are found at nearly every deposit. The proportions of these minerals vary widely. A mineral predominant at one deposit may be present only in trace amounts at another. The metallic oxides are found in both ore and host rocks. The zinc spinel, gahnite, is intermixed with sphalerite and chalcopyrite as well as with quartz-biotite-tourmaline gangue at the Headlight mine. The interest in the occurrence of gahnite lies in its potential as a prospecting guide to Precambrian sulfide deposits (Sheridan and Raymond, 1977). A green spinel was observed by D. C. Hedlund (oral communication, 1978) in outcrops of schist about 1.6 km west of the Headlight mine.

Gangue minerals vary in accordance with the host rock of each deposit. Quartz, biotite, and chlorite are nearly ubiquitous. Other gangue minerals include sericite, muscovite, tourmaline, calcite, epidote, hornblende, plagioclase, microcline, orthoclase, apatite, sphene, and zircon. Tourmaline commonly is intermixed with sphalerite-rich ores. Some of the sphalerite at the Headlight mine is poikilitic with tourmaline inclusions.

Secondary minerals at the various deposits include marcasite, scorodite, pyrite overgrowths, malachite, covellite, cuprite, idaite, chalcocite, aurichalcite, and hydrozincite.

In the Vulcan district, a variety of tellurides and other minerals are associated with a younger mineralizing event. The Good Hope mine is the type locality of three copper tellurides: rickardite and weissite (Eckel, 1961) and vulcanite (Cameron and Threadgold, 1961). Coloradoite, petzite, tellurite, native tellurium, tetradymite(?), native selenium, native copper, native sulfur (Eckel, 1961), and tellurobismuthite are also found at the Good Hope. The tellurobismuthite occurs as myrmekites within galena interstitial to the edge of larger pyrite grains and gangue. The textures exhibited by the tellurium-bearing minerals would have been destroyed by metamorphism, thus indicating a younger mineralization than the metamorphosed host sulfides.

The parallelism of sulfides to foliation and layering reflects to a large part the original compositional layering. Some of the layered sulfides ores are massive and others are disseminated. In massive layers, only a small percentage is gangue. The gangue minerals within the sulfide ores are the same as those in the host rocks, but have a tendency to be nonfoliated when intermixed with the larger percentages of sulfides in recrystallized assemblages with annealed 120° triple junctions. Grains in the sulfide-rich ore are slightly coarser (2–3 mm across) than are sulfide grains elsewhere. Distinct alternating pyrite-rich and sphalerite-rich layers may be 1 cm thick. Disseminated sulfides are interstitial to quartz in silica-rich bands in the foliated micaceous rocks. In places, sulfide minerals have migrated to noses of folds and pyrite laminae have been boudinaged.

The mineral textures that indicate that the sulfide deposits and host rocks underwent metamorphism simultaneously, include grain size and annealing of intermixed grains of gangue and sulfide, layering, exsolved phases, and poikilitic textures. Examples of equilibration include the coarse grains of sphalerite that contain minute (less than 10 microns) exsolved blebs of chalcopyrite, some of which are crystallographically oriented. Also, coarse grains of all the major sulfides commonly contain rounded inclusions of the other sulfide minerals with which they are intermixed.

Grade

The base-metal and precious-metal contents of samples of ore from the five mines in the Powderhorn quadrangle and from the two mines in the Iris quadrangle are summarized, respectively, in Tables 1 and 2. In ores from both quadrangles the principal base metal is zinc, followed in abundance by copper and a minor amount of lead. Silver occurs in appreciable amounts in most of the ores and is accompanied by a minor but noteworthy amount of gold.

The gold content of two samples from the Midland mine (fig. 1) ranges from 1.76 to 33.9 grams/metric ton*. Unlike the other mines summarized above, however, the base-metal content of the ore at the Midland mine is extremely low. The deposit consists of abundant pyrite in a magnetite-bearing quartzite.

In addition to base and precious metals, the Precambrian ores of the Gunnison region are characterized by abundant iron, generally greater than 10 percent. Ores at the White Iron, Denver City, Yukon, and Headlight mines are characterized by high arsenic with amounts ranging from 3 to more than 10 percent.

---

*Analyses by fire assay and atomic absorption methods by J. G. Crock, A. W. Haubert, and Joseph Haffty, U.S. Geological Survey.

Table 1. Analyses of Precambrian ores from the Powderhorn quadrangle

	5 samples from dumps of 5 mines[1]	
	Range	Average
Copper (percent)	0.07–7.0	2.3
Zinc (percent)	.1–>10	>6
Lead (percent)	0–0.3	0.13
Silver (grams/metric ton)	3–70	30
Gold (grams/metric ton)	0.13–2.11	0.71

Data for copper, zinc, lead, and silver from semiquantitative spectrographic analyses by N. M. Conklin, U.S. Geological Survey; data for gold from analyses by fire assay and atomic absorption methods by J. G. Crock, A. W. Haubert, and Joseph Haffty, U.S. Geological Survey.

[1]One sample from each of the following mines shown by name on the geologic map of the Powderhorn quadrangle (Hedlund and Olson, 1975): Headlight, Anaconda, Ironcap, Good Hope, and Vulcan mines.

Table 2. Analyses of Precambrian ores from the Iris quadrangle

	6 samples from dumps of 2 mines[1]	
	Range	Average
Copper (percent)	0.7–>10	>4
Zinc (percent)	0.7–>10	>6
Lead (percent)	0.1–1.5	0.7
Silver (grams/metric ton)	15–150	60
Gold (grams/metric ton)	0.29–4.17	1.76

Data for copper, zinc, lead, and silver from semiquantitative spectrographic analyses by L. A. Bradley, U.S. Geological Survey; data for gold from analyses by fire assay and atomic absorption methods by J. G. Crock, A. W. Haubert, and Joseph Haffty, U.S. Geological Survey.

[1]Four samples from the Denver City mine and two samples from the Yukon mine. Both mines are shown by name on the geologic map of the Iris quadrangle (Olson, 1976).

Genesis

As a result of their detailed mapping in the Gunnison region, J. C. Olson and D. C. Hedlund concluded that the gold deposits are "spatially and probably genetically related to a belt of Precambrian metavolcanic rocks" (U.S. Geological Survey, 1970, p. A3). They noted that the discordant veins and the stratabound sulfide deposits that have been mined or prospected for gold are related to a Precambrian greenstone belt and also are considered to be Precambrian in age. The Precambrian terrain of southern Colorado was included with that of northern New Mexico by Giles (1974) in his suggestion that this terrain may be a previously unrecognized volcanogenic massive sulfide metallogenic province.

During reconnaissance studies of Precambrian sulfide deposits in the Gunnison Gold Belt, D. M. Sheridan and W. H. Raymond observed features that suggest strongly that many of the deposits are volcanogenic (U.S. Geological Survey, 1977, p. 6). These features are summarized as follows: (1) location of most of the known deposits within the metavolcanic belt, which comprises a significant part of the region; (2) elongate stratabound deposits parallel to gradational and interfingering contacts between mafic and felsic metavolcanic rocks; (3) apparent stringing out of groups of deposits parallel to major contacts and to beds of magnetite-bearing quartzite (metachert); (4) common occurrence of sulfides as laminae and elongate aggregates parallel to lithologic layering and foliation; and (5) crude banding in some of the ores. These features are believed to be significantly similar to features displayed by sulfide deposits now considered to be volcanogenic in numerous other greenstone belts throughout the world. The sulfide deposits probably formed syngenetically during deposition of the volcanic rocks and later recrystallized at the same time as their host rocks during regional metamorphism.

In considering the Gunnison gold belt, Giles (1976) also supported the general theory that the metals originated approximately contemporaneously with their host rocks, but his ideas differ slightly from those presented above. Giles (1976, p. 129–130) thought that the genetic model developed by Rye and Rye (1974) for the Homestake deposit in South Dakota could also apply to the Gunnison belt. By this model, the gold and other metals are considered to be indigenous to the volcanics and probably volcanogenic exhalative in origin. Giles proposed that the actual deposits were formed later during regional metamorphism when the "syngenetic components migrated and concentrated in dilatant zones." Although Giles' proposal is appealing, it may apply more to the quartz-rich pods and quartz veins associated with some of the deposits than to the sulfide deposits themselves.

Economic Potential

We believe that the Gunnison belt of metavolcanic rocks has considerable potential for the discovery of minable Precambrian sulfide deposits, although a limited amount of exploration in the mid-1970's was generally disappointing. Factors considered favorable to the economic potential are: (1) the belt is moderately large in size; (2) the geologic setting is favorable and is comparable to the settings in many known mining districts in greenstone belts; (3) the geologic evidence is compelling that the deposits are volcanogenic; (4) ores of noteworthy grade have been observed both on mine dumps and in drill cores. Also, the presence of clusters of old mines and prospects in various places in the belt is significant, because massive sulfide deposits are known to occur in clusters in many productive mining regions of the world (Sangster and Scott, 1976, p. 173; Solomon, 1976, p. 35).

Drilling efforts in 1975 and 1976 by two mining companies were interpreted as showing that several of the deposits are of insufficient size to mount a major mining effort, even though the ores intersected are high in grade. Interest shown by mining companies in this region has continued.

Search for larger concealed deposits could be continued in various parts of the belt, both in areas where deposits are clustered and in areas extending laterally from such clusters. The geochemical patterns found to be most useful in mineral exploration in this region have been described by Drobeck (1979, p. 149–153). Considering the location of some of the presently known deposits, favorable areas for search might be along contacts between felsic and mafic metavolcanics and along the thin layers of metachert. As noted by Sangster (1972, p. 3) the presence of so-called "millrock" (pyroclastic breccias) may prove useful in prospecting for areas in which massive sulfide deposits are likely to occur. Solomon (1976, p. 30) noted, however, that many deposits are found in areas not having such coarse-grained volcanic rocks. The fact that the Yukon mine is in metasedimentary terrain indicates that the search need not be limited to the metavolcanic rocks.

Consideration should be given to the possibility that the original (presumably tabular or discoidal) shapes of the deposits may have been modified considerably by folding during regional metamorphism. During the reconnaissance studies forming the basis of this report and during subsequent examination of samples of host rocks and ores, several examples of tight folding were noted. More recently, detailed mapping by Drobeck (1979, p. 24, 113) in the western part of the Gunnison gold belt has shown the presence of closely spaced, tight to isoclinal folds. Also, a tight syncline in the Iris area in the eastern part of the belt has been described by Afifi (1980; this guidebook). Conceivably, some or all of the deposits may have been modified to rod-shaped lenses aligned parallel to the axes of folds. If this proves to be true, conventional geophysical methods geared to the search for tabular bodies may not be effective in disclosing the presence of rod-shaped lenses that are relatively thin in two dimensions but possibly great in down-plunge length. Exploration for concealed deposits having such form and for down-plunge continuations of exposed deposits might benefit from a search for fold axes and other B-lineations defining dominant plunge directions in the favorable areas being considered for exploration. Utilization of such information, as well as consideration of the possible effects of shearing in some areas, could be significant in determining the extent and size of ore bodies.

ACKNOWLEDGMENTS

We gratefully acknowledge the advice and help given by our U.S. Geological Survey colleagues, D. C. Hedlund and J. C. Olson, concerning the Precambrian geology of the Gunnison region. The report has benefited from reviews by D. C. Hedlund and Kenneth Segerstrom.

REFERENCES

Afifi, A. M., 1980, Precambrian geology of the Iris area; Gunnison and Saguache Counties, Colorado [abs.]: Geological Society of America, Abstracts with Programs, v. 12, p. 265.

Anderson, C. A., 1969, Massive sulfide deposits and volcanism: Economic Geology, v. 64, p. 129–146.

Cameron, E. N. and Threadgold, I. M., 1961, Vulcanite, a new copper telluride from Colorado: American Mineralogist, v. 46, p. 258–268.

Drobeck, P. A., 1979, Geology and trace element geochemistry of a part of the Gunnison Gold Belt, Colorado [M.S. thesis]: Golden, Colorado School of Mines, 245 p.

Eckel, E. B., 1961, Minerals of Colorado, a 100-year record: U.S. Geological Survey Bulletin 1114, 399 p.

Eyde, T. H., 1977, Geology, in 1976 Annual review of mining, exploration, and mineral processing: Mining Engineering, v. 29, p. 51, 53.

Giles, D. L., 1974, Massive sulfide deposits in Precambrian rocks, northern New Mexico [abs.]: New Mexico Geological Society Guidebook 25, p. 378.

——, 1976, Precambrian mineralization in the Southern Rocky Mountain region, in Tectonics and mineral resources of Southwestern North America: New Mexico Geological Society Special Publication 6, p. 127–131.

Hansen, W. R. and Peterman, Z. E., 1968, Basement-rock geochronology of the Black Canyon of the Gunnison, Colorado, in Geological Survey Research 1968: U.S. Geological Survey Professional Paper 600-C, p. C80–C90.

Hedge, C. E., 1969, A petrogenetic and geochronologic study of migmatite and pegmatites in the central Front Range [Ph.D. dissertation]: Golden, Colorado School of Mines, 158 p.

Hedge, C. E., Peterman, Z. E., and Braddock, W. A., 1967, Age of the major Precambrian regional metamorphism in the northern Front Range, Colorado: Geological Society of America Bulletin, v. 78, p. 551–558.

Hedge, C. E., Peterman, Z. E., Case, J. E., and Obradovich, J. D., 1968, Precambrian geochronology of the northwestern Uncompahgre Plateau, Utah and Colorado, in Geological Survey Research 1968: U.S. Geological Survey Professional Paper 600-C, p. C91–C96.

Hedlund, D. C. and Olson, J. C., 1975, Geologic map of the Powderhorn quadrangle, Gunnison and Saguache Counties, Colorado: U.S. Geological Survey Geologic Quadrangle Map GQ-1178.

Horikoshi, E., 1969, Volcanic activity related to the formation of the Kuroko-type deposits in the Kosaka district, Japan: Mineralium Deposita, v. 4, p. 321–345.

Hutchinson, R. W., 1973, Volcanogenic sulfide deposits and their metallogenic significance: Economic Geology, v. 68, p. 1223–1246.

King, H. F. and Thompson, B. P., 1953, Geology of the Broken Hill District, in Edwards, A. B. (ed.), Geology of Australian ore deposits: Fifth Empire Mining and Metallurgical Congress, Australia and New Zealand, p. 533–577.

Lakes, Arthur, 1896, Sketch of a portion of the Gunnison gold belt, including the Vulcan and Mammoth Chimney mines: American Institute of Mining and Metallurgical Engineers, Transactions, v. 26, p. 440–448.

Matsukuma, T. and Horikoshi, E., 1970, Kuroko deposits in Japan, a review, in Tatsumi, T. (ed.), Volcanism and ore genesis: Tokyo, University of Tokyo Press, p. 153–179.

Money, P. L. and Heslop, J. B., 1976, Geology of the Izok Lake massive sulphide deposit: Canadian Mining Journal, v. 97, p. 24–27.

Olson, J. C., 1976, Geologic map and sections of the Iris quadrangle, Gunnison and Saguache Counties, Colorado: U.S. Geological Survey Geologic Quadrangle Map GQ-1286.

Olson, J. C. and Hedlund, D. C., 1973, Geologic map of the Gateview quadrangle, Gunnison County, Colorado: U.S. Geological Survey Geologic Quadrangle Map GQ-1071.

Olson, J. C., Steven, T. A., and Hedlund, D. C., 1975, Geologic map of the Spring Hill Creek quadrangle, Saguache County, Colorado: U.S. Geological Survey Miscellaneous Field Studies Map MF-713.

Rye, D. M. and Rye, R. O., 1974, Homestake gold mine, South Dakota, I. Stable isotope studies: Economic Geology, v. 69, p. 293–317.

Sangster, D. F., 1972, Precambrian volcanogenic massive sulphide deposits in Canada—A review: Geological Survey of Canada Paper 72-22, 44 p.

Sangster, D. F. and Scott, S. D., 1976, Precambrian strata-bound, massive Cu-Zn-Pb sulfide ores of North America, in Wolf, K. H. (ed.), Handbook of strata-bound and stratiform ore deposits, chap. 5, v. 6, p. 129–222: Amsterdam, Elsevier Scientific Publishing Company.

Sheridan, D. M. and Raymond, W. H., 1977, Preliminary data on some Precambrian deposits of zinc-copper-lead sulfides and zinc spinel (gahnite) in Colorado: U.S. Geological Survey Open-File Report 77-607, 27 p.

Silver, L. T. and Barker, Fred, 1968, Geochronology of Precambrian rocks of the Needle Mountains, southwestern Colorado—Part 1, U-Pb zircon results [abs.]: Geological Society of America Special Paper 115, p. 204–205.

Solomon, M., 1976, "Volcanic" massive sulphide deposits and their host rocks—a review and an explanation, in Wolf, K. H. (ed.), Handbook of strata-bound and stratiform ore deposits, chap. 2, v. 6, p. 21–54: Amsterdam, Elsevier Scientific Publishing Company.

Stanton, R. L., 1972, Ore petrology: New York, McGraw-Hill, p. 495–577, 612–648.

Stern, T. W., Phair, George, and Newell, M. F., 1971, Boulder Creek batholith, Colorado, Part II—Isotopic age of emplacement and morphology of zircon: Geological Society of America Bulletin, v. 82, p. 1615–1634.

Tweto, Ogden, 1980, Precambrian geology of Colorado, in Kent, H. C., and Porter, K. W. (eds.), Colorado geology: Denver, Colorado, Rocky Mountain Association of Geologists, p. 37–46.

Tweto, Ogden, Steven, T. A., Hail, W. J., Jr., and Moench, R. H., 1976, Preliminary geologic map of the Montrose 1° × 2° quadrangle, southwestern Colorado: U.S. Geological Survey Miscellaneous Field Studies Map MF-761.

U.S. Geological Survey, 1970, Geological Survey research 1970: U.S. Geological Survey Professional Paper 700-A, 426 p.

——, 1977, Geological Survey Research 1977: U.S. Geological Survey Professional Paper 1050, 411 p.

PROTEROZOIC SYNGENETIC MASSIVE SULFIDE DEPOSITS IN THE GUNNISON GOLD BELT, COLORADO

P. A. DROBECK
Fischer-Watt Mining
114 Tucker #7
Kingman, Arizona 86401

INTRODUCTION

Proterozoic rocks exposed in the region south of Gunnison, Colorado contain precious-metal and base-metal massive sulfide deposits, which have been referred to in the past as the Gunnison Gold Belt. Work by several authors (Afifi, this guidebook; Drobeck, 1979; Riesmeyer, 1978; Beaty and Zahoney, 1977; Hartley, 1976; Trost, 1975) provides compelling evidence that these deposits were originally formed by subaqueous fumarolic activity during deposition of the local statigraphic successions. A feature that sets these deposits apart from many other districts of syngenetic, subaqueous, fumarolic-volcanogenic deposits is the variety of subaqueous environments in which the Gunnison deposits occur. Associations include: 1) within a series of basalt and basaltic-andesite flows (Ironcap Mine), 2) in a chert horizon near the contact of komatiitic flowrock and arkosic sediments (Gunnison Mine), 3) within a sequence of rhyolite pyroturbidites (Denver City Mine), 4) along a disconformity within argillites and siltites (Yukon–Alaska Mine), and 5) within a sequence of felsic water laid tuffs and flows (Vulcan Mine) (fig. 1). The lack of a preferred stratigraphic occurrence hampers exploration evaluations within the region.

The deposits commonly contain a simple ore assemblage with pyrite and sphalerite comprising 15 to 90 percent of the ore (usually 80–95 percent of the sulfides). Quartz ± chlorite ± calcite ± dolomite gangue usually comprises 20 to 80 percent of the ore. Chalcopyrite and pyrrhotite are usually present as accessories (rarely as much as 10 percent together) and galena is commonly absent, or less than 2 percent. Silver and gold occur in anomalous concentrations in the ores, but only a few samples showed precious metals values of interest as ores (as high as 2 oz/T Ag and .15 oz/T Au at the Ironcap deposit).

Lithogeochemical samples from mineralized areas in the belt were analyzed for Cu, Pb, Zn, Ag, Au, Se, and Te using a leach-

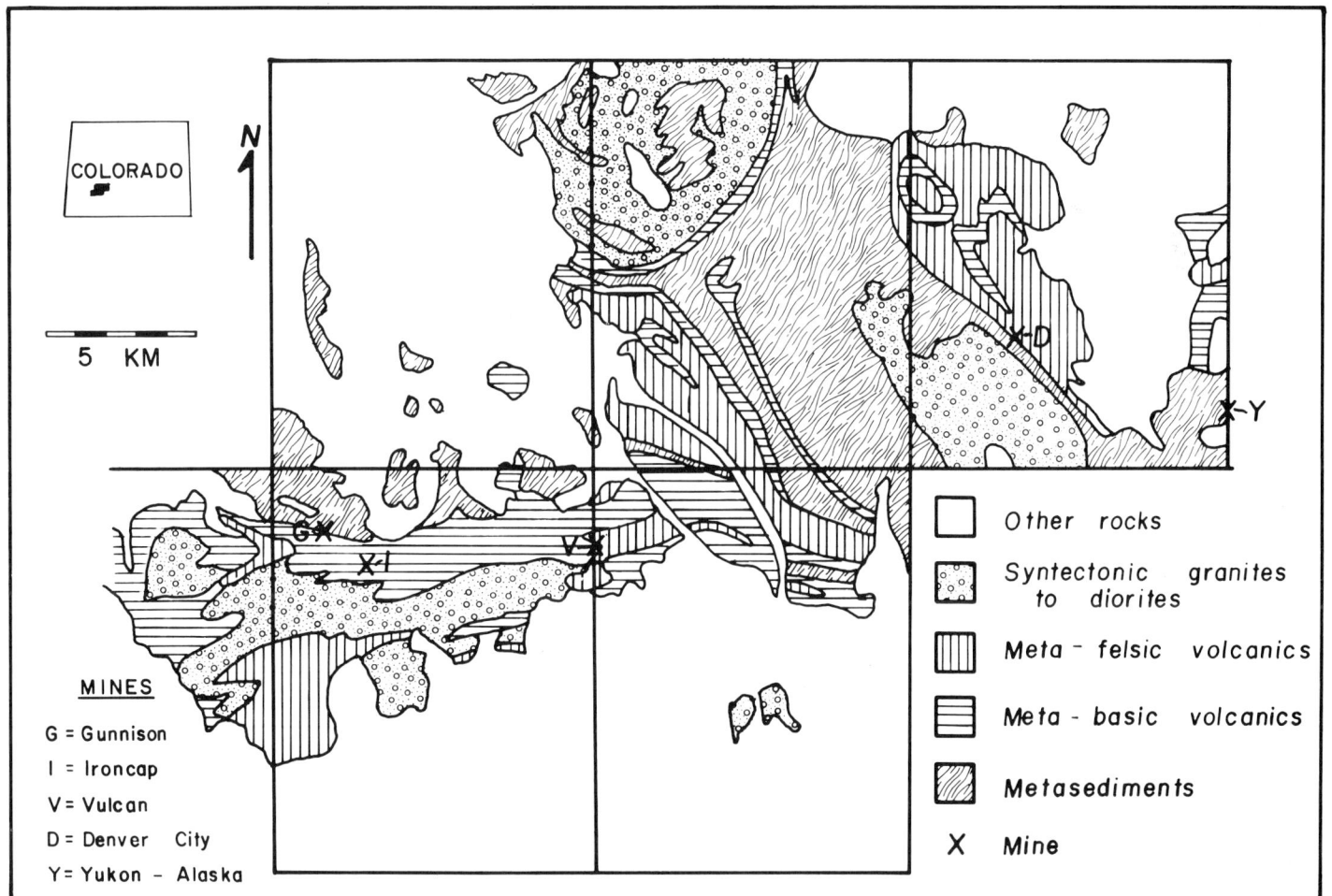

Figure 1. Generalized Precambrian geology of the Dubois Belt, southwestern-central Colorado. Sketched from Olson and Hedlund (1973), Hedlund (1974), Hedlund and Olson (1974, 1975), Olson and others (1975), and Olson (1976).

extraction technique (Clark and Viets, 1979) that measures concentrations of these elements not in silicates. Thus, the concentrations measured are less than a fire or wet chemical assay. This work showed that Cu commonly forms a large dispersion halo, especially in the stratigraphic footwall of the deposits. Pb, Zn, Au, Ag, and Se have narrower halos, being closely restricted to the visibly mineralized horizons (inferred to be the seawater interface at the time of mineralization). Te has different concentration patterns at the different deposits. Cu, Zn, Se, Ag, and Te are the most useful of the elements studied for mineral exploration here.

GENERAL GEOLOGY

There are four major Proterozoic rock types of interest to this study (fig. 1): 1) metamorphosed arkose, greywacke, and siltite with a large percentage of primary feldspar; 2) metamorphosed basalt to andesite water-lain flows and tuffs; 3) metamorphosed dacite to rhyolite tuffs, pyroturbidites, and flows; and 4) syntectonic to late-tectonic granite, granodiorite, and diorite. These rocks are informally referred to here as the "Dubois Belt" after the designation by Hedlund and Olson (1975) at the "Dubois Greenstone Belt." Afifi (this guidebook) and Vance and Blackburn (1981) found a calc-alkalic trend in the region, and Urbani and Blackburn (1974) found a calc-alkalic trend in similar rocks of 20 km NE of this study area.

Between 1730 and 1650 m.y. the region was metamorphosed and intruded by granite to diorite stocks and plutons (Hansen and Peterman, 1968; Wetherhill and Bickford, 1965). This tectonism has been referred to by Hutchinson (1976) as the Boulder Creek Orogeny. Preliminary study of the regional metamorphism indicates a "medium" grade (Winkler, 1976) was produced in much of the region, implying maximum temperatures of 500–525°C (Drobeck, 1979). No systematic study of the variations in metamorphic grade has been completed. The metamorphism was accompanied and followed by folding and faulting. The west part of the Dubois belt is dominated by shallow plunging east-west trending tight to isoclinal folds and the eastern part shows steeply plunging, northwest-trending folds (Drobeck, 1979, Fig. 1; Afifi, this guidebook). Hedlund and Olson (this guidebook) discuss the regional geology in greater detail.

DENVER CITY MINE

General Geology

This area has been geologically mapped by Riesmeyer (1978) (fig. 2), and Afifi (this guidebook) and Olson (1976). The area is dominated by steeply dipping meta-felsic tuffs and pyroturbidites, which commonly contain recrystallized pumice lapilli, and quartz and microcine phenoclasts. Thin, discontinuous purple metachert horizons imply a subaqueous environment. The mineralization is restricted to a quartz-eye rhyolite unit, and in particular, a fragmental facies of this unit (Riesmeyer, 1978; fig. 2). The rocks have been folded into steep southeast-plunging folds, and work by Afifi (this guidebook) indicates this area is on the flank of a large syncline with stratigraphic top to the northeast.

Mineralization

No production records were found pertaining to the Denver City. The deposit was developed by a now inaccessible shaft. The rich sphalerite on the dumps suggests the zinc ore was not shipped.

The mineralization occurs as a stratabound lens parallel to the dip of the host rhyolite. It is composed of massive sulfides intercalated with calcite, quartz, and fine-grained tuffaceous material.

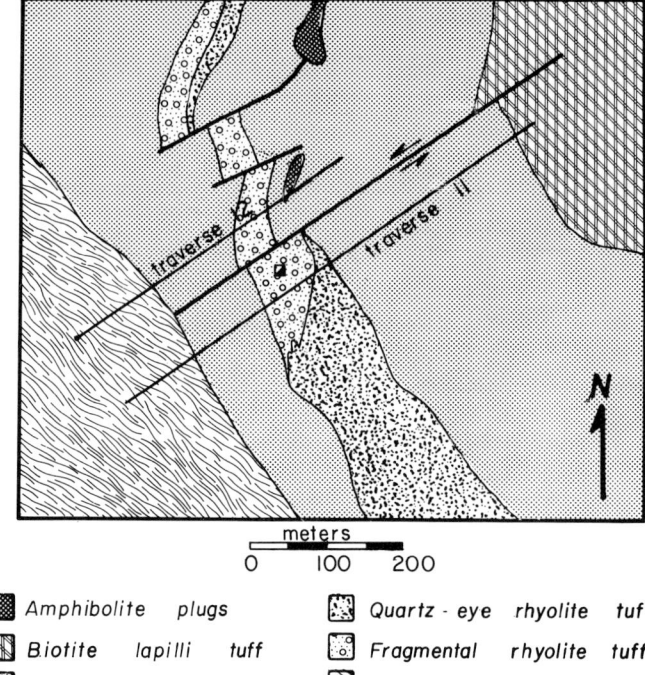

Figure 2. Geologic map of the Denver City Mine area, simplified from Riesmeyer (1978).

The massive ore is 35–45 percent quartz-calcite-muscovite gangue with 30–40 percent black sphalerite, 20–25 percent pyrite, 2–5 percent chalcopyrite, and less than 2 percent pyrrhotite. In general, where greater amounts of massive sulfide occur, the gangue becomes more calcite-rich. In places thin laminae and beds of carbonate were encountered in drilling. One sample of massive sulfide yielded 0.46 oz/T Ag and 0.04 oz/T Au by the partial extraction analysis.

The massive sulfide usually has alternating pyrite-rich and sphalerite-rich laminae, which appear sedimentary in origin. Triple junctions between the four sulfide phases are common, suggesting equilibrium was attained. Sphalerite was the first and last sulfide phase to crystallize, replacing the other phases in the latest stage. This replacement of pyrite and pyrrhotite may be a retrograde metamorphic phenomenon since the sphalerite cell can accept more iron as load pressure decreases (Scott, 1976).

Veinlet-controlled (with minor replacement) quartz-calcite-sericite alteration is restricted to a small area on the northeast side of the massive sulfide lens.

The banded sulfides, the intercalation with tuffaceous material and exhalative carbonate, the obvious metamorphic effects in the sulfides, and the stratabound, stratiform occurrence together clearly imply the deposit was formed cogenetically with the enclosing volcanic rocks.

Trace Element Geochemistry

Analysis of 31 samples on two traverses perpendicular to the strike of the mineralization showed the Cu was enriched two-fold relative to similar rocks elsewhere in the study (an average of 97 ppm versus 41 ppm). These anomalous values occur as much as 300 m from the known mineralized horizon. Directly over the known mineralization Cu concentrations rise to about twice the local background (fig. 3). Pb forms a two order of magnitude anomaly and Zn a one order of magnitude anomaly within 30 m of

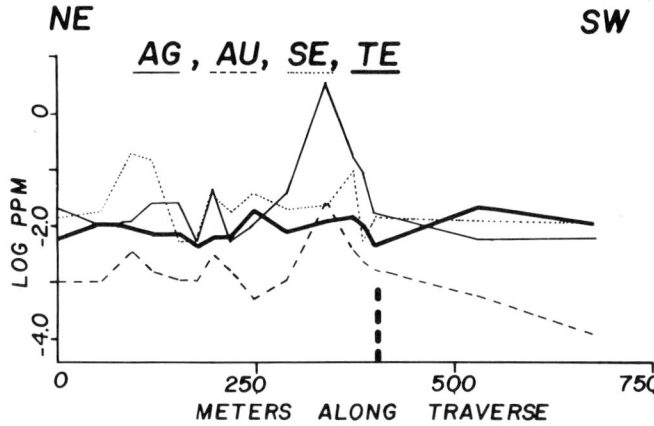

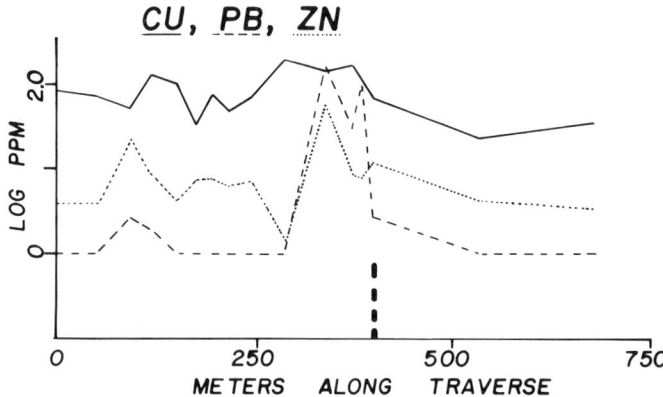

Figure 3. Trace element concentrations in samples from traverse 11 in the Denver City Mine area. Vertical dotted line notes location of mine shaft.

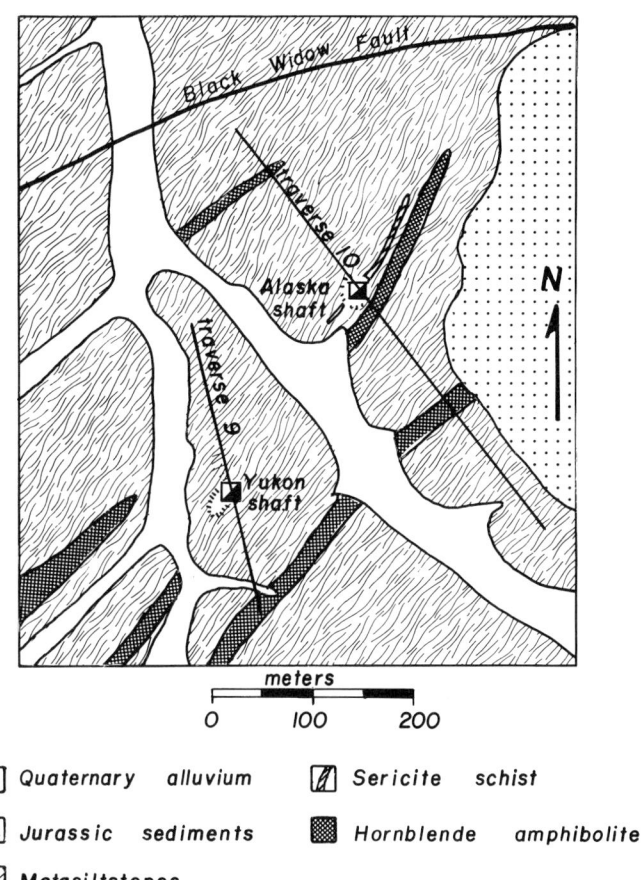

Figure 4. Geologic map of the Yukon and Alaska Mines area, simplified from Beaty and Zahoney (1977).

the known mineralized horizon (fig. 3). Se is only weakly concentrated and Te is not at all concentrated at the known mineralization. Ag forms a two order of magnitude anomaly and Au a one order of magnitude anomaly in one sample. Hence, at this deposit, Cu would have been most useful in delineating the prospect since it is so widely dispersed, and Pb-Zn-Ag are most useful in delineating drill targets. The ratio of Te/Se over the known mineralization is less than one—a characteristic of all the syngenetic mineralization in this study.

YUKON–ALASKA MINES
General Geology

This area was previously mapped by Beaty and Zahoney (1977) (fig. 4). The area is predominantly fine-grained metamorphosed argillites, siltites, and greywackes. Local relict graded bedding sequences and rare cross-beds indicate stratigraphic top is to the southeast. The stratification and foliation strike N. 30–35° E. and dip steeply to the southeast.

A 2–7-m thick horizon of fine-grained quartz-feldspar-muscovite schist occurs in outcrop next to the Alaska shaft and in subsurface on strike with the Alaska shaft. This schist is also abundant on both mine dumps. It has abundant elliptical disc-shaped weathered-out pods of quartz and muscovite 0.5 to 1.5 cm long. Though most of these pods are parallel to stratification, some are skewed to it. Hence, these are interpreted as rip up clasts of a fine-grained facies, implying a disconformity. The mineralization occurs on the stratigraphic top of this surface.

Amphibolite lenses occur throughout the area and are thought to represent sills or discontinuous basaltic flows. Minor thin metachert horizons also occur sporadically. Jurassic sedimentary rocks cover much of the area.

Mineralization

The workings at this deposit are very minor and date to the turn of the century. The Yukon Mine is developed by a presently inaccessible shaft. Reportedly, only five ore cars of 4 to 11 percent Cu ore were produced from the Yukon. The Alaska produced only ten tons of 0.70 oz/T Au ore, 15 tons of 11 percent Cu ore, and four ore cars of 34 percent Zn ore.

The mineralization at both mines occurs as one discontinuous lens of sulfide intermixed with quartz veining and interbedded sericite schist. The massive sulfide occurs as laminae 0.2 to 5 cm thick and has alternating pyrite-rich and sphalerite-rich bands. The ore consists of 25–60 percent quartz-sericite gangue, 20–50 percent sphalerite, 15–25 percent pyrite, trace to 5 percent pyrrhotite, and minor chalcopyrite, covellite, chalcocite, tetrahedrite, and galena. (Drobeck, 1979; Beaty and Zahoney, 1977). Pyrite and pyrrhotite occur as intergrowths in one sample from the Alaska dump. Triple junctions between pyrite, sphalerite, and pyrrhotite are common indicating equilibrium was attained. Broken grains of pyrite, pyrrhotite, sphalerite, and chalcopyrite occur in the gangue-rich bands, suggesting the gangue material flowed over the previously crystallized sulfide crystals and eroded them. Sphalerite was the last sulfide phase to begin crystallizing and it continued to crystallize long after the other sulfide phases, replacing them in places.

The field and textural evidence indicates the sulfides were formed as an integral part of the sedimentary sequence. The mineralization is preceeded by a local disconformity. Subsequently sulfides were precipitated as chemical sediments, becoming interlaminated with minor influxes of fine-grained sediments. The footwall of the Alaska deposit shows very minor potassic alteration (sparse 0.1 to 0.5 cm veinlets of K-feldspar ± quartz). The lack of stronger alteration implies that the fumarolic source of the sulfides was not observed in the study. It was not found along strike, and hence, is believed to occur up-dip or down-dip of the present exposed surface. The lack of associated carbonates and cherts also indicates a distant source.

Later, the deposit was metamorphosed along with the enclosing sediments, forming equilibrium textures among the sulfides. Samples on the dumps have banded sulfide and schist, which have been folded together, indicating the schist and sulfide are cogenetic.

Trace Element Geochemistry

A sampling traverse through the Yukon Mine showed no anomalous element concentrations more than 25 m from the mine itself. This lack of a dispersion halo, or any difference between the footwall and hanging wall imply that the geochemical cell that produced the mineralization was not sampled.

The sampling traverse through the Alaska Mine did show a dispersion halo of several elements. Anomalous Cu concentrations all occur in the stratigraphic footwall of the deposit and are found as much as 100 m in the footwall (fig. 5). The deep footwall Cu anomaly and relative Cu depletion in the hanging wall are characteristics found in many syngenetic massive sulfide deposits (Hutchinson, 1973). The weak anomaly at the Alaska could be a distal equivalent of a copper stringer-ore zone as is sometimes found in the footwall of these deposits (Franklin and others, 1975; Walker and others, 1975). Pb and Zn form one order of magnitude anomalies 65 m into the footwall of the known mineralization. Neither Ag or Au form an anomaly (except the high values from a dump sample). Se and Te show a two times background erratic anomaly associated with the Cu anomaly. Most samples have a Te/Se ratio less than one.

For exploration purposes, Cu, Pb, and Zn would be most useful in finding this mineralization. The footwall-hanging wall assymetry of the dispersion halo further corroborates the syngenetic model for the mineralization here.

GUNNISON AND IRONCAP MINES AREA
General Geology

This area has been mapped in detail by the author (1979) (fig. 6). The area is underlain by complexly folded and faulted Proterozoic metasedimentary and metavolcanic rocks.

The metasediments are predominantly fine-grained arkoses, greywackes, and siltites with minor quartz arenite beds. Interbedded cherts are very rare. Many sedimentary structures have survived the effects of metamorphism. Fining upwards graded bedding, ripple laminations, convoluted beds, flame structures, and rare cross-bed sets were all observed and were useful in determining stratigraphic tops. Some incomplete Bouma sequences were observed (B+C+D±E parts of a typical sequence; Walker and Mutti, 1973). These structures, and the predominance of angular feldspar in the rocks, indicate the sediments were shed from a tectonically active continental margin or island arc. These sediments

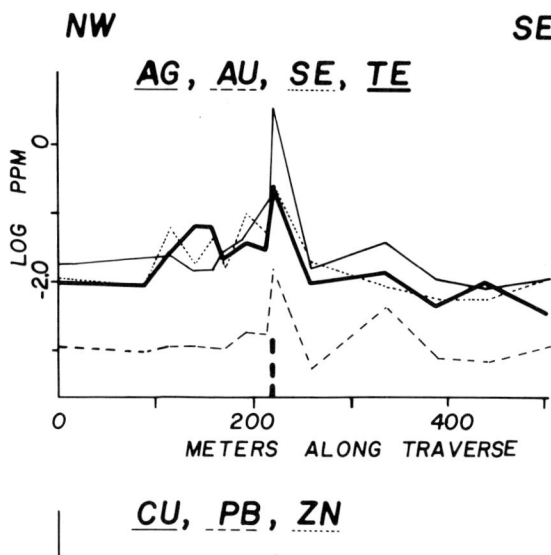

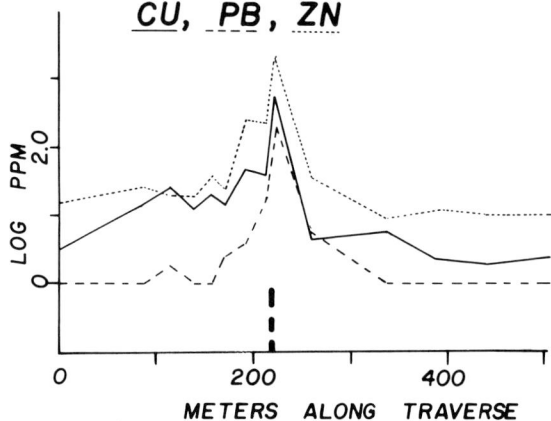

Figure 5. Trace element concentrations in samples from traverse 10 through the Alaska shaft. Vertical dotted line notes location of mine shaft.

are the predominant Proterozoic rock type from this locality north to the Gunnison River, suggesting these rocks represent thick coalesced submarine fans.

The metavolcanic rocks in this area are mostly mafic to intermediate flows that are typical of the "Dubois Greenstone" described by other authors (Hartley, 1976; Hedlund and Olson, 1975). One of the earliest flows is a green to bluish-green ultramafic schist consisting of actinolitic tremolite, chlorite, talc, and traces of pyrite, magnetite, and relict olivine phenocrysts. A whole rock analysis of this rock showed it has 46.5 percent SiO_2, 6.2 percent Al_2O_3, 22.0 percent MgO, 8.7 percent CaO, 0.13 percent Na_2O, and 0.013 percent K_2O. Following the classification of Jensen (1976), this rock is an ultramafic komatiite.

The metamorphosed basalt and basaltic andesite flows are mostly younger than the metasediments, except in the east half of the map area where they are time equivalent. Amygdaloidal horizons can sometimes be traced for hundreds of meters. Pillows are rarely formed on top of flows and indicate the sequence was erupted subaqueously. Thin, laterally extensive horizons of fine-grained schist are believed to represent reworked hyaloclastites (Silvestri, 1963). Though most of the basaltic sequence is flows, some laminated tuffs were found in the southern part of the study area.

Metamorphosed chert horizons are common in the metavolcanic rocks. They occur as 0.5 to 10 m thick beds of purplish-black quartzite commonly with sweated-out white bull quartz. Locally

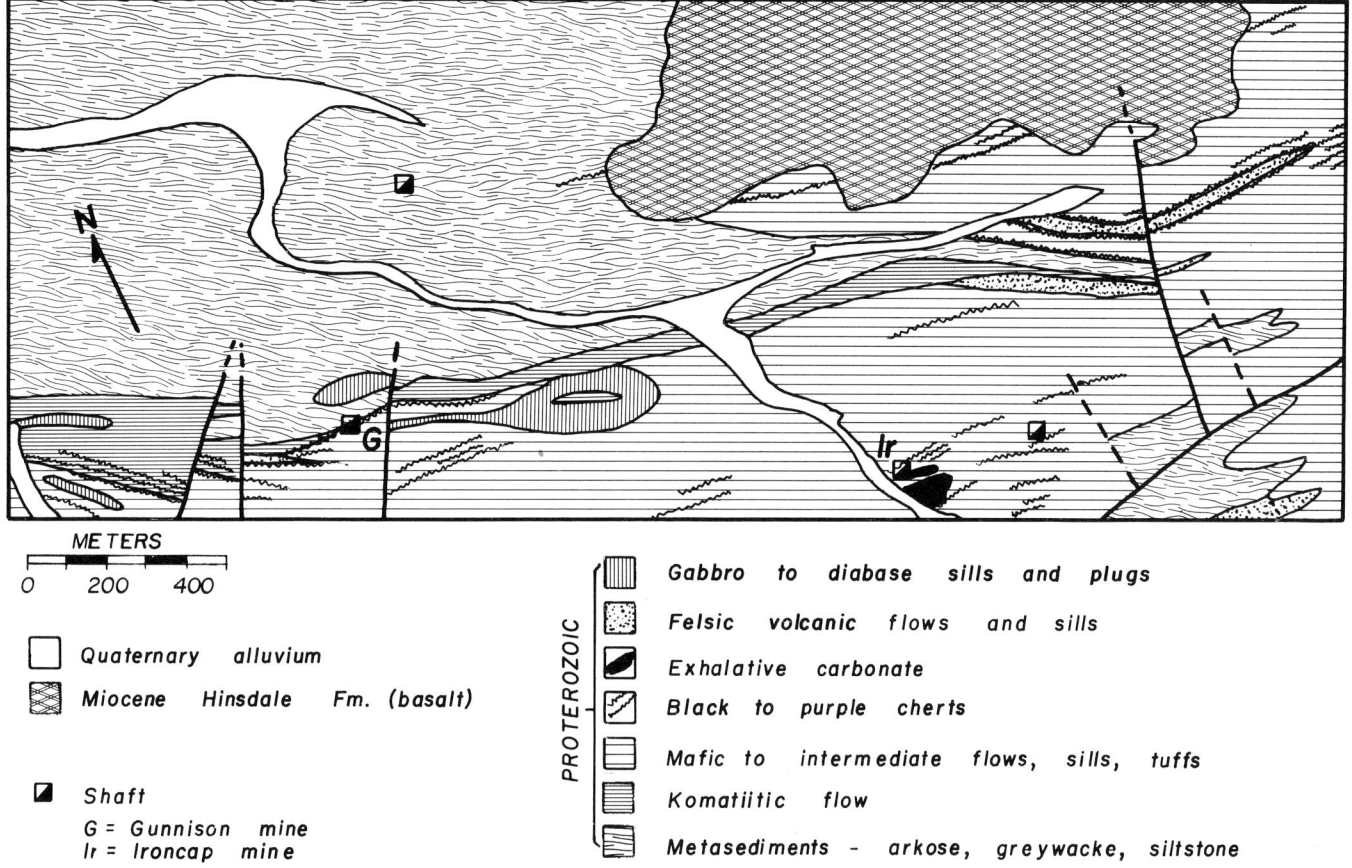

Figure 6. Geologic map of the Gunnison-Ironcap area.

they are highly magnetic, although no true iron formations were found. The cherts are believed to be chemical sediments and are closely related to the mineralization at both the Gunnison and Ironcap deposits. They carry anomalous concentrations of Pb, Ag, Au, and Se.

Carbonate exhalites were also found in the area and are closely associated with the mineralization. They are comprised of brown to white calcite, siderite, epidote, hornblende, quartz, actinolite, and minor sulfides. Well developed calcite alteration of the surrounding rocks is commonly associated with these exhalites and locally with the cherts.

The dominant structures in the area are tight to isoclinal folds plunging gently to the west-northwest. The foliation in the volcanic schists commonly subparallels axial surfaces of the folds, implying metamorphism was synchronous with folding. There are probably more folds than can be mapped since top indicators and marker horizons in the volcanic sequence are generally lacking. North-northeast trending faults cut the folds and are believed to be late Tertiary in age.

Mineralization

The Ironcap Mine has the best show of mineralization in this area. No records of the production were found but it was apparently minor. A caved shaft connects with an adit and an inaccessible winze drops from the adit. Two small shafts approximately 320 m east of the main workings are also inaccessible. They develop a correlative mineralized horizon.

The deposit occurs as an exhalite dome built around a fumarole, which contains jumbled pods of chert and tuffaceous volcanic material. The mafic volcanics are intensely altered to calcite and epidote and commonly have had all the plagioclase destroyed. Where the volcanics are still recognizable, they have numerous small calcite veinlets. The mineralization consists of laminations, veins, and veinlets of sphalerite + pyrite + chalcopyrite + galena in a quartz + calcite + epidote ± actinolite matrix. Banded textures are common. The sulfides exhibit many triple junctions and clearly have been metamorphosed with the gangue. Chalcopyrite commonly has inclusions of sphalerite and also occurs as inclusions within sphalerite. Sphalerite is less abundant in this deposit than the other deposits so far mentioned, and Cu is more abundant. A partial extraction analysis of a 1-m chip sample (representing a minimum value, not an assay) indicated 2.6 percent Cu, 2.0 oz/T Ag and 0.15 oz/T Au.

The shafts east of the main Ironcap workings have kink banded, chlorite-sericite altered volcanics with disseminated pyrite and chalcopyrite. This mineralization is considered cogenetic with, and a distal part of, the Ironcap deposit.

The Gunnison Mine consists of two small shafts sunk in a chert horizon that occurs along the metasedimentary-metavolcanic contact and is associated with a thinned portion of the komatiite flow. The stratigraphic footwall is a soft, deeply weathered biotite siltstone with minor almandite. No massive sulfide was found; only disseminated pyrite and chalcopyrite in remobilized quartz veins occur within the chert. Locally the chert has been brecciated. The chert and the remobilized quartz veins contain anomalous concentrations of Au, Se, and Te.

The stratiform and stratabound occurrences, the association with exhalites, and the obvious metamorphism of the ores indicate that both the Ironcap and Gunnison were formed as chemical sediments contemporaneously with the volcanics.

Trace Element Geochemistry

Lack of outcrop prevented rock sampling traverses perpendicular to strike through the Gunnison and Ironcap mines. A sampling traverse was made 320 m east of the Ironcap, through the weakly mineralized equivalent horizon. Only the sample from the dump on this traverse was highly anomalous in Cu or Zn. Two samples stratigraphically above this dump carried anomalous Pb, Ag, Au, and Se.

Several samples of calcite-altered metabasalt on the hill formed by the Ironcap define a +100 ppm Cu anomaly 150 × 400 m in size. Zn and Se are also highly enriched near this mineralization. The cherts near this deposit contain anomalous concentrations of all the elements analyzed.

Samples from the Gunnison Mine contain anomalous Au, Ag, and Te, but are not strongly anomalous in Cu. This is probably so because the deposit is formed on metasediments, which normally contain much less Cu than metabasalts (in which the Ironcap occurs). The Gunnison deposit is also notably more Te-rich than the Ironcap.

VULCAN–GOOD HOPE MINES
General Geology

Hartley (1976) mapped and described the geology and mineralization of this deposit. Figure 7 is a simplified version of his map.

Metabasalt and metaandesite flows and sills are major rock types here and are similar in most respects to those in the Ironcap area. Most are thought to be flows. Quartzo-feldspathic schists and fels (Winkler, 1976) are interpreted as dacite to rhyolite flows, water-laid tuffs, and tuffaceous sediments. Neither the author, nor Hartley (1976) recognized pumice or any textures indicative of ash-flow tuffs or pyroturbidites, as are found in the Denver City area. Cherts are also found in the area, although much less so than in the Ironcap area. Metasedimentary rocks include greywackes, siltites, and argillites which Hartley (1976) suggested were eroded directly from the volcanic pile.

The texturally and compositionally variable Tolvar Peak Granite outcrops in much of this area. It varies from granite to granodiorite in composition. It is believed to have intruded late during Boulder Creek metamorphism.

Hartley (1976) interpreted the structure in the Vulcan area as a steeply dipping homocline with stratigraphic top to the south.

Mineralization

The Vulcan–Good Hope deposit was the largest producer in the Gunnison Gold Belt. It reportedly produced $500,000 in gold-silver ore (approximately 25,000 gold ounce equivalents) between 1898 and 1902. The actual tonnage mined and average grade are not known. The Colorado Bureau of Mines records show that another 100 tons of 2½ oz/T Au + 12 oz/T Ag were shipped in 1919. Sporadic production continued until the 1930's, including an effort to recover seleniferous sulfur. The deposit is developed by four shafts, the deepest being nearly 200 m deep.

The deposit occurs as a lens of massive sulfide (mostly pyrite) between bleached sericite schists. Within a narrow band of quartz and bleached schist on the hanging wall are opaline chalcedony veinlets which carry silver, gold, and copper tellurides as well as native tellurium (Crawford and Johnson, 1922; Crawford, 1927; Hartley, 1976). The deposit is completely oxidized down to 30 m (water table) where a pencil-shaped body of seleniferous sulfur was found. Below this body is the massive sulfide, which extends to approximately 200 m below the surface when it pinches into low-sulfide sericite schist (Hartley, 1976). The deposit has an intense quartz-sericite-pyrite alteration envelope in which no relict textures of the rock remain. This envelope is partly surrounded by an envelope of quartz-chlorite alteration.

The origin of the massive sulfide mineralization here is believed to be syngenetic with deposition of the volcanic pile (Hartley, 1976). Triple junctions between pyrite, pyrrhotite, and sphalerite, and the coarse grained annealed pyrite imply the sulfides were metamorphosed together. The sulfides are sometimes banded into sphalerite and pyrite-rich laminae similar to that described at the Denver City Mine. Hartley (1978) noted sphalerite forms hair-line veinlets parallel to foliation and that pyrite grains tend to be elongated parallel to foliation, again indicating metamorphism of the sulfides.

The chalcedony stringer veinlets on the hanging wall, which carry the precious metal values, may be conformable to the foliation in the schists but cut across the massive sulfides (Crawford and Johnson, 1922; Crawford, 1927; Hartley, 1976). The veinlets are distinctly unmetamorphosed, showing delicate replacement textures, which would not have survived metamorphism (Hartley, 1976). A polished section from the dumps showed replacement and brecciation textures with quartz-sericite after pyrite-sphalerite.

Hartley (1976) was the first to recognize the two very different mineralization episodes here: the Proterozoic syngenetic massive sulfide mineralization, and the later gold-silver telluride chalcedony veining. He proposed that the chalcedony veining was a much later and unrelated event. Although the age of the second stage is not known, a Miocene age seems most likely since gold-silver telluride deposits of this age are known to the south in the San Juan Mountains.

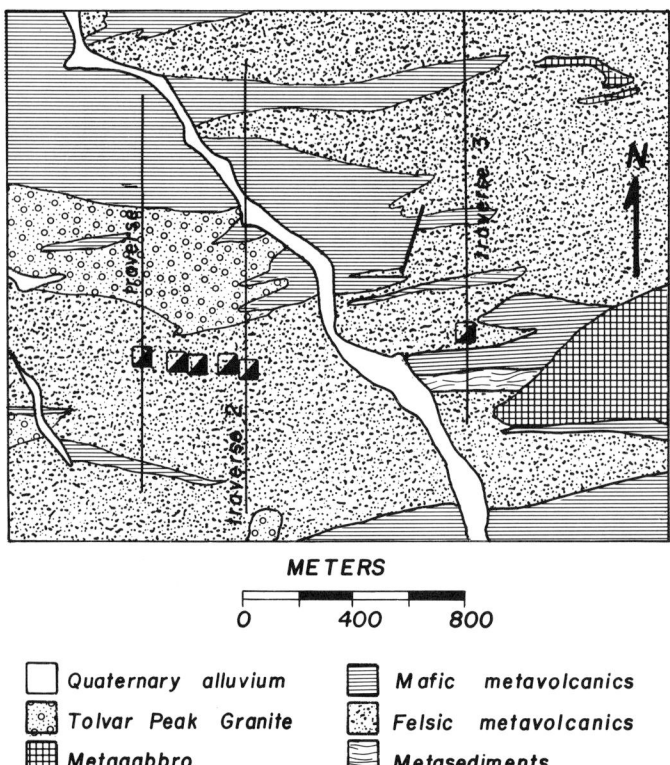

Figure 7. Geologic map of the Vulcan–Good Hope area. Simplified from Hartley (1976).

The spatial coincidence of the two styles of mineralization seems fortuitous. However, D'yachkova and Khodakovskiy (1968) have shown that decreases in oxygen fugacity are the most effective way to precipitate Te from solution (more so than drops in temperature or changes in pH). It seems reasonable that if Miocene mineralizing fluids were percolating through this Proterozoic terrain, a favorable structural discontinuity to follow would be the massive sulfide-metavolcanic contact. Furthermore, these sulfides, being very reducing, would act as a geochemical trap-precipitating tellurides.

Trace Element Geochemistry

Three sampling traverses through the known mineralization were made. These samples clearly define the known mineralization and also outine a strong anomaly 730 m north of the Vulcan–Good Hope, which was also an induced polarization anomaly in Newmont Mining's 1952 project (Hartley, 1976). Copper is strongly anomalous at both horizons, especially the north anomaly, which is 100 m wide and has four times background Cu concentrations on traverse 2 (fig. 8). No Cu zone was found on traverses 1 or 2 in the footwall of the Vulcan–Good Hope as there was at the Yukon–Alaska. This feature may be due to intrusion of the Tolvar Peak Granite in the footwall. On traverse 3, where the granite has not intruded the footwall, a Cu anomaly was found stratigraphically below the Pb-Zn anomaly (fig. 9). This pattern corroborates the syngenetic model for the massive sulfide mineralization at Vulcan.

The most noteable feature of the geochemistry is the high Te

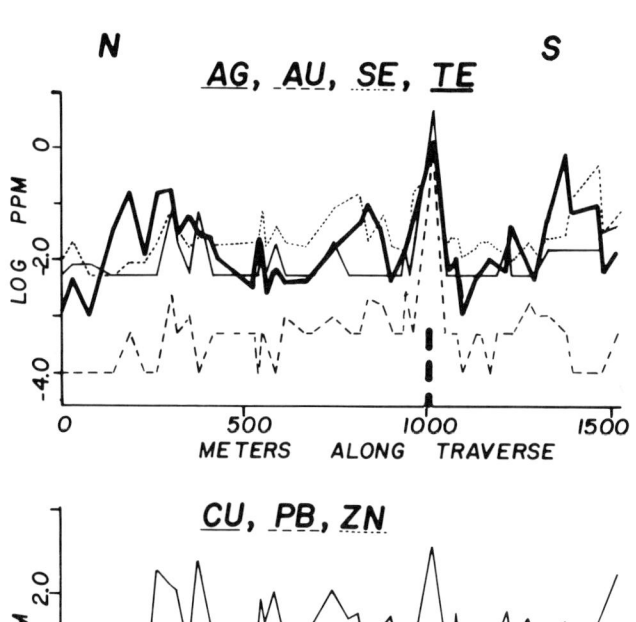

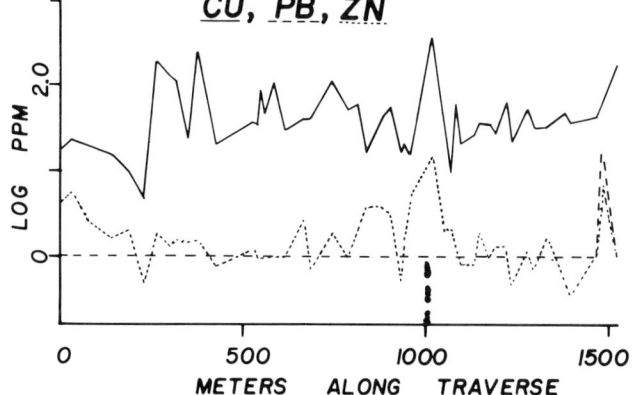

Figure 8. Element concentrations along traverse 2 through the Sulfur shaft, Vulcan–Good Hope area. Vertical dotted line notes location of shaft.

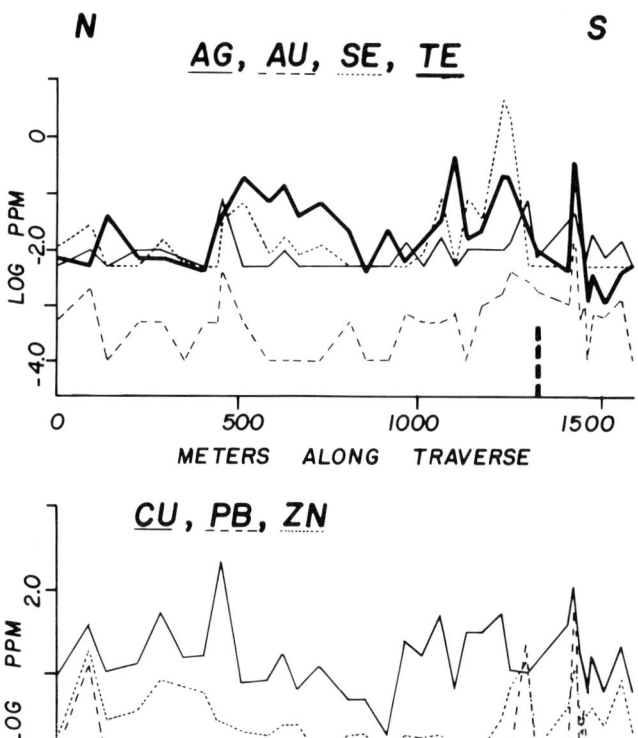

Figure 9. Trace element concentrations along traverse 3 through small shaft east of the main Vulcan–Good Hope workings. Vertical dotted line notes location of shaft.

content. The average Te content of all the samples taken in the Vulcan area is 9.3 times the average of all other samples in this study. Te clearly outlines the known productive zone on all three sampling traverses as well as the northern IP anomaly. At the core of the anomalies, Te rises to 2 orders of magnitude above background (up to 4.7 ppm against a background of 0.016 ppm).

The Te/Se ratio is highly enriched at the Vulcan–Good Hope deposit relative to the other areas studied. In most samples elsewhere in the study, this ratio is less than one and always less than 4.5 (the few samples with greater than one Te/Se all had a deficiency of Se). The ratio is greater than one in a third of the samples in the Vulcan area, even though many of these samples have high Se concentrations. In the cores of anomalies the ratio varies from 5.0 to 206. This unique Te chemistry is attributed to the later epigenetic mineralization at Vulcan, which is so different from mineralization elsewhere in the study. Thus, this ratio divides samples affected only by Proterozoic syngenetic fumarolic mineralization from those affected by Miocene(?) epigenetic mineralization.

CONCLUSIONS

The lenticular massive sulfide deposits of the Gunnison Gold Belt have several common characteristics despite their differing lithologic associations. All those studies are stratiform, stratabound, have well developed metamorphic textures, and have banded fabrics. The Denver City, Ironcap, and probably the Vulcan–Good Hope were formed proximal to fumarolic activity whereas the Yukon–Alaska was not. Both the Denver City and Ironcap are associated with well-developed carbonate exhalite zones and cherts.

Hutchinson (1973) noted that the Proterozoic deposits of syngenetic-volcanogenic origin commonly have associated carbonate exhalites. Therefore, these deposits are all believed to have originated as chemical sediments on the seafloor.

Hutchinson (1973) suggested that volcanogenic syngenetic massive sulfides of Proterozoic age can be expected to have more lead than similar Archean deposits. However, the Jerome deposit in Arizona (Anderson and Creasey, 1958), the deposits of the Pyhäsalmi-Pielavasi district in Finland (Huhtala, 1979), and the deposits of the Gunnison Gold Belt have low lead contents—similar to the Archean deposits.

The trace element geochemistry method can be used reliably to outline known deposits and can thus probably be used to locate blind orebodies. Copper was found to have the widest dispersion halo at all the deposits studied and is therefore the most useful in delineating possible project areas. Zn, Pb, Se, and Ag have narrower, and higher contrast anomalies so they can be used in delineating drill targets. It was interesting to find clearly developed footwall Cu enrichment zones, which are believed to be analogous to footwall stringer zones in other deposits. The element Te and the Te/Se ratio can be used to explore for the style of mineralization found at Vulcan and to discriminate between the two different styles of mineralization studied.

ACKNOWLEDGMENTS

This research benefitted greatly from discussions with S. B. Romberger, L. G. Closs, T. R. Bultman, A. M. Afifi, W. D. Riesmeyer, T. R. Klein, and J. R. Clark. Critical review of the manuscript by F. H. Haynes and A. M. Afifi is appreciated. The research was funded by CONOCO Metallics Division and Sigma Xi.

REFERENCES

Afifi, A., 1981, Stratigraphy, petrology, and structure of Precambrian metavolcanic rocks in the Iris District, Gunnison Mineral Belt, this volume.

Anderson, C. A. and S. C. Creasey, 1958, Geology and ore deposits of the Jerome area, Yavapai County, Arizona: U.S. Geological Survey Professional Paper 308, 185 p.

Barge, E. M., 1971, Geologic report: Vulcan deposit, Gunnison County, Colorado: Unpublished report.

Beaty, D. and S. Zahoney, 1977, Geology of the Yukon-Alaska mine area Cochetopa Mining District Saguache County, Colorado: Unpublished report.

Clark, J. R. and J. G. Viets, 1979, A sulfide-selection leach and multi-element extraction system for the study of primary trace element dispersion patterns (abs.): American Institute of Mining Engineers, Abstracts of Programs, October Meeting, Tucson, Arizona.

Crawford, W. P. and F. Johnson, 1922, Geology and cyanidation of ore from the Good Hope Mine, Vulcan, Colorado [M.S. thesis]: Golden, Colorado School of Mines.

Crawford, E. P., 1927, Selenium deposits at Vulcan: Unpublished notes.

Drobeck, P. A., 1979, Geology and trace element geochemistry of a part of the Gunnison Gold Belt, Colorado [M.S. thesis]: Golden, Colorado School of Mines.

D'yachkova, I. B. and I. L. Khodakovskiy, 1968, Thermodynamic equilibria in the systems $S-H_2O$, $Se-H_2O$, and $Te-H_2O$ in the 25–300°C temperature range and their geochemical interpretations: Geochemistry International, v. 5, p. 1108–1125.

Franklin, J. M., J. Kasarda, K. G. Poulsen, 1975, Petrology and chemistry of the alteration zone of the Mattabi Massive sulfide deposit: Economic Geology, v. 70, p. 63–79.

Hansen, W. R. and Z. E. Peterman, 1968, Basement rock geochronology of the Black Canyon of the Gunnison, Colorado: U.S. Geological Survey Professional Paper 600-C, p. 80–90.

Hartley, P. D., 1976, The geology and mineralization of a Precambrian massive sulfide deposit at Vulcan, Gunnison County, Colorado [M.S. thesis]: Stanford, California, Stanford University.

Hedlund, D., 1974, Geologic map of the Big Mesa Quadrangle, Gunnison County, Colorado: U.S. Geological Survey Map GQ-1153.

Hedlund, D. and J. Olson, 1974, Geologic map of the Iris NW Quadrangle, Gunnison and Saguache Counties, Colorado: U.S. Geological Survey Geologic Quadrangle Map GQ-1134.

———, 1975, Geologic map of the Powderhorn Quadrangle, Gunnison and Saguache Counties, Colorado: U.S. Geologial Survey Geologic Quadrangle Map GQ-1178.

Huhtala, T., 1979, The geology and zinc-copper deposits of the Pyhäsalmi-Pielavesi district, Finland: Economic Geology, v. 74, p. 1069–1083.

Hutchinson, R. M., 1976, Precambrian geology of western and central Colorado and southern Wyoming, in Epis, R. C. and Weimer, R. J., Studies in Colorado Field Geology: Professional Contributions, Colorado School of Mines, no. 8, p. 73–77.

Hutchinson, R. W., 1973, Volcanogenic sulfide deposits and their metallogenic significance: Economic Geology, v. 68, p. 1223–1246.

Jensen, L. S., 1976, A new cation plot for classifying subalkalic volcanic rocks: Ontario Division of Mines Miscellaneous Paper 66, p. 1–22.

Olson, J., 1976, Geologic map of the Iris Quadrangle, Gunnison and Saguache Counties, Colorado: U.S. Geological Survey Geologic Quadrangle Map GQ-1286.

Olson, J., T. Steven, and D. Hedlund, 1975, Geologic map of the Spring Hill Quadrangle, Saguache County, Colorado: U.S. Geological Survey Map MF-713.

Olson, J. and D. Hedlund, 1973, Geologic map of the Gateview Quadrangle, Gunnison County, Colorado: U.S. Geological Survey Geologic Quadrangle Map GQ-1071.

Riesmeyer, W. D., 1978, Geologic map of the Denver City area: Unpublished map.

Scott, S. D., 1976, Application of the sphalerite geobarometer to regionally metamorphosed terrains: American Mineralogist, v. 61, p. 661–670.

Silvestri, S. C., 1963, Proposal for a genetic classification of hyalocalstities: Bulletin of Volcanology, v. 25, p. 315–321.

Trost, P. B., 1975, Geologic report on the Vulcan-Anaconda-Headlight Mine area Dubois Greenstone Belt, Gunnison County, Colorado: Unpublished consulting report.

Urbani, F. and W. Blackburn, 1974, Investigations in the basement rocks of Gunnison County, Colorado: The igneous rocks: Neues Jahrbuch Mineral. Abhand., v. 121, p. 272–292.

Vance, R. K. and W. Blackburn, 1981, Investigation of the basement rocks near Gunnison, Colorado (abs.): Geological Society of America, Abstracts with Programs, v. 13, p. 229.

Walker, R. G. and E. Mutti, 1973, Turbidite facies and facies associations, in Bouma, A. J. and Middleton, G. V.: Society of Economic Paleontologists and Mineralogists, Short Course, Pacific Section, p. 119–157.

Walker, R. R., A. Matulich, A. C. Amos, J. J. Watkins, G. W. Mannard, 1975, The geology of the Kidd Creek Mine: Economic Geology, v. 70, p. 80–89.

Wetherill, G. and M. Bickford, 1965, Primary and metamorphic Rb-Sr chronology in central Colorado: Journal of Geophysical Research, v. 70, p. 4669–4686.

Winkler, H. G., 1976, Petrogenesis of Metamorphis Rocks: New York, Springer-Verlag, 334 p.

STRATIGRAPHY, PETROLOGY, AND STRUCTURE OF PRECAMBRIAN METAVOLCANIC ROCKS IN THE IRIS DISTRICT, GUNNISON AND SAGUACHE COUNTIES, COLORADO

ABDULKADER M. AFIFI*
Department of Geology
Colorado School of Mines
Golden, Colorado 80401

INTRODUCTION

The Iris district occurs within the Iris and Iris NW 7.5 minute quadrangles, 8–16 km southeast of Gunnison, Colorado. The area is underlain by a mass of Proterozoic ($\simeq 1700$ m.y.) metavolcanic rocks shown as Dubois Greenstone by Hedlund and Olson (this guidebook). A discussion of the regional geology of Proterozoic rocks exposed along the eastern part of the Gunnison Uplift is presented by Hedlund and Olson. Previous mapping in the Iris district was undertaken by Hedlund and Olson (1974) and Olson (1976). The geology and geochemistry of mineralized areas in the Gunnison gold belt are discussed by Drobeck (1980), and Sheridan and others (this guidebook). The aim of this report is to discuss some aspects of the geology of the small area where detailed mapping was undertaken (Afifi, 1981). Despite two generations of foliation development and metamorphism to the epidote amphibolite facies, relict fabrics and lithologies are locally identified with confidence. For this reason, the prefix "meta" often will be dropped from the following descriptions.

Figure 1 is a simplified geologic map of the Iris district. The stratified rocks are informally divided into three formations: lower metasediments, Iris formation, and upper metasediments. The Iris formation consists of pyroclastic and hyaloclastic rocks and is divided into five mappable members. In chronologic order, these are (1) dacitic member, (2) andesite lapilli tuff member, (3) rhyolitic member, (4) Dirigo Gulch (basaltic) member, and (5) alkali feldspar rhyolite member. Figure 2 is a generalized stratigraphic column for the Iris district showing the proposed stratigraphic nomenclature. The layered rocks are intruded by sheets of metagabbro which are probable subvolcanic equivalents to basaltic rocks of the Dirigo Gulch member. The layered rocks and metagabbro sheets are folded into a tight, steeply plunging fold which is called the Iris syncline. Consequently, all bedding and foliation attitudes are steeply dipping.

STRATIGRAPHY

The stratigraphy of the Iris district represents an interplay between episodes of volcanic eruptions and intervals of epiclastic sedimentation, largely by submarine reworking of nonindurated volcanic debris. Intervals of quiescence are marked by deposition of ferruginous chert. In the following treatment, the stratified rocks are described based on their principal mode of fragmentation.

Epiclastic Rocks

Epiclastic rocks include the lower metasediments, the upper metasediments, and numerous lenses of wacke and siltstone interbedded with volcanic rocks of the Iris formation. All epiclastic rocks are metamorphosed to a weakly to strongly schistose assemblage of quartz, feldspar, biotite, muscovite, epidote, and magnetite. The content of microcrystalline biotite and muscovite, derived from a pelitic component, is a reflection of original sorting. Based on sedimentary structures, two facies associations are recognized:

(1) Plane and ripple laminated siltstone, mudstone, and fine grained sandstone. These are interpreted as CE turbidites.

(2) Thinly- to thickly-bedded arkosic wacke and pebbly wacke, which commonly display broad basal scours and grading, followed by parallel stratification. These are interpreted as AA or AB turbidites.

Both associations are laterally and vertically mutually gradational. Other primary structures are slump-folded bedding, load structures, and syndepositional listric normal faults. The association of sedimentary structures indicates a submarine fan environment of deposition, with sandstone occupying submarine channels, and siltstone-mudstone forming overbank (channel margin) deposits.

The composition of most sandstones is arkosic wacke. Quartz is subordinate to feldspar in wackes, and both are probably reworked phenocryst fragments. Pebbles are of local rip-up origin. The microcrystalline matrix composed of quartz, feldspar, biotite, muscovite, and epidote represents metamorphic recrystallization of transported vitric ash.

Pyroclastic Rocks

Pyroclastic rocks include the dacitic, rhyolitic, and alkali feldspar rhyolite members of the Iris formation, in addition to minor dacitic pyroclastic rocks interbedded with the lower metasediments.

The rocks consist of metamorphosed tuff, lapilli tuff, and tuff-breccia having various proportions of lithic, crystal, and matrix components. In weakly foliated rocks, the matrix component is observed to consist of silicified and recrystallized vitric ash composed of bubble wall shards (fig. 3). The assemblage of phenocryst fragments allows the distinction of three members. The dacitic member has phenocrysts of plagioclase, orthoclase, and magnetite. The rhyolitic member has phenocrysts of plagioclase, orthoclase, quartz, and magnetite. The alkali feldspar rhyolite member has phenocrysts of alkali feldspar (perthitic intergrowth of orthoclase and albite derived from sanidine), quartz, and magnetite. Chemical data indicates that all three members constitute a calc-alkalic dacite-rhyodacite-rhyolite sequence which becomes increasingly felsic with time.

Most lithic fragments in the pyroclastic rocks are rip-up fragments of tuff, chert, or epiclastic rocks which were incorporated during mass transport. Essential fragments consist of aphyric or vitrophyric felsite (fig. 3), and fragments of long-tube pumice (figs. 3, 4).

---

*Present address: U.S. Geological Survey, P.O. Box 1488, Jeddah, Saudi Arabia.

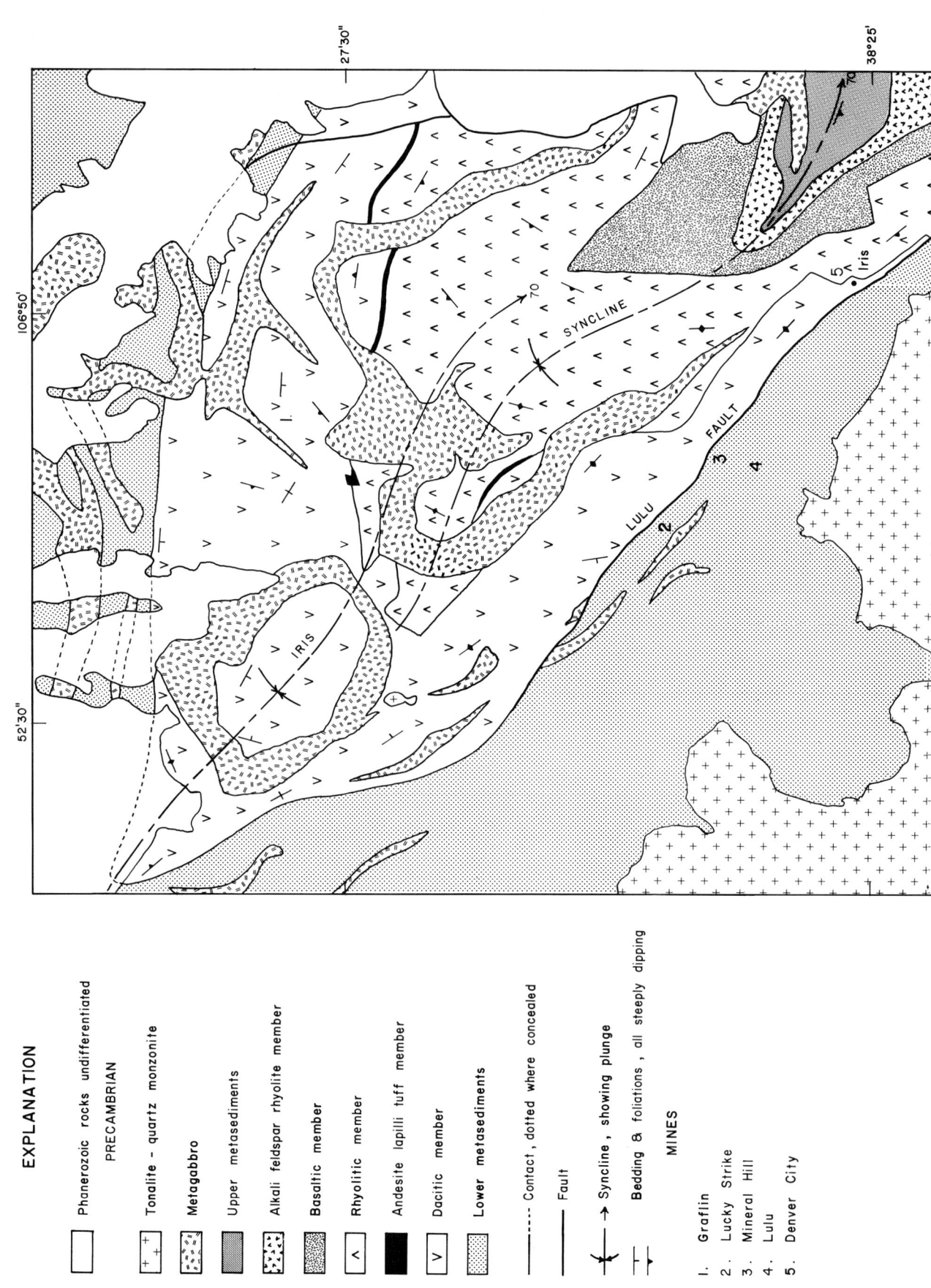

Figure 1. Generalized geologic map of the Iris district, Gunnison and Saguache Counties, Colorado.

PRECAMBRIAN METAVOLCANIC ROCKS

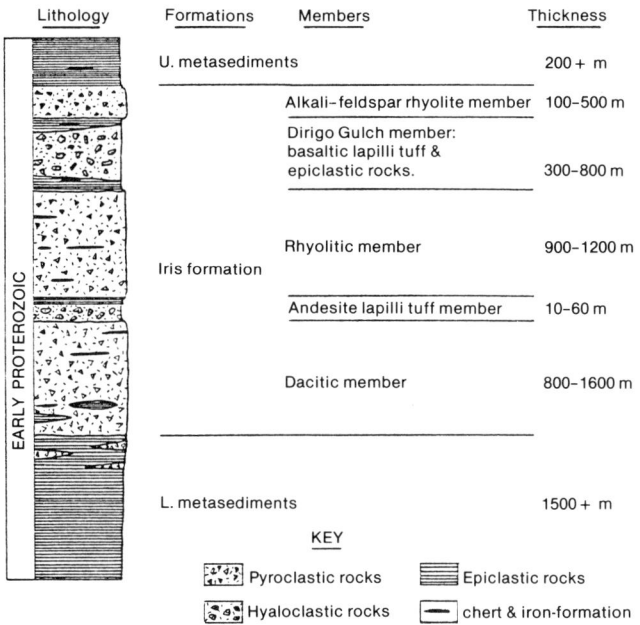

Figure 2. Generalized stratigraphic column for the Iris district. Stratigraphic nomenclature is informal.

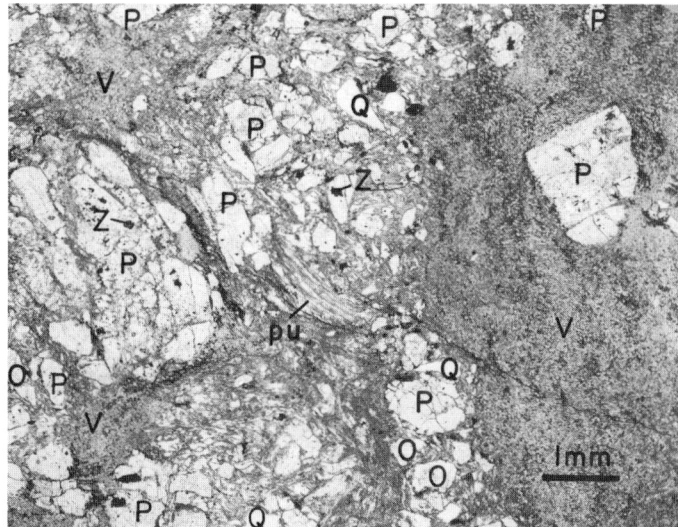

Figure 3. Photomicrograph of nonfoliated quartz latitic lapilli tuff from the rhyolitic member. Uncrossed nicols. Dense fragments are flow banded vitrophyre (V). Phenocrysts and phenocryst fragments are plagioclase (P), orthoclase (O), quartz (Q), magnetite (opaque), and zircon (Z). Matrix consists of long-tube pumice (pu), and shards, both replaced by quartz. The vitric component is metamorphosed into microcrystalline quartz, feldspar, biotite, muscovite, epidote, and magnetite.

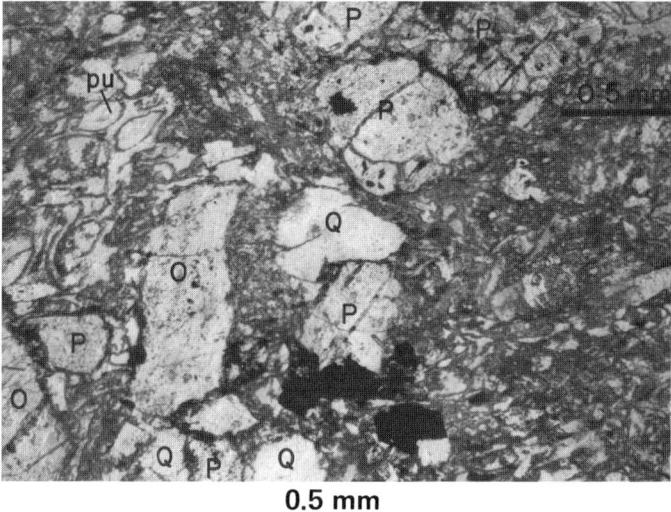

Figure 4. Photomicrograph of nonfoliated quartz latitic lapilli tuff from the rhyolitic member. Fragment to upper left is a cross-sectional view of long-tube pumice (pu). Phenocryst fragments are plagioclase (P), orthoclase (O), quartz (Q), and magnetite (opaque). The matrix consists of bubble wall shards. Shards and pumice are replaced by quartz, and are enveloped by microcrystalline biotite, muscovite, and epidote.

Although the pyroclastic rocks rarely display stratification in outcrop, detailed study of their primary structures indicates subaqueous deposition by mass-flow mechanisms as described by Middleton and Hampton (1973). The pyroclastic flows of the Iris district arrived by a combination of turbulent flow, debris flow, and fluidized flow mechanisms. Individual pyroclastic flows have scoured bases and locally abundant rip-up fragments of underlying deposits. The typical vertical sequence of primary structures is (1) a thin basal zone of reverse grading, (2) a middle massive zone, and (3) an upper zone of normal grading. The upper zone sometimes grades into parallel stratified tuff. Thickness of individual units varies from 0.5 to 60 m. The extremely thick units are actually a fining-upward sequence of pyroclastic flows which arrived in rapid succession, each carrying successively finer material. Such units probably correspond to single eruptions. The vertical sequence of primary structures in pyroclastic flow deposits of the Iris area are similar to subaqueous mass-flow deposits, including the turbidite facies association (Walker and Mutti, 1973) and subaqueous pyroclastic flow deposits (Fiske, 1963; Fiske and Matsuda, 1964; Tasse and others, 1978).

In thick pyroclastic flows, accidental rip-up fragments of wacke and siltstone underwent soft sediment compaction and are flattened parallel to bedding (fig. 5), and their undersides are indented by essential vitrophyre or pumice fragments. This compactional fabric locally resembles the eutaxitic fabric in moderately welded subaerial pyroclastic flow deposits. However, no effects of plastic deformation or welding of shards or pumice were observed in the Iris district.

Hyaloclastic Rocks

Hyaloclastic rocks include the andesite lapilli tuff member, and basaltic lapilli tuff and tuff-breccia of the Dirigo Gulch member. In both members, the metamorphic assemblage is hornblende, albite or oligoclase, epidote, biotite, magnetite, quartz, and sphene. The rocks consist of self-supported fragments of angular, sparsely vesiculated vitrophyric andesite or basalt, and medium- to coarse-

Figure 5. Massive tuff-breccia zone in a pyroclastic flow deposit from the alkali feldspar rhyolite member. Stratigraphic top is to the left. Effects of soft sediment compaction on rip-up clasts of arkosic wacke are: 1) flattening parallel to bedding (S_o), 2) sigmoidal rotation of bedding planes in some clasts, and 3) indentation of the undersides of soft sediment clasts by rigid equant rhyolite fragments (arrows). Phenocryst fragments consist of alkali feldspar and quartz, and are supported by a microcrystalline matrix derived from vitric ash.

Figure 6. Photomicrograph of meta-andesitic lapilli tuff, uncrossed nicols. Fragment to left consists of microcrystalline devitrification products of andesitic vitrophyre, chiefly hornblende, biotite, and iron oxides. This fragment contains flow-aligned plagioclase microlites, and former vesicles (V). Euhedral pyroxene fragment (Px) is recrystallized into blue-green hornblende, and has a thin skin of recrystallized former andesitic glass. Plagioclase fragment (P) is replaced by albite, epidote, hornblende, biotite, and tourmaline (T). The matrix consists of microcrystalline hornblende, biotite, albite, epidote, quartz, and magnetite. From outcrops 650 m west of Mick Homestead.

grained phenocryst fragments (fig. 6). Although all mafic phenocrysts have recrystallized into hornblende, the euhedral outline of whole phenocryst fragments has enabled distinction of the primary phenocryst assemblages. The andesite had abundant plagioclase, with subordinate pyroxene and amphibole phenocrysts. The basalt had abundant coarse-grained pyroxene, with subordinate plagioclase and olivine. Glassy fragments have recrystallized into microcrystalline aggregates of hornblende and iron-oxides. Chemical analysis indicates that the andesite has a calc-alkalic composition while the basalt of Dirigo Gulch is a Mg-rich tholeiite.

Both members are underlain by, overlain by, and laterally gradational into epiclastic rocks. Both display abrupt thickness variation which is partly due to localized deposition in small graben bounded by syndepositional normal faults. Locally, large accidental blocks of wacke are incorporated in basaltic tuff-breccia. Since essential fragments are sparsely vesiculated and glassy, fragmentation was probably due to phreatomagmatic explosions and quenching of subaqueously erupted lava. The lack of sorting, abrupt thickness variation, local incorporation of rip-up clasts, and association with turbidites suggest that deposition was by subaqueous mass flow.

Chert Beds

Interbedded with all stratified rocks are lenticular beds of magnetite quartzite metamorphosed from ferruginous chert and cherty iron formation. The unusual amount of grain growth from chert to quartzite is due to biminerallic composition of the rock. Similar grain growth has occurred in itabirite (banded magnetite quartzite) derived from iron formation (Beukes, 1973).

Chert beds range up to 5 m in thickness and 300 m in strike length. The lenticular nature of these beds is due to localized sedimentation in submarine depressions, and, to a lesser extent, subsequent submarine erosion, since rip-up clasts of chert are commonly incorporated in pyroclastic flow deposits.

INTRUSIVE ROCKS

Metagabbro

Amphibolites derived from gabbroic sills and dikes occur throughout the layered sequence. The larger sills range up to 500 m in thickness. An intrusive origin is indicated by cross-cutting relationships, chilled borders, and relict textures. The outcrop pattern of the larger sills (fig. 1) indicates that they are folded along with the layered sequence. Metagabbros are metamorphosed into blue-green hornblende, albite or oligoclase, epidote, biotite, magnetite, muscovite, and sphene. Where relict textures are preserved, three varieties are recognized: equigranular gabbro, plagioclase-phyric diabase, and pyroxene-phyric basalt. The porphyritic varieties are observed at chilled margins or in dikes. Pyroxene-phyric metabasalt dikes contain hornblende pseudomorphs of coarse-grained euhedral pyroxene phenocrysts which strongly resemble phenocryst fragments in basaltic hyaloclastites of the Dirigo Gulch member. The two rocks are identical in chemistry and are probably co-magmatic.

Large gabbro sills have differentiated in place resulting in metamorphosed differentiates which show a wide range of color index (40–90). Differentiated metadiorites have increasing amounts of plagioclase and biotite at the expense of hornblende. The final differentiates are pods of granophyric albite granite consisting of albite laths and granophyre, with minor magnetite and biotite. This differentiated sequence is similar to that of known layered tholeiitic intrusions. Chemically, equigranular metagabbros are Mg-rich tholeiites. Metadiorites have a higher total FeO/MgO than the metagabbros. The albite granites are chemically similar to keratophyres and plagiogranites.

Granitic Rocks

No subvolcanic granitic rocks are present in the Iris district, but pre-tectonic granitic plutons occur elsewhere in the Gunnison mineral belt (Hedlund and Olson, this guidebook). Post-folding Precambrian intrusions include a stock and cupolas which range in composition from tonalite to quartz monzonite.

STRUCTURAL GEOLOGY

Detailed mapping of stratigraphic units and fabric elements has revealed the existence of the Iris syncline: a major, upright, steeply plunging, tight, disharmonic fold. Due to the local development of several hinges, two synclinal surfaces are located on Figure 1 and are separated by a tight anticlinal flexure. Geometrical analysis of bedding attitudes indicates a plunge of 70° to 85° on an approximate bearing of S40°E. A consequence of steep plunge is that the geological map (fig. 1) is an approximate tectonic profile of the fold. The Iris syncline displays considerable departure from ideal cylindrical folding because of the large initial variation in the thickness and ductility of stratigraphic units.

Folding of the Iris syncline was accompanied by variable strain which resulted in ductile flattening of lithic fragments into oblate ellipsoids (fig. 7). The earliest foliation (S_1) is defined by the X–Y planes of ellipsoidal fragments, where X, Y, and Z are the maximum, intermediate, and minimum axes of those fragments. The X-axes define the orientation of the L_1 (extension) lineations. Both S_1 and L_1 define the trajectories of strain developed during folding. Figure 8 shows a diagrammatic illustration of S_1 attitudes with respect to the Iris syncline. The S_1 foliation is subparallel to bedding on the limbs, and either subparallel or perpendicular to bedding in the hinge zone. Principal elongation (L_1) is generally perpendicular to the fold axis on the limbs, and subparallel to the fold axis in the hinge zone. The Iris syncline apparently formed by a combination of tangential longitudinal strain and flexural flow mechanisms of buckling.

The lower metasediments on the southwest limb of the Iris syncline have responded to stress by tight isoclinal folding on the mesoscopic scale, resulting in the transposition of bedding. Transposition axes are steeply, but variably plunging due to common overturning of isoclinal folds.

The Lulu fault (fig. 1) has a subvertical attitude and cuts upsection through the south limb, bringing successively younger units of the Iris formation in contact with transposed lower metasediments. The Lulu fault is younger than the Iris syncline but older than Precambrian rhyolite dikes which intrude it.

Both the Iris syncline and the Lulu fault have been refolded by an open, steeply plunging, second generation Precambrian fold (fig. 8). The existence of this fold is revealed by the mapping of Olson (1976), but the axial surface occurs largely beneath Tertiary volcanic rocks separating the Iris district from Cochetopa Creek Canyon, 5 km east of the Iris district.

ECONOMIC GEOLOGY

The Iris district contains five abandoned gold mines which were active during the last decade of the nineteenth century (fig. 1). The Denver City Mine, the Graflin Mine, and the Shaunee #33 prospect (500 m east-northeast of the Lulu Mine) are classified as pre-metamorphic deposits based on criteria such as geometry, foliation development, alteration, and metamorphic mineral assemblages. The Denver City Mine is described by Drobeck (this guidebook) and is interpreted as syngenetic in origin. Mineralization at the Graflin Mine consists of foliated veinlets of biotite-pyrite-chalcopyrite and is due to pre-metamorphic fracture filling. The Shaunee #33 prospect is identified as a distal syngenetic massive sulfide occurrence. It consists of a 15–60 cm-thick, stratiform massive sulfide oxidized to hematite-limonite gossan, and has a strike length of 30 m. This deposit occurs conformably within a lens of laminated epiclastic rocks in the dacitic member.

The Mineral Hill Mine, the Lulu Mine, the Lucky Strike Mine, and numerous small occurrences are classified as post-metamorphic epigenetic deposits. Veins consist of quartz-pyrite ± biotite ±

Figure 7. Highly foliated rhyolitic lapilli tuff. Flattened and elongated tuff fragments define the S_1 foliation and the L_1 extension lineation. Later fracture cleavage (S_2) is related to second-generation folding.

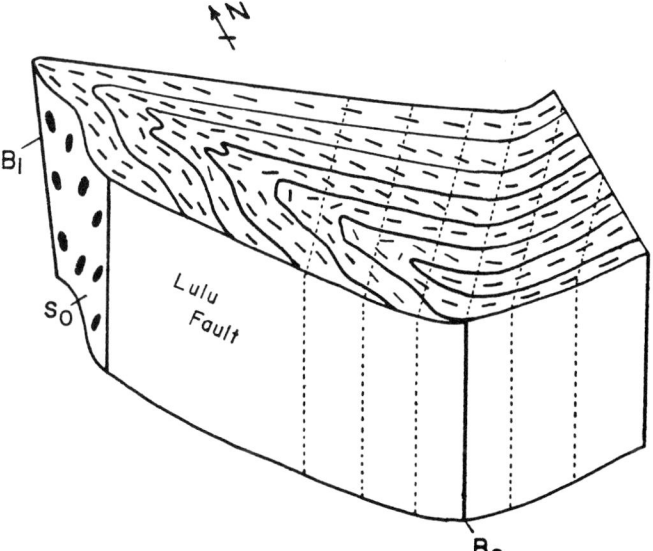

Figure 8. Schematic block diagram showing some principal structural features in the Iris area. The foreground is the surface of the Lulu fault. The Iris syncline (B_1) plunges steeply southeast within the Iris area. Second generation folding has resulted in open refolding of the Iris syncline and the Lulu fault about a steeply plunging axis (B_2). Solid lines represent bedding (S_o), dashed lines represent S_1, and the dotted lines represent fracture cleavage (S_2). The L_1 lineation is defined by elongated ellipsoidal fragments, the traces of which are shown on the S_o surface.

sericite ± tourmaline ± carbonate ± fluorite. These deposits are spatially, and probably genetically, related to a Precambrian post-tectonic tonalite to quartz monzonite stock which occurs in the southern part of the district (fig. 1).

CONCLUSIONS

The available data from detailed studies in the Iris district allow reconstruction of the following sequence of events:

1. Deposition of turbidites, which became increasingly volcanic in composition with time, signaling the onset of calc-alkaline pyroclastic eruptions.
2. Eruptions of voluminous dacitic to rhyodacitic pyroclastic debris and deposition of subaqueous pyroclastic flow deposits.
3. Phreatomagmatic eruption of andesitic hyaloclastite, coinciding with the appearance of quartz phenocrysts in the calc-alkaline magma chamber.
4. Eruptions of voluminous quartz latitic to rhyolitic pyroclastic debris and deposition as subaqueous pyroclastic flow deposits.
5. Intrusion of large tholeiitic gabbro sills and differentiation in place to produce mafic cumulates and felsic liquids.
6. Phreatomagmatic eruption of tholeiitic basaltic hyaloclastite.
7. Pyroclastic eruptions of alkali feldspar rhyolites, which represent the final differentiates of the calc-alkaline magma, and deposition by subaqueous pyroclastic flow mechanisms.
8. Cessation of volcanism and resumption of epiclastic sedimentation.

The entire sequence was deposited largely by mass flow on a submarine slope. Eruptions were subaerial or under shallow water, and deposition was probably at shallow depth. Epiclastic rocks were deposited between eruptions largely by reworking of unconsolidated tuffs. Short quiet intervals are marked by chemical deposition of exhalites, consisting of oxide facies cherty iron formation, or syngenetic massive sulfides.

The predominance of volcanic detritus indicates deposition in an environment of oceanic volcanism, comparable to primitive Phanerozoic island arcs.

Volcanism and sedimentation occurred prior to the Boulder Creek orogeny, c.a. 1700 m.y. ago (Hansen and Peterman, 1968).

Two episodes of folding are recognized, and both are correlated with the Boulder Creek orogeny, c.a. 1700 m.y. ago. The earlier generation was one of tight folding around a steeply plunging axis, and resulted in considerable horizontal shortening by internal ductile strain. This episode roughly coincided with prograde metamorphism to the epidote amphibolite facies. The Lulu fault formed after the first folding episode. The second folding episode resulted in open, regional refolding of previous structures.

Post-folding intrusions are calc-alkalic stocks of tonalite to quartz monzonite, with associated rhyolite dikes. These were probably emplaced during the Siller Plume event, c.a. 1400 m.y. ago (Hansen and Peterman, 1968).

The rocks of the Iris area are considered representative of all rock types in the Gunnison Precambrian terrain, excluding pre-folding calc-alkalic intrusions. Such intrusions occur elsewhere in the Gunnison Precambrian terrain and consist of foliated stocks of equigranular to porphyritic granodiorite to leucogranite. Some of these rocks are probable subvolcanic equivalents to pyroclastic rocks in the Iris area. It is indeed impossible to have volcanic rocks without their subvolcanic feeders, and the large volume of pyroclastic rocks in the Iris area suggest derivation from large, shallow, subvolcanic intrusions.

The recognition that the metavolcanic "pile" in the Iris area is a major syncline has led to reinterpretation of the regional structure. The outcrop pattern in the Gunnison Precambrian terrain is an interference pattern due to complex polyphase deformation. The felsic metavolcanic mass in the Iris NW quadrangle, 8 km southwest of the Iris area, is now recognized as a steeply plunging refolded major isoclinal fold.

The stratigraphic relationships established for the Iris area may apply to more deformed rocks in the Gunnison Precambrian terrain. The intermediate to felsic metavolcanic rocks are considered favorable hosts for Zn-Cu volcanogenic massive sulfide deposits.

On a more regional scale, rocks of the Iris area are very similar to Precambrian rocks of the Salida area, 70 km to the east, which have been described by Boardman (1976, 1980a, 1980b). Such similarity provides some insight on the nature of the Precambrian basement of Colorado.

ACKNOWLEDGMENTS

I wish to thank R. C. Epis, G. S. Holden, L. G. Closs, and J. C. Olson for their guidance and assistance. This study benefitted from discussions with P. A. Drobeck and W. D. Reismeyer.

REFERENCES

Afifi, A. M., 1981, Precambrian geology of the Iris area, Gunnison and Saguache Counties, Colorado (M.S. thesis): Golden, Colorado School of Mines, 197 p.

Beukes, N. J., 1973, Iron-formations of southern Africa: Economic Geology, v. 68, p. 960–1004.

Boardman, S. J., 1976, Geology of the Precambrian metamorphic rocks of the Salida area, Chaffee County, Colorado: Mountain Geologist, v. 13, p. 89–100.

———, 1980a, Evidence for two stages of Precambrian metamorphism in the Salida area, central Colorado (abs.): Geological Society of America, Abstracts with Programs, v. 12, p. 267.

———, 1980b, Geochemistry and origin of Proterozoic amphibolites from Salida, Colorado (abs): Geological Society of America, Abstracts with Programs, v. 12, p. 268.

Drobeck, P. A., 1980, Geology and trace element geochemistry of a part of the Gunnison Gold Belt, Colorado (M.S. thesis): Golden, Colorado School of Mines, 180 p.

———, 1981, Proterozoic syngenetic massive sulfide deposits in the Gunnison gold belt, Colorado: New Mexico Geological Society Guidebook 32, this volume.

Fiske, R. S., 1963, Subaqueous pyroclastic flows in the Ohanapecosh Formation, Washington: Geological Society of America Bulletin, v. 74, p. 391–406.

Fiske, R. S. and Matsuda, T., 1964, Submarine equivalents of ash flows in the Tokiwa Formation, Japan: American Journal of Science, v. 262, p. 76–106.

Hansen, W. R. and Peterman, Z. E., 1968, Basement rock geochronology of the Black Canyon of the Gunnison, Colorado: U.S. Geological Survey Professional Paper 600-C, p. 80–90.

Hedlund, D. C. and Olson, J. C., 1974, Geologic map of the Iris NW Quadrangle, Gunnison and Saguache Counties, Colorado: U.S. Geological Survey Map GQ-1134, 1:24,000.

———, 1981, Precambrian geology along parts of the Gunnison uplift of southwestern Colorado: New Mexico Geological Society Guidebook 32, this volume.

Middleton, G. V. and Hampton, M. A., 1973, Sediment gravity flows: mechanics of flow and deposition, in Turbidites and deep water sedimentation: SEPM Pacific section short course, p 1–38.

Olson, J. C., 1976, Geologic map of the Iris Quadrangle, Gunnison and Saguache Counties, Colorado: U.S. Geological Survey Map GQ-286, scale 1:24,000.

Tasse, N., Lajoie, J., and Dimroth, E., 1978, The anatomy and interpretation of an Archean volcaniclastic sequence, Quebec: Canadian Journal of the Earth Sciences, v. 15, p. 874–888.

Walker, R. G. and Mutti, E., 1973, Turbidite facies and facies associations, in Turbidites and deep water sedimentation: SEPM Pacific Section short course, p. 119–185.

THE COMPLEX OF ALKALINE ROCKS AT IRON HILL, POWDERHORN DISTRICT, GUNNISON COUNTY, COLORADO

THEODORE J. ARMBRUSTMACHER
U.S. Geological Survey
Denver, Colorado 80225

INTRODUCTION

The alkaline rocks, and especially the carbonatite stock at Iron Hill, near Powderhorn, Colorado, have been studied since 1912 (Singewald, 1912), not only because of their unusual lithologies but also because of the economically significant mineral concentrations associated with them. Various hypotheses regarding the origin of the Iron Hill rocks have paralleled the development of ideas concerning carbonatite petrogenesis from assimilation of marble followed by crystal differentiation (Larsen, 1942), to metasomatism of preexisting pyroxenite (Temple and Grogan, 1965) to formation through immiscibility of magmatic liquids (Nash, 1972). Economic minerals associated spatially and genetically with these rocks include vermiculite and minerals that contain thorium, iron, titanium, niobium, and rare-earth elements. Thorium deposits have been discussed by Armbrustmacher (1980), Staatz and others (1979, 1980), Hedlund and Olsen (1961), and Wallace and Olson (1956). Iron and titanium deposits have been discussed by Rose and Shannon (1960) and Singewald (1912). Niobium resources have been mentioned by Armbrustmacher (1980) and Hedlund and Olson (1961). Rare-earth minerals have been discussed by Olson and Wallace (1956) and Hedlund and Olson (1961).

GEOLOGIC SETTING

The Cambrian or Precambrian complex of alkaline rocks at Iron Hill (fig. 1), which is about 30 km² in area, was originally described

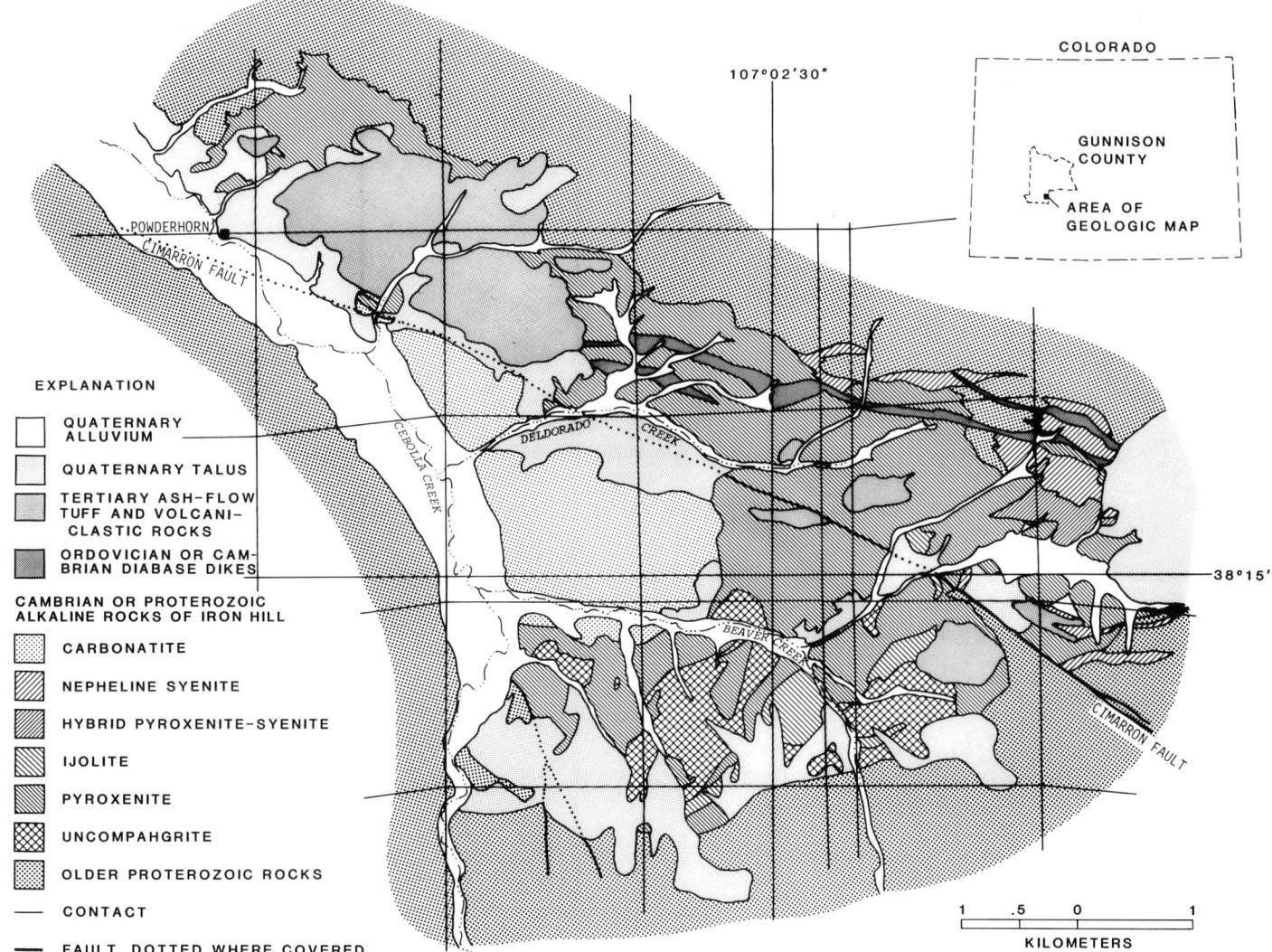

Figure 1. Geologic map of the alkaline complex at Iron Hill, Powderhorn district, Gunnison County, Colorado. Modified from Olson (1974) and Hedlund and Olson (1975).

by Larsen (1942). The complex consists chiefly of pyroxenite, magnetite-ilmenite-perovskite segregations, uncompahgrite, ijolite, hybrid pyroxenite-syenite rocks, nepheline syenite, and carbonatite, listed oldest to youngest (Hedlund and Olson, 1961). Probably prior to 570 million years ago (Olson and others, 1977), rocks of the complex were emplaced into Proterozoic X Powderhorn Granite and older Proterozoic metamorphic rocks, which are locally fenitized adjacent to the complex. Parts of the complex are covered by ash-flow tuffs, welded tuffs, and colluvium mainly of Oligocene age, and by colluvium and alluvium of Quaternary age, mainly along the drainages of Cebolla, Deldorado, and Beaver Creeks.

The complex is bisected by the Cimarron fault (fig. 1). Hedlund and Olson (1975) indicated that relative movement on the fault is such that a deeper structural level of the alkaline complex is exposed on the northeast side of the fault than on the southwest side. The interpretation of Temple and Grogan (1965), however, suggests that a deeper structural level is exposed on the southwest side of the fault. Regardless of the interpretation, nearly all the uncompahgrite, most of the ijolite, and the carbonatite stock are found southwest of the fault. The magnetite-ilmenite-perovskite segregations and the nepheline syenite seem to be restricted to the northeast side of the fault. Diabase dikes of Cambrian or Ordovician age intrude rocks of the complex on the northeast side of the Cimarron fault, although one diabase dike does cut fenitized Powderhorn Granite just southwest of the fault (Olson, 1974).

Carbonatite dikes, probably similar in age to the carbonatite stock, intrude all rocks of the complex except the carbonatite stock. They also intrude the Precambrian host rocks, especially those within the fenitized aureole. Martite-fluorapatite veins and jasper-rich veins, the latter probably representing silicified fracture zones, intersect the carbonatite stock. Rocks of the complex and the surrounding area have been mapped in detail by Hedlund and Olson (1968, 1975) and Olson (1974).

ROCKS OF THE COMPLEX

The intrusive igneous rocks at Iron Hill collectively constitute a classic example of the carbonatite-nephelinite magmatic igneous association (LeBas, 1977). Other examples include the igneous complexes at Fen, Norway; Alno, Sweden; Magnet Cove, Arkansas; and the alkaline intrusions of eastern Africa. The rocks at Iron Hill include many of the principal rock types of this classic association, which are carbonatite, nephelinite, ijolite, pyroxenite, and fenite. At Iron Hill, erosion may have removed the volcanic rocks usually associated with many of the carbonatite-nephelinite complexes elsewhere.

Descriptions of the major rock types at Iron Hill that follow are taken chiefly from Armbrustmacher (1980), Hedlund and Olson (1975), and Olson (1974).

Pyroxenite

The rock unit mapped as pyroxenite by Hedlund and Olson (1975) and Olson (1974) is highly variable in chemical and mineralogical composition. The medium- to coarse-grained, locally pegmatitic pyroxenite contains 55–70 percent clinopyroxene, 10–15 percent magnetite and ilmenite, 5–25 percent melanite garnet, 5 percent fluorapatite, and 10 percent biotite and phlogophite. Accessory minerals are chiefly sphene, brown amphibole, calcite, perovskite, leucoxene, sodic amphibole, melilite, sericite, pyrite, chalcopyrite, and pyrrhotite. Calcic plagioclase is absent. Vermiculite and magnetite-ilmenite-perovskite segregations are locally abundant. The alkali-silica diagram in Figure 2 shows the average $Na_2O + K_2O$ versus SiO_2 composition of pyroxenite analyses from Nash (1972) and Larsen (1942) and the average alkaline basalt from Nockolds (1954).

Magnetite-ilmenite-perovskite segregations

Dikes and segregations consisting chiefly of magnetite, ilmenite, and perovskite are confined to the pyroxenite northeast of the Cimarron fault. Apatite and biotite are minor constituents. The dikes and segregations are commonly less than 1 m thick but may attain a thickness of 50 m. The perovskite content, which may reach 50 percent, makes the dikes and segregations attractive titanium-prospecting targets. Seven samples of these rocks average 58.5 ppm uranium and 296 ppm thorium, and the anomalous radioactivity of these rocks is a useful characteristic in the exploration for these rocks. Outcrops of magnetite-ilmenite-perovskite segregations are too small to be shown at the scale of the geologic map (fig. 1).

Uncompahgrite

Uncompahgrite was described by Olson (1974) as a light-gray, medium-grained to very coarse-grained rock composed of melilite, variable amounts of clinopyroxene, and small amounts of magnetite, apatite, phlogopite, melanite garnet, and perovskite. The average composition of uncompahgrite is shown in Figure 2. The Iron Hill area is the type locality for this rock type (Larsen, 1942).

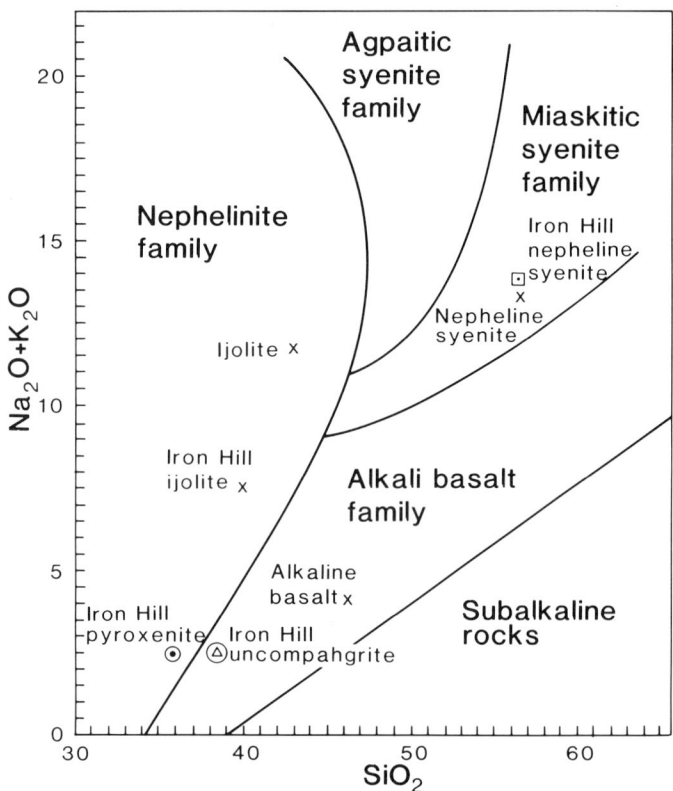

Figure 2. Average alkali and silica contents of rock types in the complex at Iron Hill. The diagram is modified from Currie (1976, p. 6). The rock types marked by x are average compositions of the data from Nockholds (1954), for comparison.

Ijolite

Ijolite is coarse to fine grained, and usually has a hypidiomorphic-granular texture (Hedlund and Olson, 1975). The rock commonly consists of 30–50 percent nepheline, 30–40 percent sodic clinopyroxene, 10–30 percent melanite garnet, and minor amounts of orthoclase, magnetite, apatite, biotite, sphene, and alteration products of nepheline. The average $Na_2O + K_2O$ versus SiO_2 of available analyses is shown in Figure 2.

Hybrid pyroxenite-syenite rocks

According to Hedlund and Olson (1975), this rock consists of brecciated pyroxenite containing numerous irregular fracture fillings and small dikes of nepheline syenite. The pyroxenite contains clinopyroxene, melanite garnet, sphene, apatite, and melilite. The syenite contains orthoclase, microperthite, sodic clinopyroxene, nepheline, and melanite garnet.

Nepheline syenite

The light-gray to pinkish-gray nepheline syenite is medium to coarse grained, and commonly has a trachytic texture. The rock consists of orthoclase, microperthite, and albite, with about 10 percent interstitial sodic clinopyroxene, and nepheline, and accessory melanite garnet, magnetite, sphene, biotite, apatite, calcite, sericite, and zircon. The average $Na_2O + K_2O$ versus SiO_2 composition is shown in Figure 2.

Carbonatite

The carbonatite stock at Iron Hill consists of light-brown to light-gray, foliated to massive carbonatite. The following minerals, listed approximately in the order of their frequency of occurrence, have been identified: dolomite, barite, goethite, hematite, calcite, quartz, fluorapatite, pyrochlore, pyrite, magnetite, biotite, rutile, fluorite, bastnaesite, aegirine, anatase, sphalerite, synchisite, zircon, magnesite(?), and manganese oxide minerals. In comparison with average igneous rocks, the carbonatite stock contains greater than 20 times more barium, cerium, neodymium, 15–20 times more lanthanum, niobium, phosphorus, and total rare-earth elements, and nearly 10 or more times manganese, molybdenum, and strontium (Armbrustmacher, 1980). The carbonatite is cut by narrow martite-fluorapatite veins and jasper veins, neither of which are shown on the geologic map (fig. 1).

PETROLOGY AND ECONOMIC POTENTIAL

Many aspects of the alkaline complex at Iron Hill suggest that it is a representative of the Ijolite Series as defined by Bailey (1974). Rocks of this series are characteristically undersaturated with respect to SiO_2 and contain fairly abundant Na_2O and K_2O. The complex at Iron Hill is also representative of the carbonatitic type of alkaline complex as defined by Rock (1976). These complexes are characterized by the occurrence of intrusive rocks such as carbonatite, ijolite, pyroxenite, melilitic rocks, and nepheline syenite, all lacking calcic plagioclase, and are also found occupying the root zones of nephelinitic volcanoes. King (1965) suggested that rocks of this type formed by differentiation from an immediate parental nephelinite- melteigite magma, which maintained SiO_2 undersaturation with a trend toward enrichment of CaO, Na_2O, K_2O, and volatile elements. With increasing concentration of these components, a point was reached where a highly mobile fraction of alkali and calcium carbonates separated from the crystallizing silicate phase to form a carbonatite melt. Initially, the melt contained abundant alkali carbonates, which, according to King (1965), allowed the carbonatite to remain as a liquid at low temperatures and pressures. The presence of fenitized country rocks reflects the alkali content of the melt and shows that alkalies were removed from the melt through reaction with the host. The final product was a carbonatite probably not unlike that found at Iron Hill. Carbon isotopic ratios from the Iron Hill carbonatite (Taylor and others, 1967) are similar to ratios found in diamond, indicating that the CO_2 in the carbonatite had a deep-seated igneous source. The carbon isotopic data and oxygen isotopic data from the Iron Hill carbonatite both fall within the field of primary igneous carbonatite defined by Taylor and others (1967). Strontium isotopic data from various lithologies within the alkaline complex, including carbonatite (Powell and others, 1966), indicate that the rocks within the complex are comagmatic. Strontium isotopic values also suggest that carbonatite-alkaline rock associations, such as that observed at Iron Hill, are mantle derived. Analyses of calcite-dolomite and pyrite-pyrrhotite mineral pairs by Nash (1972), indicated crystallization temperatures between 435° C and 290° C for late-stage carbonatites. Samoylov (1975) determined formation temperatures of Iron Hill carbonatite at 600° C, using biotite-pyroxene geothermometry, and at 400° C, using amphibole-pyroxene geothermometry.

Deposits of possible economic value of a number of mineral commodities are known to be associated spatially and genetically with the alkaline complex at Iron Hill. In discussing the occurrence of thorium and rare-earth minerals, Olson and Wallace (1956) showed that thorium mainly is concentrated in veins and shear zones outside of the complex, and rare-earth elements mainly are concentrated in carbonatite dikes and in the Iron Hill carbonatite stock. Hedlund and Olson (1961) identified four environments containing thorium, niobium, and rare-earth minerals in the Powderhorn district: (a) carbonatite, (b) magnetite-ilmenite-perovskite bodies, (c) thorite veins, and (d) trachyte dikes. The magnetite-ilmenite-perovskite segregations were discussed as early as 1912 (Singewald, 1912) as a source of iron and titanium. Rose and Shannon (1960) reported an average grade of 6.5 percent titania and 11.7 percent iron and a possible tonnage in excess of 100 million short-tons in pyroxenites containing the segregations. In the February 25, 1976, issue of the Denver Post, Buttes Gas and Oil Company announced results of a study that indicated 419 million tons of reserves averaging about 12 percent TiO_2 occurred at Powderhorn. Studies of the carbonatite stock by E. I. DuPont de Nemours and Company (Temple and Grogan, 1965) indicated a niobium reserve of over 100,000 tons of Nb_2O_5 in rocks averaging at least 0.25 percent Nb_2O_5. More recent studies of the carbonatite stock (Armbrustmacher, 1980) showed a fairly inhomogeneous distribution of thorium with values ranging between 0.0007 percent and 0.017 percent ThO_2; the average thorium content is 0.0041 percent ThO_2. The carbonatite stock contains reserves as defined by Staatz and others (1979) totaling 29,775 tons of ThO_2, 9,180 tons of U_3O_8, 2,865,500 tons total rare-earth oxides, and 412,000 tons Nb_2O_5 in the carbonatite that projects above the surrounding land surface. According to Staatz and others (1980), 13 carbonatite dikes contain reserves totaling 763 tons of ThO_2, 57 tons U_3O_8, 21,000 tons total rare-earth oxides, and 1,330 tons Nb_2O_5. Vermiculite deposits are found in altered pyroxenite, but data on reserves are not available.

REFERENCES

Armbrustmacher, T. J., 1980, Abundance and distribution of thorium in the carbonatite stock at Iron Hill, Powderhorn district, Gunnison County, Colorado: U.S. Geological Survey Professional Paper 1049-B, 11 p.

Bailey, D. K., 1974, Nephelinites and ijolites, in Sorensen, H., ed., The alkaline rocks: New York, John Wiley and Sons, p. 53–66.

Currie, K. L., 1976, The alkaline rocks of Canada: Geological Society of Canada Bulletin 239, 229 p.
Hedlund, D. C. and Olson, J. C., 1961, Four environments of thorium-, niobium-, and rare-earth-bearing minerals in the Powderhorn district of southwestern Colorado: U.S. Geological Survey Professional Paper 424-B, p. B283-B286.
——— 1968, Geologic map of the complex of alkalic rocks at Iron Hill, Gunnison County, Colorado: U.S. Geological Survey Open-File Map.
——— 1975, Geologic map of the Powderhorn quadrangle, Gunnison and Saguache Counties, Colorado: U.S. Geological Survey Geologic Quadrangle Map GQ-1178.
King, B. C., 1965, Petrogenesis of the alkaline igneous rock suites of the volcanic and intrusive centres of eastern Uganda: Journal of Petrology, v. 6, p. 67-100.
Larsen, E. S., Jr., 1942, Alkalic rocks of Iron Hill, Gunnison County, Colorado: U.S. Geological Survey Professional Paper 197-A, p. 1-64.
LeBas, M. J., 1977, Carbonatite-nephelinite volcanism: An African case history: New York, John Wiley and Sons, 347 p.
Nash, W. P., 1972, Mineralogy and petrology of the Iron Hill carbonatite complex, Colorado: Geological Society of America Bulletin, v. 83, p. 1361-1382.
Nockholds, S. R., 1954, Average composition of some igneous rocks: Geological Society of America Bulletin, v. 66, p. 1007-1032.
Olson, J. C., 1974, Geologic map of the Rudolph Hill quadrangle, Gunnison, Hinsdale, and Saguache Counties, Colorado: U.S. Geological Survey Geologic Quadrangle Map GQ-1177.
Olson, J. C., Marvin, R. F., Parker, R. L., and Mehnert, H.H., 1977, Age and tectonic setting of lower Paleozoic alkalic and mafic rocks, carbonatites, and thorium veins in south-central Colorado: Journal of Research, U.S. Geological Survey, v. 5, p. 673-687.
Olson, J. C. and Wallace, S. R., 1956, Thorium and rare-earth minerals in Powderhorn district, Gunnison County, Colorado: U.S. Geological Survey Bulletin 1027-O, p. 693-723.
Powell, J. L., Hurley, P. M., and Fairbairn, H. W., 1966, The strontium isotopic composition and origin of carbonatites, in Tuttle, O. F., and Gittins, J., eds., Carbonatites: New York, Interscience Publishers, p. 365-378.
Rock, N. M. S., 1976, The role of CO_2 in alkali rock genesis: Geological Magazine, v. 113, p. 97-113.
Rose, C. K. and Shannon, S. S., Jr., 1960, Cebolla Creek titaniferous iron deposits, Gunnison County, Colorado: U.S. Bureau of Mines Report of Investigations 5679, 30 p.
Samoylov, V. S., 1975, The temperatures of formation of carbonatites (based on geothermometric studies): Geochemistry International, v. 12, no. 6, p. 52-58.
Singewald, J. T., Jr., 1912, The iron ore deposits of the Cebolla district, Gunnison, County, Colorado: Economic Geology, v. 7, p. 560-573.
Staatz, M. H., Armbrustmacher, T. J., Olson, J. C., Brownfield, I. K., Brock, M. R., Lemons, J. F., Jr., Coppa, L. V., and Clingan, B. V., 1979, Principal thorium resources in the United States: U.S. Geological Survey Circular 805, 42 p.
Staatz, M. H., Hall, R. B., Macke, D. L., Armbrustmacher, T. J., and Brownfield, I. K., 1980, Thorium resources of selected regions in the United States: U.S. Geological Survey Circular 824, 32 p.
Taylor, H. P., Jr., Frechen, Josef, and Degens, E. T., 1967, Oxygen and carbon isotope studies of carbonatites from the Laacher See district, West Germany, and the Alno District, Sweden: Geochimica et Cosmochimica Acta, v. 31, p. 407-430.
Temple, A. K. and Grogan, R. M., 1965, Carbonatite and related alkalic rocks at Powderhorn, Colorado: Economic Geology, v. 60, p. 672-692.
Wallace, S. R. and Olson, J. C., 1956, Thorium in the Powderhorn district, Gunnison County, Colorado: U.S. Geological Survey Professional Paper 300, p. 587-592.

STRUCTURE AND PETROLOGY OF COCHETOPA PLUTON AND ITS METAMORPHIC WALLROCKS, SAGUACHE COUNTY, COLORADO

ROBERT M. HUTCHINSON
Department of Geology
Colorado School of Mines
Golden, Colorado 80401

INTRODUCTION

The Cochetopa Granite pluton and its metamorphic wallrocks are exposed in an erosional window that has been cut through the Jurassic Junction Creek Sandstone (fig. 1). The area described in this paper is bisected by northward-flowing Cochetopa Creek and includes approximately 33.7 km². Cochetopa Granite pluton includes about 14.5 km² and the metamorphic wallrocks the remainder. Nine different lithologically distinct mappable units are present as well as dikes of pegmatite and aplite.

The major lithologic units are granite-gneiss (ggn), porphyroblastic gneiss (Pgn), quartzite (qz), metadiorite (mdi), mixed zones (mz_1 and mz_2), metagabbro (mg), Cochetopa Granite (Cg), and Cochetopa granite-gneiss (Cgn). Figure 2 shows the units in geological cross section.

PETROGRAPHY
Quartzite

The quartzite unit is massive, brownish black (SYR 2/1), very fine grained, and varyingly intimately laced with fine, narrow 1–30 mm subparallel bands that are parallel to relict sedimentary layering.

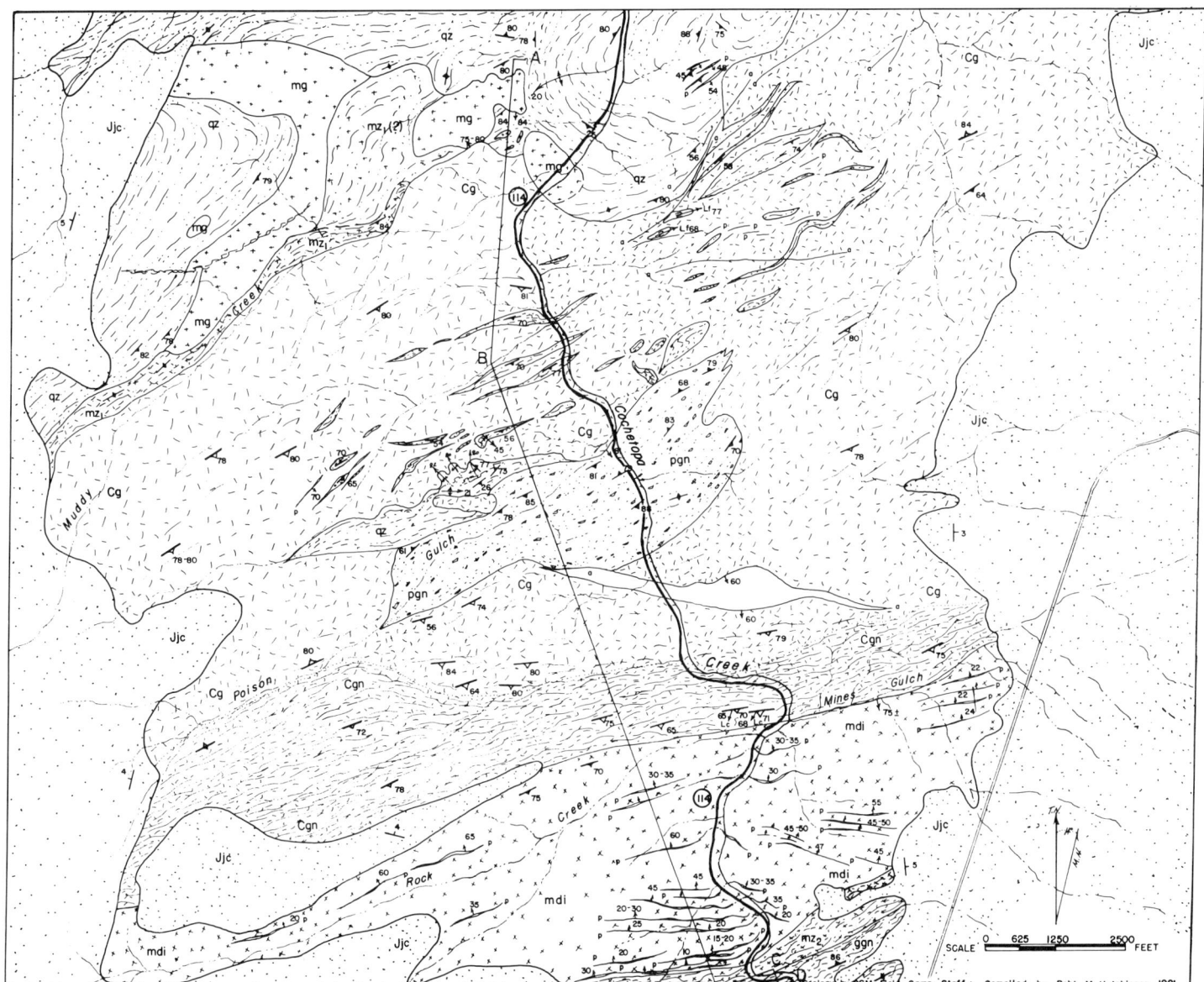

Figure 1. Geologic map of Cochetopa pluton and its metamorphic wallrocks. See Figure 2 for explanation. Section shown on Figure 2.

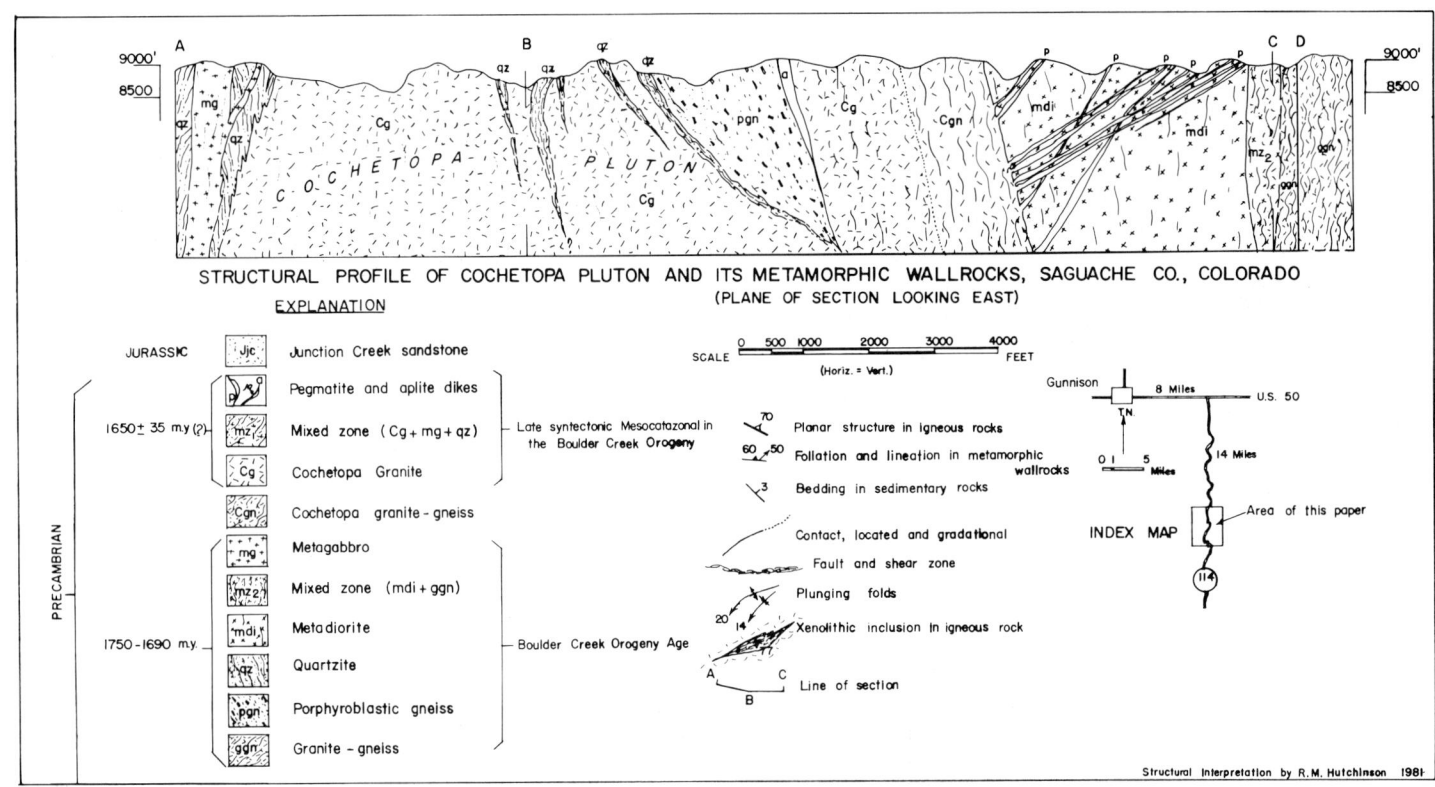

Figure 2. Structure profile of Cochetopa pluton and its metamorphic wallrocks. Line of section shown on Figure 1.

Texture of the quartzite is granoblastic, xenoblastic-granular, weakly lepidoblastic and gneissose. Gneissic layering and migmatizational layering vary in intensity throughout the unit. About two kilometers north of the area of the map shown on Figure 1, the massive quartzite is replete with circular blotchy areas of microclinization. As one approaches the Cochetopa pluton to the south, migmatization develops a banded structure and seems to become more abundant. The migmatization, however, is thought to have formed prior to emplacement of Cochetopa pluton. The quartzite is typically a biotite quartzite but also ranges to a hornblende-microcline-biotite-quartzite (Table 1 and fig. 3, photo 1).

Metagabbro

The texture of metagabbro is granoblastic, medium to coarse grained with blastoporphyritic poikiloblastic hornblende xenoblasts set in a fine- to medium-grained matrix or groundmass. The rock is greenish black (5 G 2/1). Some relict subophitic to ophitic texture is visible (Tables 1, 2 and fig. 3, photo 2). Anorthite content of the plagioclase averages about An_{46} with rare values up to An_{51}. Rock composition is intermediate between that of gabbro and diorite, leaning more toward diorite, but the rock is probably best classified as metagabbro.

Table 1. Modal composition of Cochetopa pluton and its metamorphic wallrocks. See Table 2 for rock description.

Rock Unit	qz	mgb	Cg	Cgn	pgn	aplite	mdio	mdio	mz$_2$	ggn
microcline	10	—	50	40–50	35–40	50–55	—	—	45–50	35–40
plagioclase	—	50–60	10	10–12	10–15	10	35–40	35	10–15	10–15
quartz	50–60	—	15–20	20	20–25	20–25	8–10	5–7	10–12	30–35
hornblende	2–3	30–35	—	—	—	—	25–30	50	10–12	—
biotite	25–30	—	8–12	10–15	15–20	5	7–10	5	10–15	10–12
muscovite	—	—	3	3	3	5	—	—	—	5
sphene	1	—	3–5	1	1	—	2	2	2–3	—
magnetite	1	—	trace	tr.	tr.	—	1	tr.	5	2
zircon	—	—	tr.	—	—	—	tr.	—	—	—
apatite	—	—	—	—	—	—	tr.	—	—	—
epidote	—	—	—	—	—	—	tr.	5	5	—
hematite	—	1	—	1	1	—	1	—	—	1
pyrite	—	1	—	tr.	tr.	—	1	—	—	—
fluorite	—	—	tr.	1	1	—	—	—	—	—
An-Content	—	An_{46}–An_{51}	An_{28}	An_{30}	An_{37}	An_{10}	An_{45}	An_{36}	An_{37}	An_{24}

Figure 3. Photomicrographs of rock units

Photo 1—Quartzite from the northern part of the area, very fine grained, granoblastic, xenoblastic-granular. Crossed polars, × 10.

Photo 2—Metagabbro, granoblastic, medium to coarse grained. The field of view is occupied by a poikiloblastic blastoporphyritic xenoblast of hornblende which probably was originally augite. Crossed polars, × 25.

Photo 3—Cochetopa Granite showing granulation and recrystallization effects along grain boundaries of larger microcline grains. Crossed polars, × 25.

Photo 4—Cochetopa Granite showing granulation and recrystallization effects along grain boundaries of microcline-perthite. Crossed polars, × 25.

Photo 5—Cochetopa granite-gneiss showing weak planar foliation of biotite and allotrimorphic-granular texture. Crossed polars, × 25.

Photo 6—Porphyroblastic gneiss showing an idioblastic microcline porphyroblast surrounded by fine-grained granoblastic groundmass. Crossed polars, × 25.

Table 2. Description of rock units mapped in the Cochetopa pluton area.

Rock Unit	Description
qz	biotite quartzite to hornblende-microcline-biotite quartzite
mgb	metagabbro
Cg	peraluminous biotite granite (Cochetopa Granite)
mz_1	Cochetopa Granite with metagabbro and quartzite
Cgn	muscovite-plagioclase-biotite-quartz-microcline gneiss (Cochetopa granite-gneiss)
pgn	porphyroblastic-plagioclase-quartz-biotite-microcline gneiss or blastoporphyrtic meta quartz monzonite.
aplite	granite aplite
mdio	meta diorite to meta quartz diorite
mz_2	quartz-hornblende-biotite-andesine-microcline metasomite or granitized diorite to quartz diorite
ggn	muscovite-biotite-oligoclase-quartz-microcline gneiss or granite-gneiss

Cochetopa Granite

Cochetopa Granite is holocrystalline, hypidiomorphic-granular, medium grained, averaging about 3 × 6 mm, and moderate reddish brown (10R 4/6). The rock has a pleasing uniform appearance and would make an ideal decorative facing stone if it could be quarried in large enough blocks. Euhedral wedge and diamond-shaped sphene crystals are distributed more or less uniformly through the rock and are partly altered to leucoxene. Grain boundaries of the larger microclines are weakly to moderately cataclasized (fig. 3, photos 3 and 4). Narrow, elongate, polycrystalline aggregates of individual 0.2 × 0.3 mm microcline and plagioclase register the microfracturing, granulation, and recrystallization that has occurred. The rock is a peraluminous biotite granite.

Mixed Zone Rock (mz_1)

No petrographic analysis was made of rocks from this unit. The Cochetopa Granite intruded and partially reacted with the metagabbro wallrock and to a minor extent with the quartzite. Feldspathization of the metagabbro has taken place, and the relict fine stratigraphic layering of the quartzite has been varyingly intruded concordantly by tongues and layers of Cochetopa Granite. This mixed zone ranges in thickness from 100 to 150 m.

Cochetopa Granite-Gneiss

This unit is considered a moderately cataclasized border facies of the Cochetopa Granite. Contact of Cochetopa Granite with the granite-gneiss is gradational over 180 to 300 m. The rock is holocrystalline, dominantly allotriomorphic-granular, medium grained, and moderate reddish brown (10 R 4/6). Biotite, muscovite, and anhedral, undulose quartz aggregates show increasing planar and linear alignment to the south as one approaches the contact of the metadiorite. Biotite is partly converted to muscovite. The rock is best classified as a biotite peraluminous granite-gneiss or cataclastic peraluminous granite-gneiss (fig. 3, photo 5).

Porphyroblastic Gneiss

Petrographic and fabric features seem to suggest a metamorphic rather than an igneous origin for this rock. Medium to coarse to very coarse porphyroblasts of idioblastic microcline show a weak to moderate planar alignment. They often occur in roughly aligned swarms over more than 100 m or they may be present in very minor amounts. Groundmass material is fine grained, granoblastic, xenoblastic-granular and contains an average of 20 percent biotite. Some locations may have up to 30 percent biotite. Texturally the groundmass might be described as having a salt-and-pepper appearance (fig. 3, photo 6). Except for the scattered pale yellowish brown feldspar phenocrysts the rock is olive black (5Y 2/1). The rock is best classified as porphyroblastic oligoclase-biotite-quartz-microcline salt-and-pepper gneiss. Should an igneous origin be ascribed to the rock then the best name would seem to be blastoporphyritic meta-quartz monzonite.

Granite Aplite

Granite aplite is present mainly as a large dike in the central part of the area (fig. 1). The dike is about 1600 m long, dips 60° SE and reaches a maximum thickness of about 200 m. Texture is holocrystalline, allotriomorphic-granular, very fine to fine grained and color is moderate yellowish brown (10YR 5/4). Muscovite and biotite are both present with the biotite somewhat altered to limonite (fig. 4, photo 1).

Metadiorite

Grain size in the northern part of the metadiorite body is fine to medium grained but is dominantly medium grained in the southern part. Textures are xenoblastic-granular to xenoblastic-inequigranular. Color is grayish black (N2). A weak, barely perceptible fine streaky layering or banding is best seen on some exposures from a distance of 10 m or more. Within a hundred meters of the mixed zone (mz_2) to the south, microcline enrichment appears between plagioclase and hornblende grains. The rock is a metadiorite to meta-quartz diorite. Some relict subophitic texture is present (fig. 4, photos 2, 3).

Mixed Zone Rock (mz_2)

A mixed rock zone occurs between the metadiorite to the north and the massive granite-gneiss to the south. Textural and compositional variations are large and nonuniform throughout this mixed zone (fig. 4, photo 4). Xenolithic dark ferromagnesian-rich clot-like blocks and smaller fragments are subangular to subrounded to rounded. They are distributed unevenly throughout the mixed rock and range in composition from granodiorite to quartz monzonite to granite. Grain sizes vary from fine to coarse. Biotite and hornblende tend to be finer grained than feldspars which are hypidioblastic; the entire mixture presents a blotchy, indefinite textural appearance. Some parts of the mixed zone rock take on a skialithic appearance where there has been considerable feldspar enrichment. The rock is a quartz-hornblende-biotite-andesine-microcline metasomite or a partially granitized and metasomatized diorite to quartz diorite. There is a possibility of a fault existing between the metadiorite and the granite-gneiss.

Granite-Gneiss

The southern limit of the area is occupied by a dense, massive, streaky granite-gneiss. Texture is granoblastic, xenoblastic-granular, generally on the fine side of medium grained with a moderate gneissic streaking. Color is pale reddish brown (10R 5/4). Ovoidal to elongate streaky groupings of fine-grained black biotite are nonuniformly sparsely distributed along the foliation and gneissic layering (fig. 4, photo 5). Size of the biotite clusters is usually no larger than 2 × 3 cm and more commonly is smaller and considerably more elongate. The rock is a muscovite-biotite-oligoclase-quartz-microcline granite-gneiss.

Figure 4. Photomicrographs of rock units

Photo 1—Granite aplite from the large dike in the central part of the area. Texture is holocrystalline, allotriomorphic-granular, fine grained (aplitic). Crossed polars, × 25.

Photo 2—Metadiorite from the northern part of the rock unit about 200 m south of the contact between Cochetopa granite-gneiss and the metadiorite unit. Hornblende, plagioclase, and quartz are visible. Crossed polars, × 25.

Photo 3—Metadiorite from the southern part of the rock unit about 200 m north of the metadiorite-mixed zone (mz_2) contact. Crossed polars, × 25.

Photo 4—Mixed zone unit (mz_2) from the southern part of the area. Note the variation in grain size present between quartz (clear), hornblende, biotite and the feldspars. Crossed polars, × 25.

Photo 5—Granite-gneiss from the southern end of the area. Note the weak planar orientation of the biotite and the elongate, sutured mosaics of clear quartz. The planar foliation trends northwest in the photograph. Crossed polars, × 25.

STRUCTURE

Lithologic boundaries and foliations in Cochetopa pluton and its metamorphic wallrocks have a dominant trend of N. 50–80° E. and dips generally greater than 70–75° SE. Contact of the pluton with the metamorphic wallrocks on the north is generally concordant but is locally discordant (fig. 1). Prior to emplacement of the pluton the quartzite wallrock was strongly deformed and migmatized. Cochetopa granite also intruded and partially reacted with a metagabbro as well as with the quartzite. A more or less continuous, narrow zone of mixing of Cochetopa Granite with quartzite and metagabbro (mz_1) is present.

Trend of the contacts and foliations of Cochetopa pluton and its wallrocks in the southern part of the area range N. 60–80° E. and dip generally steeper than 75° SE. Relatively large, more or less continuous dikes of granite pegmatite cut through the metadiorite and dip 10–50° north towards Cochetopa pluton (fig. 2). Planar foliation within the pluton is weak in its northern and central part but becomes increasingly stronger toward the contact with the metadiorite wallrock to the south.

Joints in Metamorphic Wallrocks

Schmidt equal-area net plots of poles perpendicular to joint sets in Cochetopa pluton and its metamorphic wallrocks show interesting and significant geometric differences. Joints in the metamorphic wallrocks have three dominant trends: (1) a joint set with a girdle maximum at N. 14° W. with dips varying 66° NE to 75° SW; (2) a joint set striking N. 60° E. to N. 76° E. with dips mainly 79–88° SE; and (3) a relatively flat joint set striking close to east and dipping 7–20° N. with a few joints dipping as much as 30° N. Some joint sets also dip 15–28° S. (fig. 5A). These three joint systems have formed in geometric response to the structural attitude of the varying lithologies present in the metamorphic wallrocks. The lithologic layering and formational contacts of the wallrocks have a general trend of N. 55–80° E. and a dip of 70–88° S.

Joints in Cochetopa Pluton

Joints within the Cochetopa pluton display a significant geometric and tectonic difference from those present in the metamorphic wallrocks (fig. 5B). Three sets of joints are present: (1) a major set oriented subperpendicular to perpendicular to the contact of the pluton with the metamorphic wallrocks; this set has a girdle polar maximum with a strike of N. 20° W. and dips ranging from 82° NE to 81° NW; (2) a set striking N. 50–82° E. dipping 30–45° SE; and (3) a set striking N. 42–70° E. and dipping 40–57° NW.

Geometric relation of these three joint sets to the sheetlike mode of emplacement of Cochetopa pluton suggests a genetic relationship between formation of the joint sets and emplacement of the pluton relative to its metamorphic wallrocks. The major joint set (1) is not only normal to the trend of the contact between the pluton and its wallrocks, but is also approximately normal to the general trend of the planar structures within the pluton.

A genetic interpretation of the orientation of joint sets (2) and (3) above would seem to indicate that they are marginal fissure-type joints related to movement of the magma sheet as it intruded upwards between the quartzite and metagabbro wallrocks to the north and the metadiorite to the south. Frictional drag along the solid wallrocks caused the magma to pull away from itself, and when the rock was solid enough to crack it did so in response to the internal stresses that accumulated during emplacement. The marginal fissures dip in the direction from which the magma column rose.

The apparent absence in Cochetopa pluton of the three joint

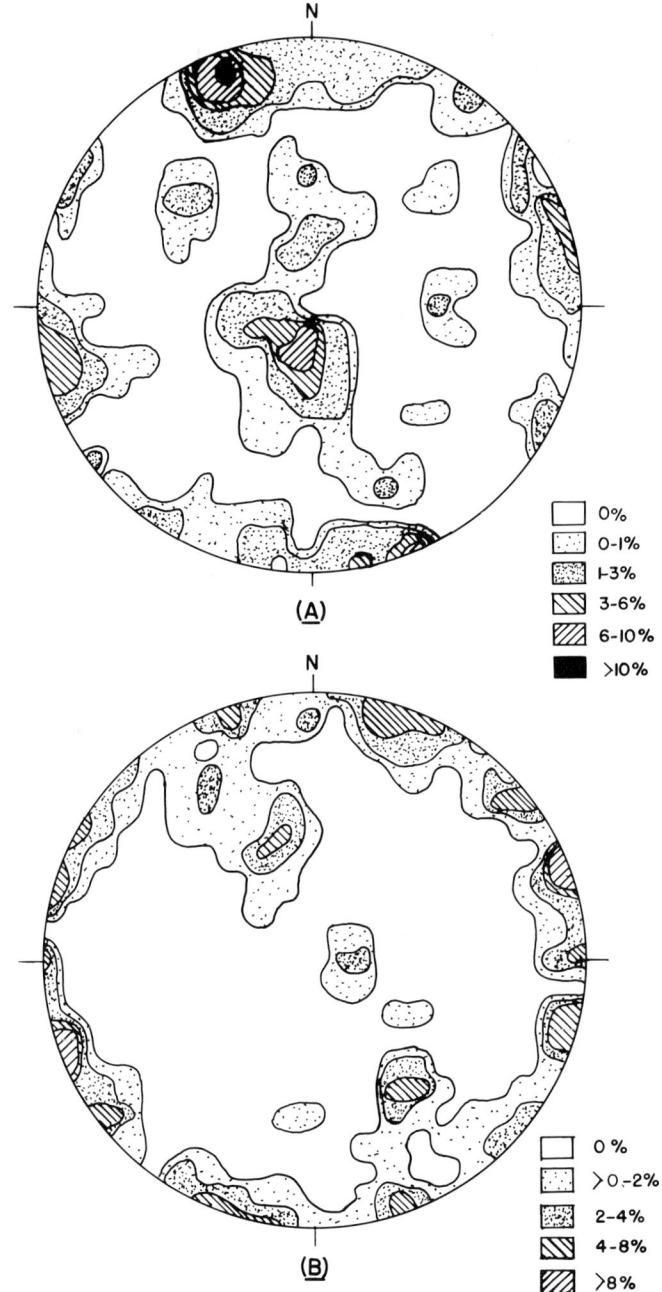

Figure 5. Petrofabric diagrams of joints in the Cochetopa Granite and its metamorphic wallrocks. A. 125 points in metamorphic wallrocks. B. 72 points in Cochetopa Granite.

sets present in the metamorphic wallrocks, and vice versa, indicates Cochetopa pluton was emplaced as a late syntectonic to possibly post-tectonic pluton during the waning stages of the Boulder Creek orogeny. Joint sets in the metamorphic wallrocks formed during the Boulder Creek orogeny and prior to emplacement of the pluton. It is believed that Cochetopa pluton then developed its own unique set of joints as it worked its way upward seeking out and following lithologic boundaries and planes of foliation of the metamorphic wallrocks.

EMPLACEMENT OF COCHETOPA PLUTON

Cochetopa pluton appears to be more lower mesozonal than catazonal, i.e., mesocatazonal, in its depth of emplacement. The granite body mainly was intruded concordantly to the structure and attitude of its metamorphic wallrocks and is an elongate, sheet-like body of undetermined length in the northeasterly direction. Thickness shows an increase from 2.2 km in the southwestern part of the pluton to 3.4 km in the northeast before it is covered by the Junction Creek Sandstone. Intense pre-batholithic folding of the quartzite unit on the northern flank of the pluton is responsible for some undulate planar and cross-cutting relationships between the granite and its wallrocks. Contact with the metadiorite on the southern flank is straight-planar and reflects the trend of the foliations in the metamorphic wallrocks.

The question of how the magma made room for itself is best answered by noting the many xenolithic inclusions of quartzite shown on Figures 1 and 2, of which about 70 percent have been mapped. Except for the large disc-shaped body of the porphyroblastic salt-and-pepper gneiss in the central part of the pluton, the xenoliths north of this body are characteristically long, narrow, septa-like inclusions of impure quartzite. These quartzite bodies show very little reaction with and minimum potash metasomatism by the surrounding Cochetopa Granite. The overall structural trend of the quartzite xenoliths is subparallel to that present in the quartzite wallrock on the north side of the pluton.

Emplacement of the magma was by forceful injection and magmatic stoping, although it was passive enough to preserve the general structural positions of the xenoliths relative to their wallrocks. The magma sheet rose slowly between the metadiorite and the quartzite units, passively yet forcefully inserting itself along planes of foliation and relict stratigraphic layering. Not only did the intrusion of granite magma completely engulf and isolate rib-like plates of the quartzite, but the emplacement of the pluton most probably made room for itself by forcefully pushing apart and opening up the many subparallel structural elements it was intruding. Evidence for shoving aside of the country rock for short distances around the pluton is hard to find because the pluton is mainly parallel to the structural trend of its metamorphic wallrocks.

Confirmative evidence that the granite magma was highly viscous and underwent high frictional drag along its wallrocks is shown by the swarm of parallel granite pegmatite dikes in the metadiorite. The dikes are fairly continuous over more than 100 m and dip 10° to 50° toward the pluton. Proximity of the pegmatite dikes to the Cochetopa pluton suggest that frictional drag of the rising magma caused a series of marginal fissure-type fractures to open up in the metadiorite wallrock and that these were readily occupied by late-stage pegmatitic solutions emanating from Cochetopa pluton.

Perhaps the strongest evidence that Cochetopa pluton is late syntectonic to possibly post-tectonic in its time of emplacement is observed in the field relations of the pegmatites to the three joint sets present in the metadiorite wallrock. It is true that the pegmatitic fluids followed the marginal fissures formed in the metadiorite wallrock, but what is more significant is that locally pegmatite dikes have departed at a sharp angle from marginal fissures and followed a pre-existing joint set. The joint set followed, in some places, belongs to that striking N. 14° W. and dipping 66° NE to 75° NW. An excellent example of this can be seen along Highway 114 in the southern part of the area. The structural relations of the granite pegmatites to the joints in the metadiorite are plainly visible in a 120-m high cliff of metadiorite.

In summary, Cochetopa Granite pluton is most probably mesocatazonal in its depth-zone style of emplacement. The evidence supporting this is as follows: (1) general concordance with the country rock structures and occurrence as a conformable sheet-like body, probably considerably attenuated; (2) exposure in a deeply eroded basement terrain of Precambrian basement rocks; (3) moderate granitization and minor migmatization in the country rock; (4) emplacement by forceful injection and magmatic stoping; (5) moderate shoving aside of the country rock for short distances around the pluton; (6) sharp contacts in the sense that aphanitic textures are absent; and (7) marginal fissure-type fracture sets, which though they are more characteristic of upper mesozonal and lower epizonal depths of emplacement, probably developed because the metamorphic country rocks were solid, thereby confirming the late syntectonic or more probably the post-tectonic age of Cochetopa pluton.

GEOCHRONOLOGY

Absolute age determinations of granitic and metamorphic wallrocks outcropping in this area have not been made. Wetherill and Bickford (1965) determined two Rb-Sr whole rock ages on granites similar to the Cochetopa Granite. Their ages were for granites exposed on Highway 50, 9.1 and 3.2 km east of the town of Parlin. Wetherill and Bickford's descriptions of the two granites closely resemble that for granite of Cochetopa pluton.

Another age determination was probably for a granite pegmatite intruding the metadiorite in the south part of the area. The Rb-Sr isochron for the whole rock samples implies emplacement of granitic to granodioritic rocks about 1650 ± 35 million years ago (Wetherill and Bickford, 1965).

Proximity of Cochetopa pluton to Precambrian basement rocks exposed in the Black Canyon of the Gunnison about 30 km northwest and the Needle Mountains area 70 km southwest lends credence to the temporal correlation of the Cochetopa pluton granite and its metamorphic wallrocks to both of these areas (fig. 6). In terms of structural position and proximity to the granite at Parlin, there is a good possibility that Cochetopa Granite pluton is also 1650 ± 35 m.y. old.

In summary, the metasedimentary wallrocks were probably first deposited as early as 1900 m.y. ago, and from 1750–1700 m.y. were involved in regional metamorphism accompanied by orogeny during the Boulder Creek orogeny (Hutchinson, 1972, 1976). Metadiorite and metagabbro are older than 1750 m.y. but younger than the metasediments. Cochetopa pluton is possibly late syntectonic but more probably slightly post-tectonic and was possibly intruded 1650 ± 35 m.y. ago.

ACKNOWLEDGMENTS

The Precambrian basement rocks exposed in the Sawtooth Mountain quadrangle were mapped by J. C. Olson and T. A. Steven (1976) of the U.S. Geological Survey. On the recommendation of J. C. Olson, the Colorado School of Mines Summer Geology Field Camp staff selected the Cochetopa pluton area as a suitable field exercise for its students. The following field camp staff members have contributed to the geological mapping: R. M. Hutchinson, Keenan Lee, R. C. Epis, L. G. Closs, G. S. Holden, T. Bultman, L. T. Grose, M. Wiltse, J. Dover, and R. Reeves. The author is grateful for the interest and encouragement of R. C. Epis to compile and write this paper. The field camp staff is greatly appreciative of the continued high level of interest and enthusiasm shown by the students while mapping the area and compiling their reports on the Cochetopa pluton and its metamorphic wallrocks.

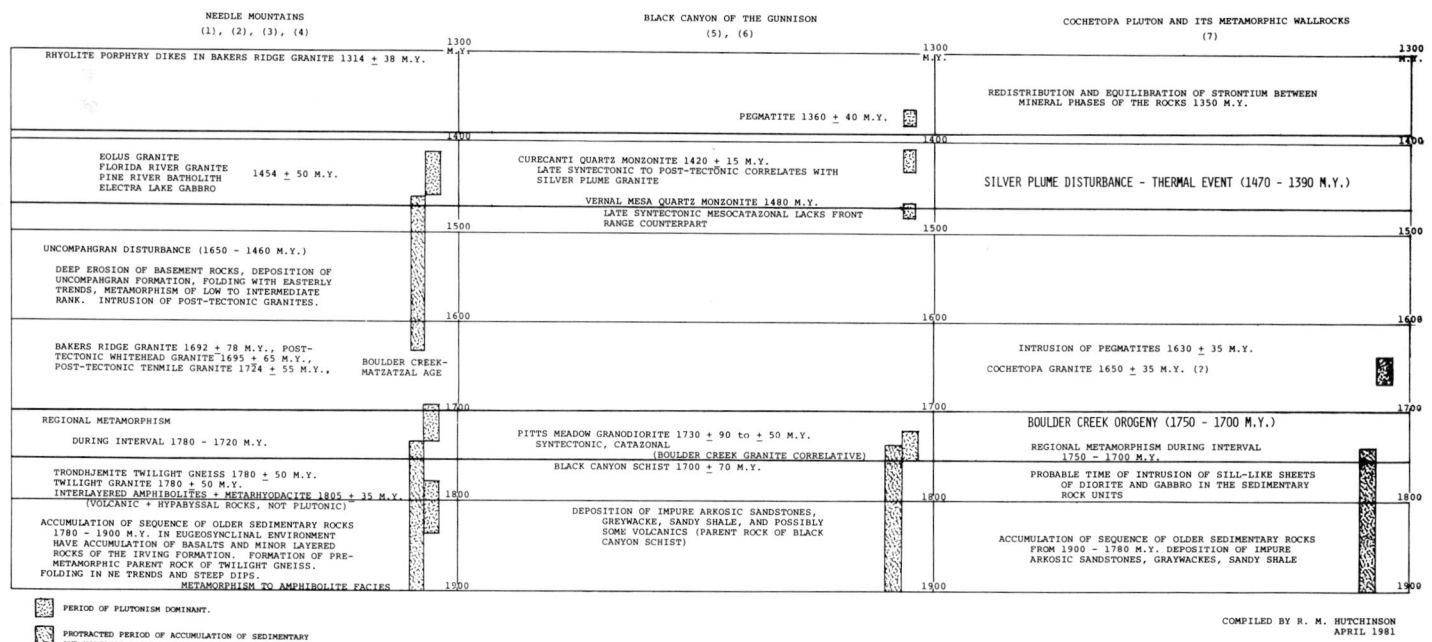

Figure 6. Geochronological correlation of Cochetopa pluton and its metamorphic wallrocks with the Black Canyon of the Gunnison and the Needle Mountains. Numbers under localities refer to references below.

REFERENCES

(1) Barker, F., 1966, Precambrian geologic history in the Needle Mountains, Colorado (abs.): Geological Society of America, Rocky Mountain Section, 19th Annual Meeting, p. 17.

(2) ———, 1969, Precambrian geology of the Needle Mountains, southwestern Colorado: U.S. Geological Survey Professional Paper 644-A.

(3) Bickford, M. E., Barker, F., Wetherill, G. W., and Lee-Hu Chin-Nan, 1967, Precambrian geochronology in the Needle Mountains, southwestern Colorado (abs.): Geological Society of America, Annual Meeting, p. 14.

(4) Silver, L. T. and Barker, F., 1968, Geochronology of the Precambrian rocks of the Needle Mountains, southwestern Colorado—Pt. 1, U-Pb zircon results (abs.): Geological Society of America Special Paper 115, p. 204–205.

(5) Hansen, W. R., 1965, The Black Canyon of the Gunnison today and yesterday: U.S. Geological Survey Bulletin 1191.

(6) Hansen, W. R. and Peterman, Z. E., 1968, Basement-rock geochronology of the Black Canyon of the Gunnison, Colorado: U.S. Geological Survey Professional Paper 600-C, p. C80–C90.

(7) Wetherill, G. W. and Bickford, M. E., 1965, Primary and metamorphic Rb-Sr chronology in central Colorado: Journal of Geophysical Research, v. 70, p. 4669–4686.

Note: Numbers refer to Figure 6.

WEST ELK VOLCANIC FIELD, GUNNISON AND DELTA COUNTIES, COLORADO

D. L. GASKILL
U.S. Geological Survey
Denver, Colorado 80225

F. E. MUTSCHLER
Eastern Washington University
Cheney, Washington 99004

and

B. L. BARTLESON
Western State College
Gunnison, Colorado 81230

INTRODUCTION

The West Elk volcanic field covers about 1,600 km² in the southern part of the West Elk Mountains (fig. 1) and ranges in elevation from about 2,100 m along the Gunnison River to 3,960 m at West Elk Peak. Tertiary volcanic deposits form a deeply dissected, south-sloping volcanic plateau whose western and northern edge is an imposing, almost continuous escarpment that culminates in the higher peaks of the Baldy Mountains. Most of the volcanic rocks were erupted locally from Oligocene intermediate-composition volcanoes, which are related in time to the larger San Juan volcanic field south of the Gunnison River (Steven and Epis, 1968; Lipman and others, 1978).

The volcanic rocks have been eroded from the northern part of the map area (fig. 2), exposing a thick section of Mesozoic and Tertiary strata intruded by many Tertiary plutons. Reports and maps of the Hayden Survey (Peale, 1876; Hayden, 1881) remain excellent first references to this region. A geologic folio (Emmons and others, 1894) covers part of the volcanic field. The southern margin of the field has been recently mapped in detail by Hedlund and Olson (1973, 1974), Hedlund (1974), and Hansen (1971). A wilderness study by Gaskill and others (1977) covers the northern part of the area. Perhaps the best general discussion of the geology is in Hansen (1965).

Most of the volcanic field lies within Gunnison National Forest. Oak brush and scattered stands of pine and fir predominate to elevations of about 2,600 m. Spruce, fir, and aspen are the dominant forest communities at higher elevations. About 6 percent of the area is above timberline. Erosion has removed all but scattered remnants of the West Elk volcanic field east of the map area, has exposed many of the intrusive structures, and has cut canyons many hundreds of meters deep into the volcanic pile. Glaciation has sculptured the higher peaks and valleys.

STRUCTURE AND GEOLOGIC HISTORY

The West Elk volcanic field is near the crest of the late Paleozoic Uncompahgre highland (Hansen, 1965) and on the flank of a later Laramide structure, the Gunnison uplift (Kelley, 1955). The Gunnison uplift is bounded on the south by the Cimarron fault, which displaced Mesozoic strata 800 m or more down to the south in Laramide time (Olson and others, 1968; Hansen, 1971). The rise of the Uncompahgre highland resulted in removal of the Paleozoic strata from this area and the gradual reduction of the highland to a peneplain eroded across Precambrian crystalline rocks (the Uncompahgran unconformity of Hansen, 1971). During Late Jurassic and Cretaceous time, about 2,200 m of continental and marine sedimentary rocks accumulated on the beveled Uncompahgran surface. Near the end of the Cretaceous and during Paleocene time, the Gunnison uplift (the area of the present Gunnison River valley) and the Sawatch Range rose to form a horseshoe-shaped upland that shed alluvial debris (Wasatch and younger strata) north and west into the Piceance basin. By early Oligocene time, erosion had greatly reduced the Sawatch Range and had cut a relatively smooth surface across the Gunnison uplift. The tilted edges of Mesozoic and Tertiary strata on the north flank of the uplift were beveled, reexposing Precambrian basement rocks along the crest (Hansen, 1965, p. 21, fig. 7). Thus, two or more major unconformities underlie the West Elk volcanic field.

In early-middle Oligocene time, granodiorite plutons were emplaced in the Elk Range, Ruby Range, and the West Elk Mountains.

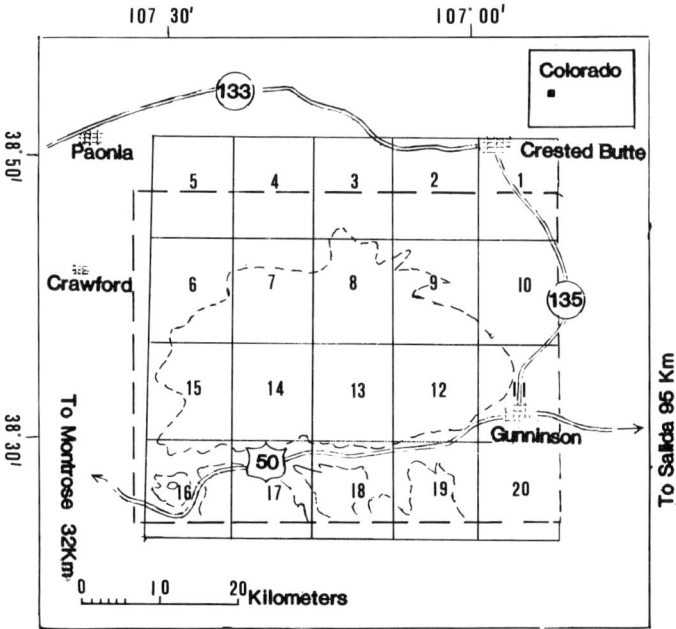

QUADRANGLE NAMES
1. Crested Butte
2. Mount Axtell
3. Anthracite Range
4. West Beckwith Peak
5. Minnesota Pass
6. Mount Guero
7. Big Soap Park
8. West Elk Peak
9. Squirrel Creek
10. Flat Top
11. Gunnison
12. McIntosh Mtn.
13. West Elk Peak SW
14. Little Soap Park
15. Lazy F Ranch
16. Currecanti Needle
17. Sapinero
18. Carpenter Ridge
19. Big Mesa
20. Iris NW

Figure 1. Index map showing area of the West Elk volcanic field (dashed lines), and 7½-minute U.S. Geological Survey quadrangle map coverage.

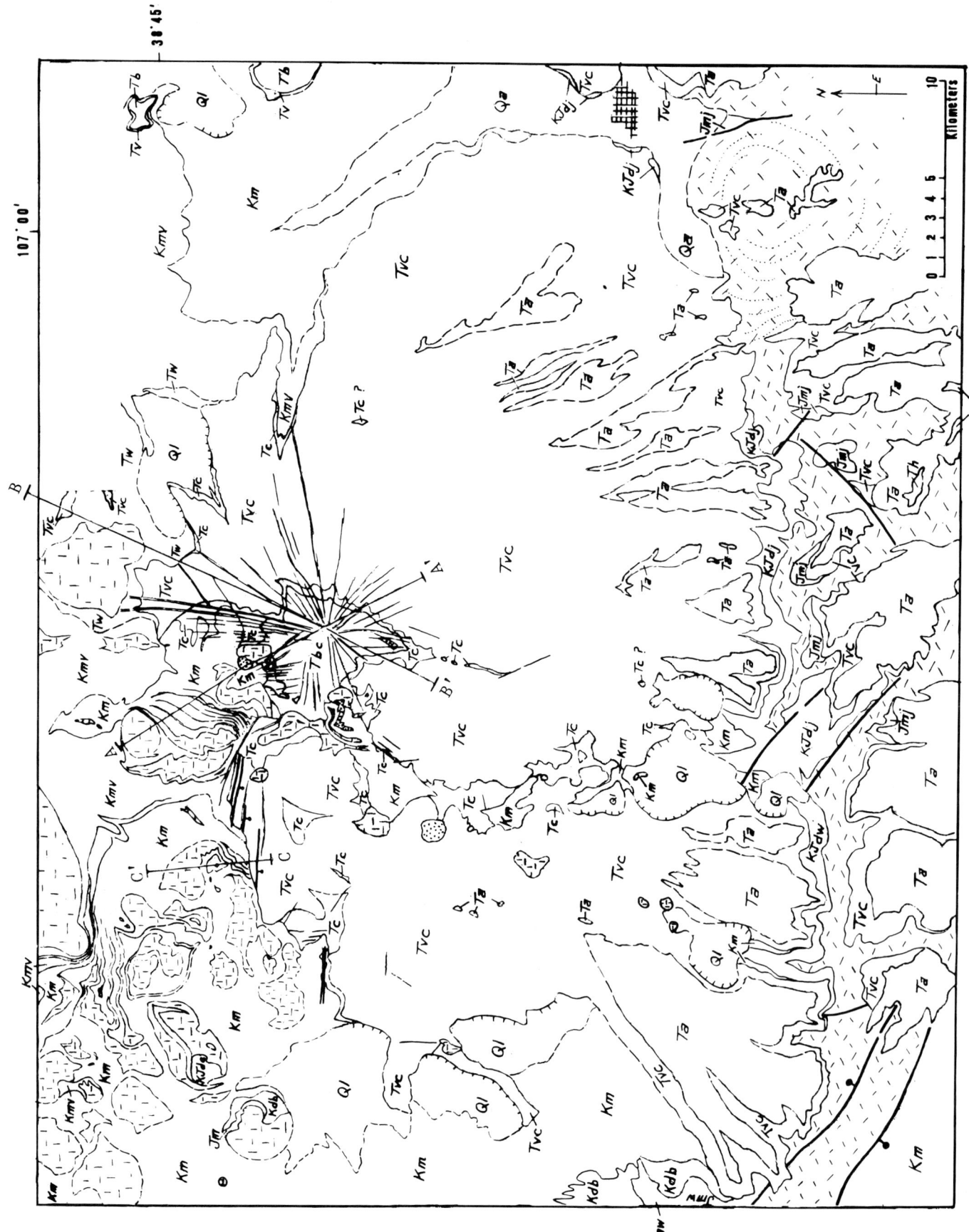

Figure 2. Geologic sketch map of the West Elk volcanic field and vicinity, Gunnison County, Colorado.

WEST ELK VOLCANIC FIELD

Explanation: Figures 2, 3, and 4. (West Elk volcanic field)

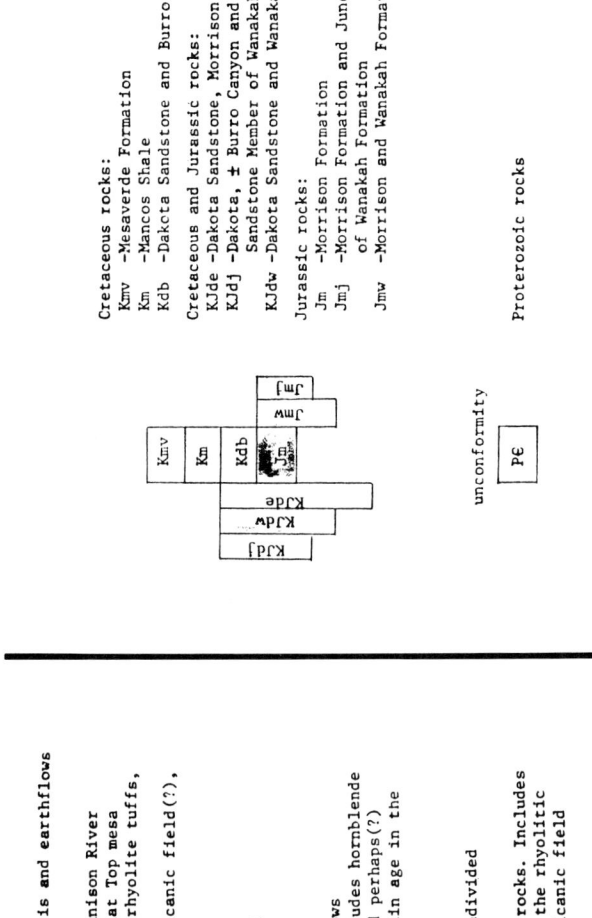

Quaternary landslides, and associated debris and earthflows

Miocene rocks:
Th — Hinsdale Formation south of the Gunnison River
Tb — Basalt flows on Red Mountain and Flat Top mesa
Tv — Volcanic conglomeratic sandstones, rhyolite tuffs, and boulder gravels
    — Rhyolite intrusions in West Elk volcanic field(?), or in adjacent areas

Oligocene rocks:

Ta — Ash-flow tuff formations, undivided

West Elk Breccia:
Tvc — Volcaniclastic facies. f= lava flows
    — Granodioritic intrusive rocks. Includes hornblende granodiorite and dacitic rocks, and perhaps(?) the rhyolitic intrusives of uncertain age in the West Elk volcanic field
Tc — Chaotic facies
Tbc — Basal cone facies
Tu — Volcanic rocks of Oligocene age, undivided

— Hornblende granodioritic intrusive rocks. Includes rhyolitic sills, and might include the rhyolitic plutons exposed in the West Elk volcanic field

Eocene and Paleocene(?) Wasatch Formation

unconformity

Cretaceous rocks:
Kmv — Mesaverde Formation
Km — Mancos Shale
Kdb — Dakota Sandstone and Burro Canyon Formations, undivided

Cretaceous and Jurassic rocks:
KJde — Dakota Sandstone, Morrison and Entrada(?) Formations
KJdj — Dakota, ± Burro Canyon and Morrison and Junction Creek Sandstone Member of Wanakah Formation
KJdw — Dakota Sandstone and Wanakah Formations, undivided

Jurassic rocks:
Jm — Morrison Formation
Jmj — Morrison Formation and Junction Creek Sandstone Member of Wanakah Formation
Jmw — Morrison and Wanakah Formations, undivided

Proterozoic rocks

unconformity

———?——— Contact, dashed where approximately located, querried where doubtful

Sedimentary formations   Volcaniclastic layered deposits   Lava flows

Generalized attitude of layered rocks

Dikes

Fault, bar and ball on downthrown side

∼∼∼Kmv∼∼∼Kmv∼∼∼   ∼∼∼Km∼∼∼Km∼∼∼

Inferred southern edge of beveled Mesaverde strata under the West Elk volcanic field

Inferred southern edge of beveled Mancos Shale under the West Elk volcanic field

Landslide scarp

Dry hole drilled for oil

Prospect

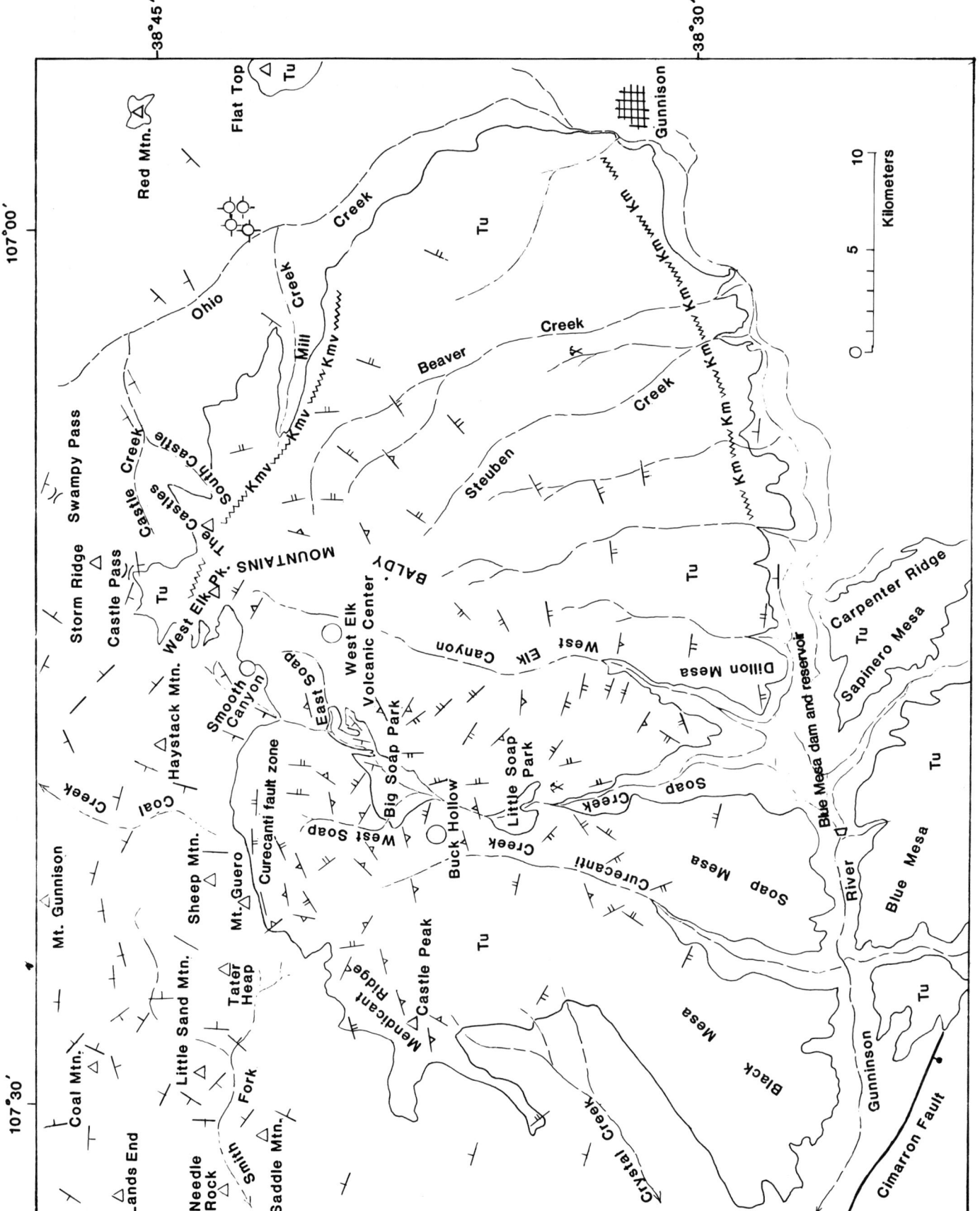

Figure 3. Map showing location of geographic features mentioned in text, and general attitude of layered rock units in the West Elk volcanic field and vicinity, Gunnison County, Colorado.

Many of these plutons probably vented, but volcanic ejecta are preserved only in the southern part of the West Elk Mountains and adjacent areas where they form the West Elk Breccia. The West Elk Breccia was erupted from numerous fissures and composite volcanoes in the area. Episodic volcanism is indicated by interbedded tuffs and gravel, and by numerous unconformities in the volcanic deposits. Potassium-argon dates in this region suggest that the West Elk Breccia and the associated granodiorite plutons are about 29–34 m.y. old (Lipman and others, 1969; Obradovich and others, 1969; Lipman and others, 1978). The southern part of the volcanic field is overlain by Oligocene ashflow tuffs erupted from the San Juan volcanic field.

The volcanic field is transected, in part, by the southwest-trending Ruby Range intrusive zone and the westerly trending Curecanti fault zone (Gableman and Boyer, 1960). These structures seem to intersect in the vicinity of the West Elk volcanic center (fig. 3). Both fracture zones are intruded by dikes that cut rocks of the West Elk volcanic field. The Ruby Range fractures seem to have been conduits for both the Storm Ridge laccolith and the West Elk volcanic center and its radial dike swarm. The Curecanti zone may be several kilometers wide, is adjacent to numerous laccolithic structures, and possibly reflects subsidence due to ejection of volcanic material.

Figures 2, 3 and 4 illustrate some of the major structural features in the West Elk Mountain region. The most conspicuous structures and rock bodies are the laccolithic mountains. Some nearly bell-shaped laccoliths have steep to nearly vertical contacts (fig. 5). Most are asymmetrical wedges having gently to steeply dipping strata overlying one or more sides, and ruptured, steeply upturned strata along the steeper face. Field relations indicate that some were fed by dikes and others by vertical pipe-like conduits. Some may be "cedar-tree structures" intruding different stratigraphic horizons (Corry, 1976). Both the roofs and floors of the laccoliths locally transect the sedimentary strata. The igneous contacts commonly follow bedding planes for a distance, but intrude along joints, fractures, folds, or bedding irregularities to higher horizons. For example, the roof of the Marcellina laccolith, north of the map area, transects more than 300 m of upper Mesaverde strata in a horizontal distance of 3.2 km. Positioning and cross-cutting relationships suggest that some laccolithic bodies were emplaced after deformation of the strata had started. Details of individual laccoliths are discussed in Peale (1877) and Cross (1894).

Figure 5. Tater Heap laccolith showing steeply dipping flatirons of indurated Mancos Shale along northwestern perimeter of the intrusion. The laccolith is composed of hornblende granodiorite.

Laccoliths intercalated with myriad sills intrude all the sedimentary formations, and some seem to intrude the volcanics of the West Elk field. At least two laccoliths (Saddle and Little Sand Mountains) intrude Jurassic strata at or near the Precambrian contact,

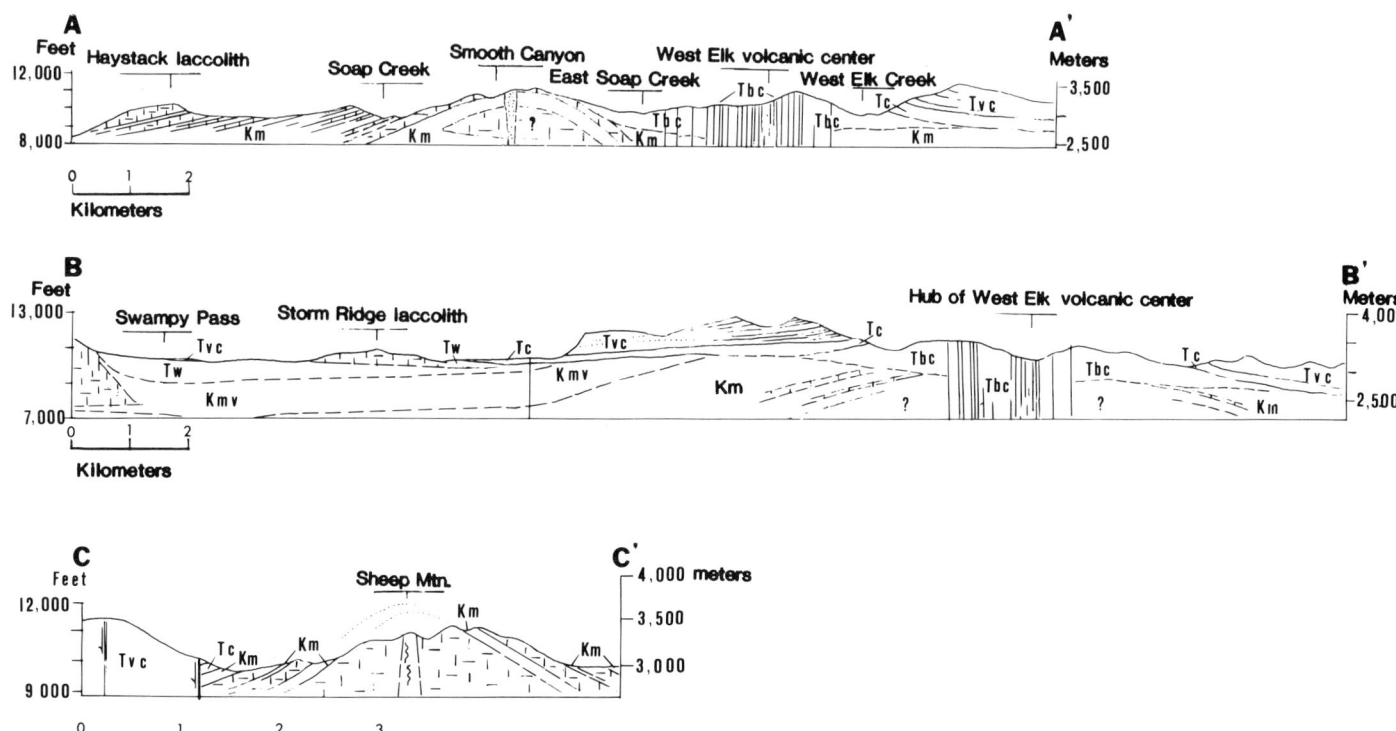

Figure 4. Cross sections through the West Elk volcanic center and Sheep Mountain (see Fig. 2 for locations).

Figure 6. Laccoliths intruding Mancos Shale. Mount Guero (right), Mount Gunnison on the horizon. View northeast from Mendicant Ridge at the northwestern edge of the West Elk volcanic field.

but most of the laccoliths are emplaced in the Mancos Shale. The largest intrude the Mesaverde and Wasatch Formations. Many are more than a thousand meters thick. The largest, Mount Gunnison (fig. 6), is exposed over an area of about 42 km^2 and has relief of nearly 1,830 m. Most of the laccoliths thin into sills on one or more sides. They commonly are surrounded by numerous sills and smaller laccolithic bodies. In general, only a thin zone of baked or indurated strata, a few meters thick, overlies the roof and flanks, but locally, the sedimentary rocks in contact with laccoliths are metamorphosed to hornfels, quartzite, and anthracite. In contrast, the small hypabyssal stocks of the Ruby Range are surrounded by broad metamorphic aureoles, 0.8 km or more wide, that grade outward from metasomatized and silicified metasedimentary rocks to slightly baked shales.

The laccoliths consist of granodiorite porphyries that contain phenocrysts of plagioclase, hornblende, biotite, augite, or hypersthene. Some contain a few rounded phenocrysts of quartz and a few large phenocrysts of potassium feldspar. Most of the laccoliths north and east of the map area characteristically contain large phenocrysts of quartz and potassium feldspar.

The most unusual structural feature shown on Figures 2, 3, and 4 is the volcanic dome and radial dike swarm of the West Elk volcanic center. The dome consists of intrusive and basal extrusive rocks at the core of the major eruptive center in the area. The apex of the dome, at the hub of the dike swarm, probably overlies a buried stock similar to those exposed in the adjacent Ruby Range (Cross, 1894; Godwin and Gaskill, 1964; Kramer, 1972).

Several hornblende granodiorite bodies intrude Mancos Shale and may intrude the volcanic pile along Soap, West Soap, and Curecanti Creeks (figs. 2, 3). These intrusives are very similar in composition and texture to most of the laccoliths and sills along the northwest margin of the volcanic field. Several are associated with dikes of the same composition. Some are sills in the Mancos Shale; others are discordant or laccolithic bodies that have spread out at or near the base of the volcanics. Stocks or laccoliths of hornblende granodiorite northeast of Big Soap Park and at the head of East Soap Creek and Smooth Canyon (fig. 3) intrude Mancos Shale and may be older than the West Elk volcanics. The body near Big Soap Park is locally argillized and contains xenoliths of Precambrian rock. The body at the head of Smooth Canyon overlies Mancos Shale and is brecciated. An altered, brecciated, granodiorite intrusion and associated dikes intrude tuff breccias south of Castle Peak on Mendicant Ridge (fig. 3). The intrusion contains large phenocrysts of hornblende (as much as 1 cm in length); it appears to be a very near surface vent for the tuff breccias.

Sheep Mountain, at the head of Coal Creek and North Smith Fork, is a distinctive symmetrical laccolith or stock surrounded by thick sills and laccoliths in the upper part of folded Mancos Shale (fig. 4). The central pluton consists of an inner, unaltered core of vertically flow-banded porphyry surrounded by altered and mineralized porphyritic granodiorite. The upper part of the pluton is argillized to light gray or white and is stained reddish brown to yellowish orange by oxidized disseminated pyrite.

The cluster of laccoliths and sills in the northwestern part of the area causes a broad magnetic high (J. G. Rosenbaum, *in* Gaskill and others, 1977) that trends north-northeast across Coal Mountain. A body of intrusive porphyry exposed on the north flank of Coal Mountain has domed and hornfelsed overlying Mancos Shale. Both the upper part of the intrusion and the overlying shale are pyritized.

Several rhyolitic plutons are exposed in the area. One is a plug-like body of argillized felsite at the head of Smooth Canyon (fig. 4). A yellowish-gray, slightly pyritized body of rhyolite is exposed in volcaniclastic breccias at Buck Hollow. This rhyolite contains traces of molybdenum and other metals. Another body of rhyolite intrudes Mancos Shale and core rocks of the West Elk center in West Elk Canyon.

The age of these rhyolites is not known. They may be the source of a biotite-rich, crystal pumice tuff that locally overlies basal lava flows of the chaotic facies of the West Elk Breccia in Mill and South Castle Creek canyons; or the rhyolites may be of Miocene age and correlate with the Hinsdale Formation.

STRATIGRAPHY

Table 1 summarizes the stratigraphic sequence. Precambrian rocks underlie the Tertiary volcanics along the Gunnison River and the southern perimeter of the volcanic field (Hunter, 1925; Olson and others, 1968; Hedlund and Olson, 1973, 1974; Hedlund, 1974). Elsewhere, Jurassic, Cretaceous, and Tertiary sedimentary rocks underlie the volcanics. The Jurassic Entrada Sandstone overlaps the Uncompahgran Precambrian surface west of the volcanic field (Hansen, 1965) and may extend northeastward under the northern part of the field. The Wanakah Formation thins eastward over the Entrada and Precambrian surface before wedging out in the vicinity of the Blue Mesa Dam (Hansen, 1965). The Junction Creek Member of the Wanakah Sandstone and the succeeding Morrison Formation, Burro Canyon Formation, and Dakota Sandstone overlay the Uncompahgran surface, but have been removed locally by prevolcanic erosion along the Gunnison River. Thick Mancos Shale underlies all but the southern margin of the volcanic field where it has been largely removed by pre-volcanic erosion. The Mesaverde Formation underlies a small area of volcanic rocks along the northern edge of the field east of Coal Creek and locally overlies the west flank of Coal Mountain. The Tertiary Wasatch Formation underlies volcanic rocks in the Castle and Pass Creek drainage basins and at Castle and Swampy Passes. Unconsolidated deposits of Quaternary age in the area include extensive talus aprons, active rock streams, and minor glacial, alluvial, and lacustrine deposits. Widespread landslides and associated mud and debris flows cover many square kilometers along the western and northeastern edge of the volcanic field, along the lower parts of Soap and West Elk Creeks, and the upper reaches of the Black Canyon.

Table 1. Generalized stratigraphic section in the West Elk volcanic field and vicinity, Gunnison County, Colorado

Age		Stratigraphic units		Description		Approximate maximum thickness in meters
Tertiary	Miocene	Hinsdale Formation and rhyolite intrusions(?)		Basalt flows, basaltic tuff, volcanic sandstones and conglomerates, rhyolitic pumice tuff, and boulder gravels		150
	Oligocene	Carpenter Ridge Tuff		A sequence of latitic welded and non-welded ash-flow tuffs with interbedded discontinuous gravel, and tuffaceous gravel deposits		70
		Fish Canyon Tuff				120
		Sapinero Mesa Tuff				160
		Dillon Mesa Tuff				55
		Blue Mesa Tuff				75
		West Elk Breccia	Volcaniclastic facies	Rhyodacite Granodiorite-dacite Rhyolite(?) Andesite Diorite	See text for description of volcanic rocks	550
			Chaotic facies			400
			Basal cone facies			600
	Eocene and Paleocene(?)	Wasatch Formation		Variegated sandstone, siltstone, shale, mudstone, conglomeratic sandstone, and conglomerate		390
Late Cretaceous		Mesaverde Formation	Ohio Creek Member	Feldspathic, conglomeratic sandstone, sandstone, siltstone, shale, and minor carbonaceous shale		670
			Undifferentiated unit, Paonia Shale Mbr., and Bowie Shale Mbr.	Sandstone, siltstone, shale, carbonaceous shale and coal		
			Rollins Sandstone Mbr.	Basal regressive marine sandstone		30
		Mancos Shale	upper member	Mostly gray, laminated, silty, marine shale. Transitional zone at top includes thin beds of sandy limestone, and carbonaceous shale. Several thin to massive sandstone beds in upper half of formation		1,300
			Niobrara Member	Includes a basal limestone unit equivalent to the Fort Hayes Mbr. of the Niobrara Fm. of eastern Colorado, overlain by a limy shale unit equivalent to the Smokey Hill Mbr. of the Niobrara Fm. of eastern Colorado		
			Juan Lopez Member	Calcareous shale and calcareous sandstone		
			lower member	Interbedded shale, siltstone, sandstone, and limestone of Benton age		
Late(?) Cretaceous		Dakota Sandstone		Thin- to thick-bedded quartzose sandstone, carbonaceous shale and silty sandstone. Generally a thin chert and quartz pebble conglomerate at base		60
Early Cretaceous		Burro Canyon Formation		Sandstone, shale, and conglomeratic sandstone		
Late Jurassic		Morrison Formation		Varicolored claystone, sandstone, siltstone. Locally contains limestone and pebble conglomerate		130
			Junction Creek Sandstone Member	Fine-grained, friable, eolian sandstone		54
		Wanakah Formation		Silty mudstone, gypsiferous sandstone and mudstone, cherty and silty limestone		45
		Entrada Sandstone		Fine to very coarse-grained, medium- to thick-bedded quartz sandstone with a few shale partings. Locally conglomeratic at base		0–(?)
Proterozoic Y and X				Crystalline metamorphic and plutonic rocks		

VOLCANIC AND ASSOCIATED IGNEOUS ROCKS

"The hills west of Ohio Creek are composed mainly of breccia . . . eroded in the most fantastic fashion. The breccia is stratified, and there are huge castle-like forms, abrupt walls, spires, and towers."

Peale (1876, p. 168, 169)

The volcanic formations in the West Elk field include the Oligocene West Elk Breccia (Emmons and others, 1894), Oligocene ash-flow tuffs (Olson and others, 1968), and patches of the Miocene Hinsdale Formation (Larsen and Cross, 1956; Olson and others, 1968). The Hinsdale consists of basalt flows and interbedded fluvial and pyroclastic materials.

West Elk Breccia

Most of the volcanic rocks are included in a single formation, the West Elk Breccia. This formation was derived in large part from the West Elk volcanic center, a deeply eroded, composite stratovolcano in the north-central part of the West Elk volcanic field. Other volcanic vents are indicated by hypabassal intrusions, extrusive domes, and local accumulations of steeply dipping, near-vent breccias south and west of the West Elk volcanic center. Eroded remnants of the West Elk Breccia are as thick as about 1,200 m. They overlie an eroded surface of Mesozoic and Tertiary strata, and locally overlie Precambrian rocks along the Gunnison River. Volcanic activity in the area is inferred to have begun with extrusion of lava domes (?), explosion breccias, and lava flows that formed part of a basal cone facies. Initial outflow aprons surrounding the basal cone facies are largely altered lava flows and tuff breccias. The greater part of the formation, however, consists of coarse, fragmental, layered breccia and a heterogeneous mélange of tuff breccia that was erupted explosively from intermediate-composition volcanoes. The formation also includes numerous andesitic to rhyodacitic lava flows, volcanic sands and conglomerates, minor ash layers, and discontinuous gravel deposits. In the northern part of the volcanic field, these deposits were widely intruded by porphyritic feeder dikes of several generations at various eruptive levels. The youngest and least altered dikes extend to the eroded top of the formation. Some of the dikes are wider than 100 m, longer than 9.7 km, and are exposed over a vertical range of more than 900 m. The West Elk Breccia has been tentatively subdivided into three facies.

Basal cone facies

The oldest and most altered volcanic rocks in the area form a basal cone unit (Tbc, fig. 2) of porphyritic, massive and brecciated, dark-gray, brown, grayish-green, red, and purple rocks of basaltic andesite, microgranular diorite, and quartz diorite (SiO_2 = 55–58 percent). This central intrusive-extrusive complex extends from West Elk Creek on the east to about Soap Creek on the west. It appears to locally underlie arched Mancos strata along the northwestern perimeter of the West Elk center. Some of these core rocks may represent lava domes and explosion breccias. The diorites probably are intrusive. The facies is widely propylitized, oxidized, locally pyritized, silicified, and laced with early mafic and later intermediate dikes. It forms a domal pile of core rocks at the West Elk volcanic center that is more than 600 m thick, although greatly reduced by erosion. There is little evidence of extrusive fabric in these core rocks.

The general symmetry of the core rocks at the West Elk center indicates that the sedimentary strata were initially domed by the dioritic magma. The granodiorite bodies along the western edge of the center intrude basal lava flows and tuff breccias, and perhaps the core rocks. They probably moved upward through narrow conduits and spread outward by lifting the near-surface strata and basal volcanics.

Chaotic facies

Altered extrusive rocks (Tc, fig. 2), associated with the initial eruptions at the West Elk center, overlie the core rocks (Tbc) and folded Mancos Shale on the periphery of the center (figs. 2, 4). These basal volcanics appear to underlie all of the northern part of the volcanic field, and are locally exposed elsewhere in the area. They extend outward over the pre-volcanic surface and form a mélange of propylitized and silicified lava flows, flow breccias, and tuff breccias that were locally fed by distinctive, dense, greenish-gray and brown siliceous dikes and dikes of intrusive breccia. These dikes are truncated at the top of the chaotic facies by an erosional surface.

Chaotic facies form a domal pile more than 400 m thick at the northwest edge of the volcanic field. Similar exposures on the northwest side of Little Soap Park are about 360 m thick. These and other exposures of pervasively altered chaotic facies intruded by igneous bodies, are shown on Figures 2 and 3 along lower Soap and West Soap Creeks and elsewhere, and seem to represent secondary eruptive centers. Where the base can be seen, or inferred, the basal extrusive rocks overlie Mancos Shale, except in a few places along the northern edge of the field, where they overlie Mesaverde and Wasatch strata.

Volcaniclastic facies

The volcaniclastic facies of the West Elk Breccia consists generally of gently dipping, crudely layered tuff breccias, local ash beds, laharic breccias, lava flows, minor tuffaceous conglomerate and epiclastic deposits. The breccias generally show large-scale stratification due to alternation of coarse, blocky, and fine-grained breccia. The volcanic fragments are generally angular and poorly sorted, and some are as much as 3 m across. The breccia beds generally dip away from the volcanic centers and are more steeply

Figure 7. Hoodoos in volcaniclastic facies of the West Elk Breccia. View west from north ridge of Mill Creek canyon. West Elk Peak in distance, Castle View Peak on right.

inclined near vents. Most of the volcaniclastic material in the southern and southeastern part of the field seem to represent a sequence of volcanic mudflows or laharic breccias (Van Houten, 1957; Olson and others, 1968; Hedlund and Olson, 1973, 1974; Hedlund, 1974).

Tuff and tuffaceous conglomerate (as much as 100 m or more thick) are interbedded with, or overlie, the laharic breccias locally in the southern part of the field and may represent air-fall tuff reworked by streams. The conglomerates contain well-rounded cobbles and boulders of Precambrian rocks, quartzite, hypabyssal porphyries, and volcanic rocks (Hedlund and Olson, 1973; Hansen, 1971).

The volcaniclastic facies has a maximum thickness of more than 500 m and contains the largest volume of volcanic material in the West Elk volcanic field. The facies overlaps basal cone extrusive (chaotic) facies near volcanic centers, but extends many kilometers to the south and southeast beyond the limits of the chaotic facies. Lava flows in the volcaniclastic facies diminish in number and thickness outward from the West Elk volcanic center, whereas the proportion of laharic and epiclastic material increases outward. The volcaniclastic rocks are petrographically similar to the flows and breccias in the basal cone unit. Locally in the southwestern part of the field (on Black Mesa), this unit contains welded and nonwelded ash-flow tuffs, as much as 60 m thick (Hansen, 1971). Along the Gunnison River, discontinuous gravel deposits containing pebbles and cobbles of Precambrian and Mesozoic rocks overlie an irregular, channeled surface eroded on underlying Mesozoic strata and Precambrian basement rocks.

The volcaniclastic facies thins southward, away from the West Elk center. The facies is locally absent, or as much as 200 m thick along the Gunnison River, where it locally overlies Mancos Shale, the Dakota and Burro Canyon Formations, Junction Creek Sandstone Member of the Wanakah Formation, and Precambrian rocks. Thick deposits of West Elk volcaniclastic material are present 9 or more kilometers south of the Gunnison River in the Carpenter Ridge quadrangle (Hedlund and Olson, 1973).

North and east of the West Elk volcanic center, the volcaniclastic facies can be subdivided into four or more mappable units separated by conspicuous unconformities. Each unit seems to represent a discrete eruptive interval represented by many individual or gradational volcaniclastic layers, consisting of alternating fine fragmental and coarse blocky tuff breccias, thin ash beds, lapilli tuffs, and many sharp depositional breaks and minor erosional disconformities. Most of the volcaniclastic layers are tuff breccias containing angular to subrounded clasts in a crystal-fragment matrix of the same color and composition. Individual layers and units are dominantly composed of one rock type.

A distinctive basal unit of the volcaniclastic facies, about 90 m thick, locally overlies basal lava flows of the chaotic facies along South Castle Creek and Mill Creek. It is composed of greenish-gray and yellowish-brown sands, pumice tuff, and thin lava flows. The unit may represent nonwelded ash-flow tuffs, pyroclastic breccia flows, and base-surge material (fig. 8; Table 2).

Some exotic pebbles and boulders of Precambrian granite; Paleozoic sandstone, limestone, quartzite, marble, and chert; Tertiary hypabyssal porphyries, and densely welded, eutaxitic crystal tuff are present in channel-fill deposits cut in chaotic facies in the South Castle Creek and Mill Creek valleys; they are mixed with ash and tuffaceous debris overlying Wasatch beds at the base of the volcaniclastic facies on Castle Pass. The exotic pebbles and boulders were probably derived from the Elk Range northeast of the area.

Figure 8. Angular unconformity in volcaniclastic facies of the West Elk Breccia at the head of Soap Creek and Soap Basin. Volcaniclastic layers and lava flows dip northeasterly away from the West Elk volcanic center. Large dacite dike in foreground intrudes the volcanic rocks. View south. West Elk Peak on the far left.

ASH-FLOW FORMATIONS

Following the eruption of the West Elk Breccia, and after erosion had planed the West Elk surface, a sequence of rhyolitic to quartz latite ash-flow tuffs of late Oligocene age blanketed the southern part of the area and the surrounding region (Olson and others, 1968; Steven and Lipman, 1976). These tuffs erupted from calderas in the San Juan Mountains. They generally thin northward, accompanied by a diminution in the degree of welding (Olson and

Figure 9. The Castles, erosional remnants of the West Elk Breccia along the northeast edge of the West Elk volcanic field. Cliff at base (chaotic facies) consists of varicolored and pervasively altered, silicified lava flows cut by feeder dikes. Light-colored beds of friable volcanic sandstones (base surge material?) interbedded with lapilli tuff (nonwelded ash-flow tuff?), lenses of conglomerate (or pyroclastic breccia flows?), and a few thin, brecciated lava flows overlie an erosional surface at top of the chaotic facies. The Castles are composed of layered crystal-tuff breccias. View west from South Castle Creek valley. Photo by W. T. Lee (1912, plate 12B) from a glass-plate negative.

Table 2. Measured section of tuffaceous, sandy beds in the basal part of the volcaniclastic facies, NW¼ Section 19, T. 15 S., R. 87 W., South Castle Creek valley.

Thickness in meters	Unit
30.0	1. Tuff breccias and tuffaceous conglomerates(?), or pyroclastic flow breccias: light brown, yellowish, and bluish-green tuff breccias, altered lapilli pumice tuffs, and interbedded, channeled, tuffaceous sands and conglomerates(?)
10.0	2. Brecciated lava flow: reddened zone at base
20.0	3. Interbedded tuffaceous, conglomeratic sandstone and crystal lapilli tuff: channeled or wind-furrowed(?) sandstone like unit 4, with andesitic pebbles, cobbles, and boulders in coarse-grained, discontinuous layers, and yellowish to greenish-gray tuff
9.2–16.0	4. Tuffaceous sandstone and conglomerate(?), yellowish-brown and greenish-gray, friable, well-sorted, fine to coarse-grained, with irregular layers of sub-rounded to sub-angular andesitic fragments that may represent pyroclastic material
5.7	5. Interbedded lava and tuff breccia: dark-gray to red and green brecciated lava(?) flows, and yellowish to greenish-gray, altered tuff breccias
1.9	6. Crystal pumice tuff, light-greenish-gray, yellowish and bluish-green, biotite- and sanidine(?)-rich, contains some heulandite
5.0	7. Tuffaceous sandstone: similar to unit 10, light-greenish-gray, yellowish and brownish-green, friable, sorted, angular-grained; slope mostly covered
9.0	8. Crystal pumice tuff: light-greenish-gray and white, fine- to coarse-grained andesitic fragments, highly altered
0.6	9. Lapilli crystal tuff: similar to unit 11, altered, contains small andesitic and vitrophyric fragments, and Precambrian granite(?) fragments
4.5	10. Tuffaceous sandstone: pinkish-brown and bluish-green, friable, well-sorted, very fine- to fine-grained, with altered biotite and sanidine(?); slope mostly covered
0.6	11. Crystal, nonwelded, pumice ash-flow(?) tuff: white to pinkish-brown and light-bluish-gray with euhedral crystals of biotite, sanidine(?), hornblende, and quartz. Pumice locally altered to montmorillonite

Base of section (unit 11) overlies basal lava flows of the chaotic facies

others, 1968). They form resistant, jointed, vertical cliffs capping the mesas and tributary divides along the Gunnison River. Typically, they "grade upward from a discontinuous nonweld base through a black or dark-brown vitrophyric zone, then a densely welded to partly welded devitrified zone, to a poorly welded to nonwelded top" (Olson and others, 1968, p. 9, 11–13). According to Olson and others (1968), boulder gravel a few meters thick underlies each ash flow, and interlayers with the Carpenter Ridge Tuff. Well-rounded pebbles, cobbles, and boulders were derived from the Morrison, Dakota, and Burro Canyon Formations, and from Precambrian rocks presumed to have come from the Sawatch Range. The ash-flows have been divided into five formations briefly summarized, from oldest to youngest, as follows (Olson and others, 1968; Hansen, 1971; Hedlund and Olson, 1973, 1974):

Blue Mesa Tuff

The Blue Mesa Tuff forms nearly continuous outcrops along both sides of the Gunnison River from Black Mesa eastward to Dillon Mesa. It consists mostly of densely welded and devitrified tuff (as much as 75 m thick), overlain by several meters of soft, nonwelded air-fall(?) and water-laid tuff. It was probably erupted from the Lost Lake caldera (Lipman, 1976; Steven and Lipman, 1976).

Dillon Mesa Tuff

The Dillon Mesa Tuff consists typically of nonwelded to moderately welded pumiceous tuff (as much as 24 m thick) and discontinuous thin beds of pumice tuff breccia (as much as 12 m thick). Locally, about 15 m of gravel, mostly derived from the West Elk Mountains, forms the basal part of the formation. The tuff was derived from the Uncompahgre caldera (Lake City area, San Juan volcanic field) about 28 million years ago (Lipman, 1976; Steven and Lipman, 1976).

Sapinero Mesa Tuff

The Sapinero Mesa Tuff is persistent and widespread, and overlies Dillon Mesa and Blue Mesa Tuffs, and older rocks in this area. The formation includes thin, discontinuous gravel deposits, and a conspicuous black vitrophyre at the base (commonly 3–15 m thick); nonwelded crystal pumice tuff (usually less than 6 m thick); and discontinuous welded tuff (as much as 60 m thick). It was derived from the San Juan and Uncompahgre calderas (Lake City and Silverton areas) about 28 million years ago (Lipman, 1976; Steven and Lipman, 1976).

Fish Canyon Tuff

The Fish Canyon Tuff is the most widespread and distinctive ash flow in the region (Olson and others, 1968). It consists largely of slightly to densely welded crystal-rich tuff that grades upward and laterally into nonwelded tuff. The unit is commonly 90–120 m thick along the Gunnison River. It was derived from the La Garita caldera (central San Juan volcanic field) and has been dated at 27.8 million years (Olson and others, 1968; Lipman, 1976; Steven and Lipman, 1976).

Carpenter Ridge Tuff

The Carpenter Ridge Tuff includes two or more ash flows, some water-laid tuff, and tuffaceous gravel (Olson and others, 1968). Most of the formation is devitrified, densely welded tuff. It is preserved only locally, but where present, it ranges from about 60 to 90 m in thickness. The formation was derived from the Bachelor caldera (Creede area, San Juan volcanic field) and has been dated at 27.5 million years (Lipman, 1976; Steven and Lipman, 1976).

Hinsdale Formation

The Hinsdale Formation is preserved in isolated knobs of basaltic lava and boulder gravel, 1 to 8 km south of the Gunnison River. It rests on a surface of low relief eroded across Oligocene volcanic and older rocks (Olson and others, 1968; Hedlund and Olson, 1973). According to Lipman and others (1978), late basaltic and rhyolitic rocks of the Hinsdale Formation range from 5 to 26.8 million years in the San Juan Mountains. The nearest dated deposit, on Cannibal Plateau, is about 18.5 million years old (Lipman and Mehnert, 1975, p. 132). Similar deposits on Grand Mesa have been dated at 8 to 23 million years (Larsen and others, 1975).

A thick Hinsdale sequence (about 50 to 70 or more meters thick) of unconsolidated boulder gravel and interbedded tuff, volcanic conglomerate sandstone and interbedded rhyolite pumice tuff underlies basaltic tuff and 12 or more basaltic lava flows on Red Mountain and Flat Top mesas about 7 to 12 km northeast of the West Elk volcanic field (fig. 2). These units overlie an erosional surface, or channels cut in Mesaverde and Mancos strata. The gravels contain well-rounded pebbles, cobbles, and small boulders derived from all or most of the sedimentary and igneous rocks exposed in the adjacent Elk Mountains. The lava flows appear to have had a nearby source to the northwest, probably along northwest-trending fissures. The rhyolite tuffs were probably erupted from one or more of the felsite and rhyolite plugs in the Elk Mountains. The lava flows have been dated at 9.7–10.9 million years by C. S. Robinson (C. S. Robinson and Associates, Lakewood, Colorado).

ECONOMIC GEOLOGY

One or more coal beds near the base of the Mesaverde Formation underlie parts of the northern and northeastern edge of the volcanic field (Lee, 1912) and a small area on the west side of Coal Mountain.

No metal production has been reported. Small vein deposits of manganese oxide were prospected in the late 1800's, along the forks of Steuben Creek and in Soap Creek Canyon (fig. 3). They occur in tuff breccia and overlying welded ash-flow tuff (Penrose, 1890; Harder, 1910; Muilenburg, 1919; Jones, 1921; Gaskill and others, 1977).

Base- and precious-metal anomalies in altered rocks associated with Tertiary intrusives, in and adjacent to the volcanic field, are discussed in Gaskill and others (1977). Anomalous values of zinc, copper, lead, silver, gold molybdenum, tin, mercury, sulfur, arsenic, boron, cobalt, antimony, fluorine, barite, vanadium and other elements are mainly concentrated on Sheep Mountain and in the area of the West Elk volcanic center. Areas of solfataric alteration occur along upper West Soap Creek and elsewhere in the area.

No oil or gas exploration has been reported in the near vicinity of the volcanic pile. Several dry holes in the Ohio Creek valley tested Mancos, Dakota, and Morrison strata, resulting in uneconomic showings of oil (fig. 3). The sedimentary section in the southern part of the West Elk Mountains is relatively thin and is intruded at most horizons by a mélange of igneous rocks.

REFERENCES

Corry, C. E., 1976, The emplacement and growth of laccoliths (Ph.D. dissertation): College Station, Texas A and M College, 184 p.

Cross, C. W., 1894, The laccolithic mountain groups of Colorado, Utah, and Arizona: U.S. Geological Survey 14th Annual Report, p. 165–564.

Emmons, S. F., Cross, C. W., and Eldridge, G. H., 1894, Anthracite–Crested Butte Folio, Colorado: U.S. Geological Survey Atlas, Folio 9, 11 p.

Gableman, J. W. and Boyer, W. H., 1960, Tectonic control of mining belts in the southwestern Colorado metallogenic province: American Institute of Mining, Metallurgical and Petroleum Engineers, v. 217, p. 296–320.

Gaskill, D. L., Rosenbaum, J. G., King, H. D., Meeves, H. C., and Bieniewski, K. L., 1977, Mineral Resources of the West Elk Wilderness and vicinity, Delta and Gunnison Counties, Colorado: U.S. Geological Survey Open-File Report 77-751, 111 p.

Godwin, L. H. and Gaskill D. L., 1964, Post-Paleocene West Elk laccolith cluster, west-central Colorado: U.S. Geological Survey Professional Paper 501-C, p. 66–68.

Hansen, W. R., 1965, The Black Canyon of the Gunnison, today and yesterday: U.S. Geological Survey Bulletin 1191, 76 p.

———, 1971, Geologic map of the Black Canyon of the Gunnison River and vicinity, western Colorado: U.S. Geological Survey Miscellaneous Geological Investigations Map I-584.

Harder, E. C., 1910, Manganese deposits of the United States: U.S. Geological Survey Bulletin 427, p. 150–151.

Hayden, F. V., 1881, Geological and geographical atlas of Colorado: Geological and Geographical Survey of the Territories, U.S. Department of the Interior, 20 plates.

Hedlund, D. C., 1974, Geologic map of the Big Mesa quadrangle, Gunnison County, Colorado: U.S. Geological Survey Geologic Quadrangle Map GQ-1153.

Hedlund, D. C. and Olson, J. C., 1973, Geologic map of the Carpenter Ridge quadrangle, Gunnison County, Colorado: U.S. Geological Survey Geologic Quadrangle Map GQ-1070.

———, 1974, Geologic map of the Iris NW quadrangle, Gunnison County, Colorado: U.S. Geological Survey Geologic Quadrangle Map GQ-1134.

Hunter, J. F., 1925, Precambrian rocks of the Gunnison River, Colorado: U.S. Geological Survey Bulletin 777, 94 p.

Jones, E. L., 1921, Some deposits of manganese ore in Colorado: U.S. Geological Survey Bulletin 715, p. 61–72.

Kelley, V. C., 1955, Regional tectonics of the Colorado Plateau and relationship to the origin and distribution of uranium: New Mexico University Publications in Geology, no. 5, 120 p.

Kramer, J. C., 1972, Geology of the Mount Owen Stock, Gunnison County, Colorado (B.A. thesis): Amherst, Massachusetts, Amherst College, 74 p.

Larsen, E. S., Jr., and Cross, C. W., 1956, Geology and petrology of the San Juan region, southwestern Colorado: U.S. Geological Survey Professional Paper 258, 303 p.

Larson, E. S., Ozima, Minoru, and Bradley, W. C., 1975, Late Cenozoic basic volcanism in northwestern Colorado and its implications concerning tectonism and the origin of the Colorado River system: Geological Society of America Memoir 144, p. 155–178.

Lee, W. T., 1912, Coal fields of the Grand Mesa and the West Elk Mountains, Colorado: U.S. Geological Survey Bulletin 510, 237 p.

Lipman, P. W. and Mehnert, H. H., 1975, Late Cenozoic basaltic volcanism and development of the Rio Grande depression in the southern Rocky Mountains: Geological Society of America Memoir 144, p. 119–154.

Lipman, P. W., Mutschler, F. E., Bryant, Bruce, and Steven, T. A., 1969, Similarity of Cenozoic igneous activity in the San Juan and Elk Mountains, Colorado: U.S. Geological Survey Professional Paper 650-D, p. 33–42.

Lipman, P. W., 1976, Geologic map of the Lake City caldera area, western San Juan Mountains, southwestern Colorado: U.S. Geological Survey Miscellaneous Investigations Series Map I-962.

Lipman, P. W., Dow, B. R., Hedge, C. E., and Steven, T. A., 1978, Petrologic evolution of the San Juan volcanic field, southwestern Colorado, Pb and Sr isotope evidence: Geologic Society of America Bulletin, v. 89, p. 59–82.

Muilenburg, G. A., 1919, Manganese deposits of Colorado: Colorado Geological Survey Bulletin 15, 76 p.

Obradovich, J. O., Mutschler, F. E., and Bryant, Bruce, 1969, Potassium-argon ages bearing on the igneous and tectonic history of the Elk Mountains and vicinity, Colorado: Geological Society of America Bulletin, v. 80, p. 1749–1756.

Olson, J. C., Hedlund, D. C., and Hansen, W. R., 1968, Tertiary volcanic stratigraphy in the Powderhorn–Black Canyon region, Gunnison and Montrose Counties, Colorado: U.S. Geological Survey Bulletin 1251-C, p. C1–C29.

Peale, A. C., 1876, Report [on valleys of Eagle, Grand, and Gunnison Rivers, Colorado]: in Hayden, F. V., 8th Annual Report of the U.S. Geological and Geographical Survey of the Territories, p. 94–176.

———, 1877, On a peculiar type of eruptive mountains in Colorado: in Hayden, F. V., ed., U.S. Geological and Geographical Survey of the Territories Bulletin 3, p. 551–564.

Penrose, R. A. F., Jr., 1890, Manganese, its uses, ores, and deposits: Arkansas Geological Survey Annual Report, v. 1, p. 456–464.

Steven, T. A. and Epis, R. C., 1968, Oligocene volcanism in Colorado: Colorado School of Mines Quarterly, v. 63, no. 3, p. 241–258.

Steven, T. A. and Lipman, P. W., 1976, Calderas of the San Juan volcanic field, southwestern Colorado: U.S. Geological Survey Professional Paper 958, 35 p.

Tweto, Ogden, Steven, T. A., Hail, W. J., and Moench, R. H., 1976, Preliminary geologic map of the Montrose 1° × 2° quadrangle, southwestern Colorado: U.S. Geological Survey Map MF-761.

Van Houten, F. B., 1957, Appraisal of the Ridgeway and Gunnison "tillites," southwestern Colorado: Geological Society of America Bulletin, v. 68, p. 383–388.

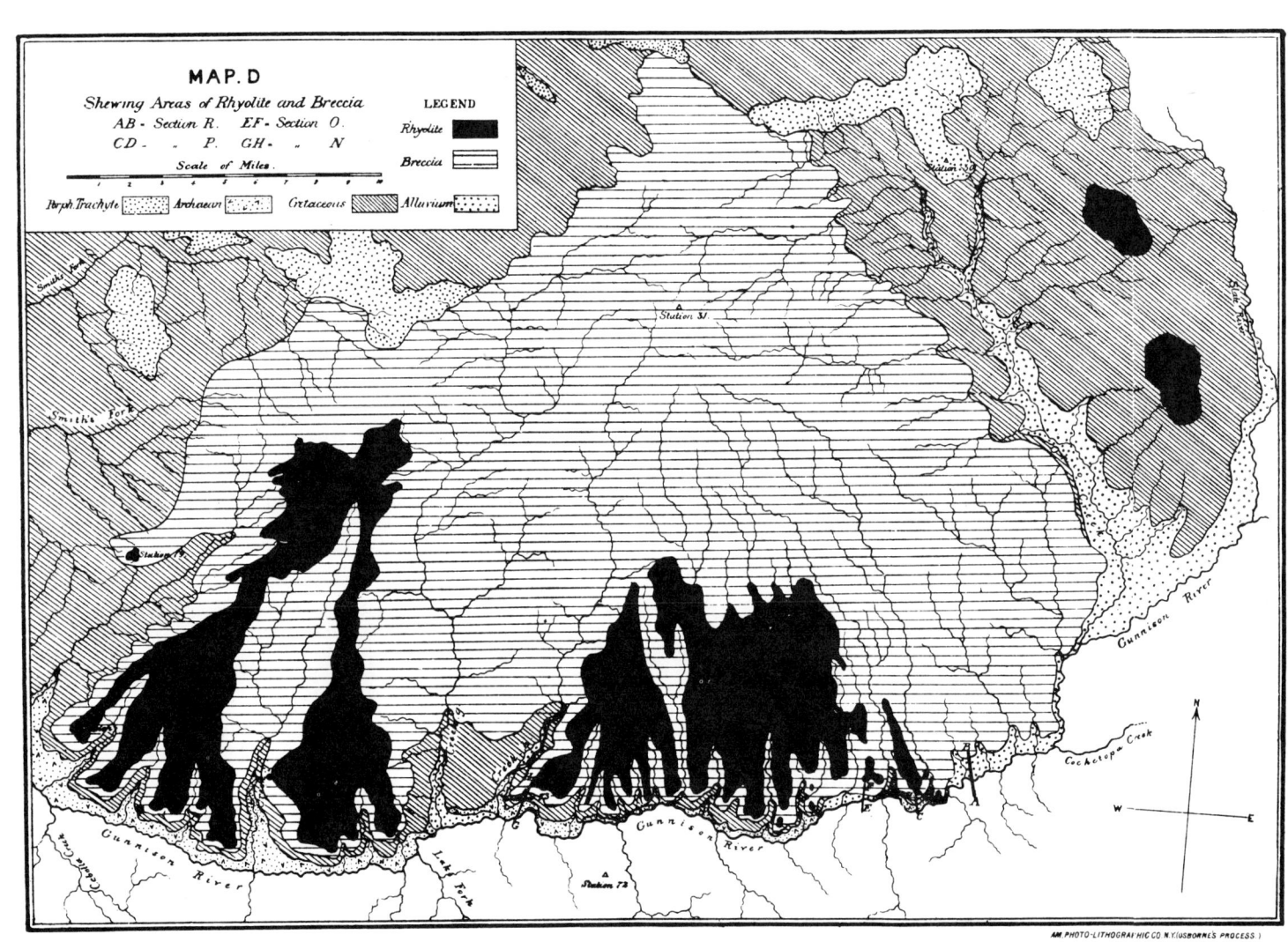

Geologic map of the West Elk Mountains and vicinity by A. C. Peale, Hayden Survey, 1874.

IGNEOUS ROCKS OF THE ELK MOUNTAINS AND VICINITY, COLORADO—CHEMISTRY AND RELATED ORE DEPOSITS

FELIX E. MUTSCHLER
Department of Geology
Eastern Washington University
Cheney, Washington 99004
and
U.S. Geological Survey
Denver, Colorado 80225

DAVID R. ERNST
Department of Geology
Eastern Washington University
Cheney, Washington 99004
now at
Noranda Exploration, Inc.
Reno, Nevada

DAVID L. GASKILL
and
PATTY BILLINGS
U.S. Geological Survey
Denver, Colorado 80225

INTRODUCTION

Late Mesozoic and Cenozoic igneous rocks of the Elk Mountains and vicinity (fig. 1) may be divided into three suites on the basis of field relations, isotope dating, and petrochemical data. Each igneous suite is associated with coeval metallic mineral deposits. In this paper we outline the chemical characteristics of each suite and summarize the nature of the associated mineral deposits. Major element rock chemical data used are from Bryant (1979), Cross (1894), Cunningham (1976), Ernst (1980), Godwin and Gaskill (1964), Mutschler (1968, and unpublished data), Vanderwilt (1937), and Young (1972). These data are available in a computer-readable data bank—PETROS (Mutschler and others, 1981).

LARAMIDE (LATE CRETACEOUS AND PALEOCENE) SUITE

Hornblende quartz diorite, quartz porphyry, aplite, and aplite porphyry form sills and fault-controlled plutons in the Aspen mining district on the west flank of the Sawatch Range (Bryant, 1979). These rocks, which have K-Ar ages of 67-72 m.y. (Table 1), were emplaced during Laramide uplift of the Sawatch Range (Obradovich and others, 1969). Westward gravity gliding of a sheet of upper Paleozoic and Mesozoic sedimentary rocks from the Sawatch Range produced the Elk Range thrust fault at about the same time.

Volcanism in the Sawatch Range probably occurred during the Laramide plutonic event since the Paleocene Ohio Creek Formation in the Ruby Range, West Elk Mountains, and Piceance basin contains clasts of fine-grained igneous rock. Volcanism probably continued into early Eocene time, since the lower part of the Wasatch Formation in the Ruby Range and Piceance basin contains tuffaceous beds and numerous clasts of fine-grained igneous rock.

Only seven major-element chemical analyses are available for Laramide rocks from the Aspen area. Bryant (1979) has pointed out that these analyses show a bimodal distribution of SiO_2 values (fig. 2). Such bimodality is not a characteristic of Laramide igneous suites elsewhere in the Rocky Mountains, suggesting either that it may represent a sampling artifact or that other Laramide plutons with intermediate silica content may be present at depth in the Aspen area.

The great Laramide silver-lead-zinc manto deposits of the Aspen district produced ore valued at more than $100,000,000. Argentian tetrahedrite-tennantite, pearcite, argentite, argentiferous galena, and sphalerite in a barite-carbonate-quartz gangue were the main hypogene minerals, but supergene native silver was locally common to depths of up to 250 meters.

MIDDLE TERTIARY (OLIGOCENE) SUITE

Middle Tertiary granodiorite rocks are widespread in the western Sawatch Range, Elk Mountains, Ruby Range, and West Elk Mountains. Available K-Ar ages (Table 1) show that they were emplaced in the five million year interval between 34 and 29 m.y. These voluminous Oligocene rocks are temporally and chemically similar to Oligocene igneous rocks of the San Juan volcanic field (Lipman and others, 1969). In contrast to the San Juan volcanic field, significant ash-flow tuff eruptions and caldera formation did not occur in the Elk Mountains area. On the basis of Pb and Sr isotopic data, Lipman and others (1978) have suggested that the San Juan Oligocene magmas were generated in the mantle and that they were significantly contaminated by interaction with the lower crust and Precambrian cratonic lithosphere.

The Elk Mountain Oligocene suite shows a typical calc-alkaline trend on an AMF plot (fig. 3). Most samples have silica contents (calculated volatile free) between 58 and 70 percent (fig. 2). The "double maxima" at 59 and 67 percent SiO_2 on Figure 2 represents in part an oversampling of volumetrically minor mafic phases of plutons, but in part, also reflects the mafic character of the West Elk Breccia (see below).

Field relations and isotopic dating suggest that the Oligocene suite may be subdivided into the following four stages. There is probably some time overlap between stages.

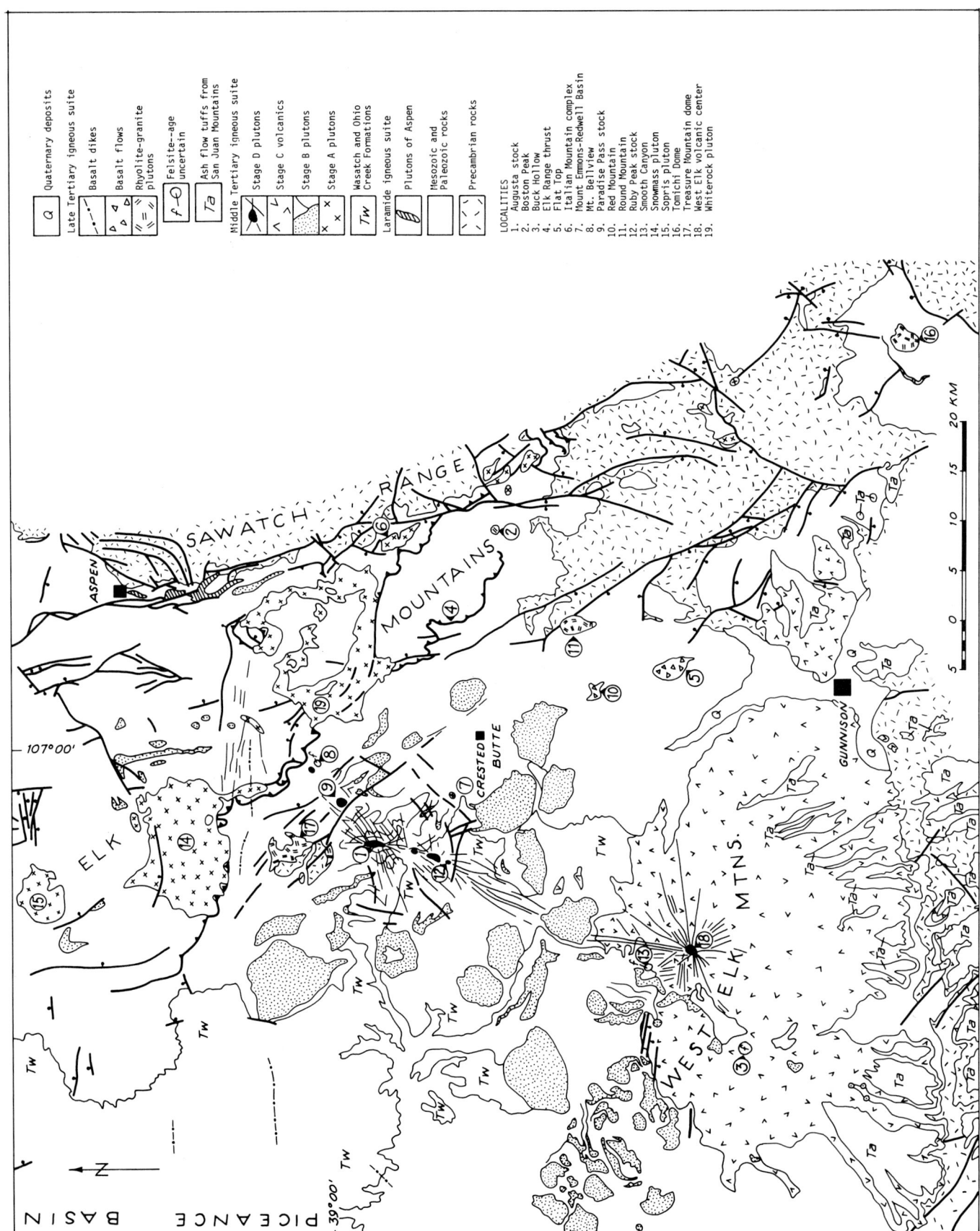

Figure 1. Geologic sketch map, Elk Mountain and vicinity, Colorado. Modified from Tweto and others (1976, 1978). Numbers refer to localities described in legend and text.

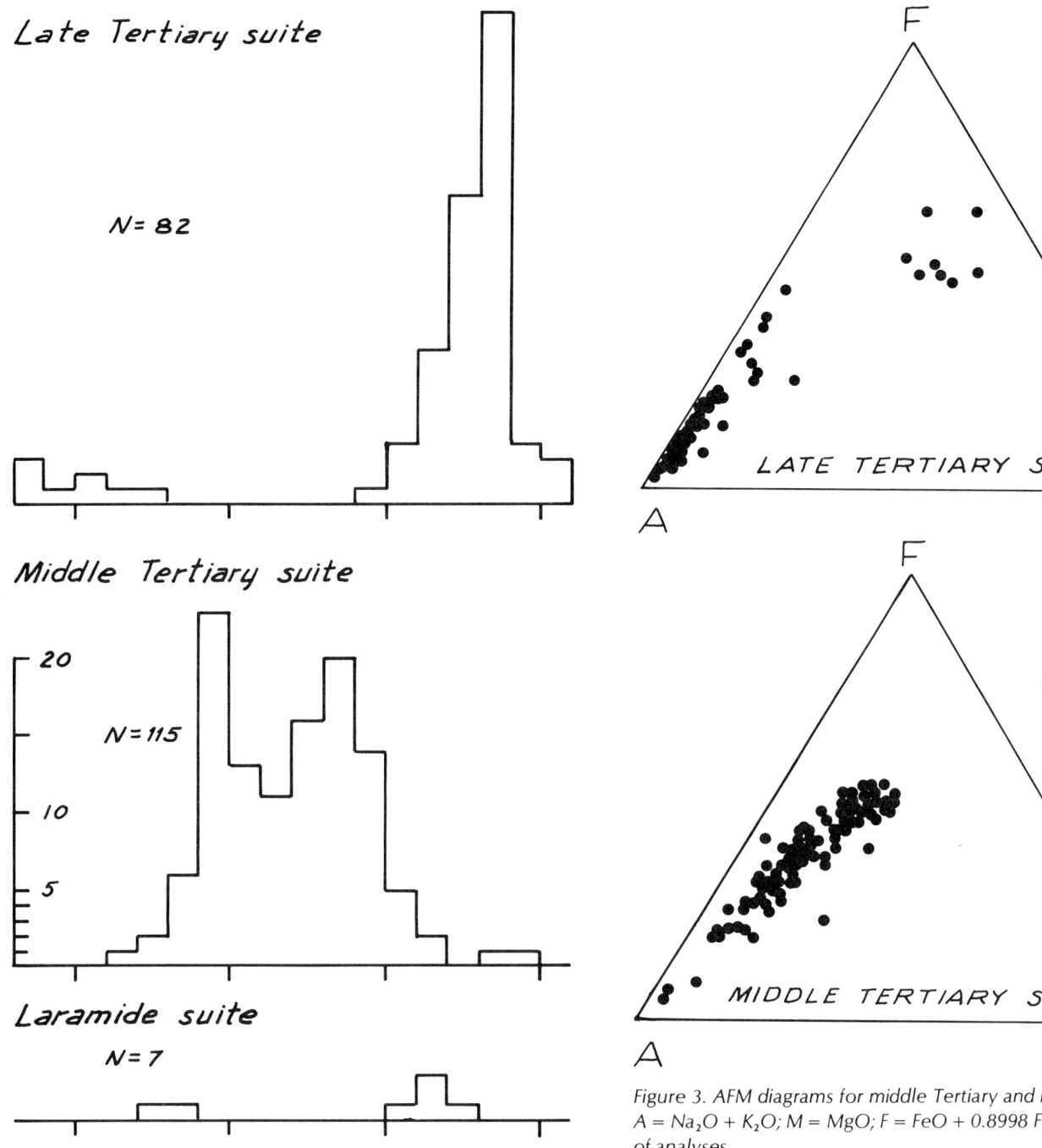

Figure 2. Histograms of SiO₂ contents for rock suites. Interval for SiO₂ is 2 percent. Plotted from analyses recalculated to 100 percent free of volatiles. N = number of analyses.

Figure 3. AFM diagrams for middle Tertiary and late Tertiary suites A = $Na_2O + K_2O$; M = MgO; F = $FeO + 0.8998\ Fe_2O_3$. N = number of analyses.

Stage A

Emplacement of large plutons of equigranular to porphyritic granodiorite in the Elk Mountains marked the onset of Oligocene magmatism. From north to south the major plutons include the Sopris, Snowmass, and Whiterock plutons, and the Italian Mountain complex (fig. 1). The Snowmass and Whiterock plutons and the Italian Mountain complex each show a chemical progression from early mafic granodiorite border phases and apophyses to late silicic granodiorites (fig. 4). Cunningham (1976) has shown that venting occurred in the Italian Mountain complex, but with the possible exception of pebble dikes which cut the Snowmass pluton (Mutschler, 1970) no other evidence of venting has been observed. Extensive contact metamorphic aureoles surround Stage A plutons.

Ore deposits associated with Stage A plutons include:

1) A contact metamorphic limestone replacement magnetite-pyrite deposit in Belden limestone adjacent to the Whiterock pluton (Bryant, 1979).

2) Disseminated pyrite-chalcopyrite-molybdenite showings straddling contacts of the Whiterock pluton (Bryant, 1971).

3) Numerous small fissure vein and limestone replacement silver-bearing, lead-zinc-copper sulfide deposits in, and adjacent to,

Table 1. K-Ar ages for igneous rocks, Elk Mountains and vicinity, Colorado.

Suite		Rock Type	Location	Age (m.y.)	Reference
Laramide (Late Cretaceous and Paleocene)		Quartz-muscovite porphyry	Aspen	72.2 ± 2.2	Obradovich and others (1969)
		Aplite	Aspen	70.0 ± 2.3	Do
				67.4 ± 2.2	
Middle Tertiary (Oligocene)	Stage A	Granodiorite	Sopris pluton	34.2 ± 0.8	Cunningham and others (1977)
		Granodiorite	Snowmass pluton	34.1 ± 1.4	Obradovich and others (1969)
		Granodiorite	Whiterock pluton	33.9 ± 1.0	Do
	Stage B	Granodiorite porphyry	Snowmass Creek sill	31.2 ± 1.1	Do
		Granodiorite porphyry	Crested Butte laccolith	29.1 ± 1.0	Do
	Stage D	Granodiorite	Paradise Pass stock	29.0 ± 1.1	Do
Late Tertiary (Miocene)		Rhyolite porphyry	Mount Emmons	17.7	Dowsett and others (1981)
				17.3	
		Rhyolite porphyry	Round Mountain	13.9 ± 0.3	Cunningham and others (1977)
		Granite porphyry	Treasure Mountain	12.4 ± 0.6	Obradovich and others (1969)
		Microgranite	Tomichi Dome		
		Rhyolite	Boston Peak		
		Basalt flows	Red Mountain and Flat Top mesa	10.9 – 9.7 ± 0.6	C. S. Robinson (personal communication, 1979)

the Snowmass and Whiterock plutons and the Italian Mountain complex. Pyrite, argentiferous galena, sphalerite, and chalcopyrite in a quartz-calcite gangue characterize these deposits. Ruby silver minerals have been reported from the Sylvanite mine adjacent to the Whiterock pluton by Emmons and others (1894). Although some high grade ore was shipped as early as the 1870's and 1880's, total value of production from these deposits has probably not exceeded $100,000.

Two unique nickel-cobalt-silver vein deposits occur in large inclusions, or roof pendants, of Paleozoic sedimentary rocks in the Whiterock pluton (Emmons and others, 1894). Pyrite, sphalerite, galena, chalcopyrite, argentite, pyrargyrite, proustite, marcasite, native silver, nickel- and cobalt-bearing loellingite, smaltite, skutterudite, and erythrite in a calcite-siderite-barite gangue have been reported from these deposits (Eckel, 1961).

Stage B

Granodiorite porphyry dikes cut Stage A plutons in the Elk Mountains. Similar granodiorite porphyry forms sills, laccoliths and dikes elsewhere in the Elk Mountains and in the Ruby Range and West Elk Mountains. Most of these Stage B granodiorite porphyry plutons are relatively silicic, containing 64 to 68 percent SiO_2 (fig. 4), but locally they contain more mafic granodiorite xenoliths similar to the early mafic granodiorites of Stage A plutons. Contact metamorphism adjacent to Stage B plutons is not as extensive as that associated with Stage A plutons.

No metallic mineral deposits are known to have formed during Stage B.

Stage C

During Stage C a group of composite andesitic stratovolcanoes developed in the West Elk Mountains. The eruptive products of these volcanoes constitute the West Elk Breccia described by Gaskill and others (1981). The bulk composition of the West Elk Breccia is less silicic than most of the granodiorites of Stages A and B (fig. 4).

The West Elk Breccia is lithologically and chemically similar to the early intermediate lavas and breccias of the San Juan volcanic field which formed in the interval 34.7–31.1 m.y. (Steven and Lipman, 1976). We have not dated the West Elk Breccia directly, but on stratigraphic grounds we believe it formed in the interval between Stage B plutons (31–29 m.y.) and Stage D plutons (29 m.y.).

In the San Juan volcanic field the early intermediate lavas and breccias were followed by caldera related ash-flow eruptions of more silicic composition. The Blue Mesa Tuff dated at $\geq 27.8 \leq 28.4$ m.y. by Steven and Lipman (1976) is the oldest of these San Juan ash-flow tuffs which overlie West Elk Breccia.

Small sub-volcanic intrusives, generally of mafic andesite or hornblende granodiorite, occur in the vent areas from which the West Elk Breccia was erupted. Some of these plutons formed early in the volcanic cycle, but the radial dike swarm of the West Elk volcanic center (here referred to Stage D) cuts some of the youngest preserved volcanic strata.

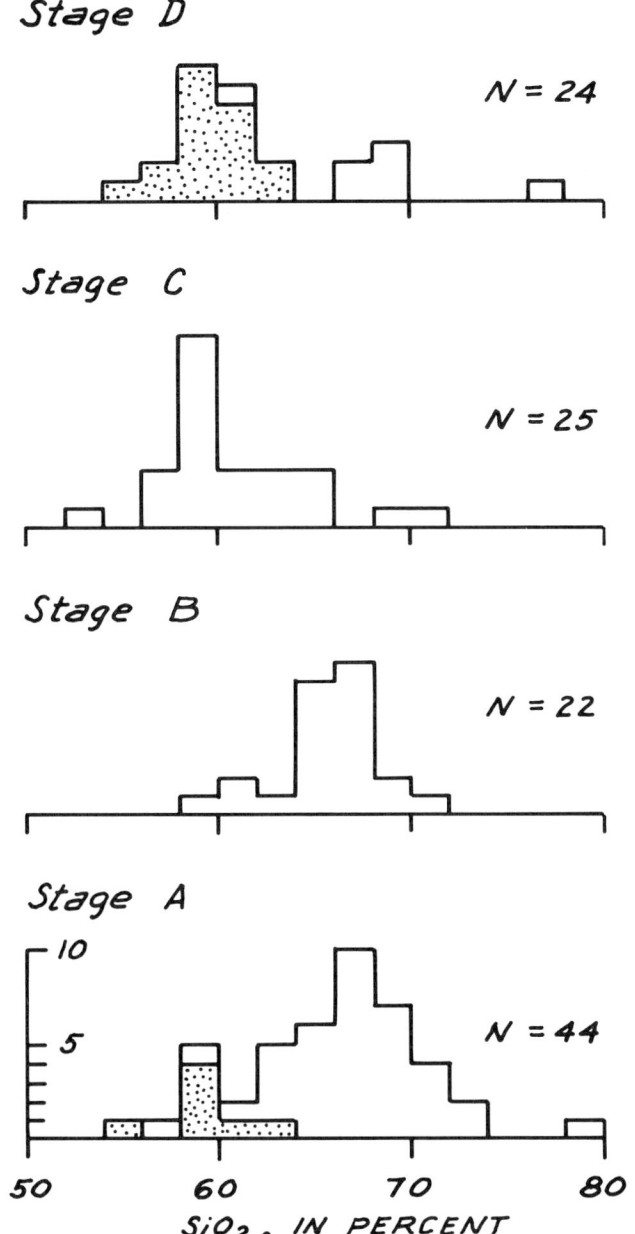

Figure 4. Histograms of SiO$_2$ contents for stages of middle Tertiary suite. Interval for SiO$_2$ is 2 percent. Plotted from analyses recalculated to 100 percent free of volatiles. N = number of analyses. Stippled areas include mafic border phases of stocks (Stage A); and mafic border phases of stocks and rocks of West Elk volcanic center (Stage D).

No metallic mineral deposits are known to have formed during this volcanic event.

Stage D

A northeast-trending zone of small stocks, several of which are the centers of radial, or linear, dike swarms extends from the West Elk volcanic field (West Elk volcanic center), along the crest of the Ruby Range (Ruby Peak, Mount Owen, Afley, Augusta, and Paradise Pass stocks), to the Elk Range (Schofield stock). The West Elk volcanic center represents the high-level intrusive center of a stratovolcano, and it is possible that some of the other stocks may be roots of volcanoes. The central stock and radial dikes of the West Elk volcanic center are mafic (58–62 percent SiO$_2$) andesites. The Mount Owen, Augusta, and Schofield stocks have borders of mafic granodiorite. These mafic borders and related dacite dikes (Gaskill and Godwin, 1966; Gaskill and others, 1967) represent the early phases of each stock, since they are cut by more silicic (66–70 percent SiO$_2$) dikes or stock-interior granodiorites.

In contrast to Stage B granodiorite porphyry plutons, the small granodiorite stocks of the Ruby Range have contact metamorphic aureoles that extend one or more kilometers into the wall rocks.

Metallic mineralization associated with Stage D plutons in the Ruby Range includes: (1) disseminated pyrite-chalcopyrite-molybdenite deposits; (2) quartz-pyrite-base metal sulfide vein and replacement deposits; (3) calcite-pyrite-base metal sulfide vein and replacement deposits; and (4) quartz-ruby silver-arsenopyrite-sulfantimonide veins and replacement deposits. The sequence 1 to 4 is both spatial and temporal—representing increasing distance from the central stock, and progressively younger mineralization.

Although Gaskill and others (1977) have reported several areas of hydrothermal alteration and geochemical anomalies, no significant metallic mineral showings have been found at the West Elk volcanic center. This may be a function of the fact that only mafic andesites are present at the West Elk center, whereas more silicic, and more highly differentiated, granodiorites occur in the Ruby Range stocks. Alternatively, the lack of mineralization at the West Elk center may be a function of level of erosion. The West Elk center has not yet been eroded to the base of its volcanic pile, whereas any volcanics originally present in the Ruby Range have been stripped away.

Mineral Deposits

Disseminated pyrite-chalcopyrite-molybdenite deposits

The Paradise Pass stock (Mutschler, 1968, 1970) at the north end of the Ruby Range shows well-developed disseminated sulfide mineralization typical of a "granodiorite molybdenite system" (Mutschler and others, 1981). Medium-grained hypidiomorphic granodiorite makes up the bulk of the stock. Thin dikes of fine-grained allotriomorphic-granular aplite and alaskite cut the stock and Mancos Shale albite-epidote-hornfels adjacent to the stock. Large areas of the stock are cut by a stockwork of quartz-sericite-pyrite veins which locally carry molybdenite and chalcopyrite. Pervasive quartz-sericite-pyrite alteration between veinlets is locally developed. The most intense alteration shows a close spatial relation to the margins of the stock (fig. 5). Comparison of major- element analysis of fresh and altered granodiorite (Table 2) show an increase in SiO$_2$ and H$_2$O+, and a decrease in Na$_2$O, in the altered rock. This is typical of quartz-sericite-pyrite alteration. Three small "pipes" or areas of almost complete replacement of granodiorite by quartz, sericite, and sulfides occur in the northern part of the stock (fig. 5).

Surface areas which contain more than 100 ppm Mo in rock are generally coincident with areas of intense quartz-sericite-pyrite alteration and are restricted to the Paradise Pass stock. Areas in which Cu in rock exceeds 100 ppm form a crude circular sheath surrounding the stock. Copper anomalies tend to extend radially outside of molybdenum anomalies.

Quartz-pyrite-base metal sulfide and calcite-pyrite-base metal sulfide veins cut molybdenite-bearing quartz-sericite-pyrite veins. A late period of argillic alteration, which is largely fracture controlled, occurred contemporaneously with the base metal event.

Isolated molybdenite-bearing quartz-sericite-pyrite veins occur in the Augusta stock, and disseminated pyrite occurs in the Ruby Peak stock.

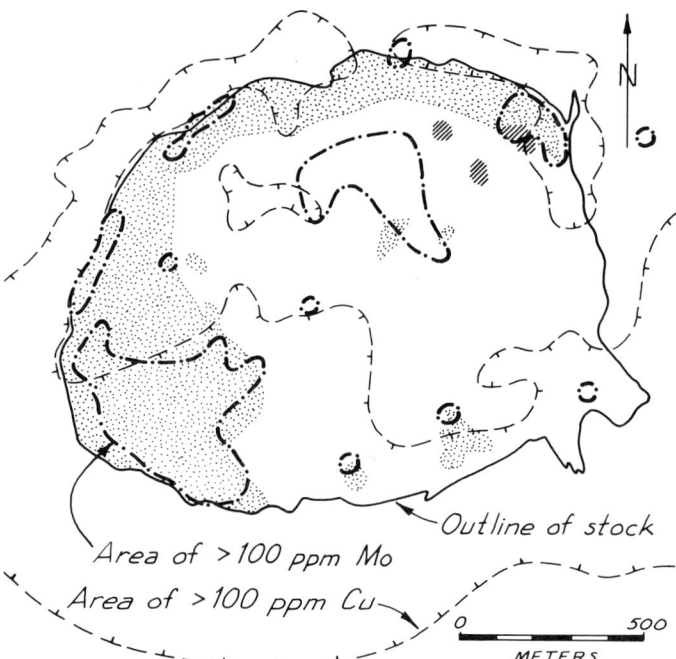

Figure 5. Sketch map showing surface alteration and metallization of Paradise Pass stock. Areas of intense quartz-sericite-pyrite alteration are stippled. "Pipes," or areas of almost complete replacement by quartz, sericite, and sulfides, are diagonally ruled.

Table 2. Chemical analyses of rocks from Paradise Pass stock. (1, 2 = fresh granodiorite; 3 = fresh aplite dike; 4 = altered granodiorite).

	1	2	3	4
SiO_2	67.40	68.00	77.20	78.90
Al_2O_3	16.10	15.50	12.40	7.70
Fe_2O_3	1.80	1.90	0.37	2.20
FeO	1.70	1.60	0.12	0.40
MgO	1.60	1.10	0.14	0.62
CaO	3.10	3.30	0.19	2.40
Na_2O	3.40	3.40	1.60	0.28
K_2O	3.00	3.40	7.30	3.30
H_2O+	0.85	0.80	0.45	1.70
H_2O-	0.10	0.17	0.06	0.31
TiO_2	0.39	0.40	0.10	0.16
P_2O_5	0.34	0.29	0.02	0.15
MnO	0.07	0.02	0.00	0.30
CO_2	0.05	0.02	0.02	0.82
Total	99.90	99.90	99.97	99.24

Ruby silver deposits

Ruby silver veins in the Ruby Range were originally prospected in the 1870's and 1880's. The entire area is pockmarked with prospects, but only two areas have produced more than a few tons of ruby silver ore. In the Ruby (Irwin) district, east of the Ruby Peak stock, production has come from northeast-, northwest-, and east-trending quartz-arseno-pyrite-pyrargyrite-proustite-tetrahedrite-galena-argentite-pyrite-chalcopyrite-sphalerite veins. In the Augusta (Poverty Gulch) district veins consisting of quartz-pyrite-calcite-rhodochrosite-galena-sphalerite-ruby silver minerals-tetrahedrite-boulangerite-jamesonite and owyheeite have been worked. These veins occur both within, and peripheral to, the August stock. Total production of ruby silver ores from these two districts probably had a value of less than $1,000,000.

LATE TERTIARY (MIOCENE) SUITE

During Miocene time a bimodal assemblage of basaltic and rhyolitic magmas reached a high crustal level, and locally vented to the surface, in the Elk Mountains and environs. Similar late Tertiary bimodal suites are widespread in the western United States and are believed to be emplaced in an extensional tectonic setting (Christiansen and Lipman, 1972; Mutschler and others, 1978). Isotopic studies of the late Tertiary bimodel suite in the San Juan Mountains (Lipman and others, 1978) suggest that the basaltic magmas were derived by partial melting of the upper lithospheric mantle, and that the rhyolites may represent partial melts of the lower crust.

In the Elk Mountains and vicinity basaltic rocks include remnants of lava flows on Red Mountain and Flat Top mesa between Ohio Creek and the East River north of Gunnison, and scattered small dikes of gabbro porphyry and lamprophyre in the Elk Mountains and Ruby Range.

Miocene rhyolitic rocks include the granite of Treasure Mountain (Mutschler, 1968, 1970), a rhyolite breccia pipe complex in Redwell Basin (Gaskill and others, 1967; Sharp, 1968), a buried rhyolite-granite plug at Mount Emmons (Dowsett and others, 1981), the Round Mountain rhyolite prophyry stock, rhyolite vents and a breccia pipe at Boston Peak (Ernst, 1980), a rhyolite and microgranite pluton at Tomichi Dome (Stark and Behre, 1936; Ernst, 1980), and small dikes and sills in the Elk Mountains and Ruby Range. Typical analyses of these rocks are given in Table 3.

Venting clearly occurred at Boston Peak (Ernst, 1980) and venting has been suggested to have occurred at Treasure Mountain (Mutschler, 1968), Redwell Basin (Sharp, 1978), and Tomichi Dome (Ernst, 1980). Any of these areas could have been the source for rhyolite pumice tuff which underlies 10.9 m.y. old basalt flows on Red Mountain and Flat Top (Gaskill and others, 1981).

Chemically the Miocene rhyolites and granites are granites in the sense of Tuttle and Bowen (1958). That is, their norms show Or + Ab + Q $\geq$ 80%, and when Or, Ab, and Q are normalized to total 100%; Or $\geq$ 20%, Ab $\geq$ 20%, and Q $\geq$ 20%. All of these rocks show significant enrichment of the lithophile elements Be, Cs, F, Li, Nb, Rb, Sn, Th, U, W, Y, and Yb. They also show significant depletion of Ba, Cu, Sr, and Zr relative to the average low calcium granite of Turekian and Wedepohl (1961). The trace element enrichment and

Table 3. Chemical analyses of Miocene rhyolites and granites. (*Total Fe reported as Fe_2O_3.)

	1	2	3	4	5	6	7	8
SiO_2	75.80	76.80	79.00	74.20	70.60	75.84	75.80	75.90
Al_2O_3	12.80	12.50	12.00	12.80	14.60	13.29	13.80	12.28
Fe_2O_3	0.01	0.35	2.10	1.40	1.60	1.02*	0.52	1.44*
FeO	0.55	0.24	0.45	1.00	0.52		0.12	
MgO	0.18	0.12	0.30	0.50	0.22	0.07	0.10	0.30
CaO	0.81	0.24	0.05	0.95	1.50	0.42	0.39	0.19
Na_2O	3.40	3.30	0.20	3.50	3.20	3.96	4.10	2.75
K_2O	5.10	5.30	3.80	4.60	4.90	4.60	4.40	4.82
H_2O+	0.10	0.31	1.85	0.10	1.00	0.81	0.45	1.47
H_2O-	0.22	0.08	0.10	0.10	0.41		0.14	
TiO_2	0.16	0.17	0.05	0.30	0.27	0.08	0.04	0.14
P_2O_5	0.00	0.00	0.04	0.16	0.10	0.02	0.00	0.01
MnO	0.00	0.03	0.15	0.05	0.03	0.09	0.13	0.14
CO_2	0.05	0.02	0.35	0.30	0.05		0.02	
F	0.25	0.01	0.10	0.10	0.08	0.16	0.21	0.13
S			0.06	0.40				
Total	99.43	99.47	100.60	100.46	99.08	100.36	100.22	99.57

1. Treasure Mountain - Granite porphyry
2. Treasure Mountain - Rhyolite porphyry
3. Redwell Basin - Rhyolite porphyry (altered)
4. Mount Emmons - Aplite
5. Round Mountain - Rhyolite porphyry
6. Boston Peak - Rhyolite
7. Tomichi Dome - Microgranite
8. Tomichi Dome - Rhyolite (breccia pipe)

Table 4. Chemical characteristics of source rocks for granite molybdenite systems. (Numbers in parentheses are alternate values.)

$SiO_2 \geq 74\%$

Molecular Al_2O_3 > Molecular $Na_2O + K_2O$

$CaO \leq 1.5\ (1.0)\%$

$K_2O/Na_2O \geq 1.25$

$Rb/Sr > 5\ (10)$

$F \geq 1000$ ppm

$Li > 30\ (50)$ ppm

$Nb > 20\ (40)$ ppm

$U > 10\ (8)$ ppm

$Zr < 100\ (150)$ ppm

depletion patterns in the Miocene rhyolites and granites of the Elk Mountains and vicinity are strikingly similar to those reported by Hildreth (1978) for the early erupted part of the Bishop Tuff from the Long Valley caldera, California. Hildreth suggested that these patterns resulted from convention-driven thermogravitational diffusion in a large silicic magma chamber. If the highly differentiated rhyolites and granites of the Elk Range and vicinity formed in a similar manner, it raises the possibility that they may represent "warts," or cupolas, extending above a single silicic batholith. Such a batholith would have to be over 80 km (distance between Treasure Mountain and Tomichi Dome) long in a northwesterly direction. If this speculation is correct it suggests that a significant part of the Tertiary batholith, which gravity data (Isaacson and Smithson, 1976) indicate underlies the region, may be of Miocene, rather than Oligocene, age.

Mineral Deposits

Many samples from the Miocene rhyolites and granites fit the chemical criteria which Mutschler and others (1981) and F. E. Mutschler, S. Ludington, and M. Ikramuddin (manuscript) believe characterize the source rocks of "granite" or "Climax type" molybdenite systems (see Table 4). Important stockwork molybdenite deposits similar to those at Climax and Henderson, Colorado have recently been discovered at Mount Emmons (Dowsett and others, 1981) and Redwell Basin (Sharp, 1978), and genetically similar, but to date uneconomic, molybdenite mineralization has been recognized associated with the granite of Treasure Mountain (Mutschler, 1976). Molybdenite deposits of this type typically have ore shells consisting of a stockwork of quartz-molybdenite veins draped above, or in the upper part of, a granite- or rhyolite-porphyry source pluton. The ore shell is typically coincident with a zone of potassic alteration and is overlain by quartz-sericite and argillic alteration zones. The potassic alteration zone and the quartz-molybdenite ore shell are formed by fluorine-rich magmatic fluids concentrated in, and released from, the source pluton; the quartz-sericite and argillic alteration zones are produced by mixed magmatic and meteoric fluids (Mutschler and others, 1981).

It seems probable that the economic potential of these Miocene granite molybdenite deposits far exceeds that of any of the older Oligocene mineralization in the Elk Mountains and vicinity.

Base-metal vein and replacement deposits are associated with both the Mount Emmons–Redwell Basin and Treasure Mountain dome centers of molybdenite mineralization. These base metal deposits are comparable to the "late barren stage" veins recognized at Climax and Henderson (Wallace and others, 1968; Wallace and others, 1978).

Base metal deposits at the Mount Emmons–Redwell Basin center include the Keystone and Daisy mines which worked pyrite-sphalerite-galena-pyrrhotite-chalcopyrite veins and small replacement bodies.

Miocene base metal mineralization related to the granite of Treasure Mountain shows a distinct zoning pattern. Skarn replacement and vein deposits showing a typical contact metamorphic paragenesis are concentrated close to the granite on the south and southeast sides of the Treasure Mountain dome. Early silicates (hedenbergite, diopside, tremolite, andradite, epidote, scapolite, and quartz) are followed by iron oxides (specular hematite with minor magnetite); followed by pyrite and pyrrhotite; followed by chalcopyrite, bornite, sphalerite, tetrahedrite, galena, and pyrite.

Quartz-calcite-base metal sulfide vein and replacement deposits occur on the outer flanks of the dome, particularly on the northeast side in the area, including Sheep Mountain, Lead King Basin, and Schofield Park. Most of these deposits are characterized by pyrite, galena, sphalerite, chalcopyrite, tetrahedrite, and marcasite in a quartz-calcite gangue. Fluorite is a ubiquitous mineral in all of the Miocene deposits in the Treasure Mountain area.

FELSITE PLUTONS OF UNCERTAIN AGE

Several rhyolitic plutons of uncertain age are present in the area. These plutons have major-element chemistries similar to the Miocene rhyolites and granites, but their trace element chemistry is not diagnostic of either the Miocene or the Oligocene suites. These enigmatic plutons include an altered felsite breccia pipe at Mt. Bellview on the western edge of the Elk Range (Mutschler, 1970) which is currently being explored as a molybdenite prospect; and rhyolite porphyry plutons in Smooth Canyon and Buck Hollow in the West Elk Mountains (Gaskill and others, 1981).

REFERENCES

Bryant, Bruce, 1971, Disseminated sulfide deposits in the eastern Elk Mountains, Colorado: U.S. Geological Survey Professional Paper 750-D, p. D13-D25.

Bryant, Bruce, 1979, Geology of the Aspen 15-minute quadrangle, Pitkin and Gunnison Counties, Colorado: U.S. Geological Survey Professional Paper 1073, 146 p.

Christiansen, R. L. and Lipman, P. W., 1972, Cenozoic volcanism and plate-tectonic evaluation of the western United States. Part II, Late Cenozoic: Royal Society of London Philosophical Transactions, Series A, v. 271, p. 249-284.

Cross, Whitman, 1894, The laccolithic mountain groups of Colorado, Utah, and Arizona: U.S. Geological Survey 14th Annual Report, pt. 2, p 165-241.

Cunningham, C. G., Jr., 1976, Petrogenesis and postmagmatic geochemistry of the Italian Mountain intrusive complex, eastern Elk Mountains, Colorado: Geological Society of America Bulletin, v. 86, p. 897-908.

Cunningham, C. G., Naeser, C. W., and Marvin, R. F., 1977, New ages for intrusive rocks in the Colorado mineral belt: U.S. Geological Survey Open-File Report 77-573, 7 p.

Dowsett, F. R., Jr., Ganster, M. W., Ranta, D. E., Baker, D. J., and Stein, H. J., 1981, Geology of the Mount Emmons molybdenum deposit, Crested Butte, Colorado: New Mexico Geological Society Guidebook 32 (this volume).

Eckel, E. B., 1961, Minerals of Colorado: A 100-year record: U.S. Geological Survey Bulletin 1114, 399 p.

Emmons, S. F., Cross, Whitman, and Eldridge, G. H., 1894, Anthracite-Crested Butte folio, Colorado: U.S. Geological Survey Atlas, Folio 9, 11 p.

Ernst, D. R., 1980, Petrography and geochemistry of Boston Peak and Tomichi Dome, and relation to other plutons in Gunnison County, Colorado (M.S. thesis): Cheney, Eastern Washington University, 52 p.

Gaskill, D. L. and Godwin, L. H., 1966, Geologic map of the Marcellina Mountain quadrangle, Gunnison County, Colorado: U.S. Geological Survey Geologic Quadrangle Map GQ-511.

Gaskill, D. L., Godwin, L. H., and Mutschler, F. E., 1967, Geologic map of the Oh-be-joyful quadrangle, Gunnison County, Colorado: U.S. Geological Survey Geologic Quadrangle Map GQ-578.

Gaskill, D. L., Mutschler, F. E., and Bartleson, B. L., 1981, West Elk volcanic field, Gunnison and Delta Counties, Colorado: New Mexico Geological Society Guidebook 32 (this volume).

Gaskill, D. L., Rosenbaum, J. G., King, H. D., Meeves, H. C., and Bieniewski, K. L., 1977, Mineral resources of the West Elk Wilderness and vicinity, Delta and Gunnison Counties, Colorado: U.S. Geological Survey Open-File Report 77-751, 111 p.

Godwin, L. H. and Gaskill, D. L., 1964, Post-Paleocene West Elk laccolithic cluster, west-central Colorado: U.S. Geological Survey Professional Paper 501-C, p. C66-C68.

Hildreth, Wes, 1979, The Bishop Tuff: Evidence for the origin of compositional zoning in silicic magma chambers: Geological Society of America Special Paper 180, p. 43-75.

Isaacson, L. B. and Smithson, S. B., 1976, Gravity anomalies and granite emplacement in west-central Colorado: Geological Society of America Bulletin, v. 87, p. 22-28.

Lipman, P. W., Doe, B. R., Hedge, C. E., and Steven, T. A., 1978, Petrologic evolution of the San Juan volcanic field, southwestern Colorado: Pb and Sr isotope evidence: Geological Society of America Bulletin, v. 89, p. 59-82.

Lipman, P. W., Mutschler, F. E., Bryant, Bruce, and Steven, T. A., 1969, Similarity of Cenozoic igneous activity in the San Juan and Elk Mountains, Colorado, and its regional significance: U.S. Geological Survey Professional Paper 650-D, p. D33-D42.

Mutschler, F. E., 1968, Geology of the Treasure Mountain dome, Gunnison County, Colorado (Ph.D. dissertation): Boulder, University of Colorado, 240 p.

———, 1970, Geologic map of the Snowmass Mountain quadrangle, Pitkin and Gunnison Counties, Colorado: U.S. Geological Survey Geologic Quadrangle Map GQ-853.

———, 1976, Crystallization of a soda granite, Treasure Mountain Dome, Colorado, and the genesis of stockwork molybdenite deposits: New Mexico Geological Society Special Paper 6, p. 199-205.

Mutschler, F. E., Finn, D. D., and Ludington, Steve, 1978, Magmatism and related ore deposits of extensile continental environments—Computer exercises in petrochemical pattern recognition and prediction: Los Alamos Scientific Laboratory Conference Proceedings LA-7487-C, p. 64-65.

Mutschler, F. E., Rougon, D. J., Lavin, O. P., and Hughes, R. D., 1981, PETROS—A data bank of major element chemical analyses of igneous rocks for research and teaching (Version 6.1): Boulder, Colorado, NOAA—National Geophysical and Solar-Terrestrial Data Center, magnetic tape.

Mutschler, F. E., Wright, E. G., Ludington, Steve, and Abbott, J. T., 1981, Granite molybdenite systems: Economic Geology, in press.

Obradovich, J. D., Mutschler, F. E., and Bryant, Bruce, 1969, Potassium-argon ages bearing on the igneous and tectonic history of the Elk Mountains and vicinity, Colorado—A preliminary report: Geological Society of America Bulletin, v. 80, p. 1749-1756.

Sharp, J. E., 1978, A molybdenum mineralized breccia pipe complex, Redwell Basin, Colorado: Economic Geology, v. 73, p. 369-382.

Stark, J. T. and Behre, C. H., Jr., 1936, Tomichi Dome flow: Geological Society of America Bulletin, v. 47, p. 101-110.

Steven, T. A. and Lipman, P. W., 1976, Calderas of the San Juan volcanic field, southwestern Colorado: U.S. Geological Survey Professional Paper 958, 35 p.

Turekian, K. K. and Wedepohl, K. H., 1961, Distribution of the elements in some major units of the earth's crust: Geological Society of America Bulletin, v. 72, p. 175-192.

Tuttle, O. F. and Bowen, N. L., 1958, Origin of granite in the light of experimental studies in the system $NaAlSi_3O_8-KAlSi_3O_8-SiO_2-H_2O$: Geological Society of America Memoir 74, 153 p.

Tweto, Ogden, Moench, R. H., and Reed, J. C., Jr., 1978, Geologic map of the Leadville 1° × 2° quadrangle, northeastern Colorado: U.S. Geological Survey Miscellaneous Investigations Map I-999.

———, 1976, Preliminary geologic map of the Montrose 1° × 2° quadrangle, southwestern Colorado: U.S. Geological Survey Map MF-761.

Vanderwilt, J. W., 1937, Geology and mineral deposits of the Snowmass Mountain area, Gunnison County, Colorado: U.S. Geological Survey Bulletin 884, 184 p.

Wallace, S. R., MacKenzie, W. B., Blair, R. G., and Muncaster, N. K., 1978, Geology of the Urad and Henderson molybdenite deposits, Clear Creek County, Colorado, with a section on a comparison of these deposits with those at Climax, Colorado: Economic Geology, v. 73, p. 325-368.

Wallace, S. R., Muncaster, N. K., Jonson, D. C., MacKenzie, W. B., Bookstrom, A. A., and Surface, V. E., 1968, Multiple intrusion and mineralization at Climax, Colorado, in Ridge, J. D., ed., Ore deposits of the United States, 1933-1967 (Graton-Sales Volume): New York, American Institute of Mining, Metallurgical, and Petroleum Engineers, p. 605-670.

Young, E. J., 1972, Laramide-Tertiary intrusive rocks of Colorado: U.S. Geological Survey Open-File Report, 206 p.

GEOLOGY OF THE MOUNT EMMONS MOLYBDENUM DEPOSIT, CRESTED BUTTE, COLORADO

FREDERICK R. DOWSETT, JR.
Mount Emmons Project
Climax Molybdenum Company
P.O. Box 579
Crested Butte, Colorado 81224

MAURICE W. GANSTER
Climax Mine
Climax Molybdenum Company
Climax, Colorado 80429

DONALD E. RANTA, DONALD J. BAKER
Climax Molybdenum Company
1707 Cole Blvd.
Golden, Colorado 80401

and

HOLLY J. STEIN
Department of Geology
University of North Carolina
Chapel Hill, North Carolina 27514

INTRODUCTION

The Mount Emmons molybdenum deposit is located beneath the upper south slope of Mount Emmons, approximately 6 km northwest of the town of Crested Butte, Colorado (fig. 1). Mount Emmons lies in the Ruby Range, which is a part of the West Elk Mountains. The Elk Mountains are situated a short distance to the north and northeast.

Mining of precious metals, base metals, and coal in the Crested Butte area has been nearly continuous since the 1870's. Molybdenum was first reported to occur in the region at Paradise Pass and at "Treasury Mountain" (now Treasure Mountain) by Worcester (1919). Extensive regional exploration for molybdenum has occurred primarily in the past 20 years.

PREVIOUS WORK

Molybdenite was first discovered beneath Redwell Basin on the north side of Mount Emmons in 1970 (Sharp, 1978). AMAX Exploration optioned both the prospect area and an adjacent block of claims on the upper south side of the mountain in 1974.

Drill hole RW 16, drilled in Red Lady Basin on the south side of Mount Emmons in 1976, intercepted the fringe of the Mount Emmons molybdenite deposit. Major geological credit for the Mount Emmons discovery is attributed to John A. Thomas and John T. Galey, Jr. of AMAX Exploration.

The subsequent drilling program initiated in January, 1977 defined the orebody with great accuracy. The geologic reserves at Mount Emmons are 155 million tons having an average grade of 0.44 percent MoS_2 using a 0.2 percent MoS_2 cutoff (Ganster and others, 1981).

REGIONAL GEOLOGY

The Elk and West Mountains of west-central Colorado consist mainly of Paleozoic, Mesozoic, and Cenozoic sedimentary rocks intruded by abundant Tertiary igneous rocks of quartz monzonite to granodiorite composition (fig. 2). The northwest-trending Elk Mountains contain a series of stocks (White-Rock, Snowmass, and Sopris) that intrude tightly folded, westward-thrusted Paleozoic sedimentary rocks (Tweto and Sims, 1963). Some igneous rocks have been dated as Laramide age in the Aspen area, but most stocks in the range are mid-Tertiary in age, ranging from 29 to 34 m.y. (Obradovich and others, 1969).

Farther to the southwest, the West Elk Mountains consist of numerous laccoliths, a cluster of small stocks, and a large volcanic center, all of which were emplaced in a thick sequence of gently dipping Cretaceous and early Tertiary sedimentary rocks (Gaskill and others, 1977). Igneous activity began in the mid-Tertiary (29 to 34 m.y.) with (1) sill and laccolithic intrusion in the northern West Elk Mountains, (2) emplacement of stocks and dikes with associated mineralization in the Ruby Range area, and (3) development of an andesitic strato-volcano and volcano field in the southern West Elk Moutains.

Late Tertiary igneous activity was relatively minor compared to the mid-Tertiary events, but has great economic significance. Four

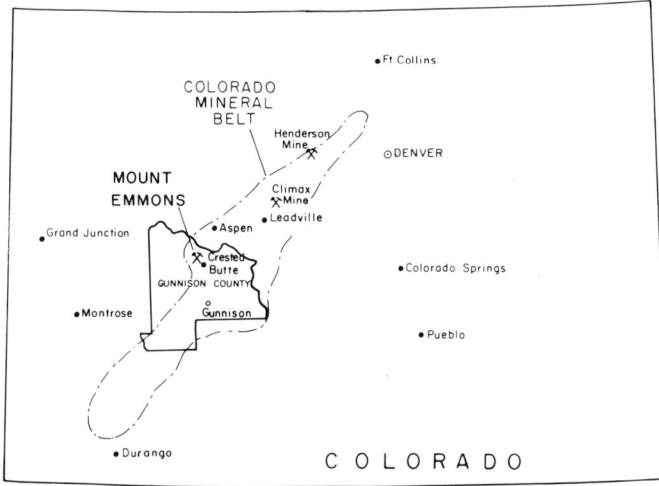

Figure 1. Location map of the Mount Emmons deposit

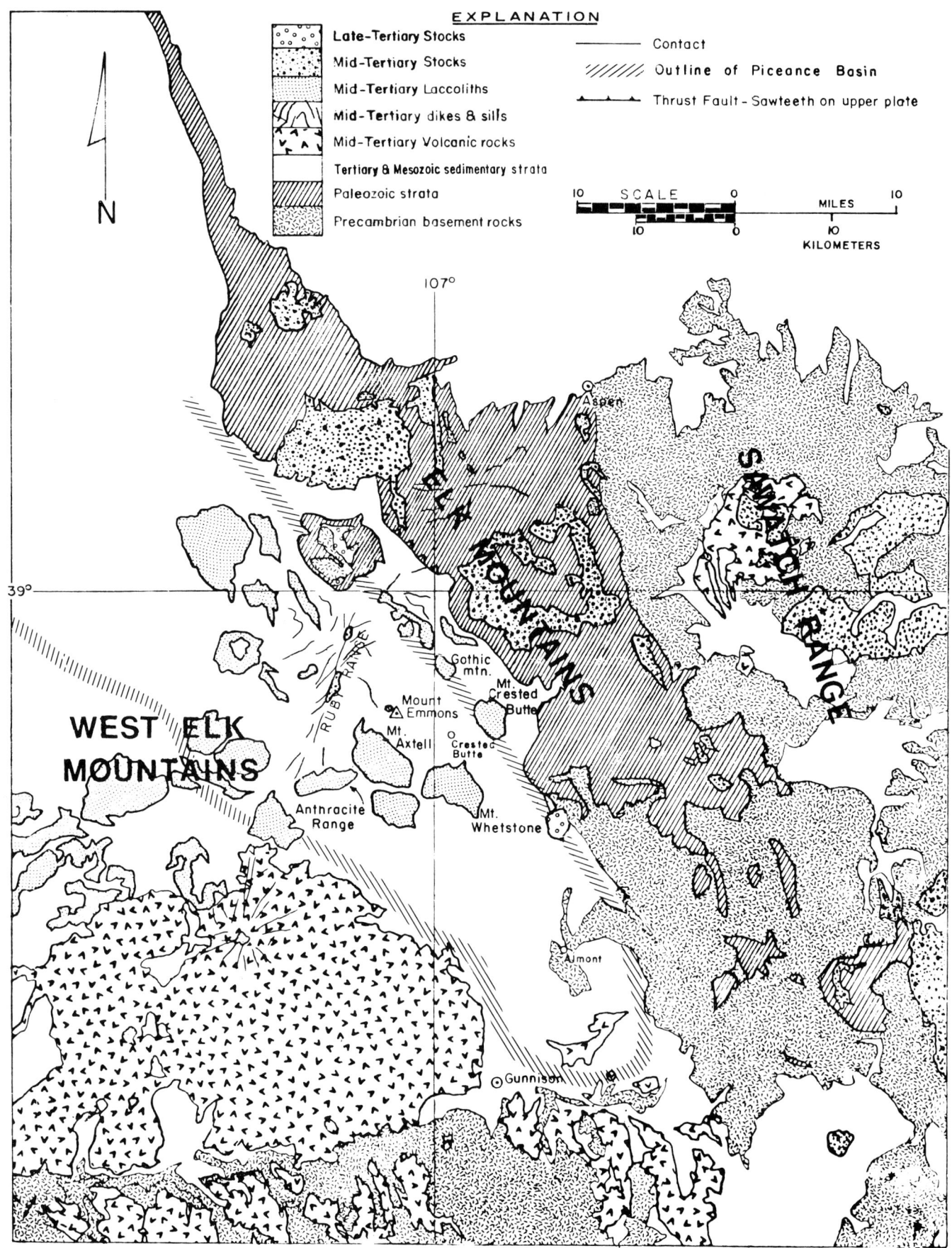

Figure 2. Regional geologic map of west-central Colorado

stocks or plugs, known to be approximately 12 to 17 m.y. old, are: (1) the granite of Treasure Mountain dome (Obradovich and others, 1969), (2) the mineralized felsite-breccia plug and underlying granite porphyry of Redwell Basin (Sharp, 1978; Thomas and Galey, 1978), (3) the mineralized subsurface granite porphyry stock beneath Mount Emmons and Red Lady Basin (Thomas and Galey, 1978; Ganster and others, 1981), and (4) the barren "rhyolite porphyry" of Round Mountain (Cunningham and others, 1977).

The Mount Emmons molybdenum deposit is located in the extreme south-central portion of the Oh-Be-Joyful quadrangle (Gaskill and others, 1967). In general, sedimentary rocks throughout the area dip gently to the south and southwest. The Mount Emmons deposit is located near the south end of the southeast-plunging Oh-Be-Joyful anticline and on the western side of the southwest-plunging Coal Creek syncline (fig. 3). Both structures are assumed to be late Laramide in age, contemporaneous with development of the Piceance Basin syncline.

GEOLOGY OF THE MOLYBDENUM DEPOSIT
Sedimentary Rocks

The sedimentary sequence in the Mount Emmons area spans from late Cretaceous to early Tertiary time. The oldest formation is the Mancos, a 1200-m thick sequence of shales with some interbedded limestones and siltstones (fig. 4). The Mancos Formation is not exposed on Mount Emmons, but may be seen in valley bottoms a few kilometers to the north, south, and east. The overlying Mesaverde Formation, also of late Cretaceous age, consists of a sequence of alternating sandstones, siltstones, shales, and minor coals. On Mount Emmons the Mesaverde Formation varies from 330 to 500 m thick. The upper surface of the Mesaverde Formation was the site of varying amounts of erosion and channel formation. The Ohio Creek Formation, dominantly a coarse sandstone with local chert pebble conglomerate and well-defined shale and siltstone beds, overlies the Mesaverde Formation. The Ohio Creek Formation is of early Tertiary (Paleocene) age and remains fairly consistent at 120 m in thickness on Mount Emmons. Capping Mount Emmons is the Wasatch Formation, also of early Tertiary (Paleocene to Eocene) age. On a more regional scale, within the Ruby Range the Wasatch Formation may reach 500 m in thickness. However, on Mount Emmons specifically, all but the basal 200 m has been eroded. The Wasatch Formation is composed of immature shales, siltstones, arkosic sandstones, and volcanic pebble conglomerates. The Mount Emmons stock has intruded the Mancos and Mesaverde sediments, strongly metamorphosing both formations up to 450 m outward from the igneous contact. Hydrothermal alteration overprints much of the metamorphic hornfels and is recognizable upward through the Wasatch Formation.

Igneous Rocks

Two stages of igneous activity are recognized in the Mount Emmons area during the mid- and late Tertiary. The rocks formed during these two episodes are described below.

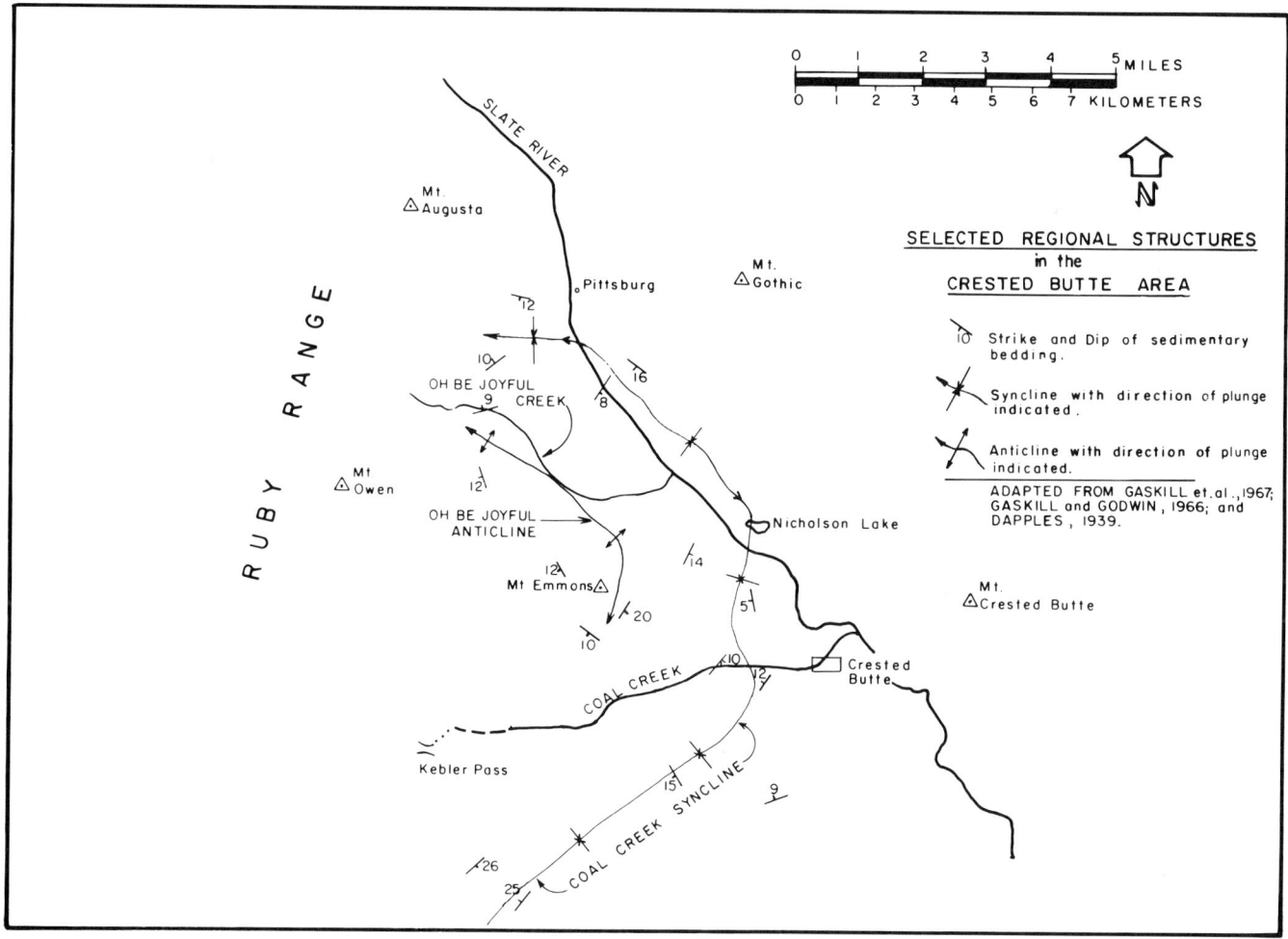

Figure 3. Structural geology of the Mount Emmons area

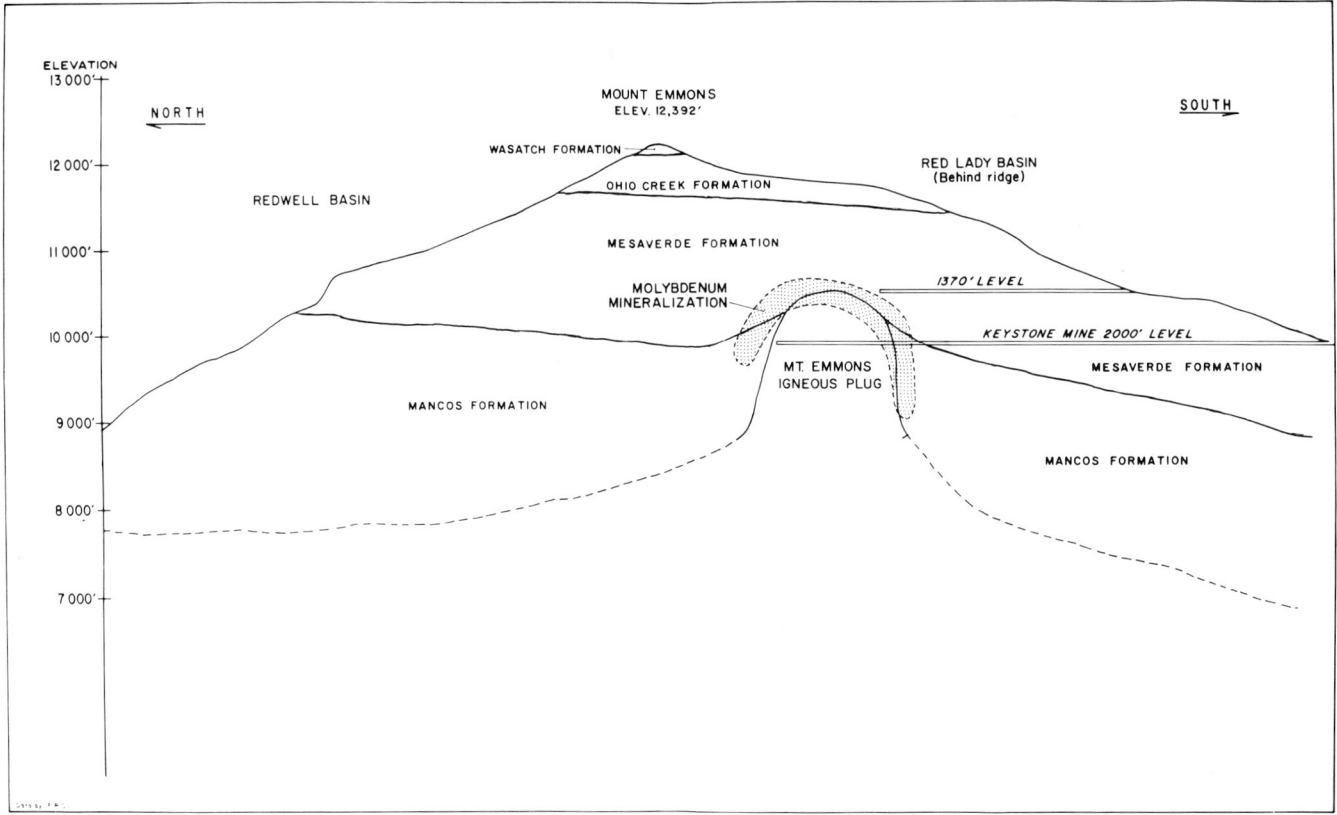

Figure 4. Generalized geology of Mount Emmons

Mid-Tertiary Intrusions

The earliest known igneous activity in the Mount Emmons area was the emplacement of sills and dikes during the mid-Tertiary intrusive events associated with laccolith development. Two compositional and textural varieties of these early intrusives have been recognized in the region.

The first of these varieties is a light green to grey rhyodacite porphyry which occurs at the upper end of Evans Basin as a sill intruded into the Tertiary Wasatch Formation. Other sills of this type have been observed in drill core from numerous locations on Mount Emmons where they intrude Cretaceous rocks.

The rhyodacite porphyry has phenocrysts of plagioclase, biotite, hornblende, and, rarely, quartz in an aphanitic groundmass composed of quartz, plagioclase, and potassium feldspar.

The second variety of mid-Tertiary igneous rock is green to grey quartz latite porphyry and latite porphyry. The quartz latite porphyry occurs as a laccolithic intrusion at Mount Axtell, and as sills and dikes in the vicinity of Mount Emmons and the Ruby Range. The quartz latite porphyry sill which forms the western ridge in Evans Basin and continues across Elk Basin is up to 200 m thick and is probably a northern extension of the Mount Axtell laccolith. The quartz latite porphyry is younger than the rhyodacite porphyry, based on crosscutting relationships and inclusions of rhyodacite porphyry in quartz latite porphyry. The quartz latite porphyry contains phenocrysts of large euhedral potassium feldspar, quartz, hornblende, plagioclase, and biotite in an aphanitic groundmass of quartz and potassium feldspar with minor plagioclase and biotite. The abundance of potassium feldspar and quartz phenocrysts varies considerably and in some areas the rock is a latite porphyry.

Late-Tertiary Intrusions (Mount Emmons Stock)

A stock of rhyolite-granite porphyry occurs below the Mount Emmons molybdenum deposit beneath Red Lady Basin (fig. 4). Three major intrusive episodes are now recognized to have formed the Mount Emmons stock. Rocks of the first igneous episode have been named the Red Lady phases; rocks of the second episode, the Keystone phases; and the third, the Union phases (fig. 5). The steep-sided stock at an elevation of 3000 m has lateral dimensions of approximately 400 to 500 m, elongate northeasterly, and enlarges slightly with depth. Similarity of rocks in the Red Lady, Keystone and Union phases suggests that they are comagmatic. K-Ar ages of 17.3 and 17.7 million years have been obtained for rocks from the Mount Emmons stock.

The Red Lady rocks have been subdivided into three separate intrusive phases: Red Lady Border, Red Lady Aplite, and Red Lady Porphyry. It was during the crystallization of these three phases that the Mount Emmons ore body and associated hydrothermal alteration patterns were formed.

The Red Lady Border phase ranges from a meter to approximately 50 m thick and is a pre-mineralization, chilled phase of the stock that now hosts about 10 percent of the orebody. The Border phase is in contact with the Mesaverde and Mancos formations and is thickest in the southeastern portion of the stock. The rock is a light buff-grey rhyolite porphyry with 10 to 30 percent phenocrysts of quartz, potassium feldspar, plagioclase, and biotite in an aphanitic groundmass of the same minerals.

The Red Lady Aplite is the second igneous phase in the stock. It has no observed chilled margin where in contact with the Border phase but does display chilled margins where it is in contact with

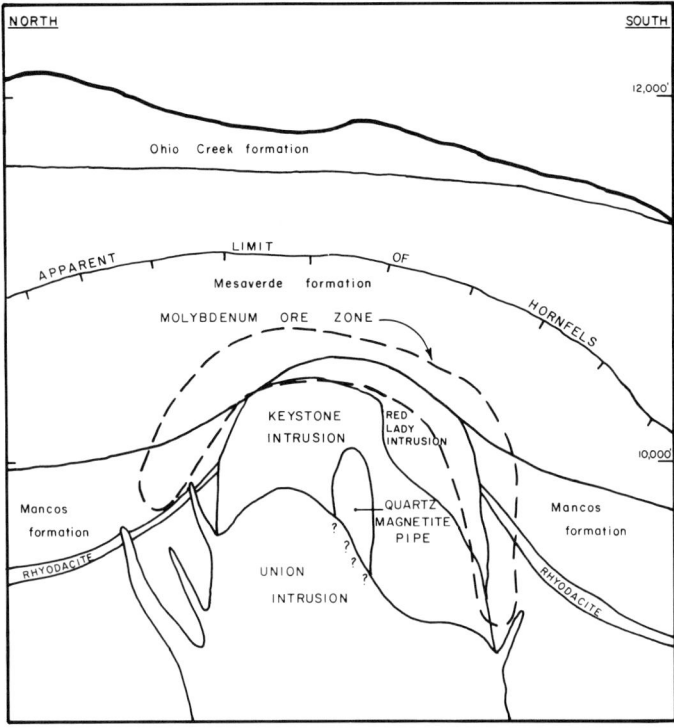

Figure 5. Geology of the Mount Emmons deposit

the Mancos and Mesaverde formations. The Aplite forms a 100-m thick zone in the upper portion of the stock. The texture of the Aplite varies from that of a fine-grained porphyritic granite to aplite to borderline rhyolite. It most typically contains 1 to 5 percent phenocrysts of quartz, potassium feldspar and plagioclase in a fine-grained aplitic groundmass of the same minerals. The Aplite hosts approximately 10 percent of the orebody.

Below the Aplite phase is the 15- to 60-m thick Red Lady Porphyry. This fine-grained granite porphyry shows no chilling at contacts with the Aplite phase but does show chilling against the Mesaverde and Mancos formations. The Red Lady Porphyry contains 15 to 35 percent phenocrysts of quartz, potassium feldspar, plagioclase, and biotite in a groundmass of the same minerals. The contact between the Aplite and Porphyry phases has been chosen where porphyritic textures predominate over aplitic textures. The Red Lady Porphyry does not contain ore-grade mineralization.

The Keystone rocks also are a multi-phase intrusion composed of several different textural units (fig. 5). The distribution and degree of continuity of these textural units are not well known at this time, but some generalizations can be made concerning their occurrence. The various Keystone phases are as follows: Aplite, Porphyry, Crowded, and Biotitic. Except for the Porphyry, the different textural varieties are generally localized within 60 m of the contacts with the Red Lady phases and the hornfels. The bulk of the Keystone intrusion is composed of Porphyry with Aplite accounting for most of the remaining volume. The Keystone rocks have chilled contacts with the Red Lady phases and hornfels and cut off veining in both cases. Numerous aplitic, porphyritic, and felsitic dikes that occur near the lower stock contacts are currently interpreted as being associated with Keystone intrusive activity.

The light buff-grey to pink Keystone Porphyry is generally porphyritic-phaneritic with 10 to 50 percent phenocrysts, averaging 20 to 30 percent. The phenocrysts are quartz, potassium feldspar, plagioclase, and biotite set in a fine-grained groundmass of the same minerals. Near the contacts the groundmass is locally aphanitic.

The Keystone Aplite is similar to the Porphyry except that it has only up to 10 percent phenocrysts, averaging less than 5 percent. The Aplite occurs as layers, pods, or bodies of indeterminate shape within the main mass of Porphyry.

The Union phases are the youngest intrusive phases recognized to date (fig. 5). The Union rocks cut off veins in the Keystone Porphyry and locally display chilled contacts with the Keystone Porphyry. The textural units of the Union intrusion are very similar to those of the Keystone intrusion making identification difficult where crosscutting relationships are not seen.

Late-stage alteration and weak molybdenum mineralization may be associated with the Keystone and Union intrusive activity.

Metamorphic Rocks

The wall rocks adjacent to the Mount Emmons stock display contact metamorphic effects to distances greater than 450 m laterally and 180 m vertically from the intrusive contacts (figs. 4, 5). Contact metamorphic rocks host 80 percent of the Mount Emmons molybdenite orebody. The sedimentary formations most strongly affected are the Cretaceous Mancos and Mesaverde formations. The Tertiary Ohio Creek and Wasatch formations may be weakly metamorphosed locally although the effects may be impossible to discern because of later hydrothermal alteration. Hydrothermal alteration has obscured the contact metamorphic changes in many areas above and adjacent to the molybdenite deposit.

The contact metamorphic rocks grade from the albite-epidote-hornfels facies into the hornblende-hornfels facies near the stock contact. The albite-epidote-hornfels facies is characterized by the assemblage quartz-potassium feldspar-biotite±sericite in metamorphosed sandstones, siltstones, and shales and by the assemblage quartz-potassium feldspar-plagioclase±epidote±chlorite ± biotite±actinolite in more mafic or calcareous shales. The absence of epidote and chlorite in more calcic hornfelses adjacent to the stock contact is an indication of the higher temperatures of the hornblende-hornfels facies. Hornfelses of both the Mesaverde and Mancos formations have veins that are contemporaneous with contact metamorphism and which contain the same minerals as the adjacent hornfels.

Within the Mount Emmons area the Mesaverde and Mancos formations vary from unmetamorphosed sedimentary rocks to totally recrystallized metamorphic hornfels. Generally, metamorphic intensity increases with depth and with decreasing distance to the stock contact. Textural changes are influenced both by the intensity of metamorphism and original sedimentary textures. In strongly recrystallized rocks, original grain size differences are often reflected in grain size differences in the metamorphic products. Original sedimentary layering is mimicked by mineral alignment and compositional banding in the hornfels. Recognition of such relict textures has made it possible to correlate rock units between drill holes and to recognize the Mesaverde-Mancos contact.

Hydrothermal Alteration and Mineralization

Hydrothermal alteration associated with the Mount Emmons stock occurs in several distinct overlapping zones (fig. 6). Altered rocks consist of the adjacent and enclosing Cretaceous Mancos and Mesaverde formations, and Tertiary Ohio Creek and Wasatch formations, as well as phases of the Tertiary Mount Emmons stock. Main stage alteration can be zoned from the Tertiary sediments inward in the following sequence:

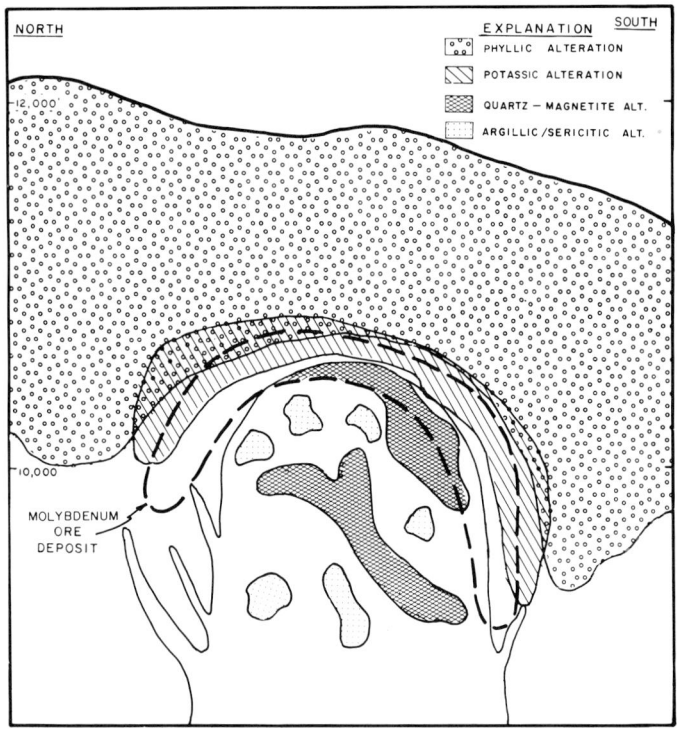

Figure 6. Hydrothermal alteration of the Mount Emmons deposit

1. An outermost zone of veins and disseminated pyrrhotite peripheral to pyrite;
2. A propylitic zone consisting of chlorite, pyrite, epidote and calcite in the Wasatch Formation;
3. A phyllic assemblage of quartz, sericite, and pyrite in the Ohio Creek, Mesaverde, and Mancos Formations;
4. A potassic zone of quartz, secondary potassium feldspar, and biotite in the Mesaverde and Mancos Formations, and in the upper Red Lady phases;
5. A zone of pervasive quartz-magnetite and local biotite and potassium feldspar within the Red Lady phases.

Late-stage hydrothermal alteration affects both the lower Red Lady phases and the upper portions of the Keystone and Union phases. Pervasive argillization mixed with sericite is the dominant late-stage alteration type. Within the Keystone phases, a deep, weak quartz-magnetite zone is present. For the most part, the Keystone and Union phases are unaltered.

Propylitic zone

Propylitic alteration effects are generally restricted to the Tertiary Wasatch Formation where it overlies the Mount Emmons deposit (fig. 4). The Wasatch is the only formation containing significant quantities of mafic minerals and calcic plagioclase, making it more susceptible to replacement by a propylitic assemblage. Minor propylitic alteration may also be seen in hornfels found in the lower lateral margins of the deposit.

In the Wasatch Formation, the propylitic assemblage is characterized by both disseminated and vein chlorite, pyrite, epidote, and minor calcite, pyrrhotite, clay, and sericite. Zonal distribution follows the northeast-southwest trend of the Wasatch in surface and subsurface exposures. Clay and sericite replacement of biotite, feldspar, and (or) matrix materials generally occurs near the Wasatch-Ohio Creek contact and probably represents a transition between the propylitic and phyllic zones.

Phyllic zone

Pervasive phyllic alteration is found in the Ohio Creek, Mesaverde, and Mancos Formations and occurs between the potassic and propylitic zones (fig. 6). Minor late phyllic alteration is also found in all Teritary intrusive rocks associated with the deposit. In both pervasive and vein alteration, an assemblage of quartz, sericite, and pyrite is characteristic, with significant fluorite commonly present.

Pyrite veinlets with quartz-sericite-pyrite envelopes are characteristics of the phyllic zone. A transition from quartz-pyrite to quartz-pyrite-molybdenite veinlets occurs as the ore zone is approached.

Within the main phyllic zone, pyrite distribution between vein and disseminated occurrences is controlled by the grain size, and possibly, the porosity of the host sediments. In coarse, porous sandstones and arkosic sandstones of the Ohio Creek and upper Mesaverde the majority of the pyrite is disseminated. In fine-grained sandstones and siltstones of the Mesaverde and locally, Mancos Formations, thermal metamorphic effects have reduced porosity and fissility, producing a more refractory and brittle rock. In these units, pyrite occurs in hairline vein stockworks, with relatively minor disseminations. Below the transition from phyllic to potassic alteration, pyrite rapidly decreases to one percent or less throughout the remainder of the deposit.

In the Mount Emmons stock, phyllic alteration is generally restricted to minor pyrite veins with quartz-sericite-pyrite envelopes, and to local replacement of plagioclase and, rarely, potassium feldspar phenocrysts.

Potassic zone

The zone of potassic alteration occurs mainly within metamorphosed Mesaverde and Mancos Formations, and partly overlaps the contact with the Mount Emmons stock (fig. 6). The zone grades into phyllic alteration above and quartz-magnetite alteration below. Most of the ore zone lies within potassically altered sediments and rhyodacite porphyry sills. Except for local recrystallization and weak flooding by potassium feldspar and biotite, hornfels matrix appears to remain intact, making potassic alteration mainly vein-related. Vein assemblages are variable, but generally contain potassium feldspar, quartz, biotite, fluorite, and molybdenite. Magnetite and pyrite may also be present.

A variation of typical potassic alteration has weak sericitic replacement of matrix biotite, plagioclase, and potassium feldspar adjacent to potassium feldspar veins. Minor sericite also accompanies potassium feldspar in the vein. Sericite in vein halos becomes diffuse within one mm of the vein.

Quartz-magnetite zone

The zone of strong quartz-magnetite alteration is primarily restricted to the upper part of the Mount Emmons stock (fig. 6). Quartz-magnetite alteration is located below both the potassic zone and the major portion of the ore zone.

The quartz-magnetite alteration is characterized by an intense stockwork of quartz veinlets with 4 to 8 volume percent magnetite. Hematite, biotite, and fluorite are minor components of the quartz-magnetite veins. Locally, the quartz-magnetite is massive with no rock fragments visible. The quartz-magnetite veining decreases greatly near the margin of the stock and the magnetite content of the quartz veins also decreases.

Within the central portion of the stock a 60-m-wide pipe-like body of massive quartz-magnetite has recently been recognized (figs. 5 and 6). This quartz-magnetite pipe cuts the Keystone intrusion. The relationships between the Union intrusion and this quartz-magnetite pipe are not known at this time.

Pyrrhotite zone

A zone of pyrrhotite mineralization is peripheral to the combined hydrothermal systems of both the Redwell and Mount Emmons deposits. It occurs marginal to pyrite from the phyllic zone of the deposit and may be related to reducing conditions in carbonaceous siltstones and shales of the Mesaverde and Mancos formations.

Molybdenite mineralization

The Mount Emmons molybdenite deposit is the only known zone of economic mineralization associated with the Mount Emmons and Redwell intrusive systems.

At its shallowest point, the upper limit of the molybdenite ore zone lies approximately 270 m below the surface of Red Lady Basin (fig. 4). Geologic reserves are 155 million tons averaging 0.44 percent MoS_2 using a 0.2 percent MoS_2 cutoff. The ore zone ranges between 75 and 120 m thick (averaging 90 m), with a cross-sectional diameter averaging 650 m. It is concentrically draped over the apex of the Mount Emmons stock in the shape of an inverted cup and extends well into the metamorphosed sedimentary rocks (fig. 5). Ore-grade mineralization is locally terminated at depth by Keystone rocks.

The majority of ore in metamorphosed sedimentary rocks lies within potassically altered rock and locally within transition zones between potassic and phyllic alteration. Molybdenite was introduced as stockwork veinlets associated with the main-stage hydrothermal event of the Mount Emmons stock. Vein mineralogy is relatively simple, consisting mainly of fine-grained quartz, molybdenite, and fluorite. Potassium feldspar, magnetite, pyrite, carbonate, and occasionally biotite, may be present in minor amounts.

At the outer margins of the ore zone, stockwork quartz-molybdenite-fluorite veins die out and grade into stockwork pyrite or pyrite-quartz-sericite veins at the transition from the potassic zone to the phyllic zone of alteration. Within the Mount Emmons stock ore-grade mineralization drops off in the outer part of the quartz-magnetite altered rocks.

SUMMARY

Intrusion of granitic magma of the Red Lady Complex into the Cretaceous and Tertiary sedimentary and igneous rocks at Mount Emmons was the initial step in the formation of the molybdenum deposit. The intrusion caused some fracturing and extensive contact metamorphism in the country rocks. The magma was rapidly chilled creating the Red Lady Border phase. Continued crystallization of the magma at somewhat slower cooling rates resulted in the formation of the Aplite. Differentiation of the magma occurred during the crystallization process causing interlayered porphyritic and aplitic textures to develop deeper in the stock.

During crystallization of the Red Lady phases, hydrothermal fluids collected near the top of the magma column. These fluids were released after a period of intense fracturing in the solid upper portions of the Red Lady intrusion and the surrounding country rock. This release of fluids was responsible for the formation of the major part of the Mount Emmons molybdenum deposit and the associated alteration zones. Continued cooling and crystallization of the Red Lady magma was accompanied by minor amounts of mineralization and alteration which crosscut earlier zones.

Renewed upward intrusive pressure within the magma chamber locally caused magma to be intruded into the Red Lady rocks, cutting off alteration and mineralization. This magma solidified to form the Keystone intrusion of variably textured granite porphyries. Minor local accumulations of hydrothermal fluids produced during crystallization of the Keystone magma affected the upper part of the Keystone rocks and portions of the lower part of the adjacent Red Lady phases.

A second resurgence of magma caused intrusion of the Union phases into the Keystone rocks. Release of hydrothermal fluids from this granite magma may have created the zones of sericitic, argillic, and quartz-magnetite alteration in the overlying Keystone rocks. Quartz-sericite-pyrite alteration in the upper portions of the Union mass was probably formed by hydrothermal fluids retained in the Union magma.

ACKNOWLEDGMENTS

The authors would like to thank the numerous AMAX geologists who have contributed to the understanding of the geology of Mount Emmons and the Climax Molybdenum Company for permission to publish this information.

REFERENCES

Cunningham, C. G., Naeser, C. W., and Marvin R. F., 1977, New ages for intrusive rocks in the Colorado mineral belt: U.S. Geological Survey Open-File Report 77-573, 7 p.

Dapples, E. C., 1939, Coal metamorphism in the Anthracite–Crested Butte quadrangle, Colorado: Economic Geology, v. 34, p. 369–398.

Ganster, M. W., Dowsett, F. R., and Ranta, D. E., 1981, Geology of the Mount Emmons Deposit (abs): American Institute of Mining, Metallurgical and Petroleum Engineers, Annual Meeting Program, p. 21.

Gaskill, D. L. and Godwin, L. H., 1966, Geologic map of the Marcellina Mountain quadrangle, Gunnison County, Colorado: U.S. Geological Survey Geologic Quadrangle Map GQ-511.

Gaskill, D. L., Godwin, L. H., and Mutschler, F. E., 1967, Geologic map of the Oh-Be-Joyful quadrangle, Gunnison County, Colorado: U.S. Geological Survey Geologic Quadrangle Map GQ-578.

Gaskill, D. L., Rosenbaum, J. G., King, H. D., Meeves, H. C., and Bieniewski, C. L., 1977 Mineral resources of the West Elk Wilderness and vicinity, Delta and Gunnison counties, Colorado: U.S. Geological Survey Open-File Report 77-751, 110 p.

Obradovich, J. D., Mutschler, F. E., and Bryant, Bruce, 1969, K-Ar ages bearing on the igneous and tectonic history of the Elk Mountains and vicinity, Colorado—A preliminary report: Geological Society of America Bulletin, v. 80, p. 1749–1756.

Sharp, J. E., 1978, A molybdenum mineralized breccia pipe complex, Redwell Basin, Colorado: Economic Geology, v. 73, p. 369–382.

Thomas, J. A. and Galey, J. T., Jr., 1978, Mount Emmons, Colorado, molybdenum deposit (abs): American Institute of Mining, Metallurgical and Petroleum Engineers, Annual Meeting Program, p. 44.

Tweto, Ogden and Sims, P. K., 1963, Precambrian ancestry of the Colorado mineral belt: Geological Society of America Bulletin, v. 74, p. 991–1014.

Worcester, P. G., 1919, Molybdenum deposits of Colorado: Colorado Geological Survey Bulletin 14, 121 p.

HYDROTHERMAL RESOURCES OF WESTERN COLORADO*

RICHARD HOWARD PEARL
Colorado Geological Survey
Denver, Colorado 80203

INTRODUCTION

In Colorado west of the Continental Divide there are 34 thermal areas containing approximately 103 thermal springs and wells (fig. 1). The surface temperatures of the waters in these areas range from a low of 23°C to a high of 80°C. The temperatures, discharge, total dissolved solids and estimated reservoir temperatures of the thermal systems of western Colorado are summarized in Table 1.

The surface temperatures of the thermal waters found in western Colorado are not excessively hot as contrasted to such higher temperature geothermal systems as hot dry rock, geopressured, and dry steam found elsewhere in the western United States. Consequently the geothermal resources of Colorado are classified as hot-water hydrothermal resources.

The hydrogeological conditions and resources of the hydrothermal systems of western Colorado have been discussed by numerous authors. For a complete listing of all authors who have written on the thermal springs of western Colorado the reader is referred to the references at the end of this paper.

With one exception, Routt Hot Springs, north of Steamboat Springs, all thermal areas in western Colorado are geologically associated with sedimentary rocks. The geological conditions of the thermal areas vary from the relatively simple structural conditions at South Canyon Hot Springs, west of Glenwood Springs and Pagosa Springs in southwestern Colorado to the highly complex structural environment which exists at Rico and Ouray in southwestern Colorado. Evaluation of the geological conditions of each thermal area has shown that all thermal waters are associated with faults and in several instances the springs are located at the intersection of two faults. This is in agreement with geological controls of most thermal systems throughout the world.

The Colorado Geological Survey, with U.S. Department of Energy funding, is currently engaged in a limited exploration program to evaluate the following resource areas in western Colorado: Steamboat-Routt Hot Springs, Hot Sulphur Springs, Waunita Hot Springs, Cement Creek-Ranger Hot Springs, Ouray, the Animas Valley north of Durango and Wagon Wheel Gap Hot Springs. Upon completion of this program in 1982, reports will be available to interested parties, which will, as accurately as possible, depict the geological and hydrogeological characteristics of each system.

USES OF THERMAL WATERS

For many years the thermal waters of western Colorado have been used for a variety of purposes. For example, thermal waters have been used for space heating at Pagosa Springs since the turn of the century; however, the main use of thermal waters has been for recreation and medicinal purposes at Juniper Hot Springs, Steamboat Springs, Hot Sulphur Springs, Waunita Hot Springs, Cebolla Hot Springs, Ouray, Orvis Hot Springs, Lemon Hot Springs, Dunton, Tripp-Trimble Hot Springs, and Wagon Wheel Gap Hot Springs.

As part of the Colorado geothermal resource assessment program the author (Pearl, 1979) attempted to estimate the size and energy contained in each thermal system in western Colorado. To make these calculations some basic assumptions about the reservoir depth, structural controls, and size of the thermal reservoir were made. These calculations showed that the energy content of the thermal systems ranged from a low of 2.1×10^{12} B.T.U.'s of thermal energy at South Canyon Hot Springs to a high of 1.43×10^{15} B.T.U.'s of thermal energy at Wagon Wheel Gap Hot Springs. The total amount of thermal energy estimated to be contained in all the thermal systems of western Colorado ranges from 1.34×10^{15} to 3.41×10^{15} B.T.U.'s (Pearl, 1979).

Earlier (Barrett and Pearl, 1978), using mathematical geothermometer models, calculated the estimated reservoir temperatures of the individual thermal systems of western Colorado. Their calculations indicate that the estimated temperatures range from a low of 20°C to a high of 225°C (Table 1). These are not exceptionally high temperatures; consequently it is projected that the ultimate use of the thermal waters will be for direct application purposes. There may be several exceptions to this. For those areas where the estimated reservoir temperatures range between

---

*Prepared in cooperation with the U.S. Dept. of Energy under Contract No. DE-AS07-77ET28365

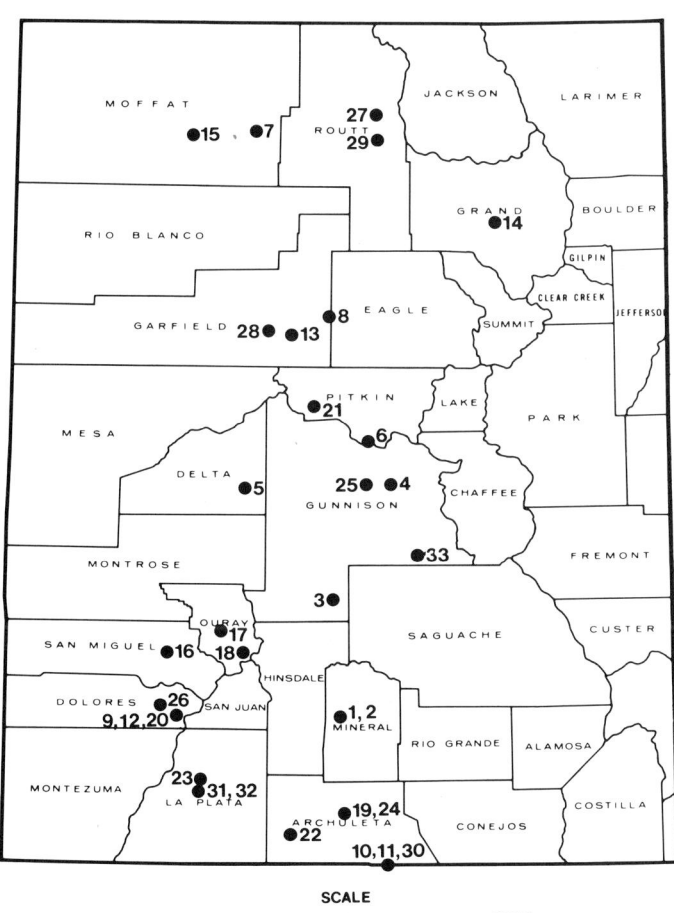

Figure 1. Thermal springs and wells in western Colorado. Numbers refer to Table 1.

Table 1. Characteristics of thermal areas in western Colorado (adapted from Pearl, 1979).

	Maximum Discharge (gpm)	Maximum Total Dissolved Solids (mg/l)	Maximum Temperature (°C)	Estimated Reservoir Temperature (°C)
1. Antelope W.S., Mineral Co.	3E	151	32	52
2. Birdsie W.S., Mineral Co.	3E	150	30	52
3. Cebolla H.S., Gunnison Co.	3	1,450	40	200?
4. Cement Creek Warm Spring, Gunnison Co.	80	390	25	60
5. Colonel Chinn Hot Water Well, Delta Co.	—	—	42	43?
6. Conundrum H.S., Pitkin Co.	50	1,910	32	50
7. Craig Warm Water Well, Moffatt Co.	24	896	39	70
8. Dotsero W.S., Eagle Co.	500E	10,000	32	45
9. Dunton H.S., Dolores Co.	25	1,260	42	70
10. Dutch Crowley Artesian Well, Archuleta Co.	—	101	70	80
11. Eoff Artesian Well, Archuleta Co.	50E	—	39	60
12. Geyser W.S., Dolores Co.	200E	1,620	28	120
13. Glenwood Springs, Garfield Co.	2,260	20,000	50	77
14. Hot Sulphur Springs, Grand Co.	150	1,200	44	150
15. Juniper H.S., Moffatt Co.	13	1,150	33	75
16. Lemon H.S., San Miguel Co.	10	2,760	33	35?
17. Orvis, H.S., Ouray Co.	1	2,250	52	90
18. Ouray H.S., Ouray Co.	200	1,500	69	90
19. Pagosa Springs, Archuleta Co.	265	3,200	58	150
20. Paradise H.S., Dolores Co.	30	6,530	46	45?
21. Penny H.S., Pitkin Co.	10	2,820	46	90
22. Piedra River Hot Spring, Archuleta Co.	50	—	42	—
23. Pinkerton H.S., La Plata Co.	54	3,900	33	125
24. Rainbow H.S., Archuleta Co.	45	161	40	50
25. Ranger H.S., Gunnison Co.	132	465	27	60
26. Rico, Dolores Co.	12	2,790	44	50?
27. Routt H.S., Routt Co.	50	552	64	175
28. S. Canyon H.S., Garfield Co.	17	800	48	130
29. Steamboat Springs, Routt Co.	140	6,170	39	130
30. Stinking Springs, Archuleta Co.	24	899	27	60
31. Stratten W.S., La Plata Co.	10	—	28	—
32. Tripp-Trimble H.S., La Plata Co.	1	3,240	44	70
33. Waunita H.S., Gunnison Co.	50	575	80	225

E = Estimated

150°C and 225°C, the resource could be used for the generation of electricity. Several thermal areas in western Colorado are currently being evaluated by major energy companies for this purpose.

With the increasing cost and growing shortage of energy, more extensive use of geothermal energy in western Colorado is envisioned for the future, especially for space heating purposes. A study by Coe (1978) showed that in 17 communities in western Colorado some or all of the total heating requirements could be obtained from nearby thermal waters. Some of the other potential uses for thermal waters in western Colorado are summarized in Table 2.

Table 2. Possible use of thermal waters in western Colorado. Adapted from Coe (1978).

Refrigeration of food products	Wood chip drying
Biomass processing for fuel and fertilizer	Feedlot warming
Agricultural product growing	Tropical gardens
Agricultural product processing	Greenhouse operations
Nahcolite-dawsonite processing	Power generation

CONSTRAINTS ON THE DEVELOPMENT OF GEOTHERMAL ENERGY

While the geothermal resources of western Colorado appear to offer great promise, their development is lagging for a variety of reasons, mainly that the resources are primarily the low to moderate type and will be used for direct application purposes. In most instances these uses are small projects with low return on investment. Consequently the major energy companies with sufficient exploration and development capital are not interested in developing them. This leaves their development to private individuals, a few small geothermal development companies, or local governments. As these entities usually do not have adequate funds available, they have had to seek outside financial assistance. During the past few years, the Federal Government has provided development monies for direct-use geothermal projects through a series of insurance, grant, or loan programs. In a number of instances, such as at Pagosa Springs in southwestern Colorado, these programs have been very successful in helping to develop a specific resource.

Another constraint to the development of the low to moderate geothermal resources of western Colorado is a definite lack of geological knowledge about each system. Prospective developers, who are not resource development oriented, are very reluctant to develop a resource when there is no information available that they can use in making reliable cost estimates regarding resource location, drilling costs, and amounts of energy to be expected.

A perceived constraint, which usually proves to be groundless, is the engineering problems associated with the use of geothermal fluids. Scaling, corrosion and noxious gases are all problems that usually can be solved with proper engineering treatment.

CONCLUSION

The hydrothermal geothermal resources of western Colorado are a largely untapped resource that appear able to supply large amounts of energy for a variety of purposes. Before this development can occur, however, better resource definition is needed to accurately define the location, size, and temperatures of the individual systems. An active group of developers are needed who are willing and able to develop and sell the low to moderate temperature geothermal resources.

REFERENCES

Barrett, J. K. and Pearl, R. H., 1976, Hydrogeological data of thermal springs and wells in Colorado: Colorado Geological Survey Information Series 6, 124 p.

———, 1978, An appraisal of Colorado's geothermal resources: Colorado Geological Survey Bulletin 39, 224 p.

Barrett, J. K., Pearl, R. H., and Pennington, A. J., 1976, Map showing thermal springs, wells, and heat-flow contours in Colorado: Colorado Geological Survey Information Series 4.

Berry G. W., Grim, P. J., and Ikelman, J. A., 1980, Thermal springs list for the United States: National Oceanic and Atmospheric Administration, Key to Geophysical Records Documentation No. 12, Boulder, Colorado, 59 p.

Blackmer, J., 1939, Geology of the Steamboat Springs area, Routt Co., Colorado, with a special emphasis on thermal springs (M.S. thesis): Boulder, University of Colorado, 115 p.

Christopherson, Karen, 1979, Geophysical evaluation, Steamboat Springs, Colorado, in Expanding the Geothermal Frontier: Transactions Geothermal Resources Council Annual Meeting, Reno, Nevada, Geothermal Resource Council, Davis, California, p. 113–116.

Coe, B. A. and Zimmerman, Judy, 1981, Geothermal energy opportunities at four Colorado towns: Colorado Geological Survey Open-File Report 81-1.

Coury and Associates, Inc., 1979, An environmental report on the construction and operation of a geothermal district heating system in Pagosa Springs, Colorado: Denver, Colorado, Coury and Assoc., Inc.

———, 1980, Direct utilization of geothermal energy for Pagosa Springs, Colorado. Preliminary design report: Prepared for U.S. Department of Energy under contract No. DE-FC07-79ET27030.

Denver Research Institute, 1980, Municipal geothermal heat utilization plan for Glenwood Springs, Colorado: DOE/ID/12049-3, U.S. Department of Energy, Division of Geothermal Energy, Idaho Falls, Idaho, 226 p.

Galloway, M. J., 1980, Hydrogeological and geothermal investigations of Pagosa Springs, Colorado, with a section on Mineralogical and petrographic investigation of samples from geothermal wells O-1 and P-1, Pagosa Springs, Colorado by W. W. Atkinson, Jr.: Colorado Geological Survey Special Publication 10, 95 p.

George, R. D., Curtis, H. A., Lester, O. C., Crook, J. K. and Yeo, J. M., 1920, Mineral waters of Colorado: Colorado Geological Survey Bulletin 11, 474 p.

Lakes, Arthur, 1905, Geology of the hot springs of Colorado and speculations as to their origin and heat: Colorado Scientific Society Proceedings, v. 8, p. 31–37.

Lester, O. C., 1918, The radioactive properties of the mineral springs of Colorado: American Journal of Science, Series 4, v. 46, p. 621.

Lewis, E. L., 1966, The thermal springs of Colorado—A resource appraisal (M.S. thesis): Boulder, University of Colorado, 91 p.

Lowther, W. H. and Knowles, R. R., 1910, The mineral waters of Steamboat Springs: Western Chemist and Metallurgist, v. 6, p. 60–65.

Mallory, E. C., Jr. and Barrett, P. R., 1973, Chemistry and spectrochemical analysis of selected groundwaters in Colorado: U.S. Geological Survey Open-file Report, 47 p.

Pearl, R. H., 1972, Geothermal resources of Colorado: Colorado Geological Survey Special Publication 2, 54 p.

———, 1979, Colorado's hydrothermal resource base—An assessment: Colorado Geological Survey Resource Series 6, 144 p.

———, 1980, Geothermal resources of Colorado: Colorado Geological Survey Map Series 14, Scale 1:500,000.

Pearl, R. H. and Coe, B. A., 1980, Potential for geothermal energy development in Colorado, in H. C. Kent and K. W. Porter, eds., Colorado Geology: Denver, Colorado, Rocky Mountain Association of Geologists, p. 247–249.

Pearl, R. H., Galloway, M. J. and Dick, J. D., 1978, The Pagosa Springs project; The first permitted geothermal wells in Colorado, in Geothermal Energy: A Novelty Becomes Resource: Transactions Geothermal Resources Council, v. 2, sec. 2, p. 517–519.

URS Corp., 1981, Problem identification and quantification salinity investigation of Glenwood-Dotsero Springs unit: Report for U.S. Water and Power Resources Services, Grand Junction, Colorado under contract No. 0-07-40-S1359, 100 p.

Waring, G. A., 1965, Thermal springs of the United States and other countries of the World—A Summary, revised by R. F. Blankenship and Ray Bentall: U.S. Geological Survey Professional Paper 492, 383 p.

THE HANGING FLUME OF DOLORES RIVER CANYON, MONTROSE COUNTY, COLORADO

ELIZABETH A. LEARNED
Grand Junction, Colorado 81501

Gold was discovered in the headwaters of the San Miguel River in 1875. Subsequent downstream prospecting led to the discovery of the gold-bearing gravels along the Dolores River, near the confluence with Mesa Creek.

In 1887, the gravels, known as the Long Tree placers, came into the possession of the Montrose Placer Mining Company, capitalized at five million dollars. In a news item in 1887, the *Engineering and Mining Journal* (E&MJ), stated this company claimed to have 2.4 km² of placer ground underlain by gravels 4 to 35 m deep, worth from 50 cents to seven dollars per m³.

After preliminary prospecting, the company decided to build a flume and ditch to a point 17 km upstream on the San Miguel River. The total cost of the project was expected to be about $75,000 and would consist of half ditching and half fluming. The company anticipated this system would provide enough water under a hydraulic gradient to operate hydraulic mining equipment.

Built in 1889-1890, the flume traversed 10 km of the Dolores River Canyon at an elevation of 30 to 46 m above the river and from 61 to 152 m below the rims of the gorge. It was 1.8 m wide and 1.2 m deep, and was set on sills fastened to the cliff with iron pins and supported on the hanging end by posts of inclined timbers pinned to the cliff. The pins, 4 cm in diameter, were placed in holes drilled to a depth of 46 cm into the sandstone. The drilling was done by hand by men lowered over the cliffs on ropes. A sawmill was established at Pine Flats, Utah near the present site of Buckeye Reservoir to cut lumber. Only the best quality 5-cm thick pine boards were used.

The operations of the Montrose Placer Mining Company were managed by Colonel N. P. Turner, an experienced California miner. Under favorable conditions, with a gang of 12 men, 76 m of flume could be erected in one day. According to legend, Chinese coolies were brought in to work on the flume and died like flies during the construction. The only Chinaman connected with the job was a cook and the only casualty reported during the construction was the drowning of a worker in the Dolores River while swimming. Construction of the flume used 13,935 m² (1,800,000 board feet) of lumber and cost a purported $173,000. It carried over 303 million liters of water per day at a grade of 79 cm to the km. The flume was one of the early engineering triumphs in Colorado.

Work at the placers began in the early summer of 1891 utilizing the latest hydraulic equipment. At that time, Colonel Turner estimated the minimum gold content at 25 to 30 cents per m³.

In August, 1891, the E&MJ—quoting local newspapers—reported that the company realized $80,000 profit after operating only six weeks. Operations were suspended in 1893 as the gravel deposits proved much less extensive, and their value proved to be only a fraction of the company's estimates. The gold was extremely fine and could only be saved with the liberal use of quicksilver.

The gold in the Lone Tree placers undoubtedly was derived from mineralized areas in the headwaters of the San Miguel River and Lake (South) Fork. No placer deposits are known upstream on the Dolores River for many kilometers from its confluence with the San Miguel.

After the flume was abandoned, ranchers in the area salvaged some lumber to construct houses and ranch sheds. Today, the flume is in a deteriorated condition, as several sections have collapsed and fallen into the river, but the basic integrity of the structure remains intact (fig. 1).

SUGGESTED READINGS

Engineering and Mining Journal, 1890, Flume work of the Montrose Placer Mining Company: Engineering and Mining Journal, v. 49, p. 563-565.
Parker, B. H., Jr., 1974, Gold placers of Colorado, book 2 of 2: Colorado School of Mines Quarterly, vol. 69, n. 4, p. 172-184.
Rockwell, Wilson, 1965, Uncompahgre County: Denver, Sage Books, p. 160-166.

Figure 1. Remains of the hanging flume today (sketch by J. D. Moore).